P9-CNB-995

Please remember that this is a library book,
and that it belongs only temporarily to each
person who uses it. Be considerate. Do
not write in this, or any, library book.

FOURTH EDITION

The Skills of Helping Individuals, Families, Groups, and Communities

LAWRENCE SHULMAN
State University of New York at Buffalo
School of Social Work

F. E. Peacock Publishers, Inc.
Itasca, Illinois 60143

To my wife, Sheila

Copyright © 1999
F.E. Peacock Publishers, Inc.
All rights reserved
Printed in the U.S.A.
Library of Congress Catalog Card No. 97-76284
ISBN 0-87581-414-X
Printing   10   9   8   7   6   5   4   3   2
Year   03   02   01   00   99

■ Contents

■ *Acknowledgments*

I would like to acknowledge the many people who contributed to this book.

William Schwartz developed the interactionist perspective upon which much of my work has been based. He died in 1982 and is still missed.

A major study of mine, cited in this text (Shulman, 1991), was supported by a generous grant from the Edna McConnel-Clark Foundation. In particular, I thank Peter Forsyth, vice president, who provided encouragement, support, and patience.

I would also like to acknowledge the contribution of the Welfare Grants Directorate of Health and Welfare, Canada, for their support of the earlier research cited in this book (Shulman, 1978; 1981). From this department, I am particularly indebted to J. Evariste Thériault. I am also indebted to the P. A. Woodward Foundation for support of my study of medical practitioners (1982).

Various colleagues have helped along the way. A number of faculty members at the School of Social Work of the University of British Columbia offered valuable advice. In particular, I found John Crane to be always ready to offer help in the area of research design and statistics. I was also fortunate to be able to consult David Fanchel of Columbia University.

Colleagues at the Boston University School of Social Work were supportive of my research efforts through colloquia and through individual consultations. In particular, Don Oellerich was always available when I needed statistical advice. More recently, a number of colleagues and I have had a wonderful opportunity to participate as faculty fellows in a faculty development substance abuse training program. This three-year project has been directed by Maryanne Amodeo and has been funded by the Center for Substance Abuse Prevention (CSAP) of the National Institutes of Health. This proved to be a wonderful learning opportunity for me as I met regularly with this group of colleagues whose practice wisdom and humor have enriched my days at Boston University. I have integrated much of what I have learned about substance abuse and its treatment in this edition.

Alex Gitterman, of Columbia University, is a colleague who has been a sounding board for my ideas about practice. Our joint editorial work and co-leadership of workshops have also enriched my understanding. My wife Sheila provided specific editing assistance and general support.

I am especially grateful to a number of social work faculty who responded to a request for suggestions for revisions. Many of their suggestions have been carried forward in this edition. For the third edition, this group included Robert Constable (Loyola University of Chicago), Ginny Raymond (University of Alabama), Ellen Bogolub (State University of New York at Stony Brook), and Ramiro Valdez (Texas Woman's University). JoDee Keller (Pacific Lutheran University), Judith L. Burke (University of Missouri-Columbia), and Ferrol E. Mennen (University of Southern California) provided additional suggestions for the fourth edition.

Richard Welna of Peacock Publishers coordinated this effort and provided excellent suggestions as well. Ted Peacock and his production staff provided their usual high level of support. I am particularly grateful, for her patience and skill, to Janet Tilden who edited this edition, and to Kim Vander Steen, who handled the production of the book.

The major study cited in this edition was implemented in the Ministry of Housing and Community Services of the Province of British Columbia. I am indebted to the many members of the Ministry staff who contributed during the key informant and data gathering stages.

Finally, I want to thank the staff and clients who participated in the studies cited in this book, the workers and students who shared examples of their practice, and my own clients who allowed me to share their experiences in the interest of helping others like themselves. These illustrations of the joint efforts of workers and clients give life to the theory and stand as a tribute to their courage and determination.

■ *Introduction*

This book is designed to be used in introductory courses on social work practice. The focus is on method—what social workers do as their part of the helping process. The author believes that the dynamics of giving and taking help are not mysterious processes that defy efforts at explanation. Helping skills can be defined, illustrated, and taught. The helping process is a complex one, and to be presented clearly, it must be broken down into manageable segments. Theories and simple models need to be developed to provide tools for understanding.

This book is built on the idea that we can identify an underlying process in all social work helping relationships. This process and its associated set of core skills can be observed whenever one person attempts to help another. These are the constant elements of the helping process. Elements of the process may vary according to the setting for the engagement (e.g., school, hospital, welfare agency), the age and stage of life of the client, the particular life problems the client brings to the encounter, and whether the client is participating voluntarily or involuntarily. The social worker will also introduce variant elements to the process related to factors such as education and experience, life events, and effectiveness of the support available to the worker.

In spite of the varying aspects of practice, when the interaction is examined closely, the similarities become apparent. This book addresses a range of helping situations in the belief that each social worker can incorporate the models into his or her own work context. In addition, findings drawn from this author's studies of social work practice, supervision, management and medical practice, as well as the research of others, will provide empirical support for the importance of these core skills that make up the constant elements of practice.

An additional assumption in this text is the existence of common elements in our work with individuals, families, groups, communities, and others in the social systems important to our clients (e.g., teachers, doctors, other social workers). The skill model developed in this book is illustrated by a range of encounters. The reader will find the core processes and skills that are identified in the chapters on work with individuals reappearing as the focus shifts to work with groups, families, communities, and organizational systems. For example, the contracting skills discussed in the beginning phase of work with individuals are also applied in first group sessions, family meetings, and community organizing efforts. These skills are common elements. In addition, the unique dynamics of, for example, first sessions with groups illustrate the variant elements.

In a like manner, the common elements of beginning work with different types of groups (e.g., persons with AIDS, children, survivors of sexual abuse, psychiatric patients, residential living groups, citizen community action groups) are presented. Unique aspects introduced by the setting and the purpose of the work are also considered.

This book represents an effort to further conceptualize and illustrate a generalist practice model without losing the detail of the specific ways we practice. The term *generalist* has been used in different ways over the years, sometimes referring to practice models so abstract that one can hardly find the social worker or client in the description. The focus here is not just on what is common about what we know, value, and aspire to, nor on our common models for describing clients (as in systems theory), but rather on the common elements and skills of the helping person in action.

Another underlying assumption of this book is that social workers need to be prepared to offer clients service in the modality (e.g., individual, group, family, community) most suitable to the client, rather than the one most comfortable for the worker.

WHAT'S NEW IN THIS EDITION

A systematic effort has been made to update the examples and illustrations used in this edition. The third edition was published in 1992. Since that time we have deepened our understanding and skill in a number of emerging practice areas. The AIDS epidemic, homelessness, problems of addiction to crack cocaine and other substances, and sexual violence have all been brought to the forefront of our practice. Our work in each of these areas has also changed at a rapid pace. For example, where just a short time ago work with persons with AIDS focused primarily on helping clients who were dying of AIDS, with the development of new drugs we now find ourselves working to help many of our clients live with AIDS. As another example, changing social policies, such as managed care and welfare reform, have had profound effects on the lives of our clients and on the nature of our practice. Illustrations drawn from these areas bring the practice theory closer to the realities of today's students and practitioners.

As in the third edition, theories and constructs about human behavior, some supported by research and others drawn from experience in practice, are shared when relevant to specific practice issues. In this way, what we know about the dynamics of helping, oppression and vulnerability, resilience, group process, substance abuse, family interaction, and so on is directly linked to the worker's interactions with the client and with relevant systems. This author's research and theory building work (Shulman, 1991), designed to develop a holistic theory of practice, has been more thoroughly integrated into this edition. This theory recognizes the complexity of our practice. Focusing solely on the social worker–client interaction ignores many factors such as supervision, availability of resources, client motivation and capacity, the impact of cost-containment efforts, and the effects of client-related traumatic experiences (e.g., the death of a client) on both worker and client. These and other elements of practice are systematically addressed.

Emphasis has also been placed on adding a strengths and resiliency perspective to constructs from oppression psychology when considering practice with oppressed and vulnerable populations. It is important to understand the socioeconomic factors that contribute to individual, family, and community problems, yet it is also essential to recognize, understand, and respect the existing strengths and resiliencies that have helped people to cope. The major ideals of this socially oriented framework for understanding individual, family, group, and community behavior are presented in the first chapter of the book and then illustrated with appropriate examples throughout the text.

A chapter on social work with communities has been included in the section of the book that focuses on social work with larger systems. Some of the issues and examples in this chapter were presented in the third edition, but they were scattered throughout other chapters. In this edition they have been brought together, along with new theory and examples, in a more structured manner oriented around community organization practice. The concept of community used in this book is a broad one, including, as examples, the milieu community in a treatment center, the residential community, the hospital ward, the housing project, and the neighborhood.

The sections dealing with the historical roots of the social work profession and the values and ethics that guide our work have been updated. Illustrations of the impact of legislation and court decisions in areas such as confidentiality, mandated reporting laws (e.g., child abuse), informed consent and duty to warn a client or third party in danger, are used to help the reader become more attuned to the ways in which our society, governments, courts, and professional associations influence our practice. The ethical dilemmas associated with the impact of private practice, managed care, and other changes are also addressed.

The reader will note that whenever possible, practice examples are used to illustrate theoretical material and ethical issues introduced in the first two chapters. This represents another change in this edition.

This fourth edition, like the third edition, provides a glossary of key terms at the end of each chapter. The index of the many case examples has been updated but is still cross-referenced by the type of problem (e.g., addiction, AIDS, sexual abuse), the processes illustrated (e.g., acting out, resistance, denial), the population (e.g., single parents, adult children of alcoholics, pregnant teens), the skills illustrated (e.g., contracting, setting limits, ending skills), special issues (e.g., race, ethnicity), setting (e.g., medical, psychiatric, residential), and modality of practice (individual, family, group, community, organization). This edition includes more than one hundred new examples, including some from the author's recent practice with foster adolescents and persons with AIDS who were in early recovery.

An additional index, specifically geared to the Council on Social Work Education's new accreditation standards, is provided in the updated teacher's guide associated with this text. This index identifies discussion and examples that deal with special populations, empirical research findings, values and ethics, and so on.

The research base and the underlying theoretical material has been updated and expanded throughout the book. Special emphasis has been placed on theory and research findings related to gender and ethnicity, thus strengthening attention to these important areas. For example, added to the four classic group development theories, all of which were considered gender-neutral but were developed by men, the reader will find a feminist approach to group development and the psychology of women that draws upon the body of theory under development by scholars at the Stone Center in Wellesley, Massachusetts.

This edition also contains an enhanced discussion (with illustrations) of issues related to diversity and practice. My interest in this area has been deepened by a number of important professional experiences. First, over the past few years I served as co-chair with Dean Wilma Peebles-Wilkens (Boston University) of the Council on Social Work Education's Diversity Videotape Project. This assignment brought me into ongoing contact with an advisory group of representatives from CSWE commissions as well as caucus groups concerned with practice issues related to women, gays and lesbians, black Americans, Native Americans, Asian-Pacific clients, the physically challenged, and Latinos. Our discussions at the annual CSWE program meetings resulted in a significant deepening of my understanding of the general issues related to diversity and the specific issues related to population groups. I have tried to incorporate some of these ideas in this edition.

In addition, as a first project for this committee, I collaborated with my Boston University colleague Cassandra Clay in the development of a series of diversity teaching videotapes sponsored and distributed by the Council on Social Work Education (Clay and Shulman, 1993). This led to us working together as workshop leaders for social work practitioners, supervisors, and field instructors. Not the least of our learning came from our efforts to develop a working relationship between my colleague—an African-American, female professor—and me—a white, Jewish, male professor. My collaboration with Cassandra has significantly strengthened my understanding of inter- and intra-ethnic issues in practice. I have tried to reflect these new learnings in this edition of the text. In particular, I address the often overlooked issues associated with intra-ethnic practice (e.g., an African-American social worker with an African-American client; a lesbian worker with a lesbian client). It has been my observation that in our efforts to focus on the important issues of inter-ethnic practice (e.g., a white worker with a client of color) we may have short-changed consideration of the special and often poignant issues facing workers who are members of the groups they try to help.

Special attention has also been given to issues related to substance abuse and treatment. Examples from this area of practice were included in the third edition, but they are now supplemented with additional examples and discussed with more in-depth analysis of the associated theory. A new chapter on variant elements in group work practice focuses on this population. This new emphasis partly reflects my recognition of the pervasiveness of the substance abuse problem in our society. In addition, the special opportunity afforded to me as a Faculty Fellow in a faculty development project funded by a grant from the Center for Substance Abuse Prevention (CSAP) has deepened my understanding of this important substantive area, and I am using this edition to begin to disseminate this knowledge.

Finally, this edition offers some advice for students and workers on the type of supervision and support they need in order to fully develop their professional skills. While the fundamental responsibility for effective supervision rests with the supervisor or field instructor, the student/worker can play a more active role in seeking the help she or he needs. With the additional pressures facing all social workers, such as the time restrictions imposed by managed care, it is extremely important that we do not allow effective supervision and consultation to disappear.

ORGANIZATION OF THE BOOK

In order to simplify the complex task of describing method, a single frame of reference—the interactional model—is presented. Introductory comments help to place this point of view in context with other models. Included are a description of a theory of the helping process, a number of models (middle-range descriptions) connecting theory and practice, and the identification of skills needed to put the framework into action.

The interactional model was developed by William Schwartz. This colleague's original thinking helped to focus my early curiosity about method. Published and unpublished works, conversations about practice, and other collaborative efforts have all contributed to Schwartz's influence on the contents of this book. The author alone, however, must take responsibility for the final shape of the chapters. While a single framework provides the unifying structure for the book, many of the skills and models can fit comfortably with other frameworks. Also, concepts from other helpful models (cognitive-behavioral, self in relationship, feminist, psychodynamic, brief treatment, and so on) are incorporated wherever they help us to understand and practice more effectively.

Part I of the book consists of a chapter introducing the major theoretical constructs of the interactional model. Part II focuses on work with individuals, examining this process against the backdrop of the phases of work: preliminary, beginning, work, and ending phases. As the helping model is developed, illustrations from a range of settings help to point out the common as well as variant elements of the work. Parts III and IV move into the more complex issues of working with more than one client at a time, focusing especially on social work with families and then groups. The common elements of the model established in Part I are reintroduced in the family and group contexts. The special dynamics of working with more than one client are introduced. Part V moves from the "micro" or "clinical" level to the "macro" level by exploring the skills involved in working with communities and with people in the larger systems and organizations important to the client. Examples show social workers helping members of a community (e.g., a neighborhood, a housing project, a ward group in a psychiatric hospital) to empower themselves by focusing on community issues related to their personal concerns. Conversations with teachers, doctors, and politicians help to illustrate effective impact with other professionals.

The book is intended to address the needs of the social work student. However, the more experienced practitioner will also find it helpful for continued learning. The book provides models that will help explain and articulate concepts that the practitioner has already developed through experience in practice. Using these models, any practitioner can be more systematic and effective. A clearly developed framework will increase consistency and help to explain more quickly why some sessions go well and others do not.

RESEARCH FINDINGS

A number of research studies, directed by the author, have also contributed to the insights shared in this book. Starting with Schwartz's framework, instruments were developed to measure social work practice skill and relate skills use to effective helping. The findings were then used to analyze the practice approach critically, to confirm some hypotheses while also generating new assumptions for future research. Each successive study built on the preceding ones and the knowledge base developed in social work and related professions and disciplines. Appendix A provides a summary of the methodology of this author's studies that are discussed in this book. The reader is referred to other publications (Shulman, 1977b; 1979b; 1978; 1981; 1984; 1991; Shulman & Buchan, 1982; Shulman, Robinson, & Luckyj, 1982) for more detailed descriptions of the methodology of each study and their findings. While all findings reported in this text are considered to be still tentative and should be considered in light of the limitations of each study, some findings have been repeated in a number of this author's studies and the studies of other researchers. Our confidence in these findings increases with each replication. A chart outlining the major constructs of the theory and citing studies that have lent support to these ideas is included in the book's teaching guide.

While the reader is urged to read the more complete discussion of methodology in Appendix A, a brief summary of the author's study most often quoted in this text follows (Shulman, 1991).

Study Design

This study was conducted in a government child welfare agency in British Columbia, Canada. Project staff reviewed family files that had been recently opened in 68 district offices. Of the 1,056 families identified as potential subjects, 348 (33 percent) agreed to participate. The final sample consisted of 305 families with 449 children served by 171 social workers in 68 district offices.

Most of the data were gathered during the first three months of the project. Home interviews were conducted with the parent(s). A mail survey of staff at all levels (workers, supervisors, managers, etc.) was carried out at the same time. Project staff also read the participating clients' files. Much of the analysis is based upon the data obtained during this time period. Follow-up data were obtained through surveys mailed to clients and staff at intervals over the subsequent 15-month period. The family files were also reviewed by project staff every three months. Twenty-three questionnaires and interview guides were developed and tested for this study.

Description of Study Participants

The five executive directors had MSW degrees; however, only 60 percent of the regional managers, 44 percent of the district supervisors, and 20 percent of the social workers held that degree. When MSWs, BSWs, and other professional degrees were included, 90 percent of the managers, 60 percent of the supervisors, and 68 percent of the social workers held professional degrees.

Two-thirds of the families were headed by a single parent. One-third of the families also reported "some" or "severe" disability with respect to physical and emotional health, learning problems, or drug and alcohol problems. Fourteen percent reported some or severe alcohol or drug problems for themselves. Eight percent reported that their spouses had similar problems. Unemployment was present for one-third of the families. Forty-seven percent of the families were living on welfare or unemployment insurance benefits. Finally, in 10 percent of the families at least one family member was a Native American (of Canadian origin).

Family problems included periodic and severe neglect of children, inability of parents to care for children (because of illness, addictions, etc.), and physical and sexual abuse. By the end of the study, 28 percent of the families had been listed on the child abuse registry. Forty-nine percent of the families had at least one child in care during the study period.

Limitations

The study is limited by the self-selection of the families involved. We compared the participating and non-participating groups on a number of variables and found no significant differences between the groups.

Our ability to generalize the findings to the broader practice of social work is limited by the setting of the study, which is child welfare. Future studies in other fields of practice are needed to determine which findings are universal and which may be particular to this setting and population.

Finally, a major limitation of the study was the introduction of cutbacks in staff and services six months after commencement of data gathering. Much of the study data were gathered during the months preceding these events and thus remained unaffected. Rather than abandoning the second phase of the study, we incorporated the impact of these cutbacks into the design. The findings of this aspect of the study take on added meaning today, as social workers are faced with an increasingly conservative climate that encourages politicians to compete in their efforts to demonstrate their ability to shred the safety net developed over the years to protect our most vulnerable populations. These findings are reviewed in the current sociopolitical context, and the call for social workers to become more actively involved in policy and political efforts is clearly articulated. This author's own experiences as a politically active social worker are used as illustrations.

PART I

A Model of the Helping Process

Part I consists of a single, major chapter that introduces and illustrates the major themes of the interactional approach to social work. Chapter 1 sets the stage for the rest of the book with a discussion of the underlying assumptions of the model, the history of the profession, and the importance of integrating the personal and professional selves. A brief summary of other theoretical approaches places the interactional model in perspective.

1

An Interactional Approach
to Helping

CHAPTER OUTLINE

Social Work Practice Theory

The Client-System Interaction

Underlying Assumptions in the Interactional Model

The Social Work Profession: A Historical Perspective

Social Work Skill and the Working Relationship

The Integration of Personal and Professional Selves

Alternative Social Work Perspectives

In this chapter we will introduce some of the central ideas of the interactional social work practice theory. A discussion of theory-building in social work will place this effort in context. We will view the client in a dynamic interaction with many important social systems (e.g., family, school, hospital). Underlying assumptions about the nature of the relationships between people and their social surroundings will be detailed. Our focus in the assessment process will be on a strengths perspective rather than on client pathology (the medical model). The role of the social work profession as "mediating the individual-social engagement" will be traced to the roots of the profession, which has historically been concerned with both "private troubles" and "public issues."

Social work practice skill will be described as the method by which the social worker strives to develop a positive working relationship with the client. This positive working relationship allows the social worker to help the client. The impact of the social worker's personal self (e.g., feelings, ethics, values) on her or his professional practice will be examined. Alternative views of social work practice will also be noted.

SOCIAL WORK PRACTICE THEORY

Before describing the **interactional model**, I want to comment on the diversity of theories guiding the helping professions. When I wrote the second edition of this book in 1988, I suggested that the helping professions were in what Kuhn described as a "prescientific stage" (Kuhn, 1962). Our profession had just begun to use theories to translate empirical research into practice. In a scientific stage, by contrast, the results of research are used to modify theories, which are then used to guide new research. In the third edition of the text, published in

1992, I suggested we were in transition to a scientific stage and to a more empirically based practice. In this edition, I will integrate recent research results from both quantitative and qualitative methods, which suggests that the helping professions have made the transition and are now in the early phase of a scientific stage.

Since we are just beginning this crucial theory-building process, there is room in the profession for a wide range of views. In recent years social work has seen a significant expansion of efforts to strengthen our theory building by employing empirical approaches. I have completed my own effort to develop a **holistic, empirically based theory** of social work practice, which has at its center the interactional approach to helping (Shulman, 1991).[1] Ideas from that model have been included in this edition, as have findings from the study associated with that effort. In particular, a greater emphasis on *resilience theory* and the *strengths perspective* as models for understanding human behavior will be noted by the reader. Discussion of these models, as well as the *oppression framework*, can be found in Chapter 2.

All practitioners eventually develop their own practice frameworks, some more and some less explicit, and judge them by how well they work in explaining their practice. The framework for social work described in this book has been most helpful to me in my practice, my theory-building, and my research. It is not dogmatically engraved in stone, however, and will continue to be used as a framework just as long as it appears to do the job. Those familiar with the earlier editions of this book will note the evolution of the framework over almost twenty years of practice, teaching, and research. Readers should test its ideas against their own sense of reality and use those portions that seem helpful. Many of the skills and intermediate models are not bound by one approach and can easily fit into other theoretical frameworks. Ideas from other models, some of which are identified and briefly summarized in this chapter, are integrated whenever they help to enrich the core framework.

Since I refer to *practice theory, models,* and *skills* throughout the text, a brief explanation of how I use these terms may be helpful. In developing his framework, Schwartz (1962) defined a practice theory as

> a system of concepts integrating three conceptual subsystems: one which organizes the appropriate aspects of social reality, as drawn from the findings of science; one which defines and conceptualizes specific values and goals, which we might call the problems of policy; and one which deals with the formulation of interrelated principles of action (p. 270).[2]

A practice theory, then, should first describe what we know about human behavior and social organizations. Based upon these underlying assumptions, the worker should establish a set of specific goals or outcomes. Finally, a description of the worker's actions to achieve these specific goals completes the practice theory. This approach to theorizing about practice is used throughout the text. For example, when we examine the beginning phase of work, assumptions about how people behave in new situations are related to outcomes the worker wishes to achieve in first sessions. These outcomes, in turn, are linked to specific activities of the worker, described as *contracting*.[3]

The term **model** is used to describe a representation of reality. One would construct a model to help simplify the explanation or description of a complex process or object. In this text, models are used to describe helping processes (e.g., the dynamics and skills required in a beginning, middle, or ending phase session), individual and social psychologies (e.g., resiliency theory), and the entities with which we work (e.g., families, groups, communities, or organizations).

The term **skill** refers to a specific behavior that the worker uses in the helping process. Many of the skills described in this text are core relationship skills, useful in the performance of professional as well as personal tasks. For example, empathic skills are needed by parents, spouses, and friends. The focus here will be on their use in relation to social work helping functions.

Finally, although I have been conducting empirical testing of the hypotheses contained in the practice theory, this work should be seen as an ongoing process. The "**grounded theory**" approach to theory building, first described by Glaser and Strauss (1967) in the field of sociology, guides this work. Formal and informal observations from practice are used to develop constructs of the theory. Formal research is conducted both to *test* propositions and to *generate* new ones. Some of the most interesting findings of my earlier study were those that did not support my initial hypotheses. These helped me to expand the theoretical constructs, leading to the development of the more general and holistic theory presented in the text that complements this book (Shulman, 1991).

Many of the core findings about skill from my earlier research, presented in the third edition of this text, have been supported by research in social work and related fields. These findings will be presented with greater confidence. Some propositions have begun to reach the stage at which they may be described, in Rosenberg's (1978) terms, as **theoretical generalizations**. These propositions have received repeated support from a number of research efforts. As these ideas are presented, supportive citations to the literature will be noted. Even these propositions must be open to modification as further empirical efforts direct. It is in this spirit of evolution that the ideas in this book are shared.

THE CLIENT-SYSTEM INTERACTION

A critical factor in the helping process is the way one views the client. In early attempts to conceptualize this process, the helping professions borrowed the **medical model** developed by physicians. Since the term *medical model* has also been used in recent years to characterize a view of the client that focuses on illness and pathology, we must make clear that it is used here in another sense. The medical model referred to here is the three-step process of thinking about practice commonly described as study, diagnosis, and treatment. In this framework, the knowing professional studied the client, attempted to make an accurate diagnosis, and then developed a treatment plan.

It is entirely possible that practitioners who are preoccupied with illness or pathology and those who use other models of viewing clients (e.g., **systems or ecological approaches** or a *strengths perspective*) may still be employing a medical model in the way they conceptualize their practice. Even practitioners who reject what they term clinical practice as "Band-Aid" help, and who advocate social action and advocacy, often employ the medical model in their thinking. The only difference, in their case, is that it is the "system" that is studied, diagnosed, and treated.[4]

One of several problems with this model was the heavy emphasis on the study phase, in which the social worker attempted to obtain a great deal of information about the client (e.g., family history, work history, medical history), in order to develop what was called the *psycho-social study* upon which the diagnosis and resulting treatment plan were developed.

Obtaining such information in the early stage was important, and in some settings, essential for reimbursement of the service, yet the question-and-answer format could lead workers to ignore the equally important processes required to engage the client and to begin to develop the working relationship.

The following example illustrates how a social work student begins to connect with her new client during their first session, loses the client as she switches to taking the family history, and then catches herself as she reconnects with her client on an emotional level.

Worker: Come on in and sit down. If you get too cold, just tell me and I will close the window.

Client: No, that's fine, it's very nice outside. So, what is your experience, your specialization? They tell me this is an important question to ask.

Worker: Well, I'm a second-year graduate student at the School of Social Work. This is my second internship. My first one was at a child welfare office. I could tell you all of the theories I have learned and books I have read, but I think it is more important for you to see how comfortable you are with me.

Client: I never had therapy before so I guess we'll make a good team.

Worker: What brought you here today?

Client: I felt like driving my car into the canal. I left my husband in Florida, and I came home. I feel like this is where I belong. Basically, I feel like I'm drowning. (Tears filled her eyes.)

Worker: Sounds like this is a very painful time for you. (Client is silent, head down.)

Worker: When did you leave Florida?

Client: Two and a half weeks ago. I went to Florida a year ago to save my marriage. I gave up everything for him—my friends, family, job—and I realize the sacrifice is not worth it. I'm experiencing the empty nest syndrome without the children. I had to adjust to his family, his way of living. There was no communication between us. I became scared! I felt more like his roommate. I always have to take care of everyone!

Worker: You sound angry.

Client: Yes, and I'm tired of it!

Worker: Since this is an intake I need to ask you some questions in order to complete the paperwork portion of our meeting.

Client: Oh, I'm sorry. Go ahead.

Worker: Don't be sorry. I just wanted you to know we needed to shift gears for awhile.

Client: Go ahead; that's fine.

Worker: Tell me about your family.

Client: I have five grown children: Pam, Jane, John, Cathy, and Tina. She's my baby. She recently had a baby and... (tears fill her eyes). That's another subject.

Worker: Seems like babies are a tough subject for you to talk about?

Client: (beginning to cry) It's OK. Go ahead, ask your questions.

Worker: They are not as important as your feelings are right now. We'll have plenty of time later to complete the forms.

When the example was discussed in class, the student worker recognized that she had switched to the questioning format just when the client expressed strong feelings of anger.

Other students in the class acknowledged that having a structured first interview in which they could focus on asking a series of questions made them feel more comfortable, while possibly making the client feel less comfortable. They could also see how important it was to stay close to the feelings of the client. Many of the questions would be answered in the course of the interview, and the social worker could always leave some time at the end to obtain the missing data.

Since assessment schemes are usually integrated into the practices of social agencies, I take the tack of trying to help my students develop a workable approach while recognizing its limitations. We develop creative approaches for obtaining the required information and skillfully engaging the client in the first interview. Involving the client actively in the process, discussing the reasons for the information gathering, and making sure that the study phase does not substitute for contracting work are essential elements. Students are also encouraged to find ways of relating to the team when discussing specific clients, such as in a case conference, which may effect a shift in attitude toward clients that is more strength-focused than pathology directed. In later chapters we will examine assessment models and systems work in more detail.

Another problem with the medical model was that it tended to make us think of clients in static terms. The emphasis was on attributing descriptive characteristics to the client (e.g., resistant, hard to reach). Even the term *therapy*, often used by social workers to describe work with individuals, families, and groups (e.g., family therapy) implies that something is wrong with the client that requires fixing. For a number of years now, dynamic systems theory has profoundly influenced the way helping professionals view their clients. One central idea has been the emphasis on viewing a client in interaction with others.[5] Instead of a client being the object of analysis, workers began to focus on the way in which the client and the client's important systems were interacting. In fact, according to this viewpoint, it is impossible to understand the movements of the client except as they were affected by the movements of others.

This shift in thinking can be illustrated using the example of a middle-aged woman admitted to a psychiatric ward of a hospital suffering from depression. One could choose to focus only on her depression and other symptoms. In fact, our current knowledge about the biological sources of some forms of depression requires that we be aware of treatment possibilities that can include the use of **psychotropic drugs**.

An alternative framework would also seek to identify those important systems in her life with which she is having to deal: her husband, her children, her job, her peer group, her parents or siblings, her society and its many sexist attitudes, and so on. In addition, one could include the hospital, her doctor, ward staff, and fellow patients. A diagrammatic way of viewing this is shown below.

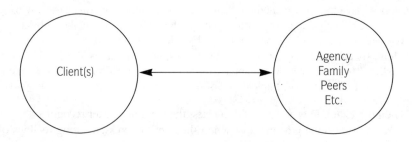

This important change in perspective leads to a change in the kind of questions the worker mentally asks. Instead of simply focusing on the state of the patient's mental health, the degree of the depression, and its possible cause (e.g., physiological, early childhood trauma, substance abuse or dependency), the worker is equally curious about the state of the interactions between the patient and each of the relevant systems. What is the nature of the relationship between the woman and her husband? Can they talk to and listen to each other? Is the relationship abusive in either an emotional or physical way? The worker would also be interested in the relationship between the patient and the hospital. How well is the patient integrating into the ward? Is she reaching out to other patients, creating an informal support group, or is she cut off and isolated?

These are not questions the worker will be asking the client in the early interviews—the structure of first sessions will be discussed later. Rather, they are examples of the potential areas of work upon which the helping process may focus. Furthermore, the worker will not focus only on the client's part in the interaction. As stated earlier, the client's movements can only be understood in relation to the movements of those around her. How well do the family, friends, and the other clients reach out to her? Part of the outcome of these interactions will be determined by the client's input, but other parts will be a result of the system's responses. In fact, the relationship will be reciprocal, with the movements of each constantly affecting the movements of the others.

If we were to apply some of the more recent "self in relation" theory, emerging from efforts to rethink women's psychology initiated by Miller (1976, 1987) and continued by Miller and Stiver (1991), Gilligan, Lyons, and Hammer (1990), as part of the Harvard Project on Women's Psychology and Girls' Development, and by others at the Stone Center in Wellesley, Massachusetts (e.g., Fedele, 1994; Jordan, 1991, 1993); we might rethink this client's situation in terms of "paradoxes." For example, Fedele (1994), in an article on the use of relational theory in group work practice, describes a central paradox first identified by Miller (1988, p. 3) as follows:

> This paradox states that during the course of our lifetime, in the desire to make connections and be emotionally accessible, we all experience harm or violation that leads to a need to develop strategies to keep large parts of ourselves out of connection. In the face of intense yearning for connection and in order to remain in the only relationships available, we develop strategies that keep *more and more* of ourselves out of connection. Simply put, the paradox is that in order to stay in connection, we keep parts of ourselves out of connection.

The relational model will be discussed in more detail as one of the group development theories outlined in Chapter 14, but for now, the paradox of maintaining connection through disconnecting offer some additional insights into the potential causes of a client's depression, rooted in current and possibly past experiences. It also suggests a line of work as we help our client to find ways of making new connections (with family members, the hospital, other women in a mutual aid support group) without the need for maintaining the disconnection defenses.

In addition, to truly understand our client, we need to understand her interactions in the context within which they take place. We are increasing our understanding of how our society's stereotypes of women and men affect relationships. In many examples, when one looks beneath the depression of some middle-aged women, one finds an understandable anger, even rage, related to sex-role stereotyping and oppression by a male-dominated society. Does the woman experience herself as able to influence her social environment, or does she feel powerless (Weick and Vandiver, 1982)? Has she experienced significant victimization in her life (Berlin and Kravetz, 1981)? Is this a situation where it is important to empower the client (Smith and Siegal, 1985)? Does our view of her situation change if we apply one of the many feminist models recently summarized by Saulnier (1996), such as "liberal feminism," "radical feminism," or "postmodern feminism"?[6]

If the client is also a person of color and economically disadvantaged, then we have the classic triple oppressions related to gender, race, and class. A severe depression in response to the oppressive conditions imposed by the increasing "feminization of poverty" (Sarri, 1985), or the impact of recent welfare reform efforts that require recipients to find work when jobs are unavailable and resources are limited, may well represent an understandable defensive reaction.

Oppression psychology, as described by Fanon and discussed in more detail in Chapter 2, suggests that prolonged exposure to oppression could lead an oppressed client to internalize the "oppressor without," adopting negative self attitudes and images. Internalized rage, often masked by depression, can lead to maladaptive and destructive behavior to themselves and others. "The oppressor without becomes an *introppressor*—an oppressor within." (Bulhan, 1985, p. 126). Such a client becomes an "*autopressor*" by participating in her or his own oppression. Ironically, and conveniently, the maladaptive behavior which results from prolonged experience of oppression is then used by the majority group to justify continued stereotyping and oppression, maintaining a vicious cycle.

If the client is also **vulnerable**—for example, lacking a strong social support system of family or friends—then the essentially maladaptive responses of the client become all the more understandable. In addition, given the client's situation, one has to be impressed by the strength the client has shown in simply surviving and continuing to struggle. By considering a *strengths perspective* and a *resiliency model* (discussed in detail in Chapter 2), the social worker can focus on that part of the client which has demonstrated a capacity to deal with life.

A worker starting from this perspective will be more interested in identifying what is right about the client than what is wrong. It is the subtle signs of life and strength that the worker will reach for in trying to help the client to overcome the effects of the oppression.

As the client-system interactions are identified, the depression may take on new meaning. The sadness and passivity are not the problems; rather, they are the symptoms of the breakdown in these important interactions and the result of the experienced oppression. The depression is not the illness to be cured, but rather a signal that important areas of interaction in the life of this woman have broken down. The worker's efforts will not be directed to "curing" the client, but rather to having some impact on the way the client and these important systems interact. The cure for the "problem" will emerge not from the professional's treatment plan, but rather from the client's increasing understanding of her situation and her own efforts to find new ways to reach out to the systems that matter to her, or to cut herself off from them and find new sources of support. Similarly, the systems may have to find new ways to reach out to this client in order to re-engage her. Both the client and the systems may find implementation of this process difficult. Here, the job of the social worker comes in.

At this point, many questions and possibly some objections may have occurred to the reader. What if the client is too weak to deal with the system, doesn't want help, and refuses to work on the interaction? Perhaps the problem is with the system. As mentioned earlier, what happens if the depression is related to biological factors for which pharmaceutical treatment is needed, perhaps in conjunction with counseling? These and other objections are pursued in some detail in the discussions that follow. For the moment, try to set them aside. At this point, the most important concept to grasp is that the person to be helped is viewed as an interactive entity, acting and reacting to the various demands of the systems she must negotiate. The systems will be viewed in this way as well.

Each client is a special case within this general model. The unwed pregnant teen in a child welfare agency might be dealing with the systems of the agency, the child's father, family, friends, societal attitudes as reflected in recent welfare legislation, prejudices towards women and sexuality in general, and so on. Of equal concern to her may be issues of income (welfare or work), housing, child care, and the medical system. If she lives in a group care home, the house parents and other residents become part of the active systems in her life. Her feelings about herself as a woman, her reactions to society's norms, and her own, often harsh, judgments of herself (the oppressor within) may all be part of her agenda, but always in relation to the way in which she deals with those systems that matter to her. Whatever the category of client discussed in this book—the child in the residential center, the husband in marital counseling, the student who is failing, the client with a terminal illness, the client learning to live with AIDS, the client in the early stages of recovery from substance abuse, or the member of a citizens' community action group—all will be viewed in the context of the interaction with their social surroundings and an understanding of the potential strengths.

UNDERLYING ASSUMPTIONS IN THE INTERACTIONAL MODEL

All models of social work practice are based upon some underlying assumptions about people and their social surroundings. These are the starting points for theory building, and they need to be made explicit. While there are many additional assumptions about people and the helping process that will be examined throughout this book, three core ideas underlying the interactional model are presented here. The first is the belief in the essential **symbiotic relationship** between people and their social surroundings. The second is the assumption that this mutual need is systematically blocked by obstacles, some raised by the client and others by the systems the client must negotiate. The third basic assumption is that the social worker must always assume and reach for the client's (and system's) strengths for change. These assumptions are explored in the sections that follow.

Assumption of Symbiosis

Now that we have placed clients in interaction with the various systems that impinge upon them, some attention must be given to the nature of this relationship. If we return to the example in the previous section of a depressed, middle-aged woman, our view of how to help this client will depend upon our assumptions about the individual-social engagement. If we examine her interactions with her environment, we can perceive a certain amount of ambivalence. Some part of her will seem to be reaching out, however faintly, towards life and the people around her. On the other hand, her withdrawal, depression, and general communications appear to signal a retreat from life. She may have experienced life as being too difficult, her feelings too painful to face, and the demands seemingly impossible to meet.

A part of her seems to be giving up and saying that the very struggle seems useless. She can be observed placing barriers between herself and these systems, including that part of the system (the worker) which is reaching out to help her. She is simultaneously reaching out for life, growth, and the important systems around her while also moving away from each.

The assumption that a part of us is always striving towards health is at the core of the practice theory formulated by Schwartz. Borrowing a "symbiotic" model of human relationships, he views the individual-social interaction as

> a relationship between the individual and his nurturing group which we would describe as "symbiotic"—each needing the other for its own life and growth, and each reaching out to the other with all the strength it can command at a given moment (Schwartz, 1961, pp. 146–147).

The term *symbiotic* is used to describe the mutual need of individuals and the systems that matter to them. This woman's needs can best be met in interaction with the world around her, not through complete withdrawal from it. In a like manner, society has a stake in maintaining this client as an active, involved, unique, integrated individual.[7] The symbiotic striving idea fits comfortably with the constructs of the relational model described earlier.

Unfortunately, the term *symbiotic* has taken on a professional connotation of unhealthy mutual overdependency, as for example, between a mother and child.[8] In the world of biology, symbiosis actually describes two organisms living in a mutually beneficial relationship. The exploitation of one organism by another would be described as a parasitic relationship.

Schwartz uses the term to underline our mutual dependency and our essential interest in each other. It is a statement of the interdependence that is fundamental to our belief in a social responsibility for the welfare of each individual. It also recognizes that each individual finds life's needs best satisfied in positive relationships with others.[9]

You may be wondering at this point how this assumption of a "symbiotic" model relates to experiences where individual-social interaction appears to be far from symbiotic and in fact, has been defined as often oppressive. Schwartz (1961, p. 15) points out that

> in a complex and often distorted society, the individual-social symbiosis grows diffuse and obscure in varying degrees, ranging from the normal developmental problems of children growing into their culture to the severe pathology involved in situations where the symbiotic attachment appears to be all but severed.

The very fact that the mutual self-interest of people and their surrounding systems is often obscured creates the working ground for the helping professional. The observation that people and their systems often appear to be acting against each other's self-interest is not an argument against the symbiotic model; rather it is an argument for some helping person to assist both to regain their sense of mutuality.

In a like manner, the worker will search for the part of the family, friends, peer group, and hospital system that is reaching out towards the patient. For instance, if the husband appears to turn away from his wife during the family session, closing off his feelings, then the worker might reach for the underlying sense of loss and hurt that he attempts to hide even from himself. When the hospital rules, procedures, and services seem to work against the best interests of a patient, the helping person will attempt to influence that part of the system which cares about the people it serves, employing a number of strategies including mediation, brokering, or advocacy.

This powerful idea recurs continually throughout this book. In example after example, you will observe that the helping person's movements with the client—the moment-by-moment interventions—are affected by the worker's view of the individual-social relationship. At critical moments in the interactions, connections will be discovered between husbands and wives, parents and children, students and teachers, community groups and politicians, individual group members and the group, and so forth, because the helping person was searching for them. This idea will be termed the **two-clients construct**, in which the social worker will always be seen as having two clients. The second client will change in each situation. For the current example, it may be the woman's family, the hospital system, friends, and so on.

The practical implications of this philosophical assumption are important. For example, in the case of our female client, the worker's belief in the importance of helping her to find her connections to people around her and the belief in this woman's partial striving for this connection will cause the worker to search for faint clues that the client is still emotionally alive and trying. The worker will not be fooled by the defenses thrown up by the client and will concentrate instead on the spark of life that still exists, often associated with the anger, even rage, buried under the depression and apathy. The work of the helping person will not be to find ways to re-motivate the client, but rather to discover and develop the motivation that is already there. For that part of her behavior which is related to the experience of oppression, always present in some form and to some degree, helping the client to understand the nature of her internalized oppressor will be an important step in helping her to take control over her life and to begin dealing with the oppressor without.

A belief in this symbiotic model does not have to ignore the existence of important tensions and real conflicts of interest between the individual and the systems. Interactions in life involve conflict and confrontation. Not all interests are mutual. Oppression happens for a reason. The effective helping person will bring out into the open these underlying differences so that the engagement will be a real human process invested with a range of feelings. This process will be illustrated with examples by which the skilled helper challenges the illusion of agreement between the parties in conflict by reaching for and demanding real work. What the model does is provide the worker with a sense of the potential common ground upon which both the client and the important life systems can build.

If we are to be effective in this role, we need to begin by recognizing that oppression clearly has some psychological and concrete payoffs for the majority group in any situation. For example, when a man uses battering and intimidation to attempt to control a woman in his life, he receives psychological and concrete benefits from the interaction. If we consider the "master-slave" paradigm developed by Hegel in 1807 (Hegel, 1966 reprint), elements of which underlie oppression theory, the insecure "master" seeks to "recognize" or define himself through the unreciprocated recognition by the "slave" (Bulhan, 1985, p. 102). In effect, the male batterer uses the subjugation of his female partner to bolster his sense of self by his partner "recognizing" him without his having to "recognize" her. *In considering such relationships, we must always be clear that our first concern should be the protection of persons experiencing oppression and the holding of the oppressors accountable for their actions. Battering is a criminal offense and must be treated as such.* Work with a battered woman often involves helping her find her own strength and the social resources needed to safely leave the abusive relationship. However, if we were to work with the male batterer, as well, we would need to recognize that this use of violence for control can have significant negative effects on him, including legal consequences, emotional damage to the self, and precluding of an intimate relationship based on mutuality and equality—a relationship of mutual recognition.

One can extend this individual psychology to a social psychology if we recognize that the wider sexist attitudes which support this brutal form of oppression can be explained by the same psychological dynamics. Not only are there psychological payoffs to sexism, there are concrete and financial privileges and rewards as well. When women are consistently paid less than men for the same jobs, profits, even in nonprofit organizations, are higher. When a "glass ceiling" stops women (and other minority groups) from advancing in business or government agencies, more senior positions are available for men and members of the majority groups. Even these gains, however, are offset by the long-term social, moral, and even economic prices paid as a result of such short-sighted practices.

On a broader scale, oppression by all majority groups against all minority groups (e.g., persons of color, women, Asian immigrants, Jews, gays and lesbians, the mentally ill, the physically or mentally challenged) results in specific economic and psychological benefits for the majority group. However, the significant personal, social, and even economic costs are often ignored. For example, when the epidemic of AIDS was viewed as only a problem affecting gays, Haitians, and I.V. drug users, many of whom live in inner-city ghettos, it was largely ignored by the United States government.[10] Some groups actually pointed to this disease as "retribution" for "immoral" behavior and saw the growing numbers of deaths as a "cleansing" of society. While these expressed views were extreme, they may have represented a more general undercurrent of racism and homophobia that fostered lethargy and inaction by the larger community.

One has only to imagine the difference in the response if such an epidemic had initially struck middle-class, heterosexual whites instead of these minority populations. This differential provision of medical research and support to these minority populations represents a deadly form of oppression. The majority group is only now coming to grips with the incredible social and health costs associated with the increase in this epidemic and its spread to the majority population. The same is true if one considers the true costs of the inadequate health care services provided in the United States to the poor and the oppressed. Lack of a universal health care system in the United States stands in stark contrast to programs developed in countries such as Canada. These examples can be added to the list of the many documented examples of racism in medicine, including the "shocking and scandalous...recently halted Tuskegee experiment on syphilis among blacks in Macon County, Alabama" (Bulhan, 1985, p. 87) in which the effects of the untreated disease on 400 black males and their families were observed for more than 40 years without the knowledge of the study participants or the provision of available treatments. (It was only in 1997 that President William Clinton publicly acknowledged and apologized for these actions on behalf of the American people.)

The existence of the many powerful examples in American history of oppression and exploitation of vulnerable populations does not change the essential, symbiotic nature of the relationship between people and their social surroundings. These instances provide evidence of how much we have lost sight of these connections. They also provide a rationale for the unique functional role of the social work profession described later in this chapter.

Assumption of Obstacles in the Engagement

Thus far we have focused on the client's interactions with important environmental systems. Both the individual and the systems are vitally linked through mutual need. Each is seen as reaching out to the other with all the strength available at the moment and with the capacity to reach out more effectively. The next logical question must be: What goes wrong? The mutual dependence can be blocked or obscured by any number of obstacles. We will briefly examine three potential obstacles to interaction between the individual and social system:

changing social systems, conflicts between self-interest and mutual interest, and the dynamics of interpersonal communications.

Increasing Complexity of Human Social Systems. One problem is the increasing complexity of human social systems. Let us take the family as an illustration of an important system. The relationships between parents and children and husbands and wives (or same-sex partners) have become increasingly difficult. Important sources of social support across generations have diminished as modern nuclear families tend to live apart from grandparents and other relatives. As society's norms and values change more rapidly than in past generations, parents are forced to reconcile their own beliefs with the shifting values of their children. The world of work absorbs more time and energy, often leaving parents less opportunity to foster family stability.

Middle-aged parents find themselves attempting to provide support for their adolescent (and often young adult) children, while simultaneously feeling responsible for the well-being of their aged parents. They have been called the "sandwich generation." It is not unusual to hear the complaint: "When will I have time for me?" Is it any wonder that members of the family may find dealing with each other very complicated?

Our definition of "family" has changed dramatically as the typical two-parent family of a generation ago has been replaced by an increasingly high percentage of single-parent families. These families, as well as low-income two-parent families, face increasing stress due to the breakdown of the formal support network—the governmental "safety-net"—as a result of budget cuts. The full impact of the "welfare reform" act of 1996 is not yet known, but early indications, often anecdotal, suggest that at least some of the families cut off from welfare have not been able to make the predicted transition to work and independence and are now far worse off than they were before.

The availability of day care, low-cost housing, financial subsidies, and adequate health care has decreased almost in proportion to the increase in need. Some political and economic leadership has stressed a "me-first" ethic that has encouraged the majority to ignore the needs of the "left-out" populations. We were at first shocked by the appearance of the homeless on our urban streets, then encouraged to be angry at them by political leaders who suggested that shelter was available for anyone who really wanted it.

Periodically, we have experienced severe problems in the economy that have undermined employment stability. Employment patterns relying on temporary workers and corporate restructuring that lays off mid-level managers are also more common. High levels of unemployment and uncertainty have led to increased family tensions. In this author's research project in the child welfare area (Shulman, 1991), workers in British Columbia, Canada, reported significant increases in the number and severity of child abuse cases that appear to be linked to economic stress—either loss of a job or fear of such a loss. Normal family tensions, such as parent-teen conflicts, become exacerbated when parents are under economic stress or attempting to cope with the "earthquake" of unemployment.

Even during stable economic conditions, a politically divided federal government, debates over a "balanced budget," pressures to provide tax breaks (which mostly benefit the wealthy), the rising costs of health care, demands for "smaller government," and the abandonment of federal responsibility to be replaced by state control over health and social welfare programs, have led to an increasing gap between the rich and the poor, the healthy and the sick, the fully participating members of our communities and those who are left out.

More generally, as the poor collected in cities, and as the institutions (welfare, medical, educational) designed to serve them became more complex, the basic relationship between people and these important systems was bound to become obstructed. One need only think of one's reactions to the first day at a new school or to entering a busy hospital in order to remember how strange, overwhelming, and impersonal the system can seem. The obstacles related to complexity are inherent, and often emerge inadvertently from the realities of the system.

Divergence in the Self and Social Interest. A second set of obstacles, mentioned earlier, is associated with the divergent interests of people and the systems that matter to them. Life does not consist only of mutual interest and interdependence. There are times when self-interest directly conflicts with the interests of others. In fact, each individual, as part of the growth process, must learn to set aside his or her own immediate needs in order to integrate into the social order.

For example, in marriage or partnerships, the male may believe he has some stake in maintaining a traditional and privileged gender role. The rules of behavior, norms, and the traditional structures in such relationships provide some payoffs for the male partner. A confident woman who is able to develop a sense of herself differentiated from her husband and her family can be a more interesting person, but she may also intimidate a partner who is struggling with his own sense of worth. Obstacles to the symbiotic relationship can be generated by the ambivalence towards change felt by family members. Rapid changes are anxiety-producing for all in our society, so we often attempt to maintain the status quo and preserve continuity.

Complex systems are also ambivalent towards the people they serve. For example, politicians may view community action pressure groups as thorns in their sides. As these groups expose important unmet needs, they also reveal problems that are difficult to handle. Government bodies face demands from many sources for a share of the economic pie, and to have this pressure heightened by citizen groups creates new difficulties.

While society's fundamental stake is in strengthening and incorporating its most vulnerable populations, it also has an element of economic self-interest in maintaining the poor and in fostering a stereotype that blames them for their own problems. It is easy to see how the need for strong, active, community pressure groups as sources of feedback for our society can be obscured by the immediate need for peace and quiet. In a like manner, large institutions such as schools and hospitals find it easier to deal with students and patients who conform, don't make trouble, and go along with the present order. They often fail to realize the price they pay in terms of effective teaching and healing.

Problems of Interpersonal Communication. A third major set of obstacles involves problems of interpersonal communication. Sharing and understanding painful or taboo thoughts and feelings is hard. People find it difficult to speak of feelings about sex, authority, intimacy, dependency, loss, sexual orientation, and so on. The powerful norms of our society are brought to bear in each interpersonal relationship, often making achievement of mutual understanding difficult. Most important conversations between people take place through the use of indirect communications that can be extremely hard to decipher.

For example, the male partner who feels hurt and rejected by his wife's apparent lack of interest in sexual relations may express this through hostile or sarcastic comments in a totally unrelated area. The wife, in turn, may be expressing her own reactions to the husband's continual criticism through lack of interest in sexual contact. Each may be feeling a powerful and important need for the other that is obscured by the built-up resentment developed by their immature means of communication.

School children who feel the teacher is always on their backs, or is racist, and does not like them respond with failure, lack of preparation, and cutting classes. The teacher, out of frustration at not being able to reach the children, responds with increased exhortation or punishment, or in some cases, by developing stereotypes based upon race, class, ethnicity, or gender. To the children the message is that the teacher does not care. To the teacher, the message is that the children (or their parents) do not care.

In most cases (not all), they are both wrong. Moreover, the children's stake in the successful completion of their education and the teacher's stake in helping students through a difficult learning process may be lost and overwhelmed by their mutual misconceptions. Instead of strengthening the relationship, the children and the teacher turn away from each other. The difficulty of overcoming these obstacles is heightened when reduced financial support for education results in larger classes and diminished support services and special programs for children with special needs.

The gay man who has been diagnosed HIV-positive may feel a strong need to repair a fractured family-of-origin relationship (in those cases where the relationship did not survive his declaration of his sexual orientation). Having been hurt deeply by family rejection, he may be reluctant to contact his parents and inform them of his illness. For the family, the crisis of their son's terminal illness may be the very catalyst needed to break the cycle of rejection and allow for some form of family re-unification and healing. An understandable fear of another painful rejection may cut a client off from his ability to communicate his need for renewed family relationships.

In the relationships between parent and child, hospital ward and patient, student and school, the person with AIDS and his family, individual and group—in each special case of the individual-social engagement—the essential mutual need is fragile and easily obscured by the complexity of the situation, by divergent needs, or by the difficulty involved in communication.

Out of this ever-present possibility of **symbiotic diffusion**, the loss of a clear sense of the symbiotic striving, Schwartz suggests, the need for the social work profession emerged. Our profession's tasks relate directly to the fact that obstacles can easily obscure the mutual dependence between the individual and important systems. When both sides have lost sight of this important connection, a third force is needed to help them regain this understanding. According to Schwartz, the social work profession, with its historical roots firmly planted in two streams—concern for individual well-being and for social justice—is uniquely suited to play this role. This idea of the third force leads to the general function of the social work professional in mediation, described later in the chapter.

Assumption of Strength for Change

Belief in the existence of symbiotic striving is closely linked to another assumption about the individual-social engagement: that both the individual and the system contain within them the potential strength to implement this mutuality. This assumption depends upon a view of people (and complex systems) as being able to act in their own interest without being bound by their past experiences. An alternative approach considers that people fundamentally act according to the sum of the strengths and skills accumulated by past experiences.[11] Causal links may be even drawn between a person's present immobility and earlier traumatic events.

While it seems logical that learning from past experiences will affect the way in which an individual attempts to negotiate new surroundings, the danger exists, with this view, of prejudging and underestimating a client's (or the system's) resiliency, strength, and capacity for change. Within the framework presented here, the individual is best described by actions and is as strong or as weak as he or she acts in the present moment. The practice implication of this attitude is that the worker must believe that the individual or the system has the capacity to move in its own self-interest, even if only by small steps, and that this movement will lead to increased strength and more change. These strengths and resiliency perspectives will be discussed more fully in Chapter 2.

Based upon this basic assumption, the interactional perspective calls for the helping person to always place a **demand for work** before the client. The demand for work will be described as the worker's efforts to have the client work effectively on her or his tasks and to invest that work with energy and affect. It is important to note that the work itself, the goals of the process (even with mandated clients), must be shared by the client as opposed to being imposed by the worker. Also, this demand must be integrated with support in what could be called an empathic demand for work. A similar demand will be placed upon the system.

A familiar expression in this connection is "reach for the client's strength," suggesting that the very act of reaching for strength—that is, believing in the potential of the work and refusing to accept even the client's own self-description of weakness—is a central part of what helps a client to act. Possibly the client has reached the present impasse precisely because all the signals received from important "others" have reinforced belief in the client's own impotence. The social worker, by contrast, will operate on a basic principle: *no matter how hopeless it seems, there is always a next step.*

In an example from my own practice, described later in this book, I confront a group of persons with AIDS in early recovery, who have apparently given up on their ability to have non-exploitive and drug- and alcohol-free intimate relationships with others, to set aside their own concerns and issues and to become a mutual support group for each other. This demand for work is rooted in the belief that even these clients, who have experienced years of polysubstance abuse, prison sentences, prostitution, and traumatic childhood experiences, still have the strength to reach out for each other within the group, which serves as a microcosm of our larger society. Their capacity for caring, as revealed in the detailed process recordings of this group, are a tribute to themselves and an affirmation of the strengths perspective.

These assumptions will interact in important ways in the models and examples shared in this book. Workers will always search for subtle connections and will always make a demand that clients and systems people act on their potential for change. This view of practice is built upon a deep investment in the concept of interdependence, a view of the client as the source of energy for change, healing, and growth, a belief in client strength, and a preoccupation with health rather than sickness.

This stance does not negate the fact that some clients and some systems, for a number of complex reasons, will not be able to use the worker's help at a given moment. The helping process is interactional, with workers carrying out their parts as best they can. Clients also have a part to play, and their strength will help to determine the outcome. Using findings from my own research (Shulman, 1991), and that of others, we will be exploring the ways in which stress, acceptance of a problem, and motivation affect the client's ability to receive help at any given moment.

Socioeconomic factors may also have a profound impact. For example, income, housing, and economic conditions may influence the results. This is all the more reason why social workers must be concerned with social policies that affect the human situation. Recognizing that a particular client may be unable to use help at that time, aware of and working for changes in social policies, the worker will nevertheless always attempt to reach for the client's strength because this is the way in which help is given.

THE SOCIAL WORK PROFESSION: A HISTORICAL PERSPECTIVE

Thus far in the discussion, we have tried to view each client as a special case of the more general individual-social interaction in our society. The issue we explore in this section is the role that the social work profession plays in this process. In considering the role of the profession, we need to examine our unique historical roots. It is beyond the scope of this book to provide a detailed discussion of the complex history of the development of the profession, but an understanding of our roots will place the helping role in perspective.

The Roots of the Profession

The profession, as we know it now, was created through the merger over the years of two basic streams of thought about the helping process. One was rooted in the work of those interested in issues of social change. An example was the early settlement house movement, most often associated with the work of Jane Addams at Hull House, founded in 1889 (Addams, 1961).[12] This movement, which began in England, was one of the many established at the turn of the century to try to cope with the stresses created by the major social forces of urbanization, industrialization, and the large-scale influx of immigrants to North America. The mission of these early, community-oriented social agencies included attempting to help immigrant and other poor families to more effectively integrate into our society. At the same time, the leadership of these movements, largely consisting of middle and upper-class liberals of the day, waged a fight against the social conditions facing these populations. Poor housing and health services, child labor, sweat-shop conditions in urban factories, all became targets for social change.

While Jane Addams was noted for her more radical approach to working with and involving actively oppressed people, it should be noted that many in the settlement house movement incorporated a "doing for" approach to the populations with which they worked. Little effort was directed at actually organizing the poor, through an **empowerment process**, to fight effectively against the forces of oppression related to class, gender, race, ethnicity, and the like. An empowerment process involves engaging the client (individual, family, group, or community) in developing strengths to personally and politically cope more effectively with those systems that are important to them. It is likely that if the leaders of these early social movements had attempted to mobilize client groups in this way, they would have been viewed as too radical and would have themselves experienced political repression.

In addition, this early movement saw as a major role the acculturation of the poor to the values and beliefs of their own upper-middle-class society. Developing an appreciation of the arts, such as classical music and literature, and participating in other "refined" activities were seen as paths for self-improvement and "building character." Workers often lived with clients in the settlement houses, with helping conceived of as practical in nature. For example, if cities were overcrowded and unhealthy, then children needed to be removed to camps in the country during the summer. It was not until the 1930s that this social-change-oriented movement merged into the mainstream of the emerging social work profession. It was this early driving concern for social justice for vulnerable populations which gave the social work profession an important element of its current identity. The early roots of the group work and community organization methods can be traced to these professional pioneers.

The other major stream of professional development was rooted in a focus on fulfilling individual needs. The founder of this stream is often identified as Mary Richmond, whose work at the Charities Organization Society is seen as having made a major contribution towards the professionalization of social work (Richmond, 1918). Her efforts were directed at moving social work beyond the notion of "friendly visitors" who were charitable to the poor toward a systematic, professional approach to helping. Richmond was interested in the helping process and wanted it to be recorded, analyzed, and then taught.

By the 1930s, two new specializations in social work had developed: group work and community organization. Group work was closely associated with the informal education and socialization movements. Early leaders included Grace Coyle (1948), Gertrude Wilson and Gladys Ryland (1949). The focus of the work was on helping people cope with the normative tasks of life through the use of the peer group. A typical group might consist of teenagers forming a social club in a community center, with the group worker assigned to help them learn to work effectively together. Activities such as games, singing, crafts, or bowling were all mediums through which group members could enjoy recreation and work on the appropriate individual and group developmental tasks.

The early community organization activity was designed to coordinate social services through, for example, councils of social agencies. A second function was to raise funds for private social welfare activities through organizations such as community chests, the forerunners of today's United Way campaigns. It would not be until the late 1950s and early 1960s, reflecting the social activist themes of the times, the civil right movement, and borrowing from community action and organizer models developed by activists such as Saul Alinsky (Reitzes & Reitzes, 1986), that community organization practice would shift to an approach that emphasized organizing and empowering clients and other members of the community to achieve social changes.

Specht (1988) describes the convergence of the three streams of casework, group work, and community organization in the mid-1930s as creating the "Social Work Trinity."[13] Social work practice had evolved into specializations: social casework, social group work, and community organization. Each drew on different theories. Community organization was related clearly enough to the organizational frameworks within which social casework was practiced to make the relationship practical even though it was not compatible philosophically and theoretically. Social group work began with a philosophical concern for social improvement and moral uplift of disadvantaged people. However, social casework focused on individual causes of problems, while social group work concentrated on citizen education for social action and social development (p. 36). Thus, these three major modalities of practice, each defined by the targeted client (individual, family, group, and community), merged to become the modern-day social work profession.

This creation of a unified profession was consummated in 1955, when seven separate social work organizations (the American Association of Group Workers; the American Association of Medical Social Workers; the American Association of Psychiatric Social Workers; the American Association of Social Workers; the National Association of School Social Workers; the Social Work Research Group, and the Association for the Study of Community Organizations) united to form a common professional organization, the National Association of Social Workers. While sharing a code of ethics, value system, knowledge and skills, social workers still differentiated themselves into groups by methodology, describing themselves as caseworkers, group workers, or community organizers.

For the caseworkers, the "friendship" of the friendly visitors became the "relationship" of the clinician with the client. The strong influence of psychoanalytic theory was evident at schools of social work, and with very few exceptions, the diagnostic model of medicine—the three-phase process of study, diagnosis, and treatment—was seen as a model of professionalism worthy of emulation.

In more recent years, the three modalities of practice have been subsumed under two more general categories. Casework, family work, and group work are often combined into "micro" or "clinical" practice. Community organization practice has become more closely linked to policy and management-oriented social work in a "macro" sub-grouping. A trend toward the de-emphasis of specialization has led to the wider use of the term "**generalist practice**," which has come to describe "a social work practitioner whose knowledge and skills encompass a broad spectrum and who assesses problems and their solutions comprehensively" (Barker, 1991, p. 91). The term **generic social work** is often used interchangeably with *generalist practice*, although if refers more specifically to the "social work orientation which emphasizes a common core of knowledge and skills associated with social service provision" (Barker, 1991, p. 92).

This historical review presents an oversimplified description of the development of the social work profession. For our purposes, the major point of this section is that the profession is the product of a unique merger of interest in individual healing and social change for social justice. This is the basis for what will be presented as the "two-client" idea, which is central to the interactional model of social work. In the complex interaction between the individual and her or his social surroundings (e.g., society, community, family, small group), the social work professional will always be identifiable because of her or his attention to both clients. While common values, knowledge, beliefs, skills, professional associations, codes of ethics, and so on, help to unify the profession, it is our shared sense of our function in society that makes social work a unique profession.

The Function of the Social Work Profession

In developing his view of the social work profession's function in society, Schwartz (1969) did not accept the broadly held idea that the profession was defined solely by a common knowledge base, values, and skills. He also rejected the notion that the profession's function could be described by statements that referred to aspirations for positive general outcomes, such as "enhancing social functioning" or "facilitating individual growth and development." He understood that a profession required a general and yet unique functional statement that would direct the actions of all social workers, regardless of the setting in which they practiced. While many variant elements of practice would be introduced by the particular problems facing the client, the mission of the agency or host setting, the modality of service (e.g., individual counseling, group, family), the age and stage of life of the client, etc., Schwartz viewed professional function as a core common element of any social work practice theory.

The term **function** is defined here as the specific part the profession, and each social work professional, plays in the helping process. For example, the analogy of an automobile engine may be helpful. If we defined the function of the carburetor as "contributing to help-ing to make car move," we would be defining function in terms of outcome. This would not provide specific direction to a carburetor, which would be left on its own to figure out how to play its part in the process. On the other hand, if we specifically defined the carburetor's function as mixing air and gasoline to create a vapor which could then by ignited by a spark plug, our anthropomorphic carburetor would have a clear idea of how to do its part. If all parts of the engine understood clearly their functional roles, and if all parts implemented that role effectively, the car would start to move. (This marks the limits of the author's understanding of automotive engineering, so he will stick to social work from now on.)

It is this sense of functional preciseness that Schwartz felt was required to help every so-cial worker understand his or her role in the many complex situations faced in day-to-day prac-tice. This professional role would travel with the social worker to any agency or host setting and would, in part, define the social worker's interventions at any given moment. We would be able to recognize a social worker in action, and distinguish him or her from other profes-sionals with similar knowledge, values, and skills, because we would see the functional role in action. Schwartz's definition of the function of the social work profession was based upon underlying assumptions about the essentially symbiotic nature of the individual-social rela-tionship. He examined the history of the profession and tried to identify the essential functional assignment that might define a unique role for social work.

His definition of the professional function is "to mediate the process through which the individual and his society reach out for each other through a mutual need for self-fulfillment." To the earlier diagram of a hypothetical client attempting to deal with a number of important systems, a third force is introduced.[14]

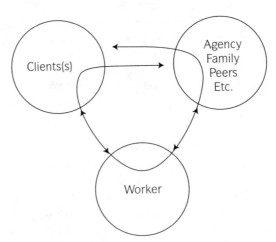

With the addition of the worker, the basic triangular model is complete. On the left is the client reaching out with all available strength, attempting to negotiate important systems while often simultaneously throwing up defenses that cut him or her off from the needed systems. On the right are the systems (family, school, hospital staff, and so on) reaching out to incor-porate the client but often reaching ambivalently. At the bottom is the social worker, whose sense of function and skills are mobilized in an effort to help client and system overcome the obstacles that block their engagement.

One could argue that this functional statement is too limited. I have already indicated that the term *mediation* is used in a broad sense and can include other activities such as confrontation and advocacy. There are times when the crucial work in the area between the helping person and the system requires conflict and social pressure. In one example, in Chapter 20, dealing with community organization practice, the social worker helps a tenant group confront the political system because of the non-responsiveness of the housing project administrator.

Even with a broad interpretation of mediation, however, one might still argue that this functional statement is too limited. The argument in response is that if the helping person is clear about the helping function and that function is specifically defined, than there is a better chance of consistently performing it. Jessie Taft (1942), one of the early leaders of the "functional school" of social work practice, stressed this view. In addition, the client who understands what the helping person does—the way in which help is given—will be better able to use the worker's services.

Work with couples in couple counseling provides a good illustration. The division between the couple has caused most people they know (family, friends, co-workers) to take sides with one or the other. An early, often unstated question on the minds of both partners as they enter the counseling process is "Whose side will the social worker be on?" Only through explanation and demonstration will the skillful worker help the couple understand that the worker's ability to help them depends upon being on both sides at the same time. Practice experience has taught most workers that the moment they identify with one side versus the other, they have lost their usefulness to the client who feels cut off.

Clarity about one's professional function and role in the helping process is essential for effective practice. When a social worker is clear about his or her part in the interaction, there will be less likelihood of the worker taking over the client's part—for example, doing things *for* the client instead of *with* the client. Once a social worker has integrated a sense of professional function, then the communications, relationship, and problem-solving skills become the tools through which the social worker puts her or his function into action.

A profession is not defined uniquely by its knowledge, values, and skills. It is differentiated from other professions by its functional role. For example, in a hospital, empathy skills are important for the social worker, the doctor, and the nurse. Each professional must harness these skills in pursuit of his or her separate functions. In the scores of illustrations included in this book, the reader will note that the moments in which social workers get in trouble in their practice are usually the moments when they lose their sense of functional clarity. For example, we will examine incidents in family work in which the social worker identifies with the children and loses the parents. Such a worker is no longer able to help the family work on its issues. One might see ongoing professional development as a continual deepening of the social worker's understanding of his or her helping function as well as understanding those situations which tend to cause functional confusion and functional diffusion. Functional diffusion occurs when the social worker tries to be everything for everyone, losing sight of the core job. This is not a terminal illness, however, and is usually cured by a dose of functional clarity.

At this point, the reader may be wondering how generally applicable this mediation assignment can be. In the rest of the book we will work toward the answer, drawing illustrations from a range of settings with varying types of individuals, families, groups, and communities. In each example, the reader should mentally step into the shoes of the worker. The argument is that the worker's sense of the next step at specific moments of interaction will be vitally affected by an internalized sense of function. These introductory comments have laid out the general model applied in each step of analysis throughout the book. A further elaboration of this function and worker tasks will be shared in the context of practice illustrations.

SOCIAL WORK SKILL AND THE WORKING RELATIONSHIP

At the core of the interactional theory of social work practice is a model of the helping process in which the skill of the worker helps to create a positive working relationship. In turn, this relationship is the medium through which the worker influences the outcomes of practice. This simple model can be visualized as follows:

While the model suggests that skills leads to relationship which influences outcomes, the double-pointed arrows imply that the model is dynamic. For example, a change in the working relationship will affect the worker's use of skill. A worker may be influenced in her or his interaction with a client by the changing nature of the relationship (e.g., a positive relationship leading to more empathy on the worker's part). In a like manner, positive or negative outcomes for the client may influence his or her sense of the relationship.

Another model incorporated into this theory has to do with the relationship between our clients' ability to *manage their feelings* and their ability to manage their problems.[15] These ideas were developed as part of the theory-building effort described in other publications (Shulman, 1978; 1981; 1991). The construct is based upon the assumption that how we feel has a powerful effect on how we act. The relationship between feelings and action is reciprocal in nature; how we act also influences how we feel.

To this feeling-behavioral connection we can add a third element: cognition. Cognition refers to the way our clients think about themselves and their environment. The contributions of cognitive-behavioral theory (Berlin, 1983a) have helped us to broaden our understanding of how a client's perception of reality can have a powerful impact on self-image, identification of the nature of a problem, and self-assessment of the ability to cope. It will be argued throughout this book that how our clients think affects how they feel, which affects how they act, in a circular and reciprocal manner. The model presented could be termed a cognitive-affective-behavioral framework without confusing it with other models that incorporate cognitive-behavioral approaches.

For example, it is not uncommon for female survivors of childhood sexual abuse to describe themselves as "damaged goods" as they enter their teenage years. These clients often respond to the oppression they have experienced by internalizing a negative self-image and assuming some form of responsibility for what was done to them. They may express feelings of guilt and concern that they may have been "seductive" toward the offending adult, thus shifting responsibility for the problem to themselves—a form of blaming the victim. This is an example of the internalized oppressor at work. Symptoms of depression and personal apathy often cover an underlying rage that the child learned to suppress in order to survive. The use of alcohol and drugs provides an escape, a flight from the pain associated with the abuse, and is an example of the self-destructive behavior described earlier in which oppressed clients become "autopressors."

The association between these perceptions of low self-image, and the feelings they generate, may lead these teenage survivors to enter into relationships and life patterns that tend to perpetuate their exploitation. For example, a low sense of self-esteem may lead to relationships with exploitive men who use physical, emotional, and sexual violence to maintain control over the lives of women. The use of drugs and involvement in the street culture may lead to prostitution. These actions on the client's part, related to the client's feelings, may in turn deepen the sense of being "damaged." Thus, a negative reciprocal relationship between how the client feels, thinks, and acts results in a deepening of the problems in living.

An intervention is needed to disrupt this vicious cycle. In the example of the survivor, as the worker helps a client (or groups of clients) to examine the underlying pain and rage, and to face the oppressor within, the client can begin to take control of the emotions and more effectively manage them rather than being managed by them. Effective practice can help the client to *reframe* the source of the problem and begin to perceive herself as a survivor rather than a victim. The principle of dealing with *feelings in pursuit of purpose*, to be discussed and illustrated in more detail in later chapters, will cause the worker to help the client to connect her feelings and perceptions with her actions. Awareness of the connections between how we think, feel, and act is an early step in taking control over these thoughts and feelings and of our resultant behaviors. As these feelings are better managed by the client and she can develop a more accurate assessment of herself and her situation, she can begin to more effectively manage her life problems. Success with her life's problems, in turn, will influence her thoughts and feelings.

For example, the teenage survivor in this illustration may begin to change her self-destructive behavior by taking some first step on her own behalf. Obtaining help with her addiction, leaving the street for a shelter, or attempting to break off from an abusive and exploitive relationship may be the first step in breaking out of her trap. Each step that she takes in her own self-interest, however small, can contribute to a more positive feeling about herself and strengthen her to take the next step. Thus, managing her feelings helps her to manage her problems, and managing her problems helps her to manage her feelings.

As this model is explored, we will see that if the worker is to help clients manage their feelings, the worker must be able to manage his or her own emotions. For example, a worker whose client is a survivor of sexual abuse, feeling the woman's pain, may prematurely attempt to reassure her that she is not damaged. Or the worker may take on the woman's anger against the men who have exploited her, which may preempt the client's essential work in facing her own anger. Both of these understandable emotional reactions by the worker may block the client's ability to manage her own feelings. The worker would need to share his or her sense of the client's pain without trying to relieve it. For example:

> As I listen to you I'm feeling how much pain you are in, how damaged you must feel. A big part of me wants to say "Don't feel that way! You are a person of value." But I know that no matter what I say the pain is there, and I can't make it go away.

The anger against the exploitive men—for example, a sexually abusive father—can also be shared, but in a manner which helps the client to face her own anger rather than doing the work for her. For example,

It makes me angry when I think of what was done to you by people you expected to take care of you and to protect you. But from what you are saying to me, it seems that your feelings are mixed right now. It sounds like a big part of you wishes your family could be different, could change, and that you could still be like a real family.

Sharing the worker's feelings, in an integration of personal and professional selves, will be a crucial element in this model.

The eight skills examined in my study (Shulman, 1991) were drawn from those that proved to be most important in my prior research (Shulman, 1978, 1979a). Twenty-two specific skills were examined in that study with 10 of the 22 associating at a significant level with developing a positive relationship and worker helpfulness. While all of these skills, and others, are discussed in the chapters that follow, a particular emphasis is placed on the eight skills examined in the more recent work. (The reader should review the outline of this research provided in the Introduction and the detailed discussion of the study methodology in Appendix A.) These eight skills have been organized into two groupings. The list below summarizes the two sets of skills:

WORKERS' SKILLS FOR HELPING CLIENTS TO MANAGE THEIR FEELINGS
- *Reaching inside of silences*
- *Putting the client's feelings into words*
- *Displaying understanding of the client's feelings*
- *Sharing the worker's feelings*

WORKERS' SKILLS FOR HELPING CLIENTS TO MANAGE THEIR PROBLEMS
- *Clarifying the worker's purpose and role*
- *Reaching for client feedback*
- *Partializing client concerns*
- *Supporting clients in taboo areas*

All of these skills are important in all phases of practice. However, each skill may have other meanings or varying impacts at different stages in the relationship. Since the helping process is so complex, it helps to analyze it against the backdrop of the phases of work. The four phases of work described in this book are as follows:

1. Preliminary (or Preparatory) Phase
2. Beginning (or Contracting) Phase
3. Middle (or Work) Phase
4. Ending and Transition Phase

Each phase of work—preliminary, beginning, work, and ending/transition—has unique dynamics and requires specific skills. Jessie Taft (1949), referring to the beginning, middle, and ending phases, was one of the first to draw attention to the effect of time on social work practice. Schwartz (1971) incorporated this dimension into his work, adding the preliminary phase and modifying the ending phase to "ending and transition" phase. The **preliminary phase** is the time period prior to the first encounter with the client. The **beginning phase** refers to the first sessions in which the worker develops a *working contract* with the client and makes a start on developing the working relationship. The **middle phase** is the period in which the work is done. Finally, in the **ending and transition phase**, the worker prepares the client to bring the relationship to an end and to make transitions to new experiences. I will use the phases of work to organize the presentation of this model, starting with the preliminary phase.

Another way of thinking about these phases is that the client (individual, family, group, or community) must make a *first decision* in the beginning phase about whether or not to face the problems and engage with the worker. Even *mandatory clients* (e.g., child welfare or probation) must make that decision in order for the work to be effective. The *second decision* comes as the client makes the transition to the middle phase and decides to deal with the more difficult and often painful issues. The *third decision* is made by the client as she or he prepares for the termination of the relationship and (in a manner often described as "doorknob therapy") raises the most powerful and difficult issues of the work. These processes are identified in the balance of this book using examples of micro (clinical) and macro practice.

We begin the exploration of these constructs in Chapter 2 with a focus on the preliminary phase of practice in work with individuals. In Part II, focusing on social work with families, Part III, addressing social work with groups, and Part IV, dealing with community and systems work, we will also use the phases of work as an organizing principle.

THE INTEGRATION OF PERSONAL AND PROFESSIONAL SELVES

Another carry-over from the medical model was the importance placed on maintaining one's professional self. Most helping professions stressed the professional role and the need to suppress personal feelings and reactions. For example, in order to work with stressful patients, one might have to keep one's real reactions in check so as to avoid appearing judgmental. A professional worker was described as one who maintained control of emotions and would not become angry or too emotionally involved, would not cry in the presence of a client, and so forth. The injunction to the worker appeared to be: "Take your professional self to work and leave your personal self at home." This image of professionalism was widely held, with many of my social work students starting their careers wondering if they would have problems becoming a social worker because they "felt too much."

The practice model presented in this text will suggest that we are faced with a false dichotomy when we believe we must choose between our personal self and our professional self. In fact, I will argue that we are at our best in our work when we are able to synthesize the two—that is, integrate our personal self into our professional role.

This conflict in view of professional self was brought home dramatically in a workshop I led on direct practice. One hospital social worker described an incident in which a mother appeared at her door after being referred by the attending physician. The mother had just been told that her seven-year-old daughter had a terminal illness. After explaining this to the social worker, the mother broke down and cried.

When I asked the worker what she did, she described how overwhelmed she felt by the mother's grief. All that the worker could do was sit and hold the mother's hand, softly crying with her. I maintain that while there would be much work to be done in this case (e.g., helping the mother to deal with the dying daughter and her family over the next few months), at this point what the mother needed most was not advice but someone to be with her. In fact, as the worker partially experienced the mother's pain, and shared it with her through her own tears, she was giving that client an important gift of her own feelings. The worker was being professional in the best sense of that word. Other workers, who might not cry with a client, might make the same gift in other ways—through facial expressions, a respectful silence, or a hand on the shoulder—each worker responding in a way consistent with his or her own personality. The crucial factor would be the worker's willingness to be honest and to share his or her own feelings.

In the case described above, the worker continued her story by telling us that her supervisor passed the open door, called her out, and berated her for unprofessional behavior. The supervisor said: "How could you let yourself break down that way? You can't help your clients if you become overwhelmed yourself." When I asked the worker what she took from the experience, she replied, "I learned to keep my door closed."

While many who hear that story are upset with the supervisor, I am not. I realize that she may have been trained, as I was, in a time when any personal expressions of emotion were considered to be unprofessional. I encouraged the social worker to talk to her supervisor since I felt it was crucial for her to obtain support from her supervisor and colleagues if she was to continue to provide this kind of help to clients. My research (Shulman, 1991) has emphasized the importance of formal and informal sources of social support for social workers. This worker was making a gift to the client of her willingness to "be with" her at a terrible moment in her life. The worker's capacity to continue to be there for the client will be somewhat dependent upon her having someone—supervisor, colleague, or both—there for her.

This artificial split between personal and professional selves was created because of the profession's understandable concerns over the inappropriate use of self by helping professionals. For example, we were concerned about *counter-transference,* a process in which workers might project onto clients their own unfinished family business (e.g., relating to a father in a family as if he were one's own parent). We were troubled by workers who used the argument of spontaneity to justify acting out with clients, such as getting inappropriately angry or judgmental, or sharing personal problems ("If you think you have troubles with your wife, let me tell you about *my* marriage"). Unethical behavior with clients, such as abusing the powerful forces of the helping bond to sexually exploit a vulnerable client, is another example. Each of these examples illustrates a lack of integration of personal and professional selves. I would agree that the concerns about the use of the personal self are well founded. Unfortunately, the adopted solution to separate personal from professional led to more problems than it resolved.

The argument advanced throughout this text will be that each of us brings our own personal style, artistry, background, feelings, values, beliefs, and so on, to our professional practice. Rather than denying or suppressing these, we need to learn more about ourselves in the context of our practice, and find ways to use our self in pursuit of our professional functions. We will make many mistakes along the way, saying things we will later regret, having to apologize to clients, learning from these mistakes, correcting them, and them making more sophisticated mistakes. In other words, we will be real people carrying out difficult jobs as best we can, rather than paragons of virtue who present an image of perfection.

As we demonstrate to our clients our humanness, vulnerability, willingness to risk, spontaneity, honesty, and our lack of defensiveness (or defensiveness for which we later apologize), we will be modeling the very behaviors we hope to see in our clients. Thus, when workers or students ask me: "Should I be professional or should I be myself?", I reply that the dualism implied in the question does not exist. They must be themselves if they are going to be professional. Fortunately, we have the whole of our professional lives to learn how to effect the synthesis.

ALTERNATIVE SOCIAL WORK PERSPECTIVES

The social work profession is in a stage of development with many emerging theoretical frameworks to draw upon. An emphasis on theory building and empirical testing of constructs about practice is evident. While this book offers one perspective on the role of the profession and the processes of helping, others compete for our attention. This is healthy. The approach taken in this book will be to borrow practice concepts and ideas from all of the models described below and to integrate them into the general framework of the interactional approach. The emphasis will be on finding "what works," rather than on maintaining ideological purity.

What are some of the models currently under consideration by the profession?

Radical Social Work Practice

In one model, there are social work theorists who call for a more radical social work approach. Advocates for these theories rightly point to persistent social problems and the lack of social justice, particularly for oppressed and vulnerable populations. These challenges to the profession have been healthy in that they have reminded us of our historical concern with social change as well as individual adaptation. This "social" aspect of social work can easily be lost as the profession moves to become more "clinical," taking on models of practice used by other professions (e.g., psychotherapy, psychology). They have also provided a needed reminder of our unique professional role, which can easily be lost if we allow our function to be solely defined by the job description written by our agency or host setting.

For a segment of this group of radical social work theorists, at times identified with what might be called "critical theory," direct practice with clients, by definition, is ineffective. For example, Galper (1976, p. 6) views social services as failing to be effective because they "derive from the existing social order, and play a role in maintaining it."[16] Problems are defined in terms of economic, political, or social contexts. These theoreticians point to the very real problems in approaches to practice which seemed to ignore social realities and issues of oppression. The reason they have had such a powerful impact on faculty, students, and workers is that they focused on aspects of our practice about which we were already feeling defensive. Workers who feel oppressed by their own agencies and somewhat overwhelmed by their clients' life situations are responsive to the charge that they are involved in "band-aid" work rather than bringing about real social change.

However, practitioners know that when they work with real clients, employing a critical analysis of the clients' problems is often just a first step. Such an analysis can lead to new and more helpful ways to intervene in the process with clients who need help *now*—today—in *this* interview, family session, or group meeting. The client cannot wait for the major changes in our society that will be needed to modify institutionalized oppression. Thus, while we need a conceptualization of practice which reframes our way of viewing client troubles and requires us to act on injustices in our society (and agencies), we simultaneously must provide services to the victims of these injustices. The real task is technical in nature. How can we integrate radical views of society, psychology, and interpersonal relationships into our ongoing practice, and how can we develop the skills to have an impact on systems as well as clients? The use of oppression psychology in this book is one example of a beginning effort toward such an integration.

Feminist Practice

A second group of models currently influencing our professional development is the emergence of a body of literature related to what is termed "feminist practice."[17] While this view can also be considered a form of radical practice, and it draws heavily on social and political issues related to gender oppression, its proponents tend to translate their ideas into specific method theory that helps to connect ideas to the realities of day-to-day practice.

In recent years, feminist approaches to practice have diverged into identifiable streams. Earlier in this chapter, I cited Saulnier's (1996) attempt to identify these various viewpoints and to analyze their similarities and differences as well presenting critiques of each. Her typology includes the following models: liberal feminism; radical feminism; socialist feminism; lesbian feminism; cultural and ecofeminism; womanism; African-American women's feminism; postmodern feminism; and global feminism. While some may disagree with the specific categorization of the models and the associated descriptions and analysis, Saulnier's contribution highlights this important area of theory development and identifies implications for social policy and social work practice.

Sands and Nuccio (1992) specifically address the emergence of *postmodern feminist theory* and its implications for social work. The authors describe how the feminist literature has identified three general categories of

> philosophical and political feminist orientations—liberal, socialist and radical feminism...
>
> *Liberal feminism* emphasizes the attainment of political rights, opportunities, and equality within the existing political system. *Socialist feminism* attributes women's oppression to the interaction among sexism, racism, and class divisions, which are produced by patriarchal capitalism. *Radical feminism* finds patriarchy an omnipresent influence that needs to be dismantled (p. 490).

They then trace the emergence of postmodern feminism from its postmodern philosophical and French feminist theoretical roots. While identifying differences in the roots and the emergent thinking of this model, they point to a shared political agenda with American feminism:

> Regardless of whether a feminist has a liberal, socialist, radical or other perspective, she has a desire to change the social and political order so that women will no longer be oppressed. Thus, organizing and taking political action to redress injustices are significant dimensions of postmodern feminism (p. 492).

An example of the specific application of this shared principle can be found in Chapter 15, in which a social worker approaches the ending phase of work with a group of survivors of sexual abuse. After many months of difficult and powerful work on the impact of the abuse on their lives, the worker suggests that they consider attending a local march against sexual violence directed toward women.

> Then group members asked me to review information about the local "Take Back the Night" march with them. We had told them about the march against sexual violence against women a few weeks before and after some exploration of their fears about participating in a public demonstration, they decided to march as a group. I supported the group's readiness to act independently and support each other in new experi-

ences. I shared with them how good I felt that they wanted to march together and gave them the information they needed.

At the next session:

> We supported the group's growing independence and shared our feelings with them. As the group processed how the march had felt for them, Jane and I shared how powerful it had felt for us to see them there, marching, chanting, and singing. We also shared that it was hard for us to see them and know that the group was ending. The group was special for us and it would be hard to let it go.

After their experience with the march, the group members decided to contribute samples of their poetry and art to an exhibit dealing with issues of violence toward women. They also decided to contribute proceeds from the sale of their art to a fund devoted to support groups for survivors like themselves. This represents an example of combining the "personal" and "political," and I would submit, it would be hard to choose which part of their work together was more "therapeutic." The cake they shared in their last session had written on it: "Survivors—Striving and Thriving!"

Another model that brings a feminist perspective to our practice, also cited earlier in this chapter, emerged from efforts to develop a new psychology of women. Much of the recent and rapidly evolving work in this area can be found in publications and a series of working papers from the Stone Center, Wellesley, Massachusetts. This framework is often referred to under the general rubric of "self-in-relation" theory. In an example of an application of this theory, Collins (1993) "reconstructs" the concept of co-dependency using a feminist social work perspective to analyze the concept and its underlying assumptions about recovery and relationships.

Many of the core constructs of this theory, and, in particular, the group work implications of the model, fit well with the interactional framework presented in this book. For example, a colleague of mine, Linda Schiller (1993) was able to use the self-in-relation framework to rethink a classic theory of group development known as the "Boston Model" (Garland, Jones, and Kolodny, 1965) and adapt it to a feminist perspective.

In another example of an application of feminist theory to practice, Holmes and Lundy (1990) present what they term a "feminist" perspective on work with men who batter. Specific prescriptions for intervention are provided based upon the underlying theoretical and ideological assumptions. Other examples that draw upon feminist perspectives include Berman-Rossi and Cohen (1988), focusing on work with homeless, mentally ill women and Breton (1988), providing an example of a "sistering" approach in a drop-in shelter for homeless women. O'Brien (1995) identified self-empowerment of a group of African-American women, who were long-term public housing residents and activists, as contributing to their resilience and effective mothering.

In an effort to merge a feminist perspective with a cognitive-behavioral approach (discussed later in this chapter), Srebnik (1994) described how internalized cultural messages negatively affect a woman's body image, then proposed interventions to influence thought patterns and dysfunctional behaviors.

While one is free to differ with the particular interventions, these "radical" approaches contribute to the general professional development by providing models that can be applied to practice with oppressed and vulnerable clients. In fact, many of the intervention constructs of the model would constitute good practice principles for any worker-client intervention.

The important point is that these theory builders have not given up on the idea of social workers playing an influential role with individual clients as well as dealing with issues of social justice.

Social Work as Psychotherapy

A third model, associated with the growth of private practice and the certification of social workers as eligible to receive third-party insurance payments, has intensified another stream of influence on the profession. This might best be described as the "social worker as therapist" model. While many social workers applaud this recognition of the competency of the profession, a serious concern about social work's continued commitment to oppressed and vulnerable populations has been raised. Many of our traditional clients are economically disadvantaged and do not have the medical insurance required to use our private services. As a field, we have found our place working in social agencies or social work departments in host institutions (e.g., hospitals, schools, residential centers). A real fear exists that our profession may abandon its important and unique roles in these settings in the search for higher status and income, and increased professional autonomy.

As some social workers increasingly describe themselves as therapists or psychotherapists, sometimes even avoiding the use of their social work title, they blur the distinctions between our profession and the others engaged in private-practice counseling activities. The very existence of a unique profession of social work could be jeopardized if we do not keep clear what it is that makes social work different. Since this private-practice movement is growing, one solution may be for the profession to identify and research the elements we would expect to see in the work of our private-practice colleagues that maintain their unique identity as social workers. Identifying themselves as social workers and affiliating with our professional associations are examples. A willingness to intervene with other professionals and systems, on behalf of a client, might be another.

Cognitive-Behavioral Therapy

A fourth emerging model is related to interest in constructs borrowed from cognitive-behavioral psychology and therapy. In cognitive-behavioral therapy,

> ...the therapist uses strategies and techniques designed to help depressed patients correct their negative, distorted views about themselves, the world, and the future, and the underlying maladaptive beliefs that gave rise to these cognitions (Elkin et al., 1990, p. 973; Beck et al., 1979).

Earlier in this chapter, I pointed out the powerful interaction between how we feel and how we act. Essentially, cognitive-behavioral approaches, building on social learning theories, suggest that how one *thinks* also interacts with behavior. When feelings and cognitive distortions combine, they can result in maladaptive behaviors which, in turn, strengthen the distortions, which then continue to affect the behavior. In cognitive-behavioral treatment models, the therapist would help the client to identify and modify cognitive distortions and would reinforce behaviors that were more adaptive for the client.

Concepts drawn from a widely recognized and researched cognitive therapy model based upon the work of Beck, who explored the causes and treatment of depression (1967, 1976), can be usefully incorporated into the interactional model of practice. Oei and Shuttlewood (1996) summarize the three dimensions of Beck's theory (p. 93). First, life experiences lead people to form assumptions about themselves and the world ("schemata" or "underlying predispositions") that are then used to interpret new experiences and to govern and evaluate behavior. "Some assumptions reached on the basis of past negative experience may become rigid, extreme, and resistent to change and, hence, are termed dysfunctional or counterproductive" (p. 93).

Second, Beck posed the existence of "automatic thoughts," short pieces of "internal dialogue" that are associated with negative emotions and can lead to self statements such as "I am a failure." According to Beck, a pattern of frequent and "highly negative automatic thoughts" can develop into a vicious cycle leading to depression, which then leads to more "depressive cognitions." Third, automatic thoughts are seen as containing "errors of logic" which Beck termed "cognitive distortions." These could include, for example, overgeneralizing, disqualifying the positive, catastrophizing, minimization, and personalization.

Beck's treatment approach, as described by Oei and Shuttlewood, "...disrupts the vicious cycle of depression by teaching the patients to questions negative automatic thoughts and then to challenge the assumptions (schemata) on which they are based" (p. 94).

Finally, examples exist that indicate how one can incorporate constructs from one model (cognitive-behavioral) into the framework presented in this book (interactional). Albert (1994) writes about a mutual aid support group for chronic mental patients using a cognitive approach. He describes a patient in a day treatment center, which had so many groups that patients often felt "grouped out," surprising staff by suggesting another group.

> She said, "We need to talk just about being mental patients, what it means, what it feels like." One patient after another seconded the motion. They wanted to address the mental patient identity. How were they thought of in their families and neighborhoods? How should they think of themselves? Was the mental patient stigma justified? Where did it come from? What were its effects? Although their patienthood was at the heart of what the ... patients had in common, it seemed to have remained an oppressive presence, at once too obvious and too painful to mention.

In one example from the group, patients are dealing with the ideation of permanent thinking—that when they are depressed, for example, treatment can seem "interminable and futile." This sense of failure and permanency, in turn, affects their ability to continue to cope.

> Sharon said, "I had the leaves raked into piles. Then the wind blew them all around the yard again. I thought, 'What's the use? They'll never get done. There will always be leaves.' Then I went back to bed. My body started feeling heavy. I couldn't get out of bed." I (the worker) pointed out that Sharon had used the word "always" when speaking about her hospitalization, too. ["I'll always go back to the hospital."] I asked, "Is it true that there will always be leaves? Is the job never done?" Sharon said, "That's one way of looking at it." I asked the group for other ways. Members suggested that Sharon think about other tasks she has completed. [disputation] Nick said, "Maybe you would have to redo the raking once or twice. Maybe even three times. But not forever. [disputation] I mean, you do what you can, then it snows and you're done." [laughter] I repeated, "You do what you can."

Cognitive-behavioral approaches represent good examples of how related disciplines can provide powerful ideas that can be integrated into a social work practice model. In addition, the emphasis by the cognitive-behavioral social work theoreticians on a **practitioner-researcher** model, in which the social worker is continuously evaluating his or her own practice, is also healthy for the field as it accelerates the movement toward development of a more empirically based practice.

While contributing to our profession's theoretical and research growth, two concerns are raised by the growth of cognitive, behavioral, or cognitive-behavioral models in social work practice. The first is evident in efforts by some theoreticians to propose such models as a social work practice theory (Thyer, 1987). Such an effort would substitute a model borrowed from a foreign discipline, one that is not rooted in the same history as the social work profession, for our own unique sense of professional function.

Examination of the literature of this approach, for example, indicates it has been applied most often to very specific problems (e.g., anxiety disorders, anger management, parenting training, depression) and populations, while social work has developed a broader constituency, including specific attention to oppressed and vulnerable populations.

In addition, the model is generally built upon a base of individual psychology. This is evident in its lack of attention to the social change aspects of practice that have been central to our profession. In an example of an exception to this criticism, Stern and Smith (1995) report on a study of family processes and delinquency in an ecological context. They tested a model "...hypothesizing that family content influences parenting, which in turn influences adolescent behavior" (p. 703). Their results for 804 adolescents and their families showed that "...the family's disadvantaged neighborhood, life distress, social isolation, and lack of partner support were associated with dysfunctional parenting that increases delinquency" (p. 703).

Stern and Smith reviewed the literature and identified a number of behaviorally focused interventions that have proved helpful in, for example, providing tools for parents to identify sources of stress from their children's behavior and parenting methods for coping with that stress. They point out, however, that

> ...our research supports the growing recognition of the importance of multidimensional approaches to intervention with delinquents and their families. It seems clear that intervention focused solely on the microprocesses in families will generally be inadequate to address the complex problems that juvenile delinquency presents. If we look at parents without considering the complex contexts in which they operate and the multiple stresses operating in them, we are likely to promote ineffective intervention models and high levels of treatment dropout. We also run the risk of blaming and revictimizing families struggling with considerable adversity who are already victimized by a society that does not adequately support disadvantaged and distressed children and families (p. 722).

In my view, if social work can hold on to the core of its unique role which always recognizes the "two-client" concept, then we can incorporate ideas from a wide range of models and theories. The task for our profession is to treat frameworks from foreign disciplines with appropriate respect, and to borrow constructs that can enhance our work, while guarding against substituting these constructs for our own model-building efforts.

A second issue related to the growth of this model is the apparent co-optation of the term *empirically based practice* by this specific framework. This has occurred somewhat by default as social work as a profession was slow in developing a solid body of research focused on practice method—what it is the social worker actually did with clients. While many outcome studies existed, they were usually weak in defining the independent (predictor) variables. For example, in Fischer's (1973) well-known article on the effectiveness of social work practice, out of more than 40 studies reviewed, not one described what it was the social worker actually did while spending time with the client. Operational definition of the worker's intervention is one of the strong points of cognitive-behavioral practice models that have allowed this framework to move quickly to attempt to fill this research vacuum.

Empirical work can be undertaken from a range of theoretical perspectives, including some that could be termed interactional. The early work of the psychotherapy researchers associated with the client-centered approach of Carl Rogers (Truax, 1966) broke ground in this area. More recently, empirical work that involves specifying worker interventions has been more evident in the field, with a wide range of research approaches and methodology emerging. The work reported in this book is one example of the use of quantitative (e.g., statistical analysis) and qualitative (e.g., content analysis of interviews) research methods for building social work practice theory. One contribution of the feminist practice movement has been to focus our attention on qualitative models of practice-research that are useful in helping us to explore worker-client interactions in ways that enhance our practice knowledge base.

Finally, the profession must guard against the tendency of proponents to oversell a particular framework or model, often by first attacking the efficacy of models currently in use. In reality, as pointed out by Oei and Shuttlewood (1996) there are many unanswered questions about what makes any form of therapy effective. Their review of the literature indicates that the evidence does not yet support the superiority of any particular form of therapy, and the debate is still intense over whether specific therapy-related factors, or "non-specific" or more general factors, may be the source of the positive results of therapy when compared to no treatment at all. They point to the most researched nonspecific factor, the "therapeutic alliance," as an example of a variable that, while defined differently, may nevertheless cross models of treatment and account for some measure of effectiveness. This concept closely parallels the idea of the working relationship at the core of the interactional approach.

It is important that we incorporate as many ideas as are helpful in developing a model of social work practice, while holding onto our unique professional identification. It is also important that we maintain the theoretical independence of the term *empirically based practice*.

Summary of Models

In summary, there are many emerging theoretical models competing for our attention. We are far from being ready to vote, as a profession, on which one will best suit us in the years to come. More likely, an integration of many of the universal constructs developed from differing points of departure will provide us with a unified practice theory. The interactional model discussed in this book may provide some of these constructs.

The framework described in this book will allow us to view relationships between clients and their important systems in an ecological context. Real conflicts between clients and systems will be identified; however, emphasis will be placed upon attempting to identify areas of common ground. Practitioners will be described trying to deal directly with clients, as well as trying to influence families, agencies, political systems, and so on. These practitioners will at times function in different roles, mediating where appropriate, confronting and advocating when necessary. In whichever role they play, however, they will keep in mind the essential common ground between the individual and society. This is the basis from which change can be brought about, and it is the real challenge for developing a radical social work practice.

CHAPTER SUMMARY

In this chapter, we introduced the interactional theory of social work practice. The client was viewed as being in a symbiotic relationship with his or her social surroundings. The mutual need between the individual and the social surroundings was described as being blocked by obstacles that often obscured it from view. An oppression and vulnerability psychology model for understanding clients was introduced. A final assumption of this model was that the strength for change was always present although not always possible to engage. An historical perspective of social work described the profession as rooted in the twin streams of concern for individual well-being and for social change. This led to our posing the functional assignment for the social work profession as that of mediating the engagement between the client and the systems important to that client. Practice method and communication and relationship skills were viewed as the tools that enable the social worker to put his or her function into action. Practice skills were described as the instruments for developing a positive working relationship that would serve as the medium through which the social worker influenced the client. Central to the effectiveness of the worker was her or his ability to integrate a personal self with the professional self. The social worker's practice was viewed as being guided, as well, by a set of professional and personal values and by a well-defined professional code of ethics. Alternative social work practice perspectives were briefly reviewed to place the interactional perspective in context.

GLOSSARY

Beginning (or contracting) phase The engagement phase of work, during which the worker contracts with the client by clarifying the purpose of the engagement, the role he or she will play, and by reaching for client feedback on the content of the work. Authority issues are also dealt with in this phase.

Demand for work The worker's confrontation of the client to work effectively on her or his tasks and to invest that work with energy and affect.

Empirically based practice theory A research-based description of a social worker's valued outcomes and interventions, which are based upon a set of underlying assumptions about human behavior and social organization and our professional ethics and values.

Empowerment process A process through which the social worker engages the client (individual, family, group, or community) in order to "increase their personal, interpersonal, socioeconomic, and political strength and influence toward improving their circumstances" (Barker, 1991, p. 74).

Ending and transition phase The termination phase of work, in which the worker prepares to end the relationship and to help the client review their work together as well as to prepare for transitions to new experiences.

Function Defined here as the specific job the professional plays in the helping process.

Generalist practice "A social work practitioner whose knowledge and skills encompass a broad spectrum and who assesses problems and their solutions comprehensively" (Barker, 1991, p. 91).

Generic social work "The social work orientation which emphasizes a common core of knowledge and skills associated with social service provision" (Barker, 1991, p. 92).

Grounded theory An approach to theory building, first described by Glaser and Strauss (1967) in the field of sociology, in which formal and informal observations from the field are used to develop constructs of the theory. Formal research is conducted to test propositions and to generate new ones.

Holistic theory Defined here as a theoretical approach that includes a broad range of variables—personal, interactional, contextual, and time related—in describing social work practice.

Interactional model A model of practice, first articulated by William Schwartz (1961), which emphasizes the interactional nature of the helping process. The client in this model is viewed as a self-realizing, energy-producing person with certain tasks to perform, and the social worker as having a specific function to carry out. They engage each other as interdependent actors within an organic system that is best described as reciprocal in nature, with each person affecting and being affected by the other on a moment-by-moment basis. The worker-client relationship is understood within the social context and is influenced by the impact of time.

Medical model The four-step process of organizing one's thinking about practice commonly described as study, diagnosis, treatment, and evaluation. Also sometimes used to describe a "pathology" model for diagnosing client problems.

Middle (or work) phase The phase of work in which the client and the worker focus on dealing with issues raised in the contracting phase (or new issues that have emerged).

Model A representation of reality.

Outreach program A program that attempts to bring services directly to clients, usually in their own homes or neighborhoods.

Practitioner-researcher A social worker who is continuously involved in evaluating his or her own practice and developing generalizations from the practice experience.

Preliminary (or preparatory) phase The phase of work prior to the worker engaging with the client. Usually used to develop a preliminary empathy about the client's issues and concerns.

Psychology of oppression A theory of the impact of societal oppression on vulnerable populations that describes both adaptive and maladaptive responses (e.g., Frantz Fanon, 1968).

Skills Specific behaviors on the part of the worker that are used in the implementation of the social work function.

Skills for helping clients to manage their feelings A collection of four worker practice skills designed to help workers and clients deal with and effectively manage their own feelings.

Skills for helping client to manage their problems A collection of four worker practice skills designed to help clients deal with and effectively manage their problems.

Symbiotic assumption The assumption of a relationship between the individual and his or her nurturing group in which each needs the other for its own life and growth, and each reaches out to the other with all the strength possible at a given moment (Schwartz, 1961).

Symbiotic diffusion Obscuring of the mutual need between people and their social surroundings by the complexity of the situation, by divergent needs, or by the difficulties involved in communication.

Systems or ecological approach A view of the client that takes into account the dynamic interaction with the social context.

Theoretical generalizations Testable propositions that receive repeated support from a number of research efforts (Rosenberg, 1978).

Two-clients construct View of the social worker as always having two clients at any moment in time (e.g., the individual and the family; the member and the group; the client and the system).

Vulnerable client A client who is particularly exposed to the impact of oppression and stressful life events because of personal and/or social factors (e.g., lack of a strong social support system of family or friends; limited economic resources).

NOTES

1. For a report of the research used as an empirical basis for the first and second editions of this book, see Lawrence Shulman, "A Study of Practice Skills," *Social Work, 23* (July 1978): 274–81.

2. For the original discussion of the framework elaborated in this text, see W. Schwartz, "The Social Worker in the Group," in *New Perspectives on Services to Groups: Theory, Organization, Practice* (New York: National Association of Social Workers, 1961), pp. 7–34. See also *The Social Welfare Forum, 1961* (New York: Columbia University Press, 1961), pp. 146–77.

3. The Teacher's Guide that accompanies this text contains an updated summary of the specific propositions in this model, along with citations for research findings supporting the constructs.

4. For a more complete discussion of the medical and the interactional paradigms, see *Interactional Social Work Practice: Toward an Empirical Theory* (Shulman, 1991).

5. For a discussion of systems theory and its impact on practice thinking, see Gordon Hearn, *Theory Building in Social Work* (Toronto: University of Toronto Press, 1958); Gordon Hearn (ed.), *The General Systems Approach: Contributions Toward an Holistic Conception of Social Work* (New York: Council on Social Work Education, 1969); Carel Germain, "Teaching an Ecological Approach to Social Work Practice," in *Teaching for Competence in the Delivery of Direct Services* (New York: Council on Social Work Education, 1977), pp. 31–39; Carel B. Germain and Alex Gitterman, *The Life Model of Social Work Practice: Advances in Theory and Practice*, 2nd ed. (New York: Columbia University Press, 1996).

6. In her book entitled *Feminist Theories and Social Work: Approaches and Applications* (1996), Christine Flynn Saulnier examines eight general models of feminist theory, summarizing and critiquing each. While some may feel such an overview is by definition reductionist, and may disagree with Saulnier's descriptions and critiques, nevertheless they provide an excellent starting point for exploring these promising alternative models.

7. This view is rooted in a school of thought developed by a number of philosophers and social scientists including John Dewey, *Democracy and Education: An Introduction to the Philosophy of Education* (New York: Free Press, 1916); and George Herbert Mead, *Mind, Self, and Society* (Chicago: University of Chicago Press, 1934).

8. A symbiotic relationship, in early psychiatric literature, came to mean an unhealthy relationship, particularly between a mother and child. This represents a departure from the original use of the term. In biology, both organisms in a symbiotic (as opposed to a parasitic) relationship benefit from the relationship. In an unhealthy mother-child relationship characterized by disabling mutual dependency, by contrast, neither party benefits.

9. Schwartz draws his rationale for the symbiotic model from such authors as Peter Kropotkin, *Mutual Aid: A Factor of Evolution* (New York: Alfred A. Knopf, 1925); Muzafer Sherif, *The Psychology of Social Norms* (New York: Harper & Bros., 1936); Gardner Murphy, *Human Potentials* (New York:

Basic Books, 1958); James Mark Baldwin, *The Individual and Society: Or Psychology and Sociology* (Boston: Gorham Press, 1911).

10. AIDS is not, in itself, a disease. Persons die from an AIDS-related illness or complication. The existence of any of a number of conditions as well as the person testing positive for Human Im-munodeficiency Virus (HIV-positive) leads to the diagnosis of AIDS. A person with the AIDS syn-drome is often referred to as a PLWA (Person Living With Aids). Since the last edition of this book, the emergence of new and hopeful drug treatments have shifted practice with many (unfortunately not all) PLWAs to learning how to live with AIDS. The long-term efficacy of these treatments is still un-known.

11. The difference noted here is essentially a fundamental difference in philosophy. The inter-actional model starts with an existential view of people that can be oversimplified to mean *you are what you do*. The way in which you act determines who you are. An alternative philosophy, which has been described as a teleological view of people, suggests *You do what you are*. Who you are de-termines how you act. In an existential approach, the emphasis would be placed on the here-and-now of life tasks in an effort to help people cope more effectively and thus influence their sense of them-selves. Again, in an oversimplification, clients become more competent in life by behaving more com-petently.

12. See K.J. Pottick, "Jane Addams Revisited: Practice Theory and Social Economics," in J.A. Lee (ed.), *Group Work with the Poor and Oppressed* (New York: Haworth Press, Inc., 1988). (Also pub-lished as *Social Work with Groups, 11* (1988): 11–24); Garvin, C., "Group Work Activities and Settings," in *Contemporary Group Work* (Englewood Cliffs, NJ: Prentice-Hall, 1981).

13. Harry Specht was my first-year field instructor at the Mt. Vernon YM&YWHA in Mt. Vernon, New York. He, and other staff at that innovative placement, provided a foundation for my understand-ing of social action as an inherent part of my role as a social worker. Harry later became the Dean of Berkeley University School of Social Work. The executive director of the Mt. Vernon Y at that time, George Braeger, who later became the Dean of the Columbia University School of Social Work, devel-oped and headed a major demonstration and research project on Manhattan's Lower East Side called Mobilization for Youth that became a model for national community action organizations and poverty programs funded during the Johnson presidential term of office. A few months before his death, when I informed Harry Specht that I often told people that he was my first field instructor, he belatedly in-formed me that I had been his first student.

14. For another discussion of this function, see William Schwartz, "Social Group Work: The In-teractionist Approach," in *Encyclopedia of Social Work, 11*, John B. Turner (ed.) (New York: National Association of Social Workers, 1977), p. 1334. See also William Schwartz, "Between Client and System: The Mediating Function," in *Theories of Social Work with Groups*, eds. Robert W. Roberts and Helen Northen (New York: Columbia University Press, 1976), pp. 171–97. For a publication containing the complete collection of published and unpublished writings of William Schwartz, see Toby Berman-Rossi, ed., *The Collected Writings of William Schwartz* (Itasca, IL: F.E. Peacock Publishers, 1994).

15. I wish to acknowledge the contribution of my friend and colleague, Alex Gitterman, who suggested these terms during a discussion of the concepts.

16. For an interesting discussion of the way in which major philosophical assumptions underlie social work practice theory, see R.G. Dean and B.L. Fenby, "Exploring Epistemologies: Social Work Action as a Reflection of Philosophical Assumptions," *Journal of Social Work Education, 25* (1989): 46–54. For a discussion of radical social work practice, see J. Galper, "Research and Writing for Radical Social Work," *Catalyst, 4* (1979): 37–50.

17. For a discussion of women's issues, see Elaine Norman and Arlene Mancuso, *Women's Is-sues and Social Work Practice* (Itasca, IL: F. E. Peacock Publishers, 1980). For further readings on the feminist perspective, see A. Ivanoff, E.A. Robinson, and B.J. Blyth, "Empirical Clinical Practice from a Feminist Perspective," *Social Work, 32* (1987): 417–23; J. A. Ness and P. Ladicola, "Toward a Definition

of Feminist Social Work: A Comparison of Liberal, Radical, and Socialist Models,"*Social Work, 34* (1989): 12–21; M.E. Swigonski, "The Logic of Feminist Standpoint Theory for Social Work Research," *Social Work, 39* (1994): 387–93; L.G. Day, "Counseling for Women: The Contribution of Feminist Theory and Practice," *Counseling Psychology Quarterly, 5* (1991): 373–84; E. Lewis, "Regaining Promise: Feminist Perspectives for Social Group Work Practice," *Social Work with Groups, 15* (1992): 271–84.

PART II

Social Work with Individuals

Part II of this book consists of four chapters that elaborate and illustrate the interactional approach to social work in the context of work with individuals.

Chapters 2 through 5 introduce the practice theory using the four phases of work—preliminary, beginning, middle (work), and ending/transition—as the organizing framework. In Chapter 2, on the preliminary phase, we examine the skills required to prepare for a new contact with a client, we explore an oppression psychology model, and we discuss the impact of ethics, values, legislation, and the court on practice. In Chapter 3, on the beginning phase, our focus is on the contracting skills for creating a clear structure for work. In Chapter 4 we examine the middle (work) phase of practice, providing a model of the stages of an individual session. Finally, in Chapter 5 we explore the ending and transition phase of practice, in which the worker and client bring their relationship to an end and prepare the client to move on to new experiences.

Each chapter describes the specific dynamics and skills associated with the particular phase. Research findings are cited to provide an empirical basis for the work. Detailed illustrations of social workers interacting with clients help to connect the theory to day-to-day realities that are familiar to the reader. These examples illustrate the constant or core elements of practice while demonstrating the many variations introduced by the nature of the client population, each client's particular problems, and the impact of the setting of practice.

2

The Preliminary Phase of Work

CHAPTER OUTLINE

Communications in Practice

The Preliminary Phase: Tuning In to Self and to the Client

Responding Directly to Indirect Cues

Oppression Psychology

Resilience Theory

Agency Records, Referral Reports, and the Agency Culture

Values, Ethics, and the Law in Social Work Practice

In Chapter 1, we outlined four phases of work: the preliminary, beginning, middle, and ending/transition phases. Now we will begin to explore the constructs introduced earlier, starting with the preliminary phase of practice.

The indirect nature of the communication process will be examined, with suggestions provided for ways in which the worker can respond directly to indirect cues. We will look at an approach for developing a preliminary empathy, prior to the first interview, with potential client feelings and concerns related to the worker, the agency or setting, and the client's problems. The importance of a social worker "tuning in" to his or her own feelings will also be stressed.

Social workers must also use theory about human behavior and development within the social environment to better understand their clients' theme of concern. Two important examples of constructs drawn from human behavior and social environment theory—an oppression model and a resiliency framework—are presented as illustrations.

In this chapter we will also consider how agency records and any other form of prior information about specific clients can provide helpful information or present obstacles to genuine understanding.

Finally, we will explore ethical and legal issues that affect a social worker's practice.

The rationale for the preliminary phase of practice is based upon the idea that preparing for social work interactions can increase the likelihood of establishing a positive worker-client relationship and of hearing and understanding what the client has to say. We will start by looking at the complexity of the human communication process in general, and then we will explore issues specific to social work practice. In this chapter we will also consider two theories of human behavior in the social environment that can help a social worker to "get into the shoes of the client" and to better understand dynamics, such as those related to gender, race, or other oppressions, which may be far from the worker's own life experiences.

Since social workers often initiate their work with a client by reviewing information from previous workers within the agency or from other professionals, some attention needs to be paid to how a worker might use and not misuse such information in preparing to engage the client. Finally, social work practice often raises ethical and legal issues for the worker. We will address these issues in this chapter under the assumption that familiarity with some of these concerns, such as the requirements and limitations associated with confidentiality, will assist the social worker in preparing for their emergence in her or his practice.

COMMUNICATIONS IN PRACTICE

Human communications can be complex under any circumstances. Let us examine the nature of a single communication. We start with a sender—an individual who has an idea to transmit. This idea must first be "encoded" and then transmitted to the intended receiver through spoken or written words, touch, or nonverbal means (e.g., facial expression, posture). The message must next be received. This involves hearing, reading, seeing, or feeling by the recipient. Next, the message must be decoded—that is, translated by the recipient from symbols to the ideas that they represent. The recipient must then acknowledge the message through some form of feedback to the sender, thus completing the cyclical process.[1]

Obstacles to Direct Communication

When one considers how complicated even the most simple communications can be, and the number of points in the process where meanings can be distorted, it is a wonder that any communication is ever completed. In the helping relationship, additional factors can complicate the process. These obstacles to open communication often cause a client to employ indirect methods of expressing thoughts and feelings.

One obstacle may be the feeling of **ambivalence** associated with accepting help. Our society responds negatively to almost all forms of dependency, stressing instead the norm of independence. Value is placed on being able to handle things on one's own. Society's pressure is counterbalanced for the client by the urgency of the task at hand. The resulting vector from these conflicting forces is often an ambiguous call for help. Particularly in early sessions, before a working relationship has been established, the client may present concerns in an indirect manner.

A second area of potential blockage to direct communication is **societal taboos**, reflecting a general consensus to block or prohibit discussion in areas of sensitivity and deep concern. The client enters the helping relationship with a conscious or unconscious internalization of these taboos, hindering free speaking. Major taboos in our society discourage "real" talk about topics such as sex, dependency, substance abuse, authority, and money. The discomfort clients experience when talking about issues and feelings in certain areas may cause them to use indirect methods of communication.

A third obstacle is associated with the feelings that accompany concerns. Feelings may be painful and frightening to the client. The raising of a concern may be blocked by conscious or unconscious defenses that the client uses to avoid moving into sensitive areas. This can lead to clients sharing the facts of an issue while ignoring their own feelings. Since all issues of concern are invested with both facts and feelings, this represents only a partial communication. In one example, described in detail later in this chapter, a client with a chronically ill child was able to share her anger but was less in touch with the pain that contributed to her rage. She was using a form of "**flight-fight**" that served as a defense from her own distress. Since it cut her off from the support she desperately needed, it was a maladaptive defense.

Finally, the context of the contract with the helping person may contribute factors that block real talk. For example, in a child welfare agency, workers carry dual functions and in some cases may have to act for the state in apprehending (removing) a child. Parents are very aware of the worker's authority and power and thus will be wary of sharing information or feelings that can be used against them. A parole officer who can revoke a parole, a nurse who can make a hospital stay unpleasant, a psychiatrist who can decide when a patient can go home, an adoption worker who can decide if a person gets a child, a worker in a mandatory group for male batterers—all these helping people have power over the lives of their clients, and this power may become the most important obstacle to real talk.

Examples of Indirect Communication in Practice

Because of the obstacles that block the direct expression of feelings, clients may use indirect means to present them, as in the classic case of the client who "has a friend with a problem." Hinting is an important indirect cue; the client makes a comment or asks a question that contains a portion of the message. The mother who asks the worker if she has children, for example, may be using a question to begin to raise, very tentatively, a more complex and threatening issue: "Will this worker be able to understand what it is like for me?" Clients may also raise their concerns through their behavior. For example, a child in a residential setting who has not been asked to go home for a family visit over Christmas may let his child care worker know how upset he is by a sudden increase in "acting out" behavior. Adults in counseling sessions who "come on" negatively may be doing the same thing.

Another illustration can be drawn from the child welfare setting. A social worker was visiting a young, single-parent mother who had three children under the age of four. There had been an abuse complaint, and the worker was called in to investigate. As the worker spoke to the harried mother, the youngest child pulled at her mother's leg until the mother said, "Leave me alone, I'm talking now." The child continued to try to engage the mother, who finally grabbed the little girl by the shoulders and shouted, "Leave me alone!"

The worker was stunned and immediately, responding to that part of her function which called for the protection of children, began to counsel the mother: "Mrs. Jones, don't you think there might be other ways in which you can tell your child you wish to be left alone?" The mother understood the implied criticism and immediately began to feel more tense and defensive with this worker.

If the worker could have been in touch with her own feelings, and those of the mother, and if it had been clear to the worker that the mother was a client in her own right and not just an instrument for providing service to the child, then she might have recognized the indirect cues of the negative behavior and responded as follows: "Is this what it's like for you all the time—no chance to be alone, to talk to other people without the kids pestering you?"

If said with genuine understanding of the plight of a single mother who is young, trying to raise kids on her own, probably struggling with an inadequate income, and so on, then there is a good chance that the working relationship might be strengthened by this direct response to indirect cues.

In one of my studies, the use of this skill contributed directly to the client's perception that the worker was there both to investigate and protect the child and to help the mother (Shulman, 1991). The worker might also acknowledge how hard it must be on the mother to have a social worker come and talk to her about these things. It might still be necessary for the worker to intervene by offering respite care to give the mother a break. Since protection of the child is of central importance, the worker might also have to remove the child with or without the mother's agreement. The impact of exercising the worker's authority would be somewhat moderated by the worker's caring for the mother as a client in her own right (Shulman, 1991).

Metaphor and allegory can be used by client as means of indirect communication. As in literature, the intent is to send a message without necessarily expressing its content directly. This is illustrated by an example from an interview with a depressed adolescent foster child who has recently lost his parents. The youngster is getting ready to leave the care of the agency because he is eighteen, and he is worried about where he will live. He has had eight changes of residence during the past year. Note both the indirect communications and the means by which the worker uses her preparatory empathy to reach for the underlying message.

> Frank asked me if I ever thought of the fact that space never ended. I said I hadn't really. I wondered if he had, and if it worried him somehow. He said it did, because sometimes he felt like a little ball, floating in space, all alone. A little bit higher and more to the right, and bye, bye world—just like a wee birdie. I said he really has been floating in space, moving from place to place, and that he must be feeling all alone. Frank's eyes filled with tears and he said, emphatically, "I am all alone!"

Nonverbal forms of communication can also be used to send important indirect messages. The client who always arrives late or early or who misses sessions after promising to attend may be commenting on his reactions to the process of helping. The children in the family session who arrive looking tense and angry and refuse to take off their coats may be saying something about their feelings about being there. The client who sits back looking angry, with arms firmly folded across his chest, may be saying, "Go ahead, try and change me." These are all important messages; however, the common element is that the clients are not using words.

The crucial point in this discussion is that it is often hard to understand what clients are trying to say because of the indirect nature of their communications. In particular, negative behavior is difficult to understand, particularly for new workers, because it throws them off balance. Developing the capacity to reach behind negative behavior for the client's real message comes with the growth of the worker's sense of professional competency.

With communications so complex, how is the worker ever able to hear what the client is trying to say? This is where developing a preliminary empathy prior to a first (or any) session through the use of the "tuning in" skill can be helpful. It can substantially increase the odds in favor of understanding, particularly in the beginning stage of work when the conversation tends to be indirect. In the next section we examine the "tuning in" skill more closely.

THE PRELIMINARY PHASE:
TUNING IN TO SELF AND TO THE CLIENT

A major skill in the preliminary phase of work is development of the worker's sense of empathy. This technique can be employed before contact with the client has begun. Schwartz termed this process "**tuning in**." It involves the worker's effort to get in touch with potential feelings and concerns that the client may bring to the helping encounter. The purpose of the exercise is to help the worker become a more sensitive receiver of the client's indirect communications in the first sessions. For a number of reasons that were discussed earlier in this chapter, some of the most important client communications are not spoken directly. By tuning in, the worker may be able to hear the client's indirect cues and then respond directly.[2] This direct response to an indirect communication is one of the skills a worker can use to help clients manage their feelings. It is called **putting the client's feelings into words**.

In the balance of this section we will explore the importance of tuning in to issues related to the worker's authority, the differences between affective and intellectual tuning in, tuning in to the worker's own feelings, and different levels of tuning in.

Tuning In to the Authority Theme

All levels of tuning in will be illustrated in this book. I believe, however, that the first question on the client's mind is: "Who is this worker, and what kind of a person will she or he be?" For that reason, I will begin with what I will be calling the **authority theme**, focusing on issues related to the relationship between the client and the social worker. An example from practice will illustrate the general issues involved. This particular experience has been shared by workers in consultation sessions so often, with only slight variations, that it probably represents an archetype. The presenter was a social worker in a **child welfare** agency. She was 22, unmarried, and new to the job.

Her first interview was with a 38-year-old mother of seven children who had come to the agency's attention because of a neighbor's complaint about her care of her children. Another worker had been meeting with her for four months but was leaving the agency. The new worker was the replacement, making her first visit. After introductions, the worker and client sat in the living room chatting for a few minutes when the client suddenly turned to the worker and said, "By the way, do you have any children?" There was a brief silence after this embarrassing question. Recovering quickly, and hiding her feelings, the worker said to the client, "No, I don't have any children. However, I have taken a number of courses in child psychology." Discussing this incident in a consultation session, the worker reported her internal feelings and her thoughts: "I panicked! I thought, 'Oh my God, she knows I don't have any children—how am I supposed to help her?'"

While I will explore the issue of the authority theme using this example, I could just as easily have provided any number of variations on the same theme: the recovering alcoholic who wonders if the worker has "walked the walk" (been an alcoholic) or "talked the talk" (been a member of Alcoholics Anonymous); the gay man with AIDS who inquires if the worker is straight; or the person of color who describes prior white workers who "didn't understand our people." These variations, and others, will be explored throughout the book. For ease of exposition, I will stay with this first common example.

The conversation in the interview with the mother shifted back to the worker's agenda of agency business and didn't return to this area. An important issue had been raised indirectly, however, and an unprepared worker had responded defensively. If we were to analyze the more subtle, indirect communications involved in this incident, we could interpret the client's question in the following manner.

> **Client:** By the way, do you have any children? (*unstated:* I wonder if this one will be like the other worker. They have all kinds of ideas about how I should raise children and have never changed a dirty diaper themselves. How can they understand what it's like for me?)

Other interpretations are possible; however, I believe that this question is central for all clients in first sessions. The crucial part of the message left unsaid was the client's concern that she would not be understood. The worker's response, a product of her own concern about her capacity to help, only confirmed the client's apprehension. It is quite normal for clients to wonder if a new worker will be like other helping professionals whom they have met: a stereotypical cold, unfeeling "expert" who thinks she has all the answers. This thought was too dangerous to express openly, so it was only hinted at. The worker's reaction was also quite normal, especially for a new worker who had not anticipated the question.

If the worker had been tuned in to the client's potential concern, not intellectually but by actually trying to get in touch with the way clients in general, and this one in particular, might feel, she might have been able to read the real question behind the question. If she had been given some help in understanding her own feelings, either by a supervisor or by colleagues, she might have been able to consider in advance how to respond directly to an indirect cue in this important area. Each worker develops his or her own unique responses, but one way to deal with this situation might be to say:

> No, I don't have any children. Why do you ask? Are you wondering if I'm going to be able to understand what it's like for you having to raise so many? I'm concerned about that as well. If I'm to help you, I'm going to have to understand, and you are going to have to help me to understand.

Such a response might have opened up a discussion of the woman's past experiences with other workers, some of whom had been helpful and others of whom had not. The response also allows the worker to share her own feelings of concern (without overdoing them). She says, "I'm concerned about that as well." This is an example of the use of a second skill in the grouping described as skills designed to help clients manage their feelings. It will be called **sharing worker's feelings**. We will argue that if the worker withholds his or her own affect, then the energy invested in suppressing the worker's feelings will not be available for investing into the affect of the client. Of course, integrating personal and professional selves requires some restraint on the worker's part. It would not have been appropriate for the worker to have said, even if it were a reflection of her real feelings, "You're absolutely right! What are they doing sending me out to work with you when I've never changed a diaper or heated a bottle?" The client does not want to hear that level of concern. These feelings need to be shared with supervisors and colleagues before the interview.

As the client begins the worker's education, the work gets underway. Instead of the working relationship being closed, the potential exists for this one to begin to grow. If nothing else, the client might end the interview thinking, as one client in an earlier study of mine said, "This worker is different. Perhaps I can train her."

Although the empathic skills will be discussed in more detail in Chapter 4, it's important to comment here on the issue of genuineness. One of the key reasons for tuning in is to combat the ease with which helping professionals can learn to say the words related to affect without really experiencing the feelings. For example, a popular technique advocated in some texts on practice involves the use of "reflection." That is, the worker reflects back to the client the affective words. If a client says, "I'm really angry at my kids," the worker might repeat, "You're really angry at your kids." If I were the client in that situation, I probably would feel like saying, "Dummy, I just told you I was angry at my kids."

The problem with a reflective response is that it is mechanical and artificial. The worker is not really feeling the client's anger. When I press practitioners on this question, they usually admit that they reflected because they didn't know what else to say. Unfortunately, the client perceives the response as uncaring. The workers would have been better off being honest and admitting not knowing what to say.

An even better response might be to remain silent for a few moments—the skill of **containment**—and to try to feel how angry parents can get with their children, and then to respond with reactions that might deepen the conversation. For example, instead of being slightly behind the client, as illustrated in the reflective response, one approach might be to try to be one half step ahead of the client by putting the client's unstated feelings into words: "That's the thing, isn't it—how can you be so angry at the kids and at the same time, love them so much?"

The exact words one uses are not crucial, since each of us develops our own personal style and way of expressing our feelings and those of our clients. What is crucial is that the worker should be feeling *something*. My students have pointed out that this is easy for me to say and hard for them to do. The fact is, most of us have not learned how to deal well with our feelings, and those of others, in most areas of our lives. As one mature student put it, "I have trouble dealing with my kids' feelings; how am I going to help this client deal with hers?"

Fortunately, helping professionals have their whole practice lives in which to develop their ability to be genuinely empathic. As they listen to clients, trying to tune in, they will discover feelings within themselves that may have been earlier ignored. In the beginning, they will borrow the words of others. It is not uncommon for one of my students to bring the audiotape of an interview into an early class, with the students using my words in his or her efforts to empathize. With some, you can even pick up traces of my New York City accent. When this was pointed out by a fellow student, in one case, the mimicking student replied, with some feeling, "I know, and I don't want to be a little Shulman." I try to reassure my students and suggest that they can borrow whatever words they need in the beginning. With continued work at developing their skills, they soon become more comfortable and are able to find and use their own voice. This point is elaborated in Chapter 4.

In describing the situation with the young mother and the new worker, I mentioned the term **working relationship**. The concept of a working relationship is central to the model, so a brief explanation is required. A generally accepted model contained in most practice theories suggests that the activities of the helping person can develop a positive working relationship with the client; this is a precondition for helping. Something about the way the worker and client talk to and listen to each other, the flow of both positive and negative feelings between them, affects the outcome. I believe that the development of a working relationship is a precondition for helping.

The reader should note the use of the word *working* to differentiate this relationship from those that may be personal in nature (e.g., parent-child, friend). This is a simple yet crucial idea. The relationship is based upon the work to be done together. The purpose of the encounter will affect the relationship directly, and the relationship will be the vehicle through which this purpose is achieved. A common misconception about practice is that the worker must establish a relationship first and then begin to work. This leads to a practice of "chatting" with a client during the first contact, discussing the weather or other superficial matters, supposedly to set the client at ease. Actually, the reverse is often true, with the worker feeling more at ease and the client more uncomfortable. I suggest in Chapter 3 that the relationship grows out of the work itself and that a worker needs to get down to business quickly. The relationship is not separate from the work, but rather, it is part of the work. The very act of defining the nature of the work together (contracting) helps to develop the working relationship.

Of course, the worker must also be aware of cultural diversity issues that may moderate the just-stated rule of getting to the work quickly. In some cultures, for example for some Asian people or Native Americans, directness might be perceived as offensive. Cultural awareness would help a worker distinguish those situations where "small talk" about families or appropriate discussion of life experiences might be exactly what is needed to set the stage for the development of a working relationship.

Lum (1996) addresses this issue in a text dealing with practice with people of color. The author identifies the many barriers that may exist in the beginning stage in cross-cultural, or what I will term inter-ethnic, practice. The author provides an example:

> A common question asked by Native Americans in formal helping situations is: "How can I tell you about my personal life, which I share with my lifelong friends, when I have just met you only a half hour ago?" Mistrust and reservation are typical responses of ethnic clients until the social worker moves out of the category of stranger. Taking the first step of professional self-disclosure sets the stage for openness and relationship-building (p. 145).

Lum provides the following "practical suggestions for professional self-disclosure":

- *Introduce yourself.*
- *Share pertinent background about your work, family, and helping philosophy.*
- *Find a common point of interest with the client. (p. 145)*

Sensitivity to issues of race, gender, ethnicity, sexual orientation, physical and mental ability, and so on, can be just as important in what I will be referring to as intra-ethnic practice—that is, working with someone who is the same as you in some important characteristic. For example, an African-American male student presented an example during a videotaped discussion of diversity issues and practice (Shulman and Clay, 1994). He was working intra-ethnically with an African-American female client. The student recognized, however, that gender and class (he was from an upper middle-class, suburban background, and she was poor and living in the inner city) meant he was also working inter-ethnically and would have to deal with these potential barriers. Tuning in to his own feelings about working with persons of color as a part of the "system" would also be essential to his development as a social worker and his ability to deal with the authority theme.

Elements of the Working Relationship

Many elements make up the working relationship. Three included in my most recent study (Shulman, 1991) are **rapport, trust,** and **caring**. *Rapport* refers to the general sense on the client's part of getting along well with the worker. By *trust*, I mean the client's willingness to risk sharing thoughts, feelings, mistakes, and failures with the worker. By *caring*, I mean that clients sense that the worker is concerned about them as clients in their own right and that the worker wishes to help them with concerns that they feel are important. For example, a middle-aged son of an aging parent would experience the elder care worker as being concerned about him as a stressed caretaker, as well as being concerned about the well-being of his aged parent. In another example, a parent who has been reported as neglectful of her child would experience the child welfare worker as attempting to help her cope with her stresses that may cause the neglect, as well as attempting to investigate the child's situation for protective purposes. In later chapters, I will show how these themes of rapport, trust, and caring are affected by issues of confidentiality, the fact that the worker may be a mandated reporter of certain abuses, and so on. For now, I simply wish to put into operation the construct of the working relationship.

Many elements of a working relationship, such as trust and a sense of caring, are also important in other areas of our lives. This is sometimes the source of confusion about the differences between relationships in general and the working relationship. As will be seen in numerous examples in later chapters, these elements take on special meaning in the context of work.

I have defined the working relationship at this point in the discussion because my research (Shulman, 1978, 1991) suggests that the ability of the worker to be tuned in to the unspoken feelings and concerns of the client in the preliminary phase of work, and then to articulate these feelings, contributes to the establishment of a positive working relationship. In fact, all of the skills for helping clients to manage their feelings, when used in the beginning phase of practice, have been found to have a positive impact on the working relationship (Shulman, 1991, pp. 78–79). This underlines the importance of preparatory empathy and the worker's ability to respond directly to indirect cues.

When I present these ideas in classes or workshops, I usually note that the eyes of the participants seem to indicate that they have begun to free-associate to their own caseloads. This may be happening right now to the reader as well. When I inquire as to what is happening, they will reveal that they are feeling guilty as they review the many times they have passed over the indirect cues of their clients, particularly in the taboo and sensitive areas such as race, gender, ethnicity, and so on. I try to reassure them with the following advice.

If they still have a client active on their caseload, they can always go back and reopen what they may feel is unfinished business. For example, the worker in the earlier example who responded defensively could return the next week (or later) and say, "I was thinking about your question last week about whether or not I had children. I think you were really wondering if I could understand what it was like for you." Three months later, it might sound like this: "I think I ducked your question when we first met about whether or not I had children. It made me feel uncomfortable. I suspect you were really wondering whether or not I would understand what it was like for you raising seven children. I wondered if during our three months together I had come across as not understanding?" I believe clients love it when a worker shares a mistake and can be perceived, as described by one client in one of my studies, as "more like a real human being."

I would suggest that skillful practice involves learning how to shorten the distance between when a worker makes a mistake and when he or she catches it. Very skillful workers catch their mistakes in the same session that they make them. I also believe that becoming an effective practitioner involves learning from **active mistakes** (as opposed to inactivity resulting from fear of making a mistake), developing more skillful interventions, and then making more sophisticated mistakes.

One example of catching one's mistakes was provided by a second-year student who was preparing to take over as a new group leader for an ongoing group of mothers with children who had a chronic disease. The group met in a hospital. This student had read my book and had done his tuning in. His field instructor had explored his feelings at being a young, unmarried male, working with an all-female group of mothers. He had role-played how he would respond to the questions: "Are you married?" or "Do you have any children?" He had prepared for everything except what actually happened.

Before he could make his prepared opening statement, one group member said, "Before you start, I want to let you know what we think of this damned hospital!" The force of the anger in her voice stunned him. She continued, "We have doctors who patronize us, nurses who push us around, and we keep getting young social workers like you who don't even have kids!" The reader can probably imagine what happened to all of his tuning in. As he put it later, "It went right out the window." When I asked him what he had felt like saying, he replied, "I may be in the wrong room!" Fortunately, he was so thrown by the comment that he did not switch to what I call a "counseling voice," the way of speaking some workers reserve for clients—a manner that they would never use with colleagues or friends. He did not suppress the feelings churning away inside of him and respond mechanically by saying, "I'm glad you could share that with me," or "Go with that feeling, Mrs. Smith." He was so thrown that he responded spontaneously, saying, ***"I may not have any children, but I have a mother just like you!"***

He was shocked, and the group members were shocked. The angry Mrs. Smith looked again at this new worker and probably saw him for the first time. Up to that moment, he had been a representative of professionals, and she was responding to a stereotype. He was most likely concerned about what he was going to put in his process recording for his field instructor. The group was an ongoing one, so other members moved in and shifted the conversation to a more general discussion. The remainder of the meeting could be characterized as an "illusion of work," a term to be more fully defined later in this text. In this case, it meant conversation without real focus, meaning, or feelings.

He returned the following week after further discussion and tuning in with his supervisor. He began as follows:

> Mrs. Smith, I would like to discuss last week for a moment. I was unready for so much anger from you, and as a result, I think I missed the pain that must be under that anger for you and for all of the group members. You must have run into a lot of professionals who simply did not understand how much it hurts to have a child who is always ill and who never gets better. You saw me, a young worker, and felt, "Here comes another one."

His comment was greeted with silence in the room. Silences will be discussed in detail later in the text. For now, I will suggest that they are full of meaning, but they are sometimes hard to interpret. Most people guess that inside the silence might be some of the members getting in touch with their pain or some positive response to the human quality of this young worker.

Mrs. Smith, who had been so angry, started to cry and said to the other women in the group, "You are all married. You have someone to help you. I'm a single parent. Who helps me cope? I never have time for myself!" Another woman responded to her: "I'm married, but big deal!" She went on to describe her husband working 12 hours a day, six days a week, since the birth of the ill child (his form of flight from pain). The group took off as the worker listened and began his education.

I don't believe he would have been able to reach for the underlying pain the first week. I am not sure he could have done it the second week if he had not risked his spontaneous response the first week. He would have still been struggling with suppressing his own feelings. Some might argue it is possible to get to the empathy of the second week without having to risk the spontaneous expression of feelings the first week. That has not been my experience. The reader will have to explore that question in her or his own practice. I believe this young worker is better able, now, to share some of his feelings when faced with anger in a first session and then more quickly move to reach for the client's underlying pain. He now makes more sophisticated mistakes.

A second line of reassurance I use is to explain to workers that they are usually more effective than they think they have been. More than two-thirds of the clients in one of my studies (Shulman, 1991) found their workers to be helpful. This is similar to the findings in my earlier work (1978). Workers tend to underestimate their positive impact on clients. They eventually communicate their caring and concern for the client. It just may take longer, with a period of testing that might not have been necessary if the worker had tuned in and responded directly.

Finally, regarding those clients whom they did not reach and who are no longer on their caseload, I suggest that they realize that they did the best they could, given the training and level of support that they had at the time. Somewhat like an artist who must hang up an early painting that reflects limited skill and knowledge, learn from it, and begin a new painting, the worker must start anew with the next client. I suggest a little guilt is helpful, since it keeps the worker in a self-discovery and learning mode of practice. A lot of guilt would be overwhelming and counterproductive. It will be hard for a worker to help a client to manage his or her feelings of guilt if the worker is overly judgmental of her or his own work.

The practice described in the preceding examples raised the following three areas for further discussion: affective versus intellectual tuning in; tuning in to the worker's own feelings; and the different levels of tuning in. Each of these is explored now in more detail.

Affective Versus Intellectual Tuning In

To tune in effectively, one must try to experience the client's feelings. One way to do this is to recall personal experiences that are similar to the client's. The client, for example, is having a first contact with a person in authority. This is true even if the client is there voluntarily and the helping person has no specific control functions (e.g., protection of children, maintenance of parole). The first encounter is also a new situation, filled with unknown elements.

What new experiences or first encounters with people in authority has the worker had? Can the worker remember how it felt, what his or her concerns were? A new school, a new teacher, the first experience of hospitalization—any of these might serve to remind one and put one in touch with feelings related to those of the client. The important point is that the worker needs actually to experience these feelings.

Supervision in practice, or field instruction in social work education, can provide important assistance to the worker or student in developing genuine empathy in the tuning-in process. [See *Interactional Supervision* (Shulman, 1993a) and *Teaching the Helping Skills: A Field Instructor's Guide* (Shulman, 1993b).]

In a preparatory consultation session with a social worker who is working with AIDS patients, family members, friends, and lovers, the supervisor attempts to help the worker get in touch with issues facing all of the parties concerned. In this excerpt, the tuning in is to a gay man whose lover has recently been diagnosed with ARC (AIDS-related complex), which is a precursor to an AIDS diagnosis.

Supervisor: What do you think John must be feeling right now?

Worker: Devastated! It must be as if an earthquake has hit him and his lover.

Supervisor: Are you really feeling devastated right now?

Worker: Really feeling it? Well no, but I can imagine how it must feel.

Supervisor: Try to take it further. Can you remember a time in your life when you felt devastated by a family earthquake? I'm not asking for the details of your personal life. I'm just trying to help you get in touch. For me, it was a breast cancer diagnosis for my sister. I can still remember the feelings well.

Worker: The closest I can remember was when my grandfather had a heart attack. We were close to each other. He was old, but I still couldn't believe it, and it took a long time until I really faced it.

Supervisor: Now you're closer. So tell me, what would you be feeling right now if you were John?

Worker: Oh my God, this can't be happening. It must be a mistake. Maybe the diagnosis was wrong. I can't believe I'm going to lose him. What am I going to do?

Supervisor: What do you mean—going to do?

Worker: We have been sleeping together for over a year. What if I have it? Am I going to stay with him? I must stay with him, he needs me now more than ever. But what about my life? I've seen so many friends in these relationships. I want to help him—I *must* help him—but what about my own life?

Supervisor: As John, how are you really feeling right now?

Worker: I'm overwhelmed, depressed, and I think I'm even angry at him for having AIDS. But how can I be angry at him when I love him?

Supervisor: I think you are getting closer to possible themes. We have to remember to be prepared for a totally different response from John. Each person may be quite different. What are your feelings right now about working with John and with his lover Rod?

Worker: I'm not sure how I feel about anything right now. I know I'm a little scared. A part of me is not sure I want to get close to this pain. I'm not sure what it will do to me. If I get close to Rod, I'm going to lose him as well.

Supervisor: I'll try to help you through this. It is going to be tough, in part, because it's the first time around for you. My problem is that I have gone through it so often, with so many clients, that I sometimes forget what it was like the first time. (silence) No, to be honest, I don't forget—I just feel like closing it off myself. We should both monitor this process and help each other if our defenses get in the way. Also, raise it at the next staff meeting. I think others can offer some support.

Perhaps the most important contribution made by the supervisor to the worker's growth was her willingness to admit that the struggle to deal with one's own feelings persists throughout one's professional life. The supervisor provided a model for the worker to emulate. She could not ask the worker to tune in to the feelings of the client unless she was simultaneously tuning in to the worker's emotional response. The suggestion that the worker reach out for additional support from colleagues was also helpful. In one of my studies (Shulman, 1991, 1993a), workers who reported access to support from supervisors and colleagues were more effective at providing that same support to their clients. The study also indicated that the supervisor would need access to sources of support as well.

Tuning In to Your Own Feelings

The AIDS example emphasizes how important it is for workers to get in touch with their own feelings. How we feel can have a great deal to do with how we think (cognitions) and how we act. The young, unmarried workers in the earlier examples could not immediately respond to the clients' concerns because of their preoccupation with their own feelings of inadequacy. The worker in the AIDS example, as he explores his own reactions to working with the terminally ill, will discover many of the same feelings of helplessness and impotency often felt by friends, lovers, and family members of a person with AIDS. Health professionals often feel quite deeply their inability to save a dying patient. Precisely because the helping person's feelings are similar to the client's, it may be difficult to listen and to respond. In a recent experience co-leading a group for persons with AIDS in early substance abuse recovery, I commented to my co-leader, a full-time, experienced staff person at the AIDS agency, that I would need his help in dealing with the serious decline in health of one of our clients. He responded, "And what makes you think it ever gets any easier for me?"

By tuning in to one's own feelings and experiencing them before the engagement, their power to block the worker can be lessened. In many ways, the helping process is one in which workers learn a great deal about their own feelings as they relate to their professional function. One's capacity to understand others and oneself can grow while engaging in this continual process. In fact, I believe this is one of the reasons many workers have entered the social work profession.

This stress on the importance of the worker's own feelings runs counter to many conceptions of professionalism. As pointed out in Chapter 1, a central construct of the medical model stresses the hiding of real feelings, which are seen as interfering with one's professional role. In a study I did of the effects of family physicians' communications and relationship skills, it was interesting to note that the strongest predictor of positive outcomes, such as patient satisfaction and comprehension, was whether the doctor felt positively or negatively toward the patient (Shulman and Buchan, 1982). Also, patients were very good perceivers of their doctors' attitudes towards them. The crucial point is that we need to learn to understand and use our feelings, instead of pretending to deny their existence. This core issue will be explored in many different ways throughout the chapters that follow.

Different Levels of Tuning In

Tuning in can be done at a number of different levels. To illustrate, we will use the example of a social worker at a residential center for delinquent adolescent boys. A first level of tuning in would be to the general category of adolescents. The literature on stages of development and the worker's own recollections can help in this process. The adolescent is going through a time of normative crisis in which he must begin to define himself in a new role. A number of central questions are dominant. He is trying to sort out conflicting messages in our society about the qualities that make a real man.

Sensitivity to underlying currents of feelings, to the ways in which clients struggle to deal with the normative crises of life, can also be enriched through reading works of fiction. The adolescent's efforts to develop his sense of differentiation from his family, to further his independence while at the same time trying to maintain some sort of relationship, has been explored with great perceptiveness by a number of authors.

Workers must tap into their own adolescent experiences in an effort to remember the feelings associated with this stage of life. Here are some examples from a training session in which workers attempted to express some of the problems of adolescence.

> There are so many things I need to know about sex and girls. When I talk to adults about these things, they make me feel dirty or try to scare me with AIDS. It's important to me that I get accepted by the guys—be one of the gang. It feels great when we hang out together, kid around, talk about girls, gripe about parents and other adults. I'd be willing to do almost anything, even things I don't feel comfortable about, to be in and not left out.
>
> I'm feeling a bit trapped by the drugs at school. I'm under a lot of pressure to use—and I've tried to resist—but it's hard not to go along. I'm worried about my friend. He's gone over the edge and could get himself in trouble. Who can I talk to? I don't want to be a fink. If I talk to a teacher, all I will get is a lecture and my friend could get thrown out of school. I can't talk my parents. My mother would have a fit, and Dad is so drunk himself most evenings I can't talk to him.

The second level of tuning in is the specific client: in this case, youngsters who are in trouble with the law. Information on the background of the boys, the nature of the delinquent acts, their relationships with their families, and so forth can all prove useful in attempting to orient oneself to the thoughts and feelings of a specific group of adolescents.

They probably feel that society is starting to define them as outcasts who can't fit in. Their feelings must be mixed.

> The hell with them; who wants to be part of all of that crap anyway! Parents, teachers, social workers—they are always pushing you around, telling you what to do. I don't give a damn.... What the hell is happening to me? I'm getting deeper and deeper into trouble, people are taking control over my life. Maybe I am a loser—how in the hell am I going to end up?

The third level of tuning in relates to the specific phase of work. For instance, an adolescent has been judged delinquent and is about to enter a new residential setting. What are the feelings, questions, and concerns on his mind about this new experience, and what are some of the indirect ways they may be communicated?

> I'm scared stiff but I'm going to act cool—I won't show it. I wonder about the workers, what kind of people are they? How do they treat kids like me? And the other kids, what will they be like? Is it going to be hard to break in? I've got to watch my ass.

Many of the general fears people bring to new situations will be present. For example, the client may be apprehensive about the new demands placed on him and concerned as to whether he will be able to meet them. At the same time, his feelings may include a sense of hope. "Maybe this place will be OK. Maybe these workers and the kids will accept me, make me feel at home. Maybe I can get some help here. Anything is better than going back home." The key element in all tuning in is the recognition of ambivalence. A part of the client is moving towards the service, hopeful but guarded. Another part is using past experiences or hearsay about the service, workers, and so on and defensively holding back.

Finally, what happens if we add race and class to the example, as was done in a presentation at a workshop I led? Consider an African-American teenager from a poor, inner-city neighborhood who has been mandated by a judge to a residential program for "delinquent boys" in a suburban to rural, middle-class, white community. The core focus of the program is on "anger management" skills.

Not only is he in a new and potentially frightening situation, he is also in a community where he will be an outsider. For teens of color, finding themselves in a white neighborhood is threatening. If the staff of the center are also white, he will probably begin (and possibly end) the experience wondering what any of this experience will have to do with what he faces when he returns to the streets of the city.

In the tuning-in exercise of workers preparing to meet new clients, I have usually observed that the first efforts at tuning in always pick up the resistance, the defensive side of the ambivalence. This often reflects the worker's frustrating past experiences. It is a statement of the worker's concerns that the client will not want help. This can be a self-fulfilling prophecy unless the worker has a sense of the client's potential for resilience and change, and a belief that part of the client is reaching out to the worker. Otherwise, the worker's pessimistic stereotype of the client will meet head on with the client's pessimistic stereotype of the worker. The tuning-in process is a first step in trying to break this self-defeating cycle.

An important objection often raised to the tuning-in skill is that the worker may develop a view of the client that is far removed from what the client actually feels and thinks. The worker may then proceed to make sure the client fits the preconceived picture. This is a very real danger if the tuning in is not tentative. In a sense, the key to the successful use of the tuning-in skill rests in the worker putting all hunches aside when beginning the engagement. What the worker responds to in the first contacts are the actual "productions" of the client. By this I mean the direct and indirect cues that emerge in conversation with the client.

For example, if the worker in the residential setting has tuned in to the front a tough kid might put up on the first day and some of the concerns that may underline this front, the worker will have to see evidence of this behavior before acting. The worker reaches only tentatively for indirect messages, prepared to have the client share totally different and unexpected responses. Each client is different, and tuning in is an exercise designed to sensitize the worker to potential concerns and feelings. It does not dictate what they must be. The assumption is that after tuning in both to the client's feelings and your own, there is a better chance that your spontaneous reactions to the client's productions will be more helpful. If it simply produces a new stereotype of the client, it will be self-defeating.

I remember one example in which a worker tuned in to what he believed would be the client's anger at having to come to counseling. Appropriately, the worker reached for these feelings. The client indicated that he was not angry, and the worker provided a second chance by suggesting that other clients had felt angry under the same circumstances. The client, with some exasperation in his voice, answered a second time, indicating he was not angry. When the worker, on automatic pilot, then said: "Well, I can't understand why you are not angry!", the red-faced client responded, "Well, damn it, now I *am* angry!" The lack of tentativeness on the part of the worker had led to a self-fulfilling prophecy.

This section of the chapter has highlighted the importance of preparatory empathy in the beginning phase of practice. In later chapters, we will return to tuning in as we explore different phases of work, different modalities of practice (e.g., family and group) and even its importance in working with other professionals. In the next section, we focus on the skill of responding directly to indirect cues.

RESPONDING DIRECTLY TO INDIRECT CUES

The importance of tuning in during the preliminary phase lies in preparing the worker to hear indirect cues in the first contacts and to respond directly to these cues. In the first example given in this chapter, the new worker would have demonstrated this skill if she had said in response to the client's question, "Do you have any children?" something like, "No. Why do you ask? Are you wondering if I'm going to be able to understand what it is like to raise kids?"

A direct response to the indirect cue would have been just as important if the worker did have children. In one example, a worker in an agency dealing with physically differently-abled children was asked by a new client if she had children. When the worker responded positively, the client asked, "Teenage children?" The worker shared that her children were teenagers. After a brief silence, the mother inquired, "A handicapped teenaged child?" The worker in this case was able to respond, "As a matter of fact, the reason I was attracted to work in this agency was that my own teenager does have a physical handicap." After a long pause, the client responded, "But not like mine!"

The client was not satisfied with the responses because the real question was not related to the worker's family situation. I believe this worker would have been better off answering, "I do have a handicapped teenaged child; however, the experience is different for each of us. You'll have to let me know what it has been like for you."

The advantage of a direct response in this example is that it opens up an area of important conversation that can then deepen the working relationship. A common objection is that the worker may "lead" the client by putting words into his or her mouth that are not really there. In addition, the argument goes, even if the worker guesses correctly, the client may not be ready to deal with that particular feeling or concern and may react defensively, be overwhelmed, and not come back. Because of this fear, the worker may be cautioned to withhold hunches and to wait for clients to raise a concern or feeling when they are ready to do so.

I argue in favor of risking more direct responses early in the first contacts. As the working relationship develops, the client is watching the worker, trying to sense what kind of a helping person this is. If there is diversity in the relationship (e.g., Latino family and white worker), the question carries even more potency. Indirect communications are employed because the client is reluctant to risk communicating directly some of the more difficult and more taboo feelings. Let us consider what happens when the worker responds directly to the indirect cues, for example, by using the skill of articulating the client's feelings. If the worker's guess is "off base," the client will usually let it be known. Even if the client goes along reluctantly, hesitation in the voice and lack of affective response will tip the worker off to the artificial agreement. The worker can then respond directly to that cue. This is an example of how the worker can learn and grow from an active mistake.

One very common example of indirect communication is one in which the client, early in the interview with a new worker, says, "I'm glad to see you. My last worker was really terrible!" There are few comments that can strike more fear into the heart of a new worker. The usual response is to immediately change the subject. Workers claim to be uncomfortable discussing another professional. In my experience, they are particularly quick to change the subject if they secretly agree that the other worker is terrible.

The mistake they make is to think the client is really talking about the previous worker. When in early contacts clients refer to other people, such as social workers and doctors who have not helped, it is usually the new worker they are really talking about, only indirectly. A direct response to this indirect cue might be: "It sounds like you experienced a hard time with John. Can you tell me what went wrong so that I can understand what you are expecting from me? I'd like to try to make our relationship a positive one." The discussion of the past relationship is cast in the context of the beginning of this new relationship. The worker is not making a judgment about the previous worker—rather, the intent is simply to acknowledge what the client has experienced.

Another early client statement, even harder for the new worker to hear, often sounds like this: "My last worker was really terrific! My kids used to look forward to his visits." Once again, if the new worker can handle his or her own feelings, then a direct response to the indirect cue might be the following: "It sounds like you and your children really got close to John. You must really miss him. Can you tell me why you felt he was terrific? I may not be able to be just like him, because I'm a different person, but it would help to know what you are looking for in a worker." Once again, the ensuing discussion moves the worker and the client quickly into the authority theme—the relationship between the giver and taker of help. The worker both acknowledges the feelings of loss and reaches for the client's concern about how well the new worker will replace the previous worker. In effect, the new worker is starting to answer the client's implied question.

Students and workers have said to me, "That sounds great, but how do you say that when you are scared spitless?" I point out that you usually don't say it the first time, but if you are good, you catch yourself before the end of the interview, or on the next contact. For example, you might say, "I was thinking about our last conversation, and I wondered if when you were talking about your problems with John, you might also have been thinking about what kind of a worker I'm going to be?"

A second objection raised by workers, particularly those with some elements of mandated authority (e.g., financial aid workers, probation officers), is that they fear the client who is positive about the last worker might may say something like this: "Well, John, he didn't hassle me. When I needed something extra, he came up with the money." Or they might say, "John wasn't all uptight about every beer I had." If the comment about the last worker is an indirect communication related to how the worker is going to enforce his or her authority, then a direct response opens up the discussion for the worker to be clear about how he or she will operate—what the client can expect from the worker, and what the worker will expect from the client.

If a child welfare client is angry at the last worker for "always trying to prove I was a bad mother and trying to take away my kids," a direct response about this worker's perspective on the use of authority would be helpful. For example, the worker might say,

> Mrs. Smith, my agency is not trying to take away children. There are too many in care already. I would like to try to help you keep your family together. I would only recommend removing your children if I felt they were in danger through abuse or neglect. And even if that ever happened, I would still want to try to help you get them back. I hope I can convince you that I really mean this.

This is an important part of the contracting process, and getting the issue on the table early can speed up the work. The issue of authority and contracting is discussed in more detail in Chapter 3.

Not only are clients responding to workers in early sessions as symbols of authority and stereotypes based upon prior experiences, they sometimes are operating on the basis of specific information about the particular worker (or agency) provided through the grapevine. For example, one parole officer reported a first session with a recently released ex-con in which they got into a battle of wills over whether or not the client's last worker had been too tough. The new parole officer tuned in, between sessions, and inquired during the next session, "Were you really asking what kind of a parole officer I'm going to be?" After a long pause, the ex-con said, "The word back at the pen is that you're a real dink." The parole officer asked what that meant, and the ex-con revealed that he had left the penitentiary with a dossier on the parole officer at least as long as the one the worker had on him. The parolee was beginning with a stereotype of the worker that needed to be dealt with early in the work. Even if the parolee had not possessed any information on this particular parole officer, there would have been a stereotype of parole officers to contend with. In reverse, the worker has to be careful not to be so worried about being "conned" that he or she relates to the client as a stereotype rather than a person.

If the client is not ready to pick up on the worker's direct response to an indirect cue, particularly in taboo areas, because of lack of trust or lack of readiness to share the concern or feelings, the client still has the option of not responding. The worker must give the client that room. The important outcome of the worker's direct responses is not that the client will always immediately deal with the concern. The crucial message to the client is that the worker does understand and is ready to deal with this taboo area when the client is ready. The message received is that the worker is prepared to discuss even tough issues (e.g., authority) or painful themes of concern. In effect, these interventions give the client permission to deal with these issues when ready, while simultaneously showing the worker to be a feeling, caring, direct person who can see the world through the client's eyes and not judge harshly.

My research findings have repeatedly supported the importance of the use of the tuning-in and direct-response skills. My study in a Canadian provincial child welfare program (Shulman, 1991) replicated earlier findings (Shulman, 1978) supporting this view. Although findings in any study are always tentative, even when replicated, these shed some interesting light on this issue. I was able to examine whether a specific skill, or group of skills, contributed to strengthening the worker-client relationship. The working relationship construct consisted of two elements described earlier as trust and caring. This working relationship, in turn, was the medium for effective helping and positive outcomes.

Clients in the study were asked to rate their workers' use of eight specific skills. The scores for the four skills most related to this discussion were averaged to create a scale called *Skills for Helping Clients to Manage Their Feelings.* These skills were the following:

- *Reaching inside of silences;*
- *Putting the client's feelings into words;*
- *Displaying understanding of client's feelings;*
- *Sharing worker's feelings.*

In one explanation, employing a technique called **causal path analysis**, I was able to determine the path of influence and strength of influence of these skills on the development of the working relationship and a number of outcome measures.[3] Findings indicated that the use of this group of skills positively affected the client's perception of the worker's caring, and in turn, the caring dimension of the working relationship had a moderately positive impact on the client's perception that the worker was helpful. In addition, caring had a small but statistically significant impact on two other outcome measures: the final court status of the child (e.g., permanent custody) as well as the number of days children spent in care.[4] These findings provide further support for the central construct of this practice model—that worker skills affect outcomes *through* their influence on the working relationship.

The average scores achieved for each skill by workers also revealed an interesting pattern. While clients reported that their workers acknowledged their feelings "fairly often," their rating of the worker's articulating their feelings for them was between "seldom" and "fairly often." Exploring silences was rated closer to "seldom" and sharing the worker's feelings was rated "seldom" by study clients. This pattern, repeated in a number of my studies, provides some sense of the degree of difficulty in developing these skills as well as support for the argument of the dominance of the medical paradigm (see Chapter 1).

Since 81 families out of the 305 in the study provided us with ratings of their workers' use of skills at the time we interviewed them, as well as a retrospective rating of skill use when they first met their workers, I was able to do some tentative analysis of the impact of time on the model.[5] Employing a statistical method called **regression analysis**, I found that the use of these skills for helping clients to manage their feelings in the beginning phase of practice did have a moderately strong predictive ability for both the caring and trust elements of the working relationship. When the use of these skills in the middle phase of practice was examined, they still had a moderate impact on relationship, although less than in the beginning phase. Both of these findings are consistent with the constructs of the practice theory.

Finally, I examined each specific skill in the study, when used both in the beginning and middle phases, and analyzed their simple correlations with the elements of trust and caring as well as the client's perception of the worker's helpfulness.[6] All four skills for helping clients to manage their feelings were found to have moderate positive correlations with relationship and outcome measures, increasing to moderately strong correlations in the middle phase of practice. In general, the positive impact of the use of these skills appears to be supported by research findings.

I would argue that for most clients, their difficulty in articulating their own feelings at the beginning of a new relationship, perhaps even being conscious of what they feel, requires that workers take the risks represented by tuning in and responding directly to indirect cues. Some additional examples of the use of these skills follow.

The first illustration is from a school counselor's initial contact with a sixth-grade child whom she had observed in the class at the request of the teacher. The child was the class clown and did not do his work, and the teacher did not know how to reach him. Using her hunches, the worker began her conversation with the child as follows.

> Class was into their art work. I walked over to Steven and asked if he would come and talk with me. He came along easily. He seemed apprehensive and nervous (the indirect cues). I tried to deal with this by saying I was not a teacher, and I had not come to check up on him. I explained that his teacher was concerned because he didn't seem to be enjoying class and had asked me to talk to him. My job was to try to help kids who weren't having fun in school or getting much out of their work. After some further conversation about my role, I said that he seemed quite bright and was able to do the work on math with the class. He agreed. I said I also noticed that when he began to fall behind or things got a bit difficult, he seemed to be really frustrated and just gave up. Steven nodded, smiling, and said that I was right, that's how it happened.

The worker had tuned in to his original anxiety and so tried in her opening statement to offer some reassurance. She began to demonstrate her understanding by showing Steven that she could sense the underlying frustration that led to his giving up.

Another example of direct responses to indirect cues comes from a recording of an interview with a single-parent mother who had just returned home from the hospital with her baby to live with her parents.

> I phoned Linda at her work on the day of the appointment to confirm the time. She said she had "forgotten" but would like to come anyway because she had a few things she wanted to talk to me about. I asked if her concerns involved her parents and the situation at home. She said they did.
>
> [Later] As the interview started, Linda sat stirring her coffee, silent, looking down at the cup. I said, "Linda, you sounded rather upset on the phone. Do you want to talk about the things that are really happening at home?" Linda started to cry and said, with a lot of emotion, "I'm breaking up my parents' marriage. They are fighting all the time. My father is screaming and swearing at both me and the baby and then at my mother."

The worker had tuned in to the difficult time the family and Linda were having during her first days at home. She "reached" for this on the phone and then did so again in response to the client's nonverbal cue at the start of the interview.

The worker's signal to Linda allowed the client to move directly into a painful area of discussion. I believe the client is often ready early in the contacts to discuss tough issues, explore taboo subjects, and even deal with the worker-client relationship if only the worker will give the invitation. Workers have said in consultation sessions that they often hesitate because they are not sure if they are ready. Thus, the worker's own ambivalence about exploring an area of work can produce the block. In the guise of protecting the client, workers are actually protecting themselves. As one worker put it, "I don't reach directly for those cues early in the work, because I'm afraid the client may take up my invitation. What will I do with all that feeling if I get it?" This excellent question is explored in more detail in later chapters.

Workers will have particular difficulty in reaching for cues in taboo areas. In another example, one student social worker in a school setting described working for weeks with a depressed teenager who seemed unable to share what was upsetting her. There were enough cues related to problems with the client's mother's live-in boyfriend to alert the worker to the possibility of sexual abuse. The worker felt uncomfortable about raising the issue directly. Finally, taking her courage in hand, the worker said at the end of an interview, "You know, a surprisingly high percentage of teenage girls and young women report that they have experienced some form of sexual abuse during their lives." The client did not respond, and the interview ended. The client began the next session with the worker by disclosing sexual harassment and abuse experienced with the mother's boyfriend. I believe the worker had signaled to the client that she was ready to hear if the client was ready to share. One of the skills examined in the study (1991), included in a grouping called *Skills for Helping Clients to Manage Their Problems*, was called "supporting clients in taboo areas." This skill, when used by the worker in the beginning phase of practice, was also predictive of more effective helpfulness in the middle phases of work.

Consider this final example, in which a white school social worker is talking to Dean, an African-American teen, about his expressed desire to return the following year to a public school in his inner-city community. He had been part of a special program that bussed volunteer teens of color from the inner city to white, suburban, private schools for enriched educational programs. Since the worker had already acknowledged and explored their racial difference early in their work together, the stage was set for the worker to reach for the underlying reasons motivating the desire to change. After tuning in to the possible reasons, the worker reaches for underlying issues, although still reluctant to name race as one of them.

Worker: I remember a couple of week ago you mentioned you wanted to go to the public schools next year. I'm curious why you would want to do that if you like getting away from the city to come to school.

Dean: I do like it here, but my brother and cousin go to public schools in the city.

Worker: Is that why you want to go to the public school?

Dean: Sort of. I don't think they get as good of an education as I do, though.

Worker: I see. I guess I'm still a little confused why you would want to go the public school. Maybe you're not sure yourself? I'm thinking that it may be difficult to come to school out here where you have a totally different atmosphere from what your brother and cousin experience in the public schools. Then you have to go back home and fit into the routine there, which is very different from what your friends at this school experience.

Dean: It really is different.

Worker: Tell me how it is different.

Dean: Well, it's like I have to act different when I am at school than when I am home.

Worker: Like you're struggling with two different identities? You are expected to act a certain way at this school, and that way doesn't fit in with how you are supposed to act at home?

Dean: Right! Here, I'm supposed to act "white," and at home I have to act "black" or people will accuse me of being too "white." I have to be mean at home, but I can be nice here.

This conversation, aided by the worker's tuning in, created the opportunity for the young man to explore with the social worker his ambivalent feelings about making the change. Of course, since social workers have experienced the same set of taboos and have observed the same set of norms of behavior as their clients, it will take training and support, from supervisors and/or peers, for the workers to feel comfortable enough to give clients permission to explore these areas of work.

OPPRESSION PSYCHOLOGY

As aids to the tuning-in process, it is important for social workers to draw upon the social sciences and the large theory and knowledge base on human development, behavior, and the impact of the social environment. This theory base can help the practitioner to understand the client in new ways and to hear underlying client communication that might otherwise be missed. Of course, as in the previous sections of this chapter, the reader is cautioned to use information in a tentative manner and to be open to totally different responses on the part of the client.

As one example of a theory that can guide our practice, I have selected the oppression psychology of Frantz Fanon. A brief introduction to the life, views, and psychology of Fanon will help to set the stage for the use of a number of his central ideas and those of others who have built on his work. Fanon, an early exponent of the psychology of oppression, was a black, West Indian revolutionary psychiatrist who was born on the French-colonized Island of Martinique in 1925. He died at the age of 36. His short life was chronicled by Bulhan (1985). At the age of 17, Fanon enlisted in the French army to fight against the Nazis in World War II. He later became interested in and studied psychiatry. While working as a chief of service at a psychiatric hospital in Algeria, he secretly provided support and medical services to the national liberation front (FLN) fighting against the French colonial government. When he resigned his position, he became a spokesperson for the FLN and was based in Tunisia. These experiences, and others, shaped his views of psychology, which challenged many of the constructs of the widely held, European-American, white, male-dominated psychology of the day. Bulhan states,

> In the first chapter of his classic *The Wretched of the Earth* (1968), Fanon elaborated the dynamics of violence and the human drama that unfolds in situations of oppression. He boldly analyzed violence in its structural, institutional, and personal dimensions....
>
> Fanon analyzed the psycho-existential aspects of life in a racist society. He emphasized the experiential features and hidden psychoaffective injuries of blacks and the various defensive maneuvers they adopted. Another unstated objective was quite personal: He himself had experienced these injuries, and writing about them was a way of coming to terms with himself (p. 138).

While Fanon's psychology emerged from his analysis of race oppression, particularly oppression associated with white, European colonial repression of persons of color, many of the key concepts can apply to any oppressed population. In doing so, it is important to recognize the significant differences in degree and types of oppression experienced by clients. The results of the oppression of African-Americans, for example, rooted in the unique experience of slavery, must be seen as one of the most critical, major social problems still facing urban areas in America.

In addition, we must be cautious in thinking about the impact of oppression, since it may be done in ways that ignore significant strengths and resiliency demonstrated by oppressed clients and communities. Such a one-sided view can lead to a practice that does not recognize or work with existing sources of support (e.g., the extended family, the church, community leadership). In the next section of this chapter we will complement this oppression model with a summary of a resiliency model that will help us to uncover clients' strengths for coping.

If we think about issues of oppression, vulnerability, and resiliency broadly, then many of the clients we deal with as social workers can be understood using such a model. The mentally ill, female survivors of sexual abuse, persons with AIDS, the differently abled (physically or mentally), long-term unemployed persons, persons of color, the homeless, aged nursing home residents, neglected and abused children, clients addicted to substances or in recovery—all of these clients and others can be understood using a framework that takes oppression, vulnerability, and resiliency into account.

These concepts will be illustrated in the examples of practice explored in this book. Strategies for social worker intervention, based upon understanding emerging from this psychology, will be directed toward helping clients deal with both the oppressor within and the oppressor without. In fact, it will be argued that unless we broaden our understanding of many of our clients' problems in living as being dynamic and systematic in nature, and related to oppression, then the social agencies, social work departments, and helping professionals who are trying to help these clients can themselves inadvertently become part of the system of oppression.

The Master-Slave Paradigm

We have already noted the influence of Hegel's 1807 (1996 reprint) formulation of the "master-slave" dialectic, which described relationships in which two people, each depending upon recognition of the self by the other, struggle to determine a hierarchy. The winner of the struggle (the master) is recognized by the loser (the slave) without having to reciprocate the recognition. While the complete exposition of the dialectic is more complex than presented here, the central idea of gaining one's sense of self through exploitation of others can be seen in many different oppressive relationships. The abusing parent and the abused child; the battering husband and his wife; societal male-female sexism; the scapegoating of religious groups (e.g., the Jews) and ethnic and racial groups (e.g., Southeast Asian immigrants, Hispanics, African-Americans, Native Americans); the treatment of the differently abled (physically or mentally); the "normal" population and the "mentally ill"; and the straight society's repression of lesbians and homosexuals, are all examples in which one group (usually the majority) uses another group for enhancing a sense of self.

Repeated exposure to oppression, subtle or direct, may lead vulnerable members of the oppressed group to internalize the negative self-images projected by the external oppressor—the "oppressor without." The external oppressor may be an individual (e.g., the sexual abuser of a child) or an aspect of society (e.g., the racial stereotypes perpetuated against people of color). Internalization of this image and repression of the rage associated with oppression may lead to destructive behaviors toward self and others as oppressed people become "autopressors" participating in their own oppression. Thus, the oppressor without becomes the oppressor within. Evidence of this process can be found in the maladaptive use of addictive substances and the growing internal violence in communities of oppressed people, such as city ghettos populated by persons of color.

Oppressed people may develop a *victim complex,* "...viewing all actions and communications as further assaults or simply other indications of their victim status. This is one expression of the 'adaptive paranoia' seen among the oppressed" (Bulhan, 1985, p. 126). The paranoia is adaptive since oppression is so omnipresent that it would be maladaptive not to be constantly alert to its presence. For the white worker with a client of color, the male worker with a female client, the straight worker with a gay or lesbian client, etc., this notion raises important implications for the establishment of an effective and trusting working relationship. These implications are explored in later chapters dealing with the dynamics and skills involved in developing a positive working relationship between worker and client.

Indicators of Oppression

Bulhan (1985) identifies several key indicators for objectively assessing oppression.[7] He suggests that "all situations of oppression violate one's space, time, energy, mobility, bonding, and identity" (p. 124). He illustrates these indicators using the example of the slave.

> The male slave was allowed no physical space which he could call his own. The female slave had even less claim to space than the male slave. Even her body was someone else's property. Commonly ignored is how this expropriation of one's body entailed even more dire consequences for female slaves. The waking hours of the slave were also expropriated for life without his or her consent. The slave labored in the field and in the kitchen for the gain and comfort of the master. The slave's mobility was curbed and he or she was never permitted to venture beyond a designated perimeter without a "pass." The slave's bonding with others, even the natural relation between mother and child, was violated and eroded. The same violation of space, time, energy, mobility, bonding, and identity prevails under apartheid, which, in effect, is a modern-day slavery (p. 124).

Bulhan was commenting on the apartheid of South Africa before the recent political changes that overthrew the oppressive, white, government domination. The model of a slave is an extreme example of the violation of space, time, energy, mobility, bonding, and identity as indicators of oppression. One can find current examples of these restrictions. Institutionalized racism in North America toward persons of color (e.g., African-Americans, Indians) currently offers examples of restrictions on all six indicators.[8]

While the slavery experience of African-Americans in North America must be considered as a unique and special example of oppression, the indicators may be used to assess degrees of oppression for other populations as well. In this way, a universal psychological model may help us to understand the common elements that exist in any oppressive relationship. Consider these six indicators as you read the following excerpt of a discussion among battered women in a shelter, as they describe their lives. (An analysis of four sessions of this group can be found in Chapter 11.)

> Candy said one thing that she didn't like was that her husband had to be number one all the time. He felt he should come first even before the children. She said, "The man's got to be number one. Just like the president, Ronald Reagan. He's a man and he's number one. You don't see no female presidents, do you?" I said, "Are you say-

ing that a man has the right to abuse his partner?" She said no and then turned to the women to say, "But, who's the one who always gives in the family? The woman does." All the women nodded to this remark. Linda said, "To keep peace in the family." Candy said, "In the long run, we're the ones who are wrong for not leaving the abusive situations." She said she finally came to the realization that her man was never going to be of any help to her. In the long run, she felt that her children would help her out if she gave them a good life now. She feels very strongly about her responsibilities to her children.

Another woman, Tina, said that when she called the police for help, they thought it was a big joke. She said when she had to fill out a report at the police station, the officer laughed about the incident. The women in the group talked about their own experiences with the police which were not very good. One woman had to wait 35 minutes for the police to respond to her call after her husband had thrown a brick through her bedroom window. I said, "Dealing with the police must have been a humiliating situation for all of you. Here you are in need of help and they laugh at you. It's just not right."

Joyce said that she wanted to kill her husband. This desire had been expressed by an abused woman in a previous group session. Other women in the group said it wouldn't be worth it for her. "All he does is yell at me all the time. He makes me go down to where he works every day at lunch time. The kids and I have to sit and watch him eat. He never buys us anything to eat.... Plus, he wants to know where I am every minute of the day. He implies that I sit around the house all day long doing nothing." Marie said her ex-husband used to say that to her all the time. She said, "But now I'm collecting back pay from my divorce settlement for all the work I never did around the house."

Then Joyce said she was going to tell us something that she had only told two other people in her life. Joyce said that she had been molested from the ages of five to seven by her next-door neighbor, Pat. He said that Pat was friendly with her parents. Her mother would say, "Bring a glass of lemonade over to Pat." The first time she did this, he molested her. After that incident, when her mother told her to bring something over to Pat, Joyce would try to get out of it, but her mother insisted that she go over. Pat had told Joyce not to tell anyone what went on. At this point in the session, Joyce began to cry. I said that I understood this was a difficult situation for her to talk about. Candy said, "Joyce, it wasn't your fault." Joyce said she had kept this incident to herself for approximately 25 years. Finally, when she told her husband, he said, "You probably deserved it." Joyce said she felt like killing him for saying that.

...Candy said she watched while her father beat her mother. She said she used to ask her mother why she put up with it. She said now she sees that it's easier to say you want to get out of a relationship than it is to actually do it...Candy said that leaving was better in the long run. By staying, the children will see their father abusing their mother. "What kind of example is that going to set for the children?" She felt her children would be happier by their leaving. Joyce said her children were happy to leave their father. She said, "They're tired of listening to him yell all the time." She said her son was more upset about leaving the dog behind than he was about leaving his father. Linda said another good reason for leaving is self-love. She said, "It comes to a point where you know he's going to kill you if you stay around."

Careful reading of the preceding excerpts provides examples of the violation for these women of their space, time, energy, mobility, bonding, and identity—the six identified indicators of oppression. Other examples with differing numbers of indicators violated, and different degrees of violation, could include an in-patient in a rigidly structured psychiatric setting; a wheelchair-bound person constantly facing buildings (e.g., work, school, social club) that are not accessible; an African-American woman who is the only person of her race in an organization, held back from advancement by the "glass ceiling" and excluded from the "old boys' network"; an unemployed, 55-year-old man who can't get a job interview because of his age; an elderly person in a home for the aged who is tied to a chair or tranquilized all day because of staff shortages; a large, poor family, forced to live in inadequate housing, a homeless shelter, or on the street. To one degree or another, space, time, energy, mobility, bonding, and identity may be violated for each of these clients.

Alienation and Psychopathology

Bulhan (1985) believes that Fanon's complete work suggests five aspects of *alienation* associated with the development of "psychopathology." Alienation is a commonly used term in psychology and sociology to describe a state of withdrawal or estrangement. Fanon's five aspects of alienation included:

a. alienation from the self;
b. alienation from the significant other;
c. alienation from the general other;
d. alienation from one's culture;
e. alienation from creative social praxis. (p. 188)

Fanon's work emphasized alienation from the self and from one's culture. These were the inevitable results of prolonged oppression and the "deracination" (uprooting) of persons of color by the oppressor. The destruction of the culture (e.g., forced use of another language) is an assault on the oppressed person's sense of self, which is already alienated by the internalization of the negative self-image. Alienation from the "general other" refers to the estrangement between the oppressed group and the oppressor (e.g., the majority group). Significant others include family, friends, neighbors, etc. The "creative social praxis" refers to organized activities of society, such as employment.

An example illustrating wide-scale oppression and these five aspects of alienation can be found in the experience of Native American groups in the United States and Canada. These "first peoples" were displaced by the immigration of European, white settlers, eventually forced off their traditional lands, resettled on reservations, and cut off from their traditional forms of activity, such as hunting and fishing. Efforts on the part of Native people to fight back were met with brutal repression. Their children, during one period in our history, were removed from their families and sent to white boarding schools. Native children in many of these boarding schools report being told to "speak white" and punished for using their Native language.

Even social welfare services, such as those designed to protect children, participated in the alienation process by the removal of children viewed as being neglected or abused (by certain white, middle-class, cultural standards) and then placing these children in white foster or adoptive homes. This was often done without first making a serious effort to use the formal and informal support system that existed in the Native community. The results of these assaults on a whole people, and the resultant alienation, can be seen in high levels of family violence, alcohol addiction, and suicides among Native peoples. The alienation is reversible, however, and significant progress has been made by Native people in opposing and changing many of the oppressive influences on their culture. For example, in British Columbia, Canada, a number of bands (tribal subgroups) take full responsibility for child welfare services and have maximized the use of Native resources for children in need. An emphasis on traditional values and a reintroduction of traditional ceremonies and events, such as the Potlatch, a large-scale meeting and celebration attended by different bands within a tribe, have been important vehicles for reversing the alienation process.[9]

In working with clients who are members of groups that have experienced long-term oppression, it is important to understand the potential impact of alienation as an underlying cause of and contributor to the current problems.[10] Cultural awareness on the part of the social worker can make a major difference in developing intervention approaches that use the strengths of the culture to decrease the alienation. Examples of this approach to practice can be found in the chapters that follow.

Methods of Defense Against Oppression

A final element of the oppression psychology theory concerns methods of defense used by oppressed people. Bulhan (1985) summarizes these as follows:

> In brief, under conditions of prolonged oppression, there are three major modes of psychological defense and identity development among the oppressed. The first involves a pattern of compromise, the second flight, and the third fight. Each mode has profound implications for the development of identity, experience of psychopathology, reconstituting of the self, and relationship to other people. Each represents a mode of existence and of action in a world in which a hostile other elicits organic reactions and responses. Each also entails its own distinct risks of alienation and social rewards under conditions of oppression (p. 193).

Bulhan sees these modes of defense as implemented in stages, although it is possible for individuals and whole groups to be stuck in a stage and not develop or take decades for a transition to take place to a new stage. The first stage involves *capitulation*, in which the oppressed people identify with the oppressor without and assimilate into the majority culture. This is associated with a rejection of one's own culture—the alienation mentioned earlier. The second stage, which he calls *revitalization*, involves a rejection of the dominant culture and a "defensive romanticism of the indigenous culture" (p. 193). The third stage, in which a clear commitment toward radical change is made, is termed the *radicalization* stage. Individuals and whole populations can move with a different timing through these stages, and some may become fixed in one or the other. Whatever stage is in effect, for an individual or a group, will have a profound effect on all aspects of alienation as well as upon the mode of reaction of the dominant culture.

While the model described above is most directly related to issues of cultural identity, elements can be applied to understand a wider model of defensive reactions to oppression. Examples in the chapters that follow will illustrate how oppression can lead to capitulation, resulting in symptoms that are then viewed as pathological. In one illustration, in Chapter 15, a group of survivors of childhood sexual abuse will describe the pattern of capitulation that led to their loss of self-identity and their identity as women. The resultant internalizing of the belief that they are "damaged goods," and the often-noted willingness to feel guilty about what was done to them, profoundly affects their current lives and relationships. A revitalization of their selves and their sense of their identity as women can be seen developing, enhanced by the social support of the group. Finally, a form of radicalization is noted when the group decides to join a "Take Back the Night" march in the community, protesting actively against violence toward women. This leads to their making a commitment to work toward changing community understanding and attitudes toward children who have been sexually abused.

This overly brief summary of some central ideas in oppression psychology theory sets the stage for the use of these constructs in later chapters. It is not the only theory that can inform our practice—there are many models that can help us to understand our clients and to develop effective intervention strategies. It is, however, a very useful model for thinking about work with oppressed and vulnerable populations, which makes up a large part of the social worker's practice.[11] As we consider the impact of oppression, it is also crucial to understand the elements of resilience that help individuals, families, communities, and entire population groups to survive and often thrive in the face of adversity.[12]

RESILIENCE THEORY

During the 1970s and 1980s, developmental research focused on "risk factors" that appeared to be associated with negative outcomes for clients. A child raised in an inner-city neighborhood besieged by drugs and violence faced a degree of risk in attempting to negotiate the passage to young adulthood and eventually, successful adulthood. If the same child also had experienced childhood trauma (physical or sexual abuse, abandonment, and so on), and had parents and family members who were active abusers of drug and alcohol, research indicated that the degree of risk for the child's negative developmental outcome increased exponentially.

Yet, a recurring anomaly in our practice experience and the literature indicated that not all children exposed to high degrees of risk and trauma had negative developmental outcomes in their lives. Butler (1997), examining the "anatomy of resilience," pointed out that

> ...a growing number of clinicians and researchers are now arguing that the risk-factor model burdens at-risk children with the expectation that they will fail, and ignores those who beat the odds. Broad epidemiological studies, they say, don't explain why one girl, sexually abused by a relative, becomes an unwed mother or a prostitute while another becomes an Oprah Winfrey or a Maya Angelou. Retrospective studies can't explain why one man, raised in a harsh, crowded household in impoverished Richmond, California, becomes addicted to crack cocaine and dies of AIDS, while his younger brother—Christopher Darden—graduates from law school, and goes on to prosecute O.J. Simpson. It's time, they say, to see what the Dardens and Winfreys of the world have to teach (p. 25).

Given the widespread nature of substance abuse, the evidence of substantial emotional, physical, and sexual abuse, the increase in the nature and degree of violence in many communities, and the growing numbers of children living in poverty, it is little wonder that research attention is shifting to attempting to understand why some children, families, and communities can still thrive under these conditions, given the risks that they face. This focus lends itself to the development of both preventative and curative approaches to clients at risk.

Rak and Patterson (1996) identified four major groupings of protective factors associated with the "buffering hypothesis": variables that may provide a buffer of protection against life events that affect at-risk children. These include the personal characteristics of the children (e.g., an ability from infancy on to gain others' positive attention); family conditions (e.g., focused nurturing during the first year of life and little prolonged separation from the preliminary caretaker); supports in the environment (e.g., role models, such as teachers, school counselors, mental health workers, neighbors, and clergy); and self-concept factors (e.g., the capacity to understand self and self-boundaries in relation to long-term family stressors like psychological illness) (p. 369).

Garmezy, Masten, and Tellegen (1984) suggested three models for understanding the relationship between risk, vulnerability, and resilience. These were *compensatory,* in which protective factors simply outweigh risk factors; a *challenge* model suggesting that limited risk factors enhance competency; and the *conditional* model, which focuses on personal factors that increase or decrease the impact of the risk factors.

Developmental Psychology Theory and Research

A landmark study in this area involved 698 infants on the Hawaiian Island of Kauai who, in 1955, became participants in a thirty-year, longitudinal study of "...how some individuals triumph over physical disadvantages and deprived childhoods" (Werner, 1989, p. 106). Werner described the goals that she and her collaborators shared as follows: "...to assess the long-term consequences of prenatal and perinatal stress and to document the effects of adverse early rearing conditions on children's physical, cognitive, and psychosocial development" (p. 106). She described their growing interest in resilience as follows:

> But as our study progressed we began to take a special interest in certain "high risk" children who, in spite of exposure to reproductive stress, discordant and impoverished home lives and uneducated, alcoholic or mentally disturbed parents, went on to develop healthy personalities, stable careers, and strong interpersonal relations. We decided to try to identify the protective factors that contributed to the resilience of these children (p. 106).

The researchers identified 201 "vulnerable" children (30 percent of the surviving children) as "high-risk" if they encountered four or more risk factors by the age of two (severe perinatal stress, chronic poverty, uneducated parents, or troubled family environments marked by discord, divorce, parental alcoholism, or mental illness). Two-thirds of this group (129) developed serious learning or behavior problems by the age of 10 or had delinquency records, mental health problems, or pregnancies by the time they were 18.

It was the other third (72) of these high-risk children, who "...grew into competent young adults who loved well, worked well, and played well" (p. 108) who attracted the researchers' attention. They identified a number of constitutional factors as sources of resilience (e.g., high activity level, low degree of excitability and distress, high degrees of sociability, ability to concentrate at school, problem-solving and reading skills, and effective use of their talents). They also identified environmental factors (e.g., coming from families with four or fewer children, spaces of two or more years between themselves and their next siblings, the opportunity to establish a close bond with at least one caretaker who provided positive attention during the first years of life). These resilient children were found to be "...particularly adept at recruiting such surrogate parents when a biological parent was unavailable...or incapacitated..." (p. 108). These children were also able to use their network of neighbors, school friends and teachers, church groups, etc., to provide emotional support in order to succeed "...against the odds" (p. 110).

The researchers concluded on a hopeful note, indicating that

> As long as the balance between stressful life events and protective factors is favorable, successful adaptation is possible. When stressful events outweigh the protective factors, however, even the most resilient child can have problems. It may be possible to shift the balance from vulnerability to resilience through intervention, either by decreasing exposure to risk factors or stressful events or by increasing the number of protective factors and sources of support that are available (p. 111).

Researchers and theorists have built upon this basic set of ideas: life stressors can lead to negative outcomes for persons at high risk; however, personal and environmental factors can buffer the individual, providing the resilience to overcome adversity.

For example, Fonagy, Steele, Steele, Higgitt, and Target (1994) used attachment theory, which focuses on the impact of early infant-caregiver attachments on a child's development and the security of such attachments. They examined the inter-generational transmission of insecure attachments, focusing on factors that might disrupt a negative cycle: in other words, ways to help mothers who had themselves experienced insecure attachments to avoid transmitting these to their own children.

Other researchers have applied the basic model to specific populations (e.g., race, ethnicity) or economic status (poverty), or community variables (e.g., inner-city, level of violence).

For example, Daly, Jennings, Beckett, and Leashore (1995) make use of an "Africentric paradigm" to describe an emphasis on the collectivity, expressed as shared concern and responsibility for others: "Scholarship using this perspective identifies positive aspects of African-American life richly embedded in spirituality and a world-view that incorporates African traits and commitment to common causes" (p. 241).

As an example, on the individual level, referring to the resilience of successful African-American males, the authors cite research findings (Gary and Leashore, 1982; Hacker, 1992) that suggest:

> Much of their success can be attributed to individual and family resilience, the ability to "bounce back" after defeat or near defeat, and the mobilization of limited resources while simultaneously protecting the ego against a constant array of social and economic assaults. To varying degrees, success results from a strong value system that includes belief in self, industrious efforts, desire and motivation to achieve, religious beliefs, self-respect and respect for others, responsibility toward one's family and community, and cooperation (p. 242).

In another example, researchers examined age, race, and setting by focusing on risk and resilience for African-American youth in school settings (Connell, Spencer, and Aber, 1994). They developed a theoretical model that they tested with data from two large samples in two cities: New York and Atlanta. Their findings confirmed

> ...family involvement as an important target for these interventions...This study's results also support efforts to develop intervention strategies for increasing poor African-

American youths' belief in their own abilities and capacities to affect their academic outcomes and for improving their relationship with peers in the school context...

Perhaps the most intriguing and disturbing implication of this study for our understanding of risk and resilience is that disaffected behavior in low-income African-American youth can lessen parental involvement, which in turn contributes to negative appraisals of self that exacerbate disaffected patterns of action and contribute to negative educational outcomes (p. 504).

An example of resilience research that examines the impact of community violence on childhood development is the work of Richters and Martinez (1993). They examined factors contributing to resilience on the part of 72 children attending their first year of elementary school in a violent neighborhood of Washington, D.C. Their findings indicated that

Despite the fact that these children were being raised in violent neighborhoods, had been exposed to relatively high levels of violence in the community, and were experiencing associated distress symptoms, community violence exposure levels were not predictive of adaptational failure or success. Instead, adaptational status was systematically related to characteristics of the children's homes (p. 609).

The authors pointed out that it was only when the environmental adversities contaminated the safety and stability of children's homes that their odds of adaptational failure increased.

Garmezy (1991) focused on resilience and vulnerability of children in relation to the impact of poverty. He states, "The evidence is sturdy that many children and adults do overcome life's difficulties. Since good outcomes are frequently present in a large number of life histories, it is critical to identify those 'protective' factors that seemingly enable individuals to circumvent life stressors." The author points to a core of variables marked by "...warmth, cohesion, and the presence of some caring adults (such as a grandparent) in the absence of responsive parents or in the presence of marked marital discord" (p. 421). Similar findings in studies examining the resiliency of children exposed to poverty and other traumas have identified emotional responsivity in the parent-child relationship (Egeland, Carlson, and Sroufe, 1993) as a buffering factor. Similar protective factors in the home were identified in a study of resiliency of low-birthweight, premature children living in poverty (Casey, Kelleher, & Pope, 1994).

In one example of a study focusing on practice with children from maltreating homes, Herrenkohl, Herrenkohl and Egolf (1994) report on a longitudinal study of the effects of abuse and neglect on 457 children. The study began in 1976 and continued with follow-up studies of 345 of the children in 1980–82 (elementary school age) and again, in 1990–92 (late adolescence). The 1980 phase included children receiving services from the local child welfare agencies for abuse (N=105) or neglect (N=86), and a control group of children in day care (N=52), Head Start programs (N=52) and private nursery schools (N=50). All of the children were rated on a number of variables and then grouped into high-functioning, low-functioning, and middle-functioning categories. School success (e.g., attendance, graduation) was one of the key outcome measures for determining success.

The authors suggest that their findings, although based upon a limited final sample, indicated that "...at least average intellectual capacity is a necessary, though not sufficient condition for minimal success for abused and neglected children" (p. 304). Chronic physical abuse by one parent, without intervention or protection from another parent, created "insuperable obstacles to academic success" for children who remained in such an environment (p. 304). Their data also suggested that "the presence of at least one caretaker throughout childhood appeared to be a necessary, although not sufficient, condition for school achievement" (p. 304). Finally, positive parental expectations for self-sufficiency on the part of parents with children who experienced severe physical health problems appeared to "stimulate the child's goal-setting and determination, with good effect on their academic work."

Unger and Wandersman (1985) explored the importance of neighbors and neighboring as sources of informal support and social networks providing a resource for coping with stress. I will return to these models and provide a review of the research in Chapter 20, which focuses on community.

Garmezy (1993), in a review of the literature on resilience and poverty, suggests that

> These findings provide new questions and new avenues for research. What factors are involved in the seeming diminution over time of resilience in some hitherto adaptive children and adults? Prolonged and cumulated stress would appear to be a prime candidate for examination. Another factor worthy of consideration would be the absence of a support structure and its availability over time. Other candidates for effecting change may be critical modifications in the child's environment such as the physical dissolution of the family (p. 130).[13]

Resilience and Life-Span Theory

Resilience theory does not apply only to children and families. Staudinger, Marsiske, and Baltes (1993), working in the area of aging, have attempted to integrate the notion of resilience with work concerning developmental *reserve capacity* emerging from the field of *life-span psychology*. Life-span theory suggests that

> development throughout life is characterized by joint occurrence of increases (gains), decreases (losses), and maintenance (stability) in adaptive capacity (p. 542).

They suggest this theory challenges a one-dimensional model in which aging, for example, might be seen as simply the loss of capacity. *Plasticity*, which can be positive or negative, is another central notion of life-span theory suggesting variable components of change that can be attributed to individuals or populations and may be associated with cross-cultural or historical differences. The degree of an individual's plasticity may be contingent on the individual's reserve capacity,

> which is constituted by the internal (e.g., cognitive capacity, physical health) and external (e.g., social network, financial status) resources available to the individual at any given point in time. It is important to note that an individual's resources need not be fixed but may themselves change over time (p. 542).

The authors describe two types of reserve capacity: "baseline reserve capacity" and "developmental reserve capacity." Baseline would be the individual's current "maximum performance potential" with current internal and external resources. Developmental reserve capacity refers to resources that can be activated or increased. The life-span theory argues that as reserve capacity increases, so does the potential for positive plasticity.

Social work intervention activities, such as case management, may be seen as focusing on helping elderly clients, for example, to use their baseline reserves while intervening to activate their clients' developmental reserves. For example, increasing the client's social network (external reserves) through involvement in a senior citizens' program could directly improve the internal reserve capacity (health, emotional state, cognitive capacity), which in turn strengthens the client's capacity for developing stronger social networks. This client would have demonstrated positive "plasticity" in the area of social relationship.

Staudinger, Marsiske, and Baltes attempt to merge these two streams—resilience theory and life-span theory—as follows:

> Mapping definitions of resilience onto the concepts of reserve capacity and plasticity suggests that resilience can be conceptualized as one *type* of plasticity. While plasticity, in principle, can be seen as encompassing the potential for any change in adaptive capacity (including increase, maintenance and decrease), resilience refers to the potential for the maintenance and regaining of levels of normal adaptation; that is, resilience is a subtype of the broader range of changes in adaptive capacity encompassed by plasticity. Like reserve capacity, resilience implies the presence of latent resources that can be activated. Unlike resilience, however, reserve capacity is not only relevant to maintaining or regaining *normal* levels of adaptation. Reserve capacity also refers to factors and resources that promote *growth* beyond the normal level of functioning (pp. 543–544).

Implications for Social Work Practice

This growing interest in resilience theory and research, and the concepts of life-span theory, fits well with evolving theory and practice in social work and with the interactional model. For social workers who have long held a psycho-social approach to understanding and working with our clients, and who have more recently embraced ecological models and a strengths perspective, these theoretical models and research findings tend to confirm what our practice wisdom and research has told us. They also reinforce the first practice principle I was taught in graduate school: "Always reach for the client's strength!"

The strong emergence of a resilience model, and the concepts of reserve capacities and plasticity from life-span theory, can influence social work practice on a number of levels. For example, in our practice theory development, as described in Chapter 1, we draw upon theories for understanding to provide the underlying propositions about people and their behavior that guide our interventions. Gilgun (1996) provides one example of an effort to integrate resilience theory with social work practice theory—what has been commonly described as an "ecological framework." She suggests that this framework leads to social work interventions that are "…wide-ranging, covering research, program development, direct practice, and policy formulation, implementation, and evaluation" (p. 399). She points out that

> developmental psychopathology introduces social work to a language replete with generative concepts and theory, while social work provides the ecological framework, strengths-based focus, and phenomenological perspectives. In combination, social work and developmental psychopathology can greatly advance knowledge to inform research, program development, direct practice, and policy.

One example of the use of resilience theory and research would be its implications for child welfare practice with African-American families. Scannapieco and Jackson (1996) review the historical response of African-American families to separation and loss, starting with slavery and continuing through the reconstruction period, World War II, the civil rights years, the 1970s and 1980s, and on to the decade of the 1990s. In each stage, they describe the resilience of the African-American family and the ways in which it coped with life stresses brought about by racism in our society. Current stresses associated with poverty, AIDS, child abuse and neglect, and reductions in services have elevated childhood risks to crisis proportions. These authors point to "kinship care" placements where the resources of the extended African-American families are used to provide some of the resilience factors described in the previous discussion of the research. The authors suggest that all members of the extended family should be involved in case planning, since any of them may need to take over as full- or part-time caregivers.

> Social work practice within kinship care programs must recognize the resilient nature of the African-American family and work with the "kinship triad," made up of the children, the biological parents, and the caregiver relatives. A system of services should be directed at this union of three to ensure a permanent living arrangement for the children (p. 194).

This same example could be conceptualized in life-span theory terminology as focusing on resources (internal and external, baseline and developmental) which have increased the positive plasticity of the African-American family, thus allowing not only for recovery from trauma but for the optimizing of individual, family, and community growth and development.

For the purposes of this chapter, I suggest that resilience and life-span theory and their related research provide an important framework for tuning in and engaging any client. If we understand that clients—even those who appear to be totally overwhelmed by the personal and environmental stress factors in their lives—have the potential for overcoming adversity if factors that enhance their resilience are strengthened and if interventions maximize their developmental resources and resultant plasticity, we will always be looking for what's right with the client, the family, the group and the community, rather than being preoccupied with what's wrong. By doing so, and representing to the client a professional who believes in the client's capacities for growth, change, and adaptation, the social worker becomes one of the sources for resilience in the life of the client.

AGENCY RECORDS, REFERRAL REPORTS, AND THE AGENCY CULTURE

One worker reported a first session with a client who had a long history of contact with the agency. Before the worker could begin, the client, in a good-humored manner, said, "I bet you read all about me."

Many helping contacts involve clients who have had prior contact with the particular setting or with other professionals. The agency file system may contain detailed recording on past experiences or a report from an **intake worker** whose job it is to make the first contact with a client and conduct some form of assessment of suitability for services. Referrals from other professionals often include descriptions of the client, family, problems, and past history. Depending upon how it is used, this prior information can be helpful or can itself become a block to the work.

On the positive side, information about the client may help the worker to develop the preliminary empathy needed to prepare for the first session. A review of past experiences with workers or a report of the intake conversation may reveal potential themes of concern to which the worker can be alert. Understanding the recent strains that have brought the client to the attention of the worker may help the worker develop a feel for the emotional state to be expected in early sessions. A summary of past experiences may yield insight into the client's attitude towards helping professionals. If the records reveal that the going has been rough, the worker may want to plan how to change the client's stereotype of workers.

On the other hand, if the prior information is used by the worker to develop a stereotype of the client, then the preparatory work can block the development of a working relationship. If the worker begins a contact with, for example, a natural parent in a child welfare setting believing that the client is defensive, resistant, hostile, and not open to help, then this "mind set" may be the start of a self-fulfilling prophecy. One stereotype (the worker's) tries to deal with another stereotype (the client's), and no real communication takes place. As one of my clients once described this problem, "It's like two ships passing in the night." In particular, the worker will miss seeing the potential resilience already demonstrated by the client's ability to survive in the face of adversity.

The agency culture will often have an impact on the new worker or student in terms of developing a stereotypical view of a particular client or clients. A common example is what I call "the agency client." This is a family or client who has been with the agency for a long time, sometimes two or three generations, and who has developed a reputation for being "unworkable" after experiences with a number of workers. These are the cases that are often assigned to students or new workers. A common experience is for the new worker or student to mention this client to a colleague who exclaims, in amazement, "They gave you the Smith family!" Even before the first contact, the worker has been set up for a negative experience.

Sadly, agency cultures can foster stereotypes of a whole class of clients—a process that at its worst can be racist, sexist, ageist, homophobic, etc. In my recent study, negative outcomes were associated with a worker's perception that Native families were more difficult to help than non-Native families. For example, there was a negative association with the Native family's perceptions of their workers' availability, their trust in their workers, and outcomes such as workers' helpfulness and Native children going into care (Shulman, 1991). These workers' perceptions may be rooted in the oppressive attitudes toward others we all must acknowledge within ourselves. When we experience difficulty in working with others who are different, our inherent racism, sexism, or homophobia may emerge as part of our efforts to explain our feelings of being ineffective.

Study findings also revealed positive practice outcomes related to workers' sensitivity to the impact of differences between them and their clients. A worker's cultural awareness and sensitivity also had positive associations with outcomes, as did the general attitude of the office involved. For example, the existence of cooperative, rather than conflictual, relationships between an office or region and the minority group's formal support system (e.g., Native court workers or homemakers, Native social workers, Native friendship centers) was positively associated with outcomes (e.g., fewer Native children going into care).

Negative attitudes and stereotypes in an office can be heightened and maintained if most or all of the staff are members of the majority group (e.g., white). Agencies have begun to understand the importance of diversity in the management and front-line staff and increasingly, affirmative action programs have been developed to address this issue.[14]

In general, if we are to avoid responding to clients as if they were stereotypes, it is helpful to remember that a client described in a report is constantly acting and reacting to systems, including the worker who wrote the report. It is simply not possible to know clients without understanding them in terms of this process. Their actions need to be viewed in relation to the actions of others. I have found it interesting to sit in on case conferences where a client is being discussed. The helping professional will report on a home visit or a contact, describe the client in some detail, review the client's history, and then offer a diagnosis of the problem, a prognosis, and a proposal for treatment. If the worker reports that the client was defensive or hostile, this is discussed. Such a conference is operating under the medical paradigm described in Chapter 1. The focus of the discussion is on assessing the client.

The change in the conversation is quite striking if I suggest we shift from talking about the client as an entity to discussing the details of the interview between the worker and the client. This actually represents a shift to what I described in Chapter 1 as the interactional model. I ask the worker to describe how the interview began, what was said to the client, and how the client responded. As the detailed description continues, the staff members begin to get a feeling for the reciprocal interaction between client and worker. The worker's and client's feelings are explored in the process, and the not-too-surprising fact is that the actions of the client are often quite explainable in relation to the worker's efforts. For example, the worker sensed the underlying resistance but did not respond by directly exploring it. Perhaps the worker read a previous report on the client and began the interview expecting trouble, thereby bringing it about. The worker's own feelings may have made empathy with the client's struggle difficult, thus closing off openings for work.

The end result of such discussion, even when the worker had been skillful in the first interview, is the emergence of a client who is more multidimensional than at first seemed. One sees ambivalence rather than just defensiveness. In addition to the anger, one can sense the underlying hurt, distrust, and bitterness that may have resulted from poor past experiences with professionals. The important point is that what might have seemed like a hopeless case changes under our hands to a hard case with some important openings for work.

If the worker using prior record material or referral material can keep in mind not only the tentativeness of the information but also the need to see the client in interaction rather than as a static entity, then this material can be helpful in the preparation process. As will be seen in the next chapter on beginnings, the important point is that as the first interview begins, the worker needs to clear his or her mind of all of these facts, opinions, and even the worker's own tentative tuning-in guesses. The preparatory work has helped pave the way; now skill will be demonstrated in responding not to what was expected but to the actual productions of the client.

VALUES, ETHICS, AND THE LAW IN SOCIAL WORK PRACTICE

In addition to knowledge and a sense of professional function, a social worker's practice will also be guided by values, ethics, and, increasingly, legislative and court decisions. In preparing to meet clients, a social worker needs to consider these areas, which will affect the process and content of practice in significant ways. While it is impossible to prepare for every situation and eventuality, familiarity with basic expectations of professional practice will alert a worker to potentially serious situations and possible missteps, thus encouraging consultation with colleagues or a supervisor.

In the first part of this section we will focus on issues related to values and ethics. In the second part, we will examine issues related to state or provincial legislation designed to govern the conduct of professionals (e.g., licensing acts) and court decisions that have more sharply defined a social worker's responsibilities in areas such as informed consent, confidentiality, and the duty to protect.

Values and Ethics

Values are defined in the *Social Work Dictionary* as "the customs, standards of conduct, and principles considered desirable by a culture, a group of people, or an individual" (Barker, 1991, p. 246). The same dictionary defines **ethics** as "a system of moral principles and perceptions about right versus wrong and the resulting philosophy of conduct that is practiced by an individual, group, profession, or culture" (Barker, 1991, p. 77).

Loewenberg and Dolgoff (1995) define professional ethics as a

codification of the special obligations that arise out of a person's voluntary choice to become a professional, such as a social worker. Professional ethics clarify the ethical aspects of professional practice. Professional social work ethics are intended to help social work practitioners recognize the morally correct way of practice and to learn how to decide and act correctly with regard to the ethical aspects of any given professional situation (p. 6).

Of course, if all situations were clear and unambiguous, and if ethical codes were explicit enough to provide specific guidelines for all occasions (and all professionals could agree on these), then ethical practice would simply involve a learning process and the strict implementation of agreed-upon standards of practice. In reality, however, it does not work that way. For example, Loewenberg and Dolgoff describe an important distinction between "ethical problems" and "ethical dilemmas":

Ethical problems raise the question: What is the *right* thing to do in a given practice situation? How can a social worker avoid unethical behaviors in that situation? Ethical dilemmas occur in situations where the social worker must choose between two or more relevant, but contradictory, ethical directives, or when every alternative results in an undesirable outcome for one or more persons (p. 8).

The authors point out difference between values and ethics. Ethics are deduced from values and must be in consonance with them. The difference between the two is that values are concerned with what is good and desirable, while ethics deals with what is right and correct (p. 21).

An example of this distinction would be everyone's general right to privacy, a value of American society. An ethical rule of the social work profession that is generated by this value is the idea of obtaining *informed consent* from clients. Informed consent is a broad concept that is defined in more detail later in this section and applies to many circumstances. One specific example, however, is the requirement that a worker get permission from a client before taping or recording an interview or allowing observation by a third party. Informed consent, in this case, is the client's agreement to the recording or observation with full knowledge of the procedure involved. In short, then, ethics are descriptions of right and correct behavior through which we put our values into action.

An Example of an Ethical Dilemma. The interplay between values, ethics, and practice is rarely simple and clear-cut. Workers are often faced with an ethical dilemma in which several possible solutions are equally desirable or undesirable. Consider, for example, a social worker assisting an elderly man and his adult child as part of an elder care outreach program that brings support services (e.g., homemaking services) to elderly people in their own homes. A not-uncommon example of value conflicts may emerge when the client indicates a wish to remain in his home while his adult children, fearful for the client's safety, urge the social worker to arrange to move the client to a nursing home. The value systems of a number of parties and organizations may be impinging upon this decision. There are the values of the elderly client, his family (the second client), the agency, the local community, our society in general, the social work profession, and the individual social worker. If any of these are in conflict, which ethical rules will guide the worker?

For example, a generally accepted social work ethical principle is **self-determination**—the client's right to make her or his own choices—which seems to provide a clear direction. The worker must support the client's decision. What happens, however, if the client is so frail that his living independently may pose some danger to himself and to his neighbors? While the client adamantly insists that he can care for himself, the apartment is in desperate need of cleaning. The client mentions he is not feeling too well today because he sometimes forgets to take his medicine. He excuses himself in order to get his pills but opens the closet door instead of the door to the kitchen, appearing momentarily confused. His still-lit cigarette sits on the edge of the ashtray, close to falling off, the long ash suggesting it may have been forgotten. Old newspapers are strewn around the floor under the coffee table.

Add to the mix a worker whose elderly grandfather, living alone and unable to safely care for himself, accidentally set his house on fire by leaving a pot on a hot stove. The resulting fire almost killed the grandfather and posed a serious threat to the neighbors.

The client in this example values his independence, and the value system of the social work profession supports his right to make the decision. The agency also values outcomes that help elderly people remain at home. The funding for the agency may even depend upon how many elderly people it can keep out of nursing homes. A recent memo from the agency director has encouraged staff to "keep the numbers up" as the agency prepares to re-negotiate with the health insurance provider the contract upon which its very existence depends.

The family members value the client's safety and their own peace of mind. The social worker's professional and personal value system, in part based upon his or her own life experience, causes him to identify with the family. The community's value system, which may even be embodied in state legislation, may make the social worker a **mandated reporter**, required to report to the proper authorities if this elderly client is a potential threat to himself or others. The degree of seriousness of the danger is ambiguous in this case, and the regulations of the legislative act are somewhat unclear in providing specific guidelines. What ethical principles can guide this social worker's actions? What does the worker do when some of the ethical principles appear to be in conflict with each other?

Factors Affecting Ethical Decision Making. Some ethical issues are reasonably clear-cut, providing unambiguous guidelines that are universally agreed upon. For example, the injunction against a social worker engaging in sexual activity with a client falls into that category.[15] Given the power differential between the helper and the client, as well as the serious potential for long-range damage to the client, such activity is universally condemned. The new National Association of Social Workers (NASW) Code of Ethics is very clear on this point:

> Social workers should under no circumstances engage in sexual activities or sexual contact with current clients, whether such contact is consensual or forced (NASW, 1997, p. 2, Section 1.09a).

In some places, recent legislation has declared such unprofessional acts a crime, with violators subject to criminal penalties. Many ethical dilemmas, however, are less clear-cut and require careful thought and even consultation before action.

Loewenberg and Dolgoff (1995) have identified some factors that may contribute to those moments when workers experience serious uncertainty. For example, in the illustration of the elderly client there were competing values (self-determination and the need to protect a client); multiple-client systems (the elderly client and the family); worker difficulty in maintaining objectivity (the impact of the worker's life experience); and ambiguity in the case (lack of clarity on the degree of danger to the client). By simply recognizing the factors contributing to the dilemma, the worker begins the processes of managing the problem rather than having the problem manage the worker.

Rather than naively operating under the assumption that social work practice is "value free," it is crucial that social workers recognize that even the very act of a social worker intervening in a situation is based upon certain value assumptions. In an increasingly complex and changing society, with value systems constantly in flux, every social worker must be knowledgeable about current ethical dilemmas and must develop a methodology for analyzing value and ethical conflicts when they emerge. Many agencies and health settings have ethics committees in place to assist in this process.

For example, in the illustration of the elderly client who is resistant to the idea of moving into a nursing home, the social worker should have a forum either in supervision or in staff groups to raise a case such as this one for consultation. An atmosphere should exist in which a social worker can feel free to share honestly his or her own personal value conflicts in such a situation and thereby sort through the conflicting pressures.

Perhaps the agency should set up a committee to examine the specific criteria used to make decisions about the degree of danger required before a worker must implement the mandated reporter role. Would a checklist based upon these criteria help to reduce the amount of ambiguity in any case? Can the worker be helped to see a role in mediating the conflict between the client and his family so that their mutual concerns can be made clear to each other? Can the client and the family members be involved in a process of decision making in which they all feel their concerns are respected? What is suggested here is not a simple answer to a complex problem, but rather a process for recognizing and dealing with the complexity itself. In addition, agency responsibility for actively assisting workers in dealing with these issues is also proposed. Appendix B contains an example of one agency's efforts to provide a simple and clear summary of a number of ethical rules for professional behavior.

A number of texts have addressed in detail the issues introduced in this section (e.g., Loewenberg and Dolgoff, 1995; Reamer, 1990; Gambrill and Pruger, 1997[16]), providing models useful for thoughtful consideration when a worker is faced with an ethical dilemma.

The Values and Ethics of the Profession. Efforts to provide direction for social workers can be found in the literature of the profession. For example, the revised Curriculum Policy Statement of the Council on Social Work Education (1992) attempted to describe core values for the social work profession:

1. Social workers' professional relationships are built on regard for individual worth and dignity and are furthered by mutual participation, acceptance, confidentiality, honesty, and responsible handling of conflict.

2. Social workers respect people's right to make independent decisions and to participate actively in the helping process.
3. Social workers are committed to assisting client systems to obtain needed resources.
4. Social workers strive to make social institutions more human and responsive to
   human needs.
5. Social workers demonstrate respect for and acceptance of the unique characteristics of diverse populations.
6. Social workers are responsible for their own ethical conduct and the quality of
   their practice; they should seek to attain continuous growth in the knowledge and
   skills of their profession.

While the development of commonly accepted values for a profession is important,
core values do not provide specific directions for actions in all situations. In the illustration of
the elderly client, a number of the values just listed may potentially be in conflict. As pointed
out by Loewenberg and Dolgoff (1995),

> There is a general consensus about social work values. For example, most profes-
> sional social workers agree that client participation, self-determination, and confi-
> dentiality are among basic social work values. However, disagreements are likely to
> occur when it comes to implementing these generalized professional values. Social
> workers may differ about priorities, specific objectives, and the means necessary to
> put these generalized values into practice. Thus the value of "enhancing the dignity
> of life" may be used by one social worker to support a client's request for an abor-
> tion, while her social work colleague may call on the same generalized value to
> support her professional decision to try to persuade the client to go through a full-
> term pregnancy (p. 20).

In another effort to develop guidelines for practice, the National Association of Social
Workers developed a professional code of ethics to provide guidelines for practice. The code
covers issues related to the social worker's conduct and comportment as well as ethical responsibilities to clients, colleagues, the profession, and society. [The full revised code (1997)
can be found in Appendix B, along with the code of the Canadian Association of Social
Workers.]

The drafters of the code recognized the difficulties involved when professionals attempted to make specific decisions based upon general principles. They also introduced the
notion of peer review and peer standards for judging ethical behavior.

In itself, this code does not represent a set of rules that will prescribe all the behaviors
of social workers in all of the complexities of professional life. Rather, it offers general principles to guide conduct, and the judicious appraisal of conduct, in situations that have ethical
implications. It provides the basis for making judgments about ethical actions before and after
they occur. Frequently, the particular situation determines the ethical principles that apply
and the manner of their application. In such cases, not only the particular ethical principles are
taken into immediate consideration, but also the entire code and its spirit. Specific applications
of ethical principles must be judged within the context in which they are being considered.
Ethical behavior in a given situation must satisfy not only the judgment of the individual social
worker, but also the judgment of an unbiased jury of professional peers.

Finally, while many of the ethical guidelines for practice with individuals may generalize to other modalities, such as family or group work, unique issues must also be considered.[17] For example, consider this variation on the confidentiality issue, introduced by the presence of other clients in group work, as raised in the Ethical Guidelines for Group Counselors:

- *Members are made aware of the difficulties in enforcing and ensuring confidentiality in a group setting.*
- *The counselor provides examples of how confidentiality can non-maliciously be broken to increase members' awareness, and helps to lessen the likelihood that this breach of confidence will occur.*
- *Group counselors inform group members about potential consequences of intentionally breaching confidentiality. (American Association for Counseling and Development, 1989)*

While a group leader can make clear his or her own position on confidentiality, the leader must also acknowledge that a "rule" of confidentiality cannot be imposed upon group members. It is up to the group itself to discuss the issue and to develop appropriate ground rules.

Complex issues associated with disclosures in multiperson practice have also been raised by researchers in the related field of group psychotherapy (Roback, Purdon, Ochoa, and Bloch, 1992). The authors conducted a multidisciplinary survey of 100 members of the American Group Psychotherapy Association. Thirty-six of the respondents were social workers. The instrument used described six hypothetical group therapy incidents that posed threats to the confidentiality of the group.

The description depicted incidents in which (a) a group member has disclosed outside the group highly sensitive material about another group member, (b) a group member has disclosed current involvement in nonviolent criminal activity, (c) a moderately depressed outpatient group member has threatened physical harm to his ex-wife, (d) a moderately depressed inpatient group member has threatened physical harm to his ex-wife, (e) an adolescent group member has disclosed physical abuse that occurred for several years but is currently not present, and (f) an 8-year-old group member has disclosed an intention to run away from home, with no evidence of physical or sexual abuse (p. 172).

Each of these illustrative examples takes on special significance because the disclosures took place in the group context. For example, in those states and circumstances where the confidential patient/therapist communications are protected, is the protection voided because of the presence of third parties?

Respondents in the study were asked three questions with regard to each incident. These included the most appropriate context for dealing with the disclosure (group, individual or both); with whom it should be discussed (therapist, group consensus, disclosing individual); who has primary decision-making responsibility for managing the situation; and what action should be taken by the group leader.

While a full report of the study's findings is beyond the scope of this discussion, a number of results provide insights into how group leaders would handle the ethical and practice issues associated with these scenarios. For example, 80 percent of the group leaders indicated they would not contact authorities in response to a disclosure of involvement in nonviolent criminal activities; however, 53 percent would encourage the group member to do so. Open-ended responses indicated that the nature of the crime (e.g., arson) and the potential threat to others would modify their response.

Almost all therapists (94 percent) reported that they would contact the authorities if confronted with an outpatient's threat to harm others, and 92 percent would do so in response to an inpatient's threat. An interesting related finding was that gender affected the context within which such threats would be handled, with male group leaders more likely to deal with them in group alone.

The same gender difference was found in the scenario in which a teenager disclosed prior physical abuse. Overall, 89 percent of the group leaders indicated that they would contact the authorities if confronted with such a disclosure. Approximately 50 percent of respondents would engage in each of the following four alternatives in response to a report of abuse that was no longer occurring:

> (a) discuss and assess the legitimacy of the allegation with the group member; (b) discuss with the member in group his or her feelings about the abuse and abide by what, if anything, he or she wants to do; (c) explain to the group the therapist's responsibility to report this information to the proper agency and proceed to do so; and (d) discuss with the group members their feelings about the abuse and honor their chosen strategy for resolving the situation (p. 178).

While the ethical issues and the guidelines for practice in situations where someone is at risk are clearer, and the social worker's responsibility as a mandated reporter removes much of the ambiguity in such a situation, the process can still be a painful one for all concerned. Consider the following example from a group of eight women who were survivors of childhood sexual abuse. It was a long-term open group and, while the group had been ongoing for two years, this was the student group leader's first year. The group was co-led by a therapist from a local social service agency and the student, a representative from the state child welfare agency.

> Confidentiality is a particularly salient issue, because, while the group was voluntary for these women, the fact of my being an employee of the child welfare agency was concerning for them until they got to know me and became comfortable with me.
>
> The week prior to this meeting was very emotional, as one of the women had talked about concerns about how her son behaved when he returned from a recent visit with his father. The description of his behavior and the things that he said pointed to the father having digitally penetrated the boy's anus after they had showered together. I reminded the group of my role as a mandated reporter, and stated that I would be filing a report alleging sexual abuse of the young boy by his father. I told the mother that I thought that it was clear to me that the fact that she brought it up in group was her way of trying to get help. I praised her courage and her concern for her son.
>
> Eileen, the mother of the young boy, did express some concern that her ex-husband, who she was still emotionally attached to, was going to be mad at her. Mary, a young woman who was in the process of filing charges against her stepfather for her past sexual abuse as a child, expressed feeling empowered by what she saw as my immediate response to protect the child, since her mother had never believed her when she told her of the sexual abuse. After a short discussion, the group ended.

At the start of the next group meeting these was a long silence of about two minutes. Several members were glancing at Eileen, and she was moving about in her seat in an agitated manner.

Worker: Eileen, you appear to be upset…is something going on for you?

Eileen: This is very hard for me…I'm really pissed at you, and I'm having a hard time confronting you. I spoke with Alice (her individual therapist) about what you did last week, and she told me that I should tell you how I feel.

Worker: You sound very angry. I would very much like to hear what you have to say. (There is about 30 seconds of silence.)

Eileen: Well, I thought what we said in group was supposed to be confidential! You took what I said in group when I was upset last week, and then used it against me. How the hell am I supposed to ever trust you again?

Worker: You feel I betrayed your trust by filing a report against Bobby and you feel that it is not safe in the group because it is not really confidential.

Eileen: Damned straight! How can I trust you anymore?…Bobby is blaming me…I know my own son. I know when he's exaggerating and when he's not.

Mary: (angrily) Right! I'm sure that's the same excuse that our mothers used when we were abused.

Worker: Eileen, I wonder what it means to you that I reported Bobby. Do you think that it means that I don't trust you to protect your son, or that I think that you are a bad mother? (Eileen starts to cry. As she sobs, others squirm about in their chairs. She looks up.) Yes, it means that I am no better than my mother!

In the worker's analysis of this incident she described how, even though she knew she was doing the right thing and that she had no choice, it was painful for her to hear the anger of the client. The worker's skill was evident in her not falling into the trap of explaining and justifying her action but instead exploring the source of the member's distress. Since the worker had clearly described her role as a mandated reporter and had stated under what circumstances she would have to disclose confidential information (see Chapter 3 for a full discussion of contracting), she could be reasonably certain that the member knew she would take action. Many non-offending parents, who were themselves sexually abused, report later that they wanted their social workers to intervene to protect their children because they were unable to do so themselves.

The Impact of Managed Care on Ethical Practice. The significant cost of health care in the United States has led to an incredible growth in **managed care**. Loewenberg and Dolgoff (1995) describe managed care as

> one major strategy developed in an attempt to control health and mental health costs; this is done by monitoring access to and the type of health care a patient will receive from a health care practitioner or from a health maintenance organization. The goal is to reduce costs by placing controls on health practitioners and by fostering competition among HMOs. Managed care plans attempt to reduce these costs through controlling the type of health practitioners utilized, limiting access to service, and prescribing the type and length of service to be provided (p. 186).

In Canada, the cutbacks in resources available to the universal provincial health programs have resulted in some of the same efforts to reduce costs and to manage care.

Loewenberg and Dolgoff address some of the ethical dilemmas facing social workers in this rapidly changing system. For example, the Code of Ethics requires that "The social worker should not participate in, condone, or be associated with dishonesty, fraud, deceit or misrepresentation" (NASW, 1997). They describe a case situation in which a client's symptoms could be defined either as psychiatric or associated with alcoholism and drugs, but the worker suspects the psychiatric assessment is not indicated. The dilemma is created by the third-party payer's rules, which would allow for more sessions if the diagnosis is psychiatric and less than is needed if the diagnosis is substance abuse. Should the social worker select the less likely diagnosis in order to assure that the client gets the needed number of sessions?

In another example provided by the authors, the Code of Ethics states that "The social worker should be alert to and resist the influences and pressures that interfere with the exercise of professional discretion and impartial judgment required for the performance of professional functions" (NASW, 1997). The authors then describe a scenario of a depressed college student who has been threatening suicide. The dilemma emerges when the claims reviewer for the third-party payer rejects hospitalization, citing recent research. The Code of Ethics holds the social worker responsible for ethical practice, and the legal system would hold the social worker responsible in the event the student did commit suicide (this issue is discussed later in this chapter).

To complicate the scenario suggested by these authors, let's add a third-party payer, or an HMO, that takes the position that the social worker (or doctor for that matter) cannot inform the client that a recommended service is not being provided; thus, a so-called "gag rule" is in effect. This would eliminate the option of empowering the client to fight for his or her own rights in the situation. Fortunately, abuse of this silencing of professionals has led to legislation in a number of states to bar such rules. But if the social worker is a "solo" private practitioner who is dependent on referrals from this third-party payer and whose participation in the panel of approved clinicians is coming up for review, the ethical issues are further heightened.

The profession is just starting to face some of the crucial debates associated with the rapid emergence of managed care and increased control over social work practice. Gordon and Klein (Gambrill & Pruger, 1997) debate whether social workers should even participate in for-profit managed care programs. Gordon argues that we should do so for several reasons, including the opportunity to influence the care provided. He draws upon his own experience to support the ability to work ethically within a for-profit structure. Kline rejects this argument and suggests that working in a managed-care program would lead to damaging effects on the client-worker relationship, raise ethical issues because of competing economic pressures, and end up with workers justifying inadequate care with simplistic clinical reasoning (pp. 52–62).

Clearly, the debate concerning these ethical issues and others has just begun. It mandates that the profession and every professional social worker attend to issues of social policy that will affect the core of our practice and our profession. In this text, when ethical dilemmas are inherent in the examples in the chapters that follow, they will be highlighted in the analysis and the discussion. In the next section, we will explore the impact of specific legislative acts and court decisions affecting social work practice.

The Impact of Legislation and the Court

Two interrelated factors are increasingly affecting practice. First is the trend toward licensing of the social work profession by state (U.S.) or provincial (Canadian) legislative bodies, and second is the growing body of case law (decisions of the courts) emerging from important legal decisions involving helping professionals.[18] Both the legislation and the case law are more sharply defining the rights, duties, and obligations for agencies, host settings (e.g., hospitals) and social workers. These two forces, for the most part, have helped to clarify social work practice guidelines and to reduce professional vulnerability. The principles of practice emerging from most of these changes reveal that many of the regulations and directives codify sound practice concepts.

In this section, we will outline several examples of the growing influence of the law on practice issues. Five topics are discussed: licensing, confidentiality and the client's right to privacy, informed consent, privileged communications, and the social worker's duty to protect a third party. Each area is explored and illustrated in the chapters that follow.[19]

Licensing and the Social Work Profession. A major effort has been undertaken by social work professional organizations to lobby for legislation that would license and regulate the practice of social work. One impetus for this movement has been a concern for the protection of the public through regulation of the quality of practice and even the protection of the title "social worker." State or provincial legislation often defines different levels of educational requirements (e.g., BSW, MSW), and supervised practice experience required for different levels of licensing. Usually, passing a knowledge-based test is a prerequisite for licensing. Such legislation also calls for a professional to continue his or her education through certified programs of continuing education. Regulations associated with the legislation may also spell out the rights, duties, and obligations of a licensed professional. The legislation usually establishes a Board of Registration that defines and enforces a Code of Ethical Practice. It is important that social workers become aware of and familiar with such legislation and the resulting codes.

Another powerful impetus for the licensing movement in the United States has been the acceptance of social work services for reimbursement by third-party payers such as health insurers. Both agencies and private practitioners increasingly depend upon direct reimbursement or the ability of a clients to obtain some portion of their fees from these third parties. Licensing and standards of practice are requirements for reimbursement eligibility.

Confidentiality and Privileged Communications. As an illustration of the influence of legislation on practice, let us examine how confidentiality and the client's right to privacy may be protected or limited. The Commonwealth of Massachusetts, for example, has legislation regulating social work practice.[20] A licensing board has been established to administer its provisions. Legislation amending that Act in 1989 was designed to further protect communications between social workers and clients. These communications are held to be privileged and cannot be disclosed by the social worker in the course of legal proceedings without the client's permission. The client's right to privileged communications strengthens the confidential nature of the professional relationship. When the client's right to privacy is protected, there is a greater possibility that the client will share private information more freely.

The statutory exceptions to privileged communications in Massachusetts arise in the following circumstances:

1. A child custody and/or adoption suit.
2. When the client introduces her or his mental health as an issue in a court.
3. When it is necessary to commit a client to a hospital in the event of danger to the client or someone else.

4. When a social worker is conducting a court-ordered evaluation.
5. In a malpractice action brought by the client against the social worker.
6. After the death of the client.
7. In the case of a child abuse investigation or certain other state investigations.

Exceptions are also found in other state regulations. For example, professionals are required to report suspicions of child and elder abuse or neglect, as illustrated in the example presented earlier in this chapter. While still leaving gray areas where professional judgment will come into play, regulations such as these are helpful guidelines to a worker and to clients. In later chapters, we will see how these requirements may be integrated into practice activity. For example, limits of confidentiality may be spelled out in the first interview with a client or at the first group session.

For now, the central idea is that legislation and case law do exist, and social workers must be aware of the rights and obligations that flow from these bodies of work. Consider the example of a social worker who is approached by a police investigator requesting information about the worker's client. The protections of confidentiality, and in some instances, privileged communications, mean the worker cannot be forced to disclose any information unless a clear exception exists or the client expressly consents. It is helpful for a social worker to be prepared to respond, for example, by stating, "I am not saying Mr. X is or is not my client; however, if he were my client, my communications with him would be confidential and protected, and I would not be able to share them with you."

Until a recent Supreme Court decision (*Jaffee v. Redmond,* 1995)[21] clarified the matter, the federal court system had held different views on whether communications between a social worker and a client were privileged. While communications with "psychotherapists" were privileged in all fifty states and the District of Columbia, the inclusion of clinical social workers was in question. Alexander (1997) points out that in this decision, the Supreme Court has recognized the "...absoluteness of social workers' right to privileged communications; social workers can no longer be compelled to disclose confidential information in civil lawsuits filed in federal court" (p. 388). For example, if a licensed social worker is treating a child protective services worker by providing counseling to assist in overcoming grief related to the death of a child on a caseload, the counselor cannot be compelled to testify in federal court.

Alexander points out that the absoluteness of privileged immunity does not carry over to nonfederal cases in state court systems. He describes one difficult situation in which a criminal defendant may request access to a sexual assault victim's records. Based upon *Jaffee v. Redmond,* the privilege is absolute in a case occurring on federal property and tried in a federal court. In most states, however, if certain standards are met by the defense (e.g., demonstrating the relevance of the information to the defense), the trial judge will review the records and decide if any information should be disclosed. Alexander emphasizes the importance of keeping these distinctions clear:

> On the whole, *Jaffee v. Redmond* recognizes and elevates the prestige of social work. The U.S. Supreme Court spoke positively of clinical social workers and stated that social workers are entitled to the same consideration in counseling that is given to psychologists and psychiatrists. However, social workers should keep in mind that *Jaffee* involves federal issues, and state laws do not provide absolute confidentiality to psychotherapists and differ in their exceptions for privileged communication. Thus, social

work agencies should provide in-service training on the conditions of privileged communications in their states (p. 390).

As pointed out by Alexander, this absoluteness of privileged communications in federal cases can raise significant moral dilemmas for the social worker. He gives the hypothetical situation of a client disclosing in counseling that he or she murdered someone on federal property, a crime for which someone else was convicted and received the death penalty. He points out that "the social worker would be bound to keep this confidence; by disclosing this information, he or she could be held criminally and civilly liable" (p. 390).

Informed Consent. The requirement that the client provide informed consent to services offers another example of how legislation and the resulting codes of ethical practice influence a social worker's obligations. Once again, guidance is available from the NASW's revised Code of Ethics:

> Social workers should provide services to clients only in the context of a professional relationship based, when appropriate, on valid informed consent. Social workers should use clear and understandable language to inform clients of the purposes of the services, risks related to the services, limits to services because of the requirements of a third-party payer, relevant costs, reasonable alternatives, clients' right to refuse or withdraw consent, and the time frame covered by the consent. Social workers should provide clients with the opportunity to ask questions (NASW, 1997, p. 2, Section 1.03a).

In Massachusetts, the code provides the following definition of "unethical or unprofessional conduct":

> Performing or attempting to perform ongoing social work services without the informed consent of the client, the client's legally authorized representative, or, in the case of an unemancipated minor client, the client's parent or legal guardian.[22]

Generally, the five elements that should be included for true informed consent are the following:

1. The worker makes full disclosure of the nature and purposes of the service, including associated potential benefits and risks. The availability of alternatives must be explored.
2. The client demonstrates an understanding of the information offered in the disclosure.
3. The client must be competent to provide informed consent.
4. The client's consent must be voluntary, with no coercion.
5. The decision must be explicit and involve either consent to or refusal of services.

While the guidelines for informed consent seem clear, one study (Lidz et al., 1984) identified a number of practical problems observed in an analysis of how informed consent actually works. For example, the study pointed out that the person responsible for obtaining informed consent was not always clearly identified. Informed consent was, in some cases, a "floating responsibility." In addition, clients reported that family members often exerted pressures on them to act in a specific manner. Was consent under these circumstances really voluntary? Workers were not always trained to educate clients. A worker's perception of the client's intelligence and ability appeared to have some influence on the disclosure process. Informed consent was often obtained after the caregiver had made an assessment and decision in favor of a specific intervention. Were other alternatives really considered? The authors also observed that a client's understanding appeared to occur over time rather than immediately. True informed consent might require revisiting the consent issue periodically as the client's understanding grows. The authors argue that it is important to review the informed consent procedures in place in any setting and to actively promote strategies to ensure that informed consent is real rather than illusionary.

The Duty to Warn. Another court decision has had a powerful impact on practice by defining the duties and obligations of a social worker in respect to her or his "duty to warn" (or, as termed in some states, the "duty to protect") a third party if information shared by a client indicates the third party may be in danger. An important California decision, *Tarasoff v. the Regents of U. California* (1976),[23] severely limited privileged communications under certain circumstances.

In this case, a client of a therapist at the Berkeley University Clinic indicated murderous fantasies about his former girlfriend, Tatiana (Tanya) Tarasoff. The therapist became concerned and notified campus police requesting that they have the client committed. After a brief confinement, the police, believing the client was rational, released him. No further steps were taken, on the orders of the therapist's superior. Neither Tarasoff nor her immediate family was notified. The family sued after the client followed through on his threats to kill Tarasoff. The court held that the therapist had been negligent in not notifying Tarasoff directly, or in not taking other steps to prevent the attack. Essentially, the court said the following:

> When a doctor or a psychotherapist, in the exercise of his professional skill and knowledge, determines, or *should determine*, that a warning is essential to avert danger arising from the medical or psychological condition of his patient, he incurs a legal obligation to give that warning.

This is another example where the evolving rules for professional behavior provide structure and clarity for the professional. In this case, if a client communicates a threat toward a specific person, and has the intent and ability to implement a violent act, or the client has a history of such acts, the social worker is required to take appropriate actions. These may include warning the victim, calling the police, asking the client to accept voluntary hospitalization, or attempting to arrange an involuntary hospitalization. While helpful guidelines have emerged from legislation and the court decisions, the worker's judgment is still required.

Given the importance of understanding evolving legal requirements as they affect the obligations of the social worker, it is important for practitioners to stay up-to-date with the law and its application to new sets of circumstances. Membership in a professional association, such as the National Association of Social Workers (NASW), can provide a means for keeping abreast. Consider, for example, a recent issue of the Massachusetts NASW Chapter's monthly newspaper, which provided advice on the duty-to-warn issue:

> A clear case of duty to warn occurs when a client reports a clear intent to harm another and has both the motivation, intention and means to fulfill this threat. It becomes incumbent on the clinician to report the client to both the police and the third party. A situation not involving weapons or arson, but where there is an explicit threat, would be the client who is HIV-positive, is aware of the risks of transmission,

knows how to avoid such risks, but has no intention of doing so and wants to infect his partner(s). A more complicated case would be in the instance of an HIV-positive client who is not overtly threatening to harm a spouse or partner but is unwilling to disclose or take precautions against the risk of transmission. Although there may be no explicit oral threat, there may be an explicitly behavioral threat. Many states now have statutes requiring duty to warn in such instances. To date, however, Massachusetts does not require partner notification. The other side of the coin, however, is that the clinician, by not disclosing, runs the risk of suit should the partner at a later point become infected and learn that she/he had not been informed by either the infected client or the client's therapists. The therapist has a difficult decision here and should probably seek legal consultation on a case-by-case basis (*Focus*, November, 1996, p. 7).

Some Concluding Comments. After reviewing the previous sections from the perspective of a student or any practicing social worker, it would not be surprising if rather than feeling more prepared to meet a client, the reader might be having second thoughts about engaging in practice at all. Ethical issues, rules of professional conduct, and the still-evolving case law in a number of areas highlight the increasing clarity as well as the growing complexity of guidelines that affect our practice. The reader should understand that developing competency in practice takes place over time. The purpose of highlighting these issues was not to discourage readers, but rather to sensitize them so that they will be more alert to the signs of ethical dilemmas or legal questions. This awareness should encourage the worker to make use of supervisors, colleagues, agency procedural manuals, and other resources whenever such an issue seems to emerge. Thus, in a case-by-case manner, as the social worker raises her or his concerns about a client disclosure in an interview or group meeting, increasing clarity will emerge concerning when such a disclosure triggers the duty to warn or the worker's mandated reporter responsibility. This is an important part of the learning process, which in the long run will significantly strengthen a worker's competency and practice effectiveness.

CHAPTER SUMMARY

It was suggested that the complexity of human communications often makes it difficult, particular in a relation to taboo subjects (e.g., authority, dependency), for the worker to hear and to understand what a client is thinking and feeling. A worker can increase his or her sensitivity to indirect communications by employing a skill called tuning in, or putting oneself in the emotional shoes of the client, prior to the first contact. It was also argued that the worker needed to tune in to his or her own feelings first, particularly those related to anxiety about the first meetings. A set of skills to help clients manage their feelings were discussed and illustrated. We explored research results suggesting the importance of using these skills in the beginning phase of practice to develop a positive working relationship and to be helpful.

An oppression and vulnerability psychology model for understanding clients was introduced. A final assumption of this model was that the strength for change was always present although not always possible to engage. This framework was balanced by a resilience model that focused on clients' strengths to overcome risk factors and to succeed in the face of adversity. We emphasized the importance of not allowing agency records or stereotypes of clients to create a self-fulfilling prophecy.

We saw that the social worker's practice was guided, as well, by a set of professional and personal values as well as a professional code of ethics, legislation, and state and federal law as clarified in the courts.

GLOSSARY

Active mistake A response by a worker than may be off target, but because it is an active rather than passive mistake (inaction), allows the worker to grow. Social workers are encouraged to make active rather than passive mistakes.

Ambivalence Mixed feelings about a problem, person, or issue. For example, a client may wish to finally deal with an issue, but because of the painful feelings associated with it, the client may also wish to deny that the problem exists.

Authority theme Issues related to the relationship between the client and the social worker.

Caring One element of the construct "working relationship." The client's sense that the worker is concerned about him or her and that the worker wishes to help with those concerns the client feels are important.

Causal path analysis A form of statistical analysis that allows the researcher to create a model of a process that involves a number of predictor variables having some impact on a number of outcome variables. The analysis allows the researcher to determine the direction (path) of the influence and the strength (coefficient) of the influence. A useful tool for empirically based theory building.

Child welfare A field of practice in social work that is concerned with the protection and care of children and the strengthening of families.

Containment The skill of refraining from responding immediately to a client's comment or question.

Displaying understanding of client's feelings The skill of acknowledging to the client, through words or nonverbal means, that the worker has understood how the client feels after the affect has been expressed by the client (e.g., a response to crying).

Ethics "A system of moral principles and perceptions about right versus wrong and the resulting philosophy of conduct that is practiced by an individual, group, profession, or culture" (Baker, 1991, p. 77).

Flight-fight The natural tendency on the part of any organism to respond to a threat by either running from it (flight) or attacking it (fight). In human relationships, flight-fight characterizes a generally (not always) maladaptive response to emotional pain that can lead to the avoidance of real work. Family violence is an example of fight, and drug and alcohol addictions are examples of flight.

Human communications A complex process in which messages are encoded by a sender, transmitted through some medium (e.g., words or facial expressions), and received by the receiver, who must then decode the message. The response of the receiver involves encoding a new message and transmitting it, which keeps the cycle going.

Informed consent "The client's granting of permission to the social worker and agency or other professional person to use specific intervention procedures, including diagnosis, treatment, follow-up, and research. This permission must be based on full disclosure of the facts needed to make the decision intelligently. Informed consent must be based upon knowledge of the risks and alternatives" (Barker, 1991, p. 114).

Intake worker Usually makes the first contact with a client and conducts some form of assessment of suitability for services.

Mandated reporter A professional who is required by law to report if certain categories of clients (e.g., children and the elderly) are at risk (posing a threat to themselves or others or experiencing serious abuse or neglect).

Nonverbal forms of communication The transmission of a communication without the use of words (e.g., through posture or facial expression, where a client sits, getting up and leaving an interview, or an affectionate touch).

Putting the client's feelings into words The skill of articulating the client's feelings, in response to tuning in or perceiving the client's indirect communications, prior to the client's direct expression of affect.

Rapport A general sense on the client's part that he or she gets along well with the worker.

Reaching inside of silences The skill of exploring the meaning of a silence by putting the client's possible feelings into words (e.g., are you angry right now?).

Regression analysis A statistical procedure for projecting the impact of predictor variables on outcome variables.

Self-determination "An ethical principle in social work which recognizes the rights and needs of clients to make their own choices and decisions" (Barker, 1991, p. 210).

Sharing worker's feelings The skill of appropriately sharing with the client the worker's own affect. These feelings should be shared in pursuit of professional purposes as the worker implements the professional function.

Societal taboos Commonly shared injunctions in our society that directly or indirectly inhibit our ability to talk about certain areas (e.g., sexual abuse, death and dying).

Trust An element of the construct "working relationship." The client's perception that she or he can risk sharing thoughts, feelings, mistakes, and failures with the worker.

Tuning in The skill of getting in touch with potential feelings and concerns that the client may bring to the helping encounter. For this to be done effectively, the worker has to actually experience the feelings, or an approximation, by using his or her own life experiences to recall similar emotions.

Values "The customs, standards of conduct, and principles considered desirable by a culture, a group of people, or an individual" (Barker, 1991, p. 246).

Working relationship A professional relationship between the client and worker that is the medium through which the social worker influences the client. A positive working relationship will be characterized by good rapport and a sense on the part of the client that he or she can trust the worker and that the worker cares for the client.

NOTES

1. For an elaboration of the idea of communication as a "transmission," see J. Reusch, *Disturbed Communication* (New York: W.W. Norton and Co., 1957).

2. The skills of tuning in and responding directly to indirect cues have been described by Schwartz in some detail. For example, see William Schwartz, "Between Client and System: The Mediating Function," in *Theories of Social Work with Groups*, Robert R. Roberts and Helen Northen (eds.) (New York: Columbia University Press, 1976), pp. 186–88.

3. See the preface of this book for a brief discussion of causal path analysis and Shulman (1991) for a complete discussion of the cited study.

4. The study in the 1991 (Shulman) book approached practice in a holistic manner. It recognized that other factors, such as client motivation, acceptance of a problem, stress, ability to use help, and socioeconomic factors all contributed to some portion of the explained outcomes. When such factors were added to the causal path analysis they increased significantly the amount of variation in court status and days in care explained by the predictor variables.

5. Caution must be exercised in considering these findings because of the smaller sub-set of the total sample as well as employing a rating that made use of the clients' memory of their workers' behaviors in their early sessions—from one to three months prior to these research interviews.

6. To determine the correlations between two sets of ordinal variables (e.g., {1} strongly agree…..{5} strongly disagree) I employed the more appropriate polychoric correlation available in a data preparation program called "Prelis" (Joreskog and Sorbom, 1988).

7. Bulhan credits the first four items in this list to Chester M. Pierce.

8. See W.J. Wilson, *Power, Racism and Privilege: Race Relations in Theoretical and Sociohistorical Perspectives* (New York: Free Press, 1973); Solomon, B.B., *Black Empowerment* (New York: Columbia University Press, 1976).

9. At one point in Canadian history, the Potlatch was banned by the federal government because of fears that Native unity might lead to aggressive pursuit of land claims. More recently, organized efforts on the part of the Canadian Native community to use confrontation, the political system, and the courts to pursue these claims have led to a number of successes.

10. For examples, see D. Lum, "Toward a Framework for Social Work Practice with Minorities," *Social Work, 27* (1982): 244–249; J.B. Robinson, "Clinical Treatment of Black Families: Issues and Strategies," *Social Work, 34* (1989): 323–329; L. Chestang, "Racial and Personal Identity in the Black Experience," in B. White (ed.), *Color in White Society* (Silver Springs, MD: National Association of Social Workers, 1984); L. DuBray, "American Indian Values: Critical Factors in Casework," *Social Casework, 66* (1985): 30–37; Man Keung Ho, "Social Group Work with Asian/Pacific Americans," *Social Work with Groups, Special Issue: Ethnicity in Social Group Work Practice, 7* (1984): 49–61.

11. For examples of social work approaches for work with gays and lesbians, see H. Gochros, "Teaching Social Workers to Meet the Needs of the Homosexually Oriented," in R. Schoenberg, R. Goldberg, and D.A. Stone (eds.), *Homosexuality and Social Work* (New York: Haworth Press, 1984); H. Hidalgo, T.L. Peterson, and N.J. Woodman (eds.), *Lesbian and Gay Issues: A Resource Manual for Social Workers* (Silver Springs, MD: National Association of Social Workers, 1985); S.J. Potter and T.E. Darty, "Social Work and the Invisible Minority: An Exploration of Lesbianism," *Social Work* (May, 1981): 187–191.

12. I am particularly appreciative of conversations I have had with my Boston University colleague, Joyce West Stevens, who has encouraged me to balance this discussion of oppression with the important notion of resilience.

13. For a general review of the research on resilience and child development, see A.S. Masten, K.M. Best, and N. Garmezy, "Resilience and Development: Contributions from the Study of Children Who Overcome Adversity," *Development and Psychopathology* (1990) *2* (4): 425–444.

14. Unfortunately, the impact on staff of the changes resulting from affirmative action is often underestimated by administrations. As a result, not enough tuning-in to potential resistance and blocking behaviors is undertaken, and a heightening of tensions often results. Since the subject of difference (e.g., race, ethnicity) is as taboo for staff as it is for clients, management and front-line staff often avoid open discussion of these tensions. When powerful issues such as these go underground, they can have a negative influence on staff relationships which then works against the goals of the original program. Training for management and staff in how to face potentially explosive issues is a prerequisite for truly effective change.

15. For a discussion of this issue, see K. Pope and J. Bouhoutsos, *Sexual Intimacy Between Therapists and Patients* (New York: Praeger, 1986).

16. Gambrill and Pruger provide a collection of "debates" about practice, coercion, self-regulation, professional education, and special client populations. For example, "Should clients have access to their mental health records?" Reading first the "yes" author followed by the "no" author with respect to each question points out just how complex are the issues involved in debates over ethics, values, and obligations.

17. For a discussion of ethical issues related to social work with groups, see D.A. Seebalt, "Ethical Dilemmas in Social Work Practice with Groups," in *Roots and New Frontiers in Social Group Work*, M. Leiderman (ed.) (New York: Haworth Press, 1988).

18. While the U.S. and Canada (except for Quebec) share a common history based on English Common Law, there are differences in legislation and case law principles between the two countries.

19. For further reading in this area, see D.J. Besharov, *The Vulnerable Social Worker* (Silver Springs, MD: National Association of Social Workers, 1985); S.J. Wilson, *Confidentiality in Social Work* (New York: Free Press, 1982); J.C. Beck, *The Potentially Violent Patient and the Tarasoff Decision in Psychiatric Practice* (Washington, DC: American Psychiatric Press, 1985); T. Gutheil and P. Appelbaum, *Clinical Handbook of Psychiatry and the Law* (Washington, DC: American Psychiatric Press, 1987).

20. Chapter 585 of the General Laws of the Commonwealth of Massachusetts, 1989.

21. *Jaffee v. Redmond*, S.Ct., U.U. Lexis 3879 (1996).

22. *Code of Ethical Practice*. MA: Board of Registration of Social Workers, 258 CMR–25, 1991. For further discussion of informed consent, see also R. Faden and T. Beauchamp, *A History and Theory of Informed Consent* (London: Oxford University Press, 1986).

23. *Tarasoff v. The Regents of U. California*, 551 P.2d 334 (1976). This case was decided by the California Supreme Court and is used as a legal precedent by other states. See J. Beck, *The Potentially Violent Patient and the Tarasoff Decision*. Washington, DC: The American Psychiatry Association Press.

3

Beginnings and the Contracting Skills

CHAPTER OUTLINE

The Dynamics of New Relationships

Contracting in First Sessions

Contracting Over Time

Contracting with Resistant Clients

Models for Assessment in the Beginning Phase

Culturally Diverse Practice

Evaluation of Practice: Process and Outcomes

In this chapter, we will explore the dynamics of new relationships in general and new helping relationships in particular. A model for contracting with the client in the first sessions will be presented and illustrated. We will describe specific skills for helping clients to manage their problems, including clarifying the worker's purpose and role, reaching for client feedback, and dealing with issues of authority. The contracting process will be viewed as flexible and changing over time. The special concerns involved in contracting with resistant clients will be discussed.

We will also explore a number of models for assessment that can be useful, in some circumstances, in helping the social worker to obtain a clearer picture of the client in relation to the environment. Issues of diversity and culturally competent assessment and practice will be addressed. Research on the intervention process will also be shared. Finally, we will look at methods that social workers can use to evaluate their practice (e.g., single-case design; critical incident analysis; records of service) that require obtaining and recording data.

During a first interview, a 25-year-old client put his social worker through an indirect test to see if she would be honest with him. The worker, responding directly to the indirect cues, asked, "Did I pass?" After acknowledging that she had passed, the client said, "I had to see where we stand. The first meeting is really important, you know."

First meetings in all helping relationships are important.[1] If handled well, they can lay a foundation for productive work and begin the process of strengthening the working relationship between client and worker. If handled badly, they can turn the client away from the service offered. In this chapter, we will explore the special dynamics associated with new relationships.

In Chapter 2, our focus was on skills designed to help clients to manage their feelings. Our focus in this chapter will be on an associated set of skills called *worker's skills for helping clients to manage their problems*. These skills are described in some detail later in this chapter. They include:

- **Clarifying worker's purpose and role.** *A simple, non-jargonized statement by the worker, usually incorporated into the opening statement to a client, that describes the general purpose of the encounter (and/or services of the agency) and provides some idea of how the social worker will help.*
- **Reaching for client's feedback.** *An effort on the part of the worker to determine the client's perception of his or her needs. The working contract will include the common ground between the services of the setting and the felt needs of the client.*
- **Partializing client's concerns.** *Helping a client to break down into manageable parts large and often overwhelming problems.*
- **Supporting clients in taboo areas.** *Helping the client to talk about issues and concerns that are normally treated as taboo in our society (e.g., sex, death, authority, dependency).*
- **Dealing with issues of authority.** *The worker's efforts to clarify mutual expectations, confidentiality issues, and the authority theme.*

Each of these skills, and others, will be discussed and illustrated in the sections that follow. Since not all clients are pleased to have the social worker and the agency involved in their lives, in this chapter we will also explore the special dynamics of working with involuntary (mandated) or "semi-voluntary" clients. While I cautioned in Chapter 1 against using the study process in a manner that interfered with the engagement process, it is important for social workers to obtain an accurate picture of the relationship between the client and the environment. We will look at a number of models for developing this framework. Issues in the beginning phase related to ethnic-sensitive practice and assessment will also be explored. Finally, since the beginning phase of practice provides a baseline for evaluation of the social work process and outcomes with each client, models for assessing changes in both will be discussed. We begin our exploration of this important phase of work by examining what we know about the dynamics of new relationships.

THE DYNAMICS OF NEW RELATIONSHIPS

All new relationships, particularly those with people in authority, begin somewhat tentatively. Clients perceive workers as symbols of authority with power to influence their lives. Clients often bring with them a fund of past experiences with professionals or stereotypes of helping professionals passed on by friends or family. So the first sessions are partly an effort to explore the realities of the situation. Encounters with people in authority usually involve risks, and clients will be careful to test the new situation before they expose themselves.

Ambivalent feelings will be present in any new situation. The client's doubts about adequacy and competency are heightened, as are fears concerning the worker's expectations. The other side of the ambivalence is hope of receiving help. Depending upon the individual and the helping context, one side of the ambivalence may be stronger than the other.

The two major questions on the client's mind in individual work, rarely spoken, are: "What is this going to be all about?" and "What kind of worker is this going to be?" The urgency of these questions stems from the client's fear of the demands to be made. People in authority often have hidden agendas, and the client may fear that the worker will try to change him or her. The client's actions will be affected by this suspicion until the two questions are answered. Fear of feelings of dependency will be present until the client can see the helping person, not in the imagined role as the all-powerful authority, doing things *to* the client, but rather as someone with skills who will do things *with* the client. Even in situations where social workers deal with mandated clients who are involuntary, it is crucial to acknowledge that it is the client who will really be in control. The worker must be viewed, in the final analysis, as helping the client to work on the client's own concerns.

Another way to consider this early process is to realize that the client is having to make what I call "the first decision." The first decision is essentially whether or not the client will engage with the worker in a meaningful way and begin to develop what has been called "the therapeutic alliance." In the middle and ending phases, we will explore the "second" and "third" decisions, but for our purposes now, the first decision is the essential one. Without a client's real commitment to the work and the worker, the relationship is doomed to failure. Clients can drop out by not returning, or they can continue to come and engage in what I have called the "illusion of work," in which they go through the motions but no real work or change is occurring. With a mandated client, this illusion can be a form of "conning" the worker where the client says what she or he thinks the worker wants to hear, not what the client really feels.

In the illustrative interview that follows, some of the concerns of the beginning phase, described earlier, are evident in the client's indirect communication. The worker heightens the client's feeling of concern by not addressing her questions about the purpose of the session and the role of the worker. The setting is a hospital and the patient a 43-year-old woman with three young children. Although laboratory tests have been negative, persistence of symptoms necessitated exploratory surgery and a possible diagnosis of cervical disk disease. Referral to the social worker was made because a long convalescence would be required, during which household duties and child care would be impossible. In his written introduction to the recording of the interview, the worker described his purpose as exploring after-care possibilities and determining whether homemaker or alternative services might be necessary.

> **Worker:** Good day, Mrs. Tunney. I'm Mr. Franks from the social service department. Your doctor asked me to visit you and to see in what way we could be of help.
> **Patient:** Is this a habit? Do you visit all the patients or only me? (She was smiling, but seemed anxious.)
> **Worker:** We interview patients whenever it seems to be indicated, when there is such a medical request.

The patient was asking, What's this all about? and expressing a natural anxiety. She might be wondering but not saying, "Oh my God! It must be more serious than they told me." The worker's response does not answer this question and does little to address the concern. Instead of clarifying the reasons for the referral, such as concern over a possible need for homemaking services, the patient is left in the dark. She responds with an unusually direct demand.

> **Patient:** All right, in what way do you think you can help me? I am in the hospital

for the second day. My children are being looked after by their father. Most
probably I will be operated on in the near future. You know this started because I felt I had arthritis. I had difficulty in moving my hands and fingers, so
I decided to come here and see what I really have. (Occasionally she works
on her crocheting while she speaks.)

Worker: I would like to ask a few questions, Mrs. Tunney. But first, tell me, do you
feel more comfortable talking while you are working?

Patient: Perhaps. I always do something with my hands...I have to....

Once again the worker has not responded to a direct question. The worker is proceeding according to his agenda, conducting a fact-gathering interview. The client is left out
of the process. As long as the patient is unclear why this worker is talking to her and what his
purpose and role as a social worker are, she will be unable to use him effectively. The client
will experience the interview as being "acted on" by the worker. Her sense of dependency will
be heightened and her fears of intrusion into her personal life increased. She will be uncertain
of what to say because she has no framework for weighing her responses. The interview
continued:

Worker: You said, Mrs. Tunney, that your husband is taking care of the children. If
I am correct, you have three. Is that right?

Patient: Yes, but the eight-year-old is a very hard one. He cannot be left alone. Fortunately, my husband's superiors are understanding people, and he can take
off time whenever he needs to, and now he needs it. Usually, he is away on
trips, and sometimes he is gone for weeks.

Worker: I understand your husband is in the army. In what capacity?

It is my guess that the client might be thinking at this point, "Why do you want to
know about my husband?" The worker's questions are designed to elicit family information for
the worker's study, but the client must wonder how disclosing this information is meant to
help her.

Clients do not usually ask why the worker wants to know. That is not polite in our society. They may even cooperate, providing answers to all of the social worker's questions. As
long as the doubt persists, however, feelings of suspicion and tension will remain. The interview continued with the worker asking questions about how the pain began, how the husband
helped out at home, where the patient was born, and if she had family in this country. The patient's responses became shorter and consisted of direct answers to the worker's questions.
When the worker suggested meeting with the husband and the children "to get a clearer picture of how we could be helpful," the client agreed and said, "Jeez! Do you do this for all of
the patients?"

The worker's summary of the first interview reported, "Inappropriate, almost childish,
smiling and expressions of distress. Distress is covered by rigid attitudes and a compulsive personality. There are rules and consequently a role distribution which for some reason she
would not negotiate."

Another interpretation of the "childish smiling and expressions of distress" would be as
signals of her feelings about the interview. These feelings can be expressed in many indirect
forms. The new boy at the residential institution who acts out his anxiety by immediately
breaking rules and picking fights is one example. The adolescent whose total vocabulary
during a first interview consists of the words "yes" and "no" and the parent who responds to

the child welfare worker with open hostility are others. When the worker interprets the behaviors as reflecting the client's personality or resistance, the worker is viewing the client as an object rather than as someone in **dynamic interaction** with the worker. As a result, the initial client behavior often becomes part of a stereotyped view of the client initiating an endless cycle. The interactional framework alternative, incorporating the notion of reciprocity in relationships, would require that the social worker understand the client's behavior as, in part, responsive to the worker's interventions. The worker's interventions are also dynamically affected by the client's responses.

There are a number of factors that lead workers into first contacts such as the one just described. First, the medical paradigm itself, borrowed from physicians, suggests a four-stage approach to conceptualizing practice. In this model, one studies the client, develops a diagnosis, plans treatment, and then evaluates the results. While this systematic approach has made important contributions to advancing our practice, the emphasis on a first stage of study encourages some workers to see the initial interview as a fact-gathering exercise in which the client's function is to provide information. This can lead to an interview somewhat like the extreme example described above.

This discussion of the medical model and the four-step process of study, diagnosis, treatment, and evaluation always provokes some anxiety on the part of students who may be placed in fieldwork agencies in which this format for a first interview is required. In some situations, workers must complete a detailed intake form that requires them to obtain a "**psychosocial history**," the client's psychological and social life story, elements of which may have some bearing on the current problems. The worker is then required to provide an initial diagnosis or assessment. In some settings, a checklist is provided to guide the worker's responses. These students often ask, "How can I conduct a first interview in the way you described if I'm expected to complete this form?"

Examination of these forms and detailed analyses of such first sessions often reveals the following. First, while protesting the rigidity of the structure, the worker often feels much more comfortable having the form to guide the first interview. Use of the form maintains control in the hands of the worker, allows for predictability in the first session, and allows the worker time to become comfortable. Of course, the opposite may be true for the client, who may feel more uncomfortable as the interview goes on.

A second observation is that with very little effort on the part of the worker, it is possible to design the first interview to simultaneously contract with the client, try to help the client feel more at ease, and obtain the required information. For example, a worker could say,

> There are a number of questions I need to ask you for us to be able to obtain insurance reimbursement, but before I do so, I thought I would explain how I might help, and find out what's on your mind.

In example after example, students discovered that this preliminary discussion often yielded much of the information they needed to obtain for the form, but it was provided in an order that fit the client's sense of urgency instead of the worker's. Time could be set aside in the second half of the interview for covering missing information by going through the form. The client was often ready to provide the data at that point, especially if the worker explained why it was required (e.g., medical insurance, obtaining a more complete understanding of the family's health experiences).

An explanation of how the information would be used is important not just to help build trust, but also because of the worker's ethical responsibility to obtain informed consent from the client. The client has a right to know how personal information will be used by the worker and the agency. The client also has a right *not* to share information of a personal nature, as a condition of service, unless that information is demonstrated to be essential to receiving service. The National Association of Social Workers' Code of Ethics (Appendix B) provides direction for a social worker on this question.

While students can change the structure of the interview and still work within the framework provided by their setting, they still have to face the question of the assessment and diagnosis. Even this can be dealt with if one thinks of diagnosis as a description of the state of the relationship between the client and the various systems to be negotiated, as well as an assessment of the client's sense of strength and readiness to cope with the problem. The discussion of the resilience research in Chapter 2 provided more than enough evidence of factors that could be included in the assessment, thus focusing on what is right with clients rather than what is wrong. Later in this chapter a discussion of assessment will provide some examples of strengths-focused models.

Diagnosis could be seen dynamically as something that changes and shifts, often moment to moment, as opposed to a fixed description of a client's "problems." Thus, in most settings, students and new workers could adopt more flexible structures for first interviews while still working within the framework of the setting. Even in those situations where a worker is required to make a specific assessment, such as a medical insurance requirement to provide a specific diagnosis, the worker needs to incorporate elements of contracting in the first session. Simply recognizing the difficulty of actually listening to a client and empathizing with him or her, while trying simultaneously to "categorize" the client, will often free the worker to respond more, with greater affect.

A second factor that can contribute to the worker's reluctance to be direct about purpose is the notion that one must "build a relationship" before the work begins. In the model described thus far, the term *working relationship* has been used. The hypothesis advanced now is that the working relationship will develop only after the purpose of the encounter has been clarified and the worker's role explicitly described. In effect, the relationship emerges from the work, rather than preceding the work.

It is true that the nature of the relationship can change over time. A client may be less likely to share a particularly difficult or embarrassing problem in the beginning, before a "fund" of positive working relationship has been developed. This is one of the reasons for the common phenomenon of clients raising "**near problems**"—defined as real issues in their lives that are near to the most difficult concerns—at the start of the work. The contracting skills described here are designed to build up this fund from which both the worker and the client can then draw. As the working relationship strengthens, clients may move on to more powerful themes of concern. I referred to this process earlier as making the "second decision" to make the transition to the middle phase and to deal with more difficult and often painful material. A finding of my research was that the skills of clarifying purpose and role, used in the beginning phase of practice, helped to develop a positive relationship, in particular the element of trust, between worker and client (Shulman, 1982; 1991).

A third factor is the worker's tendency to be embarrassed about either the client's problem or the worker's intentions. Having a problem in our society has become identified with weakness and dependency. Workers sometimes feel uncomfortable about mentioning this. Some of the client's difficulties, such as a physical or mental ability that is different from the rest of the population, are considered so difficult to discuss directly that workers have invented euphemisms to describe them. One group for teenage unwed mothers met for four sessions during which no mention was made of their pregnancy, while their midsections grew with each passing week. Children having great difficulty in school have been brought together by school counselors in "activity groups" for after-school fun activities with no mention of why they were selected. They are not usually fooled, since they all know they are considered to be "the dummies." The worker is embarrassed about mentioning the problem, and so the client gets a message that reinforces reluctance to discuss painful areas.

When workers begin their sessions with hidden agendas, they are equally ill at ease about making a direct statement of purpose. If a worker believes the client's problem is all figured out and the task is now to proceed to change the client's behavior, then reluctance to be direct is understandable.

A final factor leading to difficulty in being direct is our use of professional jargon. When I graduated with a professional degree in social work, my mother asked me at a dinner in my honor, "Now that you're a social worker, tell me, what do you do?" I replied, "I work with people to enhance their social functioning, to facilitate their growth, and to strengthen their egos." She smiled at me and said, "But what do you do?"

In fact, I was unclear about how to articulate my professional function. What made it worse was that my fellow social work graduates appeared to be clear about theirs. I thought, desperately, that perhaps I had missed a key lecture or had not completed a key reading. In reality, all the helping professions, not just social work, have had trouble with direct statements of purpose and role and have tended to obscure this confusion with jargon. Key words such as "enhance," "facilitate," and "enable," when followed with a statement of our hopes and aspirations (e.g., "enable clients to be empowered"), avoid the functional question. If, in training sessions with professionals, I restrict their use of jargon and insist that they describe what they have to offer me as a client in simple, clear sentences, they usually find it difficult to do so. The more ingenious try to avoid the difficulty by asking me, the client, "What is it that you want?" I point out at such moments that they are answering a question with a question. While it is a good question, in that it reaches for client feedback, I don't think I can really answer it without some structure from the worker. In effect, the structure provided by the worker through a clear opening statement will potentially free the client to respond. This is another example of a false dichotomy—structure versus freedom. In effect, freedom emerges from structure.

There are situations in which the client has come to the worker for service—for example, a voluntary client in a family counseling service. In such cases, the worker may well begin by explaining the purpose of the first visit as one in which the client can tell the worker what brought him or her to the agency so that the worker can see whether she or he can be of any help. The worker listens for the client's sense of urgency and when that is clear, the worker can explain how she or he may be able to help.

In the section that follows, we will present a model that depicts how to use a first session to clarify the worker's purpose and professional role directly and simply, without jargon or embarrassment.

CONTRACTING IN FIRST SESSIONS

The first sessions described in this book take place in the context of an agency or a host setting (e.g., hospital, school, residential institution). Although many of these concepts of help-ing are equally relevant to social work in individual private practice, group practice, or "fee for service" managed care clinics in which workers are reimbursed for the number of counseling hours provided, our focus in this book is on the social work that takes place in more traditional and formal settings. The unique ethical problems, for example, facing social workers who de-pend for their income on maintaining a client in treatment are variations on the issues raised in Chapter 2. Increasingly, social workers in managed care settings and programs report feel-ing caught in the middle between the client's right to know about the availability of services or the restrictions (e.g., number of sessions) being placed on services by the insurance com-pany, and the injunction of the provider that this information not be shared. The issues in-volved in private practice, and the profound implications of changes in managed care in our country, mostly go beyond the scope of this text.

The effect of the context of practice is particularly important in the contracting phase and so needs to be explored. Social workers usually work for an agency or institution (often re-ferred to as a "host setting"). The setting is more than a convenient place for sessions to take place. It has a function in society, which means it has a stake in the proceedings. In the soci-etal distribution of tasks, each setting deals with some area of particular concern. The hospi-tal is concerned with the health of patients, the school with the education of students, the family agency with family functioning, the parole agency with monitoring and assisting re-leased prisoners to function in the outside world, and so on. The mission of the setting is im-portant and affects the helping person's actions.

In the first chapter, some of the pressing life tasks that face clients were identified. These included dealing with school, family, work, the welfare or medical systems, and so on. The client sees successfully dealing with these tasks as the immediate necessity. In each case, we were able to describe some life tasks that might be important to the client.

It is these two sets of tasks, that of the agency and of the client, and their possible convergence, that Schwartz considered in developing the contracting concept (1971). Writing in the context of group work practice, he said,

> The convergence of these two sets of tasks—those of the clients and those of the agency—creates the terms of the contract that is made between the client group and the agency. This contract, openly reflecting both stakes, provides the frame of refer-ence for the work that follows, and for understanding when the work is in process, when it is being evaded, and when it is finished (p. 8).

In the beginning phase of work, the worker's function can be considered as mediating the initial engagement between the client and the service, searching for the connection be-tween these two sets of tasks. Although there may be many obstacles blocking the mutual in-terests of the setting and the client (e.g., the authority of the worker, an involuntary client, an insensitive doctor in the hospital), the worker searches for the often elusive **common ground**, the overlap between the specific services of the setting and the felt needs of the client.

Three critical skills in this phase of work described by Schwartz are those of clarifying purpose, clarifying role, and reaching for client feedback (the client's perception of his or her stake in the process). Although these skills are central to all beginning engagements, there are many variations in their implementation. For example, variant elements are intro-duced by the setting. The issue of authority, whether the client is voluntary or the worker makes the first contact, can also introduce variations. These skills are described in detail in this section and illustrated in different contexts, and the results of my research on their effects are reported.

Contracting Example

Given the dynamics of new relationships described earlier in this chapter, the worker must attempt to clarify the purpose of the meeting with a simple, non-jargonized, and direct **opening statement.** This statement should openly reflect both the stake of the setting and the possible stake of the client. For example, in the hospital interview described earlier, one way (and there can be many variations) the worker might have begun could have been to say,

> My name is Mr. Franks, and I am a social worker from the social services department. Your doctor asked me to see you to determine if there was any way I could help with some of the difficulties you might be facing in taking care of your children or your home while you're recovering from the operation. I know that can be a difficult time, and I would like to help, if you wish. I would like to discuss this with you to see if you want some help with these problems or with any other worries you might have about the operation or your hospital stay.

Such a simple statement of purpose sets the stage for the discussion that is to follow. The purpose of the visit is to discuss the service and to see how that service fits with what the client feels she needs. With this simple framework in place, the client's energies can be involved in examining areas of possible work. With a clear boundary in place, the client does not have to worry about why the worker is there. Conversation and the worker's subsequent questions should be related to this task, a mutual exploration of areas of potential service.

The worker also needs to be prepared for the client's inevitable question about how the worker can help. In this example, clarifying the worker's role might consist of spelling out a number of possible forms of assistance. For example, "I can help you examine what you may be facing when you return home, and if you think you need some help, I can connect you to some homemaking resources in the community." Another form of assistance could be presented in relation to the family:

> "If you're worried about your husband's ability to help at this time, I can meet with the two of you and try to sort this out," or, in relation to the hospital and the illness, "when you're in a big, busy hospital like this, you sometimes have questions and concerns about your illness, medication, and the operation that are not always answered; if you do, you can share these with me and I can see if I can get the staff's attention so that they can help out, or perhaps I can do so myself."

Each of these simple statements defines a potential service the client may wish to use immediately or at some future date. They may seem overly simple, but for a worried patient on the ward, these statements provide an orientation to services of which she may simply not be aware. They can be described as **handles for work** that provide a way for the client to grab onto the offer. The specific examples shared by a worker reflects his or her tuning in, as described in Chapter 2, to the particular situation faced by the client. Previous clients may have taught the worker about the themes of concern that are most common in the particular situation. Thus, the worker not only speaks directly to the heart and mind of the specific client but also normalizes the problems since they have been shared by so many clients in similar situations.

Contracting is a negotiating period in which both the client and the worker are involved. The skill of reaching for client feedback is essential. In the last example, this skill might sound like this: "Are any of these issues of concern to you, and would you like to discuss how I might help?" It is quite possible that in the feedback stage the client may raise issues that were not part of the worker's tuning-in process. The agenda for work can expand. The only limitation is that the area of service offered is bound by the tasks of the setting. The worker cannot offer services that are not relevant to those tasks. For example, the acute care hospital social worker in this example would not get involved in long-term marital counseling with this woman and her husband, even if early contacts indicated that this was needed. Instead, he might make a referral to an appropriate family counseling agency or, if it existed, to the department in the hospital that provided such services.

The boundaries to the work created by the agency service and the needs of the client help the worker to focus and also relieve the client's anxiety that private areas may be intruded upon. Contracts are negotiated continuously and can be openly changed as the work proceeds. Often a client, not fully trusting the worker, will only risk discussing the near problems in the early interviews. When the working relationship strengthens, areas of concern that were not part of the initial agreement may enter the working contract.

I want to make a distinction here between the way I am using the term *contracting* and some other uses in the field. Some refer to a specific written document, or "service plan," that the client literally signs and agrees to fulfill. In the case of an involuntary client, or perhaps a teenager in a residential setting, the contract specifies the agreed-upon goals and the way they will be achieved (e.g., a substance-abusing child welfare client might agree to attend meetings of Alcoholics Anonymous or some other self-help group). In many cases, such documents represent the agency's or the worker's perception of what needs to be done, which the client will go along with to obtain the service or to create the illusion of cooperation. While a genuine, mutually agreed-upon contract *may* be put into writing in appropriate settings, this is not required in my broader use of the term.

Some Variant Elements in Contracting

The contracting procedure is not mechanistic; variations in the first sessions are often required. As pointed out earlier in this chapter, the helping person who is contacted by a client for assistance may begin the first interview by indicating a wish to understand what brought the client to the agency—to know what is on the client's mind. As the client shares concerns, the worker tries to connect these to potential service areas and to explain available help. The important point is not the order of skill use, but the fact that the contracting is started, that it be an open process, and that both parties are involved. Some illustrations of statements of purpose and role from a range of settings might help at this point.

> **Marriage Counselor:** Living together over a long period of time can be tough, with many ups and downs. You have been describing a crisis in your marriage, which I am sure is a frightening time. It's also an opportunity for change, perhaps to make a new marriage out of the one you already have. One of the ways I may be able to help is by assisting both of you to talk and

listen to each other about the problems you are having. I can help you tell each other how you are feeling, try to help you figure out how you get into trouble, and help you do some thinking about what each of you can do to strengthen the relationship. As we work, I'll throw in some of my own ideas about living together, and some of these may be helpful.

School Social Worker: Your teacher told me you were having trouble in her class and that she thought school was not much fun for you. My job at the school is to meet with kids like you to see if we can figure out, together, what's going wrong for you at school and to see if there are things we can do to make it better. How about it—how is school for you right now?

(After some discussion of the problems, the worker tries to define her role.) If you really feel Mrs. T. (the teacher) is down on you, maybe I could talk to her a bit about how you feel and help her understand that it makes it harder for you to work. With so many kids, she may just not understand that you feel that way.

Residential Treatment Social Worker: (First contact with new resident) I thought I should tell you what I do around here so if there is any way I can help, you can let me know. My job includes being interested in how you guys are making out. For example, right now, you're new to the house and that can be a scary time; if there is some way I can help you get connected with the other staff or the kids, or if you want me to answer any of your questions about the place, I'd be happy to.

(In the course of the conversation, other functions can be clarified.) Sometimes you may have troubles on your mind and you need someone to talk to about them. For example, if it's not going well at school, or you're having problems with the guys in the house or your family when you visit, or you're mad at the staff or the rules, I'll be around to listen to your troubles, if you want me to, and to try to help you figure out how you might handle them.

Hospital Social Worker: (To a new patient on the ward) Coming into a hospital with an illness can be a very stressful time. There are so many people to deal with, questions you may have about the ward routine or your illness, and problems getting settled in. If I can help in any way, I would like to. For example, if you're feeling down about what's going on and you need someone to talk to about it, you can call me. If you're not sure what's going on with your doctor or the tests or the medicine, I might be able to give you some answers or find someone who can. In addition, if your family is concerned about what's happening, I could talk to them about it.

Child Welfare Worker: (With a young, unmarried mother who is rejected by her family) I know it's tough when you're young, pregnant, and feeling very alone. We could meet each week and talk about some of the things on your mind right now. Perhaps I can help you think them through and figure out some answers to some of your concerns, such as trouble with your parents or your boyfriend, or uncertainty about whether you can make it if you keep the baby or if you need to give the baby up. How about it, are some of these things on your mind right now?

AIDS Counselor: Most of my clients tell me that getting the diagnosis hits them like an earthquake. There are so many questions, so many issues to face, and their feelings are so overwhelming they hardly know where or how to start. I can help you try to sort things out over the next few months—the medical part, the financial issues, work, friends and family. We also offer groups that I encourage you to consider as well as individual buddies for those who want someone to be with them and help them through. It helps a lot if you have others to help you face what you're going through. You might feel a little less alone. The important thing is to try to get some control over your life for the next period of time even if you feel out of control of the disease. Does any of this hit home?

The opening statement may well have to be fashioned to deal with the specific capabilities of the client population. Young children would have to be addressed at a level of language that they can understand. In a sexual abuse investigation, for example, purpose might be explained in terms of adults touching children in places that make them feel uncomfortable. Realistic dolls are often used to help the child understand the areas of the body involved.

In a back ward of a psychiatric hospital, an opening statement to a group of patients described as "catatonic" (appearing to be completely out of contact with their social surround), describing a discussion group to provide mutual support would have little meaning. A worker who says, in a loud voice, "I'm going to try to get all of you to talk to each other" might be closer to the mark.[2]

These illustrations show how contracting can be fashioned to reflect the particular service of the setting and possible needs of specific clients. This is where the tuning-in process can be helpful. Later in this chapter, an example of contracting with a voluntary resistant client, and another with a mandated client, will provide an opportunity to discuss the importance of clarifying issues of authority, such as confidentiality and the worker's potential use of authority, which are also essential elements in the contracting process.

Research Findings on Contracting

In my study (Shulman, 1991), the skill of reaching for client feedback about purpose was significantly associated with a worker's ability to be helpful. This supports the concept that the areas in which the worker can be most effective are those in which the client can perceive some stake. Garvin (1969) found the same principle to be true for group work practice.

The four skills that make up the grouping called *skills for helping clients to manage their problems* included clarifying the worker's purpose and role, reaching for client feedback, partializing the client's concerns, and supporting clients in taboo areas (Shulman, 1991). The scale that included these skills was predictive of the development of trust in the working relationship. Trust, in turn, was the medium through which the worker influenced outcomes of service. These findings supported the idea that contracting creates a structure that is freeing to the client.

The skill of exploring taboo areas is included in this grouping since some of the most important client issues are taboo in nature. This skill helps a client to move from the near problems to the real problems.

Partializing is included in this grouping since it also serves a contracting purpose. By listing the specific issues, the worker is providing potential "handles for work" that the client can grasp. The worker is also breaking down big problems into more manageable components and suggesting that some next steps are possible. Even if a client faces a terminal illness, there is still some work that can be done during the remaining time in relation to friends, family, lovers, and the general quality of life.

CONTRACTING OVER TIME

Our discussion thus far has focused on the initial contact with the client and the beginning of the contracting process. In practice, the contracting process takes place over time, with both the worker and client deepening their understanding of the content to be covered and of the expectations each can have of the other. For example, as pointed out earlier, clients often share "near problems" in the early sessions as a way of testing a worker. If the worker deals with these in a way that helps the client to lower defenses, then more serious (and often frightening) themes may emerge. For the worker's part, even a clearly stated description of purpose and role may not be heard nor remembered by a client overwhelmed with anxiety on a first session. Thus, contracting should be understood as a process which, in some ways, may continue throughout the life of the relationship.

The worker can also feel overwhelmed in a first session, and as a result, miss or skip over clues to crucial issues related to contracting. In the following example, a client uses the device described earlier of referring to a former helping professional who was not helpful as an indirect cue to her concerns about this new worker. The strength of her feelings frightens the worker, a student with some counseling experience, who ducks the issue. The client also raises her past suicide attempts, further upsetting the student. The student starts to catch her mistakes at the end of the first session and then continues to clarify the contracting at the start of their second meeting.

> Right at the beginning of our first session, Mary indicated that she had been to see a psychiatrist over a year ago, shortly after her husband had left her. When I asked if that experience had been helpful, she described at length how terrible it had been. She stated laughingly that if she was violent she would like to go and punch him out right now. I failed to respond to this message by relating it to me, and instead, asked her to elaborate.
>
> **Mary:** He told me more or less that I was just feeling sorry for myself and that the relationship had ended, and that I had to accept it and get on with my life. I knew I was feeling sorry for myself, but I couldn't help it. I didn't need him to tell me what I already knew. I just wanted an assist—not for him to solve my problems. He wanted to give me pills but I wouldn't take them. I was afraid enough of myself that I would do something stupid—like I have…
>
> **Worker:** Like you have?
>
> **Mary:** Yeah, I've tried to commit suicide a few times—a number of times—lots of times (pause—a strange laugh)—and one of these days I'm going to succeed.
>
> **Worker:** Have you been thinking of suicide lately?
>
> **Mary:** (Silence) Yeah, that's a good question. I think I hit the age of 12 and I really felt like I was 95 in my mind.

The client continued to talk about suicide, describing how she was not afraid to die, how nobody would miss her, and so on. The worker changed the subject by picking up on the problems the client faced. The worker described her feelings as follows:

I felt that Mary was trying to manipulate me into feeling sorry for her and I was angry at her for doing this. I also felt a little bit nervous at what I'd gotten myself into—this was my first client at field placement number three (my first two did not work out). All I needed was someone to commit suicide on me. I wasn't able to empathize with Mary since I was caught up with my own feelings.

I had heard her message loud and clear that she was desperate for help; however, I didn't let her know that I'd heard or that I was prepared to help. I didn't realize at the time this was her way of saying: "Hey, are you sure you can handle me?" Although I didn't reassure her at the beginning that I was prepared to take her on, because I was feeling ambivalent myself, I had my opportunity at the end of the interview.

As we were leaving at the end of the session, Mary suddenly stated, "You know, I once called a crisis center and told the person I felt like killing myself. They told me I might as well go ahead and do it."

Worker: I'm wondering if you are worried that I might tell you something like that. I guess you're worried about if I'm going to be able to help you. You know, I can't decide for you if you want to live or die—that's something only you can decide. But if you want to live, I can help you to begin sorting through some of your problems, one step at a time. I don't have any magic cures to help you feel better—I wish I did, because I know you're feeling pretty low right now. It'll take lots of hard work for both of us. I'll try my hardest if you want to continue. (Long silence)

Mary: Yeah, I guess that's fair. At least I can talk to you.

I had some anxieties about whether or not Mary would show up the following week. She was ten minutes late, and I was on pins and needles thinking the worst had happened. I couldn't believe how relieved I felt when she finally arrived. I tried to own up to my mistake, declare myself as human, and return to some of Mary's concerns I had missed last week.

Worker: Mary, you know I was going over the tape of last week's session and I think a lot of what you were trying to tell me went right over my head. It seems like you were quite worried that you wouldn't be able to get the kind of help you needed. Who wouldn't be after the experience you had with the psychiatrist? I guess I first want to let you know that I am going to make mistakes too and I'm probably going to say things that you don't agree with, so you're going to have to let me know if you feel I've screwed up. It'll be hard, but please don't keep it in.

Mary: Well, at least you seem real and I'm glad you're not a guy. I didn't trust him. It was all a big game of verbal semantics, with him trying to guess what I was thinking and feeling and me going along with him because I wanted to give the right answers, I wanted him to like me. I didn't realize it at the time.

Worker: Do you find it hard to say things sometimes, because you're afraid the person won't like you?

Mary: Yeah, I think I do that, especially with men.

When I asked her to elaborate, she described her relationships with men, her fear of making demands, how she gets angry and "starts acting like a bitch." When I asked if that was what was happening with her current boyfriend right now, she elaborated in some detail, and we spent the remainder of the session on this theme.

The contracting process is not completed in this example. Both worker and client will have to come back to discussions of their way of working, as well as expansions of the content (themes of concern) of their work. The worker has laid the groundwork for the discussion of their process by letting the client know she will make mistakes and that it is the client's responsibility to help keep her honest. The worker's job will be to try to create the conditions that will help the client to do just that. This would be one example of the skill referred to earlier as helping the client to deal with the authority theme—the nature of the relationship to the worker. The goal is to help the client deal with the worker as a real person, not just as a symbol of authority.

The discussion thus far has described contracting work with clients who appear open to help or who have sought it out. What about work with clients who are resistant? How can you find common ground when the client appears defensive and not open to your intervention? How can you contract with a client when your function includes authority over the client's life (e.g., parole, protection in child welfare)? In the next section we will explore this variation on the contract theme, stressing the importance of dealing directly with the issue of authority. The analysis of first sessions expands to include discussion of the skills required to begin to strengthen the working relationship.

CONTRACTING WITH RESISTANT CLIENTS

All clients bring into the first interview some ambivalence towards the idea of taking help. Resistance to the worker may be very strong for some clients because of their past experiences with professionals, their particular concerns, or the problems created by the authority of the helping person. It may be expressed passively, as by an apathetic response during the interview, or by open hostility. Although students and inexperienced workers often indicate they prefer passivity over an angry client, they soon come to realize that an angry client who is openly resistant can be much easier to work with than one who sits quietly, nodding and agreeing with the worker, while inside feeling exactly the same as the openly resistant client.

Consider the following example of a mandated client, a young mother who was on probation for substance-abuse-related offenses. She was required to meet regularly with her probation officer, attend a group program, see a social worker at a court clinic, and stay free of drugs and alcohol. The social worker, a first-year student, tried to be understanding and to engage with the client but never made clear her expectations. After repeated appointment cancellations, the worker finally decided to confront the client and set limits.

[Session 4]
> In keeping with the client's pattern of canceling and rescheduling her appointments, it was no surprise that she called the Court Clinic at 12:05 today. I answered the phone, and spoke to her briefly. She asked if she could change her 12:30 appointment to 1:30 because her "kid is sick" and she was at home taking care of him. I asked her if it would be possible for her mother to watch over him while she came to the Clinic, but she told me that her mom "wasn't up yet because she takes medication."

I told Deedee that this recurring problem with her appointments cannot continue. She admitted that she realized that this was a problem and offered a variety of excuses. Yesterday, the problem was that she went into work early, today it is her son.... I told Deedee that if she would like, she could "come in at 2:30 today." "2:30 is no good," she replied, due to her work. I explained to Deedee that I was busy until then, as other clients were scheduled to come into the clinic. I was not prepared to change their appointments or to keep others waiting because of this problem. Consequently, Deedee became very abrupt and angry. She raised her voice and said, "Fuck it all. I'll try to get in. What time is it now?"

This confirmed for me that she had no idea of the exact time, she was just trying to get out of today's meeting. "My kid's sick" was the last I heard before she hung up. Deedee had tried to get me to let her off the hook for her appointment by employing her manipulative techniques, including guilt. (She told me that she didn't want to have to take "Stevie" out in the heat with a fever.) She asked if she could just see her probation officer next week as she was already scheduled to see him on Tuesday. I explained to Deedee that, regardless, she had to see me on a weekly basis.

At 12:45, and still no sign of Deedee, the telephone rang. Obviously, after some rethinking, Deedee called the Court Clinic to apologize for her behavior. She began immediately by apologizing. "Sorry, Lois. I'm so sorry. I'm disgusted with myself. I have split personalities, you know. That wasn't me. I had to cool down." I excused Deedee, and asked her when she would be coming in. She told me that she would be able to make it in at 2:30 today, as I requested. She arranged with her co-worker to fill in for her, as she would be in a few minutes late (according to Deedee, "work" now starts at 3:00). I told Deedee that her schedule was something that we were going to have to review again, as this seems to be a recurring problem. She explained that "I wouldn't want someone to do it to me" (i.e., hang up), and that she wasn't brought up that way. She told me that she hangs up on her mother, too. I told Deedee that I appreciated her apology. She thanked me once again.

The worker's beginning efforts to confront the client and to set limits opens up a discussion of the authority theme and the client's difficulty in responding to demands placed upon her by people in authority. It is not uncommon for clients who begin serious substance abuse to appear stuck developmentally at the stage of the life cycle associated with the start of the addiction. If the client sounds like a teenager in the interviews, it may well be because she is still stuck in that stage of her growth. In part, the helping process involves beginning to work through these developmental issues.

Deedee arrived promptly at 2:30. As soon as I greeted her she apologized. We were unable to sit in our usual meeting place as hearings were being held, so we sat in the hall at a table. I began by explaining to Deedee that I was concerned about her difficulties arriving at the clinic each week. I asked her what the problem was. She explained that it was nothing personal; however, she hated feeling "trapped by the court." I asked Deedee if she felt that the terms of her probation were unfair. Deedee recognized that she was the cause of these terms and admitted that they exist because of her actions. (Too bad next week she'll forget that she admitted this.) Deedee explained that she "wished all of this didn't happen." She "hates to see her friends lead a normal life"—they didn't have to comply with the terms of the court, could "go shopping when they want," and "don't have to worry about their appointments."

Deedee expressed a sense of feeling overwhelmed by having to "go to a special group program, the Court Clinic, see her probation officer, and go to work" while managing her own responsibilities.

I tried to help Deedee with this sense by partializing her responsibilities. I focused on our task of meeting weekly. I explained to Deedee that I think we would be best suited to pick a firm meeting time that would be adhered to strictly. 12:30 Fridays was agreed upon. I suggested that by having a permanent appointment, it would make it easier for her to organize her other meetings and priorities. This way, she would not have to think about or try to remember when we were scheduled to meet, thereby increasing her anxiety and frustration, and resulting in her changing or canceling our appointment.

Further, I told Deedee that she should use these meetings for her benefit, as that was their purpose. It was her chance to outline her goals and discuss any pressing issues. Deedee told me that she "loves to talk and could do so." She explained that, once her job is finished in two weeks, that she will have more time. However, she likes working as it gives her money which she plans to use for Christmas gifts. She told me that she loves to buy gifts for everyone, especially her son. I asked her how he was doing (aside from feeling sick today). She said he is "doing great" and that he knew that she is supposed to be seeing me weekly. It was "Stevie," Deedee explained, who told her to call me back and to come in today.

I asked Deedee if she hangs up on everyone, not just her mother. She said she does it all the time, to everyone when she gets mad. I asked her how she feels once she's hung up, whether or not she's still mad. Deedee told me that she "felt like running away, escaping to a far-off place." These are the same feelings she was having prior to her encounter at Burger King that led to her arrest. Clearly, Deedee was feeling overwhelmed and tried to escape today rather than confronting her anger.

I told her that her hanging up is "not acceptable," while at the same time, I appreciated her apology. I told her that next time she should tell me what's the matter instead, if possible. I realize that Deedee has certain limitations that I and others do not. Over the phone, Deedee went on to tell me that she "didn't care if I was going to give her a bad report when she hung up," and wanted to "fuck it all." She said that she was ashamed of her previous behavior, and that by coming to the court it is all just a "bad reminder" for her. However, she recalled what I said to her last week, that she "must take everything one step at a time." She mustn't look at everything that she has to do as one task, but as many smaller ones. "Stevie" helped her today by making her realize that she should and has to go the Clinic. Deedee asked me if I'd ever met him, and recalled that he used to come in for a group last year. I told her that we would arrange a time for him to come in. She told me that she was excited by that idea.

I reviewed briefly with her how the rest of her week was otherwise. No drug or alcohol problems. She asked what Dr. Simms had said about her taking the Valium last week. I explained that, while it was not condoned, she must focus on not taking any more and remain drug-free. I asked her what her plans were for the long weekend. She was planning to pick up groceries, as she had just received her check yesterday.

We then chatted briefly about what else she had to do, and Deedee asked if she could go. I reminded her that I would see her next week, and to have a good weekend and week. She said one last time that "it wasn't me before." I explained to her that over the phone it was her voice, and that's "all I have to go on." She said she understood and said I must have thought she was "crazy." I told her that today's conversation was forgotten and that from now on, this shouldn't be a problem as we have contracted an agreement and are beginning to formulate goals (who am I kidding?).

The question of how long these meetings would continue resurfaced again. At the beginning of the meeting I told her that, unless I hear otherwise from her probation officer, she would go to the group program for two months and remain at the Clinic for the duration of her probation. I feel, though, that this issue was dealt with by telling her the meetings are permanent. While I realize that today Deedee agreed with these terms, chances are that our next meeting will reflect a lack of compliance to these terms. Finally, when Deedee left she seemed to be in brighter spirits. As she said good-bye, she said, "Have a good weekend, Hon. See you Friday."

When the client has not made the first decision, whatever the specific reasons or the form of expression, an obstacle sits squarely on the line between worker and client (see Figure 3.1). Therefore, the worker's efforts to turn the client towards the service must be integrated with efforts to deal with this obstacle.

The first step in this process begins with the worker honestly facing his or her own feelings about the engagement. Workers are human, and the thought of meeting a new client who does not appear to want help or who has a reputation for being hostile (or one whom the worker anticipates may be hostile) can cause the worker to hold back on efforts to reach for the client. Workers experience difficulty in offering help in the face of possible rejection. In the example just described, the student shared that this was her only client at the time (the start of the school year at the school of social work) and she was afraid of losing her. It was this fear that caused the student to wait three sessions to confront the client. I had pointed out to her, in class, that she really couldn't "lose" the client because at this point, she didn't "have" the client.

In those situations where the worker's feeling when the client misses appointments is relief, the worker's offer of service may contain the same elements of ambivalence as the client's. This can easily lead to a self-fulfilling prophecy where the first engagement breaks down.

FIGURE 3.1

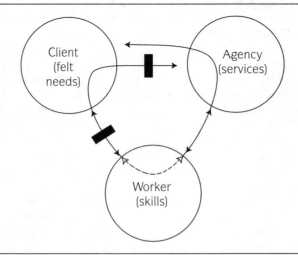

An argument has existed in the field about whether it is possible to work effectively with mandated clients. Some believe that the use of authority to require engagement so profoundly distorts the helping relationship that it can only be an illusion of work. In some cases, it is clearly true that no matter what the worker says or does, the client refuses to accept the service. In some situations, the client may not yet be ready, and in other cases, the client may never be ready. This is one of the reasons children must be removed permanently from some abusive homes, men need to go to prison for battering their partners, and some heroin addicts end their lives overdosing on the street. The worker can only do her or his best to maximize the possibility that the client can use the help, leaving the final decision to the client.

For some categories of clients, however, the requirement that forces them to seek help serves as the beginning of a process of change. Trimble (1994), writing about his development as a professional in working with men who batter, describes his own understanding of this process:

> I was idealistic when I started this work. I wanted men to come to the service because they realized they had a problem which had hurt another person physically and psychologically and had hurt themselves. I hoped they would come to realize that they needed to change themselves even if their wives would never return. In reality, few of us face our problems unless we have to. It has been my experience that most violent men who come to our group and stay long enough to make a change are there because they have to be. That "have to" is either a court order or their wives saying they won't return unless the men get some help. This does not mean that most men want to be violent but rather that most of them cannot tolerate for very long the pain and fear I mentioned earlier. Their inability to tolerate pain, fear, and loneliness forms a part of the foundation for both their violence and for the impulsivity which carries them out of the group. Because of this impulsivity an outside pressure is needed to keep them in the group past their usual tolerance level for self-confrontation (p. 261).

The skills of beginning discussion with a resistant client are the same as those described earlier: clarifying purpose, clarifying role, and reaching for feedback. A negotiating process is taking place, but this time the potential obstacles to a working relationship must be part of discussion. In effect, the worker is asking the client if they can work together in spite of the barriers that may block their efforts. Often, when an obstacle has been identified and explored, it loses its power, and the client and the worker are free to move past it into a deepening relationship.

To illustrate how this might work, let us take an example of a first session with a voluntary but resistant client in a child welfare agency. The client, Mr. Gregory, is 25 years old. He has recently separated from his wife. She has applied to place their three children in temporary care of the agency. Mr. Gregory has a long record with the agency in which different workers have consistently characterized him as hostile and defensive. This is an example of the client referred to in Chapter 1 as the "agency client." In fact, when the worker told her colleagues she was going to see him, their comment to her was "Good luck!"

This worker described the purpose of her first interview as informing him of his legal rights, describing the meaning of the agency's intervention, having him sign consent forms, and seeing if some help could be offered to him for his own concerns. The interview began with the worker's efforts to clarify purpose.

Worker: You know that your wife has signed forms to place your children under the care of this agency. I wanted to meet with you to have you sign agreements, but before that, to discuss what this means for you and your children. I know it can be an upsetting time, and I thought you might also have things on your mind you want to discuss.

Mr. Gregory: For how long are my kids going to be in care?

The worker's opening statement clarified the purpose of the interview, placing a strong emphasis on the offer of service to the client—not just as someone called in to sign forms, but as someone with feelings and concerns as a client in his own right. In a sense, her direct reaching for him represents a form of skill called *making a demand for work*. This is discussed in some detail in the next chapter, but in the present context it means the worker is gently attempting to involve the client actively in the engagement. The demand is synthesized with the worker's ability to express some genuine empathy with the client's situation. This is demonstrated in the sentence, "I know it can be an upsetting time...." (The use of empathic skills is also discussed in detail in the next chapter.) In the client's response—"For how long are my kids going to be in care?"—we see a shift back to the children—a polite way for him to refuse her offer. The interview continued with the worker responding to the direct question but also refusing to be put off by the client's first refusal.

Worker: Your wife has signed forms for six months. That means that we are responsible to look after your children for that time, but with 24-hours' notice you or your wife can have your children home at any time. If you wish, after six months, the time can be extended.

Mr. Gregory: It's a long time for the kids.

Worker: Yes, it is, and for you also.

Mr. Gregory: Yeah, I haven't seen them yet, but I hear they're doing fine.

Worker: Would you like to see them?

Mr. Gregory: I thought I wasn't allowed to.

Worker: Sure you are. You have the right to see your children whenever you wish.

Mr. Gregory: I was told that it would upset the kids, especially Alan, to see me, so it would be better not to.

Worker: Sure it will upset him. It will upset you, too. It's hard to see someone you love and can't be with.

The worker's continued "empathic demand" is contained in the phrase "and for you also." In response, the client began to explore the visiting issue. The issue of visiting is important to the client and is an example of feedback on the contracting. The worker continued her emphasis on his feelings with the comment, "It will upset you, too. It's hard to see someone you love and can't be with." This persistence resulted in his beginning to explore the difficult feelings surrounding visiting. In the next segment, the worker opened up this area by using the skill of putting the client's feelings into words. She used her "tuning in" preparation to articulate the underlying difficulty clients face in visiting children who have been placed in care.

Mr. Gregory: Yeah, Alan has been in care before, and he's confused and sad.

Worker: Yes, that must make it hard on you to see him.

Mr. Gregory: Yeah. Like what do I say to him?

Worker: Like when he asks "When do I come home?"

Mr. Gregory: Well, yeah.

Worker: What do you say?

Mr. Gregory: Oh, I change the subject and cheer him up.

Worker: Does it work?

Mr. Gregory: Not really.

Worker: What do you want to say?

Mr. Gregory: Well, I don't know when he's coming home.

Worker: I guess that hurts you.

Mr. Gregory: Well, kids don't understand.

Worker: Have you tried telling him?

Mr. Gregory: No, not really.

Worker: I think it's hard to tell your child you don't know when he's coming home, but clearing that up might make it easier for you both once it's discussed.

Mr. Gregory: Yeah, I won't feel like I'm holding out. But I won't be seeing him until he comes to my wife on the weekend. Can I do that?

The worker's persistent and genuine concern with his feelings caused the client to begin to open up and deal with a real concern. When she responded to his comment, "Like what do I say to him?" by saying "Like when he asks, 'When do I come home?'" she effectively opened the door for him to explore one of the roughest issues facing parents who place children in care—the guilt they feel that often results in difficulty in visiting. Even in these first few minutes, the relationship has opened up, disturbing the client. Before he can allow himself to go further, he has to clarify how things stand between them. The next excerpt demonstrates how this discussion of the authority theme emerged.

Worker: Whatever visiting arrangements you want to make will be done. I have to know in advance to help plan and to know where he is, since he's our responsibility. Seeing him at your wife's place is fine if your wife wants that.

Mr. Gregory (In a louder voice): I want to know something. Are you going to be my social worker? I know you see my wife and you help her. So how does it work? Are you on her side or mine, or do I get another social worker?

The directness of the client, which workers in the past may have confused with aggressiveness, is apparent. It is interesting to consider the effect of this question on the worker. When asked about her reactions to the client's question, the worker admitted to being taken aback and feeling put on the spot by his assertiveness. Clients often ask questions or make statements that throw a worker off balance. This worker responded to her own feelings of defensiveness by delivering a substantial lecture that contrasts with her earlier terse reactions.

This type of response is not uncommon when workers feel put on the spot. Rather than responding with their gut reaction—their honest feeling at the moment—they try to control the situation with the use of words. Compare the following speech, delivered quickly, with the worker's previously terse, focused, and on-target responses.

Worker: I'm on no one's side. I try to help your wife with what's on her mind. I'm here to help you with whatever you want. I do this so you can both come to the point of finally making a decision about your children—do you want them home? If yes, when and how many of them? Whatever we discuss is

> confidential, and the same goes for your wife and me. When the two of you will make decisions that will affect each other, we'll do it together. Then I won't take sides but try to help the two of you talk to each other and work together on arriving at a decision. (Quiet)

The silence which followed this speech was important, since it contained a message for the worker. A number of possibilities existed. It could simply have been that the client was confused by the words ("What did she say?"). He may have felt that he was not getting a direct answer to his question ("She must be on my wife's side"). In the next segment, the worker is seen demonstrating an important skill called reaching inside of silences. This is the worker's effort to explore the meaning of the silence to understand better what the client is thinking or feeling.

In an earlier research project of mine (Shulman, 1979b, 1981), more than 120 hours of videotaped social work practice was viewed and rated according to an observation system we developed. Silences seemed to often occur just after the worker appeared to misunderstand the client's concern. They were often, but not always, a message that the client felt cut off. Other times, the silence was not a signal that the worker was off-base, but rather that the worker had hit home. In this early study, workers responded to silences most often by changing the topic of discussion. Workers often experience silences as uncomfortable because they sense negative feedback. Silences can, of course, mean other things as well. For example, the client may be reflecting on the worker's comments, or he may be experiencing strong emotions. The different meanings of silence will be discussed in the next chapter.

As illustrated in the next segment, by reaching inside the silence, this worker demonstrated skill in catching her mistake at the same time she was making it. Workers often have the mistaken notion that in good practice one never makes mistakes. In reality, good practice involves spontaneity on the worker's part, and so mistakes will be a natural part of the work. If workers always wait for exactly the right thing to say, they will always be thinking and analyzing while the client is working well ahead of them. This was a key moment in the interview, and this skilled and experienced worker proved herself up to the challenge.

> (Silence)
>
> **Worker:** Why did you ask? It sounds like you may have had trouble with social workers before?
>
> **Mr. Gregory:** I did. All the other social workers seemed to be with my wife and against me. I was always the bad one.
>
> **Worker:** And you're worried that I might do the same thing?
>
> **Mr. Gregory:** Well, yeah, you might.
>
> **Worker:** I try to help the two of you decide to do what's best for you and the children. If you feel I'm siding or if you don't like how things are going with me, I want you to tell me because I want to help you both.
>
> **Mr. Gregory:** Don't worry, you'll know. Are you new at this job?

As a result of her "tuning in," the worker correctly guessed the meaning of his earlier question, "Are you on her side or mine?" She knew that his past experiences might well have led to the development of a stereotype about social workers and that at some point she would have to deal with this. By reaching directly for this in her comment, "It sounds like you may have had trouble with social workers before," she gave him permission to talk directly about what some clients would consider a taboo subject.

Workers sometimes express concern about exploring such a question. They feel it would be unprofessional to discuss other workers or other professionals. They say that they might be perceived as "not identifying with the agency" or as simply "trying to get on the client's side." If one views most discussion of other helping professionals as the client's way of indirectly exploring the present working relationship, then the dilemma is nonexistent. This worker picked up the indirect cue and reached for his present concerns with her comment, "And you're worried I might do the same thing?"

This client responded directly and acknowledged that this was what he meant. Many clients who lack this strength and ability to be direct might have held back at this point. Since the obstacles are powerful ones, they needed to be explored openly in first sessions. The worker needs to push, gently, a bit harder for these concerns. For example, in response to a client who says, "Oh no, I wasn't worried about you," the worker might continue, "It would be easy to understand how you might be concerned about me. After all, I'm a social worker, too, and you have had some tough experiences. How about it—perhaps you are just slightly concerned?"

The client will often sense, in this second invitation, that the worker really means that it is all right to talk about their relationship. If not, the worker can let things be and try to return to this topic at another time when the client's trust has developed a bit more strongly. Meanwhile, the client has the message that this issue can be discussed when he or she feels ready. In a first group session described in Part II of this book, the process of accepting a second invitation is clearly illustrated.

Returning to the interview, we have the interesting question by the client, "Are you new at this job?" When students discussed the possible meaning of the client's question, a number of alternatives were considered: "Maybe he was trying to figure out what kind of worker you are, because you don't talk like a social worker." "Maybe he was thinking after you have been around for a while, you'll change." This time, in contrast to her reactions to the earlier direct question, the worker tried to explore its meaning. This involved the skill of elaboration, inviting the client to expand on the meaning of his comment or question.

> **Worker:** No, I've been here for a while. Why do you ask?
> **Mr. Gregory:** Well, the last worker I had was really green. She knew nothing. She took me to court—didn't get anywhere, but what a mess.
> **Worker:** Are you wondering if I'll take you to court?
> **Mr. Gregory:** Oh, no. And if you did, I'd go and fight.

Once again, the worker reached for the implications for the here-and-now of their relationship from his description of past experiences. In the next excerpt, she tries to clarify some of the terms of their working relationship in the context of the agency and her dual responsibility of trying to offer him a service while still carrying statutory responsibility for the protection of his children. This is part of the contracting process. The terms of the relationship must be defined openly. The client may be able to overcome the obstacle posed by the worker's dual function if there is an honest discussion of it and a clear definition of the worker's responsibilities.

This is just as true with the elder care worker during a first visit who must deal with the elderly client's fears of being "put in a home" or the adoption social worker who must make a report on the suitability of the prospective parents. When these realities are openly discussed in the first sessions, when the responsibilities and mutual expectations are clearly defined for both the client and the worker, the client is often able to overcome the obstacles they pose. The worker in this illustration attempted to define this part of the contract.

> **Worker:** I think it's important for me to let you know under what conditions I'd go to court. Children can be in care of the agency either by court custody or voluntary agreement. In your case, it's voluntary, so there is no court involvement. But if I see the kids harmed when they're with your wife or you while visiting—by harmed, I mean beaten, black and blue, bones broken, or not fed or supervised for the whole weekend home, then I go to court. But only under those circumstances—beaten or neglected.
>
> **Mr. Gregory:** What if I want to take my kids home? Can you stop me, go to court and stop me?
>
> **Worker:** No. You can take your children whenever you want.
>
> **Mr. Gregory:** That can't be. What if I'm not working, can't care for them, you won't let them come home.
>
> **Worker:** I can't stop them. If, however, once they're home and they don't get fed, clothed, taken care of, then I can go to court and bring them back.
>
> **Mr. Gregory:** (Smiling) I really knew the answers to this, but I was misinformed by other people in the past. I used to sort of test my last worker to see if she would tell the truth.
>
> **Worker:** Did I pass?
>
> **Mr. Gregory:** Not you, her. (Quiet) Yeah, you passed [he smiled]. I had to do it to see where we stand. The first meeting is really important, you know.
>
> **Worker:** Yes, it is. And it is also scary, since you don't know what to expect.
>
> **Mr. Gregory:** Yeah, but it looks okay.

They talked some more about procedures, rules, regulations, arranged a next meeting, and then summed up. The worker asked if Mr. Gregory would like to meet again to discuss his children and their care. Mr. Gregory declined this invitation. He indicated he was too overwhelmed just then trying to find a new job. I was able to contact this worker a number of months after I obtained the process of this interview. Since so many people had asked me about Mr. Gregory, I asked if she had seen him again. The worker told me that a few months after this interview, Mr. Gregory had called the agency and asked for her by name. When they met, he told her he now had a job and an apartment of his own, and felt he could take his children home. He indicated that he could not handle this by himself and that he would need her help. She agreed, discussed possible support services, and soon afterward, the children returned to their father. He may have not been ready to use her help after the first interview. However, I believe that she had laid the groundwork in the first session so that when he was ready he saw her as a source of real help.

When we have reviewed this interview, a number of students and workers have commented on the client's directness. They have even asked, with a touch of hopefulness in their voices, whether clients like this come into agencies often. The key point is that he seems like such a good client only because the worker was able to respond to him with skill. Another worker, and even this worker in her early student days, would have been put off by an assertive client such as this. The interview might have had a much different ring to it if the worker had not "tuned in" and prepared herself to reach for the part of this client which, in spite of his ambivalence, was still reaching out to the agency, the worker, and his children. The directness and anger were actually a sign of his caring.

A similar analysis could be presented of a social worker in a residential setting dealing with a new resident and reaching past the bravado that is part of the front put up by the "tough" teenager. Even if the teenager does not immediately accept the worker's offer to help with the fear and stress associated with suddenly finding oneself in a strange setting with possibly threatening peers, it is important that the worker acknowledge these feelings.

Another example might be an alcohol addiction counselor who faces a client whose arms are tightly folded across his chest, thus expressing physically his feelings about being referred to the program by his boss. The worker needs to make clear her or his recognition that the client is present on an involuntary basis and that the worker is powerless to help the client without his active involvement. In a first session with men referred to a group for men who battered their wives, Trimble, quoted earlier as learning to understand the value of mandated attendance to his group, was also able to point out at the start that he recognized that the men could continue to attend and meet the requirements of the group without ever changing, thus acknowledging that control—a crucial issue for male batterers—was really still in their hands. The worker incorporated this reality into his opening statement.

> I'm sure it is possible to follow all these rules and not change, not open up to facing yourself or to the other men here. You can probably get through this group and really not change. That's up to you. The judge may order you to be here or your wife may be saying that she won't come back unless you get help. And as I have just said, we require your anger diary and regular attendance in order for you to stay here, but no one can reach into your mind and heart and order a change. That's where you have complete control (Trimble, 1994, p. 262).

In each case, the worker must "tune in" to prepare for indirect cues and to get in touch with his or her own feelings about the engagement. A clear statement of purpose and role, one that incorporates the client's potential sense of urgency, is needed. An opportunity for client feedback about purpose must be given in addition to the exploration of the potential obstacles to developing a working relationship.

As with any client, the worker begins in the first session to use skills to start development of a positive working relationship while the contracting process is taking place. These skills include elaboration, reaching inside of silence, empathizing with expressed feelings, and articulating unexpressed feelings slightly ahead of the client.

The worker attempts to carry out the helper role as well as abilities permit, making mistakes along the way but correcting them as soon as possible. The client also has a part in the proceedings: the decision to use this worker, to trust, to take some responsibility for part of the problems. If worker and client are both up to their interdependent tasks, then a foundation may be laid in the first sessions for movement into the work phase. This phase is examined in the next chapter, with a more complete discussion of many of the skills mentioned in this one.

MODELS FOR ASSESSMENT IN THE BEGINNING PHASE

While I have questioned the medical paradigm (study, diagnosis, treatment, and evaluation) that has guided our profession's practice, theory development, and research, the individual elements contained in the model can be useful tools for the practitioner. Thus, within the interactional paradigm described in this book, obtaining relevant information (study), using models to guide our understanding of our client's circumstances (diagnosis), developing intervention strategies (treatment), and assessing our impact on the process and outcome (evaluation) all play important roles. It is the four-stage, linear model, in which each stage appears to follow the other, the associated trappings also borrowed from medicine, the focus on pathology, and the underlying assumptions of where change comes from—the worker, rather than the client—that has caused me to reject it as a useful paradigm for my teaching, research, and practice. With these reservations in mind, it is important to explore some of the questions associated with assessment and to examine some innovative models for determining "where the client is."

Kirk, Siporin, and Kutchins (1989) reviewed the history of social work and diagnosis in an article focusing on the profession's apparent "ambivalence" toward a formal classification system and the impact of the Diagnostic and Statistical Manual of Mental Disorders (DSM-IIIR).[3] The DSMs are a series of psychiatric manuals used to describe and classify "mental disorders" for the purpose of developing responsive treatment plans. Referring back to the publication of *Social Diagnosis* (1918) by Mary Richmond as the beginning of social work's "distinctive model of assessment, upon which a distinctive approach to treatment was based" (p. 296), they point out that

> The conception of "social diagnosis," as Richmond named this process, was a complex one. It consisted of analysis of three interacting elements: the social situation, the personality of the client or client group, and the problem. This process of diagnosis did not result in the affixing of a label, but rather in an accurate assessment of the dynamics of the problem in its life context.... Richmond further contributed to this change by leading a movement within the social work profession to adopt a medical model for assessment and intervention and to view charity/social workers as "social physicians" who provide "social therapeutics" (p. 296).

The authors trace the evolution of social work's unique approach to assessment through a number of models leading up to the "person in situation" perspective, more recently reframed as the "ecological" approach, that has been widely adopted in the field. While their analysis raises many important questions about the suitability of the DSM system for social work assessment, and they call for work in developing a unique social work system rather than borrowing from psychiatry, they do not challenge the core of the medical paradigm in terms of the stages of the process.

Mailick (1991) called for "re-assessing" assessment in clinical social work practice, based upon changes in client populations, agency services, and treatment technologies (p. 3). For example, she highlights emerging controversies that influence assessment, associated with the "social constructivism" of postmodern theory.

> Customary ways of thinking about how information is obtained and how it can be confirmed are being re-examined. Social workers are debating whether it is the context in which information is sought, the purpose for seeking it, and the theoretical framework that shapes the investigator's search that critically influences the meaning of what is obtained. Social constructivism suggests just such an argument. For social work clinicians, it both raises the question of whether facts exist and can be discovered and challenges the usefulness of a monolithic model of assessment (p. 4).

Her proposal for a new approach to differential assessment calls for acknowledging three major determinants that contribute to assessment: the nature and scope of agency service (e.g., goals of the service, identified population, time frame of service); the theoretical and value orientation of the practice (e.g., psychodynamic, behavioral); and the unit of attention (individual, family, small group). Thus, an assessment of an individual client might read quite differently (or be constructed differently) depending upon the setting, the practice orientation, whether the service was individual or family oriented, and the time limits placed on the service.

A number of authors have developed assessment frameworks or instruments that ask the social worker to pay attention to variables that may otherwise be overlooked. For example, Gutheil (1992) points out the importance of understanding physical environment and its impact on behavior in the home, the family, the agency, and the interview. For example, the placement of the worker's chair behind a desk or the type and arrangement of furniture in a waiting room may convey a message to clients about the formality or informality of the practice. In the client's home, issues associated with personal space, crowding, privacy, and territory may influence family functioning and individual behavior. The author argues for training to help social workers be more observant and skillful in assessing physical space and its impact on clients.

Tracy and Whittaker (1990) propose developing a "social network map" as a means of assessing a client's sources of social support. This instrument, which has been developed and tested by the authors,

> allows both clinicians and clients to evaluate several aspects of informal support: (1) existing informal resources, (2) potential informal resources not currently utilized by the client, (3) barriers to involving social network resources, and (4) factors to be considered in the decision to incorporate informal resources in the formal service plan (p. 462).

The social network map provides a tool for a client to identify both the number of significant people in different domains (e.g., household, friends, neighbors) and also the nature of the interaction (e.g., concrete support, emotional support, information and advice). Given the contributions of social support networks to resilience, as reported in Chapter 2, identification of these actual and potential resources could play an important role in helping the client develop strategies for effective buffering of stress.

Finally, an example of the use of a "culturagram" to assess and empower culturally diverse families is described by Congress (1994) as a means for strengthening ethnic-sensitive practice, particularly in relation to immigrant families. The author created an assessment model that allowed social workers to move past generalizations about ethnic groups (e.g., African-American, Latino, Southeast Asian) and to recognize significant levels of diversity within diversity, as well as unique cultural factors that may be client- or family-specific. As the author points out,

> A Puerto Rican family that has lived in the United States for 30 years may be very different from a Mexican family that came to the United States without legal documentation in the past year. An African-American family that relocated from a small southern town to a northern city will be unlike a Haitian family. Use of the culturagram helps the social worker clarify differences among individuals and families from similar racial and ethnic backgrounds (p. 533).

Topics included in the culturagram include reasons for immigration, length of time in the community, legal or undocumented status, age at time of immigration, language spoken at home and in the community, contact with cultural institutions, health benefits, holidays and special events, and values about family, education, and work. Examples are provided of information gained through the assessment that helped workers to understand values, attitudes, and behaviors that would have been differently and incorrectly assessed in the absence of cultural sensitivity (e.g., a two-year-old Mexican child brought to a hospital by a mother who had not previously sought medical care—not because of neglect, but rather because of fear of deportation as an undocumented alien; a seven-year-old Haitian school child whose increasing depression was connected to his family's emigration from Haiti for political reasons and the family's increasing sense of hopelessness about returning to their homeland).

Other assessment instruments will be described in later chapters dealing with family practice, child welfare, and substance abuse. I want to end this section with some suggestions for how a worker can assess the assessment process before deciding whether to incorporate the use of any instrument in the beginning phase of practice. A worker should be able to answer yes to each of the following questions:

1. Will the information gained through this process provide specific understanding that will directly help me and the client in our work together?
2. Is the client fully aware of the reason for using the assessment tool?
3. Has the client provided informed consent for the use of the tool and is the client "in control" of the process?
4. Can the assessment process be used in a manner that does not interfere with the crucial contracting and engaging process of the beginning phase?
5. Is the use of the assessment tool critical to the work, as opposed to providing a structure that makes the social worker feel more comfortable?

If the answers to all of these questions are "yes," then I believe use of the instrument early in the working relationship can enhance the process.

CULTURALLY DIVERSE PRACTICE

Lum (1996) defines culturally diverse practice as follows:

> Culturally diverse social work practice recognizes and respects the importance of difference and variety in people and the crucial role of culture in the helping relationship. Its primary group focus is on people of color—particularly African Americans, Latino Americans, Asian Americans and Native Americans—who have suffered historical oppression and continue to endure subtle forms of racism, prejudice, and discrimination. In working with an individual, family, group, and/or community, the practitioner draws upon the positive strengths of diverse cultural beliefs and practices and is concerned about discriminatory experiences that require approaches sensitive to ethnic and cultural environments (p. 12).

Rapid changes in demographics in the United States and Canada have been brought about by a surge of immigration over the past two decades. Social workers often find themselves working with clients of different races and ethnicities whose cultures are foreign to them. Differences can also be related to gender, sexual orientation, class, physical ability, and so on, with distinct cultures associated with each population group.

Significant differences also exist within general population groups. For example, when one refers to a Native American client, one would also need to know which tribe or Nation the client comes from. An Asian-American client can be Chinese-American, Japanese-American, or a recent immigrant from Southeast Asia. While there are many shared experiences and cultures, an African-American client from the rural South may seem very different from one raised in Chicago. A black American immigrant from the West Indies will bring a perspective that is quite different from one from Haiti. Among Latin-American clients, one would expect to find differences between Puerto Rican–American clients in New York City and Mexican-Americans in southern California, or Hispanics from Central America living in Boston. Cultural "sensitivity" that leads to stereotyping of clients according to general population groups, and doesn't allow for diversity within diversity, is actually a form of cultural insensitivity.

I remember working with white child welfare workers in British Columbia, Canada, who described their Native Canadian clients as very "passive" and tending to be "silent." They would interpret this behavior as a cultural trait when they worked with Native Canadian clients on the reserves or in the cities. There is some truth to this notion in that thoughtful pauses before responding often characterize such conversations. When I conducted workshops for Native counselors, however, they had another interpretation of this behavior. One counselor told me that a Native client had noted, "When you stay very quiet long enough, the white workers get so nervous, they go 'natter, natter, natter...'" The white social workers in this example were explaining the silence as a cultural trait instead of understanding it as a form of indirect communication from this particular Native Canadian client, in this interview, with this white child welfare worker.

A lack of understanding of cultural differences can create barriers between the social worker and the client, particularly in the beginning phase of practice. As described earlier in this chapter, in the section on assessment models, a social worker risks misinterpreting client behaviors, values, and attitudes if he or she is not able to see through the cultural eyes of the client. Weaver and Wodarski (1995) point out that

> Clearly, professionals cannot be expected to know everything about every cultural group; however, rather than judging a client by dominant society standards, it is the practitioner's responsibility to seek out relevant information, just as a social worker must seek out information when a client is referred to them with an unfamiliar case situation; for example, a particular disability, a need for advocacy, a question of eligibility for an entitlement program. Often one of the best sources of information about clients' culture are the clients themselves (pp. 219–220).

In those settings and geographic locations where a particular population group is regularly a part of the caseload, then the additional responsibility for learning about the group and appropriate culturally sensitive practices rests with the individual social workers and the social work department or agency.

It is beyond the scope of this book to fully explore the wide range of diversity issues and how they affect practice. A number of excellent social work texts have addressed these areas, including books by Davis and Proctor (1989), Devore and Schlesinger (1996), and Lum (1996). In this section, we will set the stage for how one might address diversity issues, providing some illustrative examples of research and practice with different populations. Discussions in later chapters—for example, on work with families, treatment of substance abuse, group work, or community practice—will expand on this initial discussion by addressing other populations (e.g., Asian-Americans) and by identifying diversity issues as they emerge from the work.

Mexican-American

In one "cultural study," Lum discusses the Mexican-American cultural value of the family as a "...source of identity and support in times of crisis" (p. 51). The author points out,

> Mexican American familism, or concept of family identity, extends beyond the immediate family unit (*la casa*) to include two other similar but distinguishable systems—*la familia* (extended family) and *los compadres* (godparents). In times of crisis, Mexican Americans are inclined to seek the family first for support (p. 51).
>
> Mexican Americans frequently extend the definition of family membership beyond *la casa* to include individuals labeled *compadre* and *familia. La compadres* are important individuals who are often, but not always, related in some manner. ...*Familia* is variably defined in the literature. Generally, it connotes a social network resembling a modified nuclear structure. Elder males in the community may hold positions of respect and authority, and other members may or may not be related, but have some sort of significant interaction with the family (p. 52).

Lum points out that each of the three systems have a sense of responsibility that leads to a "volunteerism," with *la casa* as "the center of Chicano identity and commitment" (p. 52). Lum uses this understanding to develop guidelines for practice with Mexican-American families that take into account and work through this "triad of systems" that can provide support for the family members involved. Once again, this example emphasizes the importance of the worker respecting and involving the social support system, which has been shown to be an important element of resilience in the face of adversity.

African-American

Lum (1996) points out that from a historical perspective,

> the African American family has long existed within a well-defined, close-knit system of relationships. Authority and responsibility have been clearly assigned, and complex rules of behavior have embedded them in village and regional linkages. Family life in the United States was impaired by slavery, but the African American community has survived as an active unit to meet the needs of its members. The church is still a central community institution (p. 95).

Lum identifies underlying themes of the African-American community to include "strong bonds of household kinship, an orientation to work for the support of family, flexible family roles, occupational and educational achievement, commitment to religious values, and church participation" (p. 95).

This description of the essential values of the African-American community often clashes with perceptions of social workers who deal with clients who do not appear to fit this general model. For example, the frequency and problems associated with adolescent pregnancy in inner-city communities suggests a breakdown in this value system. Stevens (1994) studied adolescent development and pregnancy among African-American females. She suggests that current paradigms of adolescent pregnancy "tend to view the female adolescent's behavior as disordered, diseased or as an intergenerational transmission of psychological dysfunction" (p. 435).

She argues that non-pathologic analysis of problematic behaviors is required to better understand and respond to this pattern. Her findings support the following theoretical perspectives:

> (1) pregnancy can serve as a primary way of confirming existence and providing a sense of identity rather than the result of sexual acting out behavior; (2) parenthood is perceived a viable route to an adult social identity when opportunities for alternate routes of negotiating an adulthood status are blocked; (3) the adolescent does not have to disconnect or individuate from familiar relationships for the development of self (p. 434).

In comparing a group of 20 pregnant teens with 16 nonpregnant teens, she found that the "...nonpregnant females manifested a sense of care and responsibility to others in varied relationships and articulated more frequent self-expectancies for social mobility. They were actively engaged in church, work and school environments. They demonstrated civic competency by being registered voters. Nonpregnant females were less restrictive in their dating and mating behaviors and experienced multiple dating partners" (p. 449).

Stevens suggests that the findings supported the view that both pregnant and nonpregnant participants viewed pregnancy as a way of "managing concerns for personal and social maturation," providing a maturational experience and an indicator of adult status, and felt that their age group was mature enough to deal with parenting (p. 449). In summary, Stevens suggests that adolescent pregnancy, rather than being viewed as a sign of pathology, may be better explained as an alternate life-style choice. With this understanding, the social worker might well be advised to engage such a client with a non-pathologic orientation, focusing instead on both the adaptive and maladaptive aspects of this behavior. Stevens advocates for early intervention with troubled populations before sexual decisions are made (e.g., primary and middle school prevention programs). She also suggests that social workers emphasize mother-daughter dyads, the adolescent peer group, mentor-apprenticeship programs, and collaborative programs with inner city institutions.

While non-pathologic approaches to troubled clients are crucial in developing the working alliance in the early stages of engagement, the impact of long-term and persistent racism and discrimination have influenced many members of the African-American community in their perception of social workers and others from the dominant society. Davis and Proctor (1989) suggests that "persons of African descent are especially reluctant to disclose themselves to whites, due to the hardships they and their forebears experienced in the United States" (p. 23). They suggest that this represents a special case of their unwillingness to disclose themselves to any representatives of the white world.

The authors suggest that

> Practice with black families may also be facilitated by the employment of certain practitioner styles. Practitioners should keep in mind that blacks in the United States have historically received less respect from this society than perhaps any other ethnic group. Hence, a style that indicates respect for them by the therapist will be positively received. As an example of demonstrating respect, the adult members of these families should be referred to, upon introduction, by their last names. The practitioner should not supplant the family's desire to be respected with his or her desire to be informal or even to establish a positive therapeutic rapport. Specifically, in the interest of establishing rapport, informality does not automatically facilitate the establishment of a sincere relationship (p. 82).

The importance of showing respect by the use of the last name was brought home by a participant in a workshop of mine when, referring to her work with African-Americans in the South, she emphasized the relatively recent history of slavery during which slaves had their last names ignored and were referred to by first names in a manner that was demeaning. Thus, efforts by young white workers to establish informality with elderly clients by using their first names were actually perceived as insulting.

American Indian

Williams and Ellison (1996) address issues of culturally informed health and mental health practice with American Indian clients, providing guidelines for non-Indian social workers. For example,

> American Indian clients will involve themselves in interventions they perceive to be appropriate. Involving a traditional healer may increase the desirability of an intervention. Social workers should use ceremony and ritual—two important aspects of healing—in an intervention. Giving gifts, serving food, and involving family and friends emphasize the importance of an intervention. The inclusion of family members underscores that the family is a supportive and protective unit whose help is valued (p. 148).

Weaver and White (1997) raise the issue of the impact of historical trauma on Native families:

> In order to work effectively with Native families, social workers must first acquire an understanding of the historical influences on contemporary issues and problems. The root of many current social and health problems among Native people lies in the past. Specific and deliberate attempts were made to destroy Native people both physically and culturally. The impact of these actions cannot be minimized. Although Native people have survived, tremendous damage was done to individuals, families, and communities. The trauma experienced by Native families has never healed. Social workers must be prepared to acknowledge and confront the historical trauma and grief experienced by Native people if they are to successfully assist contemporary Native families (p. 67).

Weaver and White's injunction was brought home to me personally when I met with a group of Native leaders, homemakers, counselors, friendship center workers, and clients to conduct a group key informant interview in preparation for my major child welfare research project. In the early part of the meeting I listened to stories of more recent abuses experienced by Native families and communities as one by one participants shared, with great anger and frustration, their experiences with child welfare services. As I attempted to listen and understand, without defensiveness, their stories moderated and began to reflect the pain and anguish that seemed to lie just beneath the surface of their anger. Although I was in the role of researcher attempting to enlist their aid in designing and implementing my study, many of the practice principles for effective cross-cultural social work proved important.

Weaver and White (1997) point out that a "deep respect for people is a basic value for even many non-traditional Native people and Native children. In particular, a strong respect for elders is common among Native people" (p. 69). They point out that sharing and giving are highly valued and that even families in poverty will express generosity through "giveaways" that earn respect. This culturally appropriate behavior can create problems if the social work-er does not understand its meaning and importance.

> Resources expected to last over a period of weeks may be gone within a day or two because they have been shared with other relatives. From the point of view of many Native people, it is inconceivable not to share resources with needy family members. However, from the point of view of the social worker, limited resources designated for a nuclear family in need have been squandered on people that may not be deserving and in any event were not part of the case plan (p. 70).

Weaver and White point to the importance of humor, often used to teach norms and val-ues, as well as the Native sense of connection to land and the environment. Time, they point out, is measured "in terms of natural phenomena, not the movements of a clock" (p. 70). Additional strong Native values include privacy, the primacy of the group over the individual, decision by consensus, cooperation, and decentralization of power.

Differences in Native family structure, as compared to the dominant culture's extended and nuclear family models, are illustrated by Weaver and White using the Lakota Indian word for family, *tiospaye,* which includes a variety of people. In the dominant culture, they point out, this grouping would be called an *extended* family, while in most Indian cultures, the word it-self means family. In the dominant society a common question when meeting someone for the first time might be "What do you do?" while among Native people, it might be "Who are your relations?" (p. 72). The importance and influence of tribal elders and grandparents is also emphasized in the Native community.

Weaver and White (1997) offer specific suggestions for practice interventions to provide culturally competent services to Native people:

1. Seek the sanction and support of people in gatekeeping roles....
2. Include Native people in a variety of supportive roles....
3. Maintain a positive, objective approach to each Native American family assess-ment....
4. Advocacy around the issues of tribal sovereignty and treaty rights by the client should not be considered a threat to the service plan for the family....
5. Members of tribes/Nations may be able to get services or funding for services through their Nations. (pp. 77–78)

Canadian Indian

Much of the discussion of the American Indian culture can be applied as well to Canadian In-dian groups. In fact, some of the tribes and Nations extend across the border, with the Indian identity viewed as primary. In my experience with the Canadian Indian community in western Canada I found similar extensions of support starting with the family and including extended family members, neighbors, and the leadership of the band. My own child welfare research findings (Shulman, 1991) indicated that those workers who were perceived by their Native clients as understanding and respecting the Native Canadian culture were more effective in es-tablishing positive working relationships and influencing positive outcomes for the children in-volved. On a macro level, those regional offices of the province-wide child welfare agency who involved and worked cooperatively with the band leadership, Native Canadian friendship workers, homemakers, or court workers, and who involved this Native Canadian social sup-port system in deliberations on how to help the family, had a better record of maintaining children in their own homes, finding kinship placements in the Native Canadian community, or being able to return children to their own families.

Issues in Cross-Racial Practice

Proctor and Davis (1994) address their perception of the reasons for "the sustainment of race as a salient issue for practice" (p. 314) and the roots of the lack of understanding in cross-racial practice. They suggest that the higher rates of growth of populations of color when compared to white populations, the fact that nonwhites continue to be segregated from whites and the mainstream of America, and the negative connotation associated with race issues "leaves both groups uncomfortable discussing race" (p. 315). They continue,

> the combination of these social forces may be quite ominous for personal and professional cross-racial interactions. Although economic problems are likely to increase the numbers of minority group members who need social work services, the white professionals who will be asked to help them may have little prior contact with these groups and hence little substantive knowledge of them. At the same time, minorities are apt to be increasingly distrustful of representatives from "the system." As a worst-case scenario, society may confront increasing numbers of minority clients who must be helped by white practitioners who understand too little about them and for whom their clients have too little trust (p. 315).

The authors state that one of the questions on the mind of a minority client with a majority worker (actually, on the minds of all clients), is whether the helper is a person of "goodwill." This is the equivalent of the "Who is this worker, and what kind of person will she or he be?" question I posed in the previous chapter. Proctor and Davis point out that "Respect and professional courtesy are particularly important with minority clients, to whom society frequently gives less" (p. 317). They suggest that

> Signals of respect and goodwill may be conveyed in several ways. Social workers are advised to extend a warm greeting to the clients, to move physical barriers that inhibit communication out of the client's way, and to address the client by his or her last name. The client should be given an opportunity to get settled before the worker begins to talk. Privacy should be maximized, and the worker should appear unhurried with the client and refer to the shortage of time only in the final minutes of the session.[4]

If you (the reader) are thinking that these are good principles for practice with *all* clients, you are right. It is critical, however, that we understand the differential perceptions based upon race, culture, ethnicity, etc., that the client may bring to an experience. The ease with which majority workers can miss these crucial differences was brought home to me in a striking manner in a workshop I was leading for county child welfare investigators in Florida. An African-American worker was describing his experiences when he had to make an investigation call to an upper-middle-class, white family, living in a gated, almost all-white community. He described his feelings as the guard at the community entrance gate examined closely his identification card and seemed reluctant to admit him to the property. His white colleague, sitting next to him at the workshop, said, "But they want to see my ID as well." I had to point out that I suspected he experienced the examination differently because he was black. He agreed, adding, "I always wear a suit, even on dress-down day, because I know I will need to be wearing one to be treated seriously if I get a call from that community."

Davis and Proctor (1989) offer specific suggestions on managing early treatment interactions in which race is a salient factor.

> First, racial difference and its potential salience should be acknowledged. Acknowledgment, by the worker, of a worker-client dissimilarity will convey to the client the worker's sensitivity and awareness of the potential significance of race to the helping relationship. It will also convey to the client that the worker probably has the ability to handle the client's feelings regarding race. It is probably best to introduce this topic by asking if the client has racial concerns and issues, rather than problems. Obviously the most likely answer to the question, "Do you have problems with my race?" is "No"! Thus we suggest a question such as, "How do you think my being white and your being nonwhite might affect our working together?" Or the practitioner might ask, "If during the course of our meetings you have concerns or issues pertaining to race, please feel free to discuss them." If the client hastens to assure the worker that race is not an issue, the worker can reply, "I don't think it will be a barrier either. But if at any time you feel that I don't understand something you say or mean because our backgrounds are different, I hope you will feel free to tell me. I want to help and I will work hard at understanding you and your situation" (pp. 120–121).

These types of comments, when used in appropriate situations, convey an openness to the client and a sensitivity to the impact of the difference. Variations on this theme can apply to early sessions when the differences involve gender, sexual orientation, age, religion, physical or mental ability, or any factor that may create a barrier if it is not addressed.

Education and Training for Culturally Sensitive Practice

Increased attention to cultural sensitivity is evident in the social work education field and in agency training programs. There are many obstacles to such training, such as the structure and organization of the school (e.g., the absence or under-representation of black faculty and students) (Hardy and Laszloffy, 1992). New strategies for teaching clinical practice with specialized populations are emerging (e.g., working with Asian and Pacific Island Elders) (Richards, Browne, and Broderick, 1994). Proposals have been advanced for using ethnographic research methods to encourage practitioners to become sensitive observers of cultures and to learn how to form assessments within culturally relevant frameworks (Thornton and Garrett, 1995).

For many students and practitioners, a potential source of learning can come from their peers who bring life and practice experiences that can enrich the common learning process. Unfortunately, it is difficult in our society to hold conversations that allow for honest self-reflection on attitudes, values, and stereotypes, in these potentially toxic areas (race, gender, sexual orientation, ethnicity, etc.). It is necessary for a supervisor or a teacher to create an atmosphere in the class or work group that allows for such discourse while maintaining mutual respect and an openness to hear.

An effort to create videotapes for faculty and students that demonstrate this process was sponsored by the Council on Social Work Education (Clay and Shulman, 1993). The key element in setting the stage for a frank and constructive conversation was a preliminary exercise that asked participants to identify factors that made this kind of conversation hard. Participants were also asked about conditions that might make the effort easier. As the discussion on the process of talking about taboo subjects began, the social work students found themselves talking about taboo subjects. It was also important for the two faculty members to self-disclose their own struggles with these issues through the presentation of brief examples.

I will return to issues of inter-ethnic and intra-ethnic practice and culturally sensitive practice in the chapters and examples in the remainder of the book.

EVALUATION OF PRACTICE: PROCESS AND OUTCOMES

Most social workers are not going to engage in formal research studies of their own caseloads. Schools of social work and the Council on Social Work Education recognize this fact and thus focus research methods courses on helping social workers to be critical consumers of research. Agency-wide research on effectiveness of service is becoming more common as managed care, federal and state funding, and other forces are demanding greater accountability and evidence of effectiveness. The use of client satisfaction surveys can also provide any agency or setting with important information.

Yet, ongoing evaluation of one's practice is an important element in social work. The ability to adapt intervention approaches and to work in a flexible and client-responsive manner depends upon some form of feedback on how the process is going. Thought should be given to evaluation in the beginning phase of the engagement when important baseline information may be available.

Two forms of evaluation that can be useful are process evaluation and outcome evaluation. In process evaluation, the social worker measures progress on factors such as developing a good working relationship that serves as a medium for helping clients to achieve the outcomes. In group work practice, the process outcome might involve a mutual-aid support group creating a supportive culture in which to tackle difficult and taboo issues (e.g., a survivors' group dealing with disclosure issues). In another example, assisting family members to stop arguing and to start listening to each other in order to address their problems and develop solutions would be a process outcome. The distinction between process and outcomes is an artificial one, since each of the examples just listed can also be considered an important outcome in its own right.

Outcome evaluation refers to the worker's efforts to assess how well the client is meeting the objectives of the work as defined in the mutually agreed-upon contract, also known as the working agreement. For example, the client may have sought specific help in dealing with her or his family, coping with stress in the work environment, or maintaining abstinence from drugs or alcohol in the early recovery process. Most clients do not come to a social worker to develop a working relationship; they have other life-related concerns and goals in mind.

As already noted, the distinction between process and outcome often blurs. For example, learning to speak to a social worker about a personal problem in one's life is both creating the conditions for effective work on the problems and also providing an opportunity to practice the skills required to speak to others who are important in the client's life. Developing trust in the social worker may be the first step in learning to risk, to be vulnerable, and to develop trust in other relationships. The reader should note the addition of another false dichotomy to the growing list in this book: process *versus* outcome.

All too often social workers, or their agencies or funding sources, fail to recognize positive outcome points along the way. These may represent the most progress a client can make at a particular time. I remember a social worker in a residential setting for female teenage survivors of physical, emotional, or sexual abuse. She described one client to whom she had become close and who had seemed to be making progress. At the end of a year's work, in the spring, the teenager ran away. The worker informed me that this client was running from city to city across the United States. When I asked her how she knew this, the worker replied, "Because she calls me once a week, collect, to let me know she's all right!"

I maintain the staff had not failed with this client, and in fact, had taught the client that there could be adults who could care for her and not just exploit her. The client may not have been ready, at that time, to use all of the help the staff was prepared to provide. When she was ready, if ever, she would be able to build on the base they had provided. Unfortunately, the agency's evaluation model could not account for this point-in-process outcome and could only judge the work with this client as having failed.

Process Evaluation: The Record of Service

This book is filled with examples of a particular process outcome instrument called a Record of Service (Garfield and Irizary, 1971). (A complete description of this device is provided in the teacher's guide that accompanies this text.) Many of the process recording illustrations in this book follow the basic structure of this instrument. After identifying the individual, family, group, community, or other system, and providing basic information (e.g., age, gender, race), the social worker identifies the process problem. For example, one worker's case recording read as follows:

> *Problem:* Every time we get close to talking about painful areas of her life, Jane takes off into a form of flight and changes the subject or denies any serious emotional impact. I often feel she is both asking me to explore these areas and, at exactly the same time, telling me how difficult that would be for her. She seems to be stuck in the beginning phase and is unable to make the transition to the middle phase of work.

The identification of the specific problem (in process terms) is followed by a section in which the worker describes, in brief detail, how the problem came to her or his attention:

> *How the problem came to my attention:* In the first few sessions Jane hinted about issues with her family that were difficult to talk about. In one session she angrily said: "I'm not too happy with my mother's current boyfriend. He gives me the creeps when he is around and I think both of them would just rather see me out of the house." When I asked her if anything specific had happened with the boyfriend, she switched to an example where he had sided with her mother on a discipline issue which had made her angry. When I tried to get at the underlying hurt and rejection she might be feeling, she denied it. When I tried to get back to what made her feel "creepy," she changed the subject.

In the third part of this evaluation instrument, the worker examines and illustrates her interventions designed to effect a change in the state of the problem—in this case, the client's hesitancy about exploring painful emotions and disclosing details of her interaction with her mother's boyfriend. An example of one such intervention follows:

> *Third Session: I tried to indirectly let Jane know that I realized there were some issues that were hard for her to talk about.* Near the end of the session, when I felt frustrated again about her mixed signals, I said, "I have worked with many girls just like you, and one of the things I have noted is that they are often afraid to share how much

hurt they are carrying around inside. Sometimes it is easier to run from the pain or hide from it under a lot of anger. Sometimes people don't feel that anyone else really cares or could understand. Sometimes they are just afraid of opening the flood gates and that they will lose control, maybe even cry. I just want you to know that if you are feeling that way, I am prepared to hear what you have to say and I will try as best I can to understand." Jane just sat in silence, but I could tell she was taking in what I said.

A number of excerpts such as this one helped the worker to examine her interventions and to consider their results. For our purposes here, I will skip these entries and get to the next section of the practice evaluation instrument, where the worker takes stock of the current situation, referring back to the problem identified at the start of the Record of Service.

Where it (the problem) stands now: Since the session when I told her about my other clients, Jane has been more forthcoming in our conversations. In the fourth session, when she told me of another confrontation with her mother and her mother's boyfriend, I reached past the anger for her feelings of rejection. Jane cried for the first time and talked about how upset she was and how she often cried herself to sleep at night, wishing her father were still alive, and desperately wanting her family to be back to the way it once was. While Jane seems more ready to work on her feelings of loss and rejection, she still only hints at what I suspect may be possible abuse or attempted abuse by the boyfriend. We are coming to the last few sessions and I feel I have to be more assertive in reaching for this issue.

In the final segment of this instrument, the worker developed specific strategies for intervening:

Specific next steps:
    1. I'm going to continue to reach for her losses and the associated pain, providing as much support as I can along the way.
    2. I'm going to be more direct and use the same method I used in session three, but this time, I'm going to address the issue of my clients having trouble disclosing issues like sexual abuse.
    3. I'm going to explore with her what would make it hard for her to share this aspect of her life with me, or anyone else, and what, if anything, I could do to make it easier. I'm prepared to discuss her fears of her mother's or the boyfriend's reactions, the legal consequences, etc.
    4. I'm going to make sure she feels in control of the process and that I am not forcing any disclosure.
    5. I'm going to remind her that we only have three sessions left.

In this example, Jane disclosed the following week that the boyfriend had been making sexual overtures towards her whenever her mother was not around. She discussed her concerns about raising the issue with her mother, who she was sure would not believe her. Jane said she was considering running away. The worker offered to help her to face the issue with the boyfriend and the mother and ended up intervening in the family situation.

There are other instruments that can help a worker evaluate ongoing process and interaction with a client. By focusing on a specific problem, the worker can explore his or her own feelings about the issue and shape interventions to attempt to remove the obstacles to effective work.

Outcome Evaluation: The Single-System Research Design

One method of outcome evaluation that has been widely used in social work is called Single-System Research Design (SSRD). Nugent (1989) defined this approach as "systematic, objective procedures for the study of the impact of an independent variable upon a specific individual subject. Thus, they are, in effect, systematic and objective procedures for carrying out case studies" (p. 49). In the simplest form of this approach, the practitioner/researcher might obtain data on a client's behaviors, attitudes, feelings, or other outcome measures at the start of the work (the A measurement). Specific treatment would be employed, during which the same outcome measures would be obtained (the B measurement). If all other extraneous variables could be controlled, then the changes in the B measurement would indicate the efficacy of the intervention. This would be termed a simple A-B single-case design. More complex designs might obtain multiple measurements of the outcome variable before and after treatment (e.g., AAA-BBB) or even A-B-A-B single-case design that turns treatment "on" and "off."

Thyer and Thyer (1992) described the development, dissemination, and adoption of this approach as "controversial" in a bibliography of more than 250 citations of the use of SSRD by social work educators or practitioners (p. 99). In part, the controversy has centered on the apparent (or not apparent, depending upon the author) conflict between a process designed to yield information about the efficacy of practice interventions (a research tool) and the demands of delivering the best clinical services, which might be negatively affected by the research agenda. Describing the debate over whether the efficacy of SSRD as a research tool for developing practice knowledge on a case-by-case basis is negated by practice realities, or if its use as a research tool inherently interferes with good practice, is beyond the scope of this book. My focus is on the use of the method as a clinical tool for the practitioner interested in monitoring the effects of her or his interventions.

Berlin (1983b) took the same position that notwithstanding the debate on SSRD as a research or practice tool, "it is possible to keep the obligations of practice central, systematically assess the extent of change in the client's problem, and become a more sensitive, knowledgeable, credible practitioner in the process" (p. 4).

In a description of a first interview with a client, Berlin's social worker implements most of the ideas outlined in the contracting discussion of this chapter.

> In the first interview, the worker encouraged Cynthia to say more about the bad time she had been having and to tell her story in her own way. The worker then gradually asked questions to identify more clearly the nature of Cynthia's despair and the situations, thoughts, and behavior that seemed to account for it. In the next hour and a half, Cynthia and the worker put together a description of the problem that seemed right to Cynthia, was relatively specific, and by virtue of its credibility and logic, appeared to help her feel more "normal" and less out of control. They reached agreement on the target concerns, started to analyze the components of these concerns, began to speculate about contributing conditions, and set tentative goals—all in the context of trying to understand Cynthia's despair so she could find relief. By the end of the first interview, Cynthia felt somewhat reassured. The worker assigned specific tasks for Cynthia to carry out during the next week and asked her to fill out the Center for Epidemiological Study Depression (CES-D) Scale.[5]

The author acknowledges a number of problems in the validity of this approach as a research design, and also cautions against "bombarding" the client with instruments. As a tool for monitoring client progress, however (the instrument was completed at each session) it provided "objective" information to the social worker on the client's progress. She also acknowledges the need for "flexibility" in design; for example, the model might change to an A-B-C analysis if psychotropic drugs were added at some point to the treatment plan.

As with most reports of SSRD, it is hard to fully assess the nature of the practice since it is summarized rather than reported in verbatim or as a process recording. For example, we do not know if the social worker was using empathic skills in her responses, or the nature of the empathy; however, we might assume so based upon the sensitive description of the problem. Also, there is no mention of the working relationship as a key factor in the process, but again, I would assume it developed out of the clear contracting and the exploration work done by the worker. There could also be debate as to whether the use of the depression inventory in the first session might enhance the practice or inhibit it. The author argues that it was not a major impediment. One could argue it provided the client as well as the worker with a clearer measure of the nature of the problem.

While reasonable people may differ on the relative importance of process or outcome evaluation, the impact that the use of formal date-gathering instruments may have on practice, the nature of the practice itself, the potential conflict between research and clinical goals, etc., most social workers would agree on the importance of developing systematic methods for assessing what we do client-by-client, as well as research that evaluates practice effectiveness with client populations. In this section, we have presented two illustrative approaches to this task. The position taken throughout this book is that we still have a great deal to learn about what works, with which clients, under what circumstances, and so on. Contributions that enhance our understanding should be gratefully accepted, no matter what their source.

CHAPTER SUMMARY

All new relationships, particularly those with people in authority, begin somewhat tentatively. Clients perceive workers as symbols of authority with power to influence their lives. Clients often bring with them a fund of past experiences with professionals or stereotypes of helping professionals passed on by friends or family. Thus, the first sessions are partly efforts to explore the realities of the situation.

A structure is needed to free the client to accept the offer of help. The crucial skills involved in the beginning phase of practice include clarifying the purpose of the interview, clarifying the worker's role, reaching for the client's feedback, and exploring issues of authority. Contracting is never completed in the first session. It is an ongoing process, with the common ground between the client's felt needs and the agency's services evolving and changing over time. With resistant clients and clients who are mandated to be involved, it is important that the worker bring up the obstacles that may block the client's ability to take help. Mutual expectations need to be defined and are part of the contracting process.

Social workers must also take into account the impact on practice of the diversity of our client populations. Models of practice need to be adapted through ethnically sensitive variations introduced by knowledgeable and responsive social workers. Social workers also have a responsibility to evaluate their practice. There are many models available for analyzing the process of practice, as well as its outcomes.

GLOSSARY

Clarifying the worker's purpose and role   Establishing the purpose of the contact, the various services offered by the agency or setting, and the specific ways in which the worker may help.

Common ground   The overlap or commonality between the specific services of the setting and the felt needs of the client.

Contracting process   A worker-initiated effort, usually in the beginning phase of the work, to establish the purpose of the contact, to explain the worker's role, to gain some sense of the client's issues (feedback), and to deal with issues of authority.

Dealing with issues of authority   The worker's efforts to clarify mutual expectations, confidentiality issues, and the authority theme.

Dynamic interaction   A dynamic interaction is one in which the parties involved are affecting each other in a reciprocal manner, with the movements of one party affecting the other, moment by moment, in the interaction.

Handles for work   Concerns and problems, suggested by the worker in an opening or contracting statement, that offer possible areas of connection between the client's needs and the agency's services.

Near problems   Legitimate issues raised by clients early in the relationship to establish trust before raising more difficult and often threatening issues.

Opening statement   The worker's statement, during the first contact, which attempts to identify the purpose of the encounter, the worker's role, and possible areas of connection with the felt needs of the client.

Partializing client's concerns   Helping the client to deal with complex problems by breaking them down into their component parts and addressing the parts one at a time.

Psychosocial history   A term used to describe the client's story, taking into account personal, psychological, and social factors that may have some bearing on the current life situation. Usually obtained during an intake interview or early history.

Reaching for client's feedback   Inviting a client to share his or her concerns related to the purpose of the contact and the agency service. This may be a simple question or a statement of specific illustrative examples of possible concerns (*See* Handles for work).

Supporting clients in taboo areas   Encouraging a client to discuss a sensitive or difficult area or concern (e.g., sex, loss).

NOTES

1. For readings that deal with the beginning phase of work, see N. Polansky and J. Kounin, "Clients' Reactions to Initial Interviews," *Human Relations, 9* (1956): 237–264; A. Malluccio and W. Marlow, "The Case for Contract," *Social Work, 19* (January 1974): 28–36; V. Satir, *Conjoint Family Therapy* (Palo Alto, CA: Science and Behavior Books, Inc., 1967), pp. 91–160; F. Stark, "Barriers to Client-Worker Communications at Intake," *Social Casework, 40* (April 1959): 177–183; A. Pincus and A. Minahan, *Social Work Practice: Model and Method* (Itasca, IL: F.E. Peacock, 1973), pp. 141–161; M. Siporin, *Introduction to Social Work Practice* (New York: Macmillan, 1975), pp. 192–218; L. Frey and M. Meyer, "Exploration and Working Agreement in Two Social Work Methods," in S. Bernstein (ed.),

Exploration in Group Work (Boston: Boston University School of Social Work, 1965; also, Boston: Charles River Books, 1976). (Reprinted by Practitioner's Press, Hebron, CT, 1984).

2. In just such a group, a worker met with the patients each day for months, showing them magazine pictures. Initially, there was little response. Just before Christmas, while looking at a picture of a family around a Christmas tree, one patient began to cry. Another patient next to him began to cry as well. The purpose of this group—to establish contact of any kind between patients—was appropriate to the population.

3. A more recent version of the manual has been published as DSM-IV.

4. Proctor and Davis cite the work of Johnson and Fawcett (1987) and LaFromboise and Dixon (1981) in describing these principles.

5. Lenore Radloff, "The CES-D Scale: A Self-Report Depression Scale for Research in the General Population," *Journal of Applied Psychological Measurement, 1* (1977): 385–401.

LIBRARY MAIL

ADDRESS SERVICE REQUESTED

TO:

GARY LIBRARY - UI & U
VERMONT COLLEGE
36 COLLEGE STREET
MONTPELIER, VT 05602

MAY BE OPENED FOR POSTAL INSPECTION IF NECESSARY

_____ PARCEL POST   _____ EXPRESS COLLECT
_____ PREINSURED   _____ EXPRESS PREPAID
$_____ VALUE

DEMCO

FROM:

4

Skills in the Work Phase

CHAPTER OUTLINE

In the course of a training workshop, one participant expressed her feelings about the work phase in a manner that sums up the experiences of many helping professionals: "I'm good at the beginning phase and I can even deal with the endings, but I'm at a loss when it comes to what happens in the middle." After a session of discussion with social workers about the problems of contracting clearly with children in a group home, one of the participants echoed this sentiment, saying, "I'm afraid that if I make a direct and clear offer to help the kids with their problems, they might take me up on it and I would be in the middle phase. What do I do then?"

This chapter explores the answer to the question, "What do I do then?" It picks up after beginning, tentative clarity about the working contract has been achieved, as discussed in the previous chapter on the beginning phase. To simplify the presentation, the processes of the middle phase are also examined using the phases of work: tuning in, beginning, work, ending, and transitions. In this chapter, these phases are applied to each session.

A simplified, general model of a work phase interview is presented first to give the reader a grasp of the subject matter of the chapter. This is followed by a detailed analysis of each segment of the interview. Specific skills are identified and illustrated using examples from a variety of practice situations. Findings from research projects are discussed where relevant.

A MODEL OF THE WORK PHASE INTERVIEW

In Chapter 1 the idea of the phases of work—preliminary, beginning, middle, and ending/transition—was introduced as a model for understanding the dynamics of practice with clients over time. These four phases are revisited in this chapter, but this time we will use them to understand each individual worker-client encounter. Every interview, family, or group session can be understood as having certain unique dynamics associated with its beginning, middle, and ending. Specific practice skills are useful in each of the phases of a session. Some of these general skills, such as tuning in, have been discussed in previous chapters, but we will now examine them in a more specific context. For example, instead of describing general tuning in to prepare to meet a new client, the skill is called **sessional tuning in,** referring to the preliminary phase preparation undertaken by the worker prior to each encounter.

In earlier chapters, eight of the core skills of helping were combined into two groupings: skills to help clients manage their feelings and skills to help clients manage their problems. Some of these skills are discussed in more detail in this chapter, and additional skills are also examined. The skills of the work phase have been reorganized into general categories called skill factors in order to simplify the description of this phase. A **skill factor** consists of a set of closely related skills. The common element of the behaviors is the general intent of the worker using the skill. For example, in this model all behaviors associated with the efforts of the worker to deal with client affect are grouped together under the title *empathic skills.*

Table 4.1 lists the skill factors included in this work phase model.

Work Phase Summary

In this section we will summarize the work phase model. Each skill factor will then be elaborated and illustrated in the sections that follow.

In the preliminary phase, prior to each session, the worker attempts to sensitize herself or himself to potential themes that may emerge during the work. A review of the previous ses-

---

TABLE 4.1 The Work Phase Model

1. **Preliminary (Sessional)**
   Sessional Tuning-In Skills

2. **Beginning (Sessional)**
   Sessional Contracting Skills
   Elaborating Skills

3. **Middle (Sessional)**
   Empathic Skills
   Sharing Worker's Feelings
   Exploring Taboo Subjects
   Making a Demand for Work
   Pointing Out Obstacles
   Identifying Content and Process Connections
   Sharing Data
   Helping the Client to See Life in New Ways

4. **Endings/Transitions (Sessional)**
   Sessional Ending/Transition Skills

---

sion, information passed on by the client or others, or the identification of subtle patterns emerging in the work may all serve to alert the worker to the client's potential current concerns. The worker also develops some preliminary strategies for responding directly to the indirect cues. This involves the use of the skill described earlier as articulating the client's feelings.

In the beginning phase of each session, the central task of the worker is to find out what the client is concerned about at the moment. **Sessional contracting skills** are used to clarify the immediate work at hand. In some cases, the worker may bring up issues that need to be addressed, and these will then be included in the contracting discussion. Since clients often use indirect communications to indicate their concerns, care has to be taken to determine the client's agenda before moving quickly into the work. **Elaborating skills** are also important in this phase to help the client tell his or her story.

When the sessional contract has been tentatively identified, the process shifts into the middle or work phase of the session. A priority in this phase is the worker's use of **empathy** to help the client share the affective part of the message. The worker must also be ready to **share the worker's feelings** as spontaneously as possible. Since many concerns touch on taboo areas, the worker must be ready to help clients to overcome social norms that often block free discussion and to explore taboo feelings.

As the work progresses, it is not unusual to encounter some **resistance** from the client, who is often of two minds about proceeding. A part of the person is always reaching out for growth and change, but another part is pulling back and holding on to what is comfortable and known. This ambivalence often emerges just as the work in the session starts to go well. It can be seen in evasive reactions (e.g., jumping from one concern to another), defensiveness, expressions of hopelessness, or other forms. A premium is placed on the ability of the worker to "read" and explore this resistance and to make a demand for work that can help the client prepare to take the important next steps. It is important for the worker to realize that resistance is part of the work. It is normal and to be expected, and can be a sign that the work is going well. Workers often assume that client resistance is a sign that they have done something wrong. Ironically, just the opposite is often true. Lack of resistance many mean the worker has not pushed hard enough. Resistance is often a sign that the worker is doing something right.

As the work phase proceeds, obstacles may emerge that will frustrate the client's efforts on his or her own behalf. For example, the flow of feeling between the client and the worker may itself become an obstacle. As the worker makes demands for work, the client may react to the worker, and this reaction in turn will have an effect on the working relationship. Attention has to be paid to this obstacle as well as others that may emerge to block the client's work. Since the worker-client relationship is similar to others the client must deal with, discussion of these feelings can contribute to the client's understanding. These obstacles are usually brought to light when the worker notices patterns in the work.

A new skill grouping was added to this list in the third edition of the book. It is called **identifying content and process connections**. The central idea underlying this category of skills is that the process, or way of interacting between the worker and the client, may often offer clues as to the content of the work. In effect, it is argued that the client may (consciously or not) use the working relationship as a medium for raising and working on issues central to the substantive issues under discussion. For example, a client working on developing independence of thought and action may demonstrate extreme dependence upon the worker. It is as if the client were saying, "Do you want to see what my problem around dependence and independence is all about? Watch me!" The worker skill associated with this idea is that of first identifying these connections and then pointing them out to the client. The assumption is that clients who are aware of the way in which they use process to deal with content may be able to learn from the awareness and take control over their interactions with others. For example, recognition of the meaning of the dependency upon the worker may free a client to become more independent in the helping relationship by taking more responsibility for the work. In turn, this serves as a training medium for the client to practice new skills of independence—skills that can later be transferred to other significant relationships.

The client must also be allowed to have access to the worker's own relevant data. Contrary to some views, which require a form of neutrality on the part of the worker, it will be argued that worker sharing of data such as facts, opinions, and value judgments is an important part of the helping process. Legitimate questions about when **sharing data** is appropriate and how data is shared need to be explored. For example, the worker must take care to share only data that would otherwise be unavailable to the client and is relevant to the client's work. Such data needs to be shared openly and in such a way that the client is left free to accept or reject the worker's views.

A skill grouping described in the third edition as *helping clients see systems people in new ways* has been expanded and renamed, in this fourth edition, to **helping the client to see life in new ways**. It could also be called "reframing" or any of a number of terms based upon the notion that clients' thoughts (cognitions) about their problems, about themselves or other people who are important to them, have contributed to their difficulty. These skills involve helping the client to revisit these cognitions and examine them, with the goal of developing a more accurate picture. For example, a chronically mentally ill client may have a perception of himself as a failure in life. Reviewing events of his life where he has succeeded, even those he had not conceived of as successes, may help him to change his self-image. This, in turn, can have an impact on his feelings and his behaviors, helping him to cope with other areas of his life.

Endings and transitions of sessions have important dynamics and require the worker's attention. In addition, issues that have been raised indirectly throughout the session may emerge with some force when the client is about to leave (the classic "doorknob therapy" phenomenon). Finally, transitions need to be made to next sessions and future actions. **Sessional ending and transition skills** are used by the worker to bring a session to a close and to make the connections between a single session and future work or issues in the life of the client.

In an effort to describe this complex process in simple terms, I have had to oversimplify the central ideas. The work session does not proceed as neatly as we have outlined here. The skill categories are not mutually exclusive. For example, as the sessional contracting proceeds, the worker will use elaborating, empathic, and demand-for-work skills. The advantage of describing this complex process in a oversimplified form is that it gives us a model with which to orient ourselves as we explore each phase and each skill factor in further detail.

SESSIONAL TUNING-IN SKILLS

All the principles of tuning in described in Chapter 2 on the preliminary phase of work are equally applicable to each encounter with the client. This process involves an effort by the worker of self-sensitization to potential concerns and feeling that may emerge during the session. The worker must also tune in to her or his own feelings about the encounter. This is also a time when one can draw upon memories of personal experiences, the literature on human behavior, or input from colleagues and supervisors to deepen understanding of the client's struggle and, especially, of the symbiotic connection between the client and the people and systems that matter. Each of these types of preparatory work is now explored.

Tuning In to the Client's Sense of Urgency

Because of the client's ambivalence or lack of conscious awareness of concerns, client communications are often indirect. For example, a client may begin a conversation by describing "how great the weekend was compared to the week before." The client may continue to describe in positive tones the details of the "great" weekend. In the midst of all of the words is the phrase "compared to the week before." This comment is a signal to the worker of the real work of the session—a red flag meant to attract the worker's attention. The client may be ambivalent about raising the more painful feelings and unsure that the worker really wants to hear them. Thus, the client has opened the session by expressing emotions that are the opposite of what he or she feels underneath. The client waits to see if the worker will notice the **first offering**, the initial hint of a concern, and respond to it in a direct fashion. The worker significantly increases the chances of catching the crucial issue early in the work by being prepared to "hear" it. For example, in this case, the worker might be aware of events in the client's life that have taken place between sessions and may affect the client's sense of urgency.

In another example, a worker was preparing for a conversation with an ongoing client who was being seen because of an HIV (human immunodeficiency virus) positive diagnosis. Such a diagnosis is an early signal of the possible onset of AIDS. The client had called the worker for an appointment and informed the worker that his doctor had now indicated that he had developed ARC (AIDS-related complex), a set of mild symptoms indicating the next step in the progression to a full-scale AIDS diagnosis.[1] The worker in this case attempted to tune in, once again, to the shock, pain, and fear associated with this change in status from a blood test diagnosis of HIV-positive to the emergence of preliminary AIDS symptoms. First, however, the worker needed to tune in to his own feelings about another of his clients becoming progressively sicker and, even with the new drug treatments, possibly facing death. This triggered many feelings about other clients and friends who had already died. The worker found it helpful to share some of his own distress with a colleague prior to the session.

In another illustration, a social worker in a residential institution might be informed by child care staff of an incident in the house that had been difficult for a resident or told that the resident's parent had not shown up for a visit on the weekend. The worker would prepare by tuning in to the sense of rejection and hurt that the client might be feeling. The worker would also anticipate, based upon past experiences in general or observed patterns with this resident in particular, some of the indirect ways in which the feelings might be raised. For example, a pattern of "fight or flight" when faced with pain is not unusual. One resident might demonstrate "flight" from the pain through hyper-activity, or passivity and withdrawal, or the use of drugs or alcohol. Another resident might respond with "fight" by provoking a confrontation with peers, child care workers, or even the social worker.

In one example from a residential setting, a worker was told that a teenager had just heard about the death of his father, necessitating leaving the residence the next day to return home for the funeral. The youngster had appeared to take the news badly but handled it by withdrawing. The worker tuned in to the effect this had on the resident. He did this by getting in touch with his own feelings about the death of a close relative. He thought of the mixed feelings that must exist: on the one hand, wanting to be alone and not to talk about the hurt, and on the other, desperately wanting to share the feelings with another person. He thought about the boy's need to cry, despite the societal injunction that crying is supposedly not "manly." He worked hard to be in touch with his own sense of sadness so that he would be sure not to run from the sadness of this youngster.

He guessed that the cues would be indirect. In this case the youngster was hanging around in the lounge, looking sad but not saying anything. So he prepared to reach for the feelings and make an offer to talk while still respecting the youngster's right to be left alone. Even if the youngster did not take him up immediately, or at all, at least he would know the worker cared. At an appropriate time, he made his offer.

> I heard about your father's death, and I wanted you to know how sorry I am. I think
> I can understand how much it must hurt. If you want to talk with me about it, or just
> spend some time together this evening, I'd be glad to. If you just feel like being alone
> for a while, I'd understand that as well.

In this case, the youngster said he wanted to be left alone. He had heard the message, however, and at bedtime when the worker stopped by to say goodnight, he began to cry. The worker sat for a while, sharing some of the hurt and then listening as the youngster spoke of his father.

When an incident is traumatic, the worker can strategize to reach for it directly in the sessional contracting stage. If a number of less urgent themes are possible, the worker can be alert to their potential emergence. When the session starts, the worker will clear all these potential themes from her or his mind and listen to and watch the client. Tuning in is tentative, and the worker must be open to the possible emergence of feelings, issues, and responses that are completely different from those emerging from the tuning-in process.

In another example, a social worker on a geriatric ward in a psychiatric hospital is aware that a client is going to be interviewed for placement at a long-term-care facility. The worker is aware that this client has had a recent stressful experience at another residence, resulting in his being admitted to the hospital. The worker uses her tuning in to reach for some of his underlying fears as a way of preparing him for this new and frightening transition.

> I met Mr. Peters in the geriatric day room. He was sitting calmly.
>
> **Worker:** Hi, Mr. Peters, do you remember meeting me last week? My name is
> Michaele, and I am a social work intern here at the hospital. Steve asked me
> to speak with you and see if there is anything I can help you with.
>
> **Mr. Peters:** Sure, I remember you. I'm always happy to talk to a pretty girl like you.
>
> **Worker:** So, how are you doing today?
>
> **Mr. Peters:** OK, I guess.
>
> **Worker:** You don't sound convinced. Is something bothering you?
>
> **Mr. Peters:** I don't know. They tell me that somebody is coming to talk to me from
> somewhere.
>
> **Worker:** Steve told me that someone is coming to interview you for a placement at
> a nursing home. Is that what you mean?
>
> **Mr. Peters:** Yeah, if they even come. They probably won't show up. They won't
> want me either.

The worker explores the incident at the previous nursing home in which the client acted out after feeling neglected by staff. She asks Mr. Peters if he wants to leave the hospital and then explores his fears about the transition.

Worker: Do you want to leave the hospital?

Mr. Peters: Yeah, but I don't know where to go next.

Worker: You mentioned to me that somebody was coming to interview you for another nursing home; that might be a possibility.

Mr. Peters: Yeah, but they probably won't come, and I don't know about the place. It's probably not a good place.

Worker: So you seem worried that this nursing home won't be a good place for you and that they may not even come to interview you in the first place.

Mr. Peters: Yeah. I don't think they will want me.

Worker: Are you feeling alone?

Mr. Peters: Yeah—but I am all right.

Worker: Are you worried about where to go next?

Mr. Peters: Yeah. I don't know where it will be.

Worker: That must be really hard, not knowing where you are going to go next and feeling all alone.

Mr. Peters: Yeah. (Long pause. Mr. Peters was very quiet and seemed pensive. Another patient starts yelling in the hall very loudly.)

Mr. Peters: Aw, man—be quiet.

Worker: He's pretty loud.

Mr. Peters: Yeah. He needs to shut up and have some respect for the other people.

As the discussion touched on painful issues, the client used the distraction to change the subject. The worker also switched to a more neutral conversation for the rest of the interview. It would be important for the worker to reflect on her own emotions during the session and to attempt to determine what she was experiencing during the silence that caused her to collaborate with the client on the shift in focus. (In the next section, we will explore in greater detail the issue of tuning in to the worker's own feelings.) Nevertheless, the issue had been opened, and in the next interview the worker continued to explore the client's concerns and fears about a change of residence.

Tuning In to the Worker's Own Feelings

The worker's feelings can be used to facilitate the work or can block a concern from emerging. For example, when thinking about an interview, a worker may believe that she or he has "blown" it by not listening to the client, attempting to impose an agenda, and turning the client off by attempting to preach. The worker can easily tune in to the client's feelings of frustration and anger at finding another professional who thinks he or she has all the answers. The worker may plan to begin again by apologizing, pointing out how the worker had "missed" the client, and inviting the client to discuss his or her reactions.

It would be important in this case for the worker to tune in to his or her own feelings about receiving this negative feedback. For inexperienced workers, reaching for negative feedback is one of the hardest skills to develop. How will it feel if the client accepts the invitation and provides negative feedback? If the worker can get in touch with his or her own feelings of doubt, insecurity about the work, and possible panic if the client were actually to get angry, that worker will have a better chance of avoiding defensiveness. This can then be the start of the development of a new idea about what makes a professional. Instead of believing that a professional is always right and never makes mistakes, the worker can begin to be more comfortable with the notion of a professional as someone who can own up to mistakes. The worker's honesty and non-defensiveness provides a model for the client, who must develop the same ability.

Another illustration might be an interview where the helping person anticipates having to set limits or carry out the part of the helping function that involves control over the client's access to resources. For example, a social worker in an agency working with recent immigrants from eastern European countries may find out a client has lied about available family resources in order to obtain certain benefits from the agency. If it is a client with whom the worker has developed a good relationship, it would not be surprising if the worker were to feel hurt and disappointed by the client's actions. The worker may wonder if the client has "conned" him or her all along, and this possibility can increase the anger.

Client behavior is often an indirect signal to the helping person of an important work issue, of some difficulty in the helping relationship, or a way of testing limits. In this example, the deceptive behavior was related to the client's perceptions of how to deal with authority—views that had been firmly developed while the client was living under an oppressive, eastern European government. Social workers were seen as "agents" of government with significant power to control the client's life. The client was also extremely anxious about protecting whatever family resources he had been able to bring with him from his former country. Once the behavior had been confronted, the social worker could both set limits on the client in terms of the benefits and use the incident as a way of helping the client to develop a new perspective on the role of social agencies and government—an important shift in thinking required for a successful adaptation to the client's new country. I remember a group of workers in an immigrant assistance agency describing, with good humor, their first reactions when they began to work with some Russian immigrants who offered them bribes in the first interviews. They were shocked at first, until they began to understand that this was the only way one received services in the country the clients had just left. Rather than responding with anger or indignance, the social workers could use such incidents to help the immigrants with their transition.

Helping professionals are just as vulnerable as clients and will often refuse to take risks because of their fear of being emotionally taken for a ride. If the social workers in these examples can get in touch with their feelings, then there is a better chance of using the incident as a critical turning point in the relationship, rather than feeling that it signals an end to the work.

The line of argument pursued here is that the worker is a human being, like the client, with a special function and skills to put that function into action. The worker's feelings can have as profound an impact on actions as do the client's. For example, it is not unusual for a child welfare worker who has developed a beginning relationship with a mother to dread the interview following a neighbor's report of neglect of her child. As one worker put it, "I feel like a rat. I have encouraged this woman to open up to me, to share her feelings, and now I may have to take her kid away." This feeling can lead the worker to harden him- or herself, to put up a front, and at a time in the work when the most help is needed, cut him- or herself off from the very feelings needed in being helpful.

Tuning In to the Meaning of the Client's Struggle

As patterns emerge in work with a client, the worker must often step back and attempt to understand the client's struggles in a new way. For example, consider the worker meeting with a father who is attempting to deal with his 17-year-old son's efforts to break away. The battle is a classic one, but the worker must consider what the special meaning of the struggle might be for this father. Understanding the stage of life development which the father may be going through can be helpful in getting at the unique qualities of this particular father-son engagement. The literature on mid-life crisis tells us something of men's (and women's) struggle in their late thirties to work on their own sense of differentiation as individuals in their marriage. The father may be seeing signs of rebellion in his son that mirror some of his own feelings that he is still trying to deal with.

The worker who sensitizes himself or herself to the father's potential conflict will be better able to "hear" this theme if it emerges in discussion. Helping the father face his own crisis may often be the best way to help him understand and deal with his son's experience. The worker's understanding can be gained through life experience, work experience, professional literature, and fiction.[2] In many ways, the work experience is an education about life, and the worker is an eager learner. Each client will teach the worker something new. If the worker is listening and feeling, then every encounter with a client will result in some change in the worker. In fact, if the worker has not been moved, or educated in some way, something is probably wrong with the work.

One particularly important aspect of the tuning-in process in the interactional practice approach is the worker's ability to find the threads of the common ground when the parties are frustrated by obstacles. In developing his practice approach, Schwartz described method as the means by which the worker implements the helping function. He identified five general tasks of the worker that constitute social work method (Schwartz, 1961). The first of these is "the task of searching out the common ground between the client's perception of his own need and the aspect of social demand with which he is faced" (p. 17).

There are a number of ways in which the worker carries out this task, but in the immediate context of this discussion, the connection between the father and the son would need to be explored. I have already pointed out one possible connection: the son's struggle may not be so different from that of the father. Let us explore others. For example, as a young man pursues independence, some part of him will also want to hold on to the security of home, parents, and people who care about him. The connection between the son's need for security as he moves into adulthood and the father's concern about his son's budding independence may be only partial, difficult for the father or the son to perceive, but present nevertheless.

On the other side of the coin is the father's hopes and aspirations for his son's growth into adulthood. What connections exist between these aspirations and the son's effort to find some form of independence? It must be obvious that these connections are subtle and can easily be lost by both parties as they become overwhelmed by the obstacles related to their ambivalent feelings. This is why the worker must tune in to the common ground to be sensitive to it when it emerges. Under the anger and recriminations of both is a fund of feelings for each other that needs to be identified and nurtured. It will not make the son's struggle for independence or the father's struggle to let go an easy one, for both are always difficult. It may, however, allow the parties to hang on to what is important between them.

Tuning In and the Worker's Realities of Time and Stress

Workers often say to me, "It sounds great, but who can take the time?" Having time to prepare for a session is often prevented by the size of the caseload or the speed with which events happen. It is not possible to prepare for each encounter if caseloads are too heavy. It is important to acknowledge the reality faced by many social workers, particularly those in the public services. In developing the Interactional Social Work Practice theory (Shulman, 1991), we included job stress and job manageability as elements of the final model. The findings of the associated research, in a large, public, child welfare agency, indicated that 84 percent of the front-line workers felt that their jobs were stressful ("strongly agree" and "agree" combined). Only 25 percent of the workers felt that their jobs were manageable (p. 140). More recently, restrictions imposed by managed care have added to these stresses.

Given these realities, it is important for workers with heavy caseload stress to tune in whenever possible and to recognize the limits to their ability to provide service for all their clients. Workers will often admit they have time to connect emotionally with some of their clients while they drive home or as they review the work of the week. In addition, many examples can be identified where lack of a few moments of tuning in resulted in the worker missing early cues to a problem (the client's first offering), resulting in escalation of the problem until it became much more difficult to deal with. For example, when cues of stress in a foster home are ignored, the amount of time required when a worker has to transfer a foster child to a new setting can easily become a major contributor to job stress and unmanageability. Thus, workers get caught in a vicious cycle of reacting to crisis rather than providing ongoing preventative services.

It is not unusual to note a pattern in high-stress agencies, which deal with difficult problems and clients (e.g., sexual abuse, terminal illness), for workers and managers to engage in what I have come to term "agency hyperactivity." The demands of their jobs are indeed too heavy and stressful. However, some element of the "busy-ness" appears to be a maladaptive way in which staff run from the pain of their work. They can't tune in because they are too busy, and they are too busy so they can't tune in. Workers who continue to connect affectively with their clients but are lacking in support themselves are often workers who experience **burnout**.[3] Closing off one's feelings is not a solution, since that can also lead to burnout. In one of my studies, I found that the availability of support for the worker from the supervisor and/or colleagues, and the worker's willingness to use this support, were predictive of the worker's ability to tune in to the client (Shulman, 1991).

Tuning In to the Worker's Own Life Experiences

In my view, a worker's capacity for empathy expands with use. This exciting part of the worker's growth comes from the engagement. Within limits, the worker gradually can feel more often, more accurately, and more deeply what the clients are experiencing. Life and work experience contribute to understanding, and this understanding can be drawn upon when needed. Workers may discover their own feelings about many of the issues their clients deal with, some of which may touch on unresolved concerns in their own lives. This is one of the payoffs in the helping professions which, in part, may motivate many to enter the field. As I often point out in training sessions, social workers rarely come into the field because they look forward to the working hours or the financial compensation. The motivation to help others is there, but so is an understanding that we also help ourselves when we help others.

This is one sense in which the work is interactive, with the feelings of the client affecting the feelings of the worker. This idea is easier to understand when one views the professional worker not as someone who has found all of the answers to life's problems and is now prepared to share them with the client but rather as a fellow learner with a special functional role and a number of skills for implementing that function.

Because of the close parallels between the social worker's life experiences and those of the clients, it is important for the worker to guard against a process called **counter-transference**, defined as "A set of conscious or unconscious emotional reactions to a client experienced by the social worker or other professional, usually in a clinical setting" (Barker, 1991, p. 52). For example, young workers still close to the battle for independence in their own families may discover that their own feelings lead them to identify with the child in the struggle with the parent. The worker may start to relate to a parent in the family as if it were his or her own parent.

A supervisor can be very helpful to the worker in the lifelong educational process of discovering oneself through practice. A common danger, however, is that the supervisor may lose her or his sense of function and begin to relate to the social worker as a client rather than as a student or employee. Supervision can turn into an inappropriate form of personal therapy as the conference explores the worker's unresolved issues with his or her own family of origin, rather than focusing on the impact of personal experiences on practice with clients.

SESSIONAL CONTRACTING

In one sub-design of my earlier research project examining social work practice skill (Shulman, 1981), I videotaped and analyzed more than 120 hours of individual and group practice. With clients' permission, interviews were recorded by a videotape camera. The clients knew that these tapes would be analyzed at the university by some unknown researchers; however, during the interview, the client and the worker were alone in the room with the camera.

One videotape illustrated dramatically the issues related to sessional contracting. As the session began, the client touched upon a concern she was feeling about her child in a slightly indirect manner, hinting at it instead of raising it directly. The worker listened to the concern, but it soon became obvious that she had her own agenda for the session as her questions attempted to lead the client to other issues. After a few minutes the client hinted again, making a second offering of her concern, this time a little more strongly and clearly. The worker still did not "hear," since she was preoccupied with her own agenda. The client made a third attempt a few minutes later, which the worker once again missed. At this point, with a look of complete frustration, the client turned to the video camera and said, "Do *you* understand?"

This interview illustrates the problems that occur when the client and the worker are operating on two different agendas. It also raises the larger issue of control over the interview. This, in turn, is directly related to the paradigm or model that guides the helping professional in thinking about his or her work. The sessional contracting skill provides us with a good opportunity to elaborate on this general issue.

In an interactional approach, clients are seen as attempting to work on those issues of importance to them as best they can. Clients will find that their sense of urgency about problems shifts from week to week, depending upon the realities of their lives. A major assumption of Schwartz's practice theory is that clients will only invest in those areas of concern that they feel are important. The worker's task is not to decide what the client *should be* working on. Instead, using sessional contracting skills, the worker attempts to discover what the client actually *is* working on.

I have already discussed some of the difficulties clients experience in communicating their thoughts and feelings directly, especially at the beginning of each session. Clients often raise their concerns ambivalently and express this ambivalence in indirect forms of communication. For example, a client may begin a session describing how great things have been that week, while actually facing a difficult problem. An example from a couples' group illustrates this situation.

> **Worker:** Does anyone have anything they would like raised?
>
> **Fran:** We've had no problems this week; it has been really great. We have been communicating with each other better than ever before. (Silence) We had a problem last week which I used to get really angry about, but I think I was more helpful to Ted this time (looking over to her husband).
>
> **Worker**: Can you tell us a bit about it?
>
> **Fran**: It was a problem that had to do with our sexual relations (looking nervously over at Ted now), but I'm not sure Ted wants to discuss it.

Further discussion revealed that the concern was over Ted's premature ejaculations, a major concern for this couple now being raised for the first time. This client offered her concern for the first time by emphasizing the opposite to the true state of affairs.

In another example, an 18-year-old foster child, who is about to leave the care of the child welfare agency, introduces a discussion of his feelings of rootlessness and terrible loneliness by using a metaphor.

> **Client**: Have you ever thought about space, about space never ending?
>
> **Worker**: Yes, I have. Have you thought about it, and does it bother you?
>
> **Client**: Sometimes I imagine that I'm a little bird and that I'm floating up into never-ending space. A little bit higher and a little bit to the right, and it's "bye, bye world."
>
> **Worker:** You have been floating in space this year, with all of the changes you've made.

The client responded by detailing with great feeling all of the places he had stayed during the year (eight), the deaths of his mother and an uncle, and his feelings of being alone in the world. The discussion continued with a poignant description of what it was like to spend important family holidays, such as Christmas, alone in a movie theater. The worker noted, but did not respond to, the client's hinting of suicidal ideation in the comment "bye, bye world." In her next session, she listened carefully for additional hints of how deep his desperation was and asked him directly if he had considered suicide. He indicated that he had felt "low" enough but that he wanted too much out of life not to keep fighting.

Examples of indirect first offerings of concerns could be endless. A parent who is dreadfully worried about how her child is making out and feeling guilty about her own parenting raised the concern by attacking the worker's competency to help her child. A child in the residential treatment center, who the week before Christmas holidays found out his parents were not taking him home for a visit, **acted out** his feelings through behavior by fighting with other residents and staff. A mother of a young man who had just died from AIDS began her first session with a worker by talking rapidly and non-stop about all of the things she had done that week in order to keep busy, thus demonstrating to the worker her use of flight to run from her pain. The adult child of an elderly patient in a nursing home, still feeling guilty for not taking her mother into her own home, questioned the quality of care provided by the nursing staff. An attractive, female teenage survivor of sexual abuse wore provocative clothing and "came on" to her young male social worker in a residential setting, which turned out to be her way of signaling her need to work on issues of relationships with men and her own sense of self-worth as a woman.

In each case, the clients are working on important issues. Sometimes they are aware of the concern but have difficulty expressing it. Other times the feelings are there, just below the surface, but the clients themselves are unaware of the central theme. Whatever the circumstances, the clients' offerings are present, but they are hard to understand in their early forms. Because of the complexity of communication, a worker often feels that the client is not working and so decides to take over the task of determining the client's agenda. As in the example that opened this chapter, there is little possibility of the worker understanding the client's agenda without actively attempting to determine what it is.

One of the findings of a sub-design of the early research project (Shulman, 1981) concerned the question of sessional contracting. It was drawn from the practice of 11 workers, out of the 118 in the major study, who agreed to have their practice videotaped and analyzed. It would be a mistake to generalize the findings beyond this sample. In my experience as a consultant in a number of settings, however, I have found this pattern persisting.

Each videotape was analyzed by a trained rater who assigned a number representing a category of behavior (e.g., clarifying purpose, encouraging elaboration, dealing with feelings) every three seconds. A numerical record of the session was available for computer analysis. More than 120 hours of individual, family, and group practice were analyzed in this manner.

It was possible to judge whether workers were relating to the client's concerns, as judged by the raters, or working on their own agendas. According to this analysis, workers related to the client's concerns only 60 percent of the time.

We further analyzed separately each third of every session. This roughly approximated the beginning, middle, and ending phases of work. Workers began by relating to client concerns 65 percent of the time but dropped to 58 percent in the middle and ending phases. This finding was interpreted as suggesting a high incidence of unsuccessful sessional contracting in the beginning phase.

In a more recent study (Shulman, 1991), the overall score for all of the workers on the skill called *reaching for feedback* (asking for the client's perception of his or her sense of urgency) was between "seldom" and "fairly often". This skill was ranked sixth out of the eight skills studied. When time was introduced as a factor, we found that the *correlation* (a nondirectional measure of association between two variables) of this skill on the development of the working relationship was stronger when used in the middle phase as compared to the beginning phase. This finding could be interpreted as supporting the continued and increased importance of sessional contracting.

Earlier, I suggested the question of sessional contracting was related to the larger questions of control of the interview and the paradigm of the helping process guiding the worker. I believe that some of these workers operated from a paradigm of helping that gave the worker the central responsibility for determining the agenda. A good worker was seen as one who controlled the interview so as to reach selected goals for the clients. Case conferences with supervisors and colleagues might even develop an agenda for the session, with specific goals to be accomplished by the worker. Unfortunately, the client, not having been involved in the conference, would remain unaware of the plan. Workers operating from this model would find it impossible to hear the clients' indirect efforts to communicate their own sense of urgency.

Clearly, there are times when the worker must bring an agenda to the conference. Agency issues, information to be shared or obtained, and other topics may have to be part of a session. Sessional contracting suggests that the worker can openly and directly raise these issues with the client while simultaneously attempting to determine the client's perception of the sense of urgency. The sessional contract emerges from the convergence of the worker's agenda items and the acuteness of the client's felt needs. Either client or worker may have to set their own issues aside for a moment.

It becomes clear that even as we discuss specific skills, such as sessional contracting, the worker's sense of function needs to be considered. If one believes that the worker's tasks include selecting the agenda for the work, then sessional contracting, as discussed here, is impossible. If one believes that this is the task of the client, however, and one has faith in the client's ability to do this with help from the worker, then all beginnings are tentative. The worker begins each session by listening for the client's concern, and the question of control of the interview is settled. The important point is that this is a joint process since in the last analysis, no matter what the worker's view, the client will "own" the session.

ELABORATING SKILLS

When a client begins to share a particular concern, the first presentations of the problem are usually fragmentary. These initial offerings provide a handle that the worker can use to deepen the work. The elaborating skills are important in this stage, since they help clients tell their own story. The focus of the worker's questions and comments is on helping the client to elaborate and clarify specific concerns. Some examples of elaborating skills explored in this section include containment, moving from the general to the specific, focused listening, questioning, and reaching inside of silences.

Containment

As clients begin to tell their story, it is not at all uncommon for workers to attempt to "help" before the whole story is told. This is especially true for people who are new to helping. The desire to be of help is so strong that they will often rush in with suggestions that are not helpful, since they are not directed at the client's actual concerns. The elaborating skill of containment is an interesting one, since it suggests that *not* acting—that is, a worker's ability to contain himself or herself, is an active skill.

In the following example, we see a new worker in a public welfare setting failing to contain herself in response to a mother whose children have grown up and who is thinking of pursuing a career.

> **Client:** I've been thinking that now that the kids are older, perhaps I can find a job. But you know, finding jobs is difficult these days.
>
> **Worker:** I think that's a great idea. You know we have a job-finding service, and I bet if you speak to one of the workers, he could come up with something for you.

> **Client:** (Hesitantly) That sounds like a good idea.
> **Worker:** Let's set up an appointment. How about next Wednesday at three?

The client agreed to the appointment and then did not show up.

When you explore the worker's feelings in interviews such as this, they often describe what I call the "heart soaring" sensation. They are pleased at the client's interest in doing something about the problem and are feeling like very successful workers indeed. If job referral is one of the ways in which practice is evaluated, the inner response for the worker is to check off one more successful referral for the month. Containment in response to the client's interest in a job, and further exploration of the client's feelings and concerns about return to the work force, would be much more helpful. Picking up the hesitancy in the client's voice as a signal of unexplored issues would be helpful. Even when the client enthusiastically says she will go to the appointment, using the containment skill of **looking for trouble when everything is going your way** would be important. For example:

> **Worker:** You sound excited about the appointment and I'm happy for you. However, you have not been in the workforce for quite a while, and you have not had to deal with an employment interview, either. I wonder if after you leave the office you might have some second thoughts.

By reaching for the concerns, the worker gives the client an opportunity to explore them with the worker, rather than having to face them on her own the night before the interview. However, the worker can always go back and catch a mistake. At the next interview, the disappointed worker asked the client why she missed the appointment. The client said that she forgot, and this time the worker contained herself and did not schedule a new appointment. Instead, she attempted to explore further the client's perception of what was involved in taking a job.

> **Worker:** I was thinking about this business of taking a job, and it struck me that it might not be so easy for you after so many years at home.
> **Client:** That's what I'm worried about; I'm not sure I can handle work again—you know, I've been away so long. I'm even nervous about what to say at a job interview.

Feelings of fear and ambivalence are usually associated with most concerns. Workers who attempt to find simple solutions often discover that if the solutions were indeed that simple, then the client could have found them without the help of the worker.

Moving from the General to the Specific

Clients often raise a general concern that is related to a specific event. The general statement can be seen as a *first offering* by the client to the worker. It may be presented in universal terms because the client experiences it that way at the moment. The general nature of its expression may also reflect the ambivalence the client may feel about dealing with it in depth.

As one example, at the beginning of an interview a mother may state, "It's impossible to raise teenagers these days." The worker who responds to the general theme may soon be engaging in a discussion of changing mores, peer group pressure, drug availability, and so on. An example of **moving from the general to the specific** would be to ask, "Did you have a tough time with Sue this week?" The client's response in this case was to describe a fight she had with her 15-year-old daughter, who had returned home after 2 A.M. and refused to say where she had been. This second offering of the concern is a more specific and manageable piece of work. By this, I mean that the general problem of raising teenagers is pressing in our society, but this client and this worker will not be able to do much about it. However, this mother's relationship with her daughter is open to change.

Behind most early general statements is a specific hurt. If the worker does not encourage elaboration, the concern might emerge at the end of the session as a **"doorknob"** communication (offered as the client is leaving the office). The teenager in the living room of the group home who casually comments during a general discussion that "parents just don't understand" may be reacting to a letter or phone call received that morning. The patient on the ward who mentions to the nurse that "doctors must work hard because they always seem so busy" may still be reacting to terse comments overheard during rounds, which the patient was too frightened or overwhelmed to inquire about. In each case, the skill would involve reaching for more specific information.

Helping professionals have suggested to me two major reasons why they might refrain from reaching for the specifics behind the general comments. First, they have not been aware of how specific work must be. By that I mean that help can be given on the details of the problem. One cannot help a parent with the problems of dealing with teenagers through general discussion alone. The learning will take place through the discussion of the specific interactions between parent and child. The worker can help the parent develop general principles about her relationship with her daughter that emerge from the discussions of the specific events. Without the specific discussion, the worker's attempts to generalize may be perceived by the mother as theoretical advice.

For example, the parent in the earlier encounter might describe a conversation with her daughter in which she did not level about her distress and hurt but instead gave way to the surface feelings of anger. After a while, the worker may be able to help the client see how, in incident after incident, she finds it hard to be open with her daughter about certain feelings. The client may be able to understand this point because of the discussion of specific incidents. The discussion should develop an experiential base upon which the client can build the new understanding and a reframing of her perceptions about the problem and possible solutions. The client may not be able to do much about changing mores in our society, but she can conduct her next conversation with her daughter in a different way. Lack of understanding of the power of specific discussion may lead the worker to overlook the usefulness of this elaboration skill.

The second reason why workers do not reach for the specifics, even when they sense the concrete problem connected to the client's general offering, is that they are not sure they want to deal with it. Hospital social workers, for example, suggest they do not reach for a patient's comment about busy doctors because they are not sure what they can do about it. As one put it, "I find the doctors too busy to answer my questions, so how can I help the patient?" The source of the worker's ambivalence may vary, but feelings of ambivalence are common. My belief is that when workers feel more confident about offering help, they find themselves reaching more easily for the specifics.

I believe there is a third, and less obvious, reason for failure to reach for elaboration. It has to do with the parallel process between workers and supervisors described earlier. It is not uncommon for a worker or student to raise a question with a supervisor, such as, "Do you have any thoughts abut techniques for handling angry clients?" Unless the supervisor inquires,

"Did you have a tough interview?" the remainder of the conversation may stay at a general level. If the modeling is sound, the supervisor will always be moving from the general to the specific, thus teaching by modeling the skill. In turn, the supervisor is aided by having an administrator reach for her or his specific concerns behind the general offerings. My research on supervision of supervisors has indicated that this is rarely done (Shulman, 1994).

Focused Listening

Listening is something we do all the time; however, **focused listening** involves attempting to concentrate on a specific part of the client's message. I discussed earlier how complex even the most simple interchange of communication can be. In complex communications at the beginning of sessions, it is essential that the worker focus on whatever the client is working on at that particular moment. By listening to the early communications with this purpose in mind, the worker has a better chance of hearing the message.

A simple analogy is the difficulty of hearing two simultaneous conversations at a crowded social event. If one listens in a general way, all one hears is a loud buzz. If one then attempts to focus on one particular conversation, it begins to stand out clearly, and the buzzing noise recedes to the background. Similarly, when one is driving at night in a rural area, sometimes two radio stations are heard at once. The driver must tune in one station and tune out the other in order to be able to really "hear." In the same way, the "noise" of the client's early communications may make it difficult for the worker to understand the single strand representing the basic concern. Focused listening, directed to determining the concern, often makes the theme stand out clearly.

A common mistake is for the worker to take over control of the interview when the worker does not immediately understand the meaning of the communication. Focused listening would involve attempting to hear the communication as the client's effort to work, and to search for the connections when they are not apparent. The worker can ask for the client's help. For example, "Could you help make the connection for me of this discussion and the concern you raised abut your daughter at the start of the session?" Clients will often be able to do that immediately, or after some reflection. They do not get the opportunity if the worker has already decided they are simply not working and more worker activity is needed. If there is no real connection, and the client is simply evading work by changing the subject, that in itself is a message that focused listening will clarify. The client is signaling resistance to a topic, and the resistance is what the worker should hear and deal with.

Questioning

Questioning in the elaboration process involves requests for more information as to the nature of the problem. Fledgling high school journalists are encouraged to always make sure to answer the "five w's" early in their articles: the who, what, when, where, and why of the story. These are useful areas for exploring the details of a client's concern. For example, in the earlier illustration of working with the mother and daughter, we left the process at the point where the client responded to the worker's effort to move from the general to the specific by describing a fight with her daughter. Picking up the process at that point, we can see that the worker's questions are designed to elicit more detail about what happened in the encounter.

> **Client:** We had some row last night when Sue came home at 2 A.M.
> **Worker:** What happened?

Client: She had told me she was going to a movie with a friend, but when she
        didn't get home by eleven, I was really worried.
Worker: You were afraid something might have happened to her?
Client: Well, you know we have had some problems in the neighborhood with
        men.
Worker: What did you say to Sue when she came home?
Client: I let her have it good. I told her she was irresponsible and that I was going
        to keep her home for two weeks.
Worker: What did she say back to you?

As the conversation proceeded, the worker helped the client to elaborate on the details
of the interaction. A term to describe this process between worker and client would be "memory work," in which the client reaches back into her memory to recall the incident. In other situations the questioning may be directed at getting a fuller picture of the client's concern. In the
earlier example of the woman considering a return to the work force, the questions would be
designed to elicit the "what" and "why" of the concerns she might have about returning to
work.

Reaching Inside of Silences

Silence during a helping interview may be an important form of communication. The difficulty
with silences is that it is often hard to understand exactly what the client is "saying." In one situation the client may be thinking and reflecting on the implications of the conversation. In another, a discussion may have released powerful emotions in the client that are struggling to
surface. The client may be at the critical point of experiencing suppressed and painful feelings.
Silence can indicate a moment of ambivalence as the client pauses and tries to decide whether
or not to plunge headlong into a difficult area of work. This is not uncommon when the conversation deals with an area generally experienced as taboo in our society. Silence may also
be a signal that the worker's preceding response was "off base" in relation to the client's expressed concern. The worker has "missed" the client, and the silence is the client's polite
way of saying so. The client may be angry at the worker. Frequent silence in an interview may
reflect a systematic attempt to express this anger passively by withholding involvement.

Since silences have a variety of different meanings, the worker's response must vary accordingly. An important aid is the worker's own feelings during the silence. For example, if the
silence does represent the emergence of difficult feelings, the worker may have anticipated this
reaction from the content of the conversation or from the nonverbal communications sent by
the client. Posture, facial expression, bodily tension—all speak loudly to the observing worker and can trigger empathic responses. The worker may experience the same emergence of
feeling as the client. At moments like this, the worker can respond to silence with silence or
with nonverbal expressions of support. All these responses offer some support to the client
while still allowing time to experience the feelings.

If the worker senses that the client is thinking about an important point of the discussion
or considering a related problem, then to respond with silence allows the client room to
think. Silence demonstrates respect for the client's work. However, a problem can be created
if the worker extends the silence over a period of time. Silence can be particularly troublesome
if the worker does not understand it or if it is used to communicate either a negative reaction
or passive resistance. In such cases, the client may experience the silence as a battle of wills.
What started as one form of communication may quickly change to a situation where the

client is saying, "I won't speak unless you speak first." In this battle, both worker and client are always losers. During these kinds of silences the skill of reaching inside the silence is most important.

This skill involves attempts to explore the meaning of the silence. For example, the worker who responds to a silence by saying, "You've grown quiet in the last few moments. What are you thinking about?" is encouraging the client to share the thoughts. In another case, the worker could try to articulate what the silence may be saying. For example, the client who hesitates as he describes a particularly difficult experience might be offered this response: "I can see this is hard for you to talk about." Once again, the worker's own feelings guide her or his attempts to explore or acknowledge the silence. The worker must be open to the fact that the guess may be wrong and must encourage the client to feel free to say so.

It is not unusual for workers to find silences in interviews to be difficult moments. They have been affected by societal norms that create the feeling that a silence in a conversation is embarrassing, and they may feel that the most helpful thing to do is fill the gap. When one works with clients from different cultures, one is struck by the differences in these social norms. For example, American Indian clients describe how hard it is to talk to non-Indian workers because they never keep quiet. As one native worker said to me, "The problem with white workers is that they never stop 'nattering.'" She went on to point out that Indian culture respected silence as a time to reflect, but non-Indian workers would continue to talk because of their own anxiety, without giving the native person a chance to think. In some cases, the Indian client might simply be trying to translate the non-Indian worker's English into the Indian language and then trying to translate back to English.

In my early research project on practice (Shulman, 1978), the skill of reaching inside silences was one of the five skills used least often of the 27 skills studied.[4] But another analysis showed it to be the one of the most significant. The 15 workers (out of a total of 155) with the most positive overall skill scores were compared to those workers with the most negative overall skill scores. The group with the positive skill scores were found to have more positive working relationships and were more helpful than those with the negative scores. The practice skill profiles of these two groups of workers was compared according to their scores on the 27 specific skills. The skill of reaching inside silences was one of the three most important in which the positive skill group of workers differed from the negative skill group (p. 337).

In the more recent study (Shulman, 1991), reaching inside of silences was one of the four skills included in the skills for helping clients to manage their feelings. This grouping was predictive of the development of the client's sense that the worker cared, which was one element of the working relationship. When the skill was examined by itself, we found that workers were perceived by their clients to use it seldom. In fact, out of the eight skills examined, it was the seventh-least-used skill, only slightly ahead of the skill of the worker sharing his or her own feelings (p. 61).

The particular impact of each of the four skills on the development of the working relationship (caring and trust) as well as the client's perception of the worker's helpfulness was also examined (Shulman, 1991). The striking results, replicating the general findings of the 1978 study, indicated that this skill, when used in the beginning phase of practice, showed the highest correlation with the client's perception of the worker's caring (.56) and trust in the worker (.68). It was fifth in importance in terms of helpfulness (.51). The findings of both studies support the notion that the worker needs to actively explore the hidden meaning of silences in interviews.

Another finding from a separate design of the 1978 (Shulman) study yielded additional evidence that this important skill may often be lacking. In this part of the study, the individual interviews and group sessions of eleven volunteer workers were videotaped and then analyzed by trained raters using a system developed by this author. (The results of the group session analysis are reported in Part III of this book.) In an analysis of 32 individual interviews, raters scored the worker's or the client's behavior by entering a number describing the interaction at least every three seconds. A total of 40,248 individual observations were scored and then analyzed by computer. In one analysis, we were able to determine which behaviors of the workers most often followed silences of three seconds or more.

The findings were striking. Of all the entries scored, only 1,742 (4 percent) indicated that a silence of three seconds or more had taken place. Raters found that silences were followed by client comments only 38 percent of the time. A three-second silence was followed by another three-second silence 26 percent of the time. Workers' active comments in response to silences were noted 36 percent of the time. When these were examined more closely, the revealed the following results. When workers actively intervened after a silence, they attempted to encourage elaboration 31 percent of the time. Their efforts to deal with the client's feelings or share their own feelings were noted in only 4 percent of their responses. The most common active action in response to silence was, in the rater's judgment, to direct the client away from the client's presented theme of concern. This occurred 49 percent of the time.

The reader should review Appendix A for a fuller discussion of the research projects. In particular, the limitations of the project should be kept in mind when assessing the data. For example, these findings are based on one small sub-design of the project, which analyzed the practice of only eleven workers in one child welfare agency with a variety of training and experience, each of whom was under the unusual pressure of being videotaped as part of a research project. My attempt to generalize from these findings to other settings or workers is tentative—supported, however, by my observations as a training consultant and the findings of the more recent study (Shulman, 1991).

These findings are shared because they reflect statistically my own observations that workers often seem reluctant to explore silences. In addition to the reasons already advanced, workers have suggested when discussing these findings that they often perceive silences as representing a problem in the interview. If there is silence, then the worker must have done something wrong. The irony in the situation is that silence results more often from a worker doing something right. The worker often sees silence as negative feedback, even in those cases when it may stand for other things. A worker's willingness to reach inside the silence when there is a possible negative response is directly related to feelings of comfort in the work and willingness to deal with negative feedback. This aspect of the process will be discussed more fully under the skill factor called "pointing out obstacles." Understandably, a worker may be unsure about what to do with the feelings and concerns which may live within the silence and may choose to change the subject rather than reach inside the silence. At this point, after the worker has successfully helped the client elaborate concerns, the discussion needs to move to the question of feelings and how to deal with them.

When these findings are shared with workers in training sessions, their reactions may provide some clues as to the apparent low frequency of use of this important skill. Many indicate that their skill training specifically cautioned them *not* to put a client's thoughts or feelings into words. They report having been encouraged to always ask questions but to avoid the possibility of "putting words into the client's mouth" or "doing the clients' work for them." While these are legitimate concerns, these repeated findings suggest that more errors of omission may be made by workers than errors of commission.

EMPATHIC SKILLS

As clients tell their stories, workers use a number of skills designed to keep the discussion meaningful by having clients invest it with feelings. Clients often share difficult experiences while seeming to deny the affect associated with them. For some, the experience may be so painful that they have suppressed the emotion to the point that their own feelings are not clear to themselves. For others, the emotions may seem strange or unacceptable, and they are fearful of discussing them with the worker.

Whatever the reason, the affect is there, and it will exert a powerful force on the client until it can be acknowledged and dealt with. The client's sharing of feelings with the worker can release an important source of energy. The client can also learn how emotions directly affect his or her thoughts and actions, can develop skills in understanding the sensations, accepting them without harsh self-judgment and disclosing them to those who matter. This can be described as the **feeling-thinking-doing connection**. How we feel affects how we think and act, and how we act affects how we think and feel. This interaction between feeling, thinking, and doing leads to the model described in this book, in which a worker's skills for helping clients to manage their feelings takes on such importance in helping clients to manage their problems.

Taft (1933) was one of the early social work theorists to discuss the power of feelings:

> There is no factor of personality which is so expressive of individuality as emotion…The personality is impoverished as feeling is denied, and the penalty for sitting on the lid of angry feelings or feelings of fear is the inevitable blunting of capacity to feel love and desire. For to feel is to live, but to reject feeling through fear is to reject the life process itself (p. 105).

Rogers (1961) stressed the importance of the helping person listening for the affective component of the communication.

> Real communication occurs when the evaluative tendency is avoided, when we listen with understanding…. It means to see the expressed idea and attitude from the other person's point of view, to sense how it feels to him, to achieve his frame of reference in regard to the thing he is talking about (pp. 331–332).

As the worker allows himself or herself to get closer to the client, to experience the client realistically and not necessarily as the client has presented himself or herself, the worker also gives the client permission to be natural. The acceptance and understanding of emotions and the worker's willingness to share them by experiencing them frees a client to drop some defenses and to allow the worker and the client more access to the real person. The worker also serves as a model of an adult with empathic ability. The client can learn to develop powers of empathy to be used in turn with those who need support. It is not uncommon to observe a worker so identified with a child in a family conflict situation that the worker pushes the parent to understand the child's feelings while simultaneously expressing very little understanding of the feelings of the parent. Providing genuine empathy for the parent's dilemma is often the key to helping the parent to understand struggles of the child.

There are a number of reasons why it can be difficult for a worker to express empathy with the client. The capacity to be in touch with the client's feelings is related to the worker's ability to acknowledge his or her own. Before a worker can understand the power of emotion in the life of the client, it is necessary to discover its importance in the worker's own experience. Workers will often have difficulty expressing empathy with the feelings of the client in specific areas that touch upon their own lives. Workers are human, facing all of the stresses and difficulties associated with daily living, including periods of life crises. When a worker hears his or her own difficult feelings being expressed by a client in an interview, the capacity for empathy can be blunted. Another major block to empathy can be the worker's authority over the client. For example, a child welfare worker who has apprehended (removed) a child in an abuse situation may find empathic responses to the client blocked at the time when they may be most needed.

The following example effectively illustrates this difficulty and shows how it can lead to a relationship devoid of feeling—cold, and apparently uncaring. The excerpt is from a recorded interview with a mother who has undergone psychiatric treatment for a time and is separated from her husband. Her nine-year-old adopted and only daughter came into care of the agency one year before this interview because the mother had found her unmanageable. A short time into the interview, there was a pause followed by this comment:

> **Client:** You know, I'm afraid of you.
> **Worker:** Why?
> **Client:** Because you are sitting in judgment of me. You're only human—you might make a mistake.
> **Worker:** I'm only judging how we can help you—help you to improve....
> **Client:** No, you are judging whether or not I can be a mother to Fran—whether I can have my child back. (Silence) I feel at the moment I am not capable of caring for Fran on a full-time basis—I know that....(tape garbled) Don't you understand—I'm grieving—I'm grieving for Fran. Wouldn't you be upset and worried and confused?
> **Worker:** I'm worried about other things as well.

The worker was not in tune with the client's feelings. She regarded the child as her client and did not respond to the mother as a client in her own right. After some further discussion in which the worker indicated that the client was not working hard enough in her contacts with her psychiatrist, the worker asked how long she had been seeing the doctor.

> **Client:** I'm not sure—I don't remember—(with tremendous feeling)—It's absolutely terrible not to be able to remember. It makes me feel incompetent, incapable—(silence)—There are some things in my head I know can't be real—(silence)—but I feel I can be competent and capable of looking after Fran—or I wouldn't want to—because I know she is a problem to look after. But I love her even with her faults.
> **Worker:** When you think of Fran, what do you think of most—her faults?
> **Client:** No! Fran wants to laugh—enjoy people—not to analyze them. She's a baby bird, full of life, receptive, loving people. I may seem aloof, but I'm really just shy.
> **Worker:** You say Fran is sociable, but before, you told me she had no friends.

The worker ignored the client's productions, her self-depreciation, and her expression of feelings of loss and guilt. Her capacity to help this mother was minimal, since she saw her intellectually, not affectively. Smalley (1967) has described this process:

> The self of another cannot be known through intellectual assessment alone. Within a human, compassionate, and caring relationship, selves "open up," dare to become what they may be, so that the self which is known by a worker, a worker at once human, caring, and skillful, is a different self from that diagnosed by one who removes himself in feeling from the relationship in an attempt to be a dispassionate observer and problem solver. As an adolescent girl once said to her new social worker, in referring to a former worker, "She knew all about me, but she didn't know me" (p. 86).

Because of the difficulty of this area of skills, workers must develop over time their ability to empathize. The capacity for empathy appears to grow with experience. The worker who is open to this learning can learn more about life from each client, which will aid in better understanding the next client. One also learns more about one's own feelings and true reactions to the plight of others. Awareness of the sensitive areas in one's own emotional armor will help to avoid denying or intellectualizing difficult emotions when they are presented. The worker will more readily allow a client to share more difficult emotions as the worker becomes comfortable with their effect, particularly with negative affect, both worker's and client's, which is a natural part of any helping relationship.

Supervision can play an important part in a worker's emotional development. The concept of the **parallel process** suggests that the helping relationship between a supervisor and a worker, or field instructor and a student, parallels the relationship between the worker (student) and the client. Thus, a supervisor must model effective empathic skills in the supervisory relationship.

This parallel process can be illustrated if we consider the supervision session between the field instructor and the student involved in the verbatim interview just described with the mother who was fearful of losing her child. If, as they listened to the tape together, the supervisor was simply critical of the student for her lack of affective response to the client, then the student might remain stuck, showing little growth. The supervisor's words might be teaching empathy for the client, but his or her actions with the student would be repeating the student's mistake. In effect, she would be asking the student to "be with" the mother, but at exactly the same moment, the supervisor would not be with the student. In contrast, if the supervisor asked the student, "What were you feeling when she was describing her relationship with her daughter?" the crucial affective work would begin. If the supervisor could genuinely acknowledge the student's struggle to be emotionally with the parent and the child at the same time, a powerful lesson would be taught. The supervisor would be modeling by demonstrating her ability to be with the student social worker *and* the client at exactly the same time.

In my most recent supervision study (Shulman, 1991) a worker's perception of the effectiveness of the supervision was seen to be a powerful predictor of the worker's morale (pp. 153–155). Supervisory skill was also found to contribute to the development of a positive working relationship with staff and to their sense of the supervisor's helpfulness (pp. 192–193). When I share these findings with supervisors, there is usually a short period of silence. When I reach inside of the silence, one supervisor will often say, "But who listens to me?" The appropriateness of that question was suggested by other findings in the 1991 study. The skill of *articulating the supervisee's feelings*, the parallel skill to articulating the client's feelings, was found to be positively associated with relationship and helpfulness on every level of the study (supervisors-workers; managers-supervisors, executives-managers).

The three worker empathic skills described in this section are reaching for feelings, displaying understanding of client's feelings, and putting the client's feelings into words. They will be illustrated by excerpts from practice with a mother whose child is about to be apprehended (taken into care) because of parental abuse. This example provides a contrast to the earlier one and demonstrates how the functions of protection of a child and caring for the parent can be integrated. It will illustrate how a worker can be with the parent and the child at exactly the same time.

Reaching for Feelings

This is the skill of asking the client to share the affective portion of the message. It is important to clarify one point before proceeding. This process can be handled superficially, in a ritualistic manner, thus negating its usefulness. The worker who routinely asks a client, "How do you feel?" while not really being open to experiencing the feeling, may be perceived by the client as not really caring. Experienced clients have been known to say at that moment: "Stop social-working me." Of course, what they are reacting to is the worker's intellectualizing, which is not effective social work. Genuine empathy involves stepping into the client's shoes and summoning an affective response that comes as close as possible to the experience of the other.

With the emergence of technique-centered training programs focusing on developing a patterned response by the worker, the danger of expression of an artificial response is increased. One worker described how she had been taught by one program to reflect back the clients' feelings with the phrase, "I hear you saying…" When she used this technique in one interview, her client looked aghast and replied, "You heard me saying *that!*" The reaching for feelings must be genuine.

In the illustration that follows, a worker talks with a mother about her reactions to one of her five children being taken into the care of the agency after being admitted to the hospital with bruises. In discussions with the hospital social worker, the mother had admitted having beaten the child. The child welfare social worker discussed the placement with the mother.

> **Worker:** We have to be honest with you, Mrs. Green. Did the hospital social worker talk to you about the possibility of your child being placed?
> **Client:** Yes, but not with my mother. Anywhere else but there.
> **Worker:** I guess your mother has enough kids already.
> **Client:** It's not that; it's that we don't get along.
> **Worker:** Can you think of anyone else your son can live with?
> **Client:** I have a friend, Sara, who helped me when my husband died and when I had my baby.
> **Worker:** This must be a hard time. How are you feeling about the possibility of your son being placed?
> **Client:** I can't stand the idea. I don't want the other children with me if John is placed. I have often said this to the kids when I was angry at them—I told them I would place them all, and the kids remember that.

Displaying Understanding of Client's Feelings

The skill of displaying understanding of client's feelings involves indicating through words, gestures, expression, physical posture, or touch (when appropriate)[5] the worker's comprehension of the expressed affect. The worker attempts to understand how the client experiences the feelings even while perhaps believing that the reality of the situation does not warrant the reaction. The worker may believe that the client is being too self-punishing or taking too much responsibility for a particular problem. The worker needs to resist the natural urge to rush in with reassurances and attempts to help the client feel better. The worker may feel the client shouldn't feel so guilty, but the client does feel that way. Efforts at reassurance are often interpreted by the client as the worker's failure to understand. As one client put it, "If you really understood how badly I felt, you wouldn't be trying to cheer me up."

We return to the interview with the mother at the point, where she commented that "I told them [the children] I would place them all, and the kids remember that."

> **Worker:** We often say things when we are hurt or angry that we regret later.
> **Client:** I told the hospital social worker that if John was placed, all of the kids might have to be placed. I feel very strongly about this. It will hurt me to lose my kids, but I can't bear to think about getting up in the morning and only counting four heads instead of five.
> **Worker:** You mean that together you are a family and if one is missing, you're not? (She nodded when I said this and began to cry softly.)

The worker's gentle restatement of the client's feelings has communicated to the client the worker's understanding and compassion. The emotions are expressed through the tears. This is an important form of communication between worker and client. Part of the healing process includes the client's sharing of feelings with a caring person. Workers often express their fear of strong emotions. They are concerned that a client might become too depressed and that the worker's effort to bring the emotions to the fore could result in more problems. Some workers worry they will be overwhelmed by the client's feelings and feel equally depressed and hopeless, thereby losing their ability to be effective. For many workers the ultimate fear is that they might trigger such deep expression of emotion that the client might be overwhelmed and turn to a drastic act such as suicide.

The assumption here is that it is not the emotions themselves that create the problems, but rather clients' inability to be in touch with their feelings or to share them with someone important. The power that feelings can have over clients may be dissipated when these feelings are expressed and dealt with. The greater danger is not in the facing of feelings but in their denial. The only thing worse than living with strong emotions is the feeling that one is alone and that no one can understand.

As for the worker's fear of being overwhelmed by the emotions, this can be alleviated somewhat if the worker is clear about the function and purpose of the engagement. The worker's sense of function requires placing a demand for work on the client. This important skill is dealt with in some detail in the next section, but it must be noted at this point in the discussion. No matter how strong the client's feelings of hopelessness are, there is always some next step that can be taken. The worker needs to experience the client's feelings of being overwhelmed (the empathy) while still indicating a clear expectation (the demand) that the client will do something about the situation, even in those cases where doing something means coming to grips with the reality (e.g., the death of someone close) and picking up and beginning again (e.g., searching out new significant relationships). The worker can make this demand because of a belief in the client's strength and resilience.

With clarity of purpose in mind, the worker can help the client find the connections between the emotions and the purpose of the discussion. This topic is also explored in the next section under the skill of connecting feelings to purpose. The central point is that significant work with clients in painful areas can only be done after the expression and acknowledgment of feelings. The flow of affect and understanding between worker and client is a necessary precondition for the movement to follow. Workers who attempt to make demands upon clients without first having experienced the affect with them will be perceived as "not understanding," and their demands will be experienced by the client as harsh and uncaring. Empathic responses can be seen as building a fund of positive relationship that the worker can draw upon later. This fund is a buffer that helps the client to experience a worker's later confrontation as coming from caring.

Putting the Client's Feelings into Words

Thus far, I have described how a worker might reach for feelings and acknowledge those which have already been stated. There are times, however, when a client comes close to expression of an emotion but stops just short. The client might not fully understand the feeling and thus be unable to articulate it. In other cases, the client might not be sure it is all right to have such a feeling or to share it with the worker. The use of this skill involves the worker articulating the client's affect (in the words of Schwartz) "just one half-step ahead of the client." This occurs when the worker's tuning in and intense efforts to empathize during the session result in emotional associations as the client elaborates a concern.

Returning to the previous example to illustrate this point, the worker had said, "You mean that together you are a family and if one is missing, you're not?" and the client had responded by crying softly. The worker gave the client a tissue and waited a few minutes. The client was just sitting and looking at the floor.

> **Worker:** You must be feeling like a terrible mother right now. (The client nodded.) It must be really rough with all of the problems with the house, everything breaking down on you, having these hassles every day, and five kids also must make it pretty rough some times.

The client had not said anything about her parenting or about feelings of guilt, but by articulating this emotion, the worker gives permission to the client to discuss her own feelings about herself. Often, as in the first illustration in this section, the worker is so busy trying to communicate, indirectly, disapproval of the client's actions that she cannot hear the client's own harsh judgment of herself. The assumption here is that how we feel about ourselves has a great deal of influence upon how we think about ourselves and how we act. The way to begin to help this mother is to break a vicious cycle where her own guilt leads to feelings of helplessness and hopelessness and a negative self-image, which in turn leads to poor parenting, which in turn…and so on. The ability to articulate and face her feelings, sharing them with a caring and yet demanding worker, can be a beginning. The worker's acceptance of the client, including her feelings, can be the starting point for the client's acceptance of herself.

Research Findings on Empathy

The empathic skills have consistently been identified as important in helping relationships. Working in the field of psychotherapy, Truax (1966) found a relationship between therapist empathy, warmth, and genuineness, and personality change. Rogers (1969) has pointed to a number of studies in which empathy was found to be central to the worker's effectiveness. In the field of educational research, Flanders (1970) found empathy to be an important skill for teachers in improving student performance. A growing body of evidence suggests this is one of the core skills that applies to all helping functions.

The results of my own research studies supported these findings. The skill of acknowledging the client's feelings appeared to contribute substantially to the development of a good working relationship between worker and client as well as contributing to the worker's ability to be helpful (Shulman, 1978). It was the second most powerful skill, ranking only behind the skill of sharing worker's feelings, which is discussed in a later section. This finding was replicated in both the study of supervision skill (Shulman, Robinson and Luckyj, 1981; Shulman, 1984) and the study of the practice of family physicians (Shulman and Buchan, 1982).

Data drawn from the observers' scores after rating 62 videotaped segments of practice in the 1978 study (Shulman, 1981) indicated less concern with affect on the part of workers than the overall study suggested. Workers appeared to share their own feelings or to deal with client feelings in only 2.3 percent of their interventions in the individual sessions and in 5.3 percent of their interventions in the group sessions. When total interactions in the session were analyzed, including the times when the client was speaking and the worker listening, the total interventions dealing with the affect in the group sessions dropped to 1.4 percent. This figure is very close to Flanders' results when he analyzed teaching behaviors (1970).

In my more recent study of practice skill (1991), when examining the skill profile of the average worker, I found that clients perceived their workers as acknowledging their feelings "fairly often" and articulating their feelings without their having to share them between "seldom" and "fairly often." When the correlation between this skill and the development of the caring dimension of the working relationship was examined, it was the second strongest associating skill when used in the beginning phase of practice (.54) and the strongest associating when used in the middle phase (.77). Similar patterns were found in relation to trust and worker helpfulness.

SHARING WORKER'S FEELINGS

An essential skill is related to the worker's ability to present himself or herself to the client as a real human being. Some theories of the helping process which have borrowed their model from the medical paradigm have presented the ideal worker as an objective, clinical, detached, and knowledgeable professional. Direct expression of the worker's real feelings (e.g., anger, fear, love, and ambivalence) has been described as "unprofessional." This has resulted in a concept of professionalism that asks the worker to choose between the personal and the professional self.

One worker, in an example described earlier, illustrated the effect of this attempt to dichotomize the personal and the professional during a training workshop. She described her experience as a student working with a woman who had just discovered her child was dying of cancer. As the woman spoke, she was overcome with grief and began to cry. The worker experienced her own feelings of compassion and found herself holding the woman's hand and crying with her. A supervisor, passing by the open door, criticized the worker for her "unprofessional" behavior.

My view is that the worker was helping at that moment in one of the most important and meaningful ways we know. She was sharing the pain with the client, and in expressing her own sorrow she was making a gift to the client of her feelings. This worker was responding in a deeply personal way, yet at the same time was carrying out her helping function. Schwartz's practice theory suggests that the helping person is an effective helper only when able to synthesize real feelings with professional function. Without such a synthesis of "personal" and "professional," the result is a loss of spontaneity, with the worker appearing as a guarded professional, unwilling to allow clients access to the worker's feelings. The irony is apparent, for the professional asks the client to be open, honest, risking, and vulnerable in sharing feelings, while in the name of professionalism is doing just the opposite. The result is often the "mechanical" worker who appears to be always under self-control, who has everything worked out, and who is never at a loss for words or flustered—in short, an impossible person to relate to in any real way.

The client does not need a perfect, unruffled worker who has worked out all of life's problems but instead a real human being, like the client, who cares deeply about the client's success at work, expresses the client's own sense of urgency, and openly acknowledges feelings. When the client experiences the worker as a real person, the worker and the helping function can be utilized more effectively. If the worker is presented without signs of any humanity, the client will either be constantly testing to find the flaws in the facade or idealizing the worker as the answer to all problems. The client who does not know, at all times, where the worker stands will have trouble trusting that worker. If the worker is angry at the client, then it is much better for the client to have the anger out in the open where it can be dealt with honestly. Workers who fear the expression of angry feelings as signs of their "aggressiveness" often suppress them, only to have them emerge indirectly in ways to which the client finds it harder to respond. Professional expressions of anger, for example, through an unfeeling interpretation of a client's behavior, can be more hurtful than an honest statement of the feeling.

Direct expression of feelings is as important for the worker's sake as it is for the client's. A worker who suppresses feelings must use energy to do so. This energy can be an important source of help to the client if it can be freed for empathic responses. The worker cannot both withhold feelings and experience those of the client at the same time. The worker may also become cut off from important forms of indirect communication in which the client uses the worker's feelings to express his or her own. Consider the following example of this process. A worker in a residential center for children was confronted by an angry parent after an incident on an excursion in which the child was left on a bus during a field trip and lost for a period of time. This child had been apprehended by the agency because of numerous complaints of neglect and abuse. During a visit to the center, the client began a loud, angry tirade directed at the worker.

> **Client:** What kind of a place do you run here anyway? He's only been here three
> weeks, and already he's sick, had a bump on his head, and you jerks lost
> him on a bus.
>
> **Worker:** (Obviously upset but trying to control himself) Look, Mr. Frank, we do the
> best we can. You know with 15 kids on the bus, we just lost track.
>
> **Client:** Lost track! For God's sake (his voice getting louder), you mothers are paid
> to keep track, not lose track of my kid. Do you realize what could have hap-
> pened to him on that bus alone? (The client screams the last question. The

worker is feeling embarrassed, overwhelmed, backed against the wall, conscious of the other workers and the kids watching, and angry at the client.)

Worker: (With great control in his voice) You know, we simply can't tolerate this behavior in the house. You're upsetting all of the children, and if you don't calm down, I'm going to have to stop your visiting.

The truth of the matter is that the client was upsetting the worker, who did not know what to do about it. His anger was expressed in a controlled fashion, turning it into an attempt to exert his authority on the client. He tried to tame the client by using his ability to influence access to the child. The calmer and more controlled the worker seemed, the angrier the client became. With his own feelings racing away in all directions, the worker's efforts to put up a calm front actually cut him off from a professional response. He has no way of understanding, at this point, that parents who have had children apprehended also often feel guilty, embarrassed, overwhelmed, backed against the wall, and very conscious of the reactions of their children. The client was unconsciously using the incident to make the worker feel exactly how he himself has felt for the past three weeks. In this sense, the client's feelings were projected onto the worker and the attack was also a form of indirect communication. Unfortunately, the worker expended his energy on defending himself and suppressing his anger. He was not able to work with this client in a meaningful way as long as he blocked expression of his own feelings. The client needed to keep pushing him until he got some reaction. Returning to the interview, we see that the worker's attempt to "read the riot act" to the client resulted in an escalation on the client's part.

Client: You can't stop me from seeing my kid. I'm going to call my lawyer and bring charges against you and the agency for incompetency.

Worker: (Finally losing his temper) Well, go ahead and call. I'm tired of hearing you complaining all the time. Do you think it's easy to deal with your kid? Frankly, I'm tired of your telling me what a lousy worker I am.

Client: (With equal intensity) Well, how the hell do you think I feel? (Silence)

Worker: (A deep sigh as the worker seems to be catching his breath) I guess as frustrated, angry, and guilty as I do. You've been feeling this way ever since they took Jim away from you, haven't you?

Client: (Subdued, but still angry) It's no picnic having your kid taken out of your house and then being told you're an unfit parent.

Worker: Look, we can start all over. I felt angry, guilty, and very defensive when you put me on the spot, and that's why I threatened you about the visiting business. I guess I just didn't know how else to handle you. You know, we really need to get along better in spite of your being angry at the agency, for your sake, for mine, and especially for Jimmy's. How about it? (Silence)

Client: I guess I was a little rough on you, but you know, I worry about the kid a lot and when he's not with me, I feel…(Struggling for the right word)

Worker: …powerless to help him, isn't that it?

The worker's expression of his own feeling freed his energy to respond to the client's question, "Well, how the hell do you think I feel?" The results of this important step were threefold. First, the worker began to strengthen the working relationship between himself and the child's parent. This parent cared, and his anger and assertiveness could make him an excellent client to work with. Second, it allowed the worker to begin to respond empathically to the client, a crucial skill in the helping process. Finally, it demonstrated an openness on the part of the worker to admitting feelings and mistakes. The client perceived an adult, a helping professional, who understood the connection between his own feelings and his actions. It is precisely this kind of openness to self-examination that the father will need to develop if the family relationship is to be strengthened.

In the two illustrations thus far, we have seen how the worker's feelings of caring and anger, when expressed openly, can be helpful to clients. This honest and spontaneous expression of feelings extends to a broad range of worker affective responses. Another example is the feeling of investment a worker can have in a client's progress. For some reason, the idea of "self-determination" has been interpreted to mean that the helping person cannot share a stake in the client's progress and growth. Workers sometimes watch a client struggle towards change and at the points in the process when clients feel most hopeless and ready to quit, workers suppress their own feelings of disappointment. This is a misguided attempt not to influence unduly the client's choices.

The following example illustrates the importance of direct expression of a worker's feelings of hope and expectation. The illustration is of a professional working with a paraplegic young adult in a rehabilitation center. A relationship has developed over months as the worker has helped the patient deal with his feelings about this sudden change in his life. The exercise program to help the patient develop some limited functioning in his limbs has gone slowly and painfully, and with no signs of a quick recovery. The patient is disappointed by the pace of his progress and becomes depressed and apathetic, refusing to continue. It is at this point the following example begins. The reader should keep in mind that this excerpt follows months of development of the working relationship. The professional has a fund of positive feelings to draw upon as she makes this **facilitative confrontation**. It is a confrontation designed to facilitate the work of the patient.

> **Patient:** It's no use continuing—I quit!
>
> **Worker:** Look, I know it's been terribly frustrating and damn painful—and that you don't feel you're getting anywhere—but I think you are improving and you have to keep it up.
>
> **Patient:** (With anger) What the hell do you know about it? It's easy for you to say, but I have to do it. I'm not going to get anywhere, so that's that.
>
> **Worker:** (With rising emotion) It's not the same for me. I'm not sitting in that wheelchair, but you know, working with you for the past three months has not been a picnic. Half the time you're feeling sorry for yourself and just not willing to work. I've invested a lot of time, energy, and caring in my work with you because I thought you could do it—and I'm not about to see you quit on me. It would hurt me like hell to see you quit because the going gets rough.

The patient did not respond immediately to the "demand for work" expressed in the worker's affective response. However, the next day, after some time for the feelings to work through, he appeared for physiotherapy without a word about the previous conversation. Once again, we see how a worker's statement of feeling can integrate a highly personal and at the same time, highly professional response. The worker's feelings are the most important tool in the professional kit, and any efforts to blunt them results in a working relationship that lacks real substance.

Another way in which sharing the worker's feelings can be helpful in a relationship is when the affect is directly related to the content of the work, as when the worker has had a life experience that is similar to, or the same as, that of the client. Self-disclosure of personal experiences and feelings, when handled in pursuit of purpose and when integrated with the professional function, can promote client growth.

In one dramatic example, a student social worker was describing in my practice class her work with a group of young men in a residential setting who were described as mildly mentally challenged. All of these clients had recently experienced a loss of a significant family member. They had been brought together to discuss their losses because they had been exhibiting ongoing depression and denial. The group was to help them face their feelings and to accept, or at least learn to live with, their sadness. Two weeks into the group, the student's father died and she had to return home to take care of her own grieving. The clients were aware of her loss.

When she returned, she picked up with the group but did not mention the reason she had been away, even though she knew the members had been informed while she was away. One of the members said to her, "Jane, your father died, didn't he?" The worker later described feeling overwhelmed by his comment and struggling to maintain her "professional composure." She reported that the group members must have sensed her emotions, because another member said, "It's OK to cry, Jane, God loves you too!" In response to his comment she began to cry and was joined by most of the group members. After a few moments, she commented to the members that she had been encouraging them to share their pain over their losses, and then she had been trying to hide her own. The group members began their first serious and emotion-filled discussion of their own losses and why they tried to hide their feelings, even from themselves. As the student described the incident in class, she cried again and was joined by many other students and this instructor as well.

Even as I write about this incident, I can remember the many objections raised by workers when I have advanced the argument in favor of sharing the worker's feelings. Let us take some time to examine these.

Issues in Sharing Worker's Feelings

The first concern relates to the boundaries within which personal feelings can be shared. I believe that if a worker is clear about the purpose of the work with the client (the contract) and the particular professional function, then these will offer important direction and protection. For example, if a client begins an interview by describing a problem with his mother-in-law, the worker would not respond by saying, "You think you have problems with your mother-in-law? Let me tell you about mine!" The client and worker have not come together to discuss the worker's problems, and an attempt by the worker to introduce personal concerns, even those related to the contract area, is an outright subversion of the contract. If the worker, Jane, in the previous example, had started to discuss the death of her father and her own loss, rather than using the moment to return to the clients' issues and to deepen their work on their losses, she would not have been synthesizing personal and professional, she would have simply been unprofessional.

The client seeks help from the worker, and the worker's feelings about personal relationships can be shared only in ways that relate directly to the client's immediate concerns. For example, take a situation where a worker feels the client is misinterpreting someone's response because of the client's feelings. The worker who has experienced that kind of miscommunication might briefly describe the experience as a way of providing the client with a new way of understanding an important interaction.

A second area of major concern for workers is that in sharing their feelings spontaneously—that is, without first monitoring all their reactions to see if they are "correct"—they risk making inappropriate responses. They are worried that they will make a mistake, act out their own concerns, and perhaps hurt a client irretrievably. There is some basis for this fear because we do, at times, respond to clients out of our own needs. A young worker may get angry at an adolescent client's mother because the mother seems as overprotective as the young worker's own. Another worker experiences great frustration with a client who does not respond immediately to an offer of help but moves slowly through the process of change. Although the client makes progress at a reasonable pace, it still makes the worker feel ineffective. Another worker misses a number of indirect cues from a shelter resident about a serious problem with his family, whom he is about to visit over the Christmas vacation. The worker then responds to the resident's acting out of the feelings by imposing angry punishment instead of hearing the hidden message.

Spontaneous expression of feeling will lead to all these mistakes and others. In fact, a helping professional's entire working experience will inevitably consist of making such mistakes, catching them as soon as possible, and then rectifying them. A good worker will learn from these experiences something about his or her personal feelings and reactions to people and situations. As this learning deepens, these early "mistakes" will become less frequent. The worker now becomes conscious of new, more sophisticated "mistakes."

When teachers, supervisors, theorists, and colleagues convey the idea that one tries during interviews to monitor continuously one's feelings, to think clearly before acting, and to conduct the perfect interview, they are setting up blocks to the worker's growth. Only through continuous analysis of some portion of one's work *after* the interview has taken place can workers develop the ability to learn from their mistakes. The more skilled workers, who are spontaneous, can catch their mistakes during the interviews—not by withdrawing and thinking, but by using their own feelings and by reaching for the cues in the client's responses.

What is often overlooked is that clients can forgive a mistake more easily than they can deal with the image of a perfect worker. They are truly relieved by a worker owning up to having "blown" an interview, not having understood what the client was saying or feeling, or overreacting and being angry with a client. An admission of a mistake serves the simultaneous functions of humanizing the worker and indirectly giving the client permission to do the same. Workers who feel clients will lose respect for their "expertise" if they reveal human flaws simply misunderstand the nature of helping. Workers are not "experts" with the "solutions" for clients' problems, as suggested by the medical paradigm. Instead, workers possess skills that can help clients work on developing their own solutions to their problems. One of the most important of these skills is the ability to be personally and professionally honest.

Finally, there are some worker feelings that are experienced as potentially too harmful to be expressed. I can understand and agree with this view while feeling that these types of feelings are very few in number. For example, there are many feelings of warmth and caring that may flow between a worker and a client. These positive feelings constitute a key dynamic that helps to power the helping process. Under certain circumstances, feelings of intimacy may be associated with strong sexual attractions. When the ages and circumstances are right, these mutual attractions are understandable and normal. However, it could be very difficult for a client to handle a worker who honestly shared the sexual attraction. This would be one example of a feeling a worker would not want to share with a client.

Because of the authority of the worker, and the process of transference described earlier, sharing feelings of sexual attraction—and even worse, acting on them—constitutes a form of unethical sexual exploitation. Clients are vulnerable in the helping relationship and need to be protected. It is especially tragic and harmful when clients who are seeking help to heal their wounds from exploitive relationships find themselves in yet another one. It is important to underline that the problem is not that the worker experiences sexual attraction toward a client. This can be understandable, and the worker should be able to discuss these emotions with a supervisor and/or colleagues. The unethical part is acting on feelings with the client.

Workers sometimes feel in a bind if clients begin to act seductively towards them and even directly request some response from the worker. For example, a young and attractive female worker described her reactions to the "come-on" of the paraplegic male client in a rehabilitation setting as "stimulating." She felt somewhat ashamed of her feelings, since she thought they revealed a lack of "professionalism." Most workers in the consultation group where this illustration was presented reported that they, too, had experienced these feelings at times. They had not discussed them with colleagues, supervisors, or teachers because they felt a professional "taboo" against doing so.

When the discussion returned to the interaction in the interview with the paraplegic, I asked them to tune in to the meaning of the sexual "come-on" in the context of the contract. Speculation began as to the fear of the young client in this situation as to his sexual attractiveness as, in his words, a "cripple." With a new handle for approaching the issue, it was clear to the worker that the client's feelings and fears about his sexual attractiveness might be a central issue for work which the worker would miss if overwhelmed by her own feelings. This is an example of the way in which the process of an interview can be connected to the content of the work. This issue is explored in more detail later in this chapter in the section dealing with identifying content and process connections. It is an illustration of how the worker may use the process (interaction with the client) as a tool for exploring the content (the substantive content of the working contract). In this example, the worker confronted the client directly about his comments to her, clarified her professional and ethical responsibilities, and then reached directly for his issues with regard to relationships to the opposite sex. The work proceeded to explore this painful, yet crucial area of content.

Research on Sharing Feelings

Research on worker sharing of feelings has been undertaken in a number of helping professions. The findings have indicated that this skill plays as important a part in the helping process as the empathic skills described earlier. The skill has been described as "self-disclosure" or "genuineness," among other labels. The findings on this skill in my own research were among the strongest in the 1978 study. The worker's ability to "share personal thoughts and feelings" ranked first as a powerful correlate to developing working relationships and to being helpful. Further analysis of the research data suggested that the use of this skill contributed equally to the work of developing the working relationship and the ability of the worker to be helpful.

The importance of this skill was replicated in the more recent practice study (Shulman, 1991). It was one of the four skills in the grouping called "skills to help clients manage their feelings." These skills had a strong impact on the development of the caring element of the working relationship, and through caring a strong impact on the client's perception of the worker's helpfulness, as well as low but significant influences on hard outcome measures (final court status of the children and days spent in care).

When examined by itself, the skill was found to have significant correlation with caring, trust, and helpfulness when used in beginning and middle phases of practice, but it was usually at the low end of the list of eight skills. The difference in the importance of this skill in this study, as compared to the 1978 study, may be related to a change in study design.

What inferences can we take from these findings? It may be that the worker in sharing personal thoughts and feelings breaks down the barriers that clients experience when they are faced with the feelings of dependency evoked by taking help. As the worker becomes more "multidimensional," more than just a professional helping person, there is more "person" available for a client to relate to. In addition, thoughts and feelings of a personal nature appear to provide substantive data for the client's tasks and therefore contribute to the helpfulness factor. Perhaps it is the personal nature of the data that makes it appear more relevant to the client, easier to use and to incorporate into a sense of reality. This skill, like many others, may simultaneously serve two functions. A worker shares feelings freely and at the same time effectively strengthens the working relationship (the process) while contributing important ideas for the client's work (the contract).

When the skill use profiles of the average worker in the 1978 and 1991 studies were examined, I found that clients perceived their workers as seldom sharing their personal thoughts and feelings. These findings were shared with workers in a number of training groups following the completion of each of the studies. They always provoked some of the most important discussions, exploring the reasons why they found it difficult to reveal themselves to clients. The first response was to cite a supervisor, a book, or a former teacher who had made it clear that sharing feelings was unprofessional. As one worker put it, "I was told I had to be a stone-faced social worker."

After a discussion of these injunctions and their impact on the workers, I would offer to lift them as barriers to the free sharing of feelings. I would say, "Based upon my research, my practice experience, my expertise, I am now telling you that it is no longer 'unprofessional' to be honest with clients and to make your feelings part of your work." I would then inquire how this new freedom would affect their work the next day. After a long silence, a typical response from a worker would be, "You have just made things a lot tougher. Now I'm going to have to face the fact that it's my own feelings which make it hard for me to be honest. I'm not really sure how much of myself I want to share." At this point in the workshop discussion, the work deepened.

Developing the ability to be honest in sharing feelings is difficult, but it is possible; we ask clients to do it all the time. Its importance can be underlined by a client's written comment in response to our research questionnaire. She expressed, in her own words, the essence of the statistical finding on sharing feelings: "I like Mrs. Tracy. She's not like a social worker, she's like a real person." This model suggests that Mrs. Tracy was both a real person and a real social worker.

MAKING A DEMAND FOR WORK

In constructing this model of the helping process, the importance of establishing a clear contract, of identifying the client's agenda, of helping the client to elaborate concerns, of making sure the client invests the work with feeling, and of the worker sharing feelings has been stressed. At this point in the model-building process, it is important to examine the question of ambivalence and resistance. Clients will be of two minds about proceeding with their work. A part of them, representing their strength, will move towards understanding and growth. The other part of them, representing the resistance, will pull back from what is perceived as a difficult process.

Work often requires lowering long-established defenses, discussing painful subjects, experiencing difficult feelings, recognizing one's own contribution to the problem, taking responsibility for one's actions, giving up long-held cognitive frameworks about life, and confronting people and systems that are important to the client. Whatever the difficulty involved, a client will show some degree of ambivalence.

Perlman (1957) described client ambivalence as follows:

> To know one's feelings is to know that they are often many-sided and mixed and that they may pull in two directions at once. Everyone has experienced this duality of wanting something strongly yet drawing back from it, making up one's mind but somehow not carrying out the planned action. This is part of what is meant by ambivalence. A person may be subject to two opposing forces within himself at the same moment— one that says, "Yes, I will," and the other that says, "No, I won't"; one that says, "I want," and the other, "Not really"; one affirming and the other negating (p. 121).

Relating client ambivalence to the relationship with the worker and the process of taking help, Strean (1978) describes resistance as follows:

> Recognizing that every client has some resistance to the idea and process of being helped should alert the social-work interviewer to the fact that not every part of every interview can flow smoothly. Most clients at one time or another will find participation difficult or may even refuse to talk at all; others will habitually come late and some may be quite negative toward the agency, the social-work profession, and the social worker (p. 193).[6]

An example of this ambivalence at work is found in the following excerpt from a videotaped interview with an adolescent foster boy. Early in the interview, the 18-year-old youngster indirectly hinted at his feelings about leaving a group home and particularly about the warm feelings he had established for the head child care worker. The worker missed the first cues, since she was preoccupied with her written agenda resting on the table between them. Catching her mistake during the session, the worker moved her agenda aside and began to listen systematically to this theme, encouraging the client to elaborate, and reaching for and articulating his feelings. The following excerpt picks up the interview at the point where the worker responded to the client's second offering of this concern.

Worker: Is it going to be hard to say good-bye to Tom? (the child care worker)

Client: It's not going to be hard to say good-bye to Tom, but I'll miss the little kittens that sleep with me. Last night one dug his claws into me and I screamed and screamed and yelled to Tom—"Come and get this God damn kitten—do you think I'm going to go around ruptured all my life?" (At this point the client had told the story with such exuberance that the worker was laughing along with him. The client quickly reached over to the table for the worker's written agenda and said, "OK, what's next?")

When the worker was distracted by the agenda, the client continually offered indirect cues related to this important theme. As the worker began to deal seriously with the theme, that part of the client that feared the discussion and the accompanying feelings found a way to put the worker off by using the worker's own agenda. In part, the client may also be testing to see if the worker is ready for the discussion. By allowing herself to be put off, the worker sends the message, "I'm not ready, either." When this was explored with the worker, her reflections on the process led her to recognize that she was also about to end with this client—an ending she was avoiding. Once again, the ability of the worker to manage her own feelings influenced her ability to help the client manage his. The ending phase of practice is discussed in detail in Chapter 5.

The important thing to remember is that resistance is quite normal. In fact, a lack of resistance may mean the progress of the work is an illusion, with the real issues still unexplored. If this client could have easily dealt with his feelings about terminating his relationship with Tom, he would not have needed the worker's help. Termination feelings are at the core of the work for foster children who must struggle to find ways of investing in new, meaningful relationships in spite of the deep feelings of rejection they often feel. When the worker approaches the core area of feeling, it would be surprising if resistance didn't appear.

A lack of understanding that resistance is a part of the work leads less experienced workers to back off from an important area. Their own confidence in what they are doing is fragile, and so when the client shows signs of defensiveness or unwillingness to deal with a tough problem, they allow themselves to be put off. This is especially true if workers experience ambivalence about dealing with the area themselves. Communication of ambivalence in tough areas can be seen as the client's way of saying, "This is tough for me to talk about." It can also be a question to the worker, "Are you really prepared to talk with me about this?" It is one of those life situations in which the other person says he is reluctant to enter the taboo area, hoping you won't really believe him. The surface message seems to be, "Leave me alone in this area," while the real message is, "Don't let me put you off." These are the moments in interviews when the skills of making a demand for work are crucial.

The notion of a demand for work is one of Schwartz's most important contributions to our understanding of the helping process. He described it as follows:

> The worker also represents what might be called the demand for work, in which role he tries to enforce not only the substantive aspects of the contract—what we are here for—but the conditions of work as well. This demand is, in fact, the only one the worker makes—not for certain perceived results, or approved attitudes, or learned behaviors, but for the work itself. That is, he is continually challenging the client to address himself resolutely and with energy to what he came to do (Schwartz, 1961, p. 23).

The demand for work is not limited to a single action or even a single group of skills, but rather it pervades all the work. For example, the process of open and direct contracting in the beginning phase of work represents a form of demand for work. The attempts of the worker to bring the client and feelings into the process is another form of a demand for work. The earlier illustration of the first interview with the angry father in which the worker kept coming back to his feelings in the situation is a good example. Similarly, in the interview with the foster child just described, the youngster was discussing, at one point, the feeling that had grown between Tom (the child care worker) and himself, and he said to the worker,

"How does it hit people like him?" The worker's response was, "How does it hit you?" This is another illustration of the demand for work. It is important to note that this demand can be gentle and coupled with support. It is not necessarily confrontative in nature. I underline this point because of a tendency for people to see confrontation as negative and uncaring. Some models of practice, particularly in the substance abuse area, have been designed to use confrontation to "break down" defenses. It is perfectly possible for the worker to make an empathic demand for work—and, as emphasized earlier, confrontation is experienced as caring if carried out in the context of a positive working relationship.

A number of specific skills can be categorized as demand-for-work skills. Each is related to specific dynamics in interview situations that could be interpreted as forms of resistance. These are reviewed in the balance of this section. It is important to note that the consistent use of demand-for-work skills can only be effective when they are accompanied by the empathic skills described earlier. As the workers express their genuine caring for the clients through their ability to empathize, they build up a fund of positive affect that is part of the working relationship. Only when clients perceive that their worker does understand, and is not judging them harshly, are they able to respond to the demands.

The argument advanced here is that workers who have the capacity to empathize with clients can develop a positive working relationship but not necessarily be helpful. Workers who only make demands upon their clients, without the empathy and working relationship, will be experienced by clients as harsh, judgmental, and unhelpful. The most effective help will be offered by workers who are able to synthesize, each in their own way, caring and demand. This is not easy to do either in the helping relationship or in life. There is a general tendency to dichotomize these two aspects of relationship—caring about someone, expressing it through empathy, but getting nowhere. This frustration leads to anger and demands, with an associated hardening of empathic response. Precisely at this point, when crucial demands are made on the client, the capacity for empathy is most important. With this stipulation clearly in mind, in the next section we will explore four demand-for-work skills.

Partializing Client Concerns

Clients often experience their concerns as overwhelming. A worker may find that a client's response to an offer of help in the contracting phase consists of the recitation of a flood of problems, each having some impact on the other. The feeling of helplessness experienced by the client is as much related to the apparent difficulty of tackling so many problems as it is to the nature of the problems themselves. The client feels immobilized and does not know how or where to begin. In addition, maintaining problems in this form can represent resistance. If the problems are overwhelming, the client can justify the impossibility of doing anything about them.

Partializing is essentially a problem-managing skill. The only way to tackle complex problems is to break them down into their component parts and to address these parts one at a time. The way to move past perceptions of helplessness and feelings of being immobilized is to begin by taking one small step on one part of the problem. This is the sense in which the worker makes a demand for work. While listening to the concerns of the client, while attempting to understand and acknowledge the client's feelings of being overwhelmed, the worker simultaneously begins the task of helping the client to reduce the problem to smaller, more manageable proportions. This skill is illustrated in the following excerpt of an interview with a single parent.

Worker: You seem really upset by your son's fight yesterday. Can you tell me more about what's upsetting you?

Client: All hell broke loose after that fight. Mrs. Lewis is furious because he gave her son a black eye, and she is threatening to call the police on me. She complained to the landlord, and he's threatening to throw me out if the kids don't straighten up. I tried to talk to Frankie about it, but I got nowhere. He just screamed at me and ran out of the house. I'm really afraid he has done it this time, and I'm feeling sick about the whole thing. Where will I go if they kick me out? I can't afford another place. And you know the cops gave Frankie a warning last time. I'm scared about what will happen if Mrs. Lewis does complain. I just don't know what to do.

Worker: It really does sound like quite a mess; no wonder you feel up against the wall. Look, maybe it would help if we looked at one problem at a time. Mrs. Lewis is very angry, and you need to deal with her. Your landlord is important, too, and we should think about what you might be able to say to him to get him to back off while you try to deal with Frankie on this. And I guess that's the big question, what can you say to Frankie since this has made things rougher for the two of you? Mrs. Lewis, the landlord, and Frankie— where should we start?

The demand implied in the worker's statement is gentle and yet firm. The worker can sense the client's feelings of being overwhelmed, but she will not allow the work to stop there. In this example, one can see clearly two sets of tasks: those of the worker and those of the client. The client raises the concerns, and the worker helps her to partialize her problems. The client must begin to work on them according to her sense of urgency. This is the sense in which work is interactional, with the worker's tasks and those of the client interacting with each other.

When a worker partializes an overwhelming problem and asks a client to begin to address the issues, she or he is also acting on a crucial principle of the helping process. This is the principle that says *there is always a next step.* Put simply, there is no client problem to which there is not some form of next step. The next step is whatever the worker and client can do, together, to begin to cope with the problem. Even when a client is dealing with a terminal illness, the next steps may mean developing a way of coping with the illness, getting one's life in order, taking control of the quality of one's remaining time, and so on. When social supports, such as adequate housing, are not available for a client, the next steps may involve advocacy and confrontation of the system, or if all else fails, attempting to figure out how to minimize the impact of the poor housing. While the worker may not be able to offer hope of "solving" the problem, it is important that the worker help the client to find whatever next step may be available. When a client feels overwhelmed and hopeless, the last thing he or she needs is a worker who feels exactly the same.

The research finding in my more recent practice study on the skill of partializing was most interesting. Partializing was one of the four skills for helping clients to manage their problems that contributed to the development of the trust element in the working relationship (Shulman, 1991). The other skills in this grouping including clarifying purpose and role, reaching for client feedback, and supporting clients in taboo areas. The trust element of the relationship, in turn, contributed to the client's perception of the worker as being helpful. This is a logical finding, since workers who help their clients to deal with complex problems are going to be seen as more helpful.

When time was taken into account in the analysis, that is, whether a skill was relatively more important if used in the beginning phase of practice as compared to the middle phase, the importance of the partializing skill was underlined. The partializing skill, when used in the beginning phase of practice, ranked fifth out of eight skills in the strength of its correlation with the caring element of the working relationship. It moved to second place in relation to the trust element of the relationship, and to first in importance in terms of its impact on helpfulness.

This association between partializing and the working relationship replicated a finding in the earlier study (Shulman, 1978) in which the skill appeared to contribute to the outcome of helpfulness though its impact on relationship.

One explanation of the effect of this skill on relationship building may be that the worker's use of the partializing skill conveys a number of important ideas to the client. First, the worker believes the tasks facing the client are manageable. There has to be some positive affect flowing towards a worker who takes a complex problem and helps to sort it out in this way. Second, the worker conveys the belief that the client can take some next step: that is, that the client has the strength to deal with the problem when properly partialized. The conveying of a secondary message of positive esteem on the worker's part towards the client is an essential part of a positive working relationship. Finally, another secondary benefit may flow from the worker's focus on the work rather than on the client. A popular public conception of helping is of some form of "therapy" in which the problem lies with the client, who needs to be "changed." Some support was cited earlier for the positive impact that the clarification of role had on developing the working relationship. Since partializing also serves to focus the work clearly, it may be another form of clarifying role and purpose. The particular finding on the partializing skill suggests that workers might concentrate in the early sessions on helping clients to identify clearly the component parts of the concerns they bring to the worker.

Holding to Focus

As a client begins to deal with a specific concern, associations with other related issues often result in a form of rambling, with great difficulty in concentrating on one issue at a time. Once again, the skill of asking the client to stay on one question represents the use of a problem-solving skill incorporating a demand for work. Moving from concern to concern can be an evasion of work—that is, if the client won't stay with one issue, then he or she does not have to deal with the associated feelings. **Holding to focus** send the message to the client that the worker means to discuss the tougher feelings and concerns. This skill can be illustrated in the earlier interview with the single parent. After the client decided to deal with Mrs. Lewis first, because of her fear of police involvement, the discussion continued.

> **Client:** When Mrs. Lewis came to the door, all she did was scream at me about how my Frankie was a criminal and that she would not let him beat up her son again.
>
> **Worker:** You must have been frightened and upset. What did you say to her?
>
> **Client:** I just screamed back at her and told her that her son was no bargain and that he probably asked for it. I was really upset because I could see the landlord's door opening, and I knew he must be listening. You know he warned me that he wouldn't stand for all of this commotion any more. What can I do if he really kicks me out on the street?

Worker: Can we stay with Mrs. Lewis for a minute and then get back to the land-lord? I can see how angry and frightened you must have felt. Do you have any ideas about how Mrs. Lewis was feeling?

By acknowledging the distress (support) and then returning to the issue of dealing with Mrs. Lewis (demand) the worker was helping the client to stay focused on this issue instead of allowing her anxiety to overwhelm her.

Checking for Underlying Ambivalence

One of the dangers in a helping situation is that a client may choose to go along with the worker, expressing an artificial consensus or agreement, while really feeling very ambivalent about a point of view or a decision to take a next step. A client who feels the worker has an investment in the "solution" may not feel like upsetting the worker by voicing doubts. The client may also be unaware at this moment of the doubts that may appear later on, when implementation of the difficult action is attempted. The client may also withhold concerns as a means of putting off dealing with the core of the issue. In this sense, it is another form of resistance—a very subtle form, since it is expressed passively. In these circumstances, when words are being spoken but nothing real is happening, we have the "illusion of work," which is the single most dangerous threat to effective practice. Workers and clients develop marvelous ways of maintaining the illusion, each for their own reasons.

Sometimes workers are aware of the underlying doubts, fears, and concerns but simply pass over them. As one worker put it, "I knew we were just spinning our wheels, but I was afraid to confront the client." Workers believe that raising these issues may cause the client to decide not to take the next step. They believe that positive thinking is required, and they do not wish to heighten the client's ambivalence by discussing it. The reverse is true. It is exactly at moments such as these that the worker should **check for the underlying ambivalence**. When a client has an opportunity to express ambivalence, the worker has access to the client's real feelings and can be of help. The power of the negative feelings can be diminished through the process of discussing them with the worker. Perhaps the client is overestimating the difficulties involved, and the worker can help to clarify the reality of the situation. In other cases, it will indeed be a difficult next step. The worker's help consists of empathic understanding of the difficulty and expression of faith in the client's strength and resilience in the face of these feelings. There are any number of reasons for hesitation, but whatever they are, they must be explored so that they do not block the client's work outside of the session.

Workers need to struggle against a sense of elation when they hear clients agreeing to take an important next step. Schwartz described the need for workers to "look for trouble when everything is going your way." For example, in working with a client with a substance abuse problem, an enthusiastic worker might accept the client's agreement to enter a treatment program and then be disappointed when the client does not show up for the intake appointment. Careful examination of the session reveals that the client sent signals that he was still in the "contemplative" stage and not yet ready to move into the "action" stage of seeking help. Workers often admit sensing a client's hesitancy but believing that it can be overcome through positive encouragement. This is a mistake that comes back to haunt the worker when all of the ambivalence and fears emerge *after* the session.

All is not lost, however, if in the next session the worker can admit to having moved too quickly and encourage the client to explore his mixed feelings, which are normal at this stage of the process.

This example provides a good opportunity to elaborate on the earlier comment that resistance is part of the work. It would be a mistake simply to think of client resistance as an obstacle blocking progress. Resistance is not only explored for the purpose of freeing the client to proceed. There are important "handles for work" within the resistance itself. In this example, as the worker explores the client's resistance, a number of important work themes may emerge: concerns regarding acceptance of a problem with substances, how employers would view him, feelings of shame, and so on. One colleague of mine described an example in which a young university student, who had been admitted to a psychiatric unit after a suicide attempt, announced early in the first interview that she would not discuss her boyfriend or her family because that would be blaming them. This is simultaneously resistance and the expression of one of her central concerns related to her guilt over her feelings of anger and resentment. Exploring why she does not want to discuss them could lead directly into a central theme of concern.

Challenging the Illusion of Work

One of the greatest threats to effective helping lies in the ability of the client to create what I referred to earlier as an **illusion of work**. Much of the helping process I have been describing takes place through an exchange of words (although helping can be achieved through nonverbal means, such as touch). We have all developed the capacity to engage in conversations that are empty and devoid of real meaning. It is easy to see how this ability to talk a great deal without saying much can be integrated into the helping interaction. This represents a subtle form of resistance because by creating the illusion of work, the client can avoid the pain of struggle and growth while still appearing to work. But for the illusion to take place, it is necessary to have two partners in the ritual. The worker must be willing to allow the illusion to be created, thus participating actively in its maintenance. Workers have reported helping relationships with clients that have spanned months, even years, in which the worker always knew, deep down inside, that it was all illusion.

Schwartz (1971) described the illusion of work when writing about the practice of group work.

> Not only must the worker be able to help people talk but he must help them talk to each other; the talk must be purposeful, related to the contract that holds them together; it must have feeling in it, for without affect there is no investment; and it must be about real things, not a charade, or a false consensus, or a game designed to produce the illusion of work without raising anything in the process (p. 11).

The skill involves detecting the pattern of illusion, perhaps over a period of time, and confronting the client with the reality. An example from marriage counseling illustrates this process. The couple had requested help for problems in their marriage. As the sessions proceeded, the worker noted that most of the conversation involved problems they were having at work, with their parents, and with their children. Some connection was made to the impact on their marriage; however, they seemed to have created an unspoken alliance not to deal with the details of their relationship. No matter how hard the worker tried to find the connections to how they got along, they always seemed to evade him. Finally, the worker said,

> You know, when we started out, you both felt you wanted help with the problems in your marriage, how you got along with each other. It seems to me, however, that all

we ever talk about is how you get along with other people. You seem to be avoiding the tough stuff. How come? Are you worried it might be too tough to handle?

The worker's challenge to the illusion brought a quick response as the couple explored some of their fears about what would happen if they really began to work. This challenge to the illusion was needed to help the couple begin the difficult, risky process of change. In addition, their response illustrates how the resistance itself reveals a great deal about the underlying problems. They were demonstrating to the worker their manner of avoiding talking to each other about their real problems.

Pointing Out Obstacles

When developing his theory of the mediation function for social work, Schwartz broke down the function into five general sets of tasks (Schwartz, 1961). One of these was the task of searching out the common ground between the client and the systems to be negotiated. This task is evident when the worker attempts to contract with clients—to find the connections between the felt needs of the client and the services of the agency. It is also apparent when the worker attempts to alert himself or herself to the subtle connections between a teenager's need for independence and the parents' desire to see their youngster grow. These are just a few of the many moments when the common ground between the individual and the system may appear to each to be diffused, unclear, even totally absent.

Because of the complexity of relationships and the potential for the common ground to be obscured, Schwartz elaborates his mediation function with a second set of important activities, the task of **detecting and challenging the obstacles to work** as these obstacles arise. Like all Schwartz's tasks, this one is not a single activity but one that is repeated, moment by moment, in every helping encounter. Two of the major obstacles that tend to frustrate people as they work on their own self-interest are the blocking effects of social taboos and the effect of the "authority theme," the relationship between the person who gives help and the one who takes it.

Supporting Clients in Taboo Areas

In moving into a helping relationship, the client brings along a sense of the societal culture, which includes taboos against open discussion in certain sensitive areas. For example, we are taught early in life that direct questions and discussions about sex are frowned upon. Other areas in which we are subtly encouraged not to acknowledge our true feelings include dependency, authority, loss, and money. To feel dependent is equated with feeling weak. The unrealistic image of a "real man" is of one who is independent, able to stand on his own feel, and competent to deal with life's problems by himself. This does not match reality. In the real world, life is so complex that we are always dependent and interdependent upon others. The bind we experience is that of feeling one way, consciously or not, but thinking we should feel another way. The norms of our culture include clear taboos that make real talk in such areas difficult.

Money is considered a taboo subject as well. Many families deeply resent questions related to their financial affairs. Having enough money is equated with competency in our society, and the admission of poverty is considered embarrassing. Reluctance to discuss fees with professionals is another example of the effect of the taboo against open discussion about money. Clients will sometimes contract for services without asking about the fee, feeling that it would be embarrassing to inquire.

One of the most powerful taboos involves feelings toward authority. Parents, teachers, and other authority figures do not generally encourage feedback from children on the nature of the relationship. We learn early on that commenting on this relationship, especially if the reactions are negative, is fraught with danger. People in authority have power to hurt us, and therefore, we will at best hint at our feelings and reactions. It is almost as hard to reveal positive feelings to people in authority, since our peer group has taught us that this is considered demeaning. This taboo creates an important problem in the working relationship between the worker and the client, as I will demonstrate in the next section.

Loss is another major area of taboo in our society, which often overlaps with other areas. For example, the loss of a relationship because of death or separation may be considered too difficult to discuss directly. A parent whose child has been born with a physical or mental problem may secretly mourn the loss of the perfect child he or she had wished to have. A survivor of sexual abuse or of emotional or physical abuse may mourn the loss of childhood and innocence. The adult child of an alcoholic may mourn the loss of the family he or she had hoped for, but not feel free to discuss this since the family training was that the "problem" must be kept secret. Many of the messages of our society indicate that direct discussion of losses is not acceptable.

A worker who is to help a client discuss feelings and concerns in these areas and others experienced as taboo will have to create a unique "culture" in the helping interview. In this culture it will become acceptable to discuss feelings and concerns that the client may experience as taboo elsewhere. The taboo is not going to be removed for all situations. There are some good reasons for us not to talk freely and intimately on all occasions about our feelings in taboo areas. The purpose of the discussion of the taboo in the interview is not to change the client's attitudes forever, but only to allow work in the immediate situation. The way the worker does this is to monitor the interaction of the work with the client and to listen for clues that may reveal a block in the process related to a taboo. The worker's past experiences with clients and the tuning-in process may heighten sensitivity to a taboo that lies just beneath the surface of the interview. On recognizing the taboo, the worker brings it out in the open and begins the negotiation of a new norm of behavior for the interview situation. The following illustration is from an interview between a professional and a male, 48-year-old patient. It demonstrates how a helping professional can support a client in discussing a taboo subject.

Patient: I've been feeling lousy for a long time. It's been especially bad since my wife and I have been arguing so much.

Worker: Tell me more about the arguments.

Patient: They've been about lots of things—she complains I drink too much, I'm not home often enough, and that I always seem too tired to spend time with her. (At this point, the worker senses the patient's difficulty in talking. His hesitation and an inability to look directly at her are the cues.)

Worker: Often when there is a lot of difficulty like this, it spills over into the sexual area.

Patient: (After a long pause) There have been some problems around sex as well.

Worker: You know I realize that it's tough to talk about something as intimate as sex, particularly for a man to discuss it with a woman. It's really not something one can do easily.

Patient: It is a bit embarrassing.

> **Worker:** Perhaps you can speak about it in spite of your embarrassment. You know there is not much I haven't heard already, and I won't mind hearing what you have to say. Anyway, we can't do much about the problems if we can't discuss them
>
> **Patient:** I've been tired lately with a lot of worries. Sometimes I have too much to drink as well. Anyway, I've been having trouble getting it up for the past few months.
>
> **Worker:** Is this the first time this had happened?
>
> **Patient:** The first time. I usually have no trouble at all.
>
> **Worker:** It must have come as quite a shock to you. I guess this has hit you and your wife hard.

The discussion continued as the client went into more detail about the nature of the problem. Other symptoms were described, and the worker suggested that a complete physical was in order. She pointed out that it was not at all unusual for these things to happen to men of this age and that often there were physiological reasons. At the end of the interview the worker reinforced the development of the new norm in their working relationship by commenting, "I know how hard it was for you to speak to me about this. It was important, however, and I hope this discussion will help you feel free to talk about whatever is on your mind." The patient answered that he felt better now that he had been able to get it off his chest.

It is important to stress that identifying the taboo or any other obstacle that obstructs the process of work with a client is done for the purpose of freeing the client's energy to work on the negotiated contract. Sometimes all that is necessary is for the obstacle to be named to release the client from its power. In other situations, some exploration of the obstacle may be needed before its impact on the work can be reduced. For example, a client might need to talk briefly about the difficulty he feels in discussing issues related to sex. His family norms might have added to the pressure against such open discussion. The worker needs to guard, however, against a subtle subversion of the contract that can easily occur if the discussion of the obstacle becomes the focus of the work. The purpose of the helping encounter is not to examine the reasons why the taboo exists nor is it to free the client from its power in all situations. The importance and power of clarity of purpose and function is best demonstrated when they assist the worker in avoiding the trap of becoming so engrossed in the analysis of the process that the original task becomes lost.

In the original study (Shulman, 1978) the skill of supporting clients in taboo areas was one of four skills that distinguished the most effective workers from the least effective, from their clients' perspective. In the more recent study (Shulman, 1991), this skill was the sixth lowest in use of the eight skills examined. Clients reported that their workers used this skill between "seldom" and "fairly often." This is not unexpected, since worker have also been exposed to the same societal injunctions about the taboo areas as have clients. It takes experience and supervision before workers have the courage to speak directly about many of these issues.

This skill was included in the grouping of four skills designed to help clients to manage their problems. The use of these skills appeared to contribute to the development of trust in the working relationship, and in turn, to the client perceiving the worker as helpful.

The introduction of time to the analysis for this skill yielded some interesting findings. Supporting clients in taboo areas, when used in the beginning phase of work, was the third strongest (out of 8) skills correlating with the client's perception of the worker's caring (.52).

The correlation for the use of the skill in the middle phase of work was slightly higher (.58). These finding were expected, since support of any kind, particularly in sensitive and painful areas of work, could contribute to the client's perception that the worker was concerned about him or her.

When the association between the beginning phase use of this skill and trust was examined, however, it was still significant but it was only .37. The correlation was higher when the skill was used in the middle phase, jumping to .57. A similar pattern was found when the skill use was correlated with client perception of the worker's helpfulness (.39 in the beginning phase and .50 in the middle phase). One inference from these findings might be that the use of this skill in the early phases of work, before a solid working relationship has been established, primarily contributes to the working relationship though the development of a client's sense of the worker's caring. This provides some justification for the argument that it is better for the worker to risk and be too far ahead of the client than to be overly cautious.

The use of the skill may have less of an impact on trust and helpfulness early in the work because of the lower levels of trust in the beginning phase of any relationship. In short, the client needs to trust the worker somewhat before the worker's efforts to explore taboo areas have their largest impact on trust.

Dealing with the Authority Theme

Schwartz (1971) described the authority theme as referring to

> the familiar struggle to resolve the relationship with a nurturing and demanding figure who is both a personal symbol and a representative of a powerful institution (p. 11).

As the client uses the worker's help to deal with this task, positive and negative affect will be generated. There will be times when the client thinks fondly of this caring and supportive figure. There will be other times when the client feels anger toward a worker who demands that the client take responsibility for the client's own part in the events of her or his life. Workers are not perfect individuals who never make mistakes. Even the most skilled worker will sometimes miss a client's communications, lose track of the real function and begin to sermonize, or judge the client harshly without compassion for real struggles. Reactions and feelings on the part of the client will result. As one enters a helping relationship, problems with the authority theme should be anticipated as a normal part of the work. In fact, the energy flow between worker and client can provide the driving force that helps to power the work.

Two processes that are central to the authority theme are *transference* and *counter-transference*. Strean (1978) describes their effects on the worker-client relationship, drawing upon the psychoanalytic theory of Freud.

> This relationship has many facets: subtle and overt, conscious and unconscious, progressive and regressive, positive and negative. Both client and worker experience themselves and each other not only in terms of objective reality, but in terms of how each wishes the other to be and fears he might be. The phenomena of "transference" and "counter-transference" exist in every relationship between two or more people, professional or nonprofessional, and must be taken into account in every social-worker-client encounter. By "transference" is meant the feelings, wishes, fears, and defenses of the client deriving from reactions to significant persons in the past (parents, siblings, extended family, teachers), that influence his current perceptions of the social worker. "Counter-transference" similarly refer to aspects of the social worker's histo-

ry of feelings, wishes, fears, and so on, all of which influence his perceptions of the client (p. 193).

Unfortunately, the authority theme is one of the most powerfully taboo areas in our society. Clients have as much difficulty talking about their reactions and feelings towards their workers as they do discussing subjects such as sex. When these feelings and reactions are generated but not brought to the surface, the helping relationship is in trouble. These strong feelings operate just below the surface and emerge in many indirect forms. The client becomes apathetic or is late for appointments or can't seem to follow up on commitments. The worker searches for answers to the questions raised by the client's behavior by attempting to understand it in terms of the client's "personality." The answers to the worker's questions are often much closer to home and more accessible than the intangible notion of "personality." The answers often may be found in the interactional process between the worker and client.

The skill of dealing with the authority theme involves the worker's continual monitoring of the relationship. A worker who senses that the work seems unreal or is blocked can call attention to the existence of the obstacle and try to respond directly if the source of the trouble may be the authority theme. Once again, as with other taboo subjects, the worker is trying to create a "culture" in this situation in which the client perceives a new norm: "It is all right to treat the worker like a real person and to say what you think about how she or he deals with you." The worker can begin the process in the contracting stages, as pointed out in Chapter 3, in responding directly to the early cues that the client wants some discussion about what kind of worker this will be. The new "culture" will develop slowly as the client tests this strange kind of authority person who seems to invite direct feedback, even the negative kind. As the client perceives that the worker will not punish, then the ability to feed responses back to the worker more quickly will grow. As an important side product, the client is exposed to a worker who is nondefensive and is demonstrating the capacity to examine his or her own behavior and to be open to change, exactly what the worker will be asking the client to do.

The following illustration demonstrates the skill in action. It describes a brief interaction between a worker and a 14-year-old male resident in a group home. The resident had been disciplined by the worker that afternoon for a fight he appeared to have provoked with another resident. The worker's one-sided intervention had shifted the fight to a battle of wills between John and himself, which then escalated until he finally imposed strict consequences. John had been quiet and sullen throughout dinner and the early evening. The worker approached him in the lounge.

Worker: John, you have been looking mad all evening, ever since the fight. Let's talk about it.

Client: F—K off!

Worker: Look, I know you're mad as hell at me, but it won't help to just sit there and keep it in. It will be miserable for both of us if you do. If you think I wasn't fair to you, I want to hear about it. You know I'm human, and I can make a mistake, too. So how about it, what's bugging you?

Client: You're just like all the rest. The minute I get into trouble, you blame me. It's always my fault, never the other kids'. You took Jerry's side in that fight without ever asking me why I was beating up on him.

Worker: (Short silence) I guess I did come down hard on you quickly. You know you're probably right about my figuring it was your fault when you get in trouble—probably because you get into trouble so often. I think I was also a little tired this afternoon and maybe not up to handling a fight on my shift. Look, let's start again. OK? I think I can listen now. What happened?

The discussion carried on about the fight and the issues which led up to it. It became clear that there were some ongoing questions between John and Jerry that needed to be argued out. The worker suggested another meeting with Jerry present, at which time he would try not to take sides and try to help both John and Jerry work this out. John indicated some willingness to try, but with a great deal of skepticism. The interview continued, and the worker returned to the authority theme.

> **Worker:** You know, I really wasn't helpful to you this afternoon, and I'm sorry
> about that. But you know, I'm only human, and that is going to happen
> sometimes. What I'd like you to do, if it happens again, is not just sit around
> upset but to call me on it. If you do, I may catch myself sooner. Do you
> think you can do that?
> **Client:** Don't worry, I'll let you know if you get out of line.
> **Worker:** I guess this kind of thing happens a lot to you, I mean with the other staff
> here and maybe even the teachers at school.
> **Client:** You bet it does! Mr. Fredericks is always on my back, the minute I turn
> around in my seat.

In this illustration, the worker was able to catch his mistake and to have an important discussion about the way in which they worked together. His willingness to own up to his mistake and to take negative feedback contributed to a change in the subtle rules that have governed this child's reaction to adults in authority. The worker was very conscious that one of the most important outcomes of the youngster's stay in the group home may be his development of greater skill in dealing with authority people who are not always conscious of their effect on him. In many ways, the helping relationship itself is a training ground in which the client develops new skills at dealing with authority people, and that in itself is a major achievement. For some clients, particularly children in alternative care facilities, their ability to trust adults and to risk themselves is so limited that a profound change would be embodied in their ability to relate in a new way to the worker. It becomes a first step in developing their skills at dealing with the outside world, which may not always be as skillful in dealing with them as this worker had been.

The worker also demonstrated an advanced level of skill by the move at the end of the illustration when he deftly integrated process and task. Part of his work with John involves helping him to deal with the other systems of his life, such as his school. By generalizing to another situation, the worker found the work element, related to their contract, that was contained in the process. Dealing with the authority theme is not only a requirement for maintaining a positive working relationship, but it may also provide important material for helping clients to work on the substance of the contract. The process-content integration issue is discussed in more detail in the next section.

IDENTIFYING PROCESS AND CONTENT CONNECTIONS

Process refers to the interaction that takes place between the worker and the client (the authority theme) and the client and other clients, such as family or group members (the intimacy theme). Another way to describe process is that it refers more to the way of working than the substance or content of the work. **Content** is defined here as the substantive issues or themes that have been identified as part of the working contract.

At any one time, the work in an interview (or family or group session) is related to either process (authority or intimacy themes) or content, but often, because of the indirect nature of client communications, it is hard to know which is really under discussion. For example, a single parent may have contracted to work on issues related to dealing with her children, employment, and relationships with friends and family. She may begin a session apparently talking about content—how none of her friends or relatives understand her pain. The issue is a real one to her, but actually, she has been angry at the worker since the previous session when the worker had missed her signals of distress. This example emphasizes the importance of sessional turning in and worker tentativeness in the sessional contracting phase of a session, discussed earlier in this chapter. The worker who is tuned in to the client's pattern of indirect communications around issues of authority may be better prepared to hear that the discussion is really about process (authority)—her ability to understand—rather than about content (friends and relatives). If the worker prematurely assumes it is only content-related, the session may turn into the illusion of work, with the process issues buried under the surface.

Thus far, the terms *content* and *process* have been described and illustrated; however, the concept of the integration of the two remains to be explained. One major, common mistake made by workers is to fail to see the possible connections between process and content that allow for a synthesizing of the two. Workers often describe being torn between dealing with process and content. Group leaders will describe trying to "balance" the two, spending some time on process (how the group is working) and some time on content. What they don't realize is that they have fallen into the trap of accepting another false dichotomy: process versus content. (The dichotomies described earlier were personal versus professional, support versus confrontation, structure versus freedom, and so on.) Once this false dualism is accepted, there is no way to avoid being struck. Instead, the worker must search out the connections between process and content so that the discussion of process deepens the work on the content, and vice versa.

Returning to our single-parent example, the worker who looks for this synthesis may recognize (usually between sessions, rarely during a session) that the way in which the client indirectly raised her anger and hurt at the worker's lack of compassion is a good example of the way this client deals with friends and other important people in her life. When her needs are not met, she gets angry since she expects other people to intuitively sense her feelings. She does not take responsibility for being direct about her pain and thereby helping others to understand. In this case, if the worker opens up a discussion of the authority theme, this can lead to a deeper understanding by the client of the skills she must develop to create and maintain a social support system. The client can be held accountable for her own responsibility in the relationship with the worker as well as relationships with other significant people in her life. Thus, we see in this example that the content of the work can be synthesized with process issues, and the process issues can be integrated into the content.

In another illustration of the possibility of synthesizing process and task, a social worker used her discussion with a foster teenager about the termination of service to open up a discussion of the difficulty the youngster encountered in making new relationships after so many had ended badly. They were able to explore this pain over the ending with the worker as well as the many other losses he had experienced in his life. The teenager was able to see how difficult it was for him to invest in new relationships that might also end and therefore cause pain. The worker used a review of their relationship (the authority theme) to help the client understand and take some control over the feelings that affected him and his life. The importance of being willing to risk by getting close to other people was a central theme of the ending discussions, helping in the transition work. Their own ending provided an important opportunity for substantive work on how he could deal with new relationships now that he was leaving the care of the agency.

In a final example, one worker explored the difficulty a male married client has having in allowing himself to feel dependent upon the female worker and the discomfort he felt at expressing his need for help. The difficulty seemed related to many of his notions of what a "real man" should feel. The work on the authority theme led directly to discussions of how hard it was for him to let his wife know how much he needed her. In each of these examples, dealing with the authority theme served two distinct functions. It freed the working relationship from a potential obstacle and led directly to important substantive work on the contract. But this can only happen if the worker rejects the process-content dichotomy and instead searches for the potential connections between the two.

At times, the difficulty for the worker in being able to see and make use of the process-content connection is related to the emotions engendered in the worker by the manner in which the client uses process to communicate. In one example of a first videotaped session of a married couples' group I led, all five men arrived indicating they were present to do whatever they could to help "straighten out" their wives. (This first session is reported in some detail in Chapter 10.) All of the wives indicated they were depressed and seemed to accept the role of *"identified patient,"* the client in a family system who is identified as having the problem. This client often accepts the designation, which prevents the family from addressing the problems of the whole family and its dynamics. The women in the group indicated that they were being seen by psychiatrists (all male in this example) who had prescribed drugs for their depression.

When I have shown this tape in my classes, many students, particularly female students, have become very angry at one of the men, a 69-year-old who talks at great length about his wife's depression while she sits passively and silently. They become angry at me for not confronting this man at the start of the session and demanding that he speak for himself ("Tell him to use *I* statements!") The students are understandably upset about the sexist attitudes and myths that allow the male partner to deny his responsibility in the problem and to project all the difficulty onto his wife. I try to point out that in my view, the couples are letting me know in the first few minutes of the session exactly what the core of their problem is. This husband is saying to me:

> Social worker, if you want to see how we mishandle our marital relationship, just watch. I defend myself by taking no responsibility and defining my wife as the problem, while my wife accepts the blame outwardly, covering her rage with apathy and depression. So far, most helping professionals have colluded in accepting this maladaptive pattern of behavior as the definition of the problem.

I explain to my students that it is hard for me to get angry in a first session at clients who are acting out the very problem that brought them to the group for help. Understanding the connection between process and content *reframes* (redefines in a new and more helpful way) the interaction into a positive call for help. The process *is* the content.

In the detailed discussion of this example in Chapter 10, as I keep coming back to the male partner and reach for his feelings, while he is trying to talk about his wife, a noticeable lowering of his defenses takes place. For example, he says "My wife has been an in-patient for six weeks, and it has been a long time for her." I respond, "And it hasn't been easy for you either." After a short while, in a dramatic moment, he accepts some responsibility for his part in the problem when he reveals an incident of verbal abuse of his wife that causes him to cry in the session. As is often the case, during the group meetings that followed this first session, the women who were defined as the problem emerged as strong partners in the relationship and internal group leaders. In effect, the depression was their call for help—a signal of their strength rather than their weakness. During later sessions, for some of the men, a confrontation by the worker was needed as they continued to defend themselves and minimize their own part in the problem.

Once again, our ability to manage our own emotions as workers will have a powerful impact on our ability to help our clients to manage their feelings and their problems. As a male group worker in the previous example, it was not particularly difficult for me to tolerate the men's denial in the first session, to reframe the process as a call for help, and to reach for the related content. For a female worker, the struggle might be greater, as she would have experienced the oppression associated with sexism firsthand. This important understanding was reinforced for me by an incident that occurred when I was teaching a social work class on group work. By chance, the class consisted of all female students and myself, the only male and a symbol of authority. I commented on this class composition issue and pointed our that we all might want to monitor this to see if it had an impact on our work. There was no immediate response.

A turning point came in the sixth class when Jane, a student working in the criminal justice system, was presenting her work with a client who had been convicted of assaults. She related his story, in which he told how he had assaulted and raped his wife. She had experienced the manner in which he told the story as threatening to herself. It was as if he was trying to intimidate her in the telling of the story. The class discussion proceeded as follows:

> I asked Jane and the class to take a few minutes and explore what it felt like to work with clients who had done things that were very upsetting to them. In this case it was rape of a woman; in another situation it might be an adult who had sexually abused a child. We were discussing examples of male oppression of women and children. I wondered what Jane and the other students experienced as they heard this client's story. There was a brief silence, followed by Jane saying, "I was furious at him!" The class members began to tell stories of clients who had engendered similar feelings in them. Some indicated that their feelings were so strong that they didn't think they could ever work with a client like this.
>
> After several minutes, I intervened and said, "I think this is going to be the hard part for you, trying to examine the feelings provoked by clients like this and deciding whether or not you can work with them as clients in their own right." There was a momentary silence, following which one student said to me, with great feeling and anger, "You could never understand what this means to us!" I was stunned by the force of her comment. The other students stared at me to see how I would respond. I remained silent for a moment and realized that as I was giving them my sage advice about examining their own feelings, I had not been feeling a thing.
>
> I broke the silence by saying, "You are absolutely right! I gave an intellectual response just then. It was easy to do, since I have not experienced the kind of gender oppression you have. What you said just now, about my never being able to under-

stand, hit me very hard. I guess on this issue, you are going to have to help each other."

After I spoke, I could sense the tension lift. I remained silent as they began to talk with each other about how they have tried to handle these situations. One student with work experience in shelters for battered women said she had felt she could never work with batterers because of her strong identification with the women. She went on to describe how she had taken a risk and co-led a group for male batterers with a male colleague. She had been amazed to find that she could retain her anger at the men but still start to overcome the stereotype of them she had developed. She found she had been able to hold the men accountable for their actions and take steps needed to protect the women still in their lives. She was also able to see the men as clients in their own right. She said she felt she now did a better job with women after having worked with the men. Discussion continued along these lines, with some students feeling they would be able to do it and others sure they could not.

As we neared the end of the class, I pointed out that Jane was going to be seeing this client again this week. I wondered if we could help her think through how she might handle the next interview. Last time she had sat on her feelings because she needed to be "professional." What advice did they have for her now? Jane indicated the discussion had helped already. She realized that she wanted to work with this client in spite of her feelings. If she didn't reach him, he eventually would abuse other women. She felt she should confront him with his behavior toward her the previous week. Others in the class supported this. I asked her what she might say. She tried to role-play how she could get back to the issue. Other students provided suggestions and feedback. I pointed out that she could also view his behavior toward her as demonstrating how he related to women—how he tried to exercise control through intimidation. Perhaps she could use the process in their work together and generalize to his relationship with other women. She agreed that it was worth a try, saying that at least she now felt she had a next step with him.

I credited Jane and the class with their fine work. I thanked the student who had confronted me. I asked them all to keep an eye on this issue and said that if they ever felt in future classes that I was not really understanding their struggle they should say so as soon as possible.

This example is shared at this point in the book for a number of reasons. First, it is another illustration of process and task integration. The process in this class in relation to the authority theme (the relationship of the students to myself), and the impact of issues of gender (a male teacher with female students), provided a medium for an important learning experience for the class. As the instructor I had to model in the class a way of using process to deepen the work on the content, especially at a time when my own feelings were influencing me in a powerful way. This was exactly what I was attempting to help them do with their clients. As is often the case in teaching and learning, more is "caught" than "taught."[7]

SKILLS FOR SHARING DATA

In a social work setting, we define worker data as facts, ideas, values, and beliefs that workers have accumulated from their own experiences and can make available to clients.

Schwartz (1961) argues,

The worker's grasp of social reality is one of the important attributes that fit him to his functions. While his life experiences cannot be transferred intact to other human beings, the products of these experiences can be immensely valuable to those who are moving through their own struggles and stages of mastery (p. 23).

Not only is it important for workers to share data because of the potential usefulness to the client, but the process of sharing the data is also important in building a working relationship. The client looks to the worker as a source of help in difficult areas. If the client senses that the worker is withholding data, for whatever reason, the withholding can be experienced as a form of rejection. As a client might put it, "If you really cared about me, you would share what you know."

I remember an experience during my social work training when a fellow student, majoring in group work, described his work with a group of teenaged boys in a residential institution. They were planning their first party and were obviously without any sense of the quantities of food and drink required. The soda pop they ordered, for example, would be insufficient for the number of people present. When I asked if he had pointed this out to them, he replied that he had not interfered, feeling that they would learn something important about planning. I was shocked and felt that if they ever found out he knew they were underestimating quantities and had not told them, their significant learning would be about him.

While the skills of sharing data may sound simple, a number of misconceptions about how people learn and a lack of clarity about the helping function have served to make a simple act complex. The problems can be seen in the actions of workers who have important information for the client but withhold it, thinking that the client must "learn it for himself." These problems are also apparent in the actions of workers who claim to be allowing clients to "learn for themselves" while they indirectly "slip in" their ideas. This is most easily recognizable in interviews where the worker leads a client to the answer that the worker already has in mind. The belief is that learning takes place if the client speaks the words the worker wants to hear. In the balance of this section I will identify some of the skills involved in sharing data and discuss some of the issues that often lead workers to be less than direct.

Providing Relevant Data

The skill is the direct sharing of the worker's facts, ideas, values, and beliefs that are related to the client's immediate task at hand. The two key requirements are that the data be related to the working contract and that it be needed by the client for the immediate work. If the worker is clear about the purpose of the encounter and that purpose has been openly negotiated with the client, then the worker has a guideline as to what data to share. A problem is created when the worker wants to "teach" something indirectly to the client and uses the interchange to "slip in" personal ideas. This mistaken sense of function on the worker's part is rooted in a model in which the worker attempts to "change" the client by skillfully presenting "good" ideas. The problem is that the client soon senses that the worker has a hidden agenda, and instead of using the worker as a resource for the client's own agenda, must begin to weigh the worker's words to see what is "up his or her sleeve." This hidden purpose often creates a dilemma for a worker in sharing data directly. A part of the worker is uncomfortable about efforts to impose an ideology on the client, thus treating the client as an object to be molded. This ambivalence comes out in the indirectness with which the ideas are shared. If data are related to an openly agreed-upon purpose, then the worker is free to share them directly.

The second requirement for directly sharing data is that the data be connected to the client's immediate sense of concern. Clients will not learn something simply because the worker feels it may be of use to them at some future date, even if it is related to the working contract. The attraction people feel towards objects (e.g., ideas, values) is related to their sense of their usefulness at the time. One reason for the importance of sessional contracting is that the worker needs to determine the client's current sense of urgency and must share data that the client perceives as helpful.

An example of sharing data that are not immediately relevant is a practice I have observed in work with pre-adoptive couples in child welfare agencies. Individual or group work is often employed for the dual proposes of evaluating the couples' suitability as adoptive parents and helping them discuss the adoption. It is not unusual for the worker to prepare a well-developed agenda for group meetings touching on all the issues that workers feel the couples will need to face as adoptive parents. Unfortunately, such an agenda may often miss the immediate concerns pre-adoptive parents have about adoption and about agency procedures for accepting and rejecting potential parents. In the following illustration, pre-adoptive couples in a second group session respond to the worker's query, "Should one tell adopted children they were adopted? If yes, when and how?" The important point to remember is that these couples are still waiting to hear if they are going to get children and are all expecting infants. The issue of whether to tell is one that will not present itself until a few years after the child is adopted.

> **Mr. Franks:** I think you have to tell the child or you won't be honest.
>
> **Mr. Beck:** But if you tell him then he probably will always wonder about his real parents and that may make him feel less like you are his parents. (This comment starts a vigorous discussion between the men about how a child feels towards his adoptive parents. The worker uses this opportunity to contribute her own views indirectly; she already has in mind an "acceptable" answer to her question.)
>
> **Worker:** I wonder, Mr. Beck, how you think the child might feel if you didn't tell him and he found out later.
>
> **Mr. Beck:** (Recognizing that he may have given the wrong answer to the worker, who will also judge his suitability to be an adoptive parent) You know, I hadn't really looked at it that way. I guess you're right, it would be easier to tell right away.

When the group had apparently reached the consensus that the worker had intended from the start, she shifted the discussion to the question of when and how to tell. Unfortunately, the urgency of the issue of "telling" was not an immediate one. Pre-adoptive couples are more concerned with how they will feel towards their adoptive child. This is a very sensitive subject, particularly since pre-adoptive couples are not sure about the agency's criteria for acceptance. They worry that they may be rejected if they don't express the "right" attitudes and feelings. This cuts them off from a supportive experience in which they might discover that most pre-adoptive parents are "in the same boat," that it is normal for them to have doubts, and that the agency will not hold that against them. In fact, parents who are in touch with their feelings, including such feelings as these, are often the ones who make excellent adoptive parents. Because the worker was so occupied by "teaching" ideas for future use, she missed the most important issue. Compare the earlier example with the following excerpt. In this case, the parents raised the question of "Should one tell?" and the worker listened for cues to the present concern.

> **Mr. Friedman:** (Responding to a group member's argument that the kids would not feel they were their real parents) I can't agree with that. I think the real parent is the one that raises you, and the kids will know that's you even if they are adopted.
>
> **Worker:** You have all been working quite hard on this question of how your adopted child well feel towards you, but I wonder if you aren't also concerned about how you will feel towards the child? (Silence)
>
> **Mr. Friedman:** I don't understand what you mean.
>
> **Worker:** Each of you are getting ready to adopt a child who was born to another set of parents. In my experience it is quite normal and usual for a couple at this stage to wonder sometimes about how they will feel towards the child. "Will I be able to love this child as if it were my own?" is not an uncommon question and a perfectly reasonable one, in my view.
>
> **Mrs. Reid:** My husband and I have talked about that at home—and we feel we can love our child as if he were our own.
>
> **Worker:** You know we would like the group to be a place where you can talk about your real concerns. Frankly, if you're wondering and have doubts and concerns such as this, that doesn't eliminate you from consideration as an adoptive parent. Being able to face your real concerns and feelings is very much in your favor. You folks wouldn't be in this group if we hadn't already felt you would make good adoptive parents. It would be the rare situation in which we would have to reconsider.

The worker shared some important data with these clients that was relevant both to the general contract of the group and to their immediate sense of urgency. They learned that their feelings, doubts, and concerns were not unusual, that the agency did not reject prospective adoptive parents for being human and having normal worries, that the group was a place to discuss these feelings, and finally, that their presence in the group indicated that they were all considered good applicants. This comment was followed by a deeper discussion of their feelings toward their prospective child and the adoption. These included their concern over the possibility of getting a child from a "bad seed," their fears as to the reactions of friends and family, and some of their real feelings of anger about the delays and procedures involved in dealing with the agency. The data shared by the worker in these areas was more meaningful to these parents than information about future problems. Agencies often offer follow-up groups for adoptive parents at key moments along the child's developmental path that can focus more clearly on issues that are only theoretical in the pre-adoptive stage.

Providing Data in a Way That Is Open to Examination

Workers are sometimes fearful of sharing their own fears, values, and so forth because of a genuine concern over influencing clients who need to make a difficult decision. The unwed mother, for example, trying to decide whether to abort her child, to have it and keep it, or to have it and give it up for adoption faces some agonizing decisions, none of which will be easy. In each case there will be important implications for her future. The skillful worker will help such a client explore in detail these implications and her underlying feelings of ambivalence. During this work, the client may turn to the worker at some point and say, "If you were me, what would you do?" Workers often have opinions about questions such as these but hold them back, usually responding to the question with a question of their own. I believe it is better for workers to share their feelings about revealing their opinions and then to allow the client access to their views as representing one source of reality. For example,

> When you ask me that question, you really put me on the spot. I'm not you, and no matter how hard I try, I can't be you, since I won't have to live with the consequences. For what it's worth, I think the way you have spelled it out, it's going to be an awfully tough go for you if you keep the baby. I probably would place the child for adoption. Now, having said that, you know it's still possible that you can pull it off, and only you know what you're ready for right now. So I guess my answer doesn't solve a thing for you, does it?

Workers who withhold their opinion are concerned that the client will adopt it as the only source of reality. Rather than holding back, however, I believe that a worker should simultaneously allow the client access to his or her opinions while guarding against the client's tendency to use them to avoid difficult work. Schwartz describes this consideration that guides the worker's movements as follows:

> The first (consideration) is his awareness that his offering represents only a fragment of available social experience. If he comes to be regarded as the fountainhead of social reality, he will then have fallen into the error of presenting himself as the object of learning rather than as an accessory to it. Thus, there is an important distinction to be made between lending his knowledge to those who can use it in the performance of their own tasks and projecting himself as a text to be learned (Schwartz, 1961, p. 24).

Thus far I have described how a worker can provide data to clients in a way that is open to examination by making sure that the client uses the data as just one source of reality. An additional consideration is to make sure that what is shared is presented as the worker's own opinion, belief, values, or whatever, rather than as fact. This is one of the most difficult ideas for many workers to comprehend, since it contradicts the normal pattern in society for exchanging ideas. Workers have an investment in their own views and will often attempt to convince the client of their validity. We are used to arguing our viewpoint by using every means possible to substantiate it as fact. New workers in particular feel it is essential to present their credentials to clients in order to convince them that they know what they are talking about. In reality, however, our ideas about life, our values, and even our "facts" are constantly changing and evolving. A cursory reading of child-rearing manuals would convince anyone that the hard and fast rules of yesterday are often reversed by the theories of today. I have found that workers are often most dogmatic in relation to areas where they feel most uncertain.

The skill of sharing data in a way that is open for examination means that the worker must qualify statements in order to help the client sort out the difference between reality and the worker's sense of reality. Rather than being a salesperson for an idea, the worker should present it with all of its limitations. A confident and honest use of expressions such as "this is the way I see it" or " this is what I believe, which doesn't mean it's true" or "many people believe" will begin to convey to the client the tentativeness of the worker's beliefs. The worker must encourage the client to challenge these ideas when they do not ring true to the client. Any nonverbal signals of disagreement mean that the worker needs to reach for the underlying questions. For example, "You don't look like you agree with what I just said. How do you see it?" The client's different opinions need to be respected and valued. Even if all the experts support the idea, fact, or value at issue, it will only have meaning for the client if and when the client finds it useful. In many ways, the worker is a model of someone who is still involved in a search for reality. Every idea, no matter how strongly held, needs to be open to challenge by the evidence of the senses. The worker is asking the client to do the same in relation to life, and the client should not expect any less of the worker. Schwartz (1961) sums this up:

> As he (the worker) helps them to evaluate the evidence they derive from other sources—their own experiences, the experiences of others, and their collaboration in ideas—so must he submit his own evidence to the process of critical examination. When the worker understands that he is but a single element in the totality of the [group] member's experience, and when he is able to use this truth rather than attempt to conquer it, he has taken the first step toward helping the member to free himself from authority without rejecting it (p. 25).

Ethical Dilemmas in Withholding Data

The question of providing data has taken on increased complexity as governments and other funding agencies introduced economic and political issues into the equation. For example, cost-containment efforts in the health care system have led to government and private third-party payers developing standard of care that dictate how long, on average, a patient should remain hospitalized after a specific procedure. Reimbursement to the hospital is of a fixed amount, which means patients who leave the hospital early produce income for the hospital, while those who stay longer cause the hospital to lose money. Social workers often feel pressured to help "empty the bed" quicker. In some settings, the social work department has defined this as one of its major roles and may even be viewed as a "revenue-generating center" if it does its work effectively.

The ethical dilemma emerges when a patient, family members, or even the social worker feels that a patient may not be ready for discharge for any number of reasons, some unrelated to strict medical factors, perhaps more related to psychosocial issues or the availability of suitable community resources. It will be argued in Chapter 18 that the social worker has a responsibility to help the client to negotiate the system, which includes working to advocate for the client's interest. That discussion will be left for later. The question here is whether the social worker should inform the patient of his or her right to appeal a decision to discharge the patient early, even if the patient does not ask. What if the medical or administrative staff specifically asks front-line staff not to share such information unless it is requested?

Another, even more striking, example comes from the political controversy surrounding a decision of the Supreme Court of the United States (in May 1991), which supported the right of the government to cut off funding for family planning centers that informed pregnant clients, many of whom were young, poor, and persons of color, of the availability of the option of abortion. Even if clients requested information on this option for dealing with an unwanted pregnancy, or the client's health and safety might be in danger, any center that provided such information or referred a client to an alternative source of counseling, where such information might be available, would lose its funding. Many centers indicated an unwillingness to accept such a restriction on free speech and a client's right to be fully informed so that they could make a sound, personal decision on the issue. However, what if a center decided that continuing to provide family planning services to poor women was such a crucial factor that they would accept this restriction? For many social workers, regardless of their views on the issue of abortion, denying access to this information to women dependent upon public social services is sexist, racist, and classist. Should a social worker try to subvert the policy? Should a social worker refuse to work in such a setting?

The NASW Code of Ethics (1997) would define the social worker's responsibility to the client in both of these examples. The ethical worker would need to make available to the client all information required by the client to make a sound personal decision about her health care or her options in the face of unwanted pregnancy. Acting ethically, however, might require courage and might well involve personal risk. This represents another example of how practice may be affected as much by ideological, financial, and political issues as by theories of human behavior.

HELPING THE CLIENT TO SEE LIFE IN NEW WAYS

A specific form of data was viewed as important enough to be included as a separate skill category. These are the skills by which the worker helps clients to reexamine perceptions (cognitions) about themselves, their life situations, or important persons or systems in the client's life (e.g., husband, parent, the school). Concepts from cognitive-behavioral therapy approaches were discussed in Chapter 1 in the section dealing with alternative approaches to practice. To summarize briefly, clients have developed their views of life subjectively. Given the difficulties involved in communications, they quite possibly distort other people's actions or have internalized perceptions of themselves and their life experiences that lead to negative feelings and self-defeating behaviors. By exploring alternative views in collaboration with the client, the worker attempts to help a client rethink his or her life situation and correct negative and inaccurate "automatic thoughts" and perceptions.

One way in which the worker may do this is by identifying the part of the system or the important person that may still be reaching out to the client. In a way, the worker plays the role of the missing person in the interview, articulating what might be the thoughts and feelings lying beneath the surface. For example, here is an excerpt from an interview between a school social worker and an adolescent who is having trouble in a class.

> **Client:** Mr. Brown is always after me, always putting me down when I'm late with my work. I think he hates me.
>
> **Social Worker:** You know, it could be that Mr. Brown knows that you're having trouble keeping up and is really worried about your failing. He may be keeping after you to try to get you going again.
>
> **Client:** Well, it doesn't help. All it makes me do is want to miss his class.
>
> **Social Worker:** He might not realize that what he says makes you feel so badly. Maybe it would help if I could let him know that you feel he is really mad at you.

The work continued with a discussion of the student's fears of what might happen if the counselor talked to the teacher and the counselor's reassurance about how he would handle it. Mr. Brown was surprised at the student's feelings. He had been frustrated because he felt the student didn't care about school. A joint meeting was held to begin to discuss what each really felt in relation to the child's schoolwork. This started to open doors for collaboration.

After a period of bad experiences, the blocks in the reality of the relationship become the client's (and sometimes the system's) only view of reality itself. The worker needs to help the client explore this maladaptive pattern and to break the cycle that prevents the client from connecting to people and systems that are important for her or his success. At these moments a worker offers the possibility of hope and some next step by being able to share a view of others in the system that allows the client to glimpse some possibility of mutual attraction. This is only possible when workers themselves see these possibilities which have been described earlier as the areas of common ground. When a worker can help a teenager see that his parents' setting of curfew limits may be a reflection of caring for him as well as a recognition that he is growing up, the worker has not solved the problem, but at least he has put a new light on the interaction. The child care worker who helps a resident see that a parent who misses visits may not be saying that he doesn't care for the child, but rather that he really cares too much, also holds out the possibility of reconciliation.

The finding of my earlier research (Shulman, 1978) on this particular skill was not strong; however, it correlated with helping to develop a working relationship, perhaps indicating that the importance of sharing new ways of perceiving other people is not in its content but rather in its impact on the relationship with the worker. The client will have to revise some thinking about people and systems during the time between or after sessions, based upon personal experiences. It takes many years to build up stereotypes of oneself, parents, systems, and people in authority, and it will take more than the worker's words to change them. In expressing these alternative views that can help the client see strengths and mutual attraction, the worker is making an important statement about views of life. The willingness to see the positive side in people's behavior and not to be a harsh judge of people's weaknesses may say a great deal to clients about how the worker might view them. This could contribute to strengthening the working relationship.

SESSIONAL ENDING AND TRANSITION SKILLS

As with beginnings and middles, endings contain their own unique dynamics and special requirements for worker skills. I have described this phase elsewhere as the **resolution stage**. It is not unusual to find workers carrying out their sessional contracting, demonstrating sensitive work with clients on their concerns, and then ending a session without a resolution of the work. By resolution of the work, I am not suggesting that each session end neatly, with all issues fully discussed, ambivalence gone, and next steps carefully planned. A sign of advanced skill is a worker's tolerance for ambiguity and uncertainness which may accompany the end of a session dealing with difficult work. If uncertainty is present for a client at the end of a session, then the resolution stage might consist of identifying the status of the discussion. The five skills discussed in the balance of this section include summarizing, generalizing, identifying next steps, rehearsal, and identifying "doorknob" communications.

Before describing these skills, it is important to comment on the question of client activity between sessions. Workers sometimes act as if clients have no life between sessions. They review an individual counseling session or a group meeting and then prepare to pick up the next session "where we left off."

The worker needs to realize that the client has had life experiences, contacts with other helping systems (e.g., family or friends), new problems that may have emerged during the week, and time to think about problems discussed in the previous session. A worker may be surprised, after having given much consideration as to how to help a client with a particular problem, to discover that the client has resolved the issue between sessions. It would be a mistake not to recognize and legitimate these between-session activities. That is one of the reasons for the importance of the sessional contracting skill described at the beginning of this chapter.

The Skill of Summarizing

In many ways, the client is learning about life and trying to develop new skills for managing it in more satisfying ways. It can be important to use the last moments of a session to help the client identify what has been learned. How does the client add up the experiences? What new insights does the client have in understanding relationships to others? What has the client identified as the next, most urgent set of tasks? What are the areas the client feels hopeless about, at a loss as to what to do, and needing to continue to discuss? I believe the process of **summarizing** can help a client secure the grasp of learning. Sometimes the client may summarize the work, other times the worker may try, and sometimes they can do it together. It is important to note that summarizing is not required in all sessions. This is not an automatic ritual, but rather, a skill to be employed at key moments.

The skill is illustrated in the following excerpt from an interview with a mildly mentally challenged 16-year-old boy, who is discussing his relationship with his mother, who he feels is overprotective. After a painful session in which the worker has asked the youngster to examine his own part in maintaining the problem, the resolution stage begins.

> (John paused and seemed thoughtful.)
>
> **Worker:** This hasn't been easy, John; it's never easy to take a look at your own actions this way. Tell me, what do you think about this now? (Silence)
>
> **John:** I guess you're right. As long as I act like a baby, my mother is going to treat me like a baby. I know I shouldn't feel like such a dummy, that I can do some things real well—but you know that's hard to do.
>
> **Worker:** What makes it hard, John?
>
> **John:** I have felt like a dummy for so long, it's hard to change now. I think what was important to me was when you said I have to take responsibility for myself now. I think that's right.
>
> **Worker:** If you did, John, then maybe your mother might see how much you have grown up.

The worker's request for summarizing the work constitutes a demand for work. Her silence allows time for the response, and her support ("This hasn't been easy…") helps the client to face a painful realization.

The Skill of Generalizing

Earlier discussion underlined the importance of moving from the general to the specific as a way of facilitating the immediate work of the client. One example was the worker who responded to a general comment by a mother about the difficulty of raising teenagers with a specific request for information on conflicts that week. As clients deal with the specific details of their life problem by problem and system by system, it is often possible to **generalize** the learning from one experience to a whole category of experiences. This is a key skill of living, since it equips the client to continue without the worker and to use the newfound skills to deal with novel and unexpected experiences. This skill is demonstrated in the continuation of the interview with the adolescent, started in the previous section. The discussion has moved to the importance of talking more honestly with his mother about his feelings. He balks and expresses doubts about being able to do this.

John: I could never tell her how I felt, I just couldn't.

Worker: Why not? What would make it hard?

John: I don't know why, I just couldn't.

Worker: Is it anything like what you felt when we discussed talking to your teacher, Mr. Tracy, about how dumb he sometimes makes you feel in class?

John: I guess so, I guess I'm afraid of what she would say.

Worker: You were afraid then that he would get angry at you or laugh at you, do you remember?

John: Yeah, I remember. He didn't get mad. He told me he hadn't realized I felt that way. He has been nicer to me since then.

Worker: Maybe it's also like that with other people, even your mother. If you could find a way to tell her how you felt, she could understand better. Do you remember how proud you were of yourself after you did it, even though you were scared?

Generalizing from the experience with the teacher is an important learning tool. A life skill, such as the importance of begin direct with your feelings, becomes clearer as clients observe its power in different situations.

The Skill of Identifying Next Steps

We have all experienced at one time or another the frustration of participating in some form of work that goes for naught because of lack of follow-up. A good example is a committee or staff meeting in which decisions are made but the division of labor for implementing the decisions is overlooked, and no action follows. Conscious effort must be made by the worker to help the client **identify the next steps** involved in the work. No matter what the situation, no matter how impossible it may seem, some next step is possible, and the worker will ask the client to discuss it. Next steps must be specific; that is, the general goal the client wishes to achieve must be broken down into manageable parts. In the example used in this section, next steps included helping the youngster to plan to spend some time thinking of some of the things he could do differently to help his mother see another side of him, identifying what he felt about the relationship, and deciding to confront his mother with his true feelings.

The next step for an unemployed mother on welfare who needs to find a job might include exploring day care centers for her child and meeting with an employment counselor. The next step for a couple in marital counseling, who feel their relationship is worsening and they don't seem to be getting anywhere, might be to identify specific areas of difficulty for discussion the following week. In essence, the identification of next steps represents another demand for work on the client. Lack of planning by the client does not always represent poor life management skills. It may also be another form of resistance. It may have been difficult to talk about a tough subject, but it can be even more difficult to do something about it. By demanding attention to future, specific actions, the worker may surface another level of fear, ambivalence, and resistance that needs to be dealt with.

Sometimes the expression of understanding, support, and expectation by the worker is all the client needs to mobilize resources. There may be no easy way for the client to undertake the task, no simple solution, no easy resolution when two genuinely conflicting needs are evident. For the client, verbalizing the dilemma to an understanding and yet demanding worker may be the key to movement. At other times, the specifics of how to carry out the act may require help. For example, the client may need some information about community resources.

In the example of our adolescent, where the next step involved implementing some difficult interpersonal strategy, the next described skill was crucial.

The Skill of Rehearsal

Talking about confronting another person around difficult, interpersonal material is one thing, but actually doing it is quite another. A client who protests, "I don't know what to say" may be identifying an important source of blockage. A worker can help by offering the safe confines of the interview situation as a place for the client to **rehearse**—that is, practice exactly what to say. The worker takes the role of the other person (boss, teacher, husband, mother, doctor, etc.) and feeds back to the client possible reactions to the client's efforts. All too often, the worker skips this simple and yet powerful device for aiding a client by saying, "When the time comes, you will know what to say." Words do not come easily for us, especially in relation to our most difficult feelings. With the help of a worker, a client may be able to find a way of saying what must be said, and with some successful rehearsal under the belt, may feel a bit more confident about doing it. We return to the illustration at the point the teenager says that he does not know what to say.

> **Worker:** Look, John, perhaps it would be easier for you if you practiced what you would say to your mother. I'll be your mother, and you say it to me. I can tell you how it sounds.
>
> **John:** You will be my mother? That's crazy! (Laughing)
>
> **Worker:** (Also laughing) It's not so crazy. I'll pretend I'm your mother. Come on, give it a try.
>
> **John:** (With a lot of anger) "You have to stop treating me like a baby!" Is that what you mean, is that what I should say?
>
> **Worker:** Yes, that's what I mean. Now if I was your mother I could tell you were really angry at me, but I'm not sure I would understand why. I might think to myself, "That's just like John, he always runs around hollering like that." Maybe you could begin a bit calmer and tell me what you want to talk about.
>
> **John:** I don't understand.
>
> **Worker:** Let me try. I'll be you for a minute. "Mom, there is something I want to talk to you about—about the way we get along. It's something that really bothers me, makes me sad and sometimes angry." Now I don't know, perhaps that's not so good either. What do you think?
>
> **John:** I see what you mean. Tell her I want to talk to her about how we get along. That's good, but I don't like the part about being sad.
>
> **Worker:** Why not? It's true, isn't it?
>
> **John:** I don't like to admit that to her.
>
> **Worker:** You mean you don't want to let her know how much it hurts you? (John nods.) How will she ever understand if you don't tell her? Maybe there are things she would like to tell you, but she feels the same way.

As the conversation continued, the worker and John explored the difficult problem of real communication between a teenager and his mother, with this case a special variation on the theme because of the mental challenge. John tried to formulate what he would say, using some of the worker's ideas and incorporating some of his own. The worker offered to speak to John's mother or to be there during the discussion if John wished. The illustration underlines the preparation value of rehearsal, as well as the way in which role play can reveal additional blocks to the client's ability to deal with important people in his life. A worker who thinks a marvelous job has been done in helping a client achieve a new level of understanding and readiness to deal effectively with an important person may find additional work needs to be done when the client formulates the words to be used. In this case, the difficulty in sharing the client's sense of hurt with his mother was important, unfinished business.

The Skill of Identifying "Doorknob" Communications

A **"doorknob" communication** is shared as the client leaves the office with his or her hand on the doorknob. This commonly observed phenomenon, described in the literature of psychotherapy, actually refers to any comments of significance raised by the client towards the end of a session when there is too little time to deal with them. We have all experienced a session with a client, or a conversation with a friend, when after a relatively innocuous discussion he says, "There is just one thing that happened this week." Then we hear that he lost his job or found out that his girlfriend was pregnant or received an eviction notice or noticed a strange lump in his groin. When reflecting on the session, the worker may see where the first clues to the concern were presented indirectly in the beginning phase. It is also possible that there were no clues at all.

A doorknob comment is a signal to the worker of the client's ambivalence about discussing an area of work. The concern is raised at a time when it surely cannot be fully discussed. It may be a taboo area or one experienced as too painful to talk about. Whatever the reason, the desire to deal with the concern finally overwhelms the forces of resistance. Time has its impact on the interview, and the urgency of the concern, coupled with the pressures created by the lack of time, finally results in the expression of the issue. This kind of comment is actually a special case of the general problem of obstacles blocking the client's ability to work. As with all forms of resistance, it is a natural part of the process and provides the worker with an opportunity to educate the client about the client's way of working.

The skill would involve the worker identifying the process for the client. For example, in a session with a young woman concerned about her marriage, at the end of the second session the client directly revealed a difficult sexual problem between herself and her husband. The worker responded directly:

> **Worker:** You know you have just raised a really important issue which we will not have time to talk about. You raised it at the end of a session. Were you feeling it was too tough to talk about, too uncomfortable?
> **Client:** (Brief silence) It is embarrassing to talk like this to a stranger.
> **Worker:** I can understand how it would be hard to discuss sex, I mean really talk about it, with anyone. You know, it's quite common for people to be reluctant to discuss this subject directly, and they often raise these kinds of difficult areas right at the end of the session, just like you did. (The client smiles at this.) Would it help if we started next session talking a bit about what makes it so hard for you to talk about sex? That might make it easier for us to discuss this important area. What do you think?
> **Client:** That sounds OK to me. This is a hard one for me, and I would like to discuss it.
> **Worker:** I think you are making a good start even raising it at the end.

The worker did not blame the client for her difficulty and, instead, offered support for the strength she had shown in raising the issue. By identifying the doorknob nature of the comment, she is starting to build into the interview comments on the way in which the two of them work. The client's sophistication about how she works will increase, and after a number of such incidents, she can begin to understand and control how she introduces material into the interviews. In addition, the discussion of the source of the embarrassment in the interview will open up related feelings about the difficulty of discussing sex in our society, as well as the couple's problems with open communication in this area. The discussion of the process in the interview will lead directly into work on the content—another illustration of the process-content connection.

This discussion of sessional ending skills brings to a close our analysis of the work phase. The purpose has been to identify some of the key dynamics in giving and taking help that follow the negotiation of a joint working contract. The discussing of doorknob comments is an appropriate one to serve as a transition to the next chapter on the skills of the ending and transition phase. In many ways, the last portion of the work with a client may have a doorknob quality in that some of the most important and hard-to-discuss issues may make their appearance at this time. This phase of work provides an opportunity for the most powerful learning of the entire encounter. It does not always happen that way, however, and in the next chapter we will discuss why the ending phase can create problems if not handled well, or solve others if the worker is skillful.

CHAPTER SUMMARY

A session in the middle phase of practice can be understood as having four stages: preliminary (sessional tuning in); beginning (sessional contracting); middle (work); and sessional ending and transitions. The indirect nature of client communications at the start of a session, often related to client ambivalence, makes it important for the worker to tune in to potential themes of concern prior to the session and to remain tentative in the beginning phase, listening for cues of underlying issues. As a middle-phase session proceeds, the worker uses a number of skills that were grouped together in this chapter and called skill factors. These are designed to help the client tell his or her story and to do so with affect. They are also important for the worker to be able to challenge the "illusion of work" and to be able to find the connections between the process (way of working) in a session and the content (substantive areas of work). These skill factors included elaboration, empathy, sharing of the worker's feelings, pointing out obstacles to work, making a demand for work, identifying process and content connections, sharing of worker data, and helping the client to see life in a new way. A number of skills were also identified for bringing a session to a close and helping the client to make the transition to post-session activities or the next session.

GLOSSARY

Act out To communicate thoughts and feelings through behavior, often in a disruptive manner.

Burnout "A nontechnical term to describe workers who feel apathy or *anger* as a result of on-the-job stress and frustration. Burnout is found in social work and other fields where workers have more responsibility than control" (Barker, 1991, p. 27).

Checking for the underlying ambivalence Exploring client ambivalence that may be hidden by an artificial agreement.

Content The substance of the work, consisting of ideas, issues, problems, concerns, and so on, which are part of the working contract.

Correlation A non-directional measure of association between two variables.

Counter-transference "A set of conscious or unconscious emotional reactions to a client experienced by the social worker or other professional, usually in a clinical setting" (Barker, 1991, p. 52).

Detecting and challenging the obstacles to work Perceiving and then confronting directly the obstacles that impede the client's work.

Doorknob communication A client communication usually shared at the very end of a session (hand on the doorknob) or in the last sessions.

Elaborating Helping the client tell his or her story.

Empathy Helping the client share the affective part of the message.

Exploring client resistance Identifying and discussing, with the client, the meaning of the signals of a client's resistance.

Facilitative confrontation Drawing upon the fund of positive working relationship with the client to facilitate the work of the client through confrontation.

Feeling-thinking-doing connection A process in which how we feel affects how we act and think, and how we act affects how we think and feel.

First offering An indirect communication from the client that offers the worker a clue as to the nature of the client's concerns. Often followed by a second (more direct) and even third or fourth offerings designed to increase the clarity of the signal.

Focused listening Concentrating on a specific part of the client's message.

Generalizing Using specific instances to help the client identify general principles (e.g., the importance of being honest about one's feelings in different situations).

Helping the client to see life in new ways Skills designed to help clients modify their cognitions about themselves and their world (e.g., reframing a situation in a more positive way).

Holding to focus Asking the client to stay focused on one theme as opposed to jumping from issue to issue. It is one of the demand-for-work skills.

Identifying content and process connections Identifying connections between the content of the work and the way (process) of working.

Identifying the next steps Helping the client to develop ideas about future actions based upon current discussion (usually used at the end of a session).

Illusion of work A process in which the worker and the client engage in a conversation that is empty and devoid of real meaning. It may be a form of passive resistance in which the client tries to please the worker by pretending to work.

Looking for trouble when everything is going the worker's way Exploring hidden ambivalence or a negative response when a client immediately responds positively to a difficult suggestion.

Moving from the general to the specific Helping a client to share specific details that help to elaborate an issue raised on a more general level.

Process The interaction that takes place between the worker and the client during an interview, or between the client and another client, which characterizes the "way of working" as compared to the content of the work.

Parallel process The way in which the process on one level (e.g., supervisor-worker) parallels the process on another level (e.g., worker-client).

Rehearsal Giving the client an opportunity to practice a difficult next step in an informal role play, with the worker usually playing the role of the other person.

Resistance Behavior on the part of the client that appears to resist the worker's efforts to deal with the client's problems. Resistance may be open (active) or indirect (passive). It is usually a sign of the client's pain associated with the work.

Resolution stage The stage of work in which a session is brought to some form of closure or resolution, which may include recognizing the lack of closure and determining next steps.

Sessional contracting The skill usually employed at the start of a session to clarify the immediate work at hand.

Sessional ending and transition skills The skills designed to bring a session to a close and to make the connections between a single session and future work or issues in the life of the client.

Sessional tuning in The skill designed to sensitize the worker, prior to each session, to the potential themes that may emerge during the work.

Skill factor A set of closely related worker skills.

Sharing worker's data Sharing data such as facts, opinions, and value judgments.

Sharing worker's feelings Appropriately sharing with the client the worker's own affect. These feelings should be shared in pursuit of professional purposes as the worker implements the professional function.

Summarizing Helping a client to identify the main themes of discussion during a session.

NOTES

1. For an excellent discussion of themes of concern associated with AIDS, see G. Getzel, "Group Work with Gay Men with AIDS," *Social Casework, 2* (1989): 172–179.

2. For examples of efforts to understand normative life crises, see Jack Block and Norman Haan, *Lives through Time* (Berkeley, CA: Bancroft Books, 1971); Erik H. Erikson, *Childhood and Society* (New York: W.W. Norton, 1950); Barbara Fried, *The Middle-Age Crisis* (New York: Harper & Row, 1967); and Joan Huber (ed.), *Changing Women in a Changing Society* (Chicago: University of Chicago Press, 1973). One example of an author who has explored this universal struggle between a father and a son is Chaim Potok; see *My Name Is Asher Lev* (New York: Alfred A. Knopf, 1976) and *The Chosen* (New York: Alfred A. Knopf, 1976).

3. For readings related to the area of burnout, see J. Borland, "Burnout Among Workers and Administrators," *Health and Social Work, 6* (1981): 73–78; Daley, M.R., "Preventing Worker Burnout in Child Welfare," *Child Welfare, 58* (1979): 443–450.

4. *Note:* Citations for findings from the 1978 study may be made to one of two publications. When findings have been discussed in the more widely available journal article, "A Study of Practice Skills," *Social Work, 23* (July 1978): 274–281, this citation is used. For other findings, the reader is referred to the major report, *A Study of the Helping Process.*

5. The use of physical contact with a client is generally problematic for a number of reasons. For many clients, physical contact is experienced as intrusive and may, in fact, recreate feelings associated with abuse and other exploitive situations. The NASW Code of Ethics specifically prohibits such contact as a protection for the client, in particular, against any sexual involvement, which is always unethical. However, in some situations, for example the use of activities in group work (e.g., folk dancing) or touching the hand of an elderly and ill client, physical contact has another and more appropriate meaning.

6. See also Florence Hollis, *Casework: A Psychosocial Therapy* (New York: Random House, 1964), pp. 154–155.

7. This expression was used by my colleague, Alex Gitterman, during a jointly led workshop.

5

Endings and Transitions

CHAPTER OUTLINE

The Dynamics and Skills of Endings
The Skills of Transitions
Some Variations on the Endings Themes

This chapter will complete our presentation of the phases of work. Our focus will be on the ending and transition phase of practice. We will explore the unique dynamics and skills associated with bringing the helping process to a close and helping the client to make the appropriate transitions. Practice examples will illustrate how this phase can be the most powerful and meaningful phase of work as the client makes the "third" decision—the decision to deal with core issues that may have only been hinted at in the earlier phases. We will also examine the danger of this phase becoming a moratorium on work, in which both the client and the worker participate in an illusion without substance. Specific skills for increasing the possibility of positive endings and transitions will be described and illustrated.

In the beginning phase, clients face a "first decision." They must decide if they are prepared to engage with the worker—to lower defenses if needed and to begin to work. The "second decision" is associated with the middle phase of work. After clients understand that emotional pain might be involved and that they might have to take some responsibility for their own part in their problems, they have to decide if they will continue the work. This decision marks the transition from the beginning to the middle phase of practice.

The "*third decision*" is the one that clients must make as they approach the end of the working relationship, when very little time may be left. The ending phase offers the greatest potential for powerful and important work. Clients feel a sense of urgency as they realize there is little time left, and this can lead to the introduction of some of the more difficult and important themes of concern. The emotional dynamics between worker and client are also heightened in this phase as each prepares to move away from the other. Termination of the relationship can evoke powerful feelings in both client and worker, and discussion of these can often be connected by the worker to the client's general concerns and tasks. The ending phase holds tremendous potential for work, yet ironically this phase is often the least effective. Missed appointments, lateness, apathy, acting out, and regressions to earlier, less mature patterns of behavior are often characteristic of this phase of work. Moreover, these behaviors can be observed in the actions of the worker as well as the client.

In many ways the ending sessions are the most difficult ones for both worker and client. The source of the strain stems from the general difficulty we have in dealing with the ending of important relationships. The worker-client association is a specific example of this larger problem. It can be painful to terminate a close relationship; when you have invested yourself meaningfully in a relationship, have shared some of your most important feelings, and have given and taken help from another human being, the bond that develops is strong. This is true with friends, family, working colleagues—in fact, with all relationships. Our society has done little to train us how to handle a separation; in fact, the general norm is to deny feelings associated with it. For example, when a valued colleague leaves an agency, the farewell party is often an attempt, usually unsuccessful, to cover the sadness with fun. The laughter at such parties is usually a bit flat. Similarly, children and counselors who have developed an intimate, living relationship in summer camps usually end by resolving to meet again at a winter reunion—a reunion that often does not take place. When someone moves to another city, leaving a close and valued friend behind, the two may occupy themselves with elaborate plans for keeping in touch by mail, phone calls, and visits, rather than mutually acknowledging the fact that the relationship will never be quite the same.

A version of this difficulty in ending can also be seen in professional relationships. Strean (1978) has described the difficulties involved in terminating a close working relationship:[1]

> Whether a social worker-client relationship consists of five interviews or a hundred, if the worker has truly related to the client's expectations, perceptions of himself, and transactions with his social orbit, the client will experience the encounter as meaningful and the worker as someone significant; therefore, separation from this "significant other" will inevitably arouse complex and ambivalent feelings. Still, a long-term relationship with a social worker will probably include more intense emotions at termination than a short-term one. A prolonged relationship has usually stimulated dependency needs and wishes, transference reactions, revelation of secrets, embarrassing moments, exhilaration, sadness, and gladness. The encounter has become part of the client's weekly life, so that ending it can seem like saying good-bye to a valued family member or friend (pp. 227–228).

The extreme illustration of this general difficulty in dealing with endings is in death and dying, and the process of grief. Kübler-Ross (1969) has written with great sensitivity about the phases of dying and how people react to this most permanent separation. The ending of any intimate relationship may resemble, in a less powerful way, the ending process described in her book. Her phases of dying can usefully be adapted to all separations. The ending process in a helping relationship can trigger feelings of the deepest kind in both worker and client. This is the reason why there is potential for powerful work during this phase as well as ineffective work if the feelings are not dealt with. In this chapter, we will explore the dynamics of the ending phase, identify some of the central skills required to make effective endings, and discuss how workers can help clients make transitions to new experiences.

THE DYNAMICS AND SKILLS OF ENDINGS

Schwartz (1971) described the ending phase in the group context:

> In the final phase of work—that which I have called "transitions and endings"—the worker's skills are needed to help the members use him and each other to deal with

the problem of moving from one experience to another. For the worker it means moving off the track of the members' experience and life process, as he has, in the beginning, moved onto it....The point is that beginnings and endings are hard for people to manage; they often call out deep feeling in both worker and members; and much skill is needed to help people to help each other through these times (pp. 17–18).

One of the dynamics that makes endings hard has already been mentioned. This is the pain associated with bringing to an end a relationship into which one has invested a great deal. In addition to the pain, there is a form of guilt. Clients may feel that if they had worked harder in the relationship, played their parts more effectively, and risked more, then perhaps they could have done a better job. This guilt sometimes emerges indirectly with their saying, "Can't I have more time?" As with many of the feelings in the ending phase, this sense of guilt is often shared by the worker, who may feel that he or she should have been more helpful to the client. Perhaps if the worker had been more experienced, more capable, he or she could have been more helpful about some of the unresolved issues. Rather than recognizing the fact of being just a part of the client's life, the worker tends at this time to feel responsible for the client. Instead of understanding that the client will need to work continually on life's problems, the worker feels guilty at not having "solved" them all. Social work students often articulate this feeling as follows: "If only the client had a *real* worker!" Usually, they are underestimating the help that they have given.

The flow of affect between worker and client is heightened during the ending phase. Because of the general difficulty of talking about negative and positive feedback, both worker and client may have many unstated feelings that need to be dealt with in the final phase. Things may have been left unsaid because of taboos against honest talk about the role of authority. This theme needs to be discussed before the relationship can properly end. For example, there may be things the worker did and said that made the client angry. The reverse might also be true, with the worker somewhat frustrated over the client's inability to take risks and to open up with the worker. Providing this feedback, if it is related to the worker's real caring for the client, can serve to clear the air. Even if a client and worker have not been able to get along together and both face the impending separation with a sense of relief, the discussion at the end should be real. What was it about the worker that the client could not relate to? In turn, the client should know what made it difficult for the worker. There may have been misconceptions on the part of either or both parties, and discussing these can help to clear them up. This could be very helpful to the client, who may choose to enter another helping relationship at another time. The importance of feedback to the worker is also obvious. In addition, if the negative feelings are not dealt with, it is not unusual to find a client transferring them to his next worker in the way that we have seen in some of the examples in Chapter 3 on beginnings.

Even more difficult for worker and client to handle than the negative feelings may be the positive ones. It is not easy for any of us to tell someone close to us, particularly someone in authority, that they have meant a great deal to us. Moreover, accepting these feelings gracefully is something many workers find extremely hard. I have repeatedly observed workers responding to a client's genuine expression of thanks for all that the worker has done by protesting, "It wasn't really me, I didn't do that much, it was really all your work." One student in a social work training program asked during a class if it was all right for her to accept a fruitcake offered to her by an elderly client at the end of their work together. This was not a case in which a client was trying to pay a worker for her services, which were normally free. It was simply this old woman's way of saying "thank you" to a worker who cared. I asked the student if the fruitcake looked good and suggested that if it did, the student ought to take it.

When I press workers as to the cause of their embarrassment when clients express positive feelings, they usually point to the general cultural barriers against appearing immodest, as well as their belief that they could not have really given that much help. The second response reflects an underestimation of the effect of the help given. Clients respond with great feeling to a caring, honest worker. They are not usually as critical about what the worker might have done as the worker is self-critical. Mutual sharing of positive feelings is important at the end of a relationship, cultural barriers notwithstanding, because this enables both client and worker to value what has taken place between them and to bring it properly to an end. Both client and worker can carry feelings of regret for unspoken words long after they have stopped seeing each other, thus making the actual ending process protracted and more difficult. The problem with delaying endings is that it ties up energy that both parties need to invest in new relationships.

The timing of this phase depends upon the length of the relationship. For example, in weekly counseling over the period of one year, approximately the last eight weeks constitute the ending process. In short-term work—for example, six sessions—evidence of feelings about endings may emerge in the fourth or fifth session as the worker receives subtle cues to the client's reactions. While these cues mark the beginning of the ending phase, thoughts about the end are present even in the beginning. It is not unusual for a client to inquire early in the process, even after a first session that was helpful, how long the sessions will continue. Time is an important factor, and clients will orient themselves accordingly. A long break in the work phase, whether caused by the worker's illness, a vacation, or perhaps the Christmas season, can provoke ending feelings as the client associates the break in the work with the ending to come. It is not uncommon to observe apathy, withdrawal, and other premature ending symptoms immediately after such a break.

Schwartz has outlined the stages of the ending process as follows: denial, indirect and direct expressions of anger, mourning, trying it on for size, and finally, the "farewell-party syndrome." Each of these is discussed now in more detail, and the required worker skills, as suggested by Schwartz, are identified and illustrated.

The Denial Phase

Because of the general difficulty of facing feelings associated with the ending of important relationships, the first stage is often marked by evidence of denial. The client neither admits to the impending ending nor acknowledges his feelings about it. During this first phase, the client may refuse to discuss the ending, insist on a nonexistent agreement with the worker to continue the sessions long past the ending date, "forget" that an ending date has been set, or request that sessions be prolonged because the client feels "unready." Unless the worker raises the ending issue, the client may simply ignore it right up until the last session. Workers also may handle their feelings towards endings through denial and avoidance as, for example, when they leave a job. Many clients have greeted a new worker with stories of how their former workers had simply told them that they were leaving the agency during their last session. These clients are often left with the feeling that their workers did not care about them. In reality, these workers' denials are often rooted in the fact that they cared very much but were not able to face their own feelings.

It is important that workers be able to manage their feelings in this stage if they are to be able to help their clients manage theirs. Feelings about ending with the client as well as feelings about ending with the setting, supervisors, and colleagues need to be addressed. A not uncommon phenomenon in workshops I have provided for field social work field practicum instructors is for a field instructor to present his or her problem with a student having trouble ending with clients at the end of the school year. When I inquire if the supervisor has begun to discuss endings with the student, the supervisor is shocked to recognize that she or he is also avoiding dealing with endings.[2] Once again, more is being caught by the student than taught by the field instructor.

It is important that the ending process provide enough time for the worker and client to sort out their feelings and use this phase productively. A sudden ending will be difficult for both worker and client and will cut short necessary work. Since the worker wants the ending to be experienced as a process rather than as a sharp closure, the skill of **pointing out endings early** should be employed some time before the relationship is to end. At the appropriate time, given the length of the relationship, the worker will remind the client of the impending ending. An example from a child welfare setting will help to illustrate this skill. The client was a young man who had been a ward of the agency for eight years. The worker had been in contact with him for the past two years. In two months, the client would be 18 years old, and at that time he would be leaving the care of the agency. The worker set the ending process in motion by reminding the client of the ending date.

> **Worker:** Before we start to talk about that job interview next week, I wanted to remind you that we only have eight more weeks before you leave the agency. You have been with the "Aid" [the term used by clients to describe the Children's Aid Society] for a long time, and I thought you might want to talk about the change.
>
> **Client:** Only eight weeks? I hadn't realized it was coming so soon. That's great! After eight years I'm finally on my own; no more checking in, no more "Aid" on my back. You know, I'm going to really need that job now, and I'm worried about the interview.
>
> **Worker:** What's worrying you?

By commenting on the limited time left, the worker set the process in motion. The client's reaction was in part denial of the impact of the ending and in part recognition of its importance. Schwartz has described the "graduation quality" of endings, when clients feel excited and ready to test their ability to make it on their own. The quick switch from the ending topic to the job interview represented resistance. The client did not want to talk about it right then. The worker was also reluctant to discuss it and thus allowed it to be dropped easily. In addition, he had identified the issue of ending only in terms of the agency, instead of also in relation to their work together. This evasion by the worker signals his own ambivalence. Nevertheless, the statement of the impending ending is enough to set the process in motion.

In the following example, the worker presses for the ending feelings, but the client resists.

> **Jane:** I will be leaving the office at the beginning of May, which gives us four more times together. I thought we might want to talk about this.
>
> **Thelma:** I don't understand—why are you leaving?

Jane: I'm not sure if you remember, Thelma, but I mentioned to you last October that I was a student, which means I will be leaving my placement in early May. (Silence)

Jane: Thelma, you have turned quiet. What are you thinking about?

Thelma: (After a pause) I don't know what I am going to do now. I don't understand why you have to go.

Jane: Are you worried about what is going to happen with you after I leave? (Silence)

Thelma: Yes, but you are not leaving for a month, right?

Jane: Yes. I know that we have been seeing each other for many months now, and talking about my leaving is hard, it is hard for me too—but we both need to share our feelings and thoughts about this. (Silence)

Jane: I know that I am feeling a little sad, we have been through some tough times together. It's tough letting go.

Thelma: (Looking down…picked up a piece of her child's schoolwork) Hey, did you know that Gladys will be going into grade 2 next year. Ivan and I went up to the parent-teacher meeting last Friday and the teacher told us then. She even showed us some of her schoolwork. She is doing so well.

I tried to have Thelma elaborate on her feelings about the ending of our sessions, but she denied and avoided the opportunities, and the remainder of the session covered some superficial topics and how her children were doing.

Although the client moved away from the painful work, the worker's strong message through the demand for work has sent a signal that this topic must be addressed. The worker understands and accepts the client's reluctance to continue, demonstrating a respect for the client's defenses. The stage has been set, and the worker will return to the ending theme in the weeks to come.

Indirect and Direct Expressions of Anger

The denial stage of ending is often followed by the indirect or direct expression of anger by the client toward the worker. The circumstances of endings may vary; for example, the worker may be leaving the agency, as opposed to the client ending contact. While these circumstances may affect the intensity of the angry feelings, these feelings are usually present even in those situations where the ending seems perfectly reasonable. The anger may be expressed directly, by the client challenging the worker who has changed jobs, "How could you leave if you really cared for me?" The ending is perceived as a form of rejection, and the worker must be careful to face these feelings directly and not try to avoid them.

Alternatively, the cues to the underlying feelings may be communicated indirectly—for example, by lateness or missed sessions. Conversations with clients may take on an element of antagonism, and the worker may sense the hostility. Sarcasm, battles over minor issues, or indications by the client of being glad to see the relationship finally end may also be evidence of this reaction. However, under the angry feelings are often sad feelings. It is therefore important to allow the expression of anger and to acknowledge it even though the worker's instincts make it hard to do so.

The skill involved here, as with all stages of the ending process, calls for the worker to respond directly to the indirect cues to ending stages. The worker, perceiving these signals, should point out the dynamics of the stage to the client. In the case of anger, the worker should reach past the indirect cue and encourage the client to express any angry feelings directly. The worker should also acknowledge the validity of the feelings and not attempt to talk the client into feeling differently. This direct acknowledgment is important even if the client does not take up the worker's invitation to discuss the anger and instead denies its existence. When the worker **identifies the stage of the ending process,** the client can increase understanding of the experience. This can then free energies for productive participation in the ending-phase work. It is important for the worker to be honest in sharing any personal reactions to the client's anger.

The following illustration involves a worker in a residential setting who was leaving the home to attend graduate school. The day after she announced she was leaving, a young female client had a blow-up at home with her mother and her mother's girlfriend and had to be brought to the center to be "in-house." The example illustrates clearly the struggle for the worker, who must deal with her own guilt and pain at leaving a client to whom she has become very close and a setting in which she has enjoyed working.

> I was sitting with Jane, ready to check in, and I knew by the look on her face that last night was a hard one. I felt two things: first, "This is such bull—it is so easy for her to do well at home, especially since her brother is gone," and second, "I just don't want to have to deal with her being in-house." I had just announced the day before that I was leaving the program, and I was exhausted. She gave me her book, and as I was reading it she started to cry and yell, "I hate your stupid system, I hate this program, I hate you!" As I sat there reading about her night, listening to her yell at me, I thought, "This child will never change." I was ready to give up due to my own exhaustion, but I couldn't let her know that.
>
> Mom wrote that Jane had a really hard night. She refused to clean her room, started throwing things, and called Mom and her lover bitches and homos. When Mom told her to get in the time-out area, Jane hit her. When Mom's lover tried to intervene, Jane kicked her. Mom and her lover eventually left her alone (she's too big for them to restrain) and she calmed down after a while and went to sleep.
>
> I knew she was going to have an in-house suspension, and she knew too. I just didn't want to deal with it. She was still crying and saying, "I hate you! I'm glad you're leaving!" All of this process took about two minutes and then I knew I had to speak. I tried really hard to get my tone of voice to be supportive, yet confronting, and I said, "What do you think made you have such a hard time last night?" She kept crying and yelling, "I don't know!" I thought back to my announcement yesterday and remembered her reaction. "Are you mad at me for leaving?" I asked. She said, "No! I don't care! I hate you! You're a bitch!"
>
> At this point, I was thinking, "Oh yeah! Well you're a brat!" but instead I said, "I understand that you are having feelings about me leaving and that's okay. What's not okay is that you swore at me. You have a reminder for that." (We use reminders for behavior management. When a kid gets a third reminder, they get a time out.)
>
> "I know that my leaving is hard for you. Good-byes are always hard. You and I have worked together for a long time and we've had a lot of fun together. It's going to be hard for me to say good-bye to you, too. The important thing is that you tell me you're mad or whatever feelings you have. It's okay to feel that. It's not okay to swear and it's not okay to hit your mother."
>
> She just continued saying over and over again, "I hate you." I felt irritated again. I said, "We have a choice: we can make the best of the next four weeks and really talk

about what's going to be hard about saying good-bye to each other, or we can struggle and try to hate each other so it won't hurt. You know you're in in-house today because of last night, and we're going to use that time to do a little work around me leaving." With that, she cried louder and yelled, "No!" I could see how upset she was about this. She once told me I was the only person that she felt she could depend on, and here I was leaving her. I felt like saying, "Okay, I won't go back to school, I'll stay here with you." She really pulls at me. So, knowing I had to say something else, I said, "This isn't easy for me either," and then I talked with her about how I felt about leaving her and saying good-bye to·her.

We talked about fun things we did together and looked at pictures, and all through it I kept assuring her that no matter what, I would never forget her. I was trying to keep good boundaries, but I started to really feel the sadness over my leaving. I was leaving a job I love, kids I love, and a team that had become my second family. I felt myself getting too emotional, so I cut the conversation short by saying, "We are going to be able to talk about this a lot before I leave." I was torn about what to do. I thought about continuing the conversation so she could understand that someone really did care about her and that her feelings about me leaving are all very normal. But on the other hand, I felt that if I kept talking about it, I would've cried. When I said we'd be able to talk more about it she said okay, got up, hugged me, cried and said, "I'm going to miss everything about you." Well, that did it. I felt myself wanting to cry and my eyes were getting watery. I walked her over to the in-house area, got her settled, and then composed myself.

I wish that I could've let go of my own sadness. I am usually really good at sticking with hard feelings even though I can relate it to my own life. I sat through a check-in with a kid who was my absolute favorite kid I've ever worked with, and I had to tell him his mother was in the hospital. She went in while he was in school. I was his age when I found out my mother had cancer. He looked at me with tears in his eyes and said, "Is she gonna die?" I could sit with that. I was kind of annoyed that I couldn't stick with the conversation. I think this was different because it was so emotionally charged for me, the team and most of the kids. I also wish I could've addressed her behaviors more directly too.

This excerpt illustrates the importance of supportive supervision. The worker's instincts were on target; however, she was afraid of showing her emotions too directly and was concerned about crying. At the same time, the worker demonstrated good professional work as she self-analyzed her struggle with this most difficult ending. It is important that she did this, so that the process of her ending could be directly synthesized with the content of the work. Most children in residential settings are dealing with profound losses, and yet, the staff and the system often have great difficulty in dealing with losses themselves.

In the following example, the anger is expressed indirectly towards the agency. This meeting had involved a social work student worker, a single mother (Debbie), her 12-year-old son (Mike), and another worker (Liz), who would continue working with Mike in school after the worker left. The worker had been involved with Debbie on a regular basis for most of the year. There were four more meetings planned. Both Liz and Mike had left, and Debbie and the student worker had been discussing future plans for Mike. The worker initiated the discussion on ending.

Worker: I've been thinking that we have just four more meetings together. I'll be finished with school—the time seems to be going quickly.

Debbie: What do you mean? I didn't know that you were in school. Are you not coming after you're finished school? (Debbie sounded shocked; it surprised me that she actually said that she didn't know I was a student, as she'd regularly asked me how school was going.)

Worker: Seems like I shocked you and you shocked me right back when you said that you didn't know I was in school.

Debbie: Yeah, I know you're in school, it's just a surprise that the year has gone so fast.

Worker: I'm feeling both happy and sad—I'm happy about the way things have worked out, and I'm sad that I won't be coming after April.

Debbie: (Starting to speak angrily) Those jerks—you just get someone who you can talk to and then they take them away. Now I have to start all over again with someone else. You know Mike used to be angry...you know...when Trudy (previous worker) would be coming over; but with you, he's always wondering what we're going to do and he likes to see you.

I could feel and accept Debbie's anger at me for leaving and realized how frustrated she'd be, starting over again. She'd paid me quite a compliment and I appreciated it.

Worker: I remember our first meetings, Debbie, when I wasn't sure if we could work together at all. I feel that we've come through a great deal together, and it's been rough at times to talk about some of the things we've talked about. Thank you for telling me about Mike—he and you have made me feel welcome in your home. I've gotten to like you both very much and I'm going to miss you.

Debbie: Then why are you leaving? (Debbie said this quickly, then added abruptly) I know you have to leave. Who will be my new worker?

Worker: That's something I've been wondering about. You've said that you've had a hard time whenever a new worker is involved. Do you think our experience together has given you any ideas about getting to know and work with a new social worker?

Debbie: Yup—if I think he's a jerk I'm going to tell him right away instead of waiting for three months and burning up inside. I'm not going to fool around like I used to.

Worker: That's one of the things I really like about working with you, you give it to me straight. I was honored last week when you told me that you trusted me, and I saw how hard that was for you—that's when you added "almost."

Debbie: Well, I do trust you (she laughed, and added) almost.

Worker: What do you want to be able to do with your new worker?

Debbie: I guess I'll want someone to talk over what happens with Liz and Mike and also how things are going at home for me with Mike—you know, just as things come up.

I explained how cases got assigned at the office and that Sue most likely would be the new worker. Debbie had spoken with Sue a couple of times on another matter but said she didn't know her all that well. We talked a bit more about some of the issues we'd tackled, how things had progressed, fallen back and continued on. As I was walking down the front steps, Debbie called out, "At least I'll see you until the end of April" and I felt warm and sad at the same time.

A number of skills were demonstrated in this excerpt. In addition to dealing with the underlying feelings, the worker began the important transition work. In this case, the transition would be to a new worker. The worker was also using the process in their relationship to help the client work on the content—developing the insights and skills needed to get the help and support she needed. By reflecting back on their own rough beginnings, the worker asked the client to identify her new understandings and to consider how to put them into action with her next worker. In some situations, inviting the new worker to a joint session for the transition can also be helpful.

The Mourning Period

Under the feelings of anger expressed by the client, there are often feelings of sadness. When these emerge, the client begins the mourning stage of the ending process. During this stage, the client experiences fully the feelings he or she may have been struggling hard to suppress. When this happens, some clients are able to express their feelings directly to the worker. For others, the feelings emerge indirectly. A normally active and involved client suddenly seems apathetic and lethargic. Interviews are marked by long periods of silence, slow starts followed by minimal activity, and conversations that seem to trail off rather than end. One worker described arriving at a woman's home to find the blinds drawn at midday and a general feeling of gloom pervading the usually bright room. In part, the difficulty in working reflects the client's unwillingness to open up new areas just when the work seems about to end. In addition, the work left to the end is often the most difficult for the client, adding to the ambivalence. Essentially, the feeling is one of sadness over the ending of a meaningful relationship. The denial and anger are past, and the ending must now be faced.

Two important skills in this phase involve *acknowledging the client's ending feelings* and *sharing the worker's ending feelings*. The skill of acknowledging and sharing worker feelings has already been identified as crucial to the helping process but also difficult for workers to employ. In the ending phase, the difficulty is compounded by the intensity of feelings and our society's taboos against their direct expression. Workers have suggested that even when they did pick up cues to the sadness, they did not acknowledge the feelings because they felt somewhat embarrassed. "How can I tell clients I think they are sad because we won't be seeing each other anymore? It sounds like I'm taking my impact on the client and blowing it out of proportion. And anyway, how will it feel if the client says I'm all wet?" The worker feels vulnerable to the risks of commenting on the importance of the relationship. This also holds the worker back from expressing personal feelings toward the client. As one worker said, "It doesn't sound professional for me to tell a client I will miss him. He will think I'm just putting him on. Won't that be encouraging dependency?"

In most cases the reluctance to share feelings stems from the difficulty the worker has in coming to grips with his or her own sadness when separating from a valued client. The flow of affect between the two has first created and then strengthened a bond that the worker values. It is important that the significance of this relationship be recognized as it comes to an end. Often workers must take the risk of expressing their own feelings before the clients will feel free to do the same. Both may feel vulnerable, but it is part of the worker's function and a measure of professional skill to be able to take this first, hard step. Let us look at an illustration of an 18-year-old foster child about to leave the care of the agency.

Worker: You seem quiet and reserved today. You don't seem to have much to say.

Client: I guess I'm just tired.

Worker: And then again, this is almost our last session together. I've been thinking a lot about that, and I have mixed feelings. I'm glad to see you getting ready to go out on your own, but I'm really going to miss you. We've been through an awful lot together in the past two years. (Silence) How about you? Are you a little down about our ending too?

Client: (Long silence) I guess we have gotten close. You've been my best worker—although sometimes you were a real pain.

Worker: Why do you feel I was your best worker? It can be important to talk about this.

After the mutual acknowledgment of feelings, the worker takes another step by asking the client to reflect upon the relationship. The client has had many important close relationships and has seen them broken, sometimes experiencing sharp feelings of rejection and pain. It is not uncommon to develop an armor against such vulnerability, an unwillingness to risk getting close again only to experience another loss. Once again, an important synthesis between process and content is possible. Understanding this worker-client relationship can be an important aid to the client in his future efforts to make close contacts. This part of the work is discussed further in the "Transitions" section of this chapter. In the following discussion and process recording, a social work student worker described the difficulty of sharing her own feelings as she and her client approached the end of the field placement.

Beginning termination was a difficult and emotional process for both myself and my client, Joan. As I attempted to discuss the ending of our relationship, Joan stated that she wanted her next income assistance check mailed to her home address. I asked her why. Joan replied that by doing so, she would no longer have to go into the office for her check.

Worker: Joan, I don't really understand that. You've always picked your checks up. In fact, you preferred it that way, didn't you?

Joan: Well, yeah, but I'm getting tired of seeing the same people, and I think they're tired of seeing me every month. (Silence; Joan looking away)

Worker: Joan, is it that you don't want to see me at the end of this month? (Silence) Check days have been our "hi/keep in touch days." I feel like you want to avoid seeing me on my last check day here.

Joan: Maria, what am I going to do without you?

Worker: Joan, do you feel you really need me?

Joan: I need somebody to talk to. Well, sometimes I feel like I don't. Other times I feel like I'm going to fall apart. I don't know what I'm going to do without you.

Worker: Joan, I know we've been through a lot and shared a lot together, but to be honest, I feel you're much stronger now than you were in the beginning, and I feel you can make it without me. That's not to say I think things will be easy for you, but I've seen a growth in your own self-confidence. You're beginning to take more risks, make your own decisions.

Joan: Yeah, my self-confidence has increased slightly, hasn't it?

Worker: It really has, Joan. I know it's going to feel weird and empty without me, but you know you've made a lot of new friends in the past few months at the center, at your new place. Sherri has been a real support and a good friend for you, hasn't she?

Joan: Yeah, she has, she really has. But it won't be the same. I just know it.

Worker: It won't be the same for me either, Joan. You know I've never had an ongoing involvement with any client before. It feels weird to think that I won't be your worker after May. Right now…I can't describe exactly how I feel, but I know it's going to feel weird without you. I know I'm going to keep thinking about you, about how you're doing. I know I'm going to miss you and Don (her son). (Joan silent; looking down) I feel you'll make your goal (to be self-dependent and off of income assistance). It'll be slow and you'll have to take a lot of steps, but I really feel you'll do it. I wish I could be there to see that.

Joan: Yeah, I'm going to make it!

Worker: You sound determined. That's another change I've noticed.

Joan: Yeah, I am more determined. I have to get off I.A. (income assistance). The changes in me have been because of you.

Worker: Well, I may have helped you, but the changes came from you. (Joan shrugged her shoulders.) Joan, what kind of a worker have I been for you?

Joan stated: (1) that I was the first worker that ever shared personal feelings with her. She felt that this made it easier for her to discuss problems and to relate to me; (2) that I expressed a great deal of concern for her, but at times Joan felt I was overly concerned; (3) that in the first term I seemed to think I was always right, whereas in the second term I was easier to talk to, more relaxed, more open…; (4) that whenever I was late, Joan felt I was treating her like "scum," even though I did apologize to her each time. As Joan began to know me better, she realized that my apologies were genuine, that I really did care for her.

I also relayed my feelings to her regarding our relationship. For example: (1) I struggled with her resistance; (2) as I noticed more strength and confidence in herself, I felt threatened—I wanted to keep "protecting" her; (3) I've learned a great deal about single parenthood, the hardships and difficulties associated with sole child rearing, with no outside support. Near the end of the session, we began to discuss Joan's feelings regarding new beginnings with a new worker in a new office. Joan stated that prior to myself, she had two good workers. Both these workers were older and had children of their own. Joan hoped that her new worker would also be older; she felt this would help in the new beginnings. This issue was tabled for our next session. As I was leaving, Joan stated that she would see me on check issue day.

The discussion about what the work has meant is interactional in nature: both the client and the worker have been affected by the relationship, and the evaluation of how things have gone and what has been learned is important for both parties. It is important for the client to see the worker as being involved in a process of continual growth and learning—not, as many clients fantasize, as a "finished product." The worker exemplifies the value of reflection, analysis, learning, and growth. When the worker shares that at times she felt "threatened" by the client's growth, she forces the client to begin to see this worker (and possibly future workers) as human and vulnerable.

"Trying It on for Size"

Earlier I referred to the graduation quality of the ending. As the client moves to the final sessions, the worker often senses an effort to test out new skills and ability to do things independently. It is not unusual to have a client come to a session with a report of having tackled a tough problem or dealt with an issue which, prior to this time, would have first been discussed with the worker. The worker senses the client's positive feelings of accomplishment and employs the skill of crediting the client. This consists of a direct acknowledgment of the client's ability to "go it alone." In those situations when the client remains with the service and the worker leaves, discussion of the new worker often begins to dominate the conversation. Who will the new worker be, and what will he or she be like? This can also represent a "trying the change on for size" as well as being one form of expression of anger towards the worker.

I have experienced this process during my classes when I have worked with students over a long period of time. Our class/group relationship and the students' relationship with me is, in some ways, a model of the process we study, although both the content and my function differ from that found in social work practice. Nevertheless, I can remember times when I found it impossible to get into the class conversation. I would make a comment on the work under discussion, and the students would look at me briefly and then continue to talk as if I were not there. After a few such attempts to enter the conversation, I felt as if I were not in the classroom. As I sat back and listened, I could hear the students carrying on important discussion and analysis of practice within the peer group and without my help. This was a part of our ending process.

The "Farewell-Party" Syndrome

Schwartz uses this term to refer to the tendency to "pad" ending discussions by concentrating only on the positive aspects of the relationship. All working relationships have both positive and negative aspects to them. It is important for the worker not to allow the ending discussion to get so caught up in the positive feelings that an honest analysis of the content and process is bypassed. The worker should use the skill of reaching for negative evaluation to encourage the client not to hold a "farewell party."

Thus far I have detailed some dynamics and skills involved in the ending process with individuals. In Part III of the book, we will examine further illustrations in the group context and address ourselves to some of the differences in the dynamics. In addition to the process of ending, it is important that the worker pay attention to the substantive content that can make the ending important for the client's learning. In the next section of this chapter, I will review those skills of the ending phase that help the client to use the experience with the worker to make an effective transition to new situations that she or he may face alone.

THE SKILLS OF TRANSITIONS

It is important to remember that a new beginning is always inherent in the ending of a working relationship. As the young adult, the former foster child, leaves the care of the agency, he begins a new phase of his life and faces a new set of demands. Some of these are similar to those faced by any young person of the same age, but others are unique to someone who has been the ward of an agency. The ex-con who is completing the term of parole begins to function in society without the supervision and support offered by the parole officer. The patient who is leaving the rehabilitation center must face the experience of negotiating the outside world, perhaps still limited by the effects of the accident or illness. The former narcotics addict who leaves the treatment center must deal with many of the same pressures and demands on the street that helped lead to the addiction. This time, the ex-addict needs to make it without the support of either the worker or the drugs. The adolescent delinquent leaving the protection of the wilderness camp may be dealing again with a family that has changed little during his or her time away. For each of these clients, the time of ending is also the time of a powerful beginning.

The worker needs to pay attention to this process of transition during the ending phase by focusing on the substance of the work together as well as on the process of ending. In work that has gone well, clients may have discovered new things about themselves, their strengths and weaknesses, their patterns of behavior under pressure, and their abilities to handle problems. They may also have learned new ways to view some of the important people and systems they must deal with. Ending should be a time for adding up what has been learned. Since the work is never finished, clients end with new ideas as an agenda of future issues. This agenda needs to be identified. As with all phases of the relationship, the interaction between workers and clients offers fertile areas of learning related to the contract. Workers can use the dynamics of the ending process to help clients generalize from their learning to new experiences.

Finally, workers can help clients make direct transitions to new experiences and to other workers and alternative sources of support that may be available for their use. These tasks of the ending phase are examined in this part of the chapter.

Identification of Major Learnings

Endings are a time for systematically adding up the experience. The worker asks the client to reflect on their work together and to identify some of the things that have been learned. One week before the final session, the worker could ask the client to prepare to share these important ideas during the last week. In the first session, the worker asked the client for feedback on the issues that seemed to be of concern. Now that the sessions are ending, the worker and client need to review jointly where things stand on these issues and others that may have emerged during their work together. The worker's demand must be for specifics, since a general summing up is not enough. When the client says that the sessions with the worker were valuable because the client has learned so much about himself or herself, the worker might respond, "Exactly what was it you learned that was important to you?" This process helps the client to consolidate the learning. A second benefit accrues from the client's recognition of new abilities that have been developed. This can strengthen the client in preparing to end. The worker can participate in this process as well, since in any real interactive experience, the worker will learn from the client. What does the worker now understand differently about the client's problems and about the worker's personal and professional self? The summing up should include discussion of what both worker and client are taking away from the experience. The following example illustrates this adding-up process.

> Christine came in because she felt so bad that she hit her oldest daughter whenever she became angry. It was established that she wanted techniques of parenting that would prevent her from hitting her child. We openly discussed her lack of bonding with this oldest daughter, and the poor marital situation Christine found herself in. Christine tried but could not get her family to participate. This was to be the second to last session (fourth) with a follow-up in February (two months).
>
> **Worker:** Let's review a little where we started and where we are now.

Chris: The reason I came was because I had been hitting Raphaelle, much more than I felt good about. But things have been going very well. In the beginning I thought that if I can stop hitting her altogether, I would feel really happy about it. Well, I haven't struck her once, and I don't even feel like it. It is going very well.

Worker: And it's been about three months.

Chris: It almost seems so far away now.

Worker: You mean from the time we started?

Chris: Yes, it seems almost a little unreal, do you know what I mean…a little embarrassing.

Worker: Well, it has been some time since October, but it was all very real then.

Chris: No kidding. But it feels good to end, because I don't feel I need it anymore—things are going well. but it does feel good that I can come back in February.

Worker: Why did you say it is embarrassing?

Chris: It was embarrassing to even come in and state that I was hitting my children. I had to talk to my family doctor and explain it all to him. I wish I could have solved it within the family without outside help (condensed).

Worker: I guess it seems easier to solve this hitting now, eh?

Chris: Well, this is it, but I am glad I came because I might still be hitting Raphaelle. You know, just the commitment of getting help was the biggest factor.

Worker: Asking for help makes you vulnerable, but ironically it also makes you stronger. Is there anything else that's different for you and Raphaelle?

Chris: For some reason I look at her a little different. I see her having some problems, but I see her also as older. Remember how you said that she is becoming a teenager and won't take hitting anymore. I also think like she could be gone in five years. Where have all the years gone? (Showing sadness)

Worker: What is happening for you right now? (Some discussion followed about Raphaelle.)

Chris: …I guess I also feel that things aren't going so well between my husband and I.
I suppose that will always be there.

Worker: Well, you know I always did feel it was a shame that you couldn't get him to participate in these sessions. But maybe that's for another time and under different circumstances. Have things deteriorated between you two? I guess I am asking if you need to spend some time on this issue even though he won't come in?

Chris: No, not really. I guess I don't really want to dwell on the negative. I am glad for me and as you said, that's what counts.

Worker: Sure, but the door is open. I don't know how aware you were but a couple of times I really pushed hard for you to bring your husband into these sessions.

Chris: (Laughing) Oh, I felt it! (This was followed with some discussion about this issue.)

Worker: You seem to have consolidated some strengths and determination. You seem to put your foot down. I guess it will take some adjustment for your relationship (with husband). Somehow you have to find a way to support each other. You do tend, it seems to me, to walk a bit of a tightrope sometimes and as a result, you end up having to give quite a bit, even when you need to get your own needs met.

Chris: You know how you said, last time, that I am a giving person. My husband just thinks I am a selfish manipulator. I think he is more right. But it sure is nice to hear.

Worker: You mean that you are a giving person?

Chris: Yes. (A little teary)

Worker: It's hard to hear, isn't it?

Chris: It's just not something I heard before. My husband says I do some nice things but doesn't say I am a nice person. I don't think of myself as a nice person.

Worker: It can be your secret that you are a nice person.

Chris: (Laughing) What do you mean?

Worker: Well, we'll say good-bye and we'll see each other only one more time in the end of February, but you'll remain a nice person, even though I won't say it anymore.

Chris: It's nice of you to say so and it's funny but you have to hear it to believe it, but I have also thought about it as well and that makes a difference. (We reviewed some of the main themes of the sessions and discussed what was helpful and what wasn't. We contracted to see each other at the end of February. We planned to have a short session in February to see if things are still okay with her and Raphaelle.)

The following is the end of our follow-up session in February, a short half-hour session in which Christine brought in a little book as a gift.

Worker: Well, maybe we can just say good-bye?

Chris: Good-bye, John, and thank you.

Worker: You're welcome; good-bye, Christine, good luck to you and your family. It's funny, but I feel a little sad about saying good-bye.

Chris: I feel a little bit sad as well. Just a little sad but I am also happy that I came and now I don't feel I need to come anymore. I felt good about having this six weeks to see if I could keep it up.

Worker: In retrospect, that does seem like it was good. Anyway, you have our telephone number, and don't hesitate to call even if it is to say hello.

Chris: Yes, thanks a lot for that. Bye, John, and good luck with your studies. You're not a bad social worker (laughing).

Worker: Thanks, good-bye, Christine…and of course thanks for that beautiful little book.

Identification of Areas for Future Work

It is important to convey to the client that the work will continue after the ending. It is all right for the client to have unanswered questions, to be faced with unsolved problems, and not to have life all figured out. The client began the experience with certain problems or life tasks and has learned how to handle some of these more effectively than at the beginning. The experience ends with other problems or life tasks ahead. The difference now is that the client has learned how to deal better with these concerns. If some of the uncertainties and accompanying ambiguity are detailed, the worker must resist the temptation to "jump in" and try to "solve" these last-minute concerns. Part of the learning experience involves being able to live with some uncertainties. The worker's task is to help the client to inventory these unresolved issues, to create an agenda for future work, and to use their experience together to determine how the client can continue to work on these concerns. The worker must also resist the temptation to reassure the client who expresses doubts about competency. Acknowledging and understanding these fears of not being able to continue alone is more helpful. It is important for the worker to convey a belief in the client's potential to tackle future tasks without in any way attempting to minimize the feeling that the going may be rough.

To illustrate this point, we will return to the ending sessions of the 18-year-old who was about to leave the care of the child welfare agency. The worker had asked the client to identify those things he had learned as well as those areas he still felt he needed to consider. This excerpt from the last session begins as they review what the client has learned.

> **Worker:** What ideas hit you hard during our discussions together? What will stay with you?
>
> **Client:** I learned that I have to be more responsible for myself. That was important to me.
>
> **Worker:** Exactly what do you mean by that?
>
> **Client:** Well, I used to walk around with a chip on my shoulder. All my problems were someone else's fault. I was angry at my mother for giving up on me; it was always my foster parents who were the cause of my fights; and the "Aid" (Children's Aid Society)—well, I hated the place.
>
> **Worker:** And how do you see it now?
>
> **Client:** Well, I did have it tough. It wasn't easy moving from home to home, never having the kinds of things normal kids had. But I think I understand better that what happens to me from now on is pretty much up to me. I can't blame everyone else anymore. And the "Aid," well, for all my complaining, with all the changes in foster homes, the "Aid" has been the only place I can call home.
>
> **Worker:** I guess you have a lot of mixed feelings about this place, but now that you're leaving, a part of you is going to miss it.
>
> **Client:** (Silence) With all the complaining and all the crap I had to take, I'm still going to miss it. You know, I'm scared about being on my own.
>
> **Worker:** Sure it's scary. What exactly are you afraid of?
>
> **Client:** I'm going to have to make it on my own now. I'm starting this new job, and I'm worried about how I'm going to do. And what if I don't make any friends in the rooming house? There are other people my age there, but it's hard to get to know them. It's not like a group home where you spend a lot of time together and you always have the house parents to talk with.
>
> **Worker:** So you have two questions to work on: how to make it on the job and how to make some new friends.

The two critical tasks identified in this discussion are major ones for any young adult and quite appropriate to this client's phase of life. As he moves into adulthood, he must tackle issues related to how he will fit into the world of work, and he must also begin to shift his relationships from parental figures to his peer group. These tasks are made more difficult for a client who has moved through the child welfare system. His life has been marked by so many broken relationships, so many times that he has invested himself and then been hurt, that he has become reluctant to risk being hurt again. In the next segment, we will continue this illustration to demonstrate how the worker-client ending process can be directly related to the content of the work.

Synthesizing the Ending Process and Content

If we keep in mind that the worker-client relationship is one of many the client deals with in life, and is in fact just a special case among all relationships, then the experience can be used to illustrate important themes. The relationship can be viewed as a training ground for the client. Skills that have been developed in dealing with the worker are transferable to other situations. The astute worker can use "tuning in" to identify connections between the worker's own interaction with the client at the ending. For example, to return to our illustration, this client had to overcome his guardedness and establish a close relationship with the worker. It was a long time before the client allowed himself to be vulnerable, to risk being hurt. In effect, the client needed to learn what we must all learn: for our life to have meaning, we must risk getting close to people, even though this may mean getting hurt sometimes. If we go through life remembering only the hurt, then we may build a wall between ourselves and people who could provide comfort and support. The typical "graduate" of the child welfare system has been hurt so often that he or she often begins a new relationship with the expectation that it will not work out. Such children may seek out close ties (e.g., marry early) but will hold back on really investing themselves. This worker recognized that intimacy is a central issue for clients who must now risk themselves with their peers in the rooming house and elsewhere. Eventually they will face the same problem as they consider marriage.

Let us return to the interview as the worker tries to help the client learn from their experience together. This is another example of trying to synthesize process and content.

Worker: You know, I think what we have gone through together might offer you some ideas about how to handle this friendship question. Do you remember how it was with us when we first met?

Client: Yeah, I thought you would be just another worker. I wondered how long you would stick around.

Worker: As I remember it, you made it pretty tough on me at the beginning. I had the feeling you wouldn't let me get close to you because you figured it wouldn't last too long anyway.

Client: That's right! I didn't build it too high 'cause I knew it was only temporary.

Worker: It was frustrating for me at first because I couldn't seem to get anywhere with you. You seemed determined not to let anything get going between us. Somehow, it worked out. Because I feel real close to you, it's going to hurt now not to be seeing you all the time. I knew from the first day that someday we would have to say good-bye and it would be painful. No matter how much it hurts now, I wouldn't want to have missed knowing you this way. It was something special for me, and I will remember you.

Client: (Silence—obviously struggling with emotion) I'm glad you stuck with me. You're the only worker who really did.

Worker: What can you take out of our experience that relates to you and the people at the rooming house, or wherever you meet friends—at work, the Y?

Client: You mean the same thing could happen there? If I build the walls too high, they might not get through?

Worker: You said before that you had discovered how responsible you are for a lot of what happens. I think that's true in this case as well. If you're afraid of risking yourself, of being rejected, of getting close to these people and then losing them, then you will be alone. Maybe the most important thing you have learned is that you can get close if you want to, that it does hurt when you say good-bye, but that's life. You pick yourself up and find new people to get close to again.

Client: You mean like the kids at the rooming house?

Worker: Right! And on the job, and maybe at the Y, or other places where you can meet people your own age.

Client: So it's up to me.

Worker: It usually is.

In many ways the worker is sharing his own learning with the client. Every time the worker starts with a new client and finds himself investing feeling, he must do so with the knowledge that it will hurt to say good-bye. This is the gift a worker can give to a client. The best way for workers to handle their own feelings of loss is to share them in the ending and then begin with a new client.

Transitions to New Experiences and Support Systems

As the worker brings the relationship to a close, it helps to identify what it is about their work together that the client valued and to discuss how the client can continue to receive this support. The previous illustration demonstrated a worker helping a client think about how he might shift his need for support to a peer group. This suggestion made sense for his stage of development. In another case, a worker might help the client identify family or friends who could offer help if the client will use them, employing the skills developed while using the worker. In cases where a transfer is made to a new worker, some discussion of the strengths and weaknesses of the present working relationship can aid a client to develop a strategy for using the new worker more effectively. Community resources for social, vocational, and counseling needs can also be identified.

The worker can, in addition, convey to the client a sense of having used the worker for important work at a particular time of life and an awareness that the client might want to seek help at other times when the going gets rough. The counseling process is not necessarily a one-time experience that leaves the client capable of facing all of life's crises. It was helpful for getting through a particular period of life and may be needed again at some future time. The notion of a client moving in and out of supportive experiences at different points in life, and at different stages in the life cycle, is much more realistic than the idea of seeking help once and never needing it again. For example, a young child who is a survivor of sexual abuse may need immediate help to cope with the trauma and the resulting disruption of her family. New issues will emerge as she enters her teen years, and a mutual-aid support group may be helpful to her, and to her non-offending parent, during this normally difficult transition stage. As a young adult, when she is getting ready to enter into partnerships of her own, and again later, as a new parent, she may need some support in coping with the normative issues of the transitions in age and status that are compounded by the unique issues facing survivors. An ending at any one stage should help the client realize she has not "solved" her problems, but instead has learned how to use social support to cope with them. She should not see it as a sign of failure if she needs help again.

Finally, a physical transition can also be made to the new situation. For example, a joint session with the new worker can ease the change. In another example, a worker from a residential center might accompany a resident on visits to a new foster home. In many circumstances, concrete steps can be taken, in addition to conversation about endings and transitions.

The following record material provides a complete illustration of a session in which a social worker in a psychiatric residential setting tells a teenaged client that she is leaving the agency. Their relationship has been very positive, using dance therapy as a medium for helping the client express her thoughts and feelings. Even as the worker begins to deal with her own feelings and those of the client, she incorporates first steps for effecting a transfer of the work to other support staff.

> Sandra arrived in a good mood and with a bouncy step, and said, "I've been looking forward to this...I'm glad to get back." She was talkative and indicated she hadn't had enough activity or exercise over Christmas, felt sluggish—and had difficulty with her feelings. She said Christmas was hard for her—she missed me while I was on holidays, and she tried not to get into anything too heavy.
>
> As we were talking, I began to put on the videotape, and Sandra noticed the video equipment. I asked whether she was really energetic, saying, "We've been away for a while. Was it difficult to start again?" Sandra said it was a bit scary. She not sure how deep she wanted to get in—we were working on some very frightening things— she wanted to get into it but felt safer if she avoided it, too. I said, "Sounds right on—you've been taking lots of risks with me, and our dance work has been getting deeper and deeper." I pointed out that safety was a must if she was to go on with it, and we must build and establish that important trust. I said, "This was really important, Sandra, and we have to be honest with each other and not take things for granted." I stopped working on the equipment and said, "Before we go on, I've got something to tell you first—we have to talk about it—I'm going to be leaving in two months, on April 2." I choked a little as I said this and revealed feeling in my voice, and a tear ran down my face. I stopped for a moment, and Sandra stepped forward to me and put her arms around me in a hug, and I put my arms around her. We held each other for several moments. She stepped back and looked me directly in the eyes and said, "But why are you going? Why?" I answered, "Sometimes that's a hard question to an- swer." I said that we'd have six weeks together to complete our work and to say good-bye, but stopped talking when I saw Sandra's feelings were still back at the sense of loss. She said, "Just like that—you're walking out just like that!" I said, "It's been very hard for me to come and tell you. I knew it would hurt. It just seems when things start going for you, somebody important leaves. I want you to know it's not you, what we've been doing together was very important, and you're doing very well—I know it's a bad time for me to have to go. We're not finished, and we're at a critical point in your treatment. I feel terrible." She, as if in a trance, said, "Then why are you going? I don't understand. Are you going to a new job? Did you get fired?" The questions came like a barrage demanding to be answered, insisting on a response as her anger mounted. She became more direct, and her contact and communication be- came more personal and intimate.
>
> My own feelings were stirred, and I grasped in my mind for an answer that would sound "right." I replied, "I am tired, my job has been demanding, and I feel I need a change. My husband and I will be having his family to visit us this summer, and

we're thinking we might want a family of our own. I would like to be at home for a while."

Sandra said brightly, "That's nice that you want your own family—you're the same age as my mother." To which I replied, "But I'll be leaving you and that will be hard—I'll really miss you—we've become very close and you've shared a very private and special part of yourself with me." Sandra visibly appeared to sag—at which I took her by the arm and said, "Let's sit down together." She sat down, and tears formed in her eyes. I gave her a handkerchief from my purse and she wiped her eyes and began twisting the cloth. I asked, "What are you feeling now—can you get it out?" She replied initially as if not hearing me, "Why? How can you do this to me? It's like I'm losing my best friend, or my dog—You're just like my mother and now you're leaving." I said, "Like your real mother or your adoptive mother?" She said, "like the real mother I never had—you're what I would like my real mother to be like, as I imagine her." I said, "You've been very special to me, too, Sandra—I'd be proud to have a daughter like you." She said, "Not one as mixed up as me." I said, "You're putting yourself down again, Didn't you hear what I said? You've given me a lot, too—but you are not my daughter, and I am not your mother, and we must not lie about that. We must look each other in the eye and treasure the real things between us." Sandra looked up and said, "I don't know if I can, it's too hard and it hurts too much. You're the person I've really cared about here. I've never told you that. What will happen to me when you go?" I replied, "That's very honest, Sandy—I believe you can make it, but we'll have to work on it. There was lots to do yet. Do you think we can use the next five sessions to do that?" She weakly replied, "Only five left—they're disappearing already. It's all happening too fast." So she added, "We'd better get busy. I want to get as much as I can before you go. I do want to get through my fears." I hugged her and said, "You're a very determined young lady when you make up your mind, aren't you!" She replied, "That's what you've taught me, to say what I want and I'm determined toward that!"

I cautioned her, "But we probably won't finish everything—and in a couple of weeks you may need to close down, you may want to stop, but as long as you can and as long as it is safe to keep going—we'll keep working—but you must keep me informed on how you're doing and how much you can handle—you must take some control of the safety, and I'll watch closely—that must be our bargain. I want to leave you with support and with staff who can understand, but we will have to bring our work together to a safe finish."

Sandy agreed, saying, "Let's get started—I don't want to lose a day." I said, "And as if that's not enough, I have one other thing to say. You've asked me to be confidential on some of the really scary things until you felt safer to talk about it. Well, we've got to begin sharing the material with cottage staff." Sandra said, "Not yet, don't ask me this now, this was too much." I replied, "I must. I want to show your videotape to staff from your cottage. We can't keep secrets. They won't understand, and you'll need them. I'd like your permission to show the tape, and I want you to know that this material must be shared." Sandra became quite vulnerable and said, "They'll think it's ugly. I'm scared of what they'll think about me, I'll feel like something inside has been violated!" I paused and said, "I know—I'm asking a lot, maybe too much of you all at once, but I'm asking you to keep your trust in our work, that I'll treat the material as we have in these sessions with love, with care and with dignity, as something beautiful and a part of your inner world." Sandy shrugged her shoulders and said, "Now you're determined, aren't you?" to which I replied, "I am, and this sharing was part of our work. It would be wrong and hurtful to both of us to keep it to ourselves. You know I've talked to your cottage staff about what we're doing, but they have not seen the videotapes." (Long pause) Sandy said, "Oh, go ahead, you'll do it anyway, I don't feel very good about it, but you can show them if you want to." I replied, "If I would do it anyway, I wouldn't be talking to you now—we must be together on these things—that's our bargain—I would like your permission." She said, "I agree, but I don't have to like it." We both looked at each other, and I laughed, saying, "That's a deal, but I promise I'll give you time to get mad at me." Sandy replied, "I won't get mad—I like you," to which I replied, "It [the anger] will come, but we'll work on it when it comes."

As we cleaned up at the end of the session, Sandy claimed, "If I'd only known what was waiting for me when I came today!" I said, "It has been a really hard session for me, too. Are you feeling OK to go back to the cottage?" She replied, "I'm feeling OK now, but I feel a bit low." I said, "You've really struggled with hard things today. I don't expect you to be singing, but if you start to feel bad, talk to Fran or Rhonda. They'll be available for you." I walked her back to the cottage arm-in-arm and said good-bye. She replied, "It sounds so final." I said, "It does, but we've got to start—and I'll see you next week."

The tapes referred to by the worker were videotapes created by the client with the worker's help. They involved the client's use of singing and dancing to break out of her shell and to speak of very difficult experiences and emotions. The singing and dancing itself represented an assertion by the client of her own competency and willingness to risk herself and be vulnerable. This was a side of her that the worker felt needed to be shared with other workers in the system. However, the worker's own anxiety about connecting the client with social support systems may have led the worker to press too hard in insisting on the sharing. Even though they had agreed, as part of their initial contracting, on an eventual sharing of information with other professionals in the system, the client's rights to confidentiality regarding material that the worker was not required to share would take precedence. Along with the strong assertion by the worker of the importance of the sharing, the worker needed to also stress the client's right to say no.

SOME VARIATIONS ON THE ENDINGS THEMES

When I discuss endings with students and workers, such as the emotional endings just described, there is usually at least one group member who will courageously say, "These endings sound great, but what if you and the client really don't feel so bad about endings?" When I credit the commentator for being honest, another participant might follow up by commenting, "Never mind not feeling so positively. What if you don't like the client and are glad to see the relationship come to an end?" In this section, we will explore several variations on the ending model: endings in which the worker feels he or she never really was able to get started; endings when the worker is angry rather than sad about ending; endings associated with the worker's job loss; and finally, endings associated with the death of a client—in one case, a suicide, and in another, a client in the last stages of AIDS.

Ending a Relationship That Never Really Began

When students review examples of powerful and emotion-laden endings with clients, they often feel a sense of guilt if their own experiences were not similar. Examples are shared in which the working relationship never got off the ground. Intellectually, the student understands that the client may have played some part in the creation and maintenance of the illusion of work. Emotionally, however, the student often takes full responsibility for the "failure" because of feelings of guilt and incompetency. These feelings, in turn, may block the student from moving fully into the ending/transition phase of work, causing her or him to avoid the process of evaluating the experience with the client.

First, it's important for students to gain a clear perspective on the interactional nature of their practice. They will never be able to reach all clients, no matter how effective and skillful they become. Second, social workers can only do the best they can at any particular moment in their professional careers. They cannot hold themselves responsible for not being able to give a client more than they had. Instead, they should guard against allowing their feelings to cause them to underplay the help they have given—just as big a mistake as overplaying their contribution to the client. Once the worker has developed perspective and has received support from his or her supervisor and/or colleagues, then the ability to manage these feelings can help the worker mobilize him- or herself to use the ending period as a time in which to provide additional help to the client. Support is crucial to the success of this process, since students and inexperienced workers are very vulnerable at this stage in their careers, experiencing negative feedback as particularly painful.

In many cases, it is even more important to discuss the endings when the work has gone poorly compared to when it has gone well. The focus of this ending process is an honest evaluation of the working relationship. The worker needs not only to own up to his or her part in the process, but also to help the client examine the part she or he played in keeping the work superficial. This discussion, if handled in a non-accusatory and constructive manner, can constitute the worker's most important contribution to the client's growth. Significant professional growth for the worker can also emerge from this conversation.

In the following example, a worker levels with the client as the ending work begins, making the demand for work that the worker failed to make during the beginning or middle phases of practice. In this example, the client is an African-American, inner-city teenager who has been in a residential setting in a rural area of the state. The original referral was from the court system and the state child welfare agency. Problems with the law, drug use, and family members were part of the teenager's history. While the client had superficially conformed to the program, the worker, who was white, had always felt "conned" by the client but had failed to confront the issue. The dialogue has been modified a bit, since the original transcript contains segments of conversation that would require translation—that is, the use of a street jargon that the worker said was like a "foreign language" he had to learn. The use of the jargon, and the worker's feeling like an "outsider" were key signals of the core of the problem.

> **Worker:** We only have two more weeks left, and I think it is important that we discuss our time together. I realize that you are probably looking forward to finishing since I don't believe you have found the program very helpful. I have to admit to feeling the same way. I think it is important that we discuss why it didn't work out. I'd like to know what you think I could have done to be more helpful, and I'd like to let you know what I think you could have done.

Client: Man, I don't think you understood what it is like for me. This place is O.K., no hassles, no problems. But when I get back home, it starts all over. The pressure is on to use when I'm on street, and who's going to help me then? You don't have any idea at all. I mean, my ass is on the line back home, every day.

Worker: I think you're right about that; I don't have any idea. I was hoping I could help you anyway, fix you up so when you went back home, you could handle it differently. Why didn't you level with me from the beginning—why did you just play along with me?

Client: Are you kidding? You're the "Man," I'm not going to level with you.

Worker: I think I knew it was bull all along; I should have been more honest with you. I'm white, and you're black. I have a job and a safe place to live, while you're just scratching to survive. I pretended that didn't matter.

Client: Look, don't get me wrong. You're not so bad for a white dude. You just don't have a clue.

Worker: You know, it would have helped if you had taken a risk, been a bit more honest and let me know what it was really like. I understand why you didn't, why you just conned me, said the right words, and I realize I could have pushed you harder, right from the beginning. But you had a part to play as well. You can keep on playing the game when you get back home, but it seems to me, that's when you are going to need some real help the most. You going to have to trust someone sometime.

Client: What good is that going to do me? Talk isn't going to help no one. I'm stuck in that hole and I'm not getting out. So I just gotta work on survival.

Worker: It's like you're up against a stone wall, isn't it? No future, no hope—like you're trapped.

The conversation continued, with the worker listening and acknowledging feelings that were present for the client but had been only hinted at earlier. Even though it was the ending of their work together, this conversation was real and might begin to lay a groundwork for the client's future use of a helping professional. The focus turned to what resources the client might be able to tap back home when the pressure started again. The conversation also helped this worker to better tune in to the realities of oppression related to race, class, and gender, which most of his inner-city clients faced in their real worlds. This would increase the chance that the worker could make a quicker start with the next client, pushing for honesty earlier, while integrating a demand for work with support. The worker could also focus more on the realities of life back in the city instead of thinking that the client's "personality" could be changed in the country. By facing the reality that their time together had mostly been an illusion of work, the worker turned the ending phase into a positive experience—perhaps some of his best work with this client.

In another example, where an angry and openly resistant client responded to the worker's request for some honest evaluation of their work together, the client said, with feeling:

"The problem was that you were one hell of a real asshole." The worker responded, with feeling: "Well, you know, you weren't much of a bargain to work with either! The fact is, you never gave me a chance, right from square one. I made my mistakes, I'll own up to that. But you should realize that as long as you keep your wall up, and won't let anyone inside, you are going to be all alone with this stuff. And that's a shame, because I think you're really hurting and could use some help."

It is quite possible that the client did not take in a word the worker said. Even so, it was important for the worker to level with the client. The hard part for this worker is to tune in to the source of his anger and frustration. If it's rooted in a sense of failure and incompetence, the disclosure may not help. If the worker is able to see past the client's defenses, and the emotions are coming from concern for the client, then it may be the most helpful gift the worker can make. This is where supervision and/or peer support can be helpful to a worker ending with a difficult client.

Endings Caused by the Termination of the Worker's Job

With severe cutbacks in federal and state funding of social services over the past decade, and the impact of managed care in health settings, endings caused by the professional's job loss are raised more frequently in my workshops with workers, supervisors, and managers. Supervisors describe workers who are depressed, cynical, and apathetic as they enter the final phase of their work. Anger over the restriction of services and the job loss often leads the worker to want to ignore the ending phase issues, sometimes withholding disclosure of the termination of work until the last session with a client or even avoiding it completely. This lack of closure is not good for either the clients or workers.

Clients are disempowered in such interactions and are denied the chance to deal with their ending feelings, to take some control over the endings, and to make an effective transition to life without their workers. The abruptness of the ending can negatively affect the transition to the new worker or service, or make the client reluctant to become emotionally invested with any other helping professionals. Clients are also denied the opportunity to challenge, if at all possible, the loss of the services. In some situations, when clients have been made aware of what is happening, they have been able to mobilize resources (other clients, family members, etc.) to object to the losses, and have even been able to reverse or moderate such decisions.

Workers pay a price for abrupt endings as well, as they lose out on the opportunity to end professionally, which is one way to deal with some of their guilt over "abandoning" their clients. In addition, upon later reflection, workers often report how helpful it was for them to be held up to their supervisor's expectations for a professional level of practice in the ending phase, not being allowed to withdraw out of anger and depression. Of course, a crucial element in the process is the work done to create a supportive atmosphere in which workers know they can get assistance in managing their feelings. In workshops I have led for front-line workers facing potential or actual loss of their jobs, I have focused first on their feelings of anger and then on the pain and sadness that is usually also present. The guilt of workers who are remaining (survivors) needs to be dealt with so that they do not withdraw into flight (or fight) in reaction to their own anxiety. After some supportive work, staff is able to respond to my request to tune in to the impact on their clients of the cutbacks and loss of specific workers, and to strategize on how best to help clients to cope with loss while they struggle simultaneously with their own feelings.

In the following excerpt, a worker announces that she has lost her job and will be ending her work with the client, a single parent involved in family support work focusing on problems with her teenager.

> **Worker:** I'm afraid I have some bad news for you. You may know that the state was considering cutting the funds available for support agencies like ours.

Well, the cuts have come through, and because of seniority, I will be one of the first workers to lose my job. I'm afraid this means we only have four weeks left, and we are going to have to start to discuss how to end our work and connect you up to other sources of help.

Client: Oh my God, you must feel terrible. You mean they're letting you go, just like that?

Worker: Actually, we have known there might be cuts for a few months. I didn't want to worry you because we just were not sure what would happen. But now we know, and you and I have to start to face it. I am feeling terrible about losing my job, and part of the reason for that is that I am going to have to say good-bye to clients I have gotten close to—and that includes you. (Silence) How about you, what are you feeling right now?

Client: I'm furious at your agency. Just when I find a worker I can really like, they take you away. Does this mean I will get another worker? What will happen to me now?

Worker: I want you to know I have really felt close to you and it means a lot to me to hear that you will miss me too. I'm also angry, but underneath that I'm feeling a lot of sadness and loss. We need to talk about that over the next few weeks as well as where do you go from here. I must be honest, I don't think the agency really has had time to consider what we are going to do for clients like yourself. We never felt the cuts would be this bad, with so many positions lost. I will try to find out what may be available to you, and if you wish, I will put you in touch with my supervisor who is staying on. That way you can ask some of these questions yourself. If it turns out that you cannot get the help you need here, we are going to have to see what else may be available in the community. Also, we better discuss where you can get help from other sources—your family and friends, for example. I can't make any guarantees about services because every other agency is also getting clobbered, but I will make sure we spend time on how you can cope no matter what we find out. You have grown a lot in the last few months, and I think you have more strengths than even you realize.

Client: Those bastards! (Starting to cry) Don't they realize it's going to be hard on me to cope on my own? (Silence—the worker also starts to fill with emotion—the two sit quietly for a while, the client crying softly and the worker with tears in her eyes).

Worker: (After a short while) I'm not sure they do realize the impact of all of this on clients. If you want to discuss ways in which you can let them know, tell me. I'll be glad to help you communicate your views. Your needs are important, and they have to realize these decisions have serious impact on real people. In the meantime, let's start to talk about our work together, what you have learned, your strengths, areas where you still feel vulnerable, and what other sources of help you have available. I want to make sure we work hard right up to the end.

There were many points in this dialogue at which the worker could have lost her sense of professional function. When the client asked the worker how she felt about the job loss, the rest of the conversation could have revolved around the worker's reactions. It did not, since the worker came right back to the impact on the client. When the client expressed anger at the agency, the worker might have joined in the anger, focusing on her own sense of the unfairness of the situation. Instead, she shared her own feelings of loss and reached for those of the client. When the client asked, "What will happen to me now?" the worker could have expressed her resentment and bitterness by reflecting back the client's sense of hopelessness. Instead, the worker empowered the client, suggesting that she begin to actively make some demands upon the system. The worker did not try to falsely reassure the client, but did focus on next steps available to the client if the formal systems failed her. Also, when the client focused on her anger at the political neglect and lack of understanding, the worker offered to empower the client in finding ways to communicate her feelings, rather than reflecting her own sense of hopelessness by saying, "What's the use—you can't fight city hall." And finally, instead of focusing just on the social action possibilities open to the client, the worker came back to the immediate issues, leaving the door open for further discussion. All in all, this worker should feel good about her efforts to help the client cope, her maintenance of a professional role, and her commitment to the client. It was all the more admirable given her understandable anger towards the political system and the community, which lacked the will to meet their commitments to vulnerable clients.

Endings Caused by the Death of the Client

Coping with the death of a client on a caseload, or working with a dying client, can be extremely traumatic for a worker. While workers have had to deal with the issue of death and dying as a normal part of their caseload (e.g., accidental deaths, suicide, a terminal illness), the epidemic growth of health and social problems such as AIDS and crack cocaine addiction has increased the likelihood of such traumas. In the next sections, we will explore the impact of a sudden death (a suicide) on the caseload, as well as the implications of working with a client dying of AIDS.

Traumatic Events and Worker Practice. The impact of a trauma on a specific worker, or on his or her colleagues, can be significant and often subtle. For example, in one study (Shulman, 1991) we examined the impact of a traumatic event, such as the death of a child on caseload while in foster care or left at home with the biological parents. Analysis of the data indicated that not only was the practice of the caseworker affected by the trauma, the trauma may also have affected the practice of other workers in the same office and region. The incidence of traumatic events in a region was positively associated with children going into care, being less likely to return home, and staying in care longer. A traumatic event on a specific worker's caseload was also somewhat predictive of a number of worker-related measures including negative morale and decreased practice skill with clients.

This impact of trauma can be buffered by the existence of a social support system designed to aid not only the particular worker involved, but all of the other workers in the office or agency. A description of my work with such an affected office (Shulman, 1991) revealed a tendency on the part of all staff to avoid the pain associated with the traumatic event through the flight/fight syndrome. The stress was often increased when the administration responded (from their own anxiety) with the question, "Who is at fault?" Workers consistently report that at such a time, what they desperately needed was for supervisors and administrators to be asking, "How are you doing?"

It is interesting to note that a large, Canadian bank has developed a program, under the direction of a social worker, to provide support to bank branch staff immediately following a traumatic armed robbery. The branch would be closed for a day, with the social worker flown in to meet individually and in groups with all staff for a form of trauma counseling. The bank discovered that it experienced less sick leave, absenteeism, staff turnover, and even a lowering of the level of mistakes if it paid attention to the needs of its staff after a trauma. It's ironic that a corporate entity was able to recognize the benefits of support for its employees, while social and health services often seem not to understand.

The reader is referred to another text (Shulman, 1991) for more complete discussion of the impact of trauma and the importance of social support. For now, it is enough to note that an ending of a working relationship brought on by the sudden and traumatic death of a client should immediately mobilize the resources of the agency to attend to the needs of workers involved. In the next section, when the impact of a suicide on a caseload is examined, we will outline some steps to help workers not only to deal with their own feelings but also to work effectively with the feelings of clients.

Suicide on a Caseload. A client suicide can have a powerful impact on a worker, as well as other workers and clients in the system. A sudden and permanent ending to a working relationship can evoke feelings of guilt on the worker's part. Even if one logically understands that such a decision was made by the client and was not the responsibility of the worker, self-doubt often remains. This doubt can have an impact on a worker's current and future practice. In one example, a social worker in a veterans' hospital reported having difficulty ending his work with a Vietnam veteran even after five years. When the issue was examined closely, it became apparent that the suicide of another, similar client on his caseload, shortly after they had ended their work together, had made the worker overly cautious about ending before all of a client's problems had been "solved." Further discussion revealed that the worker had received very little help with his own emotions at the time of the suicide, with most of the administrative responses geared to an investigation of the circumstances (e.g., was the recording up to date; had all of the proper procedures been followed). Even colleagues seemed to shun him, turning away in a form of "flight" from his pain. For some, they simply may not have known what to say. In addition, the suicide may have been frightening to them, raising anxiety about their own clients. Lacking a defined protocol for dealing with staff in traumatic situations, and lacking leadership from supervisors and managers, the system's reaction to the suicide left the worker feeling alone and abandoned. Unable to manage his feelings, he became less able to manage his practice-related problems—particularly, ending with clients.

The impact of such an event on an entire staff system was brought home to me dramatically during a two-day workshop I led for the staff of a psychiatric ward for in-patient teenagers. During the first day, staff presented problems with one Native American patient who was emotionally isolated from other patients, resistant to work, hard to reach, and in general, considered to be the ward's "**deviant member**"—the client who acts significantly differently from other clients in the system but may actually be sending an indirect message on behalf of the other clients. (The concept of the role of deviant member will be discussed more fully in the chapters on family and group work.) In discussing this patient, I tried to help the staff see him in a new way—as a patient who could be sending a signal to staff of issues and feelings related to the ward as a **dynamic system** in which the behavior of each participant in the system (staff and clients) affects and is affected by the behaviors of all other members of the system. Staff moved quickly to integrate this new view of his behavior and to strategize about how to intervene differently with him and the other teens on the ward.

When I arrived to start the second day of the workshop, I noticed staff speaking in hushed tones at the coffee urn. When I inquired as to what had happened, they told me the client they had presented had been home on a pass the previous evening, and that he had shot himself and was dead. I felt stunned at the news, and I knew the staff must be experiencing similar feelings of shock. When the session started, I acknowledged the impact of this traumatic event and suggested we abandon the other examples we had scheduled for discussion and instead deal with this event. I told them I thought we could connect the discussion to the purpose of our workshop. I was conscious of the fact that I would be modeling for the staff a way of dealing with the group of patients they would be meeting that evening. I believed the patients would be experiencing many of the emotions that staff would be feeling in reaction to the suicide. How I handled the staff discussion should somewhat parallel the work they would need to do with the teens on the ward.

The morning's work that followed could be divided into three related phases. The first phase of this work involved expressions of grief, loss, and guilt. The second phase involved discussion of how to provide support to staff in these circumstances. In the third and final phase, we examined the impact on other clients and the implications for practice.

> I began by telling them that even though I did not know this child, except for their brief description of him the day before, I felt stunned and tremendously sad about his loss of life. I asked if we could take some time, with each person having a chance to share what they were experiencing. Staff began to speak slowly and in quiet tones as they shared how upset they were by the event. One staff member, the patient's **key worker** who had particular responsibility for providing continuity of service, began to cry. She felt guilty about not having reached him sooner—she wondered how alone he must have felt on the ward, cut off from the other patients and staff. A colleague next to her offered support by putting her arm around her. A number of other colleagues cried as well. She went on to wonder if she had made a mistake in agreeing to allow him home on a pass. She said that if she had not let him go home, he might be alive today. I acknowledged her feelings and asked if the other staff could be helpful to her. I suggested helping her might also be helpful to them, since I thought they all felt some of her emotions and doubts.
>
> One staff member pointed out that they had all participated in the decision to allow weekend passes—it was a joint responsibility. Another pointed out that the patient had done well on his previous passes and that they had no way of predicting this suicide. A third pointed out that while they might want to review their procedures for assessing a client's readiness for passes, he thought it would be a mistake to suddenly stop the leave program or become overly cautious and restrictive. Weekend passes worked well for most kids most of the time. Another staff member pointed out that this teen had brought his pain with him to the hospital—staff had not caused it. He might well have committed suicide no matter what staff had done. One staff member noted that he was a Native patient, and wondered if he had felt even more isolated on the ward with "white workers, white patients, even white walls." (I had raised issues of race and culture during the workshop the previous day.) A supervisor suggested that they put on their future agenda some discussion of the issue of race—a topic that they usually ducked. He said he often felt cut off from the Native patients and had to think about how to reach them more effectively. Some suggested the need to recruit Native staff who might be able to relate more effectively.

The conversation continued along these lines. There were long periods of silence and many moments when each staff member seemed to be lost in his or her own feelings and thoughts, as well as other moments when they seemed to be able to come together. As the conversation continued, I felt a deepening of the staff's feelings of depression and sadness. It was important to allow time for these emotions to emerge and to accept them. The initial instinct to reassure or move too quickly into next steps can pre-empt the space needed for the emotions to be felt and acknowledged. As is discussed in more detail in Part III of this text, dealing with group work and mutual aid, a powerful healing can occur when group support is available and the "all-in-the-same-boat" phenomenon is experienced. Given the brief time we had left, I decided to help the staff focus on where they could go from here as a way of coping with the loss.

> I shared my own feelings about the depth of sadness we were experiencing and then wondered if it might not be helpful at this point to discuss how to help the key worker and all of the staff over the next few weeks. I thought this might be a way of developing a protocol of how to handle such traumatic events in the future. A number of suggestions emerged, including the acknowledgment that it was useful just to have some time together to share in the grieving. One worker asked the key worker if she felt up to meeting with the teen's family; if not, she would do it for her. The key worker thanked her, but said that she felt she should do it herself. Another worker revealed a similar incident he had experienced a number of years before in another setting. He said he still felt the pain, and this incident had brought it all back. He told of having been given time off to attend the funeral and said that this had been important to him and to the family. The supervisor indicated this could be arranged if the key worker wished. She indicated that she would like the opportunity. Further discussion focused on their concerns about how the hospital administration might react. The whole group shared with their supervisor some suggestions about how he might handle the issue so that administration was tuned in to the needs of the staff over the next few weeks.

From my perspective, it is important to first focus on the needs of the staff. If those needs are ignored, then staff may not be able to focus on the needs of the remaining (and future) clients. It is also important, however, to reach for the professionalism of staff and not let them get lost in just dealing with their own pain. An important way in which workers can heal themselves and lessen their guilt over the client they feel they didn't help is by focusing on the clients they still can help. In the next excerpt, I asked staff to shift their focus from self to other—the remaining clients on the ward.

> As this discussion proceeded, one could almost sense a lifting of the pall over the room. Staff seemed energized by a focus on what they could do as next steps. I summarized the suggestions that had emerged thus far and then asked if they could give some consideration to the teens still on the ward. If staff was reacting so strongly, how would the patients, many of whom may have had similar feelings as the patient who had suicided, how would they be reacting? One participant pointed out how in the past, when there had been a suicide attempt, staff had tried to hide it from the patients. They were afraid that it might trigger other attempts. He indicated he thought that this was probably a mistake, because patients knew something was wrong and soon found out what had happened through the grapevine. By trying to hide it, they closed off the possibility of helping the teens with their reactions. He recognized that

it was his own fears he was running from. He proposed that they raise it at this evening's community meeting.

The remainder of the session was devoted to sessional tuning in to the potential re- actions of the patients and developing strategies for helping them to cope. I pointed out the parallels between their experience during the workshop and the group experience they were about to lead. They recognized the importance of sharing their own feelings, allowing time for grieving, the need to shift to the impact of this death on each of the remaining pa- tients, and some discussion of the mutual responsibility each patient and staff member had for the others. They decided to involve the patients in a discussion of what they could do if they ever felt so cut off and alone and how they could try to be more supportive of each other.

At the end of the session, I congratulated the staff on their work and their profession- alism. I told them they had a very rough shock to their systems but that I saw a lot of strength in their ability to help each other and to stay focused on their professional tasks with their clients. I wished them luck, and the session ended.

The three-step model discussed in this section—grieving, the need for support for the worker, and then moving to focusing on clients—can be helpful in conceptualizing the stages of coping with trauma of any kind.

Working with a Dying Client. With the exception of settings associated with terminal illness, such as a **hospice**—a residential setting for people who are in the final stage of a terminal ill- ness—or a medical setting, such as an oncology (cancer) ward, most social workers tradi- tionally have not found themselves dealing with dying clients. Unfortunately, with the emergence of the AIDS epidemic this has changed. I have noted the increasing frequency with which participants in my workshops raise examples of clients on their caseloads who are in some stage of this illness. While the initial success of the new triple-drug treatment has had a significant impact on survival rates, many clients with AIDS are not able to take advantage of this new treatment because they do not qualify for the trials or have other medical problems that prevent treatment.

The reader is referred to other authors for a more detailed description of the stages of death and dying (Kübler-Ross, 1969) and the worker skills required to help a client take some control over the process. For this discussion, our focus is on the impact on the working rela- tionship of having a dying client and the way in which the worker may integrate process and content. The illustrative example comes from a worker who raised in a workshop the stress involved in working with a male client with AIDS in the final stages of the illness. He was living at home with the support of his lover, some friends, and family members. The worker introduced the example by asking, "How do you work with a client when you don't know from week to week if you will ever see him again?"

When the example was explored in some detail, it became clear that one of the client's major issues was that none of the people who were important to him were willing to talk to him about his impending death. He felt he had come to grips with this ending of his life, but all of his initial efforts to raise the issue with his lover, friends, and family members were met with a wall of denial. He was angry at them for not being willing to talk with him and for trying to "cheer him up." He was afraid he might die before he could complete some work with each of these people who had been so important in his life.

When I asked the worker if she had discussed with the client her feelings about not knowing if the client would be there for the next interview, she indicated that she had not. It became clear that the worker, too, was distressed about this client's impending death. She was also having difficulty with her own ending work with him—which mirrored the client's problem with the other significant people in his life. With support from other workshop members, she strategized as to how to confront the issue with her client and how to use the conversation about their relationship (the process) to help him with his concerns about family and others (the content). The following is her report of her next conversation with the client.

> I began our conversation by telling him there was something I needed to talk to him about that was very difficult for me to raise. I told him I had been trying to help him deal with a number of people who were denying that he was facing death when I now realized I was doing exactly the same thing. I told him it was very difficult for me coming to see him each week, not knowing if he would be around for our next session. I had come to care a great deal about him and it was hard for me to face his impending death. I was going to miss him.
>
> He was quiet for a few moments, and then smiled. He told me he had been aware that I was avoiding the issue and had wondered if I was ever going to raise it. He said I had been very important to him, this past year, and that he wanted to make sure I knew how much he had appreciated my help. At this point I began to cry, unable to maintain my "professional" composure. After a while, I told him that I wondered if the other people in his life he wanted to talk with had similar feelings. Perhaps they too cared so much for him that it was hard for them to face losing him. I wondered if they were afraid they might upset him and were holding back their real feelings. I wondered if they were like me, and were simply afraid of the pain of losing him.
>
> He was thoughtful for a while, and said that was probably it. But what could he do about it, because at this point it was more painful for him not to talk about his death? I suggested that perhaps he needed to tell them that he understood why they kept avoiding the issue. Perhaps, if they knew how important this was to him and that he was really ready to face his death, and wanted them to face it with him, they might find the strength to stop avoiding it. At this point, he started to cry and I sat quietly. I asked him if he thought he might have some mixed feelings himself about having this conversation with these people. I noted that he was aware we were ducking the issue between us, but he had not raised it with me. I had to raise it with him. Was he sending mixed signals to these people who were so important to him? Could they be sensing his ambivalence? He indicated that he probably was not being as direct as he could be and was simply blaming them for changing the subject. I suggested we might discuss ways he could initiate this conversation more directly and how he could refuse to be put off by their initial denials. We worked on this for some time.
>
> At the end of the conversation, I told him that I wanted to be sure that we discussed our own work together and made sure we said all that we needed to, just in case. We agreed that we would focus on our work together next week as well as how well he did with his family members. As I left, I told him I was glad we had spoken so honestly and I would see him next week. He smiled and said, "God willing."

It was crucial in this example that the worker face her own ambivalence and start the process of expressing her real feelings. This signaled to the client that the worker was ready to face the client's real feelings about ending with others in his life.

CHAPTER SUMMARY

The ending and transition phase of practice can be the most important part of the work, during which the client deals with some of his or her most significant issues. Because of the feelings involved in the loss of a relationship, this phase may become a moratorium on work unless the worker helps the client to identify the stages of the process (denial, anger, mourning, trying it on for size, and the farewell party syndrome) so that the client can maintain some control. Specific worker skills involved in this phase include pointing out endings early, identifying the stages of the process, asking for a mutual exchange of the feelings related to ending, pointing out process and content connections, asking for an honest evaluation and summary of the work together, and addressing the transition issues as the client moves on to new experiences. Variations on the ending themes were discussed, including situations in which the work has gone badly, it ends because of a traumatic event (e.g., suicide), the worker is fired, or the client is dying.

GLOSSARY

Deviant member The client who acts significantly differently from other clients in the system (e.g., family or group) but may actually be sending an indirect signal of feelings and concerns on behalf of the other clients.

Dynamic system A system in which the behavior of each participant in the system (staff and clients) affects and is affected by the behaviors of all other members of the system.

Farewell-party syndrome The tendency on the client's part, in the ending/transition phase, to avoid the pain of ending through some form of celebration. Also, the tendency to be more positive about the experience and less likely to be critical.

Hospice A residential setting for people who are in the final stage of a terminal illness.

Identifying the stage of the ending process The skill of naming for the client the stage (e.g., denial, anger) of the ending process for the purpose of helping the client to feel more in control of the endings.

Key worker A worker, usually in a residential setting, who has particular responsibility for providing continuity of service to a particular client.

Pointing out endings early The skill of reminding clients, some time before the last sessions, that the working relationship is coming to a close.

Third decision The decision clients make to deal with their most difficult issues as they approach the end of the working relationship.

NOTES

1. For a seminal article on the use of time in social work practice, see J. Taft, "Time as the Medium of the Helping Process," *Jewish Social Service Quarterly, 26* (1949): 230–243; see also R.E. Smalley, *Theory for Social Work Practice* (New York: Columbia University Press, 1967), pp. 147–150.

2. For a discussion of this process, see L. Shulman, *Teaching the Helping Skills: A Field Instructor's Guide* (Itasca, IL: F.E. Peacock Publishers, 1983).

PART III

Social Work with Families

Part III of this book consists of two chapters that elaborate and illustrate the interactional approach to social work in the context of work with families. A distinction between social work with families and family therapy is made.

Chapter 6 sets out the basic model of family practice in the social work context. A brief summary of constructs from family therapy theory is presented. These constructs are illustrated in the context of social work with families, focusing on the family counseling and family support functions.

In Chapter 7, the agency services (rooted in agency mandate) and specific client problems come to the foreground. Illustrations are used to demonstrate how the boundaries of this working contract give focus and direction to family work in a child resources agency, a child welfare setting, a school, and a Big Brother agency.

6

Family Practice in the Social Work Context

CHAPTER OUTLINE

In this chapter, we will build on the concepts explored in Parts I and II by examining the variant elements of the helping model introduced by working with families and family problems. While the core elements of the model are the same—the phases of work concept, the importance of contracting, the skills required to build a positive working relationship, and so on—there are significant differences when one attempts to provide help to families and family members. Some of these differences are addressed in this chapter to assist the reader in making the transition from work with one client to work with more than one client at a time.

In addition to describing the purpose of this chapter, it is important to note what we are *not* attempting to do. This chapter is not meant as an introduction to family therapy. While we will draw on ideas from family therapy models, we will harness these constructs to the family support and family counseling functions.

SOCIAL WORK WITH FAMILIES

Social workers have a long history of working with families which predates the emergence of family therapy as a practice modality. *Families* are defined in this chapter to include a wide range of associations, many of which do not fit the traditional two-parent-family image. The increasing number of single-parent families, as well as families headed by gay or lesbian partners, for example, has broadened our understanding of the concept of family. The discussion in Chapter 3 of culturally competent practice also introduced the idea that even the word for *family* in some population groups refers to what the dominant culture would call the *extended family.*

Social work with families falls into two general categories. In the first, examined in this chapter, the practice is often called **family support work** or **family counseling**. This activity is usually short-term in nature and is designed to help families facing normative crises (e.g., the first child reaching the teen years or a crisis provoked by the birth of a new baby). The impact of an environmental crisis, such as the loss of a job by one parent, is another illustration of an event that may require professional intervention. The focus of the work is on helping a relatively healthy family get through a difficult time, using the experience to strengthen rather than erode the family system. Services may also be provided to couples without children. This general type of social work with families is often provided by voluntary family service agencies or through private practice.

Many of the concepts and theories introduced in the earlier chapters can also be applied to understanding the family. For example, from the life-span framework the social worker would attempt to help the family members identify the available baseline reserve capacity, both internal (within the family) and external, that could increase the family's ability to cope with the sources of stress. If, for example, the family crisis involves an elderly parent who is no longer able to cope independently because of physical deterioration, then the work might involve identifying the developmental reserve capacity potentially available through interventions such as the services of a home-care aide or housekeeper.

Other practice models introduced in Chapter 1 may also provide constructs that are useful in this work. For example, cognitive practice interventions can help family members identify automatic thinking processes that cause them to misinterpret the reality of their family interactions, thereby allowing the family members to break maladaptive cycles of blaming and conflict and to identify individual and family strengths and sources of support. Feminist practice frameworks may help members of the family identify gender-stereotypical behavior that has led to internalization of anger and frustration and the generation of interactional-related depression on the part of parents or children.

In a variation on this general theme of family practice, when the potential for child abuse or neglect is present, family support services may be provided by a child welfare agency. Most child welfare agencies deal with families facing problems on a continuum ranging from the normative problems described above to more serious issues of abuse and neglect requiring court involvement and protection of the children (e.g., foster care placement). A family support worker might be assigned to a family in addition to the ongoing child protection social worker.

For example, a social worker might work with a family by helping the parents to strengthen their child-rearing skills and to find more effective ways to cope with aspects of their life that are making parenting more difficult. Just as the worker would make referrals to other services for alcohol counseling, job counseling, and so on, he or she would also make such a referral to another service for ongoing marital counseling or intensive family therapy if needed. The focus of the work would be directed by the agency's mandate to work with families with children at some level of risk.

Resilience theory and research would offer suggestions to the worker and the family on interventions, such as the involvement of extended family members or elders, or other resources in the community (e.g., a big brother or big sister) designed to buffer the impact of a trauma, such as physical abuse, on the children or one of the parents. In this sense, the work is restorative in nature, designed to strengthen the family and to lead to more normal or positive growth and development.

In those families in which the crisis leads to the revelation of deeper, more long-term problems, it is not unusual for short-term, family support work to involve helping the family to identify the real problems (e.g., to abandon the use of a family scapegoat as the identified patient), creating a working relationship so that the family can begin to see helping professionals in a positive way, and then referring the family for more traditional forms of long-term family therapy. The professional providing this more intensive help may well be a social worker, since many are active in family therapy practice within agencies or in group or private practices as managed care providers. The family support worker, according to the job definition used in this book, does not undertake the long-term, intensive family therapy task.

The second major set of circumstances in which most workers find themselves working with families is in providing families with forms of assistance that are directly connected to the specific services offered by their agency or host setting. For example, a hospital social worker in a medical setting might work with family members on their adjustment to a patient's illness or other medical condition. A school social worker might undertake family work in helping parents and a teenager deal with serious school failure problems. A social worker in an elder care agency may work with the adult children of an elderly client preparing to make the transition to a nursing home. In this type of work, the emphasis is on a particular problem or life crisis that is in the foreground, both guiding and limiting the nature of the work. In the type of family work described earlier, the emphasis is on the family itself in the foreground with the life crisis as perhaps one of a number of issues affecting family dynamics. This second type of social work practice with families will be explored more fully in Chapter 7.

In this chapter, then, we will focus on ways of helping families through normative crises, creating the conditions for effective referrals to long-term, intensive family services for more troubled families, and working with families and family-related problems in the context of child welfare services. It is hoped that this focus will help the reader see how the ideas of the first five chapters can be useful in the family modality, as well as helping workers in many different settings understand how work with families can be an extension of their ongoing tasks, rather than the introduction of a completely different practice. Although ideas and techniques found useful in family therapy approaches were borrowed in developing this chapter, no one model of family therapy has been adopted as the sole working approach.

SELECTED CONCEPTS FROM FAMILY THERAPY THEORY

A number of factors should be taken into account when one works with families. For example, families have a history that goes back many generations. The impact of family members beyond the nuclear family, both dead and alive, can often be felt in the present. The impact of the nuclear family's relationship—or lack of relationship—to the extended family or the community may play a large part in its functioning. There is a power differential between family members. For example, children (or a spouse) may face serious threats of retribution, including physical violence, when family members return to their lives between counseling sessions. The fact that the stereotypes, roles, communication patterns—the whole family structure—has developed and been reinforced on a daily basis, 24 hours a day, over many years, can create strong resistances to the "unfreezing" process needed for change. The family has had years to develop a **family facade**—a false front it presents to outsiders—and each family member has also had time to create the external role that he or she presents to the other family members. One of the major advantages of seeing whole families, as opposed to working with one member of a family at a time, is that it allows the worker to observe many of these factors in the family interaction (e.g., who sits where, who speaks for the family).

Family therapy theory can help us to better understand family dynamics and choose effective interventions. There are many different views about how families function and what to do when one tries to help. One text on the subject (Horne and Passmore, 1991) describes seventeen different models.[1] The following discussion is limited to identifying and briefly describing key concepts from a few of these models.

One early contributor to family therapy theory, whose work has influenced many of the current theories, was Nathan Ackerman (1958). I will draw upon his framework for viewing a family and many of his practice strategies for describing the role of the worker in carrying out family work, while also integrating concepts from other theorists. Ackerman (1958) viewed family work as a special method of treatment of emotional disorders based upon dynamically oriented interviews with the whole family. The **family** is seen as a natural living unit including all those persons who share identity with the family and are influenced by it in a circular exchange of emotions. The family has a potential for mutual support that can be blocked by communication problems and anxieties of individual members. This leads to family disorders and the family's inability to carry out its tasks.

Although Ackerman does not specifically define the function of the helping person as mediation, many of his treatment skills can be explained as implementing this function in action. For example, he recognizes that treatment usually begins at a time of crisis, when the emotional equilibrium of the family has been upset. In the beginning stages of work, after contracting to help the family members work together to improve their communications and deal with the family problems troubling them, the worker employs the skill of observation to identify the idiosyncratic language of the family. Using personal emotions stirred by the feelings of the family members towards each other and herself or himself, the worker tests hunches about the family and its feelings by sharing them with family members. In this way, the worker helps the family move past the facade presented in the first stage to a more honest disclosure of their interpersonal conflicts. One example of this would be helping the family move beyond viewing the family problem as concerning a single child (the **identified patient**) who serves as a family scapegoat. This process has been described by other family theorists as **reframing the problem** to help the family see it in a new way.

The worker would identify these patterns and roles and point them out to the family members. Roles might include scapegoat, victim, persecutor, and so on. Facilitative confrontation (similar to the demand for work) is used to break the vicious cycle of blame and punishment that usually characterizes disordered family relationships. The worker challenges the illusion of work using the "here-and-now" of the family session to bring out the central issues. The process of the family session is directly synthesized with the content of the work, since the family acts out its dysfunctional patterns in front of the therapist. The therapist, in Ackerman's model, controls interpersonal danger, selectively supports family members, and attempts at all times to present a model of positive interpersonal functioning.

Another theorist whose ideas are helpful in understanding and working with families is Murray Bowen (1961, 1978, Kerr and Bowen, 1988). Bowen also viewed the family as guided in its activities by an emotional system that may have developed over years. He stressed the importance of understanding and exploring the intergenerational contribution made to the development of this family emotional system. Key concepts in Bowen's model include the importance of each individual being able to differentiate between emotional and thinking systems so that control can be maintained over behavior. (This is somewhat similar to one of the key concepts of the interactional model, in which clients are helped to manage their feelings in order to be able to manage their problems.) Bowen also stresses the impact of anxiety on the family system. Increased anxiety, resulting from a perceived threat, can lead to efforts toward "togetherness" in the family as a maladaptive means of coping. One example is the process of **triangulation**, in which two members of the family involve a third (e.g., the parents pulling in the child) as a means of coping with anxiety.

Without needing to adopt the model whole, it is possible to borrow concepts and techniques that can be integrated into effective family work at any level. Freeman's (1981) work has been useful in explicating Bowen's theoretical model and describing and illustrating the method for its implementation. In particular, his use of time in organizing his discussion of family work (beginning family therapy, the family therapy process, and the terminating stage) makes it easy to fit useful concepts within the model presented in this book.

Freeman points out that the family therapy process begins before the first interview as the helping professional responds to the call to set an appointment. Rather than rigidly requiring all members of the family to attend a first session, the therapist can carry on a skillful and sensitive telephone discussion with the caller, usually the person who most often takes responsibility for dealing with the family's problems, and thereby discover important information about who is involved in the problem and clues as to who should be asked to attend the first sessions. Instead of challenging the caller's definition of who should attend, the therapist respects the feelings of the caller and agrees, if needed, to see the parents alone, at first, to help develop a working relationship that will encourage the parents to allow the therapist entry into the family. He points out how the discussion of whom the caller sees as involved can be the beginning of helping the family members to redefine who is involved in the problem and who should attend the sessions.

Freeman describes four phases in the first interview: warming-up, defining the problem, reframing the family's thinking about the problem, and obtaining the commitment to work as a family. The warming-up stage helps to reduce family members' anxiety. Defining the problem involves a form of contracting, trying to understand how all family members perceive the problem. The reframing phase involves helping the family to see the problem in new ways (e.g., as a family problem, not just as a result of the behaviors of the identified patient). Finally, the commitment-to-work phase lays the groundwork for future sessions.

It is in the middle phase of practice that Bowen's theory adds its special emphasis on intergenerational work. As individuals take more responsibility for their own actions, and the sessions are marked by less blaming and reactive behavior, the relative calm in the family sessions allows for identification of subsystems within the intrafamilial and extra-familial networks to which the family can direct its attention. It is at these points that the multigenerational concepts are used to help families expand their boundaries. An effort is made to help the family members use the extended family as a source of support and as a means of understanding the impact of the family history. For example, in one of the illustrations provided later in this chapter, the active involvement of a stepfather in dealing with a teenage stepdaughter in a family session leads to his revealing for the first time his own childhood experiences as a stepchild. The telling of his story has an important impact on the family's ability to find areas of common ground.

Another family therapy theory, termed the person-centered approach, builds upon the ideas developed from the early work of Rogers (1961). In this approach, as described by Thayer (1982), the therapist works on establishing a healthy psychological climate which the family members can use to establish realness in family relationships, express true feelings, remain separate and yet identify with the family, develop effective two-way communication, start a healthy process for family development and problem-solving, and clarify societal effects on the family as well as clarify conflicts, seek solutions, explore values, make decisions, experiment with new behaviors, and develop a family model/direction unique to its needs and wants (p. 192).

The followers of this approach focus on the core helping skills that have been demonstrated repeatedly to facilitate change. These components of a healthy psychological climate include the therapist's genuineness (being real as a person); the therapist's caring and prizing of family members (unconditional positive regard for family members); and the therapist's willingness to listen carefully to what family members have to say (hearing and understanding family members' needs, wants, conflicts, fears, joys, loves, goals, values, hates, disappointment, dreams, sorrows, and their worlds or realities). These core conditions will be familiar to the reader from Parts I and II of this book.

Many of the core ideas in family therapy cut across theories. For example, multigenerational issues are important in most models, with Satir (1967) interested in "family fact chronology," and Keith and Whitaker (1982) referring to a "longitudinally integrated, intra-psychic family of three generations." The core issue of integration and differentiation—how to be part of a family and at the same time, a separate individual—appears in most formulations, although the terms used may differ [e.g., Keith and Whitaker (1982) refer to unification and separation].

Most theorists refer to the problem of triangulation—the effort of one party to gain the allegiance of a second party in the struggle with a third party (e.g., the parents and the therapist versus the child; the mother and an older child versus the father). Where they tend to differ is in their views of how to avoid the trap, change the pattern, or make strategic use of being the third party in the situation. The importance of developing a safe atmosphere is also stressed, although theories differ sharply in their timing and methods of confrontation designed to upset the dysfunctional patterns.

In considering family therapy models and practice strategies that might be useful for this discussion, I have selected ideas that lend themselves to integration into the general model described in this book. In particular, I have not included interventions that constitute "indirect" forms of influence in which the therapist influences family members without their knowing what is happening to them. Many of these forms of intervention are found in what has been called "strategic therapy," with Haley (1963, 1973, 1984) a leading exponent. Central to the model is the notion of the therapist developing strategies to solve the family's problems. For example, the therapist may give family members "straightforward directives" designed to influence their interactions and to resolve their difficulties. Families that are deemed to be resistant to straightforward treatment may find themselves faced with a **paradoxical directive**, a suggestion from the therapist that the family member continue their symptomatic behavior or possibly even heighten it (Barker, 1991, p. 166). The therapist makes the suggestion so that the family members may become more aware of their pattern of behavior and the subtle benefits derived from it. The eventual goal is that the family members be able to take control over how they interact. The indirect nature of the influence results from the fact that at the time the therapist makes the suggestion, the family members do not know the actual intent of the intervention.

The early work of another group of family therapists, whose model has been called the Milan approach (Palazoli et al., 1978), also incorporated strategic interventions. This group, made up of committed practitioner-researchers, revised some of their early thinking in relation to the use of paradox when the evidence did not support its efficacy.

While many interventions such as these are dramatic and artful, and may in fact accomplish their underlying goals (e.g., upsetting defenses to help families reorganize their structures), there is a price associated with such indirect forms of influence. Central to the model of practice presented in this book is the emphasis on trust and the crucial role played by the helping professional's honesty in developing client confidence. The danger in the use of indirect approaches is that if clients become aware of the therapist's use of such techniques, they may begin to divert their energy into figuring out what the therapist is trying to do to them. In some situations, the use of some of these techniques may heighten client defenses. In spite of these reservations, anecdotal reports of practice experience indicate that for some families, under certain conditions, these techniques prove effective in influencing change.

The reader is encouraged to explore the literature dealing with these approaches and to evaluate their usefulness in the crucible of day-to-day practice. As a helping profession, we are a long way from closure on many of these issues. Nevertheless, in order to be consistent with the basic assumptions of the interactional paradigm, family interventions selected for inclusion in this book must pass the test of whether the helping professional appears to be acting *with* or acting *on* the client. Indirect forms of influence, in which the social worker's real intent is not made transparent to the client, are considered for our purposes as acting on a client.

In the sections that follow, a number of constructs borrowed from family therapy theorists will be discussed and illustrated with examples of family work drawn from a variety of social work settings.

THE TWO-CLIENTS CONCEPT AND THE WORKER'S ROLE

One of the major differences in working with families rather than individual clients is that the worker is dealing with more than one person at a time. In most of the examples in Part II of this book, workers had before them a single client. Even though the model called for conceptualizing the client in interaction with important systems, the worker usually had only one person to deal with at a time. As soon as the helping unit expands to more than two (worker and client), it becomes more complex, introducing new problems, new possibilities, and new demands upon the worker's skills. One of the most common problems observed in family work results from worker identification with a subunit of the family system.

Perhaps the best way to describe the problem is to give an example of how it typically emerges in workshops I conduct for helping professionals. The workshop participant in this case was presenting an example of a general problem: "How do you work with a family if the father is unmotivated and very defensive?" In response to my request, the worker described the family as containing middle-aged parents (the father was an immigrant from Europe), a 15-year-old daughter (the identified patient, or IP, whom the parents viewed as the problem), and an 11-year-old son whom the parents described as no problem at all. The parents had called indicating they could not control the daughter and wanted the child welfare agency to "straighten her out or get her out." While the particulars may differ, this type of situation and the conversation that follows is typical of hundreds of workshops.

After the description of the family and the circumstances of the worker's involvement, I asked for the details of the first session (word for word) to the best of the worker's ability to recall. He described the father angrily taking the lead and confronting the daughter with accusations of misbehavior. These were addressed to the worker almost as a prosecuting attorney might speak to a judge. When I inquired what the daughter was doing, the worker said, "She was just sitting there, her head hanging down, very close to tears." When I asked for the worker's feelings at the moment, he replied, "I felt badly for her and could easily understand why she had trouble dealing with that father. He didn't seem to have any sense of how upset she was." I replied, "You must have also felt angry at him for his insensitivity. You were feeling her hurt and pain, and he seemed closed off from her." The worker agreed.

At one point the worker described the father berating his daughter for running around with girls who "…came in late, dressed like sluts, smoked dope, and didn't listen to their parents." I asked how the worker responded and he said, "I asked Maria [the daughter] if it hurt her to hear her father say those things, and she just nodded. I asked if she could tell her father that, and she just sat there, unable to speak and about to start crying." I said to the worker, "You wanted the father to understand her hurt. Did it seem to get through to him?" The worker replied that the father was so dense, he couldn't hear a thing. The father simply escalated the anger, saying, "In Europe children listen to their parents and respect them." I continued, "Which made you even angrier. What did you say to him?" The worker replied, "I told him that I thought he had to understand that he was in the United States now, and that teenagers here were quite different in many ways from the old country. I don't think it helped much, because he just sat there and glared at me. How do you get through to a guy like that?"

It is at moments such as these that it is possible to help workers see the problem in a new way. Using the three circles illustrated below, I asked if the worker could put himself back into that moment and tell us where he was with respect to his emotional identification. Pointing to the daughter's circle, I said, "It would be quite understandable if you were really with the daughter." The worker replied that I was right. I then asked the workshop group, "Who was with the father?" After a few moments of silence, someone said, "He was all alone."

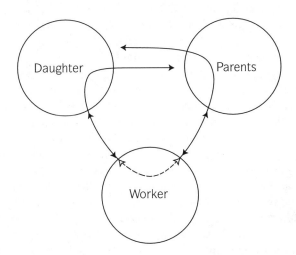

This is the moment when the "two-client" idea, proposed by Schwartz (1961) in the context of group work, becomes helpful in understanding the worker's function in work with families. In order to effectively mediate the individual-social engagement, in the special case of the family, the worker must understand the importance of conceptualizing and identifying with two clients simultaneously: the individual and the family system. Thus, in the conflict example just described, for the worker to be helpful, he must find a way to emotionally identify (be with) both the daughter and the parents in the family system. By identifying with the daughter, however understandable his reaction might have been, the worker cut himself off from the parents, particularly the father, just at the moment when the father needed him the most. His response to the daughter was helpful in that he recognized her pain and articulated her feelings. If, at the same moment, he could have understood the father's feelings and responded with genuine empathy, the conversation might have sounded as follows:

> **Father:** In Europe, children listen to their parents and respect them.
> **Worker:** So it makes it hard for you to understand what's going on now—why it
>   doesn't seem to work the same way here in the United States.

It's important to underline the fact that genuine empathy must be present if the worker uses these words at this moment. The worker must be feeling something of the father's struggle to figure out how to be a good parent when the world seems turned upside down from the way in which he was raised. As indicated in the previous section on family therapy theory, the worker will work in this first session to reframe the family's thinking about the problem, trying to help them shift from blaming and confronting the daughter to seeing the problem as one facing the whole family system. At this moment, however, the worker needs to be able to develop his working relationship with the parents, particularly the father. The worker must resist the pull described earlier as triangulation, in which the family members may attempt to align the worker with their side. Instead, the worker must align him- or herself with both clients—each individual family member and the family as a whole.

In fact, as will be apparent in the first full example described next, the father's behavior is in part an effort to find out just what kind of worker this is going to be. Since he may already be feeling guilty about his parenting (something he may not admit even to himself), he probably began the session assuming that the worker would be on his daughter's side. When the father saw the worker's informal dress and guessed at the worker's age, a part of him said, "He's not much older than she is. How is he going to understand?" When the worker responded with the lecture on American culture, the father knew he had been right.

The worker was suffering from an advanced case of **functional diffusion**. Fortunately, this is not a terminal illness and can be overcome with a dose of functional clarity. If the worker is there to mediate the individual-social engagement, and the worker can understand his responsibility to the two clients—each individual family member (including the father) and the family as a whole—then he can be with both clients simultaneously. The importance of this can be seen clearly if one realizes that in the example as presented by the worker, at precisely the moment he was trying to get the father to understand the daughter's feelings, he was demonstrating his complete inability to feel with the father. Since the worker demonstrates a model of personal functioning (what Schwartz has described as "lending a vision"), he said more to that father by his actions than through his words. He wanted the father to understand the daughter's behaviors, even those the father experienced as "deviant," but he was having difficulty in reaching behind the father's deviant behavior to understand the message he was sending.

In reality, even with functional clarity, workers will continuously find themselves overidentifying with one part of the family system and cutting themselves off from another. The countertransference process (that is, workers relating to clients as substitutes for important people in their own lives and attributing to clients feelings and reactions from their own experiences), is never stronger than in work with families. Younger workers, some not far removed from situations similar to those experienced by the teenager in the family, must work hard to deal with their own feelings towards authoritative fathers or mothers if they are ever to begin to relate to these parental types as individuals instead of as cardboard caricatures.

This is a lifelong task, as described in Chapter 1, with workers using their professional experiences to better understand their own personal lives, and using their personal experiences to better understand their professional practice. In this sense, each family we work with represents an opportunity to learn more about our own family of origin. Some family therapy theorists, such as Bowen (1978), incorporate family-of-origin work as a central part of the training for family therapists. As the therapist comes to grips with personal issues in relation to the family of origin, it can have a profound impact on work with clients.

While it seems a truism that work on one's own family issues (or any form of therapy) may add to a social worker's ability to work with others, this idea raises a controversial issue in social work training. Students have reported supervision sessions that appeared to have abandoned work on the practice problems experienced with a client, focusing instead on the student's own family history, life issues, and problems. Take, for example, a student who grew up in an alcoholic family. Instead of reflecting on the specific ways this life experience may be affecting the student in moment-by-moment interactions with an alcoholic client-parent, the educational focus of supervision may be lost as case conferences turn into therapeutic encounters. This is an example of functional diffusion on the part of the field supervisor.

In the balance of this chapter, and in Chapter 7, a number of examples will be used to illustrate the key concepts outlined in Parts I and II of this book and the first half of this chapter.

FIRST FAMILY SESSION WITH AN ANGRY FATHER

In the example that follows, we see a worker dealing with a family not unlike the one described in the previous section, with an angry, volatile father and a 14-year-old son. It is an illustration of how one can catch a mistake and correct it during the session. This worker is a social work student in a family support worker role in a large child welfare agency. Because of a complaint of physical abuse of the teenager, the social worker with the protection responsibility had made the first contact. The family support worker was called in to provide family counseling to see if the family could be helped to deal with the problem while keeping the child at home. The material that follows is from the worker's report of the first contact.

Description of the Curakis Family:

Father: A Greek store owner. Described to me as an angry, volatile, and violent man. Those who had tried to work with him described him as "a write-off," unworkable. He held very definite ideas of family life, including roles, expectations, etc. He came from a family where his father hit him often when disciplining. Obedience was valued.

Mother: A German teacher. A quiet, soft-spoken woman from an upper-middle-class background.

Son: A 14-year-old who was defiant towards his father. He smoked in front of him, in direct contravention of the father's orders. He performed well in school and had no apparent peer problems.

Precipitating Incident:

Mother sought help after husband repeatedly hit her son with his fist and once with a board. (Mother was not present during this incident. The story was shared by the son.) Father denies he hit the boy with anything other than an open hand.

History:

During the family's previous contacts with professionals and family friends, they scolded—in one form or another—the father for his behavior and showed sympathy for the boy. The most recent contact with a social worker was similar, with the additional threat to remove the boy from the house. The mother was planning to remove the child at the time of this meeting, and did do the following day against the father's wishes. The father believed the family and its functioning were his responsibility.

Both the husband and wife said that their marriage prior to the birth of their son had been fine, though Mrs. Curakis's voice was tentative. Discord arose shortly after the child's birth. From Mr. Curakis's point of view his wife was too soft; from her point of view he was too hard. Throughout the child's life they could not agree on parenting procedures.

Mr. Curakis was the boss in the house. What he said was done. His wife was able to modify these edicts to a moderate degree in regard to herself, but only to a minor degree in regard to her son. At times of discipline the father took command—often in a physical way. While this was happening, Mrs. Curakis would not become involved unless she felt that her son would be seriously hurt. However, after Mr. Curakis finished, she would take her son aside (in Mr. Curakis's absence), calm him, cuddle him, and in most instances contradict or modify what Mr. Curakis had said.

These actions on Mrs. Curakis's part were a constant irritant to the couple's relationship. She felt it was necessary to her son's development. He felt it was undermining his authority and was the reason the boy was acting the way he was. I gave the above history to indicate how—from the father's point of view and in reality—he had been undermined, excluded, and put down, and at the same time how his son was "sided with" (coalition)—against him—by family friends, social workers, his family doctor, and his wife.

It would be easy to see how the social worker in this example, based upon the agency records and the initial assessment, might begin the interview already identifying with the family members versus the father. It would also be natural for the father to assume that this worker would be like all the rest. As the interview begins, the father, son, and mother act out their issues in a conflict over smoking. The worker skillfully responds to the process by recognizing it as a communication to him and uses it to focus on the content. During the early part of the session, the worker fails to pick up on the father's escalating clues of his anger and concern about the worker siding against him. In a skillful example of catching one's mistake while one is making it, and trusting one's feelings, the worker finally reaches for the issue of the authority theme.

The Interview:

The family had just been introduced to me by the social worker. The boy walked into the interview room smoking a cigarette.

I introduced myself and began to give a brief introduction of myself and my role in the agency. As I was about two minutes into the introduction, the father began admonishing the boy for smoking. The boy said nothing at first. The father kept shouting. His statements became more derogatory and turned into a general attack on the boy's attitude. Mrs. Curakis, under her breath, said her husband's name, thereby asking him to stop.

I asked her if this is how the fights between her husband and her son often began. Mr. Curakis glared at me, at his wife, and then continued attacking his son (verbally).

Throughout the next ten or fifteen minutes, I made numerous attempts at connecting with individual family members by empathizing, understanding, etc. I connected easily with Mrs. Curakis and her son, but was unable to do so with Mr. Curakis. In fact, he was becoming more and more angry each time I spoke, regardless of whom I spoke to. But he was most hostile while I was speaking with the boy. Each time I began speaking to the boy, the father would, in a voice louder than mine, accuse the boy of some transgression. They would then get into a loud argument.

After a while, this pattern changed. Now each time I spoke to the boy, Mr. Curakis would start arguing with the boy, but ended up shouting at me. At first I did not realize this change; I only realized that I was beginning to understand what my colleague had warned me about. I was becoming impatient and angry with this "jerk." Almost mechanically, I said, "You are angry with me?" There was little or no concern in my voice and it must have sounded completely monotone.

The nonverbal cues did not seem to matter. The quality of anger changed. He was now focused on me, but he was not angry with me. For the next fifteen minutes he angrily related the years of no one understanding him, the sincere attempts he had made and was making to help his son grow up properly, the repeated incidents of "people" siding with his son against him after he had disciplined his son and how that had created the present situation, and how his wife and he could not get close because of it. I said something like, "And that makes it even more difficult, doesn't it?" in a sincere manner.

But he just continued letting it out. There was a pregnant silence—a very pregnant silence. I began to get uncomfortable and wanted to find something appropriate to say. Something that would summarize what he was trying to say. But I couldn't think of anything. Then a sentence came to mind: "And you think I'm going to be like all the rest."

"That's right!" he shouted, almost coming out of his seat. He went on for a few minutes about his concern that when I talked to his son, I was acting just like the others.

There was a long silence. I was nodding, admitting to both of us that he was right. I apologized and told him that what I had done was not what I was trying to do. I went on to say that it was my job to be helpful to both of them, and if I wasn't then I wasn't doing my job the way I wanted to. I asked him to do me a favor. If he noticed me doing that again—to anyone in the family—to please let me know. I would appreciate it.

The remaining ten to fifteen minutes of the meeting were spent, to a large degree, discussing "old" parenting issues (between Mr. and Mrs. Curakis)—nothing significant.

What was significant was that they were talking on a topic that they had avoided—except in argument—for many years. I asked them if they wanted another appointment. After a few moments' discussion they decided they did—as a family.

As they were on their way out, I said goodbye to the boy. He was a little less "cocky," but not very different. Mrs. Curakis seemed quiet, not quite at ease, but it looked like the universe she had been carrying around on her shoulders was reduced to a solar system. The biggest change was in Mr. Curakis. He shook my hand with both hands, looked me in the eyes and said, "Thank you…thank you…thank you very much." There were tears in his eyes. I put my other hand on his and said, "You're welcome." Tears welled up in my eyes.

When I walked into the front office after they left, some of the office staff shook their heads, thereby referring to what I must have gone through and what a "jerk" he was. (It seems that he had been quite gruff to the receptionist on the way in.) I told them that he was really quite a nice guy. (Pregnant silence)

Discussion of the First Family Session

In a first session with a family, as with an individual counseling session, contracting is crucial. The key questions on the minds of all the family members are, "Who is this worker, what kind of worker will he or she be, and what will happen here?" Because of the family's prior experiences with other helpers, they begin with a stereotype of the worker that must be dealt with head-on. Even though the worker in this example had tuned in to the potential feelings and concerns of the family members and was sensitive to the past experiences described in the brief history, when the father exploded at the son all of the worker's best plans, opening statements, strategies, etc., went up in smoke. His first reactions are quite normal for a new worker. His skill is revealed in the quickness with which he catches the mistake in the same session and begins to address the real issues raised by the boy who enters with a cigarette, the mother who displays her passivity, and the father who says through his actions: "If you want to see what it's like around this family, just watch."

The worker has been set up by previous workers (even the office staff) to see the father as the stereotype he presented. The father is ready to see the worker as a stereotype as well. By responding directly to the anger and the implied question about how he was going to help, the worker broke the pattern. Previous workers had found this father hard to work with because of his anger. As the worker reached past the cardboard caricature presented by the father and responded to the process of the session rather than just the content, he began to develop a working relationship with one of the most important family members, revealing a side of the father than probably had been hidden from previous workers and the family members. In fact, the father's open expression of anger will make him an easier client to work with, in some ways, than if he had hidden his real reactions and participated in an illusion of work, while all the time really feeling, "He's just like all of the rest of those workers; against me, and with the kid."

Because of the urgency of dealing with the father, and the "which side are you on?" issue, other steps were left undone. For example, the worker will need to be clearer about the purpose of these meetings and the specific role he will play. He has started this process by trying to say that he wants to help all of them and not take sides. At a next session, he might want to say something about helping the family members to talk to each other about how they operate as a family, and helping them to understand how the other family members really feel.

In addition, he will need to make sure that in his effort to be with the father, he not lose sight of the mother and the son.

The worker will need to help the family reframe the problem as well. At this point they are meeting to discuss their "problem" teenager. Even in the first session, however, the problem with the son quickly leads to the problem between the parents. It is not unusual for a family needing help to use a teenaged child as a "ticket of admission" to the helping agency. The struggle over authority and the role of the father in the family is just as much an issue for the husband and wife, but the wife has found it easier, and perhaps safer, to deal with that struggle through the child. The pattern of relationship in the family is oppressive as the father attempts to use intimidation, emotional and physical, to retain control over the family members. Some of this may be closely related to family and cultural background. This pattern will need to be confronted by the worker; however, such a confrontation may be more fruitful if a relationship can first be developed.

It is important for the worker to stay focused on how the parental struggle relates to the couple's ability to parent effectively, helping them to see the connections to their general relationship, but not embarking on a course of general marital counseling (which would be outside of the agency-family working contract). Reassurance on this point may make it safer for both the husband and wife to drop the **family facade**—the false front presented by family members to the outside world.

Another issue that was not dealt with directly in this interview was the question of confidentiality. There was a child welfare agency involved, and already a threat to apprehend (take into care) the teenaged son had been expressed. The worker will need to deal honestly with this issue, since as a staff member of the agency, the worker carries a responsibility to report to the child protection social worker information related to child abuse. This issue was just under the surface of the first interview and must be raised and clarified. Under what conditions might the family support worker have to report child abuse to the social worker in the case? Avoiding such a discussion will not make the authority issue go away—rather, it will invest it with more power to block the work.

In summary, the worker has made a start toward developing a working relationship with the family, especially its most potentially resistant member. There is much work to be done, and the outcome of the work will depend somewhat on how the worker handles his part and how ready the family members are to tackle their responsibilities.

FAMILY SUPPORT WORK OVER TIME

In the example that follows, a family support worker is brought in by a child welfare agency social worker to help a family in which a 12-year-old son is having trouble staying in school. The family has a two-and-a-half year history of difficult times with the agency staff and is seen as "hard to work with." As the worker's tuning-in comments indicated, he was aware of the past history and of the need to deal with it at the beginning of the relationship. In this case, a 15-year-old daughter raised the question for the family. He was also aware of the family's concern over the session turning into marital counseling between the mother and her common-law husband of five years.

The example demonstrates how the worker tried to develop a working contract that respected the family's concerns, and then redefined the contract as it became clear that the parents wanted help in sorting out how they dealt with the children. A central issue, not uncommon in families with stepparents, is how involved the non-biological parent shall be. Often, the stepparent is wary about "butting in," while the biological parent is concerned about not burdening the other parent. In the early sessions, the mother indirectly chooses to exclude the stepfather. After confidence grows in the new family support worker, mother and father are more open to including their relationship in the working contract.

The device to describe this practice is a *Record of Service* (Garfield and Irizary, 1971). It is an assignment used with social work students to help them assess a particular problem faced by a client (individual, family, or group) and then to describe their efforts to address the problem over time. It begins with the worker's description of the client and the time frame under discussion. A brief statement of the problem, as seen by the worker, is followed by examples of how this particular issue came to the worker's attention. Next is a summary of the work using excerpts from process recordings to illustrate the worker's efforts to address the problem. The record of service concludes with an assessment of the current status of the problem (identified at the start of the record) and the worker's strategies for further intervention.

The worker's analysis of what she or he could have done differently is included in the description. The reader will be able to note how careful self-analysis of practice can lead to significant, positive change in both the worker's interventions and the client's responses. The device provides a means for a worker to incorporate an ongoing analysis of his or her practice, which is the hallmark of a practitioner-researcher.

RECORD OF SERVICE: THE SMITH FAMILY

Client Description and Time Frame:

Composition: Natural mother Linda, 35, common-law husband of five years Brian, 29, Marie, 15, Mike, 12, and foster child, Sally, 15. The time period covered is from November through April. The setting is a child welfare agency.

History: Linda, 35, natural mother of Mike and Marie, was from a very unhappy background, having an alcoholic father, being abused by him, and living in fear. School was a bad experience, and she prides herself on being very financially successful with only a grade 6 education. She believes that Mike can do just as well if he can learn the basic "three Rs." Brian, 29, had lived with Linda for the past five years as her common-law husband. He was born and raised in Europe, immigrated to the United States when he was 15 years old, and works successfully with a small business. He only gets involved with the children if Linda is desperate. His family, which lives in town, feels that Linda has led him into a sinful life, and he visits them on his own. He cannot accept the fact that Mike has a severe learning disability and feels that he must be made to sit down and learn. Brian had not spoken to the previous worker in 2½ years except to exchange hellos.

Marie, 15, was in the process of dropping out of school and trying to get into an accelerated program in order to get school finished quickly. Sally, 15, joined the household in January, had been Marie's best friend previously and couldn't manage living with her own family. Mike, 12, had been at numerous resources and was expelled from school as he'd threatened several teachers and beaten up different children at the school. The special teacher later supplied had threatened to resign if she was required to tutor Mike. When I contacted the last resource he'd been in, I was informed that the family and Mike were "unworkable." Combined with the information at the office, I was more than a little wary about being involved.

Description of the Problem:

Linda (the mother) was in a bind; she had turned to the Agency for assistance but was very hesitant to work with an agency that she felt wasn't responsive to her needs. Both Linda and her previous worker of years had seen each other as adversaries, each trying to do what they thought was best for Mike. My record will follow how I worked to develop a culture in which Linda and the Agency could identify their common ground of getting Mike back into school.

How the Problem Came to the Attention of the Worker(s):

The Smith family was my first chance to get working with a family, and Jane, the previous worker, went over the file with me. It soon became clear that the Agency and Linda went through a definite pattern whenever the social worker found a facility that would consider taking Mike. The worker would find a facility, set up intake interviews, inform Linda, she'd agree to attend the interviews but always ended up by saying it wouldn't work. Mike would initially attend the program but after about a month, he wouldn't show up. In frustration, the worker would tell Linda that Mike had been missing, and she'd confirm that she knew this. Mike would always stop attending the facility close to the times that there were to be "family sessions" and Linda's perception of these was a time when her relationship with Brian would be examined and the two of them would be blamed for Mike's problems.

Summary of the Work:

In preparation, I did some resource hunting and came up with some possible placements from the description of what Linda wanted from conversations we'd had by telephone. I also did some preliminary tuning in (or How to Stay Alive Planning). In considering the work to follow, I came up with several taboo areas:

1. Telling Linda about parenting techniques.
2. Trying to probe Linda and Brian's relationship.
3. Trying to do a sales pitch for a resource.
4. Trying to steer Linda where I though she should go.

I realized that

1. Things must be getting desperate for Linda to call for help.
2. Linda had been through the routine many times and knew the ropes much better than I.
3. I had to level about my agenda.
4. I had to do a lot of work on the negatives before we could move.
5. I had to let the family know that there might be nothing available for Mike.

The First Meeting (I Was Nervous):

(First Session)

I was let in the door by Linda, who seemed tired, flustered, and looked as if she were in pain. They'd just finished supper and another social worker who was seeing Sally had left about 20 minutes previously. Linda offered me a seat in the living room, turned off the TV, and called Mike, who sat next to me on the couch. To my amazement Mike was a pleasant-looking 12-year-old who spoke as I'd expect a fellow his age would. I relaxed a bit, figuring he must either have been well drilled beforehand or a top-blower. Marie sat about six feet away looking at a book but was all ears. Brian sat at the far end of the dining room reading and looked up occasionally. I opened the meeting by establishing role and purpose.

Worker: Linda, you and I have spoken on the telephone and I'm wondering if the others know why I'm here tonight. What have you told them?

Linda: Well, I told these guys that we're having a new social worker to find a place for Mike to go to school. He's 12 now and needs to get something—anything—so that he'll know how to read, do some math, and get a job. We need someone to find out where he can go and still be able to stay at home.

Linda continued speaking, and Brian had stopped his reading and looked interested, so I asked him what he thought about plans for Mike. He agreed that Mike needed to be in school and hoped that I could find a place. Linda jumped in suddenly, "Brian works really hard and I do all the kids' schoolwork planning, you know." It seemed like Linda was trying to shut me off from talking with Brian, but I fought the urge to try to override her. Linda said, "Brian, why don't you make us some coffee?" He slowly disappeared into the kitchen and only appeared to deliver coffee, then returned to the kitchen. I wondered why Linda wanted Brian out of the discussion but didn't feel comfortable asking, so I turned to Mike and asked him what he'd like.

Mike: The same things you've been talking about.

Worker: Some regular schoolwork and some things to do with your hands like mechanics and carpentry?

Mike: Yeah, I'd really like that. I fix my bike all the time and I've made things, you know. Would you like to see something?

Linda: Show Frank your blue vase.

Mike got a blue ceramic vase from the knick-knack shelf and proudly showed it. It was a good job, and I told him that I liked it. Marie was getting fidgety and I thought she wanted to get in so I asked her what she thought about plans for Mike. She spoke angrily.

Marie: I don't want to talk about that. I want to talk about social workers and how they don't care about people. All they care about is making money and themselves.

She gave a rundown on all the things that had been tried, failed, and a list of social workers' faults. I was glad for our classwork on checking out previous experiences and felt Marie's strength in speaking out.

Worker: (Moving from the general to the specific) Boy (I sighed), from what you've said I'm sure you must be wondering if I'll be just like all the rest. I do want to find out exactly what Mike wants, as I know that there's no point in trying to force something on Mike that he doesn't want and that everyone doesn't agree to try. I hope that Mike and Linda will tell me, like you have, when I've missed the point or am not listening.

Marie: Well, you are different. You're the first person who's asked Mike what he wants and not just come here and told us what to do.

I thanked Marie, felt like she'd done a lot of work for me as everyone agreed to let me know if I was missing their point. I told them that I'd let them know if I thought they were missing my point or assuming without checking. This led into a discussion about years of misunderstandings and the frustrations involved.

February

As the weeks passed, no facility was available for Mike. Our first meeting in February started with Mike meeting me at the door; he had two friends with him and was eager to talk and leave. I'd been looking for a tutor for Mike and had been unsuccessful.

Mike: Have you found a tutor for me yet? It's getting to be a long time, you know, everyone says they're going to do something and then nothing ever happens.

Worker: No, I haven't found anyone yet. Right now it looks like it could be several weeks before there'll be someone. Bet you're angry waiting to see who'll come.

Mike: Yeah, you know the longer things go, the worse they'll get; sometimes I just get mad and say to Mom—just tell him to stuff it if he can't get someone to help.

Worker: I get really frustrated too, sometimes it seems like forever before there's a worker available.

In the kitchen Linda was tallying her day's receipts, so I sat down and helped sort them out.

Linda: No news, it sounds like, from your call.

Worker: That's right, you sound like you've been through this before, Linda—fed up with the whole waiting business.

With that we got into a discussion about hassles she's had with the Agency, the school system, and other agencies. She asked if I'd go with her to find out exactly what had happened when Mike had got suspended, and I agreed. Brian, who so often barely said two words, came in and sat opposite me at the table and looked as if he wanted to join the conversation.

I tried to include Brian and needed to recontract if he were to be included.

Worker: Do you know what we've been talking about so far, Brian?

Brian: Yes, I could hear from the living room and want you to know that it's no good if you get someone for two hours a day. If Mike can get into doing something he wants, then he'll leave the schoolwork and never learn.

Brian went on to explain how he'd learned English, etc., when he arrived from Europe by studying eight hours a day, and he began to attack Linda's parenting skills and blame her for Mike's failure. I could see Linda freeze up and referred to our contract.

Worker: Linda, Brian is talking now about your differences, and we've agreed that you will decide if I'm to be involved in those discussions.

I could see the smoke inside Linda, didn't want to lose Brian's impetus, but wasn't going to break my agreement with Linda.

Linda: Brian, you know I don't want to talk about this in front of others, it always leads to trouble.

Brian: We've got to talk about it or it'll always be the same, nothing's going to change if we don't try something different.

Brian was visibly shaken; he motioned to his chest indicating that he could hardly breathe and stuttered badly while he told me of an old injury that causes this condition when he's angry. I still wanted Linda to have the say as to my participation.

Worker: I still want you to ask me to wait in the living room, Linda, if you want to talk with Brian privately. I am willing to stay if you want; I might be able to help sort out some of the things both you and Brian are saying. This conversation sounds like it's been talked through a number of times without any solutions, just going around in circles with both of you getting really mad at each other.

Linda: You can stay.

They talked about the differences in their upbringings and their expectations for their own family. They seemed to exaggerate their differences and I pointed out many similarities such as the belief that you have to be tough to survive and at the same time they both wanted warmth and affection. Brian's gasping for breath made it almost impossible to get his words out. At that point it seemed like they both wanted each other's support so badly but couldn't say it.

Worker: You both sound so frustrated and both really want things to be good here. Linda, you sound like you could use some support from Brian. (I missed "vice versa.")

Linda looked startled and said, "Yes, I could." Brian was done in, but heard, and excused himself from the room. Linda talked more about how hard it'd been for her and how she felt the kids were biologically hers so she should take all the responsibility for them. I told her we could talk more about that and thanked Brian on the way out for telling his part.

Because conversations between the husband and wife had broken down and turned to blaming and recriminations, Linda had feared opening up the "taboo" area. And yet, if the family system was going to work effectively, she would need all the help she could get from the whole family to tackle their problems—Brian included. By creating a positive and safe working relationship, and focusing on the part of their relationship dealing with the children, this worker helped set the stage for Linda agreeing to open the door on this important area of work. When Linda and Brian explore their different cultural backgrounds and family histories, they may find they can better understand both their commonalities and differences. It is only a beginning, but a rather important one in reframing the problem.

Another interesting observation is to note than the worker sat down with Linda and helped her sort her receipts. Workers often complain of the difficulty of getting a family's attention with so much going on. This worker did not feel the need to ask Linda to stop what she was doing but instead sat with her and helped. In another case, this worker carried out an excellent interview with a single-parent mom while helping her fold laundry. These ongoing family activities are often a signal to the worker of the stress the family feels about the session, and sometimes it may be easier to work within the activity than to try to bring it to a formal stop.

In the excerpt that follows, the worker brings a tutor into the situation and meets with her, Linda, and Mike to discuss their working contract. When the tutor mentions the possibility of a family meeting to discuss Mike's school progress, both Mike and his mother go off into "flight" in an effort to escape the uncomfortable subject. The worker responds to the process of the session and calls everyone's attention to what happened. This allows the concerns about "family sessions" to be aired and the contract clarified. In the second excerpt, we see the worker beginning the phase of transitions and endings, getting ready to connect the family members to new sources of help after he leaves.

March

By March, I was able to get a tutor for Mike—Betty, who had worked with him two years before and was the only worker the Smiths had identified as having been helpful. We met together to draw up Betty's contract. Mike was eager to have Betty work with him.

Worker: Now, what do you two want Betty to work on during her time with Mike?

There was silence, many shrugs, looks at the ceiling and "I don't knows"; then Linda asked me, "What do you think should go down there?" referring to the contract.

Betty: No, no, no—it's not up to Frank to say what you want, it's up to you and Mike. There's no way I can work with you unless we agree on the contract. We can change as we go along, but you have to say what you want.

After more silence, Linda listed what she wanted. Betty added a weekly family meeting to discuss how things were going at school and at home for Mike and Linda. Suddenly Mike started talking about the paint on the ceiling, and he and Linda spoke at full speed about the ceiling paint.

Worker: Wait a minute, wait a minute—what's going on here? All of a sudden you two took off and I don't know what's happening. What just happened here? (Responding to indirect cues)

Linda: Oh, nothing, I'm sorry.

Worker: Mike, do you know what happened to you, you started looking at the ceiling all of a sudden?

Mike: It's the family meetings—she doesn't like them, that's what happened before, she didn't want to go to them. (Linda looked shell-shocked.)

Worker: What happened when you didn't have the sessions, Mike?

Mike: I got kicked out.

Worker: Are you worried that the same thing might happen again? (Supporting Mike in a taboo area)

Mike went on to say that he wanted to have the school work out for him. Linda explained to him what she'd disliked about previous family meetings. After some clarification of Betty's role and purpose in the meetings, Mike thought it would work and was first to sign the agreement, looking proud of playing his part. Betty and I told them that they'd both taken big steps in leveling with us and each other. (Crediting work done)

April

At a regular evening meeting in early April we'd been talking about endings, and Linda had been shocked at first that the time was so short and then angry at me for leaving and frustrated about having to start all over again with another worker.

Worker: I remember our first meetings, Linda. I wasn't sure if we'd be able to work together at all. I feel that we've come through a great deal together and it's been pretty shaky at times—you know the times we've both got pissed off. You've all made me feel welcome in your home, I've come to like you very much, and I'm going to miss you.

Linda: Then why are you leaving? I know, you have to leave. Who will be my new worker?

Worker: That's something I've been checking out. You've said that you've had a hard time whenever a new worker is involved. (Linda agreed and said that she wouldn't fool around and be nice to a new worker she didn't like.)

Worker: That's one of the things I really like about working with you, you give it to me straight. I was always confident when I felt like I'd blown it that you'd tell me. That's a feeling I enjoy. Also I was honored last week when you told me that you trusted me—I knew that was hard for you to say—that's when you added "almost."

Linda: Well, I do trust you. (She laughed and added "almost.")

I explained that I'd talked to my supervisor to find out who'd be getting the Smiths after I left, and we talked about getting together in order to clarify what would be happening. The conversation continued around some of the snags we'd hit, how things were resolved, and what obstacles might come up. It hadn't occurred to me how much I'd become involved with the family until that evening, and the conversation about leaving really hit me.

Current Status of the Problem:

Where It Stands Now: Linda has begun to see the Agency as an ally and took the opportunity to suggest a joint meeting with Debbie, who'll be the new worker, in order to establish a working contract. Brian has joined in the last four out of five meetings and has said that he's willing to help with Mike when Linda asks. She's agreed to include Brian in the weekly family sessions.

Strategies for Intervention:

1. Betty will continue working with Mike until the end of June and will be available in September for schoolwork and family sessions.
2. Debbie and I will follow up on our meeting to discuss future plans, and she'll be available to the Smiths and Betty.
3. Linda, Mike, Betty, and I will visit another possible resource this week and discuss future plans.

It's important to note that the worker's analysis of the current status of the problem does not consider it to be "solved." Very rarely are problems solved, and in fact, I encourage workers to remove that word from their vocabulary. What the worker identifies is important changes in the state of the relationship between the family and the agency and between the family members themselves. The worker has helped to build a platform for ongoing work. He has been only an incident in the lives of these clients; however, he has been an important incident. Keeping this perspective helps workers to avoid two common types of mistakes in analyzing practice: overestimating or underestimating the impact on a client.

WORKING WITH A SINGLE-PARENT FAMILY

Our view of the average family as consisting of a working father, a mother at home, and two to three children has become more myth than reality. The rate of growth of single-parent families is increasing, as is women's involvement in the work force. At one of my speaking engagements on the subject of working with single parents, I asked the audience, all helping professionals, how many of them were single parents, had been children in homes of single parents, or had close relations who were involved in single parenting. Almost two thirds of the five hundred people in the audience raised their hands.

Although there are many similarities between single-parent and two-parent families, there are also some differences that should be noted by helping professionals. Single parents have to face many of the same normative crises faced by other families (e.g., children becoming teenagers), but they have to face them alone. Most single parents are women, and a large percentage of these must either work (often in low-pay, low-status, dead-end jobs) or depend upon welfare. For many, the lack of affordable day-care facilities makes it impossible to work and improve their financial situation. Between low pay and welfare, most single-parent mothers are trying to live on income levels below the accepted poverty level—a factor that adds significantly to the stress of raising a family alone.

An already difficult situation for single parents on welfare may become even more stressful with the advent of welfare reform measures and the decentralizing of welfare programs to the states. The artificial setting of specific time limits to welfare and the limited supports (child care, training, and so on) offered to welfare parents who can move into the work force, when combined with the limited availability of decent-paying jobs, does not augur well for the future of this population of single-parent families.

Housing is another major area of distress for single parents. Many housing options are not open to them, and as a result, they need to pay more of their income for housing than the general population. A female single parent quickly discovers that her credit rating left her with her husband, even if she had a positive relationship with her local bank while she was married. She may suddenly find herself in a "catch-22" situation, needing a positive credit record to get credit, and needing credit to obtain a positive credit record. Thus, if she wishes to purchase a home, she may run into discrimination cutting her off from this avenue of improving her housing situation.

The problem of dealing with friends can also be a serious one. Many single parents report changes in attitudes towards them after a split in the marriage, with former close friends seeming to take sides. Another common factor is sometimes referred to as the "Noah's Ark syndrome," in which friends seem to be operating under the general belief that people should come "two by two." Old friends seem to slip away, and new friends seem to be harder to find. This problem, often compounded by the single parent's depression and lack of effort to create new support groups, leads to further isolation and loneliness. With all of these added pressures, a single parent often has difficulty finding time to meet her personal needs while still taking care of the needs of the children. Dealing with school meetings, dental appointments, homework, and so on is difficult enough for two parents. At the time of this writing, the Clinton administration was advocating family leave time from work to deal with child-rearing activities; however, these suggestions were meeting with considerable resistance—often from those who claimed to be "family friendly."

In addition, dealing with the feelings of one's children when one is so vulnerable can be too hard to do alone. As a result, barriers start to grow in a family, and certain areas become "taboo." One crucial taboo area may be the feelings of the children about the absent parent and the rejection they feel. As one woman said in a group I led for single parents, "It's hard for me to help my kids face their rejection because I still haven't been able to face mine." The guilt felt by the remaining parent often makes it hard to open up honest discussion with the children in the family. If the children show signs of their distress through behavior cues appropriate to their age (e.g., young children regressing and bedwetting; latency age children cutting themselves off from friends, having school trouble, and getting into fights; teenagers getting into trouble with the law), the parent often senses the cause; however, the parent's guilt can create a significant communication blockage.

Ongoing relations with the ex-spouse can also take a toll on the parent and the children. Often, the battles of the marriage or feelings concerning the split emerge around custody issues, financial support issues, and struggles over loyalty. Children already hurt by a split between their parents, for which they may feel responsible, are further distressed by feeling they must take sides and cannot be loyal to both parents at the same time.

A number of these problems emerge in the example that follows. In this case, the setting is a community care team, with the single-parent mom, age 32, coming for help in coping with her family of five children, aged 2 to 14. Kurt, the 10-year-old, is the "ticket of admission" for this family.

RECORD OF SERVICE: A SINGLE-PARENT FAMILY

Client Description and Time Frame:

The family includes Jane (mother) who is 32. She has three children from her first marriage (Judy, 14; Robert, 13; Kurt, 10) and two from her second marriage (Arn, 5; and Bobby, 2). She has separated from her second husband, Len. The time period is from February 26th to April 4th. The agency is a community care team.

Description of the Problem:

Jane is a 32-year-old-woman, a single parent with five children. She is a very reserved, dignified person who finds it difficult to ask for help, to open herself up, and share her feelings. She came in identifying her problem as depression. She also has difficulty managing her family and communicating well with them. One child, Kurt, has become the IP [identified patient] and has been acting out with attention-seeking behavior by stealing at school, setting fires, and eventually breaking into homes and stealing. Jane needs help in dealing with her own depression and in dealing with her family situation.

How the Problem Came to the Attention of the Worker(s):

During our first interview, Jane spoke of how difficult it was for her to come to the team and ask for help. She only came when she was desperate and felt there was no other way she could help herself. Jane had not been able to tell any other person the problems she was having with being depressed and in handling the children. Much of this seems to have to do with Jane being a single parent and having to take care of the children by herself. After a few family sessions, I discovered that the children, too, were responding in the same way as Jane—keeping their feelings inside—except for Kurt, who overtly displays his unacceptable behavior. I could see that they needed to learn how to express their feelings and perhaps could help each other by learning how to do this together. Jane and the children need to learn how to respond directly to each other as a way to help their communication. The problems with Kurt brought the situation out into the open, as Jane was not able to handle him or know how to respond to him.

Summary of Work (*Note:* Entries are not in chronological order.)

March 14

I gave Jane a chance to express some of her feelings to me which she finds difficult to admit even to herself. I had a guess that Jane was not only feeling depressed but also angry and was keeping this anger inside. This came out very clearly when Kurt ran away one day when he was in trouble after setting a fire in the school. Jane was very upset and kept saying how depressed she was over what had happened. I reached into what she was saying and said, "I imagine this makes you pretty angry too?" Jane said, "I do all I can and I get no thanks; I know they're only children but they're all I have. (Silence) They are quite a burden to handle." She cried a little. She began to say how angry she was that Kurt would do this to her. "I have no life of my own; they're all I have." For Jane to be able to express anger in this way was something new for her. After we had talked, she was able to gain some control of herself and begin to organize some search parties to go out and look for Kurt.

Jane also has a lot of angry feelings about having been abandoned by her two husbands and also by her parents when she was a child. "I am sick of being walked on by him. When we got married, I went out to work to help put him through school and then he just dumped all of us. He just walked out. And now he makes all these demands (to see the kids). Now we have to jump just 'cause he says to. And I really resent it. I'm really bitter about it. It's not fair." Jane's first expression of feelings to me were depression over having been abandoned by her husband. She slowly was able to turn this expression of depression into an expression of anger. Getting her to admit these feelings was a beginning step.

I began to help Jane try to understand some of the feelings the children were having, especially Kurt. In the first excerpt [above] after Jane had a chance to express some of her anger, I began to try to point out how badly Kurt must have been feeling to run away. She said she knew how desperately he was asking for help. I asked her to go over in detail what had happened in the family the night before or earlier that morning. She told of how she had been awakened early by Kurt and Arn fighting. Later, Arn told her Kurt had said, "I'm going to kill myself." I pointed out to Jane how badly Kurt must have been feeling that morning. I asked about school and what was going on there that could be upsetting him. Jane suddenly remembered that today was report card day and that the teacher had told him that if he didn't stop stealing (he had been stealing from the class), he would get a bad report card. Jane began to tune into some of Kurt's fears of getting a bad report card and how worried he probably was. She also began to tell some of the reasons why Kurt is picked on by the other children and isn't liked. Jane seemed to be more understanding of Kurt at that point and could see a little why he was behaving like he did.

March 24

Helping Jane to tune into Kurt's feelings occurred a number of times. In another instance when Kurt stole from the school and was suspended, Jane first began expressing her own feelings of depression about what he had done. I asked her how she thought Kurt was feeling and she said, "pretty badly." She told me how he had confessed to her what he had done, had started crying, and wanted to strangle himself. Because Jane was able to express this to me, she began to really feel for him and tears rolled down her face. "I feel badly that he feels so bad." We talked of how depressed Kurt is underneath and asking for help in his own way.

April 2

Another example occurred when Jane was telling me about her second marriage to Len and how he wanted a child of his own. I began to question her about how Kurt had felt at that time because he was the baby (5 years old). Jane began to describe how hurt Kurt was over Len's rejection of him when their new baby came. Len had wanted to put all three older children in a foster home to get rid of them. I pointed out to Jane how this still must be an influence on Kurt today and he probably has lots of

feelings from what happened then. Through having Jane discuss these three incidents in detail, she was able to understand some of Kurt's feelings and begin to understand what the world is like from his eyes.

March 19

Through family sessions, we (the worker who leads the family sessions, John, and
I) were able to help Jane express some of her thoughts and feelings directly to the
children. This began to open up for the family a communication pattern of talking directly to each other. An example of this occurred in our second family session. Jane
came in looking obviously upset. John asked her about this and she said, "I'd rather
not talk about it; it doesn't concern the kids." John said, "the subject matter doesn't
concern them; your upset concerns them." John asked the kids how they feel when
their mom gets upset. Kurt said, "worried." The other kids agreed; they were curious.
Jane said that if it was going to upset them, then she would tell them. It had to do with
her second husband calling her that morning. After Jane put that out, we were able to
deal with two important issues: (1) the kids should know why she's upset so they
don't think that they're the cause of her depression, and (2) how the kids should respond to her when she's depressed. Jane had been afraid to share her feelings with
the children but found that it helped them not be worried by doing so.

April 4

Another example of this occurred at our family session after Kurt had been breaking into homes and stealing. John said, "Did you [Jane] and Kurt have a talk last
night?" Jane said, "A little. I thought it was better not to say too much. I didn't know
what to say to him." John said, "Do you have any idea today what you'd like to say to
him?" Jane said, "No, I don't know what to say to him; I'm at a loss." John had to per-
suade her to try to think of what she should say. Jane finally turned to Kurt directly
and said, "I want to know why you did that." The conversation didn't end up so
well. Kurt cried, and Jane yelled at him unmercifully. A better intervention here would
have been to help her understand some of his feelings first and then begin to have
them talk directly. Because she came down so hard on Kurt, we were not able to get
him then to respond back to her.

We were able to point out the difficulties they were having in their communications with each other. During the first family session, Bobby was receiving a great deal
of attention by crying, demanding his own way, and generally disrupting the family
session. I asked whether this occurs at home. The kids all said that it did. Robert said
that Bobby demanded a lot of time at home. Judy said he was always getting into
something, you had to pick it up, and he was into something else. Kurt said that
Bobby kept getting up at night and this kept his mom up so she was tired during the
day and didn't have time for anyone else. Jane agreed with all this. Everyone decided to leave Bobby with a babysitter so that the rest of the family could enjoy the family sessions.

March 27

At a later family session, John was able to point out some communication problems
the family seemed to be having. The boys were talking about the neighborhood hockey game that they play. Arn said, "Can we have a hockey game today, mom?" Robert
jumped in with "no." Jane said, "You and Kurt have things to do first." John said,

"Does that mean that he can do it after?" Mom said yes. John asked Arn if this is what he had understood it to mean, or that he couldn't do it at all. Arn said that he thought he couldn't do it at all. John pointed out that sometimes people mean one thing and other people can take another meaning from it. The family seemed to think this happened quite often with them.

During this same family session, John was also able to point out how Jane's anger was an obstacle to communication in the family sessions. John asked the kids how they could get on the good side of their mom. They were answering with some joking about what their mom liked and how they could win her over to their side. Jane's face was very serious, and John asked what was happening with her. Jane said, "I'm mad at these two" [to Arn and Kurt]. John said, "What brought that on? Did you just get angry all of a sudden?" Jane said no. She had been angry all day because she couldn't get the kids to do anything at home. John told her that was a real shame because she had not been enjoying what had been happening with the family. She had been missing out on that opportunity. We then were able to talk about her anger and begin to help her deal with the source of the anger. Often Jane's feelings are an obstacle in ways similar to this when she will not put them out in the open and tries to hide them.

Later on in this session, John had asked the family to give things they liked about the family as a way of ending the session. Kurt said to Jane, "Good job," and patted her hand. Jane was silent. John asked her if she had heard Kurt say that. She said, "I guess I didn't." Kurt said, "Yes, you did." Jane was silent again. John pointed out to her that is the way people often respond when they hear a compliment because they think the person is trying to flatter them. "But that's the way you really see it, isn't it, Kurt?" said John. Kurt agreed. John told Jane that "one way to keep a depression going is to not hear the good things. From Kurt's point of view, you were doing a good job." One of Jane's obstacles to improving communication in the family is her own unwillingness to hear the good about herself. These obstacles to communication encourage denial and repression of feelings instead of the open and honest communication the family needs to function.

February 26

I tried to point out to Jane that the kids are concerned about her and that they have a common concern for each other. During the first family session this concern came out in a natural way, without my intervention. When we asked the children why they were here, Kurt promptly replied, "Because my mom cares what happens to the family." Later on in that session we were talking about what it's like for the kids not to have a father in the home. Kurt replied that his mom is twice as busy 'cause she has to be both mom and dad. Jane had a startled look come over her face as she realized how deeply Kurt understood her feelings. At the end, Jane said that she had appreciated what Kurt had to say as she had never realized this herself. This was a beginning step in drawing Kurt and Jane together, as she took his understanding of her as genuine concern.

March 19

In a later family session we had asked the kids to try to think of options of what they could do to help their mom since she is so down. The suggestion was offered that the three oldest go live somewhere else for awhile to give their mom a break.

Robert said, "If it will make her feel better, or if she'll recover by the time we come back, then I wouldn't mind." The kids discussed this for awhile. Jane said, "I wouldn't consider that as an option. I think that's all that's keeping me going, to keep the kids together." John said, "I bet the kids were glad to hear that, that they meant that much to their mom." Jane then said, "Well, maybe they'd rather do that." John asked her what she heard them saying. She said [about Robert] "that he wouldn't mind living somewhere else." John asked her what she thought his preference was. She didn't know so he told her to ask him. Jane said, "Do you want to go live somewhere else?" Robert said, "I wouldn't rather, but if it's better for you, I would." John said that it sounded like he was really considering her first, and would sacrifice for her if necessary. This began to show Jane that the kids do care about her and she about them. The obstacle of her not really listening (or not wanting to listen) is what hurts communication with the children.

April 4

In a later family session, Kurt had been talking about how bad he felt for not having a father. He had been crying and was expressing his deep hurt over being rejected by his real dad and his stepdad. John said, "It seems like you've been shortchanged in the dad department and not had very good luck. And you, Jane, you've been shortchanged in the husband department." In this way he was trying to draw attention to the common ground between them—they've both been shortchanged, and it's rough for them. The need that they have for each other and the help that they can give each other is the message we tried to get through to them. We gave Jane alternatives for dealing with the children when she asked for help in knowing what to do.

February 27

In the first family session the kids described the things they miss with no dad in their lives. The two older boys said that they missed having a dad to be involved with them in sports. Jane said that she finds it difficult to work with the boys. When I asked her to clarify this she said that she finds it overwhelming, finds herself inadequate for sports, etc. This theme of concern was raised several times, so I suggested that she try to find a "big brother" for each of the boys, someone who would take a special interest in them and give them a little attention. I told her that this was especially important for Kurt, whose behavior indicated that he wanted more attention. Jane has never carried through with this suggestion even though I tried to pin her down on it several times. It seems as though this is "my" idea rather than hers.

April 25

As a result of pointing out and identifying feelings with Jane (her own and Kurt's), she has been able to speak more directly with her children, especially Kurt. Jane had been telling me how her second husband was trying to get custody of the two youngest children. We had been discussing the legal details and implications of this for about a half hour. I said to Jane, "It must be hard on you having Bobby and Arn look like their dad. It must remind you of him." Jane said, "Yes, I suppose that's why it's so hard to stop caring for someone. Arn and Bobby are more special to me." I said, "Is that because they're Len's kids?" She said she guessed so. I told her that was not an easy thing for her to be saying. I asked her if she thought the other three children could sense how she felt. She said she didn't know. Maybe they could. A week later Jane told me this: "I've asked Kurt what's going on inside of him...I asked him if he thought I didn't love him or if he thought I didn't love him as much as the other kids. And he said yes. I asked him how long he felt like that, to see if it goes back a long ways to when Arn was born and Len rejected him. He said, a couple of months. I tried to explain to him that he has friends that he likes more than others, or that he gets along with better. I said I love you. It's taken me a long time to figure that all out 'cause I do love them all the same but I get along much better with Robert, Arn, and Judy. For Kurt and I, it's a real effort to get along." For Jane to speak this directly and openly with Kurt is something new. It shows her concern, her realization of mistakes in the past, and how she is trying now to share her feelings and thoughts with Kurt.

Current Status of the Problem:

Jane still appears depressed a good deal of the time, and she and the family have only made beginning steps in their relationships together. It seems that Jane is learning that it isn't easy to share feelings with another person but it can be rewarding. This past week she was able to tell a friend all about the family problems. That person became a real source of help to her. I pointed out that because she had been willing to open up, this person then was able to help her. Jane has also begun to get out of the house two afternoons a week while a homemaker comes there. It seems that as she begins to develop a life outside of her children, that it will help lift some of her depression and give her more quality time when she is home. She and Kurt still have difficulty in getting along with each other, but they have made a few positive steps in trying to understand each other.

Specific Next Steps:

1. Explore the common area mother and children share in not having a husband or father. Probably this is one of the areas that is most difficult for them to express their feelings about.
2. Help the family begin to support each other as they express feelings. Jane especially needs to learn how to listen and support the kids as they open up to her.
3. Support Jane in her efforts to develop her "own life" away from the children. Help Jane to structure her limited free time away from the home so that she is able to accomplish some of her personal goals.
4. Point out to Jane the pattern of response that she has with the children.
5. Deal with ending and who will continue work with Jane.

The workers in this excerpt were trying to have an impact on the maladaptive ways this family used to deal with pain. The losses associated with the marital breakups were artfully described when the worker pointed out that the kids were "shortchanged in the dad department," just as their mother was "shortchanged in the husband department." It is crucial for the single parent to come to grips with his or her own losses and pain, and to find sources of support, if the parent is to be able to face the pain of the children. Often, guilt over the marital breakups cuts the parent off from the underlying message of hurt sent by the children. By breaking the cycle and helping to teach family members how to be more open, honest, and supportive of each other, the workers may help release the family's inherent capacity to provide mutual support.

THE IMPACT OF CULTURE AND COMMUNITY: A WHITE WORKER AND AN AMERICAN INDIAN FAMILY

One of the greatest tragedies in North America has been the impact of the white society on its "first peoples," the Indians or Native Americans. A strong family and community tradition, a whole culture and way of life, was systematically stripped from a people in what has been described as cultural genocide. This problem is a special case of the struggle each minority group faces, whether aboriginals or immigrants. Each must find a way to preserve what is of value to its own culture and still come to grips with a surrounding and dominating culture. When the group is of another race—Indian, black, Chicano, Asian—the struggle is usually intensified by a persistent racism, sometimes subtle in nature, other times open and direct.

In the Native community, from which the family in this example is drawn, years of neglect, discrimination, and exploitation have often led to a breakdown in individual, family, and community functioning. Once-proud cultural traditions have been lost for many of the community's members. In particular, teenagers must go through a crucial step in their normative development in which they struggle to understand who they are, and how they shall be. The separation and integration issue is just as important in relation to one's culture and community as it is in relation to the immediate family. In fact, the two struggles become intertwined in important ways. The ambivalent feelings are pronounced when the subculture, the peer group for a teenager, encourages and supports deviant behavior (the extensive use of alcohol, criminal activity, and so on) and the future appears to be bleak. When a teenager looks around and sees members of the adult community who appear to have given up, it is not hard to understand an internal struggle that can lead to complete alienation from the larger society, or in a shockingly large number of cases, teenage suicide. The alternative choice of facing the problems, finding the strength to cope, accepting the role model of many of the adult members of the community who have refused to surrender to years of oppression, is also an option. For the teenagers in this situation to make this transition, they will need all the help they can get from family, community (the local band), and their cultural heritage.

In the example that follows, culture and community are key issues as Jim, a 14-year-old Native teenager, struggles with this crucial, transitional crisis. The worker must also deal with the fact that she is white. No matter what her attitudes and feelings may be with respect to persons of colour, she is an outsider—a member of the oppressor group. White workers must be alert to the fact that, as one African-American described it, "For a person of color, the antennae are always up on the lookout for racism."

In a study cited throughout this book (Shulman, 1991), the issue of race and practice in relation to Native clients was explored. Two variables included in the analysis were the worker's understanding of the Native culture (as perceived by clients) and the worker's understanding of the impact of race on the relationship (as perceived by the worker). Both of these variables evidenced strong positive associations with the client's perceptions of a positive working relationship with the worker and the worker's helpfulness. These variables, as well as those that measured the attitude of the regional staff as a whole toward Native clients, also affected other outcome measures. A first step in dealing with racism in practice is for the helping professional to abandon the denial of its existence. By facing and accepting the existence of one's own internalized racism and sexism, a product of centuries of white, male, Euro-centered history, philosophy, medicine, psychology, and so on (described by such mental health revolutionaries as Fanon [1968]), a worker begins the task of monitoring and then purging its impact on her or his practice. Each new client who is different from the worker can be part of the worker's education. The worker also has a responsibility to work on his or her own education.[2]

With a clearer sense of the impact of oppression on the psychology and sociology of persons of colour, coupled with an understanding of the resilience factors that have helped people to cope with oppression, the worker may be able to perceive problems in living in new ways. The focus shifts from personal pathology and a reinforcement of oppressive stereotyping to a practice that helps the client to perceive the devastating impact on self that can occur for any member of an oppressed group. In addition, the identification of baseline and developmental reserve capacity in individuals, the family, and the community offers opportunities to break the cycles that block growth and development.

This socioeconomic perspective is important for work not only with persons of color but with the oppressed and vulnerable populations (e.g., women, the mentally ill, Asian immigrants, survivors of the Nazi Holocaust and their descendants, gays and lesbians). Such a shift in perspective by the helping professional opens up the possibility of finding important areas of strength in the client, the community, and the culture. It also more clearly defines a professional responsibility (discussed in Chapter 18) for social workers to have professional impact on their own agencies, the community, and society in general.

Examples of adoption of self-destructive behavior and self-denigrating attitudes painfully emerge in the following example as the parents refer to their son's "crazy Indian" and "dirty Indian" behavior. Illustrations of the worker's recognition of culturally based strengths are also evident in her attention to the importance to the son of his "dancing" and "carving" skills.

RECORD OF SERVICE: A NATIVE AMERICAN FAMILY

Client Description and Time Frame:

Father is 40, stepmother is 29, and son Jim is 14. The family is being seen as part of a probation program ordered by a judge because of Jim's arrests for breaking and entering.

Description of the Problem:

Jim, in the throes of puberty, is searching very hard to establish his identity. Most of all, he wants to feel and be proud of his Native heritage, but the conflicting messages he has internalized about "being Indian" do not allow him to do so positively. His anger and confusion manifest themselves by his acting out: he has committed seven B&Es (Breaking and Entering) on the reserve, two of them specifically focusing on the Indian Band office. He has developed an alcohol problem. His acting out has alienated him from the elders of the band, who refuse to be involved in helping him with the court process, as is usually the case for juvenile delinquents of this band. I perceive his B&Es as cries for help with his home situation.

Jim's parents are disheartened and upset. They feel they have tried their best and have failed. They are considering sending him away to a residential school. Their medium of communication and major stumbling block between Jim and his parents is discussion of Native identity: all emotions, conflict, and disagreement are discussed under the heading "Indian." In my efforts to help this family, I must also deal with their feelings about me—a white, female probation officer. I realize I will have to become more than just a symbol of white authority.

How the Problem Came to the Attention of the Worker:

My first meeting with Jim and his parents was to discuss the B&E charges in the hope of sparing Jim court appearances. I had great difficulty keeping the session on focus: it was too painful a topic for everyone to discuss directly. Actually, Jim and his parents reenacted their communication pattern in front of me: the war was on. Jim's mother said angrily that these B&Es were "crazy Indian stuff." I tried to reach for the feelings of pain and disappointment behind the anger and said, "Jim's B&Es are hard on the family right now; they would be for any family, Indian or not." Jim's father said, "I knew nothing about them Indians." Jim didn't give me a chance to say anything and counterattacked by angrily saying that his parents are Honkies in disguise but he is an Indian, he is a super dancer and carver and can drink and fight with the bigger guys on the reserve any day. I said that his parents might be proud about his dancing and carving. Jim's mother said, "Honkies or not Honkies, we know that Jim is a no-good Indian." The energy they put out fighting made me believe that there was a lot of concern and care hidden behind the anger. Their faces indicated they were clearly in pain.

Summary of the Work:

Second Session:

I tuned in to Jim's feelings and tried to put his feelings into words. Jim had a tough look on his face. He slid himself into a chair, his knees up close to his chest as if to protect himself. I said, "You look angry as hell today." No response. I waited out his silence. He said with a tone devoid of affect that he had a big fight last night after Indian dancing and that it lasted until 4 in the morning. I asked him if he'd got hurt (empathizing). He said no, he never gets hurt. He was drunk anyway. I was lucky he was sober this afternoon. I said, "Alcohol dims the pain. A 14-year-old drunk is a sad story to me." He said he knew. Jim said he had also siphoned gas out of a car last night. I said, "It is a lot for one night. Are you trying to tell me how bad you can be?" Jim looked at me intently. I said that behind his tough facade I thought there was a lot of pain. His voice changed. With a defensive tone he said "Pain about what?" I said, "Maybe it is painful to feel you have to act like a hellion to get attention." He giggled and said it wasn't funny. I said, "I agree, it's not funny, it hurts." He cocked his head down. I waited out his silence. He said suddenly, "Nothing ever hurts anymore. Nobody cares about me anymore." I said, "Are you talking about home?" (recognizing his indirect communication) He said simply, "Yeah."

I recognized his indirect communication and tried to help him go from general to specific concerns. Jim had done a rerun of the above two weeks in a row; that is, enumerating all the "bad" behaviors he had got into. I said it was the third weekend that he had asked me to give him hell. He said that if I didn't, nobody would. I asked him if that's what he wanted his parents to do. He said, "No, I want them to understand me." I said that I knew things were rough for everyone at home right now; could he tell me what had taken place at home that hurt? He looked away and said in a low voice, "They called me a rotten Indian." The affect of pain was so strong that he could not elaborate on his feelings or the specific circumstances. I said, "It hurts a lot doesn't it? I wish I could take the pain away from you."

I tried to share my feelings openly. Jim said that he was sick and tired of being called a dirty Indian at home. The affect was anger. I tried to reach for the specific feeling but got nowhere. He said that all his parents talked about was "dirty Indians this, silly Indians that. Who do they think they are, anyway?" I said, "It may hurt to hear the word Indian coming from your own parents as a curse word." He asked me if I though he was a dirty Indian. I said no, he was Indian all right, "but the two words together are a terrible combination." He said, "What about a silly Indian?" I reached for his indirect communication and said, "You're checking out if I'm prejudiced, aren't you?" He said, "Yup." I said it was for him to judge. He said I would be on probation for awhile. I said I knew. He said in a low voice that he didn't think I could understand. I said gently, "Do you feel you can't win: you can't be right and you can't be Indian?" (Putting the client's feelings into words) He said suddenly, "I don't know what 'Indian' means. How am I supposed to grow up okay?" I put my arms around him and said that he was right. I wasn't sure I could understand fully what it means to grow up as an Indian. I said that his hurt was choking me up right now.

I tried to help Jim view his parents in new ways. Jim said that his parents put him through a grinder whenever he is home. I said that it sounds horrible, what does it mean? (Reaching for elaboration) He said that his parents hassle him about every little detail about what he does at night. I jokingly said, "It's not such a horrible grinder after all!" He laughed. He said that really they don't care about him, they just want him on a leash. I said, "And you want to be more independent, don't you?" (Recognizing the metaphor) He said, "Yup."

I asked him to give me an example of the grinder. He said that last night he came home at midnight. They just had to know who he was with, where he had been. I said, "That sound to me like they care about you. They worry about you, and frankly at midnight I would worry too." Jim pouted. I waited out his silence. He said, "I don't think they care. They're just angry." I said that maybe they felt both fear and anger. Did he think that they had any reason to be angry last night? He said, "Maybe so. Midnight is kind of late." I agreed. I asked him if he knew what his parents felt waiting for him. He said, "They always assume the worst. That's dumb." I said, "We all do that when we're worried." He said, "I guess I give them reasons to be angry and I don't like it." I said sadly, "and they don't, either. I bet they feel just as bad as you do about yesterday."

I supported him in a taboo area and tried to stay close to his feelings of anger and rejection. Jim said that he was going to kill his mother one of these days. She isn't his real mom anyway. I asked him if he was angry about something she had done or angry because she isn't his real mom. (Trying to partialize his concern) He said, "Both." I asked him what his mom had done for him to be so upset. He said, "She is really unreal; she phoned the school to insist that she be warned if I skipped out. It's none of her business. My dad's, sure, but not hers." I kept the issue in focus and said, "Not hers because she is your stepmom?" He said, "Yup, I'm not her son. She's got no right on me." I said sadly, "No right to care? She can't win, can she?" Jim said, "No, she can't win. She's the one who made us move from the reserve." I said I knew about that, that she wanted to make a better home for him and his dad. Jim nervously twisted his hair around his fingers and said that he would rather have his mom around than "her" care. I said that he had expressed real and deep feelings. (Crediting his work) "It's real hard to get over one's Mom's death."

I tried to help Jim identify the affect obstacle and offered to mediate with his parents. Jim said that he doesn't know how to tell his parents to stop calling him names when he does something wrong—names like "silly Indian." When they do, his blood boils and he goes out and gets drunk. He can't say anything. He just walks out. And he does start acting silly. I asked him to tell me exactly what he would like to tell his parents. He said that he just wants them to stop calling him names. But he can't say it to them. I said, "That's their way of criticizing you, isn't it?" He said, "Yeah. It's bad enough being told off when you do something wrong, but then calling me names like that, it's below the belt." I said, "It's like you're nobody all of a sudden." He said, "Yup." He had tears in his eyes.

I said, "Do you want me to help you talk to your parents?" He said, "Yeah." He couldn't do it alone. I said that I'd phone his parents, and if they agreed we'd try to talk about the name-calling and try to understand what is behind it from their side. Jim said that he didn't want to talk about the things he does wrong. I said that he forgets he does a lot of things real well too. We have to take the bad with the good. He said, "Yeah, but I'm far from perfect." I said that perfection is like a rainbow—nobody can reach it, we can only try. He said his parent didn't know that. I said I was sure they did, they just had high expectations for him. He said he didn't believe in high expectations. I laughed and said, "Baloney—you want to be the best about everything." He said, "How do you know?" I said that I had seen some of his carvings. They're beautiful. It was obvious to me that he was trying to be the best. (Emphasizing the positive) Jim had a long-drawn-out "oh." I brought the conversation back on focus and said, "So if your parents are willing, we'll talk about both sides." He said he was willing to try but that I was going to get myself into a lot of trouble with his parents. I said, "Because I'm white?" He said, "Yeah." I said I could only try, that things should go easier if I didn't take sides. (Emphasizing the contract)

Third Session:

I tried to tune in to the feelings of ambivalence of the one (Jim) and the many (the family), tried to include everyone in the commonality of the experience and clarified the contract. At the first meeting I said that they must feel a bit uncomfortable about having a white probation officer coming into their home. Mr. Jones smiled and said, "You bet, you're the first one we managed to get in here." Mrs. Jones said, matter of factly, that she didn't mind, today she'd had to clean her home for the health nurse anyway. I recognized her ambivalence and said that I know how it feels, it's a hassle to clean house because a stranger is coming in. She nodded hesitantly. I said I felt a bit like an intruder today (putting my personal feelings into words) but that I hoped we would feel more comfortable once we knew each other better.

Jim's eyes were covered by his cap and his arms crossed at his chest. I asked him what he was angry about. He said, "Nothing, leave me alone." Mrs. Jones firmly said that he couldn't talk to me like that. I said it was okay to be angry. Did they (Jim's parents) know what was making Jim so angry? (Beginning to partialize and trying to help the family members help each other) Mr. Jones said that Jim is like that around home, not to worry. I said that maybe Jim is afraid that we might all gang up on him. (Putting client's feelings into words) "It's certainly not my intention." I said that I was here to have them talk about a real painful issue: Jim can't stand being called a dirty Indian and it hurts so much that he can't talk about it usually.

I got a nasty look from Mr. Jones. Mrs. Jones said she thought it was simple: I should forbid Jim from doing any of that crazy Indian stuff, then she'd stop calling him a crazy Indian. Mr. Jones agreed with her. I said that I know they often worry about Jim, but I can't do that. That's not my role, and it wouldn't work anyway. Jim nodded sullenly. I said that I felt uncomfortable about the words "crazy Indian stuff." (Acknowledging feelings) I asked Jim if he knows what his parents mean by that. He lifted his cap from his eyes and said that he knew for sure that "all Indians are dirty, crazy, violent, and lazy drunks." Mr. Jones said, "Here he goes again, acting crazy. Everyone knows that Indians aren't violent and drunk." Jim giggled, and Mr. Jones cracked his knuckles. I said that perhaps Jim was hitting something very painful. That was the prejudice they had to live with day in and day out. Mr. Jones said I was damn right. Mrs. Jones said that's what she worried about, that Jim would become like the rest of them Indians. I said, "You are Indian and you aren't violent, lazy, and crazy. Neither is Jim." (Gentle demand for work) Mrs. Jones said no, but that's because they'd moved away from the reserve. I said that maybe it was time to look at the positive things of the present rather than the bad things of the past. (Emphasizing the positive and the potential to work)

I tried to reach their feelings in their way, to establish contact, and to help the family members help each other. Jim said, "You can't help but act on impulse, that's what my B&Es are all about." I said, "You forget to pray to the spirit of the bear, don't you?" Mr. Jones nodded and said I was right. He told us an Indian story about a little boy becoming a man becoming a bear. It was the opposite of Jim's progress at this point, but it emphasized his potential. Jim said that the story was OK, but that the elders had better ones. I said to Jim that maybe the story hit home a bit hard. (Demand for work) I got nowhere.

Jim said that he had been kicked out of English today and that he wasn't much more disruptive than some of the white kids. I said that a little more disruption is all it takes to make a difference. (Silence) Mr. Jones said that white teachers are racist. Mr. Jones said that females are more racist than men. He would fight with a white man any day, but you can't fight with a white woman. I acknowledged my feelings and said that I was afraid the arrows might start flying toward me. We all laughed at the relief of tension. Jim said that the Indians only scalp white people who have no honor. Mr. Jones grinned. I recognize their offering and said that it felt good to hear I have honor. Their feelings for me are important to me, because I respect them.

I tried to put the client's feelings into words for the benefit of the other family members so that they would gain a new understanding of each other. Mrs. Jones asked me what I intended to do about Jim's alcoholism. I said Jim was doing his best to stay away from alcohol and the reserve, but sometimes he got so depressed about feeling bad about himself that he couldn't help it. Jim said I was right. He can't control himself when his parents call him a crazy Indian. Mr. Jones said that he and his wife mean well. Then just don't know what else to say. I said, "I know, when you're worried words don't come easily." Jim said gently, "When I'm rotten, why don't you just say I let you down, Dad?" Mr. Jones put his arms around his son.

Mrs. Jones said that Jim was wasting his time carving, you can't make a living out of it. I said that I was really impressed by Jim's carvings. They are really beautiful. Mrs. Jones said that Jim spends too much time doing that. I said that it takes a lot of time to create a piece of art. Mr. Jones said he knew, because he tried when he was younger and couldn't do half as well as Jim. Jim was beaming. He asked his dad how good an Indian dancer he was when he was younger.

I offered to mediate between the family and a system that made it harder to communicate between Jim and his parents as a result of his delinquencies. Everyone was silent. Mrs. Jones, especially, looked grim. I asked if I had offended them in any way. (Silence) I said, "Anything I have done or said in relation to Jim?" "No," said Mr. Jones, "I guess we are taking it out on you." Jim says that he knows what it's all about. It's about the band. I recognized the indirect communication. "You wish you were on good terms with the band, don't you?" Mrs. Jones said it wasn't possible. There was so much politics going on. Mr. Jones said they were arrogant. Jim continued rocking in his chair and looked hurt. I said, noting his eyes, "You feel guilty about it; you want to cry. Your B&Es stand in the way, don't they?" (Demand for work) He nodded. I said that I would talk to the band office. Maybe they would agree to supervise Jim's probation once I'm gone. Mr. Jones said, "They refused in the past; why would they accept now?" I said that they had had time to get over the shock, just as Jim had had time to do a lot of growing. Jim nodded. (Crediting client's work)

Current Status of the Problem:

The problem has shifted in urgency. Jim and his parents are starting to be able to discuss the problem of Indian identity with less anger and pain and are starting to be able to discuss other issues without approaching them from a perspective of ethnic origin. Jim's parents are beginning to be able to give positive strokes to Jim for his "native Indian-oriented" achievements (e.g., his beautiful carvings and his proficiency in Indian dancing). They are striving to live together under the same roof without feeling that it is a battlefield of "good Indians" versus "bad Indians." Jim's anger has lessened, largely because he has regained the support of the elder in the band. He has stayed away from committing further delinquencies.

Specific Next Steps:

1. For the next white worker, do not shy away from discussing the racial element of the interaction, because it is a central element for Jim and his family and permeates all their lives.
2. Continue family work around communication patterns. There are a lot of feelings of anger and sadness connected to Jim's natural mom's death that interfere between Jim and his stepmom.
3. Continue to emphasize Jim's ability and desire to do well and excel rather than Jim's past record of delinquency; emphasize his parents' desire to be the best parents.
4. Make an effort to enlist the band elders to help provide a social support system for Jim and his family.

The worker in this example has made a start in breaking down the barriers between the parents and the child, the family and herself (and her white social service system), and between the family and a source of support in the Native community. Recognizing that a long history of communal support is central to the Native culture can be a crucial step in strengthening the family. One finding of the child welfare study cited earlier (Shulman, 1991) was that regions of the Provincial child welfare agency that established effective working relationships with the Native community (e.g., friendship centers, homemaker and court workers; band

Chiefs and elders; social workers) had fewer Native children going into alternative forms of care, or if they did go into care, fewer leaving the Native community. Continued work with the family would need to integrate some discussion of the socio-economic issues of oppression that had contributed to the struggles within the family so that the problem could be reframed from a personal pathology perspective to a social perspective.

PARENT-TEEN CONFLICT IN A PSYCHIATRIC SETTING

In the following example, a 15-year-old Native teenager is in conflict with her mother and step-father. The family included eight children, and the client's natural father had been sent to prison two years before. Recently, she had outbursts of uncontrollable aggressive and destructive behavior that had led to her being committed to the psychiatric department of a large urban hospital. The social worker, in this setting, worked with the patient and her family in trying to identify family issues and prepare the family for the patient's return home. In separate interviews, first with the teenager and then her parents, the worker started to develop a working relationship and tuned in to the issues for both. In his work with the teenager, it became clear she missed her natural father and consistently made negative comparisons with her new "dad." In contrast with the previous example, the worker here does not acknowledge the fact that he is white and the family is Native. While some very sensitive work of intra-family communication takes place, the lack of attention to socioeconomic issues is also evident.

In the session with the parents, the worker described how the mother, Mrs. Smith, continually interrupted and answered for her husband. An example from the first interview follows:

> My first session with Janet's parents contributed even more to my understanding of the problems they faced. My purpose for seeing them was partially upon the doctor's request for a social history, but I also wanted to give them a chance to talk about the concerns they had about Janet. During this meeting they shared their fears of not knowing how to handle their daughter without making her angry, the feeling that they were always "walking on eggshells" around her and that they were losing total control of her. Mrs. Smith was definitely the dominant personality. Mr. Smith, on the other hand, seemed content with taking more of a backseat role, allowing his wife to speak for them. However, in my zeal to understand their situation (and acquire the necessary information), I neglected the process of the interaction, which graphically illustrated several problems:
>
> (1) Mr. Smith found it hard to share his personal feelings about Janet.
> (2) Mrs. Smith generally bailed him out by doing the talking for him.
>
> The following is a very brief excerpt that illustrates these dynamics. I was focusing on their response to their daughter's anger and had explored in considerable depth the mother's reactions and feelings in those circumstances. The course of the conversation began to drift into an unrelated issue, and I made a deliberate attempt to draw it back in order to concentrate on the father's feelings.
>
> **Worker:** Before we leave this area of Janet's anger, I wonder, Mr. Smith, whether you can share with us what it is like for you when your daughter gets really angry with you and defies your authority.
>
> **Mr. Smith:** (He began very slowly.) Well, you know it's really frustrating...(his voice trailed off and for a brief moment there was silence as he pondered the question).

Mrs. Smith: (Almost immediately) It's usually worse when we are trying to get her
  to do the dishes or some other chore. I notice that this was when Henry
  finds it most difficult to handle her. He gets angry, yells, and then kind of
  clams up, almost like he is giving up. (Looking to her husband) Isn't that
  right, dear?

Mr. Smith simply nodded his head, and Mrs. Smith carried on. It wasn't until after
the interview while I was reviewing the audiotape that I noticed how often Mrs. Smith
spoke for her husband when I asked him about his feelings and how often I had
missed it. In spite of this mistake, we clarified some common areas of concern and laid
the groundwork for the first family session.

In the following excerpt the worker meets the teenager and her parents together for the
first time. He attempts to establish a working contract and to underline the mutual concern for
each other that is not apparent to the parties in conflict. In addition, he points out the pattern,
observed earlier, of Mrs. Smith answering for her husband. This brings a strong response
from the daughter and establishes a new set of ground rules for the discussion.

This session took place while Janet was still in the hospital. I greeted each one of them
as they walked into the room. During the first few minutes as we were settling into
our chairs and informally chatting, I sensed an air of tension that had not been present
to the same degree when I met with them separately. Even their laughing lacked
spontaneity and seemed to be filled with anxiety. I asked them whether they were
feeling a little anxious about this session. Mrs. Smith was the first to agree, while
Janet just smiled, trying to avoid eye contact with anyone in the room. Mr. Smith just
nodded in agreement with his wife. I asked Janet whether that smile meant that she,
too, was a little nervous. She indicated that it did. I shared with them that I was also
a little anxious. This brought a smile to each of their faces.

I wanted to go further with this, sensing it was part of the beginning work, so I
asked them what it was about this session that was making them feel anxious. There
was a silence. Mrs. Smith eventually spoke up, suggesting that possibly everyone was
unsure about what to say or what might come out of the meeting. I asked if that's how
she was feeling. She said she was, so I tried to find out what she was afraid might happen. She replied that her fear was that the family would not get back together. Sensing that Mrs. Smith was trying to reach out to her daughter early in the session in her
own way, I said that it appeared that she cared very deeply for Janet and that to lose
her would really hurt. For a moment Janet looked at her mother and then quickly returned her gaze to the floor. There was another silence. I went to Janet and asked her
what it was about the meeting that made her nervous. After a brief moment of contemplation she shrugged her shoulders and said, "I guess, the same as Mom." I tried
to highlight the common concern that I saw by saying that being part of the family appeared to mean a great deal to her, too. Finally, I went to Mr. Smith, but he was unable to articulate what he was nervous about. I shared that it was natural to feel this
way when dealing with something as important as this.

In the next few minutes, I tried to clarify for each of them my understanding of
why they were there and what I saw my role as. I said that from previous meetings
with them individually they had indicated a need to look at what made it difficult for
them to live with each other, talk to each other, and to be understood by each other,
and that they wanted to give things another try. I attempted to check this out with

them. (Reaching for feedback) Mrs. Smith said that they needed a chance to really sit down and work out some of their differences because life had been becoming unbearable prior to Janet coming into the hospital. I agreed, saying that it had been hard on all of them, but in spite of that, they had continued to care about each other. I indicated that I would try to help them to say the things they wanted to say to each other.

Very early in the interview I noticed the pattern begin to develop once again where Mrs. Smith would speak for her husband, especially in situations where he found it difficult to share his feelings.

We were looking at what it was like for them at home and what kinds of things made it difficult for them to get along with each other. Mrs. Smith had just shared how crowded and inadequate their living conditions were and how much easier it was for them to get on each other's nerves under such circumstances. I asked if the others could relate to what was being said. Mr. Smith said that the same thing was true for him and that sometimes after a hard day at work it was impossible to find that much needed time to himself. But before he could really answer for himself, his wife interrupted and without as much as a pause began to talk about how she saw her husband react. The following is a verbatim account of the conversation.

Mrs. Smith: (Looking at me) Well, I know it is hard on Henry because he gets very irritable and then yells at the kids and often frightens them. I know he doesn't mean to because he just isn't that kind of person.

Worker: Mrs. Smith, I have noticed that whenever I ask your husband how he feels about a certain situation that you quite often answer for him. I wonder whether you were aware of that? (There was a brief pause where both parents looked to each other. Mrs. Smith seemed somewhat startled at my comment, and then both began to chuckle.)

Mrs. Smith: No, I wasn't aware that I was doing that.

Worker: Mr. Smith, were you aware that your wife often answers for you?

Mr. Smith: No, I hadn't noticed it either. (At that point Janet seemed to come to life.)

Janet: Yes, you do, Mom. You do speak for Dad lots of times. Sometimes you speak for me too.

Worker: What is that like for you?

Janet: Sometimes it's okay, and sometimes it makes me angry.

Worker: When does it make you angry?

Janet: When I have something important to say.

Worker: Like to Dad?

Janet: Yeah, maybe, or anyone.

Worker: Could you tell your mom what it is like for you and how you want her to change that?

Janet: (For a minute she laughed at the awkwardness of having to speak directly to her mother, but then became more serious and demonstrated more strength than I had previously seen.) If I have something to say, I will say it on my own.

Worker: Mrs. Smith, what is going on with you as you listen to this?

Mrs. Smith: Well, this is the first time I am hearing this from her, but now that I know I'll try to be more aware of what I do.

Worker: I know that your intentions are to be as helpful as you can, but I am very interested in what your husband and daughter are feeling in some of these areas and so I would like them to answer for themselves. I don't want you to take that the wrong way, because I value what you think about things as well. Can you go along with that?

Mrs. Smith: Yes, of course. I'll try to catch myself from now on.

After this exchange, the session began to open up in a greater way and I was able to draw Mr. Smith into the discussions much more readily. Overall, it helped the work to progress much more rapidly.

In retrospect, I could have been more open with Mrs. Smith by expressing my concern that she might feel I was putting her down by implying I didn't care about what she had to say, and that I was afraid of alienating her. Second, it probably could have been useful to explore why she spoke for her husband and daughter, and what it was like for her to see them struggle to share their own feelings.

As the work continued, the worker tried to encourage the stepfather, Mr. Smith, to share more of his feelings about how difficult is was for him to be the father of a family with eight children, none of whom were his own. Because of a number of factors, some related to an unrealistic sense of what a "real man" should be like, others related to cultural factors, it is not easy for fathers to share with their children the side of them that is tender, caring, and vulnerable. In addition, as discussed in the previous example, the obstacle presented by having a white worker can also be having an impact.

As the worker provides the opportunity and the demand for Mr. Smith to increase his participation, the stereotype of the uncaring and cold father starts to break down. As this process proceeds, it leads to Mr. Smith sharing his own experiences with his father, which have had a powerful impact in shaping his views and his feelings. This process illustrates the intergenerational work described in the earlier theory section. Through the medium of discussing his own family history, he is able to communicate a greater sensitivity to the feelings of his teenaged stepdaughter. Since the family moved away from the city when the daughter was discharged, the worker also made efforts to encourage a transition to another worker as part of the ending process.

I tried to explore some of Mr. Smith's feelings about how difficult it was for him to be the father of a family with eight children who were not his own.

To see Mr. Smith with his rough, unkempt, unshaven exterior, one could be fooled into thinking he was a callous, uncaring man. But behind that was a man who was frightened by his responsibilities and struggling to hold on to what little self-worth he had left. He was faced by stresses on every side. Our conversation had shifted to Mr. Smith's role in the family.

Mr. Smith: Right now I am barely making enough money to make ends meet. That really makes it hard to satisfy the needs of the children, let alone anything extra on top of that. I don't know if Janet really understands how hard it is for us to give her any spending money. She complains that we are stingy and never give her any money to go to the movies, but she just doesn't understand.

Worker: Mr. Smith, could you tell Janet what it is like for you when you have to tell her she can't go to the movies and then she calls you stingy or gets angry with you?

Mr. Smith: Janet, it makes me angry.

Worker: What else besides angry?

Mr. Smith: (After a long pause, and in a quiet voice) A little hurt, too.

Worker: Like you're not really appreciated?

Mr. Smith: Yeah, I guess.

Worker: Janet, has your dad ever shared with you how much it hurts him, besides the anger you see?

Janet: No, he never tells me that part. He just says no and doesn't give a reason, so of course I get mad and then he gets mad and then it's over.

Mrs. Smith: We've told you before how hard it is for us, you should know.

Janet: You have, maybe once, but Dad never has.

Worker: Are you saying you would be more willing to understand if your dad would take more time to explain these things to you?

Janet: (She nodded her head in agreement.) At least that way I know.

This exchange represented a crucial point in the sessions because Janet was starting to see her stepfather as someone with more than just feelings of anger.

In between sessions, Janet went home on a weekend pass with her family. She had been making considerable progress in the hospital, and there were plans for her discharge in the following week. I briefly talked with her about what it had been like at home. She said that things had gone well, everyone had been happy to see her, and even her stepfather had been much nicer. She was looking forward to the time when she could finally go home.

Although Janet and her mother had been quite close from the beginning, I noticed a lessening of the distance between Janet and her stepfather. We began to deal with an issue in the final session that had been touched on briefly in previous sessions.

I raised the issue of Janet's natural father. It was an area that I tried to deal with in previous sessions, but up to this point they had not been ready to look at it, with the exception of Mrs. Smith. Janet and her mother had been talking about an event in the family's past. Janet made reference to her natural father with a degree of fondness. I said to her that it appeared she had a lot of good memories of him. She said that she did but had not seen him for several years. I asked her what it was like not to have seen him for so long. She paused and then replied she was getting used to it. I commented that it must still hurt anyway. Mrs. Smith joined the conversation, saying that Janet had been closest to him, and for this reason was taking it hardest of all the children. Janet retorted that she wasn't taking it hard. There was silence. Mr. Smith tried in his own way to reach out to Janet by saying that he could understand why she would find it hard to forget her real dad and accept him. I asked him to say a little more about that. Janet sat with her head down and tears in her eyes.

Mr. Smith said that the kids probably didn't know it but he too had a stepfather when he was growing up. Sensing this was probably a common experience which could draw them together, I tried to pursue it further. In the next few moments he described a very painful part of his own past that in many ways seemed to parallel what Janet was going through at this point. He shared with us how at the age of eight he was taken by his own father to live with his cousins because his father couldn't make ends meet. He was told by his father that he would return to get him as soon as possible. But he never did, and Mr. Smith hasn't seen him to this day. I tried to find out what it was like for him when he finally realized that his father was not coming back. He just avoided the feelings by saying that he waited and waited but he just didn't come back. I said it must have been a very painful time for him. He didn't acknowledge the pain and I could see it has hard for him to talk about. I asked him what it was like to talk about this part of his life. He just said, "Well, it's over now."

I told him that I thought it took courage to share this with Janet and that he could probably understand quite well what she was going through right now. I asked him where his stepfather came into the picture. He continued to relate his story to us, but carefully avoided the feelings associated with it. Janet was quiet throughout and seemed to be listening intently. He talked about how hard it was for him to get along with his stepfather, and that he was never able to talk much with him. I asked Janet if she could relate to anything that was being said. She nodded her head to say yes, but refused to elaborate. We continued with it for a while longer, and then I suggested that they could continue to share more about this in the future with each other. We spent the rest of the session talking about their transition to another helping person in the community.

The worker reached sensitively for the underlying and unexpressed emotions in the family and consistently attempted to point out the areas of common ground. In this example, in contrast to the one preceding it, there is no addressing of the fact that the family is Native. The worker did not raise the issue of being white and seemed to avoid discussing the impact of race and culture on the family. His rationale for taking this approach may have been the fact that many of the issues raised can be seen in any family—in particular, issues having to do with stepparents. The worker may well have been trying to work with the family in a manner that could be described as color-blind. And yet, the current family situation (crowded and inadequate housing, lack of income, etc.) can be viewed as the result of socioeconomic oppression. Also, the stepfather describes his own abandonment by his father as having been triggered by economic stress.

It may well be that the family members wish to deal with their current issues without regard to the issues associated with the race and oppression. This is their right. However, the worker may need to open the door and give permission for this discussion if the family is to feel free to explore it. By acknowledging issues of race and ethnicity, the worker also frees the family to use their culture and background as part of their current work. This father may well have been one of many young Native children abandoned by family members at that time in history. To turn all of the family's problems inward, to pathologize them (e.g., admitting the teenager into a psychiatric ward) without recognition of the social issues involved, may leave an important element out of the discussion. It is argued here that the worker must create the conditions for the family to explore these aspects of their life, while respecting the family members' perspectives on the matter.

CHAPTER SUMMARY

In this chapter we have explored some of the ways the core skills outlined in Chapters 2 through 5 can be applied in working with families. Our focus was on family work, as opposed to family therapy, although many of the concepts and strategies developed in family therapy theory were used both to understand family dynamics and to strategize ways to intervene. Illustrations were provided of workers dealing with an angry parent, developing an ongoing working relationship, bringing a stepfather into active family involvement, helping a single-parent family cope with their unique stresses, and assisting a Native family in dealing with their culture and their community.

GLOSSARY

Family A natural living unit including all those persons who share identity with the family and are influenced by it in a circular exchange of emotions (Ackerman, 1958).

Family facade A false front presented by the family in early contacts with the worker. The facade demonstrates how the family collaborates in hiding its problems from the social environment.

Family support (family counseling) Usually short-term in nature, and designed to help families facing normative crises (e.g., the first child reaching the teen years, the birth of a new baby, loss of a job). The focus of the work is on helping a relatively healthy family get through a difficult time, using the experience to strengthen rather than erode the family system.

Functional diffusion A loss of functional clarity that causes a worker to diffuse her or his activity and implement a role or roles inappropriate for the moment.

Identified patient (IP) The client in a family system who is identified as having the problem.

Paradoxical directive Suggestion from a therapist that the family members continue their symptomatic behavior or even heighten it. The therapist makes the suggestion so that the family members may become more aware of the pattern and the benefits derived from it. The eventual goal is that the family members be able to take control over the process (Barker, 1991, p. 166).

Reframing the problem This process is described by family theorists as helping the family see a problem in a new way. One example of this would be helping the family move beyond viewing the family problem as concerning a single child (the identified patient) who may be serving as a family scapegoat.

Triangulation A process in which one party attempts to gain the allegiance of a second party in the struggle with a third party (e.g., the parents and the therapist versus the child; the mother and an older child versus the father) as a means of coping with anxiety.

NOTES

1. For examples of the work of a range of family therapy theorists, see Murray Bowen, "The Family as a Unit of Study and Treatment," *American Journal of Orthopsychiatry, 31* (January 1961): 40–60; Virginia Satir; *Conjoint Family Therapy* (Palo Alto, CA: Science and Behavior Books, Inc., 1967); Frances H. Sherz, "Theory and Practice of Family Therapy," in *Theories of Social Casework*, ed. Robert W. Roberts and Robert H. Nee (Chicago: The University of Chicago Pres, 1970), pp. 219–264; Nathan Ackerman, *The Psychodynamics of Family Life* (New York: Basic Books, 1958); David S. Freeman, *Technique of Family Therapy* (New York: Jason Aronson, Inc., 1981); Gregory Bateson, Don Jackson, Jay Haley, and John H. Weakland, "Toward a Theory of Schizophrenia," *Behavioral Science, 1* (1956): 251–264; John H. Weakland, Richard Fisch, Paul Watzlawick, and Arthur M. Bodin, "Brief Therapy: Focused Problem Resolution," *Family Process, 13* (1974): 141–168; Richard Bandler, John Grindler, and Virginia Satir, *Changing with Families* (Palo Alto, CA: Science and Behavior Books, 1976); Salvador Minuchin, *Families and Family Therapy* (Cambridge, MA: Harvard University Press,

1974); Salvador Minuchin and Herman C. Fishman, *Family Therapy Techniques* (Cambridge, MA: Harvard University Press, 1981).

2. See, for example, L.E. Davis and E.K. Proctor, *Race, Gender and Class: Guidelines for Practice with Individuals, Families, and Groups* (Englewood Cliffs, NJ: Prentice-Hall, 1989); A. Gitterman, *Handbook of Social Work with Vulnerable Populations* (New York: Columbia University Press, 1991); W. Devore and E.G. Schlesinger, *Ethnic-Sensitive Social Work Practice*, 3rd ed. (New York: Macmillan, 1991); and M.P. Mirkin, *The Social and Political Contexts of Family Therapy* (Boston: Allyn and Bacon, 1990).

7

Problem-Centered Family Practice

CHAPTER OUTLINE

Mandate, Client Problem, and Family Counseling
Hiding the Family's Secrets: Dealing with Taboo Areas
The Child Welfare Setting
Family Practice in a School Setting
The Single-Parent Family and the "Big Brother" Service

In this chapter we continue our discussion of work with families, focusing on practice in which the agency mandate or the client's particular problem is in the foreground, giving direction to the family work. Thus, the counseling focuses on a specific problem or issue, such as a physical or mental illness of a family member or a child's problems in school. The work with the family explores the impact of the particular problem on the family and the ways in which the family can be mobilized to cope with it more effectively.

MANDATE, CLIENT PROBLEM, AND FAMILY COUNSELING

In this chapter we will continue to explore social work with families. Our argument will be that the mandate of the setting, and the specific client problems related to that mandate, give focus and direction to the family practice. In effect, in this chapter we will revisit the contracting idea introduced in Chapter 3. It was argued in that chapter that the worker's practice with a client must be centered on the common ground between the service of the agency or host setting (e.g., a school) and the felt needs of the client. This apparently simple, but actually complex and powerful idea, provides a boundary and structure that frees the client and the worker to be more effective. The worker needs to be asking himself or herself, at all times, "How does this conversation with family members relate to our service and the family's particular problem?"

It is important that the work be guided by the specific agency function and not be subverted by the worker or the clients and turned into family therapy. Fear of this outcome often causes clients to be defensive and resistant in early sessions. A family that is meeting with a school social worker about their child's educational problems will not necessarily appreciate the conversation turning to the parents' marital problems. Identifying marital stress as a factor affecting the child's schoolwork would be appropriate, as would a discussion of how to handle its impact on the child. It would also be appropriate for the social worker to offer to assist in making a referral for the couple's marital problem.

The client's fears of invasive practice are not completely unfounded. Social workers who are unclear about the boundaries of their practice sometimes use the initial reason for the contact as an entry for family therapy. In one extreme example, a child welfare agency family support worker described working with a couple on their sexual dysfunctions. Although the worker was originally referred to the family to help them with parenting problems that had led to suspected child abuse, the sessions with the couple had revealed sexual problems that the worker had undertaken to treat through counseling.

When I inquired as to the connection between this work and the agency mandate, the worker admitted that there was no connection. She went on to say that she had taken a course in counseling people with sexual problems, and this seemed like a good chance for her to practice. This worker's subversion of the working contract was inappropriate for many reasons, not the least of which was that while she was busy doing sexual counseling, she was ignoring the parenting-focused work that was in her domain.

Workers have argued that in rural areas, with few services available, they often must be all things to all people. The problem is a real one, and I can appreciate the dilemma. In some cases, workers may have to provide a range of services as the "only game in town." Even in these situations, I believe there is a responsibility for social workers to try to close the gap between client needs and available services through professional impact on the community. The strategies and skills for this aspect of social work are discussed in more detail in Part V of this book. My assertion here is that in trying to provide all services to all clients, we often become less effective in providing the services that are clearly our responsibility.

Each of the illustrations that follow will highlight this crucial idea.

HIDING THE FAMILY'S SECRETS: DEALING WITH TABOO AREAS

Family members often have a **family secret** that they feel is so terrible, no one is willing to talk about it. At times, an unspoken agreement exists in which all family members agree not to deal directly with a sensitive and taboo concern. Family violence, alcoholism, and sexual abuse are examples of family secrets often hidden behind a family facade. At times, the secret is maintained through coercion as the oppressor in the relationship uses emotional or physical threats. Other common secret areas are associated with physical and mental illness. Examples include family members who try to hide the onset of a potentially life-threatening illness, such as AIDS, cancer, or Alzheimer's. At times, the secret of the illness may be known by all family members but is still treated as a taboo subject. Each family member may fear that the others are not emotionally able to handle an open discussion. While genuinely wanting to protect the other family members, the guardian of the secret is also protecting herself or himself.

The problem is that family secrets that are kept out of sight and not discussed can impair a family's ability to function in a healthy manner. The inability to discuss the subject area, the norm of behavior that has declared such discussion to be forbidden, works to block the family members' ability to deal with the issue and discover their own inherent strengths.

In one example, a young mother suffered from a degenerative illness that had already caused her to go blind. She had experienced strokes and memory loss, and the prognosis was for an early death. The father was no longer in the picture, and the family living in the home consisted of the mother (Ruth), her eight-year-old son (Billy), and the maternal grandmother (Millie). A norm of behavior had evolved in which all of the family members agreed, in a covert manner, not to speak of the illness or its symptoms, and in particular, not to speak of the mother's future. The child was seen as too young to be able to understand. The grand-mother worried that discussing the illness would make the young mother more depressed and perhaps even trigger a stroke. The young mother worried about the burden the illness placed upon the grandmother and its impact on her health. Both mother and grandmother were deeply concerned about what would happen to Billy if the other died first.

The tensions and stress in the family were carefully covered up. There was no way for the feelings to remain under the surface, so the child, Billy, signaled the underlying problems. His behavior acted out the anxieties he felt about what was happening to his mother and his family. As his behavior problems worsened and his mother and grandmother were at a loss as to how to handle them, they sought help from a child care resource to arrange a temporary placement in a foster or group home. It's important to note that the mission of this agency is to provide assistance to families in dealing with their children's behavior problems or re-sources for substitute child care. It is not, for example, a hospital social service department, for which the issue of the illness itself might be central.

The first response of the agency, and the family worker involved, was to respect the grandmother's injunction against getting into the health issues. The grandmother involved the workers in a conspiracy of silence on the core issues. Given the child-focused service of the agency, the worker's agreement was understandable. Her early efforts focused on helping the mother and grandmother try to deal with Billy's behavior, and helping Billy to control his activities. Since this missed the real meaning of the deviant behavior and played into the fam-ily's use of Billy as the identified patient, very little progress was observed, and both the mother and grandmother expressed feelings of dissatisfaction with the results.

The family worker realized that the core issue was the family secret and made a num-ber of efforts to open it up. She pointed out to the mother and the grandmother that Billy's be-havior might well be related to his anxiety as he sensed something wrong in the family. However, at the first sign of resistance from the grandmother, the worker backed off. The worker had to examine her own feelings about issues of death and dying that contributed to her willingness to go along with the illusion of work. As long as the family members sensed the worker's discomfort and resulting ambivalence, they would resist as well. By backing off, the worker was indirectly signaling to the family members her lack of readiness to help them with the issue. Once the worker had dealt with her own feelings, she could begin to see the resistance as a sign that the work was on target, although entering a taboo and painful area. When the meaning of the phrase "Resistance is part of the work" became clear to the work-er, she made a demand for work on the family members by persisting in raising the underly-ing issue.

Recognizing she would need to confront the family about their conspiracy to keep the family secret, she took her courage in hand and challenged the obstacle. She confronted the mother and grandmother and tried to support them in opening up discussion between each of them and then between them and Billy. She explored the resistance by asking "What makes it hard for you to talk about this with each other?" The taboo subject was at least out in the open, yet the grandmother refused to continue this line of discussion and closed off further dis-cussions by saying, "When the time comes, we shall deal with it." The mother, on the other hand, with the worker's support, responded by dealing more openly with Billy on the issue of her death. This discussion seemed to help the situation and resulted in a decrease in the child's acting-out behavior. However, the mother was more reluctant to act when it came to discussions with the grandmother.

Although the worker was unable to help the family face the future at this time, a beginning was made on creating conditions in which the unspeakable could be spoken. Given the service of the setting, the work was successful in that the child was freed of the responsibility of signaling the family distress. The denial on the part of both mother and grandmother was strong, but in these circumstances, very understandable. In the last analysis, it was really up to them to pick the time and place for facing a harsh reality.

THE CHILD WELFARE SETTING

A child welfare agency offers a good example of a setting in which functional clarity is crucial in practice. Examples of contracting with the natural parents in a family, and in particular, dealing with the issue of the authority of the worker and the agency were discussed in Part II. In this section, family practice variations associated with work in a child welfare setting are explored through examples involving practice with two foster-parent families, with an 11-year-old child in residential care, and with a teenaged mother. In each of these examples, the work involves helping the client deal with her or his family-of-origin issues at a point when she or he is not living with the family. The examples illustrate the fact that clients take their families with them wherever they may go, and that their families of origin can have ongoing and continued influence on their current experiences.

The Foster Parent

Child welfare family work often involves collaborative work with the foster (or group home) parents or child care workers in residential settings. The role of the social worker in relation to the alternative parent is often misunderstood by both the worker and the parent (Shulman, 1980). On one end of a continuum, the foster parent may be viewed as a client. On the other end, workers may ignore important signals from the foster parents of their need for support and help. In reality, foster parents (and other alternative caregivers) are collaborators in the process of trying to buffer the traumatic experience of children who find themselves in short- or long-term care. The positive impact of alternative caregivers described in Chapter 2 in the section on resiliency research, and the potential contribution to the foster child's plasticity described in the life-span theory and research, suggest that attention to the foster parents as contributors to the child's developmental reserve capacity can contribute significantly to the child's growth. The social worker can play an important role in mediating between the foster parents and the child, the agency, the natural family, the foster parents' own family, and other systems in the community (e.g., health care providers, the school).

In my own work with foster parents and from my research studies, I have identified a number of areas in which problems may emerge. For example, the foster parents may feel unappreciated and undervalued when the agency and the social worker make decisions without consulting with them—the people who may know the child best and will have to deal with the results of these decisions. Difficult foster children can also raise problems in the natural family between a foster mother and father, or in relation to other children in the family. Foster parents have described feeling torn between their own childrens' needs and the demands placed upon them by needy foster children. Of all the issues raised in my workshops, two of the most difficult ones have to do with over-identification with the foster child resulting in unrealistic expectations for a return home, and identification with the child that results in anger and rejection of the biological parents. The next examples illustrate these two problems.

In the first example, the social worker tries to help a foster parent of a nine-year-old child deal with his struggle over having been removed from his family. The social worker's role is to try to provide a source of support for the foster parent as she attempts to help the child. By recognizing the foster parent's caring for the child and her difficulty in dealing with the child's pain, the social worker strengthens her in her difficult role.

> Mrs. Edwards, foster mother of seven weeks to nine-year-old Tony, phoned me at 9 A.M. She told me in an angry, excited voice, "I had to call you and tell you that you need to hear the things that Tony told me this morning before he went to school. You people have things all wrong. I am convinced that the agency and that private school have done this boy and his family a grave injustice." I immediately thought to myself, "What has this kid cooked up now?" I said that this sounded serious and asked her to tell me more. She said that Tony insisted that his father had never beaten him and that his mother had never locked him out—he had just refused to go in the house and had gone away. Furthermore, Tony told her that he had decided to leave his last foster home two weeks early because he didn't want them to adopt him.
>
> I asked Mrs. Edwards why she thought Tony was telling her these things. She replied, "Because he wants me to help him get home—he trusts me and he's hurting so bad that I told him that I'd get you to listen to him." I promised Mrs. Edwards that I would listen to Tony, but not on the phone as she suggested, because he played games on the phone and got her and himself upset in the process. I arranged to be there at 2:00 to talk to her before Tony got home from school.
>
> When I saw Mrs. Edwards, we went over Tony's stories again. It appeared to me that Tony was using the information shared with him by another worker a month previously (when he decided to go home and not wait to be adopted) in an attempt to force me, through Mrs. Edwards, to get him home now. I reminded Mrs. Edwards of the tiny boy she had told me about, whom she had once fostered. He had been hospitalized after a beating from his mother, but had welcomed his mother when she had visited him in hospital. Mrs. Edwards responded that it was the same with Tony—blood is thicker than water, but she felt it would help Tony for me to listen to his story—he needed to be believed. I had told her that I felt that Tony needed most to know that she and I were on his side and would help him to get home, but that going along with his tall tales was not helping him to wait or helping him learn to get along with people. Mrs. Edwards replied, "But he's only a little boy, he feels all alone and wants to get back to his mother." I said, "You really hurt when Tony is hurting, don't you?" She agreed that she was a "softie" and that Tony really got to her with his constant appeals for help to get home.

The worker in this prior excerpt avoided the mistake of identifying solely with the needs of the child. The "two-client" idea, in relation to work with foster parent, is illustrated when the worker is able to understand Tony's needs and those of the foster parent at the same time. In addition to providing emotional support, the social worker offers resources including herself to help the foster parent help the child get through the stress of the court process. Foster parents are often told by the agency that they are the "most important members of the foster care team," while simultaneously being excluded from any significant planning or decision making. This foster parent is brought into a collaborative process, discussing a plan with the social worker. The worker also conveys the importance of involving the child in the discussion.

We discussed how the agency might see Tony through the waiting period until court on November 30th. A child care worker to take responsibility for Tony after school is not acceptable to her—Tony needed to come home to her and discuss the school day and do his homework. Talking to a psychiatrist not connected with the agency or with the court appealed to Mrs. Edwards, although she felt Tony should not be told that he was seeing a psychiatrist. She agreed when I pointed out that this would not be fair to Tony or the psychiatrist and could not work because of Tony's alertness. We decided to ask Tony what he thought about this idea.

I suggested to Mrs. Edwards that Tony took advantage of her fondness for him and her wish for him to be happy. She replied that she knew he did, but he made her feel like she was the only one he could rely on. I told her that he could rely on me too, and that I could understand why he had doubts, since I had been absent during the most upsetting month of his stay in care—in other words, I had deserted him when he needed me. I told her I would try, with her cooperation, to spend more time with Tony and to reassure him that he would go home. I did not mention that she had balked at many of my attempts to see Tony during the early weeks of his placement in her home. Mrs. Edwards said that this should help a lot.

I told her why I thought that Tony was attempting to discredit the evidence used in court, pointing out that this was a plucky attempt on his part to take the responsibility for having been left in Canada by his parents, but reminding her that this information was in writing from Tony's mother, and that, although I was committed to returning Tony home, it could only be done through the court. Mrs. Edwards said she understood this.

Tony arrived home from school, gave me a fleeting greeting, collected his Halloween candies, and ignored Mrs. Edwards's request that he tell me what he had told her that morning. He finally went outside, and Mrs. Edwards turned to me in consternation and commented that she couldn't understand this behavior. I told her that it was OK if he wasn't ready to share this with me, as he probably hadn't decided whether he could trust me or not. After two more excursions in and out of the room and a brief period at his homework, Tony offered me a candy and sat down with us. Once more Mrs. Edwards urged him to tell me what was on his mind. Tony looked me straight in the eye and said, somewhat defiantly, "I told her I left Susan's two weeks early because I didn't want to be adopted by them." I told Tony that this wasn't the way I remembered it happening, and reminded him of visits and discussions about his leaving Susan's home, including his statements to me at the time. Tony wiggled a bit, conceded that was the way it had happened, shot Mrs. Edwards an amused glance, and looked at the floor. Mrs. Edwards's mouth was open. Then Tony looked up and told me firmly, "But my father never beat me!"

I told him that I wasn't going to get into a discussion of what had gone on in his family, because he had made his choice to return home and my job was to help him do this. I put it to him, "The fact is your mother left you in Canada, didn't she, Tony?" He nodded, looking at the floor once more. I went on to say, "The law in Canada is that, when children are left by their parents, it has to go to court and the judge has to decide if you will go home or go for adoption. I'm asking the judge to send you home because your mother wants you and you don't want to be adopted." I asked Tony if that was what he wanted. He said yes, with fervor. I told him OK, we all agree that's what we're working for. Now what can we do about the time between now and November 30th? Tony observed brightly, "It's my birthday on November

7th and I'm having a party at McDonald's." I said that would be great, but what I meant was that things had to be a lot more peaceful in the Edwards home if Tony was to go home in good health and well-behaved. Tony glanced at Mrs. Edwards, who chimed in: "I've been telling Donna that you're a hard boy to live with sometimes."

I told Tony that I felt that a lot of his behavior towards Mrs. Edwards and towards the girls (her children) was way out of line, so much so that I wondered if he really wanted to stay there until he left for home. Tony had been looking at me, but when I referred to the misbehavior towards the girls, his eyes glistened and he smiled a smug secret smile which caused Mrs. Edwards to widen her eyes in dismay. I told Tony that it was up to him to improve his behavior, since I knew that he was capable of this, and that I wanted to be able to tell his mother that he was happy, healthy, and well-behaved when he left for home. When I asked Tony if he thought he could make this effort, he looked at Mrs. Edwards with an appealing smile, and told me, "Yes, I'll try." We discussed whether or not it would be helpful to him to talk about his situation with someone outside the department and the court and, despite Mrs. Edwards's encouragement to do so, Tony declared that he didn't want to talk to anybody else. He then asked for permission to go outside and play.

Mrs. Edwards and I had a brief discussion of our talk with Tony, and she acknowledged that she had been taken in by him and that she now realized it had been deliberate. I, in turn, tried to get across to her the need to provide a structured, calm atmosphere in order to keep Tony on an even keel until he returned home. Although Mrs. Edwards verbalized intellectual understanding of this need, I was not assured that she could put it into effect because of her own emotional needs.

The worker has begun to address the meaning of the behavior on Tony's part but needs to further focus on the connection between his acting out and his hope that he can return home. Teenagers have sat on the front porch of a new foster home, suitcase in hand, refusing to enter and demanding that they be returned to their natural parents. Foster children of all ages often act out in their alternative care setting, thinking that if they are rejected there they will most certainly be returned home. When their acting-out behavior affects the foster parent's own natural children, it can lead to a call to remove the child. More often than not, rather than them returning home, the acting-out leads to being placed in a new foster home. Foster parents need help in understanding the meaning of the behavior, and the children need assistance, from the social worker and the foster parent, in dealing with the pain of rejection.

In the next example, erratic visiting has upset a young teenager in care and angered the foster parents. It's important that the social worker help the parents deal with their own feelings so that they will be ready to help the child with his. The anger toward the biological family, is in part, a cover for their pain at sensing the child's hurt. One of the roles of the foster care social worker is to help the foster family tune in to the meaning of the "deviant" behavior of the biological family. Before that can be done, the worker has to demonstrate a capacity to tune in to the foster parents. The worker's report follows:

> I drove up to Ann and Tom's home. Kevin was standing outside with a friend. He ran up to my car and said, "I'm not going."
> I didn't understand. "Going where? What do you mean?"
> "I'm not going away this weekend. No one can take me."
> I said, "I'm taking you."

He said, "No. No one can take me at their house. My grandmother is taking two of my sisters, and she's tired and can't handle any more. My aunt is going away and my other aunt just moved and doesn't have a telephone."

I said, "I'm sorry."

He shrugged, looked away, and said, "That's okay. I've got stuff to do around here this weekend."

I said, "I was looking forward to taking you up. I also wanted to meet your grandmother."

He asked, "When can I go home?"

I asked him, "To Edison?" [where his mother and stepfather live] He nodded his head "yes." I asked him if he had talked about this with his mother and stepfather. He looked at the ground and shook his head "no." I asked him how his conversations with his stepfather were going. He said, "Good." I asked him if they had discussed the fight or had they just blown it off like it didn't happen. He said they had blown it off. I told him to talk about it with his mother and stepfather and see what they said. Then, if everyone felt comfortable, I would talk about it with his child welfare worker and maybe we could arrange a visit.

He walked back over to where his friend was waiting for him and I went inside to talk to Ann and Tom. Ann immediately started talking about how she couldn't believe that his family had cancelled his visit.

She said, "They just don't want him. How could you do that to a child?"

I said, "He must be very disappointed."

She made a noise and said, "Yeah, he is."

Then she started talking about how a previous foster child was supposed to come visit her this weekend as well as Tom's son. She also made a comment about how it would be difficult to keep Kevin occupied to keep his mind off his disappointment.

I said, "It [Kevin's family cancelling the visit] must be hard for you too. You have other plans, and you thought that Kevin was going away for the weekend."

She reluctantly agreed. She said, "I just wish they had given us more notice. He has been planning on going all week, and they just call up the night before and say, 'You can't come.'"

I said, "You are right. Their not giving more notice is not fair to you or Kevin. I will call them next week and discuss visitation. You shouldn't be expected to always conform to their schedules; they need to compromise and work with you. Kevin's feelings need to be considered, too."

She appeared relieved that I would address this. Tom entered the room and also began discussing how "Kevin's family doesn't want him."

He said, "That kid isn't going home, I can feel it in my gut."

Ann expressed her anger and repeated, "How can you do that to a kid?" several times.

I listened to them, but added, "We can't assume that his family doesn't want him."

I asked Ann if she voices these concerns to Kevin. She said she does not. I told her that as a person she was free to vent her frustration with his mother with me, but as a professional, she must try not to let her anger at his mother get in the way of working with his mother. She said she understood.

Tom expressed his feeling that Kevin needed to face the reality of not being able to go home because his family did not want him. I told him that I did not know what was going to happen when it was time for Kevin to leave our program, but I would ask the child welfare worker what the alternative to his going home would be.

I also stated that he and Ann could help Kevin by developing some of his independent living skills. I took out a skills assessment, and we went over it together. We targeted some of the areas where Kevin might need their supervision, such as nutrition, what to do if there is an emergency, etc.

While we were going over this, Kevin came inside to tell Tom something. Tom asked him, "Are your ears ringing?"

Kevin looked confused and said, "No."

Tom said, "Well, we are in here saying a lot of good things about you."

The worker was supportive and offered to intervene with the biological parents around visiting issues and setting limits. She could, however, have taken this conversation even further. After tuning in to the foster parents, the worker could have explored with them the meaning of this erratic behavior. Were they cancelling the visit because they didn't care, or because they cared too much? What were the stresses the family faced that influenced their capacity to take care of him? In addition, since contact between foster parents and biological family members can become extremely negative in such circumstances, it would be helpful for the worker to consider with the foster parents how they might deal with the interaction. Was there a way to recognize the biological family's difficulty while simultaneously sharing their own issues around the missed visits and short notice? The foster parents want the biological family to be more understanding of the child's feelings, and one way to do this would be for the foster parents to express some understanding of what the other parents were going through. The interview continues with the worker addressing the feelings of the foster child. However, the intensity of those feelings results in the worker changing the subject to one less painful to the child (and to herself). This is an example of a situation in which the worker's use of an assessment tool blocks the immediate work instead of deepening it.

Kevin smiled and ran out. I followed him outside a few minutes later to talk to him. We sat down, and I started by telling him a few of the things Ann, Tom, and I had discussed such as his family contacting him earlier in the week if he couldn't go there for the weekend. I then said to him, "you must be disappointed about not going home."

He said, "Yes."

I reminded him that I was not opposed to his visiting Springfield (an aunt's home town) if it could be worked out between him and his mother and stepfather.

He said, "My aunt didn't call like she said she would."

We were silent for a minute. Then I told him that I had brought him some exercises to work on since he wasn't in school.

He asked me, "What does this have to do with school?"

I said, "Well, it's not reading, writing or arithmetic, but these exercises will give you something productive to do."

He said, "Well, if I get real bored, I'll take a look at them."

At this point, Ann yelled out the window at his friend who was still in the yard, the friend started walking away, Kevin asked him where he was going, and he responded that he'd be back in a minute.

I said, "I know there are a lot of distractions and you probably want to get back to what you were doing, but I have one more thing I want you to look at." I pulled out a family assessment. I said, "This is something to help you figure out ways your family interacts with each other. I made two copies for you so you could do one on your foster family and one on your other family."

He said, "I don't know about my other family. I haven't been there in so long."

I said, "Well, do the best you can. We might be able to figure out things that need to happen in both families to help you feel more safe and comfortable."

He said, "Okay. Leave it here and I'll do that one this week."

Kevin started telling me about some of the yard work he and Tom are doing. Then I told him I had one other thing on my mind that I wanted to talk about with him before I left. I told him I had been thinking about our conversation from last week, and I wanted to talk with him about keeping himself safe. He listened to me, then told me he wasn't normally in the situation like the one we talked about last week. I said, "Okay, but still think about what I said." He said, "Okay."

I went inside to tell Ann goodbye. I also told her that I had addressed "safety" with Kevin. I told her to do the best she could and have a good weekend. Then I left.

Working with the Child in Care

In the next illustration, an 11-year-old boy in residential care is helped by the worker to explore the connection between his feelings of loss and rejection and his ability to cope in the setting. The example also illustrates how work with children can often take place in non-structured settings. This could be called "steering wheel" (the car) or "fast food" social work. In residential treatment settings, where so many other children are around and competing for attention, a child needs to use these opportunities to capture the worker for his or her own needs. The issues, as in the example that follows, are often raised indirectly.

On October 15, Danny and I visited his grandmother. She is a terrifically "grand-motherly" lady who obviously cares for Danny a great deal. She, in fact, has no use for her daughter for rejecting Danny. Danny's birthday was the next day, and the occasion for our visit was to pick up his present and for me to meet her. We spent about two hours there—a very pleasant afternoon—and Danny was relaxed on the drive home.

Our conversation turned to Halloween, which Danny said he was looking forward to because he didn't get to go out last year. I asked why. He said that last year he'd stolen 50 cents from a friend of his and his mother found out and put him to bed right after supper. I asked him if he'd repaid the money, and he said yes he did when he got some money later that week. I asked why he'd taken money from his friend, and he said, "Well, he had money and I didn't." When I glanced at him he hung his head. I said, "Oh." But before I could make a further comment, he said that one time he'd stolen $4.65 from his mother and bought a whole shoe box full of bubble-gum cards. He said his teacher at school had found out about how he'd gotten them and made him rip them up and throw them away. His mother hit him and sent him to bed. This was relayed rather bitterly by him.

I was unsure at this point just where our pleasant driving-along conversation was headed, but I decided to explore how he was feeling about how he was handled by his mother vs. how the teacher handled him. When I asked him how he felt about having to throw the cards away, he said "awful," because he wanted to give the cards to friends. I asked him if he thought it was fair, and he said yes, that he shouldn't have been allowed to keep them. When I asked the same questions about what his mother had done, he said that he got hit a lot whenever he'd done anything wrong, and it hurt when he got hit, but it also made him mad. I asked him if he'd ever expressed this anger directly to his mother and he said no, because, if he did, she (or her boyfriend) would have probably hit him more. He went on to say that Dale (his mother's boyfriend) had noticed 25 cents missing one night on returning from work and had really gotten angry and, although it was past midnight, Dale went into Danny's room and pulled him into the kitchen by his hair and in the final pull Danny crashed into the table and knocked over a glass which broke. Danny said he then had to sweep up the mess and was hit by his mother with a yardstick and sent back to bed.

At this point in the interview, the worker is probably feeling the pain involved in the child's description of the abuse. An understandable resistance to exploring this pain, coupled with lack of clarity about his role, causes the worker to respond as a "teacher-preacher," using the description as an opportunity to teach a lesson. This misses the signal of the child's real work, illustrating the problem described earlier as *functional diffusion*. Fortunately, the worker catches his mistake as the child gives him another chance, making a "second offering" of the theme of concern.

Danny's voice in this recital was getting more and more strained, and he sounded angry. I didn't answer for a couple of minutes (for one thing I wasn't sure of how to respond) and Danny calmed a bit. Then I said, "Well, it sounds like Dale and your mom were really fed up and angry with you stealing from them and other people. I guess I wouldn't like it much if you stole a lot around me either." He said, "I wouldn't steal from you, and besides you don't hit me." I said, "No, I wouldn't hit you, even if I was really mad at you for stealing."

I obviously still wasn't getting his point, however, because he was very tense and tight in the seat. He then said, "What would you do if your kid was fighting at school and got hurt and had a bloody nose and you had to leave work to take him to the hospital?" This came out in a rush and he started to go on with his "hypothetical" example when I interrupted him and asked if that had happened to him, and he said "Yes."

Worker: What did your mother do, Danny?

Danny: She got mad at me for fighting.

Worker: Well, I wouldn't be very happy if you got into a fight at school.

Danny: I don't blame you. Kids shouldn't fight.

Worker: I guess I'd also be concerned about how your nose felt. It must have hurt a lot if you were going to the hospital.

Danny: That's what I mean!

Worker: (To myself) I think I finally got it.

Danny: All she did was nag me about how she had to leave work to take me to the hospital and how it upset her to do it, and she never once asked me how I felt about having a sore nose!

Worker: That must have felt really awful.

Danny: Yeah!

Worker: Like she didn't care about you, only the problems you caused her.

Danny: Yeah, all she did was nag, nag, nag about having to leave work and how it was stupid to fight....

Worker: I guess you already knew about the fighting; you had the sore and bloody nose to prove it.

Danny: (laughing) Yeah, and it was the only time she ever had to do anything like that, but she acted like I did it all the time and I didn't. I know you're not supposed to fight, but kids do anyway sometimes.

Worker: It must have been hard for you to act like a kid around his mother.

Danny: Yeah, especially with Dale sticking his nose in all the time.

The issue of his painful relationships with his family has emerged, although it has been timed to surface just as the worker drives into the center parking lot. This is often the way in which the client asks, "Do you really want to hear about this? Do I really want to talk about this?" If the worker uses the arrival as an excuse for backing off, the message to the client will close down the discussion. By continuing the discussion, the worker is saying to the client, "I am ready if you are."

At this point we were a block away from the center, but instead of turning right onto the side street, I turned left into the parking lot of a park. He asked why I'd done that and I answered that it seemed to me that we were having a pretty good talk and that I wanted it to finish a bit more naturally than by pulling into the parking lot and getting mobbed by the rest of the kids. He said, "Okay" and settled back in his seat.

Worker: What do you mean about Dale "sticking his nose" into things?

Danny: My mom and Dale would have meetings to discuss things and then they would vote on it.

Worker: What did you vote on?

Danny: We voted on my bedtime. I wanted to stay up til 9:00, but my mom wanted me to go to bed at 8:30, so we voted on it and he voted for her.

Worker: Wow, that sounds like they were sort of ganging up on you and pretending to be fair.

He agreed and said that they did that a lot. I asked if he was glad to be away from his mother, and he said yeah—that she didn't know how to treat kids and that all she did was nag or get mad and then stay mad, and he alluded to an incident that we had talked about before. I said that he must have gotten pretty angry sometimes when he was at home. He said yes and was sobbing. He said that he wished that she was right here now so he could tell her how much he hated her. I said he could hate her all he wanted and I didn't blame him.

He said that sometimes he felt like going by where she lived and throwing rocks through all the windows. I said it must have been hard to be angry a lot of the time he lived at home and not be able to tell anyone. He said that he'd like to tell her now and talked about how he'd like her to be a target in a shooting gallery so he could shoot at her. He laughed then and said that was a joke. I said he was saying that he was really angry, joke or not. He had relaxed somewhat by this time and said yes he was angry.

Having listened to the child's pain, the worker now makes a connection between his family experiences and life at the center. The child has another social worker whose focus is on the ongoing relationship to family members. This worker is concerned with the relationship of the child to the center (e.g., staff, other residents) and to other parts of the child's life, such as school. The next comments attempt to connect the discussion of the family experience to life at the center.

I said that he got angry a lot at little things around the center and sometimes screamed and raged on at the adults. He agreed, and said he thought it was good at the center because he could get mad and nobody held it against him, I said yes, it was okay at the center to get angry and let people know about it, but maybe sometimes he wasn't yelling at the person he was really angry with. He said yeah, that sometimes he was really feeling angry with his mom and the least little thing would set him off. I said that he must have his mother and home on his mind a lot, and he said that he thought about it "sometimes," especially bedtime, but during the day too.

I said that I thought I understood some of how he felt and that I was feeling right then really sad and hurt for him, and is that what he felt like, especially before he got angry, did he feel sad and hurt by his mother? He said yes, that most of the time before he got angry he felt hurt and that would help get him mad. I said that maybe he could come and tell me when he was feeling sad or hurt because he was thinking about his mother and home. He perked up a bit at this and said sure, he'd try to do that, but why? I said that maybe if he did that then he wouldn't have to get angry with the wrong person. He said maybe, but what would I do? I said, "Well, if you come and tell me when you feel hurt and sad, maybe we can just sit and feel hurt and sad together." He looked at me for a couple of seconds and smiled and said, "OK." I gave him a small hug, and we started back for the center.

In this last excerpt, the worker focused on helping the child to develop more adaptive ways of obtaining social support when he is hurting. The flight-fight mechanisms for dealing with pain are counterproductive. The child needs to learn how to make close connections with others who can help to fill the gap in his life left by parental abuse and abandonment. The worker has made a nice connection between the feeling of the client and the purpose of their work together.

A Teen Parent and Her Family of Origin

The problem of children having children is a growing one in North America. The stress of having to meet one's own, teenage developmental needs, while simultaneously trying to meet the needs of a child, often results in a call for help through behaviors that bring the child welfare agency into the picture. In the following example, a family support worker attempts to help a teenaged mother cope with her own feelings of rejection by her family of origin so that she can receive the support she needs as a parent under stress.

The following excerpt is taken from the fifteenth session of counseling with Mary, a 17-year-old who is the mother of a two-year-old daughter.

Mary says that she has had little contact with her original family since she became pregnant. She has not wanted to talk about her family with me and has focused on her relationships with her boyfriend and foster mother. I felt that she might be ready to talk about her family, and I was looking for signals from her.

Mary said that her father was shopping in the same store as she was this week. I asked what had happened. She answered, "Nothing." I smiled and asked her what happened when nothing happened. She laughed and said he pretended that he didn't see her. I asked her how she felt when he did that. She said, "I didn't care. He makes me laugh because he is so messed up." I said that when she says nothing happened, she seems to mean that they didn't speak to each other. I said I wonder if it really feels like nothing happened when her father passes her as if she didn't exist. She said that she really doesn't care.

I said that I have known Mary since September and have seen her go through some really difficult situations. She has had some big fights with people close to her, she has had her boyfriend sentenced to 12 to 15 years in jail. However, in all this time, only once have I seen her with tears in her eyes. She asked, "When was that?" I answered that it was after the sentencing when she said that her child would not have a father just like she didn't and that it was so important to her that her daughter have it better than she did. Mary thought a moment and said that I was right. She really has a lot of feelings, but she can't talk about it. I asked her why she thought it was so difficult to talk about it. She said because it is so painful. I agreed with her. I asked her what she thought happened to painful feelings that a person can't talk about. I asked her where the feelings go. She said that she keeps them buried inside. I asked her if they stay buried.

She smiled and said she had a dream about her father after she saw him in the supermarket. In the dream, her father and mother were both in the store and, when they saw her, her father gave her mother some money and said to buy Mary whatever she needs. Mary said she knows what the dream means, but she doesn't want to talk about it. I said that she may not be able to talk about it today, but that she has done some really important work today. She took a tremendous step in moving from her statement that she has no feelings to saying she has a lot of feelings, but it is a difficult and painful subject to talk about. I said that she is sharing some feelings with me, but she is also saying that she needs to go slowly because it is so hard for her. I said that I will try to help her progress at a pace that is OK for her. I said that we know that there is some important work for us to do even if it is just a little bit at a time. Those bottled-up feeling are fighting to get out.

Mary was silent for a little while, and then she changed the subject. This was the first time that Mary discussed her father beyond the statement that they don't get along. I felt comfortable with the way I had handled this situation. I challenged her to work, gave her support, recognized her difficulty, gave her praise for beginning, and gave her permission to proceed slowly with my support. Finally, I gave her the opportunity to choose to continue or to change the subject knowing that we have agreed that it is an important area for us to work on. In the two sessions we have had since this meeting, Mary has been able to talk in detail about her family relationships.

Emotional support is one way Mary can get the help she needs in order to provide the parenting needed by her toddler. In this author's research project (Shulman, 1991), it was clear that concrete support was also crucial. To meet her own developmental needs, this client will require adequate financial support, child care, alternative schooling possibilities, respite care (someone to give her a break from child care duties), and so on. If this mother chooses to keep her child, the "goodness-of-fit" between her developmental needs and these formal and informal resources may make the crucial difference between success and failure (Germain and Gitterman, 1980).

FAMILY PRACTICE IN A SCHOOL SETTING

In this section, we examine an example of family practice in a school setting. The 15-year-old high school freshman has been diagnosed as having an Attention Deficit Disorder that has affected his ability to negotiate his educational experiences. The social worker in this setting attempts to mediate between the client and his family as well other professionals in the system. Family members and teachers often fail to understand the impact of this disorder and attribute the problems to "lack of trying" or "laziness." The illustration, in the form of a record of service, examines the social worker's efforts over time as she becomes clearer about her specific role in this educational setting. Her early use of activity (checkers) is, in this case, her way of structuring time because she has not effectively contracted in the first session. With effective contracting, activities can be used with children and teens as a medium to create a comfortable setting for conversation. In spite of the lack of contracting, the client raises a number of themes of concern.

Client Description and Time Frame:

The client is a 15-year-old freshman, male, Jewish student. The time frame was from October 19th to March 22nd.

Description of the Problem:

Jack is a young man who experiences considerable difficulty in navigating his family and school systems due to the effects of Attention Deficit Disorder.

Summary of the Work:

October 19th (Second Session)

I wanted to find out how Jack was adapting to his new school. We began by talking about the fact that Jack had been absent last week. Since he is a freshman, I wanted to find out if he knew what he had to do to get his absence excused and if he had gotten his make-up work from his teachers. When I asked Jack how his classes were going, he said that he had received a supplemental (warning notice) in civics. We talked about how he could get help on his homework from the remedial services teacher. I should have asked Jack more about the situation—how he was getting on with his teacher, how his parents reacted to him getting a supplemental. I could tell he was becoming uncomfortable, but rather than acknowledging that, I allowed him to change the subject. We talked about the World Series and the earthquake out in San Francisco.

October 26th (Third Session)

I asked Jack to choose the activity and take some responsibility for the session. I asked Jack to choose the game, he decided on checkers, and we began to play. After a few minutes, Jack asked me if I had taken drafting in high school. I said that I hadn't, was there a special reason he was wondering about it? Jack replied, "Because I'm having trouble in drafting—I can't finish any of the assignments." I asked him what about drafting was keeping him from finishing the assignments, and he said, "It's just too hard." I asked him what part of it was hardest for him, and he said, "The measuring. If you have one line out of place, you get a zero." I said that I had taken mechanical drawing in junior high and that it is difficult and frustrating because it is so precise. Jack agreed but said that it wasn't really a big deal, because drafting was only the first six weeks of his Exploratory Shop Class and it was almost over anyway. I said if it was frustrating him I thought it was important. I offered to act as the mediator, but I didn't make Jack part of the process. I suggested that I talk with his drafting teacher and remedial services teacher to see if we could work together to make it easier for him. Jack agreed that I could do that.

This interview led to a lot of running around. However, I did not take time to tune in with the other members of the system. I had my own agenda. After having seen the difficulty Jack had with hand-eye/fine motor coordination last week when we played the game with the blocks, I was not surprised to hear that he had trouble in drafting. I spoke with the drafting teacher, who showed me one of Jack's papers. All of the lines were crooked, and I could tell that Jack had erased many times to try to get the lines straight. The drafting teacher said he couldn't understand why Jack couldn't make the lines straight. I said that Jack obviously has some trouble with this and that we need to find out how to help him. I did not empathize with the teacher. In fact, I felt annoyed that he hadn't recognized the trouble Jack was having and told someone in the Special Needs Department.

I then went to talk with the school psychologist about all of the testing in Jack's file. I wanted to know why Jack was having trouble and what we could do to help him be more successful in drafting. The psychologist took one look at the test results and said that a child with Jack's deficits shouldn't even be in such a class, that all of the testing showed that he wouldn't be able to do it. I was somewhat flabbergasted by this statement and confused by the fact that Jack was put in this class in the first place if the testing showed he couldn't do it. I was intimidated by the psychologist's authority. I asked her if there were any more tests to be done or any methods we could use to help Jack learn to measure. She said that all of the testing had been done, and that Jack should be removed from the class. I knew that she was giving up on Jack, and I felt uncomfortable about this, but I didn't verbalize it.

I then spoke with Jack's mother (who would have to give permission for Jack to drop the class). She said she wanted him to stay in drafting, that he probably wasn't trying hard enough. She said that he usually didn't try hard enough and wasn't motivated. I did not explore this statement or reach for the mother's feelings. At this point, I was identifying so strongly with Jack's predicament and how nobody wanted to help him, that I was very angry with all of these authority figures. I said that I would see if Jack's remedial services teacher could help him learn how to measure. I was very surprised that Jack's mother would not acknowledge that there must be more of a problem than just not trying hard enough when a 15-year-old can't draw a straight line, but I did not try to find out what was going on.

I then went to see the Remedial Services teacher, who said that she had her hands full helping Jack with his other classes and didn't know anything about drafting anyway. I didn't offer the teacher any support. She suggested that I ask Jack's Special Needs math teacher to help him. So I went to see the math teacher, who said that he would help Jack learn how to measure. Jack remained in drafting class and did a little better during the remainder of the six-week period until they switched to a new area of study.

Over the next several weeks, we settled to an illusion of work. Jack and I continued to play games in our sessions. Jack was very uncomfortable and restless if we did not play a game, but when we did, he would open up and talk about himself. It became apparent that his mother hassles him a lot, always trying to get him to try harder. Jack became more able to talk about his feelings.

Last week in January

Jack's mother called me and said that she was concerned because Jack had not been bringing any homework with him from school, and she thought he should have some. She said that Jack told her that he did his homework in Remedial Services, but she didn't know how that could be so, since he was getting such awful grades. I offered to act as the mediator between the systems, but I didn't actively include all of the parties involved. I said that I would mention her concerns to Jack, and if Jack agreed to it, I could go around and find out if he had been doing his work. She said that would be helpful to her, that it was really hard for her to get time off from work and come in to school. I told her I would call her back in a couple of weeks.

February 1st

I worked to maintain Jack's trust by including him. I told Jack that his mother had called me about him not having any homework. I told him that I had been careful not to reveal to his mother anything that we talked about in our meetings. Jack said that it was fine with him if I checked around with his teachers about his homework, because he was doing it anyway. We talked a little about how hard it is when your parents don't believe you.

I spent the next couple of weeks going around to all of Jack's teachers. I started out with the Remedial Services teacher and the Special Needs math teacher, both of whom said that Jack wasn't the best student, but he came to class and handed in his assignments. At this point I think I was still over-identifying with Jack. I was looking for evidence that would show he was doing his best, so I didn't explore very much with these teachers. When I talked with the mainstream teachers, they all said that Jack was doing OK work (in the C range), handing in his assignments, and behaving well. I found out that Jack did have some difficulty with hearing and remembering instructions given verbally by the teachers and that he would sometimes blurt out answers before the teacher finished asking the question. I knew from the research I was doing into Attention Deficit Disability that these were common symptoms, and I found myself a little annoyed that none of the teachers seemed to be helping Jack with this (for example, by writing things down on the board).

Before I had the chance to call Jack's mother back, she called me, saying that she had found two supplemental reports in Jack's pocket when she was doing the laundry. The supplementals were from the Remedial Services teacher and the Special Needs math teacher. I told her I was surprised that he had received supplementals in those classes because I had just spoken with those two teachers within the last couple of weeks and they had given me no indication they were planning to send home a notice. I volunteered to take the role of the mediator, this time making suggestions that all parties take an active role. I suggested that perhaps it would be a good idea if we set up a time for a meeting. The meeting would include the two teachers, Jack, his mother, and me. I explained that maybe if we sat down together, we could figure out some strategies to help Jack do better. Jack's mother agreed that a meeting was a good idea, but she said that she thought the problem was that Jack wasn't motivated enough. We agreed upon a time for the next week, and I told her I would call back to confirm after I had spoken with the teachers and Jack. The teachers were open to the idea of a meeting, and in our next session Jack and I talked about it.

March 8th

Jack started out by saying that things were going better in school lately except that he didn't like Remedial Services. I asked him what he did not like about it. I made a demand for work, asking Jack to define his own needs. He said, "Well, she makes up all of these rules…like we have to come in and sit down and go right to work. We can't talk to each other at all. In classes like shop we get to talk to each other while we work." I asked him if it was hard for him to sit there and work the whole time without talking. He said that it was hard and usually he ended up forgetting and talking anyway. I said that it's hard when people expect you to do something that's really hard for you, and he agreed.

We went on talking about the meeting. Jack asked if everyone was going to yell at him and be mad that he was not doing better. I told him that I couldn't promise that there wouldn't be any yelling, but that the point of the meeting was to find out what we need to do to help him to learn better, and that sometimes when people care they yell. I tried to reframe the situation. We then went on to talk about how this can tie in to his mother nagging him about school, that maybe it wasn't just because she wanted to bug him, but that she really cares about him. We talked a little bit more about what Jack could expect the meeting would be like, and I told him that his input would be very important, that he had just as much to say as anybody else and that I would support him.

I later called Jack's mother back to confirm the meeting, and talked with her a little more about the purpose of the meeting. I found that we really had the same objective in mind, even if we had a different way of looking at it. I spent a lot of time over the next week doing research on ADD and tuning in to Jack, his mother, and the teachers.

March 16th

Jack's mother arrived early for the meeting, which gave us a chance to get a little bit acquainted. I wanted to establish a rapport with Jack's mom, to tune in to her position and try to get her to work with me. I said that I was really glad that she had come in, that I could tell she was really concerned about Jack and I thought it was very positive that she was so invested in making sure that Jack did well in school. I told her that a lot of parents aren't that interested in how their kids are doing, and that having a parent who really cares makes a big difference for the kid. I also said I thought it must be really frustrating for her. I had seen Jack's file and it was filled with years and years of evaluations and testing, yet things were still difficult. Jack's mother agreed, and seemed to relax a little.

Jack and the teachers arrived and we sat down in the conference room. I wanted to defuse any of the defensiveness people were feeling and set the stage for some work to be done right at the beginning. I introduced Jack's mom to the teachers and said I wanted to thank everyone for taking the time to be here, that our objective was to figure out how to help Jack to do better in school. I said that I knew everyone was working really hard already on this and that we weren't here to criticize anyone or get down on Jack, and I thought that if we worked together we might come up with some new ideas. I said that Jack's input would also be important and I wanted him to share his ideas with us too. I said I thought we could start out by hearing from the teachers. I asked them to tell about how Jack was doing, and to not only talk about the things that needed improvement but also the things that Jack was doing well. Each teacher took a turn, and when they brought up behaviors that were related to the ADD, I made a point of stating that those behaviors were tied to the ADD and not lack of control on Jack's part.

Jack's mom spoke next, saying that she still thinks that the problem is that Jack needs to be more motivated and try harder. I made a demand for work, asking Jack to say what he really felt. I asked Jack what he thought about that. He said it was probably true. I said that I thought he was trying pretty hard already and that some of the things he was being asked to do were difficult for him. Jack looked relieved and agreed that he does try, and no matter how hard he tries, everyone always asked him to try harder.

We then went on to talk about ways to help Jack to remember to bring his books and pencil with him to class, and how his mom could help him at home. The teachers came up with some really good ideas, and as the meeting ended, everyone thought the strategy was worth a try. We agreed to reevaluate the situation in about a month, and the teachers left. Jack, his mother, and I continued to work a little longer, talking about how they relate to each other at home. Once again, I tried to reframe their views of each other, and I gave them some suggestions about working together. This seemed quite successful, with Jack and his mom laughing a little and expressing some affection to each other

March 22nd

I asked Jack to evaluate the meeting, to continue participating actively. We began by talking about the meeting with Jack's mother and teachers last Friday. I asked Jack what he thought about the meeting. He said that it was OK. I said that I thought it had gone well, that we had made some progress, but I had wondered what it had been like for him to sit in the meeting. He said that it hadn't been as bad as he thought it would be. I said that it is hard to sit in a meeting when it is about you and that I thought he had done really well. Jack smiled. I asked him how things were going now with his mom. He said they were still arguing a little over school, but that the new ideas were helping.

Current Status of the Problem:

A couple of weeks later, Jack's mom called me again to talk about how things were going. This time, I found myself really empathizing with her on the phone. In talking with her, I found out that in all the time that Jack has been diagnosed with ADD, no one has ever given her any real information about it or suggestions on how to deal with a kid with Jack's special needs. All this time I assumed somebody had given her that information and advice. I offered to photocopy an article I had about "Guidelines for living with a child with ADD" and a list of some good books on the subject. She sounded really interested, and I mailed the materials off to her.

It then occurred to me that if nobody had spoken about these things with Jack's mother in all this time, probably nobody had spoken with Jack, which turned out to be the case. Since then, Jack and I have done some work on what ADD is, what might cause it, and what the treatment is. Jack said that all this time he thought that the ADD symptoms he experienced meant that he was stupid. I've learned never to assume that the obvious work has already been done. Even though we have not yet had our meeting to reevaluate the situation, Jack already seems to be doing better and feeling better about himself.

Strategies for Intervention:

1. Work with Jack on strategies for coping with the ADD symptoms (i.e., ideas for helping him to remember things and helping him to expand his attention span).

2. Find information about a support group for parents of ADD children for Jack's mother. This would help her to learn more about ADD and talk with other parents about strategies for coping with and helping Jack.

3. Work with Jack on expressing his feelings with his mother in a more constructive way to help their communication. Also, help Jack speak up more to his teachers and ask for them to repeat directions or write them down on the board.

4. Continue to work on the idea that the ADD symptoms are not Jack's fault.

5. Help Jack learn to work effectively with his parents and teachers.

6. Work on termination/transfer issues, including any ideas for talking with Jack's classroom teachers for next year and preparing them for his special needs.

By staying focused on education-related issues, and by bringing into the picture as many members of the family and school system as possible, the worker was mobilizing all parties involved in an effort to help Jack overcome the deficit and make it at school. The repeated statements by the mother that all Jack needed to do was to try harder may have been a signal to the worker of an important area for discussion with the mother—her feelings about his academic problems and her difficulty in accepting that he may have physical barriers to success. The worker might want to explore the meaning of education to the mother's family and the cultural significance of education as well.

THE SINGLE-PARENT FAMILY AND THE "BIG BROTHER" SERVICE

One problem facing a female single parent, if the father is out of the picture, can be the lack of adult male authority figures for her children. In addition, the tasks facing a single parent may make it difficult to spend as much time with a child as one wishes. As one parent put it, "When do I have time for myself?" The changing nature of the family structure and family mobility increases the chance that a single parent may find himself or herself socially isolated, lacking the kind of social support once offered by the extended family. One organization providing a service to meet this need is the Big Brothers agency. The equivalent for girls would be the Big Sisters service. These are social service agencies that attempt to match children with adult volunteers. The social worker's role in these agencies can include screening and evaluation of the parents, children, and potential volunteers as well as ongoing monitoring of the relationship.

The Acting-Out Parent

In the next example, an acting-out parent is sending strong signals of her own distress through her complaints about the service and the Big Brother. There is a good chance that the client is demonstrating to the worker, through the process of their interaction, the way in which she is pushing other people away just when she needs support the most. The worker maintains her focus on the family issues related to the service while recognizing the need to empathize with the parent.

> Mrs. Stevens arrived on time for her office appointment. The purpose of our meeting was twofold. First, we were meeting to discuss her concerns about her son's (Richard's) one-year match to "Big Brother" Ted. Second, I wanted to meet with her to begin to establish a positive working relationship. Previous conversations with Mrs. Stevens had consisted of her yelling and hanging up on me.

Upon Mrs. Stevens's arrival, I greeted her warmly and accompanied her into my office. She immediately began to talk about changes at her workplace that might result in a layoff of several of the employees. From experience with Mrs. Stevens, I knew that being passive is totally useless and it was necessary to set limits with her ventilation or she would go on and on. However, I also supposed that no one ever listens to her and she needed the opportunity to ventilate. So, I listened to Mrs. Stevens for a few minutes, asked her how the changes at work might be affecting her current position, and empathized with her fear that she too might be laid off.

At a pause in her conversation, I stated that I was glad that she told me about what was going on at work and that I would be happy to talk with her to discuss her work concerns, but I thought she and I needed to discuss what we had originally planned to discuss—her son's match—since she and I only had an hour to meet today. Mrs. Stevens agreed, and without pausing, she began to tell me about how inconsiderate Ted, her son's Big Brother, is of her son's feelings. She cited several instances in which Ted did not do enough for her son. For example, Mrs. Stevens did not think it would be too much for Ted to call Richard during the week on some mornings just to say hello. Or another example, Mrs. Stevens thought that Ted's plans to take Richard out for a few hours on a Sunday afternoon was unfair for Mrs. Stevens because it interfered with her ability to make her own plans on Sunday. As Mrs. Stevens spoke, she became increasingly angry, kept citing the same examples over and over, and stated that I didn't understand, the agency didn't seem to care, and she wanted to file a child abuse report against the agency because we're responsible for letting the Big Brother hurt Richard over and over again.

I felt myself growing more impatient and angry with Mrs. Stevens, which is how many people probably feel when dealing with her. I was determined not to engage in an argument, which would not be constructive. Instead, I listened to her and asked her to clarify exactly what it was that the agency or I didn't understand. She replied that Richard takes it out on her whenever Ted does not come through with their original plans. Mrs. Stevens expanded her response by telling me how her other children have abandoned her and Richard and that there has been no stability in Richard's life. I added that it sounds as if there had been no stability in her life either and I empathetically identified the stresses of being a single parent.

I assured Mrs. Stevens that even though she seems very angry with the agency and myself, I will continue to try to help her and Richard to the best of my ability. Somewhat jokingly, I said that no matter how much she yells or how frequently she hangs up on me, I will not go away. Mrs. Stevens smiled. I took the opportunity to add that, in order for me to best help her, she and I need to talk and discuss, not argue and yell. Mrs. Stevens simmered down and again cited the same examples as previously, regarding Ted's "failure to come through," in Mrs. Stevens's eyes.

I calmly and slowly acknowledged Mrs. Stevens's concerns and even repeated them back to her, one by one, so that she knew that I had heard what she said. I then clarified the role and responsibilities of a Big Brother, carefully pointing out how Ted has fulfilled that role, and areas that he needed to work on, agreeing with some of Mrs. Steven's concerns. I next explained very clearly what my plan of action would be, making sure that she was aware of my every step so that she would not feel like she was being left out.

Mrs. Stevens seemed to respond well to clarity and structure. She stated that she did not think that Ted liked her or Richard and probably does not want to remain a

Big Brother. Mrs. Stevens could not substantiate her feelings that Ted didn't like her, however. I asked Mrs. Stevens if she agreed with my course of action (re: my meeting the following week with Ted and Richard). She said it was fine with her, but she didn't think it would be of any help. She did not think it would be a waste of time either, but was agreeable to "giving it a shot" to meet with Ted and Richard. Mrs. Stevens did not want to take any responsibility in terms of stating she wanted to end the match, nor did she express support for trying to salvage it. I pointed this out to her, and she said that she did not want to end the match because "Ted is better than nothing." I summarized our meeting and concluded it by agreeing with her that Ted has been of value to Richard (and pointed out how so) and that I am clearly aware of her concerns and will discuss them with Ted. I will speak with Mrs. Stevens after my meeting with Ted and Richard.

Despite Mrs. Stevens's hostile tone throughout most of the meeting, she stood up, patted me on the shoulder, and said, "Good luck."

While the worker needs to stay within the boundaries of the agency service, additional help can be supplied to Mrs. Stevens through referral. In addition, although the worker handled the confrontation with Mrs. Stevens over her angry acting out with gentle good humor, she will need to confront her on the impact she is having on the worker, and in all likelihood, the Big Brother Ted.

An Ending and Transition

In another Big Brother example, we see a worker dealing with an ending and transition as a change in job status causes her to transfer the case. Since the clients using this service have usually experienced important losses in their lives, it is particularly important that the worker pay close attention to the demands of the ending and transition phase of practice.

> **Worker:** I have some news that I need to tell you.
> **Client (Mother):** Don't tell me you're leaving the agency.
> **Worker:** No, I'm not, but I will become supervisor of our new office, which will cause me to have to transfer the families I've been working with in this area.
> **Client:** I'm so happy for you, but it will be difficult for us not to have you as our social worker any more.
> **Worker:** I have mixed feelings also, because I'm excited about the new position, but it will be hard for me to give up certain people, like you.
>
> After hugging, I said I'd be in touch to arrange a meeting with her and the kids to begin talking about the change. Later that week, we set up an appointment. Mom came in talking about what a difficult time her son was having due to rejection from his father, and now her son's Big Brother was also rejecting him. I asked if he was also feeling rejected by me. Mom said that he was angry about finding out about the change by getting a letter, as he no longer felt special. I apologized for that and explained that I had meant to tell him myself, but didn't get a chance before the letter was sent. I added that he is special and that I was planning to tell him and apologize.
>
> After discussing more issues related to her son's depression and making suggestions for follow-up treatment with the next worker, I asked how the mother was feeling about meeting another worker. She replied that she was ready. I commented on how nonchalant and accepting she seemed about the change, and mentioned that I was feeling sad. Mother acknowledged that, like her other son, she tends to deny dif-

ficult situations and then "fall apart" later on. I said that I hoped I wasn't pressuring her, but that I thought it was important for her to recognize how she was acting. She started to cry, and said she was glad to have known me. She spoke positively about our relationship and how much she has grown through her involvement with the agency. I told her that I would miss her cooperativeness, kindness, and appreciation, and that the next worker would be lucky. Mention was made that it had been difficult to keep the professional and personal issues separate and how our relationship would change now. We then embraced again and made introductions to the next worker. Mom did call once after the day of my meeting with her child, but has not called since.

While the focus of the work is clearly on the match between the child and the volunteer Big Brother, the worker is often also providing an important support service to the parent. At minimum, having a professional "friend" with whom to discuss the child's progress can take a significant load off a single-parent client.

CHAPTER SUMMARY

In this chapter we focused on variations on the themes of family social work. Particular emphasis was placed on the importance of contracting and boundaries for service. The common ground between the services arising from the agency mandate and the client's perception of need was brought to the foreground and served to give direction to the work. Examples were presented focusing on the impact of a catastrophic illness, child welfare issues, family practice in a school setting, and Big Brother services for single-parent families.

GLOSSARY

Family secret An explicit or unspoken agreement in which all family members agree not to deal directly with a sensitive and taboo concern. Family violence, alcoholism, and sexual abuse are examples of family secrets often hidden behind a family facade.

PART IV

Social Work with Groups

In Part IV we explore the interactional model of practice in the context of social work with groups. In Chapter 8 we discuss the group as a mutual aid system, and in Chapter 9 we review the principles of group formation. In Chapters 10 and 11 the beginning phase of group work practice is examined in detail. In Chapters 12, 13, and 14 our focus is on the middle phase of practice, with special emphasis on the importance of working with two clients: the individual and the group. In Chapter 15 we elaborate on the ending and transition phase of practice in relation to groups, and in Chapter 16 we look at variant elements of contracting introduced by different types of groups. Finally, in Chapter 17 we turn our attention to the unique aspects of group work with substance abusers and their families, as well as young people in groups for the prevention of substance abuse.

8

The Group as a Mutual Aid System

CHAPTER OUTLINE

The Dynamics of Mutual Aid

Obstacles to Mutual Aid

The Function of the Group Leader

The "Fear-of-Groups" Syndrome

Our approach to group work starts with the assumption that a group has the potential to serve as a mutual aid system for its members. Our focus in Parts II and III was on the worker's efforts to assist individual clients to negotiate systems that were important to them. In this first chapter of Part IV, we will explore the dynamics of mutual aid that can occur when a group of clients with common concerns is brought together for the purpose of helping each other. The reader will find that many of the processes and skills discussed in Parts II and III are equally applicable when employed in the group context. We will also explore some unique features involved in the use of group method, as well as specific obstacles to mutual aid. In this chapter we will outline the mutual aid processes and examine the function of the social worker in the group. We will also look at the concerns often experienced by workers as they prepare to lead their first group session.

In our previous discussions of the underlying assumptions of the general helping model, our focus was on the client in interaction with the various surrounding systems: family, agency, school, and so on. It is easier to perceive the similarities between individual and group work when one realizes that the group is a special case of the general individual-social interaction. In a sense, the group represents a **microsociety.** The potential for the "symbiotic" relationship described in the first part of this book is also present in each small-group encounter.[1] In a seminal article entitled "The Social Worker in the Group," Schwartz (1961) defined the helping group as follows:

> The group is an enterprise in mutual aid, an alliance of individuals who need each other, in varying degrees, to work on certain common problems. The important fact is that this is a helping system in which the clients need each other as well as the worker. This need to use each other, to create not one but many helping relationships, is a vital ingredient of the group process and constitutes a common need over and above the specific tasks for which the group was formed (p. 18).

The idea of the group as a "mutual aid system" in which the worker helps people to help each other is an attractive one,[2] yet it raises many questions and doubts in the minds of workers whose experiences in groups, as members and leaders, have led them to question the potential of group work for mutual aid. Exactly how can a group of people sharing the same set of concerns help each other? Isn't it a bit like the blind leading the blind? How will clients be able to talk about their most intimate concerns before a group of strangers? What about the coercive power of the group? How can individuals stand up against the odds? What is the job of the group leader if the members are helping each other? These questions and others are legitimate. They sometimes reflect workers' past group experiences, which may have been hurtful, nonproductive, or boring—far from being enterprises in mutual aid.

My response is that the potential for mutual aid exists in the group, but simply bringing people together does not guarantee that it will emerge. Many obstacles can block the group members' ability to reach out to each other and to offer help. Many of these are similar to the obstacles described earlier, but their effect can be magnified in the group context. Because all members will bring to the group their own concepts, based upon past experiences with groups (e.g., school, camp, committees), and because many of these past experiences may have been poor ones, the group worker is needed to help the group members create the conditions in which mutual aid can take place. The tasks of the group worker in attempting to help group members develop the required skills are related to these obstacles. Creating a mutual aid group is a difficult process, with members having to overcome many of their stereotypes about people in general, groups, and helping. They will need all the assistance they can get from the group worker. Since the worker has also been affected by past group experiences, one of the worker's early tasks requires facing her or his own feelings and examining stereotypes. Without this self-examination, the worker may be unable to convey to the members a belief in their potential for helping each other. Faith in the strength of the group will make an important contribution to the group members' success in their struggles.

In the balance of this chapter, we will begin to address the worker's hesitancy and questions by listing some of the ways in which group members can help each other; these are the processes of mutual aid. The obstacles that can emerge to block this potential are briefly reviewed. An overview of the function of the group worker is then presented. In the other chapters in Part IV, we will elaborate upon the model and illustrate the skills of the group worker in action.

THE DYNAMICS OF MUTUAL AID

In the chapters that follow, the mutual aid process will be described in detail and illustrated with examples from a range of groups. To assist the reader in conceptualizing mutual aid in a general way, a number of illustrations are described here. In particular, illustrations from a recent group for persons with AIDS in early recovery from substance abuse, co-led by this author, will be shared. A more complete discussion of this group will be presented in Chapter 17.

Sharing Data

One of the simplest and yet most important ways in which group members can help each other is through the sharing of relevant data. Members of the group have had different life experiences, through which whey have accumulated knowledge, views, values, and so forth that can help others in the group. For example, in a married couples' group described in detail in later chapters, one of the couples is in their late sixties. They have experienced many of the normal life crises as well as those imposed by societal pressures (e.g., the Great Depression of the 1930s). As other group members who are in their fifties, forties, thirties, and twenties describe their experiences and problems, this couple is often able to share an insight which comes from being able to view these crises from the perspective of time. As the group leader, I often found myself learning from the experiences of this couple. We created in the group a form of the extended family in which one generation passed on its life experiences to the next. In turn, the older couple was able to use the group not only for their immediate problems but also as a place for reviewing their 50 years together. (This may be an important part of their work at this stage in their life cycle.)

In another group, working mothers are able to share ideas that have proven helpful in organizing their daily routines. They share the names of community services that they have discovered, and each mother taps the experiences and the ingenuity of the others. Whether the data consist of specific tips on concrete questions (jobs, available housing, money management, and so on), values, or ideas about relationships, each member can contribute to the common pool of knowledge. The worker will also contribute data which, when combined with that of the others, provides a rich resource for the members.

In a group of clients with AIDS who were in early recovery from substance abuse (referred to as an AIDS/Recovery group), specific information about the recovery process and coping with AIDS and its treatment was shared on a regular basis. For example, one client told another, "This is the start of your second year in recovery—the feelings year—so don't be surprised about all of the pain you are feeling because you don't have the drinking and drugging to cover it up." At another meeting, clients shared their experiences with the new triple-drug therapy and provided information for those who were not in the trial groups about how to get connected. In the example that follows, group members provided tips to another on how to increase one member's chances for acceptance into a special housing program for people with AIDS.

> I pointed out that, earlier, Theresa had mentioned her interest in getting into this independent living facility. I wondered if we might help her just by addressing that issue, as well. She told us she was concerned about putting an application in because she didn't think she had established enough credibility in her single-room occupancy housing. At this point, Jake and Tania started suggesting strategies and ideas about how to approach the living facility and what would maximize her ability to get in. They strongly encouraged her to make an application right now, since there were openings and a few months down the road these openings might close, and there would be no place for her. They said they thought it would be wonderful if she could move into the building.
>
> Tania pointed out that the building—if you looked at it—the building was supposed to be for people with AIDS, but, if you took a look at it, your guess would be that it was essentially for gay men. She said she was the only woman in the whole building—the only single woman in the whole building. She said to Theresa that if worse came to worst, you could always tell them it's discrimination, and that'll get their attention. She said, "That's how I got in."
>
> They continued to talk with Theresa about ways she could demonstrate her responsibility, things that she had done, her commitment to recovery, the fact that she wanted to leave this other place. Even though it was supposed to be a safe single-

room occupancy, everybody knew drug dealing was going on there all the time, and it was scary to be there. She took it all in, thanked them for their advice, and said she was going to apply.

The Dialectical Process

An important debate of ideas can take place as each member shares views on the question under discussion. Group members can risk their tentative ideas and use the group as a sounding board—a place for their views to be challenged and possibly changed. It is not always easy to challenge ideas in the group, and I will discuss later how such a "culture for work" can be developed. When this kind of group "culture" is present, the argument between two or more members takes on a **dialectical** nature. Group members can listen as one member presents the "thesis" and the other, the "antithesis." As each member listens, he or she can use the discussion to develop a personal "synthesis."

An illustration of this process in the couples' group occurred when one couple in their fifties discussed a problem they were experiencing with their grown, married children. They described their negative perception of the way in which their children were handling their marital difficulty and how this was affecting their marriage. As they spoke, I could see anger in the eyes of a younger couple in their twenties. They were experiencing difficulty with the wife's parents, whom they viewed as "meddling" in their lives. When I reached for the verbal expression of the nonverbal cues, the battle was on. The older couple had to defend their perceptions against the arguments of the younger couple, who could see the problem through the eyes of their children. In return, the younger couple had to look at their strained relationships with the wife's parents through the eyes of the older couple, who could understand her parents' perspective. For each couple, the debate led to some modification of their views and new insights into how the respective children and parents might be feeling. It was obvious from the discussion that other group members were making associations to their own experiences, using the dialogue taking place before them.

It is important to note that confrontation is a part of mutual aid. Instead of being suppressed, differences must be expressed in an arena where they can be used for learning. I believe that group members often present strongly held views on a subject precisely because they have doubts and desperately need a challenging perspective. The skills involved in helping group members to use these conflicts constructively are explored later. This example also illustrates the fact that the group can be a laboratory for developing skills such as asserting oneself, so that the individual members can become more effective in their external relationships. The conversation between the older and younger couples constituted a rehearsal for the important discussion that needed to take place with their respective children and parents. The group members were able to use the experience for this purpose when the leader pointed this out.

Discussing a Taboo Area

Each group member brings to the group the norms of behavior and the taboos that exist in our larger culture. Norms are the rules of behavior that are generally accepted by a dominant group in society. These norms can be recreated within a social work group or other system. The existence of the norms is evident when the group members behave as if the norms exist. For example, one norm of group behavior may be to avoid discussion in an area of societal taboo.

In the beginning phase of work, the group recreates in this microsociety the general community "culture," consisting of norms, taboos, and rules that the group members have experienced outside the group. Thus, direct talk about such subjects as authority, dependency, and sex is experienced as taboo. One of the tasks of the group leader will be to help the group members develop new norms and feel free to challenge some taboos so that the group can be more effective. Each client will feel the urgency of discussing the subject somewhat differently from the others, and each group member will experience the power of the taboo differently. As the work proceeds and the level of comfort in the group increases (the skills for helping this to happen are discussed in later chapters), one member may take the first risk, directly or indirectly, that leads the group into a difficult area of discussion. By being first, the member allows the more fearful and reluctant members to watch as the taboo is violated. As they experience positive work, they are given permission to enter the formerly taboo area. Thus, all the group members are able to benefit from the particular sense of urgency, the lower level of anxiety, or the greater willingness to risk of the member who leads the way.

In my AIDS/Recovery group, one member spoke about her own abusive past history and how she had escaped her family and turned to the streets and "to every kind of drug and drink you could imagine." She went on to describe her experiences prostituting in order to raise money for drugs and how she was not proud of herself or what she did. She said, "While I was on the street I was with many men but I was really with no man." These revelations opened the door for other members to share their own sexual experiences, often degrading and exploitive, as they went on "coke dates" to raise money for their drugs. The ability to discuss their emotions in a supportive, non-judgmental environment appeared to have a cathartic effect, creating a culture in which other taboo issues were discussed, such as their own illnesses, their rejection by friends and family, painful losses of people close to them, and their own fears of debilitation and death associated with AIDS.

The "All-in-the-Same-Boat" Phenomenon

After the group enters a formerly taboo area, the members listen to the feelings of the others and often discover emotions of their own that they were unaware of, feelings that may have been having a powerful effect on their lives. They also discover the reassuring fact that they are not alone in their feelings, that group members are "all in the same boat." Knowing that others share your feelings somehow makes them less frightening and easier to deal with. When, as a group member, one discovers that one is not alone in feeling overwhelmed by a problem, or worried about one's sexual adequacy, or wondering who one is and where one comes from (e.g., a foster teenager), or experiencing rejection because of "the virus," one is often better able to mobilize oneself to deal with the problem productively. Discovering that feelings are shared by other members of the group can often help release a client from their power. Guilt over "evil" thoughts and feelings can be lessened and self-destructive cycles broken when one discovers they are normal and shared by others. For example, a parent of a differently abled child who hears that other parents may also feel that their child's condition represents "God's punishment" may be better able to cope with their guilt. This can be one of the most powerful forces for change resulting from the mutual aid process. There is not the same impact when a worker in individual work tries to reassure the client that the same feelings are shared by others. Hearing them articulated by others in the group sessions makes a unique impression.

In another example from the AIDS/Recovery group, one member talked of her fears of being rejected by her boyfriend because she had AIDS and he didn't. Even though the boyfriend knew about her AIDS and seemed to accept it, she was afraid to ask for a stronger commitment from him because she thought he would turn her down and she would lose him. Although she was an attractive young woman, she feared that no one else could ever love her because of the "virus." A male member of the group responded, saying, "That's the thing you fear most...the rejection. I just disconnect my telephone and stay in my room because I know if I get close to someone, I'm just going to be rejected again."

Developing a Universal Perspective

Expanding one's perspective is a special case of the all-in-the-same-boat phenomenon just described. Many clients, particularly those belonging to oppressed and vulnerable populations, may internalize the negative definitions assigned to them by the larger society. Thus, battered women, survivors of sexual abuse, persons of color, the mentally ill, or people with AIDS may assume the blame for their troubles and see their difficulties as a product of their own personal shortcomings. This can be reinforced by mental health professionals who focus on personal pathology while ignoring the socioeconomic factors that created and constantly reinforce the negative self-image.

In a mutual aid group, as common experiences of oppression are shared, it becomes easier for clients to recognize that a source of their problems in living may be external to themselves. Early in the women's movement, this process was exemplified in the "consciousness-raising" groups designed to help women become more aware of gender stereotyping and oppression issues that affected their lives. With a more universal perspective on one's problems, the additional burden of taking all of the blame for one's troubles may be lifted. The anger against the oppression—anger that often lurks just beneath the outward signs of depression, submission, and apathy—can be released and converted into positive energy for dealing with personal as well as social issues.

In an example described in some detail in Chapter 15, a group of young female survivors of sexual abuse support each other in recognizing the social roots of the gender oppression and violence they have experienced. In a pivotal meeting, the worker announces that a "Take Back the Night" march will occur in their town the following week and wonders if group members might want to participate. An important discussion between the women, which highlights how these women have been taught to accept their "victim" status, leads to their decision to attend the march as a group. This group experience, resulting from their ability to universalize their perspective, may well have been one of the most therapeutic aspects of the group practice.

In an example from the AIDS/Recovery group, one woman talks about the sexual exploitation she has experienced both from her "Johns" while prostituting and from her boyfriends over the years. A transgender female member of the group angrily declares that in her experience, sex is all most men are interested in and they will use and exploit you and your feelings, if they can, in order to get it. To underscore her point, she declares, "and I know, because I have been both!" This leads to a discussion among the men and women of the group about intimate relationships, how hard it is to find people who really care, and how painful it is when you lose someone who does.

Mutual Support

When the group "culture" supports the open expression of feelings, group members' capacity to empathize with each other is evident. With the group leader setting the tone through expression of personal feelings and understanding of others, each member is able to observe the powerful effect of empathy. Since group members share some common concerns, they are often able to understand each other's feelings in a deeper way than the worker. This expression of empathy is an important healing agent for both the group member who receives it and the one who offers it. As group members understand the feelings of the others, without judging them harshly, they begin to accept their own feelings in new ways. For a member struggling with a specific concern, the acceptance and caring of the group can be a source of support during a difficult time.

I have just used the expression "the acceptance and caring of the group," which introduces a new concept to be explored in detail in later chapters. The important element here is the group, the entity that is created when people are brought together. This entity, which we will call the *group-as-a-whole*, involves more than just the simple sum of the parts (members). For example, support in the mutual aid group often has a quality that is different from support received in interaction with a single empathic person. It is more than just a quantitative difference of more people equaling more empathy. At crucial moments in a group one can sense a general tone or atmosphere, displayed through words, expressions, or physical posture, that conveys the caring of the "group" for the individual. This seems to have a special meaning and importance to the individual group member. The properties of the group-as-a-whole are described in detail in Chapter 14, in which we will explore the idea of working with the group as the second client.

In the following example of support, also from the AIDS/Recovery group, the client who is reluctant to confront her boyfriend for fear of losing him asks the transgender member how she looks:

> Once again, Theresa asked Tania how she looked. She said, "You're a woman. I know, as a woman, you will be honest with me and just tell me what you think. Do you think I look okay?" Tania seemed confused and said, "Well, sure, you look wonderful." I said, "I wonder if Theresa is really asking, 'Am I pretty enough? Am I attractive enough? If my boyfriend leaves me, can I find someone else who could love me even though I have AIDS?'" She said, "That's it," and came close to tears. She said, "I'm so afraid, if I lose him, I won't find anyone else." She said, "I know I could have guys, and I know I could have sex, and I like the sex. I sure missed it during the time I was in prison, but can another guy love me?"
>
> The group members tried to reassure her that she was a wonderful person, on the inside as well, not just on the outside. Tania said, "It's not what you look like on the outside, it's what you're like on the inside." And she said, "And you, honey—you've really got it where it counts."

Mutual Demand

Earlier in this book, we saw how the helping relationship consisted of elements of both support and demand, synthesized in unique, personal ways. The same is true in the group context. Mutual aid is provided through expectation as well as through caring. One illustration is the way group members confront each other. For example, in the couples' group two male members were able to challenge a third who was maintaining that the source of the problem was his wife, that she was the identified "patient," and he was coming to group merely to "help her out." Both of the confronting group members had taken the same position at our first session and had slowly modified their views. They had lowered their defenses and accepted the idea that the problem was a "couple" problem. This demand on the third member had a different quality coming from group members, rather than the group leader.

As the group culture develops, it can include expectations that members risk their real thoughts and ideas, listen to each other, put their own concerns aside at times to help another, and so on. These expectations help to develop a productive "culture for work." Another group expectation can be that the members will work on their concerns. At moments when clients feel overwhelmed and hopeless, this expectation may help them take a next step. The group cares enough about them not to let them give up. I have witnessed group members take some difficult action, such as confronting a boss or dealing more effectively with a close relative. When the action was discussed the following week, they indicated that one of the factors that had pushed them to make the move and take a risk was the thought of returning to the group and admitting that they hadn't acted. Mutual demand, integrated with mutual support, can be a powerful force for change.

In the AIDS/Recovery group, members often used their insights and understanding about the recovery process, gained through participation in twelve-step groups such as Alcoholics Anonymous (AA) and Narcotics Anonymous (NA), to confront each other when their behaviors threatened their recovery. In one example, a group member who had just spent two weeks in a detox program after relapsing into cocaine use described how hard it was for him not to "hang around" the pool hall where all of his friends were. He described how he wavered each day, wondering if he could connect up with them and not relapse again. One of the other members, using an analogy obviously known by the others, said, "You know, John, if you hang around a barbershop long enough…" (pause) and the rest of the group, in a chorus, replied, "you're gonna get a haircut!" The group members all laughed, and John replied, "I know, I know, you're right, I would definitely be risking my recovery."

Individual Problem-Solving

A mutual aid group can be a place where an individual can bring a problem and ask for assistance. For example, in one group a young mother discussed the strained relationship between herself and her mother. Her mother lived nearby and was constantly calling and asking to come over. The group member had been extremely depressed and was going through periods where she neglected her work at home (dishes piling up in the sink, and so on). Each time her mother came over, she felt, because of her mother's actions, that she was being reprimanded for being a poor housekeeper and a poor mother to her young children. The resulting tension produced many arguments, including some between the husband and wife. The client felt her mother still treated her like a child even though she was 27.

As the client presented the issue, at first indirectly and later with much feeling and tears, the group members reached out to offer support and understanding. They were able to use their own experiences to share similar feelings. The older members of the group were able to provide a different perspective on the mother's actions. They could identify with her feelings, and they pointed out how uncertain she might feel about how to help her daughter. Conversations and incidents described by the client were discussed, and new interpretations of the interactions were offered. It became clear that the client's perceptions were often distorted by her own feelings of inadequacy and her harsh judgments of herself. The problem was described by the worker from a new perspective, that of a normative crisis in life as the young couple sought new ways to relate to her parents, and the parents, in turn, struggled to find ways of being close while still letting go. There were other issues involved as well, related to some of the reasons for the client's depression, such as her feelings of being trapped at home and trapped as a woman. These emerged in later sessions.

It is important to note that as the group members offered help to the individual with the problem, they were also helping themselves. Each group member could make associations to a similar concern. All of them could see how easily the communications between mother and daughter were going astray. As they tried to help the client clarify her own feelings, understand her mother's reactions in new ways, and see how the mutual stereotypes were interfering with the ability to communicate real feelings, the other group members could relate these ideas to their own close relationships. This is one of the important ways in which giving help in a mutual aid group is a form of self-help. It is always easier to see the problem in someone else's relationships than in your own. The general learning of the group members can be enhanced through the specific problem-solving work done with each member. The group leader can help by pointing out the underlying common themes.

Rehearsal

Another way in which a mutual aid group can help is by providing a forum in which members can try out ideas or skills. In a sense, the group becomes a safe place to risk new ways of communicating and to practice actions the client feels may be hard to do. To continue with the previous example, as the session neared the end, the group leader pointed out that the client seemed hesitant about taking up the issue with her mother. The following excerpt from the process recording starts with the client's response.

> **Rose:** I'm not sure I can talk with my mother about this. What would I say?
> **Worker:** That's a good question. How about trying it out right here? I'll pretend to be your mother calling to ask to see you. You can practice how you would respond, and the group can give some ideas about how it sounds. Does that sound all right?
> **Rose:** (She stopped crying now and is sitting straight up in her chair with a slight smile on her face.) OK. You call me and tell me you want to have lunch with me and that I should keep the kids home from school so you can see them.
> **Worker:** (Role-playing) Hello, Rose, this is Mom.
> **Rose:** Hi, Mom. How are you and Dad feeling?
> **Worker:** Not so good. You know, Dad gets upset easily, and he has been feeling lousy. (The client had indicated that her mother often used her father's health to try to make her feel guilty.)
> **Rose:** That's it! That's what she would say to make me feel guilty. (The group members are laughing at this point.)

The discussion picked up, with the group members agreeing about how easy it is for others to make us feel guilty. The worker inquired how Rose would feel at that point in the conversation. It became clear that the rest of the discussion would consist of her indirect responses to what she perceives as her mother's "laying on a guilt trip." After some discussion of what the mother might have been really feeling and having trouble in saying (e.g., how much she and her father really care about Rose and how much she needs to see her—an admission she might find hard to make), the group strategized with Rose about ways to break the usual cycle of indirect communications. The key moment in the role play came when the mother asked Rose to keep the children home for her lunch visit. Rose had complained that the mother never wanted to see her alone, it was always with the children. She was always asking to have them at home when she visited. She thought her mother didn't trust her with the kids and was always checking up on her.

> **Worker:** (Speaking as the mother) I wonder, Rose, if part of the reason I always ask to have the kids there is that I'm uncomfortable when we get together. I'm not sure what I would say to you for a whole two hours. I want the kids around to help fill the conversation.
>
> **Rose:** You know, I'm not sure what I would say to my mother either. I really don't know what to talk to her about.
>
> **Fran:** (Another group member) Can you try to tell your mother that you get upset when she asks to keep the kids home because you want to have some time alone with her? Maybe your mother could understand that. (Silence)
>
> **Worker:** Rose, do you really want to spend some time with your mother?
>
> **Rose:** I'm not so sure I do.
>
> **Worker:** Then that's the first step. When you're sure, I think the words will come more easily. If you tell your mother how you really feel, it could be the start of some honest talk between you. Perhaps she could share some of her real feelings in response, instead of always doing it indirectly and in ways which are open to misinterpretation. Maybe if you could do this, then your mother would see this as a sign of your maturity.

Rose tried to articulate her feelings more clearly but was obviously still having difficulty. She reported the following week that she had talked with her mother about how it made her feel when the mother tried to do things for her (e.g., wash the dishes when she came over), and the mother had responded by describing how she never really knew what to do when she came over—should she help out or not? Rose felt it cleared the air, even though other issues and feelings were not discussed. The interesting thing about the role-playing device as a form of rehearsal is that is often reveals the underlying ambivalence and resistance that the client feels but has not expressed in the discussion. The rehearsal not only offers the client a chance to practice, it also reveals to the group, the worker, and the client some of the feelings that need to be dealt with if the client is to succeed in his or her efforts.

In the AIDS/Recovery group, at one point the client who had raised boyfriend problems used the group to consider how to approach him with her concerns. One member helped by role playing how Theresa could handle the conversation:

> We returned to Theresa, and I said, "Is the question really, Theresa, that you're afraid that he might not stay with you—that, if you actually confront him on this issue of the other women, that he might leave you?" She agreed that it was her concern. At this point, I wondered if it might help Theresa to figure out what she might say to her boyfriend. Theresa said that would be helpful because she didn't know when and how to say it. Then she laughed and said, "Maybe I should say it in bed." Tania said, "Oh no. Don't say it before sex and don't say it after sex." And I added, "And don't say it during sex." Everyone laughed at this point, and Tania did an imitation of having a conversation with Theresa's boyfriend, while pumping up and down as if she were in bed having sex with him.
>
> Tania said, "You have to find a quiet time, not a time when you're in the middle of a fight, and you have to just put out your feelings." I asked Tania if she could show

Theresa how she could do that. She started to speak as if she were talking to Theresa's boyfriend. I role-played the boyfriend, and said, "Oh, but Theresa you're just insecure, aren't you?" Tania did a very good job of not letting me put her off and, instead, putting the issue right where it was—whether I was prepared to make a commitment or if I was too insecure.

Theresa said, "I know I have to talk to him, but, you know, he's told me that he's not sure he wants to be tied down, that he likes to have his freedom." Jake nodded his head and said, "Yeah, that's the problem, they want their freedom and they don't want to make a commitment, and you're afraid, if you push him, he'll leave you because you got the virus." Theresa said she realized she had to sit down and talk to him because it couldn't keep up the same way. She would just get too angry and do something crazy and screw up her recovery. She said when she had a fight with him on Thanksgiving, he did call his sponsor and came back much more gently. She felt she had gotten through to him, but she had to find another way to get through to him and talk to him. Otherwise, this thing was just going to continue and it was going to tear her up inside.

The "Strength-in-Numbers" Phenomenon

Sometimes it is easier to do things as a group than it would be as an individual. In one example described earlier, a group of female survivors of sexual abuse attended a "Take Back the Night" march. In another example, described in detail in Chapter 20, individual tenants in a housing project found it difficult to stand up to the housing authority on issues of poor maintenance service. When organized into a tenants' group, the "strength-in-numbers" phenomenon worked to decrease their feelings of isolation and individual risk involved, which encouraged the group members to make demands for their rights. An individual's fears and ambivalence can be overcome by participation in a group effort as his or her own courage is strengthened by the courage of others.

Summary of the Dynamics of Mutual Aid

A number of examples have been shared to illustrate how the dynamics of the mutual aid process can work. Sharing data, the dialectical process, discussing taboo areas, the "all-in-the-same-boat" phenomenon, developing a universal perspective, mutual support, mutual demand, individual problem solving, rehearsal, and the "strength-in-numbers" phenomenon are some of the processes through which mutual aid is offered and taken. It is important to note that we are not suggesting that working in groups is a preferred method. The choice of individual or group work is influenced by many factors, particularly the comfort of the clients in dealing with their concerns on a one-to-one basis as opposed to within a group setting. As I will explain in detail later, it is often helpful for a client to have both individual and group work available so that both experiences can be used productively. Each would have a slightly different focus, and each could be expected to provide important stimulation for the other. For many clients, the group can offer (under certain circumstances) unique forms of help in dealing with their life problems. I have attempted to identify some of these mutual aid processes, but it is important to realize that groups will not provide this kind of help just because they have been brought together. In the next section, we will examine some of the obstacles that can make mutual aid a difficult process indeed. These obstacles, and others, will be explored in detail in later chapters.

OBSTACLES TO MUTUAL AID

In the early phases of a group's development, one potential obstacle to mutual aid is the apparently divergent interest each group member brings to the engagement. Even in a group with a narrow, clearly defined purpose, some group members may perceive their sense of urgency differently from the others. Even though the mutual threads of concern may exist, group members may not identify their common ground. Various group members may feel their concerns and feelings are unique and unrelated to those of other members. The "symbiotic attractions" between members may be partial, subtle, and difficult to perceive. In many ways, the group is a microcosm of the larger society, and this diffusion of interest between "self" and "other" reflects the individual social encounter in society. Thus, as each member becomes oriented to the group engagement, that member will be asking, "How am I the same or different from the other members?"

One of the early tasks of the group leader will be to help group members begin to identify their common ground. As the group develops a mature way of relating, individual members can begin to understand that they can learn and grow by giving help as well as receiving it. As each individual member develops the skills required to offer and take help, these same skills will be found to be related to their individual concerns outside of the group. For example, group members who learn how to get in touch with their feelings and to share them in the group may be able to apply these skills in other intimate relationships. Nevertheless, at the beginning stage and periodically during the life of the group, the inability of members to perceive their connections to the others will present an important obstacle.

A second set of obstacles will emerge from the fact that even a small group can be a complex system that must deal with a number of developmental tasks if it is to work productively. As soon as more than one client is involved, a new organism is created: the group-as-a-whole. This group is more than the simple sum of its parts (that is, the individual members). For example, this new organism needs to develop rules and procedures that will allow it to function effectively. Some will be openly discussed, while others may operate beneath the surface by mutual consent of the members. Roles may be subtly distributed to group members, such as scapegoat, deviant member, internal leader, and so on. Some of these role assignments will represent ways by which the group-as-a-whole may avoid dealing directly with a problem. For example, the group **gate keeper** may intervene to distract the group each time the discussion approaches a painful subject. Many of the unstated rules for relating will be counterproductive to the purpose of the group. These factors, and others to be discussed later, are properties of this complex organism called the group and must be dealt with by the leader if the group is to function effectively.

A final major source of potential problems for the group is the difficulty of open communication. I have already discussed some of the barriers that make it difficult for clients to express their real feelings and concerns. These are related to a social culture that has implicitly and explicitly developed a number of norms of behavior and identified taboo areas in which honest communication is hard to achieve. Each group member brings a part of this culture into the group, and thus the group culture, in early phases of work, resembles the culture of the social surroundings. This often makes it difficult for group members to talk with and listen to each other in areas of central concern. With the group leader's help, group members will need to develop a new culture in which norms are modified and taboos lose their power, so that members may freely communicate with each other.

I have just outlined three major areas of potential obstacles to mutual aid: the difficulty individual members have in identifying their self-interest with that of the other group members, the complex tasks involved in creating a mutual aid system, and the difficulties in communicating honestly. The existence of these potential obstacles helps to define the job of the group leader. These problems are not arguments against the use of groups as mutual aid systems; rather, they represent an agenda for the group worker. If groups were not faced with these problems, and if people could easily join together to offer aid and support, then there would be no need for a group worker. Essentially, what we find in the small group, which is a special case of the larger individual-social engagement described in Chapter 1, is the same potential for diffusion of the "symbiotic" relationship. Once again, the functional role of mediation will be used as a starting point for describing the tasks of the helping person—this time, however, in the context of group work.

THE FUNCTION OF THE GROUP LEADER

In the earlier discussion of Schwartz's mediation practice theory, the function of the helping person was illustrated using three circles. The client was on the left, the systems to be negotiated on the right, and the worker in the middle. Since the group is a specific case of this larger engagement, the same diagram can be drawn with the individual on the left and the group on the right.

The general function of mediating the individual-social engagement is now translated into mediating the individual-group interaction. This leads Schwartz to argue one of his most central and exciting ideas about group work: that the group worker always has "two clients"—the individual and the group. The function of the worker is to mediate the engagement between these two clients. As the group process unfolds, the worker is constantly concerned both with each individual member and with the other client, the group. For example, as an individual member raises a specific concern, the worker will help the member share that concern with the group. The discussion in Chapter 4 on the work phase detailed how difficult it often can be for clients to describe their concerns. All the worker skills described earlier (e.g., reading indirect communications, helping clients move from the general to the specific) will now be employed to help individuals express their concerns to the group. As the leader helps the one (the individual) talk to the many (the group), the interaction will also be monitored to see if the members appear to be listening and relating to the individual. If they seem to be turned off, the worker will explore their feelings and reactions. Perhaps the individual's problem is painful to the group members, raising related feelings of their own and making it hard for them to listen. Whatever the realities may be, the group worker, with a clear sense of function, will pay attention to both "clients" at exactly the same time.

Attention to the second client—the group—will require that the worker help group members to deal with the obstacles described earlier. For example, if the group culture is making it difficult for members to discuss their real feelings about a specific issue, then the worker can call this to the attention of the group members. An effort to bring the obstacle out in the open is a first step in helping the group members become more conscious of their own processes. With the assistance of the group worker, group members can discuss how the blockage of open communication in a sensitive area frustrates their work. With understanding may come growth as the group becomes more sophisticated about its ways of working. A new agreement, including new norms that are more productive, can be openly reached. In many ways the group worker serves as a guide for the group members faced with the complex task of developing an effective mutual aid system. The important point is that this is the members' group, the work to strengthen it is theirs, and the group worker is there to help them to do it.

In a general way, these two areas of work characterize the group leader's responsibilities: helping the individual and the group relate effectively to each other, and helping the group become more sophisticated about its way of working, so that it releases the potential for mutual aid. Of course, this process is more complicated than this simple explanation implies. In the remaining chapters of Part IV, we will explore the underlying assumptions about how mutual aid groups work and the tasks and skills required of the group worker. Once again, the process will be analyzed step by step. For example, the chapter on the preparatory phase will include a discussion on setting up a group, dealing with questions of group composition, recruitment of members, and the important work required with fellow staff members to gain their support and avoid possible "sabotage." The dynamics of initial group meetings will be discussed and illustrated using examples from a number of groups. The discussion of the work phase will include a chapter on the individual-group interaction. In a second chapter we will explore the role of the individual in the group, and in a third we will examine the tasks of the group-as-a-whole and explore how the worker can assist in the group's development. In a fourth chapter we will look at variations on the central ideas, using groups from a wide range of settings. A consideration of group endings and transitions will complete Part IV.

THE "FEAR-OF-GROUPS" SYNDROME

In every group work training workshop I have led, there is a moment, usually early in the first morning, when I can sense a general unease in the group. Sometimes the first clue of what I call the **"fear-of-groups" syndrome** emerges during the introductions, when participants will indicate they have never led a group, expressing this fact in a tone of voice that suggests that if they had it their way, they would never lead one. When I explore these clues, I often hear that the worker was sent to the workshop by an administrator or supervisor who decided that group work would be a good idea. More recently, the pressures of managed care have led agencies to try to expand their group services, often for the wrong reasons.

Whether the participants are in the workshop voluntarily or not, whether they are experienced workers or new workers, the underlying feelings are often the same: they are scared stiff of the idea of being responsible for leading a group. As one experienced social worker said in one of these workshops, "There are so many of them (the clients) and only one of me!"

A common concern is of having to practice with a group of people who are judging your work. Group work practices is seen as more exposed than individual work. If an individual client does not return after a few interviews, workers can always chalk it up to the client's "lack of motivation." If ten clients don't return to a group session, however, the worker feels he or she has failed.

Another concern involves the potential for direct negative feedback from clients. Anger from a single client or couple is one thing, but facing an angry group is something else. Of even greater concern is the possibility of a boring group. Workers feel completely responsible for the success of a group and dread the possibility of long silences, rambling conversations, individuals who dominate the discussion, or the sight of ten pairs of eyes glazing over.

Lack of control is often cited as a fear by beginning group workers. One workshop participant put it this way: "When I'm conducting an individual interview I know where it is going and can keep track of what is happening. In a group session, the members seem to take control of the session away from me. It feels like I am on my motorcycle, pumping the starter to get going, and the group members are already roaring down the road." It takes some experience for a new group worker to realize that it is exactly at moments such as these, when the group members take over the group, that the worker can relax in the knowledge that the group is well on its way to success. One of the benefits of caseworkers doing groups is that they begin to realize they can also let go of control in their one-to-one interviews.

The complexity of group work also intimidates workers. Whereas before they needed to concentrate on the relationship between themselves and the client, they now have to also concentrate on the relationships between group members. As they gain group work experience they become more conscious of the entity called the group-as-a-whole, which I will discuss in detail in a later chapter. In their one-to-one interviews they just had to concentrate on the individual, but now they must also pay attention to the group and somehow develop the ability to observe both the one and the many at the same time.

All of these concerns are understandable. Upon reflection, however, experienced practitioners soon realize these concerns are similar to those they experienced when they first began to practice. Skills in work with individuals, which they now take for granted, seemed out of reach in their first interviews. They are continually learning more about the dynamics of the relationships between themselves and clients, as well as the dynamics of family relationships or couples. With some confidence in the skills they have, they are less concerned about those they need to learn and are more able to tolerate areas of ambiguity. The difference with group work is that they are often starting with no confidence at all.

I try to reassure these workers that they already know more about group work than they realize. Much of what they have learned about helping can be applied in the group situation, as will be illustrated in the chapters that follow. The areas of uncertainty represent exciting opportunities for new learning that can take place during the rest of their professional lives.

For the new worker or student, I suggest starting with individual work to develop some beginning confidence in basic practice skills, and then broadening these skills in the group context. This does not mean students cannot begin their learning with group work practice. I have seen many students develop quickly while working in the group medium. For their own comfort in the beginning of their practice, however, it is often easier to start by talking to one client at a time. If this can be supplemented with an opportunity to work as a co-leader or observer with a more experienced group worker, then the learner has the best of all learning possibilities.

With both the new and experienced worker, I try to point out that the root of their fear is a misconception about their complete responsibility for the group work process. In fact, it is when they realize that they only have responsibility for their part, and in fact, some of the most important helping in the group will be done by group members, that they can view group work in its proper perspective. Certainly they will be more helpful to the groups they lead later in their careers, as they develop an increased understanding of group processes, more skill, and greater confidence. They can, however, still give a great deal to their first groups as they develop their group work skills.

New group workers tend to underestimate the amount of help they can give to their group members in the same way they did when they began their work in the one-to-one context. Continued group experiences will do a lot to correct this misconception, and the marvelous feeling a worker gets when he or she sees the power of mutual aid that can be released in group work practice helps to make up for the worker's anxiety along the way.

Finally, it is important to recognize that clients have a right to receive the modality of service that is most appropriate to their particular needs. Consider, for example, populations of oppressed and vulnerable clients, as well as client populations of those who do the oppressing (e.g., male batterers), where mutual aid groups may well be the service modality of choice, providing a crucial complement to individual counseling. These clients should not be restricted to what may turn out to be less effective agency service simply because their social worker did not receive training in group work practice or feels more comfortable facing one client at a time. As the reader explores the many examples of mutual aid in the chapters that follow, the obvious healing power of groups will make the case for overcoming one's fear of groups.

CHAPTER SUMMARY

In this chapter, we explored a number of ways in which clients can help each other in mutual aid groups. These included sharing data, the dialectical process, discussing taboo areas, the "all-in-the-same-boat" phenomenon, developing a universal perspective, mutual support, mutual demand, individual problem solving, rehearsal, and the "strength-in-numbers" phenomenon. Three major areas of obstacles to the mutual aid process in groups were defined and illustrated. These included the difficulty members may have in identifying their common ground; the tasks that must be accomplished by a group in order to develop a positive culture for work; and the general difficulty of open communication. The role of the group leader was defined as an extension of the mediating function described earlier in the book into the group context. The group leader was seen as mediating between two clients: the individual and the group-as-a-whole. A number of common fears of new group leaders, referred to as the "fear-of-groups" syndrome, were discussed, as well as ways in which they may be overcome.

GLOSSARY

"All-in-the-same-boat" phenomenon A mutual aid process in which group members gain support from discovering that other group members have similar problems, concerns, feelings, and experiences.

Developing a universal perspective A mutual aid process in the group in which members begin to perceive universal issues, particularly in relation to oppression, thus allowing them to view their own problems in a more social context and with less personal blame.

Dialectical process A mutual aid process in which group members confront each other's ideas in an effort to develop a synthesis for all group members.

Discussing a taboo area A mutual aid process in which one member enters a taboo area of discussion, thereby freeing other members to enter as well.

"Fear-of-groups" syndrome The anxieties experienced by workers as they prepare to work with groups for the first time.

Gate keeper A group or family member who may intervene to distract the group or family session each time the discussion approaches a painful subject.

Individual problem-solving A mutual aid process through which group members help one member to solve a particular problem, receiving help themselves while offering it to another.

Microsociety A description of the small group as a special case of the larger individual-social interaction in our society.

Mutual demand A mutual aid process in which group members offer each other help by making demands and setting expectations on personal behavior.

Mutual support A mutual aid process in which group members provide emotional support to each other.

Rehearsal The process in which the client has an opportunity to practice a difficult next step in an informal role play, with the worker usually playing the role of the other person. (Also, a mutual aid process in which group members help one another).

Sharing data Skill of worker in sharing data such as facts, opinions, and value judgments. Also, a mutual aid process in a group when members share data with each other.

"Strength-in-numbers" phenomenon The mutual aid process in which group members are strengthened to take on difficult tasks (e.g., challenging agency policy) through the support of other group members.

NOTES

1. The mutual aid model of group work practice is used to organize the discussion in this book. Schwartz draws upon the work of Kropotkin in developing the "mutual aid" concept. See P. Kropotkin, *Mutual Aid: A Factor of Evolution* (New York: Knopf, 1925).

2. For some examples of other orientations towards group work, most of which include mutual aid within their models, see J.A. Lee, *Group Work with the Poor and Oppressed* (New York: Haworth Press, 1988); U. Glassman and L. Kates, *Group Work: A Humanistic Approach* (Newbury Park, CA: Sage Publishers, 1990); L.N. Brown, *Groups for Growth and Change* (New York: Longman, 1991); K.E. Reid, *Social Work Practice with Groups: A Clinical Perspective* (Belmont, CA: Brooks-Cole, 1991); H. Falck, *Social Work: The Membership Perspective* (New York: Springer, 1988); C. Garvin, *Contemporary Group Work* (Englewood Cliffs, NJ: Prentice-Hall, 1981); P.H. Ephros and T.V. Vasil, *Groups That Work* (New York: Columbia University Press, 1988); A.S. Alissi, *Perspectives on Social Group Work Practice* (New York: Free Press, 1980).

For examples of the rich literature on social work with groups upon which current theorists have built, see G. Wilson and G. Ryland, *Social Group Work Practice* (Boston: Houghton Mifflin, 1949); E. Tropp, *A Humanistic Foundation for Group Work Practice* (New York: Selected Academic Readings, 1969); M. Hartford, *Groups in Social Work* (New York: Columbia University Press, 1972); B. Levine, *Fundamentals of Group Treatment* (Chicago: Whitehall Press, 1967); G. Konopka, *Social Group Work: A Helping Process* (Englewood Cliffs, NJ: Prentice-Hall, 1971); A.F. Klein, *Effective Group Work* (New York: Association Press, 1972); H. Northen, *Social Work with Groups* (New York: Columbia University Press, 1969); H. Philips, *Essentials of Social Group Work Skill* (New York: Association Press, 1957); R.D. Vinter (ed.), *Readings in Group Work Practice* (Ann Arbor, MI: Campus Publishers, 1967); S. Bernstein (ed.), *Further Explorations in Group Work* (Boston: Boston University School of Social Work, 1970); S.D. Rose, *Group Therapy: A Behavioral Approach* (Englewood Cliffs, NJ: Prentice-Hall, 1977).

9

Group Formation

In this chapter, we will explore in detail the steps required to establish a group and to increase its chances for success. Work with the staff system is dealt with first, since much that follows depends upon these efforts. Next, issues related to group formation (timing, composition, and so on) are explored. The impact of ethnicity and culture in the group formation stage is discussed, as well as problems of recruitment. Finally, we return to the tuning-in skill, this time applying it to a first session in the group context.

PREPARING FOR GROUP WORK

The preparatory phase can be one of the most complex in work with groups, as a number of crucial issues must be dealt with before the first meeting takes place.[1] The literature on group work pays surprisingly little attention to the problems of this phase, beyond discussion of questions of group type (e.g., educational, therapeutic, support), structure (e.g., frequency and number of sessions), group composition, and so on. As one example of a problem that is often ignored, it is not unusual for a worker to decide that a group would be helpful for clients and then to approach colleagues for appropriate referrals. General agreement may be reached at a staff meeting to support the group; however, the worker waits two months without getting a single referral. In analyzing examples of this kind, I have consistently found that the worker had left out the important step of involving the colleagues in a meaningful way. I could often determine the moment in the staff meeting when the groundwork was laid for the frustration that followed.

In like manner, a worker may launch a group and prepare for a first meeting with ten group members who have promised to attend. The evening of the meeting arrives, and after waiting 35 long and painful minutes for latecomers, the worker must face the reality that only two members have come. Once again, the source of the disappointment can often be traced to steps that were left out in the preparatory work with clients as the worker or other workers began the referral process. In analysis of interviews and telephone conversations, it

319

is often possible to identify the moment the worker sensed the ambivalence of the prospective group member but did not reach for it.

In the sections that follow, these and other group formation issues will be discussed, with an emphasis on describing and illustrating strategies that may increase the possibility of launching effective mutual aid groups.[2]

WORK WITH THE STAFF SYSTEM

An important first principle is to recognize that a group in an agency or institution must be related to the service. If a worker attempts to establish a group because of a desire to develop new skills or because he or she has decided (without involving the rest of the staff) that there is a need for such a group, the work may be doomed to failure. A common example is the student who is placed in an agency for practicum experience and is taking a course in group work practice. A requirement for the class is to have a group, so the student endeavors to set one up in the field. Quite often the group never even has its first meeting because the student's need for it is not a sound reason for developing a group. The idea for a group must begin with the identification of an area of clients' unmet needs that the group method may be able to meet. The group must reflect the consensus of the department or team involved so that it is not seen as being personally "owned" by the group worker.

The difficulty or ease involved in establishing a group may depend upon the group experience of the agency. In those settings where groups are a common form of service and where all staff members take their turn at leadership, many of the problems of formation may be minimized. In other agencies, where groups are unusual as a form of service, these problems may be intensified. For example, a worker who attempts to introduce group work into a setting that has never had groups must recognize that a threatening situation may be created for other staff. Many workers are frightened by the idea of facing more than one client at a time. If they do not have a fund of good experiences to draw upon or if they unsuccessfully attempted to establish a group when they were students, they may be hesitant about working with groups. The worker attempting to initiate a group service must recognize that, on some level, colleagues may wonder whether, if the service is successful, they will be asked to carry a group next. This fear is often expressed indirectly with comments such as, "Groups would be great in this agency, but do we really have the time?" The development of group service can have an important impact on the staff system, and the worker should make use of the tuning-in skill in preparing to negotiate the establishment of the group.

Staff resistance can also be noted when the administration of an agency or organization, because of the pressures of managed care or other cutbacks in resources, has decided to move into group work as a cost-cutting measure. In reality, group practice may actually increase costs, since it rarely serves as a substitute in those situations where individual work is required. In many cases, issues that emerge in the group for one client may generate the need for more intensive individual work, rather than less work, for other group members. Group work should be the practice modality of choice only if it is the best modality for the particular population and problem. When cost-cutting is the only rationale offered, then staff resistance due to fears about competency is often masked by staff anger at the "top down" imposition of group practice. Whether the reasons for developing group work practice are sound or spurious, there is little question that there has been an explosive expansion of the use of group work in social work practice. Since simultaneously there has been a documented decrease in group work content in social work education programs, any system considering moving into group practice must also consider the need for staff training and consultation to ensure the quality of the practice.[3]

In the rest of this section, excerpts from an effort by a hospital social worker to establish a ward group are used to illustrate the dynamics and the skills involved in preparatory work with staff.

Achieving Consensus on the Service

There are many ways in which the idea of a group may emerge in an agency: client feedback, a worker discovering a common concern among a number of individual clients, or a staff team discovering an important gap in the service. Wherever the idea of a group is initiated, it is important that all staff involved have the opportunity to comment honestly on the potential service. A common mistake is for a worker to decide on the need for a group and then to set about "selling" colleagues on the idea. Rather than presenting their own views on the need for it and inviting feedback and discussion, workers may try to influence their colleagues, creating the illusion that they are involving others in the process. In the following illustration, a young social worker, relatively new to the hospital, approaches a long-time head nurse about the possibility of forming a group on the ward. She has been warned that the nurse has a reputation for being tough and uncooperative on projects such as this, and she has therefore steeled herself for the task of convincing the nurse of the need for the group. The illustration demonstrates the problems generated when one tries to "sell" an idea.

> I said to Miss Ford that I had been doing some thinking which I would like to share with her. I told her that I had been on the ward quite a bit and felt quite at home on it. I said to her that I, as everyone else on the ward, am here to try to service the patients to the best of my ability. I then asked her what she thought of a group having any value on the ward. She said that it has been suggested before, so that it was nothing new. She said that the room full of ladies could do with something of that sort but that that's the only ladies' room there is. I asked if she thought that only ladies could benefit from a group experience and she said "no," but that she was thinking in terms of room number 1403. She asked what the group would be about and for. I said that I'm open to suggestions but that perhaps the basic purpose could be for the patients to discuss their hospitalization, frustrations, etc. It would be open to all patients.

Although the worker said she wanted to explore the nurse's views, she really did not mean it. The nurse quickly sensed her purpose when she did not explore the suggestion that the patients in room 1403 might benefit from a group. The worker was still reacting, on an emotional level, to the nurse's first comment that the idea had been suggested before and that it was nothing new. Had the worker not been so set on convincing the nurse, she could have asked for an elaboration of the comment. What had that earlier effort been like? Had there been any problems? The worker is new on the ward, and the nurse might have shared some past experiences that could have provided helpful feedback. Because the worker began with a stereotype of the nurse as being "resistant," however, she did not reach past this first comment. The same lack of genuine interest in the nurse's views is demonstrated when the worker challenges her suggestion that the ladies in room 1403 might need the help. As the worker will find out at a later date, this room contains patients with terminal cancer. It represents a room full of problems for which the nursing staff has genuine concern but few ideas of how to help. It could represent an important area of missing service, but the worker does not know this because she has cut off the nursing supervisor's participation in the process.

After the nurse has received the signals confirming her own stereotype of workers as outsiders who do not really appreciate the problems of the ward, she responds rather perfunctorily, asking questions sharply and crisply about the worker's proposed group.

> Miss Ford asked how the patients would know or how I would tell them. I told her that in order to make it a voluntary thing, perhaps written invitations to each patient would be a good idea. She asked when and where it would be held. I told her that I hoped she could help make that decision, especially the time, because I realize they are busy. As far as the room goes, perhaps an empty bedroom or the sunroom. She said that by October 16th all rooms should be filled up. I suggested we could decide on that at a later date. I asked if she could, however, talk to the doctors and staff about this, get some ideas, and we could discuss it again next week at rounds. She said that would be fine.

At the end of the worker's process recording, she included the following comment:

> Miss Ford did not seem too enthusiastic and was quite resistant (mentioning no rooms, how would patients know, etc.). However, I feel she can see some value in a ward group. Next week I plan to give her some examples of why I can see a need for the group.

If the worker had done that, it is likely she would have met the same resistance. If she had continued to accept the nurse's superficial agreement, she would have proceeded to set up her group and, most likely, been surprised on the day of her first meeting. Either the room would have been unavailable or the worker would have discovered that half the patients she had selected for the group session had been "inadvertently" scheduled for blood tests, X-rays, or other medical procedures that took them off the ward. There would have been profuse apologies by the nursing staff, and the problem would have repeated itself the following week. The worker would eventually have given up, adding one more story to the collection of examples of how "resistant" Miss Ford was to any new ideas.

The missing skill in this interview was described in Part II as "looking for trouble when everything seems to be going the worker's way." In this case, the worker sensed the underlying negative reaction in the interview but did not reach for it. For example, she could have said, "Miss Ford, you don't seem too enthusiastic about this group. Why not?" This direct response to the indirect cue would have opened up Miss Ford's real feelings and reactions and might have turned a one-way selling job into an honest exploration of mutual thoughts about a new service. In many ways, the nurse's relative directness about her feelings should have been an aid to the worker. At least her feelings were almost out in the open. By contrast, there are many instances, as when a worker is describing a group to fellow workers at a team meeting, when the worker might find an artificial agreement expressed through apparently unqualified support. Once again, the skilled worker would not leave the session without first reaching for the underlying reservations. For example, the worker might say, "It's great to see such quick support for my idea, but you know, it's going to cause some problems and inconveniences for the rest of you. Don't you think we should also talk about these?"

The worker often senses, as did this worker with the head nurse, the underlying resistance but fears to reach for it. The belief is that if one leaves the negatives unexpressed, they will perhaps go away. They never do. These reservations, negative reactions, fears, and the like all come back to haunt the worker in the form of conscious or unconscious sabotage of the worker's plans. If the group is to become a reality, the worker must insist that it be a service of the team, the agency, or whatever, not just the worker's personal group that happens to be taking place in this setting. Without real support from the rest of the staff, the worker will be alone when problems emerge. I have seen excellent work done with school principals, for example, when after the principal has given perfunctory agreement to allow a group to meet in the school, the worker has asked, "Would you be very upset if we couldn't offer this group to your kids?" After a moment's pause, the principal has responded, "The only reason I OK these groups is that the people at the board like to see them in the schools. Actually, staff and I often find they are more trouble than they are worth." Only at this point does the real discussion begin, and the worker can start serious contracting with the agency or setting. If this stage is skipped over in the worker's eagerness to gain a toehold, then the lack of real investment will hurt when the going gets rough in the group.

Fortunately, as in work with clients, workers usually have the opportunity to go back after making a mistake and to try again. After some consultation and discussion of the first process recording of the interview with the nurse, the worker strategized to return to Miss Ford and instead of trying to convince her, own up to her mistake and try to start over again. You will notice the change in the nurse's attitude as the discussion becomes real.

> I told Miss Ford that I felt I may have been too pushy about the ward group. I said that I had asked for her participation and interest, yet I hadn't given her a chance to express herself, and I wasn't really listening to her. I then apologized and suggested that we might go back to the beginning. I said I was interested in knowing her true feelings regarding the group. She said she thought the group would be very good for most patients, but she was worried about the manpower of nurses. She said it was difficult enough to get all the nurses to attend her ward conference without having them attend a patients' group. I asked if she was thinking in terms of all the nurses going to the group at once. She said she didn't know and wondered what I thought. I said that the decision of nurses was up to her. I suggested that it might be just as effective to have one nurse drop in on the group or have the nurses rotate.

This may have been the issue on the head nurse's mind when she commented on the group having been tried before. It is important that the worker pay attention to the problems created by the group for the ongoing system. The worker must be able to empathize genuinely with the day-to-day difficulties of other staff members. Often, the recognition of these problems can lead to alternative solutions or to the willingness of the staff to extend themselves. As in all human relationships, it is important that the worker really understand how the other staff member feels. The discussion in the interview turned to the issue of purpose and contract.

> I suggested that one important gap existed between patients and doctors or patients and nurses. I explained further that I believed that if a patient could release some of his anxieties or fears about his medical problems or share his hostilities in the group, he might be an easier patient to cope with. Rather than expressing his feelings in an undesirable way, he might be happier on the ward and easier to deal with. Miss Ford agreed with this and then asked about the resident on the ward. How could we keep him involved? We discussed this for a while.

Although the worker's contract statement is still unclear, reflecting her own lack of clarity, the general sense of the group dealing with issues related to hospital and illness and with

communication between patient and staff is clearly suggested. This is important, since workers who propose groups in a setting without connecting the purpose of the group to the
general service of the agency are often seen as simply requesting space. When administrators
and staff members perceive the connection between their service and the purpose of the
group, they will be more likely to invest themselves in the group's development. A worker offering to lead a group for children who have been identified by teachers as having trouble at
school will be more easily accepted by the staff than one asking to lead groups for general discussion (e.g., "I would like to work with children who need a socialization experience").

As the discussion with Miss Ford continued, note her more active involvement:

> Miss Ford asked how the patients would know about the group, who would go, etc.
> I suggested that the nurses see all the patients, and they could tell who could bene-
> fit from a group experience, who was ready to go. She asked how patients would find
> out about the group. I suggested we stick notices to their bedside tables. She said it
> would not be a good idea because the tables must be washed. She suggested we
> put them in the bathrooms where the beauty salon advertises. I said it was a good
> idea, and we went to the bathroom to select the best spot. I then brought up the sub-
> ject of confidentiality.

The worker has used her "tuning-in" preparation to anticipate another sensitive area for
discussion—the issue of confidentiality. Although the nurse has not raised this issue, it is a
good bet that she is wondering what would happen if patients complained about the nursing
staff. This issue is often a difficult one for workers. It is often an important underlying negative when a worker proposes a group in a hospital, school, or residential setting, or when the
worker is sharing clients with another worker and the worker will continue to see the client
on an individual basis. The group worker often suggests the need to maintain confidentiality
to staff, not reporting group discussion, so that the group members will feel free to talk. In my
experience, when group members talk negatively about staff, they are often hopeful the worker will help improve a bad situation. It is true that they are concerned about how the information will be used (e.g., the possibility of retribution from the teacher, nurse, etc.). They are
not, however, raising the concerns just for the sake of ventilating feelings.

From the point of view of the helping function outlined in this book, the mediating approach, acting as a communication bridge between clients and the agency system, is very
much a part of the work. If the worker begins work with staff by stating they will not be included in discussion of group content, their fears and anxieties may lead to direct or indirect
efforts at sabotage. In one such case, a worker in a home for unmarried mothers had completely ignored the housemother's concerns, particularly her fear of complaints, and had indicated that all discussions would be confidential. When the worker arrived, the housemother
rang a bell and shouted, to the worker's consternation, "Group therapy time." In other examples, the worker's colleagues have described the group to their individual clients in a way that
served to heighten the clients' fears of involvement: "We are going to offer this group for single mothers, but you don't have to go if you don't want to."

If the worker's sense of function involves a commitment to helping in the process between client and system, including the agency, then this must be part of the contract. Nurses,
child care workers, teachers, and other counselors must be viewed as colleagues, with each
having a part in the operation. Discussions should focus on how the group worker and the
other staff members will handle feedback. The meaning of the feedback and the way in

which clients might use either the individual worker or the group worker as a channel must be recognized. The agreement can include ways to achieve the optimum outcome, in which each will attempt to assist the clients' efforts to provide direct feedback to the other. I have found that this discussion often takes much of the threat out of the possibility of negative feedback and, instead, turns it into an important technical issue for both workers. The details of how the fears of the group members can be handled and how a worker can effectively share feedback with other staff will be dealt with in later chapters.

When I explore why workers are reluctant to follow this course of action—that is, to treat other system people as colleagues and work out agreements for mutual sharing of relevant information, they usually express concern about the client's acceptance of such a contract. While there is some basis to this concern, I often find, in addition, their own fears about confronting a colleague with "bad news." How do you tell a fellow staff member, with whom you have coffee each day, that his client doesn't feel he understands her? Confidentiality can then serve as a protection for the group worker. Often workers reveal that they have developed stereotypes of their colleagues as "lousy" workers (poor teachers, insensitive doctors, and so on), so what good would sharing be? I can understand their reticence to take on this function, yet if the group worker accepts that the nurse on the ward, the teacher, a fellow social worker, or whomever, is actually closed to change, such acceptance means that an important part of the service to clients will no longer be available. The worker will inevitably be in a serious quandary when the strength-in-numbers phenomenon leads the group members to share their real feelings. A situation will have been set up that makes it impossible for the worker to do anything about the problem except empathize, ignore it, or defend the system. This often leads to apathy and disengagement on the part of the group members.

The question of confidentiality has broadened during this discussion to encompass a much larger issue: the function of the helping person within his or her own helping system. This will be explored in detail in Part V of this book. For now, I would summarize my view as being that this concern may be a central issue for other staff members when group formation is discussed. I would want it out in the open, and I would want to contract with both staff and group members for freedom of communication of group content in a responsible manner. Returning to the interview, we find that this is precisely what our worker on the hospital ward does.

> I then brought up the subject of confidentiality. I asked how Miss Ford felt it should be handled. For example, if one patient or more complained about a certain nurse or herself, would she like to know or not? Rather than directly answering, she told me about a patient on the ward who would complain of different shifts of staff and play one against the other. I asked her if the gist of her story was that it was better to know the complaints so that they can be investigated and dealt with. She said "yes." I told her I felt the same way and that I would like to know when patients made complaints about me.
>
> We then talked about where the group could be held. I again suggested the sun porch. This time, Miss Ford said that it would be all right because patients used it anyway. We then discussed further clearances in the hospital and set up a meeting with the nursing staff to clarify the group's purpose and to select members.

The result of this effort was active involvement on the part of Miss Ford in the establishment of the group. The front-line nursing staff quickly picked up the message of positive support for the group and offered their assistance to the social worker. The group was established and became integrated into the program on the ward, with nursing staff becoming involved as co-leaders.

Identifying Group Type and Structure

Staff colleagues can also be helpful in considering the question of the group type and structure. For example, will it be a group of fixed membership meeting over a period of time, or will it be an **open-ended group** in which different members arrive and leave each week? Special problems and dynamics associated with open-ended groups will be discussed in later chapters; however, for some purposes and settings they provide a better alternative than a fixed-membership group. One ward group in a hospital consisted of women who arrived for a two-day preparatory stay, a one-day exploratory operation to determine the possibility of cancer, and a two-day recovery period. Participation of both pre- and postoperative patients lent itself to the mutual aid process as those who had just gone through the experience were helpful to those preparing for it, and those who were newly admitted began the process of preparing to leave the hospital by helping those who were leaving.

In contrast, a group for teenaged survivors of sexual abuse will need some time to establish the levels of trust required to explore painful and formerly secret experiences. An open-ended group with a continually changing membership would not be appropriate for such a population. Some members might be added after the initial sessions, but at some point, such a group would need to be closed.

Groups are sometimes formed from ongoing natural groups, such as in a residential setting. A group home is a good example, since it represents a living group, operating seven days a week, 24 hours each day. For two hours twice each week, house meetings are held at special times within the ongoing group life to focus on issues of group living, such as problems among residents and between residents and staff. These meetings represent structured incidents in the life of the ongoing group designed to improve the ability of all concerned to live and work together.

Another issue is related to the content of the group meeting. People can provide mutual aid through means other than just talking. Mutual aid can be provided through other "mediums of exchange" between people (Shulman, 1971). For example, senior citizens in a residential center might use activities that they have developed to structure their time, provide enjoyment or education, give them the opportunity to develop new skills, or just to enjoy the company of others. In Chapter 16 I will discuss the place of program activities in the life of the group and the worker's tasks. In the formation stage, it is important to consider whether interaction through activity represents an important part of the purpose of the group and fits within the general function of the setting.

A ward group in a psychiatric hospital involved in planning recreational activities for patients provides an example in which activities relate both to patients' need and to the service of the setting. On the other hand, community-center-type activities offered during the school day to a group of children who are not doing well in their classes may be viewed by the school staff as a "reward" for acting badly, even if the worker argues that the students are helped indirectly. When these activities are used in work with children as a substitute for discussions about class problems or because the worker is concerned that the youngsters would not come to a "talking group," they may frustrate the essential work rather than assist it. This issue will be discussed in some detail in the section on work with children, but for now the important point is that a decision on group type (talk, activity, or both) needs to relate directly both to the service of the agency and to the needs of the group members.

One widely used framework for describing group types was developed by the group work faculty at Boston University.[4] They identified four general types:

1. *Support and stabilization groups* are best suited for persons experiencing a life crisis such as divorce, bereavement, or economic instability. As the name implies, group support is used to help members stabilize and begin to cope with the stress.
2. *Growth and education groups,* more familiar in traditional group service agencies, are applicable to persons experiencing major life developmental challenges or transitions (e.g., teenagers) or persons with delayed development of skills because of isolating, regressive, or stagnating influences (e.g., long-term chronic care mental patients). The focus of the group is on learning specific competencies and social skills related to the developmental tasks.
3. *Task and action groups* include committees, grassroots community organization groups; hospital ward government, and so on. Their focus is on tasks to be accomplished, rather than support or individual development of the group members.
4. *Recapitulation and restitution groups* are more closely related to the classical psychoanalytically oriented insight groups for adults or play therapy groups for children. Their focus is on recapitulation of life events and restitution of member strengths and positive self-esteem.

While the various types of groups are helpful in conceptualizing the central purposes of the group, the authors point out that no group is ever a "pure form" of the model. In fact, most groups can be seen to contain elements of two or more of the "classical models."

Group Versus Individual Work with Clients

Another issue that can create problems for the group worker is the compatibility of group and individual work. Some group workers take the position that group members should not be seen individually because that will lessen the intensity of the group experience. Individual counselors, as well, are often worried that clients will use their group session to discuss central issues. This can lead to a struggle over "who owns the client," a misunderstanding of the interdependence of individual and group work, and an unacceptable attitude to client participation in decisions about service.

On the first issue, clients may use both individual and group help for different issues, as they see fit. For example, as the group works on the concern of a particular member, the discussion may raise a similar concern for the client, who may want a chance to discuss a special case of the general problem and may not have enough time in the group to do this. Individual sessions can provide this opportunity. Group discussion, rather than robbing the individual work of its vitality, will often enrich the content of the individual counseling sessions. As clients listen to issues, as they understand how others are experiencing problems, they may be put in touch with feelings of their own that were not previously evident. Finding out that others have fears related to taboo areas, such as sex, may greatly speed up clients' willingness to discuss their own concerns in individual work.

In like manner, the work in the individual sessions can strengthen a client to raise a personal concern in the group. For some clients it may be too difficult to start to talk in a group context about some of their most private feelings and concerns. As they find they can share these with an individual counselor and not be harshly judged, they may be more willing to share these feelings in the group. Thus, the group and individual work can be parallel and interdependent, with the client free to choose where and when to use these resources for work. The question of client choice raises the second issue. In my view, these choices, at any particular moment, rest with the client. Feeling comfortable about dealing with issues in one context or the other, the client will make these decisions. I may share my opinions, offer support, and even provide concrete help (e.g., role-playing in an individual session to show how the client might raise an issue in the group).

With two and possibly more helping people working with the same client, good communication between the helpers becomes essential. Structures should be established that guarantee regular communication so that each understands how the client is choosing to deal with issues and so that the workers can help each other in their related work. For example, in a couples' group that I have led, two co-leaders sat in on each session. They were seeing most of the couples on an individual counseling basis. In the "tuning-in" session we held prior to each group meeting, they summarized the specific concerns dealt with in the individual sessions. We used this preparatory work to anticipate potential group issues. I maintain a policy of not directly raising concerns in the group that were discussed in the individual work unless the couples wish them raised. Through the tuning-in process, I became more effective at picking up their indirect cues. Since co-leaders sat in on the sessions, they were able to incorporate content from the group experience into their individual work. If they were not able to sit in, I shared copies of my group process and couple summary reports so that they would be aware of the couples' progress. When sessions were videotaped, the tapes were also available for their use. Rather than competing for client ownership, we had three professionals, each providing a service through different modalities. As pointed out in the earlier discussion on confidentiality, without freedom to share information this open communication would not have taken place

Agency Support for Groups

In addition to support from colleagues, help from the agency administration may also be needed. For example, special expenses may be incurred in carrying out a group program. Mothers' groups held during the daytime may require baby-sitting services. Recruitment publicity, transportation expenses, coffee, and other items may be involved in some group programs. In addition, the worker developing a group may need support in the form of a reduced individual caseload and group work consultation from an outside consultant if one is not available on staff. These issues should be discussed when the group is formed.

In some settings, where groups have not been an integral part of the service, the approach to group work programs may require that the worker take personal responsibility for their implementation. For example, workers are encouraged to develop groups if they can do so "on their own time." Many workers, eager to see the service begin or to develop new skills in work with clients, accept this responsibility and soon regret it. If a service is part of the agency function, it should not have to be carried as a personal "hobby" by the worker. Groups take time, and if workers do not see that the group is viewed as a part of their responsibilities, the additional demands upon them and their feelings about these demands will often affect their work with the group.

Even when agencies support the development of group services, they sometimes do so for the wrong reasons. Administrators may believe that seeing clients in groups can save time and so encourage a swing to group programs as a way of providing more service to clients without increasing staff. With **cost-containment** programs on the rise, there are some situations in which seeing clients in groups does save time. For example, orientation meetings for prospective adoptive parents or new foster parents can be an effective way of starting communications with more than one person at a time. As pointed out earlier, however, more often than not the development of group services tends to increase the staff's workload, since new issues and concerns may be discovered that require additional individual work. Groups should be viewed as an important service in their own right rather than as a service substitute. A worker in a group will need time to follow up with individual members, to meet with other staff, to develop a system for recording the group work for agency accountability, and for personal learning.

To start a group service on a sound agency footing is better, even though the formation process may be slower and more frustrating. Time taken by the group worker to interpret the group's purpose as well as to identify the special needs and potential problems related to instituting new group services will pay off in the long run. In those cases where doubts exist about the benefits of group practice, the worker can propose the group as an agency experimental service to be closely evaluated. Records can be kept on the costs and benefits. The agency staff and administration can use the first groups as a way of developing experience with a new form of service. The important point is that the service be the agency's, not the personal project of a concerned worker. With the latter, it is not unusual to have a good first group only to discover that the service dies when the worker is no longer able or willing to provide it personally.

GROUP COMPOSITION, TIMING, AND STRUCTURE

A conversation I had with a group of students and health professionals helps to illustrate some of the myths and questions involved in planning a group. I led a group for five couples in marital difficulty that was videotaped and simultaneously observed on a monitor in another room. After each session, I met with the observers and my co-leaders to discuss the session. At the end of a first session that was marked by excellent group member involvement (excerpts from transcripts of this group are shared in later chapters), I was peppered by questions on how the group had been formed. The first request was for my principles of group composition that had led to such a lively, interactive group. One couple was in their twenties, another in their thirties, a third in their forties, a fourth in their fifties, and the oldest couple was in their late sixties and early seventies. I explained, much to the disappointment of the group, that these were the only five couples referred for the group.

Another student asked how I had decided on five couples. I pointed out that we were using a studio, and with myself and my co-leaders, there was only enough room for five couples. Another effort to tease out principles followed as they inquired how we decided on the number of sessions. I pointed out that there were many long-standing issues involved, and a short-term group did not seem to offer enough time. "How did you settle on exactly twenty-three sessions?" was the next question. Once again I disappointed the group by explaining that we decided we couldn't do the advance work needed to start the group before October 15. We simply counted the weeks until the end of the academic year. We then went on to discuss the differences between what I felt to be the myth of scientific group composition versus the reality of how decisions were made.

The students wanted prescriptions and rules, and I argued, perhaps more strongly than was needed, that the rules were not really that clear. In reality, we often "take what we can get." Our experiences, and some research findings, have provided us with some guidelines. For example, we know that extremes often lead to problems. Groups can clearly be too large to provide opportunity for everyone to participate or too small to provide a consistent core of members. While groups can tolerate some degree of age range, as in my married couples' groups, extremes for some populations, such as teenagers, can create serious problems. For example, a 12-year-old foster child faces life tasks that differ significantly from the concerns of a 17-year-old who is preparing to leave the care of the agency upon turning 18. One person of color in an all-white group may experience a sense of isolation that the addition of another might well alleviate. A group of survivors of sexual abuse may have significant difficulty in achieving intimacy if it is structured as open-ended, with new members constantly joining the group and other members leaving it.

The literature provides a fund of observations on questions of group composition and structure, but unfortunately it also provides conflicting scientific evidence in support of rules. For example, there are conflicting studies on the optimum size for effective discussion groups, with support for different numbers argued persuasively. A balance has to be struck between ignoring these issues completely and depending too much upon rigid rules and structures.

The position argued here is that each setting must develop its own rules, based upon its experiences as well as those of others. Given this reality, a worker must address a number of questions, using the experiences of colleagues and of other settings to develop some tentative answers. Each group represents an experiment that can contribute to the fund of experience the worker will draw upon in starting new groups. Some of the questions requiring discussion are highlighted in the remainder of this section. We will not provide definitive answers to these questions, but rather, a way of exploring the issues.

Group Member Selection

The crucial factor in selection of members is that there be some common ground between their individual needs and the purpose of the group. Whether this purpose has been defined broadly or narrowly, each member must be able to find some connection between a personal sense of urgency and the work involved. Even if this common ground is not apparent to the prospective members at the start, the worker should have some sense of its existence. In the example of the couples' group, each couple was having severe marital problems. Another point in common was that all five couples had some commitment at the start to trying to strengthen their marriages. Couples who had already decided to separate and who needed help in doing so without causing additional pain to each other or their families would not have belonged in this group.

In an AIDS/Recovery group I co-led, the five members included one white, gay male, a transgendered woman, a heterosexual woman, and two African-American males. While their life experiences differed significantly, all of the members shared in common the disease of AIDS and all were in relatively early recovery (one week to a little more than one year) from poly-substance abuse (alcohol, cocaine, heroin, etc.). Group members differed in their status with respect to AIDS. Two members were on an experimental treatment that had lowered their AIDS viral loads (counts) to almost zero and had raised their T-cell (protective) counts to near normal. One client was waiting for her viral load and T-cell count to reach the point at which she could enter the experimental clinical trials with the new drugs. Another client was eligible, but refusing treatment. The health of the fifth had been damaged so badly by her use of hormones and illegal substances that she was too ill for the experimental treatment. For this client, her viral load was climbing each week, her T-cell count was nonexistent, and she was experiencing a range of opportunistic infections common to later-stage AIDS. In spite of these significant differences, each member was able to relate to the others on the basis of their shared struggle with AIDS, with early substance abuse recovery, and with the interaction between the two.

In organizing a community action group, the fact that members live in the same community, share the same services, face the same problems, and use the same institutions (e.g., schools) can help bind them together and foster a sense of mutual need.

As the group leader defines the purpose of the group and considers potential members, common sense can help to identify potential differences which might create difficulty in reaching group consensus on the focus of the work. As mentioned previously, for example, although 12-year-old foster adolescents may have their wardship status in common with 17-year-old wards, their issues and concerns may be quite different. Combining these two age groups in a group to discuss life problems and issues related to being "foster" could create unnecessary obstacles. On the other hand, I have seen groups developed by a child welfare agency to promote better communications between teens and staff and to provide social and recreational activities in which a wide age difference between teens appeared to have a less negative impact. The older teens provided leadership for the group and looked upon themselves as "big brothers" and "big sisters" to the younger ones.

Group purpose will be important in thinking about age and group composition. For example, in the couples' group described earlier, the differences in the ages of the five couples provided unexpected dividends. Each couple was experiencing the crises associated with their particular phase of life and phase of their marriage; however, there were common themes cutting across all phases. In many ways, the older couples were able to share their experiences and perspectives with the younger ones, and the group often took on the appearance of an extended family. After one session in which some of the problems associated with the older couples' life phases were clearly delineated, the husband in the youngest couple said good-humoredly, "I'm beginning to wonder if this is what I have to look forward to going through!" The wife of the oldest couple, who had been married 49 years, responded, "But you will have the advantage of having had this group to help you face these problems."

Whether to include males, females, or both will similarly have to be determined according to the group's purpose. I find some of the other factors often discussed when deciding on group membership, such as judgments about a member's "personality," somewhat questionable. For example, I have seen a group meticulously assembled with a proper number of relatively passive schoolchildren balanced by a manageable number of active ones. The theory was to guarantee interaction, with the active members stimulating the passive ones. In addition, some limit on active members was thought to help the leader with potential problems of control. Unfortunately, nobody informed the group members about their expected roles. The leader was observed in the first session desperately trying to deal with the acting-out behaviors of the "passive" members while the "active" members looked on in shock and amusement. The fact of the matter is that clients do not act the same in every situation. A passive client in an individual interview or classroom may act differently when exposed to a new context. Clients will not remain in the "diagnosed" box long enough to be clearly identified. Their reactions will be somewhat dependent on the actions of those around them, particularly the group leader.

Race, ethnicity, and language issues also need to be considered when composing a group. Davis (1979, 1980, 1981, 1984) has addressed the impact of race on group composition and practice, basing his observations on anecdotal as well as empirical evidence. In reviewing the literature on the impact of racial composition, Davis (1981) identified a number of observed processes that emerge when a racial ratio changes and minority membership is increased. These included such processes as *cleavage, tipping points*, and *white flight*. In **cleavage,** the group splits into distinct racial subgroups. The **tipping point** is the number that creates in majority members anxiety, resulting in aggression toward members of the "out" group. He suggested that white persons are so often in the majority that when they are placed in a group in which they are in a smaller than usual majority—for example, with more than 10 percent to 20 percent persons of color—they may experience a mental state of being in the "psychological minority," at times leading to a **white flight** reaction (Davis and Proctor, 1989, p. 103). Conversely, members of the minority group faced with this ratio may experience being in the "psychological majority" even though their absolute numbers are less than 50 percent.

As with many such observations, these concepts of psychological minority and majority may not significantly affect the decisions related to the composition of one's group. Rather, they serve to attune the group leader to potential group dynamics resulting from a composition that may affect the group's functioning. Awareness of the process by the group leader, as well as a willingness to address these issues when and if they emerge, may help the group cope more effectively.

In summarizing the literature on race and group, Davis and Proctor (1989) suggest that

> There is some evidence that whites and minorities may prefer different racial compositions: neither whites nor minorities appear to like being greatly outnumbered. The language spoken in the group may also be important. For example, if some members speak Spanish, while others do not, the nonbilingual speakers may become isolated (p. 115).

Davis and Proctor (1989) also summarize the findings on group leadership:

> Leaders who differ in race from their group members may receive less cooperation. Biracial co-leadership may enhance communication in racially heterogeneous groups. However, biracial co-leaders must remain alert to the possibility of one leader being perceived as the leader and the other as his helper (p. 116).

Finally, in addressing the paucity of empirical research, they suggest that

> There is no evidence which suggests that group treatment is more or less suitable for any particular ethnic group. Furthermore, there is little evidence that either racially homogenous or racially heterogeneous groups are superior in their outcomes....Very few studies have attempted to assess the effects of the group leader's race on group member outcomes. Furthermore, reports from studies involving the race of the leader are mixed. However, these studies are consistent in that they have found that prior group leader experience in working with minorities appears to have beneficial effects for the group (p. 117).

Group Timing

There are a number of time-related factors to consider when setting up a group. How often will the group meet? How long will the meetings last? For how long will the group meet (e.g., six sessions, four months)? Once again, each of the answers must draw on common sense, the experience of the agency, and the literature, and all must be related to group purpose. In the married couples' group, we chose to meet once each week, for two hours each session, over a period of 23 weeks. Meetings had to be held in the evening so that the working partners could attend. The group was designed to provide long-term support to the couples as they dealt with their marital problems. The alternate option of intensive weekends, for example, was not considered. For couples in crisis, it seemed that the intensive, short-term experience might open up more problems while leaving the couples unable to deal with them. On the other hand, weekend workshops for marital enrichment groups, in which the relationships are strong to begin with, may be beneficial as educational and skill-development experiences.

The decision to meet weekly was based on the recognition that longer breaks between meetings might diffuse the intensity of the experience, making each session seem like a new beginning. Two hours seemed to be enough time to allow for the development of central themes and issues in the beginning phase of each meeting, while leaving enough time to deal effectively with specific individual and group concerns. More than two hours might be wearying for both group members and group workers.

Whatever decisions are reached for a particular group, discussing and clarifying the plan with group members is important. Group members have a sense of the group's time frame and will be affected by the particular phase of the meeting or the phase in the life of the group. As pointed out earlier, the "doorknob" phenomenon can accelerate the presentation of important issues; however, the members need to know when the time to reach for the door is close at hand. It is possible for group members to work more effectively if they have less time to carry out their tasks. Reid and Shyne (1969), for example, have discussed the impact of time on both the worker and the client in their work on short-term treatment. There is a limit, however, to how much can be dealt with, so judicious balance needs to be developed, allowing enough sessions to deal with the anticipated themes of concern. This limit will come from experience as an agency evaluates each group, using the group members as part of the evaluation process. Group members can be used quite effectively in setting up the initial parameters by exploring their reactions to time proposals before the group is established. Feedback on the day of the week or the specific time for starting may help a group worker to avoid unnecessary conflicts.

An expression borrowed from architecture, "form follows function," is useful in thinking about time in the group formation stage. The form of the group in relation to time needs to be connected to group purpose. Agency conceptions about time can change as experiences with new group services are evaluated. In one example, I served as a consultant to an agency providing extensive group services to persons with AIDS (PWAs) as well as their friends, lovers, and family members. Under the original plan developed by the agency, a group would start with clients diagnosed as HIV-positive and continue as members progressed through the stages of the illness (AIDS-related complex, or ARC) and AIDS itself. The group would continue as a mini-community as members became progressively more ill and most finally died. This structure seemed to make sense if the purpose of the group was to provide an alternative source of support for its members, many of whom felt cut off from other systems in their lives (e.g., family, work, friends). In reality, the groups did not work this way. Most of the groups began to dissolve as some members died or became seriously ill.

The experience caused a re-thinking of group purpose. Rather than the agency providing the substitute community, the groups were conceptualized as time-limited, with a focus on helping the members deal with transitions to the various stages of the illness (e.g., one group for recently diagnosed HIV-positive clients; another group for clients facing the onset of serious medical problems). This was not always easy to do, as the course of the illness was not always smooth nor predictable. However, instead of the agency attempting to provide the substitute community—a task that would eventually overwhelm the agency, given the number of potential clients involved in the pandemic of AIDS—the focus changed to one of helping group members mobilize existing support in their own family, friendship, and community systems. Analysis of process in the groups indicated that group leaders had been too quick to accept their group members' contention that such support was closed to them and that only the group could provide it. Work in the groups became more demanding, and members were asked to look closely at their own efforts to connect with their social support systems. The move to time-limited groups had an important and positive impact on the nature of the work. Once the "function" of the group had been clearly defined, the questions of "form" were easier to resolve.

In my more recent experience co-leading a group for persons with AIDS in early recovery from substance abuse, new issues of timing presented themselves. For example, with a number of our group members on the triple-therapy drug regime, and with their resulting improvement in health, we were viewing the group as one of the ongoing support systems designed to help the members cope with (for most of them) living with AIDS rather than dying from AIDS. Also, the recovery issues required more long-term support than if the members were dealing with AIDS alone. This group began in October of one year, focusing on helping members get through the extremely stressful holiday season of Thanksgiving, Christmas, and New Year's Eve. The group reconvened in the new year and continued until a summer break period with the understanding that the members would assess the need to reconvene in the fall. Individual group members received ongoing support from my co-leader, who served as their substance abuse counselor.

Group Structure, Setting, and Rules

There are a number of questions related to group structure and setting in the formation stage. For example, the meeting place needs consideration. Ease of access by public and private transportation might be a factor. Holding a session on sensitive and potentially embarrassing work (e.g., child abuse) in a public setting where members might fear being identified could be a mistake. The room itself should offer group members face-to-face seating (e.g., in a circle or around a table) and privacy. Comfortable chairs and surroundings often add to the group members' comfort during the first sessions. Work with children, on the other hand, where activity is going to be part of the work, may require facilities that are relatively "activity proof," so that members and the group worker can relax without constant worries about order and decorum.

Finally, group "rules" need clarification prior to the first group meeting. For example, limits on physical activity may be set with children's groups. Even with some adult groups it may be necessary to clarify the boundary on the use of physical force. In a group session for prison parolees described in Chapter 14, for example, one member pulls out a knife and begins to clean his fingernails in a manner meant to be threatening to another member. The worker must re-contract with the members on the issue of bringing knives to the session. Expectations about attendance are also important. The expectations the members have of the agency and the group and those the worker has of the members should be discussed. In addition, what can each member expect from the others (e.g., confidentiality of material shared)? In my couples' group, for example, the three rules discussed in the first session are that each member is expected to come each week as long as he or she is not ill, that a couple wanting to quit the group will come back for one additional week to discuss it, and that confidentiality will be respected by group members. In the example of my AIDS/recovery group, meeting were held in a "clean and sober" residence (three members lived in this house). Members were not to bring substances to the group or be under the influence of substances when they attended.

There are many differences of opinion on the question of group rules. For example, some would argue that group members should not have contact with each other outside the meetings. The field of group work is far from the point where we can come to agreement on these questions. My general bias is that group members own their own lives and that my group is simply an incident in their week (I hope, an important incident). I would, therefore, have difficulty insisting on a rule preventing them from having contacts outside the group. In fact, in many groups the bonds of mutual aid that have developed through telephone calls and informal contacts outside the group have been powerful supports for individual members. Workers in some groups, who fear that group members may get involved in "acting out" outside of the group (having sexual contact, for example), appear to me to take more responsibility for their lives of the members than they should. In some groups, such as the AIDS/recovery group, such outside activity could be a distinct threat to the members' recovery at a particularly vulnerable time in their lives. These issues need to be discussed as part of the structure of the group.

In addition, group members should be free to bring their outside interactions into the group if they wish, since they can represent an important entry into the content of the group work. In general, the rules stated in the beginning of the group should be firmly rooted to the reality of the situation rather than the arbitrary authority or personal preferences of the group leader. They should be seen by group members as emerging from the necessities of the work.

A number of issues related to group composition, timing, setting, rules, and structure have been raised in these sections for the purpose of alerting the reader to questions requiring consideration prior to the start of the group. My opinions on these questions have been shared not as the truth, but rather as an illustration of how one practitioner develops his own views from his experiences and those of others. As with all the ideas shared in this book, the reader will have to test them against her or his own sense of reality and ongoing group experiences.

WORK WITH PROSPECTIVE MEMBERS

After agency administration and staff support have been mobilized, potential obstacles to cooperation identified and discussed, and decisions made on the formation questions, then one more step remains: recruitment of group members. In contrast to individual and family work, very rarely does a group of clients arrive at the agency and request services. It may happen with some naturally formed groups, as when a group of teens in a school or a group of tenants in a housing project approach the social worker for help. These are the exceptions rather than the rule. Most group work practice requires **outreach,** where the social work service must be brought to the potential clients. Recruitment of group members is therefore a crucial element in the formation stage.

This process can also be complex, since clients feel the general ambivalence about taking help described in Parts II and III as well as unique concerns related to the group context. I should point out that there are workers who deal with groups in settings less focused on personal problems, such as community centers or community organization agencies, and do not have to deal with the same reluctance to join a group activity. Nevertheless, some degree of ambivalence is usually present when people consider joining any group. I will focus this discussion on examples of mutual aid groups designed to deal with problems of living (e.g., marital difficulties, parenting skills, alcohol or drug addiction, school difficulties) in the belief that some of the principles can be applied to other types of groups as well.

Clients may become prospective group members by identifying themselves in response to posters, newspaper stories, letters from the agency, or other means of publicizing the existence of a group service. If handled well, the steps involved in making potential group members aware of the group can help to turn the potential client towards the service. For example, posters or letters should be worded clearly, without jargon, so that the prospective member has a clear idea of the group's purpose. It may be helpful to identify some of the themes of concern that may be related to the client's sense of urgency. If the embarrassment of the workers, discussed in the chapter on contracting with individuals, results in the use of euphemisms, or if the workers have the idea of changing the client "up their sleeves" and try to hide this by general and vague offers of service, prospective group members may be turned away. It can be helpful to test the letters or posters with colleagues and clients to get their sense of the meaning and suggestions as to how to make the wording direct but still non-threatening.

Other clients are referred by colleagues or other helping professionals or are selected by workers from their caseloads. Whatever the case may be, even when the client has initiated the contact, the gap between thinking about joining a group and arriving at the first meeting can be a big one. Many of the skills already identified can be helpful in increasing the chances of a successful start. Two areas I will now examine are work with colleagues after they have agreed to recruit group members (a real agreement), and telephone or in-person contacts between the worker and prospective members.

Strategizing for Effective Referrals

A worker may have done an effective job with fellow staff members on the establishment of a group and still be disappointed by a relatively low number of referrals. An important question often overlooked is how the colleague will conduct a referral interview. It is a mistake to assume that even a motivated colleague will be able to make an effective referral without some joint work and strategizing as to how it might be done. For example, the colleague may have a general sense of the group contract but be unable to articulate it clearly. One who has not worked with groups may not be sensitive to some of the underlying feelings and ambivalence that the client may share indirectly, thereby missing a chance to help overcome some of the obstacles blocking access to the group.

It is often helpful to suggest a "tuning-in" session, either one-on-one or with a staff group, in which workers pool their efforts to sensitize themselves to the concerns clients may have about joining the group and the indirect ways these may emerge. Staff can then share strategies for reaching for the underlying concerns. In addition, a brief role-play of the referral interview may reveal to the group worker that the colleagues are not able to articulate purpose, and work can then be done on this skill. Such a process may also bring to the surface ambivalent feelings on the part of the worker or unanswered questions that need to be dealt with prior to the actual referral interviews.

An example of this process is a referral workshop that I conducted for social service professionals in connection with the establishment of a new and (at that time) experimental group service for men who had physically abused their wives or mates. Recognizing the importance of professional referrals to launch the program and knowing that the referral process might be extremely difficult in this situation, we provided an opportunity for "tuning-in" and joint strategizing. To keep the discussion focused on skills, I asked for examples of difficult referrals of a similar nature.

One worker described from memory a referral he had recently attempted with the common-law husband of a client. The client was a prostitute who had been beaten by the husband who was also her pimp, but she had refused to report the incident or leave him (the existence of many situations such as this had led to the project to establish mutual aid groups for the men involved). As the worker's interaction with the husband was analyzed, it became clear that he had never mentioned the physical abuse, attempting instead to lead the husband indirectly to agree to seek help. When this was mentioned during the analysis of the example, the worker revealed that he had feared angering the husband and risking that the husband might then take the anger out on the wife. An important discussion followed in which other workers spoke of their fears of possible retribution not only on the partners but also themselves. Their dilemma was discussed and strategies developed for broaching the subject directly without exacerbating the partner's defensiveness. Without this preparatory work, workers would have been blocked, thus offering this group indirectly because of their fears.

Let us consider another illustration of the problem of stating group purpose. In a role-play it became clear that one of the workers was describing the group in a way that would lead the prospective member to believe his worst fears—that the group was designed solely to chastise him for his behavior and to educate him to appreciate his impact on his woman. When I pointed out that the worker seemed angry at the prospective group member, my comment released a flood of feelings, echoed by many in the room, of anger at the men. All of the professionals had agreed earlier that these groups could not be effective unless the men could *both* be held accountable for their violent actions toward women and also see the group as designed to help them as clients in their own right. This intellectual agreement evaporated in the role-play. It was replaced with an essentially punitive and thereby ineffective offer of service. The ability for the workers to discuss and be in touch with these natural yet often denied feelings might help ensure a presentation of the group that might turn prospective members towards the service rather than reinforce their resistance. It was recognized that for many of these men, even the most effective offer of service might not elicit a response. For some, it would take their partner leaving them or a court order to get them to come to the first meeting. Although this group example may be an extreme one, I believe that in most cases the worker forming a group would be well advised to take some time with colleagues to discuss the technical aspects of making the referral.

Worker Skills in the Initial Interviews

Group workers often have initial contacts with individual members, in person or by phone, to discuss their participation in the group. These interviews can be seen as part of the exploratory process in which the worker describes what the group has to offer and checks with the client to determine what may be needed. The skills described in Part II of clarifying purpose, clarifying role, and reaching for feedback are useful in this interview. Describing the structure of the group (how it will work) as well as timing helps to provide the information needed for the prospective member to make a decision about using the service.

In addition to the normal "tuning in" to the client's feelings about beginning a new relationship, it is also important to "tune in" to the specific concerns related to beginning in a group. The general population has been exposed to a number of reports on groups ranging from "group psychotherapy" to "encounter." In addition, clients may bring stereotypes of groups based upon their past experiences (e.g., class groups at school, camp experiences) that will have some effect on their feelings about attending.

Questions about how people with the same problems can help each other will also be on their minds. Much of this hesitancy and fear may be just beneath the surface. It can be expressed in indirect ways, and the worker must listen for it and reach directly for the indirect cues. In the following example, a worker has been describing a foster parents' group to an agency foster parent and has found the parent apparently receptive. The cues emerge when the worker gets specific about the dates.

> **Worker:** We are going to have our first meeting in two weeks, on a Wednesday night. Can I expect you there?
>
> **Foster Parent:** (Long pause) Well, it sounds good. I'll try to make it if things aren't too hectic that week at work.

If the worker quits right there and accepts the illusion of agreement, she may be guaranteeing that the parent will not show up. Even though workers can sense the ambivalence in the client's voice, they often refrain from reaching for the negative attitude. When I have inquired why workers refrain from exploring such cues of uncertainty, they tell me that they are afraid that if they bring the doubts out in the open, they will reinforce them. They believe that the less said, the better. In reality, these doubts and questions are valid, and the worker is missing an opportunity to help the client explore them.

Without this exploration, the client may simply not show up at the first meeting despite having promised to attend. When the worker later calls, there is much guilt on the client's part and profuse explanations of his absence (e.g., "I really meant to come, only it got so hectic that day it just slipped my mind").

Returning to the interview with the foster parent, note the turn in the work when the worker reaches for the cue.

> **Worker:** You sound a bit hesitant. Are you concerned about attending the group? It wouldn't be unusual; most people have a lot of questions about groups.
>
> **Foster Parent:** Well, you know I never do too well in groups. I find I have a lot of trouble talking in front of strangers.
>
> **Worker:** Are you worried that you would have to speak up and be put on the spot?
>
> **Foster Parent:** I don't mind talking about fostering; it's just that I get tongue-tied in a group.
>
> **Worker:** I can appreciate your concern. A lot of people feel that way. I can tell you right now that except for sharing your name, no one will put you on the spot to speak. Some people always talk a lot at the early meetings while others prefer to listen. You can listen until you feel comfortable about speaking. If you want, I can help you to begin to talk in the group, but only when you're ready. I do this all the time with people who feel this way.

Foster Parent: You mean it's not just me who feels this way?
Worker: Not at all. It's quite common and natural. By the way, are there any other concerns you might have about the group?
Foster Parent: Not really. That was the biggest one. Actually, it doesn't sound like a bad idea at all.

Once again we see the importance of exploring the indirect cue so that the worker has a clearer idea about the source of the ambivalence. Many workers would hesitate to explore the cue because they would feel it was a sign of polite rejection of the group (and the worker). When asked why they assume this unnecessarily, they often reply that they are unsure about their own competency and the quality of the group. They respond to the client's ambivalence with their own feelings. In the case just cited, the fear of speaking in the group needed to be discussed. Knowing that the worker understands and that it is all right to feel this way can strengthen the client to overcome an obstacle to undertaking group experiences. In other cases, it may be memories of past group experience, or horror stories recounted by friends or relatives about harsh and confronting group encounters, or embarrassment about sharing personal details with strangers. The workers need to clarify the reality when possible, empathize genuinely with the fears, and still attempt to help the client take the first difficult step. With this kind of help from the worker, many prospective group members will be able to overcome their fears and doubts and give the group a try. A source of great support for the client is knowing that the worker understands his or her feelings.

One other not uncommon type of resistance occurs when a group is offered to the caretaker, support person, or relative of a client. In one example, a worker was recruiting a group for relatives of elderly Alzheimers patients who were caring for their family members at home. In the face of the initial, hinted reluctance, the worker said, "You sound hesitant about coming to the group, Mrs. Smith. Can you tell me why?" The client responded, with some feeling, "Just one more thing on the list for me to do to take care of my mother. I don't have time for myself!" The worker replied, "Mrs. Smith, I think I can appreciate how demanding caring for your mother must be. But I don't think I made the purpose of this group clear when I described it. This group is not your mother. This group is for you. Other group members will also be feeling overwhelmed by the demands made upon them by their relatives with Alzheimers, and part of what we can discuss is how you can get the support you need." By reaching for the lurking negatives and the ambivalence, the worker creates an opportunity to clarify group purpose to a potential member.

A common trap that workers fall into when they hear the indirect or direct cues of some reluctance is to try to "sell" the group even harder. Consider the following example of a worker in a convalescent home recruiting an elderly resident. In this case, the worker's honest caring and enthusiasm may well help the potential member consider the group, but her work would be stronger if she explored and acknowledged the obvious resistant responses. Also, the worker's focus on discussion of the "good old days" brings a response that surprises the worker but may actually suggests a different group purpose: to talk about both the good and the bad old days.

Purpose of the interview: To explain the group and to invite 92-year-old female resident to attend. The prospective member is white, with a diagnosis of progressive dementia and agitated depression. She has been living in the nursing home for three years.

Mrs. Franks was sitting up in a chair listening to music upon my arrival. I knocked on her door, entered, and introduced myself. She asked me to have a seat, which I did. I asked her how she was doing. She responded rather cheerfully that she was OK, but a little tired. I asked her if she generally napped in the afternoons (a common practice in the nursing homes). She replied, "Well, on Sundays I don't really have anything to do." "Oh," I replied, "so Sunday is your day of rest." We both laughed, and she agreed. "What do you do during the rest of the week?" I asked her. "I have my duties," was her reply. "Do you ever get down to any of the activities?" "Oh sure," she said.

"One of the reasons that I stopped by was to invite you to an activity that I am organizing. Beginning next week, we are going to be having a group called 'Jog Your Memory.' There will be five or six women in the group and we'll spend some time talking about the good old days. Do you think that you might be interested in something like that?"

"Well, I didn't have any good old days."

"Nothing good happened in your life?"

"Oh, sure," smiling. "There were many good times. Some days were good, some days were bad."

"Each week there will be a different topic and we'll see what kinds of memories it brings back."

"Well, it sounds nice, but I don't think that it's for me."

"Well, it's going to be a small group of ladies, and we'll meet for about a half hour each Tuesday, just down the hallway in the nursing home."

"Oh, it sounds nice. We need something like that."

"Do you think that you'd like to come? I would pick you up and bring you back, so you wouldn't have to worry about that."

"Oh, wonderful. I might be older than some of the others though."

"Don't worry about that, Mrs. Franks. All of the ladies are in their 80s and 90s, and one woman is even over 100."

"My goodness." We laughed.

"Mrs. Franks, I am glad that you are interested in the Jog Your Memory group. I think you will enjoy it."

"Oh yes, it sounds like a wonderful opportunity. Thank you so much for thinking of me."

I smile at Mrs. Franks and touch her hand.

"You're welcome. Today is Friday. I will come back Tuesday morning to remind you about the Jog Your Memory group. I will also let the nurse know, so she'll be sure that you are up."

Once again, the worker's caring comes through and may well lead to Mrs. Franks attending the group. The odds are good, since this is a residential setting.

Now that the worker has completed the group-formation tasks and the clients are ready to attend, the worker needs to pay attention to the beginnings and the dynamics of first sessions. These topics are explored in the next chapter.

CHAPTER SUMMARY

In this chapter we explored three major areas of work involved in the formation stage of group work practice. The first focused on the skills required to work with one's setting and colleagues in order to engage them as active partners in the development of the group service. Strategies were suggested for coping with underlying obstacles that can lead to sabotage of group work efforts. The second area involved issues of group composition, timing, and structure. A model was suggested for exploring issues in advance in order to maximize the possibility of success in forming the group. The final area of work examined and illustrated the skills required to recruit members who may be ambivalent about attending a group session. In particular, the skill of looking for trouble when everything was going the worker's way was identified as important for avoiding the illusion of agreement, in which the client promises to attend but doesn't show up.

GLOSSARY

Cleavage A process in a group in which the members split into sub-groups in response to a changing racial ratio. In particular, an increase of the minority or "out" group members past the "saturation point."

Cost containment Efforts on the part of administrators to lower the cost of services. Often introduced because of reduced funding by private and government agencies or third-party payers such as health insurance companies.

Open-ended group A group in which new members can join at any point while ongoing members may leave at different times. For example, a ward group on a hospital may have new members join when admitted to the hospital and others leave when discharged.

Outreach Process in which the social work service is brought to the potential clients.

Tipping point The "saturation point" in the changing racial ratio of a group that leads majority group members to respond with anxiety and aggression toward the "out" group. Can generate such processes as "cleavage" and "white flight."

White flight The process of white members leaving a group when the racial composition ratio of the group changes, resulting in an increase in minority group members past the "tipping point."

NOTES

1. For discussion of group formation issues, see A. Gitterman, "Developing a New Group Service," in A. Gitterman and L. Shulman (eds.), *Mutual Aid Groups, Vulnerable Populations, and the Life Cycle,* 2nd ed. (New York: Columbia University Press, 1994), pp. 59–80; M. Hartford, *Groups in Social Work* (New York: Columbia University Press, 1972); G. Konopka, *Social Group Work: A Helping Process* (Englewood Cliffs, NJ: Prentice-Hall, 1971), Chapter 6; D.S. Whitaker and M.A. Lieberman, *Psychotherapy Through the Group Process* (New York: Atherton, 1964), Chapter One; L.N. Brown, *Groups for Growth and Change* (New York: Longman, 1991); P.H. Ephros and T.V. Vasil *Groups That Work* (New York: Columbia University Press, 1988); and U. Glassman and L. Kates, *Group Work: A Humanistic Approach* (Newbury Park, CA: Sage, 1990); J.A. Lee, *Group Work with the Poor and Oppressed* (New York: Haworth, 1988); W. Schwartz, "Group Work in Public Welfare," *Public Welfare, 26* (1968): 322–68.

2. A helpful illustration of the introduction of a mutual aid model of group services in a drug abuse prevention program can be found in M.H. Phillips and M.A. Markowitz, *The Mutual Aid Model of Group Services: Experiences of New York Archdiocese Drug Abuse Prevention Program* (New York: Fordham University Graduate School of Social Work, 1990).

3. This author is the chair of a Commission for Strengthening Group Work in Social Work Education, sponsored by the Association for the Advancement of Social Work with Groups (AASWG). For information on the work of this Commission and the resources available for group work training and education, see the AASWG home page on the Internet:

http://dominic.barry.edu/~kelly/aaswg/aaswg.html

or contact John Ramey, General Secretary, AASWG, e-mail: (jramey@uakron.edu); telephone: 1-800-807-0793.

4. See *A Curriculum Guide for Field Education*, 11th ed. (Boston: Boston University School of Social Work, 1990); S. Bernstein (ed.), *Explorations in Group Work* (Boston: Boston University School of Social Work, 1965; also, Boston: Charles River Books, 1976, Hebron, CT: Practitioner's Press, 1984), pp. 31–34.

10

The Beginning Phase with Groups

CHAPTER OUTLINE

The Dynamics of First Group Sessions

The Couples' Group

Recontracting

Co-Leadership in Groups

In this chapter we will examine the dynamics of the first group session. The contracting issues explored in Parts II and III with individuals and families will be revisited, but this time, we will explore the variant elements of practice introduced by working with a group. A detailed example of a first session with a married couples' group will be used to illustrate the concepts. We will examine the issue of recontracting when the initial contract was not clear, looking at examples of social workers modifying their working agreements with their own groups as well as with ongoing groups. Examples from a work training program for teenagers, a shelter for battered women, and a psychiatric ward are presented and analyzed. The example from a psychiatric ward also illustrates recontracting work with co-leaders and the system. The chapter ends with a brief discussion of issues raised by co-leadership and strategies for dealing with them.

Many of the issues related to beginning work that we described in Chapter 3 are equally applicable to first sessions with groups, with an important addition: the individual client must also deal with a new system—the group. The first two central questions for the client in the individual context were "What are we doing here together?" and "What kind of person will this worker be?" In the group context, a third question is added: "What kind of people will these other group members be?" Many of the uncertainties and fears associated with new beginnings will be present in a first group session, but they will be increased by the public nature of the engagement. For example, the client's fear of being manipulated by someone in authority may be heightened by the thought that any potential inadequacy displayed, and the resultant humiliation, may be witnessed by peers. For this reason, among others, special attention to first sessions is important, so that a proper stage can be set for the work that will follow.

In this chapter we provide an overview of the general structure of a first group meeting, reviewing some of the underlying assumptions outlined in Chapter 3 and considering some of the unique dynamics associated with group work. The tasks of both the group members and the group worker are outlined, and a number of specific skills are identified. With this overview as a backdrop, the dynamics of a first group session are illustrated using a detailed analysis of a first session of a married couples' group. The issue of *recontracting* is also explored. This is the process in which the worker reopens the issues of contracting by providing a clearer statement of purpose or exploring the group members' resistance or lack of connection to the service. We will discuss the not-uncommon situation in which a worker joins an ongoing group in which a clear working contract has not been developed. The skills in working with the co-leaders and the group in initiating a recontracting process are illustrated using a detailed example from a student's experiences. The chapter ends with a discussion of the potential problems involved in co-leadership and strategies for dealing with them.

THE DYNAMICS OF FIRST GROUP SESSIONS

Clients begin first group meetings, as they do all new encounters with people in authority, with a certain tentativeness. Their normal concerns about adequacy and being up to the demands that will be made upon them can be heightened by the fact that the encounter is taking place in public view. Most clients bring to first meetings an extensive fund of group experience (e.g., classrooms, summer camp), many of which are associated with painful memories. We have all either witnessed or experienced the excruciatingly difficult moments in a classroom when an individual student has been singled out to answer a question, solve a math problem on the board, or give some indication of having completed the assignment. One could feel the embarrassment of a classmate when exposed to sarcasm as a punitive weapon in the hands of an insensitive teacher. In fact, whereas new encounters in a one-to-one counseling situation generate fears of the unknown, new group encounters tend to reawaken old fears based on past experiences.

The requirement of early clarification of purpose, described in individual work, is also central in the group context. The clients' first question will be, "What are we here for?" Once the boundary of the group experience has been clearly described, it will be easier for members to select appropriate responses. When the expectations of the group worker and the setting or agency within which the group takes place are clear, the group members' feelings of safety can increase. If purpose remains ambiguous, then all the fears of inadequacy will be increased. As the group starts, the group members will watch the group worker with keen interest. Having experienced the impact of powerful people in authority, they know it is important to "size up" this new authority figure as soon as possible. This leads to the clients' second central question: "What kind of person will the worker be?" Until the group members can understand clearly how this worker operates and the way in which they will be affected, they will need to test the worker directly or indirectly. Defenses will remain in position until members are certain that their individual safety is ensured.

All these dynamics are similar to the ones described in Chapter 3 on the beginning of any new helping relationship. The major difference in the group setting involves the presence of other clients. As the group session proceeds, each group member will also be appraising the others. Many questions will arise: Who are these other people? Do they have the same problems as I do? Will I be embarrassed by finding myself less competent than they? Do they seem sympathetic and supportive, or are there people in this group who may attack and confront me? While the client's primary concern in the first session is the group leader, questions about fellow members follow closely behind. Not only do members wonder what they can get out of the experience to meet their own needs, but they also wonder why it is necessary to get help in a group: "How can other people help me if they have the same problems as I have?"

With some of these issues in mind, the worker should design the structure of first meetings to meet the following objectives:

(a) To introduce group members to each other.

(b) To make a brief, simple opening statement that tries to clarify the agency's or institution's stake in providing the group service as well as the potential issues and concerns that group members feel urgently about.

(c) To obtain feedback from the group members on their sense of the fit (the contract) between their ideas of their needs and the agency's view of the service it provides.

(d) To clarify the group worker's task and method of attempting to help the group do its work.

(e) To deal directly with any specific obstacles that may obstruct this particular group's efforts to function effectively: stereotypes group members may hold concerning group work or people in authority, or group members' feelings of anger if attendance is involuntary.

(f) To begin to encourage inter-member interaction rather than discussion only between the group leader and the group members.

(g) To begin to develop a supportive group culture in which members can feel safe.

(h) To help group members develop a tentative agenda for future work.

(i) To clarify the mutual expectations of the agency and the group members. For example, what can group members expect from the worker? In addition, what expectations does the worker have for the members (e.g., regular attendance, meetings starting on time)? Such rules and regulations concerning structure are part of the working contract.

(j) To gain some consensus on the part of group members as to the specific next steps; for example, are there central themes or issues with which they wish to begin the following week's discussion?

(k) To encourage honest feedback and evaluation of the effectiveness of the group.

At first glance, this list of objectives for a first meeting may appear overwhelming. Actually, many of them can be dealt with quickly, and most are interdependent in that work on one objective simultaneously affects the others. Obviously, however, these objectives cannot be achieved in the first session unless a clear structure for work is provided. The approach to creating such a structure, which is illustrated in detail in the remainder of the chapter, is offered as a general statement recognizing that the order of elements and the emphasis may vary depending on the worker, the group members, and the setting.

The next section illustrates a first meeting using excerpts from a videotaped recording of the first session of a married couples' group. In the next chapter we will examine some variations on this basic structural theme.

THE COUPLES' GROUP

The group was conducted under the auspices of a community mental health setting. Five couples were referred from a variety of sources. All had experienced problems in their marital relationships, and in each of the five couples, one partner was identified as the "patient."

The youngest couple were John and Louise, in their twenties, with two young children. Rick and Fran were in their thirties and had been married for seven years with no children. Len and Sally were in their late forties, had been married for 20 years, and had children in their late teens and early twenties. Frank and Jane, in their fifties, were recently married after prior marriages and divorces. Jane's teenaged sons were living with them at this point. Finally, Lou and Rose were in their sixties with a number of married children, who in turn, had children of their own. Louise and Rose had recently been inpatients at a psychiatric hospital. Sally had been seen at the hospital and was considering entering as an inpatient. Frank, Jane, Rick, and Fran had been referred to the group for marital counseling. Each of the couples had been interviewed individually by one of my two co-workers in the group; however, they were meeting me, the senior group worker, for the first time that evening. My two co-workers, one male and one female, were also present.

The Initial Stage

The group meeting room was carpeted and had comfortable chairs set in a circle. The session was recorded on video cameras placed in an adjoining studio.[1] Cameras and cameramen were on the other side of one-way glass partitions. The couples had met the co-workers in another part of the clinic and had been escorted to the meeting room so that they all arrived at once. The purpose of the videotaping had been explained to the couples, and they had signed consent forms prior to the first session. The group workers had tuned in to the impact of the videotaping and had therefore strategized to reach for their reactions at the beginning of the session. As the couples arrived, I met them at the door, introducing myself to each partner and encouraging them to take a seat. Len, Sally's husband, had to miss the first session, as he was out of town on business. Frank and Jane, who had expressed the most ambivalence and uncertainty about attending the group during the week, were not present at the beginning of the session. After everyone was comfortably settled, I began by suggesting that we go around the room so that the members could share their names, how long they had been married, and whether they had any children. I said this would be a way for us to get to know each other.

> **Louise:** I am Louise Lewis. We have been married six years, and we have two children.
> **Worker:** Go ahead, John (speaking to Louise's husband sitting next to her), please share it with the group members. (Points to the rest of the group.)
> **John:** My name is John. (Pause)
> **Worker:** (Smiling) With the same kids!
> **John:** (Laughing along with the rest of the group) Yes, I hope so.

The group members continued around the circle, giving their names and the data on their families. The advantage of introductions is that they help group members break the ice and begin to speak from the start. In addition, the worker conveys to them the sense that knowing each other will be important. Often during these introductions someone will make a humorous comment followed by nervous laughter; however, even these first contributions can help the members settle down. It is important that a minimum of relevant information be requested at this point, since discussion of contract has not taken place. Group members will have the opportunity later to share the reasons why they have come. This will come after clarification of group purpose, which will provide the necessary structure. An alternative approach would be to make a brief statement of purpose before asking for introductions. This could be particularly important if group members had no idea of the purpose of the group.

Following the introductions, I brought up the videotaping issue.

> **Worker:** I realize you discussed the taping with my co-workers, but I thought I would like to repeat the reasons for taping these sessions and also to give you another opportunity to share your reactions. As you know, this is a training institution and we are involved in teaching other health professionals a number of skills, including how to work with groups. We find it helpful to use videotapes of groups such as these so that new group leaders can have examples to assist them in their learning. In addition, the co-leaders and myself will use these tapes each week as a way of trying to figure out how to be more effective in helping this group work well.

I went on to explain that if segments of the tape were kept, they would have an opportunity to view them and could decide if they wanted them erased. I asked if there was any response, and after a few moments of silence and some verbal agreement that there was no problem, I proceeded. I believed the tapes were still on their minds and would come up again; however, they were not quite ready at this point to accept my invitation.

With this acknowledgement of the taping issue, I moved to begin the contracting process. The first skills involved were similar to those described in Chapter 3: clarifying purpose, clarifying role, and reaching for client feedback. I had prepared an opening statement in which I attempted to explain the stake the clinic had in providing the group, to identify their potential interest in the work of the group and to state our roles as workers. This statement had been reworded a number of times with the assistance of my co-leaders until we felt it was jargon-free, short, and direct.

> **Worker:** I thought I would begin by explaining how we view the purpose of this group and the role that we would be playing, and to get some feedback from you on what you see the sessions to be all about. All of the couples in the group, and there may be one more here later this evening, are experiencing some difficulties in their marriages. This is a time of crisis and not an easy time. The way we see it, however, is that it is also an opportunity for change, for growth, and a chance to make a new marriage right within the one you presently have. Now we know that isn't easy; learning to live together can be tough. That is why we have organized this group. Essentially, the way we see it, it will be a chance for you to help each other—a sort of a mutual aid group. As you listen to each other, as you share some of the problems, some of the feelings, and some of the concerns, and as you try to help each other, we think you will learn a great deal that may be helpful in your own marriages. So that's pretty much the purpose of the group. Now, for our role as group leaders, we have a couple of jobs. The first is that we are going to try to help you talk to and listen to each other, since it's not always easy to do that, particularly with people you don't know. Secondly, we will be sharing our own ideas along the way about close relationships, some of which may be helpful to you. Does that make sense? Do any of you have any questions about that? Does that sound like what you thought you were coming to? (Most heads were nodding up and down, there were murmurs of "yes".)

Worker: I thought to get us started, it would be worthwhile to take some time to do some problem swapping. What I would like you to do is to share with each other, for a little while, some of the problems and difficulties you have found between you as couples. I would like you also to share some of the things you would like to see different. How would you like the relationship to be? We can take some time to find out the kinds of issues that you're concerned about and then move from there. Would someone like to start?

The purpose of the problem swapping is twofold. First, it provides the feedback necessary to begin to develop the client's side of the working contract. These are the issues and concerns that will be the starting point for the work of the group. It is quite possible that in the initial stage, group members will share "near" problems that do not bear directly on some of the more difficult and hard-to-talk-about issues. This is their way of testing, of trying to determine how safe it is to use the group. The group worker has to respect and understand their defenses as an appropriate way to begin a new experience. The second function of the problem-swapping exercise is to encourage inter-member interaction. For most of their lives clients have participated in groups where the discussion has essentially been between the group member and the leader, the person in authority. This is a long-standing habit. They will need to learn new ways of relating in a group, and the problem-swapping exercise is a good way to start.

As each individual member shares a problem or a concern, the group worker pays attention to his two clients. The first client is the individual who is speaking at the moment. The second client is the group. Attention is paid to the group by monitoring their reactions as revealed by their eyes, their posture, and so on. The mediation function of the group worker can be seen in action during this exercise as he encourages individual members to speak to the group and share the concerns they are bringing to the forefront and at the same time helps group members respond to the individual. As group members hear others describing problems, they become better able to identify those issues for themselves. In addition, when they hear their own concerns echoed by other group members, there is some relief at finding out that they are "all in the same boat." The onus that each member may feel over having somehow failed as a human being and as a partner in a marital relationship can begin to lift as they discover that their feelings and their concerns are shared by others.

Silence is not unusual at this point in the first group session. This silence can represent a number of communications, a different one for each group member. Some may be thinking of what they are willing to share with the group at that time. Others may be shy and afraid to be the first one to speak. Still others are expressing their wariness of being put on the spot if they raise a concern, since they do not know how other group members or the leader will react. These are the moments that inexperienced group leaders dread. The silence, they feel, confirms a recurring nightmare they have had about their first group session. They are worried that after they have made their opening statement and invited feedback, nobody will speak. It is not unusual for group leaders to take over the group at this point and to offer subjects for discussion or, in some cases, to present prepared films or presentations. This, of course, leads to a self-fulfilling prophecy, where the message conveyed to the members by the worker is that although their participation is being asked for, there is no willingness to wait for it. An alternative, after a brief delay, is to explore the silence by acknowledging that it is hard to begin and that it is difficult to discuss such subjects with people one doesn't know. Often, this supportive comment frees a member to risk. If not, the group leader can ask if members might discuss what makes it hard to talk in a first group session. As the members discuss why it's hard to talk, they inevitably start the problem swapping as well.

In the case of this couples' group, Lou, the member in his sixties, had a strong sense of urgency about beginning to work and was ready to jump right in. He was seated directly to my left. As he spoke, he directed his conversation to the other members. He began by describing the problem as his wife's depression. The effect was flat in his voice, and his wife sat next to him stonefaced, without any change in expression. This is a position she held throughout the session, almost until the end, not saying a word, although she appeared to be hearing everything said by others. As Lou spoke, the rest of the group listened intently, obviously relieved that he had started.

> **Lou:** To begin with, as you heard, we have been married for 45 years. Our relationship has been on a rocky road due in a great degree to tragedies that have happened to our family. While that was a real contributing factor, social conditions, economic conditions, and family relationships were also contributing factors. I'm making this very brief because most of this will come out later on. I think the outline on this will be enough for us to get our teeth into. As a result of the things I have mentioned, Rose, particularly, went into some real depressions. All the threads of her family seemed to go. As a result, it became difficult for her to operate. The problems were so strong, she decided she had to go to a psychiatrist. She went and I went with her for two and one-half years. The psychiatrist opened up some doors for her but not enough to really make her free to operate. The unfortunate thing about her depression is that it developed into hostility towards me and the children. Now as soon as the depression lifted, as far as she was concerned, things straightened out. As soon as her depression lifted, we had no problems. (This is said emphatically, facing the group worker.) We had differences of opinion, but we had no problems.

> **Worker:** It sounds like it has been tough for her and also tough for you.

> **Lou:** Oh, yes! The unfortunate thing as far as we were concerned is that we did not have a psychiatrist who understood what the relationship was. He took our problems as a family problem. His suggestion after a while was that if we weren't getting along together, we should separate. I felt I really didn't like that because I knew that wasn't the problem. The problem was getting Rose out of her depression.

Lou had begun presenting the problem the way one partner often does in a couples' group. The problem was essentially the other partner who, in some way, needed to be "fixed." This is the way one partner often experiences things, and it is important that the group worker attempt to understand and express that understanding of the members' feelings as they are presented. When I show this tape to students, one will often confront me for "allowing" Lou to talk about his wife as the "identified patient." Many students in the class identify with his wife and become angry with Lou for not taking responsibility for his part in the problem. I point out that in the first few minutes of this session this couple is acting out the very problem they have come to get help with. Lou is saying, "Do you want to see how I deny the problem and blame it all on Rose? Just watch me!" Rose is saying, "Yes, and watch how I sit here passively, letting Lou talk about me." I point out to the student that it doesn't make sense for me to get angry at these clients for having the very problem the group was established to deal with. Also, before I confront Lou, I have to build up a fund of support. In this case I attempt to do that by my comment about this experience being tough on his wife, and on himself. He talks about his wife, while I come back to him. Later in the session, this same client drops some of his defenses.

Some observers wonder about my letting Lou continue to talk instead of immediately involving other members. It seemed obvious to me that the second client, the group, was listening to what Lou had to say and did not mind his going on at some length. Group members begin first sessions with various patterns of behavior. Those who are used to being quiet and withdrawn in new situations will begin that way. Those who are used to speaking and jumping in quickly, such as Lou, will begin that way. Each member is entitled to his own defenses in the beginning, and it is important that the group leader respect them. When a group member speaks for a period of time, keeping to the subject, usually only the leader feels nervous. The other group members are often relieved that someone else has begun the discussion. In this case, the tuning-in work from the individual session had alerted us to Lou's strong feelings toward helping professionals who he felt had not been helpful. I had strategized to reach directly if I felt there were indirect cues related to us, the group workers. I did so at this point in the following way:

> **Worker:** Are you worried that I and the other group leaders might take the same position with you and Rose?
>
> **Lou:** Well, I don't know (voice slightly rising with annoyance). I'm not worried; I'm past that stage (accompanied with a harsh laugh). I'm just relating what happened, because I know where I'm at (said emphatically). To be very frank, my opinion of psychiatrists is very low, and I can cite two hours of experiences of what I have been through, my friends have been through, to show you exactly what I mean. This was a good case in point, his making a suggestion that we should separate because of the problem.
>
> **Worker:** After 45 years I can imagine that must have hit you as a terrible blow.
>
> **Lou:** Well, sure it did.
>
> **Worker:** Lou, do you think we could move around the circle a bit and also hear from the others as to what they see some of the problems to be?

In retrospect, I think Lou responded somewhat angrily partly because of the way I made my statement, "Are you worried that I and the other group leaders might take the same position with you and Rose?" I wanted to open up Lou's concerns about what kind of workers we would be; however, my attempt was not direct or clear enough. Instead of asking for further elaboration from Lou, or perhaps, asking if others in the group had similar experiences or relations, I suggested we allow others to exchange problems by "moving around the circle." It is important to encourage such an exchange of problems; however, further exploration of the authority theme was also important. Fortunately I had an opportunity to "catch my mistake" later in the session when I returned to the initial concerns raised by Lou. Lou responded to my suggestion that we "hear from the others" by turning to his wife.

> **Lou:** Sure, you're on. Go ahead, dear. (He turns to his wife.)
>
> **Rose:** I think I'll pass right now (said in a slow, even way, with no evidence of affect).
>
> **Worker:** That's fine. How about some others? You don't have to go in order, and you know, you can also respond to what Lou just said if you like, as well as

adding some of you own issues. We won't solve all of the problems tonight; I hope you realize that. (Some laughter by the group members) But what we would like to try and do is get a feel for how they seem to you right now. That can help us get a sense of what we need to talk about, and I think Lou has helped us get started. (At this point, John takes off his coat and seems to settle back in his chair.)

Louise: (John's wife, who is now speaking directly to Lou) I can understand what Lou means because depression has been our problem as well. I have gotten into such a state of depression that I can't function as a mother or a wife. I feel I have lost my identity. (This is all said with a very flat affect.) And I don't think that separation is the answer either. And I have had some pretty bad psychiatrists as well, so I can really feel for you when you say that, Lou. I can understand that. But the problem is to be able to sort out and find out what feelings I really have and recognize them for what they are and try to get myself out of the hole that I fell into, and that's the tough part.

Worker: How does it affect your relationship with John?

Louise: It's very strenuous. There is a lot of strain and tension when I'm sick and down and I put the responsibility for taking care of the household on John's shoulders. There is a breaking point for him somewhere there; I want to catch it before we get there. (Pause, worker is nodding and other members are listening intently) That's about it. (Brief silence)

John: Our biggest problem, or Louise's biggest problem, is due to her migraine headaches. She's had them ever since she was five years old. This is where the whole problem stemmed from, those migraine headaches. And this new depression which she seems to have gotten in the last few months.

Worker: Anything special happen within the last few months?

John: No, it has been actually a very quiet time this summer.

Louise: I think it is things that have been festering for a long time.

Worker: For example?

Louise: I don't know. I can't put my finger on what they are.

Worker: (Speaking to John) This depression came as a surprise to you, did it?

John: Yes, it did.

Worker: How do you see the problem, John? What would you like to see different in the relationship?

John goes on to describe how they don't do much together as a couple anymore and that he would like to see Louise get back on her feet so they can have some fun the way they used to. Discussion continued around the circle, with Fran and Rick looking at each other as if to ask who would go first. I verbalized this, and Fran begged off, saying that she didn't feel comfortable starting right away and that she would get in a bit later. Her husband, Rick, responded to my question by saying he was wondering why he was there because he knows that he has, or rather, they have, a problem, but what the problem is, is hard to define. Fran coached him at this point by whispering in his ear the word "communication." They seemed to agree that that's the problem, but when I asked for elaboration, Rick said, "That's not my problem, that's Fran's problem." Rick then took a further step for the group by entering a taboo area.

Rick: I guess if you get right down to basics, it would have to be sexual intimacy. I have been going along for a little over seven years, and now I find that I'm all alone. Fran's gone on a trip, and we're really in the very rocky stages of breaking up. (Some shaky emotion in his voice as he is speaking.) For the last six months, we have sort of been trying to recover, but it's still pretty shaky.

Worker: It must feel pretty dicey for you right now.

Rick: Right. (With resignation in his voice)

Worker: What would you like to be different? What would you like to see changed in your marriage?

Rick: (After a deep sigh to get his breath) There are times when everything is just fine, it seems to be going along smoothly, but just to say what I would like would be tough to put my finger on.

Worker: How would you like the relationship to be with Fran?

Rick: I think I would like it to be peaceful at all times. We have been getting into a lot of fights and just recently we have been getting into a lot of physical fights. A peaceful relationship, that's what I would really go for.

Worker: How about you, Fran, do you have any ideas now?

Fran: No, can we come back to me?

Worker: Sure.

The discussion continued with Sally talking about her marriage. This was difficult because her husband, Len, was not present. She described it from her perspective. Her description was filled with interpretations that had obviously been gleaned from years of involvement in various forms of analysis. The group listened intently to her stories. She also responded to Louise's comments about migraine headaches, mentioning that she had had them as well, and then she and Louise exchanged some mutual understanding. After Sally finished her description, there was a long silence as the group seemed unsure about where to go.

Worker: (Turning to Lou) I didn't mean to stop you before, Lou, if you want to get in again.

Lou: No, that's OK (laughing). I could go on for hours.

Worker: Oh, they won't mind, you know (pointing to the group), they would be glad. (Most of the group members laugh at this.)

Lou: I want to give others the opportunity to speak because, after all, I have been married over 45 years, so I have an accumulation of incidents.

At this point, I picked up the theme that had been common to many of the presentations: "helping people" who had not really helped. I had reached for this theme earlier in the session in relation to the role played by me and my co-workers, but Lou had not accepted my invitation. I believe the relationship between the group and the group leader is a central question at the beginning of each new group. Some discussion needs to take place on this issue so that the group can begin to work on what was called in Part II the "authority theme," the relationship between the person who offers help and the person who takes help. It is a powerful factor in the first group session, and for the group to develop properly, the worker must begin to deal with it.

During the problem-swapping exercise, I had attempted to express my empathic responses to the concerns as they were raised, taking care not to express judgments on their feelings and actions. Even this brief period had built up a sufficient fund of positive relationship that I was able to reach for some discussion on this difficult theme. If the group was to start to develop as a healthy organism, it would need to begin to sort out its relationship to me as the leader and the person in authority. Since this is a taboo subject, it would require considerable effort on my part to make it clear that the topic was open to discussion. I decided to return to the theme of helpers who had not helped. It is important to note that I returned to this issue directly by pointing out to the group members that I thought such a discussion might be important, so that they could be involved with full knowledge of the process. The group discussion that followed, led by Lou who was an internal leader on this issue, was a critical factor contributing to a striking change in the group atmosphere and to its successful beginning.

> **Worker:** I have noticed a theme that has cut across a number of your presentations that I think is important for us to talk about. A number of you have commented on helping people who have not been very successful—psychiatrists you have had in the past, doctors, and so on. (Group members all nod, saying yes.) Can you stay on that for a minute in terms of the things in your experiences that you found difficult? The reason I think it is important is because it would be a way of your letting me and my co-leaders know what you would not find helpful from us.

This is the second time I reached for some comments about the group members' concern about us. This time, since a relationship was beginning, and since I reached in a way that was less threatening, they were ready to take me up. Lou volunteered to begin the discussion. He took us back to the year 1940 when he had his own business. He described some of the pressures on him concerning economic conditions and a rash he developed on his leg. His doctor referred him to a psychiatrist who was brand new at the hospital. It was his first job. Lou's enthusiasm and feelings while describing this experience captured the attention of the group. They smiled and nodded agreement with his comments as he continued his story.

As he was about to describe his encounter, the door to the group room opened and the fifth couple, Frank and Jane, arrived late. It is not unusual for group members to arrive late for a first session. It usually presents a dilemma for the group worker: What do I do? In this case, I had the new couple introduce themselves, and I asked the other couples to give their names as well. I then briefly summarized the contract, explaining that we had been hearing about some problems to help get a feel for the concerns that had brought the couples to this session, and pointed out that one theme that kept recurring had to do with helping people who had not been very helpful. I said that we were focusing on this right now and that just before they had entered, we had been with Lou in 1940. With that, I turned back to Lou to continue, and the group picked up where it had left off. I think that it is important to recognize the entrance of the new group members and help them connect to the group but, at the same time, I think it would be a mistake to take a great deal of time to start again. As will become clear later in this group session, these group members were late for a reason; their lateness was their way of handling a new and frightening experience.

Lou continued his story of his first encounter with the young psychiatrist, indicating that the psychiatrist had tried to lead him indirectly to recognizing that he had a marital problem. As Lou put it, "I was talking about the economic conditions and the problems of the time, and he kept coming back to the wife and the kids, and the wife and the kids, and the wife and the kids...until I said to him, 'Are you trying to tell me my problem is with my wife and my kids?'" Lou went on to say that when the psychiatrist indicated it was, he stood up, called him a charlatan and quickly got out of the office as the enraged psychiatrist came out from behind the desk shaking his fist at him.

> **Lou:** OK. I knew that my wife and my family were part of the problem, but I also knew that they were not at the core of the problem. They were a contributing factor because of the social and economic conditions. I went to this guy to get rid of this rash on my leg and not to have him tell me that my wife and my kids were giving me the problem. It took a while for the rash to go away, but eventually it did. That was item number one. I am going to skip a lot of the intervening incidents that had to do with families, and I will go to the one which we just experienced recently. We went to a psychiatrist in the community for two and one-half years... (and then with emphasis) two and one-half years! I knew I had to go with her to give her some support plus I wanted to find out what made her tick. I couldn't understand her depression. I had been down in the dumps and felt blue, but I had never felt depressed as she seemed to feel. He asked her a lot of questions, asked me a lot of questions, tried to have us do some play acting and had us try and discuss the problems. "You're not communicating" was his term. I didn't know what he was talking about when he said we didn't communicate, so we tried to communicate. But nothing really came of it because we saw we weren't communicating.

As Lou related his experiences, he was describing a number of techniques that apparently had been used to try to help him and his wife deal with their problems. The central theme appeared to be that of a helping person who had decided what the problem was and was now acting in order to educate them as to its nature.

Lou was resentful of this approach and resisted it in most of the sessions. And yet, part of him deep inside knew that there was a problem that he attempted to deal with in his own way. He described an incident when he had taken a tape recorder home and recorded a conversation with his wife, listening to it later. His description of the aftermath of this tape recording contained the first overt expression of the sadness and pain the couple had felt but were not ready to share. In this case, I believe it was necessary for Lou to share first the anger and the frustration at the helping people who had not understood him before he was willing to share his hurt and pain.

> **Lou:** We talked for about 15 minutes, and I realized when we played the tape back, that I was screaming at Rose. Now I never realized that I was screaming at her. But I heard my voice. (Lou clears his throat at this point and begins to choke up, obviously feeling emotions and trying to fight back his tears.) This is a little rough for me, can I have some water?
>
> **Worker:** (Getting a glass of water from the decanter) Sure you can, Lou, take your time.
>
> **Lou:** It's kind of tough to get over the fact that I was screaming at her. Then I realized that when I was screaming at her, I was treating her like a kid. I took this tape to the psychiatrist, and he couldn't hear the screaming. He got nothing out of it.
>
> **Worker:** He didn't seem to understand how it felt to you to hear yourself screaming?

Lou: That's right. He didn't even hear me screaming. The other thing he tried to get us to do which I found really devastating is he tried to get us to reverse roles; she should be me and I should be her. OK, we tried it. But while we were doing it, I was thinking to myself: "Now, if that isn't stupid, I don't know what is." (Turning to me at this point) But you're a psychiatrist, you know what the score is. How can you reverse roles when I'm not feeling like she's feeling and she doesn't feel like I do? How can I communicate? Well, it was things like that that had been going on for two and one-half years, and when we had finished, I was nowhere nearer being helped to be able to live with Rose than I was when we started. Now that's two and one-half years! It isn't that we didn't try; both of us used to discuss this. Rose went back to the doctor, but I said I wouldn't go because I found I was just getting more frustrated.

At this point, there was some discussion on the part of group members about the use of the tape recorder. Rick thought it was a good idea and wondered if Lou had tried it again. Lou said he hadn't. The conversation returned to his feelings of frustration and his sense of not having been helped.

Lou: I felt stupid. The psychiatrist kept telling me something, and no matter how hard I tried, I simply couldn't understand.

Worker: You also seem to be saying, not only couldn't you understand him, but he didn't seem to be understanding you.

Lou: Well, yes. Peculiarly enough, that thought had not occurred to me. I felt, well you are a professional (facing the worker at this point), so what you're doing, you're doing on purpose. You know what you're supposed to be doing. And whether you understand me or not is immaterial. That's not what the game is. It's my responsibility to understand what you, if you are the psychiatrist, are saying. (There was anger in his voice.)

Worker: If you're asking us (referring to the other co-workers) in this group, that's not the way I see it. I think that if we can be of any help to you or the other group members, the help will be in our listening and in our trying to understand exactly how you see it. The gimmicks and the things that seem to get tried on you is not my idea of how we can help. You'll have to wait to see if I mean that.

Lou: Yeah, we'll see.

Worker: I think you folks have a powerful lot of help to give each other. And essentially, what I will try and do is to help you do that. And I'll share my own ideas along the way. But I have no answers or simple solutions.

Lou: Then, well, OK.

(General silence in the group as the members appear to be taking in the meaning of the words)

Co-Worker: I'd like to know, Lou, as we go along, how you see things. So, if you're feeling stupid or whatever, you'll let us know.

Worker: It might be because we've said something dumb (some subdued laughter in the group).

Although I had described the group as a mutual aid group in the opening statement, it was only at this point that the members really began to have a sense of how the group might work. Also, the clarification of the group worker's role contained in this exchange was actually "heard." Lou, playing the role of an internal group leader, was able to articulate the fears and concerns that group members felt about the potential power invested in the group worker's role. He provided the opportunity for an initial clarification of who we were as group leaders and what we did. Skills of accepting and understanding his feelings and his frustrations, and of helping to connect his past experiences to the present moment, were crucial in this session. The feeling in the group was that we had moved past the first step in building our relationship. The authority theme was not finished as a topic of discussion; however, one could sense that an important start had been made. Following this exchange, the group members were able to move into work on their contract with more energy, involvement, and inter-member interaction.

The Work Continues

With a two-hour session it was possible to move past problem swapping and clarification of purpose and worker role into beginning efforts to focus on an example of what the work might consist of. Interestingly enough, Frank and Jane, the couple who had arrived late, provided an opportunity to do this. Frank began to share, with some elaborative assistance from the group worker, a problem that they were experiencing in relation to his wife's teenage sons who were living with them. It was an interesting example of a group member raising a problem tentatively, moving quickly back and forth between the implications of the difficulty for the couple and his relationship to the children. He spoke of the sexual difficulty they had, while attributing most of it to a medical problem he was having treated and also to the lack of privacy in their home. The bedroom door was not locked at any time, and the children would wander in without notice. As Frank was sharing this dilemma, he phrased it in terms of his problem with his stepsons, but one could hear throughout the discussion hints of the implications for his relationship to his wife. Each time the worker would acknowledge, even gently, the implication for the relationship, Frank would back off slightly, and both he and Jane would be quick to reassure the group of the positive nature of their communications.

It is not unusual for group members to use the early sessions to raise "near" problems in a way that presents them as issues and at the same time defends them from discussion. This matter was discussed in Part II in relation to the ambivalence of the client to deal with real concerns. It is also necessary for the group members to test the reaction of a group worker and the other members. Group members often feel it would be unwise to rush right in until they know how their feelings and thoughts are going to be treated, whether they will be met with support or confrontation, and whether it is OK to share their real feelings and concerns. Not only are the group members worried about the worker and the other members, they are also concerned about their partners. Each of the couples has developed a "culture" in their marriage that has included certain norms, behaviors, taboo areas, rules for interaction, and so on. The group will in many ways be a place for them to learn how to change that culture, or at least those parts of it that are not conducive to strengthening their marriage. With so many factors to consider, however, it is not unusual for group members to come close to a concern while watching to see how the partner, the other group members, and the group workers will react. Timing is important in a first session, and it would therefore be a mistake for a group worker to attack defenses at a point when the group member greatly needs them.

As Frank began to describe his efforts to deal with the children about this issue of privacy, the worker suggested that they might use this as an example of one of the ways in which the group members might help each other: (speaking to the group) "Perhaps we can use this as an example of how we can be helpful. Frank can describe the conversation he had with his son, and the rest of the group members might respond by suggesting how they would have reacted if they had been the son. We could do some thinking with Frank about how he might handle this kind of an issue." The group members agreed, and Frank went into some details of a conversation in which he sarcastically implied to the son that they needed some privacy. After a number of group members supported his right to privacy, the co-worker pointed out that it would be difficult to take his comments seriously because he always seemed to be joking as he described things and never seemed as if he could really get angry. This triggered a response on the part of his wife, Jane.

> **Jane:** Aha! That's it exactly. Frank has trouble getting angry. Ever since he has been a kid, he has been afraid to be direct and angry with people. I keep telling him, why don't you let yourself get angry and blow off steam? He says that he feels that it is just not the thing to do. You just don't do it. I do it all the time. I didn't use to, but now I do, and I get angry at least a couple of times a day.
>
> **Frank:** You know the kids are scared of you because you get angry so much.
>
> **Worker:** (Noticing that Sally appears to want to say something) Go ahead, Sally, get in.
>
> **Sally:** (Laughing as she speaks to Frank) You've got to meet my Len! (The whole group, including Frank, erupts in a great roar of laughter.) You sound like two of the same kind, and you're hard to live with.
>
> **Worker:** Frank, what made it hard for you to speak seriously to your son right then?
>
> **Frank:** I don't know. Well, you know the image of a stepfather like in the fairy-tale books, he is like a monster. I've got a nice thing starting to build with these boys, and I don't want to ruin it.
>
> **Worker:** You are afraid they would get angry if you were direct and honest.
>
> **Jane:** (Laughing, but with a touch of anger) It's all up in your head.
>
> **Worker:** You know, Jane, I think Frank really is worried about that.
>
> **Frank:** I do worry about that. I really do.

In response to the worker's question, "What are you afraid might happen?" Frank goes on to describe the relationship the children had with Jane's former husband, of some of his fears of being unable to prevent the continuation of the same coldness and the problems that he envisioned in that relationship.

> **Frank:** It was because I didn't want to hurt that relationship that I more or less…symbolized what I really meant.
>
> **Worker:** You kind of hinted at what you felt rather than saying it directly.
>
> **Frank:** Well, it's like you are in a washroom and you saw a fellow peeing on the floor. You would probably say, "Hey, you missed, fella." (Group members roar with laughter at his story.)

Frank went on to describe how he finally had to speak directly with the son. He described, much to his wife's surprise, a very direct conversation in which he explained the problem to the son. Frank's point was that since that time, the son had been much more understanding about not interrupting. At this point in the group session, Lou, who had been listening intently, moved in and took responsibility for the group process. In a striking illustration of internal leadership at an early stage in the group development, Lou moved directly from the general discussion of anger and indirect communication to the implications for each couple. The worker had noticed during the discussion that on a number of occasions Lou had attempted to whisper to his wife, Rose, and to ask her a question but she had refused to respond, and instead had sat impassive and expressionless. Lou now used the group and this theme to deal with his concern—a concern that was common to all members. I believe that he was able to make this direct intervention and assume some leadership responsibility in the group because the way had been cleared through our earlier discussion of the role of the worker. This was an example of Lou accepting the worker's invitation for the group members to begin to own their own group.

> **Worker:** (Noting Lou's indirect communication of his desire to get into the discussion) Were you going to say something, Lou?
>
> **Lou:** Something has come up here which I would like each couple in turn to answer if they can. (Turning to John, he asks his name, which John gives him.) I would like each couple to add to this in turn if they can. John, do you get really mad at Louise? I mean really mad, peed off? Do you yell at her, do you tell her off?
>
> **John:** Not really.
>
> **Lou:** Why not?
>
> **John:** That's my style, that's the way I have been all my life.
>
> **Lou:** Louise, how about you?
>
> **Louise:** I'll probably hold back until as long as possible and then usually end up to where I'm in tears, or slam cupboards or dishes, or give John a cold shoulder rather than coming right out and saying that I'm angry. (As Louise is speaking, Lou is nodding and saying yes.)
>
> **Lou:** Why? By the way, I am referring to Rose and myself right now when I'm asking this question and I...want to...hear from everyone.
>
> **John:** It happens sometimes, but it is really rare that we actually yell at each other. (Louise shakes her head, agreeing.)
>
> **Lou:** Are you afraid to get angry, either one of you?
>
> **John:** I don't think I'm afraid. I don't have a problem yelling at other people. It's kinda strange. I don't know why.
>
> **Lou:** How about you, Frank and Jane?

Jane and Frank both discussed her getting angry regularly, blowing her top all the time. She indicated that it worried her. Frank said he had trouble getting angry directly at Jane and gave an example of her not sharing her load of chores (they are both working) and that he had been getting angry at that because it was setting a bad example for the kids, but that he had not told her. He paused when he said that, and then said, "I guess I hadn't said that to you until tonight." As the conversation went on, the group worker was monitoring the members, making sure they were involved and paying attention. Occasionally he would comment on some of the feelings associated with the comments.

> **Lou:** (Directly to Jane) You have no aversions about getting mad, I mean spontaneously mad?
>
> **Jane:** What other way is there to get mad?

Lou: You don't build anything up and then have it boil over?

Jane: Not anymore, not now.

After a pause, the worker turned to Lou and said, "Stay with it." Lou responded, "Fine, because something is happening here that happens to us (pointing to his silent wife, Rose) and I would like to hear from everyone in the group on this." At that point he asked Fran, who had declined to speak thus far, if she got mad.

Fran: I hold it for a little while, and then I start and I pick, and I can't stop at the issue. Often I can't even determine what the issue is at the time. Since I can't figure out what it is, I go through the whole gamut to make sure I get to the right one. And—maybe I should let Rick speak for himself—my opinion is that he's quiet. He listens to all of this without a comment back. That really drives me out of my mind. I can't stand the silence. If only he would yell! Even if I'm wrong, then I know I'm wrong. But like I said, I go over the whole ballpark because I know I may hit the right one, since the right one is in there somewhere. There's not much of a reaction, because Rick is the quiet type. He doesn't like to argue or fight. And the quieter he seems to get, the angrier I get. I have to push even harder. It's just recently, the last couple of months, that we've started to fight physically. We've been married for seven years, and this is just coming out now. Well, I didn't think that Rick had a breaking point and that he could get that mad. And I wasn't even aware that I could get that mad, but I can. I'm the pusher, I'm the one—the things that I could say could definitely curl your hair.

Rick: She basically said it all for me.

Fran: And that's usual, too.

Lou: (Smiling in a supportive way) Your hair looks pretty straight to me, Rick.

Rick: (Sighing) It's been a long day. Yes, I am the quiet type, and I have a very long fuse, but once it gets to the end, look out. I've done some stupid things in my time, and they usually end up costing me. I guess I just reach my breaking point and take the frustration out somewhere. If it happens that Fran is taking hers out on me, I try and cool it as long as I can, but then I can only take so much of that, and we end up going at each other. That's about it.

Lou: Let me ask you a question, Rick. When Fran is at you like she does, is it that you don't want to or are you afraid of hurting her feelings so that she'll come back at you again and this thing will snowball, or is it that you have a reluctance and you feel you'll let her get it off her chest and then things will calm down again? Which of these is it?

Rick: I guess I'm just hoping that she'll get it off her chest and things will calm down again. But it doesn't work that way.

Worker: (Turning to Lou) If I can just ask Rick this before you go on, Lou—what's going on inside of your guts when Fran is pushing that way? What do you feel?

Rick: (Takes a big sigh before he speaks) Well, I guess I'm trying to just block everything out of my mind. That's the reason I become quiet, even go to the point of reading the newspaper and just completely try to wipe it out.

Worker: Because it hurts?

Rick: Right.

Lou continued, turning to Sally, who also described how she saw herself in Fran since her husband, Len, is like Rick, the quiet type. She described a number of similar examples, finally ending by saying, "I don't think I have ever found his boiling point. Heaven help me if I ever do."

> **Worker:** That must be as hard as having found it.
>
> **Sally:** Yes, I guess it is. The problem is that you hoard the hurts and when you get a chance, zap, you give them right back. The sad part is that I really don't think Len has a mean bone in his body.

There is a long silence after this as the group waits in anticipation. The next speaker should be Rose, Lou's wife, who has not said a word nor changed her expression during the entire session. She has been watching and listening intently. Because of her silence, her comments at this point have a stunning impact on the group members as well as the group worker.

> **Rose:** Well, I think there is a common thread running through with everyone and part of it is anger, and there may be some recriminations amongst the couples here. Some people have learned to live with it, but obviously, those of us here have not. And no matter how long you're married, it's still something you don't know how to handle. I found that I got very angry here and…
>
> **Worker:** You mean here tonight?
>
> **Rose:** Yes, but I wasn't going to interrupt my husband to tell him that I didn't want him to say that or I didn't like what he was saying. So, I'm back to zero, not just one. I can pack my bags and go back to the hospital. (At this comment, her husband, Lou, flinches almost as if in pain and looked towards the worker.) And I don't feel comfortable talking about it.
>
> **Worker:** It's hard even now, isn't it?
>
> **Rose:** Yes, but I made up my mind I was at the point where I would pack my bags or talk.
>
> **Worker:** I'm glad you talked.
>
> **Lou:** (His face brightening) Well, I have been thinking that that was about the only way I could get Rose to talk and to burst open.
>
> **Rose:** Sure, well, I knew that's what was going on.
>
> **Lou:** She wasn't going to say anything to me. I asked her during the group if she was mad, and she said she was. I asked if she would say something, and she said no.
>
> **Rose:** Right, I said no.
>
> **Lou:** Plus the fact that what goes on is that all our lives both of us have always been afraid of hurting each other.
>
> **Rose:** So, we kept quiet. Or else one spoke and said too much. I always felt that Lou had spoken lots more than I did. Now, I had an opportunity to do a lot of speaking at the hospital for five weeks, and certainly I found it helped me quite a bit. I told myself and the people there that I was going to try and remember to use everything they taught me. And there's really no way. Because different things come up and, say, they're not in the book that I went by.
>
> **Worker:** I guess you have to write your own book, then.

Rose: That's right. I'm not very quick on my feet, and I don't think my mind operates very quickly either. But how to deal with anger seems to be everyone's particular problem. (A pause in the group as Rose's words sink in)

Worker: It's close to the end of our session, and I wonder if what we haven't done is identify a common theme and issue that we might want to look at in more depth next week. Perhaps you could be prepared to share some of the incidents and difficulties, because I think if you can bring some of those arguments from the outside into here, where it is a little safer, and where there are people around to help, maybe it's possible to learn to do what Rose did just now without hurting. Perhaps it is possible to say what you are really thinking and what you're felling without having to store up the hurts. My own feeling is that any real, intimate relationship has to have both some loving and some fighting. That comes with the territory. But it's a hard thing to do. We simply haven't learned how to do it. So maybe this could be a safe area to test it out. Does that make any sense to the rest of you? (Group members nod.) Maybe we could pick up on this next week as something that we're interested in. How do you find a way of saying what you're really thinking and feeling towards each other without wiping each other out?

Jane: Is there a way to do that?

Worker: I think so, but why don't we test that out here in the group? If there isn't, though, then I think we're in trouble, because I don't think you could really care for each other if you can't also get angry at each other. Does that make some sense to the whole group? (Once again, there is some nodding in agreement.) What we could do is different couples could bring some examples. Maybe you'll have a hard time during the week that's tough to handle. Well, we could go over that with you here in the group and see if we can find a way of helping you identify what you were really feeling and also be able to say it directly and clearly in a way that keeps communication open. I think this is the way it would work. Even if one couple raises a specific example, the rest of us could learn in helping them with that example. So, you would get something out of each week's session even if you weren't talking about your own marriages.

With a clear contract and some work in the beginning of the session that helped create the safe conditions within the group, group members felt free to begin to risk themselves. The group has moved directly to one of the core issues in marital relationships. What is striking is the way the group members themselves directed the emergence of this theme. Each group is different, since it reflects the strengths and experiences as well as the weaknesses of its members. Lou brought a sense of urgency and a willingness to risk himself to the group that helped it not only tackle the issue of authority directly and constructively but also helped it to move past its early defenses into the common concerns they had about their relationships with teach other. Although the particular way in which this group worked during its first session is unique, I do not believe the level of its work or the speed with which it began is at all unusual. I believe it reflected the sense of urgency of the group members, the clarity of group purpose, and worker role. The members were willing to attack the issue of authority directly, and the worker consistently tried to articulate the feelings expressed by the group members, even being slightly ahead of them. Given these core conditions, the impetus of the group members carried them toward productive work.

The Ending and Transition Stage

Now that the session was nearly over and a consensus had been reached on a theme for additional work, the ending and transition phase of this session continued with an opportunity for evaluative comments. The worker wished in the first session to encourage members to talk about the way the group was working.

Worker: We have five minutes left. This was our first session. I would like you to take a few minutes to share with each other and with us what your reactions are. What are your feelings and your thoughts? How has this session hit you? What will you be saying to each other on your way home in the car about this evening's session? It's important that you say it now.

Rose: Well, I have the feeling that the first thing out the door, Lou is going to ask me what it is he said that made me angry. I can't define it right now. I'd have to pull it out of my head.

Louise: That's tough. That's really tough trying to figure out what it is that makes you angry. I feel that way, too. When I was an inpatient and someone showed me that I was angry at a resident and why I was angry, well that was fine; I was able to do a little bit of yelling and get it off my chest. But it's not always easy to put my finger on what it is I'm feeling.

Worker: Maybe that's what we can do here—help you figure out what those feelings are. (Turning to Lou) What's your reaction? I'm really interested in your reaction because I have a feeling that you came in here thinking about all of the people in the past who haven't been helpful. Where do we stand so far?

Lou: So far I feel that we're beginning to break a little new ground. Actually, the most important thing that happened to me tonight was Rose getting mad.

Worker: Is it easier to handle it when you know where she stands?

Lou: No, not really, I don't know where she stands. I knew she was mad; I asked her to tell me what she's mad about, but she said no. The reason I am feeling good about this is that she has just gone through five weeks as an inpatient, and I can assure you (voice cracking) I've just gone through the same five weeks.

Worker: I think these things change step by small step and perhaps tonight made a beginning. Perhaps if you aren't too harsh with yourself and demand too much, you have a chance of doing it. I am glad it hit you that way. How about the others, what will your reactions be tonight?

Frank: Whew!

Jane: (Laughing) I think we were so apprehensive about what would happen here tonight it wasn't funny.

Worker: What were you afraid of?

Jane: Well, I guess it was the fear of the unknown, and yet when we got here, we immediately started to sense that here are people who are concerned, who care, and this came right to the fore.

Lou: Larry, I'd like to make a comment here. Our youngest son is 36 and one of the things he complained about to us was that "You never taught me how to argue with my wife." I wondered where in the world did he get the idea that it was necessary to argue with each other. As time went on, I realized that we used to argue and keep things on the inside. My son today is having problems, and he even called me last night on the very same subject. The important thing he said was, "You haven't taught us how to argue." Oh, yes… not only that but, "You haven't taught us how to argue and to win the argument." (The group roared with laughter.)

Other members of the group were given a chance to comment. Frank pointed out that he and Jane were late partly because they were ambivalent about coming. He had been telling my co-worker all week that he wasn't sure whether he really belonged here. As he described his conversations, he laughed along with the other members of the group. They all acknowledged that coming to the first session had been frightening. Frank went on to say that what impressed him was the people in the group; they all seemed to be a really "super bunch," and that helped a lot. Lou commented that it was reassuring to find out that he wasn't alone and that others had the same feelings.

After some additional positive comments, I pointed out that it would also be important to share their negative reactions or questions; these were tough to share but were also important. Sally indicated her concern about whether or not the group would really help, if anything would really change. She was also worried about her husband Len having missed the first meeting. We talked about this, and I asked the group to strategize how we might bring Len into the second meeting quickly, since he would be feeling a bit like an outsider, having missed this first session. I then told Sally that there were no promises, no sure answers or easy solutions. Marriage is hard work, as she knew, but perhaps through the group we might be able to offer some support and help with their difficult tasks. She nodded in agreement. Fran and Rick responded that they had felt a bit shy and found it difficult to talk in the group. John and Louise jumped in and reassured them, saying that they thought they had participated quite a bit. I pointed out that they had risked some very difficult and hard-to-talk-about subjects in the discussion with the group and gave them credit for that. Rick said that after a week or two he would probably find it easier getting in; I told him to take his time, that he would get in as he felt comfortable.

As the evaluation seemed to be coming to an end, I pointed out that there were three rules we would follow in the group. I explained that members were expected to come each week and that it was OK to come even if your partner could not make it because of illness or some other reason. I said that material they shared with each other should be treated as confidential so that they could all feel that the other couples in the group would not be talking about them to outsiders. I also asked that if they wanted to drop out of the group at any time before the 23 sessions we had planned were over, they would agree to come back and discuss it with the group before quitting. All agreed that these seemed to be reasonable rules. I then complimented them on what I thought was an excellent start. I told them I could understand how nervous they must have felt at the beginning, since I felt a little of that nervousness, too, but that I thought they were off on some important work, and that boded well for our future. The session ended at this point, but people did not leave immediately; instead they milled around talking to other members and the workers. Then, slowly, the group members left the room.

This has been a detailed description of the first session of one kind of group. Perhaps the reader will immediately be thinking about some of the differences in the groups he or she has led. For example, these were generally articulate group members. They had volunteered to come to the group session and were not there under duress. The group leaders carried no additional functional responsibilities in relation to the members (e.g., a child welfare protective function). Of course, there are differences between groups depending upon the setting, the members, the purpose, and so forth. Some of these are illustrated in the next chapter with brief excerpts from first sessions of groups from different contexts. Nonetheless, the basic dynamics and skills involved in effective beginnings with groups cut across these differences. You will find in our examples that when these principles are respected, they more often than not lead to an effective start. When these principles are ignored, they haunt both the group leader and the group members. First sessions are important because they lay a foundation for the difficult tasks to follow. If handled well, they can provide a fund of positive feeling as well as a clear framework, both of which will influence the remaining sessions.

One final note concerns a comment made by more than one social work student after watching the videotape of this session. Students are struck by Lou taking the initiative in asking the couples about anger in their relationships. The video images reveal my facial expression, which clearly indicates my delight at his moving into a leadership role. At one point I am asking Lou if it is all right for me to interrupt him and ask a member a question. The surprised students will ask, "Why did you let Lou take over your group?" My response is that it is not my group. The group belongs to the members, and the fact that they accepted my invitation to take over in the first session was a very positive sign and an indication of the strength of the group members. This exchange often triggers an important discussion of the fear of an inexperienced group leader of "losing control of the group." It takes some experience and growing confidence for the group leader to realize that the process of "letting go" is central for leading effective groups.

RECONTRACTING

Another common student reaction to the videotape of the couples' group just described is to feel somewhat intimidated. As they often put it, "My first session didn't go that way!" I reassure them that neither did my early efforts. Even if the neophyte group worker has done excellent preparatory work, is clear about the working contract, and has role-played an opening statement with a supervisor, unexpected events and problems may occur. Retrospective analysis often reveals that the worker has left something out or the words did not resemble the carefully constructed and rehearsed opening statement. New group workers are understandably nervous leading their first groups and should not be too hard on themselves. They also need to realize that they usually have an opportunity to recontract with a group if they don't get it right the first time. Even if they are able to begin exactly as planned, group members may not hear nor understand the opening statement. Contracting in an ongoing group always takes place over a number of sessions. The next three examples illustrate recontracting efforts.

Another common problem may be encountered when workers join an already functioning group and have to recontract around their role as leader and the purpose of the group. Joining an ongoing group as a co-leader and discovering that the contracting was never done or has been done badly can also be disconcerting. One student put it this way: "This sounds great in class, but I don't think the psychiatrist running our group has ever read your book!" In some circumstances, the ongoing group leaders have adopted a group practice model that operates under assumptions that differ from the interactional, mutual aid model put forward here. The student needs to be reassured that there are many frameworks for helping and that this group provides them with an opportunity to see another model in action. Also, elements of the interactional model can often be integrated easily into other frameworks. In some examples, there simply is no model at all. Groups can be disorganized, unfocused, with members and the group leaders unclear about the purpose. Group sessions can resemble individual counseling in a group, with each member being "helped" by the group leader in turn. In the second set of circumstances, it becomes the social worker's job to try to influence the process with co-leaders and members to recontract for a more effective group. The third example in this section illustrates this process in a psychiatric setting.

Recontracting with Your Own Group

It is usually possible to come back at a later session and initiate the contracting discussion. In the following illustration, a worker recontracted during the second session of a discussion group for adolescents who were attending a training workshop that was established to deal with work-related problems. The first meeting had been difficult, marked by acting-out behavior from the members, with the worker finding herself playing a police role. The acting-out behavior, in fact, reflected their lack of understanding about the purpose of this mandatory group and their resultant anxiety.

> **Worker:** OK. Let's get started. I overheard Roy sigh as he sat down and say, "Boy, is this boring." (When I commented on this, Roy grinned and looked surprised.)
>
> **Worker:** I don't think he is the only one who feels this way. Last week, after our meeting, Jimmy expressed doubts about whether this could be a good group. (Silence)
>
> **Jimmy:** I just meant that Lou (another staff member) could make us shut up and stop fooling around if he were here.
>
> **Worker:** Is that what you want me to do?
>
> **Jimmy:** Well, yeah. (Others agreed with him.)
>
> **Worker:** I don't think it's the leader's job to force everyone to listen and get involved. I'll help but not take that on entirely as my own job.
>
> **James:** You know, what we need in the workshop is filing cabinets to store the cards in. (Everyone agreed, and they all started talking at once.)
>
> **Worker:** Things are getting out of hand again. (Silence)
>
> **Roy:** Say something, will you!
>
> **Worker:** What do you want me to say?
>
> **Roy:** Anything!
>
> **Worker:** I guess it's hard for us to get down to what we are really here to do.
>
> **Roy:** Well, what are we here to do? I didn't even know about this until last week when Dennis told me it was time to go to the group about the workshop.
>
> **James:** I know why we are having the meetings. To get the filing cabinets and stuff like that.
>
> **Worker:** I think that's part of it, James. But there is another part to these meetings. It's a place where we can talk about what is going on in the workshop, what some of the problems might be for you down there, and also make connections from the workshop experience to the world of work outside. That is where you are all going eventually. You can relate past experiences you have had out there to what is going on here. (They all agreed this would be a good idea.)
>
> **James:** I'm here 'cause I got fired for always coming in late.

The worker's courageous invitation for feedback opens the door for the direct discussion of the working contract that was missing from the first session. The group members immediately took up her offer to expand the discussion to include their work experiences in general.

In the more detailed example that follows, we will see the worker with an open-ended group in a shelter for battered women begin a first session with a mixed message about the contract. In her opening statement she briefly mentions a number of powerful themes related to the abuse and oppression that have brought these women to the shelter. In her structuring of the first session, however, she moves immediately to her agenda of providing information on "independent living skills." Rather than structuring time for problem swapping, which would have allowed the women some control over the agenda, the worker makes the decision for them. If one applies the oppression psychology outlined in Chapter 2, encouraging these women to take control of their own group could be seen as an important step towards "independent living."

A number of group members signal that they are at a different place in their needs related to this group. While independent living skills, job opportunities, and so on, are all important for these women, at this moment their sense of urgency may be more connected to their abuse and their living situations. The worker continues to control the first session, providing a sermon about the importance of "community support." As we will see, her understanding and skill evolves over the next few sessions as she recontracts with the women.

Session 1

As I was setting the room up for the group session, one resident of the shelter arrived. She helped me arrange chairs and, as other residents arrived, she introduced me to them. I had planned to go around the room so that each woman could tell me her name, her length of stay at the house, and the number of children in her family, but I decided against it since we had already been introduced. Now I feel that I still should have asked them for a little more information about themselves. I did tell the women a few things about myself and then I stated the purpose of the group. I said, "The purpose of this group is to provide you with some helpful information that you can use once you leave the house. The group will also provide you with an opportunity to talk about your feelings, experiences, and concerns that you might have about the different topics we'll be discussing. Tonight's topic is independent living skills." I went on to say, "Some of you are here because of abuse either by a boyfriend or a husband. You may find tonight that you have some feelings in common with each other. Some of you may be here for reasons other than abuse, and you may have your own set of circumstances that you'll want to share. My role is to help you to talk and to listen to each other. So I hope that we can all learn tonight not only from the material I have brought but also from the comments that we share with one another."

I began by giving the women information about two job training programs. One woman, Linda, talked about a job training program that she had attended and how she had landed a job afterwards. Two other women talked about the skills they had, one in accounting, the other in word processing and stenography. Four out of the seven women were interested. The other three women showed no interest at all. I didn't ask them why they seemed uninterested. I feel that I should have confronted them.

From there we moved on to the subject of community support. I stated that many people think asking for help is a sign of weakness. People, in many cases, think it's important to handle problems on their own. I said I disagreed with this type of thinking. I said people who think this way are oftentimes worse off because individuals aren't always equipped to handle situations that come up on their own. I said that people who look to their community for support could be better off in many ways. I then asked the women if they had any ideas or suggestions on where to find community support when they leave the house. No one had any suggestions off the bat, so I mentioned places such as churches, local community action programs, etc.

Although the worker wrote "...we moved on to the subject...", she should have written "I moved on..."; clearly, the members did not move with her. In the next excerpt, an internal leader emerges to move the women to a discussion of the "here and now" of their experiences in the house and the pain of the abuse they carry with them.

One woman said she was very glad to be at the house. She said she came into the shelter wondering what the other women would be like and found out that many of the women were just like her. She said, "It feels good to be with people who have the same problem." She said that when she lived with her husband, he would be on her mind all day long. She would worry about what he would be like when he came home. Before she came to the house, she would stay with her parents when her husband became abusive. Eventually, her parents would talk her into going back with her husband. She said, "Here at the house, you get support. You're told he has a problem, not you." She said she was very glad to hear that. I said, "So it sounds as if you're relieved to be here." She said, "Yes."

Another woman said she used to wonder what her husband would find wrong when he came home. She also said he wouldn't allow her to talk with friends. I said, "You probably feel good that you don't have that pressure over you now." She agreed. In addition, she said she planned to attend Al-Anon meetings for support once she left the house.

In the next excerpt, one of the members sends a signal to the worker that the session is not meeting her needs. The worker's written comment about "reaction formation" indicates that she noted the negative feedback and reacted with internal anger and an external smile. The worker's early anxiety about doing a good job makes it hard for her to hear negative feedback. The group members' anxiety about their dependency upon the shelter may make it hard for them to share it. The discussion finally turns to money and issues of economic oppression that are closely tied to a major source of anxiety experienced by these women—economic survival. The worker does not understand the meaning of the "flight" behavior and thinks that she will need to do a better job at setting out the rules—a step that would cut off the expression of feeling, rather than dealing with it.

One woman who had left the group for 15 minutes came back and said, "What did I miss out on?" Angela, one of the uninterested women, said, "Oh, you only missed out on some boring information." I should have asked her why she found the information so boring. Instead, I just smiled at her (reaction formation?). Then Janice, a night staff person, joined the group. Everything was fine until she started talking with the woman next to her. They continued to talk between themselves for about five minutes. I didn't know how to handle this situation.

When we started to talk about the area of financial management and I mentioned budgeting, one woman said, "What do I want to know about budgeting? I don't have any money to budget." Then she said that actually she did want to know about budgeting. She felt that someone should have sat down with her at the welfare office and shown her how to get the most for her money. Angela said she was always worried about having enough money to make ends meet, and she didn't see what good a budget would do. Angela has four children, one of whom is handicapped. The group began to talk about how she could get help for the handicapped child with cerebral palsy. The women suggested that she or her social worker call a cerebral palsy foundation. I turned to Angela and said, "You must get very discouraged at times." She agreed.

As the discussion continued about financial management, the discussion became somewhat chaotic. People were talking at once, cutting each other off. The women were skipping from topic to topic. I finally asked them to please talk one at a time. For the most part three women were doing all the talking. I could see that the other women were not paying attention. Next week I'd like to lay down some ground rules for discussion and emphasize the fact that everyone has important comments to make and we should take the time to listen to one another.

With hindsight, the worker might have been able to address the second client, the group, by acknowledging that the discussion was hitting home for all of them. She could have identified the flight behavior as an understandable expression of the anxiety associated with the economic oppression and humiliation of being on welfare. These women had to demonstrate remarkable courage to overcome the economic restraints that our society places on them when they consider fleeing an abusive home. Inadequate financial supports function as a societal "shackle" helping to keep women chained to oppressive family situations. The worker might have responded to the group with the same empathy she had demonstrated moments before when she said to Angela, "You must get discouraged at times." The worker is surprised when another staff person intervenes with the offer of going to church the next Sunday. There is the possibility that this staff member responded to the group's anxious flight with what she felt might help.

Suddenly, Janice, the staff person, asked if anyone wanted to go to church the following Sunday. This question was somewhat disruptive because we were talking about managing money at this point. She may have been responding to our discussion earlier about finding community support. It's difficult to say. The discussion became focused again when Linda asked for information about apartment hunting. One woman said that transportation was a big problem. Everyone chimed in on this. One woman said they should write a letter to the governor asking him to supply a car for the shelter. The women got excited at this point. I agreed that it sounded like a good idea, and I asked who would be in charge of writing the letter. Pam volunteered. Janice, the staff person, said they could talk about the letter the next day at the house meeting.

I told them that we had discussed a number of important issues. I said I hoped they would be thinking about questions and ideas for next week's session on single parenting, and said I would see them next Wednesday night.

In the second session, once again the worker has planned an agenda for the session without the involvement of the women. Even the best plans can go awry, however, and the worker has problems with a film projector. The worker has a hidden agenda of selling to the mothers the importance of providing emotional support to their children, but the women need support for themselves to strengthen them for their children. The "deviant" member of the group the previous week, Angela, who had said that the group was boring, sends another signal this week through her nonverbal behavior of sitting outside of the group. The worker is still too insecure to reach for it. The response of the other women, to bring Angela into the group, may represent their understanding of her role and importance. This time, the worker does reach for Angela's individual needs by providing some concrete help. This is an effort at relationship building and an expression of individual caring, but it does not deal with Angela's message on behalf of the group-as-a-whole.

Session 2

I started the group by asking the women if they had any questions about the material I had handed out the previous week. No questions. I told them, as I had the previous week, that tonight's topic would focus on parenting. I said that I has planned to show a 15-minute film called *Special Times,* but the projector I had rented didn't work correctly. Since I had watched the film twice, I said I would go over the main points of the film and we could have a discussion focusing on these points. I said, "Before we get started, let's go around the room so that each of you can tell me how many children you have, their names and ages." After the women told me about their families, I asked Angela to move in closer because she was outside the circle of the group. She said she was fine where she was. Two of the women got up, went over and picked up the love seat that Angela was sitting on, and moved her closer to the rest of the group. Everyone, including Angela, had a good laugh.

At this point, I mentioned to Angela (the woman who, last week, had said the group was boring) that I had called the Cerebral Palsy Foundation. "They gave me a few referrals that might be helpful to you." I said that I could make another call for more information or I could give her the number to call. I said, "You can think about it and let me know at the end of group whether you want to call or if you'd like me to call." Angela talked for five minutes about the problems she was having finding services for her handicapped son. Everyone in the group listened.

When Angela finished, the focus on parenting began. I told them the movie's main point is that a parent should set aside a special time—one or two hours every week—to spend with her child. The parent and child should plan ahead for this time. Additionally, the parent should ask the child what he or she wants to do. The child should decide. Angela said, "My son would say, 'Ma, take me to Zayre's and buy me something.'" Everyone laughed. I said that there had been a scene in the movie where a mother initially felt uncomfortable with this special time. The son said he wanted to browse through the sports department at the store. They spent an hour looking at sports equipment (not necessarily buying anything). The time they spent together was enjoyable for both of them.

Linda said, "One day I brought my child to the store. I put her on the swing set in the children's department. She had a great time. While she was on the swing, I went to the sewing department and bought some material." I said, "Well, you know, there is a scene in the film where a mother and daughter are at a park. The mother is reading a book while the child is playing on the slide. The narrator says, 'Let's do this scene over.' When the scene is shown again, the mother and child are sliding on the slide together. The narrator says, 'The important thing to remember is that you do things together during this special time. Change your role from parent to that of a close friend.'"

Linda said she didn't remember her mother ever getting on a slide with her; however, she said she got the point. She said, "You don't care if the kid's face is dirty and you're not on their back saying don't do this and don't do that." I said, "You can see how important this special time is especially since most of you, as single parents, are the ones mainly responsible for disciplining your children. It's good for both you and your child to get a break from this role." Cindy said, "Yes, I'm always disciplining the children. Then when they go with their father, they're like angels." At first, she couldn't understand it. Then Kathy, the counselor, said, "Did you ever stop and think that maybe they're afraid he won't come back to see them if they don't act very good?" Cindy said she had never thought of that. She said now she sits her children down and says, "You have to listen to me. I'm your mother. I know what's best for you." These talks are helping her relationship with her children.

I told Cindy that I had read a little about single parenting. One writer had mentioned that sometimes the child will act very good with the parent who is not living in the household in hopes that the parents will get back together. The children think that somehow they can be responsible for the parents getting back together. She said, "You know, one time when Julie was only two, Matt and I happened to be with her one day together. We were walking and she was between Matt and me. We were both holding Julie's hands. Julie started swinging our hands back and forth. Then, she took our hands and brought them together." Cindy said, "I couldn't believe that at that age she knew that things weren't right between us and she wanted us back together."

I said that what Cindy had just mentioned brought us to another major point of the film. The narrator says that children should be encouraged to talk openly about their feelings. Cindy picked up on this point and said she agreed one hundred percent. She said when the children ask her questions she tries her best to answer them. "They ask me if I still love Daddy. I tell them that I do love Daddy, but in a different way. I tell them that it's not good for Daddy and me to live together." She said that her children listen to her. Linda said that she agreed with Cindy. She said that she's trying to explain to her daughter the changes that have taken place since they've come to the house. "My daughter doesn't know where she is or what's going on. She's clinging to me like a leech all of a sudden. I don't understand it." I asked Linda when she came to the house. She said one week ago. I said, "When parents split up, oftentimes the child is afraid that the parent the child is living with will also leave. Your daughter may be very afraid that you're going to leave her."

The next major point that the film made is that special time can take away the worries that parent and child have. I said, "I think all of you worry more than the average person because of abusive situations that you've been in. That's why special time is very important for you and your child. You can both put your worries aside." Cindy said, "The other day I took my two daughters to the beach. They were looking at snails, examining them closely." Pam broke in and said, "If that was my son, Jason, he wouldn't have looked at the snails, he would have eaten them." Everyone laughed. Cindy continued, "My daughters didn't fight, they didn't make a lot of noise. It was wonderful." I asked her how she felt. She replied, "I felt very relaxed." Pam jumped in to say, "One of the first days here at the house, I was playing with a couple of the kids. We started wrestling; we were laughing and playing for about an hour. We had so much fun. I felt great for the rest of the day. When I put Jason to bed at night when I'm relaxed, he falls asleep right away. I rock him and he falls asleep. If I'm aggravated or tense, I'll put him to bed and he won't fall asleep. He knows that something is wrong."

Linda said she feels that she is yelling at her child 24 hours a day. "My daughter does things that she never did before we came here." She said the other day her daughter was walking by Pam's son, Jason, and she slapped him on the face. Linda said she felt terrible about this. Pam said, "Don't worry about it. How do you think I feel? My son (who is big for his age) goes around trying to hug everyone. He's so big he knocks the kids over and they begin to cry. I feel the same way you do." I said, "Just the fact that you're expressing how you feel about your children's behavior makes it easier for you to understand one another." The women began to talk about how they discipline their children.

After a few minutes, I said, "Can we come back to Linda for a few minutes? I think she's very concerned about the changes she sees in her child since she came to the house." Linda said, "I wish I knew I was doing the right thing coming here with my daughter. I wish there was some research that said, 'It's better to leave your husband when the child is such and such an age—then I could feel better. I don't want to be yelling at my child all day long." Vicki said, "But, Linda, every situation is very different from the next. It's not easy to say that for everyone who leaves her husband, the children should be a certain age. It takes time for a child to adjust to a new situation and a new environment." Angela said, "Look, as long as the kids aren't killing each other, I leave them alone. If one kid takes another kid's toy, at first they cry. But two minutes later they're playing with another toy." I was getting ready to ask Linda if she thought she should be back home with her husband. But I didn't have to say anything. She said, "Well, I guess my only other choice is to go back home and have my child see my husband beat me up." I said, "Yes, that's right."

I wrapped up the discussion about the film by naming different activities that they might want to consider for special time. Then, I asked them how they thought the discussion went. Everyone thought it was a great discussion. They said they never have an opportunity during the week to get together to talk. At this point, Cindy started to talk about one of the children and the funny things he says and does. We sat and laughed for about ten minutes. I felt very pleased that everyone seemed so relaxed—much more relaxed than last week. As everyone got up to leave, Cindy said, "This was a good discussion, even though you were only able to get a few words in." Linda said, "Yes, you might not think so, but you're really helping us." I thanked her and said I was glad that I could be of help to them.

The closing comment by Cindy, abut the worker only being able to "get a few words in," reflects her sense of the worker's viewing her role as "teaching." In many ways, these women used the film as a starting point and took the discussion to their own issues related to their stress and its impact on their children. As the worker felt more comfortable, and started to refrain from giving advice, the members took over and the power of mutual aid became apparent.

In the next session, marked by changes in the group composition, the worker still begins with an agenda; however, this time, she acknowledges that it is up to the group members to decide what they wish to discuss.

Session 3: Stress Management

Three women who had been participating in the group left the shelter. A new woman, Jennifer, joined the group this week. This week, the group consisted of only three women. I told the group that tonight's focus would be stress management. I said I would give them a definition of stress, and then they could take a stress test to find out where they stood currently in terms of stress in their lives. Afterwards, I said, we could have a discussion about stress and, possibly, the ways it has affected their lives. I said, "But, it's up to you to decide what you want to discuss."

After the stress test, we were talking about good and bad ways of coping with stress. When alcohol and other drugs were mentioned as a bad way of coping with stress, all the women agreed in unison. From this comment, a group discussion got off the ground that lasted for an hour and a half. All of the women's partners had problems with drinking or drugs or both. They talked about how their men spent most of their money on alcohol and cocaine. The new woman, Jennifer, said her boyfriend sold her TV set and spent $180 of her money for drugs. She left him after this incident but went back with him again. Now, she has left again. Pam said that when her boyfriend spent money that was supposed to be spent for the baby, she became very upset. That's when they would have big fights. Angela joined in to say that her husband spends all day in the bar. She said the last time she was in a shelter he called up. He was crying on the phone and he promised to get help. She went back with him, but he never went for help. I asked her how she felt about him when he didn't go for help after he had said he would. She said, "You want to know how I feel? I'd like to get a gun and shoot him. That's how I feel. Then, I wouldn't have to worry about him giving me no more trouble."

I wanted to respond to Angela's strong statement, but Pam jumped in at this point to talk about her feelings concerning another issue. Pam said she was having a hard time making a decision about visitation rights for her husband. She said she wants to deny visitation rights for her husband but she feels guilty about doing this. I told her I remembered her talking the previous week about an incident where he took the child, drank, and then called her up to pick the child up. She said, "The only reason he took the baby is because his mother told him he should. He took the baby to a bar with him." Angela said that she had just met with her lawyers and made an agreement that her husband could only see the children when he stopped drinking. Pam said, "Maybe I could do the same thing." She seemed very pleased to hear this information since it provided her with a possible solution to the dilemma she was facing. Jennifer thought that an arrangement of this type was a good idea. She said, "You know what my boyfriend does? He'll be smoking cocaine and he'll blow the smoke in my face and the baby's face. Now, that's not right."

Angela said, "You know, I was talking with Kathy (counselor) this week and she said to me, 'Did you ever think about why alcoholic men are attracted to you?'" Angela went on to say that this question bothered her and that she had been thinking about it. She said her father was an alcoholic and her mother always backed down to him. "In other words, if my father told her to shut a light off, she'd shut it off, even if she wanted the light on. Of course, if she didn't shut if off, he'd beat her up." She said she ended up doing the same thing with her husband. She said no matter what she did, she came out a loser. If she talked back to him, he'd slap her. If she didn't answer him, he'd yell at her for not answering him.

All the women agreed that they dealt with the same type of behavior from their partners. Jennifer said, "Only we know what it's really like because we've lived in this situation. Someone else might try to understand, but they don't know what it's really like." She went on to say that her boyfriend would come home and start arguing with her. When the baby would wake up, he'd blame her for the baby waking up. Pam said her husband did the same thing. I said, "Looking back on this situation, do you see that it wasn't your fault for the baby waking up?" They said yes, now they did, but back then they weren't so sure. I said, "We've been talking about very stressful situations. Do you feel that you have less stress since you've left your partners?" They said they all felt less stress in their lives now.

The women mentioned that their partners didn't like their having friends. Jennifer said her boyfriend also didn't like her seeing her family. She said that her stepbrother had raped her from the time she was 8 until she was 12 years old. She said her boyfriend would say, "They don't care about you. Look what happened to you." She said, "My family couldn't help what happened to me." I asked Jennifer if the stepbrother had lived in the same house. She said, "Yes." I said, "That must have been terrible for you." This would have been a good time to ask her if she thought that experience may affect the relationships she now has with men (abusive). At the time, I wasn't quick enough to connect her statement with purpose. The other women went on to talk about their partners' reactions to their having friends.

As the evening drew to a close, I said that we had talked about many issues. The women thought the discussion went very well. I finished up by mentioning four or five good ways to cope with stress. Overall, I thought the group went well. However, I don't think I said enough in the group to connect their feelings with purpose. Additionally, once the women started to talk, I found it difficult to break into the discussion. I'm perfectly happy not to be in control of the group; however, I just want to make sure that I do say the right things so that the women will work on their issues.

The worker's questions about her practice show an increasing sophistication about her role in the group. Rather than feeling responsible for all of the group's work, she is now feeling the freedom of letting go and exploring what kind of interventions she should be making to help the women to deepen and grow from their work. The discussion represents just the beginning of recognition of the pattern of "master-slave" relationship which has dominated their lives: the physical abuse designed to coerce conformity; the tendency to internalize the negative self-image and to take responsibility for problems; the no-win situations where no matter how they respond they are wrong; the attempts to isolate them from other contacts; the effort to prevent them from having any control over their lives. Exploring these patterns, and the roots they have for many of the women in early childhood abuse and exploitation, is a beginning for them in their efforts to overcome the "internal oppressor" in their struggle with the "external oppressor."

In the next session, there are six new women, giving the worker an opportunity to start again. The worker's continued growth is evident when this session is compared to her first session of only three weeks before.

Session 4

This week's group session consisted of six new women. Because of the new group composition, I told the women some information about myself, and then asked them to tell me their names, how many children they have, and how long they've been at the shelter. Then, I stated the purpose of the group session. I said, "This group will give you an opportunity to talk and to listen to one another. This is what's called a mutual aid group. All of you here are experiencing some difficulty in your lives because of abusive relationships. This is not an easy time for you. In fact, it's a time of crisis. Because you've experienced similar difficulties, this group session will give you a chance to help each other. As you listen to each other, share some of your problems and feelings, I think you'll learn a great deal from each other."

"In order to get the group discussion started, I'd like you to do some problem swapping—share with each other some problems and difficulties you've experienced in your abusive relationships. If you want to, you can share some of the things you'd like to see differently in your lives now. By problem swapping, we'll find out what your major concerns are, and then the discussion can focus on these issues. There's no sense in having a discussion if it's not about issues that you're concerned with." I said, "Who would like to start?" Joyce said, "My problem right now is that I don't have any money and the last time I tried to apply for welfare, they told me I wasn't eligible." The women talked about this for a few minutes and tried to offer Joyce suggestions about receiving welfare. Next, Linda said that her life was very disorganized. At this point, she doesn't know where she's going.

Candy said one thing that she didn't like was that her husband had to be number one all the time. He felt he should come first, even before the children. She said, "The man's got to be number one. Just like the president, Ronald Reagan. He's a man and he's number one. You don't see no female presidents, do you?" I said, "Are you saying that a man had the right to abuse his partner?" She said no and then turned to the women to say, "But, who's the one who always gives in in the family? The woman does." All the women nodded to this remark. Linda said, "To keep peace in the family." Candy said, "In the long run, we're the ones who are wrong for not leaving the abusive situations." She said she finally came to the realization that her man was never going to be of any help to her. In the long run, she felt that her children would help her out if she gave them a good life now. She feels very strongly about her responsibilities to her children.

Another woman, Tina, said that when she called the police for help, they thought it was a big joke. She said when she had to fill out a report at the police station, the officer laughed about the incident. The women in the group talked about their own experiences with the police, which were not very good. One woman had to wait 35 minutes for the police to respond to her call after her husband had thrown a brick through her bedroom window. I said, "Dealing with the police must have been a humiliating situation for all of you. Here you are in need of help, and they laugh at you. It's just not right."

Linda talked about a woman in California who had been stabbed several times and the police didn't do anything about the incident. I brought up the recent case in Connecticut where an abused woman sued the police force and won millions of dollars. I said, "Because of this case, Connecticut police are now responding more quickly to abuse cases." I said, "I know this doesn't help you out now with your situations, but things are changing a little at a time." I thought this story would provide the women with some reassurance and let them know that some public officials do not think abuse is a laughing matter.

Joyce said that she wanted to kill her husband. This desire had been expressed by an abused woman in a previous group session. Other women in the group said it wouldn't be worth it for her. "All he does is yell at me all the time. He makes me go down to where he works every day at lunchtime. The kids and I have to sit and watch him eat. He never buys us anything to eat." I said, "What would you do? Eat before you would go to see him?" She said, "Yes. Plus, he wants to know where I am every minute of the day. He implies that I sit around the house all day long doing nothing." Marie said her ex-husband used to say that to her all the time. She said, "But now I'm collecting back pay from my divorce settlement for all the work I never did around the house."

Then Joyce said she was going to tell us something that she had only told two other people in her life. Joyce said that she had been molested from the ages of five to seven by her next door neighbor, Pat. She said that Pat was friendly with her parents. Her mother would say, "Bring a glass of lemonade over to Pat." The first time she did this, he molested her. After that incident, when her mother told her to bring something over to Pat, Joyce would try to get out of it. But her mother insisted that she go over. Pat had told Joyce not to tell anyone what went on. At this point in the session, Joyce began to cry. I said that I understood this was a difficult situation for her to talk about. Candy said, "Joyce, it wasn't your fault." Joyce said she had kept this incident to herself for approximately 25 years. Finally, when she told her husband, he said, "You probably deserved it." Joyce said she felt like killing him for saying that. Candy said, "See, you can't depend on nobody else but yourself. You're better off just not talking to anybody because when you get down to it you can't really rely on anyone but yourself."

I said that I thought there were people that Joyce could talk to, including professional people. I said it was unfortunate for Joyce that when she finally decided to talk about her experience, her husband didn't give her the support she needed. I said that we were listening to Joyce and realized what a terrible experience she had suffered as a child. After Joyce talked a little more about the situation and calmed down, I asked if anyone also had experienced or seen abuse in their families when they were growing up. Candy said she saw her father beat her mother. She said she used to ask her mother why she put up with it. She said now she sees that it's easier to say you want to get out of a relationship than it is to actually do it.

Candy said, "I want to know whether we're better off leaving or staying in our abusive situations." I said, "Why don't we list on the blackboard the benefits of leaving and staying and see what we come up with." Candy said that leaving was better in the long run. By staying, the children will see their father abusing their mother. "What kind of example is that going to set for the children?" She felt her children would be happier by their leaving. Joyce said her children were happy to leave their father. She said, "They're tired of listening to him yell all the time." She said her son was more upset about leaving the dog behind than he was about leaving his father. Linda said another good reason for leaving is self-love. She said, "It comes to a point where you know he's going to kill you if you stay around." Linda said her boyfriend told her that he'd be happy to go to jail over killing her. Other good reasons for leaving that the women mentioned included: leaving an uncomfortable lifestyle, getting away from the pressure involved in an abusive relationship, and not having to take physical or mental abuse.

In her next comment, the worker demonstrates how far she has come from her early efforts to preach to the women, reaching for the reasons a woman might find to stay in the relationship.

At this point, no one had mentioned reasons for staying in an abusive relationship, so I prompted the women to comment. The women said that money, belongings (many women leave their possessions behind when they seek shelter) and the convenience of the relationship were reasons for staying. Linda said, "Sometimes it's easier to stay because at least you know what's going to happen to you. If you leave, you don't have any idea what's in store for you. It's very hard."

Since group time had run out, I finished up the session by saying that it looked like the reasons for leaving an abusive situation outnumbered the reasons for staying. Candy said, "Yes, It's easy to see that leaving is the best thing to do." I said, "Even though we can see from the list that leaving is better than staying, that doesn't mean it's easy to follow through on a decision to leave. There are many women who decide to go back to their partners after they've left." I told the women that I thought they were very strong for having made the decision to leave, and I wished them luck with their new way of life. I thanked them for participating in the group session and said their discussion seemed to help everyone in the group.

On two nights of the six group sessions, I brought in speakers, one from Chilton's Credit Bureau to talk about establishing credit, one from Displaced Homemakers to talk about assertiveness. Unfortunately, I can't report on the credit session because I took care of a woman's child so she could participate in the group; however, the women said they enjoyed this session very much. The other session on assertiveness came at a transitional time at the shelter. As a result, only one woman attended the session.

This example illustrates how the working contract with a group can evolve over time, and how the group process can educate a worker to deepen his or her understanding of group dynamics, group skills, and the themes of importance to the clients. In the final example in this section, group leaders of a parenting group for men and women must struggle with a number of issues. First, the group is split between mandated clients who have abused their children and are required to attend as part of a child welfare case plan, and another group of clients who have been identified as at-risk for abusive behavior and have been referred by the case managers. Second, the group leaders do not start with a clear idea of group purpose, approaching the group as a course in parenting rather than as a mutual aid support group that includes parenting content. After identifying the illusion of work, particularly on the part of the mandated clients, the workers attempt to recontract with the group.

> **Group Purpose:** Parent education for clients who have abused their children and for parents who are at risk for abusing and neglecting their children.
>
> **Group Members:** This group has 13 members, ranging in age from 21 to 35 years old. Eight have been mandated by the Child Protective Services to attend the group as part of their case plan for reunification with their children. The other members have been referred to the group by case managers in the sponsoring agency. This second group of parents have received or are presently receiving 60 days of voluntary case management services to prevent the possibility of abuse and neglect of their children. There are three men in the group: a single Caucasian man and two Latino men who are attending the group with their wives. They are nonvoluntary group members. There are four African-American women (two are nonvoluntary members), four Caucasian women (two are nonvoluntary members) and one Southeast Asian woman. The majority of the members live in an inner city and are welfare recipients.
>
> **Dates Covered in Record:** March 7th to April 21st
>
> **Group Task:** Structure-maintenance
>
> **Problem:** The structure of the group seems to be preventing group members from becoming a mutual aid group with members supporting other members. The fol-

lowing obstacles may have been perpetuating the problem: (1) Group members were not interviewed by facilitators prior to the first session to screen out members who may not be appropriate due to characterological or substance abuse problems. (2) The mixture of voluntary and nonvoluntary members seems to have created two different sets of norms for behavior. (3) The curriculum developed for the group is in a teacher-student format, which has prevented interaction between the group members.

How the Problem Came to My Attention: During the first four sessions the parents would only talk when questions were directed to them by the cofacilitators. They seemed locked into the agenda that was established during the first session for parenting education. The group members were not open to discussing feelings about parenting and did not offer any support to other members. They kept their answers to questions as general as possible so that it could be any parent having difficulty with parenting. I realized that I would have to change the agenda and open each group session with a parent's issue. The group needed to develop its own leaders rather than having the cofacilitators lead the group.

Summary of the Work:

March 7 (first session)

During this session, the cofacilitators attempted to establish the contract for work. I explained to the group that it was both an education and support group. I stated that I was very much aware the parents need support around parenting because of my experiences in working with parents for the past few years.

I also presented the group with a tentative agenda and told them it had been established as only a guideline for topics because the group would only meet for 10 weeks. I said that the members could change the topics and discuss issues that were more important to them. Specific topics that the parents were interested in that appeared on the agenda were communication, anger, cycles of violence, and ways of coping. I explained that the leaders were not authorities on parenting and also explained that in this state everyone is a mandated reporter in cases of abuse and neglect. I stated that in cases where abuse and neglect had to be reported, we would support the parent as they made the phone call to child protection services.

When we asked the clients for feedback about the contract for the group, several members replied that parent education that teaches specific parenting skills does not work. Also, one of the nonvoluntary members stated that she "had to be here." I stated again that I did not intend to teach specific methods but rather to look at the communication between parent and child and also find ways of having parents meet some of their needs as adults to eliminate some of the stress related to parenting. The session ended with parents seeming more relaxed about attending the group. What I missed was not focusing on the parents' feedback about what topics they were interested in, why they felt parent education classes did not work, and what it feels like when someone tells you that you need to attend parenting classes.

The group leader's retrospective analysis is on target as she identifies the major gaps in the first session and her unwillingness to explore the resistance of the mandated members who had their children removed and the "semi-voluntary" members who may have feared losing their children. Also, the diversity in the group between members and between the group leaders and the members was not recognized as a potential barrier. While the group members are more active in the second session, one still senses they are saying what they think the group leaders want to hear, thus maintaining an illusion of work.

March 14 (second session)

This session focused on developing a definition for parenting based on the group members' input as to what a parent is expected to do. The purpose was to find a common ground for expectations for parenting roles and stress related to parenting. Parents actively contributed to the definition of parenting and seemed to enjoy the interaction with cofacilitators in developing a written definition for parenting. What the members had developed was an idealistic expectation of their role and responsibility as parents. When I asked if it was realistic, Christy replied that it was her responsibility to care for her daughter and meet all of her needs physically, emotionally, and socially. When I asked if doing so created stress for her, she had replied yes, and most of the group members agreed with her through nonverbal expressions. Rather than raising the issue of the stress related to parenting that the group members experienced, I said that the next week we would focus on the stress that can occur when parents meet their children's needs and do not address their own needs. Again, I missed the opportunity to have the group members establish the agenda for the group sessions.

March 21 (third session)

Again this session I focused the group on the tentative agenda. The teacher-student format was still present, and I was creating an illusion of work. The session began with having the parents identify their physical, emotional, and social needs as adults. The members broke into subgroups to identify the physical, emotional, and social needs of children within several developmental age groups. When the group came back together, the similarity between the lists were noted. John said that he liked doing that exercise and working with other parents in small groups; he had never done that before. Rather than exploring the issue of working together with other parents, I stayed focused on the stress parents feel when they are trying to meet their children's needs and neglect their own. As with previous sessions, there was nonverbal agreement by the group members. I had missed an opportunity to explore what it meant and how it felt to work together with other parents.

In the next session, the worker moves closer to the realities of the parents by using a check-in to request the problem swapping that was missed in the first three meetings. In retrospect, however, the group leader identifies (hindsight is wonderful) how she had remained in a "teaching" mode.

March 28 (fourth session)

I attempted to get the group more involved by asking a specific question for "check-in." I asked each member to describe a stressful incident with their child this past week. Every member was able to describe an incident. Rather than trying to find a common concern for all the parents or staying with the specifics of one incident, I moved from the specific and generalized stress to the cycle of violence and how stressful incidents can be dealt with either through discipline or punishment that included both abuse and neglect. Again, I went into a teacher format and asked parents about the different ways children are abused both physically and verbally. The group members willingly contributed to developing another list.

Diane stated that she neglected her children by allowing them to do anything that they wanted because they would not listen to her. Rather than exploring this issue further and exploring it with other group members, I ended the session with asking the group members what they would like to work on next week because it was parents' choice. Samantha said that she would like to work on communication with her child because he does not listen to her, only her mother, and other group members were in agreement. This time the group is asking me to listen to them.

In the next session, the group leader both apologizes to the members and redefines the nature of the work as a mutual aid group focusing on specific examples of the stresses they face. In many ways, the group leader is modeling for the members how one catches a mistake and goes back and tries again— one of the skills the parents need to master. After a brief silence, a group member accepts the worker's invitation, and the real work begins.

April 7 (fifth session)
I began this session by apologizing to the group. They had been telling me about stressful issues in their lives and I was not listening to them. I asked if they would be more willing to discuss one or two specific stressful incidents for parents rather than have everyone talk about a specific incident during check-in and not having the time to explore what can be done to change it. My question was met with silence. Christy broke the silence by telling me that her boyfriend told her she can't parent and the parenting classes were not doing her any good. She went on to say that she thought he was right; her daughter had got a knife off the kitchen table and could have hurt herself if she (Christy) wasn't there. Audrey described an incident when her children got into her medication for seizures and although she caught them before there was any harm, she spent most of the day crying because they could have been hurt. It seems that when children are not safe, you question your ability to parent.

Lori stated that her mother blames her when her baby cries and takes over caring for the baby: "She won't show me how to parent; I'm really mad at her." I said that this sounds similar to the issue that Samantha brought up last week about her child listening to her mother and not listening to her. I asked if she ever told her mother how she feels. She said, "I try to, but she won't listen." Rose talked about her experience with trying to tell her mother her feeling about her mother taking over responsibility for raising her five children. She said it did not work. Diane said, "I told my mother I'd raise my own children, she raised hers." Mary agreed with her (both Diane and Mary are nonvoluntary clients).

The session ended with my summarizing the session, stating that there seems to be lots of doubt about ability to parent and also anger toward people who take over parenting roles rather than helping us. I also included sessional contracting and stated next week we can discuss what it feels like when people tell us, both verbally and nonverbally, that we can't parent. Also, there is the expectation that we should know how to parent because we have children. Christy said that next week we are supposed to finish cycles of violence. I replied that this issue seems to be a concern for most of the members. Before I could get a consensus from group members about the topic, the nonvoluntary members had left in unison; they were not going to stay one minute beyond the ending time. It seems that I have touched on the taboo subject and there is ambivalence about discussing it.

As the recontracting starts to move the group into real work, one group member raises the issues of confidentiality and authority. Although addressed briefly in the opening statement of the first session, the concerns reemerge as the group prepares to move into the work phase.

April 14 (sixth session)

The conversation prior to the group session was, "Who is your child protection worker?" with Mary saying, "my worker must call every week to make sure I am here." I addressed the issue and said that I contacted the child protection workers when someone was not in the group. I also told them that their workers were only informed about attendance and subjects discussed in the group. Because I do not work with each one of them individually in their homes, I do not know if the things discussed in the group were being used in the home.

I brought up the issue of doubts about parenting, and Brenda replied that she could parent and did not know why she was here. Samantha said that she sometimes doubts her ability to parent because her son does not listen to her, only her mother: "it seems like he's trying to get me. He always acts up when we get in the store." Diana said people start criticizing you when your children don't behave. I said it seems like you're embarrassed that you can't do what people expect you to do. Brenda said that she would just leave the store. Samantha said that she promises to buy him something when she finishes if he behaves, and Diana says she does the same thing too, but most of the time she feels like her children are trying to get to her too. Samantha said that she was about ready to give up. She can't do it all by herself. She needs to be both mother and father because her son's father died when he was two weeks old. She also stated that she almost lost her son to spinal meningitis at age 1 and that he is now on meds for hyperactivity and they don't work. She also said that he has learning disabilities and acts like he is three but he's almost six; she needs to protect him. I replied that with all had happened to her and her son it would be normal to be protective. Samantha replied that she spoiled him, and now she has no time for herself.

Diana stated that she spoiled her firstborn and that's why she can't deal with him. She said she held him all the time. She said that he also slept with her because she was afraid of crib death, and at age five he still wants to sleep with her. Samantha said she did the same thing because she wanted to protect her child. Maryann said that she spoils her seven-month-old daughter: she holds her all the time and buys her pretty dresses. "She cries every time I put her down; she's spoiled." I said that it seems that the children have responded to your need to protect them and learned behavior that will get your attention. My cofacilitator stated that it may be time to set some limits on children's behavior. I stated that it may be time to take a few minutes for yourself as a parent and teach the child to engage in activities for short periods of time without you. Samantha stated that she was willing to give it a try.

Lori brought the subject back to her mother spoiling her three-month-old baby: she won't let him cry, and holds him all the time. Because the session was coming to an end, I asked the group if they would be willing to help Lori work through issues with her mother because she has brought the topic up during several sessions and we never seem to get to it. The group agreed that it would be fine.

April 21 (seventh session)

Although the sessional contract was for helping Lori to deal with her mother's taking over her parenting role, Christy began the session by telling the group members that her boyfriend does not help her with caring for her daughter. The rest of the group fell into the same conversation. Audrey stated that she made sure her children knew their father, but he never helped with raising them. She also reported that her mother did not help her either and that she needed her mother's help because she had a stroke and lost mobility in her right side. Diane said that she always found losers for boyfriends who expected her to take care of them. Lori stated that she had bought alcohol and drugs for the father of her baby.

At this point in the meeting a group theme of lack of support has emerged. However, the worker is concerned about following through with the apparent agreement the previous week to help Lori with her specific concerns. Rather than just stating the dilemma and asking the group to address it, the leader switches the conversation back to Lori. In response, the group members scapegoat Lori, who they feel has more than enough support as compared to themselves. This scapegoating process, in retrospect, is also a form of communication to the leader.

> I stated that there seems to be a lot going on about receiving support from others, but I told Lori that we would look at her issue with her mother this week. (What I missed was the connection between all the support that Lori gets from her mother and how the other group members do not feel supported in their relationships with significant others.) When I asked Lori how her relationship with her mother was this past week, she said that it was resolved but that her sister refused to help her with the baby: "She's on school vacation this week, and she should be helping." She said her sister refused to get her something she needed when she was changing the baby. Brenda said, "You should be able to care for the baby by yourself, I did." Christy said that you need to get everything ready to change the baby before you do it. Lori was being scapegoated, and I immediately went to protect her. I said, "It sounds as if Lori is being attacked. Do you ever remember a time when you tried to do something for your first child and did not have everything you needed?" What I missed was the connection between the group and Lori. Most of the group members did not feel that they had someone to help them with caring for their children. It may have been more effective to ask, "How many of us would have liked to have someone available to help us with caring for the baby?"

Where the Problem Stands Now:
The group is now interacting with each other and are no longer looking to the facilitators to dominate the group discussions. Also, individuals within the group are taking various roles during their interactions. There still seems to be a split between voluntary and nonvoluntary members. The voluntary members are more open to discussing issues and feelings.

Several nonvoluntary members have taken roles that prevent the group from moving into discussing taboo subjects any further. Brenda frequently takes either a defensive member role or gatekeeper role to prevent the group from moving on to the taboo subject of abuse and neglect. Mary has been the quiet member since the group began. Both Diane and Mary knew each other before the start of group, and although Diane has begun to open up in the group, about halfway through each session she turns away from the group and writes in her notebook or stares out the window. John is the deviant member; he arrives late to every group session and acts as if it is not necessary for him to be there. It's as if he speaks for all the other nonvoluntary clients. The group has come together with its own agenda, but as it stands now, there is still some ambivalence about interpersonal relationships for some members.

Specific Next Steps:
1. I need to address the issue of the relationship between voluntary and nonvoluntary members by expressing my feelings about what is going on and how they are working together.

2. I also need to be aware of how individuals within the group are playing roles to prevent the group from discussing taboo subjects and use supportive confrontation so the group can develop a new set of norms that support the parents in working on their issues with their children.

3. I need to tune in to my own feelings about confrontation, knowing from my own experiences that I avoid confrontation and tend to be a caregiver and gate-keeper in my own personal life.

4. I will continue to tune in prior to each group session and process the group after each group session. Without doing this, I know that I miss the interactions that prevent the group from forming a culture that is needed to address taboo areas, as well as power and intimacy themes.

5. I will also ask myself, "Whose agenda is the group working on?" knowing that I have a tendency to push my own agenda.

6. I have learned that I will always need to work on my skills, and being human I know that I will never reach perfection.

Joining an Ongoing Group

Contracting issues are complex when starting a new group. They grow more complex when a worker joins an ongoing group that may have been operating for some time without a clear working agreement or with one that does not lead to effective mutual aid. In this situation, the new group leader has to deal not only with the members of the group but also with the on-going leaders, who have an investment in the current status. Students often raise this as a per-plexing problem when they report sitting in on group discussions as co-leaders and observing clearly the problems associated with poor contracting, co-leader conflict over the contract, or simply a lack of understanding of the mutual aid process. Tensions develop as the students read about alternative models and listen in their classrooms to presentations that directly apply to their own groups. And yet, as a "mere student," they feel intimidated about inter-vening and effecting change. In a situation such as the one in the following example, their stress is increased when the team leader is also of another discipline—in this case, a psy-chologist—which introduces issues of status and power.

This example simply represents a special case of the general problem in which the ser-vice offered in the setting does not meet the needs of the clients. As such, the definition of the social work function presented in this book—mediating the individual-social engagement—places this problem on the student's agenda for **systems work**: the set of activities in which social workers attempt to influence the systems and systems people who are important to their clients. Systems work was introduced in Parts II and III. It was discussed again in the chapter on group formation, where we saw how important it was to include all staff in establishing a new group. The issue will be addressed in detail in Part V of this book.

In the example that follows, two students attempted to be involved in the group for-mation process, with little success. Staff in the setting—a psychiatric hospital—had developed ideas about the limitations of the patient population. Under continued pressure by the students, a group was started, but its purpose and structure reflected the culture of the system. Al-though this is not actually an example of joining a group in process, the principles are close enough to make it useful for our purposes in this section. The Record of Service device helps to describe the effort over time as one of the social work students analyzes her own early ef-forts to influence her colleagues and develops interesting strategies for change that minimize defensive and territorial responses.

RECORD OF SERVICE

Client Description and Time Frame:
This is an open-ended, support and stabilization group for chronic mentally ill patients on an inpatient unit of a large psychiatric hospital. The age range of the members is 33 to 64 years. The group is predominantly male (currently eight males, three females), all white, with various ethnicities. The period of time covered in the record is from January 18th to April 26th.

Description of the Problem:
The major problem this group faced from the beginning was a lack of agreement on the group's purpose, goals, and structure by the treatment team putting the group together. This resulted from uncertainty and disagreement as to what would be the most appropriate group format on the part of some members of the treatment team. The problem was reflective of and exacerbated by a hospital culture that was very hierarchical and did not easily tolerate discussion or disagreement among team members of various professions. Also, since specific alternative recommendations for group purpose, structure, and so on were coming from social work students, I believe the resistance to change was also a function of the challenge to the team culture. We were making our own recommendations, rather than just following the team leader's guidance. This restrictive hierarchical culture is an issue that is faced by both clients and staff in this setting, so resolution of the problem at the group level meant confronting the culture on the treatment team level as well.

How the Problem Came to the Attention of the Worker(s):
This problem was first noticeable in my first semester at the placement, when development of a group kept being delayed—sometimes because there was "no one available" to co-lead the group, sometimes because we "just didn't get to that item" on the agenda of our weekly team meetings, and sometimes for no stated reason at all. Another student and I were both trying to begin groups, and it became increasingly clear that there was a resistance to beginning this process that was not being admitted or dealt with. In addition, once the groups did get a start date, there was continued reluctance to plan for them, to discuss what type of groups they would be, to discuss group composition, or to engage other staff from the dorm in the process of setting them up. The psychologist, Dr. Brown, expressed frequent concerns about our trying to do too much, or not being realistic in our expectations for the group, and cautioned frequently that "people with schizophrenia are different and the books don't tell you all of it."

Summary of the Work:
I attempted to get clarification on the proposed purpose whenever new groups were recommended. Throughout the first semester, whenever possibilities for groups were mentioned, I expressed enthusiasm for getting started and asked about purpose, structure, and composition. It often seemed that a major purpose for the development of many group ideas was the fact that another student and I both needed to have a group experience at our placement, and our supervisor was trying to insure that this happened. Specific concerns about group purpose and structure, therefore, often seemed to be secondary in our conversations to the possibility of getting a group at all. For example:
Supervisor: We may have a group for you. I was talking with Edward (the team leader, Dr. Brown) about a family group that you and Evelyn (a social worker on the team) could run.

Worker: Great! What kind of family group would it be?

Supervisor: Well, we're not too sure about the specifics yet, but it would be to help people deal with their families. Maybe we'd have a little party and have them serve refreshments to their families at the end.

Worker: So, would it be family members and patients?

Supervisor: Well, it's hard to get families in. It might just be for the patients to talk about problems with the families. But we don't know if it's going to happen yet. We have to check Evelyn's schedule to see if she'll be available to do it with you.

As noted above, purpose and structure were my concern, but my supervisor's interest was more in just getting a group started, and my questions about purpose and structure seemed to feel like pressure to her, or perhaps just irrelevant to the major concern, which was getting a group.

Once the group was decided on, I repeatedly brought up issues of group purpose and structure in group supervision meetings and in meetings with my co-leader, initially just by asking for clarification, but later also by making recommendations. I asked about purpose and structure when the group was first decided on, and was told not to worry about it, that we'd be lucky just to get the members to stay in the room. I was also told that my co-leader (the team leader) would be there and I should just follow his lead. When I pressed further for information, my supervisor tried to make it irrelevant.

Worker: Well, I can do that (follow his lead), but I think it's important to know what we're trying to accomplish so I can be more effective in helping to guide the group.

Supervisor: You probably won't get much of a chance anyway, in the beginning. They (the group members) are going to look to Dr. Brown mostly in the beginning.

When I continued to press at another time for group purpose, just before we were to begin our first group, Dr. Brown finally asked what I would suggest:

Worker: Well, we could say something like, "This is a place where people can learn how to support each other and how to get along better."

Dr. Brown: Hmm. I think that might be too frightening for them to hear. Schizophrenics have a hard time with relating to others, and they may just get scared if we try to tell them they have to talk to each other. I don't think we really need to tell them anything. We can just make it very general.

Worker: Like what?

Dr. Brown: Well, we could say there's just so much to talk about and we don't get enough chance to talk that much, so this is a chance for us to be with them.

I did as he recommended at that point, but continued to bring up the topic in future group supervision meetings.

By this point in the process the student was expressing, in class, increased feelings of frustration and anger. She decided to use this Record of Service to focus on her work with the system, recognizing that influencing her co-leaders' and supervisors' perceptions about the group would require at least as much thought and skill as did her work in the group. This represented an important shift in her thinking from complaining about the existence of the problem to recognizing her functional responsibility to try to influence the system. At first, she still had difficulty tuning in to the concerns and feelings of her co-leaders. The important change in her work, however, was her focus on taking some responsibility for her part in the interaction, which she can control.

> I did eventually get some general answers about my co-leader's (and by extension the hospital's) purpose, but I failed to tune in adequately to the team leader's place in the agency and its implications for what he could feel free to do. In the example above, Dr. Brown gave evidence of an important concern: the psychological feelings of safety of the clients. In the following excerpt, Dr. Brown notes other concerns.
>
> **Dr. Brown:** I think you'll find that they don't react the way you're expecting them to. If we push them too far, I'm not sure what they'll do.
>
> **Worker:** Right. I wouldn't want to push them too far. But I think they may be able to handle some attention on relationships, and then we can see what happens and back off if someone is getting too upset.
>
> By trying to convince him to do it my way, I failed to really give attention to his concerns or to explore what he thought might happen so that we might come up with some way to avoid it that really worked and that felt right to both of us. Since I wasn't really respecting his concern or trusting that it was a valid one, I was dismissing its importance and missing an opportunity to really tune in, to reach for the negatives, and to show empathy for the needs of the organization as well as of the clients. If I had this part to do over again, I would have asked for more information about his concerns, acknowledged them, and then tried to work with him to solve the anticipated problems. In fact, I did get to do it over again in a later session, and did better at tuning in at that time:
>
> **Worker:** I thought it was great how they were able to challenge each other and really interact with each other.
>
> **Dr. Brown:** Yeah, but I was concerned. Fred seemed to be getting upset at what was going on.
>
> **Worker:** Does he have any history of having problems when he gets anxious like that?
>
> **Dr. Brown:** Yeah, actually he was at XXX (a forensic psychiatric unit) a number of years ago for attacking somebody with a knife.
>
> **Worker:** Well, no wonder you're so concerned! I didn't know about that.
>
> **Dr. Brown:** Yeah, it was a few years ago, but you never know with some of these people.
>
> **Worker:** We have never really talked about what we would do if someone became violent in the group. I've had some training in nonviolent self-defense, but what is the procedure on this unit?
>
> We were then able to talk about procedures, and about other concerns about what could happen in the group. Again, I think I could have paid a little more attention to Dr. Brown's concerns by asking, "Do you think something like that might happen during group?" rather than by talking about procedures right away, but it did seem at least to acknowledge the importance of his concerns in a way I hadn't done before.

It is important that the tuning-in and empathic responses to colleagues be genuine. Perhaps because of training that has often led professionals to respond with a pseudo-empathy (speaking the words without feeling the feelings), an acute sensitivity to being "social worked," in the worst sense of the word, will result in a negative response. In this example, as the student was better able to examine and manage her own feelings in the situation, her capacity for genuine empathy increased. In the next excerpts, the student describes a strategy she has developed for influencing the team leader. Instead of confronting him with his "deficiencies," she invites him to join her in her own analysis of her work. She does this through the sharing of her process recordings, which include her own self-analysis of her practice.

> After the first session, I began to share my thoughts on what I would like to be doing in the group with my co-leader via process recordings. I began writing weekly a description of what happened in group, the main themes I saw, my overall impression, and my plans for follow-up, and I gave a copy of this to my co-leader each week. I hoped that if I shared my thoughts with him in a written format, he might be better able to take in my ideas without having to respond to them right away. I also felt that I could show in more depth in these recordings the scope of what I envisioned for the group, and that by giving me a chance to show him the things I would have liked to say, even when I wasn't yet able to say them, he might come to trust my judgement more. An example of what I shared with him follows, from the ninth group session:
>
> **Description:** Helen started talking about her family and how her children and grandchildren kept her young. She also spoke about her job at the library and specific things she did there. I said it sounded like she really loved her job, and she agreed. She spoke more about this, addressing most of this to me, and I felt uncomfortable that the rest of the group was not being included, so I responded to her several times but then didn't pursue it further, hoping that others would be able to jump in then.
>
> **Reaction/Analysis:** Not a great strategy, I see now! Perhaps I could have said how I felt and brought it to the group more, or said I thought it was interesting what Helen was talking about and wondered how other members were feeling as they heard Helen talk about her job, or asked her if she wanted anything from the group.
>
> The second example, which is from an earlier session, shows my thoughts about my working relationship with my co-leader, as well as some ideas on group structure. I hoped that by sharing some of my own transference issues with him, I might reduce any threat he might be feeling from me and engage him more easily in working through our differences to work together more effectively.
>
> **Description:** Dr. Brown described why Fred was not on the unit today. There was no response to this, so I went on, saying, "We went over some ground rules last week, and I'd like to just review them quickly again today. The first is no smoking, which has already been mentioned. The second is that it's okay to leave if you have to go to the bathroom, but then we expect you to come back. Um, what else? Oh yes, we talked about confidentiality, that what we talk about here stays here, and that we won't talk about people who aren't here."
>
> **Reaction/Analysis:** We had agreed to review the rules at the beginning of each of the first few group sessions at least, but we hadn't decided who would do what of these tasks. I felt Dr. Brown was giving me some space, so I went ahead and started. I noticed partway through that I wanted to share the task with my co-leader, but we hadn't discussed it, so I wasn't sure if he'd jump in or not. I was glad when he did. I was also concerned about the confidentiality rule because, although we had discussed it in supervision group last week, I hadn't discussed it specifically with Dr. Brown. I guess the question arises as to whether or not I believe he can take care of himself in a situation like that. Clearly there's some transference here of me seeing him

as a dad who would quietly disapprove but never talk about it directly. I guess we should talk about whether we can feel free to disagree or at least clarify things in front of the group (I hope so), and I need to trust Dr. Brown to discuss any differences that may come up openly with me, whether in group or later, and I need to trust myself that I can stand it if he disagrees with me sometimes.

This strategy seemed to work well. When I saw Dr. Brown after he had read this, he said he had enjoyed reading it and looked forward to getting more. We then spoke more about the group and our plans for the next session. Although we rarely talked about the specific content of the recordings, it seemed that giving Dr. Brown the recordings did help him get to know me better and trust me more, and gradually we did come to work together much better. I believe these recordings had a major impact on our relationship developing as well as it did.

I pointed out evidence of successful client interaction whenever I could to my co-leader to support the notion of mutual aid. After one session in which a lot of participation happened, I mentioned in the "Overall impression" section of my weekly recording my positive views of the ability the group shows to do mutual aid:

"Very exciting session! Lots of participation, including real, relevant concerns about what the group will be like. Also, lots of evidence of people supporting each other (Ben trying to support Martha, Robert supporting Gene), and willingness of members to discuss and challenge (Ben, Martha, Jack, and Hilary on poverty, Martha and Jack on why people don't come, Robert on difficulty following conversation). Overall, it's much more participatory and interactive than I had imagined it would be. I see a lot of potential for this group!"

In our meetings as well, I consistently pointed out the positive evidence I saw of the effectiveness of the group, and Dr. Brown would usually acknowledge the evidence, and acknowledge that he hadn't paid so much attention to that. I started to listen better to my co-leader and became better able to hear his concerns and really take them in. We then became better able to work together to come up with strategies for working in group that achieved both our goals.

I continued to press for a more mutual aid focus, and more empowerment of group members to help each other and take control of the group. As my co-leader and I continued to talk about purpose and structure, he gradually became more willing for me to try to promote interaction and a mutual aid focus, and often agreed to suggestions I made for ways to let group members decide how to run the group (regarding how to handle members who leave, for example). In fact, in the tenth session, Dr. Brown joined me in helping people talk to each other and in beginning to encourage members to take some control over their group (this time, when a new member showed up at group, instead of Dr. Brown telling the group he could stay, as he had done in previous sessions, he asked the group if it was okay if the visiting patient stayed!)

As my co-leader and I started to agree more on the goals, purpose, and structure of the group, I brought up the changes in how we were using the group to the group, often using the introduction of new members as an opportunity to restate, review, and clarify any changes in those aspects of the group. For example, in session 14, after asking a new member to introduce himself, and having others introduce themselves to him, I continued as follows:

Worker: Michael, I know you've been to the Tuesday community meeting. I'd like
   to tell you a little about this group because it's different from the Tuesday

meeting. In this group, we talk about all different kinds of things, but it's a smaller group, and people talk to each other more and try to help each other here. Sometimes someone will talk about a problem and others will try to help them figure out how they can make things better, or sometimes people will just talk about how they feel about something and they might find out that other people feel the same way.

Michael: Oh, like a support group?

Worker: Yes, have you been in groups like this before?

Finally, when problems came up for individuals in the group, I encouraged a mutual aid focus. A pivotal session was one in which Gene, a patient whom I see individually, stated that he was going to leave the hospital in three days to get his own room. Although I was concerned abut the inadvisability of this move, my co-leader and I focused on the meaning to the group.

Worker: That's an important thing to be announcing here. I wonder how other people feel about you leaving.

Gene: Well, I just wanted to tell you and Dr. Brown.

Worker: Well, we can talk about it more later. But, since you're here now, I wonder if you were wanting to say good-bye to people in this group.

Other members then began to give Gene feedback, some supporting his move and initiative, some expressing concerns for him. And, instead of his being isolated by making this dramatic statement, as he had been in the past for similar statements, the group members were able to engage with him this time and help him think about his decision in a more realistic and fuller way.

Current Status of the Problem:

Tremendous progress has been made in getting the team leader to accept some different possibilities for goals and formats for use with these patients. Through much discussion, he has been able to accept the possibility of their interacting with each other in a safe and empowering way, and, even more significantly, has begun to look at the system practices that work against the patients' being able to function independently in any areas. He has begun seeing possibilities for them to have more independence in the group that he didn't see before, and is showing interest in continuing to encourage that kind of independence. The structure of the group has been pretty well set by now, although the goals and purpose still need to be more clearly stated to group members and to the entire treatment team. There is a lot of work yet to be done, but a lot has been accomplished toward creating more empowering and effective goals and structure.

Strategies for Intervention:

1. Use the remaining group supervision sessions to review with all involved group staff (myself, my co-leader, the two co-leaders of the other similar group on the ward, and my supervisor, who will be replacing me as co-leader of this group), the progress of the group to date—what worked, what didn't, and so on—and discuss ideas for any changes that are needed now or in developing future groups.

2. Write up a summary report of my impressions and analysis of the group to date, along with the recommendations below, and any identified at the meeting above. Present this to my co-leader and my supervisor.

3. Continue to point out positive results of the mutual aid focus in group supervision meetings, team meetings, and planning sessions with my co-leader.

4. Help group members use mutual aid to deal with my termination (and ask my co-leader to do this as well).

5. As I sum up my work with the group, point out how group members have been able to use mutual aid to help each other, and express hope that they will continue to do so.

This example has not only illustrated a recontracting process over time, it has demonstrated the importance of the "two-client" idea, with the agency or setting as the second client. The attitude toward group work practice in the setting was a reflection of the general attitude toward work with psychiatric patients. The student social worker was helpful to individual members of the group; however, her most important social work impact was on the system. Rather than just remaining distressed and angry about the deficiencies of the system, she began to see addressing these problems as central to her role as a social worker. The effects of her impact on the system would be felt long after she had left her placement. She had also learned that in order to empower the client, the social worker (and other staff) must first deal with her or his own disempowerment.

CO-LEADERSHIP IN GROUPS

The previous example brings us to the question of co-leadership. Whenever the general subject of co-leaders is raised by workers, I inquire if they have had experience working with another staff member in a group. Almost invariably they have, and the experience was usually a bad one. The list of problems includes disagreement on the basic approach to the group, subtle battles over control of group sessions, and disagreement during the group session over specific interventions—particularly those introduced by a co-worker that seem to cut off a line of work one feels is productive. Underlying all of these problems is a lack of honest communication between co-workers both within and outside the group sessions. Workers often feel embarrassed to confront their co-workers outside the session and believe it would be unprofessional to disagree during the session. This stance is similar to the "not arguing in front of the children" syndrome that many parents experience. There is an unreasonable expectation that they must appear to agree at all times. This lack of honesty usually reflects the insecurity of both workers and often leads to defensiveness and the illusion of cooperative work.

Co-leadership can be helpful in a group. A group is complex, and assistance by another worker in implementing the helping function can be a welcome aid. In my couples' group, one co-worker was female. She was able to add perspectives to the work that were strikingly different from mine. For example, she reacted with a different mind set to issues raised in the group related to women. Our ability to work well together was based upon a number of factors. First, there was a basic agreement about an approach to the helping process. While our theoretical frameworks differed and we used different conceptual models for understanding client behavior and dynamics, we shared similar attitudes toward clients and a commitment to mutual aid and the importance of reaching for client strength. Within this common framework, our different conceptual models served, in fact, to enrich our work with the group.

Second, we structured time to discuss the group. We met before the start of the first group sessions to prepare strategy and also met before the start of each session to "tune in," using the previous session as well as any additional knowledge gained from individual contacts with couples. Time was set aside after each session to discuss the group. (In this case, the discussion took place with a group of students training at the school of social work who viewed the group sessions on a video monitor.) Every effort was made to encourage honest communication about the sessions and our reactions to each other's input. This was not simple, since I was the senior group worker, and it was not easy for co-workers to challenge me. As our relationship grew and trust developed, more direct communication was apparent. Finally, we had an understanding that we would feel free to disagree in the group. In many ways, the co-worker and I were a model of a male/female relationship in action. It would be a mockery of our effort if we supported honesty and willingness to confront while maintaining professional "courtesy" toward each other in the group. Observing that co-leaders could disagree, even argue, in a group and still respect and care for each other can be a powerful object lesson for group members.

Group members are very observant, and they can pick up subtle cues of tension between leaders, no matter how hard workers try to hide them. This was pointed out in the midyear evaluation of this couples' group. A third co-worker in this group was a former student of mine, and although he participated in the sessions up until that point, the presence of the other co-worker and his feelings about working with a former teacher inhibited him. We had discussed this in the sessions with the student observers, who had been quick to pick up his hesitancy. In the midyear evaluation session of the couples' group, I inquired how the members felt we could improve our work during the second half of the year. Illustrating the perceptiveness of group members, Rose, our member in her late sixties, turned to my co-worker and said, "I hope you don't take what I'm going to say personally. I think you have a lot to give to this group, and I would like to hear more from you. I don't think you should let Larry (the senior worker) frighten you just because he is more experienced." He responded, "You know, Rose, I've been worried about my participation, too. It is hard for me to get in as often as I want to, and I'm going to work on it."

As a final comment on co-leadership, I believe it is very difficult, but not impossible, for two beginning group leaders to work together. Their own anxieties are so great that they often become more of a problem for each other than a help. Working with a more experienced worker provides learners with an opportunity to test their wings without taking full responsibility for the outcome. When mutual trust and sharing develop between co-workers, the workers can be an important source of support for each other. The feelings of warmth and caring that develop between members and between the group worker and members must also exist between co-leaders as they tackle the complex task of working with groups. Of course, the problems of co-leadership, only partially elaborated in this brief discussion, must be kept in mind.

CHAPTER SUMMARY

The core skills of contracting in first sessions, introduced in Parts II and III, were reexamined in the group work context. Clarifying purpose, the group leader's role, reaching for client feedback, dealing with the authority theme, and so on, were all illustrated with a detailed analysis of the transcript of a first session of a married couples' group. Recognition that contracting does not always go well the first time, or that it may take a number of sessions for the group to deal with all the issues, was central to the discussion of recontracting—the process in which the worker raises contracting issues with an ongoing group. In particular, strategies and skills for working with co-leaders and the system in the recontracting exercise emphasized the social worker's ability to see the system as the "second client."

GLOSSARY

Recontracting The process in which the worker reopens the issues of contracting by providing a clearer statement of purpose or exploring the group members' resistance or lack of connection to the service.

Systems work The set of activities in which social workers attempt to influence the systems and systems representatives (e.g., doctors, administrators, teachers) that are important to their clients.

NOTES

1. The setting, names of the members, and some of the details of the discussion have been changed to protect the confidentiality of group members. The process is described as it was recorded on a videotaped record of the group maintained for teaching purposes with the permission of the members. The videotape is available from McGill University, Montreal, Canada. (Shulman, L., 1979b, "Program 2: Leading a First Group Session." *The Skills of Helping*. Videotape series. Montreal: Instructional Communications Centre, McGill University.)

11

First Group Sessions: Some Variations

CHAPTER OUTLINE

First Sessions with Children and Adolescents
The Impact of Authority on the First Session
Client Problem Impact
Impact of the Setting of Service
Impact of Time

In the previous chapter we explored a number of common dynamics and skills related to first group meetings. These were illustrated using a first session of a group for married couples. However, not all groups are composed of articulate adults or of clients attending voluntarily. In this chapter we will consider the most important variant elements that may affect the worker's strategy. Basically, these can be broken down into the following five categories: the age and relative articulateness of the members, the authority of the worker, the specific concerns of the clients, the setting of the encounter, and the impact of time. Each of these variations will be illustrated with examples from first sessions of appropriate groups. These groups include adolescents and grade-school children; women on welfare; prospective adoptive parents; parents of children with cerebral palsy; foster parents; depressed psychiatric outpatients; widows in a community center program; a residential lounge committee; a ward group in a general hospital; and finally, the first session of a short-term group with single parents. Throughout these very different examples, the core ideas of the contracting process will become evident.

FIRST SESSIONS WITH CHILDREN AND ADOLESCENTS

The problem of lack of clarity of purpose or embarrassment about making a direct statement of purpose, discussed in Part II, is even more common in the group context. The presence of more than one client may increase the reluctance of the worker to be direct. In the examples that follow, you will note a correlation between directness and honesty in the contracting and a more effective start to the group.

Foster Adolescents in a Child Welfare Setting

In this first extract, note the worker's reliance on safe and generalized topics in her opening statement to a group of foster adolescents in a child welfare agency:

I opened the discussion by telling all the members that what was said in these groups would remain confidential. Neither workers nor foster parents would ever know what was being discussed. In addition, I pointed out that the same sort of commitment would be required on their part. I then mentioned the kinds of things we could discuss; for example, the trouble they have making their allowances stretch and whether or not the clothing allowance was sufficient. There followed a great period of silence, at which point I suggested that if they could think of nothing else, perhaps they would like to talk about the lack of conversation (which seemed to be a little too far advanced for the group to handle).

Nothing in the worker's statement recognized that they were all foster children. The examples she used could have been drawn from any discussion group for teenagers, and yet they all knew that they were foster children and that this group was sponsored by a child welfare agency. The worker omitted any comment about her role in the proceedings. The silence probably reflected their confusion about the group's purpose and their reluctance to begin. The worker's comment about the silence could reflect her own anxiety about their lack of immediate enthusiasm. In the rest of this session, the discussion was marked by wide shifts in subject matter, with youngsters talking about related topics (e.g., trouble with foster parents) and totally unrelated ones (e.g., TV shows).

In an illustration from another group, we see how the lack of clear contracting in the opening of a session came back to haunt the group leader. In this case, the group consisted of older teens who had recently left the care of foster parents or group homes and were starting to live on their own (although still legally wards of the agency) or who were about to do so. The age and relaxed attitude of the members encouraged spontaneous conversation that lulled the worker into skipping the contracting work.

> There was no official opening as the group began prior to the arrival of the last member. They discussed common issues such as Grade 13, schools, and then talking somewhat about their present life-styles living in a foster home or living on their own. When Frank entered late, he picked up on the flow of the conversation. Because of the easy flow, I did not intervene with an official contract, preferring to encourage them to interact with one another.
>
> **Connie:** How long have you been in care?
>
> **Diane:** Since I was three.
>
> **Connie:** That is a long time.
>
> **Carol:** Since I was 15. I just made it, because I was almost 16 years old.
>
>   (A short silence followed.)
>
> **Worker:** And you, Connie?
>
> **Connie:** I'm not sure. I came and then went again. About six years old, I guess.
>
>   (Discussion followed about where they lived and how they felt about their foster parents.)
>
> **Connie:** Did you notice those ads on TV asking for foster homes?
>
> **Worker:** How did they strike you?
>
> **Connie:** What do you mean?
>
> **Worker:** Well, you are a foster child. I was wondering if they affected you?
>
> **Connie:** I think it's a good idea. If you need a foster home, that's a good way to get one.

The discussion continued, covering many issues without staying on any one for very long. The worker's request that Connie elaborate on the effect of the TV ads was politely declined because Connie had no way of knowing why the worker was asking. The issue of contract became explicit at the "doorknob" as the worker attempted to end the meeting.

Worker: What about next week?

Diane: I want to come back. I have a lot to learn about loans and money and how to manage. We could meet until we are tired of meetings or don't have anything else to say, but I don't want it to be like last year in a group where we really didn't talk about anything. It got boring.

John: Well, I don't know. I like to hear from the other kids, but I don't have any real problems since I was discharged.

Diane: Well, what is the purpose of this group? Why are we coming?

Worker: We thought you might be having some problems because of your discharges, and we wanted to give you a chance to help each other. We were concerned with how you are coping with your problems.

Carol: At first I thought maybe you were checking up on us to find out how we were doing.

Worker: Sounds like you were rather suspicious.

Carol: Yes. (Laughter followed.)

Worker: No, we really do care. We just want to help you in any way we can.

Carol: Yes, I can see that now.

The worker could have eased their concern about the purpose early in the session by interrupting their conversation with a brief statement about purpose. Only at the end of the session did members have a clear framework for selecting their responses and understanding why the worker asked certain questions. This worker caught her mistake in the same session.

Ten-Year-Old Girls in a School Setting

With some groups, the intensity of the issues or the particular strengths of the members will cause an **internal leader** to emerge and to raise the work in spite of the lack of contracting. An internal leader is a member of the group who assumes a leadership role in a situational or ongoing basis. The term *internal* distinguishes this leader from the worker, who is an **external leader** with authority derived from the agency and his or her professional function. The notion of the "role" of internal leaders is discussed in more detail in Chapter 13. In the following example, the group worker is unclear in her contracting with a group of 10-year-old girls in a school setting, and two internal leaders, Harriet and Vera, emerge to give direction to the group. The worker misses some of their early signals of issues for discussion. Fortunately, instead of reacting to these two members as competing for her leadership role, or seeing their behavior as "deviant" (which is often the case with an insecure group worker), this worker relinquishes control of the group's direction to the members. The contracting begins as the members use a book device introduced by the worker to start the feedback process.

(The girls came in and sat in chairs in a circle, squirming around, flinging their legs over the chair arms. During the following conversation, the girls took off their shoes and sweatshirts. Vera and Harriet pretended to remove their shirts with their sweatshirts.)

Harriet: Is this group going to be boring?
Worker: Do you think it'll be boring?
Harriet: No.
Vera: Can we have parties?
Worker: Well, what would we do at a party here?
Vera: Food, talking, dancing, and music.
Worker: Yes, yes, yes, yes. Well, yes, I guess we can have parties here.
Vera: Today?
Worker: No, not today.
Harriet: Can we dress up like hookers?
Worker: Is that fun?
(Several): Yes!
Worker: Who does that?
Vera, Harriet: Me!
Worker: Oh, two me's!
Worker: Let me tell you about the group. (Harriet mimics.) Harriet, stop. (Harriet continues.) Harriet, that's enough. OK? It's so you'll have a place that's special, just for you guys. This is your group, with me—our group. We're going to think about fun things that we can do together, and we'll do them. And it's also a place where you can bring things to talk about—things that happen at school or at home, at the Community House, at church, with friends... because this might be a time in your life when lots of things are changing, or maybe about to change, and it can help to talk about it. I'd like this to be a place where you can say things and know that no one's going to tell them to anyone outside the group. Now let me show you this; this is our book, for this group open to page with three headings: "Things we want to do," "Things we want to talk about," "Things we want for snack." (I put the book on the floor in the center of the circle and bring out Magic Markers.)

The worker has given a general statement of contract but has not included any "handles for work" that would operationalize the concept of "things changing in your life." She also is misleading in her statement about confidentiality, since she cannot guarantee things will not be shared outside of the group. The internal leaders return to the confidentiality issue, but the worker does not respond.

Vera and **Harriet:** We can't talk with Olive (absent today). She tells, she blabs, she says she won't, but she does. (All nod.)
Worker: I hope we can work together to help Olive. (To Fran, who is quiet) What does your sweatshirt say?
(Conversation about people's clothing. At one point, Fran touches Harriet.)
Harriet: Don't touch me.
Vera: (To worker) What color is your shirt? (Points, then pokes finger up into worker's face) (Laughter) That's the oldest trick in the book!
Worker: Well, it didn't feel good to me.
Vera: Oh, I'm sorry.
Worker: OK. (Reorienting around book)
Vera: (To worker) My mom likes you, and she told Jean (the worker's supervisor).

Worker: That's nice. I liked meeting your moms. I've seen everyone's mother but Harriet's; she's coming next week.

Vera: Harriet doesn't want you to meet her mother.

Worker: (To Harriet) Why not?

Harriet: She asks dumb questions—don't tell her I said that!

Worker: I won't. Like what?

Harriet: Like she asked my teacher, "Are you a good teacher?"

Worker: And the teacher could only give one answer, huh? She had to say "yes." She couldn't very well say, "No, I'm a lousy teacher." (Laughter)

(Vera seems ready to write in the book. Worker encourages others to take a turn, but they seem content to let Vera do it. Under "snack" she writes Oreos, pretzels, Pepsi, pizza... Then she moves to "What to talk about.")

Vera: What we want to talk about...hmm. (Laughter) (Mouthing words to worker) Sex!

Worker: (Whispering to Vera) What about sex? Boys or bodies?

Vera: Both.

Worker: How do you want to write it? (Vera considers, writes "sex.")

Worker: That's the simplest, isn't it? (Vera later adds "boys and bodies"—laughter, long and loud—particularly from Harriet.)

Harriet: (Laughing) Sex, we want to talk about sex!

Worker: Harriet, Harriet, you need to be quieter.

Harriet: (More laughter) Sex!

Worker: Do you want us to leave that on the paper, or does it make you too uncomfortable? (More laughter)

(Vera moves on to "Things we want to do": cooking, drama (plays), art... Worker adds some possibilities, some contributions from others, but most are from Vera.)

The worker, having passed the first test with her "boys or bodies?" comment, encourages members to open up with other, perhaps more painful, issues. Interestingly, the worker's own ambivalence is noted in her suggestion to modify the issue "family problems" to "families." It is further evidenced when the worker seems to try to slow the girls down when they want to start the discussion. Again, a member asserts her own (and the members') control over the process.

Vera: We can talk about family problems, too.

Worker: Yes, you could just write "families."

Vera: OK, family problems.

Worker: Yes, put down "families."

Fran: Can we talk now?

Worker: Let me show you the next page. This is our group book, and this page is about who each of you is. (Page is divided into quarters.)

(Girls each choose a quarter. Vera describes the game as "4-square." Then each chooses a Magic Marker. Worker asks each to write her name, and nickname if she has one. Two volunteer preferred other names).

Fran: Don't laugh, but my baby cousin calls me _____ instead of my real name because she can't say it. (No one laughs.)

(They write their schools, ages—all are 10—birthdates, grade in school.)

Vera: (To Fran) You were held back in school, right?

Fran: Yes. But I was the youngest in my class before.

Worker: So you were young for your old grade and now you're with kids more your age.

(Write names and ages and relationships of siblings, amid discussion of "I hate...." and "We fight...." As we write and talk, Harriet several times slaps herself for saying or doing something "bad.")

Worker: (To Harriet) You don't have to hit yourself.

Harriet: Yes, I do.

(One suggests writing down names of best friends, which precipitates a discussion of the changing nature of friendships and alliances in the peer group. The group then moves on to boyfriends.)

Vera: I'm a two-timer!

Harriet: I'm a two-timer, too!

Worker: I think at this age you're allowed to be a two-timer.

(Several): Are the boys gonna see this?

Worker: No.

(Several): Don't let them! They might tell.... Are the mothers going to see?

Worker: No, this book is just for the group. The rest of the time it'll be locked up in my office.

Harriet: My mother better not see it—she'd kill me!

Worker: Why? Are you not allowed to have boyfriends?

Harriet: No, I'm not allowed to have boyfriends.

Vera: (Circling two boys' names) These are my babes.

Worker: Are boys babes or only girls? (Lots of laughter) No, really—I don't know how you use the word.

(Vera stands up, does some gesture and line about how the boys look at girls' behinds. Lots of laughter.)

Harriet: (To Vera) Don't do that. What's next?

Fran: Let's talk.

Worker: Well, I thought we could think of a name for the group, and make a cover for our book.

Fran: No, let's talk.

Worker: OK, what would you like to talk about? (Putting book aside)

Fran: I want to talk about what Harriet wants to talk about.

Vera: Sex.

Worker: (To Vera) Do you really want to talk about that already?

Vera: Yes. (General agreement)

Worker: OK. What shall we say about sex?

Harriet: Well, I don't get my period.

Vera: I know it all already; my Dad tells me everything. He told me about the birds and bees.

Worker: (To Fran) Harriet doesn't get her period, and Vera's Dad tells her everything. How about you?

Fran: (Indicates she'll pass)

Vera: I don't get my period, either.

Fran: Me neither.

Vera: Neither does Olive, but she'll lie.

Harriet: Yeah, she'll tell the kids in school, "This girl Harriet gets her period." But I don't!

Vera: We can't talk when she's here; let's talk now.

Worker: I didn't get my period till late. I was 14, and I thought everyone else got it before me. But that's how it was.

Harriet: You get your period?

Worker: Sure, most adults do—most adult ladies.

Harriet: I know.

Vera: I don't want a period; you get cramps.

Worker: Oh, not always. I didn't used to, not when I started. That didn't happen till later; it sometimes did. But it's different for different people. Do you know someone who gets cramps?

Vera: Yes, my stepmother. We were going to go to the beach, but she couldn't.

The discussion about a stepmother triggers a painful theme for Harriet. Also, as the session is coming to an end, the "doorknob therapy" phenomenon is noted, with a member raising a most difficult issue as the session closes. She sends her first, indirect signal to the worker by kicking over a chair. The worker does not reach for the meaning of the behavior and instead brings out the snack. Harriet will escalate the responses until the worker gets the message and responds.

(Harriet kicks over a folding chair; worker brings out snack.)

Vera: (Holding up cup of juice) To a good group!

All: To a good group!

(Harriet starts talking about her stepmother.)

Harriet: My stepmother hates me.

(Worker looks pained—girls laugh; Harriet spits out juice.)

Harriet: One time she said to me, "I wanna rip the fuckin' balls out of her head."

(Worker shows reaction of puzzlement/annoyance at the statement. Girls laugh.)

Fran: (Points) Look at her!

Harriet: Then she said, "I know you don't have any balls, but I wanna rip the fuckin' hair out of your head." Excuse my language. And once when I was in the bathroom, I heard her say to my father, "When is she gonna get the fuck out of here?"

Worker: Sounds like she doesn't want you there at your father's.

Harriet: My Dad hates me. What did I do to make him hate me?

Worker: Maybe you didn't do anything. Maybe his life just went another way, but it hurts.

(Meanwhile, nervous laughter from others.)

The worker is tuning in to Harriet's pain but misses the signal from the second client, the group, that they are feeling anxious about the themes raised by Harriet.

Worker: Vera, it's hard enough for Harriet to say, without you laughing.

(Harriet is also laughing, hard, almost crying, pounding her empty cup into the floor, then throwing it at the worker. She picks up the jug of apple juice, looks at each person, and begins to pour it onto the floor. All come forward to intervene, and Harriet puts the juice down. Worker gently takes Harriet by shoulders.)

Worker: Harriet, you can't do that. If you're mad, you can tell us you're mad.

(As the worker goes back to her place in the circle, Fran, next to Harriet, mimics the worker, holding Harriet's shoulders kindly. Harriet lets her.)

Worker: See, Harriet, Fran's also trying to help you calm down.

Vera: (Helping dry rug) Look at what we put you through....

Worker: No, it's not that, we just can't do something like that.

Harriet: I'm sorry. I spilled the juice on purpose.

Worker: Yes, OK.

Vera: Harriet said "f" three times.... My father lets me swear, only not gross words, like c-u-n ... yuck.

Worker: That's a slang word. Does your mother let you?

Vera: No. Can I say something dirty?

Worker: (To Fran and Harriet) Is it OK or...? (Nods, affirmation) OK.

(Vera tells about her father's collection of hats, including one with a raised middle finger, one with bird droppings painted on, and one with "boob inspector" and two plastic "boobs" on it. Harriet laughs and laughs and gleefully repeats.)

Worker: If I saw someone wearing that on the street, I'd feel uncomfortable.

Harriet: Not me, I'd laugh and laugh. (As she does)

Vera: My father was going to wear it when he took me to the dentist.

Worker: What did you say?

Vera: I said, "Don't, you'll embarrass me."

Worker: (To Fran, who has been listening intently, but not saying much) Did you have something you wanted to say?

Fran: I'm not sure...

Worker: We'll have more chances next time. It's almost time to go now.

Fran: (Starts to get giggly and jumpy) Sex! Can we write "sex" on the walls?

Worker: No, we can't write anything on the walls. Only in our minds, not really on the wall.

Harriet: (Accusingly, to worker) Now you put it in my mind!

(Worker laughs, accepting the joke. Discussion continues about how they want to stay longer, and can we keep talking?)

Worker: You can keep talking downstairs, but I need to work.

(Someone asks, as we're all cleaning up, whether we'll meet all year.)

Worker: Yes, from now until April, though we'll take a break around Christmas, because my school has vacation.

Fran: (Worriedly) Are you a teacher?

Worker: No, I'm a student. I'm going to school to learn to be a social worker, and two days a week I'm here, working. On Fridays, from 3 to 4, I'm here with you for our group.

Vera: (To worker) Will you swear here?

Worker: Would it be weird for you if I did?

Vera: No.

Worker: I don't think I will, but I might. I sometimes do.

(General glee): So we can swear here?

Worker: Yes, but you have to be able to turn it off when you're with people who don't like it.

(Discussion of what to do next time gets loud.)

Worker: We might want to start thinking about some rules, like one at a time talking.... I was thinking that next time we might go out for a walk. Is that OK?

Harriet: Just around the block, then we should come back and talk.

(We finish planning where we'll walk next week, if the weather is good.)

It's clear that even with the uncertain contracting, the lack of worker clarity about her role as a social worker, and the unresolved issue of confidentiality, the group members were anxious to have an adult they could talk to about the themes of sex, family problems, friends, and school. It's interesting to note the worker's continued ambivalence, evident in her suggestion that they go on a walk at the next session. The internal leader, Harriet, is willing to compromise but insists that the walk be a short one.

Unmarried Pregnant Teens in a Shelter

In the next example, the contrast is sharp as an experienced worker begins with a clear statement about group purpose and her role. The group members, unmarried and pregnant adolescents residing in a shelter while awaiting the birth of their babies, took up her offer immediately.

I started off the group session by welcoming everybody. I also asked their permission to use the tape recorder for my own learning. (They agreed.) I said that they were probably wondering what the group was all about. We had found that upon entering the home, many girls became more aware of the difficulties of their pregnancy and the decisions they had to make. We believed that by talking about common problems together, they could help each other. I said that I was there to help them get started and to clarify agency policy. This was their group—I wondered where they wanted to start.

Carol (who had been told she had to attend the group) immediately jumped in. She wanted to know if it was true that there were financial resources available to help you keep your child. I said that the city welfare and mothers' allowance were available. Leslie said that she had looked into this, and she proceeded to explain how this operated. I asked Carol if she was thinking of keeping her baby. She said she wanted to, but she also wanted to attend school. I wondered who would care for her child while she attended school. Carol said, "Probably a day care center."

An animated discussion began about day care. Andrea said she was giving up her child because she did not feel that you should keep your child if you were not home to care for it. Kate said she was planning to give up her child because she was not ready to stay home with it. I wondered if Carol was saying that this was a very difficult decision and that she felt like keeping and relinquishing her child at the same time. Carol said that she was not responsible enough to care for a child and that a child limited your life. Andrea felt that you might grow to resent the child, which would be unfair. She did not feel ready to be a parent. Carol said that she could be quite rational about the baby, but she was afraid of the emotional appeal of the baby. I wondered if others in the group felt the same way. There was some nodding of heads, and Andrea and Kate said out loud that this scared them. I said that I could understand this feeling.

Carol said she should have gone on the Pill. She proceeded to explain that the youth of today are sexually active. She said she kept putting it off (taking the Pill).

Several of the girls said together, "It couldn't happen to me." Everyone laughed or smiled. (Marie, Lisa, and Connie had not said anything, but they appeared interested and laughed with the rest of the girls.) Kate said that she had approached her mother about taking the Pill but had received a cold, negative response. Andrea said she does not know how she could have been so naive as to think it would not happen to her. She said that the hard thing now was that her parents were blaming themselves for her pregnancy. She said that she had tried to tell them that she was responsible for her own actions, but she did not think she was successful. She feels to blame now that all of the other kids in the family were having their freedom curtailed because of her. Carol said that her father had not spoken to her since learning of the pregnancy, but her mother had been telling Carol's 13-year-old sister not to follow in her sister's footsteps. A discussion followed about why each of the girls came to the home.

As the group members sensed their ability to use this group to deal with their concerns, they quickly accepted the worker's invitation to make it "their group." The worker concentrated on helping them to elaborate on their thoughts ("I asked Carol if she was thinking of keeping her baby"), gently confronting them ("I wondered who would care for her child while she attended school"), articulating their feelings, particularly the ambivalence ("I wondered if Carol was saying that this was a very difficult decision and that she felt like keeping and relinquishing her child at the same time"), generalizing to the group ("I wondered if others in the group felt the same way"), and acknowledging their feelings ("I said I could understand this feeling"). As the session drew to an end, the worker identified the themes of concern raised by the members, attempted to develop a consensus on where to start the next session, complimented them for their work, and reached for their evaluation.

I said that we had covered many topics—day care, the Pill, family, abortion, welfare, and so on. I said they had worked well. Kate said, "Is it over? It went so fast!" I said that I was pleased that Kate seemed to be saying that she got something out of the group. How did the rest feel?

Carol said it helped her to know that others felt as she did about abortion. She was not the only crazy one. Kate said that it helped to talk. Then, she turned to Linda and said, "How come you didn't say anything?" Andrea said, "That's because you talked too much." I said some people found it easier to talk in a group than others. I wondered where they wanted to start next week. Kate made several halting attempts until she was finally able to say that she was interested in how others would see her after this was all over, particularly men. The agreement to tackle this subject seemed unanimous.

Setting Limits: An Adolescent Acting-Out Boys' Group

Ambiguity in contracting is common in work with children's groups. A good example is the "activity group" in a school setting for children who are having difficulty with schoolwork or peers. A common problem with such groups results from having borrowed a traditional view of group work from the original group settings, which were leisure-time agencies, settlement houses, community centers, and the like. In this view, while members attended programs for what seemed like recreational purposes, the group leader actually had a "hidden agenda" related to agency purposes. In the school setting, the group worker might contract with the school administration to lead "clubs" that were designed for "teaching the youngsters how to get along better with each other and how to manage their own activities." A worker would argue that this would help the children get along better in school. The group would be viewed by the worker as a medium to "change the group members' patterns of behavior." The assumption is that a transfer of training will occur, and the learning from the group experience will make the child a better student. A further assumption is that the worker can influence the group members indirectly by using the group activity as a medium for the "real purpose." The validity of both assumptions is questionable.

I have written elsewhere about the ways in which group members can use activities (singing, games, crafts, and so on) as important tools in their work (Shulman, 1971). There are many routes whereby group members can provide mutual aid for each other; certainly, it would be a mistake to view words as the only significant medium of exchange between people. The argument here challenges the view that program activity is the worker's tool for "changing" group members. For instance, worker may withhold the real purpose of the group, leaving the members unclear as to the reason for the activity. When the youngsters look around during the first session, however, they know who the other children are and that they are the "losers," the "bad kids," or the "dummies" in the school. Because the contracting is not straightforward and honest, they become more anxious, often acting out their anxiety in disruptive behavior. The worker may assume that this behavior is intended to "test" authority or view it as an example of why the members have been referred in the first place. Early sessions may involve a great deal of limit-setting by the worker, resulting in a battle of wills between the leader and the group. An alternative pattern is that the youngsters may involve themselves quickly in the group activities, which they say are "a lot more fun than school." The worker then finds it harder to deal with school problems directly. Since the worker's promise to the teachers and the principal was that the group would "change" the child's school behavior, the worker may be in trouble with the school staff when this does not happen and may then have to defend the rationale for the group against attacks by staff who view the group activities as "rewards for the kids' bad behavior."

By honestly contracting with the school and the children from the beginning, much of this difficulty can be avoided. Group work is not magic, and the youngsters will not be "cured." The group worker can help children who are having difficulty making it in the school by providing them with an opportunity to talk about whatever goes on in school that makes it hard for them. For example, students often feel their teacher is "down" on them or does not like them. Efforts by the teacher to encourage better levels of work may be experienced by the students as "being picked on." The group might provide a means for helping the members to see the teacher's actions in new ways and to figure out how to talk to the teacher more directly about their feelings.

In turn, the group worker can meet with the teachers to help them understand the students' perspective. This might help the teachers reach out in a different way to these particular children. The group worker has a part in these proceedings, the teachers have a role to play, and most important, the children will also have to work on improving their situation at school. Other issues may include peer relationships (e.g., fights or feeling of rejection that interfere with school activity) or the impact of the family (e.g., how hard it is to concentrate in the mornings when you have just had an argument with your mother and the teacher does not understand how upset you are).

In classrooms where racial, ethnic, or class difference is a factor—for example, the white teacher with a class of students of color—students may perceive racism in the teacher's attitudes toward them. Given the pervasiveness of subtle and not-so-subtle institutionalized racism in our society, they may be accurate in their perceptions. This would then set an agenda for the social worker for action with the system, as will be discussed in Part V. In other cases, this may be a misperception caused by the students' having their "antennae up" and thereby perceiving racist attitudes and actions. Given their persistent experiences with racism and oppression, this sensitivity is understandable and necessary for survival. Once again, the worker may be able to offer to help break the taboo against open discussion with the teacher that may impede efforts in the classroom. Of course, if the worker is also a member of the majority group, work on the relationship between the worker and the group members would be essential in the early sessions.

The important point is that both the school staff and the group members understand that the group is formed to help them use school more effectively and to make learning more fun. When teachers see that this focus is central to the work, they are more willing to accept the idea that change may come slowly. They can see the group as essentially related to their educational purposes and therefore worth an investment of time and effort. When group members are clear about the real purpose of the group, they are better able to use both it and the worker to deal directly with their school concerns. In some cases, group activities may be part of the way the group operates, and the leader can contract to help the members see how their attitude to issues in the group (e.g., cooperation on projects) often reflects the patterns they have developed in the classroom that get them into trouble.

In the example that follows, the worker makes an effort to clarify the real purpose with a group of 12- and 13-year-old sixth-graders described by the school staff as "disruptive and non-cooperative." The members respond to the worker's offer in two ways: first, they verbally describe their unhappiness with school as the worker encourages them to elaborate in this problem-swapping part of the contracting; second, they *act out* their anxiety through behavior that simultaneously shows the worker (the process) why they have been referred (the content). It is a new group worker's nightmare come true as she struggles to deal with the members' verbal and physical attacks on each other. In this excerpt, we see the worker integrating two roles. First, she must set limits on behavior in order to protect the individual members (and the existence of the group itself). Simultaneously, she reaches for the meaning of the group members' behavior and points out the process-content integration.

> All five children know each other and are in classes together. Four are white, one Hispanic, and all come from troubled families. Juan has been physically abused by his estranged father. Greg has an older brother who is very violent and has terrorized this particular junior high school. James lives with his aunt, not his living parents. Jason (absent from the first meeting) has been sexually abused by his father. Collin's parents have separated. Three of these kids have had core evaluations and have been slotted for Special Education classes that have not started yet because of hiring difficulties within the school.
>
> **Worker:** I think that some of you could be nervous about being here. I want to try to reassure you and remind you that you are not in trouble, you have not done anything wrong, and this group is not detention or punishment. (James interjects.)
>
> **James:** We think it's great to get out of study period.
> (The others concur.)
>
> **Worker:** I hope this group becomes more than a way to get out of study period. The guidance director, Mr. Sher, and your teachers, Mr. Zacks and Ms. Trem-

ble, are concerned because they want you to get more out of school and they feel you all can do much better. They thought I might be able to help you talk about some of the things that might be bothering you about school. You guys will be responsible for bringing up problems and solving them. My job will be to make sure we stay on the subject. Together, maybe we can think of ways to make things better for all of you at school, so let's get started. What is it like to be in sixth grade and in a brand new school for six weeks? (Greg raises his hand after I said the word *like.*) Greg, thank you for waiting until I'd finished, but it is not necessary for any of you to raise your hands in order to speak. I will ask that one person speak at a time and people should really listen to each other.

Greg: School sucks! (As Greg finished, the others chimed in.)

Collin: Yeah! School sucks! (Both Greg and Collin are trying to see whether I will react to the vulgarity. I did not react.)

Juan: It's so boring.

James: It's not as boring as elementary school.

Juan: That is true; at least you are not stuck in the same room all day.

Worker: In what ways is school boring?

All adolescents begin talking at the same time, attempting to provide me with vignettes as to their own or present company's antics, making sure to hurl insults at each other; i.e., Greg stood on his chair and began to boisterously accuse Juan of never doing his homework. Juan snapped back that Greg was retarded and could not sit still. I told Greg to sit down in his chair and Juan not to name call. Collin asked permission to go to the bathroom (but didn't really need to go and did not ask again during the meeting). Then James spoke to me, stating that sometimes he finds school work boring because he does not understand it. As I was focused on James and about to respond to him, Greg pulled the chair out from under Collin in such a way that Collin landed on his coccyx and was in severe pain.

Worker: (Shouting) That's it! I want everybody to sit down and be quiet for a minute! (I gave Collin a brief neurological exam. I used to be an Emergency Medical Technician. Collin was okay. As his pain lessened, I helped him into his chair, and I sat back down.) I am sorry I yelled at you guys, but I felt things were getting out of hand. I got angry because I felt you guys were hurting each other with words, and, Greg, I know you did not mean to hurt Collin, but you've all got to stick to our original agreement—no physical abuse. I think you guys were trying to hurt one another to avoid talking about what is hurting you inside about school. I wonder if this isn't what happens in class when things get uncomfortable.

The worker had to shout in order to get the group members' attention. In retrospect, given the reasons for referral for this group, this kind of acting-out behavior could be expected. If possible, having a co-leader might have helped the group leader feel more comfortable. The limit-setting intervention is familiar to the group members; they have experienced it in most of their classes. What may be different is the way in which she apologizes for getting angry and then explains the limit as coming from concern about the members and her desire to provide a safe place in the group. The limit emerges from the reality of the group experience and is not expressed, as they may have often heard it, as an arbitrary imposition of authority (e.g., "In my class I will not tolerate this kind of behavior!"). Also, the worker does not fall into the trap of using this incident as an opportunity to "preach" or "teach" about "proper" behavior, as she so unsuccessfully tried earlier ("Greg, thank you for waiting until I'd finished, but it is not necessary for any of you to raise your hands in order to speak. I will ask that one person speak at a time and people should really listen to each other."). If these children could work in this manner, they would not be in the group. Instead, she honestly expresses her own feelings, reinforces the element of the working agreement against physical abuse, and starts to identify for the boys their maladaptive pattern of reacting. It will take some time until they learn to manage their feelings without using fight or flight to avoid their pain. Some may not be able to do it and may have to leave the group. However, with her first reactions, she is letting them know that this group (and she) will be different.

Contracting with 12-Year-Old Boys in a School Setting

In the following example, a new group worker begins to clarify purpose directly with a group of 12-year-old grade-school boys who are in trouble in their school. In this example, the boys were able to respond without acting out.

> **Worker:** I'm Frank, a social worker with the Riverview Youth Services. We try to help kids who are having troubles with their school and their families. The reason I'm meeting with you guys is that your teachers feel you're not having as much fun out of school as you can. I thought we might be able to help by talking about some of the problems and seeing if we could figure out a way of making school more fun. What do you think?
>
> **Kevin:** Yeah, I know what you mean.
>
> **Worker:** This is going to be your group. You guys will make the decision about what we talk about and what we do, and you will have to come up with the answers to your problems yourself. I make suggestions and I'll make sure we don't go flying all over the place so that nobody gets hurt.
>
> **George:** (Smiling) Like if we get into a rumble?
>
> **Worker:** Yeah, I'll make sure no one gets thrown through the window. (The members laugh.) What we will talk about is how to make school more fun.
>
> **Kevin:** I was in a group last year. A few of us used to go to a classroom, and Mr. Kent used to help us with our math.
>
> **Worker:** This group won't be like that. I'm not a teacher, so I won't be teaching you math or spelling or anything like that. But what we can do is talk about problems you might be might be having with teachers or with other kids that are making it hard for you to learn.
>
> **Dave:** I was having problems in my class. I had the same teacher as my older sister, and she used to always get A's.
>
> **Worker:** And you don't.
>
> **Dave:** Yeah!
>
> **Worker:** It must be hard having the same teacher when she expects you to do the same as your sister.
>
> **Dave:** Yeah, 'cause I'm different.

The group members were trying to sort out what type of group this would be and what kind of authority person this leader would be. They attempted to match this experience with others in their lives. The worker used this to help describe what they would do. Further clarification might consist of examples of how the help could work in the group. For instance, the worker could prepare a sample problem, a hypothetical situation for them to discuss (e.g., suppose you had a fight with a kid during recess because he was bugging you in class, only the teacher didn't see that part, she only saw you hit him). The examples help the youngsters get a sense of the type of problems they might bring to the group and how other group members and the worker can help them "think it through and come up with some ideas about what to do."

In the group just described, the discussion moved to the issue of confidentiality as the worker discussed the importance of his being able to share information with teachers and the principal. Group members expressed fears that he then explored, working out an agreement as to how he would communicate and how they could be involved in deciding what teachers and their principal needed to hear. They agreed that it would not do much good if their complaints were not heard, and the worker assured them that he would try to do it in a way that did not get them into more trouble. In Part V of this book we will look at systems work and some of the dynamics involved in providing feedback to teachers, doctors, and other system representatives.

THE IMPACT OF AUTHORITY ON THE FIRST SESSION

The authority of the worker is always an issue in the first session. In some settings it can take on increased importance when the agency, and therefore the worker, carries functional responsibilities that may have a profound impact on the client. Examples of workers with these additional functions include parole officers, child welfare workers in abuse situations, welfare workers dealing with income assistance, and adoptive workers who make judgments about who can or cannot receive a child. Normal concerns about the authority of the worker are heightened by fears of sanctions, and these fears can create a powerful obstacle that may block effective work. As with other obstacles, if the worker can reveal their existence and explore them with the group members, then the power of the obstacle can often be diminished.

Involuntary Groups: Addiction and Family Violence

A **mandatory client** group is one in which the members are required for some external reason to attend. For example, it may be a condition for getting their driving license returned, staying out of jail, keeping their children, or having their spouse return home. The common element is that group membership is involuntary, and the members have not requested the service. They usually start the group presenting either passive resistance (e.g., silence, apathy, creating an illusion of work) or active resistance (e.g., anger, confrontation, open denial of the problem). For the novice group worker, a first session of an involuntary group can increase the normal anxiety associated with new groups. The problems of engaging a reluctant client are similar to those raised in Parts II and III; however, in the group modality, the difference is characterized by the following statement of a young worker: "There are so many of them and only one of me!" Most new workers are so pleased at any conversation at all that they are perfectly willing to accept an illusion of work—a conversation in which the group members are "conning" the worker, each other, and even themselves.

The problem is that with the kinds of issues usually associated with involuntary groups (e.g., addiction, family violence, sexual abuse), the denial itself is a problem. The requirement by the external authority that the group members attend, "or else," is a crucial part of the helping process and the only way to reach many of these clients. As long as the boss, spouse, agency, or court allows the client to continue to get away with behavior that is oppressive and dangerous to themselves and others, they will not seek help. Demanding that they face the problem is the beginning of the helping process. The tendency on the part of the client to minimize the problem (e.g., "I only drink on weekends"; "I only hit her with my open hand"; "How can I raise my kids properly if I don't punish them to teach them right from wrong?"; "The Bible says that to spare the rod is to spoil the child") is at the core of the issue. One cannot begin to work effectively with these clients until their denial is dealt with. In this author's study (Shulman, 1991), acceptance of a problem strongly and positively influenced client motivation, which in turn had a positive impact on the client's ability to use help. Ability to use help influenced the working relationship with the social worker, as well as other outcome measures.

Some of the more recent conceptualizations about the nature of change and the change process can be helpful when working with involuntary clients in that they try to reframe denial in a manner more amenable to intervention. The model developed by psychologists Prochaska and DiClemente (1982) describes the stages of change for people who are involved in addictive behavior. Their model is incorporated into a practice theory called *motivational interviewing*, in which the helping professional adapts her or his intervention to match the client's readiness for change (Miller and Rollnick, 1991). This model views clients as being at different stages of readiness for change and suggests that resistance is often the result of a counselor using the wrong strategy with respect to the client's stage of change.

DiClemente et al. (1991) suggests that

> A therapist can be understood as a midwife to the process of change, which has its own unique course in each case. The role for the therapist is to assist the individual, couple, or family in negotiating this process as efficiently and effectively as possible. In fact, the therapist can be a help or a hindrance to the process.... Skillful therapists will best facilitate change if they understand the process of change and learn how to activate or instigate the unfolding of the process (p. 191).

The stages-of-change model suggests that clients can be in one of five stages, described by DiClemente as follows:

Pre-contemplation: Resistance and the "Four R's." Individuals in precontemplation about a problem behavior such as smoking are not even thinking about changing that behavior. In fact, they may not see the behavior as a problem, or at least they do not believe it is as problematic as external observers see it.... There are many reasons to be in precontemplation. These can best be summarized as the "four R's": reluctance, rebellion, resignation, and rationalization (p. 192).

Contemplation: A Risk-Reward Analysis. Contemplation is often a very paradoxical stage of change. The fact that the client is willing to consider the problem and the possibility of change offers hope for the change. However, the fact that ambivalence can make contemplation a chronic condition can be extremely frustrating. Contemplation is the stage when clients are quite open to information and decisional balance considerations (pp. 194–95).

Determination: Commitment to Action. Deciding to take appropriate steps to stop a problem behavior or to initiate a positive behavior is the hallmark of the determination stage. Most individuals in this stage will make a serious attempt at change in the near future, and many have made an attempt to modify their behavior in the recent past (p. 197).

Action: Implementing the Plan. What do people in action need from a therapist? They have made a plan and have begun to implement it by the time they come to the session. Often, making a therapy appointment has coincided with other change activity. Clients in the action stage often use therapy to make a public commitment to action; to get some external confirmation of the plan; to seek support; to gain greater self-efficacy; and finally to create artificial, external monitors of their activity (pp. 198–99).

Maintenance, Relapse, and Recycling. The action stage normally takes three to six months to complete. This time frame is supported in our research on addictive behaviors, but may vary with the type of problem. Since change requires a new pattern of behavior over time, it takes a while to establish the new pattern. However, the real test of change for most problem behaviors, especially the addictive behaviors, is long-term sustained change over several years. This last stage of successful change is called "maintenance."…Relapse, however, is always possible in both the action and maintenance stages (pp. 199–200).

By recognizing the difficulty associated with the change cycle, and by acknowledging relapse as part of the cycle, this approach allows the client to identify what she or he has learned from the relapse and to "recycle" into the stages to begin the action phase again, ideally this time in a stronger position to effect a longer or permanent "maintenance" of the change. This model is elaborated in Chapter 17 in our discussion of group work with substance abusers in recovery. For now, it is important to recognize that it is quite possible for members of any group to be in different stages of change, ranging from precontemplation to recycling, and that in the case of involuntary groups, many of the members may be in the precontemplative stage, not yet acknowledging the existence of a problem or the need to change. One way to view the requirement to participate in an involuntary group is that it may serve as the stimulus to help move a client from the precontemplative stage into, at least, the contemplative stage. While clients may not accept the idea that they have a substance abuse problem, for example, they can see that the use of the substance has led them to a conflict with the legal system, their boss, child welfare, their spouse or partner, and so on. One of the advantages of group practice is that a client in one stage of change may be motivated by listening to a client in a later stage to more seriously consider moving to the action stage.

Most new group leaders are preoccupied with the potential negative impact of group members on each other and often miss the real strengths of mutual aid groups with these populations. Once the worker deals openly with the authority issues in the first session, it may well be the other group members who will be most effective in identifying each other's stage of change, or if needed, confronting denial. By surfacing the involuntary nature of the group and encouraging a discussion of its impact on the potential for group effectiveness, the worker may be able to minimize this obstacle. In reality, while members may be forced to attend, they cannot be forced to participate in a significant way or to make real changes. The group leader's open recognition of this fact of life in a first session one may help to lower the barriers. For example, in a first session with men who batter, Trimble (1986) included in his opening statement the following comment:

> I am sure it is possible to follow all of these rules and not change, not open up to facing yourself or the other men here. You can probably get through this group and really not change. That's up to you. The judge may order you to be here or your wife may be saying she won't come back unless you get help. And as I have just said, we require your anger diary and regular attendance in order for you to stay here, but no one can reach into your mind and heart and order a change. That's where you have complete control (p. 234).

This honest recognition by the worker that change is in the control of the client helps to set the stage for the work to be done. The task of the group leader is try to find the faint lines of connection between the real, felt needs of the involuntary client and the potential services offered by the group. To do this, she or he must be ready to confront the illusion of work.

An illustration of a worker's changing recognition of the meaning of denial, his recognition of his contribution to the resistance of the client, and his growing skill in involving the group members, is provided in the Record of Service of work with a mandatory substance abuse group that follows. In this case, the worker confronts the members early in the group, in an angry manner, failing to also provide the support the members need to face the problem.

Using the stages-of-change model, this form of confrontation of clients in the precontemplative stage, all exhibiting symptoms of the "four R's" described earlier (reluctance, rebellion, rationalization, and resignation) may serve to stiffen their resistance. Miller and Rollnick (1991) describe it as the "confrontation-denial trap" (p. 66). Essentially, as the group leader insists on the presence of a problem and the need for change (the problem-change side of the argument), the client will take the oppositional "no problem" side of what will become an increasingly escalating battle. Another trap in early sessions is the "expert" trap, in which the group leader appears to have all the answers and tries to "fix" the client. A third, and very common one is the "labeling" trap, where the worker attempts to pressure the client to accept the socially unacceptable label of "alcoholic." Finally, Miller and Rollnick describe the "premature-focus" trap, where the counselor attempts to hone in on the substance abuse problem when the client needs first to deal with broader issues (pp. 66–69).

Gradual recognition by this worker that the source of his anger is his taking responsibility for the outcome rather than focusing on the process frees the worker to concentrate on helping the members to confront and support each other.

RECORD OF SERVICE

Client Description and Time Frame:

This is an educational and therapeutic group for clients that have alcohol and drug problems. This group is open-ended and each member contracts for 25 sessions. It meets once a week for 90 minutes. The clients are court-mandated due to alcohol- and drug-related crimes. All the members are on probation or parole of at least one year. Presently the focus in on denial within the group as a whole. Members are approximately 25 to 40 years old, and it is an all-white, male group.

Description of the Problem:

My own frustration is getting the group to confront one another on their own alco-holism and drug addiction. The denial in this group is very high. Most of the members do a lot of rationalizing and intellectualizing. They rely too much on me to do the con-fronting. Even the two members that are presently sober are not confronting the oth-ers' denial. I feel like I am doing all the work.

How the Problem Came to the Attention of the Worker(s):

On 9/6 I presented my group to our clinical supervisor and my co-workers. As I pre-sented it, I began to realize how frustrated I was with this group and how much of the work I was doing. Part of my frustration was because of the group's denial about their drug and alcohol use, as well as their lack of participation. As people gave me feedback, it became clear that there was not a lot of interaction among the group members. The supervisor suggested that I restate some of the rules and goals of the group, to get a sense of what the group members are feeling about this group at the present moment.

Summary of the Work:

August 28th (third session)

It was at this particular session where I was becoming very frustrated. I failed to in-terpret their resistance and came on too strong. In this group there was a lot of resis-tance and denial. John stated, "I went out over the weekend and got drunk." I tried to confront this and I felt like I was hitting a stone wall. He did not see this as a problem, and some of the other group members supported this type of behavior. I confronted those that continued to use but kept on stating that they did not have a problem, and they had a right to use.

I felt myself getting mad at the group, and they clearly sensed this. John asked, "Why are you picking on me?" Gary stated, "You don't have a right to tell us what to do." Gary was telling me that I cannot control their lives. Outside of the group they can do what they want. This made them more resistant, and one individual seemed to get a little angry with me. Steve, who is a marijuana addict and admits to that problem, has stopped using, but continues to drink. I confront him on this, and he stated, "I don't have a drinking problem, so why is it a problem if I drink?" The tone throughout the session was my confronting and them denying. I really felt that I missed tuning in with their feelings about loss of control. For the next year or so the court will be in con-trol of their lives. At the end of the group, I felt exhausted. I really never came to re-alize it until after I presented my case to the staff and our clinical supervisor.

Armed with the advice of supervisor and colleagues, the worker decides to stop push-ing the clients and to relinquish control of the group. This leads to a more comfortable meet-ing for the group leader and more active involvement in discussion by group members. However, the discussion is an illusion of work. A more helpful response at this point would have been for the worker to explore with the members what makes it hard for them to face the problem. In addition, a focus by the worker on the negative consequences of the behavior may miss the important positives associated with the behavior that the client would have to give up. In referring to clients in the contemplative stage, Miller and Rollnick (1991) suggest using early sessions to explore "both sides of the coin," for example, by asking "Tell me about your use of cocaine. What do you like about it? And what is the other side? What are your worries about using it?" (p. 72). This approach involves support integrated with con-frontation and an effort to avoid the confrontation-denial trap.

September 11th (fourth session)

In this group session, I decided to just let them speak about anything they wanted. The focus was on President Bush's war on drugs. Bob, who is here because of a co-caine problem, stated, "All drugs should be legalized." A lot of the members took this topic and ran with it. It became clear to me that when we discussed things other than their drug use, they seemed more open to speaking. Now the challenge came for me to integrate this with their own drinking and drug use. In this session I missed the opportunity to do this.

September 18th (fifth session)

In group tonight, I had two new members beginning. I decided to have all the members speak about their drug and alcohol use, both past and present. Having the two new members was a benefit. This was one of the best groups in a while. The two new members were both sober. One stated, "I am an addict and I need to stay drug-free." This was helpful for other members to hear, because for them it seems to become more real. As I went around, some of the other members were now able to say that they may have a problem. A couple of the older members have also been sober for the last couple of weeks. In this group, people seemed to be more open. I still am confronting them on their denial, but not in a direct way. One tactic I have used is to ask all the members to stop using for a month, just to see how it feels for them. The ones still using refused, but were willing to compromise. They agreed to cut their use in half. I told them that I felt that was OK. To me this seemed like a good intervention.

September 25th (sixth session)

The focus in this group session was on the difficulties of getting off of drugs. The members spoke about how some drugs are very difficult to get off of, particularly co-caine. There are two members, Bob and John, who continue to use. An interesting thing happened: a couple of the group members confronted them. This felt good, be-cause for a change I did not have to do the confronting. It is now where I am begin-ning to feel that some of the denial is beginning to break down. The walls are slowly beginning to crack. I have to admit that part of the reason is because of the new members, who have brought in a positive attitude. There has been less silence in the group over the last couple of sessions.

Current Status of the Problem:

I feel that this group is now beginning to head in a more positive direction. My role now in this group is to try and keep it heading in that direction. I feel that one thing I have learned is that it is unproductive to confront in a negative way. It only gets my-self and the other group members frustrated. Another ongoing problem is trying to keep this group feeling safe for the members. Since it is an open-ended group, there are new members coming in every 10 weeks or so. At times this is helpful, but other times it seems like the group digresses. In the last few weeks, having a couple of new members begin was very productive for the group.

One thing I hope to do is to keep this group continuing to look at their own drinking or drug use in a more honest way. I need to let them decide when they are ready to get sober and not try to force it on them. I need to realize that the most I might be able to do is to educate them and at least give them respect and under-standing about their addictions. It will be important for me to understand that at this time and space they are not ready to stop and the reality is they may need to get into more trouble before they are willing to come to the realization that they are addicts and have to take more responsibility for their actions.

Strategies for Intervention:

1. To keep them focused and looking at their present and past drug and alcohol use.
2. To have them continue with the AA meetings and have them talk about the meetings in the group. I should continue to do some education on AA.
3. For me to continue to confront, but in a more constructive way. To do a little more education on denial and rationalization.
4. To continue to encourage group members to confront one another and to provide a safe atmosphere to do so.
5. To work with my co-worker and supervisor, so that I continue to look at my own transference and countertransference.

The struggle to synthesize support and demand, particularly with populations in denial (or the precontemplative stage), is a central one for all new workers. This skill comes with experience. The first step requires that the worker look closely at his or her own feelings and begin to manage them effectively. This frees the worker to deal with resistance using affective energy which comes from caring for the client. In the example of work with men who batter, described at the beginning of this section, Trimble (1986) illustrates this synthesis by responding in the following way to a new group member's refusal to disclose the specifics of the violence committed toward his wife:

> I know it's hard to face it, to realize you hurt someone you love. Many men feel guilty and don't want to talk. But you can't change a problem that you try and forget. The basic goal here is to help you stop being violent. To do that, we start by asking you to tell exactly what you did when you were violent with your wife (p. 236).

Parole Group for Ex-Convicts

Issues of authority are important for all groups in the beginning phase. For some groups, authority issues are central and are directly connected to the content of the work. In the example explored in this section, the group members are on parole from prison. This counseling group was integrated into the parole service. While the group leader is not a parole officer (PO), he is part of the parole system and is required to report serious parole violations (e.g., commission of a crime; a threat to harm someone) and group attendance. This issue of the authority of the group leader is difficult for workers who want to create conditions in which group members feel free to risk discussing their mistakes and failures as well as their successes. This was found to be one of the crucial elements of an effective working relationship (Schulman, 1991). Group leaders also feel some discomfort over the "policing" part of their role.

This problem is confounded for the student social worker in the following example because he is also an ex-convict and has been on parole. He completed college through a day pass release program while in prison and worked after his release as a paraprofessional. He applied to a school of social work and was placed, at his request, in a parole agency. As will be seen in the excerpts that follow, his prior life experiences are both a help to him and a hindrance. The struggle with authority faced by the group members, for example, has been (and, at times, still is) his struggle as well. This is an extreme example of "meeting your own problems and issues coming around the corner."

The process recording excerpts have not been edited. Some of the language may prove to be offensive to some readers. However, accuracy in reporting was considered to be a primary consideration with this example. In addition, the illustration raises the issue of the use of what might be termed "unprofessional" language by the worker. This issue can be argued from different perspectives; however, in this case, this language is genuine for this worker and any attempts to speak differently would quickly be perceived as artificial by the group members. In turn, a worker who attempts to use the vernacular of the clients when it is not part of his or her persona would also be perceived as phony by his clients. The longer-term issue of the use of this language for this worker, who has chosen to enter a professional community where it might be considered unprofessional, remains to be examined.

Session 1
Rick arrived at twenty minutes past seven. I waited for the others to arrive, then collected the guys in the waiting room and started the group. I wanted to raise the issue of poor attendance over the last few weeks at the start of the meeting and then restate the contract.

"Well, we've had a couple of weeks off, except for me and Rick. We had a great meeting by ourselves. Right, Rick?" "Yeah, we was bad mouthin' you guys all night." They laughed. "Look, I gotta tell you guys; you put me in a tough situation. I gotta tell Gomez (the parole officer) who makes it and who doesn't." "Yeah, I know," said Ted. "I been having trouble with my chick, you know." "I hear that, Ted, but it doesn't make it any easier for me. Before we get into this, Rick, why don't you introduce yourself to the guys?" "I know Rick. We were in a group behind the walls," Ray said. I responded, "Small world, huh? Ted—This is Rick, he's going to be hanging out with us for awhile."

"Let me run this down again. This is a place where you guys can talk, every Tuesday night, seven thirty. You want to unload? This is a place to do it. If you've got problems with women, you can run it here. You want to stop drinkin' or get off the dope, we'll work on it here. The agency is offering this group so you guys can do the right thing and stay out of the joint, and stay on the street where you belong. How are you guys dealin' with bosses, cops, citizens in general, your POs, all the assholes and all the good guys? It doesn't make any difference what it is. This group is here so you guys can help each other."

"I don't need no fuckin' help," said Rick. I said, "Let me run on this and then we'll hit on that, Rick." He nodded. "When you come in, go to the desk and square your bill. And remember, Gomez will know if you come or not. What we talk about will be reviewed by my supervisor and my interdisciplinary team that's to help me work with you guys. Otherwise, that's it."

The new member, Rick, begins with what is for this population, characteristic bravado. He denies he needs the group and insists he will not return to prison. The group leader reaches for the fear he believes is under this front for Rick and for all of the other members.

"I don't give a fuck where it goes. I don't need to be here. I'm comin' cause I gotta do the right thing to keep Gomez off my back. I ain't goin' back, man." (Rick has just completed seven years in prison.) "I was walkin' from prison, at the fuckin' fence; I see my ride. And who grabs me? Two fuckin' cops tellin' me I got more time to do in another prison. (Pause) Ain't that a bitch?"

"I'd be bullshit," I said. Rick replied, "I don't give a fuck. Two years. I can hold my breath for two years." I said, "It doesn't bother you? Hey, it bothers me and it didn't happen to me." Rick responded, "Fuck it, I can take it. I'm just not going to fuck up this time. I messed up every parole I ever had. They cut me loose. I go straight to the dealer, cook it up and bang; it don't matter where I am." He makes a motion to his arm. "Not this time," Rick added. I said, "It sounds like you're in for a tough fight to stay straight." "Hey, I'm livin' now like I was back in the joint. I go to work, go home, catch the tube and hit the rack," said Rick. I said, "Are you afraid you're gonna fuck up, Rick?" Rick looked at me like he was hit with a sucker punch. "Huh!" he replied.

"How about you guys, are you afraid of fuckin' up and goin' back?" I asked. Ted replied, "Hey, I know where he's comin' from. I've fucked up more paroles." He shook his head. "I don't know." (Ted has a 20-year sentence; he has gone back on a parole violation three times in the past eight years for an average of 12 to 18 months a stay. He originally served two years on the first sentence.) "The PO just put me on quarterly (visits) because I been comin' to counseling. I've been clean. I try not to fuck up. I don't know. Maybe I'm burnt out and too old."

I asked, "What about you, Ray? You been out, what, three weeks?" (Ray just finished serving two years for cocaine possession. Over an ounce. His reports state that he started using heavy when he broke up with his live-in girlfriend and eventually got a habit.) He replied, "I'm doing pretty much the same, tryin' to stay straight. Stayin' away from my old friends cause they've all fucked up. Shit, it's not hard to stay away from them. They're all doin' time. I wanna stay straight, but, shit, I gotta get laid, man. I ain't had a piece in two years, three weeks, four days and (he looks at his watch) twenty or so hours. I'd get a hooker, but fuckin' AIDS. It scares the shit outta me."

The issue of relationships with women is raised by Ray. The men only see such relationships in terms of sexual exploitation, with little if any understanding of the intimacy issues involved. The commonly held cultural norms for this group of clients, a slightly more extreme reflection of the sexist attitudes in the larger society, prevent them from talking about their own vulnerability. In the next segment, the worker attempts, with little success in this first session, to reach for their fears of not knowing how to relate to women.

Rick interrupts Ray: "Wait a minute; back up, we're talkin'. My PO gives me lotsa room. It's all right, cause I'm not going to fuck up this time." I said, "Yeah, but Jesus, Rick, you're isolating yourself, not socializing at all. And Ray, you're doing the same thing. What's out here that bothers you guys so much? Don't you trust yourselves?" Rick said, "You know, they just gave me the key at work. I mean, I lock the place up, man." Ted said, "They're closin' down in a couple of months. They probably want to cut a loss." He laughed. Rick did, too.

"What about you, Ted? What's your social life like?" "Well, I got the kid; I just broke up with the old lady; I gotta get a fuckin' lawyer and... (pause) ...but I go to work and hang out at _____ (a bar). I'm seein' this chick; you know, work, home, sometimes a date." I asked, "But how long did it take you to get in the grove?" "I was lucky. I had this lady waitin' for me the last time."

Rick starts up again. "Man, they tell me to go to this boozeless bar, but that's shit. The girls in there are young, man. With my luck, I'll bump into a smokin' 16-year-old wantin' to do me and—it's all over. They'll be kickin' my fuckin' motel door in." (Laughter) Ray jumps in, saying that he's heard different—that they're not all young in those bars. I said, "It sucks not having a woman around for a long time. It gets kind of lonely." Rick responded, "I don't know about that lonely shit. I'm just sick of pullin' my dick." "I hear that," said Ray. Ted was laughing too hard to respond. "So you guys think you're out of practice in pickin' up the chicks or what?" I asked. Ray and Ted looked at Rick, and Rick shrugged uncomfortably. "You guys seem smooth enough to me. It's just a matter of getting by that rejection shit," I said. Conversation around women went on superficially.

The worker invited them to open up on the issue of being "out of practice," but in the face of the silence, he tried reassurance, which shut the door to the topic. The next theme to emerge is triggered by their discussion of their tattoos ('toos) and the image of themselves held by the straight society. The worker is aware that the tattoos were an important device for presenting the tough front required to survive in prison. Now that the men are on the outside, the 'toos are a brand they can't remove. The tattoos are a symbol of their being outlaws. While they discuss how others just see their 'toos, the underlying issue is their own deeply held, negative self-images. It will take many sessions before sufficient trust develops in this group for the members to begin to share the physical, emotional, and sexual childhood abuse that they have all experienced. This is explored later in the book in the sections dealing with the work phase in the group (Chapter 12).

Rick states that he is very much aware of what people are thinking when they see his tattoos. "How do you want to be perceived by people, Rick?" I asked. "I'm a good fuckin' guy. I don't like people being afraid of me. They see these things and right away they think con—or bikie. I just want to be trusted," he said. "What about you guys, how do you deal with the way people think of you?" Ray says almost immediately, "Shit, I been lookin' for a job for two fuckin' weeks and tellin' these guys I been on parole and not gettin' the fuckin' job. The first interview I go to and I don't fuckin' tell 'em, I get the job. Fuckin' Chamber (PO), he tells me I gotta tell 'em. 'Shit,' I says to him, 'Can't I tell 'em after I get the job?'" Ted says, "Man, I got no problem. I see my boss when he shows me the job. Then I don't see him again until payday. I don't know the guy."

I asked, "What about other people, citizens (all others who are not ex-cons), what about the way they look at you?" Ted said, "I was embarrassed about havin' to keep goin' back, you know, my family an' shit." I said, "And your friends or people you just know?" I said, "Rick, what can you do about being able to take your shirt off and not be worried about how those 'toos look to people?" Rick replied, "You know, I usually wear long-sleeve shirts. Today at lunch, I just wore this (a short-sleeved shirt) at the diner and this guy I work with comes in. He didn't even recognize me. He just sees my 'toos. Then he looks at me an says, 'Shit, Rick, I didn't recognize you.' I laughed. What else could I do? I don't know. He's all right, you know. He don't give a fuck." I said, "And most people won't give a fuck once they know you for who you are. There was a time when those 'toos did something for you." Rick asked, "What do you mean?" I said, "You were trying to convey a message, say something about yourself, and your tattoos did it for you. Rick, once you believe in yourself so will other people because I see a good guy sitting there." There was a long silence.

I continued, "Prison does this, you know. We start believing all that shit that society says we are. Everytime you get sentenced, it's confirmed. Screws shake you down, shackle and cuff you. Like animals, we were put behind bars They pissed in our food and looked up our ass. Hey look, I carry it too. But you gotta beat it. Don't buy into it or they get the last laugh. (Pause) Can you guys dig this shit or what?"

Ray said, "I hear you. Half the people out here would rather see you dead. They don't cut you no slack." Ted said, "You're right, but I'm being cool." Rick jumped in, angry but seemingly controlled, stating that he wasn't going back to prison. He ran down some of his experiences. He than restated how he wasn't going back. I told him that I could feel his anger. He said, "This ain't anger." I said, "What do you call it?" Rick replied, "I don't know, but it ain't anger." I asked Ted, "Ted, when your lady said she wasn't going to let you see your kid again, how did you feel?" "I was bullshit," he responded. I asked, "Do you think it was anything like Rick was just feeling?" "Yeah," he said in agreement, "only a lot more."

Rick angrily said, "You mothas are always talking the same shit—that I'm not gonna make it cause I got a lot of hostility inside." I answered, "I'm not saying that you aren't gonna make it, Rick, quite to the contrary. I'm sayin' you can use that anger as positive, driving energy and not just stay out of prison, but be able to accomplish any goal you set." They began to talk about guys they knew who did just give up. They either gave up and started using drugs or did a score and got busted seemingly on purpose.

The conversation shifted, and the worker decided to ride the next 20 or so minutes out and let them talk about whatever they wanted. Near the end, he decides to return to the authority theme.

I said to the members, "Look, I've got to tell you I have a tough time; on one hand, I'm an ex-con; I don't want to talk to the PO and tell him if you guys are here or not. On the other hand, I'm a clinician with this agency. That's who I am now. So I've got to." Ted said, "Come on Tom, I didn't mean to put you on the spot like that." Rick said, "Hey man, I wouldn't want you to be anything else but a clinician. I might need a letter from you some day and if you're not a social worker or somethin', it don't mean shit to them." "I hear you, Rick. But I'm not just here to write letters. I'm here to help you work with each other." The meeting wound down slowly. Talk of guys who missed it came up and then the guys who came but wouldn't come in to the meeting. I closed by recapping and predicting how they might be feeling through the week about what was said tonight.

This group continued to meet over a number of months with mixed success. Some members were able to maintain their attendance and the conditions of parole, while others broke parole and returned to prison. Overall, the group eventually reached a remarkable level of intimacy, considering they had all been socialized in the prison system where any vulnerability was seen as a sign of weakness that would be attacked. Although the worker began the tasks of dealing with issues of authority with this group in this first session, it was a theme that returned on a regular basis.

Public Welfare Clients

In the following example, an African-American public welfare worker leads a group for welfare mothers, who are also African-Americans, for the purpose of providing mutual aid on the problems of living on welfare. After some angry discussions about husbands who leave them all the bills and courts that garnish their wages if they work, they get to the authority issue in relation to welfare workers. Once again, the relationship to the group worker is raised indirectly by referring to another social worker. In addition, the taboo area of racism is broached as members describe a white welfare worker as racist.

Mrs. Smith: I didn't know about legal aid until I got involved in the welfare rights group.

Mrs. Martin: Your caseworker doesn't tell you anything. They always say they don't know. Well, what do they know? They're supposed to be trained and have an education.

Mrs. Smith: They (caseworkers) are too young; they're not mature, and they are not exposed to life. What do they know about life and especially our problems?

Mrs. Brown: How can I tell that child (the caseworker) my real problems if I don't think she cares?

Mrs. Smith: (To the worker) Can't you get some older people to work instead of those young children?

Worker: Are you saying that because your caseworker is young, she is not capable of being a good caseworker?
(Silence)

Worker: Sometimes, you know, it's harder to teach an older dog new tricks. We find that young people are not as set in their ways. Of course, there are exceptions to this rule. (Silence—a long one)

Worker: Are you trying to say something to me that you really have not stated?

Mrs. Martin: She (the caseworker) is prejudiced. She doesn't like blacks.

The worker caught her own initial defensiveness towards the anger directed at the other worker and reached inside the silence for the unstated communication. Other group members countered Mrs. Martin's opinion of this worker, offering examples of situations in which she had been helpful. Most of these were younger women. The group member has risked a powerful issue in sharing her feelings about the worker's prejudice. The group worker was also African-American, and this may have been the reason for the member's honesty. The group worker remained defensive, however, and began to challenge Mrs. Martin, thus cutting off an important area for discussion.

Worker: Have you ever discussed this with your caseworker?

Mrs. Martin: I sure did. I told her off good.

Worker: In the same manner in which you're speaking now?

Mrs. Martin: I sure didn't bite my tongue.

Worker: Then you were rude to her, yes? (Silence)

Worker: How would you feel if you were the caseworker and she spoke to you in that manner? (Silence) Respect has nothing to do with age or color; it's a two-way street.
(Silence)

One of the members commented to Mrs. Martin that she thought she was wrong about the worker, and this statement was followed by a quick change in the discussion. The group worker had not allowed this difficult area to be opened up and had not demonstrated an understanding of the client's perception. She felt required to identify with the other worker, and perhaps even more so because she was African-American and the other worker was white. This is an example of an intra-ethnic dilemma that can occur when a worker is dealing with someone who is the same as them (as opposed to inter-ethnic). Workers of color have often told me that they feel a particular defensiveness in this area because they may privately agree that the other workers in their own agency can be racist, or at least, not ethnically sensitive in their practice. Before they can help their clients deal with inter-ethnic issues, they must face their own.

In addition, in this example, the worker did not reach for the implied question about her role and her authority. The discussion continued with complaints about the amount of money available, the difficulty of making ends meet, and so on. As each theme emerged, the worker responded with a lecture or some advice, which was followed by silence. Each silence contained the message: You really don't understand.

As the group members sensed the worker's honesty and directness, however, they began to take her on. For example, when they complained about making ends meet, the worker asked them if they made out a list of what they needed at the end of the month before they went shopping. The response was, "I need everything by the end of the month; the cupboard is bare. I don't need a list!" This was said with good nature, and the group members laughed in agreement. Their energy level was high, and as the worker accepted their comments about her suggestions, laughing with them rather than getting angry, they warmed to her and took her on with even more gusto. Finally, after one piece of advice near the end of the meeting, there was a silence and the following exchange:

> **Mrs. Smith:** You see, Mrs. Powell, you just don't understand.
> **Worker:** I was wondering when someone was going to say that. (The group members all broke up in laughter.)

Even though the worker responded defensively at times and missed the indirect cues about her authority, the group members seemed to sense her honesty and her genuine concern for them. Her willingness to enter exchanges with them, to give and to take in the discussions, and to maintain her sense of humor helped to overcome her early efforts at preaching and sermonizing. The group continued to meet, and as the worker become clearer about her function and demonstrated her capacity for empathy, the work improved. The important point is that group members can forgive a worker's mistakes if they sense his or her genuine concern and honesty.

It is not always necessary to discuss the worker's authority in the first session. For instance, in the example that follows, the worker's direct offer to use the group as a means of improving communication between welfare clients and the agency was accepted immediately, without a discussion of her authority. The members moved quickly past the problems of policy to other issues they shared in common. The problem swapping revealed a range of more personal concerns, setting a broader agenda for future discussions. The worker with this group was white and the group members were African-American; however, the session demonstrated that each group is unique, and anticipated issues may not always arise in a first session.

> Our first meeting was held at the local welfare director's office. I began the meeting by stating that everyone was familiar with who I was, and then I asked each person to give her name and tell us how many children she had. Each member of the group was aware of what the group was all about, because I had previously discussed it with them. After the introductions, I said, "I'm concerned because I don't think there is any communication between the welfare board and the people. I'm hoping that our getting together will help us to overcome this. Before we go any further, I want to say that it's important to keep to ourselves what is said here. This goes for me as well as you. I've noticed that many of my clients are concerned with bud-

geting, the new revisions which went into effect in March, and the food stamp program." Before I could go any further, Mrs. Davis jumped in with, "I think the food stamps stink. You can't buy toilet paper or napkins or tissues." Mrs. Martin stated that she thought they helped her. Mrs. Smith said she didn't use them because she could get her friends to take her to wholesale houses where she could get her meats and canned goods so much cheaper. Besides, she didn't like to shop in the neighborhood supermarkets because around the first of the month, the prices there went up. The other two women agreed with this. Then Mrs. Martin brought up the fact that in predominantly black neighborhoods, foods that are usually eaten by blacks are much higher priced. I had a puzzled look on my face, and Mrs. Martin told me that it is a known fact that blacks like okra and black-eyed peas. Mrs. Smith said she noticed the higher prices, too. The group then began talking about how much it costs to feed growing boys and girls. Then Mrs. Davis said, "Something else that's been bugging me lately is the drug business with the kids. I'm so afraid that my children are going to try it someday." Everyone then launched into a discussion of raising children. All three felt that if you give a child love and respect, they'll turn out OK. Mrs. Martin stated that she wished she could find a man to marry so her sons could have a father. Mrs. Smith said she had been single for so long that she didn't want a man around. Mrs. Davis stated that she would like to marry someone again, but she was afraid.

At this point, the meeting had gone for over an hour, so I stopped the discussion and said that I thought we'd better close the meeting. I asked them how they felt about continuing this. Mrs. Martin stated she would like to because she wants to participate in things like this and see how other people manage their problems. Mrs. Davis said it felt good to blow off steam. Mrs. Smith sat there and smiled. We all decided we would like to make our group a little larger, and I said I would try to find more people who were interested. We decided to meet again in two weeks. Mrs. Smith asked if I could explain at the next meeting what would happen to her monthly check if she started working. The other two said they would be interested in that also. I agreed, and the meeting was adjourned.

Authority and the Adoption Process

One of the areas in which the impact of authority is evident is in work with prospective adoptive parents. When requests outnumber the available children, particularly if couples want "a little white girl with blue eyes and intelligent parents," preadoption groups are often experienced as one of the hurdles to be overcome. Rather than viewing it as a potential source of mutual aid, couples approach the group with trepidation and fear. Spouses will caution each other on the way to the first meeting "not to say anything dumb" that might disqualify them as applicants. Competition can often be sensed as couples silently eye each other, measuring their own chances in comparison. The difficulty can also exist for the group leader who has the dual function of leading a mutual aid group and assessing the prospective parents. Workers feel deeply their responsibility toward the child, and they fear the possibility of making mistakes that could lead to an adoption breakdown at a future date. Unless the issue of "being judged" is dealt with at the start of the first session, the discussion in the groups may become an illusion of work in which the members vie to say what they perceive the worker wants to hear. In the following excerpt, the worker contracts but does not reach directly for the unstated concern.

> **Worker:** We at the agency felt this might be a hard time for you and that you might have a number of concerns and questions about adoption. The group will be an opportunity for you to discuss these concerns with other people who are in the same situation. I realize this is not always easy to do, and I will be here to help you.

Because the question of the worker's authority was not raised, the group began a generalized discussion of how to tell the child about being adopted, whether the child's biological parents or the environment they create would affect the child more, how husbands would help their wives (they were adopting infants), and concerns about "how the agency matches the children to the parents." Each of these issues, as will be discussed later, is related to a real concern these couples have about the adoption procedure and their future child. However, they are not sure whether they can raise their real feelings because they do not know by what criteria they will be judged. Discussion remains on the intellectual level of "biological" versus "environment" because that is safer, at this point, than discussing their fears about the possibility of receiving a child from a "bad seed." As the session ends, their discussion about matching finally leads to the central issue of the authority theme in the following way:

> Mrs. Epstein said that by watching the parents in the group, we really couldn't determine what kind of parents we will make. I agreed that was not my role. Mr. W. said that people might decide they do not want to adopt, but how does the agency reject people? I said, "I guess you may be wondering if you're accepted yet?"

The worker discussed their status and reassured them that they wouldn't have gotten this far if the agency did not feel they were good prospective adoptive parents. The discussion was dropped, however, and the conversation continued in a superficial manner. As an alternative response, the worker could have introduced the topic of criteria used for making such decisions. For example, the couples might be greatly relieved to hear that having doubts, questions, and fears (e.g., the "bad seed") was not unusual and certainly did not disqualify them. In fact, the worker might underline the value of prospective parents' being "in touch" with how they felt. Workers often duck this discussion because they are also unclear about criteria. In addition, the worker could clarify under what circumstances she might have to raise questions about their suitability. Note the difference in the opening comments in another preadoption group:

> Mrs. O'Hare spilt her coffee and went into the other office for paper towels. Within a minute Mr. O'Hare followed her. I recognized that he was uncomfortable in the group and talked with him while his wife was cleaning up. I went with them to rejoin the group. I also recognized that Mr. and Mrs. Thomas, who were one of the last couples to arrive, seemed tense and flustered. Mrs. Thomas said her husband hadn't come home for supper and had met her at the door. I commented about whether he might be working late as we were entering. Mr. Thomas looked a little sheepish. Mr. Aronson arrived and apologized to the group. I opened by welcoming everyone and requesting that we all introduce ourselves and give the following information: whether you have children, if adopted or natural, age and sex; child desired—age, sex, anything else specific. Everyone responded quite comfortably to this, with the men speaking for both (as is usually the case).

I explained the purpose of the meeting as being an opportunity for them to share thoughts and feelings about adoption. Discussion in a group might be helpful to them in sorting out what their attitudes are, what they're comfortable with, and whether adoption is for them. I wondered if they might be feeling uneasy about sharing their concerns with us. We recognize their feelings about this and it being part of our getting to know them. We're not looking for perfect people, but we want to get to know them and what they are suited for. They might find it helpful to discuss questions with others who may be having the same concerns.

The information from previous visits with them is confidential, and what they share of what they've told us is up to them. It's their group. Our role as co-leaders is to see that we stay on topics related to adoption and to clarify policy matters, but we hope that they'll be free in talking about what's on their minds. I asked the group's permission to take notes of tonight's meeting. The purpose of this recording was to use it in a group learning session on how to work with groups. Confidentiality of the group members was noted—they would be identified only by initials. Staff members from other departments—unmarried parents, workers, and so on—would be present. Through this learning session, we hoped to improve how we work with groups.

Mr. Aronson wondered if what they said was confidential or part of the assessment of them. I replied that the groups are part of the total study and process of getting to know them, but the recording as we would use it would not identify anyone. It will be about how we work in a group and not thoughts and feelings they were expressing. The group laughed. I asked if they felt free to move ahead. They nodded and said yes.

Mr. Thomas began by asking how long it takes to get a child and what the ratio of applicants to children is. Mrs. Thomas followed his question by asking when they would know if they were approved. I explained that we try to let people know what we are thinking all along. Adoption brings happiness to many, but it's not right for everyone. There was also an explanation of our contacts with our clients and what happens following the group sessions.

The group members' response to this opening was to move immediately into questions of criteria and procedures involved in adopting. After some discussion, the focus shifted once again to a more general discussion rather than the specific concerns of the couples. In addition to dealing with the authority theme, the worker must stress that the purpose of the group is to deal with the concerns and feelings of the preadoptive parents. Sometimes, group leaders have a different purpose and view the group as a medium for "educating" the parents. They then develop set agendas for a preadoptive parent "curriculum." For example, such a worker might begin by discussing "how to tell your child he is adopted," even though all the couples are awaiting infants who will not need to be told for a number of years. As one listens to such discussions with an ear for the themes important to these couples in their immediate situation, one can often hear subtle undercurrents. For example, when they discuss whether the child will love them as parents once the child knows about being adopted, they are often indirectly expressing their own concerns about how they will feel towards an adopted child.

Even though the worker has been honest about the judging function, the group will still need help to enter taboo areas. They will need support to open up potentially difficult and dangerous subjects, and yet these are precisely the concerns they need to share to discover that they are "all in the same boat." Once the worker is clear that the group is offered to the couples as clients in their own right, then attention can be directed to their concerns. In the next example, the worker's empathetic responses open up an important discussion about how friends and relatives respond to the adoption. The supportive atmosphere established by the worker has encouraged members to share problems rather than to attempt to convince the worker that everything is going well.

> **Mrs. Thomas:** We have a problem with a grandmother who is against the idea of adoption, but we feel that once a child is placed with us, she'll love the child the same as she does the others.
>
> **Mrs. Charles:** People can change their opinions also. When my husband's grandmother first heard of me being adopted, she regarded it as very hush-hush. Now that she knows that we are adopting a child, she thinks it's great—she's going to be a great-grandmother, and she is very thrilled about that.
>
> **Mr. Charles:** At work, many people are asking me how the adoption is proceeding.
>
> **Worker:** What do you say?
>
> **Mr. Charles:** I say that we're going to more meetings.
>
> (Laughter)
>
> **Mrs. Kurtz:** It's a necessary thing in getting ready for adoptive parenthood.
>
> **Worker:** Are many of you feeling that this is a hard way to get a baby?
>
> **Mr. Kurtz:** It's more difficult; it's easier to have your own.
>
> **Mrs. Kurtz:** For you men, maybe. (Laughter)
>
> **Mrs. Charles:** What I find so difficult is not knowing how long we'll have to wait. When a woman is pregnant, she knows it's nine months, but this way, it's unknown just how long it will be.
>
> **Mrs. Garvin:** I was taking a friend's baby for a walk, and someone said to me, "Don't you wish it was yours?"
>
> **Worker:** How do you feel when people say things like that?
>
> **Mrs. Garvin:** It bugs me.
>
> **Mrs. Thomas:** They're giving you a dig, don't you think? People ask at work, "When are you having a family?" and "Are you pregnant?" It bothers and hurts me, too, but they don't seem to realize it.
>
> **Mr. Garvin:** Even my brothers-in-law, who are really good fellows, they tease me about why we aren't having any children. I know that they're kidding, but on a down day, it can hurt.
>
> **Mrs. Thomas:** Have you told anyone it hurts? I told a friend that it hurt me when he kept asking about us having children. He is a reference for us, and now he is the most interested and considerate person to talk to about our adoption. He's always asking me how things are going with the adoption, and he seems to really care.
>
> **Mrs. Kurtz:** I like the way you said that.
>
> **Worker:** I think it's good that you were able to say that it does hurt.
>
> **Mrs. Thomas:** It's a door closed if a couple are not able to have children born to them. You feel so alone and that you're the only person that this has ever happened to. My husband and I both love children so much and we've always wanted to have children, and when we think of a life ahead of us with just the two of us, it seems so shallow. We have to adopt, and that's why we

> are nervous. We were nervous when Mrs. Smith came to our home because
> we want to be accepted—this is our only way.

The examples in this section have illustrated how the worker's authority is a crucial issue in first sessions of a group. It will remain an issue throughout the life of the group, as is discussed in Chapter 14. However, the impact of authority is heightened in the early sessions before the development of a working relationship, which can cause it to be a major obstacle to group development. Openly recognizing and clarifying the issue of authority diminishes its power to obstruct.

CLIENT PROBLEM IMPACT

The specific concern facing the group members needs to be stated clearly and without embarrassment in the group leader's opening statement. It is helpful to provide examples that can serve as "handles" for the group members.

Parents with Children with Cerebral Palsy

In the next example, a worker begins a group for parents of children with cerebral palsy.

> Everybody had already introduced themselves, so I began by saying I wanted to give them an idea of what the group was about and then find out what they thought. I said that bringing up a teenager can be difficult, but when the teenager has cerebral palsy, a whole new set of difficulties and problems arises. In this group we are bringing parents together who are in a similar situation to discuss these problems. Hopefully, this will enable you to go back to your children with some new ideas of ways of coping with them. I also said that when I was talking to parents on the phone, they had mentioned several areas that were important to them right now. For example, what about starting high school? At this point Mrs. Boehm jumped in and said, "You know, that's exactly what I've been thinking about." She went on to describe her ambivalence about whether or not to send Stevie to a regular high school (he's 12). She talked about her desire for him to be with normal children, but she didn't really know if he'd be able to do it—it was a hard decision. She talked about this for quite a while. Finally, I said that the whole idea of the future for her son seemed to be an important thing to her now. She said, yes, it just began to be important in the last six months or so when she realized that he was getting older.

Foster Parents: The Late-Arriving Members

In the following excerpts, the worker contracts with a foster parent group under difficult circumstances. Only one couple was present at the starting time, although six were expected. The worker must have experienced a terrible, sinking feeling as she waited for additional members to arrive.

> I welcomed them and after chatting for a few minutes, I said that we were obviously going to be late in starting the meeting, as no one else had arrived. Name tags for six couples were on a small table. Mr. Leon examined the names carefully and read them aloud to his wife. They recognized one couple's name, who had also taken part in the May orientation meeting. I said the name tags were for the six couples who had said

pretty definitely that they would attend. Mrs. Leon said she wondered where they all were. I said it would be disappointing if there were not enough people present to go ahead with the meeting as planned.

Mrs. Casey arrived, breathless and apologizing for being late. I welcomed her and said we could begin by reviewing the purpose of the meeting. I said it was hoped that meetings would provide an opportunity for new foster parents to meet each other, to identify and share their common concerns, to plan with them an agenda for the subsequent three meetings; that we had resource people in the agency who were willing to meet with the group; that we might also consider using audiovisual resources like films or tapes. Mrs. Casey said she enjoyed the meetings and that it was a shame the others had not come. Mrs. Leon said it was too bad, that a foster parent group needed more than three people. Mr. Leon got up and took another look at the name tags and began intoning their names again.

Mrs. Peters arrived, flustered and breathless. She said her husband had been driving around for half an hour trying to park. Finally, he dropped her off and was still trying to find a parking place. I welcomed her and introduced the others. Mrs. Peters said she had gotten the impression there would be more people. I said I had, too, and there was some laughter. I began to feel more relaxed. There was a general interchange at this point about each other's families, their own children and foster children.

The worker's good-natured response to the member's question about the low attendance helped everyone to relax. It is important to acknowledge feelings of disappointment and help members discuss their reactions when attendance is low, whether at a first meeting or any other meeting. At the same time, it is also important to convey a sense of willingness to go on with the work in spite of the low attendance. The people who have arrived have come because of their need for the group. It would be a mistake to spend the entire evening discussing why other members have not shown up.

Outpatient Psychiatric Group: Initial Resistance

In the next extract, a worker contracts with a group of patients from an outpatient clinic of a psychiatric department in a general hospital. All of the group members have suffered severe depression and are socially isolated. The worker is thrown off balance a little when, in response to her opening statement, a group member expresses reservations about the group.

The members came in and sat down. They were early. They looked anxious and did not speak to each other. I brought some coffee in, and Mr. Crane immediately got up and served everybody. After people were settled, Miss Nann said, "After this comes the chicken." I said, "I see you're expecting a party." She replied, "Isn't it a party?" I began the meeting by introducing myself and suggesting the others say who they were. I then stated the contract: "We are here for two reasons. First, to discuss the problems which result from your loneliness and depression in order to gain some understanding of these problems. Second, we are going to try to find solutions to these problems." Mr. Crane began to talk about what he thought having a good time was. That consisted of being together with people and not getting too personal. Then he talked about how much he enjoyed playing cards. Miss Nann talked about how much she enjoyed cards, too, and they had quite a discussion about this. I asked the group for their reactions. Mr. McIver said he hadn't come here to play cards or to talk about cards. He had come to gain some understanding of his problems and for the group members to be honest with each other. Mrs. Wilson backed this up and said there were plenty of other groups they could join to play cards, and Miss Nann and Mr. Crane could join them if they wanted. Miss Nann seemed taken aback by this.

The worker had made a direct offer, and Mr. Crane and Miss Nann have expressed reservations. Other members of the group used the worker's invitation to attack the position of the first two members. The worker used her tuning in to the anxiety felt by all group members at a first meeting to search out immediately the connection between these two subgroups. She did this by recognizing that Mr. Crane and Miss Nann were simply expressing the concerns they were feeling about starting in a group.

> I said, "I feel both sides are right. On the one hand, Mr. McIver and Mrs. Wilson were saying they are here to talk about problems, and Miss Nann and Mr. Crane are basically saying how hard it is to do this." I then made a few comments about how anxious people must feel coming to a first meeting like this. Mr. Crane said, "You're right, it is hard. It's like walking down the street and telling the first guy you meet all your problems." I said, "It takes time to get to know one another." Mr. McIver said, "Let me make a suggestion. Maybe everyone could tell a little bit about himself, and then we would be one step further." The group agreed and began talking about their problems of loneliness and sadness. I was somewhat taken aback at how fast things were proceeding but figured they wouldn't share anything they didn't want the group to hear.

The worker's directness in her opening and the skill she demonstrated in understanding the meaning of the early resistance to discussion helped free the group members to begin. Her feeling of being taken aback is related to the process by which the group members were taking over the group and quickly making it their own. Workers often feel lost when this happens, out of control, and unsure of themselves. One worker described the feeling as follows: "I feel I'm on my motorcycle, hitting the starter bar with my foot and unable to start the engine, while all my group members have started theirs and they're off down the road zooming away." It is exactly at this moment, when the worker sees that the group members have made the group their own, that the leader should feel relieved.

Women with Recent Multiple Sclerosis Diagnosis: Crying in the First Session

This group consisted of women, in their twenties to forties, all white and middle-class, who had recently been diagnosed as having the progressively disabling disease of multiple sclerosis (MS). This is the first session in which the women focus on the shock of the recent diagnosis and side effects. The group leader begins with a request for introductions and a sharing of information about the illness. As is often the case, the sharing moves deeply into the work before the leader has an opportunity to make an opening statement. In retrospect, a brief statement about purpose and role prior to the introductions would have been helpful. As one member moves quickly and emotionally into the work, the group leader responds with support.

> This was the first group meeting. As members arrived, those who had previously been in a group exchanged greetings with the leader. The newer people sat down quietly. Members were asked to introduce themselves and to share information on their

illness. Specifically, members were asked to inform others when they were diagnosed, current status of their condition, and what they hoped to get out of being in the group. We went round in a circle. It was Cathy's turn. She appeared somewhat startled that it was her turn.

Cathy was asked to introduce herself. The group's attention focused on her as she tearfully began talking about herself. She related how she had been diagnosed with MS a few months ago and that she had been confused since then. "It must have been a very upsetting time for you; could you tell us more about it?" She related further how she had begun developing symptoms and after seeing doctors was diagnosed by a doctor who told her in a definitive way that she had MS. "It sounds like you heard about your illness in a very abrupt way and without any preparation or understanding of the implications it could have on your life."

Cathy went on to talk about her frustration with the illness. She described how her family and friends did not seem to understand what she was going through. "It would seem that the illness has not only been difficult for you, but also for others who are close to you." Cathy responded by saying that people did not know what to say to her nor did she know how much to tell them. "That is an understandable reaction when you first discover that you have MS." Cathy said that she felt very alone. Silence. She went on to talk about how she could not remember things and would say incorrect words for what she meant to say. "That must be very frightening. You have brought up one of the side effects of this illness. In this group you will find that others may have had similar experiences, and it may be helpful to find out how they have coped."

Jane pulled from her purse a sticker note-pad and declared that she used these everywhere to help her remember. Others agreed that these pads are very useful. I said, "You have made an important step in coming here tonight and sharing your feelings with the group."

A member crying in a group may be experienced by the others as an uncomfortable and embarrassing situation. Some models of practice argue that the group leader should control such expressions of emotion in a first session, so that they will not frighten other members. Unfortunately, this approach sends the wrong message to the group members. They perceive the workers as being uncomfortable with the emotions, which reinforces the norms leading to an illusion of work. Rather than subtly controlling the expression of emotion by ignoring it, changing the subject, moving to other members, and so on, the worker needs to reassure the member and the group that the expression of strong feelings is natural and appropriate. In understanding and accepting these feelings, the worker demonstrates a way of working that will help the group members create a new "culture" in which all the emotions of sadness, anger, joy, and so forth can be freely expressed.

When a group has begun with a particularly strong first session, in terms of emotion and quickly getting to core issues, it is important for the worker to use some time at the end of the session to discuss the members' reactions. At times, members will feel embarrassed after a session at having expressed strong feelings or ideas that they may feel are only theirs. Some attention to this issue often results in other group members reassuring the exposed members that they are not alone. For example, in the MS group, the worker could have said near the end of the session,

I would like to take a few minutes to talk about your reactions to this first session. You all shared some strong feelings this evening about what you are going through—particularly you, Cathy. In my experience, sometimes people feel uncomfortable when they share so much or have cried at a first meeting. They wonder what the other group members are thinking and feeling. Could we talk about it for a moment?

Inevitably, some members will come to the support of the individual who cried and reassure him or her that they shared in the emotions. Some members may raise their concerns about how they are going to feel if so much emotion is shared at the meetings. This provides the worker and the group an early opportunity to discuss the impact of emotions on their lives and on the group itself. Whatever the outcome of the discussion, it is usually better to have it at the session, than to have the individual (Cathy) or the other client (the group) worrying about these issues on their own.

IMPACT OF THE SETTING OF SERVICE

All groups exist within an environment with which they are in constant interaction. It is not possible to work with a group by inviting the members into a meeting room, closing the door, and pretending the system surrounding the group is not there. For example, in residential settings such as group homes, hospitals, or prisons, the members are bringing into each session their common environmental experiences. A suicide attempt on a psychiatric hospital ward will affect the content and process of the ward meeting that follows. Convicts in a group session will have to overcome the culture in the prison that makes it extremely risky to be honest and vulnerable. Members of a foster parent group may want to focus in their first sessions, not on issues of parenting, but rather their complaints about agency policies and social workers. In many different ways, the setting of service will have some impact on the nature of the group contract.

The dynamics and skills involved in helping group members with the task of negotiating their environment are explored in detail in Chapter 14. In this section we will focus on contracting and beginning phase issues in groups where relating to the environment is central to the work.

Patient Ward Group: Dealing with the Hospital

In this first illustration, a social worker in a hospital contracts with a patient ward group to discuss their illness and hospitalization. He views the hospital as a complex system that patients must negotiate, and he sees the group as a vehicle for helping them do that.

> I introduced myself to the patients and asked them to go around and introduce themselves, which they did. I asked whether they had been told anything about this group. They hadn't. I told them we get together to discuss what it means to be a patient in the hospital, how it feels being in a strange place away from family and friends. I said that often patients found it difficult getting used to a hospital experience, and sometimes it helped to talk with other patients. Often they have the same feelings of anxiety, fear, and uncertainty; we get together as a group so that we can freely talk about hospital experiences and feelings around being a patient. I mentioned that they will probably notice that I take notes from time to time, the reason being so that I can look back on the session to see where I could have been more helpful to them.
>
> Mrs. Jones began talking about the doctors and how they change, just after you get used to one doctor. I said that it must be a frustrating and anxious time when the doctors change. She agreed. Mrs. Beatty said that this is her first hospital experience and

it was upsetting. Mrs. Carter said that she's used to hospitals and she felt she adapted well. Mrs. Victor said that the system didn't bother her. I asked Mrs. Beatty why she felt so upset about the hospital. She said it was strange and she felt all alone. If it hadn't been for Mrs. Carter "adopting" her, she would never have stayed after the first hour. I remarked that it must have been terribly frightening, this being her first time here and her not knowing the ropes. She agreed.

Mrs. Carter said that the hospital system didn't bother her, but she's scared they won't find out what's wrong with her. She was very sick at home, and she hopes they'll be able to do something. I said that it's a natural feeling to worry about one's illness, particularly when the diagnosis is not known. At this point, an orderly came to take Mrs. Jones to X-ray.

Mrs. Carter said that when you're not told what's happening, you feel bad. I asked in what way she felt bad. She answered that all of a sudden you're told to go through a difficult test or examination, about which you know nothing, and you feel horrible. I remarked that you need time to adjust to the idea of a test and prepare yourself for it. She agreed. I asked whether the others had similar experiences. Mrs. Beatty said one day a doctor came in for a heart examination. She was very upset because no-body had told her anything about it and she was thinking she must have had a heart condition; otherwise, why would she have to have this examination? The nurse explained that this is just routine and that every patient who is on the ward gets cardiac and respiration examinations while they're here, and it certainly does not mean that there is anything wrong with her. I asked Mrs. Beatty how she felt now, knowing that it's a routine examination. She said, much easier; she would have felt less upset had she known this before.

In addition to helping the patients adjust to the difficult situation and clarify their concerns, the worker can use this group as a vehicle for change within the hospital. Serious illness often makes patients feel out of control over their lives. When a system appears to treat them as objects, their feelings of helplessness and impotency are increased. These feelings can have an impact on their use of the medical services (e.g., following the treatment plan), their satisfaction with services, and their ability to hear, understand, and remember what is said in conversations with medical personal (Shulman and Buchan, 1982). Involving staff in the group sessions can help to bridge the gap between the providers and consumers of service. In Part V of this book, I will explore ways in which a worker can use patient feedback to affect the way in which the system relates to the client. This is the mediating function outlined in Part I shown in action with the second client, the system. As will become evident, before workers can empower their clients, they must feel empowered themselves.

Teen Boys in a Residential Setting: Empowerment for Change

In the next example, a worker meets with a somewhat reluctant group of boys who are living in a residential institution. They have been elected by a resident executive committee to serve as a lounge committee whose purpose is to provide feedback to the administration on ways in which the new lounge could be run more effectively. They are apathetic because they feel powerless to affect the institution.

I began this meeting by explaining why I felt an active lounge committee was needed. I said that the guys probably had a lot of beefs regarding the lounge and that this was an opportunity to do something about it. Billy agreed that there were a lot of beefs but felt little could be done about them. I asked why he felt this way. The boys shared their feeling that the administration was really inflexible and uninterested in their views. Their past experiences had confirmed this. I said I could appreciate why they felt a bit hopeless; however, this lounge committee was a new attempt that the administration was supporting. It might still be impossible; on the other hand, if they acted together as a group, I thought they could accomplish something. If no ideas and suggestions were forthcoming, how could the administration act on them?

I encouraged them to try it out, and if they found it was hopeless, we could simply quit. At this point their beefs about the lounge emerged.

In the last example, the focus of the work shifted from individual personal needs and concerns to tasks related to the benefit of the group. This is also true in work with community action or tenants' groups where the focus is not on mutual aid for meeting individual needs, but rather mutual aid for impact on systems related to group needs. For example, in a group for immigrant parents designed to assist them in dealing with the school system, it would be inappropriate for members to discuss their marital problems or other areas of concern that might be personally important but are unrelated to the contract. If the group contracts to band together to improve communications with the school staff, then this boundary serves to guard their contract. The worker can offer to refer members to other services for help in other areas. Nonetheless, as they work on their social action tasks, all of the principles of group dynamics, process, and the requirements for worker skill are just as relevant in these groups as for those designed to deal with personal problems.

An artificial dichotomy is often put forward between so-called "task" groups versus "therapy" groups. All groups are task-centered groups. The differences may be in the nature of the tasks, with some groups focusing on personal tasks and others on public or social tasks. The teenagers in the just-discussed residential group had all experienced some form of oppression as children, ranging from emotional abuse and neglect to physical and sexual abuse. Their normal developmental tasks call for them to come to grips with issues of authority structure, and so on. Empowering them to find ways to influence their residential setting may be the most "therapeutic" experience they can have. Creating a sense of empowerment in their lives can positively affect their resilience, alter their negative self-perceptions, and promote the development of the skills needed to negotiate other areas of their lives.

Alternative Public Day School: Parents of Children with Emotional and Behavioral Difficulties

In the final example in this section, the not-uncommon phenomenon of clients in a first session externalizing by angrily raising issues of dissatisfaction with the setting (e.g., the school, hospital) or professionals is evident. Some of these will be legitimate concerns that should become part of the group's agenda. This behavior may also represent a form of avoidance of painful, personal issues. In this example, the group leaders do not begin with an opening statement but instead ask the group members how they wish to use the group. The group members new to the school accept the workers' offer to provide feedback on the group's contract by externalizing until one member, at the end of the meeting (doorknob), angrily brings home the pain they must all feel. The two student group leaders are too overwhelmed at this, their first group meeting, to be able to identify these themes as a way of helping the group to reach a consensus on purpose. Their anxiety over this session also leads them to miss the cues about "helping professionals" that may actually refer to them. However, the student-author's openness to listening and her astute post-meeting analysis bode well for her development and the group's potential for success.

> **Agency Type:** Alternative public day school, Meeting #1
> **Purpose:** Parent support group for parents of children with emotional, behavioral and learning difficulties
> **Gender of Members:** Male and female; **Ages:** 38–55
> **Cultural and Racial Identification:** White, middle-class American

After introductions in which each member stated his/her name, I said that we needed to discuss how the group wanted to use the one-and-a-half hours each week. I asked them if they would like to choose the issues and topics for discussion or if they would prefer that Dave (co-leader) and I prepare an agenda. Linda, a new parent who was sitting to my left, turned her body towards the group and said in an agitated voice, "I don't know about the rest of you, but I've had enough of psychiatrists, doctors and teachers telling me what to do and that it's my fault that my kid is screwed up!" Several other parents joined in, "Boy, I sure know what you mean!" Karen, another new mother, said, "Can you believe that Kirk's teacher in public school last year, told me, in front of Kirk, that he's a bad kid who's going to end up in jail if I don't get him help? Like he hasn't been to shrink after shrink since he was eight!" I looked to Dave to respond, but he remained silent.

Sharon, a parent whose child has been at the school for four years, turned to Karen and calmly and empathetically began telling stories about ways she and her family had been treated in the past by schools and professionals, but that this school was different. She said that the teachers and staff really cared about her son. Carol, another returning parent, agreed with Sharon and emphasized how much her son loved his teachers and counselors. Both Linda and Karen began to agree with Sharon and Carol. They said that they had noticed that, in the first month at this school, their children did seem happier. For half an hour the parents exchanged humorous accounts about their children while Dave and I remained silent.

Finally, I said, "We have about 15 minutes left and I want to make sure that, before we end, we are clear about the way we will use this time as a group. It sounds like you all would like to bring in your own issues and topics to discuss. Does anyone have any comments or questions about this decision?" Jack, a new parent who had been silent throughout the meeting, began speaking to the group in an angry voice, while next to him, his wife, Joan, began crying. "What I don't understand is how all of you can laugh when you know you have a sick kid. It's not funny. Your kids are not normal members of society!" The room went dead silent as each member avoided eye contact with anyone. After a minute of silence, I said, "I think people have different ways of dealing with pain. Some use anger, tears, laughter. Each of these emotions has been expressed here tonight. Does anyone have a response to Jack?" Sharon said, "I get angry and sad all the time, but sometimes I need to laugh. If I didn't have humor in my life, I wouldn't be able to get through the day." The other parents nodded in agreement. Jack was looking around the room, but not at the group. Joan was staring at the floor. Both remained silent. After a brief silence, Dave (the co-leader) said, "Looks like we're out of time. Thanks for coming, and we'll see you next week."

Summary of My Thoughts:
These parents were ready to participate in the group. Because this was the first meeting of the group, my role as leader was to provide structure and create a safe envi-

ronment in which they could begin to develop as a group. This analysis has made me aware that not listening to my own anxieties, thoughts and feelings prevented me from "tuning in" to the needs of the group and of the individuals in the group. There were times throughout the session when I wanted to remain silent but did not. At other times, I wanted to speak. Instead, I was quiet.

I realize that if I had had a theoretical framework to work from when I began this group, I would not have felt overwhelmed. I would have been more responsive to the group process and my role in this process. Finally, I would have communicated with my co-leader prior to the group meeting.

Hindsight suggests that an opening statement encompassing the range of themes that emerged directly and indirectly may have facilitated a less confrontational start to this meeting. Also, with more experience the workers would have understood that the process—the husband expressing his anger while his wife cried—was also raising a theme about how couples handled the pain of having children with these problems. There is a good possibility that a similar "division of labor" between the parents existed, in one form or another, for each of the couples.

In this section we have identified setting-related factors that may influence a first session. The argument is that the function of the group worker is the same, whether a leader of a hospital ward group or an organizer of a public housing tenants' group. The method used to pursue that function and the interactional skills required are also equivalent. Of course, when working in a community setting, the worker will also need other areas of knowledge (e.g., how political systems operate) and unique, specific skills (e.g., procedures for dealing with the press). Each setting requires specific knowledge and specific skills, but the core social work function and the interactional skills are the same.

IMPACT OF TIME

Time can have an important impact on the worker's activities in the first session. For example, some groups meet for a single session and must incorporate the beginning, work, and ending/transition phases in that time frame. This type of group is discussed in Chapter 16. In this section, I will discuss the variations in a first session of a short-term group—one that is designed to meet for only a single or a few sessions.

In the first session of my married couples' group described in the previous chapter, I could use the entire session for contracting and setting the stage for work in the knowledge that we had many sessions to follow. My work was affected by this knowledge, as was the work of the group members. For example, I did not feel the need to confront defenses and instead could concentrate on providing a clear framework and as much support as possible. The group members could take their time, as well, starting with "near problems" designed to test the waters until they felt safe.

This contrasts with another group I led, for single parents, in which the entire group experience needed to be contained in three 3-hour sessions, consisting of one evening and a full day.[1] I will use this group to illustrate the differences in a first session when time is limited.

The group was set up by community professionals in a small, rural town. They felt the need for a mutual aid group for single parents, and I was invited to fly into town to spend one evening and one day. A number of local helping professionals also attended the group, with two purposes in mind. First, they could provide ongoing services to the group members after the sessions were over. I felt it was important that resources be readily available to pick up with clients on issues that might be raised through the group meetings. Their second purpose was to observe my group leadership so that they might be better equipped to start mutual aid groups of their own. The group was advertised as open to the public, and a number of community professionals suggested it to their clients. I met the fifteen group members who attended for the first time on the night of the first session. In this section, I will focus on the implications for the first session only.

I had tuned in to the possible themes of concern prior to the group meeting and had prepared an opening statement that I hoped would focus us quickly on their most central concerns. I also tuned into the difficulty involved in getting started in such a new group, in a small town where people tended to know about each other, with an "expert" from out of town (who would not be around long), and the difficulty in opening up issues in a short-term context. I decided I needed to move quickly from the problem-swapping stage into work on specific issues, since we did not have the luxury of a long contracting phase. In addition, I felt we needed to demonstrate how helpful the group could be, quickly, if I expected members to risk. Finally, I prepared by tuning in to my own hesitations about risking in a first session and prepared to raise the issue directly with the group when and if I sensed defensiveness and/or the illusion of work. The following passage is excerpted from my recording of the session dictated immediately following the meeting.

> I explained the purpose of the group as providing an opportunity for single parents to discuss with each other some of the special problems they faced because they were alone. I explained that my role was not as an expert with answers for them, but rather, I would try to help them to talk and to listen to each other, and to provide help to each other from their own experiences. In addition, I would throw in any ideas I had that might be helpful. I then offered a few examples of possible concerns around dealing with friends and relatives after the split in the relationship, problems in relating to the ex-spouse, the financial strains, and problems that often accompanied being a single parent and the difficulties presented by the children. There was much head nodding as I spoke. I finished by describing briefly the phases that parents and children commonly go through after a separation (denial, anger, mourning, and finally, coming to terms with it). I then invited the participants to share their own experiences and suggested that these could form an agenda for our work that evening and the next day.
>
> There was a brief silence, and then Irene asked how long it took to go through the phases. I asked her why she was asking, and she said it was three years since her separation and she doesn't think she has passed through all of them yet. The group members laughed in acknowledgment of the meaning of the comment. I said I thought there must have been a great deal of pain and sadness, at the time of the split and since then, for it to still hurt after three years. I asked Irene if she could speak some more about this, and she continued, in a more serious tone, by describing her ongoing depression. She described days in which she feels she is finally getting over things and picking herself up, followed by days when she feels she is right back to square one. Others in the group agreed and shared their own experiences as I encouraged them to respond to Irene's comments. I told them it might help just to know that they were "in the same boat" with their feelings.
>
> I then asked if the group members could be more specific about what made it difficult. This resulted in a number of areas raised by members, which I kept track of in

my written notes. They included most of the problems I had raised in my opening statement. There was much emotionally laden discussion of the first area, problems with friends and family, with a great deal of anger expressed towards others who "didn't understand" and related to them in ways that hurt.

Dick, a young man in his mid-twenties, spoke with great agitation about his wife who had left him with their six-month-old baby only six weeks before. The group seemed to focus on Dick, who expressed a very strong sense of urgency and was clearly still in a state of shock and crisis. I had earlier noted that Dick was the first to arrive that evening and during the pre-meeting chatter, he had told the person next to him all of the crises he had gone through just to get there that night. I pointed out to the group that it seemed that Dick was feeling this concern about friends and relatives rather strongly, and in fact he had had a great deal of difficulty even getting here tonight. I asked if they would like to focus on problems with friends and relatives first, using Dick's example to get us started. They all agreed it would be helpful, including Dick.

My effort to move us more quickly into the work began with my contracting statement and continued when I responded to Irene's joking comment about "not getting through the phases yet" by reaching for the underlying hurt and bitterness. If we were to move quickly in the group, I felt I had to send an early message that I was ready to deal with the difficult feelings as soon as they were. The group responded by immediately moving into the painful feelings as well as the anger. Feeling the need to get into substantive work early in this first session, I moved to obtain group consensus on an initial theme of concern and to bring Dick's urgency to the group members' attention. Thus, we were moving into the work phase less than an hour after my opening statement. In the continuation of the first session description that follows, Dick's resistance to taking personal responsibility for his problems emerges. I responded with a demand for work, pointing out that we had very little time in which to work.

> After Dick described the details of his separation and his current living situation with the six-month-old child, he went on to describe the problems. He emphasized the difficulty of living in a small town, and in his particular case, being in a personal service occupation that put him in daily contact with many town residents. He said, "Sure, I feel lousy, depressed, and alone. But some days, I feel I'm getting over things a bit, feeling a little bit up, and everywhere I go people constantly stop me to tell me how terrible things are. If I didn't feel lousy before I went out, I sure do by the time I get home."
>
> Dick added a further complication, in that the baby had a serious case of colic and was crying all the time. He told the group that everyone was always criticizing how he handled the baby, and even his mother was telling him he wasn't competent and should move back home with her. He continued by saying he was so depressed by this that he had taken to not talking to anyone anymore, avoiding his friends, staying home alone at night, and going out of his mind. Others in the group shared similar versions of this experience. I said to Dick, "And that's the dilemma, isn't it? Just at the time you really need help the most, you feel you have to cut yourself off from it to maintain your sense of personal integrity and sanity. You would like some help, because the going is rough, but you're not sure you want to have to depend on all of these people, and you're not sure you like the costs involved." Dick nodded, and the other group members agreed.

After providing recognition and support for these feelings, I tried to move the group members into examining what they could do about them in terms of how they handled their conversations with friends and relatives. I encountered a good deal of resistance to this idea, with Dick balking each time I tried to get him to look at how he might have handled a conversation differently. He evaded this by jumping quickly to other comments or examples, or by expressions that seemed to say, "If you only knew my mother/friends, you would realize it is hopeless." When Rose, a member of the group in her early fifties, confronted him from the perspective of his mother—she had children close to him in age—he rejected her comments.

> I pointed out what was happening. I said, "It seems to me that when I or a group member suggest that you (Dick) look at your part in the proceedings, you won't take in what we are saying." I said I only had a day and a half with the group, so I really couldn't pussyfoot around with them. I wondered if it was tough for Dick, and all of them, to take responsibility for their part in their problems. Dick smiled and admitted that it was hard. He already felt lousy enough. Others joined in on how easy it was to blame everyone else and how hard it was to accept any blame themselves. I agreed that it was tough, but I didn't think I would be of any help to them if I just sat here for a day and a half agreeing about how tough things were for them. The group members laughed, and a number said they didn't want that.
>
> At this point, Dorris, one of the three workers participating in the group, surprised us all by saying that she had intended to listen and not talk during the session, but that listening to Dick's problem made her want to share hers. She said she had come to the group as an observer, however, she was pregnant and unmarried, and therefore, was about to become a single parent. She thought she was having the same problem in communicating with her mother as Dick was having with his. It was a classic example of a conflict between a mother who is hurt and embarrassed, and a daughter who feels rejected at a critical moment in her life. At my suggestion, Rose offered to role-play the mother as Dorris tried to find a new way to talk to her mother. The group was supportive, but at the same time, following my example, they also became quite confrontative with each other, in a healthy way.
>
> Dick listened and participated in the work on Dorris's problem, and as is often the case, was able to learn something about his own situation as he watched someone else struggling with the same concerns. When I asked him later if he had taken something from it, he said it had helped him a lot to see how he was holding back his real feelings from friends and his own mother. I pointed out to all of the group members what a shock their situation was to their friends and close relatives, and how, at first contact, they could not respond in a way which met their needs. I said, "This does not mean they don't love you. It just means that they have feelings and aren't always able to express them. Your mixed messages also make it difficult."
>
> Cerrise, another worker/observer in the group, joined the discussion at this point and described how she had felt when close friends had split up their marriage. She realized now that it had taken her a couple of months to get over being so angry at them for ending their marriage, because she loved them both. She hadn't been able to reach out to them to support them, but she was lucky, because they had not given up on her and she had been able to work it out. Dick said that hearing that helped a lot. That was what was probably going on with some of his friends.

Carrie, who was both an unmarried parent and a worker in the community, described her own experiences with her mother when she split up. She shared how she had involved her mother in the process, had let her know her feelings, and that she wanted her mother's love and support, but felt she had to handle the problems herself. Dick listened closely and said that this was probably what he had not been able to do. We did some role play on how Dick could handle the conversation with his mother—how he could articulate his real feelings. The group was supportive and helpful.

When I asked the group how they felt about this discussion, thus far, Dorris said it was helpful because I kept stressing the positive aspect, the reaching out and caring between people. Most of them were so upset, they could only see the negatives. The discussion turned to how much they needed others to talk to about what they were going through. As the session neared the end, in typical "doorknob" fashion, Dick revealed that a close male friend of his, in a similar situation with a young child, had told him he was considering committing suicide. He went on to tell us, with tears in his eyes, that the friend had just killed himself. I said, "It must have hit you very hard when that happened, and you must have wondered if you could have done something more to help." Dick agreed that was so, and the group members offered him support.

After some time, I asked Dick if he was worried about his own situation, since he had many of the same feelings as his friend. He said he was worried, but that he thought he would be strong enough to keep going, to have a goal in life, to make it for his child. I told him he had shown a lot of strength just coming to the group and working so hard on his problem. Carrie said that he was not alone, and that he could call her if he needed someone to talk to—as a friend, or as a worker. Rose pointed out that there was a single-parent social group at the church, and Dick said he had not realized that. Others in the group also offered support. I asked Dick how he felt now, and he said, "I feel a lot better. I realize, now, that I'm not so alone." Irene, who had opened the discussion by saying she had not yet gone through all of the phases, summarized the evening's work when she said, "I guess we are all struggling to find ways of saying to friends and close relatives, "Please love me now, I need you." The discussion ended, and we agreed to pick up again in the morning.

This example has illustrated how a group can move quickly into the middle phase of practice, in a first session, if the worker makes a demand for work. We will return to this group example, in Chapter 12, to explore the middle and ending phase work that followed this opening session.

CHAPTER SUMMARY

In this chapter we have seen a number of examples of contracting in first sessions. The age and relative articulateness of the members, the authority of the worker, the specific concerns of the clients, and the impact of the setting and time have added their own variation to the central theme. In addition, each worker brought a unique personal style to the beginning. The common elements, however, should also be clear at this point. These common elements represent the science of our work. In the chapters to follow, we will examine the core dynamics of groups at work and explore the specific functions and skills of the group worker. In the next chapters, we will attempt to answer the question of what to do after the first session.

GLOSSARY

Act out To communicate thoughts and feelings through behavior, often in a disruptive manner.

External leader The group leader who derives his or her authority from external sources such as the sponsoring agency. This is in contrast to the *internal leader*, who is a member of the group.

Internal leader A member of the group who assumes a leadership role in a situational or ongoing basis. This role needs to be confirmed by the other group members.

Mandatory client An involuntary client who is required to engage in services, usually by an agency policy (e.g., pre-adoptive groups), a court (e.g., male batterers), an employer (e.g., alcohol counseling) or a family member (e.g., spouse of a client with an addiction).

NOTE

1. This group example can be found in L. Shulman, "Healing the Hurts: Single Parents." In A. Gitterman and L. Shulman (eds.), *Mutual Aid Groups and the Life Cycle* (Itasca, IL: F.E. Peacock Publishers, 1986).

12

The Work Phase in the Group

CHAPTER OUTLINE

Sessional Contracting in the Group
The Work Phase in a Group Session
Sessional Endings and Transitions

In this chapter, we will focus on the interaction between the individual and the group and the way in which the group worker assists this interaction. Using time as an organizing principle, we will first examine the beginning phase of group sessions, emphasizing the way in which the worker helps individuals present their concerns to the group and simultaneously assists the group members to respond. Next, we will look at the work phase, illustrating the dynamics of mutual aid and the way in which group members can help each other and themselves at the same time. Finally, our discussion of the ending/transition phase will stress the importance of resolution and transition to next steps or next meetings. Each of these phases and the requisite skills will be illustrated with record material from a range of settings. While the focus of this chapter is on the individual-group interaction, it is important to recognize that *both* clients—the individual and the group—require further examination. In the next chapter, we will analyze the individual's role in the group, and in succeeding chapters we will concentrate on the group as a whole.

A problem raised frequently by beginning group workers, particularly those who have worked with individuals, is that in an attempt to deal with an individual's concern, they find themselves doing **casework in the group**. This is a common pattern in which the group leader provides individual counseling to a client within a group setting. This contrasts with an effort to mobilize mutual aid for the client by involving the other members. Suppose, for example, a member raises an issue at the start of a session and the worker responds with appropriate elaborative and empathic skills. The group member expands the concern, and the worker tries to help deal with the problem while the other group members listen. When this problem has been explored, the worker then begins with another client as the others patiently wait their turn.

After the meeting, the worker worries about having done casework in front of an audience. In reaction to this feeling of uneasiness, the worker strategizes not to be trapped this way during the next session, thus making a different kind of mistake. Vowing to pay attention to the "group" aspect of group work, the worker attempts to do so by refusing to respond with elaborating skills when an individual opens the session with a direct or indirect offering of a concern. For example, one member of a parent group might say, "It's really hard to raise teenagers these days, what with all the changing values." The worker quickly responds by inquiring if other members of the group find this to be true. One by one they comment on the general difficulty of raising teenagers. The discussion soon becomes overly general and superficial, and meanwhile the first group member is anxiously waiting with a specific concern about a fight with her daughter the evening before.

When trying to deal with individual concerns, workers may find themselves doing casework in the group, and when trying to pay attention to the group, workers may find themselves leading an overgeneralized discussion. Both maladaptive patterns reflect the worker's difficulty in conceptualizing the group as a system for mutual aid and in understanding the often subtle connections between individual concerns and the general work of the group. Schwartz's notion of the "two clients," discussed earlier, can help to resolve the apparent dilemma. He suggests that the worker simultaneously must pay attention to two clients, the individual and the group, and the field of action is concerned with interaction between the two. Thus, instead of choosing between the "one" or the "many, the worker's function involves mediating the engagement between these two clients. This is a special case of the general helping function for social work defined in Parts I, II, and III.

The worker's tasks in addressing these two clients are examined in this chapter against the backdrop of time—the beginning (sessional contracting), middle (work), and ending/transition phases of a group session.

SESSIONAL CONTRACTING IN THE GROUP

In Chapter 1 we examined some of the barriers to open communication in the helping situation. These included ambivalence towards taking help because of the resultant feelings of dependency, societal taboos against discussion of certain topics (e.g., sex), the client's painful feelings associated with particular issues, and the context of the helping setting (e.g., the impact of the helping person's authority). These blocks often cause a client to use an indirect form of communication when sharing a problem or concern. For example, clients might hint at a concern (state a specific problem in a very general way), act it out (begin a session by being angry at the worker or other group members, using the anger to cover up the pain), employ metaphor or allegory as a means of presenting an issue (e.g., by telling a seemingly unrelated story), use art or other mediums (e.g., a child might draw a picture of an abusive parent) or send the message nonverbally (e.g., by sitting quietly with a pained expression or sitting apart from the group with an angry expression). The indirectness of these communications may cause the group members and the worker to miss important cues in the early part of the session. Alternatively, a member might raise a concern but do it in such a way as to hide the depth of feeling associated with it, thereby turning off the other group members. The worker's function is to assist the group in interpreting individual members' indirect communications.

Reaching for Individual Communication in the Group

Because of the problems involved in individual-group communication, the worker should, in the early stages of each meeting, concentrate on helping individual members present their concerns to the group. The beginning of each group session should be seen as a tentative, slow process of feeling out the group, endeavoring to determine which member or members are attempting to capture the group's attention for their own issues, and exploring how these issues may represent a theme of concern for the group. In a like manner, the group itself may be approaching a major theme of concern for that week, and the individual offerings may thus present specific examples of the central concern of the group.

Whether the concern originates with the member or expresses the feelings of many, the worker's efforts in the early stages should be focused on answering the question, "What are they (the group members) working on in this session?" It would be a mistake for workers to rush in with their own agenda simply because the first productions of the group members are unclear. Likewise, it would be an error for the worker to believe that simply because the group had agreed to deal with a specific issue or an individual's concern at the end of the previous meeting, this will be the issue for the current session. Even if the discussion picks up exactly where the members had agreed it would, the worker should monitor the conversation in the early part of the session with an ear either for confirmation of the theme or hints that members are just going through the motions. In structured groups where an agenda for each session may be pre-planned and a topic assigned for discussion, the group leader must still remain alert to the possibility that another or a related issue is emerging and must at least be recognized.

The important point is that the worker should be aware that even though the conversation may not seem directed towards the group's purpose, it is always purposeful. For clarity of exposition, I will focus here on examples where the early discussion is directed towards presenting a specific theme of concern. In Chapter 14, however, I will explore examples where the purpose of the early conversation is to raise an issue concerning the working of the group or the leader. In both cases, the worker should be asking herself or himself during the early discussion, "How does this conversation connect to our work?" or "What is troubling this particular member?" By doing so, there is a better chance of helping the individual relate a concern to the group.

Married Couples. An illustration from the couples' group described in Chapter 10 can demonstrate this process as well as the importance of sessional tuning-in. The session was the eighteenth. At the previous one, Louise, who was present without her husband John, had revealed that he had a drinking problem. There was general agreement to pursue this concern with John present the next week. In my tuning-in session with co-leaders prior to the start of the session, I had learned that Fran and Rick had had a particularly difficult week and had threatened separation during their individual counseling session. Rick had questioned returning to the group. The couple previously had made substantial progress in the group and in a related sexual therapy group program but had hit a critical point and were regressing. Over the course of the sessions I had observed that this couple had a characteristic pattern of presenting their concerns in the group: Fran would express her own concerns and fears indirectly as she responded to other couples in the group, and Rick would physically retreat. Having accomplished the preparatory work, we stratagized to reach for Fran's indirect cues if they were evident, and we prepared to help the group discuss priorities for this session. The session began with some hints from the group about the ending process, a topic to which I had planned to respond directly. After I acknowledged the group's sadness, and my own, about ending and the members had briefly discussed their feelings, there was a silence that was broken by John:

> **John:** I know about your discussion about my drinking last week, since I met with Larry (the worker) and he filled me in. If you have any questions, let me have them.

At this point there was some relaxation of tension, and group members offered supportive comments for John for his having raised this difficult concern. I noticed that Fran and Rick had turned their chairs so that they faced apart from each other. Rick was staring into space with a bland expression. Fran turned to face John.

Fran: I want you to know, John, that I think it's great that you have come here prepared to talk about this problem. It takes a lot of courage on your part. It would have been a lot easier if you simply stayed away or refused to discuss it. That would have been the coward's way out.

Worker: Fran, I wonder if that's what you think Rick is doing right now, in relation to you? His chair is turned away from you and you seem to be upset with each other.

Fran: (After a period of silence) I don't understand how you do this, how you read my mind this way. It must be a form of magic. (Pause) But you're right, we had a really bad fight this week, and we're not over it. Rick didn't want to come this week, and he won't talk to me about it. (Fran shows signs of becoming upset emotionally.)

Worker: How do you see it, Rick?

After Rick's confirmation of the seriousness of the situation, both he and Fran state they are concerned because this was supposed to be the week for John and Louise. I raised the issue with the whole group and they decided to stay with Rick and Fran because of the degree of urgency in their situation. John and Louise felt they could wait another week. The session turned out to be an important turning point for the couple (Rick and Fran), as well as one that yielded important insights for the other couples into their own relationships.

There was no magic in picking up Fran's cues; tuning-in and the identifying of a pattern over time had helped. Also important was the recognition that often early comments from members are indirect efforts to raise themes of concern. Another example from the same group was the issue raised by Lou, the member of the group who was in his sixties. In this illustration, the problem of identifying the issue was compounded, since the nature of the concern was not clear to the member and was presented indirectly as a part of an angry attack upon the group leaders. In the previous session, a videotaped segment of a meeting when one of the couples had blown up at each other had been viewed by the group with the couple's consent. Lou was upset that this painful exchange had been replayed in the group. He began with an angry attack on helping professionals, denouncing "the way they played games with people's lives." He was extremely upset at the way workers encouraged the expression of bitter feelings between couples, feeling that this tore them apart emotionally. He argued that this was not necessary. I reached for the specific meaning of his opening comments.

Worker: Lou, I think you're talking about us and last week's session—when we watched the tape. (I had missed this session due to an accident but had reviewed the videotape. The session had been led by my co-leaders.)

Lou: Of course I am! I've never been more upset. I tore my guts watching what you people put them through.

Lou went on to attack the helping professions in general as well as us in particular. The co-leaders responded by attempting to explain what they had done. We were generally made to feel defensive and incompetent. Group members will often make the workers feel exactly the way they feel themselves. When they are unaware of or unable to express their own pain and the hurt under their anger, one way to deal with it is to project it onto the leaders or other members. Bion (1961) described this process as "projective identification," in which the client communicates his feelings by stimulating the same feelings in the worker. The difficulty for the worker is that there is always some element of truth in the attack, which is usually aimed at an area in which the worker feels less confident. In this situation we stayed with the issue raised by Lou.

> **Worker:** Lou, you're angry with us and also feeling that we really hurt Len and Sally last week. Obviously we missed how hard it hit you to see their pain. Why don't you ask them how they felt?
>
> **Lou:** Well, am I right? Wasn't that terrible for you to go through?
>
> **Len:** It wasn't easy, and it hurt, but I think it helped to get it out in the open. It also helped to have all of you care about us and feel the pain with us.
>
> **Lou:** But there must be some way to do this without having to tear your guts out. (Lou seemed a bit taken aback by Len's comments, which were echoed by his wife.)
>
> **Worker:** When you attacked us, Lou, I have to admit it hit me hard. A part of me doesn't want to get at the anger and pain that you all feel, and yet anther part of me feels it's the way back to a stronger relationship. I have to admit you shook me.
>
> **Rose:** (Lou's wife) I think you have to understand this has been a hard week for us.
>
> **Worker:** How come?
>
> **Rose:** We just got word that Lesley, our granddaughter who lives in London, is splitting up with her husband.

Lou and Rose have spoken before in the group about their children and the pain it has caused them to see each of them experience difficulties in their own marriages. Lou has been particularly angry with helping professionals who have helped neither him nor his family members. This was the first grandchild to experience marital problems, and it signified to Lou and Rose the continuation of the family's instability into another generation. Under much of the anger is their pain as well as their feelings of defensiveness and doubt, to which Rose responded by clarifying Lou's signal.

> **Worker:** It must have hit you very hard, Lou, having the first grandchild experience marital problems.
>
> **Lou:** (Seemingly deflated, the anger gone, slumped in his chair, speaking with a tone of resignation and bitterness) After 45 years, you learn you have to live with these things. It's just another notch that you have to add to all to the other hurts.

The discussion continued with Lou and Rose describing their feelings of helplessness as they watched their family disintegrating and their desire to show the children that it did not have to be that way. The group members commiserated as they described their feelings of impotence to affect the lives of their children and their grandchildren.

In the first illustration with Fran and in the second with Lou, the individual was reaching out to the group indirectly through her or his opening comments. With Fran, the concern was presented in the guise of a response to a group member, while with Lou it appeared as an attack upon the leaders. In both cases, the communication had two meanings. The first was the actual statement of fact, while the second was a disguised call for help. Unless workers are tuned in, listen hard for potential offerings from group members, and are clear about their own function in the group, it is easy to miss the early, indirect productions of group members. Of course, the member will often present a concern more directly, thus making it easier for the group to hear. And sometimes an issue may emerge at a later point in the meeting.

Male Batterers.   In the following excerpt, a member moves from the general group discussion to a specific concern. The conversation in the group and the feelings expressed generated a spontaneous response from a group member which, with the worker's help, evolved into a specific issue. The group was a support group for men who batter their wives or the women they live with. This mutual aid group was set up in recognition of the fact that in addition to holding the men accountable for their family violence, some form of intervention was need-ed to break the cycle of destructive relationships with their wives and women in general. The group was formed to help the men discuss their common concerns, concentrating on their abusive relationships with women. In this illustration, the general topic of relationships with children triggered Frank's specific concern, which the worker helped him elaborate.

> Frank said he was having a hard time finding things to do on his own. He had gone, alone, to see the movie *Short Eyes* the other night. He had left half or three-quarters of an hour into the movie. He said it was about prisons, and it had really made him uncomfortable. The movie had made him feel "boxed." Sid then said, "I feel con-fined in other ways." Frank said that he got the feeling that his wife had felt confined as well. Sid nodded and said that might often be true in relationships. He, Sid, had felt there were certain ways he had to be when he was in a relationship, I asked him what he meant. Sid said he felt that he "had to hold out in expressing certain feelings." He meant, he explained, that there were certain feelings he couldn't express. Frank said that he had felt the same way. But now, his marriage was over, and he was finding it a lot harder than he thought it would be to get over it. He said he knew it was fin-ished but that didn't make it easier to accept. I said to Frank that it had taken me longer than it had my wife to get over the marriage ending.
>
> Rod said to Frank, "It'll pass." I said to him, "What do you mean?" Rod went on to discuss how he took the few dollars he had and his three children and packed up and crossed the country to begin again. They celebrated Christmas by decorating a tree with tin cans and exchanging food wrapped as presents. However, the family had good memories of these hard times and talked about the fun involved. The other members were fascinated with the story. It was at this point that Frank moved to his specific concern about his family.
>
> Frank used this as a means of bringing up something that had been worrying him over the last week. It seems his wife had taken in two young men (about 17) who were friends of his daughters (aged 13 and 14). Rod didn't feel this was a good situ-ation and wanted to know what Frank could do about it. He looked particularly at me and asked if I knew what he could do. I said I would have to know what was going on in more detail. Rod was very interested in this situation, taking the same stance that children were all-important to him and that he "would do anything, anything, to keep mine." He said that he had even spent a night in jail, charged with five counts of kidnapping. Gerry had appeared upset while Frank and Rod were speaking; he had

been told that he could be charged with kidnapping if he attempted to remove his son from his wife's custody. Rod's response was that all Gerry had to do was cross the provincial border and he would be OK.

At this moment in the group, the worker was so identified with the men that he missed an important intervention. Rod's advice to Gerry needed to be confronted by the worker. In addition to pointing out that it would *not* be OK to cross the border, the worker needed to make clear his ethical and legal responsibilities to report (duty to warn) any serious threat to commit a crime. This was an early effort in working with men who batter. In later groups, greater clarity was achieved about the worker's primary responsibility to protect the partners in the relationships. After such an intervention, the worker can then proceed to discuss the legal rights of the fathers and appropriate alternatives, as in the following continuation of the discussion.

> I explained that generally the parent who had the most involvement with the child or children was the one who received custody. Unless there was evidence of unfitness, this generally meant the mother. Rod was nodding away at Frank, who said several times to him, "You don't know how bound I am," referring to the legal restraints applied to him by family court. I went on to say that the legal system was now changing somewhat and that either parent was denied access only on rare occasions, that even if one parent had custody, the other wasn't totally without rights.
>
> I told Frank that if he were really concerned about the situation, I would be willing to help him talk to his court worker about it. He felt reassured about this and said that maybe he would try some things on his own. He went on to say that until he had become involved in this group, he would have responded differently to the situation. I asked him how he would have handled it before. He said that he would have just charged right into a confrontation with his wife and probably achieved nothing except to raise bad feelings.
>
> Gerry appeared to be calmer by now. I asked him if he was still upset. He said that when he and his wife separated, he was really concerned about what would happen to his son. He was afraid that if his wife took up with another guy, his son would somehow be damaged. Frank and Ron were both nodding at Gerry. I asked Gerry if he was still afraid of this. He said no, that he and his wife were still working on things but they were getting along OK.

As one individual begins to explore a concern, associated feelings and issues will often be triggered for other members. It is important for the worker to recognize these issues and feelings as they emerge but at the same time, to keep the group focused on the original concern raised by the first member. In this case, it is important to come back as the worker did to Frank for further elaboration.

> Frank looked at Sid and Gerry and said that he wanted to know if they felt that being brought up in families where separations had occurred had affected them. He wanted to know what it had been like for them. I asked him if he was concerned about his children, and he said yes.
>
> Sid and Gerry talked about their perceptions of growing up in separated families. Both indicated that it hadn't been any real big deal. Gerry said his mother tended to "bad-mouth" his father, but not vice versa. Frank seemed a bit upset at that, saying that was probably to be expected. Sid indicated that he had had contact with his biological father only twice—once when he was in his teens and then when he had sought

him out several years ago. He said he was the only one of the children to have contact with their biological father. Frank was thoughtful after hearing this. I asked him what was going on. He said that he was concerned about his future relationship with his son and daughters.

The process of exploring Frank's indirect communication had been a slow one, but Frank was able to begin to talk about an area of concern that struck at the heart of his feelings of guilt at having "abandoned" his children. As will be illustrated in a later chapter when further illustrations are drawn from this group, a central theme throughout the work was the difficulty these men had in dealing with their feelings of dependency. The worker who led this group (a new experience for him) learned a great deal about the underlying feelings of men who use violence, aiding his ability to "hear" more clearly the indirect offerings of members in the next group he led. In this sense, each group is an educational experience for the worker, and the worker's ability to understand the themes expressed will increase with experience.

Veterans with HIV/AIDS. In the following brief excerpt, the disclosure by one member of the loss of a friend to AIDS opens the door for other members to share their own powerful feelings and their fears. (*Note:* This meeting took place before the encouraging results of the new triple-drug therapy.)

> **Group Purpose:** Open-ended mutual aid group for male veterans with HIV/AIDS (10th meeting)
> **Age Range:** 26–45
> After establishing a working contract for the session, I asked the group members to share some of their struggles living with the virus. John, a member who attends group regularly, began the session by sharing his feelings surrounding the recent loss of a close friend to AIDS. I acknowledged his pain by responding, "It must have been very difficult to find out that your close friend died of AIDS." John nodded. Another member of the group shared his experience of losing his first friend to AIDS. After the second member had shared his story, there was silence in the room. I recognized the silence and invited the group members to share how they were feeling at that moment. George was the first one to speak. He said that he felt that his "body was a stick of dynamite...waiting to blow up." I asked him to explain what he meant by saying his body was like a stick of dynamite. He explained that he had not become sick from the virus yet, but he feels that once he begins to get sick his body will disintegrate— like the explosion of a stick of dynamite. Other members in the group nodded in agreement. I noticed the nonverbal agreement of the members and invited anyone to respond to George's analogy.

Acting-Out Behavior: Children, Teens, and Adults

The examples discussed thus far have involved relatively articulate adults who are able to raise their concerns through verbal means. In many groups, particularly those involving children, clients will act out using behavior to signal their concerns. A problem occurs when the group leader is using a behavioral model of practice in which the behavior itself is seen as the "problem" and the underlying communication is completely missed. In this model, group leaders are often advised to ignore the "negative" behavior so that it will not be "reinforced" and encouraged. The acting-out group member is seen as "seeking attention," and if the leader ignores such behavior and instead responds to and rewards positive behavior, the member's pattern of participation will be modified and the negative behavior "extinguished."

Since the behavior is often an expression of the client's underlying feelings of pain, rage, and fear, it represents the client's effort to raise a problem. Ignoring the behavior is counterproductive. An alternative is to restrict behaviors that may threaten the safety of the client, other group members, the worker, or the group meeting room, and to simultaneously reach for the underlying issues. There is a good chance that the client is in the group precisely because of this maladaptive pattern of expressing feelings. The group leader's insensitivity to the message actually replicates the way in which significant others (parents, friends, teachers, and so on) have responded to the client. In such situations, the client will escalate the signals of the message—for example, by increasing the level of acting out—until someone hears.

The following example involves a group for 10- and 11-year-old children who had lost a close family member. They were referred to the group because of behavior problems in school and elsewhere that signaled their inability to cope with the death. The group members called themselves the "Lost and Found Group," since they had lost someone close but had found each other (Vastola, Nierenberg, and Graham, 1994). The authors describe how Mark, at the start of a group session following one in which members had begun to open up and discuss their losses, sends a mixed message using paper and pen. He repeatedly writes "Bob," the name of his grandfather who had recently died.

> **Carl:** Mark, your grandfather died?
> **Mark:** I don't want any damn body talking about my grandfather or I'll kick their butt.
> **Leader:** You sound pretty angry.
> **Mark:** I'm not angry. I just don't want anybody talking about my grandfather.
> **Leader:** It's very difficult.
> **Mark:** It's not difficult. I just don't want anybody saying that he died. (His anger is escalating.)
> **Gloria:** Nobody wants to talk about nobody dying.
> **Dick:** Yes, we don't want to talk about that.
> **Leader:** How come?
> **Gloria:** That's why he (Mark) is running around. You can't force him if he doesn't want to.
> **Leader:** Are you saying that perhaps that's what makes you run around—so you won't have to talk about something upsetting?
> **Mark:** Nope.
> **Leader:** Maybe you feel it's too hard to talk about.
> **Mark:** No, it's not hard for me to talk about anything…but that reminds you, and you could be dreaming.
> **Carl:** Yup, you dream for about a week when you talk about your mother, then it takes about five days to try to get over it, but it comes back again and it stops and it comes back again…. Nightmares, I hate. I hate talking about my mother. (p. 87)

Through his behavior, Mark has demonstrated his difficulty in dealing with the loss. The group members move to his defense, because this is their problem as well. The issue of role in the group is discussed in detail in Chapter 13. The group leader's persistence sends a message to Mark (and the group) that she will not back off from this difficult issue. As she explores Mark's resistance by acknowledging the difficulty and asking what makes it hard to talk about his loss, the members begin to open up.

In the preceding example, the worker was prepared to deal with the taboo subject of death and grieving—a very painful topic when children are involved. By responding to the behavior only, and attempting to set limits and stop Mark from running around the room, the worker would actually have been signaling her own resistance to the discussion. The fight over the behavior would have been a means of avoiding the pain for both Mark and the worker. This is why it is so important for social workers to have access to support for themselves as they attempt to deal with these powerful issues (see Shulman, 1991).

This need for support was illustrated in a consultation session I conducted for workers in a residential setting for acting-out teenage boys and girls. The setting had adopted a reward-punishment system, with levels of each related to the behavior of the residents. Residents could earn or lose points depending upon their behavior. When acting-out behavior was observed in the residence or the group meetings, a standard response was to send the resident to a "time-out room." This was a locked room that isolated the resident.

Workshop participants described an incident in a group for 13- and 14-year-old boys whose purpose was to deal with house issues and "socialization." At the start of the group, one member who was consistently confrontational and hard to handle in the residence, and was an avid body builder, arrived dressed in a "muscle shirt" and began striking body-building poses, which set the group members off into laughter and mimicking behavior. The workers felt distressed by his behavior and ordered him to take his seat. They operated under the assumption that they were being "tested" and that establishing control and structure was crucial. Instead of sitting down, the resident pulled out a bar of soap and began a mock shower in which he cleaned himself, with particular attention to his pubic area. As the group's reaction seemed to escalate, the worker quickly intervened and ordered him out of the group and into the time-out room.

My first question to the staff was to inquire as to whether any of the residents had experienced sexual abuse. Their response was that all the residents had some form of sexual abuse in their history. A flood of stories emerged of the many oppressive experiences these children had undergone prior to coming to the residence, including examples of additional sexual abuse and exploitation on the street (prostitution) and even in foster homes. As I explored the feelings of the staff, it became clear that this area had been a taboo one for staff discussions, which were usually concerned with how to better set limits. Staff felt uncomfortable opening the door to discussions of sexual exploitation and did not feel support from each other, supervisors, or administrators.

Once the feelings of staff had been explored, we were able to return to the group session, this time attempting to tune in to the meaning of the resident's behavior when considered as a form of communication—in particular, from a teenaged survivor of sexual abuse. Staff were quick to see how the muscle-building and flexing might be related to the desire of a young male to be able to protect himself from further abuse. The cleansing of the pubic area took on another meaning as staff considered how often these children feel "dirty," a form of internalizing of the oppressor without, as described in Chapter 2. While these were speculations only, and needed to be pursued directly, they offered the staff some handles to use in exploring the underlying, maladaptive acting-out behaviors exhibited by most of these children.

Further inquiry on my part revealed that some staff suspected that sexual abuse might be continuing even in the house, with the stronger residents abusing the weaker ones. It is not uncommon for survivors to become abusers themselves. This had also been a taboo subject because of the implications. This acting-out behavior could be both a call for help with the past abuse and an effort to indirectly raise the current experiences. Staff used the rest of the meeting to develop strategies for responding directly to many of these indirect communications. I do not believe this would have been possible had the staff members not continued to build their own support system along the way.

The final example of behavior as communication comes from the beginning of a session of an ongoing, open-ended group for friends, lovers, and relatives, who were grieving the loss of someone from AIDS. A woman who had just lost her son was attending her first meeting. The meeting started with a **check-in** ritual in which each member briefly shared what had happened to him or her during the preceding week. The new member began with an extremely rapid, non-stop monologue about how busy she had been keeping herself since her son died. She described a daily, hectic round of activity, showing very little emotion other than the hint of an underlying anxiety. She had clearly been in flight from her loss during the week and was indirectly communicating this flight by her opening conversation. It was as if she was saying, "Do you want to see how I am coping? Watch me!" The leader responded by cutting her off, after a while, pointing out that they needed to hear from all of the members as a part of the check-in. Later analysis by the leader revealed that he had sensed her anxiety and simply had not been able to deal with it. Had he been able to be honest about his feelings at the moment, he would have shared how he experienced her presentation— being uncertain about how to help, feeling her sense of overwhelming loss, and wondering about proceeding with the check-in. Any or all of these comments might have opened the door for further discussion and expression of emotion.

The group members joined in the collusion, in a flight process of their own. They were at a different stage in their grieving, and this new member's behavior may have reawakened feelings they would have preferred to have left behind. This example also reveals some of the problems associated with rituals such as check-in, which can take on a life of their own when adhered to dogmatically. Instead of providing an opportunity to deal with individual members' concerns, they can become a way to avoid deepening the work. In retrospect, the leader could have acknowledged the indirect communications of the member and raised, with the group, whether they wanted to respond right away or wanted to continue check-in. Either way, acknowledging the feelings underlying the individual's acting out of her pain would have laid the groundwork for dealing with her loss and the feelings evoked in the second client, the group.

The emphasis in this first section has been on helping the individual reach out to the group. In many cases, particularly when the feelings expressed reflect those held by the group members, the worker's second client—the group—paradoxically appears to turn away from the individual. In the next section, we will discuss the meaning of this dynamic.

Reaching for the Group Response to the Individual

It is easy to see how a worker can become identified with a particular client's feelings as a theme of concern is raised. If strong emotions are expressed, the worker may feel supportive and protective. Not surprisingly, if the other group members do not appear to respond to the individual, a common reaction from workers is to feel upset and angry. The worker is shocked and surprised to observe group members apparently not listening, to see their eyes glazing over as they appear to be lost in their own thoughts, or to witness a sudden change in subject or a direct rebuff to the client who has bared some innermost feelings. At moments such as these, the worker's clarity of function and the notion of "two clients" can be most critical. Instead of getting angry, the worker should view the group members' response as a signal, not that they are uninterested in what is being said, but that the theme may be having a powerful impact on them.

The tasks of the mediation function, as outlined by Schwartz, call for the worker to search for the common ground between the individual and the group at the point where they seem most cut off from each other. This clear sense of function directs the worker to empathize with the group members' feelings underlying their apparent resistance at precisely the same time as expressing empathy with the individual client. The group leader must be with both clients at the same time.

Teen Boys in a Residential Treatment Center. The following illustration of this process is drawn from group work with 14- and 15-year-old boys in a residential treatment center. One of the members, Jay, tries to use the group for some help in discussing his feelings about his parents. In this first excerpt, he is shocked when his brother (a member) tells him that he has just heard from a relative that their father may not be Jay's biological father. As Jay attempts to come to terms with his reactions, the worker pays close attention to the part of the group that has difficulty in dealing with this issue. The group discussion has been general thus far, dealing with questions about prostitutes.

> **John:** Right. Take my mother, for instance. We know that she's—she's married and going out with some guy. My old man knows it. She left him once, you see, and now she's back again.
>
> **Frank:** (John's brother) John, you want to know something? (hesitant) I don't want to bother you but—I heard—from someone—I don't want to say who.
>
> **John:** (Impatient) Ahh, come on.
>
> **Frank:** That you aren't dad's kid. That it was Mom and some other man. I'm not saying it's true or anything.
>
> **John:** (Jumps in) Oh, I wouldn't doubt it. My mother knew Bill (her boyfriend) before my old man and her were married. Bill had already given it to her before.
>
> **Mike:** Maybe your old man doesn't know.
>
> **John:** For all my old man knows, she could have said he was drunk one night— and what could he say?
>
> **Mike:** (Who had started to get restless) Let's do something else, let's listen to some music for a while now.
>
> **Worker:** Why do you want to do that?
>
> **John:** Why? Why? Why does Mike want to stop? (The others mumble something, a few yeahs.)
>
> **Mike:** We'll talk about it afterwards.
>
> **John:** (Angry) Why? You only get in here once a week. God, I'm not going to quit. You can quit if you want.
>
> **Mike:** Not quit!
>
> **John:** If I found out that my old man—that Bill (his mother's boyfriend) was my real father…

Frank: (Interrupts, soft voice) How would you feel?

John: (Pause) I'd go see him. I'd go see him—and talk it over with him—and find out what happened. I'd really want to know—I mean, that's —that's a really good thought. I never thought of that.

(Several of the boys talk at once for a couple of seconds. Meanwhile, Mike has not been paying any attention.)

Worker: Mike, you don't seem to want to talk about any of this.

Mike: Well, it's none of my business.

While John was speaking, the worker had been watching the group members, closely observing their facial expressions. This is the skill of **monitoring the group**. When she spotted the signal of Mike turning away, she reached for it directly. In some ways, Mike was expressing the discomfort felt by all the boys as they explored a sensitive and personal area that hit home for them as well. The worker acknowledged this as a potential obstacle, thereby freeing the communication process.

Worker: I think it's hard to listen to such a personal problem. What makes it even tougher is that all of you have a lot of mixed feelings about your folks. But you know, this is what the group is all about, and I think John really needs some help on this one.

John: But I want you to listen. (Said very emphatically) At least—at least—

Don: (Interrupts) You can get some ideas.

John: I can get some ideas—what I should do. What would you do if you found out your old man wasn't really your old man?

Mike: Like you were—sort of like a bastard?

John: No. Well, let's say—that your mother had got it from another man. He wasn't your real father. What would you do?

Mike: You, you were an illegitimate child (half statement, half question).

Frank: Yeah.

John: What would you do? (Pause)

Worker: How would you feel?

Don: (Emphatically) I'd feel rotten.

Mike: I, I, I, I'd feel—I'd feel dirty.

Worker: How would you feel, John?

John: I don't know what I'd feel really. I think I'd really feel—I mean, really feel...

Mike: (Interrupts) John?

John: Bad. I—you know, I don't know what I'd really do if I ever found out that this wasn't really my father.

Mike: What do you feel like right now?

Frank: (Interrupts) But John, just think back, in a way...it could be true.

John: The way I think is, it could be true. The time I was born was when my parents really started to break up—they really started to have fights and all that stuff. And after I had a heart attack as a baby...

Mike: (Interrupts) You did? (Group talks about John's heart attack and illness for a few minutes.)

John: But he's the worst-off guy of all of us, this guy right here. (Points to Don, whose parents are both dead)

The subject is changed, and the meeting ends shortly thereafter.

The worker was unable to help at this point beyond assisting John to share his concerns with the group members and encouraging the group members to stay with him. She tried to help John explore his feelings, and the boys in the group commiserated with him. This, in itself, was helpful; however, neither the worker nor the group members knew where to go at this point. The subject was dropped and was not picked up again for three sessions. At the start of the fourth session, the worker noticed that John was unusually quiet and commented on it. This is an example of the skill of **monitoring the individual**. Not only does the worker monitor the second client—the group—but she or he also pays attention to each individual member. This skill comes with practice. When these two skills have been integrated, the leader can monitor the group and each individual member simultaneously.

John was reluctant to take up the worker's offer, and the group members seemed ready to drop the issue. Nevertheless, the worker persisted, reminding the group of how they had helped John in the past. John finally revealed that his mother was leaving home.

John: (Points at Frank) You know what it's all about. (Pause. Don and Frank say they think they know.)

John: Ma's leaving home again. It's the second time. She's leaving home again. She told—I heard—a while ago I—I heard her talking about it. (Pause)

Frank: Your father's house is up for sale. (Pause) That would give her a chance to leave, anyway. (Pause)

Frank: She's leaving now—she said in two weeks. (The boys talk for a few minutes about the woman she is going to stay with. John looks at the books, lies down on the floor.)

Worker: (To the group) You're not helping John.

Frank: (Quickly) Oh, I'm thinking about it.

Mike: Get it off your chest, John.

Don: That's how you go crazy, if you don't.

Mike: It's just going to build up and you'll explode and become a paranoid, or schizophrenic—right, Joanne? (the worker) Do you know what a paranoid or schizophrenic is? (Worker answers, "Yes.")

Frank: (To John) You didn't feel that bad about it last time.

John: (Talks very low, can hardly be heard.) Then I wasn't old enough to really understand—but this time, for some reason— (Frank talks about what it was like when his father walked out. Mike, too.)

Mike: John, I've just found an article you should read. It's called "How to deal with your tensions." (Laughs. Everyone ignores this.)

Worker: Mike, I think it's hard for you to stay with John's feelings because they hit you hard as well.

Frank: When you get older, you realize more—you think and put the pieces together.

John: When you're older, you think about the future, not the past.

Frank: Sometimes it haunts you—the future. You're scared. (Pause. John is quiet.)

Worker: You told John to get it all off his chest. It looks like it's very much still there.

Carl: I think you should find out the truth...and ask.

John: I don't want to do that. I'm afraid to find out what happened—that my father might not be—my real father. I don't know what I would do. I've never lost my temper—but there's always a first time.

Worker: You're afraid of what you'd feel. (Half question, half statement)

John: If this guy was my father...he's rotten...he broke up my family. (Silence) Maybe the others aren't interested. I don't want to bore them. (Worker asked what the others said to that. They denied it.)

John: They can say that but they may not feel that inside—they got their own problems.

Carl: I don't find it boring. I'm just trying to think of a solution.

Don: It's my problem, too.

Carl: Same here. I—you don't know what's going to happen if you ask something.

Don: I think it's better to find out the truth, because sooner or later it's going to hit you. The more you wait, the harder it's going to hit.

Carl: I think so, too. (Just then the bell rang, indicating the end of the meeting. Before everyone left, the worker asked them if they wanted to continue talking about this the next time, and they said yes.)

Psychiatric Day Patients. The following example is from an adult, day treatment outpatients' group for clients with a chronic mental illness. The focus is on family issues. In this fifth session, a member raises her depression on the fifth anniversary of the brutal death of her child. The group members respond with silence, and the worker intervenes to support the second client.

At the beginning of our meeting, after group introductions and as people settled into their seats, Joan began speaking. She looked straight ahead of herself, eyes downcast most of the time, and occasionally made eye contact with me (one of the co-leaders) or looked furtively around the group as she spoke.

Joan said, "Well, I just want to tell everybody that the fifth anniversary of my daughter's death (the daughter was raped and murdered) is coming up this week and it's bothering me a lot. It always has bothered me. I try to deal with it OK, but I just don't always know how. I get to thinking about it, and the more I think, the more I'm afraid that I'm gonna lose it or do something against myself. I've tried to come to terms with it, but it's always hard when it comes around to when I lost her. So anyway, I've made arrangements to use the 24-hour bed (an emergency bed in the center) 'cause I'm too afraid when I get to feeling like this."

There was complete and utter silence in the group. I remained silent for a few moments as well. As I looked around the group, the members too were looking straight ahead or acting uncomfortable and as if they didn't know what to say. I said, "Wow, that's some pretty heavy issue that you're bringing up. It seems like it's hitting people pretty hard." The group was still silent, and I paused, although, just as Elizabeth was about to say something, my co-leader said, "I'm wondering what people in the group are thinking or feeling about what Joan has just said, and if it's difficult to respond to it." There was a little more silence, and Joan went on, "Maybe I shouldn't have brought it up. Everybody here already knows that this is a problem for me. It's just that I felt so close to her. She was the one whose birth I remember. She was the one, instead of whisking her away and doing what they have to do right after they're born, they put her on me and I felt so much closer to her than the others. I remember it so much better. But maybe I just shouldn't bring it up here."

I waited a little and looked around the group once more and then said, "You're talking about a pretty big loss, here, and especially with it being your daughter, it's very appropriate to bring it to this group. Everyone has had some losses with people close to them; maybe some of them don't seem as earth-shattering as others, but we all know the experience of loss in our families, one way or another."

Then Elizabeth, who had been about to speak earlier, said, "Whew. That's just it. Thinking about your daughter and the 24-hour bed; that's pretty serious." Wendy spoke up, saying, "Yeah, that's scary. I mean I've been thinking about my accident (she had been in a car accident a few days before, and has a long-standing fear that she may kill herself in a car) and thinking about losing my sons in the divorce like I did. It really troubles me." I said, "So, we're not only looking at family losses, but also at what we do to deal with them and look for ways to cope with them and feel safe."

With the worker's help, the group members revealed that their silence did not reflect lack of feeling or concern for Joan. In fact, it was the opposite, as Joan's feelings about her loss triggered many of their own. Joan was reassured that the group was the place to bring these issues, and she was helped by knowing she was not alone.

As I have described the sessional contracting phase of a group meeting, many of the dynamics and skills discussed in Parts II and III of this book have reappeared. The worker's sessional tuning in, sessional contracting, elaborating, empathy, and demand-for-work skills are as important in helping the individual present concerns in the group session as they were in individual work. This is the common core of practice skill, the generic element. The worker's function is also the same, since the work is focused on helping the client negotiate important systems in life. The variant elements of the work derive from the presence of one of these important systems—the group—and the need for the worker to pay attention to its responses. The core skills are important in implementing this aspect of the functional role as well.

Reaching for the Work When Obstacles Threaten

In the analysis of work with individuals, the connections between the process (way of working) and the content were explored. For example, the flow of affect between the worker and client—the authority theme—was identified as a potential obstacle to work as well as a source of energy for change. Attention needed to be paid to these feelings; they had to be acknowledged before the work could proceed. This same issue was highlighted in our analysis of first group sessions, when the importance of discussing the worker-group relationship was underlined. In the group context, one also has to deal with the interchange that takes place between the members—what Schwartz refers to as the "intimacy" theme. While both of these issues, authority and intimacy, are discussed more fully in the next two chapters, they need to be mentioned now in the context of sessional contracting. For example, it may be important to discuss the process between members as a way of freeing individuals to trust the group enough to offer concerns in painful and sensitive areas.

In the example that follows, a youngster in a group for boys at a residential center wants to discuss a difficult issue but is hesitant about revealing himself to the group. By pausing and encouraging the group to discuss briefly the intimacy theme, the worker frees the member to continue.

I began the meeting by asking if there was anything that anybody wanted to ask or say before we got started. Mike said, "Well, I have some things, but I am not sure that I want to talk about all of it." I said that Mike wanted to get at what was bothering him but he wasn't going to be able to do it right away. Perhaps he needed to test the group a bit to see if he could trust them? He said, "I don't know if I can always trust people." Terry came in here and said, "This is our group here, and we can say what we want to. What goes on in here does not go outside to others, isn't that right? If we have something that we want to talk about, something really personal, we won't let it out of our own group, right?" Terry got verbal approval from all the boys in the group. I also felt that Terry was demonstrating the basis of our contract. I said that I agreed with what Terry had said. To clarify the point further, I said that I saw our purpose as being able to talk about some of the feelings that we have around being here in the Boys' Center and that out of this might come family problems, work problems, and the problems of what is going to become of me—for example, am I really worth anything? Steve elaborated this aspect by referring to his willingness to share his feelings with the group.

The next move by the worker was important. After acknowledging the problem and restating the contract, the worker returned to Mike and his specific issue. This demonstrates the importance of not getting lost in a discussion of process. There are times when it is necessary to discuss obstacles and to explore them in depth, as will be illustrated later; however, in most cases the recognition of the obstacle is all that is needed. Workers can be "seduced" into expanding the discussion of the obstacle unnecessarily, thus subverting the contract of the group and substituting a focus of group members attempting to understand how they work as a group rather than discussing their concerns. This worker properly returned to the member, Mike.

After this brief return to the contracting, I asked Mike if he thought he might feel like sharing some of the things he had said at the start of the meeting that were bothering him. He said that he thought that he could talk about part of it. John said that he thought that he knew what it was that was bothering him. I let this hang. I wanted to see if Mike would respond to John or if the others would respond to either John or Mike to help us work on what Mike had come up with. Terry reiterated what he had said earlier: "What is said in the group is for the group." John said, "I think that it is about your family, isn't it, Mike? " Mike: "Yes, that's part of it." I asked John what he meant by Mike's family. John: "Well, Mike doesn't have any parents, and we are all the time talking about troubles with our family, or we always have someplace to go if we make a weekend." [receive permission to take a weekend away] Mike: "Yeah, that's part of it. Like I make a weekend and I stay here."

Another way in which process and content are synthesized was described earlier in the discussion of the meaning of resistance. For example, the client may appear to hold back from entering a difficult area of work, and the worker senses the client's reluctance to proceed. Such resistance was viewed as central to the work and a possible sign that the client was verging on an important area. The need to explore the resistance was suggested. In much the same way, a group may resist by launching a tacit conspiracy to avoid painful areas. This is often the reason the members of a group hold back in the early stages of a group meeting. Once again, the worker's task involves bringing the obstacle out in the open in order to free the group members from its power.

In the following example of work with mothers of children who have been diagnosed as hyperactive, the early themes had centered on the parents' anger toward school officials, teachers, neighbors, and other children, all of whom did not understand. They also acknowledged their own anger at their children. The worker empathized by saying,

"It is terribly frustrating for you. You want to be able to let your anger out, but you feel that if you do so, it will make things worse." After a few comments, the conversation became general again.

I told the group members that they seemed to be talking in generalities again. Martha said it seemed they didn't want to talk about painful things. I agreed that this appeared to be hard. Every time they got on a painful subject they took off onto something safer. I wondered if the last session had been very painful for them. Martha said that it was a hard session, they had come very close, and she had a lot to think about over the weekend. Lilly said that she felt very wound up over the last session, so much so that she had had trouble sleeping at night. I asked her to tell us what made it so upsetting for her. She said that she had felt so helpless when they had been talking about the school boards and the lack of help for children like her own. Doreen said it really wasn't so helpless. She had talked to a principal and had found out some new information.

It is interesting to note that when the worker asked, "What made it so upsetting?" the answer to the question designed to explore the resistance brought the group back to its work. This is a simple, effective, and usually underused technique for exploring and moving past resistance. When a client says: "I don't want to talk about that!" the worker's response: "What would make it hard to talk about that?" is often all that is needed. As the client talks about what makes it hard to talk about *it*, they usually find themselves talking about it. In the current example, later in the same session, the worker picked up on the acknowledgment of the members' anger toward their children and the difficulty of talking about that anger with similar results. It is easier for workers to explore resistance if they do not view it as a commentary on their lack of skill.

One final connection between process and task has to do with the power of specific examples in the work of the group. We saw earlier how the skill of elaboration, called "moving from the general to the specific," could also have a powerful impact on deepening work with individuals. *This skill is even more essential in work with groups.* Because of its numbers, a group can sustain a general discussion about problems to an extraordinary length. The problem identified at the beginning of this chapter, that of responding to a member's general comment by asking all the other group members if they too feel that way, and then forgetting to return to the original member, is one of the most common problems in the sessional contracting phase of group work.

In the following example, the group is for mothers of sixth-grade boys who were underachieving in school. The purpose was to discuss how they could more effectively help their youngsters with their schoolwork. After the members had engaged in a general discussion of their feelings when faced with their children's resistance to homework, their own memories of failure at school, their identification with their children's feelings, and their recognition that they sometimes push their children because of their own need for success, the worker recognized the need for more specificity in the work. She began by focusing the members on the need to deal with specific methods.

I said that I thought it would be useful if they described what actually happens at home concerning the issue of homework—how they handle getting the kids started on and completing assignments, and then discuss the pros and cons of the various ways of handling this.

I told them that they had come up with some good ideas during the past meetings and that if they could apply these with their own children, they might begin to resolve some of the difficulties they had been describing. I said that it seems to me that they already have found some alternate ways of dealing with their children related to schoolwork and homework, and it is just a matter of seeing where they can be applied in their own particular situations.

Next, she made a direct demand for work.

I asked that each describe as fully as possible what goes on in their home concerning getting the children started on the homework and also to describe the means they may use to get them to complete it.

The members needed help at this point to get into the details of their experiences, for it is only in analysis of the specific details that the worker and the group can provide the required help.

To summarize, in this section we have seen how individuals reach out, often indirectly, to raise their concerns with the group. We have also explored the group's ambivalent responses. The worker's function in mediating this engagement and the importance of paying attention to the process in the group have been analyzed, concentrating on problem areas such as members' reluctance to trust the group, the resistance that sets in when the work gets difficult, or the difficulties involved in helping in general terms, rather than specifically. In the next section of this chapter we will focus on the mutual aid process in the middle stages of sessions, examining how individuals and the group are helped and outlining the tasks of the worker in this process.

THE WORK PHASE IN A GROUP SESSION

A number of mutual aid processes were described in Chapter 8, including sharing data, the dialectical process, exploring taboo areas, the "all-in-the-same-boat" phenomenon, mutual support, mutual demand, individual problem solving, rehearsal, and the strength-in-numbers dynamic. In this section we will look at some of these processes as revealed in recordings from work-phase sessions of groups. The first set of excerpts will help to illustrate how general themes of concern are presented and discussed over a period of time, emphasizing how individuals use the general discussion for help with their specific concerns. In the second set of excerpts, we will see how individual problem-solving can influence the general concerns held by group members.

It is important to note that work in a group is not neat and orderly, with general themes or specific problems presented at the start of the meeting, worked on in the middle segment, and then neatly resolved toward the end. In reality, themes and problems may emerge only partially in early sessions and then reemerge later in new forms as group members become more comfortable with each other and with the worker. For example, in the early sessions of an unmarried mothers' group, most of the conversation involved sharing the hurt and bitterness the young women felt over the reactions of the child's father, their own parents, friends, and others. It was only as trust developed within the group and their feelings were accepted and understood that the members began to consider doing something about their relationships with significant others.

The process of change is a slow one, and group members need to explore their thoughts and feelings at a pace appropriate for them. Difficult issues may take weeks or months of "working through" before the group member is ready to face a problem in a new way. The worker needs to be supportive during this process but at the same time a half step ahead of the client, thus presenting a consistent yet gentle demand for work. In the sections that follow, we will illustrate the process of helping group members work on themes over time as well as confronting members to take personal responsibility.

Helping the Group Work Over Time

To provide a sense of time and process, we will look at two examples of work with a support group for unmarried, pregnant teenagers. The first involves recent work with Puerto Rican 14- to 16-year-olds living at home. The second consists of work with a population of pregnant women, ages 14 to 18, living in a Canadian shelter while awaiting the births of their children. The differences in ethnicity, ages, living circumstances, and the cultural mores of the times add variations to what appear to be some universal themes.

Puerto Rican Pregnant Teens Living at Home. The members are 14 to 16 years old, and are American girls of Puerto Rican descent. If we think of the major developmental themes facing adolescents at this age, the transition through puberty and emerging sexuality is a central one. While this may be a universal, life-cycle-related theme, it emerges in different ways within different ethnic groups. Devore and Schlesinger (1991) describe this stage for the Puerto Rican female child as follows:

> As the Puerto Rican female child learns the female role by imitating her mother, she receives much affirmation from the entire family. Gradually she takes on more female responsibility in caring for young siblings—the babies—but there is no talk of sex. She gains knowledge from friends with similar meager experience and from overheard conversations of adults (pp. 69–70).

The lack of appropriate sexual information, or the inability to make use of this information, has led to pregnancies for these group members. The members find themselves facing the responsibilities of adults with the bodies, hearts, minds, and developmental needs of children. They find it easier to express their anger at their boyfriends, who emerge relatively unscathed from the experience, than to honestly share their pain. Within their ethnic group, Puerto Rican girls may be taught to adhere to the concept of *"marianismo,* referring to the importance of motherhood and of deferring to men in their culture" (DeVore and Schlesinger, 1991, p. 229). The responsibility of caring for the family's babies is illustrated as one member must bring her four-year-old brother to the meetings. Her anger at the impending changes in her life and the way in which they are already affecting her choices is acted out toward the child.

The time frame is the first month of meetings.

RECORD OF SERVICE

Description of the Problem:

This group of young, pregnant women of Puerto Rican descent have had no difficulty verbalizing their anger at their boyfriends, parents, and friends. They are expressive of their feelings of victimization. The challenge for this worker is assisting them to move beyond their anger and be able to feel their pain and sadness. It is my hypothesis that it will only be after experiencing their grief as well as their anger that they will be able to move out of the victim role, recognize their part in the negative aspects of their relationships and find solutions for action to make changes they desire in their lives.

How the Problem Came to the Attention of the Worker(s):

During the first few sessions of this group, an underlying current was established of angrily trashing men. In particular, they tended to focus this anger on their boyfriends. Beatriz emerged as the leader of this pattern, though the others eagerly joined in. In the second group session (10/9), Valerie brought her four-year-old younger brother, whom she was looking after that day. During the course of the session, even though it was obvious that Valerie was very depressed and upset about something, she resisted looking at her own feelings, and exhibited great anger at Dennis. At one point she exploded, striking him. After I asked her what she was feeling, she admitted she was having a bad day and looked like she wanted to cry. However, she almost immediately regained her composure and put up her tough defensiveness again. At this point Yardy defended Valerie's behavior toward Dennis, saying it was just discipline. Not much later in this same session, Valerie actually stood up and said the she was sorry, but she needed to leave immediately.

In session three (10/16), in response to finding out that her boyfriend had been cheating on her, Beatriz exhibited no pain, but said instead that she couldn't wait until after her baby is born, so that she can "show him some."

Before proceeding, it is important to raise the issue of the striking of the four-year-old child. Valerie acted out her issues by hitting her brother. The worker had been shocked and upset at the behavior but had withheld her response for fear of cutting off the beginning relationship. This was a mistake, since it was important to consider the implications for protection of the child. In addition, Valerie may have been saying to the worker, and the group, "This is going to be what it is like for me with my own baby." If the worker could have responded honestly, using this as an opportunity to deal with the topic of confidentiality, it would have been helpful. It might have also opened up the issue of how these children having children were using flight and fight to run from their pain. Valerie will give the worker another opportunity at a later session.

Summary of the Work:

October 2nd (first session)

I attempted to open up the conversation to explore a range of emotions. Early on in the first session, Beatriz expressed anger and the desire to break up with her boyfriend. I asked her what it would feel like to break up with him. She replied that it would be easy and that she didn't care about him. When I suggested that, as well as those types of feelings, mightn't it also be somewhat painful and difficult, she replied firmly that it wouldn't be at all, as she didn't really care about him. (They have been dating for two years.) This told me a lot about Beatriz. I saw right away how tough and hardened she was and how difficult it is for her to admit her vulnerabilities. This was an important signal early on that painful feelings would not be easily accessed in this group.

I pointed out the commonality and intensity of the feelings in the group. I said, "Are you angry, Beatriz? You sound like it." She replied with an enthusiastic "Yes!" Then I said, "In fact, it sounds like something you are all feeling is very angry—am I right?" Once again, a round of enthusiastic agreement. It seemed helpful to put into words the emotion that was present in the room. They all seemed to experience some relief in having it named and noticing that they were all feeling the same. At the time I did not realize how this one emotion would dominate the group, and how by openly noticing the anger now, it would help me later to be able to point out how other emotions were so blatantly missing from the group culture.

Valerie shared some very rejecting behavior by her mother since she had become pregnant. I asked how this made her feel. She said that it made her feel very alone, and like she didn't have a mother. Valerie took the lead at that point as the person who was the most willing to share deeply about painful feelings. She created an opening for Yardy to share about some of the rejecting behavior of her mother.

October 9th (second session)

I ignored strong signals that Valerie was giving me and stuck to concrete questions. Valerie arrived with her younger brother and within the first few minutes threatened to hit him. Just before this, she said that she had broken up with her boyfriend that week. I ignored her behavior toward her brother and asked her another question about her situation with her boyfriend. My thinking was that if she could talk about her boyfriend, it would relieve some of the pressure and her attitude toward her brother would shift. However, I was wrong. She did not answer my question and instead yelled at her brother again. Then she sat with her eyes down. I asked Yardy a question. In fact, I think I was shocked and immobilized at her aggressive behavior and the possibility of abuse happening in the group itself. I was reluctant to make her upset or step in and set limits around her treatment of her brother.

I attempted to open up a space for Valerie to share her painful feelings. As Valerie grew tenser and tenser during the session, I noticed out loud how tense she seemed and told her in a gentle voice that I was wondering what was going on with her. She told us that she had a toothache that had been bothering her for three days. She also said that she was supposed to have started high school that day (under a special mid-year promotion program), but that she hadn't been able to because she had to look after her younger brother. Seconds later she leapt from her chair and hit Dennis.

I didn't know what to do and was frozen in my chair. The group stopped dead while I was in shock and trying to figure out what to do. I was torn between acting parental and setting limits around abuse in the group, and helping her reach for her feelings.

I shared my feelings and attempted to help Valerie reach for her pain. I said that I felt very tense when she hit Dennis and I was wondering what was going on for her just beneath the surface. Valerie was not able to talk about her pain. I think if I had a second chance, I would have acknowledged out loud all the different, difficult things that were going on for Valerie that gave her a reason to be upset, i.e., her toothache, missing her first day of high school, being pregnant and the fight with her boyfriend. I would have attempted to articulate for her the underlying pain, saying something like, "All of these things have happened and I imagine you may be feeling very alone right now, like there is no one there to support you. And yet you are expected to look after somebody else. I imagine that might be very difficult." I also would have arranged for Dennis to either leave the room and have someone else look after him, or have him come closer to me, giving him a coloring book or something to do near me, and I would have taken over looking after him for a while.

I attempted to define a group norm that would be different from the norm in their homes. Valerie said that when she felt like this she didn't like herself and she just preferred not to say anything at all. I then said that, as the group continued, I hoped that it would become more and more a place where people felt that they could say anything on their minds and express whatever mood they are in. I told her that I wouldn't judge her for being sad or angry or depressed or whatever mood she was in on any particular day. This kind of expressed permission may be something the group needs to hear often at the start, since I imagine it contradicts the situation at home. It may also address their reluctance to express themselves fully that may evolve from their mothers' unavailability to all their feelings (transference).

October 16th (third session)
I intellectualized and jumped in, cutting off the group process. We were talking about hitting people and whether it was okay to do that. I suggested that perhaps it was never a good idea, and I asked them why they thought I said that. Yardy said that it didn't work—it wasn't effective. Beatriz said that she thought it made things worse. Yardy said it was better to talk things through. When Beatriz said that didn't always work, I jumped in and said that I hadn't said it would be easy, and that hitting always created bad feelings. Beatriz replied that men deserve it sometimes and then went on to complain about men, something she frequently does. I notice that I jumped in, wanting to be right, and I stopped allowing the group to explore the issue themselves. I notice that this whole session was very different from the last one. For one thing, Valerie wasn't there (she was at the dentist), and a new member had joined the group. This week I kept the group more intellectual, posing questions and asking the girls to think about things from different perspectives. I notice that there is part of me that is put off by Beatriz' constant raving against men. I know that I am looking for a way into her deeper self, and I haven't found that way yet. This is probably why it is bothering me so much.

October 23rd (fourth session)
I try to call Valerie during the week to touch base with her. Interestingly enough, her phone number has been changed and is now unlisted. I have no idea whether or not she will come. Sure enough, she does not show. One of the other members also cannot come due to an appointment at the hospital. There are only two members present, and it is an educational group, with one of the nurses coming in to talk about fetal development and birthing. It is a good group; the girls are excited to be learning these things—new to both of them. There is little chance, however, to open up deeper feelings. There is a lot of giggling and squeamish faces as they look at the pictures and try to imagine themselves pushing out a baby.

October 30th (fifth session)
During the week, Carmen gives birth to a baby girl. I make plans for us to go to the hospital to visit her. I have written a letter to Valerie, telling her we will be celebrating both her and Yardy's birthday at the next meeting and I hope she can make it. Sure enough, she comes early to the group and is in the waiting room! I am very glad to see her. It turns out that she had come to last week's session. She had gotten a ride with her boyfriend, and they had had a fight in the car, and they ended up driving back to her house. This taught me that the circumstances in these girls' lives are complex and play a larger role in their getting to group than I had thought.

I let Valerie know that she was missed. I told Valerie how disappointed the group was that she didn't come the week before. Beatriz agreed and said that the group wasn't as good without her. By doing this I emphasized that she was important and that her open display of strong emotions two weeks before had not created negative reactions in the group or from me as leader. By fully welcoming her back, I set a group norm that it is okay to display strong feelings and/or not be able, for whatever reason, to attend group for a few weeks and you will still be accepted for who you are and remain part of the group.

Although the trip to the hospital [to visit Carmen and her baby] did not allow for an in-depth talk in which we were able to have a conversation about painful feelings and the group's tendency to avoid them (a conversation I know we will need to have at some point), I felt it was essential to set a culture of being there for each other at those critical and special moments just before, during, and after giving birth. As each girl picked up Carmen's baby and held her, they expressed a lot of feelings about being pregnant themselves. They were able to see the eventual end result of their pregnancy and ask Carmen lots of questions about her experience. As we were leaving, Yardy asked Carmen, "Are you still going to be able to be part of the group?" and Carmen responded, "Of course, I'll bring my daughter!" I knew, in that moment, that they had become a group. I knew this because the girls named it and gave it a life.

Current Status of the Problem:
Although I do not feel that we have cracked the shell of defensiveness and entered a new arena of free expression of painful feelings, I believe that this will happen in the next stage of the group. It has taken these first five meetings for the group feeling to gel. There is now a bond established, created in part by the return of Valerie to the group after we had all given her up as possibly lost, as well as Carmen's commitment to be a member of the group after having given birth. Given the fact that it is a small miracle that these girls get themselves to each group meeting, given the complexity of the circumstances in their lives, I think we have done well. I know I underestimated all the factors that would make it difficult for them to get to group, especially before it became clear to them what was in it for them. I also think I underestimated the influence of culture in their ease with anger and the unfamiliarity with expressing their pain, particularly in front of others.

On the other hand, the stage we are at could be considered normal for a group that has only had five sessions. It takes this long to establish a group bond and a culture of safety in which deeper sharing can take place.

Strategies for Intervention:
1. For the next two to three meetings, we will not go out anywhere, but stay in and "talk." This is so we can get down to the next level of work.
2. The next time someone in the group points to painful feelings but indirectly expresses them through other channels, I will confront the group with their pattern of avoiding painful emotions and ask them why they think they do this.
3. I will support the "emotional leader" of the group (which thus far appears to be Valerie), in any risk-taking she does in sharing painful or difficult emotions.
4. I will tell them that I think it is helpful and important for them to share their pain with one another.

5. I'll ask them to look and see how the norm of falling back on anger and blaming appears in their families and, in particular, with their mothers, and have them look and see how that has been helpful and unhelpful.

6. I will model unconditional acceptance of their feelings when they do share them in the group, creating a culture of acceptance of it.

Canadian Pregnant Teens in a Maternity Home. Excerpts from another group for young, pregnant women, ranging in age from 14 to 18, provide additional insights into the development of themes over time. In this example, from a group that met a number of years ago, the young women come from mixed backgrounds and are living in a Canadian maternity home prior to the birth of their children. After working with many groups of this type, the workers have identified themes of concern that are common to most young women going through this experience. Although the order in which these are raised and the particular variations of the content may change, the themes are basically the same: family relationships; relationship with the father of the child (and other men); relationship to the peer group; the pregnancy and the birth of the baby; legal rights and obligations; the decision to keep or relinquish the child; feelings of loss if they relinquish the child; problems of maintenance if they decide to keep the baby; anticipated relationship problems when they return to the community (e.g., how they will relate to friends); pregnancy-prevention measures; their feelings about sex; and throughout all the discussion, their own feelings about themselves. The worker describes the group as follows:

> Most began at the shelter feeling uniquely alone, rejected, and depressed. The group meetings were led by workers from a local child welfare agency. The sessions presented an opportunity for the members to talk about their hopes and fears and to discover that they were not alone. The support and caring in the group made the problem easier for them to bear and provided important help as they clarified their thinking about central issues in their lives.

The difference in cultural mores should be taken into account, since this group was conducted some time ago, prior to the "sexual revolution." Openness about unmarried pregnancies was less commom—which was the reason many of the young women were in the shelter. Facilities to allow pregnant girls to continue their schooling were relatively unavailable. Gender oppression was common; the young women received negative responses to their pregnancies, some of which became internalized in poor self-images. In the early sessions, a common theme was their anger towards the putative father of the child.

> Sally had trouble putting her feelings into words, but she wondered how you could get the baby's father "to feel as you do about the baby?" She said her boyfriend was sympathetic and visited her often, but she felt he did things "from his head, not from his heart." I asked the girls if they could help. Sherry said she felt the same about her boyfriend. He even denied that she was pregnant when his mother asked him. The other girls generally felt it was unfair that the boy could act as if nothing had happened. The boys didn't have to come to a home or get fat bellies or feel embarrassed to walk down the street. They agreed, after a question from me, that this made them really angry. Lisa thought the boys should take some responsibility. Fay and Bernice thought they'd like to have their boyfriends talk to the social worker. Maybe they'd find it easier to talk to someone else. Fay thought her boyfriend had been very patient

with her. She was always in a bad mood when she saw him and was ready to snap his head off. The girls expressed their resentment and anger towards the fathers again but seemed unable or unready to pursue the subject.

The members' anger and resentment towards the fathers is mixed with the hope that their attitudes might change. Perhaps after the birth or a conversation with the worker they might be able to return to the relationship that existed before the pregnancy. The same hurt and anger was expressed in early discussions about their own parents. The worker attempted to reach for the guilt that she felt was beneath their hurt and anger, but the members refused to acknowledge it at this point.

Jane said she'd like to ask a question. Did any of the girls feel closer to their parents since their pregnancy? She said her parents' letters made her cry—they were so beautiful. Bernice and Lisa agreed. Sally, Sherry, and Florence felt closer to their mothers, not their fathers. Nan could talk to her mother, used to talk to father (parents just divorced). Carla said her father told her she had disgraced the family—told her mother she'd have to go away. She thought her mother felt differently but now says her mother is "just acting a part." She told her mother how hurt she was by her father's rejection, and her father tried to be kind when she was at home at Thanksgiving, but he just ignored her pregnancy—acted as if nothing were different. She had always been her father's favorite until now. Jane and Sherry said their fathers were the same—ignored their pregnancy as if it could go away. Jane said her father said they would now be grandparents and he could have been so proud, but he couldn't be now. Fay spoke at length of her father's stupidity. She and Carla both thought their parents were from the Middle Ages—had no idea of what their lives were like. I asked if they couldn't share with their fathers how they felt. Carla and Fay thought it would be impossible for them. Lisa thought she would have to make the opening gesture. The girls generally felt they just couldn't talk to their parents.

A central theme for all the group members was the unborn baby. The decision whether to keep it or not is always a difficult one. The members feel trapped, believing that no matter what they decide, they will feel guilty. They want to do what is best for the child, and at the same time they recognize their own needs. It is important that they have a chance to explore this decision in depth, to get in touch with their real feelings during the process, to test out their ideas against reality, and to come to an answer that they can live with. At first, the discussion in this area was superficial, as the members attempted to convince themselves that they were clear about what they would do and that the issue was resolved. Nonetheless, they often hinted at their real feelings during conversations about related subjects, such as the discussion of the adoption process. In the next excerpt, group members questioned one member who stated she would like to "forget all about her pregnancy and the baby and start a new life."

Dana said she always thought she was adopted because her own mother didn't love her. The girls wanted to know what adopting parents knew about them apart from height, color of hair and eyes, etc. They wanted us to be sure we'd tell them they loved their babies. Rita wasn't entirely convinced but agreed she wouldn't want to have her child learn about adoption accidentally. Rita said she guessed she just wanted to forget all about her pregnancy and her baby and start a new life afterwards. Once again the girls said she wouldn't be able to forget—explained why they felt this way. They, too, wanted a "new life," but couldn't forget their baby.

In the following excerpt, the dilemma of whether to keep or relinquish the baby is challenged by one member, who attacks the adoption "dream"—the belief that everything will work out. The worker reaches directly for this underlying feeling.

> I asked Sherry to tell the girls about her concerns about adoption. She said she wondered how adoption workers could be sure the adopting parents would carry out the girls' wishes as to their preferences in adoptive homes. Several of the girls responded to this. They felt the adopting parents would do what was best for the baby in view of their love for the baby. This didn't satisfy Sherry. She wondered how we would know what was happening when the baby was five or six or so. I asked if Sherry couldn't trust the agency to choose good parents. She said she trusted the agency but maybe not the adopting parents. I wondered if she were really saying she wanted to be the baby's parent. Sherry agreed.

It was important here for the worker to be clear about her helping function because, in so many cases, the worker may feel the client should not keep the child, and if she acts on this feeling, she may cut off the client's ability to explore her true reactions. In those cases where the worker clearly cannot let the client keep the child (such as when the situation raises questions about protection of the infant), she must level with the client about her dual roles. In situations where protection is not an issue, the worker needs to help the clients explore this ambivalent set of feelings, so that the final decision can be made in full recognition of the mixed feelings rather than after denying one part of the client's emotions. Sherry elaborated her concern, and the worker identified the dilemma for all.

> She wanted the baby so much but didn't think it was fair to the baby to keep it. She asked if her worker could go ahead with a ten-day hospital placement even if she changed her mind in hospital. She knew she wanted a ten-day placement but feared her emotions would take over and she wouldn't be able to carry through with her plan. I suggested she might need more time than ten days, that babies were adopted up to the three-month period and later. She couldn't accept this. She knew a ten-day placement was best for her baby, but she was frightened for herself. Fay said she'd tell her (Sally) what she really wanted to do if she wavered. (Fay and Sally are expecting on the same date.) Jane (adopted herself) said she was really sold on adoption— knew how carefully applicants were screened. She agreed it would be hard. I said that the decision was a very difficult one because of the girls' mixed feelings, wanting to keep, but feeling adoption in their circumstances was best for the baby.

At a later session, the worker attempted to acknowledge the many hurt and angry feelings the group members had expressed about the reactions of others in their lives. The worker also knew, however, that under the anxiety about the harsh judgments by others was the group members' own harsh judgment of themselves. If they were to deal with their boyfriends, their parents, and the decision to keep or relinquish the child, they first needed to face their real feelings. The worker hoped that through the process of mutual aid, they would begin to modify their attitude to themselves. At this point, the worker, using the fund of positive feelings built up in the group during the first weeks and the effective relationship developed through her sympathetic attitude, makes a demand for work:

> I reviewed last week's discussion—felt the girls had expressed a lot of anger versus boyfriends, about families, even about adopting parents who would be caring for

their babies—felt their anger was justified—it wasn't fair that they received all blame, had the pain of birth while their boyfriends continued normal activity and parents condemned them. I commented that there was a lot of hurt mixed with their anger. The girls agreed, either nodding or commenting. I asked what the girls themselves felt about their pregnancy. This, they themselves saw, had been missing in last week's discussion, what they felt re: pregnancy, baby, and themselves. Carla said she hated her pregnancy—felt she was missing out—not working…

Fay said she was ashamed of her pregnancy, but not ashamed of their babies—it wasn't their babies' fault. Jane said she "wasn't going to play house again." Carla said she hated her baby, but then she didn't really mean that. She was close to tears here. Lisa suggested Carla could tell her mother how she felt, and her mother could tell her father so he would understand how she was feeling. Carla felt she was missing her best year—was getting behind in her schoolwork. Fay said the trouble with Carla was that she "hated" herself, so that anything anyone said to her made her think they were hating her. Carla said she was pleased with the girls' support, she knew who her real friends were, but feared going back in the community afterwards. What would people say? The co-leader suggested people weren't as curious as Carla feared. Fay disagreed. I suggested that they were maturing, had indeed helped each other noticeably in today's session. I summarized the work, as we were nearing the end.

As trust developed within the group, the conversation became more real and the group members shared feelings, some of which they had not been sure they could safely discuss. How could someone simultaneously love and hate her unborn child? As the group members and the leader accepted these feelings and did not judge a member harshly for them, similar feelings were expressed by all the young women. The worker suggested the use of a film at the next meeting, describing some actual case histories of clients facing a similar decision. The impact of the film was powerful, as the group members identified with the unmarried mothers on the screen. The discussion moved to a new level of feeling as the ideas they had discussed, sometimes intellectually, became very real for each of them.

The film was shown in a darkened room, and as the film played, the girls were in tears, and they sat in the darkened room for several minutes afterward without speaking or moving.

We finally moved to our group session room, and some of the girls started talking while coffee was being served. Lisa said it was hard to believe that her baby was "real." She commented on the film baby's fat legs and pigeon toes. Dina said suddenly her pregnancy was real—she was aware of what she had to face. Carla said she was "mixed up"—Jane, Pam, Rita looked closed in on themselves.

I asked the girls how they were feeling. They answered, "scared, depressed." Jane answered, "aware." Fay said she was surer than ever now that it was right to give up her baby "right away." She thought the girl in the film must have been hurt when she gave up right away, and another asked how she could possibly bear to do that. Lisa said she thought the girl in the film had been wrong to keep the baby for two years—asked if we'd noticed the baby's bewildered face when he moved toward adopting parents.

After a short silence, the worker acknowledged the pain experienced by the group members as they discussed the film.

I suggested that the film had been painful for them. Sherry said the film made her feel better about adopting parents. Carla said she was different from other girls about her baby—couldn't feel the baby was real. Sally said she felt good about both her pregnancy and her baby. She would likely have to give up her baby, but she always thought pregnant women were beautiful, and she was happy. Sherry said the film made her think about other things she didn't want to think about. I suggested that this was "hurting." Tears came to Sherry's eyes and she ran from the room. We could hear her sobs, and Sally left to be with her. I said it was sad that Sherry couldn't stay with us. There was nothing the matter with tears or expressing their feelings. Carla said they tried not to cry in front of each other or everyone would be crying. She said that Dina, her roommate, heard her sniffling sometimes at night.

The worker moved at this point to help the group members explore using each other for mutual support. They have felt alone in their feelings and have not been able to share them with friends, parents, or even the other group members. Attuned to the powerful healing process of mutual aid, the worker encouraged them to use each other in the group, a microcosm of the outside world they would need to draw support from in the future, no matter what their decision finally was.

I wondered if it didn't help to know the other girls were feeling the same way. Carla said it did help to know this, but they were all in the same boat and they kept up for each other. I asked if they felt better after their tears. Carla said she did. I asked how they "hid" their tears. Carla said she got "snappy." Fay made jokes and got "mad," too. I wondered if it might be better to let others know how they really were feeling. Jane and Fay said it didn't make them feel better to cry. They liked to be alone when they were depressed. Jane said she'd had a bad three days this week, but Dina dragged her out to decorate for Halloween, and she went and was "feeling better." She could understand how hard it was for Jane when she still had two months to go. She'd thought the time would never pass, but now she had only two weeks.

I suggested that this had been a rough session, a painful session. They were becoming more "aware" of the decision they were facing. I asked that someone tell Sherry and Sally that we were sorry—suggested that we break a few minutes early. Carla wasn't ready to stop. She said that she was all mixed up—felt in a daze—didn't know what to do about her baby. Her parents said not to keep the baby, but her girlfriend said she'd help her. She, herself, didn't feel she was ready to take her baby— she wanted to work and have a life of her own. I said she sounded as if she had mixed feelings, and suggested we start with this next week. Two or three girls said they wished it were "all over." They wanted to get it over with. I said that it was very hard, but again suggested we wait until next week.

The worker arrived at the next session to find three of the group members in the hospital, one having given birth, another in labor, and a third with an infection. The early discussion in the group centered on the excitement and the anxiety all group members felt at the moment. The home and the group had become like a family, and they all felt an investment in each other. After this early discussion, the worker inquired as to the impact of the film. She felt moved by the reactions of the members, concerned by the depth of feeling evoked, and was uncertain and worried at the power of the feelings and their effect on the members. The group members reassured her, and Carla particularly indicated that the week had been spent in important thinking and some resolution.

The girls all spoke in favor of the film. They agreed they were deeply involved with the unmarried mother in the film, related to her feeling of loneliness and loss when she walked along the street at the end of the film. But they all felt that they had become aware of their baby as a real person for the first time. Carla and Dina said they had thought a lot about their decision in the past week. I suggested they were taking responsibility for making the best decision for their baby and also for themselves. For example, Carla had suggested this last week when she said she wanted to do what was best for her baby but also wanted a life of her own, to work, to date, to be a normal teenager. Carla agreed with my comment. She said she thought adoption was the best for her baby, and she planned to return to her home and to her job.

Sherry told the group that she and her boyfriend have decided to get married and keep the baby. The worker acknowledged her excitement and told her that she was happy for her. Other group members indicated that the last session had helped them in making their decision.

Jane, Connie, Carla, Dina, and Rita plan to give up their babies. Each of the girls spoke of their own plans for themselves. Jane goes back to university, Dina, Connie, and Rita back to school, and Carla back to work. I suggested that after a painful session last week, they seemed to have really worked out their decisions.

Sherry explained why she had been upset the week before, and the worker asked the group members to explore the question of the appropriateness of sharing their feelings in the group as well as the issue of being able to use what they have learned outside.

I hoped that the girls felt it was all right to express their feelings of anger and sorrow here. They seemed to feel they could trust the group with their feelings. Carla said this was very true. She felt very close to the girls in the home—felt they accepted her no matter what. I asked if the girls felt they could carry this over to relationships with people outside the maternity home—their parents, their boyfriends. Carla felt it was "safer" in the home, because everyone was in the same boat. Jane said you tried in the "outside world," but people laughed at you or "put you down," and you started to build a wall around yourself, so you wouldn't have to be hurt.

Jane wished there weren't a wall between her and her parents. She wondered how she'd tell them her baby had been born. Would she say, "Look, you're grandparents"? She laughed but was close to tears. I suggested that the girls might help her. Carla thought she might say, "It's all over." Dina wondered if Jane could tell her parents she'd like them to visit her in the hospital. Dina said her mother didn't care what happened to her. Carla asked if I would speak to her mother and find out how she was feeling. I asked if it would help if I were to be the middle man. Carla said if I could find out how her mother felt, she would be able to talk to her. Dina, Pam, and Debby would like me to talk to their mothers. I said there was a possibility of a group for parents of girls at the maternity home. All thought this would be a great idea. Connie said her sisters told her their mother said not to mention her pregnancy unless she did. She thought the girls had to make the first move.

The group members have moved from their early feeling that it was hopeless to talk to parents to planning how they might do it or enlisting the aid of the worker. Other sessions included further work on their relationship with their families, discussions of how to handle boys, particularly sexual demands, clarifying their legal rights and learning about adoption procedures (this included a visit to the group by an adoption worker). In one session, three of the members who had given birth returned to discuss the experience with the group members. In the final group session, the members began with a party and a gift for the worker inscribed "Happiness Is Togetherness." The discussion then moved to their thoughts about what would happen after the group.

> Dina repeated her concern about her behavior afterwards. She wanted to be herself, but she also wanted to be different. I asked what she meant by "different." She said she wanted to make friends with kids her own age, not older boys. She wanted to be part of a different kind of group. She wanted to act less on impulse, but wondered if she could do all this and still be herself. Jane said last week she had suggested that she planned to be "more reserved." That wasn't exactly the right word nor what she meant. She planned to think things through more carefully, make her own decisions rather than just going along with the crowd without thinking where they were leading. Dina was still concerned that she would have to be "different." I asked if anyone else could help Dina.
>
> Pam thought they should be ready to "walk down the street with their heads held high." I wondered if she might be saying they should be feeling good about themselves. Pam agreed and thought then you would be able to be yourself, and your "real friends" would accept you as you were. Pam said she could count on the fingers of one hand the number of "real friends" she had. She said she had lots of acquaintances. I asked what qualities she found in her "real friends." Pam said they were the people with whom you could be yourself, who could accept you, even knowing your faults. She thought a good friend should be honest, that from them you could expect to be told faults and then be able to act on the advice. She gave several examples. Jane, Carla, Helen, and Dina all felt their pregnancies had shown them who their "real friends" were.

Further discussion included practicing specific strategies for handling questions at school and from the family. As the session neared its end, the worker attempted to summarize the process of change over time.

> I suggested that they were all expressing mixed feelings—planning to return to their homes and communities, but not yet parted from their group at the maternity home. I attempted to summarize the sessions: the beginning ones when they had raised all the subjects we had been talking about since; the anger expressed against parents and putative fathers in the second session; then their acceptance of the pregnancy; their feeling of responsibility in making the best decision for themselves and their child; the growth I thought was evident in the girls, the better feeling about themselves, as they were getting ready to return to their homes and families, boyfriends, and work or school better able to face new experiences, new problems.
>
> I said they had been a great group and wished them "good luck." I thought they were a "great bunch of kids." Dina said, "At least the leader thinks we're all right." The girls were all very kind in their reaction to the group sessions, thought nothing should be changed in the next group, wondered why we had to stop now. I said it was hard, but with Christmas coming and their Christmas concert, the co-leader and I would be seeing them then, and in interviews. Pam still had questions, was concerned that she had no area worker. I answered briefly, suggested we could go on with these questions in the next group, which began in January. Jane, Dina, and Lisa asked to see me afterwards, and the group session ended. Jane was all excited. She

had finally had the courage to agree to see the baby's father. She was both excited and scared, but thought it better than facing him first on her return to university.

Focusing the Group on Problem-Solving Mutual Aid

The excerpts from the previous group illustrated how group members deal with general themes of concern, the discussion of the general themes having had an impact on their specific concerns. Mutual aid is also offered in relation to specific concerns raised by individual members. As group members help an individual to look closely at a particular problem and find a new way of dealing with it, they are helping themselves to deal with similar issues in their own lives. Thus, mutual aid can also start with a specific issue and move to a general concern.

This process will now be illustrated using excerpts from a group offered in a family agency. The five women and two men in the group were separated, divorced, or widowed. All of them had experienced heavy depression and difficulties in their interpersonal relationships. The group contract was to discuss these concerns and to find some solutions. The session began with a young woman, Sheila, asking for help. The first response from group members was to offer consolation. The worker asked for elaboration while offering empathic support.

> Sheila suddenly broke in and in a choked voice said, "I am feeling so down tonight."
> Bob quickly responded, "You, too?" Sheila continued that she had called Don in Montreal; he had been busy and had not wanted to talk to her. I said, "You sound very hurt." Tears filled her eyes, and Sheila said, "Yes, I am. I blew up and acted like a baby and now I have to apologize when he comes down on Saturday." Roberta and Bob rushed in to support Sheila saying they would be hurt, too, if they called someone and he was too busy to listen. Libby nodded but said nothing. I asked Sheila why she had called and why she blew up. She softly and sadly replied that she had called Don because she was lonely. Evelyn questioned if she had told Don this. Sheila hadn't. Bob asked why. Sheila smiled and said, "That wasn't the only reason I telephoned. I sometimes call to check up and see if he is really working." Roberta said, "You can't dwell on the fact that he had an affair, and Joan is going to have his baby."
>
>   Sheila began to talk about Don and Joan and the baby. I suggested, after listening a few minutes, that it seemed to me that Sheila's relationship with Don right now was important, rather than again talking about what had happened in the past. I asked the others in the group, "What do you think?"

The worker refused to allow Sheila to discuss ground that had already been covered in the group. Instead, she made a demand for work by focusing Sheila on the here-and-now details of her discussion with Don. A major step in such work involves asking the group members to take some responsibility for their part in their problems. Our defenses often cause us to explain our problems by projecting the blame onto others in our lives or justifying the present difficulty by describing past reasons. In this case, the worker focused the client and the group on the immediate situation in the belief that this was the only way to help. The client's responses elaborated on the specifics of the concern.

> Sheila did not wait for a response and replied directly to me, "I feel so tense. I don't know what to talk to Don about. I don't want it to be like it was before we separated." I said, "You sound scared to death." Sheila became very sad and nodded. Evelyn added, "I have felt the same way with Jacques. I was his shadow. When he left and

moved in with a girlfriend, I thought I could not exist on my own. I have learned to do so. Sheila, you talk as if you had no life of your own." Libby continued, "Do you always do what Don wants?"

Sheila then revealed the reason she was angry on the telephone with Don. She had earlier thought of going on a trip to England on her own and had wanted Don to say no. He had not, and when financially she had been unable to make the trip, she had called Don expecting him to be very happy that she was staying. He was busy and had not said much. Sheila then accused him of not caring and had hung up crying.

As the details emerged, so did a fuller picture of the problem. The worker recognized a common problem in intimate relationships—that is, one partner feels that the other should "divine" what she is feeling and wants to hear and then is hurt when it is not forthcoming. This is a specific example of the general problem of the difficulty of risking oneself by sharing real thoughts, feelings, and needs directly with those who are important to us. As a group member began to provide feedback to Sheila on her part in the proceedings, she cut him off, and the worker moved quickly to point this out.

Bob started to say that Sheila had put Don on the spot, when Sheila interrupted and continued talking. I stopped her and said to the group, "Did you notice what just happened?" Everyone except Sheila and Bob smiled but said nothing. I said to Sheila, "Bob was trying to say something to you when you cut him off." She cut in to say anxiously, "Did I? I'm sorry, Bob." Bob quietly said, "My God, I didn't even notice. It has happened to me so often, I guess I just expected to be cut off." She picked this up and said Don and Bob were alike and that Don let her get away with talking too much and cutting him off. Roberta commented, "Don seems hard to get close to," and there followed a few more comments on how Don seemed unapproachable.

The worker then challenged Sheila's view of the event and asked her to take responsibility for creating part of the problem. Since the worker had already built a positive working relationship with the group members, Sheila was able to accept the confrontation and to examine her own actions. As the group members worked on the details of this specific example, it is easy to see how they were also working on their own variations on the theme.

I then went back to Sheila's telephone call and asked Sheila why she had called Don at work when he was likely to be busy, rather than calling him at home. She stumbled around and didn't answer the question. I kept pressing her with the same question and then asked the group if they had any ideas on this. Bob said, "I don't know what you are getting at." I said, "Let me check this out with all of you. My feeling is that Sheila called Don when she knew he would be likely to be busy and set it up so that he would probably be annoyed with her. Once again, she gets very hurt." Evelyn added, "You did that with Don around the trip. Had he told you not to go to England, you would have been angry. If he told you to go, you would have said he did not care. I did the same thing with Jacques, and I never knew what I wanted. I was the little girl who asked her father's permission for everything."

Sheila said, "I guess I set things up so that I am the sad little girl and everyone feels sorry for me, just like I am trying to do tonight. How do I stop?" Bob said, "How do we stop hating ourselves—that is what it comes down to." Sheila continued thoughtfully, "You know I took the job at the airline so that Don and I could travel, and he really doesn't like traveling. I also bought him a bicycle to go cycling, but then found out he hates it." I said, "It sounds like you assume things about Don but somehow never check them out with him. How come?" There was a short silence, and I continued, "Is it because when, as Bob said, we hate ourselves, we are too scared to say what we feel, or want?"

Sheila talked about how horrible and stupid she feels she is, and the group members gave her much support. They also reminded her of the one area where she feels she has accomplished something—teaching piano. She brightened and talked of her love of music and how she enjoyed teaching.

Roberta then remarked on how much everyone needs to be told they do some things well. She recounted an incident at work where she had been praised and how pleased she was. The others in the group, except Libby, agreed. She said it depended on whether or not you believed it. Sheila agreed and stated it was hard for her to accept praise. Evelyn went back to Sheila's relationship with Don, saying Sheila had given indications that she knew the marriage was breaking up, although she had said Don's decision to separate was a complete surprise. Sheila said she partly knew, but did not want to admit it to herself. She had been withholding sexually, although they had had good sexual relations prior to marriage. I asked if she often gets angry at Don, and Sheila replied angrily, "I get furious at him, but I end up being bitchy, which I don't like. I am also scared he will leave." As the end of the group session was approaching, the members began making some suggestions around dealing with Don on the weekend. She should be a little more independent, say what she is feeling and not always what she thinks she should say.

As the group members work on a specific problem, workers should share their own thoughts and ideas that may help to place the problem in a new perspective. To do this, they must draw upon their own life experience, the information they have gathered by working with people, either individually or in groups, who have had similar concerns, and the professional literature. For example, in this brief excerpt, group members were learning something about taking responsibility for one's own actions, the difficulties involved in interpersonal communications, and specific interactional skills that might promote more effective interpersonal relationships. These agenda items were set in the context of their own experiences as they explored their often mixed feelings about themselves and others. Workers frequently carry out the function of providing data that have been unavailable to the client and that may provide help with the problem or issue of the moment. In working with a couples' group, for example, the leader could draw upon communications theory, "fair fighting in marriage" ideas, developmental life theory, game model theory, gestalt, and other orientations. As workers deepen their own life experiences, as they use group experiences to learn more about the complexities of life, and as they review the literature, they can enrich their contributions to the group members' struggle.

SESSIONAL ENDINGS AND TRANSITIONS

In Chapter 4 we discussed sessional endings and transitions, pointing out that each session required a resolution phase. A number of skills were identified as helpful in this stage, including summarizing, generalizing, identifying next steps, rehearsal, and exploring "doorknob" comments. Each of these skills from work with individuals is just as applicable in the group session, as the worker helps members resolve their efforts. Even if the work is not finished, this fact should be pointed out. In the illustration that follows, a worker with a group of mothers with children diagnosed as hyperactive helped the members move toward more realistic next steps in their work as a mutual aid group. In making this demand for work, the worker was endorsing the power of resilience, suggesting that no matter how hopeless the situation may seem, the group members could begin by taking steps on their own behalf.

> There was a lot of exchanging of problem situations, with everyone coming out with her problems for the week. There seemed to be some urgency to share their problems, to get some understanding and moral support from the other members. Through their stories, themes emerged: an inconsistency in handling their children's behavior (lack of working together with husband); the tendency to be overprotective; and their hesitancy at trusting their children. The issue of "nobody understanding" was again brought up, and I recognized their need to have someone understand just what it was that they were going through. Betty said that her son was never invited to play at the neighbors' houses, because he was a known disturber. Others had the same experiences with neighbors who didn't want their hyperactive son and daughter around. I expressed the hurt they were feeling over this, to which they agreed.

After further discussion about the impact of their children on others (teachers, neighbors, other children) they moved to the impact upon themselves.

> There was a discussion of how their children's behavior affected them. Rose said that she ends up constantly nagging; she hates herself for it, but she can't stop. Her son infuriates her so much. Others agreed that they were the biggest naggers in the world. I asked what brought the nagging on. The consensus was that the kids kept at them until they were constantly worn down and they gave in to them. Also if they wanted the children to do something, they had to nag, because the children wouldn't listen. I said that the children really knew them, how they reacted, and also exactly what to do in order to get their own way. They agreed, but said that they couldn't change, they couldn't keep up with the badgering that these children could give out.

The group members have expressed two divergent ideas: on the one hand, they "couldn't change," and on the other they could not "keep up with the badgering." They quickly moved to a discussion of medications as a source of hope for change. The worker pointed out that their hope in this solution was mixed with their recognition that the drugs were addictive and that they could not provide an answer in the long run. This is an example of a process in groups that Bion (1961) calls "pairing," in which the discussion of the group members appears to raise the hope that some event or person in the future will solve the problem.

For these group members, drugs provided this hope but also gave the group members an opportunity to avoid discussing what they could do to deal with the problem. In a way, it represented a "primitive" group response: attempting to deal with the pain of a problem by not facing it. As the session moved to a close, the worker sensed the heaviness and depression of the group members caused by their feelings of hopelessness. She had empathized with these feelings but now needed to make a demand for work on the members, asking them to explore what they could do about the problem. When the members raised another hope for a solution in the form of an outside expert who would help, the worker pointed out their real feelings that no "outsider" could help and that they needed to find the help within themselves. In this way, the worker helped them resolve a difficult and painful discussion by conveying her belief in their strength and her sense of the concrete next steps open to them.

> There was further discussion around the children's poor social behavior and the mothers' own worry about how these children will make out as adults. What will become of them? Will they fit in and find a place for themselves in society? I was feeling the heaviness of the group and pointed out what a tremendous burden it was for them. Our time was up, and I made an attempt to end the meeting, but they continued the discussion. I recognized their urgency to solve the problem and the need to talk with each other and get support from each other. Marilyn said that it was good, she came away feeling so much more relieved at being able to talk about how she felt, and she certainly was gaining some new insight into herself.
>
> Discussion diverted to the problem with the children and how they were to deal with it. I asked what they wanted to do. Edna suggested they ask a behavior modification therapist to help them work out solutions. Others thought it was a good idea. I said that was a possibility, but I wondered if in wanting to get an "expert" involved, they were searching for someone to solve their problems for them. They agreed. I asked if they thought all these experts could do this. They said that it hadn't happened yet. I wondered if we could use the group for the purpose it was set up, to help each other problem-solve. I suggested that next week we concentrate on particular problems and work together to see what solutions we could come up with. They seemed delighted with this and decided that they should write down a problem that happened during the week and bring it in. Then we could look at a number of problems. Consensus was reached as to our next week's agenda, and the meeting ended.

This illustration of one form of sessional ending and transition work brings to a close our description of the work phase in a mutual aid group. Having presented the general model of the individual-group interaction, we can now examine the elements in depth and explore some variations on the theme. In the next chapter, we will examine the individual's role in the group, concentrating on how members are informally assigned to play functional roles such as scapegoat, deviant, and internal leader. In Chapter 14 we will explore the needs of the group as a whole and the way in which the group leader can help the group work on its central tasks. In Chapter 15, we will focus on the ending and transition phase of work with groups. In Chapter 16, a number of variations on the mutual aid theme will be illustrated using work from a range of groups.

CHAPTER SUMMARY

Our discussion in this chapter illustrated a number of points. First, we saw how the group worker needs to work with the individual and the group as they reach out to each other in the beginning stages of a session. Second, we found that mutual aid deals with general themes of concern as well as specific problems of individuals. The examples in this chapter illustrated how groups can move from the general to the specific and from the specific to the general. The last excerpt illustrated the importance of striving for resolution as meetings draw to an end.

GLOSSARY

Casework in the group A common pattern in which the group leader provides individual counseling to a client within a group setting. This contrasts with an effort to mobilize mutual aid for the client by involving the other members.

Check-in An exercise used in some groups at the start of the session, in which each member briefly shares what has happened to him or her during the preceding week.

Monitoring the group The skill of observing the second client—the group members—watching for verbal and nonverbal clues as to their reactions while a member is speaking.

Monitoring the individual The skill of observing individual group members, remaining alert to verbal and nonverbal clues signaled by each individual. This is an acquired skill that comes with practice. When this skill is integrated, a group leader can simultaneously monitor the group and each individual.

13

Working with the Individual in the Group

A central idea in the interactionist model has been the notion of "two clients": the individual and the group. In Chapter 12, the interdependence of these two entities was illustrated. In this chapter and the next, an artificial separation of these two clients is employed to deepen our understanding of each in interaction with the other. In this chapter, we will focus on the individual within the group, discussing how clients bring their personalities to bear in their group interactions. The concept of role is used to help describe how individual personality is translated into group interaction. A number of common patterns of individual-group relationships are described and illustrated (e.g., scapegoats, deviant members, defensive members, quiet members). As these individuals are isolated for closer analysis, it will become clear that it is often impossible to understand individual clients without considering them in the context of their group interaction.

THE CONCEPT OF ROLE IN A DYNAMIC SYSTEM

Two ideas central to the discussion in this chapter are **role** and **dynamic system.** Ackerman (1958) described the ways in which the term *role* has been used and proposed his own definition:[1]

> Sociology, social psychology, and anthropology approach the problems of role through the use of special concepts and techniques. They apply the term in two distinct ways, meaning either the "role" of the person in a specific, transient, social position or the characteristic "role" of the individual in society as determined by his social class status. Working in the psychodynamic frame of reference, I shall use the

term to represent an adaptational unit of personality in action. "Social role" is here conceived as synonymous with the operations of the "social self" or social identity of the person in the context of a defined life situation (p. 53).

Ackerman suggests that the individual has both a private "inner self" and a social "outer self" that emphasizes externally oriented aspects of his personality. I shall use this idea of social role in the following way. When clients begin a group, they present their "outer self" as their way of adapting to the pressures and demands of the group context. Their pattern of action represents their "social role." Ackerman argues that incongruity between the reality of the "inner self" and the "outer self" that is presented can be a source of tension. In many ways, the task of the group worker involves helping individuals find the freedom to express their "inner selves" in the group. For the purpose of this chapter, the central idea is that each individual member brings to the group an established pattern of translating a unique personality into social action.

When considering oppressed and vulnerable groups, it is possible to integrate Ackerman's notions about role with the oppression psychology concepts described in Chapter 2. The outer self of survivors of oppression represents their adaptive behavior to the defined situation of oppression. The incongruity between this outer self, which they present in social situations, and their real inner self can be understood as one of the defense mechanisms employed in an effort to cope. This resulting incongruity is a form of alienation from self-identity, as described by Fanon (1968). The effort in the mutual aid group is to help group members use the group to integrate their inner and outer selves and to find more adaptive mechanisms of coping with oppression, including personal and social action. The small group is a microcosm of the larger society. Understanding a role played by a survivor of oppression within a group context is enhanced if we consider the impact of oppression.

Keeping in mind the concept of individual roles, we can view the group as a "dynamic system" in which the movements of each part (member) are partially affected by the movements of the other parts (other members). This view is rooted in the work of Kurt Lewin (1935, 1951b), who is often considered to be the founder of group dynamics. Thus, members bring their "outer self," as described by Ackerman, into this "dynamic system," and the individual's "social role" is his unique manner of adapting to the perceived demands of the group. This process of adaptation is necessary for all group members, and the model presented thus far provides a general description of the individual-social interaction in group. For our purposes, however, I will concentrate on patterns of interaction that are identified as specific social roles emerging over time and requiring special attention by the group worker.

Patterned social roles are most easily illustrated using an example from a formal, organized group, such as a tenants' association. In order to function effectively, the association usually identifies specific tasks that must be assumed by group members and then assigns these jobs by some form of division of labor. For example, the association may need a chairperson, a secretary, a treasurer, and a program coordinator. The essential idea is that group roles are functionally necessary and are required for productive work. In taking on any of these roles, specific members will bring their own sense of social role to bear. For example, the role of chairperson could be implemented differently by various members, depending upon their experience, their background, their skills, and their sense of social role. Since the group is a dynamic system, the chairperson's implementation of this role will also be somewhat affected by the group and its individual members. The actions of the chairperson are best described as the product of the interaction between the individual's sense of social role, the role of chairperson as defined by the group, and the particular dynamics of the group and its members.

The roles just described are of a formal nature; in addition, every group creates roles to help in its work even though these may never be openly acknowledged. For example, in a group led by a worker who chairs the discussion as an "external" leader, one or more "internal" leaders may emerge as if they had been formally elected. The individuals who assume internal leadership in a group often bring a concept of social role that includes this function. Group members, by their positive responses to internal leaders, will encourage their assumption of this important role.

Other functional roles can emerge in a group that are less constructive and reflect maladaptation on the part of the group rather than healthy development. One such role, that of the scapegoat, its discussed in detail in the next section of this chapter. For now, it is enough simply to point out that scapegoats are often selected by the group because they have the personal characteristic that members most dislike or fear in themselves. Thus, a group of young teenage boys who are worried about sexual identity may select the youngster who seems least "macho" or least sure of himself as the group scapegoat. The group members, of course, do not have an election for such roles. It is not as if the group members held an informal meeting in the coffee shop, prior to the group session, and asked for volunteers to be the group scapegoats, internal leaders, deviant members, and so on. If the group has a need for these roles, however, they will select members to fill them through a subtle, informal process. The dysfunctional aspect of employing a scapegoat is that it often leads the group members to avoid facing their own concerns and feelings by projecting them upon the scapegoat.

Individuals do not raise their hands and volunteer to act as scapegoats, pointing out that they have successfully played the scapegoat role in their families and social groups for most of their lives. The scapegoat in the group usually subtly volunteers for this role, since it is consistent with that individual's concept of his or her "social role." Adapting to groups by playing this social role is as dysfunctional for the individual scapegoat as it is for the group as a whole. Once again, the idea of the group as a dynamic system helps us to understand the process of scapegoating in a dynamic way.

In the sections that follow, we will look at informal roles developed in groups, such as scapegoats, deviant members, internal leaders, and gatekeepers. In addition, we will examine the patterns of social role demonstrated by individuals who are defensive, quiet, or overly verbal (monopolizers). In each case, the focus is on analyzing the dynamics as a reflection of the individual's social role within a group that is a dynamic system. In addition, the skills of the group worker as he or she implements the individualizing part of his work will be discussed and illustrated.

THE SCAPEGOAT IN THE GROUP

The discussion of individual roles in the group begins with the **scapegoat** because it is both one of the most common and one of the most distressing problems in work with groups. The scapegoat is a member of a group who is attacked, verbally or physically, by other members. These group members are usually projecting onto the member their own negative feelings about themselves. The scapegoat role is often interactive in nature, with the scapegoat fulfilling a functional role in the group. Whether it is overt scapegoating in groups of children and adolescents or the more subtle type experienced in adult groups, the impact on the group members and the worker can be profound. We will explore this role in some detail as a means of introducing a number of key concepts in conceptualizing social role in the group and the function of the group worker. These central ideas will re-emerge as we examine other roles. The discussion can then serve as a general model for analyzing individual roles in the group.

First, one must consider the history of the term *scapegoat*. In a recent scholarly work on the subject, Douglas (1995) attributes the origin of the term to the fifteenth-century biblical scholar and translator Tyndale. Tyndale's translation of sections of Leviticus referred to an ancient ritual among the Hebrews practiced on the Day of Atonement. Two live goats were brought to the altar of the Tabernacle. One was sacrificed for the Lord. The second goat, after the high priest transferred his own sins and the sins of the people onto it, was taken to the wilderness and allowed to escape. Douglas suggests, "If Tyndale had read into the Hebrew idea that the goat was 'suffered to escape,' then his coining of the word 'scapegoat' becomes much clearer" (p. 8). Douglas describes the scapegoat ritual as

> ...essentially a process of purification, which means in essence that its practitioners felt that they were contaminated by the transgressions of their daily lives and that the ritual of scapegoating was one that would disperse that contamination and reinstate them as clean in their own eyes and, more importantly, in the eyes of their god (p. 14).[2]

Whole populations, such as African-Americans, Jews, and homosexuals, have experienced extreme forms of scapegoating as part of the systematic oppression described in Chapter 2. These have included the projecting of negative stereotypes as an underlying justification for slavery as well as more current forms of economic and social oppression; anti-Semitism and the Holocaust in which millions of Jews (as well as many homosexuals, Gypsies, and others) were systematically killed; gay-bashing activity in which gays and lesbians are physically attacked on the street or are the butt of homophobic jokes. The idea advanced in Chapter 2 of oppression as an expression of the oppressor's insecurity (as well as economic self-interest and other self-serving concerns) can help to explain the scapegoating process in a group. The notion of oppressed people internalizing the negative self-image (the oppressor within), after prolonged experience of oppression from the oppressor without, can also help explain the behavior of a group scapegoat. It's important to note, however, that none of these oppressed groups ever "volunteered" for the role; it was always imposed upon them by the oppressing group. This distinction is crucial so that we avoid making the mistake of "blaming the victim" for his or her own oppression. In addition, each of these groups have demonstrated remarkable resilience in the face of oppression.

Bell and Vogel (1960) have described the dynamics of this phenomenon in the family group, emphasizing the functional role played by the scapegoat in maintaining equilibrium in the family by drawing all of the problems onto him- or herself. Many scapegoats in groups have been socialized into this social role by their family experiences and are ready to play it in each new group they enter.

Scapegoating is also discussed by Garland and Kolodny (1967), who provide an interesting analysis of the forms of scapegoating prevalent in practice.[3]

> No single phenomenon occasions more distress to the outside observer than the act of scapegoating. Frequently violent in its undertones, if not in actual form, it violates every ethical tenet to which our society officially subscribes. As part of that society, the

group worker confronted with scapegoating in the midst of interaction often finds himself caught up in a welter of primitive feelings, punitive and pitying, and assailed by morbid reflections on the unfairness of fate which leaves one weak and others strong (p. 124).

In an article addressing the scapegoating phenomenon (Shulman, 1967) this author discussed the common mistake in practice, when faced with these feelings, of moving into the interaction between the scapegoat and group in a way which "preempts" the opportunity for either to deal with the problem. Most often, the worker protects the scapegoat from the force of the group members' attack, thus causing the hostility to take more covert forms. Appeals to fairness or requests to give the member a chance do not seem to help, and the worker is usually left feeling frustrated, the scapegoat hurt, and the group members guilty.

Scapegoating Examples

The examples that follow illustrate the scapegoating process, some of the pitfalls the worker faces, and effective strategies for intervention. In the first example, involving residential treatment work, the worker over-identifies with the scapegoat and loses the group. In the second example, we well see a new worker's interventions with a group of teenage girls over a period of time. She starts by developing insights into the scapegoating process and tuning in to her own feelings. Her protective responses toward the scapegoat are more subtle. She never directly confronts the process, but she does deal with the concerns of the second client, the group, which leads the group to have less need for a scapegoat. The final example of pregnant teenagers in a shelter takes the work further as a more experienced worker confronts the scapegoating process head-on, providing significant help to the group and the scapegoat simultaneously.

Boys in a Residential Treatment Center.   The following example from a residential center for teenage boys illustrates the dilemma for a group leader. John was scapegoated by the group members because of his small size, his social discomfort and lack of skills, and his general self-effacing demeanor. The pattern became apparent soon after John arrived; he did little to stop it and sometimes seemed to provoke it. His response was usually to cry and run away. This incident took place in the lounge as John was hanging around trying to get into the general banter of conversation.

> **Lou:** Why the hell don't you buzz off and stop bothering us?
>
> **Frank:** Yeah, John, you're such a putz I don't want you hanging around me. I can't stand to see your face. (John doesn't leave, just hangs his head and looks sad.)
>
> **Worker:** Come on you guys, stop picking on John. He isn't bothering you. Why do you always jump on him?
>
> **Lou:** (Defensively) He's a creep. You don't understand what he's like. He's a creep in school also, and all the kids hate him.
>
> **Worker:** Maybe that's what goes on at school, but it's not going to happen here. (The boys mutter angrily under their breath about "getting him later" and leave the room.)

When group members scapegoat another member, they usually attack the aspect of the other that they most dislike in themselves. One should think of this as a form of communication to the worker of the group members' feelings towards themselves. The boys who are angry at John for his general social ineptness are very much involved in attempting to develop their own sense of social competency. Attacks on a youngster for his behavior often represent a call for help by young men who are struggling to develop their own sense of sexual identity in a society where most adults seem to be too uncomfortable to talk to them about such issues. The anger directed towards the scapegoat is often a signal of the hurt and confusion felt by the group members.

This is not an unusual type of exchange. It is seen all the time in classrooms, residences, children's groups, and (in more subtle forms) in adult groups. When the worker was asked about his feelings during the exchange, he said, "I was mad at the guys for being so hard on John. I felt furious and frustrated because I knew they would just get him later, and I couldn't seem to do anything about it." A diagrammatic way of describing this incident is shown below.

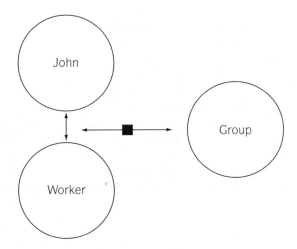

It was the worker and John versus the group. What began as a problem between the group and John had changed to a problem between the group and the worker. When I inquired as to where the worker was, emotionally, he described himself as "with John." My next question greatly affected the worker. "Who was with the group?" Analysis of examples such as this demonstrates that the answer is "no one." In a variation on this theme, if the scapegoat is overtly obnoxious to staff as well as group members and the worker finds himself clearly identifying with the group and its anger towards the scapegoat, then the worker often remains passive or offers subtle support to the group in its attack on the individual. Once again, when I inquire who is with the scapegoat in these situations, the answer is "no one." It is at moments such as these that a new insight into the scapegoating dynamic and a sense of clarity of function can help the group worker to be "with both clients" at precisely the same time.

As we think about scapegoating in the social work group, the concepts of social role and the group as a dynamic system provide us with clues to the meaning of this interaction. It is impossible to understand the behavior of the scapegoat simply as a manifestation of his or her "personality." Rather, it is a result of the interaction between the scapegoat's sense of social role and the group's functional needs. The relationship between the individual role and the group need is clearly evident if the group loses its scapegoat—if, for example, the member leaves the residence or drops out of the group. As though operating on an unconscious command, the group immediately searches for a new candidate to take the scapegoat's place. One member is usually waiting to do so.

Adolescent Girls in a School Setting. In the example that follows, a white worker leads a group of African-American and Hispanic adolescents in a school setting. The example demonstrates a typical attempt to intervene in order to protect the scapegoat. The worker tries to deal with the problem indirectly because of her concern over the possibility of hurting the scapegoated member.

RECORD OF SERVICE

Client Description and Time Frame:

A seventh-grade girls' peer support group of 12- and 13-year-old adolescents (3 African-American and 2 Hispanic girls) from a racially mixed, low-income part of the city. The time frame is from 12/5 through 2/6.

Description of the Problem:

This group is projecting its dependency needs onto one individual, causing the group to remain in the beginning stage of development. This individual, Rachel, acts out these dependency needs for the group. Rachel does her own thing, not involving herself in any group activities, keeping to herself. Thus, the group temporarily remains in the power and control stage, as described by Garland, Jones, and Kolodny (1965),[4] a stage in which authority, permission, autonomy, and confidentiality are crucial issues for these adolescent girls. The group's investment in the role of the scapegoat both hinders and helps the development of the group as it pushes towards its next stage, intimacy.

How the Problem Came to the Attention of the Worker(s):

On January 23, I observed that Rachel sat away from the other members of the group and refused to join in the group activity (which was painting) and was unwilling to speak. This behavior brought a negative reaction from the group and the other girls hypothesized about why she was acting as a loner. The group soon ignored this behavior when Lisa brought up a "hypothetical" situation in which she was involved. Lisa stated that she was tired of a girl whom she used to be friends with and now does not like anymore. Lisa asked the group for advice about what to do and how to tell this girl. At this point, I saw that the girl she was discussing was Rachel. When questioned by the other girls as to who this girl was, Lisa would not say. At this moment I was very unsure of my position as a worker and what I should do about the situation. My first instinct was to see this as an issue that needed to be dealt with by Rachel and Lisa only, but, in thinking about it further, I decided it was indeed a group problem, especially considering our group goal of improving peer relations! It became clear to me that this need for the role of a scapegoat was an issue for the entire group!

Summary of the Work:

December 5 (first session)

We were discussing the purpose of the group, and I asked them what they thought some of the rules should be. Most of the members jumped in and offered suggestions, many of them expressing concern about confidentiality and "secrets." Rachel and Kim sat on either side of me, neither of them saying anything, but nodded when Lisa and Amy asked them what they thought of a rule or idea they suggested. I attempted to engage Rachel and Kim in conversation, and gave the group permission to make their own rules. I asked them both what they thought we should do as a group if someone broke our rule of confidentiality. They both replied by looking confused and shrugging their shoulders. Rachel said, "I don't know...what do you mean?" Lisa immediately jumped in, asked Rachel if she was "deaf or what?" and gave her idea of a "punishment," causing Rachel to sink in her chair and look down at the floor.

I could sense what was going on, but did not know how to respond to it. Looking back, I can see these were all issues related to the theme of authority. I did not want to discourage anyone from saying what they wanted, and did not want to push anyone into talking if they did not want to. I was simply thrilled that anyone was saying anything, and that they were enthused about the group.

December 12 (second session)

Kim had a problem and I supported her bringing it to the group. Kim told the group that she had a problem and that she wanted to ask everyone what she should do about it. She had been involved in a fight earlier that week and now she had to go to court. She said that she was afraid that she would be sent to a school where "they are real strict and don't let you do nothing you want to do." She asked me what she could do about this and asked if I could help her by talking to the principal for her. I told her I was glad that she brought this to the group. I asked the group what they thought about the situation. Lisa stated that, if the situation happened to her, she wouldn't worry about it because she knew her mother would not get mad at her and would not care. I completely missed the boat on this statement! Kim was discussing the entire incident with Mary, and the group became interested in the details of the fight. I became interested in who did what to whom and who was responsible for what, trying to determine if Kim was indeed going to be punished severely by the court system.

Kim told the group that the reason she got into the fight was because someone in the school had spread the rumor that she was pregnant. She said that she had to let everyone know that she was not, and so she had no choice but to get into this fight with the person who started the rumor. The group agreed that she did have to fight this girl because, after all, she had no business saying such things and she ruined Kim's reputation. (I missed an important issue the group was raising and asked the group to work on the more obvious issue). I asked the group about other things they could do to avoid fighting in such a situation, and did not focus in on the pregnancy issue which, in retrospect, I think was the real problem. Almost everyone in the group was actively involved in a discussion of who can and cannot be trusted in their class, and who the people are in the school that spread rumors. I missed the significance of Rachel not participating in the discussion. I realized toward the end of the group that Rachel did not participate actively in the conversation and, in fact, had sat next to me again. I also was able to recognize the fact that I was quite uncomfortable in addressing the issue.

At a later session, the worker writing this record realized that she had missed the central theme of concern for Kim. While Kim raised her problem in terms of the fight and the discipline, this is actually a first offering of her deeper concern—the fact that she is pregnant. The issue does not resurface until the fifth session.

December 19 (third session)

I avoided an issue that I was having a difficult time dealing with. The fact that Christmas is often a sad time for many poor people was an issue that I was unable to confront in this session. It was the last day of school before Christmas vacation and only four of the members were there. We had a Christmas party and spent most of the time talking about what they would be doing with their time off. When I asked them what they would be doing, Lisa said nothing, and that it would be boring. I allowed counter-transference to take over and I felt very guilty that I was excited about my own vacation and Christmas. I tuned out as a result of this guilt. Mary seemed very quiet; I assumed that it was because Kim was not in school that day (they are best friends). Cindy said that she was going to stay home, watch TV, and sleep.

Rachel asked if we could "have group" even though they did not have school. (She was sitting next to me again and I was aware of her need to be close to me and have me recognize her presence.) I used this as an opportunity to tell them that I would be on vacation and that we would not meet until the second Monday that they would be back in January. I then stated that, if I was going to be around, I would love to get together with them, and that maybe we could do something on a Saturday to make up for lost time. Lisa stated that under no circumstances would she want to get out of bed during her vacation or on a Saturday. I did not verbalize the feelings of the group. Rachel asked me where I was going and why I couldn't come back early. Mary immediately jumped in and told her that I obviously had another life and had important things to do. Lisa said that I was lucky to be leaving "this dirty and boring city." Although my first instinct was to side with Rachel and protect her, I reminded the girls that this was their group to do what they wanted with and it was up to them if they wanted to meet on a Saturday. In retrospect, I realize that I missed the issue they were raising: the fact that Christmastime is not fun for them and that they recognize differences between me, a middle-class, white worker, and themselves.

January 23 (fourth session)

Before group started, Rachel came in and told me that Lisa had been acting unfriendly towards her and that this upset her a great deal, since they were supposed to be best friends. We discussed some ways that she could confront Lisa on this and the friendship in general. Rachel told me that she wanted to meet two periods a week instead of one. I encouraged her to bring this up in group.

When everyone arrived for the group, the girls all asked why Rachel got to get out of class early to come and talk to me. They appeared annoyed that Rachel may have received "special attention," but soon forgot this discussion when Lisa brought up a problem. I supported Lisa for coming to the group for advice, but missed an underlying issue. Lisa told me that she had a problem this week and asked if we could please talk about her this week. She went on to say that this was a hypothetical situation and that it did not involve anyone they knew. Lisa said that she has a friend who is always doing everything she does, is always wearing the same clothes she wears, says the same things she says, and even likes the same boys she likes. I sensed that Lisa was talking about Rachel, and I felt a strong urge to protect the individual being scapegoated.

The group members jumped in on this subject and stated how they all hate this behavior. Rachel sat in the corner of the room, watching the group and looking out of the window. I suggested that maybe this friend really likes Lisa a great deal and she wants to be like her. Kim jumped in and agreed with me and told Lisa that she should be complimented. I made a demand for work. I asked the group what they would do in this situation. I made the assumption that I was the only one who knew the entire picture and acted accordingly. Everyone was very involved in the pictures they were drawing and did not seem to feel like discussing the subject.

In retrospect, I see that the group knew exactly what was going on and that it was my own feelings of discomfort that allowed me to avoid the issue. I avoided the main issued being raised in an attempt to protect the scapegoat. Lisa insisted on getting my opinion on the subject, even though I threw it out to the group for answers. I picked up on a conversation that Kim and Mary were having, and began talking with Cindy about a teacher they disliked. Lisa put her problem back on the table for discussion. I was feeling very annoyed at her insistence and I told her that we had answered her question and that she could come and discuss it with me later if she wanted to. As the members left that day, Lisa pulled me aside and told be that this person was Rachel and that she did not want Rachel to know. I was able to support her as an individual group member and told her that I would be free to speak with her later that morning and gave her a pass to get out of class.

The pattern of scapegoating is not directly addressed. Rachel, the group members, and the worker all know it is going on. The worker's reluctance is rooted in her not wanting to hurt Rachel, yet the persistent pattern of scapegoating is more painful than any direct discussion might be. Workers are also often afraid to open up an issue such as this because they are not sure what will happen and where it will go. The worker's indirect efforts to deal with the problem match the group members' own use of indirect communications, thus frustrating the growth of the group. As the group culture becomes more positive, the group members are able to deal with some of their issues and lessen their need for a scapegoat.

January 30 (fifth session)
I supported Kim for bringing a problem to the group. Kim brought up a problem she was currently dealing with and asked the group for advice. She said that she has a friend who thought she was pregnant. Her friend's cousin told her to drink "this awful stuff" to get rid of the baby. She said her friend did not want the baby, but that her friend's boyfriend wanted it very badly. Now her friend does not know what to tell her boyfriend. I reached for the group's feelings. The group immediately confronted Kim and wanted to know if she was speaking about herself. Kim said it was a friend. I said that this must be very difficult and was a scary situation to be in. I verbalized the group's non-verbal behaviors. I acknowledged that there seemed to be a great deal of tension around the subject of pregnancy and that it was a difficult topic of discussion. Cindy said that her mother would kill her if she ever came home pregnant and that she felt sorry for this girl. I pointed out to the group that the problem was not only an individual issue, but also an issue for the group. The members appeared uneasy discussing the topic of pregnancy and even willing to change the subject and talk about something else.

The group tried to avoid the issue by concentrating on who in the school they thought could be pregnant. I made a demand for work. I stated to the group that a member had raised an important question and that it was an issue that demanded their attention. I asked the group what they would tell their boyfriends in a similar situation. Lisa stated that she would simply dump him and not tell him, since he must be crazy to think a 12-year-old should have a baby. Rachel stated that she did not have a boyfriend, and Mary said that she would tell him and hope he did not leave her. At this point, Kim broke in and told the group that it was her whom she was talking about. I said that everyone might be feeling a great deal of emotion and that it must have taken a great deal of courage and trust to come to the group with this issue. The members focused in on the situation, giving Kim advice, and reflecting the situation onto themselves, talking about what they would do in such a situation.

In this session the group did not appear to need the scapegoat; the conversation was intense, and everyone worked together on the issue at hand. I began to feel that the group was progressing, and I felt much more in tune with my own feelings about things that happened in the group. I was able to catch myself quicker and did not feel such a strong urge to protect everyone.

February 6 (sixth session)
A girl, Sandy, was very interested in joining our group and, since she was a good friend of the other members, I considered it and brought it up in group. I encouraged the group to state their feelings. The group had very divided reactions. Kim said, "There is no way I'm going to stay in this group if Sandy comes here…it's either her or me!" I reminded the group that they are in control. I told them that this is their group and that they are the ones who make the rules, and that the decision about Sandy is up to them. Rachel said that she liked Sandy, but that she knew that Sandy already came to the Collaborative for individual counseling. "She already gets to come down all of the time, so why should she get to come when we are here?" I made a demand for work and asked for clarification. Rachel stated that it is not fair that some people get to come to talk one-on-one whenever they want, and that they can come only one time a week for only one period. Mary said that she likes Sandy also, but that she has too many problems and would not fit in with our group.

I missed the racial issue that came up in Lisa's next statement because I was so wrapped in the issue at hand. Lisa (who is also African-American) said, "You dumb nigger, what do you think this group is for, anyway?" I used the current issue to talk about how they may be feeling about the group. I told the girls that it is okay if they want to keep the group the way it is now, and that they all seemed to be happy with the way it has been going. I then suggested that many of them need a place to come and talk about their feelings and that they've found this to be a good place to do that. Rachel (sitting next to me) said that she was glad that they could keep me "all to themselves." Lisa said, "I don't think that's fair; we don't need to be here as much as Sandy does…I don't see why this is so important to you, Rachel."

I verbalized the feelings that appeared to be present. I said I think that you are all saying that you don't want Sandy in the group, because you all need this group for yourselves and that, because you like it so much, you would rather not let someone new in. We have a great group here and you are happy with who we have in the group now. It's not easy to show that you need something and like something. Sometimes when you are a teenager you need to be really independent and don't want to rely on anyone. That's okay to do; it means that you are growing up! But it's also okay to need to talk about these feelings and to need your friends. Lisa said that she could not wait to grow up so that she could move out of the house and be on her own. I focused on what she was saying. Mary said yeah, she didn't always like it at home either, so growing up and moving out as soon as possible was a good idea. I made a demand for work. I asked them what it was like for them at home and how it felt to want to leave.

As soon as a reason for scapegoating was identified, the group steered away from Rachel and did not seem to need to scapegoat her. Instead, they began discussing their home situations and saying to me indirectly that they did, indeed, need someone to talk to about growing up. They were able to begin to show me their individual dependency needs and not feel like they had to scapegoat Rachel for outwardly showing hers.

Current Status of the Problem:
The group began entering the intimacy stage and, although power and control remain essential issues in the group, they are not issues that dominate our entire group sessions. We are able to do "real work" and discuss issues that they want to talk about. Scapegoating still occurs at times, but I am able to recognize it and address it at some level. I have found that, when I call attention to the scapegoating, it is no longer an issue (at least at that time). Rachel has been integrated into the group more often and has not been in the role of the scapegoat in our last few sessions. The group is able to discuss issues that are of concern to them, such as boys, friendship, and the violence that they frequently see in their neighborhoods.

Other issues are still very difficult for them to talk about, such as racism, what it's like to be Black or Hispanic in the city, and the fact that I am a middle-class, white worker in a group for minority girls. The theme of authority remains an issue for the group, as they have a difficult time understanding that they have control of this group. I need to work on letting them know this more often. It is when the members fully understand and accept the purpose of the group that they will no longer need the role of the scapegoat and will be able to completely move into the stage of intimacy.

Strategies for Intervention:
1. I will be aware of the group's occasional need for a scapegoat and will investigate the reasons behind such a need.
2. I will verbalize and bring out in the open issues that are hidden and are under the surface.
3. I will continue to make demands for work and challenge the group to explore their feelings on issues that are difficult for them to discuss.
4. I will let the members know that the group and I are there for them and that it is okay to express dependency needs.
5. I will try to make myself and the group available on an occasional Saturday and vacation day so that the members recognize that the group is also important to me.
6. I will continue to address the power and control issues that the group has and will let them know that the group belongs to them.
7. I will empower both the individual members and the group to feel comfortable with both their emerging feelings of independence and their dependency needs.
8. I will challenge the group about their need for the role of a scapegoat and bring to the surface my feelings about what is happening.
9. I will encourage Rachel's need to be dependent upon me and the group, yet at the same time look for meaning in her need to take on this role.

10. I will make quicker verbalizations of what I am observing, pointing my impressions out to the group.
11. I will continue to make the group aware of the fact that I will be leaving in May and will challenge them to discuss their feelings about this.

It is interesting to note that this student-worker identifies race as an issue for the girls in their lives and an issue between the girls and herself. She even includes it in her assessment of where the problem stands; however, she identifies it as an issue that the members are having difficulty discussing. And yet, her list of strategies for intervention somehow does not include any in this area. This is an agenda item for her own professional growth. Her struggle in dealing with this crucial issue is not uncommon, and she will need support and supervision to recognize that her group members' difficulty in exploring the potentially explosive area of race is a reflection of her own reluctance. When they are clear that she is ready, they will respond. This would be important to free her to attend to the meaning of the clues that emerge, including the African-American member's use of the self-derogatory term "dumb nigger" to refer to the scapegoat.

By understanding the dynamics of scapegoating, the worker can more easily avoid the trap of siding with either the individual or the group. This natural response misses the essential message: that the group and the scapegoat are using the process as a means of raising a theme of concern. The process can best be understood as an attempt, albeit maladaptive, to offer a theme of concern. The worker cannot get too upset with either the group or the scapegoat, since scapegoating may be the only way they know to deal with their thoughts and feelings. The worker's task involves helping the group and the scapegoat to recognize their patterns and assisting them in finding a new way of dealing with concerns that are common to both. The worker can view both the individual and the group as clients in need, better understanding and empathizing with the feelings common to both. This is illustrated clearly in the next example, in which a group of young, pregnant teenagers attack a member for having the same feelings that are central to their own struggles.

Pregnant Teens in a Shelter. In the following illustration, a group worker in a home for unmarried pregnant teens deals with the group's attack on a fellow member. In the previous chapter, we saw an example of the same worker in the same house working with a different group whose members had the strength to deal directly with their own feelings about giving up their unborn children. With the worker's help, they were able to move past their early, glib acceptance of the need to relinquish the child and face their real feelings of guilt, depression, and loss. In the following illustration, the members were more immature and needy and were less able to face their feelings. The group was not as sophisticated in its ability to offer mutual aid, and the sessions and the living situation were marked by incidents of anger and attack. Individual members expressed their own feelings of hurt by directing anger at each other and through the scapegoating process. The pain of the expected loss was the same; only the means of communicating it was different.

In this group, Susan was one of the youngest (14 years old) and least prepared members in terms of her readiness to keep her baby. She was dealing with more extreme versions of the problems facing all of the group members. However, she insisted she would keep the baby. The group members began a concerted campaign, attacking her ability to keep the child and expressing a great deal of anger at her position. When discussing this recording with the worker, I asked how she had felt during the first part of the discussion. She admitted to feeling overwhelmed by Susan's wanting to keep the child, and yet she felt for Susan as she was being put on the spot. She remained passive in the beginning, essentially because she agreed with the position of the group members and hoped they would convince Susan. She had explained to the group her responsibility to evaluate Susan's plan and that the agency could decide it was not appropriate. The style of the recording reflects the fact that it was written by an observer.

> Susan stated that she intended to finish school and would keep her baby.
>
> Janice stated that such an idea was not feasible.
>
> June gave examples of some friends who kept baby and it didn't work out. There was some suspicion of child beating. The husband beat wife and child.
>
> Shawn asked how Susan could possibly study when she had a baby to care for.
>
> Susan replied that the child would be in a foster home until she completed Grade 10.
>
> Debbie said she felt this would not be fair to the child.
>
> Shawn said she visited her mother weekly as a youngster but never got close to her mother.
>
> Janice expressed her feelings about the importance of a child's first year of development, which Susan would miss if the child were placed in a foster home.
>
> Susan said that perhaps she should drop out and get a job.
>
> Janice felt that Grade 10 was not much and wondered what type of work she could do. Said she is giving up her baby and returning to college to complete her education.
>
> Susan plans to marry her boyfriend when she is 16 (she is 14 now).
>
> Debbie felt that Susan would really be shortchanging herself by keeping the baby and not getting more education.
>
> Janice stressed how much they all cared for her and that's why they were trying to make her look at things more reasonably.
>
> Shannon suggested that if Susan wanted to get married at 16, that would be fine; in the meantime the child should not suffer but be given a chance at a good life.
>
> Susan insisted that they weren't going to change her mind. She had thought things through and wants the baby and will do all she can to have a good relationship with the child, something she herself never had because her own mother was in and out of hospital due to nervous breakdowns. She doesn't think that having a child in a foster home for its first year would be harmful.

The more Susan defended her position, the harder the group members pushed her. Susan dug in and refused to listen to their arguments. This often happens when a client is feeling insecure about a position. The more unsure Susan felt, the more difficult it was for her to accept the challenges. The worker sensed Susan's discomfort and reached for her feelings in the interaction.

> Worker asked Susan how she herself felt about the girls' pouncing on her like this.
>
> Susan said she is used to it, as they are always trying to get her to change her mind. She is stubborn about wanting the baby and intends to give it a good home. She had a very bad upbringing, and her mother used to get violent with her.
>
> Debbie expressed the feeling that it was risky with the added responsibility of an infant at such an early age. Her brother was having problems in his marriage.

Shannon pointed out that perhaps staying at home with the baby will make a wife dull, as interests are limited when a wife is preoccupied with child rearing.

Susan stated she had a good relationship with boyfriend.

Janice made the suggestion that boy-girl relationship can be very different when it becomes husband-wife relationship.

Debbie said that since Susan's boyfriend was in the army, he would be away a lot and the whole responsibility would be hers.

Janice stressed that keeping baby would be a very limiting thing for Susan; she may not be able to get the beautician course she wants. There are so many opportunities opened to young people, it would really be too bad to limit oneself. It's selfish to want to keep a baby, as she would not be able to offer the child very much while adopting parents had so very much to offer.

Susan became angry and insisted she could keep her baby.

Worker interpreted the other girls' pouncing on Susan as being an indication of how much they care and are concerned what will happen to Susan and the baby.

The worker tried to protect Susan from the anger of the group while at the same time supporting the group's position. This is an example of "being with" the feelings of the scapegoat but not those of the group. The group pressure continued.

Janice felt very strongly that it was crazy to consider keeping a baby at fourteen.

Shannon said that Susan's decision was an indication of her immaturity.

Susan defended herself by saying she was not immature but stubborn.

In the next excerpt, the worker regained her sense of function and began to help Susan deal with the group. She tried to assist her in communicating her feelings to the group members. She then pointed out the connection between Susan's feelings and those of the others. The worker did not blame the group members for their angry reactions, but instead expressed her understanding of how hard it would be to hear one's own feelings expressed by someone else. This is an example of being with both clients, Susan and the group, at the same time.

Worker expressed concern that Susan may be feeling that girls were attacking her decision. Perhaps Susan could share feelings as to why she wants to keep the baby.

Susan said that she would feel very badly giving baby up, she would always think of it, and feel guilty. She feels so strongly because she has to fight for two, as her boyfriend isn't here to express his feelings.

Worker stressed that the feeling Susan has is one that is common to all the girls. She said that they all initially wanted to keep their child and wondered if it was hard to hear Susan express those same feelings.

Debbie said she still wants to keep baby but feels adoptive parents can give it more.

Shannon feels that the best thing for her child is to be placed in an adoption home, but she still can't bring herself to sign the papers and won't until after the birth.

The worker's comment allowed the members to begin to express their own deep feelings of hurt that persisted in spite of their expressions of certainty about the decision. In addition, the worker had the task of asking Susan to consider why she was having such a hard time listening to the group members. This is a demand for work on the scapegoat which may be more effective after other group members have acknowledged similar feelings. Susan was unable to share her own doubts at this point, but I believe she heard the worker.

> Susan said she had never thought of giving the child up and was upset that girls (Pam and Terry) tried to give her all the negatives.
>
> Worker asked why Susan didn't consider the possibility of some of those problems happening to her. She can appreciate Susan's feeling for her boyfriend. Her life was without much love, so her boyfriend's offer to love her is naturally important. She asked if Susan wanted this so badly it made it hard to face the problems.
>
> Janice stated that she was telling her how she felt because she thinks of Susan as a kid sister, and she sure would be upset if the kid sister made a decision to keep. There was some talk about the fears and anxieties of pregnancy, labor, delivery, the pain involved, fear of needles, etc.
>
> Janice said that she planned to keep her baby but her family (particularly a sister who is a social worker) made her realize how selfish that would be.

The worker had observed the scapegoating pattern and strategized to pick it up at the next meeting by asking the group members to explore their reactions to the previous session. She planned to ask the group members why they were "so angry" and forced them to examine their own feelings. The worker asked how the group felt about the session last week. She said that they discussed some pretty heavy stuff and she wondered how they were feeling about it. The girls didn't really pick up on the feeling level.

> Janice said that there was a good article in *Redbook* on the importance of the child's first three years of life, and she passed it on to Susan to read. She wondered if Susan bothered to read it.
>
> Worker glanced at article and asked Janice to summarize it for the others.
>
> Janice felt it was too long and had too much in it but stated that it was important for a child to identify with parents at an early age, and moves should be eliminated, as it confuses a child.
>
> Worker again wondered why the girls were so angry last week, explained that their voices were really angry and they sounded a lot like "parents" might.
>
> Debbie stated that she had a brother that age and feels that she would be very upset and angry if he were in the same situation. She thus identifies Susan with her own brother.
>
> Janice has a sister that age. Knows she would have similar feelings and feel the anger.
>
> Debbie feels that the girls should ease off and lessen the pressure on Susan to change her mind about keeping the baby.

The members responded by talking about their siblings, which still evaded the question of their own feelings. They were, however, beginning to see how counterproductive it was to pressure Susan. The worker then made a demand for work as she once again reached for their feelings.

> (Continued references still seemed to be directed at Susan and her unrealistic plan to place the baby in a foster home for one year.)
>
> Worker interjected that perhaps there were other ways to approach the subject with Susan. She asked the girls to put themselves in her place and realize that Susan was being very emotional about keeping her baby and the guilt she would feel at giving it up.

Janice said that they all felt that way.

Worker picked up on this, saying that perhaps it was because they all shared Susan's feeling that they were so angry. They would all like to plan to keep their babies. In addition, Susan wasn't really listening to or answering the girls.

Janice wondered how boyfriend will feel at being trapped so young.

Worker suggested that the girls try to recall how they felt when they first learned of pregnancy, besides the feeling of panic.

Debbie said she felt like Susan, determined to keep her baby.

Janice mentioned feeling scared at first.

Carol said she had considered keeping but knew she couldn't.

Worker stated that they all had the feeling in common. They all initially wanted to keep the baby but realized it wasn't feasible. She continued that all the arguments girls were proposing were valid, but they all came on so strong that perhaps a person would hold to an idea just to prove her point, and in Susan's case, an easing off may be more beneficial, as the ultimate decision will have to be made by Susan.

With the pressure off Susan, the members explored their own feelings. Susan was able to listen and for the first time began to share the doubts she felt.

Pam feels pregnancy had made her feel old because others in the family have children at a much later age. She feels that panic is the first reaction, followed by grief at the fact that you are stuck and don't know what to do, how to get out of the predicament. The feeling of wanting the child is normal. She considered very closely whether she wanted her child to have a father, as he offered to live with her. However, in view of his drinking and running around, she doesn't want him back.

Worker stressed that it was an indication that they were moving from the feeling of wanting to keep the baby to considering what was the best plan for the baby.

Susan agreed that they all shared similar emotional and physical stages. She admitted that her boyfriend was away a lot and he himself brought up the idea that perhaps he can give up the army and go into the police corps. He still has four years to go in the army.

Worker suggested that as Susan was raised in an army family, she could share the feelings of what it was like.

Susan said that it didn't bother her until two years ago when her mother had a nervous breakdown.

Worker asked Susan to consider the stresses she will have in looking after the child. She emphasized that the girls were all working out their own ideas and were interested in helping Susan sort out her feelings, as this was helping them in their decisions.

When the common feelings were pointed out between Susan and the other girls, the scapegoating diminished considerably. The challenge to Susan's plan continued off and on, but without the earlier anger. At the end of the sixth session, Susan announced that she had decided to give up her baby. She said the group had "helped" her reach the decision, but she shared with them the feeling that it would not be easy.

Geriatric Reminiscence Group. Scapegoating is most often associated with groups for children and teens because it is most obvious in those age groups. Scapegoating can also take place with adults, however, as is illustrated in this final example of work with a geriatric reminiscence group.

Type of group: Geriatric reminiscence group

Age range of members: 68 to 101 years old

Gender, ethnic, sexual orientation, racial information: Male and female, primarily working-class. Most have only an 8th-grade education. Predominantly Italian, some Irish and Latino. All have physical problems. Some have slight mental retardation, chronic schizophrenia, dementia, and Alzheimer's.

Dates covered in record: 1/21 to 3/31

Group task: Structure-maintenance

1. *Problem:* The task this group faces is to reminisce about the past, which can bring forth both good and bad memories. The group has not yet developed a culture to talk, not only about the good times but the losses, such as death, functioning and mental capacities, as well. The group-as-a-whole goes into flight instead of talking about difficult or painful issues. The behavior itself is not the problem. The problem seems to be the communication within the group. Deviant behavior is a signal of this problem. The problem I face is helping the group find a way to talk about painful issues without scapegoating occurring.

2. *How the problem came to my attention:* The problem of using a scapegoat to avoid talking about feelings came to my attention early in the life of the group. Throughout each group session, everyone was easily engaged and ready to share. Once a topic or an issue was touched upon that seemed sensitive or emotional, immediately "the fun would begin." Different member at certain points in the conversation would start making fun and picking on other members. When I addressed the jokes and the fun poking, the acting-out members often started talking in Italian. I realized that these issues needed to be addressed if the group was going to be effective.

3. *Summary of the work:*

1/21: This was the first group session and I was a little bit disappointed. My co-leader and I named seven clients that we wanted in our group and, when we arrived at the daycare center, there were 17 members waiting for us. My co-leader and I attended daycare since last semester, so most of the members knew us quite well. I told the group that this was a reminiscence group, in order to clarify the purpose. I explained what reminiscing meant and told the group that, although we would be talking about the past, it could be any topic that they wanted to discuss. Most group members stared at me without comment. I became anxious by the silence, so I continued to talk. One group member started to discuss the news from that morning. Instead of clarifying the purpose again, I allowed the conversation to occur. At the time, I did not think about bringing the topic of the conversation to the past. In retrospect, I realize that I should have mentioned that the past does not include two hours ago. Because I did not do this, it became a common theme in the group. I left the group feeling that not much work was accomplished.

1/28: When my co-leader and I arrived, the conversation of the group already had begun. After being filled in by the group members that the conversation was about the North End in the "good old days," I helped facilitate conversation. I asked the group if their parents were born in the North End. Florence state that her parents were from Canada. Another group member started talking about Italy and how her parents came to America. Mary stated that she lost her mother many years ago, so why bother talking about her. I replied by saying that one of the ways memories can be kept alive is by sharing them with others. Right after I made my comment, Joe walked in. Mary looked at Joe and started singing, "Joe, Joe from Buffalo. He kisses girls, then says hello." The group started laughing and another member started singing a different rhyme. I had to get in touch with my own feelings because, on one hand, I wanted to laugh with the group, and avoid the work as well. On the other hand, I realized that I was there with a purpose. I tried to bring the focus back to the group. I told Joe that we were discussing the North End and where our families of origin came from. I then asked him if he would like to share with the group when his family came to America. Mary looked at me and stated with anger, "Isn't the group over?" It was.

In the next excerpt the group leader must deal with her frustration at her co-leader, who joins in the separate conversation. Starting to demonstrate greater confidence in her role, the writer pulls the co-leader in and responds to the apparently random conversation about food by skillfully connecting it to the purpose of the group.

2/4: When my co-leader and I arrived, there were 19 members waiting for us. Vinny started talking about a show that was on television last night. I asked the group what they wanted to talk about. Someone mentioned food and eventually the group was out of control. Everyone was yelling out their favorite foods without listening to one another. I had to control my own feelings because my co-leader was having a private conversation. After pulling my co-leader into the conversation, the discussion of food continued. I reached for feelings and asked if everyone was hungry. After laughter and agreement, I hoped to bring the topic back to the group purpose and examine what members had and lost. I stated that sometimes food and smells provoke a lot of memories. The group remained silent for a while and then members started sharing their memories. After two minutes, the group was chaotic again. Members started talking about Paul Revere and Bingo. I became frustrated and copped out. I did not raise the real issue of reminiscing until the end of the group and by then I was so frustrated with the group and my co-leader that I honestly just wanted to leave.

2/18: Before the group meeting, my co-leader and I realized that, although the conversations were funny and people were socializing, we were not accomplishing the group's purpose, which was to reminisce about the past. After getting seated, I stated, "Is everyone ready to work today?" Florence replied by saying, "What's the job?" The group started laughing. I stated again that the purpose of the group was to reminisce. Grace began by talking about birth order. The group talked about family, siblings, and children. The topic then turned to the discussion of medical care and how much things have changed with technology. I was actually amazed. The group was communicating, listening to one another and sharing opinions. I encouraged the communication to continue. Everyone was listening and respecting one another. When the group was over and I was getting my coat on, Lena grabbed my arm and stated, "Oh yeah, Joan, what does reminiscing mean?"

2/25: I started the group by asking if anyone knew what reminiscing means. My purpose for doing this was because that is where the group left off last week. A group member volunteered with an answer by saying, "Thinking and talking about stuff from long ago." Other members chimed in to give their definition. I asked the group if they knew why we reflect on memories from the past. Rose stated, "More importantly, do you all know that Paul has a girlfriend?" Everyone started laughing. I asked Rose how that was relevant to the conversation. Rose stated that the present was better than the past. I questioned her statement. I asked if the past was too painful to talk about. Rose told me that the past was dead. Another member asked Paul if he was in love. I ignored the comment and asked the group if they thought that Paul wanted his love life told to everyone. I now realize that I was adding to the "flight" behavior. Fran looked at me and then said something to Rose in Italian.

When the group starts to talk about Paul's "love" they are actually working on an important issue—their own lost loves. The worker's first response is to experience only the flight; however, she quickly catches this mistake and finds the connection between the joking and the theme for the day. Her acknowledgment of ethnicity issues helps the group members to discuss the sensitive area of inter-ethnic romantic relationships.

I tried to turn an awkward moment into work and asked the group if anyone would like to talk about their first love. Fran turned to me and stated, "You're Jewish, aren't you?" After I answered yes, Fran turned to Rose and continued having a conversation in Italian. I avoided questioning Fran's comment because I knew they were angry and looked at my co-leader for help. My co-leader asked the group to share one trait that makes them different. Everyone started saying what makes them different from others. After the conversation ended, I took a chance and stated, "Everyone has different abilities and traits. One thing that makes me different is that I am Jewish while most of you are Catholic, but we are all the same inside." Fran seemed to get a kick out of my statement. She came over to me, gave me a hug, and then stated, "My first love was Jewish, but I was not allowed to date him." From there, the work began.

3/4: Everyone seemed uninterested and was quiet when my co-leader and I arrived. We started by discussing the upcoming Academy Awards and movies from the past. No one seemed to want to participate. I asked everyone why they seemed down. No one responded. The group remained silent. One member reacted into her pocketbook and took out her wedding picture. She told the group that she had been 20 years old at the time. Maria looked at the picture and stated, "You should have stayed 20. You seem happy there. Now you're a miserable old lady." In shock, I asked Maria why she said this. Shirley (the woman in the picture) said, "Forget about it. Let's talk about something else." I would have liked to explore Maria's comment, but Shirley seemed uncomfortable. My co-leader asked the group what they wanted to talk about. Frank stated, "We talk about the same things over and over. Let's play cards." I asked if the past was too painful to talk about. Mary commented, "Why talk about the past? Who cares about the past? I agree with Frank. Let's play cards." Before I could respond, Rose states, "I live in the future, not the past." I tried to get Rose to elaborate. I asked her to describe her future, but she could not. I tried to keep a focus on the group and stated that, if we played cards today, then tomorrow that too would be in the past. I asked if that would be difficult to talk about. The group said no. Ethel said in a strong voice that so many people have so little time left that it is better to plan tomorrow than think about yesterday. I thanked the group member who stated this comment and acknowledged the fact that it took a lot of courage to make that statement. I then commented that it must be tough having so many losses. I shared my feelings and then tried to reach for mutuality. Lena said, "Enjoy it while you're young because it goes by too fast." With that comment, I truly empathized with what the members were feeling. I realized that they did not want to discuss the pain because they could almost count the time they had left. They would rather enjoy the time that they had left. I voiced my thoughts to the group. The response I received was, "Exactly. Now let's play cards."

3/18: My co-leader and I reached for common feelings of sadness and loss within the group. We mentioned that there would only be four more group meetings and that then the group would end. My co-leader explained that school would be over and so would our internships, which would be another loss in their lives. Mary said, "Four weeks is far away. Why are you bringing this up now?" I shared my feelings with the group. I explained that termination is a process and that, although I would be leaving, I would miss all the members and wanted to start preparing myself to leave. I explained that it would be a loss for me as well. The group expressed sadness. Joe said, "Oh well, just another person leaving my life." I validated that loss is difficult and facilitated a conversation on loss and sadness. Group members openly shared their sadness and grief with the group. Mary shared with the group, "I may give these girls a hard time, but it is only because I know I can, because I know they care." I allowed the group to connect in their sadness. The group turned its focus to friends that have left through the years. Frank seemed to get uncomfortable and started singing. I confronted Frank about his feelings and universalized to the group. As my co-leader and I left the group for the day, the group continued to share feelings with one another.

3/30: The group started talking about Easter Sunday. The conversation was very general. My co-leader and I tried to move them from general conversation to specific thoughts and feelings. We mentioned that there would only be two sessions left. The group did not seem to want to continue with this topic. I asked the group what they would like to do for our last session and where they pictured themselves in the future. The group mentioned that they enjoyed reminiscing (I found this to be quite funny, since that is the one thing they mostly wanted to avoid) and asked if the activities director would continue the group. I reached for feelings and feedback. I was interested in what the group felt that they got out of the group. The group shared with my co-leader and I that "sometimes the old days are fun to remember." The group mutually decided that, for our last session on April 16th, they were all going to bring in pictures from different stages in their lives. I thanked the group for sharing their memories with me and encouraged the group process and the friendships to continue.

4. *Where the Problem Stands Now:* The group seemed to have developed some sort of group culture along the way, only I am not sure when it happened. The communication in the group has gotten better and the scapegoating has lessened, although it still occurs. The group has mutually decided that they can discuss the good memories, but not the painful ones, although they are now able to acknowledge that sadness and losses do exist.

I was very happy to hear that the group members wanted the group to continue, which only proves that sometimes you do not realize the impact that you make. Instead of going into flight and completely avoiding the topics that are painful or denying that they are sad, the group now communicates by saying, "Oh, let's not talk about that. That makes me think about too many heartaches." The group has connected to one another, and friendships have emerged as well.

5. *Specific Next Steps:* Although I am leaving the group, these are things that I hope will occur and that I would like to do if I continued as the facilitator:

1. Continue a demand for work.
2. Continue to encourage the group to share.
3. Confront the deviant behavior.
4. Use deviant behavior to explore underlying feelings.
5. Point out patterns of flight or avoidance.

6. Have group explore sadness and pain to bring resolution.

7. Help clients further explore mutuality.

8. Help members use their humor to further explore sadness.

9. Encourage members to share more memories by bringing in photos, letters, cards, etc.

Dealing with the Scapegoating Pattern

Work with the scapegoating pattern involves a number of steps. First, the worker observes the pattern over time. Second, the worker must understand his or her own feelings in the situation to avoid siding with or against the scapegoat. By using the tuning-in skill, the worker can attempt to search out the potential connections between the scapegoat and the group. If the worker is not clear about these, the group can be asked to reflect upon the question. The next step involves pointing out the pattern to the group and the scapegoat. Thus, the worker asks the group to look at its *way of working* and to begin the struggle to find a more positive adaptive process.

As the worker challenges this scapegoating process, it is important not to be critical of either the group or the scapegoat for having developed this way of dealing with their underlying feelings. In fact, it is the worker's capacity for empathy and understanding of how hard it is to face these feelings that allows making this demand for work. The two thrusts of the worker's efforts involve asking the group to consider why they scapegoat and also asking the scapegoat to reflect on reasons for volunteering for the role. Discussion of this process is designed to free the members to explore further the underlying feelings. It would be a mistake to turn the sessions into ongoing discussions of the individual's life pattern of being a scapegoat or the group's analysis of its process. When the discussion is honest, invested with feeling, and touching all the members, then the group will no longer need a scapegoat. The discussion may help them to moderate their harsh judgments of themselves that lead to the need for a scapegoat. In turn, the scapegoat may discover his or her feelings are not unique.

THE DEVIANT MEMBER

One of the most difficult clients for workers to deal with is the **deviant member**. In this discussion, the term is used broadly to describe a member whose behavior deviates from the general norm of the group. This deviation can range from extremely inappropriate and disconnected behavior (e.g., a participant who attends the first meeting and evinces strikingly bizarre behavior) to one whose actions deviate only mildly or sporadically (e.g., a member who stares out the window while the rest of the group is deeply involved in a discussion). My major assumption is that deviant behavior is always a form of communication. The problem for the worker is that it is often difficult to figure out what the member is saying. This difficulty is compounded by the fact that the deviance is often experienced as directed towards the worker (e.g., acting-out behavior in a children's group may be seen as "testing my authority") and thus activates powerful emotions in the worker. A second major assumption, related to the earlier view of the group as a dynamic system, is that deviant behavior in a group may be expressing a communication that has meaning for the group as a whole. That is, just as the group may use a scapegoat as a means of dealing with difficult feelings, a deviant member may be serving an important social role for other group members. In this section we will explore these two assumptions.

Deviant Behavior as Communication

It was suggested earlier that deviant behavior could be considered on a continuum ranging from extreme to slight deviations from the norm. On the extreme end would be a client or group member who evinces bizarre behavior that is totally inappropriate for the group. This can happen on occasions when meetings are open to the community or screening of prospective members has not taken place. When this happens in a first session, the impact on the worker and the group is profound. As the member speaks, one can sense the group shrinking in embarrassment and at times in fear. It is important for the leader to take responsibility for gently, but firmly, asking the member to withhold comment, or in extreme cases, to leave the session. Group members are not prepared, in an early session, to deal with extreme deviance and are dependent upon the group worker to clarify the boundaries and to enforce the limits if needed.

Foster Parents. In one such example, a woman attending a foster parent recruitment session responded to the worker's opening contract statement and requests for group feedback by beginning a long, and essentially unrelated, tale of personal tragedy. When the worker tried a number of times to clarify the contract or to discover how the woman's concerns might relate to the discussion, she met with no success. The woman refused to allow others to speak and went on in detail about her personal problems and her fears that people were after her—even that the room was bugged. The discomfort in the eyes of the group members was clear. The worker, herself uncomfortable, finally moved to control the situation.

> **Worker:** Mrs. Pane, it is obvious that you're having a tough time right now, but I simply can't let you continue to use this group meeting to discuss it. I'll have to ask you to leave, but I would be glad to talk with you further about your concerns at another time.
>
> **Mrs. Pane:** You f—ing workers are all alike. You don't give a s—t about us, you're no different from the rest. You took my kids away, and I want them back.
>
> **Worker:** I'm sorry, Mrs. Pane, I can't talk with you now about that. You will have to leave, and I can discuss this with you tomorrow.

Mrs. Pane finally left, and the worker turned to the group to acknowledge how upset she was feeling about what had just happened. The group members expressed their own feelings. After emotions had settled, the worker picked up the group members' reactions to Mrs. Pane as a parent of children in the care of the agency. This led to a discussion of parents, their feelings about placements, and contacts between natural parents and foster parents. The worker followed up the next day with Mrs. Pane and did get to see her. There was a long, sometimes rambling and disjointed conversation during which the worker consistently tried to reach Mrs. Pane and acknowledge her feelings. Mrs. Pane turned to the worker as she left and said, "I'm sorry for what I said last night. You know it's just that I'm so angry—I miss my kids so much." Mrs. Pane's behavior at the meeting was an extreme example of the use of deviant behavior to express deeply held feelings. The worker could not allow the session to be captured by Mrs. Pane and, using all of her courage, she acted to protect the group's contract.

Most workers will not experience such extremes of deviant behavior. This example has been included because workers often fear that such an experience will happen to them and because it demonstrates how even bizarre behavior contains a message for the worker. On the other end of the continuum is an example drawn from another group for foster parents who already had children in their homes. The worker was well into the presentation of introductory material on the agency and fostering policies when a member arrived. She was dressed elaborately, wore a big hat, and sauntered up to the front of the room. All eyes in the group followed her as she made a grand entrance. The worker was shaken by her entry, but continued to speak. As the woman sat there, the worker noticed what appeared to be a scowl on her face and occasional grimaces in response to the worker's comments. The worker later described how she tended to "speak to this member" as the evening drew on. After the session, unable to contain herself because of the implied negative behavior, the worker inquired why the member seemed so antagonistic. The member, who had not said a word during the evening, was surprised by the worker's question. She explained that she was not angry at all, and that in fact, she was having a really hard time with her new foster child, since it was her first time fostering, and she was looking forward to these sessions to help.

Elementary School Boys. It is striking how often group leaders are surprised to find similar reactions and feelings underlying initial deviant behavior that they have felt to be attacks upon them. All that is needed, at times, is to confront the group members directly and to inquire as to the meaning of the behavior. The skills are twofold in nature. First is the **ability to tolerate deviant behavior** and second is the **ability to reach for the underlying message**. Consider the following example from a group for children who are having trouble in school. The meetings are held at the school in the afternoon, and John starts acting up as he enters the meeting room. He picks a fight with Jim, knocks over the desk, and appears ready to tackle the group worker next.

> **Worker:** John, what the hell is up? You have been roaring mad since you walked in here. (John remains silent, glaring with his fists clenched.) Did you just come from a fight with someone? Or was it Mr. Smith [the teacher]? Did you have an argument with him?
>
> **John:** (Still angry, but slighttly more relaxed) He's always picking on me, the bastard.
>
> **Worker:** OK, now slow down and tell me what happened. Maybe we can help you on this one. That's what the group is all about.

The worker was able to reach for the meaning behind this behavior instead of getting caught up in a "battle of wills" with John because he understood his function, was clear about the purpose of the group, and understood that children often raise their problems indirectly through acting-out behavior. The group member does not always immediately respond to the worker's efforts to reach past the behavior; however, he often understands the worker's meaning and will sometimes pick up the invitation later. Clarity of function is important, because if the worker is concentrating solely on his limit-setting function (e.g., stopping the fight), he may miss the other part of the work. The skill often involves setting the limit and reaching for the meaning of the behavior at exactly the same time.

Boys in a Residential Center. The following illustration comes from a living group in a residential center. Frank is a 16-year-old resident who has been away from home for a year and is preparing to visit his family over the two-week Christmas break. He had been given a number of hours of community work to do as a result of a conviction on a break-in charge. However, he was slow in fulfilling the requirements of the session, and the worker found himself having to threaten to cancel the visit home. Frank continued to be slow in completing the work as the days progressed, and the worker felt backed into a corner and deliberately provoked by Frank. After using a training workshop to tune into the feelings Frank might have about the visit, the worker had a hunch that Frank might be using the situation to avoid a difficult encounter. In essence, Frank's behavior signaled a problem. The worker confronted Frank:

> I spoke to Frank in the kitchen about how I felt he was using this community service as cover-up for more important feelings about going home for Christmas. I went on to say that I wasn't going to enforce this consequence and would rather like to help Frank with his hopes and fears about going home, especially since it was a Christmas visit. Frank dropped his peanut butter sandwich and ran out of the kitchen shouting "No way!"

The worker was not deterred by Frank's first response, and in fact, had prepared himself for the possibility of resistance. He approached the youngster later in the evening, in his bedroom, just before lights out. This is often a time when children in a residential center are ready to talk, as workers on the night shift can attest.

> I made another invitation to Frank to share his feelings, explaining that I understood it was not an easy area to talk about. He began by showing me the gifts he had bought his dad and his brothers. He asked me if I thought they were appropriate. He then went on to say he was uptight about whether he could act in a consistently mature fashion while at home. Acting his age was always his problem, and although he thought he had grown a lot in the past year, would his dad recognize this? We talked about this for a while and over the next few days; other staff spoke extensively about Christmas and his family with Frank. At one point, Frank came to me to ask how I was going to spend Christmas this year, which was a most unusual conversation for him to initiate.

Key moments will often bring out specific deviant behavior that the worker can learn to anticipate. In residential centers, holidays are difficult both for youngsters who are visiting their families and those who are not. There is always an increase in acting-out behavior at these times. Close examination of the impact of external circumstances often reveals the reason for the deviant behavior. While the thrust of the argument concerns the importance of understanding deviant behavior as a communication, it is important to underline that in those circumstances where setting limits is part of the worker's function, the worker still needs to set them and implement appropriate consequences. While Frank was allowed to go home for his visit, he still had to meet his responsibility for the hours of community service.

The Deviant as a Functional Role

As mentioned earlier, deviant behavior may be saying something related to the feelings of the group as a whole.[5] This notion is rooted in the idea of the group as a dynamic system in which the movement of one member is somewhat affected by the movements of the others. The deviant member can be viewed as simply a member who, for a number of reasons, feels a particular concern or emotion more strongly than the others in the group. This greater sense of urgency causes the deviant member to express the more widely held feeling, often in an indirect manner.

Staff Meetings. An example that may strike home to the reader and therefore help to illustrate this concept relates to staff meetings in agencies. When communications between staff and administration are poor, it is often considered taboo to raise certain issues or challenge directly the authority of the staff leader. Under such circumstances, the lack of open communication is dysfunctional for the organization, since serious problems may be ignored or ineffective policies set. It is not unusual for a staff system informally to develop a "deviant" member who directly or indirectly challenges the authority of the leadership. The administrator experiences this staff member as a "problem" and often attributes the attacks to the staff member's "problems with authority." What does not come out is that after the meetings, other staff members have approached the deviant member and offered words of encouragement, such as "I'm glad you said that. He really needed to hear it from someone." They may directly or indirectly conspire to encourage a staff member to "speak out" before a group meeting. What the group leader/administrator is missing is that the deviant member actually speaks for many on the staff. This staff members seems like the "enemy" when actually, since open communication is essential to administrative success (even though the administrator may not see this), the staff member is an "ally." If changes do not take place and the deviant member eventually leaves the agency or is fired, the role is filled very quickly by another staff member.

Schwartz (1968) refers to the function of the deviant member in the client group as follows:

> Such clients often play an important role in the group—expressing ideas that others may feel but be afraid to express, catalyzing issues more quickly, bringing out the negatives that need to be examined, etc. This helped us to see that such members should not immediately be thought of as "enemies" of the group, diverting it from its purposes, but as clients with needs of their own, and that these needs are often dramatic and exaggerated versions of those of the other group members (p. 365).

Psychiatric Hospital Group. It is critical, therefore, that the group leader not dismiss a deviant group member too quickly as simply acting out a personal problem. This would constitute the mistake of attempting to understand the movements of one member of a dynamic system (the group) apart from the movements of other members of the system. While it may be true that this member brings this particular social role to bear in all groups, the person cannot be understood simply as a separate entity. The first hypothesis should always be that the member may be speaking for the group as a whole. In the first session of the couples' group described in detail earlier, the member (Lou) who attacked "professionals" was carrying out the important task of dealing with the authority theme, an issue for the whole group. In the following excerpt, a member attacks the purpose of the group in a counseling session at a psychiatric hospital:

Mr. Wright: (Who had been quiet for most of the first two sessions, although he seemed to have a critical look on his face) You know, I think this is really all a bunch of crap! How in the hell is it going to do us any good sitting around and talking like this?

Mrs. Samuels: Well, you know, you really haven't had much to say. Maybe if you spoke up, it would be more worthwhile.

For most inexperienced workers, the force of the attack would be taken personally because the worker feels fully responsible for the success of the group. It would not be unusual for the worker to view Mr. Wright as negative, hostile, and resistant, and to set out to challenge him or encourage the group members to "take him on." For example, "Mr. Wright doesn't seem to think the group is too helpful. Do the others feel that way, or do they feel the way Mrs. Samuels does?" If Mr. Wright's behavior is viewed in the context of the dynamic interaction, and if the worker sees him as a potentially ally, he might instead help him to elaborate.

> **Worker:** I think it's important that we hear Mr. Wright out on this. If there are problems with the group, maybe we can work them out if we can talk about them. What's bothering you about the group?
>
> **Mr. Wright:** Well, for one thing, I don't think we are leveling with each other. We're not really saying what's on our minds. Everybody is too busy trying to impress each other to be honest.
>
> **Worker:** You know, that often happens in the first few sessions of a new group. People are unsure of what to expect. How about it, have any of the others of you felt that way?
>
> **Mr. Peters:** I didn't last week, but this week I thought the discussion was a bit superficial.

By treating the deviant member as an ally rather than as an enemy, the worker gave permission for the group to begin a frank discussion of how they were working. Others in the group felt the freedom to express their dissatisfaction, and as a result, the group members began to take responsibility for making their group more effective. This kind of discussion is essential for all groups, but it is often considered impolite to be direct in such areas. Members feel they do not want to "hurt the worker's feelings." As the group proceeded, the worker found that Mr. Wright, rather than not wanting to work, had a number of pressing issues he wished to deal with. His sense of urgency had forced him to speak out. Often in a group, the member who seems most negative and angry is the one who wants to work the hardest. It is easy to understand, however, how the worker's feelings might make it hard to see Mr. Wright in a more positive way.

Parenting Group.   Expressions of deviant positions in a group are often a lever for the group leader to deepen a discussion. For example, in one group on parenting skills, a major argument occurred when Mr. Thomas expressed the view that "all of this talk about worrying about the kids' feelings is nice for social workers but doesn't make sense for parents. Sometimes, the back of the hand is what they need." The other group members pounced on Mr. Thomas, and a verbal battle royal ensued. Once again, for new workers who are not clear about their function, the expression by Mr. Thomas of an idea that ran counter to the worker's view of "good parenting" would arouse a strong reaction. The worker would be particularly angered by the jibe about "social workers" and might set out to "educate" Mr. Thomas. Instead, this worker saw Mr. Thomas as expressing a feeling that in part was true for all the parents but was not considered "proper" in this group. The worker reached to support Mr. Thomas.

> **Worker:** You are all attacking Mr. Thomas's position quite strongly; however, I have a hunch there must be many times when all of you feel the same way. Am I right? (Silence)
>
> **Mr. Fisk:** There are times when the only feelings I'm interested in are the ones he has on his behind when I let him have one.

Mr. Thomas, with the worker's help, gave permission for the parents to begin to discuss the reality of parenting, which includes anger, loss of temper, and frustrations that are normal for all parents. She continued by asking Mr. Thomas why he felt he had to express this position so strongly.

> **Worker:** You know, Mr. Thomas, you come on so strong with this position, and yet you don't strike me as someone who doesn't care about how his kids feel. How come?
>
> **Mr. Thomas:** (Quietly, looking down as he spoke) Feelings can hurt too much.
>
> **Worker:** What do you mean?
>
> **Mr. Thomas:** It wasn't easy to talk with my kids when their mother died.
>
> **Worker:** (After a silence) You really know what that is like, don't you? (Mr. Thomas just nodded.)
>
> **Mr. Simcoe:** I've never had to handle something that tough, but I know what you mean about it being hard to listen when your kids are pouring out the hurt.

In summary, the deviant member who challenges the authority of the leader, provides negative feedback on the work of the group, raises a point of view contrary to the group's norm, or fights strongly and with emotion for a position may be playing an important functional role in the dynamic system of the group. The deviant member can be an ally for the worker if the worker can deal with personal feelings and then listen to the deviant member as a messenger from the group. In this last example, we can see the way in which a "deviant member" can turn into an active participant over time.

Veterans' Outpatient Clinic: Management of Chronic Pain

Age: 31–58; Gender: Male; Ethnicity: Caucasian

Dates Covered: 10/3 to 12/12

Group Task: Individual need satisfaction

1. *Problem:* This group consists of nine men, all veterans, all suffering from chronic pain. The source of each men's pain differs, but they have come together to learn techniques for trying to decrease their constant, chronic pain. The members, with one exception, seem happy to be a part of this group. The member about whom this report will focus is George. At our first meeting, he sat as close to the door as he could, wore dark sunglasses and a baseball cap with the visor tilted down over his eyes. His arms were tightly clasped around his chest. The major problem that I could see immediately was George's nonverbal message that being in the group was difficult for him. I, as the solo leader, needed to tune in to what George was saying and not saying. Also, I needed to figure out how much of George's message was unique to him and how much reflected the consensus of the group as a whole. Was George, as the possible deviant member of this new group, going to serve a functional role with this group as a whole?

2. *How the Problem Came to My Attention:* By his nonverbal messages, George was quite transparent. Sitting as close as he did to the door indicated to me that he was ready to race out of the room at any time. His dark sunglasses and visored cap, being worn in a room in an outpatient clinic, told me that he wanted to be invisible or perhaps that he wanted to observe this new group situation without being seen. By clutching his chest tightly with his arms, George was keeping himself safe and defended from this potentially dangerous group meeting.

3. *Summary of the Work with Process Excerpts:*

First session: I was quite nervous anticipating this first meeting. I was quite new to this placement and had only minimal contact with the clients—veterans. This members were all recommended to the group by their primary doctor. The group's description was "Pain management—coping with chronic pain." Early in the first session, after introductions, I sensed that some of the group members joined in order to be "free from pain." I felt this reflected George's expectations of me and the group. I told the group what I had in mind for our meetings. I gave them an overview of the "guest speakers" whom I had arranged to come to speak. Some of the people scheduled were: a pharmacist, a nutritionist, etc. This took some of the pressure off of me, that I was not doing this group by myself. Other professionals, actually, more experienced people than I, would be a part of some of our meetings. The scheduled "experts" would have concrete suggestions for these men in their struggle to deal with their pain. My role, as a neophyte group leader, would be that of a discussion leader rather than an expert. Although I realized that the men perceived me as an "expert," I felt quite inadequate initially. When each veteran introduced himself in terms of his injuries, number of surgeries, and list of daily medications, I sensed a kind of contest was in play: Who hurt more? Who took more codeine? etc.

Fifth session (of eight):

George: "I was told this was gonna be a pain relief group—it seems to be more of a therapy type group. This really pisses me off. I don't like opening up in this kind of setting, and my pain is just as bad as ever."

(I felt kind of angry at George here. What did he want, anyway—a miracle? He made me feel that I had failed the group. I bet he makes people feel inadequate frequently. He has a powerful effect on me and the group. He's so angry. What exactly does he mean by "relief"? Can he give me concrete suggestions on what would be helpful to him?)

Frank: "No way this was supposed to be a 'pain relief' group. I didn't expect any major pain relief."

Worker: "Frank, I hear you saying you didn't expect pain relief. But it sounds like George did expect relief from his pain." I tried to validate both members' statements. "I'm sorry that this group hasn't filled your expectations, George." Then I restate the goals for the group in hopes of clarification for George.

Worker: "George, I know it's difficult for some of us to open up. I think you've shared quite a bit with this group." He needs to learn how to vent anger in a healthy manner, not by attacking and criticizing others.

Ken: "What works for me is accepting what I can't change and being grateful for what's good in my life."

George responds, "You a minister or something?" Here George's anger is being channeled into attacking—this is surely unhealthy to group cohesion.

Worker: "George, you sound angry today. What makes you so angry? I think the remark you just made to Ken was hurtful. Ken, do you agree with me?"

Ken: "Not really—he has done it before. I'll get over it." Here I needed to restate the boundaries (maybe at the onset of each meeting, actually) so that members treat each other with respect in order to keep the group feeling safe. George needs these boundaries to feel more in control, and I must keep setting limits for him and also modeling respectful behavior myself. In hindsight, I maybe wouldn't have been so punitive toward George and thus given the group the opportunity to speak to George's rudeness. I think I intervene too much.

George: "To tell ya the truth, I'd rather be alone than at this meeting getting picked on."

In the next comments, it is clear that the worker is feeling defensive and holding back her anger at remarks that she is taking personally. By sitting on her feelings instead of trying to express them more directly, she cuts herself off from her capacity for empathy and ends up suggesting that George take his problems to the individual therapist. Perhaps if she could have expressed some of her frustration at trying to help and just getting anger in return, she might have broken the cycle while demonstrating how to express hurt and angry feelings in an appropriate manner.

I felt quite insulted. Here I thought I was trying to help this guy, and all I get is angry barbs that I felt were directed toward me personally and professionally. "You sound really depressed today, George. More so than I've ever seen you. What would you think about discussing this with Cheryl?" (his individual therapist). Maybe by mentioning Cheryl, I might get him grounded a bit. Also, I felt that, if indeed George was increasingly depressed, then his reactions in group were originating more internally than from group per se. George responds to my suggestion, "Yeah, I'll ask her."

Last meeting (of eight):

Worker: "Should we wait for the others?"

George: "Hell, no. They might not show up. They don't feel like us guys do about this group. I haven't missed once."

Here our man, George, who started out with sunglasses on, a hat covering his eyes and great resistance, now is comfortable expressing his identification with the group. He had perfect attendance. "Before we have our farewell party, I'd like to hear from each of you about how these meetings were for you. And if you have any criticisms or suggestions for me." I was giving them permission to tell me positive and negative suggestions.

George was the first to respond. "The first day, I really didn't want to be here—but Cheryl coaxed me to give it a try. I don't do good with groups—but I gotta tell you, it's been OK. I learned some stuff. My pain is not different, but I think I'm more relaxed. I'm sleeping much better." A certain sign that group helped.

"George, it sounds like there were parts of being in the group that were helpful for you. I think you've been an important member of this group. You've shared your symptoms, coping skills, gripes—you've opened up a lot to this group. And yes, I do remember you felt quite uncomfortable the first day and sat nearest the door. Remember?"

George: "Yeah, I thought I'd have to make a quick exit, but I never did."

I paraphrased and reflected to the group, in an attempt, during this final session, to begin summing up what work has been done.

Worker: "Ken, other than your brother, have you any more family?" God, did I step on a minefield, unknowingly.

Ken: "No, he and I were orphaned when I was six months old and he was 19 months. We lived in an orphanage until I was seven and he was eight. Then we were adopted by some people—they were terrible drunks and I still don't understand why they took us in—Dave and me. We were better off in the orphanage. My adoptive parents beat us a lot and the day I turned 17, I enlisted and never saw them again."

George: "Hey, guy, me too! My father was a bastard. A mean drunk. Man, did I hate the guy. I never shed a tear when he kicked the bucket. I could never feel relaxed in my own house or my bedroom, cause I never knew when he was gonna make me take the trash out in the pouring rain or some idiot thing like that. He made me full of shame. I never had any friends cause I was so ashamed of my father and his boozing."

Here we were, in the last minutes of the group meetings, and the common theme of being Adult Children of Alcoholics is just being brought to the surface. I said, "Oh, George and Ken—it sounds like your early years were painful and full of shame."

Frank: (Another member) says, "We're still in pain [how true]. My father and mother were the drinking Bobbsey twins. Us six kids had to do all the stuff at home—even clean up their puke. I hated them both. They ruined me and my sisters. I'll never forgive them their drinking. They were bums and never should have had kids. I've tried to be a good husband and father and bread-winner all through my pain."

These men have many common experiences, including a painful childhood. This information will be helpful to me in preparing for subsequent groups—what are the common threads? I responded, "Yes, Frank, I can see that you've been a hard work-er and your wife and daughters are very devoted to you. Wow, you men have been through your own personal wars and then you enlisted in the service and went to Vietnam, and now your legacy is chronic pain. Speaking for myself, I have a lot of feelings about you men. Firstly, respect for what you've endured lifelong. Sadness, also. But more importantly, faith and hope that you are all willing to work on the pain management and stress relievers. There's very little we can do about your alcoholic parents and the scars they left on you. But one major technique for releasing those memories and maybe in the process, a little of your pain, is to talk about it. This hour today has been a very emotional time for me and I suspect for all of you. Forums such as this, after you've built up trust among each other, can be very healthy and kind of cleansing." Because we were terminating today, I self-disclose a bit more than usual; also I praised them sincerely for their hard work and left them with some final suggestions. This may possibly be the first positive termination they've ever ex-perienced. I modeled healthy transitioning.

4. *Where the Problem Stands Now:* This group became nicely cohesive. They dis-covered they had much in common and shared willingly with one another. The mem-ber who progressed the most was George. He was talking in the last session about getting together with Ken to show him his collection of model airplanes (Ken was a bomber pilot). George was not hiding behind sunglasses or a hat with a visor. He still suffers with his pain daily, but I feel he will carry his feelings of success in this group with him for a long time. He trusted enough to share painful memories and discovered others had similar experiences. He is sleeping better, which certainly will improve the quality of his life overall. After the final meeting of this group with the revelations that took place, I can certainly see how oppressed George has been his whole life. What looked to me initially like deviant behavior in meeting #1, now looks quite like adap-tively defensive mannerisms. George has spent his life fighting. He became quite used to risking alienation due to his external persona. After this group experience, I predict that he will need his old defenses less, as he begins to trust more.

It would be a very new pattern for George to show his airplane models to Ken. No one has ever seen them, according to George. He stated in one meeting that he had never showed them to anyone for fear of being belittled for doing a "kid's hobby." Showing off his hobby may lead to his opening up other areas of himself and his life.

THE INTERNAL LEADER

The role of internal leader is played either by a single member or different members at different times. The worker in the group can be considered the **external leader** who is a part of the group but at the same time derives authority from an external source (the sponsoring agency). The **internal leader** derives authority from the group members.[6] It is easier to understand this distinction if we consider organized groups in the community (e.g., social action) or recreational groups (e.g., senior citizen clubs). These usually have a formal set of officers who are elected by group members to carry out the internal leadership role. As will be illustrated in a later chapter, the tasks of these leaders are often similar to those of the workers. All groups develop their own internal leaders, even in those situations where there are no elections and the discussions are largely directed by the worker. These leaders help to give voice to the different aspects of the group members' feelings and assist in helping the group resolve its struggles towards growth. They are usually individuals in the group who develop a higher status in the eyes of the members because of their abilities and skills in areas valued by group members. When such leaders take risks—for example, move into new areas of emotional expression—other members of the group will often follow their lead.

Group workers who are unsure of their function often experience internal leaders as a threat to their own authority, even viewing them as "deviant members." Actually, if the mutual aid process is central to the work, when workers observe the emergence of an internal leader, then they know the work is going well. This mistake of viewing the internal leader as a deviant member is most evident in work with teenagers and children, when the internal leader challenges the authority of the worker.

The Internal Leader—The Worker's Ally or Enemy

The following excerpt is from a first meeting of a group I led during my first year of social work professional training. I share this personal example for a number of reasons. First, I believe it is important for students to realize that we all start out with similar feelings, making most of the same mistakes. Many students who read examples of my more recent work with married couples, single parents, or persons with AIDS are not aware of the many mistakes I made, and still make, during my professional development process. Secondly, this particular group—acting-out adolescents—can be one of the most painful and stressful groups to lead. I still remember vividly dreading the early sessions, which seemed like perpetual battles of will—battles both I and the group were destined to lose. Third, it provides a good illustration of how an internal leader may, at first, be experienced by the worker as "the enemy" rather than as an ally. Finally, it is an example of a community center group in which activities are a central part of the work. These were the kinds of groups that have often made up the bulk of early group practice of social workers.

Acting-Out Adolescents in a Community Center Group. The group consists of acting-out adolescents (13 and 14 years old) who were members of a community center club. I had been warned that they were a difficult group and that they had given other workers a tough time in the past. Although the group was set up so that the club members planned their own activities, the agency had structured the first night by planning a mass sports program in the gym. The first issue on the group members' minds was, "What sort of worker will this be?" but my preparation had mistakenly led me to think that I must "demonstrate my authority in the first session and assert myself as leader," which in effect began the battle of wills.

> Only five boys had shown up by 7:45, so we spent the first ten minutes talking about the club last year. At this point, Al showed up and completely changed the tone of our meeting. It seemed as if the first five boys had been waiting for the catalyst that had finally arrived. Al was bubbling over about the school football game he had played in that afternoon. It was their first win in three years. When I asked how it had gone, he described it abruptly. He then wanted to know what we were doing that night. When I explained the prearranged evening program he became very negative about it. "Rope jumping (one of the competitive events) is for girls," he replied. I told him boxers use rope jumping for training, and he replied, "I'm not a boxer, and I'm not a girl." Although the other boys had not been overly enthusiastic about the evening program when I had described it earlier, their tone changed sharply as they agreed with Al.

Lack of clarity of function and initial nervousness led me to defend the program and to see Al as competition. Contracting was unclear, and an important discussion about the role of the worker in relation to the group members was missed because of my own fears and misconceptions. As the meeting proceeded, I got myself deeper into trouble:

> I tried to discuss at least next week's program with the guys. Girls from another club started pressing their faces against the window of the door, and before I could stop him, Al was racing to the attack. The contagion was immediate, and what had been a quiet group of boys was now following their leader. I jumped up and asked them to ignore the girls. Instead, they chose to ignore me. I went over to the door, closed it, and politely guided them back to the desk. This time, when they sat down, Al's feet were on the table (one of the wooden-finish types). Five more pairs immediately joined Al's (the testing was in full swing). I asked them to remove their feet, since they could damage the table. Joe and Ken responded, but the others didn't. I tried to maintain a light and firm stand. They slowly responded, stating that last year's leader let them keep their feet up that way. Another said there were a lot of things their leader let them do last year that I probably would not. I said that I would only allow them to do these things which were acceptable to the agency. One of the boys asked me what an agency was. I explained I meant the center (first week of field work and already I'm overprofessional). It was time to hit the gym for the games (much to my relief).

It is clear that my sense of function, that of "taming the group," led me to miss important issues. The discussion of the last leader's role would have been a helpful one. In addition, for this age group, relationships with girls was an emerging and uncomfortable theme. Al was the only club member to dance with girls later in the evening during the social dance part of the program. He asked about having a party with a girls' group, and I put off his request by saying, "We would need to plan this ahead of time." Al provided leadership in a number of areas, expressing the feelings and concerns of the group, but because I missed the importance of his role, the result was a battle over "who owned the group." Because I missed the signals, the indirect testing continued. Al led the members in throwing paper around the club room and leaning out of the windows, spitting on other center members as they left. I kept trying to set limits while not allowing myself to get angry (not thought to be professional). Finally, my natural instincts got the better of me.

> I said I would like to say a few words before we finished. I was attempting to reestablish the limits I had set earlier, but my own feelings got the best of me. I explained that this evening was really difficult for me and that probably it was so for them too. I said that if we couldn't relax enough to discuss further programs, there probably wouldn't be any. At this point, I said something that surprised me as I said it. I said their behavior better improve, or they could find themselves a new leader. They replied by saying that compared to the group members who hadn't shown up this evening, they were well behaved. My reaction to this group was mild panic.

It is easy to understand my panic in this situation. My idea of being professional was to be able to "handle" the group without losing my temper. Actually, in these moments at the end of the meeting when I revealed my real feelings, I was making a start at developing a working relationship with the group members. After a few more sessions of off-and-on-again testing, I moved to discuss the issue of the authority theme and to help the group members develop their own internal leadership and structure.

> I told the boys that since I had been with them for five weeks, they might be interested in hearing what I thought about the group. They perked up at this. Bert said, "You love us," and everyone laughed. I said that during this time I had been able to talk to each one of them individually and seemed to get along well. However, when we got together as a group, we couldn't seem to talk at all, right from the beginning. In spite of what they said, I thought that each one of them was concerned about stealing, acting wise all the time, and being disrespectful. Al said (very seriously this time) that it was different when they were in the group. I asked why that was so. Bert asked all the guys if they had stolen anything, and they all agreed that they had. After some discussion I told them I though they were really afraid to say what they thought in the group. Bert said he wasn't afraid. I asked about the others. Al mockingly put up his fists and said, "I'm not afraid of anyone in the group." I laughed with the rest and said I thought it was easy to be brave with your fists but that it took a lot more courage to say something you thought the other guys would not like. I said it was their club, and although it was important to me, it was really more important to them. Joel made a wisecrack, but he was silenced by Ken, who said, "That's just the kind of thing he (the worker) was talking about."
>
> As the discussion continued, the boys explained that they often didn't like my suggestions for activities, and I encouraged them to say so in the future, since it was their club. A surprising amount of feeling emerged about the kidding around in the group, much of it directed at one boy who acted out a great deal but was not present that night. They talked about how they could plan their own programs. The group members suggested that I could bring in ideas from other clubs and that they would then decide what they wanted. At this point, Al suggested they have a president. After some discussion about the respective positions, a president (Al), vice-president (Bert), and treasurer (Ken) were elected. A social committee was also formed to speak with the girls' club to discuss a party.
>
> At this point in the meeting, I realized we were actively talking about something with no kidding around and no testing of me. I felt at ease for the first time. I com-

mented to them about this. Al said, "We won't be able to do this all the time." I said I realized this and that there still would be a lot of kidding around. It would be OK as long as they could pull themselves together at times to get their work done. Al said that would be his job, and that I could help by telling them when they got out of hand. I agreed.

At the end of the process recording I commented that, as I left the building, "All of the boys gave me a warm good-bye." From this point on, much of the focus of the work shifted to helping the group members develop their own structure. For example, there were meetings with Al before sessions, at his request, to help him plan the agenda and to discuss his problems in chairing the sessions. For myself, these sessions were a painful initial lesson on the need to clarify my function and the recognition of the group's internal leadership.

I experienced Al as the groups' deviant member, when in reality, he was their internal leader. I had told them it was their group while the paradigm of practice guiding me had me believing it was really my group for implementing my "social work purposes." I encouraged them to plan activities when I already had the "appropriate" activities in mind. I experienced Al as my enemy, when in reality he was my major ally. This group provided a very painful but important lesson in my development. Further illustrations of my work with this group are included in Chapter 18, in which I describe what the group taught me about helping clients to negotiate the system—in this case the community center.

THE GATEKEEPER

The section on the deviant member pointed out how this client is often the one who feels a sense of urgency more strongly than the other members about a particular issue. In a sense, the deviant behavior is an effort to move the group towards real work. The internal leader often serves this function in a healthier, more direct way. A group can be ambivalent about work in the same way an individual may be, and members can take on the function of expressing that ambivalence for the group. This is sometimes seen in the form of a **gatekeeper** role, in which a member guards the gates through which the group must pass for the work to deepen. When the group discussion gets close to a difficult subject, the gatekeeper intervenes to divert the discussion.

In one group, for example, every time the discussion appeared to approach the issue of the authority of the worker, one female member would light up a foul-smelling cigar or in some other way attract the group's attention (and ire) in her direction. The group would rise to the bait, and the more difficult authority theme would be dropped. The worker pointed out the pattern, describing what he saw: "You know, it seems to me that every time you folks get close to taking me on, Pat lights up a cigar or says something that gets you onto her back. Am I right about this?" The group rejected the interpretation and turned on the leader with anger, thus beginning to deal with the authority theme. Later in the session, Pat commented that the worker's observation might be accurate, since she had always been fearful of seeing her parents fight and probably did the same thing then. It was not appropriate in this group to discuss the reason for the pattern, either Pat's or the group's, nor was it necessary to have the group members agree with the observation. The mere statement of the pattern offered the group an opportunity to face the worker directly, and Pat no longer needed to carry out this role.

The Use of Humor as a Form of Flight

Humor is often used to protect the gates in difficult and painful areas. A group member, usually one who has learned to play this role in most areas of her or his life, will act out, crack a joke, make a face, etc., in an effort to get the group members and the leader laughing and distracted. It should be pointed out that humor can also be used to help advance the work of the group and does not always represent a means of gatekeeping. It helps, at times, to be able to laugh when facing painful work. Staff groups, for example, often use macabre humor (e.g., stories about clients that one would never tell in public) to deal with their tensions. When this is the only form of tension release, and the underlying feelings resulting from the stresses and traumas are not dealt with, the use of this kind of humor is maladaptive and can lead to worker burnout, rather than preventing it. With the client group, the worker needs to observe the pattern over time and to note the results of the use of humor. If the humor consistently results in an illusion of work, then the gatekeeper function is a more likely explanation.

Teenagers in a Residential Setting: Question About Sex. In the following example, a worker in a residential setting picks up directly on the sexual innuendo involved in an apparently casual conversation in the lounge. The boys are young teens.

> **Frank:** (Watching a television show) Wow! Look at the build on that broad. Boy, I
>   wish I could meet her after the show.
> **Lou:** You wouldn't know what to do with her if you had her, you big jerk. Besides,
>   your pecker isn't big enough. (At this comment there is general kidding
>   around and teasing of a sexual nature.)
> **Worker:** You know, you guys kid around a lot about this sex business, but I bet
>   you have a lot of questions on your mind about it—a lot of serious ques-
>   tions.
> **Frank:** What kind of questions?
> **Worker:** Well, I'm not sure about your questions, but I bet you are interested in
>   what would make you attractive to women, sexually, and how you actually
>   handle sexual relations as well as other relations with women. It's probably a
>   tough area to talk about seriously.
> **Lou:** My old man never talked to me about sex.
> **Terry:** (Who has a pattern of clowning in the group) Did you hear the story about
>   the kid who asked his father where he came from? The father gave him a
>   15-minute sex talk, and then the kid said, "That's funny, Jimmy comes from
>   Chicago." (Some of the boys laughed and others groaned.) I got another
>   good one....
> **Worker:** Hold it, Terry! There you go again. Every time we get to some serious dis-
>   cussions in tough areas, you start with the jokes. And the rest of you guys go
>   right along with it. What's wrong? Is it tough to talk about sex without kid-
>   ding around?

The boys returned to the conversation with a number of serious questions specifically related to sex and others related to the whole question of intimacy with women. Terry sat quietly during the discussion and did not participate. The worker picked up with Terry alone later about his discomfort in such discussions. The worker asked if it was related to some of his difficult sexual experiences. Terry's mother had been a prostitute, and he had been a male prostitute for a time when he was 12. He could not talk about this in front of the other boys, and the worker had respected this. In most cases the gatekeeper carries out this functional role because he feels the resistance aspect of the group's ambivalence a bit more strongly than the rest of the members. In a sense he is the spokesman for this feeling, in the same way the internal leader or the deviant may speak for the opposite pole.

Lunchtime Elders' Group: Issues of Loss. In the following illustration, we will follow the work of a group worker who takes over as the new worker for a lunchtime elders' support group. Mario, the most recent member, takes over the role as gatekeeper using humor to deflect work from painful areas, especially those related to losses. It is interesting to note that the group appears to have a stake in maintaining Mario in this role.

RECORD OF SERVICE

Client Description and Time Frame:
An elders' lunchtime support group. Age Range: 67 to 85 years (4 Irish females, 1 Swedish male, 1 Italian male); Dates Covered: Sept. 24th to Nov. 5th

Description of the Problem:
The problem is the exclusionary relationship between the group and a new member, Mario. Mario often serves as a gatekeeper in the group, providing a distraction when the conversation approaches painful areas. Our challenge is to create an environment where the group and Mario together feel safe sharing feelings, offering suggestions and giving support to each other.

How the Problem Came to the Attention of the Worker(s):
Over the course of the first three group sessions which I attended, I noticed that Mario would frequently be the only one silent when others shared opinions; the one to interrupt a conversation by telling a joke; and the one to physically leave the table during an emotional life event story shared by another member. Before my first meeting, I knew that Mario was the most recent member to join the group, the other having been together since the group's inception 15 months before that time.

Summary of the Work:
Before focusing on my work with this group, I want to describe how I encouraged the group to tell me about work they had done before I met them. I wanted to establish trust between myself and the members, and felt that the first step was becoming acquainted. During the first two sessions, I explicitly asked about the previous co-leader and what she had done which they liked. Although I had anticipated a comparison between myself and previous co-leaders, I did react with a pang of anxiety when members told me about a wonderful meal the previous co-leader had made for them. I also felt put on the spot as members fired questions at me about where I'm from, where I go to school and how long I would be with the group.

I acknowledged that the group had recently lost a previous co-leader. I purposely related that loss to other losses they have had, hoping to communicate that I am in the group to work and that taboo subjects can be discussed here. Much time before my first session was spent "tuning in" to the issue of a new co-leader, and related themes of loss and intimacy. I brought up the subject, in part, to "prove" to this well-established group and co-leader that I was there to work, and that I had some valuable insights to offer. As a result of my raising this issue in the group, one member dubbed themselves the "love 'em and leave 'em" group.

In a later session, the group reacted strongly to my suggestion that it must be tough to be talking about loss of spouses and siblings or to talk about losing memory or dying, in front of co-leaders who are significantly younger than all group members.

Once the group summarized the work they did before I met them, and after I shared some of my background and intentions to stay until May, I was able to sit back, slightly, and watch. Before long, I noticed a pattern with Mario. He was the one to assist with weekly meal preparation while the others sat at the table conversing. He was the one to bring in cookies from home without request from the group.

He could not seem to tolerate silence, choosing instead to tell a joke or to chastise the co-leaders for not "keeping the ball rolling." His jokes were often ill-timed and inappropriate. For example, during a discussion about anniversaries of a loved one's death, Mario interrupted to tell a joke about "dumb Irishmen" who mistook a crematorium for a cemetery.

I had to get in touch with my own feelings, realizing that Mario's behavior elicited in me feelings of pity or hostility toward him. After several instances when I neglected to confront Mario's disruptive behavior, I realized that my only reason for the neglect was that I felt sorry for him after he shared with the group that he was an orphan and that he is agoraphobic. I also found myself wanting to verbally challenge him or put him down after he suggested that he prepare a meal with the co-leader, and I sit down with the others. I took the suggestion as a challenge to my authority. I believe it was, given the fact that Mario made this suggestion my first week with the group.

I initially looked at the deviant behavior as a manifestation of some "flaw" in Mario's personality. Rather than explore why Mario challenged my position and what that meant in the context of the group, I blamed Mario by labeling him as some sort of over-possessive personality. Developing a tolerance for deviant behavior became easier once I purposely explored the message indirectly presented in the behavior. Using supervision, my co-leader, and readings from class, I began to realize that Mario could be speaking for the group. In the fourth session, when Mario interrupted a member who was talking about illness in the family, I asked Mario directly if illness in the family was a difficult topic for him to discuss. What followed was his sharing with the group some feelings of sadness and anger surrounding his weekly visits to his wife in the nursing home. Mario's input then led to a discussion of other losses in various members' lives.

Once I recognized my own reactions in relation to events in the group, I tried to share my reactions. Although I often didn't figure out my reactions right away, I made a conscious effort to do just that. Then, when I did recognize my reactions to Mario's attempted diversions, I said so to the group. I said, "It was distracting for me when Alice was interrupted by Mario's question."

I made an effort to point out patterns of behavior to the group. As I noticed the regularity with which Mario succeeded in diverting the group's attention away from an emotion-laden issue or a confrontation, it became easier to point out patterns to the group. When I saw Mario offering second helpings or dessert to co-leaders and other members, I would simply comment, "You certainly like to take care of people here."

Later, when Mario pulled out his weekly contribution to the cost of the meal during a "heavy" conversation in the group, I said, "Mario, I noticed that often when we talk about death or other uncomfortable subjects, that you choose that moment to pay your money."

When caught off-guard, I did find myself doing "casework in the group." Despite tremendous effort to decipher what message Mario may be conveying about his own discomfort or that of the group, all that flies out the window when Mario goes "one step further" to divert attention. He twice stood up from the group and left the table during very emotion-laden sharing. On the first occasion, Mario decided halfway through the session that the table should be cleared (a task previously reserved for the final few minutes of the session). As he stoop up, my co-leader said, "Mario! What are you doing?!" I added, "I think that's very rude of you to leave the table when Alice is trying to tell us about her husband's death!"

I did notice that no group member attempted to intervene. What I wish I had said was, "It looks like the group wants Mario to clear the table, and change the subject." I wish I had said something like that, calmly, to suggest to other group members that the group was their responsibility, too. Instead, I just got lost in my surprise and anger.

While this worker is making important observations about Mario's pattern of behavior, she is still, at this point, tending to see Mario's behavior as unrelated to the dynamics of the system. The group members do not stop Mario because they have a stake in maintaining his gatekeeper role. He protects their feelings as well as his own. Since the worker is part of the dynamic system of the group, she must ask herself: "Now why do I react in the way I do to Mario? Am I also maintaining him in his role?" On reflection, the skill of identifying Mario's behavior by the worker probably reflects the part of her that truly wants the group to deal openly with loss and pain. However, workers are not immune to ambivalence, which may be reflected in her anger at his behavior. In a dynamic system, the end result often tells us much about the purpose of behaviors.

Over time, I became better able to get feedback from the group about (1) their reactions to Mario's behavior, and (2) whether they also felt similar to Mario at that time. In more recent sessions, when Mario suggested that he needs to "keep the ball rolling," I bounced the comment back to the group. I asked them if they felt like someone needed to "keep the ball rolling," more than it was. I also encouraged Mario to ask the group if they felt like he was monopolizing the conversation. For example, after Mario shared some memories of what it was like as a young boy without parents, having panic attacks, he expressed fear that he was a "complainer." Rather than answer for the group, we asked the group if they felt Mario was a complainer. The feedback Mario received was honest and constructive, indicating that the group appreciates the times when Mario is able to share some feelings about his own life.

I am learning how to relate back to the group most of what is shared in the group. After the confrontation between the co-leaders and Mario when he began to clear the table, my co-leader asked Mario if he was annoyed. "Of course not! You're my only friend!" he asserted. I then initiated a discussion in the group to explore how members felt toward each other, toward the co-leaders and to the group as a whole.

We also defined "friendship," according to our own experiences. This became a seized opportunity to gently confront Mario with his perception that friends are people who like you if you dress clean and do things for them. The group began to give Mario feedback that they like him, even if he doesn't bring in cookies or cook the meal.

I often counted on the co-leader's absence from the group to bring up something I had noticed in the group or Mario's behavior. I noticed after several sessions, that I was most likely to speak up in the group if the co-leader were out of the room for a moment. (She generally calls during the group any member who does not show up for the group and does not call.) I realized that this was an insecurity on my part. The group had told me that I was my co-leader's vice-president, helper, cook, secretary, etc. I must have internalized some of this. When my co-leader left, I generally took greater risks in asking a question or making a comment to the group. Often, the resulting conversation was lengthy and "responsible." The lesson here was to make a greater effort in general to speak up and share opinions.

In addition to requesting group feedback to Mario's behavior, I have started to see some initiation of feedback from members. I have done my best to reinforce this behavior. During the most recent session, Mario was very quiet. Just as I was preparing to point this out to the group and inquire into the situation, Theresa asked Mario why he was so quiet. "To tell you the truth, I didn't know how to tell you this. I fell on Friday getting off the bus from visiting my wife. A three-point landing!"

In addition to general groupwork practices of encouraging mutual aid in the group, I have also created a mental list of topics specific to Mario to explore in the group as soon as the group provides an "in." For example, when Jim talked about a fear that he has, I encouraged Mario to use his experience with agoraphobia to make some suggestions, and suggested that he tell the group a bit more about the illness.

Also on my list was ethnicity. This has come up once, in discussing upcoming holidays and the importance to each member and his/her family. A short discussion ensued in which traditional Irish and Italian meals were discussed. Ethnicity is still on my list. So, too, is Mario's experience as an orphan and as a husband of an Alzheimer's patient. My goal is to encourage sharing among members and point out the similarities among members who may still see Mario as "different"—"an outsider." There should then be less of a need by both the group and Mario for his deviant behavior.

Current Status of the Problem:

There is decided improvement in Mario's ability to share his own problems in the group. On several occasions he has revealed self-perceived "weakness" in his life: the agoraphobia, his sense of inadequacy in caring for his wife, his shame at being an orphan, and his disappointment in his children remaining distant from him since his wife moved to the nursing home. Likewise, the group has enthusiastically and emphatically listened to Mario's revelations. They have offered verbal support, indicating, for example, that it must be difficult for Mario to get a break on a hard day since he is afraid to leave his home to go for a walk.

Mario continues to have difficulty listening to others' problems. He continues to tell jokes or otherwise attempt to distract the group if a subject is hitting too close to home for him. A difference may be that now Mario is a little more aware of his actions as he engages in the activity. He sometimes comments that he's "not trying to change the subject, but he just remembered X." The group is barely beginning to take any responsibility for preserving its "work" phase. This may well be a sign that there remains a need to periodically escape from the pain associated with the work involved.

Strategies for Intervention:

1. I am going to continue to work on my own skills of acknowledging my own feelings in the group, so that I will share more. I think such a role model is crucial in a group where the members are expected to share their feelings.
2. I will confront the group when they "let Mario get away with X disruptive behavior," thus enlisting their help in controlling the behavior.
3. I will explicitly present to the group my theory that they see Mario as different from themselves. If I am wrong, they will certainly let me know.
4. I will explicitly suggest that Mario's distracting behavior is a useful tool for the group in avoiding sometimes painful work.

The Record of Service reveals the rapid professional growth of this student as she begins to see her group as a dynamic system with every member's behavior affecting and being affected by the interaction with the others. Her observations about the group's use of Mario in the gatekeeper role are crucial. Next in her development, she will have to come to grips with those moments in her work where her own resistance to the pain results in her using Mario as well.

THE DEFENSIVE MEMBER

Although defensiveness on the part of a group member has already been discussed in connection with other roles, it deserves some special attention. One often notices a group member who seems to be particularly defensive about admitting the existence of problems, accepting responsibility for his or her own part in the problem, or taking any suggestions or help from the group members after a problem has been raised. The defensiveness often results in the group members increasing their efforts to attack the defense, directly or indirectly, or eventually giving up and ignoring the member. One classic pattern is for a group member to listen to others describe serious difficulties and then have the member exclaim, "I'm not sure what the difficulty is that everyone is having. We don't have that kind of trouble." The reaction of the other group members to such a comment is usually clearly seen in their eyes.

A Three-Stage Change Process

Lewin (1951a, p. 254) described a model for change that can be applied on a number of levels (e.g., the individual, the group, the family, the organization). Stated simply, the individual personality in relation to its environment has developed a **quasi-stationary social equilibrium** in which some form of balance has been worked out. For the defensive member, denial has worked as a way of dealing with painful problems. The three steps for change involve "unfreezing" this equilibrium, moving into a phase of disequilibrium, and freezing at a new quasi-stationary equilibrium. The important point is that defenses have value to the individual, and to expect the unfreezing process to be an easy one misses the essence of the dynamics. The more serious the issue—the more deeply the individual feels a challenge to the sense of the core self—the more rigid will be the defenses. Defensiveness on the part of a group member, like resistance, discussed in Parts II and III of this book, is a signal that the work is real. The challenge of the group member or the leader to the individual's position is needed to begin the unfreezing process. However, the individual will need all the support, understanding, and help possible to translate unfreezing into movement into a new level of quasi-equilibrium.

Workers often underestimate the difficulty of what they and group members are asking people to do in the way of making substantial change. The difficulty of this process needs to be respected. It requires a delicate integration of support and demand to create the conditions in which the group member may feel free enough to let down the barriers.

A Defensive Father in a Parents' Group. In the example that follows, a father has described a conflict with his 18-year-old-son that has resulted in the son's leaving home and the family's being in turmoil. As the situation is played out in some detail, a number of other parents point out how the father has been stubborn and failed to listen to what his son is saying. They try to pin him down to alternative ways of relating, but to each, he responds in a typical "yes, but..." pattern, not able to take in what they are saying. Finally, after a few minutes of this, the group grows silent. The worker intervenes by pointing out the obstacle.

> **Worker:** It seems to me that what has been going on here is that Ted has raised a problem, you have all been trying to offer some answers, but Ted has been saying, "Yes, but..." to each of your suggestions. You look like you are about to give up on him. Are you?
>
> **Alice:** We don't seem to be getting anywhere. No matter what anyone says, he has an answer.
>
> **Worker:** Ted, I think you must feel a bit backed into a corner by the group. You do seem to have a hard time taking in their ideas. How come?
>
> **Ted:** I don't think they can appreciate my problem. It's not the same as theirs. They all seem to be blaming me for the fight, and that's because they don't understand what it really is like.
>
> **Worker:** Maybe it would help if you could tell them how this struggle with your son makes you feel.
>
> **Ted:** I gave this kid so much, raised him since he was a baby, and now he treats his mother and me like we don't matter at all. I did the best I could—doesn't he understand that?
>
> **Worker:** I think it's tough when you feel you love your child the way you do and you still see him as your kid, but he seems to want to pull away. You still feel responsible for him but you also feel a bit impotent, can't seem to control him anymore. Can any of you appreciate what Ted is feeling right now?

The group members moved to support Ted in his feelings, with others recounting similar experiences and feelings. The focus had shifted for a moment to the common feelings between group members rather than the obstacle that seemed to frustrate them. The worker sensed that Ted needed to feel understood and not judged harshly by the other parents, precisely because he tended to judge himself more harshly than any of them. Having established this support, the worker reached for the feelings underlying the resistance.

> **Worker:** Ted, if I were you, I think I would spend a lot of time wondering what went wrong in the relationship. I would be wondering how this could have happened when I had tried so hard—and if I could have done things differently. Is that true for you?
>
> **Fran:** (Ted's wife) He stays up nights these days, can't get to sleep because his is so upset.

Ted: Sure, it's tough. You try your best, but you always wonder if you should have been around more, worked a little less, had some more time...you know?

Worker: I guess that's what makes it hard for you to believe that anyone else can understand, and you feel so lousy about it yourself. Can the rest of you appreciate that it would be tough to listen if you were in Ted's shoes?

Ray: I think we are in Ted's shoes. When I see him getting stubborn in this group, I see myself and my own defensiveness.

The group discussion focused on how hard it was to take advice in the group, especially when you felt most uncertain yourself. As the conversation shifted, one could sense Ted physically relaxing and listening. After a while, he brought it back to his problem and asked the group to take another crack at it. He said, "This is really tough, but I don't want to lose the kid completely."

In some cases, defensive members need more time to back off and feel safe enough to "move." Workers will often find that the member has thought deeply about the way he reacted after the meeting, and unfreezing and readiness to change are apparent in a later session. This is the client's part in the procedure, and once again, the worker can only take responsibility for establishing the best possible conditions for change—the rest is up to the client and depends upon many factors. The findings in this author's recent study (Shulman, 1991) indicated that a client's acceptance of a problem contributed to her or his motivation to change as well as ability to use help. For some clients, the stress of the issue was so great, or the issue so loaded, with so much at stake, that they were unable to use the worker's or the group's help at that point. Although such situations are frustrating and often sad, they are a reality. This is one of the most important insights a new worker needs to develop so that he or she can avoid taking responsibility for the client's part in the proceedings. It is often the internal guilt on the worker's part, because of lack of clarity on this point and the worker's feeling of failure, that leads a worker to feel angry at a defensive client for not cooperating. It is interesting to note that the anger from the other group members appeared to be a result of their seeing some of their own feelings and attitudes exaggerated in the defensiveness of the member. In fact, the more they push him, the more they heighten his defensiveness. The issue of the functional role of the defensive member is explored more fully in the next example.

Denial in a Living-with-Cancer Group. The following illustration explores the denial exhibited by cancer patients and their family members in a group designed to help them cope with the impact of the life-threatening disease of cancer. A special focus will be on the role of one defensive member named Al, who helps the whole group avoid the taboo subject of death. In addition, the impact of gender and ethnicity is illustrated in the members' different responses to the disease of cancer. The men in the group (only two) respond by using increased work activity as part of a strong pattern of denial of their emotions about their wives' cancer. At one point, Al says, "You have to understand what it's like to be an engineer. Engineers are used to working with problems that can be resolved, and her cancer is a problem that I can't resolve."

As an Hispanic mother and daughter describe their reactions and those of their husband/father with cancer, one can see a contrast with the white members of the group and the influence of culture, as described by Schaefer and Pozzaglia (1986).

Unlike their uninhibited expression of grief and sadness, Hispanics try to control their anger. This, however, is not necessarily the case with white, middle-class families who are more comfortable in openly expressing their anger at the disease and their frustration with the hospital system. The Hispanic family's strong belief in God and His will is used to explain why the child is ill and minimizes their anger (pp. 298-299).

The reactions of shame to the diagnosis of cancer of the Hispanic father, who contemplates suicide rather than becoming a burden on his family, can be partly explained by what has been described as *machismo* (Devore and Schlesinger, 1991): "As macho, he is the head of the family, responsible for their protection and well-being, defender of their honor. His word is his contract" (p. 81).

RECORD OF SERVICE

Client Description and Time Frame:
A weekly support and education group for cancer patients and family members of patients. It is a six-week, time-limited closed group. The setting is a large teaching hospital, and the group is offered free of charge through the social services department. *Age Range of Members:* 30–78 years old. Ten group members are Caucasian-American. Two members, a mother and daughter, are Latin-American. There are ten women and two men in the group. There are five patients and seven family members. *Dates Covered in the Record:* February 1st to March 8th.

Description of the Problem:
The problem is the group's avoidance of discussion of painful issues that would lead to a discussion of the taboo subject of death. The taboo needs to be breached so that the group may begin to redefine its norms to include direct discussion of the reality of cancer. Though there is reality-based discussion of living with cancer, there is resistance to discussing the reality of dying from cancer. An additional problem is our collusion as co-leaders in the process of avoidance.

How the Problem Came to the Attention of the Worker(s):
As an observer of a previous six-week cancer group, I was witness to and aware of the incredible courage and depth of hope displayed by two patients in the group. They and their struggle were an inspiration. As the group ended, I wondered if they had gotten what they needed from the group. I had a sense that they had never faced up to the harsh reality and finality of cancer as they had maybe hoped they would in the group. I felt they may have been cheated of an opportunity to confront the reality of the disease. Though raising the more painful issues seemed taboo, I suspect it is part of the reason the group members chose to attend the group. As a co-leader of this new group, though aware of the issue of false hope, I found myself again caught up in the gifts of inspiration shared among members. In an attempt to refocus the group on more painful issues, I felt a resistance to their discussion and retreated myself from making interventions, thus colluding with group members in their hopefulness and avoiding discussion of the virtues (?) of cancer.

Summary of the Work:

February 1st
I overlooked the group's response to a member as an introduction of a major group issue: the desire to resolve the unreasonable. I kept my observation to myself. Rosina

and her mother, Maria, talked quite a bit about their father and husband who has lost interest in everything since diagnosis of cancer. They talked about what he had been like before cancer and how he had changed. People were trying to be very helpful and supportive in giving advice to them. I wondered if this may have been group members' responses because, if you give advice and people accept it, then you have helped and possibly resolved a problem—the very thing you cannot do with cancer.

I failed to reach for the feelings underlying the statement of hope. Faith, a daughter of a non-local patient, said her mother described cancer as the great liberator and she said that this part of the disease was contagious. Both she and her mother are becoming more assertive as well as expressive. She talked about friends who are there for her parents and how wonderful they are. I wondered (to myself) what about cancer was liberating.

I allowed the group to gloss over the pain and return to the hope. I succumbed to my own fear of discussion of death. Frances (a patient attending the group with her daughter, and widow of a cancer victim) began to talk about her husband after Rosina said her father would rather have died of a heart attack than lived feeling like a burden to her and her mother. Frances said her husband felt the same way. He had lung cancer (here, she pointed to Sara, who has lung cancer) and was given a year to live. He died in seven months. She said she was working when he was first diagnosed; but one day she came home and found him trying to commit suicide. She said, "We held each other and cried and I said 'We're going to fight this thing on my shirttails'...and we did...one day at a time." Sara, always an inspiration, said, "You need to fight, you need to find something to make every day count," and she began to talk to Rosina and Maria about ways they could help their father and husband make every day count. I wondered (to myself) if the return to advice giving was the group's response to the pain of Frances' disclosure about her own husband's painful and conflicted death.

February 15th
I failed to recognize the underlying disappointment that there may be no resolution and note the pain masked by a hopeful discussion of drugs and experts. As in the two previous groups, Doris talked about her allergic reaction to the chemotherapy drugs. She focused on how much she had been "digging" for information, calling the manufacturer, and even the inventor. She was discouraged to find out she was the only patient to have such a severe reaction to the drug, but seemed to feel better by taking some action. Group members seemed to admire her initiative.

I missed the connection of an individual's themes to the purpose of the group. Al, Doris' husband, talked about what a hard week it had been for him. He had overslept that morning after working night and day for three weeks on a contract that was meant to be in the mail that day.

I missed the group's attempt to resolve the problem with more advice about drugs and experts. I was caught up in the hope of resolution. Faith asked Doris if the dosage of the drug might be diluted. Christine shared that her mother was participating in a drug study and gave Doris the name of the physician conducting it.

I thought about reaching for feelings, but held back. Doris talked about having no pain and discomfort except for the rash on her legs. I wondered what it was like for her to have no pain and discomfort and still be sick with colon cancer.

I would have liked to support a group member's progress, but remained silent. Faith read a poem from her mother. She began to cry as she read it. She reiterated her mother's description of cancer as a blessed, terrible happening. Faith said she had been crying daily for 10 weeks. She said in all that time she thinks it never quite sunk in that her mother has cancer and she said the word which she previously could not say. She said she was angry about it.

I attempted to generalize to the rest of the group. I said I wondered if anger was something they had all experienced. There were many nods. Maria asked Faith who she was angry at and why she was angry. Faith talked about how her mother had not taken care of herself, though she did not directly say she was angry at her mother. She said she did not know whether or not to blame God. Al said, "You can't blame the person with the disease and you can't blame God. It's nobody's fault, it just happens." Christine asked Maria if she was angry. Maria said, "No, never." She had never been angry at God or her husband. She talked about how wonderful their life had been and said she thought God needed to give them some pain and that whatever happens they will accept. Rosina said, "You haven't always felt this way. In the beginning you were really depressed and feeling badly when he was sick." Maria said, "That's true." Rosina said she even got sympathy pains. Maria said they don't talk that much about his cancer. They just hold hands and that's enough, they don't have to talk about cancer.

Al said he understood where she was coming from, but that you cannot sacrifice and change your life because of your husband's illness. He said, "I haven't. I go to work and do what I need to do and, of course, I've given up some things." "Not many," Doris said. "No, not many," he said, "You just have to go on with your life, otherwise you'll just get depressed. You just can't let yourself get depressed." I attempted to bring the reality of the disease into the room and connect his intellectual discussion with the emotions he was trying to avoid. I said, "I understand what you're saying about needing to have a life of your own, but what do you do with the feelings...you may not want to get depressed, but the disease is depressing." Al responded somewhat angrily, saying, "I only allow myself 15 minutes of depression a year. Any more than 15 minutes is too long."

I backed off in response to his response and remained silent. Al said he gets depressed around Christmas, but always brings himself out of it. Grace (co-leader) said his feelings around Doris's disease are coming out somehow and that it sounded like he was avoiding them by being away so much. He denied this and talked about how crucial it is that he put in the evening and weekend hours at work. Christine said, "With all due respect, I don't know about your relationship, and I think I'm talking to you so much because I'm thinking of my parent (her mother has colon cancer like Doris), but I think Doris is asking you to spend more time with her and be there more."

All group members got involved in this discussion, speaking for Doris to Al who, when people said they did not want to attack him, responded by saying this was nothing, he was used to handling this kind of argument at work all the time. He defended his need to be at work. Sara said, "But Doris needs you there too." I missed an opportunity to ask if Al may have been speaking for the whole group and allowed the discussion to return to a struggle between the group and Al.

February 22nd

I attempted to connect present group activity and previous content with the issue of avoidance. Al talked for a while about the pressures on him at work. He talked about having spent 35 years building his career. Sharon (Frances' daughter) said, "I'm sitting here listening to you, Al, and I'm not sure what went on last week (she and her mother had been absent due to poor weather), but I can say that I see a lot of myself in how you're dealing with this." She talked about when her father had gotten sick. She was in Washington and her parents were in Pennsylvania. She talked about the sense of relief every time she got on the plane to go back to D.C. She did not want to and couldn't face her father's illness. She said when her mother called and said, "You'd better come," she even waited then to go to Pennsylvania. She said, "I know about career pressures. I work for an agency that regulates the type of company you work for and I know about those pressures. When my mother got sick, it was the same time that a promotion came up that I'd been working toward for years and I passed it up because I needed to be with my mother."

I failed to point out Al's need to see himself as different as a common reaction to defend against a painful reality. Al said, "But there's a difference, you're at the beginning of your career, I'm in the last ten years of it where my entire pension and retirement are determined." Sharon said, "None of us know if we're even going to be here tomorrow."

At that point, Sylvia and Sid came in with their daughter, Laura (not a member of the group). Grace briefed them on what was going on, and everyone quickly introduced themselves. Sid asked what they had missed last week, because they had also been absent. Al laughed as he said, "They all ganged up on me." He had already been through this with the other people who'd been absent the previous week. Sid said he was sorry he'd missed it. Al said, "So you could join in?" Sid said, "Who knows, maybe I would have joined in with you against everyone else." (These two were the only men in the group.) Frances asked Sylvia (the patient) how she was doing. She said her treatment had been going well, though she had been sleeping a lot. Laura said that she always sleeps a lot and said she even falls asleep at movies.

Then Doris and Al got into a discussion with them about how he loves movies and she hates to go to them. I said I wondered, as I thought Sharon had been saying to Al, if there was a tendency to avoid thinking, feeling, and talking about cancer—even in the group right now. I wondered if people found that they tended to or felt like avoiding it all. Frances said, "You avoid it and then don't know that you're doing it." Al said, "I'm not avoiding it, it's just my way of coping. You just can't think about it all the time."

I failed to clear a space for Al to be able to connect his feelings about his past losses with his current situation by tuning in to Doris's fear of that connection. Al said, "This isn't the first time I've been through it." "But it's not the same," Doris said. "But I was ten when my father died of cancer," said Al. "You were just a child, it's not the same." "My mother died of leukemia," said Al. "But you weren't in the house, your brother and sister took care of her." Al said, "That's true." I neglected to share my thoughts about how he managed to distance himself from his mother's illness as he seems to be trying to with Doris. Frances said, "It's different when you're living with the person than if you're away." I said it's different and it's the same. Al said, "No, it's definitely different when you're living with the person."

I mistook Sylvia's successful attempt to steer the conversation away from the topic of how difficult it is to live with a cancer patient as an inappropriate interjection into the conversation. Sylvia asked if anyone had seen the show *20/20* that week. Group members said they had not. Sylvia said it had been about chemotherapy drugs.

I responded to my own desire to avoid pain instead of tuning in to the probable pain of many of the group members. I allowed an eloquent expression of a painful ex-

perience to be perceived only as moving and inspiring. Frances asked Maria how her husband was doing. Maria and Rosina looked at each other and Rosina said it had been a discouraging week for them. Her father was no longer responding to the chemotherapy. Maria talked some but mostly cried as Rosina talked about a new lump her father had found behind his ear. Frances said that was the last thing he needed, to find that lump. She said her husband had gotten a great big tumor on his neck and couldn't stand it so she had to shave him. She spoke eloquently about her husband, her experience with him and his death.

I overlooked Frances's own need to confront her own cancer, which she only talked about in terms of beating. The group was engrossed. Al asked, "How do you do it?" Frances looked at him and said "Sometimes you just hold each other and cry." She said again, "I told him to grab on to my shirttails and we'll make it though this thing." After a while he said, "I'm not going to make it." She told the story of how he had died, in the hospital, not at home, I wondered how everyone felt. I imagined that everyone was moved by Frances's story, but that they also related it to themselves or their own loved one. We missed the boat.

March 1st

Grace mentioned that this was the fifth group and that we had one more left before the end. Doris said, "That's a bummer," and that was all that was said by her or anyone about the group ending. *I failed to tune in and connect Al's feelings to Doris's illness.* Al talked about what a tough couple of weeks it had been. He said it had been emotionally draining, and he attributed it mostly to work.

I attempted to confront the group's denial around its ending, but was unable to connect their difficulty in confronting the group's end with how it related to cancer and the pain of having to say untimely good-byes. In the middle of the group, I said that Doris had said it was "a bummer" that the group was ending next week and I wondered how others were feeling about it. *After an attempt to confront the denial, I copped out and colluded with it, allowing their discussion of how they could keep the group going.* Sid asked if it could be extended. Doris said that it was a bummer and that she always felt better after the group. Then everyone talked about ideas for how it could continue rather than talking about what it was like that it was ending. I wished I had said, "But this group as it exists now is ending next week."

Grace said how the tone of the group seemed different tonight and wondered if it had anything to do with the two unexplained empty chairs. *I missed the opportunity to comment on the very depressing reality and finality of cancer that group members were now unavoidably facing in the form of two glaringly empty chairs and ask how it related to themselves.* Rosina and her mother, Maria, were unexplainably absent after having spoken of their father and husband's turn for the worse the previous week. Frances, often the "cheerleader" and major source of group inspiration, said they were occupying her mind. The conversation for the next ten minutes revolved around the group's concern for the missing members and their loved one.

March 6th

I listened intently to information I wished had been shared earlier in the six weeks. I felt sad that I had not helped facilitate its earlier entrance into the group. At the end, Christine talked about what had gotten her to come to the group. She said she didn't know if people could tell what kind of person she was, but that she went on a cross-country bike trip alone and hiked and camped and was very independent. She's also organized and likes to keep things in order and be healthy. She said a few weeks after hearing her mother's diagnosis, she had a terrible headache one night and realized she hadn't eaten in three days. She said she made some cream of wheat but couldn't eat it. She looked around her apartment. There were clothes in every room and dirty dishes in the sink. She said she didn't know who was living in her apartment. She saw the flyer the next day and said, "I've got to get into that group."

I regretted that I had not trusted and acted on my instincts, which told me that this group was not dealing directly enough with the issue of death. Christine said the group had been keeping her in touch with the disease, but that she wasn't really facing that her mother could die from this. She said she talked to her boyfriend and he got so upset and said to her, "I can't believe you're in this group and you're not dealing with death." She said it as if she were the only one in the group who was not. I looked at Grace and thought that Christine said what I had been thinking throughout the six-weeks group. We had five minutes left of our final group. Sadly, this group did not confront death.

Current Status of the Problem:
This group ended, though they have made a commitment to informally continue their meetings. Possibly they will begin to confront their own avoidance, particularly if members begin to become sick. I am looking forward to the start of another six-week group March 22nd. I hope to be more cognizant of the ways in which avoidance surfaces and be more assertive in noting and helping the group to confront their avoidance without letting the discussion drop. I am also more acutely aware of how attractive it is to collude with the hope of group members as a defense, not only against their fear, but of my own fear of death and dying. I want to support their struggle to heal from the disease without cheating them of an opportunity to talk openly about the painful reality of cancer. I feel better prepared to facilitate that process having taken a closer look at the issues of avoidance.

Strategies for Intervention:
1. Be more active about listening for and speaking to the underlying messages of group members as they relate to cancer.
2. Point out a pattern of flight and be persistent in raising the issue.
3. Believing that death is something that group members are thinking about, I plan to raise the issue, breach the taboo, and bring it into the group for discussion.
4. Communicate my need to confront the issue of avoidance with my co-leader.
5. Notice my own discomfort with discussing taboo areas and share it with the group in an effort to help group members free up their energy that is bound up in their discomfort.
6. Do not fall into the trap of believing that group members are doing my job for me by asking questions of each other.

The worker in this illustration has used the experience to deepen her understanding about her clients and herself. As is characteristic with new workers, she is overly critical of her work, focusing on what she did not do while not crediting herself enough for what she accomplished. A little guilt is helpful for professional growth; however, it is important not to undervalue one's work along the way. In exploring the worker's hesitancy about dealing with the subject of death, it became obvious that a missing piece was the support system for staff that is essential in such emotionally draining practice. Case-related stressors on staff can have a direct impact on practice (Shulman, 1991). Davidson (1985) examined the impact of the special stresses affecting social workers who work with cancer patients and their families. He hypothesized that workers experience their work as stressful and lack adequate support to help them cope with the emotional impact of working with clients affected by a chronic and life-threatening illness. Pilsecker (1979) found that social workers, like other hospital staff, used strategies to deal with their painful emotions, including reduction of their direct involvement with patients. By recognizing, accepting, and trying to meet their own needs, social workers can become better able to be supportive of clients.

THE QUIET MEMBER

The **quiet member** is one who remains noticeably silent over a period of time. In small groups, it takes only a few sessions for the worker and the other group members to notice that someone has said very little or nothing at all. For the group members, a quiet member can create problems, since they do not know what thinking and feeling goes on behind the facade. There is a tendency to believe that the quiet member may be sitting in judgment of them, does not share their problems, or feels that others in the group talk too much. Workers, too, are often uncomfortable, feeling that a member who is not speaking may not be involved.

The silence of a member in a group is similar to the silence in an interview. It is a form of communication, but once again, it is hard to know exactly what the message is. For some group members, it may simply mean they are uncomfortable speaking in the group. This is one of the most common explanations. Others may feel left out or uninvolved in the group because they feel their problems are different. Some may be sitting in judgment of the group's activity (as was the case in one of the deviant member illustrations). In my experience, that is the least often stated reason for silence but interestingly is the interpretation most often put on silence by the active group members and the worker, probably reflecting their own feelings. Let us examine the quiet member who is afraid to speak, then the quiet member who is left out, and finally, the way in which the worker can help the group when they react to a quiet member.

My first assumption is that it is a mistake to believe that all members need to speak equally. The reality is that social roles developed by individuals include patterns that involve active participation through speech as well as active participation through listening. A member may be getting a great deal out of a discussion without directly participating. The worker who counts interventions and only feels that the group is successful if all members speak equally is, in my view, mistaken. On the other hand, there is a sense of mutual obligation in a small group in which members who risk themselves feel that others should do the same. In fact, the silent member often feels uncomfortable about "taking" and not "giving." In addition, many silent members have been so used to being quiet in groups for so long that they have not developed skills required for intervention. Others will tell you that they are always too slow with their thoughts. The group moves too fast for them, and by the time they can get in, the idea has been stated and the group has moved on. Others say that after they have been quiet in a group for a number of sessions, they are afraid the group members will "fall out of their chairs if I open my mouth." So although all members should be able to move into a group at their own pace and although equal participation is not a goal, the quiet member often needs some assistance in participating in the group.

Workers sometimes try to deal with this problem by direct confrontation or indirect means. Both tactics may backfire. For example, if a member has been quiet because of discomfort in speaking, a worker who suddenly turns and says, "I notice you haven't spoken yet in the group and wondered what was on your mind?" may find the member even further immobilized. The embarrassment is often great at a moment such as this and simply adds to the original level of discomfort. This direct confrontation is exactly what quiet members may have feared would happen.

The indirect means can be just as devastating. The worker has noticed a member not verbally participating in a discussion and turns and says, "What are your ideas about this question, Fran?" A member who is afraid of speaking anyway often finds that any ideas she did have completely disappear in this moment of panic. The other indirect technique, of going around the room to get all opinions when it really is only the quiet person's opinion the worker seeks, may be experienced as manipulative and artificial by members.

The task, then, is to be direct and at the same time non-threatening. My own strategy is based upon the belief that people have a right to their defenses and their characteristic patterns of social interaction. As the worker, my job is to mediate the engagement between each member and the group, so I would feel a responsibility to check with a quiet member and see how that engagement was going. If there was an obstacle between the member and the group, I could offer to help. The following conversation took place after the second meeting of a group. Richard had been particularly silent in both meetings, although his eyes seemed to indicate he was involved.

> **Worker:** Do you have a second to chat before you go?
>
> **Richard:** Sure, what's up?
>
> **Worker:** I noticed you haven't spoken in the group these two sessions, and I thought I would check to see how it was going with you. I know some people take longer than others to get involved, and that's OK. I just wanted to be sure there were no problems.
>
> **Richard:** Well, you caught me.
>
> **Worker:** What do you mean?
>
> **Richard:** I managed to get through all of my years in school without ever saying anything in class, and now it looks as if I've been caught.
>
> **Worker:** Is it hard for you to speak in a group?
>
> **Richard:** I always feel unsure of what I'm going to say, and by the time I've figured it out, the group has gone past me. Sometimes, it's just hard to get in with everyone speaking at once.
>
> **Worker:** Look, I can tell from your eyes that you are actively involved in the discussion. However, after a while, you will probably feel uncomfortable not speaking, and then it will get harder and harder to talk.
>
> **Richard:** That's the way it usually is for me.
>
> **Worker:** Not just you, you know. Lots of people feel that way. If you would like, I can help by watching for you and if I sense you want to get into the conversation by the look on your face, or your body, or if you give me the signal, I can reach for you and help you in. Would you like me to do that?
>
> **Richard:** That sounds OK. If I give you a signal, you'll call on me?
>
> **Worker:** Exactly! I find that has helped people in the past.

At the next session, Richard avoided the worker's eyes for the first 15 minutes, probably afraid of giving a false signal. The discussion was heated, and the worker kept watching Richard. After a while, the worker noticed Richard leaning forward a bit, with his eyebrows arched, looking at the worker. The worker simply said, "Come on in, Richard." The group paused, and Richard began to speak.

Another type of quiet member is one who feels that his particular concerns and issues may not be of interest to the group or that his problems are different from those of the others. Such members do not share problems with the group members, and after a while, they feel left out and the group wonders what is happening.

In the following example, Mrs. Trenke, who had shared some difficult experiences with the group, stated that she felt let down when the group did not respond to her feelings. Mrs. Davidson, who had been quiet in the group, supported Mrs. Trenke's comment.

> The worker said, "Maybe we could hear how Mrs. Trenke felt let down by the group?" Mrs. Trenke continued, "I felt that I was not a part of the group, that I was not going to get anything out of it." Mrs. Davidson cut in, "Yeah! We didn't listen to other people's troubles because we had enough of our own!" The worker turned to Mrs. Davidson and said, "Have you felt let down and left out of the group?" "No," said Mrs. Davidson, "I don't feel I have the same situation—they have husbands." (Mrs. Bennet reached out and touched Mrs. Davidson on the arm.) The worker asked Mrs. Davidson how she felt about not having a man. Mrs. Davidson replied, "Sad, depressed—I wonder if he could be proud of the kids as I am?" She went on to say that maybe things would be different if her husband were alive—maybe they could have made a go of it. The worker said he felt that Mrs. Davidson had been cut out of the group for some weeks. Mrs. Davidson agreed.
>
> Mrs. Bennet said that was probably due to the fact that she had not been able to share with the group the concerns she had. All agreed. The worker cut in after a silence and said, "I felt the group would like to know what it is like, what it feels like to be alone—what do you need help with?" Mrs. Bennet cut in, "There you go on that feeling theory again." The worker asked if it worried Mrs. Bennet when we talked about feelings? "No," she said, "but is it important?" The worker said that it seemed important because everyone in this group was having trouble talking about and sharing feelings while at the same time they were interested in what others were feeling. "Do you see what we have done here? When we began to find out about Mrs. Davidson's feelings, someone suggested and we all agreed to avoid it. Let's go back to Mrs. Davidson's feelings!"
>
> Mrs. Davidson said, "I feel like a s-h-i-t (spelled out) at home with the kids." The worker cut in and said it was OK with him if she said *shit*—why did she feel that way? "It rips me right across here (indicating mid-section) when they are fighting—I've had nothing but fighting all my life—first in my own home—then with my husband—now with my kids." "How do you see the fighting—what does it mean to you?" asked the worker. "I feel on my own, all alone." Mrs. Trenke cut in, "I know that feeling—I had it with my husband—we used to argue.... What can I do? Why is it always me?" The worker asked if Mrs. Davidson could share a specific problem with the group, and she did. It involved setting limits, then wavering on them and letting the kids have their own way.

As is often the case, simply acknowledging the lack of involvement by the member is enough to encourage the sharing of her concerns. Sometimes the initiative for reaching out to a quiet member starts with the group. It is not unusual, after a period of time, to have a group member turn to one who has been silent and ask, "What have you been thinking?" Once again, the worker's concern for the two clients and clarity of function can help assist the group and the member in an important discussion.

> **Ray:** I have been thinking about you, Fred. You have not said anything in the group so far. How come? (All eyes turned to Fred.)
>
> **Fred:** (Looking very uncomfortable) Oh, I've been listening.
>
> **Worker:** (Addressing Ray) Does it concern you when Fred doesn't speak?
>
> **Ray:** Yeah, I begin to wonder if I'm talking too much or he thinks I'm making a real ass out of myself.
>
> **Worker:** Have others in the group wondered about that as well? (Nodding of heads) I think it makes other people uncomfortable when you don't speak much, Fred, because they can't figure out what you're thinking. Could you react to that?
>
> **Fred:** Actually, I've been sitting here thinking how much all of your problems are just like mine. I've wanted to share some, but I don't feel comfortable talking in a group.
>
> **Worker:** This wasn't easy for you right now, was it?
>
> **Fred:** No, it wasn't easy at all, but I'm glad it came out.
>
> **Ray:** Maybe if I shut up a bit, you would have more of a chance to talk.
>
> **Worker:** I don't think so, Ray. Some people speak more in a group and others do a lot of work by listening. You also seem concerned about what others have to say, so I hope you wouldn't feel you needed to hold back. How about the rest of the group?
>
> **Lou:** You raise interesting points, Ray, and it helps the group keep going. I would miss you if you just clammed up. (Ray smiles at this.)
>
> **Worker:** I can watch the talk in the group, and if I see someone trying to get in, I'll help make room for him. Is that all right? (Members of the group nodded in agreement.)
>
> **Fred:** I'll get into the conversation. I just need some more time.
>
> **Ray:** That's OK. Don't feel pressed. You can get in when you feel comfortable.

Once the communications had been clarified, the problem of the silent member receded. Fred did get into the discussion the following week, raising a concern to the group and meeting with a positive response.

THE MONOPOLIZER

The previous section on the quiet member brings up the opposite side of the issue: people who talk a great deal and are sometimes referred to as **monopolizers**. My observation is that people who talk a great deal are often more of a problem for the worker than quiet members. In first sessions, in particular, group members are pleased to see someone pick up the discussion. It can become a problem when the person talking does not also listen to others, cuts them off, and creates a negative reaction in the group. The group worker who sees this happening can raise the issue directly. Usually the discussion between the member and the group helps to ease the problem. If the group worker inquires why the member acts this way in the group, the individual will often reveal that talking is a way of covering up feelings, avoiding a problem, or expressing concern about actions in the group. It often turns out that the overly verbal member's words are a way of handling the same feelings expressed in a quite different manner by the member who is quiet.

In the examples that follow, we see different types of monopolizers and some of the ways workers attempt to intervene in dealing with them.

Parents of Children with Traumatic Brain Injury

This first brief excerpt illustrates how immobilized both the group leader and the other members can feel when faced with a monopolizer. This member, Dawn, acts out her anxiety by responding to a doctor's presentation with an unstoppable stream of talk.

> *Agency type:* A hospital and rehabilitation center for children and adolescents
> *Group Purpose:* To educate the group members about their children's medical and therapeutic conditions, as well as to inform them of safety precautions for children who have had a traumatic brain injury
> *Gender of members:* 3 males and 11 females (including worker)
> *Age range:* mid-twenties to early forties
> As soon as Dr. Thomas began to explain that children who have experienced traumatic brain injuries tend to be impulsive, Dawn, started to describe what happened with her child to demonstrate that she agreed with the doctor. She went on and on for almost 10 minutes, and nobody intervened. Then, she started to talk about her other child, Lisa, and what happened at home during the past weekend. I turned to Dawn and said, "Dawn, I know you have many things to say, but why don't we go back to Eileen's behavior?" Dawn replied, "I know. I know. But let me finish. This is related to Eileen, too." People in the room rolled their eyes, but I did not object. She spoke another three minutes or so, and finished her story by saying, "So I told my children that school is always number one." I jumped in and said, "Good. Why don't we ask Melissa (the hospital tutor) about school?" People, including Dawn, laughed. When Melissa finished reporting about Eileen's school issue, I encouraged Dawn to ask Melissa questions. Then, I announced to the treatment team that we were running out of time so I would like to ask everyone to be short and precise. They nodded.

In retrospect, this first meeting was focused almost entirely on the concerns of one member. The other group members signaled their displeasure by rolling their eyes, yet the group leader, perhaps feeling unclear about how to intervene, let Dawn continue unchecked. The leader would have been helpful to Dawn and the other members if she had intervened more directly and firmly. The monopolizer, in a session such as this one, will often feel embarrassed afterward for having dominated the conversation, and the other members will wonder about the value of the group. It is up to the group leader in a first session such as this one to take responsibility for providing structure. In doing so, the leader needs to be both direct and empathic, saying something like this:

> Hold on a second, Dawn. I know your child's injury and this discussion provokes a lot of feelings in you, and you probably feel you want as much help as you can get for your own child. But we need to allow room for everyone to ask their questions and make their comments, so I'll play traffic cop if it's OK with the rest of you.

If Dawn continues to test, such as by saying, as she did in the session above, "Let me just finish…" the worker needs to say something like "Nice try, but we need to give someone else a chance." Continued persistence would require some discussion of how it is possible to be so full of one's own feelings that it leaves very little room for anyone else's. There is also a good chance that Dawn has also just acted out the problem she has with friends and other family members of overwhelming them with her issues and not being able to respond to theirs.

If these interventions are handled directly, openly, without anger and if possible, with non-humiliating humor, they will reassure the group members that the worker will not let them subvert the purpose of the group or act out their anxiety. The problem is that such interventions go against societal norms, which encourage passively allowing the monopolizer to go on at length, intervening indirectly with little success, or intervening from anger as the group leader feels frustration at one member's dominating the group. In most cases the monopolizer wants the worker to set limits, because structure helps to bind anxiety and helps the member feel more in control over what must be a devastating situation. In this case, the other members reacted negatively to the monopolizer. In the example that follows, the group members encourage monopolizing as it serves the functional purpose of allowing them to avoid dealing with their own painful feelings.

Men's Counseling Group

Age Range of Members: 20–25 (two Caucasian-Americans, one Latino-American, and one African-American)

Dates Covered in Record: 10/30 to 12/4

1. Problem

The problem is the relationship between the group and one of its members, Ruben. Ruben is a monopolizer, often dominating the discussion. He also takes on the role of the gatekeeper in the group, where he shifts the focus of conversation when it gets close to difficult topics. The challenge is to create an atmosphere in which all the group members feel listened to and supported and also feel safe to discuss feelings around difficult subjects.

2. How the Problem Came to My Attention

During the first two sessions, it was obvious that Ruben spoke more than the other members. In fact, he spoke almost the entire session. When someone else did get the opportunity to speak, Ruben would say afterwards, "I know how you feel. I…" and proceed to talk about himself again. Another pattern that I noticed emerging was that whenever someone started to talk about something difficult, like worrying about not "making it" professionally or losing their passion for their art form because of the rigors of school, Ruben would shift the focus away from the "feeling." He would often intellectualize and say things like "Everyone goes through it, you just have to work through it." When this would happen, I also noticed that the group willingly accepted this shift and avoided talking about how scary these feelings must be for them.

3. Summary of the Work

11/6: I tried to indirectly confront Ruben's monopolizing behavior.

For almost the entire first two meetings, Ruben had dominated the discussion. I was unsure how to deal with this behavior. I did not want to alienate him, but I found myself getting angry because he would barely allow anyone else to speak. During the third meeting John started speaking. After he had said a few sentences, Ruben (who was sitting to my immediate left; John was to my immediate right) started to talk and cut him off. Rather than bringing this to his attention, I stayed facing John, even though he had stopped talking. I had hoped to give John the message that I was interested in what he had to say. Much to my surprise, after a few uncomfortable moments of not knowing what to do, John looked beyond me and towards Ruben. My attempt at indirectly dealing with the behavior failed miserably. I can see now that this was a passive-aggressive act on my behalf stemming from my own uncertainty and anger towards Ruben's behavior. I also believe that there were obviously real authority issues being played out at this stage.

11/13: I decided to address Ruben's behavior directly.

The next time someone was speaking and Ruben cut him off, I intervened and said, "I'm not sure if you realize it, but Ray was speaking and you interrupted him before he had finished." I was able to say this in a non-punitive manner, and Ruben responded, "I'm sorry, I have a tendency to talk too much sometimes. Go on, Ray." For the rest of this meeting Ruben participated but did not dominate the discussion as he had previously. He did, however, continue to shift the focus of the discussion. Often another group member would be speaking and Ruben would interject by saying, "I know what you mean, that's happened to me." He would then continue and shift the focus of the conversation in a very subtle way that at this time I was unable to pinpoint. I found myself getting increasingly frustrated at this behavior, but I realized that this dynamic was not just about Ruben, because the rest of the group was allowing this to happen. I was then able to see Ruben's behavior as fulfilling a role within the group rather than as representing a character flaw in him.

11/20: I made a conscious effort to observe Ruben's behavior and see if there was a pattern to when he would jump in and shift the focus of the conversation.

The group had become very good at allowing everyone the chance to speak, offering support and appropriate feedback to each other. This would occur around issues like dating, families, and "partying." These all seemed appropriate topics for this multi-issue, college-age men's group. However, the thing that made this group unique is that they are in a performing arts college. On top of their academic classes, they had long hours of rehearsals, lessons, and private practice sessions. They were constantly auditioning for roles in school productions. It was around this topic that Ruben would act as the gatekeeper and lead the group in flight from the feelings arising from these discussions. During this session, John was telling how he really felt like he "screwed up" an audition. The group was able to support him around this. He then said, in a very somber tone, "I wonder sometimes—like, if I'm good enough to…" and before he could finish, Ruben interrupted and said, "John, you have a great voice, you just have to keep practicing." Ray then said, "We all go through this, it will pass." On the surface it appeared that the group was supporting John, but they really had shifted the focus away from how John was feeling. The feelings that John was touching on were feelings that they all had probably experienced, but they were obviously uncomfortable acknowledging and/or expressing them. The fact that the group had such difficulty discussing these feelings told me that this was probably just what they needed to do if we were going to become a true work group.

11/22: I made an attempt to point out this pattern of behavior to the group.

Ray was sharing with the group his frustration over not getting the lead in a school production. He then started saying that he was not as confident about getting work after graduation as he once was. Ruben again jumped in offering false reassurance, but did not validate Ray's feelings or let him explore them further. I said, "Ray was sharing something very scary with the group, something that probably all of you have thought about—about not making it professionally. Ruben, you offered him support, but at the same time, you didn't let Ray really express how he was feeling. I've noticed that this happens quite a bit. I wonder if it might be really hard for you (looking at the group) to hear these feelings because they bring up your own fears of not making it." I said this last sentence to the whole group because I realized Ruben's role as the gatekeeper was serving a purpose for him as well as the group as a whole. The group acknowledged what I had said through some head nodding and some verbal confirmations of, "I think you're right." Although I was pleased that this happened, I knew that it was only the first step in getting the group to tolerate this type of discussion.

12/4: I shared my own feelings with the group, hoping to model for them and encourage them to do the same.

I spent some time between our meetings and tried to "tune in" to what the specific feelings might be that the group experiences around fear of not making it. Bernie was telling the group that he begin singing at eight years old and, ever since, it is all he has wanted to do. I said, "Listening to you say this makes me realize just how important performing is for all of you. Sometimes when I listen to you guys talk, I get a little scared, thinking what would happen if you didn't make it." After a moment of silence, John said, "I don't know what I would do, maybe I would be a minister like my father. I think I could be good at it." Ray responded, "But, is that what you really want to do?" Bernie then spoke: "I know what I would do." Everyone turned towards him. He said, "I would kill myself. I wouldn't know what else to do. I love to sing and it's really all I know how to do." Ruben responded to Bernie's statement, "You could always teach." I felt that this did not validate Bernie's feelings and it was Ruben's attempt to move away from them. I then said to Ruben, "I wonder if it is particularly difficult for you to think about this because it is so close for you, being a senior this year." He denied that this was the case, and I backed off. Unsure of what to say next, I turned my attention back to Bernie. He was able to elaborate on his feelings and feel supported by other group members. I attempted to encourage mutual aid in the group. I asked the group if others had experienced what Bernie was describing. John said that he feels similar to Bernie and added that, because of the rigorous practice sessions, he fears that he may be losing his desire to play and often feels like he is "just going through the motions." Bernie and Ray agreed that this is also what they fear most. A lengthy discussion followed on this fear of losing their desire for their art.

12/4: Hoping that someone else would do it, I failed to call Ruben's behavior to the group's attention.

I felt the group was doing good work on exploring these feelings. It then appeared that Ruben shifted the discussion by talking about his girlfriend. He said that he thinks she is beautiful but that he is not as attracted to her as he used to be. He went on to say that he is also having trouble motivating himself to practice. He said, "I'm just not into it." Initially, I thought that this was a change in the topic, but then felt that it could be tied into the previous discussion. I commented to Ruben that, "It sounds like you feel you are losing your passion." He looked pensive and replied, "Yes, that's exactly how I feel." I then said, "That seems to be a theme today, it sounds a lot like what we were talking about earlier." Ruben seemed to really appreciate this connection and was able to say, "I guess what I'm feeling isn't that different from what you guys are."

12/4: I attempted to connect what was going on in the room to the feelings.

Once Ruben had started to make this connection, I tried to get him to recognize further the connection between his feelings and how he acts in the group. I said, "it seems that this is a very difficult subject for you to tolerate. Usually when the group begin to talk about it you seem eager to change the subject." Ruben replied, "Well, I'm the only senior here, and after this year I'm on my own. Sometimes I'm glad to be getting out of school, but other times—I'm not so glad." Ray then said to Ruben, "That must be really hard. I still have another year after this one and I'm already scared." Ruben showed some acceptance to this by nodding, but I still sensed that he had the need to see himself as different from the rest of the group. This is most likely due to the fact that he is unable, at this time, to confront the feelings that the rest of the group is expressing.

4. Current Status of the Problem

Ruben's relationship with the rest of the group has improved a great deal. The group has learned to regulate itself quite well, needing less intervention from the leader with regard to Ruben's monopolizing behavior. Ruben has made an obvious effort to listen more and speak less. On two separate occasions, when he did start to monopolize again, one of the group members called it to his attention. He was able to recognize it and stop without getting angry or defensive. As for his role as gatekeeper, we have made less progress. The group still needs an occasional diversion away from difficult feelings, and Ruben usually takes the lead. However, the group has been increasingly more able to tolerate my intervening and calling it to their attention. During our most recent session, John, noticing that I was about to speak, said, "I know, we're doing it again." The group laughed in recognition of being caught in flight. This told me that they were becoming more aware of their actions in relation to their feelings.

5. Specific Next Steps

1. I will try to become more aware of my own feelings in the group and to use them to tune in to what is going on for the other group members.
2. I will encourage the group members to confront each other more, and allow them to engage less in the illusion of work.
3. I will continue to work on my skills of acknowledging my own feelings and expressing them in the group.
4. I will continue to confront the group directly on issues of flight.
5. I plan to take more chances with making my observations known to the group. I will say what my hunches are at the time they are happening.
6. I will begin to reach for the feelings behind the feelings to help the group members learn to better identify and express their own feelings.

CHAPTER SUMMARY

In this chapter, we have examined a number of common examples of individual roles in the group, exploring the worker's helping role in relation to them. The concept of social role has helped to explain patterned reactions by scapegoats, deviants, internal leaders, gatekeepers, defensive, quiet, and monopolizing members. In each case, as we examined the individual, we found that the view of the group as a dynamic system forced us to attempt to understand the individual member in terms of the dynamics of the group. In the next chapter, we will explore in more detail the dynamics of working with this second client, the organism called the group-as-a-whole.

GLOSSARY

Ability to tolerate deviant behavior and to reach for the underlying message A skill that enables the worker to understand deviant behavior and to attempt to reach for the message behind it.

Deviant member The client who acts significantly differently from other clients in the system (e.g., family, group) but may actually be sending an indirect signal of feelings and concerns on behalf of the other clients.

Dynamic system A system in which the behavior of all participants in the system (staff and clients) affects and is affected by the behavior of all other members of the system.

External leader. The social worker, who is a part of the group but at the same time derives authority from an external source (the sponsoring agency).

Gatekeeper A group member who may intervene to distract the group each time the discussion gets close to a painful subject.

Internal leader A member (or members) of the group whose authority comes from the group itself. Different internal leaders may emerge to deal with specific issues.

Monopolizer A member of a group who talks a great deal and appears to monopolize the conversation. Usually, someone who does not listen well to others.

Quasi-stationary social equilibrium A term used by Lewin (1951a, p. 254) to describe a stage in the change process at which a person is in balance with his or her social environment. This balance can be upset by external or internal forces, resulting in a state of "disequilibrium" that can lead to change and a new quasi-stationary equilibrium.

Quiet member A member of the group who does not speak over a period of time.

Role In the psychodynamic frame of reference, the term is used here to represent an adaptational unit of personality in action.

Scapegoat A member of a group who is attacked, verbally or physically, by other members who project onto the member their own negative feelings about themselves. The scapegoat role is often interactive in nature, with the scapegoat fulfilling a functional role in the group.

NOTES

1. For other examples of role in the group, see L. Shulman, "A Game-Model Theory of Inter-Personal Relations." *Social Work, 13* (1968): 37–43; R. Linton, *The Study of Man* (New York: Appleton-Century-Crofts, 1936), pp. 113–19; K.D. Benne and P. Sheats, "Functional Roles of Group Members," *Journal of Social Issues, 4* (1948): 41–49.

2. Douglas's combining of his scholarly interest in the origins and theory of scapegoating with his understanding of group process and group practice makes for one of the most interesting and informative discussions of the topic currently available.

3. For discussions of the scapegoat role, see L. Shulman, "Scapegoats, Group Workers, and the Pre-Emptive Intervention," *Social Work, 12* (April 1967): 37–43; F. K. Taylor and J. H. Rey, "The Scapegoat Motif in Society and Its Manifestations in a Therapeutic Group," *International Journal of Psychoanalysis, 34* (1953): 253–264; A. Gitterman, "Group Work in the Public Schools" in *The Practice of Group Work*, ed. W. Schwartz and S. Zalba (New York: Columbia University Press, 1971), pp. 45–72.

4. The Boston Model of the stages of group development is discussed in detail in Chapter 14.

5. See E. Rubington and M. S. Weinberg, *Deviance: The Interactionist Perspective* (Toronto: Collier-Macmillan, 1968).

6. For a discussion of leadership, see L. Petrullo and B. M. Bass, *Leadership and Interpersonal Behavior* (New York: Holt, Rinehart and Winston, 1961).

14

Working with the Group as the Second Client

In this chapter we will take a more detailed look at the group as an entity, exploring its properties and dynamics and developing a strategy for the worker's intervention. The model of an "organism" is used to depict the group as something more than the sum of its parts. Next, we will trace the tasks of the group as it attempts to deal with the relationships of members to the worker (the authority theme), relationships between members (the intimacy theme), and its internal structure (e.g., culture, communication patterns, roles). Finally, we will discuss the task of the group in relation to its environment. The role of the worker in assisting this second client—the group—is described and illustrated using examples from practice.

It is not easy to describe this second client called the group-as-a-whole. In part, the difficulty comes from the fact that one cannot actually *see* the properties that describe a group. When we watch a group in action, what we are seeing is a collection of individuals. Compare this to a classroom chair. When we are asked to describe its properties, visual references such as materials (plastic, wood, chrome), parts (back, seat, legs), shape, size, and so on, immediately come to mind. With a group, it is more difficult to describe the properties because most of them cannot be seen. For example, **cohesion** in a group can be defined as a bond between members—a sense of identification with each other and with the group-as-a-whole. An observer cannot see "cohesion," but if we observe a group for a time, we can see all of the members *acting as if* the group were cohesive. Shared norms of proper behavior and taboo subjects that are not to be discussed are other examples of properties of groups. We can't see a norm or a taboo, but we can see a pattern of behavior from which we can infer that a norm or taboo exists. Our focus in this chapter will be on the unique properties that help to define the group. After reviewing this chapter, the reader will find it easier to observe and describe this second client, the group-as-a-whole.

A large body of group theory and research is available to the practitioner who wishes to better understand group dynamics. Our focus in this chapter is not on describing this body of literature, but rather on the practitioner's use of theoretical models and research results to develop his or her own integrated model of group practice. To illustrate this process, I have selected three classic theoretical models and one relatively new framework for discussion in relation to the group tasks: developmental (Bennis and Shepard, 1956); structural (Bion, 1961) environmental (Homans, 1950); and self in relation (Schiller, 1993; Fedele, 1994). As will be seen in the discussion, each of these theories has ideas relevant to all of the group tasks.

THE GROUP AS AN ORGANISM

When attempting to describe something as complex as a group, it is helpful to use a model. A **model** is a concrete, symbolic representation of an abstract phenomenon. To develop a model for describing a group, we must find an appropriate metaphor. Two common metaphors are the machine and the organism. Many theorists interested in human social systems have adopted the **organismic model** as the most appropriate. The choice of an organism rather than a machine as a model reflects the organism's capacity for growth and emergent behavior. These terms, *growth* and *emergent behavior*, describe a process in which a system transcends itself and creates something new that is more than just the simple sum of its parts.

To apply this idea to the group, we need to identify what is created when a number of people and a worker are brought together that goes beyond the sum of each member's contribution. What properties exist that are unique descriptions of the group, rather than descriptions of the individual members? An example of such a property is the creation of a sense of common purpose shared by all the members of the group. This common purpose is a catalyst for the development of a tie that binds the group members together. Group culture is a second example. As the group process begins, activities in the group are governed by a group culture made up of a number of factors including accepted norms of behavior. In a first session, the group culture generally reflects the culture of the larger society from which the members have been drawn. As sessions continue, and with the intervention of the worker, this culture can change, allowing new norms to emerge and govern the activities of the members. Thus, common interests and group norms of behavior are two examples of properties of the group that transcend the simple sum of its parts, the individual members.

A third example is the group's relationship with its environment. As the group is influenced by its environment—for example, the agency, school, or hospital—or the worker as a representative of the agency, it must develop adaptive behaviors to maintain itself. This pattern of adaptive behavior is yet another example of a property of the group.

To summarize, one cannot actually see a group as an entity. That is why a model, such as the organism, is helpful. What one can see, however, are the activities of a group of people who appear to be influenced by this entity called the group. For example, when group purpose is clear, one can explain the actions of the group members as contributions in pursuit of that purpose. Again, the behaviors of the members are influenced by group pressures, expectations, and the members' sense of belonging. The fact that a member's behavior changes as a result of believing in the existence of the group makes the group real. In the balance of this chapter, we will refer to the group as an entity, employing the organism as a metaphor, and will focus on the group's developmental and environmental tasks.

DEVELOPMENTAL TASKS

Two major group tasks have already been discussed without having been specifically described as such. It might be helpful at this point to review these as illustrations of how a group can have tasks that differ from the specific tasks of each member. In the chapter on group beginnings we addressed what could be called the group's *formation* tasks. The group needed to develop a working contract reflecting the individual members' needs as well as the service stake of the sponsoring agency. In addition, a group consensus needed to be developed. This consensus reflected the common concerns shared by members as well as agreement as to where the work might start. Reaching consensus on the work is a task unique to work with multiple clients (group, family, couples, and so on), since individual clients simply begin where they wish, with no need to reach a consensus with other clients. Initial clarification of mutual obligations and expectations was also a part of the group's formation task. The effectiveness of the group depends upon how well it accomplishes these formation tasks. The skills of the worker in helping the group to work on these formation tasks were described as contracting skills.

A second critical group task involves *meeting individual members' needs*. For the group to survive, it must have individual members. Members feel a sense of belonging and develop a stake in the work of the group when they can perceive that their own, related needs are being met. If these needs cease to be met, then members will simply drop out of the group, either by not attending or not participating. In the chapter on the work phase of the group, we saw how easy it can be for the group to miss the offered concerns of a member or to turn away from these concerns when they hit the group members too hard. In still other examples, individual members did not immediately see the relation between the work of the group and their own sense of urgency. In the chapter on the individual and the group, we saw how members can play functional roles in the group, some of which cut them off from being able to use the group to meet their own needs. In each of these cases, workers were shown attempting to help the members use the group more effectively, or helping the group reach out and offer mutual aid more effectively, and usually doing both simultaneously. All these efforts were directed toward helping the group with its task of meeting individual members' needs. Thus, the tasks of formation and meeting individual members' needs must be addressed if the group is to grow and survive. Other sets of tasks linked to the developmental work of the group are those in which the group works on its relationship to the worker (the **authority theme**) and relationships between members (the **intimacy theme**). Schwartz (1971) describes these two critical tasks as follows:

> In the culture of the group two main themes come to characterize the members' ways of working together: one, quite familiar to the caseworker, is the theme of authority in which the members are occupied with their relationship to the helping person and the ways in which this relationship is instrumental to their purpose; the other, more strange and threatening to the caseworker, is the theme of intimacy, in which the members are concerned with their internal relationships and the problems of mutual aid. It is the interplay of these factors—external authority and mutual interdependence—that provides much of the driving force of the group experience (p. 9).

The group's ability to deal with concerns related to authority and intimacy is closely connected to the development of a working culture: common interests and group norms of behavior. Finally, the group needs to develop a structure for work that will enable it to carry out its tasks effectively. For example, responsibilities may have to be shared through a division of labor, and roles may need to be assigned formally or informally.

These four major task areas—the relationship to the worker, the relationship between members, the development of a working culture, and the development of a structure for work—will be addressed in this chapter. Obviously, there is a great deal of overlapping of these tasks in that work on one area often includes work on the others. The division is somewhat artificial; nonetheless, it is helpful in the exposition of the argument. Discussion of these tasks will draw upon elements of group theory from four major models, focusing on constructs that seem relevant. For example, Bennis and Shepard (1956) have addressed the themes of intimacy and authority in their model of group development, and a number of their key concepts are useful in explaining group process. Their observations, however, are based upon their work with laboratory training groups (T-groups), in which graduate students studied group dynamics using their own experiences as a group. As a result, a number of ideas in their theory may be group-specific and will not apply to groups of the type discussed in this book. Our analysis will illustrate how a practitioner can use what he or she likes from a good theory without adopting it whole.

Dealing with the Relationship to the Worker

In the early phase of the group development it needs to sort out its relationship to the worker. Much of the beginning energy will be devoted to this theme. An early question has to do with issues of control. The dynamics of "transference" and "countertransference" present in work with individuals are also found within the group context. Members will bring their stereotypes or fantasies about group leaders to the first meeting, and these will generate a fear of a powerful authority person "doing something" to them. Thus, in my description of the first session of the couples' group in Chapter 10, the 70-year-old member named Lou raised the authority issue by sharing his negative experiences with helping people. Open discussion of the implications of this issue for the present workers helped the group members to relax and become more actively involved in the session. But such an open discussion does not "resolve" the question. In fact, the issue of the relationship to the worker is never really resolved in the sense that all the feelings are worked out and all the questions answered. What one *does* achieve is the ability of the group and the worker to address this issue openly as it emerges. The comfort of the group may increase, but the theme remains. In the second session of the couples' group, the members were watching to see if I would carry out the role I had described in the first session. Once again, Lou signaled the members' concern about this issue.

> One couple was presenting a problem that they were having that involved the husband's grown children from another marriage. I noticed each spouse was telling the group things about the other, rather than speaking directly to each other. I interrupted Frank and suggested he speak directly to his wife. After a noticeable hesitation, he began to speak to her, but soon returned to speaking to me. I interrupted him again. Once again, he seemed slightly thrown by my action.
>
> As this was going on, I noticed that Lou was looking distressed, staring at the floor, and covering his mouth with his hand. After watching this for a time, I reached for the message. "Lou, you look like you have something to say." He responded, "No, that's all right. I can wait till later." I said, "I have the feeling it's important, and I think it has something to do with me." I had been feeling uncomfortable but unaware why. Lou said. "Well, if you want to hear it now, OK. Every time you interrupt Frank that way, I think he loses his train of thought. And this business of telling him to speak to Jane is just like the stuff I described last week." I was surprised by what he said and remained quiet while I took it in.

Frank said, "You know, he's right. You do throw my line of thought every time you interrupt that way." I said, "I guess I ended up doing exactly the kind of thing I said last week I would try not to do. I have not explained to you, Frank, why I think it might help to talk directly with your wife rather than to me. I guess you must feel my comments, since you don't really understand why I'm suggesting this, as sort of pushing you around." Frank said, "Well, a bit." Lou said, "That's exactly what I mean." I responded, "I won't be perfect, Lou. I will also make mistakes. That's why it's so important that you call me on it, the way you just did. Only why wait until I ask?" Lou said, "It's not easy to call you; you're the leader." I said, "I think I can appreciate that, only you can see how it would speed things up if you did."

This second week's discussion was even more important than the first because the members had a chance to see me confronted with a mistake and not only acknowledging it but encouraging Lou to be even more direct. The point made was that they did have rights and that they should not let my authority get in the way. Of course the reader may be thinking it would be hard to reach for such negative feedback, or to encourage it, when one is just beginning as a group leader. That's the irony of the situation; one needs this kind of honesty from group members most when one is least confident and prepared to hear it. Beginning group workers should expect to miss these signals in sessions, but as their confidence grows, they should start to reach for the negatives later in the same session or in the session that follows.

There were many other times when similar discussions arose, for example, about the agenda for our work. When I appeared to return to an area of work without checking on the group's interest, members would participate in an obvious illusion of work. When I challenged the illusion, we were able to discuss why it was harder for them simply to let me know when they thought I was leading them away from their concerns. Issues of control also emerged in connection with responsibility for the effectiveness of the work. The authority theme is one that the worker must also raise with the group members. In this example, there had been an unusually long period when one couple was endlessly discussing an issue without getting to the point. I could see the reactions in the group and inquired as to what was going on.

> Fran responded by saying it was getting boring and she was waiting for me to do something. Since this was a middle-phase session, I found myself angry that everyone was waiting for me. I said, "How come you are waiting for me to do something? This is your group, you know, and I think you could take this responsibility, too."

The resulting discussion revealed that members felt it was risky to take each other on, and so they left it to me. We were able to sort out, for a time, that members, too, needed to take responsibility for the group's effectiveness. These excerpts help to illustrate the two sides to the members' feelings: on the one hand, they were afraid of the worker and the worker's authority, and on the other, they wanted the worker to take responsibility for the group. These two sets of feelings are attributed by Bennis and Shepard (1956) to two types of personalities in the group: the **dependent member** and the **counterdependent member**. They believe that the question of dependency is a major area of uncertainty for members and that the first major phase of group development, the **dependence phase**, involves work on this question. They describe three sub-phases within this first phase. In the first subphase, **dependence-flight**, the group is led by the dependent leaders, who seek to involve the worker more actively in control of the group. In the second subphase, **counterdependence-flight**, the counterdependent leaders move in to attempt to take over the group. They describe much anger towards the trainer in this phase.[1] Two subgroups develop, one arguing for structure and the other against it.

In the third subphase, **resolution-catharsis**, group leadership is assumed by members who are **unconflicted** or independent. According to the authors, this "overthrow" of the trainer leads to each member taking responsibility for the group: the trainer is no longer seen as "magical," and the power struggles are replaced by work on shared goals. While many of the specifics of the model are restricted to the particular groups observed, the general outline of this struggle over dependency can be applied to all groups.

Issues of control are just one aspect of the general theme of relationship with the worker. A second area concerns the worker's place as an outsider to the group. This is particularly noticed in those groups where the worker has not had the life experience central to the group members' themes of concern. For instance, in a group for parents of children who have been diagnosed as hyperactive, the question of whether the worker who has no children can understand them and their problems is a variation on the similar question raised in the discussion of the beginning phase in work with individuals. The following excerpt illustrates this aspect of the authority theme struggle in the group context:

> Discussion got back again to causes of hyperactivity. Ann, who had thought it was hereditary, explained that her husband thought that he had been hyperactive as a child, except that nobody gave him the title. Marilyn said that her husband had also said that he had been like her son and had felt that her son would grow out of it. The group picked up on this idea and seemed to like the possibility. I was asked by Betty what I thought. I said I didn't know the answer, but that from what I did know, not enough research has been done. The group began throwing questions at me, related to general conditions, medications, and I couldn't answer them. I admitted that I knew very little about hyperactivity. I was certainly nowhere near being the experts that they were.
>
> Someone asked if I had children. I said that I didn't. Beatrice wondered what work I had done with hyperactive children and extended this to children with other problems. I answered as honestly as I could. She wondered whether I was overwhelmed by their feelings. I replied that she and others present were really concerned about how I felt towards them, and whether I really understood what it felt like to be the mother of a hyperactive child. She agreed. I added that last week when I had said I was feeling overwhelmed, I was really getting into what it felt like to have such a child. It was pointed out to me that I was the only one in the group who didn't have a hyperactive child, that I was really the outsider. Beatrice offered to lend me her son for a weekend, so that I could really see what it was like. Everyone laughed. (I think they were delighted at this.) I said that they were telling me that it was important that I understand what it's like, and I wondered whether I was coming across as not understanding. They didn't think so. I said that the more they talked, the better the feeling I got about what they were going through. Towards the end of this there was a lot of subgroup talking going on, and I waited (thankful for the break).

The third area of the authority theme has to do with the group's reaction to the worker as a person who makes demands. For the group to be effective, the worker must do more than contract clearly and be empathic. The group will often come up against obstacles, many of which are related to the group members' ambivalence about discussion of painful areas. As the worker makes demands, negative feelings will inevitably be generated on the part of the group members. If the worker is good at what he or she does, there should be times when the group members are angry at the worker for refusing to let them off the hook. This is one side of the clients' feelings towards someone in authority who makes demands upon them. The other side, of course, is the positive feelings associated with the worker's empathic nature and the fact that the worker cares enough about the group to make these demands. The angry feelings also need to be expressed; otherwise they can go under the surface and emerge in unconscious expressions such as general apathy. Of course the worker has to feel comfortable in the role to be willing to deal with this negative feedback. In the same group of parents of hyperactive children, the worker picked up the signals of this reaction and reached directly for the negative feedback.

> Millie began talking about her son's learning disability. After a little while I cut in and asked the group what was happening here, to the conversation and to the members. (My feeling was that they were way off the track again.) Marilyn said that they had gotten off the subject again, they were supposed to be discussing how they felt, and their attitudes. I added that indeed this was what was happening; it seemed that they were unable to keep on talking about themselves. Millie and Marilyn thought that it was probably because it was hard to accept the fact that they get angry. I started to say something in response to this, and I noticed that Claudette kind of sighed and made a face. I pointed this out to her, and suggested that perhaps she didn't want to discuss some of the things I thought they should. She nodded.
>
> I told the group that perhaps this was a good time to talk about how they felt about my forcing them to look at themselves, to keep on the subject, and to talk about what they didn't want to talk about. I said that they must have some feelings about me; perhaps every time I open up my mouth and point this out to them and try to refocus them, they say to themselves, "Why the hell doesn't she get off our backs and let us talk about something easy?"
>
> Beatrice said that she had the feeling that was true, every time I brought them back to talking about how they felt, she could feel people moving back in their chairs, as if they were looking for a place to hide, and then they hide by talking about school, teachers, and so on. She said that her own behavior has changed considerably with these sessions, and although it has been hard, she's been able to see herself a little more clearly. But not everyone in the group has moved at the same pace; some people are really changing their attitudes because they are willing to risk and look at themselves, and others still hide behind the facade. I said that I agreed. Often I felt how terribly hard it was for them to face things, and I kept pushing them at it. Sometimes I pushed them hard, like two sessions ago. And then other times I feel it is too hard, and like last week, I hardly said anything and really let them talk about anything and everything. I don't think that is being helpful to them if I let them do that, even though I can feel their hurt so much, and my own gut reaction is, "I should let you alone; it hurts too much to look at yourselves." People nodded in agreement.

A fourth issue here is the need for the group to come to grips with the reality of the worker's limitations. Members hope that the worker, or some other expert, will be able to solve their problems. This is, in part, a result of the dependency of the group emerging. When the group members realize the worker has no "solutions," then their own work really begins. However, this realization is painful for the members and often for the workers as well. At the end of one particularly painful and depressing discussion in the same parents' group when the members recognized that the drugs and the professionals were not going to "make the problem go away," a member appealed to the worker to cheer them up.

> We were way over our time, and I started to sum up some of the feelings that came out today. I said that they had really been saying all along how helpless they felt that they couldn't do anything to help the children, and how hopeless they were feeling, that there wasn't a solution for them. Marilyn said to me that that's how they felt, depressed and helpless. She said that I always came up with something at the end to make them feel better. I had better come up with something really good today, because they needed it. I said that I was feeling the same way, thinking to myself, "What can I say that's going to take the depression and hurt away?" I told her that I didn't have a magic formula, that I wished that I could suggest something. I knew how much she and all of them wished that I could help them with a solution. Rose said that they were feeling depressed, but they shouldn't blame themselves. I said that perhaps part of the depression was related to the fact that they themselves hadn't been able to help their children more, and they felt terrible about it. She seemed to be so terribly depressed, more than ever before. I know because that's exactly how I felt.
>
> There was not too much discussion on the way out, as I was at a loss to know what to say to them (usually we joke around a bit). Marilyn said to me I let her down, I didn't come up with my little blurb to pep them up. I said that she was feeling very depressed and she looked to me to say something to make things easier. I said that she wanted a solution, and I didn't have one. She said to me that perhaps I had, and I was holding back. I said to her that she was very disappointed in me that I hadn't been able to make things easier. I wished that I did have the magic solution that they all wanted so desperately, but I didn't have one. After this, the members left.

A final aspect of the authority theme requires the group to deal with their reactions to the worker as a caring and giving person. The group members watch as the worker relates to them and to the others in the group. They can see the pain in the worker's face if he or she feels the hurt deeply and, after a while, they can sense the genuineness of the empathy. This side of the worker provokes powerful responses in the group, and a mutual flow of positive affect is the result. An interesting discussion in my couples' group[2] illustrates the awareness of group members of this issue and the importance of this aspect of the authority theme. It was the session before the Christmas break (the eighth), and one member arrived late and distraught. She sat down in the empty chair to the right of me, and for the first time in the group, she shared a frightening problem she was facing. Until then, the member had appeared to be "without problems," since her husband was the identified patient. I comforted her during the telling of her story and tried to help her, verbally, nonverbally, and through touching the back of her hand, communicating my empathic responses to her feelings. The group also reached out with support. In the second part of the session, after the immediate issue had been somewhat resolved and the member was in better shape, we carried out a midpoint evaluation of the group. In discussing the way in which we worked as a group, one of the members raised the authority theme.

> Fran said, "I knew that this was Jane's night to get help the minute she walked in the door." (Jane was the member who had been crying.) When I inquired how she knew, she said, "Because she sat in the crying chair." She went on to point out that all of the

people who had cried in sessions, four of the ten group members, had all sat down in that chair at the beginning of the session. In fact, some had sat apart from their spouses for the first time in the group. Other members nodded in recognition of the accuracy of Fran's observation. I inquired if they had any thoughts about why that was so. Rose said, "Because that's the chair next to you, and we sit there to get some support when the going gets rough." I responded, "Could you talk a bit about what it is about me that causes you to sit there or feel I can support you? This is important as part of our evaluation, but also, it can tell us something about what it is you might want from each other."

The request for specifics was designed to encourage discussion of the members' feelings about the worker reaching out to them with caring. In addition, as is often the case, the process in the group can serve to assist group members in understanding their own relationships more clearly. The record continues:

Louise said, "It's because we can feel free to say anything to you, and you won't judge us. We can tell you our feelings." Rose continued, "And we know you really feel our hurt. It's not phony—you really care." Lou said, "It's safe next to you. We can share our innermost feelings and know that you won't let us get hurt." As I listened to the members, I felt myself deeply moved by the affect in their voices, and I shared that with them. "You know, it means a great deal to me to have you feel that way—that you can sense my feelings for you. I have grown to care about you quite a bit. It's surprising to me, sometimes, just how hard things in this group hit me—just how important you really have become."

The authority theme is a two-way street, and the worker will have as much feeling towards the members as they have towards the worker. The counter-transference dynamics described in Chapter 4 are also present in the group. These feelings need to be made a part of the discussion. The honest feelings of the worker, freely expressed, are often the key to aiding the group as it comes to grips with its relationship to the worker.

In summary, some aspects of the authority theme to be dealt with during the life of the group include the worker's control, responsibility, and status as an outsider and the group's reactions to the worker's demands, limitations, and caring. Although the phases in which a group deals with issues are never neat and orderly, one can detect a pattern: as the issues of authority are dealt with, the group becomes more ready to turn to its second major developmental task, the relationships between members (the intimacy theme).

Dealing with the Relationships Between Members

Once again, Bennis and Shepard's (1956) theory can provide some helpful insights. In addition to concerns about dependency, a second major area of internal uncertainty for group members relates to **interdependence**. This has to do with questions of intimacy and the group members' concerns about how close they wish to get to each other. In Bennis and Shepard's model, the group moves from the first phase, concerned with dependence and marked by a preoccupation with authority relations, to a second phase concerned with interdependence and characterized by issues of peer-group relations. The two sets of member personalities that emerge in relation to this issue are the *overpersonal* and *counterpersonal* group members. These parallel the dependent and the counterdependent personalities of the first phase. Once again, three subphases are identified: the **enchantment-flight** subphase, in which good feelings abound and efforts are directed towards healing wounds; the **disenchantment-flight** subphase, in which the counterpersonals take over from the overpersonals in reaction to the growing intimacy; and finally, the **consensual validation** subphase, in which the unconflicted members once again provide the leadership needed for the group to move to a new level of work characterized by honest communication between members.

While the specifics of the Bennis and Shepard model relate most directly to the dynamics of T-groups (training groups), ambivalence toward honest communications between members can be observed in most groups. After dealing with the authority theme, the group often moves through a phase marked by positive feelings between members, not at all unlike the enchantment-flight subphase. As the work deepens and members move beyond simply supporting each other and begin to confront each other, more negative feelings and reactions are engendered. As members begin to rub up against each other in their work, these feelings are quite natural and should be an expected part of the process. However, group members have learned from their experiences in other situations (family, groups, classes) that it is not polite to talk directly about negative reactions to the behavior of others. This conditioning is part of the worker's experience as well, and it is not unusual for the worker and the group to get angry at members but nonetheless withhold their reactions.

Without direct feedback from the group members, it is difficult for individuals to understand their impact upon the group, to learn from that understanding, and to develop new ways of coping. It is the worker's task to draw these interpersonal obstacles to the attention of the members and to help the group develop the ability to discuss them. Workers often fear "opening up" discussion of the angry feelings they sense in the group because they are concerned that things will "get out of hand," they will be overwhelmed, individuals will be hurt, and the life of the group will be threatened. Actually, the greatest threat to the life of the group is from over-politeness and the resulting illusion of work. The expression of angry feelings can free the caring and positive feelings that are also part of the intimacy of the group.

Of course, the worker needs to take care that the contract of the group does not get subverted so that the discussion becomes centered on intermember relationships, thereby losing sight of the original reason the group was formed. This is one of the major criticisms of the type of groups (T-groups) studied by Bennis and Shepard. A second possibility to which the worker must be alert is that the member involved may attempt to use the group to deal with a personal pattern of behaving in groups, another attempt at subversion of group purpose.

In the following illustration from a counseling group for college students experiencing difficulty in adjusting to their first year on campus, one member developed a pattern of relating in which she consistently cut off other members, did not really listen to them, and attempted to raise her own questions and concerns directly with the worker. The worker sensed she was relating only to him. The other group members showed elevating nonverbal signals of anger at her behavior that she did not perceive. The record starts after a particularly striking example of this behavior.

> I noticed all of the group members had physically turned away as Louise was talking. Their faces spoke loudly of their negative reaction. I decided to raise the issue: "There is something happening right now that seems to happen a lot in this group. Louise is asking a lot of questions, cutting some people off as she does, and I sense that the rest of you aren't too happy about that. Am I right?" There was silence for a moment, and Louise, for the first time, was looking directly at the other group members. I said, "I know this isn't easy to talk about, but I feel if we can't be honest with each other

about how we are working together, we don't stand a chance of being an effective group. And I think Louise would want to know if this was true. Am I right about that, Louise?" She answered, "I didn't realize I was doing this. Is it true?" Francine responded, "Frankly, Louise, I have been sitting here getting angrier and angrier at you by the minute. You really don't seem to listen to anyone else in the group."

The worker opened the door by pointing out the pattern in the group and breaking the taboo against direct acknowledgment of an interpersonal problem. This freed members to explore this sensitive area.

After Francine's words there was a moment of silence, and then Louise began to cry, saying, "You know, I seem to be doing this in all areas of my life. All of my friends are angry at me, my boyfriend won't speak to me, and now I've done it again. What's wrong with me?" The group seemed stunned by her expression of feeling.

Since this was the first real discussion of an interpersonal issue in the group, it was important that the worker clarify the boundary of the discussion, using the contract as his guide. The group felt guilty, and Louise felt a bit overwhelmed. The worker acknowledged both of these feelings:

"I guess you all must feel quite concerned over how strongly this is hitting Louise?" Members nodded their heads, but no one spoke. I continued, "Louise, I'm afraid this has hit you really hard. I should make it clear that we won't be able to talk about the other areas in your life that you are finding tough right now—that wouldn't be appropriate in this group. I'd be glad to talk to you after the group, however, and maybe, if you want, we could explore other avenues of help. For right now, could you stick to what is happening in this group? How come you seem to be so eager to ask all the questions and why do you seem so cut off from the group?" Louise was thoughtful for a moment and then said to the group, "I guess it's just that I'm feeling really concerned about what's going on here at school and I'm trying to get some help as quickly as possible. I want to make sure I get as much from Sid [the worker] as I can." I paused and looked to the group. Francine responded, "You know, that's probably why I got so mad at you, because I'm the same way, and I'm sitting here feeling the same feelings—I want to get as much help as I can as well." Louise: "Well, at least you were straight with me, and I appreciate that. It's much worse when you can sense something is wrong, but people won't level with you."

After the exchange between Louise and Francine, the group seemed to relax. Louise's readiness to accept negative feedback without defensiveness had an impact on the group. In other circumstances, members may feel more vulnerable and would need all the help the worker could give in terms of support. When Louise was able to express the underlying feelings she experienced, other group members were able to identify with her, and this freed their affect and concern. Louise could sense their concern for her, making it easier for her to feel more a part of the group rather than relating only to the worker. The worker proceeded to underline the importance of honest communication between members and then guarded against preoccupation with process by reaching for the implicit work hinted at in the exchange.

"I think it was really tough just now, for Louise and the rest of you. However, if the group is going to be helpful, I think we are going to have to learn how to be honest with each other. As Louise pointed out, it can be tougher not to hear sometimes. I think it is also important that we not lose the threads of our work as we go along. I noticed that both Louise and Francine mentioned their urgency about getting help with their problems right now. Could we pick up by being a bit more specific about what those problems are?"

Francine accepted the invitation by expressing a concern she was having about a specific course. From this point on, Louise was more attentive to the group and appeared a good deal more relaxed. The few times she interrupted, she good-naturedly caught herself and apologized. The worker spoke to her after the session and arranged an appointment for personal counseling. A change in the group was also evident as members appeared more involved and energetic in the discussion.

It is important for a group to develop a climate of trust that will allow members to lower their defenses. A powerful barrier to trust can be raised and maintained by what is left unsaid by members. Group members can sense both positive and negative reactions by other members. The effect of these reactions is increased when they remain beneath the surface. On the other hand, open expression of these feelings can free members, who will feel more confident when they will know where they stand with the group.

In the following example involving a group for fathers whose children are attending a special clinic for children with behavior problems, the worker had noted a pattern of withdrawal by group members. He had observed indirect cues (such as facial expressions) of feelings toward Mr. Abrams, who had not shared his problems as the others had done. In addition, Mr. Wilson, who had spoken often, had hinted that he feared he might have been speaking too much. At the start of this session, there were a number of indirect cues leading the worker to believe members were questioning the way the group operated. After a dispirited opening marked by a rambling discussion, the worker asked the group members to reflect on the way they worked as a group, explaining that he felt the discussion tended to be "impersonal" at times and that he thought they had reactions to each other's ways of participating.

> Mr. Wilson quickly challenged the view that the group should be personal. When I asked him to say a little bit more about this, he explained that he felt he could come here and talk about these things very objectively, but then he was pretty sure that he would never see these men during the week. He was supported very strongly in his feelings about the "impersonal" nature of the group by Mr. Lewis, Mr. Abrams, and Mr. Russel, with Mr. Moran playing a quiet, listening role. Mr. Moran still seemed to be a little bit confused about where this discussion would lead but said that he would prefer to sort of listen until he got the "hang of things." I encouraged each of the three men, in addition to Mr. Wilson, to talk about how they saw this. All said that there was not much investment of feeling in the group, although each of them said that they certainly liked everyone who came and really looked forward to the sessions. At this point I wondered whether in addition to the feelings of liking and friendship, there might also be some feelings of dislike or perhaps some people whom they liked more than others. Mr. Russel was the first to comment on this, bringing out a great deal of his feeling, while looking at Mr. Abrams, about people who just rambled on about subjects and on the other hand persons who could really talk about themselves but also give a lot of opportunity for other people to identify with them. He said that his preference was for the latter person in the group, and he could recognize that there were times when he wished the former would keep quiet.

Mr. Wilson responded to this by saying that certainly there were differences in how much one participated or what one thought of somebody's participation but that he didn't see this as really being based on competition of any sort. He pointed out that for him there were various ways of participating, that it wasn't always a matter of talking or not talking about one's own problem but that one could sit back and listen and get perspective from the way in which other people spoke about their problems. He said that at the beginning, particularly, this allowed him to get help without exposing problem areas that he felt he could not share with the group. Gradually, he said, as he felt more at ease in the group and really could see where it was helpful to him, he began to share some of these problems as well. He pointed out that of course his feeling of liking was for a person who could help by talking or commenting on problems which he brought up and that he felt this was rather selfish of him, but that after all this was why he was coming to the clinic.

After Mr. Wilson had spoken, the worker asked if what he had said was true for the others as well—they weren't always motivated to talk about their own problems, and there were times when they could gain by listening to others. All the members agreed verbally. Mr. Wilson continued on the question of the impersonality of the group, using as an example that he was not missed when he did not attend a session. He also raised his concern about "talking too much" and was surprised when one member contradicted him. It is just as important that group members give each other positive feedback and express their feelings of affection for each other as it is that they express negative feelings.

Mr. Wilson said that he was fairly confident that he wasn't really missed and that the group proceeded anyhow, even though when he was there he did a great deal of talking and that perhaps it was even better when he stayed away. To this, Mr. Russel, with a great deal of feeling, looked right at Mr. Wilson and said in a fairly strong and loud voice, "I miss you when you're not here, and I can tell when you're not here. It makes for a difference in what we talk about. It's not that I don't get anything when you're not here, because I do, but we talk about different things sometimes when you're not here." I pointed out that, as we talked, they were able to recognize that it was with a great deal of feeling that they came to the group and that these feelings were not related specifically to the content and that they had really an investment in each other as well as in the clinic.

Mr. Wilson again started off and reacted in a very surprised way to Mr. Russel's statement that he really had missed him and could see in looking back over his own participation in the group that he had similar feelings about people being present or not being present. Mr. Abrams, too, felt that there were differences in how he felt about other men in the group and that while he didn't want to talk specifically about which ones they were, he knew that this was so. He went on to say that, however, in spite of the difference, most of his feeling was in a positive direction and he did like most or all of the men in the group. Mr. Moran entered the discussion at this time, trying hard to make a point. When I recognized him, he said that he could now get an idea of what I had been driving at when I focused the discussion as I did on how people felt about each other in the group.

Mr. Moran continued by discussing his role in the group. He explained that he was quiet in the beginning because he had wanted to make sure that they might have some of the same feelings before he ventured his own opinion. He explained that, at this point, he felt they were enough like him that he was willing to jump in more quickly and risk his ideas.

There was further discussion, at the worker's request, of the topic of competition in the group that had been mentioned by Mr. Moran. Mr. Wilson once again raised his concerns about "talking too much," and the members reassured him that they were interested in what he had to say.

As the members of this group began to express some of the feelings they had towards their own participation and the participation of others, their honesty helped Mr. Abrams, a usually defensive member, to bring his problems to their attention for the first time. When all of these negative and positive feelings remained under the surface, they served to block the ability of the group members to develop a real sense of trust.

Mr. Abrams said that now that we had discussed what had happened in the group, he had something else he wanted to bring up. In a very sharp contrast, he said that as long as we were talking about feelings, he wanted the group's opinion about something that he was struggling with. He said that in his contacts with the clinic, he had been "accused" of withholding a great deal of his feeling, particularly in regard to his children. He wasn't quite sure about this and what effect it had on the children, but that he was just wondering if any of the others had ever felt the same way. When I asked what it was tonight that enabled him to ask the group this, Mr. Abrams replied that he sort of felt that all of the men would really understand and would be able to help him to look at this.

Mr. Russel, Mr. Lewis, and Mr. Wilson all reacted visibly to this, each looking up, Mr. Russel smiling, Mr. Lewis nodding his head, and Mr. Wilson leaning back in his chair and looking directly at Mr. Abrams. Mr. Russel responded first. With a broad grin and in a very pleased and warm tone, he welcomed Mr. Abrams to the group. When Mr. Abrams wondered what he meant by this, Mr. Russel went on to explain that it seemed that Mr. Abrams no longer had to hide the fact that he really had some problems of his own. Mr. Russel said that it seemed to him that any time Mr. Abrams had talked before this, he talked in a very general way and that it was really hard to feel that he had any real problems, but now it seemed that he was bringing them out into the open more. Mr. Lewis confirmed this, saying that if nothing else tonight, he could really tell that Mr. Abrams was concerned about his feelings with his children as well as "what the book says one should do."

Although previously unspoken, the group's feeling that Mr. Abrams was remaining outside their work was evident in their reactions to his comments. His lack of emotional and personal involvement had been an obstacle to the group's movement. By pointing out the need to discuss the way the members worked with each other and by holding the group to this discussion, the worker played a key role in helping the members to talk about their relationships. This freed Mr. Abrams and the other group members to risk discussing ideas in more intimate ways. As the next excerpt reveals, the connections between Mr. Abrams's feelings and those of the group became evident.

Mr. Wilson looked up, paused, and then asked Mr. Abrams if he could say more about what he meant, to which Mr. Abrams replied that what he thought he was asking about had to do with the difficulty or the ease with which one really showed how one felt. He said that tonight the group seemed able to do it, and this is what encouraged him to bring his concern and the question that had come from the case-worker and that at this point he wanted to understand how this might influence his son and his daughter as well as his own participation in his family life. With this, Mr. Wilson nodded and said this is really what he thought Mr. Abrams was driving at and that he had a notion that this was something that was not only Mr. Abrams's problem, but that as far as he was concerned, this seemed to be the way that most men in the group felt. He asked whether this was not so. He said that for him, this had been and still continues to be somewhat of a concern and that he could feel what Mr. Abrams was driving at.

As Mr. Wilson stopped talking, he looked up and all of the others in the group very thoughtfully looked at him, looked at each other, at me, and finally at Mr. Lewis. I remarked that if this was so, it gave us something else that could be of some help because as we had discussed that evening, the group was one place where they could really show how they felt and look at some of these feelings in order to understand better what motivated them. Mr. Moran summarized this by saying that he thought that if the group could continue with this topic of discussion, he would have a much better understanding of what role feelings played in the behavior of his children, how these were influenced, what they represented to him and consequently, would give him a much better understanding of how he behaves, as well as what makes his children tick.

The session ended soon after this conversation; the worker acknowledged that the group had worked hard and set an agenda to continue with Mr. Abrams's concern. This excerpt demonstrated the group's need to deal with the intimacy theme as well as the connection between the process of the group and the content of the work, a connection that Mr. Moran pointed out in his last comments.

Workers usually experience intermember issues as particularly difficult. Although as they develop group experience, they become proficient at reaching for issues related to the authority theme, it takes longer before they will risk dealing with questions involving the intimacy theme. So powerful are the taboos and so strong is their fear of hurting, and being hurt in reaction, that they will try many indirect routes before finally risking honesty. The reluctance may be partly rooted in the worker's feelings that it is her or his responsibility to "handle" anything that comes from reaching for intermember negatives. As has been illustrated in this excerpt, a group that has developed even a small fund of positive relationship is better equipped for handling its own problems. What is needed is the catalyst of the worker's intervention to give them permission and to support them as they enter the formerly taboo area.

These descriptions of the difficulties group members face in dealing with two major developmental tasks, the relationship with the worker and the relationship between members, have referred to a yet more general task, the development of a culture for work. In the following section, we will explore the question of group culture in more detail.

Another theoretical model (mentioned in Chapter 1) that helps us to understand the intimacy theme has emerged more recently from the work done at the Stone Center in Wellesley, Massachusetts, which is dedicated to studying the unique issues in the development of women and methods for working effectively with them. The center has built upon the early work of Jean Baker Miller, whose publication entitled "Toward a New Psychology of Women" (1976, 1987) laid the groundwork for the relational model.

Much of the recent and rapidly evolving work in this area can be found in publications and a series of working papers from the Stone Center. This framework is often classified under the general rubric of "self-in-relation" theory. One example of a group work elaboration of this model is a working paper by Nicolina Fedele entitled "Relationship in Groups: Connection, Resonance and Paradox" (1994). Fedele draws upon three central constructs repeatedly found in relational theory: paradox (an apparent contradiction that contains a truth); connection ("a joining in relationship between people who experience each other's presence in a full way and who accommodate both the correspondence and contrasts between them"); and resonance ("a resounding; an echoing; the capacity to respond that, in its most sophisticated form, is empathy") (p. 7).

Fedele, referring to therapy, identifies a number of paradoxes: "Vulnerability leads to growth; pain can be experienced in safety; talking about disconnection leads to connection; and conflict between people can be best tolerated in their connection" (p. 8). She also identifies the paradox between "transferential" and "real" relationships in therapy as well as the "importance of establishing a mutual, empathic relationship within the context of the unequal therapist-client relationship" as additional primary paradoxes in therapy. She says,

> These dilemmas are dramatically apparent in group psychotherapy. The therapists and group members collaborate to create an emotional relational space which allows the members to recapture more and more of their experience in their own awareness and in the group. The feelings of the past can be tolerated in this new relational space. It allows us to reframe the experience of pain within the context of safety. The difficulty of creating an environment that allows vulnerability in a group format involves the complexity of creating safety for all participants (p. 8).

In applying this theory to group therapy, she identifies the "basic paradox" of a simultaneous yearning for connection accompanied by efforts to maintain disconnection as a form of protection from being hurt—a need generated from earlier painful experiences. The paradox of "similarity and diversity" describes a tension between connection around universal feelings and fears of isolation because of difference. She points out that "the mutuality of empathy allows all participants to feel understood and accepted. The leader, creating a safe relational context, fosters connectedness within that safety by working to enlarge the empathy for difference" (p. 9). Another related paradox is the fact that the very process of sharing disconnection can lead to new connection. For example, "When members phone the leader to report anger or dissatisfaction with the group, the leader can encourage them to share this experience in the group. Often, if one feels the disconnection, it is very likely that one or more of the other members experience similar feelings and resonate with the feelings of dissatisfaction" (p. 10). Thus, when these are shared feelings, disconnection can lead to connection. Finally, the paradox of "conflict in connection" describes the importance of managing conflict and keeping anger within the context of safety and acceptance of divergent realities. She points out that "One way to view anger is to see it as a reaction to the experience of disconnection in the face of intense yearning for connection" (p. 11).

In describing the second major construct of relational theory, the idea of "connection", Fedele says,

> the primary task of the leader and the group members is to facilitate a feeling of connection. In a relational model of group work, the leader is careful to understand each interaction, each dynamic in the group as a means for maintaining connection or as a

strategy to remain out of connection. As in interpersonal therapy groups, the leader encourages the members to be aware of their availability in the here-and-now relationship of the group by understanding and empathizing with their experiences of the past. But it is the yearning for connection, rather than an innate need for separation or individuation, that fuels their development *both* in the here-and-now *and* in the past (p. 11).

Finally, the third major concept of "resonance" asserts that the "power of experiencing pain within a healing connection stems from the ability of an individual to resonate with another." She suggests that resonance manifests itself in group work in two ways:

The first is the ability of one member to simply resonate with another's experience in the group and experience some vicarious relief because of that resonance. The member need not discuss the issue in the group, but the experience moves her that much closer to knowing and sharing her own truth without necessarily responding or articulating it. Another way resonance manifests itself in a group involves the ability of members to resonate with each other's issues and thereby recall or reconnect with their own issues. This is an important element of group process in all groups but is dramatically obvious in groups with women who have trauma histories. Often, when one woman talks about painful material, other women dissociate. It is a very powerful aspect of group work that, if acknowledged, can help women move into connection. It can also cause problems if women become overwhelmed or flooded. The leader needs to modulate this resonance by helping each member develop skills to manage and contain intense feelings (p. 14).

Many of the core constructs of this theory, and in particular, the group work implications of the model, fit well with the interactional framework presented in this book. For example, a colleague of mine, Linda Schiller (1993) was able to use the self-in-relation framework to rethink a classic theory of group development known as the "Boston Model" (Garland, Jones, and Kolodny, 1965), adapting it to a feminist perspective.

In the example that follows, from a support group for women with cancer, it is possible to use the relational model to explain the patterns of interaction over time. One can see examples of paradoxes, connections, and resonance in each session of the work.

Women's Breast Cancer Support Group

Members: Four 45- to 58-year-old white females from different ethnic and socioeconomic backgrounds. All of these women have been diagnosed with breast cancer and are either in the midst of treatment or have just finished. The group was created in response to inquiries made by each of the members to the outpatient oncology clinic in the hospital. All members are voluntary.

Dates Covered in Record: 11/14 to 12/5

Group Task: Individual need satisfaction

1. *Problem:* The task of this group is for members to reach out to one another in order to find support around painful issues in dealing with their cancer diagnoses. One member in particular seems to be expressing the pain and anger for the group. The problem that I began to recognize was that this member was carrying a great deal of emotion about her cancer diagnosis. She demonstrated her emotion through anger and distrust projected onto group members and the medical staff in general. I suspect that all members shared similar feelings to some extent, but were unable to recognize

them as related to their illness. My co-leader and I found ourselves faced with two problems: (1) we needed to find appropriate ways to address the emotions expressed by the angry member, or what appeared to be the deviant member, in order to get at the underlying message, and (2) we needed to help the group as a whole find the freedom to express and address their painful feelings rather than allowing this individual member to bear the responsibility.

2. *How the Problem Came to My Attention:* Through conversation and telling of individual stories, it seemed apparent from the beginning of the group that this particular woman was distrustful of people in general. I had originally suspected that she was someone who generally did not find people trustworthy throughout her life. After the second session, I began to wonder if this quality was not somehow related to her recent cancer diagnosis as well. She called my co-leader and expressed a desire to quit the group because her "ways of dealing with her illness were diametrically opposed to the other members' ways." At this time she also mentioned the name of one member specifically. Although she continued coming, it was apparent that she was carrying anger with her, especially towards the member she had named. She would roll her eyes or mutter something under her breath whenever this woman spoke. The other members did not acknowledge this, nor did the woman to whom the behavior was addressed.

3. *Summary of the Work*

Session 1: For the first session, although I was very anxious about its newness, I was truly excited about the nature of this group, as the women attending had taken the initiative to request its formation. I felt that it was going to be an exciting and rich experience for all of us. My co-leader and I began the group by introducing ourselves and then having each of the four members introduce themselves. I then went over confidentiality issues as well as the rules and the purpose of the group: This was a support group for women with breast cancer. It was created because of their requests in the oncology clinic, and I hoped that it would become a safe place for each of them to share their experiences and feelings around their illness as well as a place in which they could learn from one another. My co-leader then stated that she, too, hoped to make this a safe place for the women to share their stories, and then she invited each one to talk about her experiences.

Each member told her story, offering an account of what she had been through. I noticed that none of the women expressed their stories with much emotion, only offering descriptive accounts of their experiences. However, one woman, Joan, did stand out in her account She expressed an air of distrust in the medical system and said that so far she had not found any of the doctors or nurses helpful. "I do my own research and reading. I can't count on them to give me the answers. They're in and out in a flash." Another woman, Judy, added that she had a similar experience in the past and ended up switching doctors. Joan snapped at Judy, making an excuse for not being able to switch doctors, and said, "I just deal with it." I made a mental note of this exchange and gave some thought to Joan's account of her experiences as well as her stating that change was not possible. I, at this time, thought that she seemed to be a person who did not trust others, probably because of her own life experiences. I did not make a connection between her feelings about the medical staff and her cancer at this time, not did I think much about why her reaction to Judy was so strong. In retrospect, I would guess that Joan was offering the group some insight into how she was feeling in the group and about her cancer.

Once each woman had shared with the group, my co-leader asked if any of them had been in groups in the past. Only one woman had been in a prior group, and she talked about how each member in that group had died. The room was silent. *Instead of letting the silence stay and then addressing its meaning, I asked the woman what it felt like to be starting another group.* She commented that it was a little scary and added, "But we have to keep going on. We have no other choice." I then asked the other members what it felt like to hear her talk about the other group. They all commented about how it must have been an awful experience for her. My co-leader pushed, "Does it make *you* start to think about your own mortality?" A couple of members said that they had not really given it much thought, and Joan said that it did make her think about it but that was all. Instead of pursuing this, both my co-leader and I let the conversation drift back to the members telling Barbara how it must have been hard to be part of that group. Again, Joan had given us an opportunity to recognize her as really wanting to do the work in the group. First, she brought up the anger and then acknowledged thinking about death. Both are very real issues for all the members in this group. We failed to pick up on her desire to work.

Due to time constraints, we ended the meeting. My co-leader offered a summary of what she felt she had heard as being common in each woman's experience as they had portrayed them to the group and used this as a way to reiterate the goal of finding support from each other within the group. Death and anger were not mentioned. We both thanked them for coming to the group.

Session 2: This session began with all members arriving on time. We asked each member to give a brief check-in so that everyone could get an idea of how the others are doing. Joan was the last one to check-in, and she brought up the fact that her daughter was going through chemotherapy at the time and that she was presently taking care of a depressed friend. This opened up a discussion for all the women to find something in common. It turned out that each of them was caring for elderly parents; thus, all these women were acting as caretakers while dealing with their illnesses. I asked, "What's it like to have to not only worry about your own health and ability to live from day to day, but to have to worry about taking care of someone else as well?" Barbara said, "You gotta do what you gotta do." Everyone agreed. Judy then began to change the subject and talk about how when she's not caring for her mother she is working on a proposal that addresses research around tobacco- and cancer-related issues. She wanted to know if any of the other women would be interested in helping her out. Barbara and Gayle inquired about it, while Joan sat quietly, appearing to be somewhat annoyed. *Neither my co-leader nor I said anything. I did not realize at the time that this was Judy's way of avoiding the work of addressing painful feelings, the group's way of going along with it, and Joan's silent plea to do the work.*

The women continued to talk about their own efforts in keeping busy, and then Joan chimed in, "I haven't been able to go back to work because of the amount of chemotherapy I receive. I have enough trouble trying to take care of everyone else and myself." Judy responded by stating that she knew how she felt because she wished she had more time to work on her proposal. She then went into how long a proposal takes to draft. Joan rolled her eyes. The other members seemed to fall into Judy's trap again. My co-leader said, "I've noticed that the group sort of shifts a focus off issues that seem to bring up some painful emotions for each of you. Have you noticed that, Sandra? Has anyone else noticed that?" Gayle asked what she meant. She explained, without using names, that whenever the group got close to having to share how experiences or "realities" were affecting them, they seemed to shift to talking about less emotional topics. She then said, "I wonder why this happens." *Here we began to point out the pattern that the group was establishing in addressing painful issues. What we failed to do was to recognize and to use Joan's experience in the group as a way to name the painful feelings that the members were avoiding discussing.* Gayle stated that she hadn't noticed this. Judy and Barbara stated that they had not noticed either. Each of them was sort of smiling an embarrassed smile. Joan would not look at the group, she just let out a very heavy sigh that caused everyone to look at her. No one said anything. *Once again, we had missed an opportunity and had failed to answer what seemed like Joan's plea for work.* We let the group sit for a little while and think.

Barbara commented on how quiet it had gotten. This broke the silence, and the other members began to admit that they "might" have been avoiding painful issues. Joan still sat quietly. I remarked that she had been very quiet for a while and that our time was running out. I wondered if she wanted to share anything with the group. She said no. My co-leader said that she imagined her silence meant something. She said, very angrily, that it was sometimes easier to "just not talk." The group then began to inquire and stated that the reason they were together was to help one another and that if they could help her they wanted to. Joan just shook her head and said that she was fine. We, again, avoided bringing up the anger that was present. Maybe we (my co-leader and I) did not want to deal with it?

The group then began to talk about some side effects from their chemotherapy. Judy was the only one in the group without hair. She expressed feeling fine about not having it: "It will grow back." Others talked about hair thinning and other side effects that they had read about. Joan joined in the conversation minimally. *We still ignored the possible significance of her deviation from the group norm.*

The group ended, and that afternoon my co-leader got a call from Joan saying that she felt her way of dealing with things was very different from the group's, especially Judy's, and that she felt as though she wanted to quit coming. After talking it through with my co-leader, Joan decided to return to the group for at least one more time. *When my co-leader and I discussed this, I did not see that Joan's phone call was probably a plea, again, for us to help her work with the group on addressing the pain she was feeling.* We simply chalked it up to her not getting along with one of the members and feeling as though she was just not getting the kind of support that she needed from the group. My co-leader expressed to her that the group was as much hers as anyone else's and that she hoped she would bring her concerns up to the group during the next session. *In retrospect, what I think we were missing was that Joan was representing the ambivalence of the group to face painful issues. In addition, we failed to really note what Judy represented to her, and possibly other members.* Judy is the only one who has completed chemotherapy and/or radiation, she is the intellectualizer (or initiator of flight), her baldness is a reminder of what might happen to others in the group, and she is getting back into her work and other parts of her life that she has put on hold, unlike the other members who are still faced with much uncertainty.

Session 3: The group opened again by checking in with each member. Joan appeared somewhat more cheerful than I had expected. Barbara brought up feeling worn out about caring for her mother and herself. This opened up a discussion around how they each were giving support to other people. Directing the question to any member, I asked, "Who gives *you* support?" Judy began to talk about how her friends used to provide her with transportation and/or come over with meals when she was sick from treatment. Each of the other women shared their "support" stories as well. I finally stated that the kind of support that they had all just talked about was support around real concrete needs: food, rides, and so on. I then asked who gave them emotional support. The room got silent. Judy began to intellectualize. Joan rolled her eyes and shook her head. *I pointed out that they were "doing it again," referring to their established pattern of avoiding painful issues.* Everyone but Joan smiled embarrassedly. I said to them that everyone was smiling but Joan, and I wondered what they were really feeling. They were silent. I said that I imagined it was hard for each of them to be here and to talk about their illness, especially while they are still in treatment. *Here I failed to acknowledge or name the ambivalence and did not make its connection to Joan's desire to quit the group.* Judy offered a reminder that she was finished with her treatment. My co-leader took this opportunity to ask the group what it was like for them to still be in treatment and to have a member present who was through with it. Joan remained quiet. Gayle got tearful and began to pour out that she was "scared shitless" of what might happen to her hair, of how sick she might become and of how there's no real guarantee the chemo would work. I stated that I had just seen more emotion pour out of her than I had seen before. I named what I saw: "You seem like you're feeling sad and scared and angry all at once." She had tears rolling down her cheeks. I looked at Joan, who was tearful. My co-leader asked the group, "What do you do with all of these feelings every day?" Joan made a sound of irritation. My co-leader asked her what that sound meant. Joan just shook her head. My co-leader stated that Gayle's outpour of emotion was understandable and that she though it must be hard for her to carry those feelings around. *I then took the opportunity to narrow the focus to the anger, since it seemed to be an emotion shared at that moment by more than one member (both Gayle and Joan). At this time, I ended up taking advantage of an opportune moment to address Joan's anger without making her feel alone with it.* When I mentioned that it must be hard to deal with the anger, and asked how they managed it, Joan started right in about how angry she was at the hospital and her depressed friend. The discussion continued until Gayle said that she just wished that she could get back to where she was before she got sick. Through this discussion the group was able to talk about their anger, an emotion that all of them admitted to feeling. They acknowledged that it "might" be about their "unlucky" confrontation with cancer, but no one would give a definitive "yes" on that.

As the group ended that day, there was a sense of peace in the room. At this time I was not sure what we had accomplished. But upon reviewing my notes from this session it appeared that much work was done in breaking through the obstacles that the literature speaks to. *By reaching for the underlying feelings and the meanings of the nonverbal messages, we were able to open up some painful areas that the group obviously felt ambivalent about sharing. We were also able to take the individual's issue (the anger) and bring it out as a common feeling among all the group members, rather than leaving it in one person's possession.* One thing that was not addressed, though, was Joan's anger directed at Judy. I think the leaders were too afraid to touch this.

Session 4: The group started as usual with check-ins. The members shared some events that had taken place that week regarding new drugs that two of them were put on. A discussion opened up around side effects again, and this led Joan into discussing her anger about her visit with her doctor that week, as he had been "in and out in a matter of minutes." The group started to ask her questions about why she could not switch doctors if she was so unhappy. I noticed that Joan's response was somewhat different from how she had responded the first time that the group had confronted her regarding switching doctors. She was less hostile, and her anger did not seem to be directed at the members. She was able to discuss with them the possibility of switching but came to the conclusion that she would rather still do her own research than switch doctors mid-treatment. At this point, Barbara said to Joan, "You seem so angry at the doctors. I wish that your experience with them wasn't so dreadful. It makes it much easier if you feel like you are in good hands." The group began to discuss this thought, and Joan sat back and listened. She did not appear angry, just deep in thought. My co-leader asked her what was going through her mind. Joan said, "I just feel like my life is in their hands. They have all the power, the cancer has the power, the drugs have the power, I have none."

For one of the first times, the group started to talk about feeling helpless to their cancer diagnoses. *After we had recognized and called attention to Joan's nonverbal messages, the group was able to benefit once again from Joan's ability to bring a common issue to the forefront.* In addition, the members were beginning to feel comfortable in bringing up the issues themselves. This was evident when Barbara commented to Joan about her anger. No one other than the leaders had pointed this out before.

4. *Where the Problem Stands Now:* At the time that these excerpts were compiled, it was apparent that the group had begun to address painful issues with one another. The leader's push to address one member's obvious feelings of pain allowed these issues to emerge. The group also began to point out each other's nonverbal reactions, thus opening up deeper levels of discussion and understanding. Although the issues were constantly put in our (the leader's) faces, it took Joan several tries to finally reach us. The group continues to need prodding and reminders that they are "doing it again." Joan continues to display anger, but the group has begun to talk to her directly about this. However, the fact that her anger is often directed at Judy has never been brought up. My co-leader and I have begun to discuss our hypotheses about Joan's anger being directed toward Judy. So far, however, neither of us has brought this observation to the forefront, not has any of the group members. What is clear, still, is that Joan seems to carry the group's internal struggles. What I hope is that the group will somehow find a way to share that responsibility and Joan will no longer be responsible for vocalizing their needs. Not only will the group benefit from this, but this will help to decrease the alienation that I suspect Joan has felt as her "deviant" way of dealing with issues has set her apart from the group.

5. *Specific Next Steps:*

(a) I will continue to zero in on nonverbal messages and bring them to the attention of the group.

(b) I will continue to encourage group members to discuss painful issues and to point out the obstacles that are created to avoid this work.

(c) I will continue to collaborate about and review sessions regularly with my coleader so that we can gain greater insight from one another regarding group process.

(d) I will continue to search for connections between an individual's behaviors and those of the group's in order to help the members become more aware of internal struggles.

(e) I hope to create an educational session for members to have their questions answered by a physician in order to address feelings of disempowerment and helplessness.

(f) I will continue to work on my group skills and to actively engage in seeking materials to increase my awareness about specific group tasks and problems.

Developing a Culture for Work

The term *group culture* has been used thus far in its anthropological/sociological sense, with a particular emphasis on group **norms, taboos,** and roles. In Chapter 13, we addressed the concept of role in some detail, so our focus here will be on norms and taboos. Hare (1962) has defined group norms as

> rules of behavior, proper ways of acting, which have been accepted as legitimate by members of a group. Norms specify the kinds of behavior that are expected of group members. These rules or standards of behavior to which members are expected to conform are for the most part derived from the goals which a group has set for itself. Given a set of goals, norms define the kind of behavior which is necessary for or consistent with the realization of those goals (p. 24).

Taboos are commonly associated with primitive tribes who developed sacred prohibitions making certain people or acts untouchable or unmentionable. The term *taboo* in modern cultures refers to social prohibitions related to conventions or traditions. Norms and taboos are closely related, since a group norm may be one that upholds the tradition of making certain subjects taboo. As groups are formed, each member brings to the micro-society of the group a strongly developed set of norms of behavior and shared identification of taboo areas. The early culture of the group is constructed as a reflection of the members' outside culture. As Hare points out, the norms of a group should be consistent with those necessary for realization of its goals. The problem, however, is that the norms of our society and the taboos commonly observed often create obstacles to productive work in the group. A major group task then involves developing a new set of norms and thereby freeing group members to deal with formerly taboo subjects.

We have already been dealing with the problem of assisting group members to develop their culture for work. For example, the subjects of authority and dependency are generally taboo areas in our culture. One does not talk freely about feelings on these subjects. As one example, group experiences in classrooms over many years have taught us not to challenge the authority and alerted us to the dangers involved if one admits feelings of dependency upon a person in authority in front of a peer group. The discussion of the authority theme in the first part of this chapter described the worker's efforts to help the group discuss these taboo areas and to develop a new set of more productive norms; the same was true in the discussion of the intimacy theme. It is important to note that the effort is not directed at changing societal norms or exorcising group members from the power of taboos. There are sound reasons for norms of behavior, and many taboos have appropriate places in our lives. The focus of the work is on building a new culture within the group, a necessity for effective group functioning. Transfers of this experience beyond the group may or may not be relevant.

For example, members in a couples' group had to deal with taboos against open discussion of sex, an area critical to the work of the group. The frankness of the group discussion freed the couples to develop more open communications with each other outside the sessions.

This change in the culture of their marriages was important for them to develop and was therefore an appropriate transfer of learning. On the other hand, if the couples used their new-found freedom to discuss issues of sexual functioning at neighborhood cocktail parties, they might quickly discover the power of peer-group pressure.[3]

It is critical that workers pay attention to the group norms and systematically assist the group to examine them and decide which ones lend themselves to effective work. Research in group dynamics has shown that group norms can have a powerful effect upon group members even in more impersonal laboratory groups established for the experiment.[4] For example, in a study by Sherif and Sherif (1956), subjects were shown a stationary point of light in a darkened room. Because of what is known as the "autokinetic effect," subjects imagine some motion in the light. Each subject estimated the movement and gradually developed a range of estimates. Subject then had the opportunity to make the estimates in groups of two or three, and then return to the individual estimates. A norm of the range of movements was developed in the small groups that then continued to influence the individuals' judgments in individual sessions. In addition, if the first judgments were made in a group, individual judgments converged more rapidly.

Another experiment, by Asch (1951), showed the power of group influence on individual judgments. A naive subject was included in a group of seven to nine members made up of "coached" subjects. All were asked to match lines from a card to a standard. The coached subjects gave accurate responses on six of the tries but made unanimous inaccurate responses on twelve of the attempts to match the lines. A control group of all naive subjects also participated, but their judgments were written and not shared with each other. Subjects in the experimental group made errors on their matching 37 percent of the times, while control group subjects made almost none. In follow-up interviews, subjects described as "yielding" indicated they knew the group was wrong in its estimates, but they did not want to deviate from the group. If laboratory group norms can affect individual participation, then the impact of groups such as the ones described in this book must be powerful.

To illustrate the worker's function of helping the group work on its important tasks, we will examine the efforts of a worker to develop a **group culture** for work that encourages the expression of painful feelings. A second example highlights a discussion of the taboo against open expression of sexual issues. The final example focuses on the impact of oppression on a group of gay veterans who are HIV-positive or have been diagnosed with AIDS. The group theory outlined by Bion (1961) is used in this section to illustrate again the way in which practitioners can draw upon the literature to build their own models of group functioning.

Parents of Hyperactive Children: Accepting Difficult Feelings. The first illustration is of a worker's efforts to help a group of parents of hyperactive children share their painful and angry feelings about their children's problems. This group was cited earlier in this chapter in connection with the illustration of the necessity for group members to deal with their feelings towards the worker that resulted from her demands for work.

RECORD OF SERVICE

Client Description and Time Frame:

This is a group for parents of children with a hyperactivity diagnosis. It is a gender-mixed group. All of the members are white. The setting is an outpatient clinic at a general hospital. The time frame is five weekly sessions.

Description of the Problem:

Members found it very difficult to talk about their own feelings about their hyperactive children. Instead, they continually focused on what other people felt about the children, such as teachers, neighbors, husbands, relatives. Despite their reluctance to focus on their feelings, they occasionally gave me clues that this was their underlying concern, and as this was also part of the contract, I felt we had to explore their feelings and work on them.

How the Problem Came to the Attention of the Worker(s):

During the first few meetings, the members continued to talk about how important this group was for them, as it gave them a chance to get together to discuss their problems related to their hyperactive children and get support from each other. The feeling was that no one, not even their husbands or wives, understood what they were going through and how they felt. Anytime they would begin talking about their own feelings, they resorted back to discussing medications, school, etc.—in other words, a safe topic. Yet the need to talk about how they felt was always raised by members in different ways. This pattern began in session two, when one member raised the question of hyperactivity due to emotional deprivation at an early age—the group superficially touched upon it and dropped the subject, resorting back to something safe. As their pattern of flight became more obvious to me, I was able to help them understand what they were doing, and thus help them deal with their feelings.

Bion (1961) is helpful in explaining such difficulties with emotions, a characteristic common to groups. His work was based upon observations of psychotherapy groups, led by himself, in which he played a relatively passive role, concentrating on making interpretations of the members' behaviors. Once again, as with the earlier theory, some elements of his model are group-specific, while other aspects lend themselves nicely to generalizing. A central idea in Bion's work is the existence of the **work group**. This consists of the mental activity related to a group's task. When the work group is operating, one can see group members translating their thoughts and feelings into actions that are adaptive to reality. As Bion describes it, the work group represents a "sophisticated" level of group operation. Most groups begin with a more "primitive" culture in which they resist dealing with painful emotions. Group development is therefore the struggle between the group's primitive instincts to avoid the pain of growth and its need to become more sophisticated and deal with feelings. The primitive culture of the early stages in the group is a mirror of the primitive culture in our larger society, where the direct and open expression of feelings is avoided.

In the example of the parents' group, the worker described how the problem came to her attention, pointing out how the more painful subjects were dropped as the group took "flight" into a discussion of more superficial issues. This conforms to one of Bion's key ideas—the existence of **basic assumption groups**. He believes that the work group can be obstructed, diverted, and sometimes assisted by group members experiencing powerful emotional drives. His term *basic assumption group* refers to the idea that group members appear to be acting as if their behavior were motivated by a shared basic assumption about the purpose of the group—an assumption other than the expressed group goal.

One of the three basic assumption groups he identifies is the **flight-fight group**. In a primitive group, when the work group gets close to painful feelings, the members will unite in an instantaneous, unconscious process to form the "flight-fight" group, acting from the basic assumption that the group goal is to avoid the pain associated with the work group processes though flight (i.e., an immediate change of subject away from the painful area) or fight (i.e., an argument developing in the group that moves from the emotional level to an intellectual one). This process in the group context parallels the ambivalence noted in work with individuals when resistance is expressed through an abrupt change of subjects. Bion's strategy for dealing with this problem is to call the group's attention to the behavior in an effort to educate the group so that it can function on a more sophisticated level.

As we return to the worker's record of service on this problem, we see that her early efforts were directed at systematically encouraging the expression of feelings and acknowledging these with her own feelings in an effort to build a working relationship. As the pattern developed, the worker drew upon this working relationship to point out the pattern of avoidance and to make a demand for work to the group.

Summary of the Work:

Session 3

I listen to what the members are saying, and I encourage them to talk about their feelings toward their hyperactive children. Marilyn told us that since she had begun coming to the sessions, she noticed that she had changed her attitude in relation to her hyperactive son, and now he was responding more positively towards her. She had always thought of him in terms of being a normal child, and it had frustrated her that he was unable to react as normal children do. In fact, she had set up expectations for him that he couldn't meet. *I encouraged her to continue talking about her feelings toward him.* She said that she supposed she really couldn't accept the fact that he was hyperactive, and then after coming to the meeting she began to accept this. I asked how she felt now. She felt better, but the hurt is there.

By the fifth session, the group had come close to discussing some of the more difficult underlying feelings but each time had used the flight mechanism to avoid the pain. Some of the feelings experienced by these parents ran so counter to what they believed they were expected to feel that they had great difficulty in admitting the reality to others and at times even to themselves. The worker had developed a fund of relationship during the first sessions through her efforts to understand the meaning of the experience for the members. In the following excerpt, she draws upon that fund and makes a demand for work on the members by pointing out their pattern of flight. Even as she does this, she tries to express her empathy with the difficulty the group experiences in meeting this demand.

Session 5

The group sometimes picks up on their feelings, and I try to put a demand for work on them; that is, to stick with the subject and to really talk about their feelings. I point out their underlying anger and don't allow them to take flight. Betty started talking about George and the school again, and the others became very supportive, offering concrete help. She expressed anger at the school but also talked about George and how he didn't fit in—he couldn't read and cope with the courses, and he didn't care. I detected that some of her anger was directed towards him, and I asked how she felt towards him as this point. She said that she pitied him. I wondered if she wasn't also feeling somewhat angry at him for causing her so many problems and irritating her so much. I said that there were times when George made her very angry. Mildred agreed that she reacts negatively, too.

The worker's synthesis of empathy and demand helped the group to modify its culture and to create a new norm in which they would not be judged harshly for their feelings, even those they felt were unreasonable. As feelings of anger toward their children were expressed, the group moved to a new level of trust and openness. With the help of the worker, they described moments when they felt like "killing" their child and, under her gentle prodding, they explored how having an "imperfect child" is experienced as a reflection on themselves as bad parents. There is an important connection between their harsh judgments of themselves for having such children and their attitude towards their children. Their attitude, in turn, affects the child's sense of acceptance by his or her parents, which can lead to further acting-out behavior. Understanding and accepting these feelings is a first step toward breaking this vicious cycle. The worker's comments at the end of the session are designed to acknowledge the important change in the discussion.

> *I recognize how hard it is to talk about their feelings, and how much pain they feel. I credit them for their work, and try to create feeling among them that I understand.*
>
> Denise had been talking about her own feelings about her son, and seemingly had her feelings well under control. She had said that she was very sensitive and had trouble talking about it. I said that perhaps she was saying that she, too, had feelings that the others had mentioned, but she found it very hard to discuss. The others said that it was hard to talk about it, to admit that these children weren't the same as the others, that you wanted to be proud of them but couldn't. I agreed that it was hard—they were living the situation twenty-four hours a day, and they had feelings about these children...
>
> The members discussed how much they were criticized by their relatives and were very upset. I said that people just did not know what it was like to be a mother of a child like this, and also they did not feel the pain and frustration that they felt. I waited, and there was silence. I noticed that our time was long ago up and said that they had done some very hard work. It was not easy to talk as they had today, to share the feelings of depression and hostility towards their children and to admit that they had wanted to kill them at times. I wondered how they felt now. Marilyn said that she couldn't understand everything I tried to get them to do, but I made her think and try new things, and also I made her look at things differently. I said that it wasn't easy for them to do this, I knew that, and I often felt their pain.

We have already seen in an earlier excerpt from this group how the worker needed to help the group articulate its angry feelings in response to her demands for work. Bion might describe those exchanges as examples of the "flight" pattern of reaction in the "flight-fight" group. Another basic assumption group, as described by Bion, is the **dependent group**, in which the group appears to be meeting in order to be sustained by the leader. This is another form of avoidance of the "work group" and was illustrated in the earlier excerpt by the group wanting the leader to "cheer them up." The third and final assumption group in Bion's theory, called the **pairing group**, is one in which the group, often through a conversation between two members, avoids the pain of the work by discussing some future great event. The discussion in this group of "new drugs" or "outside experts" who would provide a solution to their problems is an example of the pairing group in action. In the next section, the worker identifies the current status of the problem.

Current Status of the Problem:
The group is beginning to work on their feelings, although not everyone is as willing to take a good look at themselves. They are starting to share with each other the

pain, guilt, and anger they have toward their hyperactive children. Also, they're sharing feelings of helplessness, wanting to be the perfect mother, knowing that they're not, and wanting to find ways to deal with their children better.

Strategies for Intervention:
1. Keep the focus, and continue making the demand for work. Continue making this a work group and not a fight-flight group.
2. I feel the deviant member, Denise, in expressing her own resistance to looking at her feelings, is really expressing what they all feel. Use the deviant member's behavior to point out their own underlying feelings.
3. Continue to recognize their feelings and credit them for their work. In crediting, make them aware of their progress as a means of encouragement.
4. Credit the internal leaders for taking over leadership and focusing the group on the work.
5. Help the group work on solutions to their feelings and problems. The group needs this if they are to lose their feelings of helplessness—they want to learn how they can function better as mothers and help their hyperactive children.
6. Help the group move into the ending and transition stage.

Married Couples: Legitimizing the Expression of Anger. In a second example of a worker helping a group change its norms to develop a culture more conducive to work, a worker in a married couples' group (not the one described earlier) notices the group members' reluctance to get involved when couples share very personal and angry feelings. She brings this to their attention.

By the sixth session (following Xmas vacation, during which the group had adjourned for two weeks) most of the group's work seemed to involve each couple presenting problems that had been decided upon by both partners and within limits felt by both to be fairly comfortable. If there was intra-couple disagreement and challenge—even that conflict seemed to be on safe topics—e.g., related to problems of the others in the group or, if pertaining to their own marriage, then almost always at the level of the more reluctant spouse. Don, at the fifth session, challenged Liz directly. Liz responded to his charge that she was "always covering up the truth" by a return challenge, asking him why he had married her—daring him to share with the group the real reason, her pregnancy.

When he tried to evade her by deliberately misinterpreting her question, she stuck with it and said she had always suspected that he had felt an obligation to marry and had never really loved her. The group seemed reluctant at first to step into this interchange—they seemed to be giving the couple a chance to "unsay" what had been said. I pointed out the difference between their reaction to this problem and others they had picked up on unhesitatingly, and asked if they agreed that there was a difference. A few members did, and I asked why they thought they hadn't wanted to get involved. Most felt it was "extremely intimate," and that made the difference. I agreed that it was and that I felt it really took guts to bring up something intimate. I said that often problems were not brought up because they were so very personal and that we were so used to keeping anything personal as private as possible. The group talked about family and friends and "how far" one could go in these relationships and how this group was different from "out there." Something clicked for Reisa, because without even checking it out with Jack, she told the group that she and Jack had been forced to marry because she had been pregnant, too. They talked about her family's reaction and how this had affected their marriage and their feelings about their first child.

Married Couples: Dealing with Sexual Taboos. To complete this discussion of group culture, the problem of taboos must be addressed. I described earlier how the skill of helping individual clients to discuss subjects in taboo areas was important to the work. Because of the social nature of taboos, their impact in the group is magnified. Many of the taboos have their early roots in the first primary groups, such as the family, and thus they can represent a powerful obstacle to group work. Sometimes it is enough for the worker simply to call the group's attention to the existence of the obstacle, but in the case of some of the stronger taboos, such as sex, more help may be needed.

In the couples' group described in Chapter 10, sexual concerns between members were hinted at in an early session. The hints were at the end of the meeting. I pointed this out to the group members and suggested that we pick up on this at our next session. The group agreed enthusiastically. I did not expect it to be that easy, since the strength of the taboo in this area would still be operating and simply calling the group's attention to the subject probably would be insufficient. At the start of the next session, the members immediately began to discuss an unrelated area. I called their attention to the existence of the taboo. I asked the group members to explore the obstacle that made it hard for them to discuss sexual subjects. As they discussed what made it hard to talk about sexuality, they were talking about sexuality:

"At the end of last week we agreed to get into the whole sexual area, and yet we seem to be avoiding it this week. I have a hunch that this is a hard area to discuss in the group. Am I right?" There was a look of relief on their faces, and Lou responded, "Yes, I noticed that as well. You know, this is not easy to talk about in public. We're not used to it." I wanted the group to explore what it was about this area that made it hard. "Maybe it would help if we spent some time on what it is about this area, in particular, which makes it tough to discuss. That might make everyone feel a bit more comfortable."

Fran responded, "When I was a kid, I got a clear message that this wasn't to be spoken about with my parents. The only thing said to me was that I should watch out because boys had only one thing on their mind—the problem was, I wasn't sure what that thing was." Group members were nodding and smiling at this. Lou said, "How many of you had your parents talk to you about sex?" The group members exchanged stories of how sex was first raised with them. In all cases it had been done indirectly, if at all, and with some embarrassment. Those with older children described their own determination to do things differently, but somehow, their actual efforts to talk to their children were still marked by discomfort. At one point, Frank described his concerns as a teenager: "You know, from the talk I heard from the other guys, I thought everyone in the neighborhood was getting sex except me. It made me feel something was really wrong with me—and I made sure not to let on that I was really concerned about this." The conversation continued with the group members noting that they had been raised in different generations, and that while some things were different in terms of attitudes towards sex, other things, particularly the taboos, were the same. I could sense a general relaxing as the discussion proceeded, and members discovered that there were many similarities in their experiences. I said, "It's easy to see how these experiences would make it difficult for you to talk freely in this group; however, if we can't get at this critical area, we will be blocked in our work."

By encouraging discussion of the taboo and the reasons for its power, I was helping the members to enter this area. It was important that I did not blame or criticize them for their difficulty in getting started, but at the same time I needed to make a demand to move past the taboo.

> "I can imagine that this difficulty in talking about sex must carry over in your marriages as well. I believe that if you can discuss some of the problems you are having here in the group, we might be able to help you talk more freely to each other—and that might be the beginning of a change." Rick responded, "We can never talk to each other about this without ending up in a fight." I asked Rick if he could expand on this. "We have this problem of me wanting more sex than Fran—sometimes we can go for months without sex, and I'm not sure I can take this anymore." Fran responded, "A relationship is more than just sex, you know, and I just can't turn it on or off because you happen to feel like having sex."

The rest of the evening was spent on Fran and Rick's relationship. The group was supportive to both as the couples' early conversation centered on who was to blame: Fran for her "frigidity" or Rick for his "premature ejaculation." During the next few sessions, the group kept discussing the sexual area as members explored the intricate patterns of action and reaction they had developed that led them to blame each other rather than take responsibility for their own feelings about sex. Once the taboo had been breached, and group members found that they were not punished, it lost some of its power and the discussion became more personal. It is again interesting to note that the process and the task are intermixed. As the group members discuss their difficulty in speaking about sex (the process), they are actually beginning to work on their concerns about sex (the task).

Homosexual Veterans with AIDS—Dealing with the Effects of Oppression. The final example of this section focuses on the impact of societal oppression on the development of a group culture. In this case, the group members are gay veterans who are HIV-positive or have been diagnosed with AIDS. The general principles of oppression psychology, as outlined in Chapter 2, can be applied to the gay and lesbian populations. Once their sexual orientation is established, these clients find themselves treated as outsiders by the larger, heterosexual population. They experience prejudice, discrimination, and assaults on their minds, hearts, spirits, and bodies. They can be the butt of nasty private and public humor (e.g., television and movie stereotypes), which if expressed about other oppressed groups—for example, persons of color—would be considered racist and unacceptable. Only more recently, as a result of growing militancy, organizational skills, and self-assertion by organized gay and lesbian groups, have laws been passed in some states to ban discrimination on the basis of sexual orientation. The tendency to internalize the negative self-image of the oppressor society and to adopt defensive strategies, some of which are maladaptive, can be seen among some members of these populations as well.

Passing for heterosexual by staying "in the closet" about one's sexual orientation has been one means of surviving in an oppressive and often threatening society. While major strides have been made in establishing a general culture that supports open declaration of a gay or lesbian sexual orientation, leading many individuals to "come out" and declare themselves, many still keep their orientation hidden from friends, family, co-workers, and the community. Such denial leads to a sense of alienation, described by Bulhan (1985), from self, culture, and community, which can cause emotional pain and damage. When the disease AIDS strikes, the negative connotation attached to the illness by our society increases the experience of oppression. The long period of time in which this disease was ignored by local and federal governments, a situation that changed only with the spread of AIDS to the majority, white, heterosexual community, is a powerful sign of the depth of oppressive attitudes. Against this backdrop of oppression there have been encouraging signs of organized resistance by the gay and lesbian community, conforming to the third, and healthiest stage of reaction to oppression, as described in Chapter 2.

A stark reminder of this discrimination was faced by every member of the group discussed in the following Record of Service. They had all served in the armed forces of the United States, where public acknowledgment of their sexual orientation would have led to dismissal. This policy, while modified slightly by the "don't ask, don't tell" policy, is in force at the time of this writing, although it is under judicial challenge. For most of the men in this group, their homosexual orientation was kept secret from the army, from friends, and from their families. Now that they are HIV-positive or diagnosed with AIDS, they face many difficult struggles that have been put off in the face of an oppressive homophobia.

RECORD OF SERVICE

Client Description and Time Frame:

Support and stabilization group for men, 28–65 years old. All the members have HIV infection and consider themselves to be gay in some capacity. All the members are United States veterans. *Dates Covered in Record:* 10/16–11/20.

Description of the Problem:

The group members resist openly addressing issues around HIV/AIDS infection. Although the members identify with being gay, discussions of homosexual life-style issues are purposely avoided. Most importantly, the painful feelings associated with watching a fellow group member's health decline are suppressed by the group and not discussed. [The group described here preceded the emergence of the "triple-therapy" drug treatment and the associated diminishing of symptoms of AIDS and increased hope for an eventual cure.]

Summary of the Work:

October 16th

I wanted the group to address their feelings on seeing one of the group members with advanced stages of AIDS. I knew that Mr. Rooney was having a hard time coming to group due to the fact that some of the members had the physical signs of advanced AIDS. Roughly half the group members were fairly new to this ongoing group of two years. I hypothesized that they too were struggling with their own acceptance of their diagnosis and were very disturbed at the sight of Mr. Jergen, the member with advanced symptoms, who was hacking, wheezing, and struggling for air when he spoke.

Mr. Rooney, one of the new members, was so uncomfortable with this that he had skipped the meeting prior to this one. When I confronted him about this outside of the group, he confirmed my suspicions and only reluctantly agreed to attend the session today. Having just been released from the hospital with a bout of shingles, Mr.

Rooney discussed this experience with the group. In being careful not to single out Mr. Rooney, I asked the group how it feels to see each other becoming sick and being forced to spend time in the hospital. Silence. Mr. Bane asked how bad Mr. Rooney's outbreak of shingles was. Just then, Mr. Downey arrived 20 minutes late, weighted down with lots of packages.

I copped out and allowed the "flight" reaction and the distraction of the late arrival to gloss over my demand for work. Jerry (co-leader) allowed this to take place also in asking what Mr. Downey had brought in all of his packages.

The student writer of this record is also gay and has experienced many personal losses to AIDS. Examination of the working circumstances in this hospital revealed a lack of social support for staff that contributed to their participation in the same "flight/fight" behavioral reactions as many of their clients. The worker's retrospective analysis helps him to understand his own participation in the illusion of work. In the next excerpt, the fight reaction, also designed to avoid pain, emerges as the members attack the poor quality of medical care they feel they are receiving. Since institutional oppression in relation to medical care is a reality for this population, some of what Fanon referred to as "adaptive paranoia" is understandable and necessary. Persistence of this angry reaction on the part of the group members, in the face of evidence to the contrary, can be understood as the "flight" reaction. The worker misses the underlying meaning of the struggle and instead, confronts the group trying to help them see the facts in the case. It is only in retrospective analysis that the worker recognizes the pain and fear that lay just below the anger. In effect, his effort to convince the group members represented his own version of fight/flight.

November 6th
I was forced to confront behavior that allowed a misunderstanding to continue. Mr. Williams needs an operation on his hernia and financially cannot afford to seek alternative medical services outside this agency. After several weeks of scheduled pre-op, appointments, and what was perceived by Mr. Williams as bureaucratic red tape, his operation was canceled. During this period, Mr. Williams took every opportunity in group to discuss the delays he was experiencing, his blame on the system and the inconvenience of having to live with the hernia. For a while the group began to become incensed with what this implied, i.e., discrimination around not treating someone with HIV infection.

At this juncture Jerry (co-leader) and I became involved in attempting to come up with a rationale for the indefinite postponement of Mr. William's surgery. It was the opinion of the chief of infectious diseases that Mr. Williams's overall health, even without regard to the HIV, was so poor that his risk was greater to have the surgery than to live with the hernia. This was then explained to Mr. Williams's satisfaction by the chief of infectious diseases (Dr. Smith). During the very next group session, Mr. Williams, when asked by Jerry as to his health, began again with blaming the system for his inability to get his surgery. It was at this point that I reminded Mr. Williams of his discussion with Dr. Smith and assured the group that no discrimination had occurred around his HIV infection.

It was during this session that Mr. Tippet had returned to group from a three-week vacation. He asked Mr. Williams whether or not he had received his operation. Mr. Williams shook his head in disgust and said that the "bureaucrats still haven't gotten it together." Mr. Tippet was enraged at the seemingly bad treatment Mr.

Williams had received from the hospital. I waited for a group member to confront Mr. Williams. Mr. Tippet went on about the injustice of it all and looked at me. I said, "It was my understanding that Dr. Smith spoke to Mr. Williams and explained that there were other serious medical considerations apart from HIV that put Mr. Williams more at risk by having the surgery." I asked Mr. Williams for validation. He nodded in agreement. Mr. Tippet thanked me for the clarification and said he felt better about the hospital.

I felt that Mr. Tippet could not be allowed to continue to think it was the fault of the system for the indefinite delay in Mr. Williams's surgery, especially when the rest of the members were made known of the truth during Mr. Tippet's absence. I was shocked and upset to think that Mr. Williams would choose to continue in this behavior. I could not allow this misconception to continue. It would have created a collusion between Mr. Williams and the rest of the group, with the exclusion of Mr. Tippet. If I had this to do over again, I would have put aside my own feelings, considered the second client and said something like, "It must be very difficult to be forced to manage several different ailments at the same time." Nearly all of these gentlemen could relate to that scenario.

The worker was surprised when the other group members did not confront the member who was angry at the system. This is not surprising at all, if in the terms of Bion's theory, we consider Mr. Williams the group's fight/flight leader. Rather than confronting this member, the group will generally encourage his angry reactions. In the next excerpt, we see the impact of the oppression on the group members' ability to openly deal with their disease and their sexual orientation.

November 13th
I wanted to allow the group to explore the feelings attached to the stigma around the HIV infection and the homosexual orientation. Mr. Tippet revealed that only one member of his family knew of his disease. Several other members expressed the same personal situation. Mr. Tippet said that he could only see himself telling one of his sisters about his HIV infection. I said, "Should you decide to tell her, what will you say if she asks how you think you got it?" Mr. Tippet replied, "Well, I'll tell you, Dan; once a man reaches the age of 62 and never marries, then I think it's pretty easy to figure it out." I smiled and asked how he thought his sister would react to the news. Mr. Tippet said he thinks she would be "OK" with it. I asked what the others thought. Mr. Bane began with his own situation regarding disclosure to his brother in a letter he had sent to the Midwest. I allowed him to go on and Jerry subsequently questioned him further regarding the particulars around the disclosure.

I should have encouraged the group at that moment to look at the feelings associated with the taboo of homosexuality and the attached stigma of an AIDS diagnosis. Something like, "How hard is it for us to talk about this now? Maybe if we can talk about where these bad feelings about being gay come from, then discussing HIV infection with loved ones may not seem like such an impossible task."

November 20
I wanted to attempt to re-explore the feelings behind seeing a few of the members develop full-blown AIDS. Two of the veteran group members had been unable to attend the last few sessions as it became just too much for them logistically to come in. My supervisor and I paid one of these gentlemen a home visit. Mr. Jergen agreed on the

next Tuesday to attend the group in conjunction with his scheduled appointments with the HIV clinic. With the aid of a wheelchair he came in early to attend group with the intent to say good-bye to the other members.

During the session, Mr. Jergen explained that he was taking his leave of the group as it had become too much for him physically to attend. He went on to say that his absence recently illustrated this but that he agreed with my supervisor and me, and he wanted to come in one last time to terminate with the group.

I asked the older members of the group how it feels to see the other original members getting sick and dropping out. Mr. Meany, who rarely speaks up, said that he has been in group for over a year and a half now and that, "At first you tend to feel bad for those who become sick and scared for yourself. You don't want to face it." He went on to say that, after one becomes sick a couple of times and gets well again, you begin to see others getting sick in a different way. Mr. Meany said, "You still feel for those that are too sick to come to group, but you begin to count your blessings that you feel good today." Silence. I thanked Mr. Meany for his input.

Mr. Victor (who is asymptomatic) said he was also taking his leave of the group because he wants to be around other HIV-infected people that aren't sick. He wants the more upbeat experience from "The Center" downtown. He went on to say that he still feels he needs the support but that he has been with this group for almost two years and believes it is time to move on. Jerry (co-leader) said we are sorry to see you go and hope that you decide sometime in the future to come back. Mr. Victor said that he may do that. Much to my surprise, the remaining time in the session was spent vividly discussing the gay affairs each member had while they were in the service.

Current Status of the Problem:

The group has managed to get at some of those feelings associated with witnessing the decline of a fellow member's health. Mr. Meany's comments were a beginning for the group to attempt to break through that negative group norm. In their defense, there exists no similar example in modern history of how to act when faced with a disease that has the stigma AIDS carries and offers, in most cases, only a slow and, in many instances, painful progression towards death.

Society tells us at best to pity those afflicted with this disease and, at worst, to blame the victim. These men take with them into group the views of our society and an internalized guilt (stigma) for being "deviant" in their homosexual behavior. I believe, based on the last process excerpt (November 20th), that ground has been broken in beginning to discuss openly issues around homosexuality and the inevitable progression of the disease which afflicts all the members in some capacity.

Strategies for Intervention:

1. Allow the group to become stabilized as old members are leaving and new ones are becoming acclimated.
2. Continue to explore group culture around avoiding discussion of the progression of the illness and encourage participation towards reversing this.
3. Continue to examine the origins of the taboos around homosexuality and help facilitate open, honest discussions of gay themes.
4. Consider making the group one that's time limited with a specific set of goals that need to be addressed before termination. This type of group more accurately mirrors life experiences in that there is a beginning, middle, and end to all that we do. This population especially needs to feel that they are completing specific goals in

the time that they have left. The time-limited group provides the HIV client with a reference of having completed the tasks the group set out to accomplish.

In addition to this list of strategies, the worker should have added a fifth: Attempt to develop a support group to assist me, my co-leaders, and other staff in the system to deal with all of the losses we are experiencing. The need for such help became obvious to the worker after a subsequent meeting, when the very ill member, who was attending a session in conjunction with a clinic visit, deteriorated so quickly that he had to request admission to the hospital. This had a powerful impact on the group and the worker. In fact, he reported that shortly afterward he had an argument with the patient's admitting nurse, which he later recognized was caused by his struggle to deal with his own pain. This led to first steps to begin his work with the system.

In a later chapter, the issue of dealing with AIDS in the present context will be examined when my work with a group of persons with AIDS who are also in early substance abuse recovery is shared. For at least three of these members, who have benefited or expect to benefit from the new therapies, the issues shift to those associated with living with AIDS and how to manage their lives rather than managing their dying.

The final two brief excerpts in this section focus on helping young people deal with the impact on their lives of violence in their families. In these brief excerpts, the workers attempt to help group members share with each other the pain and post-traumatic stress that has become a part of everyday life for many of our most vulnerable children. In the first example, the worker helps the group members discuss violence in their homes directed toward their mothers. In the worker's analysis of her practice, we see how the violence also affects her feelings and actions. In the second example, the worker and the group try to help an older teen in a juvenile delinquency detention center deal with the result of his having accidentally shot and killed his best friend. As with the first example, we clearly see how hard it is for the workers to stay with the pain expressed by the group member. In the second example, one worker reaches for the member's underlying feelings while the other moves away from them, focusing instead on questions of responsibility. Both examples underline the importance of support for helping professionals so that they can manage their own feelings while helping clients to manage theirs.

Inner-City Elementary School: The Impact of Violence in the Family

Purpose: Discussion group (with special attention to violent school behavior)
Gender of members: Female; *Age range:* 9 to 10 years
Meeting #2
Cultural, racial, or ethnic identification of members: Two are African-American, and the third is African-American and Hispanic

I asked if anyone had something they wanted to talk about today. Both Shaquandra's and Asia's hands shot up. I told them to decide who goes first. They pointed at each other and said, "You go first." Maria said nothing. It went back and forth for a few minutes with, "You," "No, you," "No, you," when finally Shaquandra said, "Oh, I will." She launched into a long, detailed account of how her stepfather tried to kill her mother. He was hiding in the room and she tried to get a gun but she could not get it because he pushed her down. She was talking very rapidly and staring blankly. She made no direct eye contact with anyone.

Finally, she paused, taking a deep breath. I said, "Wow, that's a lot of information all at once—sounds scary." She said, "Yeah." I asked her how that felt to her. She said,

"It feels bad. I'm scared of him, but he's going to jail." Asia quickly chimed in, "Yeah, it feels bad." Then she launched into a similar story about an uncle who tried to kill her mother, but Asia hit him. "He's going to jail too, but I'm scared if he gets out he'll try to kill my mother again." I asked how it felt to hit him. She said it felt good. I said, "Wow, you girls have a lot to deal with. It must be hard for you. Did you know that sometimes when kids have a lot going on at home, they sometimes have unhappy times at school?"

SUMMARY

The major thing I would want to do if I had a chance would be to encourage a fuller development of statements the girls made. Due to my inexperience, and its having been only the second group meeting, I was feeling my way and did not explore as much as I would now. At the time, there was no group stimuli for my last worker intervention statement. I think it meant I was scared, so I threw in a safe (for me) training manual statement! The Student Support Program at the school prepared a manual with suggested wording of statements for working with the kids. Statements such as "Did you know that when kids are unhappy at home, they often have problems at school?" is vintage Multicult, which I took verbatim. In retrospect, I would still want to tie the school behavior together with the home problems at some point, but I would not feel so compelled to run away from the violence issues. I have a much better comfort level with tougher issues now.

Residential Center for Young Men in the Criminal Justice System

Meeting #33

Purpose: To provide education and support to male juvenile delinquents with histories of anger and violence control problems

Gender of members: Male; *Age range:* 14–18

Cultural, racial, or ethnic identification of members: Caucasian, African-American, Native-American, Hispanic, Cape Verdian

Excerpt:

Jon (co-leader) reminded Bill of family group when his mother was so angry with his apathy and resistance to treatment that she threatened to "leave her kids and get on with her life." There was silence in the room as Bill stared at the floor. In a soft voice, I said, "Bill, I was wondering about last week in family group…what was it like to hear your mom talk about stepping over the spot where Jim died?" Bill looked up at me as a group member asked, "Where did you shoot him? It was in your house?" Bill's gaze returned to the floor and he replied, "Yeah, it was in my living room…my mom had new carpeting put in and stuff, but it's that spot, we know where it is."

I asked, "Had you considered what she continues to go through on a daily basis, or was that the first time you had heard she is stepping over it to close the drapes every night?" He raised his voice and responded, "I don't know, it made me mad to hear that she wants to sell the house or burn it or something! That made me mad." I replied, "She has a lot of memories there that she faces each day." There was silence. "I used to sit on that spot on the floor and think about Jim." "You have memories too, Bill?" He shared the moment of Jim's death on his living room floor. "I held on to him so tight…they pulled me off…the paramedics, they had to hold me so they could take him away…I just want him back." Bill began to sob uncontrollably. Jon encouraged Bill to feel the pain because that would be the only way it would go away. The group supported Bill with, "Let it go, Bill," and "It's okay, guy, we're here for you." Jon then said, "You killed your best friend, Bill. You were out of control. You killed him and you cannot afford to forget that." The group remained silent.

The Impact of Ethnicity on Group Culture

One of my important learning experiences occurred when I had the opportunity to serve as a consultant for one month for the Hong Kong government department of social services. I provided training workshops for a number of groups of social service professionals on how to organize and lead mutual aid groups for clients. Although I had tried to get ready by reading about ethnic sensitive practice and tuning in, nothing quite prepared me for the emotional impact and challenge to my adaptive skills as I led a number of short-term training groups for Chinese social workers. I quickly understood that the process in the training groups would parallel what these social workers would face as they attempted to lead their client groups. Also, I realized that although the month would be a difficult one, I would probably learn at least as much as I would be able to teach. I was aided in my education by the staff of the Hong Kong Social Service Department.[5]

My first important insight was that fundamentals of human and group behavior were universals across cultures; however, the roots of these norms, taboos, rules of behavior, and so on, can be traced to very difficult sources, and the intensity of their impact and the way they emerge will vary with different cultures. For example, I had prepared for the fact that the authority theme would be central in this group, as it is in all groups, in the beginning phase of work. With the Hong Kong groups, however, I was the "Professor," to be accorded status and deference in a manner that persisted for the life of the group. Participants would not openly disagree with me, not so much because they feared my authority (as a Western group member might), but because as a symbol of authority I deserved respect and they would not want me to "lose face" in the group. In addition, as the "expert," I was expected to provide information, in a formal manner, which they were expected to learn. In a paper on group work, student Mary Wong[6] points out that

> Chinese tradition allows great prestige and authority to the group leader. This echoes exactly the same position of the father in the Chinese family. As a person of knowledge, the group leader is entitled to respect and obedience from the group members who come to learn from him/her. Respect involves more than just ordinary politeness; it also involves agreement with the leader's view or at least abstention from open expression of disagreement. To disagree with a leader is to challenge his/her social role and hence harm his/her prestige (p. 9).

Wong traces these values toward authority, and others that stress harmony and order in all personal relationships, to the three major streams of thought in Chinese history: Taoism, Buddhism, and Confucianism.

> The main theme of Taoism is to follow Tao—"the way" or "logo." The way to reach Tao is through "Wu Wai," which…in Taoist context…means acting in a harmonious fashion with nature. In order to be Wu Wai, an individual must be "Yau"—soft but flexible. To achieve Yau and consequently Wu Wai, a Taoist must be human and possess a tranquil mind. The Taoists hold that human nature and the universe are made up of two opposing forces—Yin and Yang. These forces depict the shady or north (Yin) slopes of a hill and its sunny or south (Yang) slopes.

The Yin/Yang concept of the dual nature latent in all things pervades the Chinese view of life and everyday language, for nothing is so dark that it has not a sunny side, so cold that it has no warmth, so soft that it has no hardness, and so forth.... Water is a significant imagery for Taoists. It manifests Taoists' tendency to be non-aggressive, to absorb attack, and to live in atonement with conflicting forces (p. 4).

The second major influence on Chinese thought is based on Confucianism, which like Taoism is concerned with "maintaining balance among conflicting forces while exerting as little direct action as possible" (p. 4).

Confucianism stresses the reliance on Jen (human-heartedness or benevolence).... Jen with regard to Heaven is to serve the Heaven like one serves one's own father and to act in accordance with the natural law. Jen with regard to self is loyalty...to the Heavenly nature that makes human beings human, which involves cultivating the self, to examine oneself and find sincerity. For Jen with regard to others, one must treat others exactly the same as one would like to be treated.... Jen with regard to others implies a reciprocal relationship where the individuals involved trust each other and are trustworthy (p. 4).

Jen is seen as an expression of harmony in human relations, a desired state to which all should aspire. These converging philosophies led to the development of a strict sense of social order that provided the basis for family relationships. Knowing one's place, showing obedience and loyalty to parents, maintaining harmonious and non-conflictual peer relationships, and respecting hierarchy according to age all contribute to a general cultural stance that will be expressed in the social work group. Many of these elements can be found in all social work groups; however, their impact may be significantly different because of cultural factors.

A second major insight was that principles of good practice also applied across cultures but that I needed to make serious efforts at adaptation in order to respect and work with ethnic and cultural differences. For example, rather than opening each training group session with problem swapping and discussion, I prepared a brief and expected presentation. However, I did not abandon my requests for active discussion and involvement; I just delayed the demand and responded to their expectations of me. I also respected their early resistance to disagreeing with me; however, I pointed out my awareness of their reluctance and my hope that during our work together, we might find a way for them to provide feedback. Here is an excerpt from my notes from one of the early groups.

I am very pleased that I will have an opportunity to share my ideas about leading mutual aid groups with you. However, I have a problem with which I will need your assistance. These ideas were developed in my work with groups in a Western culture. I believe many will be useful for your groups as well, some will need to be adapted to respect your Chinese culture, and others may not fit at all. I understand and appreciate that your respect for me as a professor and your thoughtfulness will make you hesitant to disagree or suggest different ideas. It is my hope, however, that as we get to know each other, you will see that I very much value your ideas and will find your opinions to be helpful to me. I am prepared to teach what I know about group leadership, but I am also hoping to be a student as well.

There was no response to this offer, but I believe it was heard and understood. After the session, one group member, who had been educated at Berkeley University, where the cultural expectations governing the interchange between faculty and students was somewhat different, approached me privately to reassure me that it would take some time before I could expect a response and that I should not be discouraged.

I continued to try to find ways to encourage the group members to participate and provide feedback within their own cultural tradition. For example, when our groups had reached the point where they felt safe enough to share some of their difficult experiences leading groups, and we had reached a point in analysis of an example where the skill of reaching for feelings or making a demand for work was appropriate, I would comment as follows:

> If I were faced with this problem in a group I was leading back home, I would probably say the following at this point: (I would then share my specific intervention). Can you help me to see how we could modify this so that we can accomplish the same end but do it in a way that would be comfortable for your culture and your groups?

This often generated an excellent discussion in which the workshop members artfully found their own ways of making the same intervention. Because my request was presented in a cooperative, rather than confrontational, manner, workshop members appeared to feel free to respond without fearing that they would be offending their group leader. An important additional benefit here was that I was modeling the same respect for culture in the workshop group that they would need to demonstrate in their own client groups.

Language was another area where it was important to understand the impact of culture. Hong Kong is bilingual, with all students learning English as well as Chinese. However, after working for years in Chinese only, many participants could understand English well but were embarrassed to risk speaking the language. I encouraged them to feel free to speak in either language, since I had the assistance of the training staff to help in translation. When no one spoke in Chinese after two sessions, at the end of the second session I acknowledged the discomfort they may have felt at using their own language. So strong was the sense of embarrassment about not being able to speak English well, that it was not until the fourth session that some participants felt free enough in the group to accept my invitation and to use Chinese. After a few had broken the barrier, others were quick to join in and I found myself often, and with good humor, having to slow them down so my translator could keep me involved.

Respect for authority was also evident in the pattern of participation within groups that included supervisors or administrators as well as front-line workers. It quickly became apparent that most front-line workers would refer questions and discussions to senior (and older) group members. Only after this pattern had been pointed out in the group did supervisory staff begin to play a less active role that encouraged front-line workers to become more involved.

The desire to create a harmonious atmosphere was also evident in the group members' reluctance to criticize in any way the comments or presentations of their peers. Once again, pointing out the process and relating it to the same dynamics that would be occurring in their client groups allowed for a discussion of the importance of honesty and for the development of group guidelines for providing feedback in a respectful manner designed to allow a participant to maintain "face."

One area in which the taboos and the resultant barriers never lowered in these sessions related to issues of oppression. Hong Kong was a British colony at the time I visited, with many of the issues associated with colonial occupation of Asian people by white Europeans. When one example dealt with a Chinese client who spoke no English and was being tried in criminal court with an English judge, prosecutor, and defense attorney, all speaking only

English, there was no response to my efforts to raise concern about the implications. Issues of racism were never discussed in the workshops, even though early on I pointed out that I was a white, Western professor, and that this might cause a problem. Sexism was also a generally taboo subject even though institutionalized sexist attitudes, stereotypes, and practices existed in this society. Denial of the existence of problems such as sexual violence or incest was strong, even though these problems were documented. It was clear that feelings of shame associated with revealing some "family problems" to an outsider were very difficult to overcome. Devore and Schlesinger (1991) describe this phenomenon with Asian clients as follows:

> Many people don't perceive problems as being lodged in or "belonging" to individuals, as is characteristic of mainstream culture. Problems may be seen as "belonging" to the family or the community. If something is wrong, the family is shamed. (This is the case with many Asians.) (p. 204)

One final tradition was observed with each of the groups I led: I was taken out to a celebratory luncheon banquet following the last session. This is one ethnic cultural practice I made no effort to modify, and in fact would like to see imported into my Western classes.

This personal example has been provided to introduce the idea of respect for ethnic and racial variations in understanding and supporting the development of an effective group culture. In the example that follows, the experience of leading a group for Vietnamese men illustrates many of the cultural issues raised in this introduction. The additional element of these men having immigrated to a strange country, under difficult and often violent conditions, adds other issues to the analysis.

Asian Immigrant Men: Social Support for Psychiatric Patients. In addition to many of the cultural issues raised in the preceding discussion, this group of Asian men must also face the problems of having immigrated to a new country and having been diagnosed with a mental illness. Both categorical definitions—Asian immigrant and mentally ill—make them subject to potential oppression. The history surrounding their immigration must also be considered. Devore and Schlesinger (1991) describe the issue in reference to an immigrant family.

> As social workers apply the assumptions for ethnic-sensitive practice in work with the Nguyen family, they realize that history has had an immediate impact upon their lives. A past and present history of oppression, war and their aftermath, have caused them to migrate to a new country. Their ethnicity causes immediate strain as they confront an entirely new environment in which they are dependent upon the church and the welfare system for support (p. 308).

Another issue introduced by this illustration is the use of an interpreter in practice. Contracting between the leader and the interpreter is crucial so that cultural norms, to which the interpreter may also be subject, do not negatively influence the group process. For example, the worker must encourage the interpreter to share everything that is said by the group members, without modifying it to make it more acceptable to the leader. In particular, any expression of negative feedback concerning the worker or the agency must be encouraged rather than diverted. When workers feel intimidated by being "left out of a conversation" or by their lack of ethnic understanding, a defensive and overbearing reaction to an interpreter may lead to sabotage rather than effective collaboration. Some workers take the tactic of demanding a literal translation by their interpreters of everything they say. This can be a mistake, because the interpreter should really be seen as a co-leader who, in collaboration with the work, will develop effective intervention strategies for this population. Often, interpreters are former clients who have had a first-hand experience with the immigration process and can be extremely helpful to the non-immigrant worker. At the same time, the leader needs to be involved so that the interpreter, often lacking in social work training, does not lead his or her own group session. The worker wants to avoid the situation I faced in one group session I led, when a group member spoke in a foreign language in an animated fashion for over two minutes, but the translator only commented, "She said yes!"

The following record of service demonstrates an effective and non-competitive working relationship between the social worker and the interpreter.

RECORD OF SERVICE

Client Description and Time Frame:
This group is composed of six Vietnamese men ranging in age from 26 to 55. The men have all been coming to the clinic regularly for individual therapy for at least two years. Five of the men are single, living alone or with other Vietnamese families. One man is married with two children. Four of the men have been diagnosed with schizophrenia, and two with depression and organic brain damage. The group was created as a short-term psychotherapy group pilot project to meet every other week for six 90-minute sessions. The dates covered in the record are March 3rd to April 14th.

Description of the Problem:
The group members are still testing the safety of the group environment. Trusting the other members is difficult. The members have been able to share intimate concerns and they have raised "taboo" subjects, but they are extremely hesitant to engage in mutual aid, helping each other. A group cohesiveness that may foster the phase of intimacy has yet to be adequately developed. This problem could be due in part to the leader's inadequate acknowledgment of the theme of authority.

How the Problem Came to the Attention of the Worker(s):
The group members have needed to describe their individual differences in each session. As we have tried to universalize and point out common themes, the individuals seem to guard against being identified as belonging to a group of "sick" and crazy men. We have identified this through remarks made between sessions: "Everyone has too many problems, and it gives me a headache to think of other people's problems," and "How can Son feel as lonely as I do? He has a family here, how can he possibly be lonely?" The members have also tended to scapegoat Son, ignoring him or giving him quizzical looks when he denies his problems. Scapegoating could be symptomatic of our inability to address the authority theme. Furthermore, the men always wait for the leaders to start the group, and they address the leaders more than the other members of the group, displaying an inability to trust the other members.

Summary of the Work:
March 3 (First Session)
My co-worker, Toan, and I began the first meeting with a 20-minute opening statement. We explained that we would use a process of mutual aid, but we began in a very authoritative manner. When group members began talking about their illness and pain, we failed to provide support for individuals, as we focused mainly on the second client, the group. In the opening statement, we proposed that the purpose of

the group was for the men to get to know each other, to share common problems, and to discuss ways they each solve problems: We pointed out commonalities: all of the men are from Vietnam, they miss their country and family members they have lost, they are frustrated because their English-speaking ability is poor, and they all have a mental illness.

We raised the issue of confidentiality by explaining that we wanted everyone to feel free to talk openly, so other group members should not discuss issues outside of group. We also confronted the Vietnamese cultural norm of avoiding discussions of personal matters with strangers, a taboo subject. We validated the discomfort the men may feel discussing taboo subjects, but we countered the idea of personal matters being taboo by citing an old Vietnamese saying, "First strangers, then friends." We also addressed the subject of trust by acknowledging that all of the men have experienced much hardship and trauma in life and we understand they may feel unsure about trusting the group; we assured them that we would proceed at their pace.

The six men sat through the long opening statement very quietly. *We made a demand for work by asking for their participation.* The men introduced themselves, and then Hung asked how they could trust one another or be sure the other members would keep issues confidential. We attempted to establish a process of mutual aid by asking the members to speak to each other and then by throwing the question back to the group. Everyone remained silent. We acknowledged the silence and verbalized the group's uncertainty. Toan validated the feeling, saying he understood the insecurity; he imagined everyone had the same question in mind, but no one had any answers. After going around the group to find out what people were thinking and calling on members for three-quarters of the session, the group members started talking on their own. We failed to partialize and ultimately failed to give support to individual group members.

Doan took out his bottle of medication and said he would have died without the pills; he explained that he had been coming to the clinic for six years, and he monopolized the group for several minutes. Hung interrupted and told the group that he had attempted suicide last summer because he felt so sad, especially since he had just recently become sick. The other men supported him by acknowledging his fear, and they encouraged him to feel lucky that he is in America. Dinh said his concern at the moment was different, he was about to be evicted from his house and he did not know where to go. Juan said he has been sick for awhile and he wanted to know how long his illness would last. Luu said he felt too nervous to say anything, and Son said everything was fine for him. In their own ways everyone was testing us, the leaders, and the other group members. I wish we could have responded to the underlying questions of group purpose and goals and our role.

We felt overwhelmed by all of the problems, as did the men, but we did not acknowledge the feeling. We suggested that these were the kind of problems they could work on next time We asked what the group thought about this session, but everyone remained silent. Although we had explained that Toan would translate for me, he translated very little in the first meeting and, as a result, the group rarely looked at me.

March 17 (Second Session)
Four men showed, everyone except Hung and Doan, the most talkative from first meeting. The content themes of the session were loss, missing Vietnam, and hopelessness about life as a "sick" person in America. *We tried to promote a group culture*

for discussion of problems that concerned them all. After a review of the previous session, we attempted to explore the men's reactions. We also acknowledged the absence of two members, but we did not discuss the significance. As we expected, the men were polite, saying only positive things. We failed to point this out.

Son guided us into an intense issue indirectly dealing with how the group members had perceived each other. He stated that being with other Vietnamese men reminded him of his family, his father and brothers, and this has made him homesick. The other men looked uncomfortable being equated with family. *We did not acknowledge the men's reaction to Son's statement.* Son then dominated most of the session talking about why he misses Vietnam. Son was opening up two taboo issues—transference and the interrelationship of the group members—and a personal issue. He said he misses sitting around in restaurants drinking iced coffee with other men, and he misses the ease of life in Vietnam. Since Toan and I felt we failed to provide enough support to individuals in the first session, we focused on Son, and explored his feelings, thinking he was expressing a common issue. This time we failed to monitor the emotional level of the group and the group's reaction to the subject. When we finally brought Son's sadness to the rest of the group for their response or support or identification with the problem, the members all expressed themselves through somatic complaints: headaches, sleepiness, and so on. They did not respond verbally to Son.

Son picked up the discussion again by saying he felt life is so difficult in the U.S. People don't have time for you, so life seems hopeless. *I failed to point out that this statement could have reflected Son's disappointment that the rest of the group didn't respond to him.* The group seemed disengaged this time: movement and energy level felt high, and everyone was shifting in their seats. I asked what was going on for the group members, because I sensed people felt uncomfortable. Dinh said he had a headache because he still needed to find a place to live. I failed to realize that the group's expression of discomfort and somatic complaints were culturally acceptable reactions to Son. Since I felt Son had not received support from the group, I thanked him for sharing difficult feelings, and I once again asked the group to contribute their feelings. In response to my request for verbalization of feelings, the group members entered a discussion about the difficulties of life in America.

The men contributed hesitantly at first, and then in a more lively manner. They discussed their feelings about not knowing English, not having a family, and being so sick it is difficult to get a job. *We pointed out that they all share similar concerns, but we failed to acknowledge differences; for example, we ignored the fact that Son is the only one with a family. I think we should have acknowledged this and asked Son and the group to respond to the difference.* The men shook their heads, acknowledging the common problems; however, when Toan said everyone was in the same boat, the men became more distant again. For the rest of the session, the men addressed Toan when they spoke instead of looking at each other. We failed to address this change. I reached for the feeling in the room by saying that the men had expressed a lot of hopeless feeling. Individually, the men started expressing the reasons they felt hopeless and different from the other members. Luu started talking out his frustration with his roommates. We attempted to contain verbalization of problems by partializing and refocusing. We failed to support Luu. We acknowledged that all of the men had many concerns, but we proposed concentrating on one problem, thinking of ways to solve it.

Toan suggested that we focus on Son's sadness, but the group returned to Dinh's issue of being evicted. I sensed this was an "authority" issue, but I felt I couldn't do anything about it because Toan translated after the dialogue had ended. At least we allowed the group to have control. I wish we could have supported their effort verbally. *We made a demand for work by asking the men if they had any suggestions for Dinh.* Juan recommended he get a roommate so he could share expenses, but Dinh replied that he felt too uncomfortable living with others. Luu identified with this by saying he felt that he has always been exploited by his roommates, the same issue he had raised previously. We tried to return to Dinh's issue; Son and Luu remained silent until the end of the meeting. We were clearly too attached to our agenda of solving problems and, as a result, we failed to support the other members of the group. At the end, Son reflected that he sometimes thinks about things too much; everyone laughed. At first I thought Son was expressing a group issue, but more reflection suggests that Son was actually minimizing his contribution and excusing himself for expressing his feelings. I wonder that everyone's laughter suggested or meant. We failed to explore this.

In between group sessions we heard that two of the group members had expressed the feeling that the group was difficult. They felt everyone had too many problems, and thinking about other people's problems gave them a headache.

March 31 (Third Session)
Three men showed up. *We reached for the common feeling of loneliness expressed by the group members, and also explored individual symptoms of illnesses.* Hung, who had missed the second meeting, brought up the issue he had raised during the first session. He said he had felt so sad and lonely he felt like killing himself. He reviewed the course of his illness and admitted that it has taken him a while to accept that he has a chronic illness. Last summer, when he stopped taking his medication and became suicidal, was when he finally accepted his illness. I think Hung was testing us all, seeing if he could talk about his problem. We, however, failed to recognize this at the time. Hung said he felt it was difficult to be sick in America.

I asked if anyone else would talk about his illness. Dinh explained that he has been sick for many years, since he was sixteen. When he first became sick, he said, he would wander around at night singing outside the houses of his relatives. He said everyone thought he was crazy. Hung observed that being sick is not easy anywhere, not in Vietnam, not in America. He said it's difficult no matter where you are if people think you are crazy. I validated the difficulties of having an illness that is severely stigmatized. Son was sitting, showing nonverbal involvement, occasionally glancing at the other men, but he did not talk. Toan was translating more so I could be more active and the other men were looking at each other and at me and Toan. I tried to involve Son in the discussion by asking him for his thoughts. He resisted. He was drinking iced coffee (we had brought this) and, as a result, he said he felt good, he felt like nothing was wrong; he denied feeling sick at all.

The other men subtly turned away from him when he spoke. I failed to notice their reaction to Son and I think I erred in siding with him, favoring him, because I probably sensed he was being scapegoated, and I also felt allied with him because I see him individually. Toan, unfortunately, followed my lead. If we could repeat the session, I would want to acknowledge the other men's feelings about Son's denial, maybe even their feelings about my mistake of indulging Son, and their feelings about the fact that Son has a family and children and they don't. Instead, I confronted Son's denial by reminding him that last meeting he had discussed feeling sad and lonely, similar feelings the men were discussing this week. (Since Son is also brain injured, I should not have brought up something he raised two weeks ago because he may not remember.) Hung, serving as the internal leader, picked up the discussion by saying he felt that the worst part of being sick was that his old friends did not understand his illness and, therefore, would not act as friendly with him. I verbalized the feeling of loneliness due to non-acceptance.

Hung talked a bit more about feeling lonely, misunderstood, and frustrated. Dinh said he too feels lonely and misunderstood; he agreed that life is difficult when others believe you are crazy. Once again we tried to reach Son, but he said he feels accepted; he thinks his family understands him. *We failed to interpret Son's denial or the meaning it has for the group.* We explored the men's loneliness by asking them questions about their unique feelings. We made a demand for work by asking them what they do to cope with the loneliness. Dinh said he prays to Buddha and chants when he feels lonely, and he sings in the streets, but he said that these things don't really help. Hung said he tries to be around people when he feels lonely—he said it might be easier to be around people in Vietnam. Son said he crawls under a blanket and goes to sleep when he feels lonely.

I validated that feeling lonely is difficult, and then I universalized and said that we all have different ways of coping. We shared our personal feelings with the group. I asked Toan to share what he does when he is lonely. He said he reads, watches TV, and listens to music. I said I eat. Hung looked surprised and asked how Toan could feel lonely if he is here with his family. Toan explained that everyone experiences loneliness. We failed to reach for Hung's profound sense of isolation. I universalized more and said that America is a lonely country, because it is fast-paced and people don't always help those in need. We supported the men's efforts to make themselves less lonely by coming to the group and sharing their feelings. We failed to demand more work and reach for more mutual aid—ways they could help each other feel less lonely. We also missed acknowledging how difficult it is for the men to participate in the group. We could have reached for those feelings.

In between sessions, Hung told his clinician that he couldn't understand how someone like Son could feel lonely, especially when he has family. Hung did not come to the next session; neither did Luu or Doan, who was hospitalized for detox.

April 4 (Fourth Session)
By partializing and providing structure to the process, we facilitated a discussion of feeling and coping mechanisms for a common concern expressed by the group. We opened the meeting by acknowledging that each group has had different people and we realize this may make the group a bit uncomfortable. Then we updated Juan on the last group. Everyone was extremely silent, so Toan restated the goals of the group. He did not allow for the group to take control of the silence. We said that Doan was in the hospital, but we failed to reach for the group's reaction to this news. We didn't ask for the meaning of the silence. We checked the ambivalence of the group about discussing personal problems. The group remained silent. Toan asked what everyone was worrying about right now.

Dinh said he was wondering what he would do if he got sick on a weekend or at a time when Toan could not be reached. He said, if he went to a hospital ER room alone where no one knows him, he would not be able to explain to them what was happening, especially if he were sick. He worries that, when he is sick, he will have no one to take care of him. Juan chimed in, saying that he hates hospitals and he began a story of his experience being restrained in the locked in-patient psych unit. He agreed that it is horrible to be in a hospital without being able to explain what is wrong. We acknowledged that all three men had a common experience of being on an in-patient unit, and I partialized by saying it seemed that they were talking about two things: (1) what it is like to be in the hospital and to be sick, and (2) how to get help when you are feeling sick, and I suggested we talk about the issues. I missed the boat!

A third very important issue they were raising was their feeling of dependence on Toan. The issue could have also been a metaphor of the authority theme. What would the group do without Toan to fill in the silence and take control? Could they do something on their own? *I wonder what would have happened if we had related the question to group process by reaching for their feelings of discomfort and anger that Toan is not always available. We avoided the confrontation.* Juan and Dinh discussed together their experience of being in the hospital. (Son had to leave early.) They were sharing together and looking at each other shyly, and also looking at me and Toan. They also started speaking in English a little bit. I explored early warning signs and symptoms of getting sick, and pointed out that, if they could recognize that they may be getting sick, they may be able to help themselves before a crisis ensues. *We made a demand for work by posing the original question: What do you do when you are sick and you need help?* We asked the men to think of ways they can help themselves, and we also made suggestions of how they could help themselves.

In the end, I encouraged them to think of ways they could help each other—mutual aid outside the group. We pointed out that both men were feeling alone and scared that they would have no one to call for help if they got sick. I asked them if they may be able to help each other. Dinh said people are a great source of emotional support when you're sick, and Juan said he felt it's hard to bother people when you are sick. We had to end on that note. I felt like we failed to wrap up the discussion adequately. The men looked like they connected on this topic, but we could have reached for more feeling and discussion about the meaning of mutual aid and the meaning of their closing comments. We also failed to connect the whole discussion of hospitals to the fact that Doan was in the hospital. Once again we had missed identifying the difference between Son's reality and that of the other men.

Current Status of the Problem:
The group members are still testing the safety of the group; however, they have more readily identified with one another and have acknowledged that they share common concerns. A group culture for sharing and mutual empathy has developed, and the intensity of involvement has deepened. The group members have taken more ownership of the group by raising issues. However, when the leaders make a demand for work or ask the group to problem-solve, the group members participate; they do not confront the leaders.

The group is still dealing with characteristics of the power and control stage. On the surface, the authority theme remains untouched; the group members will treat the leaders with respect accorded that of "doctors," as would be expected in Vietnamese culture, but, in more subtle ways, the group is testing the permissiveness and limits of support of the leaders and their fellow members. The rebellious testing is demonstrated through irregular attendance and by the group taking control of the direction of the session either by talking or remaining silent, instead of relying exclusively on the guidance of the leaders. However, the group members still wait for the leaders to begin the session and, in Vietnamese fashion, the sessional contracting is done in a formal meeting style.

In their transition to the stage of intimacy and mutual aid, the members are demonstrating ambivalence about the level of intensity they want to have in the group. For example, two members who brought up important issues one week and discussed their feelings failed to show for the following session. The members are still scapegoating Son by not listening as closely, and he continues to deny his illness, loneliness, or any other feelings expressed by the group. The leaders have not brought the group's behavior in this matter to the attention of the group.

In summary, the group has established a supportive group culture while at the same time working through issues characteristic of the power and control stage of group process. Unfortunately, the group has only two remaining sessions, so the next step is probably to work on termination issues.

Strategies for Intervention:

1. To remind the group we have only two sessions left and allow time to discuss the meaning of this for them.
2. To remind the group that the purpose of meeting was for them to support and help one another—recontracting.
3. To help the two clients, the individual and the group, in a smoother fashion.
4. To confront the members with inconsistent attendance about the meaning and feelings behind their absences and, at the same time, support them for attending.
5. To confront Son and the group about the scapegoating.
6. To reach for feelings.
7. To communicate with Toan more about his thoughts about group process.
8. To demand work regarding problem solving about the concrete issues raised.
9. To ask Toan if he thinks Son is being scapegoated because he is more brain-damaged than the others and, as a result, less able to relate, or because he is married.
10. To continue to give all the members a lot of positive reinforcement for helping themselves and others by participating.
11. Find someone at the clinic to start a new group for these men after I am gone.

As we have seen in previous records of service, less-experienced workers appear to be over-critical of their practice. When one considers the cultural obstacles faced by the worker in leading this group, and the fact that every word of the discussion, from the worker's point of view, must flow through an interpreter, then progress in developing a mutual aid system is well underway.

HELPING GROUP MEMBERS DEVELOP A STRUCTURE FOR WORK

As a group develops, it needs to work on the task of building a **structure for work**. I am using the term *structure* to describe the formal or informal rules, roles, communication patterns, rituals, and procedures developed by the group members to facilitate the work of the group.

Research on Group Structural Variables

Group variables such as role, status, communication patterns, and decision-making processes have received a great deal of study by small-group researchers. In one of the best known of these efforts, Whyte (1943) spent one year as a participant observer with a group of young men (ranging in age from early 20s to 30s) he called the "street-corner boys." His findings on group structure indicated that position (rank or status) of the members was related to the degree of origination of group action they contributed. Once a group hierarchy was established, a great deal of energy was invested in maintaining it. In addition, if one could influence the top two or three high-status members, one could influence the entire group. Members of this group developed a subtle and complex system of mutual obligations and reciprocities, and position in the group also depended upon how well one discharged his obligations. A member's position in the group was directly related to his resourcefulness, fair-mindedness, and skills in things valued by the group (e.g., sports).

In a second example, Bavelas (1950) worked out an innovative research design in which four- or five-person groups were established to work on a set task. The communication patterns of each group were rigidly controlled by the experimenter. The patterns tested included a circle, a line, a star and a Y pattern. For example, in the Y pattern, communications were organized so that three of the members of the group had to communicate with each other only through the fourth member, who was located at the branching point of the Y. Groups were tested on their speed at solving the problem, the number of errors they made, the satisfaction of the participants, and their recognition of leadership in their groups. Findings indicated the following: The Y pattern was fastest, with the central person identified as the leader. The circle pattern was least productive, with no leader. On the other hand, the group with the circle pattern had the highest morale, and the group with the Y pattern had the lowest. In addition, as might be expected, the central people in the patterns had the highest morale and the end people the lowest. One additional finding was that after many trials, leadership emerged in the circle groups, and their time on the trials improved.

In a study by Deutsch (1949), ten groups of five college students each met once per week for five weeks to discuss human relations problems. After the first week, pairs of students were randomly assigned to groups that were influenced by the experimenter's directions into either cooperative or competitive patterns. His findings indicated that the cooperative groups had stronger individual motivation to complete tasks, a stronger feeling of obligation, greater division of labor, more effective intermember communications, more friendliness, and more group productivity.

Finally, Bales (1958) developed a system for observing and analyzing problem-solving behavior in groups called Interaction Process Analysis (IPA), in which observers could record one of 12 categories of interaction taking place in a group. Ad hoc groups of college students were brought together to solve a series of human relations or construction problems without a formal leader. One of the central findings was that the groups appeared to develop two types of internal leaders: a "task specialist" and a "social-emotional" specialist. The task specialist intervened to help the group complete the test activity, while the social-emotional specialist paid attention to problems of group maintenance.

The group worker function described in this book, and in the illustrations that follow, requires that she or he integrate these two activities.

Young Recovering Addicts: Developing the Rules for the Group

Group structure includes the formal and informal rules for group operation. Some rules are established by the agency or host setting and are not in the control of the group members. At times, the group leader may try to help a group change a rule (see Part V on helping the client to negotiate the system) when conflict is persistent. In other cases, the rules emerge from the members themselves. In the following example, one member of an outpatient group for recovering addicts raises the issue of bringing her baby to the group sessions. Underlying the issue of structure are a number of other concerns for this client as well as some questions for the workers about the need for additional agency support for the group.

The setting is an outpatient alcohol and drug clinic in a hospital. This is a group for young recovering addicts. The purpose of the group is for the members to learn from and support each other as they cope with a sober lifestyle. Two men and two women are at the first meeting, with the possibility that up to four more members will be added. The members range in age from 19 to 27 years. The two women are black; one of the men is black and the other is white. I am co-leading the group with another white woman, who is a counselor at the clinic.

The process recording picks up at the point at which we had just finished going over the group rules and the group members were quiet. Beth (my co-leader) asked the group if they wanted to add any more rules. There was a brief silence, and then Amanda said (to Beth), "You know what I would like to have for a rule." Beth nodded and said that maybe Amanda could explain what she meant to the group. Amanda turned back to the group and said that she had a three-month-old baby. The social service department had the baby now, but she hoped to get the baby back soon. She was not sure that she could find someone she trusted to watch the baby while she came to group. This was her first child, she had been separated from her for so long that she didn't want to leave her. She said that she would worry about the baby while she was in group and that she had asked Beth in the pre-group interview if it might be OK for her to bring the baby along, but that we (Beth and I) had told her that she couldn't bring the baby. Amanda looked at Beth.

Beth said that traditionally the clinic hasn't had very many female clients and that this issue hadn't come up before at the clinic, so she hadn't given Amanda an answer right away, but she had talked to me and to the other staff members, and that she and I had thought that it could be disruptive and distracting to have a baby in the group. Amanda, still speaking to Beth, said that probably the baby would just sleep most of the time. Beth said that the problem was that the baby wouldn't be three months for very long. Beth said that maybe Jen (another member) had some thoughts about the issue. Amanda turned to Jen. Jen smiled and said that she could remember when her daughter and her son were babies, and that she had never wanted to leave them. She said that it's hard to leave your baby, but if there's a baby in the room, it's hard to ignore it even if it is asleep, because babies are so cute you always want to pick them up or play with them or touch them, so having a baby in the group could be disruptive.

Amanda appeared to take this comment in thoughtfully, and then she turned to Leo and Herb and said, "What do you think?" There was a brief silence and then Leo said that he didn't personally have children, but that he had a real soft spot for children and old people. He said from what he could tell it was going to be hard for Amanda to leave her baby, and he could see why. He said it seemed like Amanda was between a rock and a hard place, because if she brought the baby, it might distract her and the rest of the group, and if she didn't bring the baby, it might also distract her because she would be thinking about her baby and worrying about it. He said that it was important for Amanda to take time to focus on her own recovery, and bringing the baby to the group could get in the way of that as well as being distracting.

Amanda seemed satisfied with this, and turned to Herb, who said that he basically agreed with Leo. Herb said that he liked kids a lot, but that he thought that a baby probably would be distracting and that it would be good for Amanda to take the group time to focus on herself. Amanda said that she could understand where everyone was coming from, but that she still felt like she didn't want to leave her baby, but that she'd do the best she could to get a baby sitter. Leo suggested that maybe Amanda shouldn't get too worked up just yet because it would be a few more weeks before she got the baby back and maybe a solution would turn up between now and then. He finished off by saying, "Easy does it," prompting Herb and Jen to follow quickly with two more AA slogans and everyone, including Amanda, wound up laughing. Then there was a brief silence.

I agreed with Leo and said that it was good this issue had come up because it might be the first time it had come up in the clinic, but that it almost certainly wouldn't be the last time. I said that I thought it showed a gap in the clinic's services and it was something Beth and I could explore a little more and see if we could find a solution. The members nodded, and Beth mentioned that there was a baby-sitting service in the hospital during the day, but that there clearly was a gap in the availability of services at night time. Amanda said that she had not known about the daytime service and it made her mad to know it wasn't offered at night. She said she thought that probably a lot more women would come to the clinic if there was someone here to watch their kids. The other group members agreed. Beth said that maybe something could be worked out such as cooperative baby-sitting, and she asked me if I would bring that up at the staff meeting on Monday morning since she isn't there on Mondays. I said I would be sure to, and I'd let them know what happened.

As is often the case, the discussion of the rule can be seen to be raising a number of issues for the client, including the problem of caring for a baby and not losing it to the child welfare agency again. The workers' involvement of the group in the discussion, while not abandoning their responsibility to enforce an agency policy, makes issues of group structure the province of all of the members as well. Most important, the worker's sense of the mediating role between client and system leads her to begin to immediately identify potential systems work on the issue.

Developing a Group Structure Over Time: Teen Psychiatric Group

In this chapter, and the previous one, we have described working with the two clients, the individual and the group. In reality, it is not possible to deal with them as separate entities. The following example is a report of a group worker's efforts, over time, to help a group develop a "structure and culture for work." She does this by paying consistent attention to the individual-group connection.

RECORD OF SERVICE

Client Description and Time Frame:
The setting is an outpatient clinic at a general hospital, and the clients are teenagers referred by their psychiatrists. The time period covered is six weeks.

Description of the Problem:
The group members' struggle to share real feelings with each other is an ongoing process. Dave, the deviant group member, expresses the widely held feelings of the

group, communicating indirectly by being loud and over-active, and so hiding the deep feelings behind his actions. On occasion he alienates group members. His anxiety and concerns are similar to what each member is feeling, so I hoped I could reach beyond his behavior to help Dave communicate and relate effectively to the group, and also help the group see past Dave's behavior to the commonality of their feelings.

How the Problem Came to the Attention of the Worker(s):

At our first session, all the group members were uptight. Dave's uncooperative behavior was the manifestation of all the members' anxiety. Both verbally and non-verbally, he brought up many of the concerns of the group. For instance, the day the group started, all members were sitting on cushions on the floor. However, Dave perched on a table and refused to sit on the floor. "I'm here just to listen—I won't be doing any talking. My psychiatrist made me come to this group." Thus, Dave started to articulate concerns felt by all members:

- The concern of being involved with a psychiatrist—am I nuts?
- Is this a group for crazies?
- I'm not going to share my feelings with anyone here, it's too risky.
- Am I going to be accepted by other group members?
- I am here involuntarily.

and the authority theme. I felt that if I could reach beyond the deviant behavior to bring out the common feelings of all the group members, Dave could become an important ally to me in the group.

Summary of the Work:

(First Session)

I tune in to the group's feelings and unasked questions. The first week of the group, when Dave made his comment, "I'm just here to listen—I won't be doing any talking. My psychiatrist made me come to this group," I was in a dilemma as to which lead to take, he had given me so many. I turned to him, saying, "Yeah, it's tough, isn't it, when you come into a group like this and you don't know anyone." There was a slight pause, then Dave said, "Yeah." I tried again and said, "I guess all of you were wondering and maybe feeling anxious about what the kids were going to be like in the group." (Expressing commonality of feelings.) Connie jumped in and said, "You know I figured you had to be whacko to be in this group." Wanda agreed, "I really thought this was a group for crazy kids, you know, but when I walked in—you all looked— well, normal." I said that it's hard to come to any group, but especially at a psychiatry clinic, and I could understand them being concerned. Several other members agreed, and Brian said it was easier now that he had met the others.

(Second Session)

I help the group deal with the authority theme. The concern with the authority theme was especially apparent in our first few weeks. Dave, as usual, had a greater sense of urgency and neatly brought it to the fore. He marched into the group session the second week and said, "Anyone mind if I lead the group today?" No objections. "Good, we won't allow psychiatrists in." I asked Dave what he meant. "My psychiatrist is about to drive me crazy, I just saw her for an hour." I asked what it was about his psychiatrist that made him feel that way. "Well, she lays trips on me." I asked if other people felt the same way. They all nodded. "I can't talk to my social worker," said

Connie. "I can't talk to people who haven't done drugs or gotten drunk," said Gayle. "They don't treat us like we know that we're doing," said Chris. I said, "Are you afraid Tom (co-therapist) and I won't treat you as if you know what you're doing?" Silence. I added that it was important that they all understood that this was their group, and we were here to help them talk to each other, and listen, and maybe give suggestions, but not to dump on them. The group did not take me up right away on this.

(Fourth Session)

A few weeks later, Tom and I raised the idea of having a parents' night (a Clinic policy), where the parents came and participated in the group. The group was immediately against this, and led by Dave, unanimously voted against our suggestion. "This is our group," Dave said. "If we don't want to have a parents' night, we won't have it." I said I'd clear it with the head of the Clinic that we would not plan a parents' night, as the group didn't feel they wanted it. I did so over the next week.

Later, I explored what it was about having parents come that the group didn't like. "I wouldn't say a word," said Gayle, "I can't talk to my parents." Chris said, "I always fight with my parents, and we'd get into a big battle." "My parents wouldn't come," said Tracy. "Sound like most of you have real difficulties talking to your parents," I said. "No kidding" was the generally fervent reply. I asked Gayle to tell us a bit of what goes on at home for her. (*Bringing the problem from the general to the specific.*) Gayle started talking and led us into an excellent discussion of problems with parents. Several of the members made suggestions to Gayle about how she could do things differently.

(Fifth Session)

I reach beyond Dave's behavior to the feelings. Dave was seeking attention, singing nursery rhymes into the microphone and being flippant. The group members were trying to ignore him. I confronted him on his behavior. "Dave, it seems you act out just to bug the group, but I'm sure something's going on." Gayle said, "Dave talks too much. He always seems to be doing something. I bet he's not showing his real self." Chris suggested, "Maybe he's insecure." I said, "Dave, I'm sure it bothers you that people are getting angry with you, is it something to do with being accepted in here? Seems you set yourself up to get put down." No reply. Gayle said, "You want us to know you and like you; you won't admit it, but it's true." Gayle had hit it beautifully, whereas I had missed the right words. Dave looked at her, then quietly said, "I guess you're right. I guess I feel uptight when I come in here." I then added I was sure each person was feeling what Dave was feeling; he just showed it differently. Gayle said, "Sure, I wonder what you guys think when I talk." I said that perhaps the group could help each other in that regard. I said I thought it was important for them to recognize that they were all wondering about each other, and that they were all tense, and each of them understood how hard it was to really express how they were feeling.

I share my feelings with the group. Through the weeks, I had been encouraging the group to give feedback to Tom and me. At the fifth session, I said, "Okay, we're halfway through our sessions now, and we'd really like some feedback on the group, what we've done, where we're going." (*Alerting group endings, demanding feedback.*) I said sometimes I felt frustrated at the flight behavior, and sometimes their rambunctious moods. The group started to talk about the help they gave each other and how they felt. A constructive mutual exchange occurred. I said I thought they should know that after the group ended, Tom and I would no longer be at the Clinic. They asked what would be happening. We explained. I said it would be hard for us to leave, and hard for the group to end because I felt really good about the work we had all done together. There was a silence. Then the group began to deal carefully with the ending.

(Sixth Session)

Dave was flippant and inappropriate more than usual. He obviously had something on his mind. I confronted Dave: "You're really high today, Dave, bouncing all over the room. What's going on?" The group picked up my use of the word "high," and a discussion ensued on whether Dave was stoned or not. I asked the group to get back to the question. I said maybe it would help for all of us to talk about what was going on for Dave, even if it was hard. The group settled down and waited. I said we knew by now that when Dave had something on his mind he got really hyped and so communicated his uptightness by being noisy, and that we hoped he could feel he could talk to us. Chris picked that up and encouraged Dave to talk, "Is something going on, Dave?" Connie said, "What's going on?" (Pause.) Dave looked down. Then he said, "I moved yesterday." I encouraged him to continue. "I moved from Franklin House into a foster home." I commented that was a big move. "Well," Dave said, "I was in Franklin House for eight months. I really liked it there." I tuned in to his feelings of loss, "It hurts, doesn't it, when you have to leave someplace familiar? You've had a lot of moves." Chris asked what it was like to move into a foster home. The group began to reach out supportively to Dave.

I explore the obstacles to working. Ingrid, sitting quietly in the corner, was confronted by Chris about never speaking in the group. Ingrid felt put on the spot, and was able to say so. I asked her what made it hard for her to talk in the group. She said there were too many people around. I guessed she wasn't used to talking in a group, probably not even in school. She said right. Tracy agreed, and said it was easier for her to talk to friends at school whom she saw every day. Chris said sometimes she felt her problems weren't very important and not worth talking about. There was a thoughtful silence.

Then Carol, who has a speech difficulty that makes her almost incomprehensible, started talking. It was the first time she had spoken in the group. She said she felt uncomfortable talking in the group because she was afraid she'd get laughed at. There was a long silence. I said, "I guess Carol's really hit the nail on the head for all of us, eh?" There were nods. Chris said, "No one will laugh; we're here to help each other." I said, "The concerns you have, Carol, are the same as the feelings Ingrid has, but she expressed them by being quiet. Dave, on the other hand, is loud. You are each wondering how the others will react." Gayle asked, "What can we do to make it easier?" Carol said she felt worse because she felt the group couldn't understand her speech. Tom said that if she spoke really slowly that we could all pitch in and help. The group started shouting encouragement to each other. I said I guess they were all feeling the same inside, even if it showed in different ways, and if they knew that, maybe it would be easier to talk, to take the risk. They all laughed and agreed.

(Seventh Session)

I point out to the group that when it's hard to talk or accept what's being said, "flight behavior" can result, breaking the opportunity to work. Carol, painfully, was talking. She was difficult to understand. Dave decided he wanted to talk about points of interest, rather than difficulties. The group started talking about their various weekends. I said to the group, "How come you changed so quickly from listening to Carol?" There was an uncomfortable silence. I said I had noticed that they became restless when Carol spoke and it seemed as if they felt uncomfortable listening to her. Carol started crying and said it was the same as at school, no one understood her. Chris asked Carol how long she had her speech difficulty. Carol said since birth. The group started to reach out for her. Dave said he had a hard time understanding her, and the group agreed. Brian said, "Let's make sure that Carol has the opportunity to speak." Gayle said, "I guess it's hard to talk about difficult things for all of us, but with Carol, it's doubly difficult to talk about difficult things." I agreed, but said I thought they were doing a great job at this point. (*Crediting the work.*)

I offer the opportunity to work. Connie was having extreme difficulties with her parents, so much so that her social worker was looking for a foster home for her. She was, however, unable to express her deep feelings of pain. As she described her difficulties, I noticed Dave was remarkably quiet. I reached for Dave: "You're in a foster home, maybe you can tell Connie and the group about it." Dave explained the technicalities. I reached for the feelings: "What's it like, Dave, to live in a foster home?" Silence. Dave said, "It's okay." I asked him what that meant. Dave started talking about being kicked out of home and having to go into the foster home. "It's the shits, Connie. I got kicked out, but it sounds like you could still work it out. It's really hard." I said, "And it hurts like hell to have your parents to the point where they're willing to let you go." Connie started to cry. "I'm so scared, I don't know what to do." Chris said she had learned to talk things out at home, and maybe the group could help. Tracy said she was learning to work out problems with her parents. Dave said how he was settling in with his foster parents and things were better for him and he hoped Connie could work it out without having to leave home. I encouraged the discussion of specific issues for Connie at home. Honest and deep feelings were shared by all the group.

Current Status of the Problem:
The group is becoming more at ease sharing real feelings with each other. They are more comfortable in taking each other on. Dave still acts out periodically, but he is doing it less frequently. The group calls him on his behavior and demands to know what's going on: "Hey, Dave, what's really going on today?" The more reserved members of the group are becoming more verbal, as each member learns to look beyond behavior to common feelings of anxiety, fear, and anger, and to accept and respect different personalities. The group is mutually supportive, and especially protective of Carol, who is encouraged to talk by all members. There are still times when work is avoided and members are not willing to risk. But a culture for work is developing and a common feeling expressed that the group members own the group, are learning to relate effectively with each other and can share common feelings and experiences.

Strategies for Intervention:
1. To continue to point out that when hard-to-talk-about issues are raise, fight and flight behavior can result.
2. To continue to reach beyond any deviant behavior for the common feelings.
3. To continue reinforcing Dave for the valuable work he has done: his particular sense of urgency has helped him raise many relevant issues. He is indeed an ally!
4. To continue to demand work and to keep the work around being honest and congruent in feelings.
5. To continue to deal with endings in the group.

HELPING GROUP MEMBERS NEGOTIATE THE ENVIRONMENT

The discussion thus far has focused on the internal tasks of the group. However, a group does not exist in a vacuum, but is located in an institution or agency, or in a community. In the description of the group as an "open social system," presented at the beginning of this chapter, the term *open* was used to imply that the boundary between the group and its environment was not closed. In fact, the activities of the group will have some effect on the relationship between the group and the environment. In turn, the interaction with the environment will have an impact on the internal operations of the group. In this section we will explore an additional group task: negotiating the environment.

With the exception of the chapter on contracting, I have been discussing the group almost as if it exists cut off from the external world. In the contracting chapter I focused on finding the common ground between the service of the agency and the needs of the group members. Contact between the group and its external system continues after the beginning phase and is one of the ongoing realities to which the group must pay some attention. Two aspects of this group-environment interaction are considered in this section. First, the group-environment relationship in terms of mutual obligations and expectations is discussed. The example is from a community center setting in which an acting-out group of young teens finds itself in trouble with the agency because of its aggressive behavior. The second example concerns a group of sixth-graders in an elementary school. Their relationship to the school they are leaving and their fears about attending a new school illustrate the fact that negotiating the system can be a central theme of work for the group. There are, of course, other examples of group-system relationships, and some of these will be discussed in Chapter 18, where our focus will be on the work carried out with the system and its representatives. For now, these two examples are used to illustrate the interdependence of the group and its environment and the role of the worker in mediating the engagement.

Adolescents: Acting-Out Behavior in the Community Center

The first example involves the young teenage club described earlier in my discussion of internal leadership in the group. The setting was a middle-class community YM&YWHA (Young Men's and Young Women's Hebrew Association), and the group had a long history of acting-out behavior at the center. This group was one of my first as a social work student. I was in the building working on recording one evening when I was told by a staff supervisor to "get the kids in my group in line, since they were acting out in the game room." He was obviously angry at them. My first reaction was panic; I had been working hard to overcome our rocky start together, trying to undo my earlier mistakes of attempting to impose limits and establish my authority. I had just been getting somewhere in this effort and saw this confrontation as a potential step backward. When I explained this to the supervisor, his reaction was, "What's wrong? Do you have trouble setting limits and using your authority?" As any student in training knows, a supervisor questioning your "problem" evokes a powerful response. I decided to face my responsibility, as defined by the supervisor, and went off to do combat in what I knew would be a battle of wills. Feeling upset about what I was doing only made me come on stronger.

> I found the guys running and screaming in the halls, and I yelled at them to "cut it out." They slowed down for a minute and I said to them, "Look, if you guys don't cut it out, I'm going to throw you out of the building." I continued, "What kind of way is

that to behave, anyway? You guys know better than that. I thought I was getting somewhere with you, but I guess I was all wrong." My words seemed to be an additional catalyst and I found myself chasing them through the building, catching them one at a time, and escorting them outside.

My mistake was a natural one. I was not clear about the concept of deviant behavior as communication at that time, so I did not attempt to find out what was wrong—why they were so agitated. Even if I had been clear about that, my functional confusion would have prevented me from dealing with them effectively. In the same situation today, I would be able to explain my functional role more clearly to my supervisor, suggesting that I speak to the boys to see what was going on and to try to cool them down long enough to talk to the supervisor about what was happening in the building and why. If I were unsuccessful, then the supervisor could throw the group outside and I would go with them. I would have explained to the supervisor that at the point the boys were thrown outside, I would be available to them to figure out what had happened and to find a way to deal more effectively with the Y, since they would want to be accepted back. The Y was concerned about this group's behavior, and this would be an opportunity to do some work on the relationship between the group and the Y.

I am not suggesting there would never be a time when I felt bound to set limits on the boys and act on behalf of the agency or society. In the course of our time together there would be many such occasions. For example, if physical violence were threatened, it would be my job to set limits and try to stop it so that we could develop safety for all members in the group. However, at this moment, when they were thrown out, they needed their worker the most. As I found out later, that day had been report card day at school, and most of the boys in the group were afraid to go home that evening and face their parents because of bad grades and reports of similar behavior problems in school. A marvelous opportunity for work had been missed. In Chapter 18, this group–environment mediation role will be further illustrated in a number of contexts.

A group theorist who could have helped me conceptualize the problem differently is Homans (1950). In his classic book *The Human Group*, Homans presents a general theory of human interaction using five well-known field studies of social interaction to illustrate his ideas. He describes three major elements of behavior, which he terms interaction, sentiment, and activity. *Interaction* refers to any contact between people, *sentiment* to feelings or drives, and *activity* to any action. Thus, Homans could take a descriptive social study and break it down into these three components: interactions, sentiments, and activities. His interest centers on the interdependence of these elements of social behavior; for example, how sentiment in a group can affect interaction and, in turn, how interactions can affect sentiment.

In the group example just described, the boys' feelings (sentiments) about their poor grades affected the way they related (interactions) to each other, which in turn generated behavior (activity) of the acting-out type. Homans's second major theoretical contribution is important here. He viewed activities, interactions, and sentiments within two interdependent systems—the "internal" system and the "external" system. The internal system consists of the interactions, sentiments, and activities *within* the group and their mutual interdependence. The external system consists of the same three basic elements (interaction, sentiment, and activity) between the group and its environment—in this case, the Y. It is important to note that Homans does not use the term *external system* to refer to the system itself—in this case, the

Y. *External system,* to Homans, would be the three elements of interaction, sentiment, and activity *between* the group and the Y.

The boys had developed a pattern of acting out within the Y that generated negative sentiment on the part of staff, which in turn affected the interactions between Y staff and the group, which in turn generated more negative sentiment, and so on. Any effort to deal with the group members' behavior within the group must take into account the impact of the "external systems" of the school and the agency.

I have oversimplified Homans's theory, but I think the central elements demonstrate once again how a theoretical construct can help a worker conceptualize a problem in a new way.

Sixth-Grade Girls and the Transition to a New School

The next example, involving a group of sixth-grade girls, illustrates the task of negotiating the environment in a slightly different way. The two aspects of the environment that these girls must deal with are the school they are leaving and the junior high school they will be attending. The worker picks up this theme at the start of the meeting.

> The girls began talking about going to a new school next year. Jean expressed her fear of leaving Bancroft, and I asked her why she felt this way. She said that she was happy at Bancroft and that she really does not want to leave. She also added that she did not know what Strathearn was like, and she had heard that they had some very strict teachers. I replied by saying that it seems as though Jean was worried about much more than just the strict teachers at Strathearn, and from what she said I got the feeling that she is telling us that it is scary to be leaving Bancroft, a school that you have been at for many years and where you know the people, and now you have to go to a completely new school with many new people and many unknown things before you. Jean agreed that she was quite scared of leaving Bancroft and having to meet new teachers and new kids. I asked the others in the group how they felt about having to go to a new school next year. All the others shared Jean's feelings and expressed their fears about leaving Bancroft. Mary said that she was worried about the first day at Strathearn and what it would be like. I asked them if any of them remembered their first day at Bancroft and what it felt like. Vera and Soula, who had come to Bancroft two years ago, said they had been frightened, but after the first few days began to feel less frightened, especially when some kids began to talk to them.
>
> Betty said that she thinks that it is harder to make friends in Grade 7 than in Grades 4 or 5. I asked her why, and she said that she thinks kids are friendlier when they are younger and that older kids do not always want to be friends with you. I asked Betty whether she had ever experienced this herself. She said that she had moved to a new street this year and tried to become friends with a group of girls on her street, but they did not want her as a friend. I said that she must have been hurt when this happened, and Betty replied that she felt lousy, but she was able to make friends with some other girls on the street. A few other girls related their attempts to make friends on a new street, or in the hospital, with some of their attempts being successful and others unsuccessful. They were able to understand how Betty had felt.

By asking the girls to think about their first day at the elementary school, the worker was hoping to help them generalize from that experience to the new one that they faced. It was important that the worker neither underplayed the realities of their concerns nor allowed the group members to overplay them. Simply having them expressed this way was helpful, as it let the girls know that others felt the same way. In this case, it was possible for the worker to try to arrange a visit to the new school. The worker felt that fear of the unknown was part of the problem, and by helping the group members to meet some of the junior high school staff and students, these fears might be lessened.

> I said that from what they are saying, making friends can be easy at times, but sometimes it is not all that easy, and it is never a very happy thing when you try to become friends with people and they turn you down. I said that it is possible that it is harder to make friends as you get older, but I reminded them that in going to a new school they will probably be going with some of their old friends so it is a little easier than going in without any friends at all. Dmitra asked whether they would be in the same class with their friends. I said that I really did not know but would think that some would be together whereas others would not. Taxia and some others said that they did not want to be separated from their friends. I said that I could understand their feelings of wanting to be together and that this would make it less frightening for them, but the decisions for this are really not in our control but are decided by the principal and the teachers at the new school. I continued by saying that I realize that they are all worried about the unknowns of a new school and about being separated from their friends. These are real worries, and I can feel for them.
>
> I told them that I had an idea that might help to reduce some of their worries, and I wanted to share it with them for a few minutes. I asked them whether if it was possible for us to arrange a visit to Strathearn to see the school, meet some of the teachers and students, they would be interested. All the girls were extremely excited and expressed their enthusiasm about the idea. I told them that I was glad that they wanted to go and I would try very hard to see if it could be arranged, but I could not assure them that we would definitely go. The girls were able to accept this and told me that they hoped it would be possible. I then said that we would talk more about this next week, once I knew if it was at all possible, but perhaps now we could continue our discussion where we had left off before I introduced the idea. Lola began to speak and said that she wants to make some new friends next year but she is worried about what the kids at the new school will think of her. I encouraged her to elaborate on this point. She was concerned with what kids might think about her looks, the way she dresses, and just her in general. I asked her how she thinks other feel about her now. She said that she thinks other like her, but sometimes she is really not sure. At this point others in the group responded to what Lola said and began to express positive, warm feelings toward Lola and told her that they liked her. Lola seemed to feel better when she heard this. I credited Lola and the others for being able to express and share feelings that are often difficult to express. I them asked whether others were worried about what other kids at the new school will think about them. The girls continued this discussion for some time.

With these excerpts, I have completed my outline of the properties and dynamics related to the worker's second client, the group. In Chapter 16, we will look at different types of groups, identifying some of the variant elements.

CHAPTER SUMMARY

The worker's second client, the organism called the group, must go through a developmental process. Early tasks include problems of formation and the satisfaction of individual members' needs. Problems of dealing with the worker as a symbol of authority (authority theme) must be faced, as well as the difficulties involved in peer-group relationships (the intimacy theme). Attention needs to be paid to the culture of the group so that norms can be developed that are consistent with the achievement of the group's goals. Taboos that block the group's progress must be challenged and mastered if the discussion is to be meaningful. A formal or informal structure must be developed. This structure will include assigned roles, assigned status, communication patterns, and a decision-making process. Effective work in the group will develop a sense of cohesion, which in turn will strengthen future work. Finally, the group exists within a dynamic system—the environment—and one of the worker's tasks is to assist with the interaction between the group and its social surroundings.

GLOSSARY

Authority theme Issues related to the relationship between the client (individual, family, or group) and the social worker.

Basic assumption groups Bion's (1961) idea that group members appear to be acting as if their behavior were motivated by a shared basic assumption about the purpose of the group—an assumption other than the expressed group goal.

Cohesion The property of the group that describes the mutual attraction members feel for each other.

Consensual validation The third subphase of the interdependence phase of group development (Bennis and Shepard, 1956), in which the *unconflicted* members once again provide the leadership needed for the group to move to a new level of work characterized by honest communication between members.

Counterdependence-flight The second subphase of the dependency phase of group development, as described by Bennis and Shepard (1956) in which group members are in flight, exhibiting behaviors indicating fear of the leader's authority, while attempting to take over the group.

Counterdependent member A member of the group who, during the counterdependence-flight subphase of group development, acts as if she or he is not dependent upon the group leader and attempts to take over the group (Bennis and Shepard, 1956).

Dependence phase The first phase of the group development, according to Bennis and Shepard (1956), which is marked by a preoccupation of group members with issues involving authority.

Dependence-flight The first subphase of the dependency phase of group development, as described by Bennis and Shepard (1956) in which group members are in flight, exhibiting behaviors indicating dependence upon the leaders.

Dependent group One of Bion's (1961) *basic assumption groups.* The group appears to be meeting in order to be sustained by the leader rather than working on its purposes.

Dependent member A member of a group who, during the dependence-flight subphase of group development, acts as if she or he is dependent upon the group leader, wanting the leader to take control of the group (Bennis and Shepard, 1956).

Disenchantment-flight The second subphase of the interdependence phase of group development, according to Bennis and Shepard (1956), in which the *counterpersonals* take over from the *overpersonals* in reaction to the growing intimacy.

Enchantment-flight The first subphase of the interdependence phase of group development, as described by Bennis and Shepard (1956), in which good feelings abound and efforts are directed towards healing wounds.

Flight-fight group One of Bion's (1961) *basic assumption groups.* In a primitive group, when the work group gets close to painful feelings, the members will unite in an instantaneous, unconscious process to form the "flight-fight" group, acting from the basic assumption that the group goal is to avoid the pain associated with the work group processes through flight (i.e., an immediate change of subject from the painful area) or fight (i.e., an argument developing in the group that moves from the emotional level to an intellectual one).

Group culture The norms, taboos, rules, and member roles that guide the generally accepted ways of acting within the group. In a group's early stage, the group members usually recreate a culture representative of the larger community. This culture can be modified over time to become more conductive to effective work.

Interdependence phase The second phase of group development, according to Bennis and Shepard (1956), which has to do with questions of intimacy and the group members' concerns about how close they wish to get to each other.

Intimacy theme Concerns related to the interactions between the members of a group.

Model A symbolic representation of reality.

Norms of behavior The rules of behavior generally accepted by a dominant group in society. These norms can be recreated within a social work group or other system. The existence of the norms is evident when the group members act as if the norms existed.

Organismic model A metaphor used to illustrate a system's capacity for growth and emergent behavior, encompassing a process in which a system transcends itself and creates something new that is more than just the simple sum of its parts.

Pairing group One of Bion's basic assumption groups, in which the group, often through a conversation between two members, avoids the pain involved in the work.

Resolution-catharsis The third subphase of the dependency phase in group development, according to Bennis and Shepard (1956), in which group leadership is assumed by members who are *unconflicted* or independent. This overthrow of the trainer (of a T-group) leads to each member taking responsibility for the group: the trainer is no longer seen as "magical," and the power struggles are replaced by work on shared goals.

Structure for work The formal or informal rules, roles, communication patterns, rituals, and procedures developed by the group members to facilitate the work of the group.

Taboo In modern cultures, the term refers to social prohibitions that result from conventions or traditions. Norms and taboos are closely related, since a group norm may be one that upholds the tradition of making certain subjects taboo.

Unconflicted member A member of the group who is independent and unconflicted about authority.

Work group The mental activity related to a group's task (Bion, 1961). When the work group is operating, one can see group members translating their thoughts and feelings into actions that are adaptive to reality. As Bion describes it, the work group represents a "sophisticated" level of group functioning.

NOTES

1. It has been my personal observation that the anger in many T-groups, or encounter-type groups, such as those studied by Bennis and Shepard (1956), was actually related to the group leader's extremely passive behavior at the start of the group. According to this theory, a passive leader would force a group to come to grips with its own responsibility for owning the group process, thus freeing the group from the restrictive impact of the leader's authority. I observed that the more passive the leader, the more power he or she accrued as group members became more dependent, rather than less so. Also, the lack of any external purpose other than the experiential learning in which analysis of the group process was the purpose also influenced the group members' behaviors. Most of the patterns of behavior observed in these groups were exacerbated by a lack of external purpose and the passivity of the leader. Bennis and Shepard would disagree with this interpretation. In spite of these differences, the fundamental phases described in this theory appear to be universal in nature.

2. See Chapter 10 for the detailed contracting session of this group.

3. Or, in some neighborhoods, they might get invited to many more parties.

4. For example, see P.A. Hare, *Handbook of Small Group Research* (New York: The Free Press, 1962).

5. I am particularly indebted to the staff at the Lady Trench Training Centre of the Hong Kong Social Welfare Department (Miss Stella Leung, Mrs. M.Y. Li, Mr. Liu Kwong-yuen, Mr. Y.F. Cheung, and Mrs. A. Mak) as well as Social Welfare Department administrators, supervisors, and workers (Mr. Stephen Law, Mr. Alexander Fung, Mr. Lau Kai-chuen, Mr. Kwok Ka-chi, Mr. Carlos Leung, Mr. Stephen Lam, Mr. Lai Cham-kun, and Mr. Billy Ho), all of whom added in one way or another to my education. In addition, the Dean (at the time, Dr. Richard Nann), and the faculty, staff and field instructors at the University of Hong Kong School of Social Work helped to deepen my understanding of Chinese culture.

6. A student paper on group work in the Chinese culture which was kindly shared with me by Mary Wong to help in my preparation.

15

Endings and Transitions with Groups

CHAPTER OUTLINE

Ending and Transition Phase Summary

Endings and Transitions: Group Illustrations

A Termination Session: The Worker Leaving the Group

The dynamics and skills involved in the ending and transition phase were discussed in detail in Chapter 5. All of these processes are equally applicable to work with groups. They are summarized in this chapter, and the variations that apply in group work are presented and illustrated. The chapter concludes with a full description of an ending group session that demonstrates the unique aspects of ending in groups.

ENDING AND TRANSITION PHASE SUMMARY

The ending stages of work with individuals, described in detail in Chapter 5, are also apparent in group sessions. First, there is the **denial** stage, in which group members appear to ignore the imminent end of the group. This is followed by **anger**, which emerges in direct and indirect forms. The **mourning period** is usually characterized by apathy and a general tone of sadness that one can feel in the group. Next, the group attempts to **try the ending on for size**. For example, one notices that group members are operating independently of the worker or spending a great deal of time talking about new groups or new workers. The **farewell-party syndrome** is seen when group members appear to protect the preciousness of the group by avoiding its negative aspects. It is not at all unusual for group members to attempt to avoid the pain of the ending itself by suggesting an actual farewell party.

Worker strategies for dealing with endings in group work are also similar to those described in work with individual clients. The worker should bring the ending to the group members' attention early, thereby allowing the ending process to be established. The stages should be pointed out as the group experiences them, with the worker reaching for the indirect cues and articulating the processes taking place: denial, anger, mourning, and so on. The worker should also put personal feelings and recollections into the discussion, since the group ending has meaning for the worker as well. Discussion of the ending feelings should be encouraged, with the worker participating fully in the exchange of both positive and negative reactions. The worker should also attempt to make the group's evaluation of their work together specific. For example, when a member says, "It was a great group!" the worker should ask, "What was it about the group that made it great?" There should also be an attempt to reach past the "farewell-party" syndrome to encourage members to share negative feedback.

In the group context, since members will have different reactions, the worker should encourage the expression and acceptance of differing views. The worker must also pay attention to the transitional aspect of the ending phase. For example, if members are continuing with other workers, how can they begin the relationship in a positive manner? If members have finished their work, what have they learned, and how can they use their learning in their new experiences? If they have found the group helpful, how can they find similar sources of support in their life situations? In this way, the worker can ensure that the ending discussion deals with substantive matters as well as the process of ending. In some situations, help can also take the form of a physical transition (e.g., a visit to a new school or institution). Finally, the worker should search for the subtle connections between the process of the group ending and the substantive work of the contract. For example, endings for a group of unmarried mothers may coincide with separation from their child. As a second example, foster teenagers who have provided mutual aid to each other have learned something about giving and taking help from their peer group. These and other connections can help to enrich the ending discussion. Illustrations of these dynamics and skills, drawn from the group context, are provided in the next section.

ENDINGS AND TRANSITIONS: GROUP ILLUSTRATIONS

The ending phase of work offers a powerful opportunity to deepen the work by integrating process and content. By that I mean recognizing that the losses involved in ending a group often provoke issues of intimacy and loss in other areas of the client's life. By constantly searching for the connections, however faint, between the dynamics of the ending process and the substantive work (content) of the particular group, the worker can help the members to use the ending as an important learning experience. In the example that follows, a worker opens up the discussion of her leaving with a group of persons with multiple sclerosis (the group will be continuing). The announcement of the impending ending initiates a powerful conversation about intimacy and loss related to the illness. It is also important to note that the worker brings the group members back to their own endings in the here-and-now of the group experience.

Ending Session with Patients with Multiple Sclerosis

Worker: As you know, I only meet with you one more time after today. You all will continue to meet until June. What are your thoughts about the group ending in a couple of months?

Bob: I am not looking forward to the summer because of the hot weather...it makes my MS flare up.

Albert: I know...I always feel tired and run down when it gets too hot. And then the group breaks up and I don't have anyone to really talk to about my MS. I used to look forward to the summer, but now I almost dread it.

Bob: I'm going to miss everyone too. I don't have anyone to talk to either. My wife is great, but she doesn't really understand what I am feeling.

Worker: Do you guys keep in touch even when the group is not meeting during the summer months?

Albert: Not really...

Fred: I often talk to Rob from the other group pretty regularly.

Bob: Albert, you live not too far from me. We should get together once in a while this summer. Or at least talk on the phone.

Albert: I like that idea...I do want to stay in touch.

James: (Who had been quiet up to this point) I used to dance and run track...and now I can't anymore. People look at me like I'm weird.

Bob: I always liked to dance too.

Worker: James, you said people look at you weird. What do you mean by that? How does that make you feel?

James: I get mad because I am not weird. I am just in a wheelchair. They don't know what I used to be able to do. All they see is what I look like on the outside.

Worker: You're right. Strangers do not know who you are or what you are like, as we do. They don't know you as a person, and it isn't fair that they should judge you by your appearance or being in a wheelchair.

Fred: That's the trouble...no one can see the MS. They can't see the pain we feel in our legs, or the burning we have in our joints.

Albert: (He is one of the members whose MS is not as extreme. He still walks.) People don't even know anything is wrong with me because I am not in a wheelchair. But I still experience the MS symptoms. When they flare up, I get tired and sometimes walk off-balance, like I am drunk or something.

Worker: It must be hard for you, Albert, because people cannot see your illness, and may not understand when you try to explain your physical symptoms.

Albert: Yeah, that happens a lot. When people find out I have MS, they don't believe me because I am not in a wheelchair and they automatically associate MS with being in a wheelchair.

Fred: I went through that a lot when I was first diagnosed. I fought going into this wheelchair for as long as I could. I was luck to be able to work until I was 60. But a short time after I retired, I had to get the chair.

James: Yeah...when I first got those symptoms, the MPs on base used to stop me to ask if I was drunk because I staggered so much. That's when I first realized something was wrong. And then it just kept getting worse until I wound up in this wheelchair.

Worker: You guys have lost important things associated with your identity because of this disease. Many of you had to quit working before you wanted...some of you lost important relationships.

James: That's what I miss...having a girlfriend. (He pauses.)

Worker: (After it looks like he won't continue on his own) Tell us more, James.

James: I just miss the company. I don't care about the sex. I just wish I had the companionship. Someone to talk to, who will do things with me. I love my son and my parents, but I wish I had someone more my age to be with. (James is a young guy, in his early thirties and, in addition to being confined to a wheelchair, he has speech difficulties and shaking in his arms and neck. In retrospect, I wish I had explored more about how the change in his appearance and increasing disability affects his romantic possibilities. He has an eight-year-old son, but I don't know what his relationship with the mother was or if she left him when he became disabled. I'm sure this is something all the men have had to face—changes in their manhood, and how society views a disabled man.)

Fred: I know, James. Companionship is important.

Bob: There are a lot of symptoms of MS that people don't see and we don't talk about. Like our bladder and bowel problems. It's very degrading and embarrassing not to be able to control them all the time. (The others all voiced their agreement.)

Worker: I know you were interested a few weeks ago in having Dr. C. (urologist) come to speak to you about these problems. Did she ever come?

Albert: Not yet.

Worker: I will talk to the RN again and try to schedule her as a speaker in the future. (I bowed out of a sensitive and embarrassing subject here as well. I probably should have explored their feelings more around this subject, too.)

Worker: I want to talk some more about our ending. I know I've been mentioning it the last couple of times we've met. It's really hard when people come and go from your life.

Albert: Yeah, it is. It seems like we just started with you and now you are leaving already.

Worker: I want you to know that it is hard for me too. I am in a field where I will have to say good-bye many times to people whom I have grown to care about. But I believe that when I leave here, I will take a part of you all and internalize it, especially your courage. I have learned a lot from all of you about what it is like to live with MS, and how hard it is to deal with all the symptoms. But mostly I have seen how courageous and positive you are in light of all you have been through, and that encourages me. I believe I will be able to help other people in your position because of what you have taught me about dealing with a chronic disease like multiple sclerosis, and I thank you for this group and this experience.

Bob: I know you are going to do well. You are a kind person, and genuine and caring. I think I speak for everyone when I say we've enjoyed having you here.

(The others nodded and voiced their agreement.)

Worker: Thank you. That's nice to hear. I've really enjoyed being a part of this group and getting to know all of you.

(The time was up and we finished by saying good-bye and talking about meeting again in two weeks.)

As the ending approaches, there is always unfinished business between the group and the worker that needs to be explored. In the following illustration from a group home for pregnant teens, we see the worker reaching for the cues that represent both the anger and the positive feelings. We also see the worker sharing her own feelings.

Pregnant Teens in a Group Home

The session opened today with a review of last week. I told the girls that Mrs. Banes (co-worker) and I had felt their sadness and depression last week, but only afterwards had we realized that they were angry, too. I commented that their depression seemed to be a result of their frustration and anger. I asked if they knew why they were angry. Monique said last week she was fearful of the possibility of a Caesarean section. Ginny said she had been fearful of going to hospital. Nicky said they'd felt depressed before the session. I suggested that when we left last week, Mrs. Banes and

I were also feeling sad and depressed, in part because of the feelings resulting from our coming separation.

Alison commented that the group seemed so small; so many girls had left. I wondered if this, too, didn't give them a feeling of loss. They were coming so close to the end of their pregnancy, and for them, in addition to the loss of the group, they were also preparing for the loss of their baby. I thought it was no wonder they were feeling angry. I also said I wanted them to know we would miss them—we had become very close to the group—they had shared so much of themselves. I said, "We are a part of all that we have met." I suggested that they were a part of Mrs. Banes's and my experience and we would not forget them, nor would we forget what we had learned from them. They had shown us how they could grow and mature, they had shown us courage in reaching their decision, they had taught us the importance of communication with each other and between teenagers, and their parents, and so on.

Ginny said it was hard to put into words what she had gained from the group, but she felt better about herself and better able to cope with things in the future. Alison said she had been feeling very sorry for herself when she arrived at the home. Through the group she had learned that she wasn't the only one, that she was lucky compared with some of the other girls. Nicky said she was learning to look at other people's problems, trying to understand them. Mona thought other decisions would be easier when they had made the tremendous decision about their baby.

After some discussion about what they had learned in the group, the workers asked if the members would like to have the workers visit them and their babies at the hospital. The responses were positive, and the group then moved into a discussion of the future. The worker acknowledged the graduation quality of the discussion as they prepared for their transitions:

Alison can hardly wait to get back home. She is very homesick. Ginny is still concerned that her parents may not be ready to let her make her own decisions. They were afraid she might get hurt again. Mona said they couldn't stop her getting hurt. She thought parents made a mistake to make early childhood "like a fairy tale." Then when you got out in the world, you discovered the real world wasn't like that. She thought parents tried to be too protective. After all, Nicky said, you had to learn by your mistakes. I said sometimes it was hard for parents to let their children go. Alison thought it was a little like their giving up their babies when their parents had to let them grow up and go out on their own. Even when their parents knew their decision to let their children go was right, it still hurt to let them do it.

Mona and Margaret thought you had to reach the point when you made your own decisions, even if you made mistakes. Mona said she was sure now she wouldn't get too involved with a boy too quickly. Nicky agreed. She said she was going to have the "light" approach. She was going to be very sure of the boy before she entered a serious relationship. Nicky thought she didn't want to get married for a long time. She said the last nine months have taught her she wasn't ready to settle down yet. She wanted to have a job, get nice clothes, travel.

Mona said she was hoping to choose a new career, get more training. Nicky was afraid she might have chosen the wrong field of study. She wasn't sure now she wanted to be a secretary. She'd like a job that would let her travel. Several of the girls thought she could travel. If she were a good secretary, she could get a job in another country too.

I said I thought the girls were sounding much less depressed. They were already thinking about new decisions, their future, and showing their increased maturity. Alison asked when the next group would be starting. Nicky said the new group would be a bunch of "teeny-boppers." She said even though some of the new girls in the home were 18 or so, they acted like children. She didn't think they were showing much "respect" for the "old-timers." Alison wanted to know if they could come to the next group if they were still there. I assured her they were welcome and said we were having difficulty "ending." I said I thought they'd been one the very best groups I'd been with. Monique, Alison, Ginny, and Nicky said they had all looked forward to their Thursdays with us, and were going to miss us. Nicky wanted to know in what way they had been a "best" group.

I said perhaps it had been because we'd been together for twelve weeks, but I felt I could see their noticeable gains in maturity. I felt very close to them all. I thought they had a better feeling about themselves and had made wise decisions for their babies. Monique said she was glad she had thought through her decision so carefully. She said on the day she left the hospital, she had felt, "I just can't leave my baby behind," but then had said to herself, "Your situation hasn't changed; you can't keep your baby." She said she had been very blue when the group began today, but was feeling ever so much better. The other girls agreed. We wished them good luck. The girls wondered when they'd be seeing us again. I said Mrs. Banes and I would be seeing them in individual sessions and said we were having trouble stopping today. Endings were hard for all of us. Alison and Nicky commented on Mrs. Banes, "the silent member." We said good-bye. The girls' supper bell had rung, and we were very late.

In the next example, we see the variation on the theme with children's groups, when the anger in the ending phase can emerge through acting-out behavior.

Children's Group in an Elementary School

Sometimes the expression of anger can emerge indirectly as acting-out behavior. This is particularly true of endings in children's groups, as the members seem to revert to the behaviors exhibited in the beginning sessions. In the following illustration, a student worker returned after a two-week absence from her group of grade-school children who had been meeting with her weekly because of trouble in school. The group had only two weeks left until its last meeting. The worker reached for the cues of the anger expressed in the children's behavior.

The children were sitting in the middle of the room in a circle waiting for me. This was different from usual. There was a big table at the back of the room, and we usually sat around it. The boys started cheering and clapping when I came in. I said hello and told them that I was glad to see them too. I had missed them, and it was good to be back. They asked me a lot of questions about where I had been, what I had done, and so on, and I had to give them a rather detailed description of my vacation. After a while of this joking around, I said that it had been a long time since I had seen them last, and I asked what was new.

They started talking about Chang, the Chinese boy in the class whom they hated, and how they had beat him up. While I was trying to get the story straight about what had happened, a couple of the kids started becoming rowdy and rude, cutting each other off more than usual and cutting me off, too. I was surprised because although they had the habit of interrupting each other and me as well, they were never so belligerent. George continued telling me about the fight he had with Chang, and how he had given him a bloody nose and sent him to the hospital for stitches. (I later found out the stitches part of the story was exaggerated.) Warren, Bobby, and a couple of others joined in and they all proudly described in detail the way they had beat Chang up. I wanted to remark on this and finally had to tell them to hold it, I wanted to say something. They quieted down a bit, and I finally was able to say what I had wanted—that I couldn't get over how excited and proud they were about what they did to Chang and I asked why?

They totally ignored my question and continued in depth about the fight. I waited for a while and tried again to say something, but they were so noisy, I couldn't finish my sentence. There was a lot of horsing around, and they continued extolling the merits of beating Chang up. I tried to speak but kept getting cut off. I let them continue for a couple of minutes and kept quiet. Finally I was able to ask them what was happening. I said that I got the feeling they were mad at me because they wouldn't let me speak. Jimmy nodded yes. Costa said, "We've wasted time, we've spent enough time talking about Chang, we only have a half hour left and then next week and that's all." I said that I thought maybe they were angry at me because I went away for two weeks, and maybe the group didn't go so well while I was away. They nodded yes. I said maybe also they were angry because the group was ending next week. John said he didn't want the group to end.

The worker has astutely picked up the ending stage being acted out both in their behavior in the school and the process in the group. She chose to focus on the underlying meaning for the group and reached for the anger toward her. In retrospect, since the children were also describing an incident of a racist physical attack, the worker needed to at least acknowledge her distress over the idea that a child was "hated," potentially because he was Asian. While she might need to wait until later to go into this in more detail, it would be important not to let the discussion continue without her comment. Children need adult models, with whom they identify, to make clear a value system that may not be expressed in their own homes or communities. The skill involves the worker "lending a vision" by sharing her own views without falling into the trap of preaching or teaching and missing the underlying anger over the endings.

George asked why it had to end, was I leaving the school? I said no, I'd be in the school until the end of May, but did they remember that in the first session we had all agreed that we'd have six to ten sessions and then it would end? They agreed. Costa said, "We'll miss you. I know we fool around a lot, but we'll really get down to talk about something properly." I said that I guess that they were sad the group was ending, and they thought that it was ending because I was punishing them for being noisy and rowdy. They nodded. I said that this wasn't so; it was ending because I had other things that I had to do in the school. But, I said, the group was not supposed to end, it was supposed to continue with their teacher leading it, as we had all agreed. There was a lot of complaining about their teacher and what had happened when I wasn't there, how she had made them do health instead of having a discussion.

I said that they were saying that the group wasn't the same when I wasn't there, and I got them to elaborate on how the two sessions had been during my absence. The boys felt that it was terrible. Jimmy complained that next week would be their last session, so they had better make the most of it. I said that in part they were angry with me because I was saying that I could no longer come in after next week and maybe they were feeling let down and deserted. They quietly nodded. I said that I could understand how they felt; I was also sad that I would no longer be able to come in on Tuesday mornings, because I really enjoyed working with them, but I would still be in the school for a while and they could come to see me alone if they wanted to, and I would come in from time to time to see them. One of the boys asked if I would come to their next party, and I said that I would love to. I added that besides talking about me and them, I knew that they were angry at Mrs. Morris, and I wondered if we could talk about that and see if we could work something out.

Mrs. Morris was a classroom teacher who had offered to continue the group. The worker focused on the transition question, realizing that she might be able to help the group members continue their work after she was gone. A detailed discussion of the group sessions that had occurred while she was away revealed that the youngsters had been so upset at her absence that they had not given Mrs. Morris a chance. They had acted out, causing her to abandon the group meeting and turn to a general health discussion. The worker strategized with the boys about how they could handle things differently with Mrs. Morris. She also offered to meet with Mrs. Morris to assist in the transition.

In these last sessions there are, in addition to issues related to the worker, questions of unfinished business between members. These issues, particularly the negative feelings, often emerge only towards the end of the group. There is a tendency for workers to pass over these issues in order to end the group on a high note. However, the worker who trusts in the group will encourage exploration of the negative feelings as well as the positive ones, as illustrated in the next example.

Welfare Mothers' Group

In the following illustration, a group of mothers on welfare is in its twelfth and final session. Hurt feelings of one member, caused by the actions of another, were shared:

> **Sara:** (To the worker) I got a lot of help here—like when I used to do this in June—I felt like you cared—(to the group)—and we helped each other....
>
> **Connie:** (To Sara—interrupting) Stop puttin' us on—I don't put nobody on and I don't want nobody puttin' me on.
>
> **Sara:** (To Connie, puzzled) Me—what are you talking about?
>
> **Connie:** (To Sara) You know perfectly well what I'm talkin' about—walkin' right out this door—that day when I was so desperate for money—
>
> **Sara:** (Looks down, ashamed) Oh!
>
> **Connie:** (To Sara) To feed my kids on and you offered me five dollars...
>
> **Sara:** Yeah.
>
> **Connie:** (To Sara, anger building, but controlled anger) ...and I called you and asked—now if it's not gonna cut you short, and you said to come over in the morning—you said you'd loaned it to your sister and she'd have it back in the morning—and when I got there, I knew you was home—I heard you when I first walked up to the door—but did you answer—no—and all you would'a had to say was, Connie—I'm sorry—and invited me in for a cup of coffee—I'd rather talked anyway—(to the group and worker)—that's why I didn't come back for so long—probably never would'a if you (the worker) hadn't kept comin' by. (Laughs)

Sara: (To Connie, some anger) Well—why didn't ya say something about it last week, if you was so mad?

Connie: (To Sara) Oh, I just said to myself forget it—it's not that important. And I should'a known better than to believe ya to begin with.

Worker: Why do you say that?

Connie: (To group) That's the way women are—we see one of us down, and it seems the best thing is to stomp on 'em.

Peggy: (To Sara, gently but firmly) That hurts—if somebody promises you something and then doesn't do it— (pause)—what was the matter with you?

Sara: (To Peggy, sheepishly) Well, I wanted to loan her the money…(to Connie) I wanted to help you. I was so mad at my sister for not giving it back to me—I still don't have it back—I felt so bad—(smiles)—and I didn't have the guts to tell you—(pause) I wish I had—cause I've felt real bad about it—real bad— ever since—I'm sorry—
(Sara smiles at Connie, and Connie smiles back. Group collectively lets out its breath and relaxes.)

Peggy: (To Sara) All right, you didn't have the guts to be the good guy—(to Connie) and she didn't have the guts to come back and tell you off— (group laughter)

Worker: I'll carry it a step further—you're each ahead. Connie did have the guts to give Sara a chance to talk about it, and Sara had the guts to be honest and say she felt sorry.
(Group makes comments of general agreement with worker, "Yeah," "Better late than never," and so on.)

It was important that this unfinished business related to the intimacy theme emerged, even though it is likely the worker was holding her breath along with the group members.

Men's Support Group

The worker must avoid the temptation to allow group members to ignore problems in the group. In the next illustration, the worker encouraged group members to share negative reactions to the helping efforts. The worker asked the group, "How can I be more helpful to groups in the future?" The group was composed of men who had been violent with their wives or the women they had lived with.

Worker: What I want to ask you is what do you think I could have done better? What did I do that I shouldn't have done? That kind of thing. I would like some feedback about me in relationship to the group and what's been going on here.

The members responded to the worker's question by referring to a co-worker, who was not present. The worker brought it back to himself.

Charles: I always felt like he was giving me the "third degree," but at the same time it brought out answers that probably wouldn't have come out any other time. I didn't feel like he was pushing, but at the same time he asked penetrating questions. And you had a choice, you could either lie about them or you could just fade out and go around them—or tell the truth; most of the time instead of hiding it I would answer his questions and I think I got a lot more said that way than talking on my own.

Worker: Do you think I could have asked more questions?

Charles: Yeah, you could have, but...I don't like criticizing.

Alan: I don't see where you could have asked that many more questions. I think you've done well at bringing things out. It always takes somebody to start it...and I think you've tried to get it going.

Charles: Yeah.

Alan: I think it has slipped quite a few times, but I don't think that is necessarily your responsibility; I think that's the group's.

Charles: Yeah. For some reason we did seem to digress quite often, I felt. But I think it's my responsibility just as much as it is yours. Alan thought maybe we could have talked about some things more.

Worker: How do you mean "slipped?" Do you mean we got off the topic?

Charles: Yeah,

Ben: We used to bullshit a lot!

Alan: But I feel that's really good because you have to be comfortable with the people you're talking with, therefore you have to bullshit sometimes. You have to get off the subject in order to get back on to it because we always manage to get back onto the topics. I think it's good to get off the subject— it's a rest...

Ben: I'm just questioning how much we do, that's all.

Alan: Yeah, well, we did quite a bit...but I think we got things done.

Charles: But we always noticed it, eh? If it got carried too far, one of the group would say something about it; but I think it helped in a way because it made things more relaxed. We weren't always discussing somebody's hang-up or anything.

Worker: I won't say that I don't mind being criticized because I do...(laughter) OK! But at the same time, I recognize that...Larry, the consultant in this outfit, says, "We make mistakes, we learn from those and then we make more sophisticated mistakes—that kind of thing." I need that kind of input, not only for me as an individual, but for other guys who are going to be leading these groups.

Charles: Well, I think you're OK then—you haven't reached the sophisticated stage yet.

Worker: You mean I'm just making the gross mistakes?! (laughter)

Charles: No, you're just making the everyday, ordinary ones.

Worker: Like what?

Charles: I don't know, I haven't noticed you making any mistakes...

Worker: What would you like to see me doing differently?

Ben: Going back to what I said earlier this evening about becoming more aware of how pervasive (maybe) this anger is, how it manifests itself in different ways, and one way is just kind of a sense of being uptight. And it seems to me that the only way I'm gonna change is that I first have to become somehow aware. I mean, I don't know how you ask questions to help another person become aware, but I think that's the kind of question that is helpful and maybe you could have asked more of those. Now, specifically, I can't say because I don't have a firm grasp on that. Do you (turning to John) have any idea of what I am talking about?

John: Yes. Maybe we are putting too much responsibility on the worker? I don't think so. If I could do everything myself, I wouldn't be here in a group.

Worker: I agree with that.

Ben: And I'm not sophisticated enough, I guess, to have penetrating questions...or to draw out...to help me become aware, I guess that takes...first of all that you have the knowledge or something and being able to see more than I can—or at least have an idea, so that you can ask the questions that will help me rather than telling me, but help me become aware of what, you know, uh...Because I'm just seeing now that I don't think I'm very aware of all the waves in my life—and I don't know why, but I think it's important that I gain that knowledge for myself. I'm not sure how to go about it. Because I don't think that my being is just going to change in the sense of my violence towards women—just towards women; I think it has to change in other areas, it will carry over. (Pause)

Worker: (Speaking to Alan): I was really moved when you talked about your feeling of being set up and you were obviously very upset talking about it. Maybe I could have reached a bit more, I don't know, helped you get in touch with...

Alan: Yeah, I think that you might have and I probably showed it too, because I was uptight that night, I was getting into it—I think maybe you should have pushed me a little more. It was a very touchy subject for me, because it's a helpless...I never really had a totally helpless feeling in my entire life; I've always been able to do something about it, but this is one thing that I can do nothing about; every time I try it gets worse, and the frustration that comes from that really gets me. I get hit by this almost every day...the feeling that I can do nothing.

By making a demand for work, the worker demonstrated that he really wanted the feedback, and the members responded. Of course, the worker had to have enough confidence in himself to invite the negative responses and to stay with them when the members tested him to see if he really meant it. In addition to making the ending discussion honest and receiving important professional feedback, the worker was demonstrating a view of manhood that said it was all right to make mistakes and to accept criticism. This was critical for this group because of their tendency to avoid owning up to their own mistakes and taking responsibility for their abusive behavior.

Hearing-Impaired Teenagers' Group

In the next illustration, a worker helps a group come to grips with her leaving and prepare for the arrival of a new worker. The group consists of teenagers who are hearing-impaired. The beginning phase of work had been difficult, since the worker had needed to develop a way to communicate with the members and to help them communicate with each other. Their concern about the new leader was heightened by their fears that an "outsider" might not accept them because of their handicap. The group had operated using a combination of discussion and activities. The planned activity for that evening was tobogganing:

When I arrived, the members were already there. The usual greetings were exchanged, and we sat down to wait to see if more members would come. Billy said, "I think we should wait ten minutes and then go." Kathy said she had spoken to several members, and they had indicated they wouldn't be coming, as it was such an awful night. I remarked that it was pretty cold for tobogganing. It was too bad we didn't know what the weather would be like. Billy said he had brought his toque, which would keep him warm. He proceeded to model it, which caused all of the members to laugh.

At this point, Billy asked when the new leader was coming. I said that Barbara would be coming next meeting. Stephen said, "Is she like you?" I replied that she was a social work student like I was, she was young and very happy to be coming to the group. I turned to Kathy and said, "We are talking about the new leader who will be coming to our meeting next week." Kathy turned to Amelia and Anna and indicated by sign language that the new leader would be coming next week. Amelia mocked a crying gesture, which bought a chorus of smiles from the other members.

Stephen said, "Has she ever worked in a group like ours, like with deaf people?" Billy turned to Stephen, and said, "Well, Lucille never worked with deaf people before us." Kathy replied, "That's right."

Amelia, Jo-Ann, and Anna were craning their necks to find out what was going on. I pointed out that some members were being left out of our conversation, and we had to try to remember to include everyone. Billy made a mock gesture to the effect of "here we go again," and he motioned the three members to move in closer. I said, "It's tough work letting everybody know what's going on," to which Billy replied, "Yeah!"

I remarked that Billy and Stephen seemed sort of worried about the new leader coming in. Kathy smiled the sort of smile that says, "You hit the nail on the head." Stephen said, "We just want to know what she's like." I said that I think Kathy was thinking that, too. I said, "Was I right, Kathy?" to which she nodded her head.

Amelia mumbled something that I didn't understand. Billy turned to her and then translated to me. Amelia had said it was like starting our group all over again. Jo-Ann asked what was starting over? Kathy explained to Jo-Ann what was going on. Jo-Ann shook her head. Anna, who is totally mute, was looking as if she were in another world; I was aware that she was understanding nothing. I smiled at her, and she grinned back. Billy looked at me and said "I'll explain to Anna."

I then turned to Amelia and said, "You're nervous, like maybe it was like when you came to the meeting with me for the first time." Amelia mumbled, "Nervous? Nervous?" and turned to Stephen with a puzzled expression. Stephen very slowly said, "Remember what it was like the first time we came here?" Amelia gave him a look that said "I sure do." I said I guessed it was like that again, knowing a new leader is coming. Stephen nodded and said, "How come you're going?" then in a joking way added, "I guess you don't like us anymore." I said, "Of course I still like you." Stephen then patted Billy on the back. Billy said, "A good group, aren't we?" I smiled and said we'd been through an awful lot together. Kathy nodded her head, and this was a message that quickly got translated to all the members. Kathy said, "Gee, I wish we could have a social worker that would stay in our group." Stephen said, "Yeah." I said I guessed that maybe people were also angry because I was going. Stephen said, "No, no, that's not right." Billy said, "We've had a good time in this group." I said, "Just the same, I understand it's a hard thing to have to face going through getting to know a new leader again." Kathy said, "Yeah, we just got to know you." Amelia made another mock gesture of crying. In the meantime, Jo-Ann and Anna were talking in sign language and I think were quite out of the conversation.

The worker's direct reaching for the anger at her leaving was too difficult a demand for the members. In flight from the painful feelings, they played a trick on her instead of responding directly:

> Jo-Ann then said to Billy (in sign language), "When are we going to go tobogganing?" He translated for me. I said we had somehow passed the ten minutes Billy had suggested we wait, and I asked her, "Are you ready to go?" Jo-Ann shook her head. I said, "You had a tough time knowing what was going on," and repeated this several times until she understood. She smiled and nodded and then smiled at Anna. Billy and Stephen then said they were ready to go. Billy poked Kathy and said, "Ready?" Kathy nodded. I said I thought Anna was being left out. Billy translated it to her, and she nodded.
>
> I said I would go and get the two office toboggans and I'd be back in a minute. When I came back, to my dismay the group had all disappeared. I looked in several rooms and then decided to sit down and wait. In several seconds, Billy came whistling in. I jumped to my feet and said, "Gee, what happened to our group?" Billy, in a mischievous way, said, "Gee, I don't know. I just went for a walk." He said, "Why don't we look in the hall?" I said I guessed the members would come back, at which point he, in an insistent way, said, "No, let's look in the hall," which we did. Five beaming faces appeared with Kathy saying, "Surprise!" Everyone laughed, as did I; however, I said, "How come the group wanted to leave?"
>
> Stephen said, "We wanted you to come look for us." Amelia grinned and said, "Were you worried?" I said, "Did you want me to be?"—to which there were several nervous titters. I then said, "I think this group wants to leave me before I leave them," to which there were vehement no's. Billy said, "We were just joking." I said, "Still, I wasn't sure that everyone knew why I was leaving." Stephen said, "You're going back to Saskatchewan, isn't that where you were from?" I said I would be working on my research till June. Kathy said, "We'll still have a good group." Stephen poked Kathy and said, "You'll still be here." Kathy said, "All of us members will be here." I said that I thought they could continue to have a good group, but that would depend a lot on them. Billy nodded his head as if he understood. Kathy said, "Like you always say, we got to work at it." The group members laughed and shared this last piece of information, and then we got ready to leave.

These examples have provided a number of illustrations of ending work during a specific meeting. In the next example, we will follow a group of survivors of childhood sexual abuse over four sessions as the ending work emerges over time.

Adult Survivors of Childhood Sexual Abuse: The Last Six Sessions

As the previous examples illustrated, the ending and transition phase of a group takes place over time. The stages are noticeable over the last three or four sessions for an ongoing group, beginning with the worker's reminder that the group is coming to an end. This example provides excerpts of the ending work in a group for adult survivors of childhood sexual abuse. The time period covers the last six sessions of the group.

The members of this group have all experienced oppression on a number of levels. They have all been sexually exploited as children, most often by people whom they knew and should have been able to trust. As women, they have continued to experience oppression in relation to their gender. Some of the members are Hispanic and must face racism, which when combined with sexism makes for a powerful influence on their lives. Finally, some are lesbians or bisexual, which also places them in a group that commonly experiences prejudice and oppression. Thus, it is understandable that all of the group members carry a great deal of pain and internalization of their oppression.

As the group members move into their ending and transition phase, and review and evaluate their work together, one cannot help but be impressed with their courage, their love for each other, and their social worker's conviction about their inherent strength not only to survive oppression but to overcome it and fight it. In many ways, the work of the group followed the three developmental stages described in Chapter 1, in which oppressed people attempt to free themselves from the oppressor within and the oppressor without.

RECORD OF SERVICE

Client Description and Time Frame:

This 24-week group for adult survivors of child sexual victimization is a combination of support and stabilization and growth and education models. It is offered by a community rape crisis center and is led by two co-workers. The time frame of the meetings was from August 28th to October 16th.

The seven members range in age from 22 to 28. All members are women from working-class or middle-class backgrounds. Two members are Hispanic, and the rest are white and from various ethnic groups. Two women are lesbians, one is bisexual, and four are heterosexual.

Description of the Problem:

As the group begins its ending stage, members are reluctant to face the pain and loss of the impending termination and the potential effect of this transition on their lives. As survivors of sexual abuse, many of the women feel acute fear and discomfort when confronted with strong feelings. They have described families of origin in which the development and ending of relationships has been poorly modeled and they have learned to keep silent about their feelings and fears. The tasks of the workers will be to help build a group culture in which the taboo subjects of endings and losses can be explored, freeing the members to grapple with the tasks of termination. We must help the group to establish a norm that supports intimacy and risk but also profoundly respects each member's need for safety and self-protection.

How the Problem Came to the Attention of the Worker(s):

As my co-worker Jane and I prepared for termination, we tuned in to the potential problems of this stage, using both general knowledge of survivors' issues and our knowledge of the work and struggles of this particular group as a guide. Since the first sessions, safety had been vital to meaningful and productive work in the group. Members had worked hard to recognize when they felt unsafe or at risk and had learned to take steps to protect themselves. Since bonding and connection had been central to the group's creation of a safe and trusting culture, we hypothesized that the group might begin to feel unsafe as members began to separate. We believed that the group might need to create a different "safe culture" which could tolerate the coming ending. On August 28th, we learned about the group's norms for saying good-bye and about subjects and feelings related to endings that were forbidden. Members responded with silence when asked direct questions about what the group's end meant to them and informed us that they usually run away from and ignore endings.

Summary of the Work:

(August 8th)

I tried to reach for the pain behind a group member's description of self-hurting behavior. Linda was describing how she felt compelled to binge on salted and high cholesterol foods lately and how it was very dangerous for her high blood pressure. I observed that in the past she had done this when she was having really strong feelings and asked how she was feeling these days when she seemed compelled to binge. She began to cry and said, "There's just so much pain, so much loss." She described her fear of losing her whole family if she confronted her mother (the perpetrator of her sexual abuse), the death of a cousin who had been missing and whose body had been found, the anniversary of a rape in which she had nearly been killed at age 18, her loss of me as her individual therapist, and the impending loss of the group, the first people who had ever believed in and supported her. In the face of this she said that she was really isolating herself and wanting to eat.

I felt guilty for "abandoning her" at this difficult time and felt an impulse to fix things for her. I decided this was a signal that I should involve the group rather than respond as her individual therapist. *I tried to enlist the support of the group to combat her isolation.* I said, "Linda, it sounds like you're feeling overwhelmed by all this pain, and at the very time you could use some support, you're all alone. Is there any way the group can help you right now?" She responded that she isolates most when she's most in pain but that the group could help by reaching out to her, that she needs to be with people when she feels this way. Some group members responded with expressions of support and offers to talk on the phone or be with her. People shared how hard it was to see her pain but how important it was that she share it.

I used Linda's expression of loss to raise the issue of termination again for the group. I said that Linda had shared feeling really sad about the group and I wondered how others in the group were feeling about the end approaching. There was silence. I waited, thinking they might need time to respond. Jane, the co-leader, asked group members how they usually say good-bye. Group members responded: "I just take off, usually." "Hey, I don't say good-bye, I say see you later." "I never say good-bye, I just disappear." "I try to pretend nothing's changed." Jane said that she felt it was important for members to understand how they usually cope with good-byes so that they can make choices this time about how they want to handle this ending. Issues of trust, intimacy, and loss had been important in the group's work, and we could do vital work in these areas during our final weeks. Time was up, and I said that we would be spending more time next week talking about the approaching end of the group and how people wanted to work on it.

(September 11th)

I reframed a member's inability to reach a stated group goal and attempted to unite ending process with content. A major goal for Martha had been to spend time in the group telling the story of her abuse, but each time she had planned to do it she had felt unable to go through with it. She had felt flooded with fear and pain. The group had processed why it was so difficult and suggested different ways she could prepare and cope with this "disclosure," but to no avail. This time, what came up was that she felt unable to risk and be vulnerable in the group when it was so close to ending and she could be rejected and abandoned by the group members. She said that it no longer felt safe in the group. I said that perhaps what she was telling us was that this goal was not right for her right now, that keeping herself safe was most important and that she was making choices about how she needed to protect herself. Since child-victims often learn that they are not worth protecting and can never feel truly safe, safety and self-protection had been important in the group's work.

I offered the group a new norm for endings. I said that we needed to strike a careful balance as we approached the ending, trying to work as hard as we could and risk as much as we could but also respecting each person's needs for safety. I said that if she wanted to do her disclosure we would help her, but that no one would force her to do it. Martha and the group discussed this for awhile, and then Jane talked about Martha's goal and goals in general and how it was important for us to review them and take stock of the work we needed to address in the next four weeks.

I attempted to demand work from the group, evaluating progress and exploring feelings, but blew it by asking for too much information at once. I asked if we could spend some time right now hearing from everyone about what they had accomplished so far, what they still needed to work on, and how they were feeling about the group ending. I immediately sensed my error, but didn't know how to correct it. The group was silent. Jane then said that she understood how hard it was for the group but that it was important for us to take stock of where we were. We could still accomplish a lot but we needed to know...Jodi burst in and said," I just feel like telling you to shut up. You both keep talking and talking about this and I'm feeling really angry. I wish you would let us move on to what we want to talk about and stop wasting time."

I attempted to address her anger directly and put it in context. I said that she was clearly feeling really angry, and that it felt to her like we were pressuring the group. I waited and then said that people often feel very angry when they face losing something that has been really important to them. I wondered if some of her anger was related to the ending itself. Rita said, "But we're not losing the group. We'll still see each other." Others agreed. *I confronted the group's denial.* "That's true," I said, "You can choose to continue your friendships as individuals and as a group, but this Monday night group is special, the way we work together here. It's like it has its own identity. That's what going to end." Michelle said that she wouldn't know what to do with herself on Mondays anymore. Others joined in, saying how they would miss the group. Both workers reflected these feeling and shared their own feelings about the group ending.

I attempted to correct my earlier mistake and reach for more feelings. I said that I had asked for rather a lot at once during my earlier question about goals. This was really hard to talk about and might require some reflection. Perhaps group members could review their progress and future needs during the week and we could set aside time to discuss them next week. We would also need to talk in more depth about the final session. For now, I wondered if we could just spend some time talking about how it felt right now to be dealing with this. We discussed this for the last few minutes of the session.

(September 19th)
I renewed the previous week's demand for work. I reminded the group that we had planned to spend some time this week taking stock of what the group has meant to people and where we needed to put our energy during these final four sessions. People had put quite a bit of thought into this, and the group spent some time eval-

uating and prioritizing. Martha had clarified the issue of disclosure for herself. She had discovered that in trying to force herself to discuss the abuse before the group "audience" while feeling unsafe, she had been recreating the dynamics of her abuse as a child in which her father had taken her to bars where she had been sexually abused by various strangers while others observed. With the support and understanding of the group, she was able to carry out a disclosure related to this specific abuse, checking with the group whenever she began to feel unsafe. *We credited her growing ability to protect herself while achieving her goals.* Both Jane and I offered positive feedback about Martha's growth and her ability to both keep herself safe and move forward with her goals.

Later, Jane raised the issue of the final session, explaining to the group that it is generally structured around feedback, both negative and positive. She asked the group to consider a structure that has worked well for other groups, in which each group member in turn gives feedback to each of the other members and the workers. Past groups have chosen to write a special message to each individual so that the feedback would be kept and remembered. Some members were eager to do this, while others expressed considerable anxiety about evaluating themselves and others. *I reached for feelings while giving the group responsibility for its own structure.* I said that some people seemed eager to do this while others seemed really uncomfortable with it. Ultimately the decision of how to handle the last session lay with the group, but I wondered if we could explore how people felt about it right now. What made it seem scary, what seemed positive about it? This was explored for awhile.

Then group members asked me to review information about the local "Take Back the Night" march with them. We had told them about the march against sexual violence against women a few weeks before and after some exploration of their fears about participating in a public demonstration, they decided to march as a group. *I supported the group's readiness to act independently and support each other in new experiences.* I shared with them how good I felt that they wanted to march together and gave them the information they needed.

(September 25th)
We supported the group's growing independence and shared our feelings with them. As the group processed how the march had felt for them, Jane and I shared how powerful it had felt for us to see them there, marching, chanting, and singing. We also shared that it was hard for us to see them and know that the group was ending. The group was special for us, and it would be hard to let it go.

I fell for the illusion of work and let the group get off the track. Rita had been talking for some time about her problems and conflicts with her parents. At first both workers and group were active in discussing her problem, but I gradually began to feel that we weren't going anywhere and my attempts to involve the group proved fruitless. They seemed to have "checked out." I now think that some of the anger Rita was expressing was indirectly aimed at the leaders and/or the group, but I missed this at the time because she had ample reason to be angry with her parents.

I tried to regain focus by demanding work of another member. I had noticed for some time that Linda seemed very agitated and seemed to be struggling to contain herself. Rita had come to a long pause, and I asked, "What's going on with you, Linda?" Linda seemed startled. "Who me? Why? What's the problem?" I answered, "Well, Rita's been talking for a while now about her family and I know your family has been a source of a lot of your pain. You seem really upset right now and I wonder what's happening." Linda began to talk of having a great deal of pain all the time. She said that her losses had totally overwhelmed her lately and she just didn't know how she was going to make it. I immediately felt the group come back to life. I checked with Rita that we could move to Linda's issue. It would have been better to clarify what had occurred with Rita first, but I wasn't sure how to handle it.

Linda and various group members talked for some time about how hopeless she felt. *I reached for her ability to cope with her pain.* "I'm just hearing that you have so much pain and sadness right now, Linda, and I wonder, what are you doing with all this hurt?" She said that she was crying a lot, just letting herself feel the sadness, and that she was also writing in her journal and writing poems. She mentioned that she had just written a poem today about her pain and where it was taking her. Several people asked her if she would read it, and she did. It was called "Children of the Rainbow," and it described how beams of light are shattered and broken as they pass through a drop of water and how they emerge to form the vibrant colors of the rainbow. The poem said that she and all survivors in recovery are like beams of light; if they can make it through their pain, they will become vibrant, beautiful, and whole. Several of us had tears in our eyes (me included) and there was a powerful silence when she had finished.

I remained silent to let the group control this moment. People thanked her for sharing such a personal, painful, and hopeful part of herself. I had been Linda's individual worker for some time and I was finding it very hard to leave her and leave the agency. *I acknowledged her feelings, shared my own, and credited her ability to cope.* I shared that I found the poem very moving, that I could feel that she had incredible pain, but that her art and ability to create were powerful vehicles for carrying her forward and transforming her pain. The group ended soon after.

(October 2nd)
We credited a member's growing independence. Martha told the group that she had confronted her father with the abuse since the last group. We were all amazed, since this had been a goal that Martha had not hoped to attain for several months, if not years, in the future. Her abuse had been very sadistic, and her father had continued to hold incredible power over her when he was able to have contact with her. She had been with Linda before he called and described "just feeling very powerful and safe. I was able to see Linda and my roommate right there, and I could hold the whole group right in my mind and feel you supporting me and helping me to be safe. I've never felt anything like that before. And he was weak! He was the one who seemed powerless." Martha had burned a picture of her father after the call as a way of exorcizing his control over her, and she had brought the ashes to group. Later the group gathered and flushed the ashes down the toilet. Both leaders credited Martha's incredible and rapid growth and related it to the ending and how she had taken control of how she wanted to accomplish her goals and approach the end of group. The group gave Martha feedback and discussed how it felt to be part of her sense of safety.

I miss two important opportunities to discuss anger in relation to the group's ending. Linda discussed feeling intense anger lately and feeling like she was about to explode and be violent. The group and both workers addressed her anger extensively, relating it to her abuse and her current pain and exploring coping strategies. Although I mentioned her several losses as being related to her anger, I neglected to focus on the group's ending as a major source of her pain and thus missed a potentially important piece of work.

Next, Donna raised the issue of her psychiatrist and how he had told her to get on with her life and stop indulging herself with her depression and dwelling on her abuse. The group responded with explosive anger. I allowed my own anger and the real differences between my approach and the approach of the psychiatrist to blind me to the part of the group's anger that might have been directed at me had I invited it. We did good work in helping Donna evaluate her therapy, but we missed another chance to explore the group's anger about the ending and our role as workers. I think that this group felt so special to me and I was finding termination from individuals, the group, and the agency so hard, that I kept myself unaware of their anger.

(October 16th—Final Session)
We assisted the group in sharing feedback and establishing closure, but neglected to reach for negative evaluation. Each member and each worker had prepared written feedback for the other members and workers, and members took turns reading their messages to each other. (Workers passed out written individual feedback and gave verbal feedback to the group as a whole.) The material was very personal and moving and related the work of the group to strong feelings about ending. Workers assisted members in preparing to read and helped the group to respond. Some members cried and expressed deep feelings of pain and loss. Workers also responded directly to their own feedback.

A few of the women chose to hand out the personal feedback and speak to the group generally while members read the personal material. Although I believe that the material was genuine, it focused on positives only, and both workers missed the opportunity to reach for negative feedback, falling for the "Farewell Party Syndrome." Although this important task was not accomplished, the workers did accomplish their goal of creating a safe culture in which members could risk being intimate and trusting as the group ended. *I reinforced the culture that permits people to risk even as they are separating.* Martha had read each note and closed with "Love, Martha." At one point, Rita said, "This is really hard, but I have to ask. You said "Love" to everybody, but you didn't say it to me. I'm sure you just forgot, but I have to say, it hurts. Don't you love me too?" She began to cry with these last words. Martha had clearly just forgotten and turned to Rita, saying, "I'm so glad you told me. I was just finding this all so hard that I didn't even realize...I do love you. I'm sorry it hurt that I forgot you. Here, let me write it on yours."

I asked Rita how it had felt to risk this question, saying I remembered that she had entered the group six months ago saying she never let herself be vulnerable with others. Rita responded that this was a safer place than she had ever been before. She had shared her story, her shame, and had been vulnerable with people here. She knew she could trust us. "It's true," added Martha, "I've never been anywhere that was safe the way this is, even more than individual therapy." Michelle added, "This place is like the safe home we never had. You guys were almost like parents for us. You were honest with us and we learned to be honest with each other. And it never mattered, we could feel good, feel bad, disagree with each other and be mad, but it was okay. We could learn to be ourselves. You were there for us the way our parents should have been." Soon after, we ended the group. There was a long "group hug" at the suggestion of the members, and we ate some cake a member had ordered. The message on the cake said, "Survivors—Striving and Thriving!"

The metaphor of the poem in which survivors in recovery are viewed as "beams of light; if they can make it through their pain, they will become vibrant, beautiful, and whole" is extremely powerful and moving. It captures beautifully the struggle of these young, oppressed, and vulnerable women to free themselves from the self-image of being "damaged goods" that had been imposed upon them by those who should have been nurturing them. Their courage in joining a "Take Back the Night" march, when they felt so personally uncomfortable in doing so, was an affirmation of their willingness to fight and overthrow their oppressors. It was a social parallel of their individual revolutions against oppression described in one member's efforts to confront her offending parent. The unique power of mutual aid groups is amply demonstrated in their content of their work together and in the "Survivors—Striving and Thriving" lettering on the cake at their final session.

In the next section, a detailed analysis of a single session in the ending phase of a group of teenagers in a residential setting completes this chapter. Many of the youngsters in that group have experienced emotional, physical, and sexual abuse in their families of origin. The example illustrates all of the ending phases described thus far.

A TERMINATION SESSION: THE WORKER LEAVING THE GROUP

A description of a group meeting with teenaged girls in a residential treatment center concludes the discussion of endings and transitions. It provides an illustration of some of the unique dynamics that emerge when the group continues and the worker leaves. The session takes place one week after the worker has told the group members that she is leaving the agency for another job. This worker in this example demonstrates both an advanced level of skill in group work and skill in dealing with endings. Of particular interest is the impact of the worker's sharing of her own powerful feelings. The entire meeting is presented, together with a detailed analysis of the skills employed. The process in the meeting is classic, as one can see elements of all the ending dynamics in one session.

> Three of the girls came in with each other and seemed in a very happy mood. They said that they'd had a good week in school. I said, you know, that sounded real nice and that this was one of the enjoyments of finally being a senior, and we kind of teased about that. I asked about where Gladys and Beth were, and they said that they had to speak with a teacher about some arrangements and that they'd be there in a little while. The three of them continued talking about school and the rehearsals and the senior trip and stuff like that. Then Beth came in, and she was singing "Everything Is Beautiful," a rock-and-roll song. She took her seat and was laughing with everyone.

The good feelings expressed by the group members were the opposite of the worker's expectations and represented a denial of the ending. Since there were only a few meetings left, the worker had strategized to reach past the denial for the opposite feelings she knew would be there. The members responded to her demand for work.

> After a while I said, "Hey, it's great to see everybody in such a good mood, and I hate to be a party pooper, but I feel that I have to say that this is our next-to-last meeting, and a lot of things between you and I will be drawing to an end." Margie said, "You have a hell of a nerve." I said, "You mean about my leaving?" She said, "Yeah, that and a whole lot of things." I said, "OK, let's hear 'em. I'm sure that my leaving and the ending of the group has caused a lot of reactions in all of you." Nobody picked up on

that, and Margie said, "Are we going to have a group next year?" A couple of girls said, "Yeah, we want to have another group next year," and Beth said, "Let's have a party in honor of your leaving."

The group's anger was expressed in Margie's comment "You have a hell of a nerve." The worker acknowledged this anger and encouraged the members to continue. The anger they felt and the pain underneath it were too much for them at this point, so they backed off. They began, instead, to discuss the continuation of the group and a "farewell party." The worker allowed them to move away from the anger, but held them to discuss the importance of the group.

> There was a lot of mixed-up talk, and I tried to pick up about continuing the group. I said, "You're saying that the group has meant something to you and that you want to continue even without me." Beth said, "Naw, the group wasn't all that good," and Margie said, "Sometimes it was and sometimes not. Sometimes the meeting was very good, and sometimes they were a waste of time." I said, "Can you tell me more about that?" Margie said, "Well, sometimes it just seemed like we weren't in the right mood and we couldn't get down to work." Jill said, "Yeah, we were just fooling around all over the place," and Donna said, "Like the mood we were in Sunday night," and they all began to talk about a riot that had happened in the cottage, and they started fooling around. I said, "Hey, can we get back to the thing about the group, and what you thought about it, and what it meant to you? I think it is important for us to take a look at it now that you're nearing the end."

The members attempted to evade the discussion once again, and it was a mark of the skill of the worker that she did not let them put her off. She made another demand for work and insisted that the group discuss their specific reactions to their time together. As the members described the mutual aid they had experienced, the worker attempted to explore this aspect of their learning; however, they were not ready for this discussion and still needed to express their angry feelings.

> Donna said, "Well, the best meeting we had was just with three of us—me, Jill, and Gladys. That's when we really talked about ourselves." Margie said, "You mean without me and Beth, is that what you mean?" Jill said quickly, "No, I don't mean that. We did have a good meeting with everybody, but I guess that was really the best," and I said, "Well, what made it the best?" Donna said, "Because we talked about our families, and we got to understand how we were feeling," and Margie said, "Yeah, I agree. The best meetings were when we talked about our families, and the worst meetings were when we talked about the cottage and the cottage parents." And I said, "How come?" Gladys said, "Because we couldn't do anything about the cottage parents or even about the cottage, and at least when we talk about ourselves and about our families we can understand more, we can know why we are like we are," and Beth said, "Yeah, we can help each other." I said, "You have helped each other a lot. Is that something important that you've gotten from these meetings?" Nobody picked up on that.
>
> Beth began talking about a party that they had been to, and all of a sudden in the midst of a whole big discussion Beth turned to me and said, "You're leaving, you God-damned fink." And everybody stopped, and everybody looked at me. I said, "I'm leaving, and I guess that makes me a fink." And everybody began, saying, "Why are you leaving? Why do you have to leave us? Why can't you stay?" Then a whole torrent

of emotion came pouring out. Finally Jill said, "Why are you leaving?" I said, "I tried to explain the reasons on Friday, but if you'd like me to I'll explain them again now. But I don't know if it's the reason that really matters, it's more how you feel knowing that I'm leaving, for whatever the reason." They said, "No, no, we want to hear the reasons, we don't understand." I said, "OK, let me try to explain. I'm leaving because I've been here for a number of years and I feel that it's time for me to move on, to move into another situation. Working here has meant an awful lot to me and you all have meant an awful lot to me. Yet I feel that a combination of things, the long traveling, working a lot of nights, have become very hard for me and I feel like I want to work nearer to where I live, and that I want to have a new kind of experience and not work in a residential treatment school. That's pretty much the reason. If there's anything you don't understand, ask me and I'll try to explain more."

As the anger emerged, the worker struggled with her own feelings in order not to block its expression. Her acceptance of their feelings demonstrated in her response, "I'm leaving, and I guess that makes me a fink," freed them to explore the feelings of dependency and hurt that were below the surface feelings of anger. Although she had explained her reasons for leaving the week before, the group members had been too shocked to heed and understand. She agreed to explain them again while acknowledging that their feelings were what really mattered, rather than her reasons. As the group members began to express their emotions toward the worker, she asked them to identify the specific things about her they had found helpful These would be the qualities they must look for in other workers. She also stayed with their hurt feelings, reached for their fear about establishing a relationship with a new worker, for their sense of rejection, and for their anger. Most important, the worker also shared her own pain at leaving them. The open expression of her feelings provided the impetus for the members to respond with theirs.

Beth started to cry and said, "You can't leave. We need you." I said, "You mean you won't be able to make it without me?" Margie said, "You're the best social worker I ever had. I won't be able to talk to anybody else." I said, "We have been real close, me and every one of you, and I guess the thought of starting over with somebody else scares the hell out of you. What do you think there was about me that made it easier for you to talk to me?" Beth said, "It's because you cared about us. It's 'cause we knew that even when you were mad at us, you were really sticking up for us, and you were really with us." Donna said in a soft voice, "Yeah, but if you cared so much, you wouldn't be leaving." And I said, "That's a thing, isn't it? How could I leave you if I really care for you." Gladys said, "We know you care for us. We know you're leaving because you really feel that you have to." And then she just kind of shrugged, and I said, "But the words don't help very much, huh? They don't take away the bad feeling." Beth said, "That's right, what good does it do me to know that you care if you're not here?" And Jill said, "Yeah, you've been my social worker for a whole year. I don't want anybody else." There was a lot more talk about the idea that they didn't want anybody new.

I said, "You're angry as hell at me. You have a right to be, and even though your anger hurts me and a big piece of me wants to say, 'Don't be angry at me,' I can understand that you are, and I know the kind of pain that must be underneath, and I feel some of that pain also. It's hard as hell for me to leave you." Beth said, "If it was hard for you to leave us, then you wouldn't leave us." Margie said, "No, Beth, that's just not the truth. It was hard for me to leave home...."

At this point in the session, the pain of the discussion caused the group to adopt its pattern of using a scapegoat when things got rough. Gladys, the group scapegoat, began to cry, expressing many of the emotions felt by the other members. Their anger at her was an expression of their anger at the same feelings within themselves. The worker demonstrated her group work skill, at a time when she herself was feeling somewhat overwhelmed by emotion, by paying attention to her two clients—Gladys and the group. In the next excerpt, we see an illustration of the worker's functional role, as outlined in the earlier discussion on scapegoating.

> Gladys put her head down and began to cry, and one of the kids hollered, "Oh, cut it out. This hurts us as much as it hurts you." I said, "Maybe it hurts each of you in a different way, and this is how Gladys is reacting." She picked up her head and said, "Oh, leave me alone. None of you care about me," and Margie said, "Yes, we do, you don't want help. You just want to feel sorry for yourself." I said, "You're all getting so angry at Gladys, and it seems that all she's doing is acting out how you feel. Is it that you hurt so much that you don't have room for anybody else's hurt?" Jill said, "She cries all the time. Who gives a damn about her?" Donna said, "I care about her, but I don't know what to do." Beth said to her (by this time Gladys had moved away from the table where we meet and was sitting alone on a chair, crying), "Gladys, why don't you come over here?" and Gladys just shrugged, and one of the other kids said, "Aw, leave her alone," and there was kind of an uncomfortable quiet in the room, and I said, "I don't think that you feel right leaving her alone," and Beth said, "Hell, what can we do?" and I said, "What do you feel like doing? Do you feel like reaching out to her?" Beth got up and walked over to Gladys and put her arms around her and said, "You're scared because everybody's leaving, right?" Gladys nodded her head. Beth said, "We're all in that situation, too. She's leaving us, too. Miss S.'s leaving us, too. Not only you." Beth said, "But maybe it is different for Gladys." Gladys said, "You have a mother and father. Every one of you has at least a mother or a father. Who do I have?" Beth said, "You have foster parents." Gladys said, "Big deal. They don't want me." There was a hush in the room at the pain of those words, and I said, "Wow, you really know how that feels."

The worker's trust in her group was rewarded as they reached out to Gladys to offer aid. As they spoke to Gladys, they were really speaking to each other and to the part of them that was facing the same set of problems. The faith of the worker was important at this point, because with her help they were able to experience the power of mutual aid in the peer group. As they move into their young adult years, they will have to seek out support and help from their peers; this was possibly the most important learning for them.

> Beth said, "I think I know how it feels. I think I know how bad it feels. And if you want to cry, that's OK, but you gotta live. You gotta pick yourself up. You gotta face it." Gladys shook her head. "No," she said, "I can't." I said, "It seems that she can't pick herself up." Donna said, "Even when you're alone, you have to trust yourself." Margie said, "That's pretty hard to do." Beth said, "But you're not alone, Gladys, you have us. We'll help you, and somebody else can help us." Donna said, "And maybe we'll also have to help ourselves." Gladys said, "I know what you mean. I know that in the end I do have to help myself." I said to her, "But are you scared that you won't be able to do that?" She nodded her head yes, and once again she began to cry. Beth said, "We'll help you, too. Just like we did here this morning." And I had tears in my eyes,

too, and I said, "Wow, you kids are fantastic." And they all kind of laughed, and somebody said, "Maybe we'll become social workers, too," and that kind of broke the tension of the moment, and we never really got back to the thing of them helping each other.

The feelings associated with endings stir deep and powerful emotions in all of us. When this example, and the earlier ones, are used in my workshops, workers have been visibly moved by the power of the feelings expressed; they have perhaps moved you, the reader, as well. Workers also react to the degree of skill demonstrated by this worker and the workers in the previous example involving the survivors' group. They reflect on endings they have not handled well by missing the cues or not facing their own feelings with enough honesty. This record represents an advanced level of skill. This same worker handled endings quite differently in her training days; she would have cut and run at a number of key places in this meeting. There were many group endings along the way in which she made mistakes, learned from them, and ended her next group with more skill. This process is a painful one, but it represents the only way to develop professional skill. It is a process that continues throughout a professional's working life.

CHAPTER SUMMARY

In this chapter, we reviewed the ending and transition phase of practice and strategies for intervention, as described in detail in Chapter 5. These concepts were then illustrated using examples from the ending phase of a variety of groups. A more detailed ending example, which covered the last six sessions of a group for adult survivors of childhood sexual abuse, helped to illustrate the phases and skills involved. Finally, a detailed analysis of the next-to-last session of a group for teenaged girls in a residential setting illustrated the special dynamics when the worker leaves and the group continues.

GLOSSARY

Anger over the ending A stage in the ending/transition phase whereby individuals, family members, or group members appear to be angry at the worker because of the ending of the relationship.

Denial of the ending A stage in the ending/transition phase whereby individuals, families, or group members appear to ignore the imminent end of the sessions.

Farewell-party syndrome The tendency on the client's part, in the ending/transition phase, to avoid the pain of ending by planning some form of celebration. Also, the tendency to express only positive reactions about the experience, rather than being critical.

Mourning period A stage in the ending process of a group, usually characterized by apathy and a general tone of sadness.

Trying the ending on for size A stage in the ending/transition phase in which one notices clients, or group members, are operating independently of the worker or spending a great deal of time talking about new groups or new workers.

16

Some Variant Elements in Group Practice

CHAPTER OUTLINE

The Open-Ended Group
Residential Settings
The Single-Session Group
Activity in Groups

Our focus in Part IV has been on the common aspects of group work, yet there are variant elements that must be taken into account. Four areas raised most often are open-ended groups, residential settings, single-session groups, and activity-oriented groups. These four variations are discussed in this chapter.

THE OPEN-ENDED GROUP

The term **open-ended** refers to a group in which the membership is continuously changing. New members arrive and old members leave throughout the life of the group. This is in contrast to a **closed** or fixed-membership group, where the same people meet for a defined period of time. Members may drop out and new members be added in the early sessions, but in general, the membership of a closed group remains constant. The decision to run a group as open-ended or closed depends upon a number of factors, including the nature of the contract, the characteristics of the clients served, and the structure of the setting. For example, in a couples' group dealing with marital problems, the difficulty of discussing personal issues such as sexual incompatibility would be compounded if membership in the group were constantly changing. The same would be true in a group for survivors of sexual abuse, where disclosure of traumatic experiences is difficult in a group context. A stable membership is essential for such groups to develop the necessary mutual trust and culture for work. On the other hand, an open-ended group is more appropriate for teenagers in a group home, where residents are entering and leaving at different times. The problems associated with shifting membership in this type of group are outweighed by the advantages of having all the residents present. Thus, the decision to operate open-ended or closed groups must be made with the unique characteristics of members, purpose, and setting in mind.

There are some advantages to an open-ended group. For example, a group that has developed a sound culture for work can bring in a new member quickly. As the new members listen to the discussion, their own willingness to risk may be accelerated by the level of openness of the others. In addition, those who have been in the group for a while are able to assist new members with issues they have already dealt with. A technical problem associated with open-ended groups is that each session may be a new beginning for some members, an ending for other members, or both. In short-term groups, where members do not remain for a long period of time, the worker can take responsibility for bringing in new members and acknowledging the departure of the old ones. In groups with longer-lasting membership, the group members themselves can discuss this process and develop a system for dealing with the changing group composition. Either way, the skills involved require that the worker be able to state purpose clearly and briefly to a new member so that the ongoing work of the group can proceed in spite of the changes.

Hospital Group on a Gynecological Ward

The following example involves an open-ended group on a gynecological ward of a general hospital. The women on this ward have all been admitted to the hospital for operations because of suspected cancer of the uterus. The usual routine is that they stay for two days prior to the operation, one day for the operation, and then, depending upon the results, they may be released from the hospital in as little as two days. Thus, some group members are in the preoperative state, while others have completed the procedure. The worker restated the group's purpose at the start of each meeting.

> **Worker:** This group meets each day at the same time to give you a chance to talk with each other and with me about your feelings and concerns about being a patient in the hospital. We realize your illness and hospitalization have caused a great deal of stress, and we feel your having a chance to discuss your reactions may help. In past groups we have discussed the food, hospital procedures, how patients get along with staff, and of course, your concerns about your illness.

The particular theme for each group changed each day with the composition of the membership. When appropriate, the worker arranged for attendance of the dietitian, nursing staff, or doctors to facilitate communication between patients and the hospital system. In the following illustration, we see how one member, who has just been told she has cancer, uses the group to deal with her initial shock even though it is her first day of group attendance:

> After some preliminary chatter, I turned to Mrs. Bourne (an elderly, delicate-looking lady) who had been silent. She didn't respond. I pointed out that she still seemed too shocked. The group members asked about her family. She said she had a son and daughter. Her son has just gone to South Africa. They said she has to tell her daughter. She should be told, and talking about it with family would make her feel better. She said her daughter would cry. I said it is a hard thing to face. Mrs. Powers suggested having your chaplain talk to you at this time. It was helpful. She had found it supportive. Mrs. Bourne remarked that there was no use having the priest talk to her. She is disenchanted with her religion. Mrs. Powers then went into a brief monologue on cancer being just another disease like alcoholism and other illness and how it used to be something to be ashamed of and now it's treated openly as a disease. She expressed her present despondency because it has reached a point where they may not be able to operate on her present cancer. Someone asked how her husband feels. He

feels terrible. They asked about the children, but she has none. She said at the end she was depressed and wanting to get this all over with. It was no pleasure for her husband, and she's not getting any younger. Then she immediately changed her mood and said you need a sense of humor, to which all the ladies agreed. Our time was up.

At this point it was too difficult for Mrs. Bourne to take in the words because of the shock of the diagnosis. However, she had been able to begin the process of talking with others about her first reactions. The worker picked up with her after the session for individual work in this area, and other group members offered their support through their informal contacts on the ward. The report of this group session was also used later for work with the medical staff on the problem of how staff communicate diagnoses to patients. Examples of using a ward group to provide feedback to the system are shared in Chapter 18.

Just as each group meeting may be a new beginning for a member, other members are leaving, and the ending process must be taken into account. The worker can deal with this by calling attention to the departure of each member at the start of their last session or sessions, depending upon the length of their attendance. There can also be some time allowed at the end of the last session for them to say their farewells and for the group to say good-bye as well. The following excerpt illustrated a worker structuring this process at the start of the session:

> **Worker:** This will be Mrs. Lewis's and Mrs. Peter's last day with us. We have enjoyed having both of you in this group. If it's all right with the rest of you, perhaps we could leave the last five minutes of the session to say good-bye and to give both ladies a chance to share their thoughts and feelings about the group.

The open-ended groups, particularly short-term groups, are characterized by the need for more worker guidance. Since the group may have little continuity, the worker needs to actively provide the structural supports. This does not mean, however, that the group members are excluded from taking some responsibility for dealing with structural issues. One common example is when a new member joins a relatively stable open-ended group. Often, the new member initially feels very much like an outsider. In turn, the ongoing group members may resent a new member and be concerned about the possible impact on the group dynamics. Ongoing members may not be direct about their feelings, since they sense it is not OK to feel that way. Their heads may say, "Since I am receiving help, shouldn't it be available to others?" At the same time, their hearts are saying, "I like the group just the way it is, and I'm afraid a new member will screw it up!" Unless this issue is openly explored, their real feelings may be acted out in the manner in which they relate to the new member. The worker may have some ambivalence as well, accepting the agency policy of keeping the group open, yet feeling concerned that a "good group" might change with the addition of an unknown new member. The result may well be an illusion of work, in which the worker announces a new member is coming the next week and the group quickly moves on to a different topic. Or, if the group raised objections, the worker may side with the new member and completely miss the concerns of the second client, the group.

The alternative is for the worker to tune in to his or her own feelings, as well as the feelings of the group members, and to use the skill described earlier as **looking for trouble when everything is going the worker's way.** This is illustrated in the next example.

Bringing in the New Member to an AIDS Group

The following example from a group for persons with AIDS illustrates how the worker asks the group members to take real responsibility for bringing in a new member.

Worker: I wanted you to know that we have a new member joining the group next week. As you know, agency policy is that we stay open to new members if we have room. I'm not asking for a vote here, but since we have been maintaining a regular membership recently, I wondered how you all felt about adding someone new.

John: It's not a problem. After all, we were all new at one point or another.

Worker: I appreciate that thought, John, but in my experience, even though it isn't completely rational, ongoing members sometimes resent and even fear adding someone new to a group that's working well. I wonder if anyone feels that way.

Ted: Does it mean we are going to go back to square one—I mean, starting all over? I've gotten to trust these guys, and I'm not so sure a new member is a great idea.

Worker: That's exactly what I meant, Ted. How about the rest of you? You have worked hard to build a good group here, and it wouldn't surprise me if the new member might make a problem for you.

Rick: I'm not sure I want to see someone going through what we all went through when we first had that diagnosis. I mean, I'm past all of that now, and I want to work on other issues.

Worker: I think it's also a little scary to have someone come in who may reawaken all of the fear and anxiety. I hear three issues: Is the new member going to set us back to going over old issues? Are we going to lose our sense of trust in the group? And, How are we going to feel facing all of our initial feelings again? Let's discuss these and see if we can come up with a way to bring this new member in and cope with it effectively. I am willing to work with him in advance to help in the entry to the group, but I think you are all going to need to help as well. The faster we integrate him, the better chance we will not lose what we have.

At the worker's suggestion, the group members used the rest of the time to tune in to some of their own feelings when they first joined the group and what it was that either helped them to connect or put them off. As the members were able to put themselves in the shoes of the new member, they developed some strategies that both the worker and they could adopt in greeting the new member. These included acknowledging that he was coming into an ongoing group and that it might take some time for him to feel connected; making some room for him in the first session to handle the initial shock issues, while still making sure that they picked up on their own ongoing issues; letting him know he could get involved as he felt comfortable; and offering to provide a "buddy" from the group whom he could contact by phone if he wished.

After some further discussion, the worker raised another potential underlying issue associated with the entry of the new member. This was the fact that the space had opened up because of the sudden and unexpected death of one of the ongoing members. Even though it had been discussed when it happened, he explored with the group members how their ongoing feeling of loss might affect their ability to attach to each other and to the new member.

It was not necessary for the worker to have this conversation for every new member who joined. Rather, the worker monitored the changing composition of the group and periodically raised the issue when circumstances required it. This concept is clearer if one is able to conceive of the group as it was described in Chapter 14—as an organism that is more than the sum of its parts. If one thinks of the group as an entity independent of its members, existing with a continuously changing membership, then the need to address its tasks in relation to new members is clear. In the next section, which deals with a group in a residential setting, a variation on the new member theme is also explored.

RESIDENTIAL SETTINGS

The issue of the impact of the environment on a group was explored in Chapter 14. In this section we will examine some of the unique dynamics when group members live together in a residential setting. In all other groups, when the group ends, members return to separate lives. In residential settings, they will continue to have contact with each other between sessions. The group members' ongoing relations may be affected by each group meeting. In turn, the informal contacts may well provide the substance for each meeting. The example used to illustrate this process is a group for elderly persons in a housing complex.

Housing Complex Group for Elderly Persons

When elderly people leave their own homes to move into a residential complex, they are making a difficult transition stage in the life cycle. Familiar housing, neighbors, friends, and relatives may all be gone, leaving the person feeling lonely and lost. Recognizing the stress associated with this stage of life, the following group was organized specifically to deal with the issue of "Getting Along with Your Neighbor." In this example, the new group members are also new to the complex. The relationship to the group may well parallel their relationship to their new community.

> **RECORD OF SERVICE**
>
> **Client Description and Time Frame:**
> This was set up as a Growth and Education/Support (short-term: six weeks) group for clients who ranged in age from 70 to 81 years old. Six were women and three were men; the group was primarily Jewish, with one Christian woman. All members were white. The dates covered in the record are from March 27 to April 24.
>
> **Description of the Problem:**
> The group, called "Getting Along with Your Neighbor," was designed for residents of a Jewish-sponsored, elderly housing complex, to talk about their issues and concerns related to living in a community setting. The early culture of the group was a reflection of the culture of the housing community, and this has created some obstacles to mutual aid and productive work. Lines of division are made between the new (three months to one year) and long-term (five to eleven years) residents, between men and women, and between those who have developed support systems and those who have not. Other aspects of the culture that hinder mutual aid are judgment, gossip, and false assumptions. The taboo areas of loneliness, loss, and despair are fears

they all have in common at this stage in their life cycle. Yet, unless the group norms shift, they will have difficulty offering support to each other in a meaningful way.

How the Problem Came to the Attention of the Worker(s):

The members of the group were having difficulty listening to each other without disagreeing, negating, or judging the others' comments. The lines were revealed almost immediately when one of the male members (Lou), a newcomer to the housing complex, said in the first session, "What I see is a big division between the men and the women. Most of us are lonely and we need to get the men and the women together here." Some of the responses he got back were, "Speak for yourself!" "Who needs men?" "He's new here," and "If you don't have any friends here, it's your own fault, there's plenty of opportunities to meet people." The longer-term residents were defensive of their relative stability and were threatened by the more obvious vulnerability of the newcomers. This dynamic was repeated, with variations on a theme, for the first several group sessions.

Summary of the Work:

March 27th (First Session)

As a way to begin to shape the culture, in my opening remarks, I stated some rules and guidelines along with the group's purpose. After welcoming everyone, I asked if anyone had been in a group before, and most of them raised their hands. I said that the name of this group is "Getting Along with Your Neighbor," and the purpose of being together is to talk about the benefits and difficulties of living in a community setting and the quality of relationships with others. I said that the group was their group, that the purpose was certainly broad enough so that the specific focus of discussion could be up to them. I explained that there were two main rules of the group, the first being confidentiality, that whatever is said in the group stays in the group; in other words, you can say you are in this group, but don't mention specific people or what someone else said. The other rule is, although this is a group about getting along with your neighbor, please do not mention specific people that are not in this group. This way, we avoid gossip and make it safe for people to share here. All agreed to these ground rules.

I tried to open the discussion by asking what I thought was a fairly tame question to "break the ice." I asked the members to go around and say briefly how long they had lived in these apartments and where they had come from. After everyone had stated this, Lou said, "I'm here on behalf of the men's group, and we feel that the men and women are divided here. Most of us are lonely, and we need to get the women and men together. It's not natural to drift apart." Marie said, "Speak for yourself, I'm not lonely." Bea said, "Who needs men?" Anne said, "How long have you lived here?" I could see the group splitting on this issue.

I tried to introduce a way they could communicate that would allow for diversity of opinions. I suggested that they only try to speak for themselves and not for others. I added that each person is entitled to their opinions and feelings and that we need to respect that in this group. *Although they were not afraid to speak up, there was no affective empathy for each other in their communication. I missed a lot of their initial hints of issues to "reach for" because I felt overwhelmed, and I stayed general.* Murray said that he had been here a year and still hadn't met many people, and that the people here keep to themselves and barely say hello. Eva said she had many friends,

"You just have to put yourself out there, it goes both ways." Mini said, "I agree with Murray. I've had a difficult time because of cliques." Bea said, "This is a wonderful place, you can't complain." I said, "What are some of the ways to meet people or feel more involved in activities?"

April 3rd (Second Session)
I wanted to help them to begin to recognize some of the assumptions and expectations they bring to their everyday interactions. Murray said again that he didn't find this a friendly place and that he would say hello and some people would walk right by. Ruth said, "Sometimes they can't hear you. I don't take it personally, I say hello to everyone anyway." I said, "It sounds like there are lots of different ways to interpret another's behavior." Eva said, "Not everyone is going to be your friend. It's got to be mutual." I asked, "What kind of behavior is supportive?" Bea said, "I like my friends to call me up and ask how I'm doing today." Mini said, "I don't have that kind of relationship with anyone here. I would feel like I was intruding to call up every day." Morris said, "I think there's a difference between friends and acquaintances."

I tried to take care of both the individual and the group as a whole, in an effort to make it a safe environment. Lou said, "The women, many of them, just sit around and play cards, and I think a man in their life, to call up and say 'how are you,' would make them feel good." Bea said, "Who cares if they play cards all day; if that's what they want to do, they're entitled." Marie said, "I had enough cooking and doing laundry, thank you." Lou said, "They are addicted to cards, some of them." I said, "Lou, you are going to have to speak for yourself only. I think that's why you get jumped on, because of the way you're saying it."

I felt stuck on how to handle the male/female conflict, so I just let them talk. Murray said, "What do you think if a man comes up to you and says hello?" Mini said, "I'd say hello back." Lou said, "If I'm the only one in an elevator with a woman, she looks at me like I'm going to molest her or something." Marie said, "Don't be ridiculous!" Lou said, "I'm serious." Eva said, "Some of the men here do just want to get their slippers under your bed." Murray said, "I'm just looking for friendship, but it seems the ladies don't really want to talk to the men." Mini said, "You have to understand, we were brought up not to be aggressive with men. I envy your (the worker's) generation, which is much more outgoing. Women don't go to men first, and if they do, people talk."

I wanted to bring out this part of the housing culture that potentially hinders their sense of freedom. I said, "So how does gossip or fear of gossip affect your behavior?" Murray said, "I invited this one lady to my apartment for a cup of tea and she said she doesn't go to men's apartments." Eva said, "You have people who meet here and become a couple. People talk at first, but so what?" Ruth said, "I don't let it bother me." Bea said, "If you want to be human and you want to talk to somebody, you've got to stick to your convictions regardless of what people are going to say."

April 10th (Third Session)
I felt there were things not being said in the group, that the discussions were fairly general and safe, and that the members might be ready to self-disclose more. I wanted my explicit and implicit behavior to allow for this. I asked if anyone had anything on their mind that they've been thinking about between sessions that they wanted to share with the group. Bea said she had lost her sister-in-law this week and wanted to thank the people who were supportive to her, that it really made a difference. I said,

"Last week we talked about being supportive vs. being intrusive. I hear you saying that you appreciated people reaching out to you." She said, "You know, I've been thinking about this adjustment that the new people are saying. But your whole life is an adjustment, from the moment you are born till the moment you go. When I first came here, I was walking with a cane. I had big plans for when I retired, I was going to travel and volunteer. But as you see, I'm now in a wheelchair. But you can't dwell in the past. I have a lot of friends here; you just have to put yourself out." Her sharing changed the mood of the group; the members were really listening.

Lou got up out of his chair and went to shake Bea's hand. Lou said, "You are an inspiration, Bea. I know, because my wife—God rest her soul—she died last year. She was in a wheelchair, and she was so ashamed that she wouldn't even go out of the house. So I congratulate you for being out there and participating in things." Lou sat back down and his eyes teared up. I said, "Lou, thank you for being so open with us."

April 17th (Fourth Session)
I realized that I was uncomfortable when Lou spoke because he tended to make the room defensive. I decided to model non-judgmental, patient listening as a way to help further the group. Lou said, "We have the settled residents and the new residents; I think we can all agree on that. The settled residents are more contented, they have had sufficient time to make lifetime friends. In other words, they are established here. Now we have the new residents. I'm here four months, and I'm lonely. Settled people know the ropes; I, on the other hand, lack that. There are a lot of people in my position, and I think the staff should do something further than the twice-a-year orientations. Maybe make a list of newcomers so we can contact them over the phone."

I attempted to stay focused on the real work here. I said, "Let's keep whatever specific planning you might organize for later. I like what you are saying, though, because I think it would be useful to get a discussion going that helps us understand each other better." Bea said, "We all came in new like you. This place is not a country club, they don't have to provide you with friends; that's up to the individual. When I came here five years ago, I went downstairs every day and talked to people. You can't expect the staff to provide for your social activities, your loneliness, your moods. It's an apartment building." I said, "Is that what you are saying, Lou?" Lou said, "Well, you see, this lady, God bless her, is not the shy type. Now there are many people that are, and don't have the nerve that this lady has." Ruth said, "Anyone who is lonely, it's their own fault. You have to reach out." I said, "What was it like when you first came?" Ruth said, "I was shy, I didn't want to push myself on people. But I made the effort." Mini said, "You were working when you first came here, that's the difference."

I attempted to help them break out of the debate nature of their interactions. I said, "Instead of putting blame or having a debate, let's see if we can just hear the experience of each person. They are just different perspectives. Given that the group is about getting along with your neighbor, hopefully that means having a better understanding of each other and being able to support each other in some of the difficulties." Marie said, "In every stage of life we are so different. We don't have the pep, we don't have the ambition to say—come over for dinner, I'll cook and bake." I said, "So what's it like for you now?" Marie said, "You just have to be content to sometimes be alone. Sometimes you're much better off alone. You don't have to dress up, don't have to get everything ready to serve, and do the dishes and everything. I really have to push myself to do things now."

Mini said, "I was told I was going to have a hard time adjusting here because I was working until I was 77 and my job ended, a sister died of cancer, and my daughter moved to England. The curtain went down, just like that, and I'm still adjusting. But I think this is my problem and not the problem of the housing. Here and there I make acquaintances, but it's going to take awhile. But it's OK." Lou said, "We forget; we say we'll never forget our problems, but we do. What I'm trying to bring out is that a newer person is faced with conditions the settled person had faced many years ago, and that it's a faded memory. I think about others, it's the way I was brought up, to look out for my fellow man. The way I see it is that the staff's purpose is to serve the residents, and maybe we can do something to help out the new residents."

April 24th (Fifth Session)
As the group began to develop an acceptance of each other, differences that occur in the housing came to light. I wanted to support them to extend their capacity for empathy to those outside the group. Murray said, "Then you have the Russians who you can't communicate with unless you speak Yiddish." Ruth said, "It's even worse with the Chinese, because we can't speak at all." I said, "We've talked about the difficulties in being a newcomer here. Can you imagine what it must be like to be uprooted from your country at this age, to a totally new culture?" Marie said, "It must be so difficult." Murray said, "There's only eight or nine in an English class. You'd think they'd make more of an effort to learn the language." Ruth said, "Learning a new language is very difficult at this age." Mini said, "It's frustrating because I can speak a little Yiddish but the conversation only goes so far and we are stuck."

I said, "We communicate in many different ways and, although we don't always speak the same language, we can show respect for one another just in our body language." Towards the end of the session, I asked the members their ages, initially just out of curiosity. Lou was talking about a 96-year-old man he knew in the building, "He showed me some pictures, and in one year you can barely recognize him. But his mind is very clear, that's what impresses me." I asked if anyone would be willing to share their age here. Mini said, "Sure, I'll tell you. I'm 79." They each proceeded to give their age proudly. Bea said, "Ruth, you're 70, what a baby!" Marie said, "Anne, I didn't know you were 80. That's remarkable." I said, "So is it both inspiring, but also difficult to live in housing with people mostly 70 and above?" Marie said, "No, I love 'em."

I attempted to reach for their feelings about aging. I said, "You see people aging here." There were several nodding, confirming statements all at once. Bea said, "That's the part…" Marie finished, "…that's most difficult." Ruth said, "Yes. For me it's seeing the people move on, unfortunately, and their health." Mini said, "Susan, you are really confronted with your own mortality in a big rush. If you lived downtown, you'd see an occasional old person. But when everybody is in various stages of active and not active, it hits you, as it has to if you are thinking at all. This is what you have to learn to live with, the moment." Bea said, "After living in a place like this, it's true." Mini said, "You see very few kids around." Ruth said, "That's before the Chinese moved in!" Lou said, "When we were young, we had different problems, we had a family, most of us. And when you go to an advanced stage, it seems your perception changes. People think of looking in the obituary. When you're young, you don't even know it exists. Then you get a call that so and so is in a nursing home." Marie said, "Or you get a call and they're gone." Lou ended with, "I think we're fortunate to have the Jewish Community agency. It provides us with good housing. So all in all, I think we are very fortunate to be here."

Current Status of the Problem:

There has been a gradual shift in the way the members of the group interact with one another. They have begun to develop a more sophisticated level of group operation. At this point, there is much more of a sense of group cohesion; the divisions I mentioned in the problem statement do not seem to carry the same weight as they did early on. The long-term residents do less idealizing of the housing and are able to offer support from their experience. The newer residents are gaining some strength; they are seeing themselves in the process of an adjustment. Both have increased their level of self-disclosure, and the procedural norms have loosened up for more spontaneous interaction.

The group culture now supports members to give more empathetic listening. They have increased their ability to experience a common ground while still maintaining individuality, though the sense of interdependence is still somewhat suspect. The issues of loneliness and loss are still potent, of course, but they have developed an increased capacity to share this with each other.

Strategies for Intervention:

Since there is only one session left, I am somewhat limited here in planning for next steps. Nevertheless, it is an important session:

1. I will continue to reach for the meaningful issues for the group members.
2. I will continue to model non-judgmental acceptance and appreciation of others.
3. I will continue to help create a safe environment for self-disclosure.
4. I will encourage dynamic member interaction.
5. I will terminate by having the members express what they have or haven't gotten from being in the group.
6. I will encourage them to recognize the growth that was made in the group in their way of relating to one another.
7. I will let them know that it has been a privilege to work with them in the group and that they each made a difference in coming here.

In this example, the process of relating in the group modeled the content related to the group's purpose. The group became a microcosm of the housing community, with members having a chance to work on their connections. With pain from so many losses a constant companion for people in this stage of life, it is important to provide the help they need to continue to invest in new relationships.

THE SINGLE-SESSION GROUP

It is not uncommon for some work to be done on a short-term, or even a single-session, basis. Examples include informational meetings (e.g., foster parent recruitment) or educational sessions (e.g., a session at a school designed to help parents assist their children with homework problems). These groups will often be larger than the small, face-to-face groups I have been describing thus far. Workers leading such groups often feel that the time limitations and size of the group will eliminate the possibility of group interaction or involvement, so they substitute direct presentation of the information to be shared, followed by a question period. Sessions structured in this way can be quite effective, but one drawback of straight didactic presentation is that people do not always hear, understand, or re-member the material presented. It is not unusual for questions to be raised at follow-up sessions which suggest that, although the worker has shared the data, the group members have not taken it in. The challenge for the worker is to structure a session so that information can be presented in a way that allows participants to interact with the data and make it more meaningful. Size of group and restricted time do not automatically rule out active participant involvement, and many of the principles discussed thus far can be adapted to such situations.

The worker should begin by thinking about each group was if it were a "small group" and by attempting to adapt the basic model to the group's limitations. For example, the idea of phases of work is still helpful, but the beginning, work, and ending/transition phases all must be encompassed in one session. Contracting in the opening phase of a session is critical, as is demonstrated in the following example from a foster parent recruitment meeting.

Information Group: Foster Parent Recruitment

I explained that the agency was holding these meetings to encourage families to con-sider providing a foster home for our children in care. The purpose of this first session was for us to share some information about fostering with the group, to try to answer their questions, and to discuss the concerns they may have on their minds that might help them to determine if further exploration were feasible. I pointed out the group was large (over forty), and I realized that might make it hard for them to talk, but that I hoped we could treat this evening as a conversation rather than a lecture—I would be interested as much in hearing from them as in sharing my own information. I then asked if this is what they had understood to be the purpose of the meeting. There was a general nodding of heads, so I continued. I said I thought it might be helpful if I could begin by asking them what some of their questions were about fostering—some of the things that were on their minds. I would keep a list of these and try to make sure we covered them in our discussion. There was silence for a moment, and then a hand was raised.

In this example, the worker chose to obtain feedback from the group before beginning her presentation. This can be termed the **listen first—talk later** approach to leading an informational group session. One advantage to this approach is that it helps the worker identify and address members' needs. If someone has an urgent concern about the subject, it can be hard for them to listen to any other conversation until that concern has been dealt with or at least acknowledged. Once they know they are "on the agenda," their energy is freed to invest in absorbing other data. The amount of time taken to raise questions or, in other groups, swap problems, is determined by the overall time available. For example, in a two-hour meeting one would not want to spend more than fifteen minutes contracting and problem swapping, while in a three-hour session, more time might be used to explore issues and develop a group consensus on the agenda. Timing is always important in group sessions, but it naturally takes on a special urgency in a single-session group. The worker needs to develop the ability to keep track of time and to point out continually to the group the relationship between time and their work. For example, the worker might say, "You are raising so many good issues I think we could probably meet for a week. However, we only have two hours. I wonder if it is possible for us to focus on one or two central concerns and dig into them?" Or the worker could explain, "I would like some time at the end to discuss this evening's program, to evaluate the session, and to see what you feel you have gotten out of it. Can we be sure to leave the last 15 minutes to do this?"

Workers often suggest a number of reasons for not involving clients in single-session or large groups more actively in the work. First, they are concerned that they have so much to "cover" they do not have time for group process. But as most of us have noticed in our own educational experience, a teacher who is busy "covering" the agenda does not necessarily teach us anything. We are often better off narrowing the field of work and limiting our goals. Effective work with a manageable agenda is preferable to going through the motions of trying to cover a wide area. The first skill in handling such meetings, then, is to narrow down the potential area of work to suit the time available.

A second area of concern advanced by workers is that the group may raise questions they are not prepared to answer. This is particularly true with new workers, who are nervous enough as it is. They may have little experience in the field and have prepared extensively to deal with the specific areas they have predetermined as important. Their notes are written out in detail, and the last thing they want is someone asking a question for which they are unprepared. This is understandable, since it takes confidence to allow the group to shape the direction of the work. When workers realize they are not being judged by group members on whether or not they have all the answers but rather on how well they involve the group in the process, they are often more willing to risk opening up the session in novel and unexpected directions. When they do so, they find they can learn as much from such sessions as the group members. Each session helps the worker to tune in and prepare for the next one, so that the ability to deal with the real concerns of the group grows with experience.

A third area of concern, particularly with large groups, is that a singe member may take over the group for individual or personal issues unrelated to the contract. The section on deviant members already illustrated how it may be necessary for the worker to be assertive in such a situation and to guard the contract vigorously. This ability also comes with experience. Once again, the worker has to be willing to risk the hazards of such an approach if the benefits of more member involvement are to be gained.

An Informal Event Group: Remembering the Holocaust

A short-term, informal, spontaneous group can be brought together to deal with an event or immediate circumstances. For example, social workers have reached out to relatives and friends in the waiting room of an emergency ward to form an informal group to help them cope with their immediate stress. School social workers have organized groups for students following the tragedy of a classmate's suicide. Groups have been held in residential settings or schools following a natural catastrophe (hurricane, earthquake, flood) or the assassination of a political or movement leader. In each case, the work is short-term and focuses on the impact of the event and ways in which group members can more effectively cope with it.

In the following example, a worker works with a spontaneous, hallway group of elderly members of a Jewish community center day program. As part of a program designed to focus on the World War II Holocaust, when millions of Jews, as well as others, were killed, the center staff had mounted a photo exhibit during Yom Hashoah—the day set aside for remembrance. An informal group had begun discussion in the hallway, and the student social worker was present. She noticed Sara, who often played the role of group scapegoat, expressing angry feelings.

Sara: Why are we talking about this nonsense? Photo whatnots. Didn't used to be what we did for Yom Hashoah. We didn't used to have a bunch of foolishness pictures—it was taken more serious.

Victor: (Referring to Sara) She doesn't know how to talk. There were community gatherings to remind us about what happened. Yom Hashoah isn't taken seriously now.

Worker: Somehow I get the feeling that we're not just talking about this particular day being taken seriously.

Sara: No, we're talking about death gonna happen again if we don't do something about it.

Robert: (To Sara, laughing mockingly) Well, what could *you* possibly do about it anyway?

Worker: I wonder what's going on that people are talking to Sara this way.

Victor: Because she is so strange!

Worker: I wonder why people are talking this way to Sara right now. To be honest, people seem angry.

Robert: (To worker) Yeah, sure we're angry. You want us to dance? I would never dance with Sara!

Worker: I wonder if people are actually angry about the Holocaust not being taken seriously.
(Silence)

Worker: Or maybe angry that nothing stopped it from happening in the first place.

Sara: (To worker) Gei kaken ("Go shit"). You're a nice girl, but... (to Robert, loudly) Did you live in the War?

Robert: (Stands up, loudly to Sara) "I'll tell you something! I saw my father shot, my mother was gassed, and my sister (makes gesture of hanging by a rope). You never had such a life! (Puts hands in pockets, jingles change, and begins to sob quietly, turns back to group)
(Silence)

Sara: (To Robert) That's a terrible thing. I wish I could say something to make you feel better.

Remembering an event as powerful and awful as the Holocaust is bound to generate many reactions to the associated pain. The "flight-fight" reaction in the group was maladaptive in that it turned survivors of oppression into antagonists, just when they needed each other the most. The worker's brief intervention illustrates the beginning of helping them to rediscover their connections.

In summary, clients in a single-session group, even a large group, can be involved actively in a group process with beneficial results. I have asked groups with as many as 900 people to attempt a discussion, with some degree of success. There are many situations where direct didactic presentation at the beginning of a session can be extremely helpful. However, the worker must keep the presentation of material to a reasonable time (more than forty minutes may be too much) and should monitor the group's reactions as the presentation progresses. The ability of group members to work effectively and with feeling in a single-session group, when the proper conditions are set by the worker, has never ceased to amaze me.

ACTIVITY IN GROUPS

Activity group is a term usually applied to groups involved in a range of activities other than just conversation. *Program* is another term used to describe the activities implemented in such groups, such as the expressive arts (e.g., painting, dancing), games, folk singing, social parties, cooking—in fact, almost any recreational or social activity used by people in groups. In one of my earlier articles (Shulman, 1971), I examined the ways in which people relate to each other, suggesting that to dichotomize "talking" and "doing" is a mistake. Relationships between people were best described by a **mixed transactional model.**

In the complex process of human interaction, people express feelings, ideas, support, interest, and concern—an entire range of human reactions—through a variety of mediums. The concept of a mixed transactional model implies that all of these mediums—words, facial and body expressions, touch, shared experiences of various kinds, and other forms of communication (often used simultaneously)—be included when considering the means by which transactions are negotiated and consummated. We should not fragment human interactions by forcing them into categories such as "talking" and "doing" but should focus instead on the common denominators among transactions, defined here as exchanges in which people give to and take from each other. As group workers, we are concerned with helping people who are pursuing common purposes to carry out mutually productive transactions.

In my analysis of the ways in which shared activity might be used by group members for mutual aid, I rejected grandiose claims that suggested specific activities might lead to "creating spontaneous or creative individuals" or "strengthened egos" and instead suggested the need to describe the specific and immediate functions that activity must play in the mutual aid process. Five of these identified functions were: (a) **human contact**—activities that focus on meeting a basic human need for social interaction (e.g., golden age clubs for isolated senior citizens); (b) **data gathering**—activities designed to help members obtain more information central to their tasks (e.g., teenagers preparing for employment arranging a series of trips to business or industrial complexes) ; (c) **rehearsal**—a means of developing skills for specific life tasks (e.g., a teenage party in an institution creating an opportunity for members to practice the social skills necessary for the courtship phase of life); (d) **deviational allowance**—activities creating a flow of affect between members that builds up a positive relationship, allowing members to deviate from the accepted norms and raise concerns and issues that might otherwise be taboo (e.g., young teenage boys who have gotten to know each other and the leader over a period of time through many shared activities might be more willing to accept a worker's invitation to discuss their real fears about sex); (e) **entry**—specific activities planned by a group as a way to enter an area of difficult discussion (e.g., the playacting of young children as they create roles and situations that often reveal their concerns of the moment).

There are two general categories of groups in which activities are used as a medium of exchange. In the first, the activities themselves constitute the purpose of the group. Examples might include a teenage club in a community center or a patients' committee in a psychiatric hospital charged with planning recreational activities or an evening lounge program. The group exists for the purpose of implementing the activity. A second category includes groups established for curative purposes, in which an activity is employed as a medium of exchange with specific healing goals in mind. A dance therapy group in a psychiatric center is an example of this type of group. These two categories will be covered separately because each raises special issues.

The first type of group—for example, a teenage club—can often be found in the agencies that gave birth to group work practice in the social work field: community centers, Ys, and national youth organizations. In addition, such groups are being used in other institutions as a vehicle for involving clients in planning their own leisure-time activities. The most typical problem with this type of group is that the worker or the agency ascribes therapeutic purposes to the group that in effect constitute a hidden agenda. The group members may think they are attending a Y teenage club, but the workers view the group as a medium through which they can effect changes in the members. This view reflects an early and still dominant view of program activity as a "tool of the worker," which grew out of the social work profession's early efforts to distinguish the social worker with groups from the recreation worker. The professional worker, so the thinking goes, would bring to bear special skills in selecting programs that would result in the desired behavioral changes.

Take, for instance, the problem of the child who was scapegoated in a group. In this early model, the worker might ascertain what area of skill this child had and then select or influence the group to choose the activity at which the scapegoated child would shine. This approach was rooted in a relatively unsophisticated view of group process and a sense of worker function that called for use of direct or indirect influence in the attempt to "change" the group members. This attitude was mentioned earlier in our discussion of children's groups developed in schools for youngsters in trouble that attempted to aid them in their school problems by involving them in "clubs" and activity groups as mediums for the worker to "change their behavior."

My own training was rooted in this view of practice. In one setting, my agenda involved attempting to influence group members (teenagers) toward their religious association. The agency was sponsored by the Jewish community, which was concerned that second-generation teenagers might be "drifting away." Program was the tool through which I was to influence the members by involving them in agency-wide activities—for example, in connection with religious holidays and celebrations. When such activities were conducted with the direct involvement and planning of the members involved, they offered powerful opportunities for deepening a sense of cultural connection and community. Unfortunately, at times I was so busy attempting to covertly "influence" the membership that I ended up missing the indirect cues group members offered about their real concerns related to their identity as a minority group in a Christian culture. There were important moments when the concerns of the community and the felt needs of the group members were identical; the common ground was missed because of the misguided view that I was to use program as my tool to accomplish the agency's ends.

My argument is that program is an effective tool, but that it is the members' tool, not the worker's. A group of teenagers in a community center or a residential setting sharing a "club" in which they plan their own social and recreational activities is an important service in itself. It does not have to be embellished with "professional" purposes. The worker's function in such a group is not to secretly influence members but rather to help them to develop their own club. The worker's suggestions for activities related to the group members' needs can be shared freely, as a worker with any group would share relevant data, but it is the group members who must sort out those activities and decide which ones they wish to pursue. They will need the worker's help in doing so as they struggle with all of the tasks of the group, as outlined in the previous chapter. If the agency has other agendas it feels are important for groups, then these must be openly presented in the contracting phase, and the group worker must attempt to find whatever common ground may exist. However, just as the worker will guard the group's contract from subversion by members, it must also be guarded from subversion by the agency. Members will learn a great deal about relationships, problem solving, and other areas as they work to create and run their groups; however, the worker must see the club as an end in itself, not a tool to be used for hidden professional purposes.

The second category of activity group is the type in which specific purposes other than the activity are the major focus and the activity is used to help achieve these ends. This is illustrated in the following three examples. In the first, the workers help a group of eight- and nine-year-old children deal with the trauma of separation and divorce through activities using drawing and puppets as mediums of expression. In the second, teenagers in a residential setting use music and dance to work on developing their confidence. In the third example, a group of Vietnamese women use cooking and food as their medium for sharing the traumatic experiences associated with their transitions to a new country and culture.

Children Dealing with Their Parents' Separation and Divorce

Type of Group: This is an ongoing group to give children the opportunity to discuss their fears, to face change, and to find solutions to the painful crisis of family disruption.

Members: eight- and nine-year-olds, white, lower- and middle-income children; two girls and one boy

Dates: 10/31 to 11/28

Group Task: Structure-maintenance

1. *Description of the Problem:* The task this young group faces is understanding that the sharing of feelings, thoughts and attitudes with each other about the theme that unites them (having lived through the separation and/or divorce of their parents) can be a powerful mechanism through which each member can identify and relate to others, recognize that their experience is not unique and that divorce is a change with both positive and negative aspects to it, thereby decreasing each member's sense of isolation, loneliness, guilt, and grief. Two major challenges are faced by members within this group. The first is the likelihood that each child is unaccustomed to or discouraged from sharing his/her feelings, particularly with regard to separation/divorce, in their respective families. The second is being more accustomed to speaking *to* teachers and *to* parents (people in authority) to have their needs met and questions answered rather than looking to their peers.

Given the ages of the children, it seems appropriate that looking to adults to provide some guidance and support is natural and healthy. However, the challenge for me, as the worker, is to create an environment in which increased communication and the sharing of affect between the children can be encouraged, as opposed to allowing only the continuation of the more familiar process of the children's dependence and reliance on authority figures to meet their needs. My role is to continually find ways to foster and strengthen the members' ability to speak with, and find support and solace from, one another. My hope is (1) the members can begin to feel freer to acknowledge their feelings with regard to the endings of their families as they once knew them, and the reconstruction of their newer families, and (2) the members, through this group experience, can practice new ways of sharing, cooperating, and finding within and among themselves a greater capacity to cope with the struggles that life presents.

2. *How the Problem Came to My Attention:* I noticed in the first group session, and again in the second, that the members seemed most comfortable speaking in response to a question or statement that my co-leader or I would raise. I was aware that the group takes place immediately after the children leave school, an environment in which it is expected that they speak only when they raise their hand and/or are acknowledged by their teachers. Given their ages and the newness of being in this particular kind of group experience, I suspected that the children may have been unaware as to what was expected of them. As a result, in both the first and second sessions, I made requests for the members to share with one another to encourage not only communication, but collaborative problem solving. They were able to do this when it was suggested, but unless the suggestion was explicit, I noticed that the members looked to the leaders for instructions on how to proceed. I knew that it would be essential to continually set a tone where discussion between the members could occur to best create a sense for the members that they were in this group for a shared purpose—a purpose, I realize, of which they may have been unaware, but which would need to be clarified through the leaders' function of helping the members put their thoughts and feelings into words, pictures, or play and helping the members reach out in new ways by bridging connections between their shared experiences.

3. *Summary of the Work with Process Excerpts:*

First Session: I was anxious about starting a group whose members were so young. My co-leader, Joanne, had a lot of experience working with children and did not share my anxiety, which relieved me to an extent. She had available to her written activities for children from a former group she had run, and she and I together modified the activities to meet the needs of this group, knowing that it was important to allow for input from the members as well. Two of the members showed up early. For the first session we had expected three members and had been told one member would arrive late. We had a snack prepared and tried to make the two members comfortable, explaining that we would wait for the third member to arrive before actually starting group. *I felt a need to reach out to these two members.* I introduced myself, asked their names and ages and where they went to school, and encouraged them to help themselves to the snack. Henry (nine) and Stacy (eight) were initially shy, but with this invitation helped themselves to juice and crackers. Stacy began talking about her family. Time passed; the third member never arrived. Joanne and I decided to formally start the "group," recognizing with only two members, we might need to alter some of our planned activities to decrease the intensity for these two children. *I asked if they knew why they were here.* I wanted to get a feel for what they had been told about the group and note any reactions. Both were able to share that it was because their parents were "going through a separation." I was confused, because my understanding was that in both these families the separations had occurred long ago and that in Stacy's family, the divorce had been finalized. *I tried to assess what I suspected was denial by eliciting information from them concerning these separations.* I wasn't sure if it was denial operating or a misunderstanding of the term "separation." Not wanting to assume that it was denial or to confront it so early in the group's life, I asked each child who s/he lived with. Then I asked when this change in their living situation happened. Both Henry and Stacy were able to respond to these questions and clearly understood their parents were, in fact, separated. Maybe they were thinking that it was the divorce that was in progress, but Henry's father had literally walked out four years earlier, and Stacy's parents had been divorced for several months, following a separation two years earlier. *I chose not to ask at this time what it had been like to make these changes in their living arrangements.* It may have been a missed opportunity to discuss how their parents' separations directly affect them, but because it was the first session and because at least one member was missing (we were working on getting more members), I did not seek further elaboration.

We began our first activity, which involved having the members draw or write their responses to benign questions: something they like, something they don't like, an animal each would like to be and one they wish they had, and then share their work as an effort to increase their comfort level with sharing. Henry drew a picture of not liking when kids fight, which he said was happening at school. I wondered, given this was a group dealing with separation and divorce issues, if he also had not liked when his parents fought—how that felt, the position it put him in. Stacy said she does not have to worry about this because "everyone in my class likes me."

I tried to encourage mutual aid. I wanted to set a precedent in this first group that there would be an expectation that members would speak with one another and that by doing so, members might find new ways of problem solving. I asked Stacy if she could give Henry some advice about how to avoid getting into situations where fighting might occur. Her response to Henry was to fight back if you had to. She said that is what her father had taught her to do. A wish that both Henry and Stacy had was illustrated by a great amount of money (green rectangles). *I missed the significance of this wish until a review of the literature helped me to understand how money, in the children's minds, could fill the void that each of them feels.*

The next activity involved each member drawing a picture of his/her family. Henry had great difficulty here. He drew a door, then a window, then asked to go to the bathroom. Stacy drew her entire family: all five members were smiling, Mom and Dad were next to each other, and a big heart encircled all of them. Henry's seeming inability to draw his family members and Stacy's wishful illustration seemed to reflect some avoidance and some denial, respectively. (Henry did complete his drawing upon his return and drew a smiling child with his mother's arm around him.)

Because of their ages and the fact that this was the first group session, as with issues mentioned earlier, I chose not to explore the significance of how this activity was played out. I knew these would be ongoing and necessary themes to explore, as the artwork demonstrated, and that my co-leader and I would need to help these children name their feelings if the group was to be effective. I was able to identify many messages in the session, but unsure as to when to probe and when to just let the members be. I knew, too, I would need to pay attention to my own resistance or hesitation to explore these emotional, painful issues.

The group leader's recognition of her own resistance to explore painful issues is an important step in helping her to reach for the members' underlying feelings of hurt, anger, and tremendous loss. At times such as these, it becomes important to explore one's own resistance through supervision or consultation. These children are very astute observers of adults around them and have already received the message that the feelings are taboo and not to be discussed. When they perceive that these adults are ready to hear them, the chances of their responding are greatly increased.

Second Session: Henry, Stacy, and Tara (nine) participated in group today. *Because Tara had missed our first group, I asked Henry and Stacy if they could share with her what took place in the first session.* Rather than my telling Tara what had occurred the previous week, I hoped that this would be a non-threatening attempt to encourage intermember communication; my intent was to set the tone right away in that the two initial members would recognize that this new member was an equal participant in the group and to encourage her sense of inclusion. Henry and Stacy could feel important sharing with her, while Tara could feel the other members, and the leaders, were reaching out to admit her. Both Henry and Stacy were able to tell Tara the activities we had done, and Henry even recalled the details of each of the drawing activities. Joanne and I asked the members if they could recall why each of them was here. Tara was able to say, as Henry and Stacy had the week before, that she knew it was because her parents had separated. We gave Tara an opportunity to draw her responses to the previous week's activities while Henry and Stacy embellished their pictures. Repeating the previous week's activities felt awkward to me, but my co-leader, and I to an extent, felt it was important for each member to participate in this early task. After Tara was done, the members shared their drawings with one another. *I frequently asked members if they could tell the others what something represented to him/her in the drawing.* I understood that this was like a first group, since Tara had not been able to come the week before, and that it might take a while for members to become comfortable sharing with one another without prompting from a leader. Still, I continued to make a demand that they speak to one another. I felt that my co-leader was excellent at drawing each child out, but the result seemed to be that the child would respond to her. I seemed to be more focused on drawing each child out in an attempt to increase dialogue with his or her peers. I am aware that this is a function of the training I have received and my belief that peers engaging one another can provide a more powerful mechanism for support and growth than that provided by the interaction between members and leader.

For this session, the plan was to focus on the word "divorce." The children were asked to brainstorm words that come to mind when they hear this word and determine whether the words have positive ("good") or negative ("bad") meanings to them. The members eagerly responded to this activity. Each took turns writing a word/phrase on the blackboard, and after they finished, we discussed what they had written. Their list was quite comprehensive: the "good" list included "no more fighting" and "parents still love us," and the "bad" list included "separation," "lots of crying," "children feel sad," and "some people think it's their fault." Because "children" was a big word and Stacy had trouble writing it, Henry suggested that she simply write, "we feel sad." I heard this as his ability to identify with her statement and bring its context closer to home.

When Henry wrote, "Some people think it's their fault," I asked him, "Which people?" I wanted to reach into his words and bring what he was saying closer to the group. He responded by mentioning "the children," which led us into a discussion as to whether each of the members had ever felt it was their fault that their parents had separated/divorced. None of them believed that it was; each sounded as if s/he was repeating messages that they had heard from their parents not to feel responsible. How much each of them really believed it was or was not their fault was not clear to me at this time.

Following this discussion, the members drew pictures illustrating aspects of what had just been discussed. Henry's picture was incredible; the top of the page said, "separation" and under this heading, he drew a crying child, alone, in the middle of the page with Mom walking off the right-hand side of the page and Dad walking off the left side. All you could see was one leg and one hand of each parent. It was a powerfully vivid and moving depiction of Henry's understanding of "separation."

The last portion of group involved reading a series of statements and the members deciding if these statements were true or false. Somehow, animal puppets had gotten passed around, to the leaders as well, and we all agreed to respond through the puppets. I did not know if it was due to difficult subject matter or the lateness of the hour, or perhaps a combination of both, but the group seemed to all be responding at once. *I asked that one puppet speak at a time.* While recognizing that this exercise was the most sensitive one in which the group had participated so far, I wanted to review the rule that we had discussed last week and at the beginning of this group that one person talks at a time. I hoped that stating this through "one puppet," as opposed to "one person" would honor the acceptability of "working" through the puppets and keep the members engaged, while pointing out the need to be respectful.

I saw that the use of puppets seemed to be very freeing for each of the members; they were immersed in their puppets, but were able to remain attentive to the activity. As well as each member had done up to this point, the use of puppets seemed to elicit much more spontaneity and free associating. Each child had much to say about each statement and was clearly speaking from his or her realm of experience. Again I noticed, however, that discussion seemed to travel between each member and my co-leader or the members and me. *I once more tried to encourage discussion between the members.* Each time someone responded to a statement, I would say, "Stacy and Henry, Tara thinks this statement is true because…what do each of you think?" My effort at this time only resulted in their responding to me.

I wished that this last exercise could have been given more time. The statements had evoked a lot of feeling and a lot of sharing, but the session was over. In comparison to the previous week's session, I did feel discussion of feelings associated with "separation" and "divorce" had taken place and that through their words, pictures, and puppets, much had been shared. It was only the second group, and the first group for the three members together. I am actually struck, as I write this, at the courage and vulnerability the members displayed. I hoped that next week's session would provide another opportunity for the members to share their feelings and recognize their capacity for mutual aid.

The leader has noted the difference in interaction between her and her co-leader. She strengthens their work together by raising the issue in a non-threatening manner. Crucial to this conversation is her recognition that they both are contributing to the group's development and that they can learn from each other.

Third Session: Prior to this session commencing, I spoke with my co-leader and mentioned that, while writing this record of service, I became aware of the different functions she and I seemed to play in the group. She found my observation interesting. I told her if this was a group for adults, I would think downplaying member-leader interaction would be important and that encouraging mutual aid would be critical. In a group for children, however, I wondered if both functions were in fact necessary to model healthy adult interaction for the children on the one hand and help the children learn to enhance their interpersonal skills with peers on the other hand. We did not get to finish this discussion, but I did notice that she made different kinds of interventions in this group session than she had previously. Simultaneously, I felt freer to explore each member's comments in more depth than I may have in previous weeks, while still continuing to make demands for mutual aid.

All three members were present for this third session. After everyone had had a snack, *I asked members if they could recall what we had done the previous week.* I wanted to see what the members would find significant to mention and if they would specifically mention our activity around "divorce." I was impressed, as I had been the week before, with the members' ability to cite details from what we had all done together in our previous session. *I then asked members if they had thoughts or feelings they wanted to bring up since the last meeting.* I wanted to demonstrate that while we only meet weekly, our work together continues between meetings, and to give them permission to share anything that might have arisen for each of them. No one felt a need to respond to this question. *My next question was to ask the members if family members had asked any of them what was happening in their group.* I again wanted to see if there had been carry-over from the group meetings into their homes. Surprisingly for me, each child said no one had discussed group with them. Henry, however, did offer that his mother had stopped smoking since our last meeting. He sounded proud of her, and this led into a discussion of when our partners make us proud of them versus when they make us sad or angry at them. Although the members had started off quietly, ten minutes into the group, each child seemed ready to share.

In this session, the focus was to acknowledge that divorce means change and that change is something that occurs all the time. Joanne asked the group what changes when parents separate or divorce. I overheard Stacy and Henry both say the word "disappear." *I commented that they had both used this word and asked each of them to share what they meant by this word.* I was trying to create a bridge by showing the members there was similarity in their response. Stacy said that things disappear, like the couch or the television—one parent gets the couch, one the television. I looked to Henry for his response, and he immediately offered that a parent can disappear. Because I had learned through Joanne that Henry's father had left four years earlier, I knew there was a lot of feeling behind what Henry had shared. The two other members in the group had both parents very much in their lives, as well as brothers and sisters and new partners for their parents; for Henry, it was only his mother and him. I do not believe the other members were aware of the significance of Henry's remark and therefore were not sensitive to what he had shared. I struggled with how to proceed. *I chose to mention how divorce can be different in different people's homes.* I discussed that for some people divorce may mean new people in their lives if mom or dad gets a new boyfriend or girlfriend and that this can be positive or negative; I also said that it can mean being single for a parent, which can be lonely for the parent and maybe for the child; and I added that it can mean leaving a place one has lived, their school, friends, grandparents, other family members, or perhaps moving to a place where one is closer to their relatives or family friends. This created discussion among the children as they began to relate stories about their parents' partners, their grandparents, and friends they knew who were also experiencing parental separation/divorce.

Our activity for this session involved giving each member a sheet of paper with three faces on it, one face reflecting happiness, one face reflecting sadness, and one face reflecting fear. Each child was to write underneath each face the best, worst, the scariest thing about divorce. The children immediately responded to this task; all were clearly concentrating and very focused on what they were writing. When they were finished writing, they shared what they had written. All of them agreed that "no more fighting" was the best thing about divorce, a theme they had perhaps recalled from the previous week. A variety of answers were written, and *both Joanne and I encouraged each of the members to think about if what their co-members had written applied to them*. My purpose here was to demonstrate once again that similarities in their experiences might exist. Not surprisingly, there were several examples with which the children could identify. They all agreed with Tara's comment that another "best" thing about divorce is that "your parents still love you" and with Henry's comment that a "worst" thing about divorce is that "some kids think it's their fault." While a number of these themes had been discussed the previous week, it revealed to me that the members were incorporating some of what was being shared in our group. In addition, this week it seemed there was more feeling behind the words. I wondered if Joanne and I were functioning well as leaders and creating a safe environment in which the children's feelings could emerge, as the group seemed to be feeling more comfortable with one another, and in turn, more comfortable sharing.

Fourth Session: With the Thanksgiving holiday occurring this week, I thought it would be appropriate to focus our fourth session on how the members were feeling about the upcoming holiday and what it represented to them in terms of how and with whom they had spent it in the past, what has changed for each of them and what they anticipate for this holiday. *I spoke with my co-leader about this idea,* and she agreed that it would be useful and that we could modify any activity to include this event. As has been described, each week so far had revisited discussion about expressing feelings of sadness, anger, and happiness in response to divorce. While in some ways it seemed redundant, my co-leader and I recognized that the purpose of this group was to get the members to feel increasingly comfortable acknowledging and voicing their feelings. The Thanksgiving holiday seemed a perfect vehicle to elicit current struggles each member might be experiencing.

When this session started, I notice that all three members immediately began chatting, eating their snack, and asking what we were going to do in a more animated display than I had seen in previous weeks. *I used this opportunity to get right down to work, and I asked what was happening this week that made this week special.* Each child mentioned that it was Thanksgiving. I asked if they could tell the group how each one would be spending the time. All three members began speaking at once. *I asked the group if we could review the group contract.* Tara and Henry raised their hands. I explained that hand-raising was not necessary, but that it seemed that they had the right idea. Tara said that only one person should speak at a time. I commented that it seemed all three of them had something interesting to say and that I did not want to miss anyone's contribution. Stacy asked if she could go first, since she was the youngest. Each child described how they would be spending the holiday and then drew a picture of how they envisioned feeling on that day.

All three members reported that the previous Thanksgiving had been their favorite Thanksgiving; Joanne and I looked at each other skeptically, since we knew that for Stacy in particular, her parents' marriage had already been in serious trouble. *I tried to confront the denial and avoidance I was sensing by reaching for more feelings.* I asked the group what had made the previous Thanksgiving so special. Each child commented that they were with family and had good food. Stacy talked in great detail about her grandmother's soup. I recalled Stacy's difficulty focusing on her personal situation in our first group session. *I tried to verbalize the pain members of the group may have been feeling and missed an opportunity to point out to the group that talking about painful emotions seemed to be difficult for them.* I mentioned that holidays can be very special since for many people they are spent with loved ones, but that they can also be difficult when families change or when someone wants to be in two places at once. The members continued to draw. Tara commented that she has an aunt who draws well, but not as well as Henry. Despite the members' inability to tolerate what I was attempting to raise, this was the first time I had heard an unsolicited comment from one group member to another. While this may have demonstrated a member's aligning with another member rather than dealing with the issue at hand (flight), other examples of this interaction occurred in the session that supported my initial sense that the members seemed more connected and willing to speak to one another. Nevertheless, Joanne and I looked at one another and agreed we needed to move on to another activity; the members had become very absorbed in their artwork and needed a push.

Joanne and I took turns creating vignettes, and the members had to decide whether someone described in the vignette would feel happy, sad, angry or disappointed. We spontaneously created scenarios that seemed relevant to what the children might be facing this week. *I went first and offered: "Mary's father is supposed to pick her up at 10 a.m. on Thanksgiving. He calls her at 11 a.m. to say he can't make it because he's decided to go to his girlfriend's house. Mary feels_____."* The scenarios became more complicated as Joanne and I introduced step-parent and step-sibling issues and other conflicting themes that might involve the members. Each child responded quite positively to this activity. They were spirited and engaged, and each contributed sound reasons for feeling as the character might have felt. Often the members personalized the scenarios by saying how he or she would feel. After Joanne and I had each done two scenarios, Tara asked if she could make one up. Stacy followed. She described a situation where a mother's boyfriend was angry at a child and threw the child down the stairs. She wanted to know how the mother should feel.

Henry and Tara responded together that the mother would be sad the child was hurt. *I felt an urgent need to make a stronger statement, as well as model for the members the acceptability of their own strong feelings.* I added, in a very firm voice, that if I was the mother, I would be furious that my boyfriend had hurt my child and that no matter how my child behaved, no child deserved to be hurt and that my boyfriend's behavior was absolutely unacceptable. Recalling the activity we had played in a previous session, Stacy acted like the judge and said I had given the best response for that scenario. It was a scenario Joanne and I would need to be alerted to.

The scenario raised by Stacy must also raise a warning flag for the workers. The possibility that the child is raising an abusive situation would need to be explored further in an individual session. The social workers leading this group are mandated reporters, and even an indirect communication of possible abuse must be explored, and if confirmed, shared with the appropriate child welfare agency.

The children's vignettes were complicated and revealing. Each member seemed to be an internal leader—creating a vignette and listening to each person's discussion as to why someone might feel as s/he did. This activity seemed to reduce the amount of denial and avoidance I had sensed earlier; by removing the focus from the three members, which in a group of three may have simply been too intense, the members could be more spontaneous in exposing their feelings. Time had run out, and the members did not want to leave. *I told the group that everyone had made wonderful, creative, and sensitive contributions and that we would talk more next week.* I wanted to praise and reinforce their willingness to take risks and to take ownership of their group by conceiving their own stories. I also hoped to imply that next week would provide another opportunity to do more of the same.

Fifth Session: My co-leader and I decided to focus this week's session on anger. Prior to group, she and I had agreed that we would use vignettes again since it seemed to be an effective way of getting each of the members to reveal their own feelings, sometimes in the guise of sharing through what the characters might feel and sometimes through making identifications with the characters as to how they, the members, would feel.

The group opened as it did last week; the members were snacking and chatting with each other and seeming comfortable as they discussed how they had spent their Thanksgiving holiday. The members asked what we were going to do today, and Joanne responded that we would be talking about anger. *I felt a need to review why we were all together and to remind the group that there was a shared purpose to our meeting.* I asked the group what we had been discussing in our previous weeks together and what it was that brought us all together. Tara immediately responded "divorce." I nodded and then asked if anyone could be more specific. Stacy said we talked about "happy, sad, mad." I asked the group if this is different from what they do in school and if it is, in what way. Everyone said it was different and that in school people do not discuss their feelings. I asked the group why they thought this was so. A silence followed. *I thought the members might be feeling uncomfortable and that their silence reflected their own discomfort and sense of isolation regarding their ability to discuss their family situations freely at school, and perhaps even in the group. I missed an opportunity to acknowledge their discomfort and instead tried to educate them and normalize their experience about the common occurrence of divorce.* I asked the members if they knew other children at school whose parents were separated and divorced, in an attempt to normalize their experience. My co-leader pointed out that almost half of all marriages end in divorce. Not surprisingly, the intellectualized response by my co-leader, and perhaps by me, generated little response, and my co-leader and I moved on to our planned activity.

The workers have taken the children to the edge of an important discussion. The question about what makes it hard to talk about these subjects is on target; however, the children's silence in response moves the workers away from an important discussion. This is the moment when reaching into the silence, perhaps by offering some specific possible reasons why it is hard, may help the children deepen the conversation. The group leader shows important insight in her learning process as she recognizes her own intellectualizing response. It is possible that one of the reasons it is so hard to talk about these feelings relates to the anger that is the focus of this session.

We asked the children what makes them angry about divorce. They were able to come up with several responses. *I tried to draw them out in an effort to have them reveal more depth that they had in previous sessions, and I pointed out connections to other responses when similarities were evident to me.* Joanne and I then took turns creating vignettes that we knew would resonate for the members in our group. What followed was a lengthy discussion about absent parents, new partners in their parents' lives, and contending with the children of these partners. This presented an opportunity for helping the children to engage in some problem solving. Tara and Henry both described wanting to kill a new baby that was born to "Walter's mother and her boyfriend," characters in a scenario. *I thought it was important to acknowledge the expression of their feelings and again tried to elicit from them* why might they want to kill this baby, who else might they be angry at, what would happen if they really did kill the baby, and what might their loved ones feel about them. Following this opportunity for them to play out this scenario, I asked if it was really okay to kill a baby. The members all said no. *I then asked if anyone could think of other solutions to this dilemma, since killing a baby is really not okay. I hoped that this would instill confidence in the members' own capacity to problem-solve.* Henry and Stacy smiled. Tara, who had a newborn in her home, did not. Henry, an only child, said maybe "Walter" could play with the baby; I asked Henry what that would do. He replied, "Walter might like it." I acknowledged that Walter might enjoy having a younger sibling after all, even though his feelings might remain mixed. This seemed to give Tara permission to discuss that it is hard having only younger siblings and that she wished she were not the oldest in her family.

 I tried to articulate the idea that members in the group have had different experiences in their families from which they draw their feelings and attitudes, in an effort to increase members' sensitivity to the experiences of others and to demonstrate tolerance. I commented to the group that it sometimes sounded like Henry found it lonely to be an only child and that Tara, having two sisters and now a newborn would often prefer more privacy. Both children nodded.

 One of the vignettes created a scenario of a friend wanting talk to someone about his parents' divorce. *I wanted to show the group that each of them, not only in the presence of the group, but outside the group, had a lot to offer.* I asked the group who this friend could speak with. Henry said that he would tell this person to speak to a counselor or teacher. I said that this was a very good suggestion. I then highlighted for the group that each of them could be very supportive to a friend because of their own experience of having gone through a similar situation and that it might help the friend to feel less alone. As had been discussed earlier in the group, we again began discussing why talking about these feelings is difficult. I noticed that all three children had moved into the corner and were focused on a doll house, standing with their backs turned towards Joanne and me. *This time I was not going to miss the opportunity to acknowledge their discomfort.* I said to the group, "I have asked all of you a question. Is it hard for you to talk about this stuff right now?" I was stunned by the honesty of their reactions. Henry immediately nodded, and Stacy and Tara said, "Yes." *I chose to reach further to have them identify their discomfort.* "How come?" I asked. There was no answer, and this session was over. *I again wanted to praise their willingness and bravery to take risks and share their feelings.* I commented, "That's okay. You've all been doing a great job today talking about issues that are hard for everyone. It's not easy, and you've all been very brave."

 4. *Where the Problem Stands Now:* Each week the group members have appeared increasingly comfortable with one another, as evidenced by their spontaneous interactions when they enter group. They seem to recognize that they share similarities as children of divorced parents. Even though the children admit that it is hard for them

to discuss painful events they have experienced, they have each shown a greater willingness to tolerate sensitive issues. It is my hope that the structure and maintenance Joanne and I strive to continually sustain has resulted in a group culture that is different from what they may experience elsewhere and that it has made the members feel safer to express themselves when they choose.

The members still look to Joanne or me to guide the session, but this may be a function of their developmental stage and being more accustomed to looking to adults for guidance, rather than to themselves. Movement towards mutual aid is apparent, however, as I have noticed that greater interaction does take place between the members, with less prompting from me, as we progress into each session. The members are increasingly showing that they can share and cooperate with one another. Perhaps because this group is so small, or that we have not yet faced it, power and control struggles have been negligible; the only manifestation of this kind of struggle that I have been aware of has been when the children, together, decide they no longer want to discuss the issue at hand and begin to play with or focus on something else. I am trying to not only recognize this, but as I did in this last session, point out to the members areas that are troublesome for them. It is my hunch that, many times, they are able to identify certain feelings and are conscious of holding back, but remain confused as to how to express themselves. If their attention is directed to these areas, the members may slowly become less constricted and freer to externalize through an appropriate means of communication the confusion and the turbulence they feel inside.

5. *Specific Next Steps:*

1. I will continue to discuss with my co-leader the importance and value of encouraging mutual aid, as opposed to only encouraging member-leader interaction.

2. I will continue to be sensitive to the age and developmental stage of the group members so as not to create any unreasonable exceptions for myself or for them.

3. I will continue to recontract—to remind the members that they are here because they are all children who have experienced separation and divorce.

4. I will continue to create an environment that feels safe for each member so that s/he can feel increasingly safe to disclose aspects of his/her inner self and know that s/he will be heard.

5. I will be sensitive to each member's outside reality in terms of defenses, learned behaviors, and coping mechanisms each may have developed, while encouraging them to adopt a different way of relating while within the group.

6. I must make demands for work (reach for feelings of sadness, loss, anger, frustration, confusion) and continue to help the members explore painful themes that are difficult for them to examine and verbalize.

7. I must stay in tune with my own need to intellectualize or avoid painful feelings so as not to sabotage the critical work of this group.

8. I will try to listen for and understand the underlying messages members may be communicating.

9. When silences occur, or lapses in process (reluctance to draw, to participate in an activity, and so on), I will mentally make note of the seeming resistance to understand what is happening for the members while gently helping them to identify, or identifying for them, what the group might be experiencing.

10. I will continue to demonstrate support to any of the members who demonstrate initiative and take risks by sharing their feelings and thoughts with the other members.

11. Similarly, I will continue to credit the group's efforts at working together.

12. I will continue to reveal and create connections for the members as I see and understand them.

13. I must take a more active role in acknowledging my own feelings with the group to demonstrate my own humanity and to help model for them the sharing of feelings.

14. As I sense the members' feelings emerge, I must help the members put their feelings into words rather than internalize them or put them into actions.

15. As I prepare the group for its eventual termination, I must continually work to reflect the value of connection and to instill in each member an enhanced sense of being able to trust, interact, and depend on others for support and validation, as well as a firmer, more confident sense of self on which to rely.

Teenage Girls' Dance Group in a Residential Setting

Our next illustration involves a dance therapy[1] group in a psychiatric setting. Group members were girls aged 13 to 16 with various levels of disturbance. Their worker described their common characteristics as poor body awareness and image, concerns over their sexuality, and significant problems in expressing feelings. Staff felt these clients were "overloaded" with talking groups yet unable to make effective use of groups that were verbally oriented. The worker contracted with the members to develop a weekly dance group in which she would help them develop the ability to express their feelings through dance. She openly explained the purposes of the group and her hopes that through these activities they might discover new feelings and insights and that this could lead to their ability to talk with her and other staff about things that concerned them. She also explained that as they developed confidence in their bodies, they would find it easier to develop confidence in other areas of their lives. Her contract included the agreement that they would select the music they wished to use and would take control over what they wanted to express, the concerns they wished to work on, and so on. They would use video equipment to record sessions and then view their tapes, and group members would be expected to provide critical feedback to each other on the dance techniques as well as the related discussion. A critical factor to be underlined at this point was that the worker was suggesting the use of activity as a tool for the members' use. The group members, not the worker, would be in control over the medium, so that they would experience the activity as something they did with the other group members and the worker, as opposed to something the worker was doing to them.

In the following illustration from this group, two of the group members are sick. The worker continued with the remaining member, Sandy, aged 16. The opening of the session demonstrates the group member's control as she selects the music and decides to use singing as a medium instead of dance.

> Sandy arrived early today and ready for work. She noted the others were absent and said, "Good, I can have a one-to-one with you—there are some things I want to work on." I asked what, to which she replied, "'The Dog'—with the Harmonica Man Music, but I'm a bit tight, a bit scared, can we start with something else?" I agreed that it made sense to loosen up a bit and not rush into the heavy things right away. At times Sandy becomes impatient, and there is a need to slow the process down and give her controls within which to work.
>
> We looked at the records, and she picked out "I Can See Clearly Now" and said she wanted to work with it. I asked if we could use the video, to which she agreed.

When I asked how she wanted it, Sandy said she didn't feel like dancing but she would like to sing, but wasn't sure she would sound or look very good. I suggested that we use the music as an exercise and try it several different ways. In the first of three versions, her affect was flat, she was unable to look directly into the camera, and her body movements were stiff, with nervous gestures with the hand-held mike. Her voice was also flat and hushed. After looking at it on replay, Sandy was disappointed, to which I replied, "Let's keep going—add something into the next taping—pretend you're on TV, that you're a professional singer, try looking into the camera, sing to somebody, and don't worry how your voice sounds; let the feeling come out."

The second version began to come alive. She smiled, looked into the camera, and began to build up some confidence. Sandy became more stylized in her singing and began to move the mike back and forth. She tossed her hair and did stepping movements as she sang. On viewing the replay, Sandy was really surprised to see the changes in her appearance and wondered if she should go on to something else. I suggested she stay with this piece and do another version—putting as much as she could into it—exaggerating—really feeling the music. She shared that it is one of her wishes to be a rock singer. She liked the feeling of being the center of so much attention and of being able to really sing about what is inside. I said, "OK—let those feelings go—let them out, let's see what really does come out."

In the third version, Sandy was like a person totally removed from her former identities. There was a surging sense of power in her voice, a ventilation of emotion that reached a climax in which she threw her hair back, holding the mike up over her mouth, and she held a high note strongly until her energy dissipated and she gasped for air, choking forward. The jerking movement and relaxation of the tension was clearly orgasmic in quality. She appeared to be stupefied at her own power and physical reaction—grabbing her throat and trying to regain her balance and composure. She lost several lines of the music, then began again to complete the song. Her outpouring of feeling, movement, and charisma was definite and exciting. While her voice lacked true singing quality, its impact was unmistakable. In replaying the tape, she became a little giddy and excited with the results and expressed concern with the voice quality and that maybe she'd overdone it. I reassured her that we were learning and experimenting and she should not make a final decision on the results yet. I gave her feedback as to how much more animated and alive she was than the first and second version and just how much feeling she had inside. I asked how she felt after letting the feeling go, to which she replied, "I feel just exhausted—so much rushed out at once." I suggested we move on to something else and asked if she felt ready for the "Harmonica Man Music." She said she would try but wasn't sure if she could get into it now. She said the music frightens her, but she is also haunted by it and wants to understand why it has this effect on her. I replied that we must move slowly—take one step at a time.

It is interesting to note how the words of the music can be used to express, in a poetic manner, the group member's inner feelings and aspirations. For example, the words of the song Sandy selected are as follows:

I can see clearly now—the rain is gone
I can see all obstacles in my way
Gone are the dark clouds that had me blind
It's gonna be a bright, bright sunshiny day.[2]

Sandy used this music to begin to express the part of her that was reaching for growth—the hopeful part. The second song, to which she danced later in the session, enabled her to express some of her fears, which up until that point she had not felt free enough to share with the staff. The discussion of these feelings followed her improvised dancing as she and the worker attempted to understand the reactions evoked by the music.

Another group, in the same setting, decided to develop a dance routine that the three members would perform at the institution's annual Christmas party concert. The dance involved dressing in Tahitian costumes and performing a dance before staff and other residents. The three girls in the group had all been shy, concerned about their bodies and their sexuality. The idea of performing was quite frightening. At the last moment, Jeannine decided she could not go on, and the other two girls performed the dance with the worker. This illustration is from the first meeting after the concert. The two girls who danced are preparing to leave the institution, and the discussion at the start of the meeting began with their impending endings. The discussion shifted to the Christmas concert and revealed the learning that had taken place for the girls who danced and the one who did not.

> To this point, none of the girls had mentioned the Christmas party concert or the Tahitian dance performed by Terry, Joanne, and myself. I said, "We've done a lot together over the last few months, and I'm realizing our group, too, will be ending , and we won't be able to continue on as we were before Christmas." There was silence. Joanne and Terry both indicated the Christmas concert had been exciting but a real struggle, and they hadn't believed they could do it.
>
> Jeannie, who had been quiet throughout the discussion, looked up, twisted her fingers, looked down, then looked straight toward Terry and Joanne and said quietly, "You looked really beautiful—I wished I had been up there with you, but I couldn't stick with it—I was having a bad time before Christmas. I was scared, and I couldn't do it—but you guys did—and they (the kids in the cottage) loved it. You were good." Jeannine was choked with emotion as she spoke. She was soft-spoken and looked vulnerable. Joanne burst into smiles and chatter, saying, "Were we really? Gee, I was so nervous and I made so many mistakes—you know I had to be on medication, I was so anxious I didn't think I could do it—but Sharon (the worker) came over and I did it!" Terry asked Jeannine, "Did they really like it?" She added, "It was the hardest thing I've ever done—I can move my hips to the music, but I don't do steps and I usually get mixed up." The girls went on to compare notes on their highly successful performance and remembered their encore and the kids whistling and applauding. Terry added, "I didn't believe I could do such a dance in front of the boys, especially from our own cottage. I was afraid they'd laugh." I said, "I had the jitters, too—I knew you could do it, but for a while there it was touch and go for all of us!" The girls started to laugh saying, "You weren't nervous, too!" I reminded them the rehearsals had been difficult, and it was natural to get nervous before a performance.
>
> I looked at Jeannine, who was glowing with the excitement, and said, "That was very special of you to tell Joanne and Terry they looked beautiful. I wish you could have been up there doing it with us, too." I moved and put my arm around Jeannine. "It's not easy to watch others do something you couldn't follow through on—but you know, it feels like you really were up there with us in spirit." Jeannine nodded her head, saying, "I do that all the time—I know the steps, but I just wouldn't do it." Terry and Joanne listened to Jeannine, attempting to reassure her by pointing out

their own misgivings. I said, "I'm really proud of all of you; you've worked so hard, and it sounds like you want to get more for yourself, Jeannine."

I looked at Jeannine and asked, "What about you—do you want to continue in the dance group?" Jeannine was embarrassed and quiet but said, "If there is a group, I'd like to stay—but maybe I will be the only one." I indicated that I would be glad to work with her, even alone.

In the weeks that followed this session, Jeannine struggled to take new risks in the dancing area with the encouragement and support of the new group members. A close working relationship usually developed between the group members and the worker that encouraged them to use her for discussions in sensitive areas, such as trouble with other staff or their fears about leaving the institution. At times, the worker would point out the connections between their fears of risking new dances or exposing themselves to criticism (e.g., using the video) and similar concerns in other areas of their lives. Thus, the work moved between activity and talking, and the supposed dichotomy between the two was proved to be false. Similar creative group work has been demonstrated using other mediums, showing the potential power of mutual aid offered without words.

Activity Group for Vietnamese Immigrant Women

The group in this example was set up for the purpose of aiding Vietnamese immigrant women in dealing with their transitions to a new country, language, and culture. Each meeting began with tea and ethnic food prepared by the members. The food activity provided a medium for maintaining old customs as well as for discussion of difficult issues. Conversation was in English, as much as possible, to provide an opportunity to practice this second language. Written English exercises were also integrated into the group's activities. The contract included using the time to discuss their weekly experiences related to the transition. In this session, held close to the Christmas holiday, the worker explores their feelings of loss. This is also an example of practice without a translator with the worker depending upon an internal leader for help.

Session 5

We began the group as we always do, with food and tea. We then talked about the week's activities (letter from Vietnam, one woman's daughter had a cold, one woman had been to a Housing Authority meeting). My opening statement for the group went something like this: "Last week when I brought in the picture of a Christmas tree, you talked a little about your feelings about being away from home during the holiday season. I thought maybe today you might like to talk a little more about those feelings." I looked around the room to see if the women had understood what I had said. It's still very hard for me to "read" their expressions. I then said, "It must be difficult coming to a new country and having to learn so many new things." Hoan was nodding her head, so I asked her what was the hardest thing for her. Hoan said she didn't realize snow was slippery, so during her first snowstorm in America she slipped and fell on a sidewalk and broke her wrist.

Thu asked something in Vietnamese, and the four women spoke together in Vietnamese for about five minutes. I feel certain that none of the women understand everything I've said. I think this is their way of processing all the pieces they do understand and putting them together to form a whole.

When they stop talking, I always ask if there's something I've missed. They always smile, and then Hoan gives me a brief synopsis of what they were discussing. (Hoan is the spokesperson for the group. She's the oldest, as well as the one who speaks English the best—I'm not sure which is the most important in making her the spokesperson.)

Hoan told me they had been discussing coming to this country. I asked her what she meant. (I am always unclear where the group is when we reconnect in English.) Hoan said it was very difficult to leave Vietnam. I said it must have been difficult to leave her family. She said it was, that she had many brothers and sisters still in Vietnam. I asked her why she had left Vietnam, and she said it was because of her son (age 16) and her daughter (age 18), who is the Thu in the group. (Thu is developmentally delayed from a fall she had when she was three years old.) She didn't want her children to have to grow up under the Communist rule. She said she probably wouldn't live another 15 years, so she didn't care for herself, but she cared very much about her children.

Toi spoke up and said she had left Vietnam because of her children, too. She has five children; two are by her first husband, a Vietnamese man who was killed in the war. Her other three children are by her second husband, an American GI. Her Amerasian children bore the brunt of a lot of racial criticism by the Communists. Toi went to the Communist government and asked them if she could leave the country to go to America with her three Amerasian children. (Her other two children are still in Vietnam with relatives.) After a two-year bureaucratic struggle, she moved to the U.S., only to find her American husband had divorced her last November.

Hoan said that it really hurt Toi to find out her husband had divorced her. I said that would hurt me too. Hoan said it took her seven months to leave Vietnam. First she fled to Cambodia, then to Thailand, then to the Philippines, then to California, and finally to Boston in November of 1984. I said it seemed like a lot of things happened in November—Toi's divorce and Hoan arriving in the United States.

Again, there was discussion in Vietnamese. After a few minutes, Hoan told me they had been talking about Vietnam. I asked her what she meant by Vietnam (trying to reconnect with them again). She said they all wished things were different—that the Communists weren't in power.

Toi said she wanted to bring her other two children to America, but that she didn't think the Communists would let them leave. I asked her if she had made a formal application for immigration and she said yes, but that it had taken her two years to leave the country when the government had wanted her and her Amerasian children to leave. I asked Toi if there was a lot of discrimination in her country against Amerasian children, and she said yes. I asked her if she faced any discrimination here and she said sometimes. Hoan said Toi has had windows broken in her apartment. I asked Hoan if she had felt discrimination and she said no, she was an old woman and people left her alone.

The phone rang, and they lapsed into Vietnamese again. When we reconnected, Hoan said she knew we didn't have much time left, and could I go over the English paragraph she had written. The rest of the session was much less intense and formal. We did some grammar and some English pronunciation, and I left a short time later.

In later group sessions, the women used the activity group meeting to explore current issues of cultural clash, as they attempted to help their children integrate into a new country while holding on to some of their own culture; their own struggles with changing gender roles and rules in relation to their families and husbands; and the painful memories of their passages—in particular, the experiences of those who had endured the atrocities committed on the "boat people."

CHAPTER SUMMARY

A number of variant elements in group practice were described in this chapter. These included the unique processes and skills required in working with an open-ended group, in which members join and leave the group continuously, the impact of working with a group where members are in a residential setting together and have frequent contact; single-session groups that meet for informational proposes or in response to a particular event or trauma; large groups; and the use of activities in groups as "mediums of exchange" between members. The argument was made that the core dynamics and skills discussed throughout this book were applicable, with variations on the themes, to all types of mutual aid groups.

GLOSSARY

Activity group A term usually applied to groups involved in a range of activities other than just conversation. *Program* is another term used to describe the activities implemented in such groups, such as the expressive arts (e.g., painting, dancing), games, folk singing, social parties, cooking, and so on.

Closed group A fixed-membership group where the same people meet for a defined period of time. Members may drop out and new members be added in the early sessions, but in general, the membership of the group remains constant.

Data gathering One of the functions of activities in groups designed to help members obtain more information central to their tasks (e.g., teenagers preparing for employment arranging a series of trips to business or industrial complexes).

Deviational allowance When group activities create a flow of affect between members that builds up a positive relationship, members can be freed to deviate from the accepted norms and raise concerns that might otherwise be taboo.

Entry A function of activity in groups, planned as a way to enter an area of difficult discussion (e.g., the playacting of young children as they create roles and situations that often reveal their concerns of the moment).

Human contact One of the functions of activities in a group. A meeting of a basic human need for social interaction (e.g., golden-age clubs for isolated senior citizens).

Listen first—talk later An approach used in work with information groups, in which the leader first listens to the group members' questions, issues, and concerns, and then presents the required information.

Looking for trouble when everything is going the worker's way The skill of exploring hidden ambivalence when a client immediately responds positively to a difficult suggestion.

Mixed transactional model Defined here as exchanges in which people give to and take from each other through different mediums of exchange, including words, facial and body expressions, touch, shared experiences of various kinds, and other forms of communication (often used simultaneously).

Open-ended group A group that is structured so that new members can join at any point, while ongoing members may leave at different times. For example, a ward group in a hospital may have new members join when admitted to the hospital and others leave when discharged.

Rehearsal In activity groups, a means of developing skills for specific life tasks (e.g., a party for teenagers in an institution that creates an opportunity for members to practice the social skills necessary for the courtship phase of life).

NOTES

1. For readings related to dance therapy, see Sandel (1975) and Lefco (1975).
2. Johnny Nash (words and music), "I Can See Clearly Now." New York: CBS, Inc., 1972.

17

Substance Abuse and Group Work Practice

CHAPTER OUTLINE

The Literature on Substance Abuse

Group Work with Substance Abusers

Group Work with Clients with a Dual Diagnosis

Group Work with the Substance Abuser's Significant Others

Group Work and Substance Abuse Prevention

Our focus in this chapter will be on group work practice with the client population associated with substance abuse of alcohol and other drugs. We will see how the general principles of group work outlined in the preceding chapters can be adapted to address the unique issues and concerns of a particular population. To begin, we will develop a theoretical base for practice with this population. We will then explore practice with substance abusers who are at different stages of the change process. Next, we will examine the impact of dual diagnosis on the group process. This is illustrated with detailed excerpts from the author's work with a group of persons with AIDS in early recovery from substance abuse. Since substance abuse powerfully affects those who are close to the abuser, we will also examine group work with significant others such as the abuser's partner or children. In the final section, we will explore the use of groups in substance abuse prevention activity.

There are two reasons for including a special chapter on group work and substance abuse in this edition. First, the prevalence of the problem and its often obvious but sometimes subtle associations with many other areas of our practice (e.g., family violence, geriatric social work, child welfare, school social work) brings it to the forefront as an area of practice concern. Second, the documented tendency of helping professionals to avoid direct practice with this population or to ignore signals of its presence in clients with whom they do work requires that we examine the issue.

THE LITERATURE ON SUBSTANCE ABUSE

More than a decade ago, Googins (1985) identified a syndrome that he termed "Avoidance of the Alcoholic Client." He argued that while "problem drinkers" comprised 12 percent of the population (21 percent of men and 5 percent of women), social workers and their organizations tended to avoid offering service to this population or even recognizing the problem in their clients when it was masked by other issues. While this "avoidance" has been somewhat abated by programs such as the United States Department of Health and Human Services Center for Substance Abuse Prevention (CSAP) program for social work faculty development, Googin's original assessment appears to hold true today.

In attempting to understand the widespread reluctance of social workers to deal with this specific social problem, Googins identifies a number of "myths" surrounding alcoholism. For example, informational myths leave many people unable to appreciate the fact that alcohol is a drug with properties and characteristics common to all drugs. Googins also identified "attitudinal myths" that lead to a moralizing approach that labels alcoholics as "morally inferior." Other attitudes, according to Googins, lead to labeling alcoholics as "undesirable, untreatable, and unmotivated" (p. 163).

Among organizations that have labored long and hard to fill the treatment gap in the substance abuse field have been self-help groups such as Alcoholics Anonymous (AA), Narcotics Anonymous (NA), and a number of groups focusing on family members and friends of addicted persons, such as Alanon.[1] While these groups differ in some ways, common themes include a focus on achieving and maintaining sobriety and helping others to do so, the use of structure to help bind anxiety, and the use of traditions and slogans to support recovery efforts. AA, for example, describes its purpose as follows:

> Alcoholics Anonymous is a fellowship of men and women who share their experience, strength, and hope with each other so that they may solve their common problems and help others recover from alcoholism. The only requirement for membership is a desire to stop drinking.... Our primary purpose is to stay sober and help others to achieve sobriety (AA, 1984, p. 2).

Many of these self-help groups adhere to **12-step models** that identify the route to achieve and maintain sobriety. My co-leader in a group for persons with AIDS in early recovery, described later in this chapter, and members of this group would often refer to these steps as guidelines for behavior when faced with difficult choices in their relationships with others. For example, steps 8 and 9 provide a means for members to deal with their guilt over their past behaviors by having "made a list of all persons we had harmed, and become willing to make amends to them all," and "made direct amends to such people whenever possible, except when to do so would injure them or others." These principles were invoked one night when men in my group for persons with AIDS in early substance abuse recovery talked about their guilt over having had unprotected sex with women after finding out that they were infected with AIDS.

AA follows an **"abstinence" model**, which suggests that this problem is a disease. One of the many AA sayings that guide members in their recovery is that "For an alcoholic, one drink is too many and a thousand are not enough" (p. 10). While there are disputes in the substance abuse field about the **"disease model,"** a focus on abstinence, the emphasis on spirituality, and other issues in 12-step programs, this structured recovery program and philosophy has worked for many and was reported as being crucial by three of our AIDS/Recovery group members who attended AA and NA meetings while also attending our group. In addition, when the recovery of any member of our group appeared to be threatened, group members and my co-leader drew upon their 12-step experience to protect the member's recovery.

There are other approaches to dealing with addiction, some of which are critical of the 12-step model. For example, the Relational Recovery movement (Trimpay, 1996) rejects the disease model of addiction and many of the central structures and approaches employed in 12-step programs. Advocates object to what they call the "jargon" of **"relapse," "triggers," "enabler,"** "alcoholic," "addict," and other recovery group movement concepts.

Their central theme is that addictions can be conquered through use of "thinking" skills that radically reframe the problem of "addiction" by defining it as a "beast" that exists within the person. They describe an **"addictive voice"** (AV), which is "your body taking to you, in thoughts and feelings, telling you to drink or use drugs. It is the *sole cause* of your substance addiction." (p. 36) Central to recovery is the use of an "addictive voice recognition technique" (AVRT) to recognize those thoughts and feelings that constitute the "addictive voice" as it constantly attempts to take control of the individual. This movement suggests that those thoughts and feelings that support abstinence are the real "you" speaking in a struggle with the enemy, the beast expressed by the addictive voice that encourages continued use.

It is beyond the scope of this book to describe in detail these approaches or others that offer aid in fighting addictions, or to enter into the debate as to their relative efficacy. The real question may be which approach is most appropriate to a specific person at a particular time in his or her life. The two self-help approaches described here do agree on the importance of abstinence from substance abuse as central to dealing with addictions. Even this concept, however, has been challenged by proposals for **"harm reduction"** models that advocate attempting to help addicted persons moderate the negative impact of substances on their lives, rather than calling for abstinence. This debate exists within the professional treatment community as well. For example, an analysis of data from a 1988 national survey of outpatient substance abuse treatment units indicated a general rejection of the disease model by social-work-trained managers, when compared with non-social-work managers. Social-work managers were also more likely to support continued treatment in the face of relapse and efforts at harm reduction activities when AIDS was involved (Burke and Clapp, 1997). We will avoid this debate as well.

Our focus in this book will be on developing an integrated approach involving social work groups, led by professionals, with a strong mutual aid component. Concepts and strategies employed by other models will be used when they are judged to increase the effectiveness of the practice.

Matano and Yalom (1991) address the issue of integrating approaches in their efforts to synthesize an "interactional" approach to group therapy and the methods employed by traditional chemical dependency groups. While their interest is in a group therapy model in which the interpersonal interactions of the group members are used to develop insights and influence changes in interpersonal behaviors—a model somewhat different from the mutual aid support group described in this text—their principles for successful integration of approaches are relevant to this discussion. The authors suggest that

> an interactional approach can be effectively applied to alcoholics if the following guidelines are observed: (1) recovery is always accorded priority, (2) the patient accepts identification as an alcoholic, (3) anxiety is carefully modulated, (4) the proper distinction is made between what the alcoholic is and is not responsible for, (5) the therapist is thoroughly familiar with Alcoholics Anonymous language, steps, and traditions. It is important that therapists not permit misperceptions of AA to be used as therapy resistance and that they be able to harness the wisdom of AA for psychotherapeutic ends (p. 269).

Issues of diversity must also be taken into account, since attitudes towards the use of substances and issues of addiction and treatment may vary widely depending upon factors such as ethnicity, country of origin, immigration stage (e.g., recent immigrant versus second-generation), and community factors. For example, in an article dealing with the use of foreign language interpreters, Amodeo, Grigg-Saito, and Robb (1997) identify difficulties non-English-speaking clients may experience in substance abuse interviews. Among these, they cite

> worry about reports to referral agents...fear that the human service worker, interpreter, or both, will be disapproving or angry with them...shame and embarrassment about having to discuss with strangers an issue that is generally not discussed openly in their culture... (p. 81).

The authors describe the difficulties that may be experienced by interpreters which, in turn, may affect their translation (e.g., annoyance or embarrassment at the client's behavior, leading to the impulse to reprimand the client). They describe strategies to increase the effectiveness of the clinician-interpreter-client relationship. They also stress the importance of increasing knowledge and skill in cross-cultural work and the value of attracting bilingual, bicultural workers to the field.

For the reader who is interested in exploring the literature involving substance abuse issues, I offer three suggestions for good places to start. Stephanie Brown (1985) provides a developmental model of recovery with a discussion of stages of recovery and an integration of concepts from AA and psychotherapy. Miller and Rollnick (1991) have edited a collection focusing on motivational interviewing as an approach to helping people prepare to change addictive behavior. Finally, Marsha Vannicelli (1992) provides an excellent discussion of issues in conducting long-term group psychotherapy with substance abusers, adult children of alcoholics, and other family members.

GROUP WORK WITH SUBSTANCE ABUSERS

In this section we will examine work with two distinct groups. The first consists of clients who are actively abusing and could be defined as being in the **pre-contemplation** or **contemplation** stages of change described earlier in this book. These clients have not yet accepted the idea that they have a problem or are just starting to think about the nature of their substance abuse. The second group consists of persons in recovery who have accepted their addictive behavior and are attempting to deal with it.

Group Work with Active Abusers

Court-Mandated Group for Drunk Drivers: First Meeting. In the first excerpt, we see a fairly typical start to a first meeting of a court-mandated group for persons convicted of driving while intoxicated (DWI). Resistance and denial is in the air as the young female worker begins the session. Instead of confronting the resistance head on and initiating the inevitable battle of wills, she recognizes it as a symptom of the stage of acceptance most of the men are in. She uses an exercise to help the group begin to explore their resistance and thus is able to capture their energy in pursuit of the group's purpose.

> *Purpose:* To introduce clients to support services; to encourage clients to explore their own use of substances and the role that alcohol and/or drugs play in their lives; to avoid re-arrest.

Gender of Members: Male

Age Range: 27 to 55 years

Cultural, Racial, or Ethnic Identification of Members: two Irish males, one Indian male, seven European-American males

Excerpt from Process Recording:

After going over the contract, I passed out a sheet that stated the purpose of the group and the topics to be covered. While some group members appeared to be reading the topics, others folded the sheet in half without a glance. I asked the group how they felt about the topics and if they had any questions. After a moment of silence one group member angrily stated, "You know, I shouldn't even be here. I was set up." *(Nervous laughter from other group members.)* He proceeded to tell his arrest story, while other group members appeared attentive. When he finished, I said, "It must be hard for you to be here when you don't even feel that the arrest was justified. I wonder if other people are feeling the same way." Another member spoke up, saying, "Well, what I don't understand is why we're going to talk about things like alcoholism and AIDS in a class for drunk drivers" *(referring to the handout).* "Yeah, we made one mistake, and now we're all alcoholics." Other group members joined in, expressing similar dissatisfaction with the topics. I replied, "You're raising some important points. It sounds like one of the things you're especially concerned about is being labeled. I wonder if we can come up with a list of some other things that you don't want to have happen in this group." As I wrote on the board "Don't Want" and under it put "to be labeled," I asked members for further suggestions. Another member said "to feel guilty. I don't want to feel guilty for what I did." As I wrote, "to feel guilty" on the board, I asked him if he could say more about this. He responded, "I mean, I know it was wrong, and I don't want to have people keep telling me it's wrong." Another member added, "Yeah, I feel like a criminal!" "Well, we are criminals, what do you expect?" another member commented. I asked, "Is it hard to see yourself in that way?" "Yeah, well, I guess we are criminals, but there are worse things we could have done."

In the excerpts that follow, we see the beginning phase and the transition to the middle phase in a group in which a number of the men have begin to face the fact they have a problem, confronting the profound negative impact on their lives of their abuse of alcohol. One man, the "deviant member" Phil, holds out and refuses to engage. While the leader misses his early signals and sees him as the "enemy" to the group, internal leaders emerge to help both the man and the leader understand the behavior as a signal of the intense pain and guilt associated with a traumatic event. Once again, the "deviant member" is someone in the group who faces the same issues as the other members but who feels them more strongly. This recognition allows the whole group to move into a deeper level of work.

(Second session)

The group was struggling with their denial, Tom was starting to open up, but Phil was attempting to sabotage the movement of the group. It does appear that Phil is the gatekeeper, for every time the issue of drinking and driving is brought up he tries to prevent the process from occurring. I encouraged Tom to speak about his drinking and driving. Tom started talking about how he had three arrests in one year for drunk driving. I asked Tom if he could share with the group how he feels about this happening. He started to speak, but Phil jumped in and said that no one wanted to hear about this story. I tell Phil that Tom has the floor and ask him not to interrupt. I am starting to get upset that Phil is constantly interrupting, but I am hoping someone else will take a risk and say something.

Tom continues, saying he knows he needs help because he must have a problem, otherwise why all the arrests. Phil jumps in, but this time Pete speaks up and says that he has had enough of Phil and wants him to stop being rude. Inside I am excited that Pete, after having made overtures before as the internal leader, has stepped up to question Phil's behavior. I had asked myself how I might handle this challenge to my leadership (as a first-time leader) and my authority, but I realized the group had moved forward in the mutual aid process and that the group's work was going well. This was a good opportunity to point out to Phil, and to the group, that he was diverting the group's attention away from the emotional issue of drunk driving. I asked the group if they think this is a sign that they are beginning to be a more cohesive group, and they replied yes, except for Phil.

(Third session)
While I think the group is starting to make progress, the illusion of work is holding them back. I make a demand for work by saying we are to discuss triggers that can cause them to drink. Jim speaks up and asks what I mean by triggers. Pete answers that was the Lone Ranger's horse. Tom jumps in and says that is what you use to shoot a gun with. I realize now that the group may have been in Bion's enchantment flight phase, but I am not sure if this is where the group is or if the humor is a defensive tool to change the subject. I reply that this subject may have hit a sensitive spot, so I ask the group for feedback. Phil says that Jim asks the dumbest questions and wonders how Jim ever got his license. This is not the first time that Jim has been attacked when sensitive emotional issues are being brought to the surface. I am feeling some counter-transference issues rising in me, about Jim being a scapegoat, and I tell the group that they must be feeling pretty powerful when they attack Jim. I ask why they feel it is necessary to do this. (In retrospect, I see that I have taken Jim's side and have forgotten the group as a whole. I am surprised I did not lose the group at this point.)

Pete, the internal leader, makes a leap of consciousness and apologizes to Jim for acting the way he did. Tom, Sam, and Phil all say the same. Pete continues and says that he had never considered anyone's feelings before and asks me why. I open it up to the group. The one member who has been noticeably quiet, Bob, speaks for the first time since the beginning of the first session. He says it has to do with the topic of the day—triggers. Bob says that everyone has triggers that can set them off, but he sees triggers as coming from his past. He lived in an alcoholic and abusive home. I was taken aback by Bob's speaking up and what he had to say. I asked him if there was more he would like to say. He said he grew up never being allowed to say much, nor have an opinion, without suffering a negative consequence. It has taken him this long to overcome his fear enough to talk in the group, but after hearing the apologies to Jim, he feels safe in the group. I said he was very brave to speak up and describe his feelings.

(Fourth session)
I told the group that the last session showed the group is moving, and they should feel good about the work they have accomplished. I had a feeling that there was more work to be done with the issue of triggers, so I brought this out to the group. Pete said

he had done some thinking over the week and wanted to know if the group could help him. All responded with a yes, except Phil. Tom asked Phil why he wouldn't, and Phil said he just didn't want to talk today. Bob said he thought Phil was struggling with his own triggers, and asked Phil if the group could get back to Phil's not wanting to talk after helping Pete. Phil, in a very quiet, subdued voice, said okay.

Pete said he wanted to revisit triggers because he feels that is where his major stumbling block is. Discussion was fruitful, and the group was beginning to take on a life of its own, dealing with intimacy and interpersonal relationships. Bob, Pete, and Sam were willing to look at these issues, while Phil and Tom were resisting any further intimate movements. The group went back to Phil not wanting to talk, with Sam showing empathy and caring by saying that maybe Phil has some painful memories that have been triggered. The group as a whole struggled around how to help Phil. It seemed that the group had finally found a common ground to focus on—triggers. Other members took turns expressing how they have been affected by their triggers, how alcohol had taken over their lives, and the consequences. Bob talked about how he had lost his job, Sam said he had lost his job and his wife had divorced him, Pete said he had to go through bankruptcy, Jim finished by saying he had to spend eight months in jail for his drunk driving and this has affected how his children see him now. This was done with a lot of expressed emotions, with all members sitting in their chairs, but all leaning towards one another, as a way to begin to connect to the pains they had experienced due to alcohol.

They now turned to Phil, who looked like he had seen a ghost, and they asked if he was ready to share his triggers. Phil said he had thought this group was foolish and felt that he had everything under control. We all sat with Phil's emotions. He started to cry, saying that he had for the first time since coming to group realized he was not alone in this fight over alcoholism. He said he felt this was a place for him to finally talk about his haunting nightmare. We all waited patiently, and I was overcome with the power of this group. Phil said that his trigger for all his years of drinking was he had never been able to forgive himself for driving the car and getting into an accident that had killed his wife. The group all sat in silence and cried for Phil and for their own losses.

Where the Problem Stands Now:

I believe we have created a new phase of work whereby the group is able to open up and express their painful feelings. I am surprised at how much progress they have made in moving to the middle phase of group work. The difficulty of denial, defensiveness, challenging me to be in control, members wanting to take control, and the different roles each member has played has been fascinating. There has been a slow change in the manner in which the members have interacted with one another, each playing a dramatic role in moving the group to its current place.

The culture of the group has grown to the point where they can begin to use empathic listening skills. This was not present in the beginning phase. I knew the group had the opportunity to experience the finding of a common ground, but I was not sure how we were going to get there. In retrospect, the problem statement does not have the same meaning as in the beginning. I now see their denial and resistance as a tool they use to cope, with alcohol being the method they use to hide their fears and feelings. The group had begun to deal with some of their most sensitive issues and losses in a more honest and trustful way than they had initially presented. The members carry within them a history of pain and denial, and their allowing this to surface has been a thrill to observe. I know there is much more work to be done, but to have experienced Phil's growth to the point of allowing others access to his feelings will stay with me forever. Just as the members are taking risks, I hope that I too can do the same in my role, challenging each of them to work more on their issues.

Strategies for Intervention:
   1. I will continue the demand for work, keep the focus, and try to create an atmosphere where work, not infighting, will occur.
   2. I will continue to point out to the group how they are playing different roles, and use these opportunities to point out their underlying feelings.
   3. I will continue to reflect back to the group that it is their group, not mine.

Resistance is also noted in the excerpt from a middle-phase group meeting that follows. The worker must deal with older teen members who admit having used drugs prior to the meeting. She must also face the challenge from one member for her to disclose her own drug use. While substance abuse is included in the contract in this group, it is only one issue among others. The worker is attuned enough to recognize that the members' disclosure of drug use prior to the meeting is a "first offering," a way of both testing the worker and raising the issue. All of the members of the group have been assigned to a diversion program in a special school as an alternative to sentencing to a detention center. While the group members are older than those in later examples of work with teens, their behavior seems more adolescent. This is not unusual for older teens who are "stuck" in the stage of the life cycle that coincided with the beginning of their serious substance abuse.

High-School Students in a Diversion Program

   Agency Type: Mental health agency serving young children to elders. Clinicians within agency lead/co-lead a number of school-age groups from the elementary to high-school level.

   Group Purpose: The group is made up of the students enrolled in the Diversion and Mainstream class at the local high school. The purpose of the group is to provide a safe haven where members can discuss their concerns, question, thoughts, and feelings. The group focuses on issues related to self-esteem, conflict resolution, peer and familial relations, and substance use/abuse.

   Gender of Members: Male; *Age Range:* 17–18

   Cultural, Racial, or Ethnic Identification of Members: One is African-American, one is Hispanic, and the remaining five are white.

   Meeting 13:
After a brief check-in with members, Don, Matt, and Jake began discussing their drug use prior to the start of the school day. I questioned their ability to participate in group while under the influence of drugs. Jake reported that it was easier to come to school high than straight. Others laughed. Mike jumped in, responding, "You guys are stupid, man. How the hell can you come here high? That's fucking stupid!" I asked Mike if he has had an experience with using before school. Mike shook his head. Members laughed at Mike and called him a "fat fuckin' liar." Referring to the contract, I emphasized the issue of respect for one another. Bob (a usually silent member) disclosed his history of drinking before school and firmly stated his decision against drugging. I thanked Bob for sharing and asked if he could say more about his expe-

rience. Before Bob could answer, Matt turned to me and questioned my history of drug use. I remained silent as I looked at my co-leader.

While not falling into the trap of a battle of wills over the drug use prior to the meeting, and demonstrating some level of attunement as the worker starts to explore the reasons for this behavior, she does not ask the members to elaborate on the joking, yet very serious comment of needing to use drugs in order to come to school. The group must also deal with the issue of limits and the worker's expectations that members will not be high during meetings. This is acknowledged by the group leader, but the limit is not clearly set. Finally, the authority theme test experienced by the worker in the request for her drug history is, in part, an accurate perception. However, the question may also be an attempt to get at the experience of others who may have used drugs but are not currently addicted. An honest response could take many forms. For example, "I don't feel comfortable answering that question, and yet, I am asking you to share your experiences." Or "I did experiment with drugs, as all of my friends did, but at one point I decided I had to take control of the drugs before they took control of me." Or "I think I faced many of the same pressures you experience around drugs. I also didn't think any adults could understand and that most of them were just preaching to me and were hypocritical, since they used alcohol." There is no correct response to this question, only honest responses that may differ for each of us. The important thing is to address the real meaning of the question without turning our response into a disclosure designed to increase our own comfort at the expense of our group members.

Group Work with Persons in Recovery

Gender should be taken into account in considering the different meanings of group processes for men and women. For example, Hardesty and Greif (1994) described the common themes in groups for female IV-drug users who were HIV-positive. Drawing upon their work with a mandatory women's group in a methadone-maintenance clinic, they point out that

> Substance abuse spanned a number of generations. Members discussed with the group their long histories of physical abuse and neglect at the hands of family members, friends, and strangers, which left an indelible impression of worthlessness that the women carry into their current relationships with their parents, friends, lovers, and children. Because of their belief in their own worthlessness, they fiercely guard secrets of shame and inadequacy (p. 290).

The authors describe the unique advantages of a women's group in creating a safe environment for disclosure of family-of-origin issues. The women in the following group clearly expressed their struggle with feelings of low self-worth that resulted in a vicious cycle of behaviors that maintained and often intensified their internalized negative self-concepts.

A link for women between post-traumatic stress disorder (PTSD) and substance abuse was documented in a recent review of the literature (Najavits, Weiss, and Shaw, 1997).

> Various studies have found frequent histories of childhood physical and/or sexual assault among women with current substance abuse, ranging from 32% to 66%.... Moreover, if a woman experienced both physical and sexual abuse as a child, her likelihood of using illicit drugs was almost twice as high (44%) as if she had earlier type of abuse alone (23%).
>
> Women with substance abuse have also been found to have high rates of repeated trauma. In both studies of women in an inner-city neighborhood and a diverse out-

patient sample of cocaine-addicted subjects, the average number of lifetime traumas among women was five. Moreover, the likelihood of PTSD diagnosis was increased in women exposed to a greater number of traumas and more violent traumas (p. 276)

The authors point out a number of differences between men and women documented in the studies, suggesting that PTSD in men is more often associated with victimization or witnessing of violence, in particular war experiences, while for women it is associated with physical and sexual abuse and trauma. "Female substance abusers have also been found to have significantly higher rates of repeated trauma and family perpetrators than male substance abusers." The authors describe women with PTSD and substance abuse diagnosis as also having more comorbid disorders (mood, anxiety, and medical problems) as well as concurrent life problems (homelessness, loss of custody of children, and so on). They cite other studies that describe the women's "intense stigmatization, blame for failure in maternal roles, frequent sex-for-drugs exchanges, and the downward spiral of The Life, in which crack is used to manage the symptoms of trauma, retraumatization occurs in the context of crack use, and the cycle repeats" (p. 278).

These research findings come alive in the process recordings in this section involving groups for women and in the next section's example of an AIDS/Early Recovery group. In each instance, we can see the internalized oppressor at work in the lives of these women as well as the sources of strength for change.

Maintaining Sobriety for Women Trauma Survivors

Group Purpose: Learn new coping skills to help in maintaining sobriety. Members support each other in the use of the newly learned coping skills.

Members: 25- to 47-year-old white females, primarily low-income single mothers. Most are of European descent. All are substance abusers who have had at least three failed attempts at remaining abstinent from drugs and/or alcohol. All are also survivors of childhood trauma.

Dates: 2/1 to 4/19

Group Task: Structure-maintenance

1. *Problem:* The original task of this group was to be accomplished in eight weeks; after four weeks the group was extended to ongoing. The group faces the task of learning coping skills to deal with intense and overwhelming feelings that do not involve the use of alcohol or drugs. The task is complicated by the fact that all the women are trauma survivors and have used alcohol or drugs to numb their feelings since they were very young, beginning between the ages of 9 and 12 years old. It is my opinion that the group is having difficulty getting through the beginning stage and creating a group culture that allows the members to share openly. Since all the women are trauma survivors, I anticipated that it will be more difficult for them to trust each other and become a cohesive group. I pushed the group to move into the work phase of the group too soon, which resulted in the members engaging in flight or fight.

2. *How the Problem Came to My Attention:* During the initial interviews the women all seemed to be excited about learning new coping skills and expressed a strong desire to stay abstinent. When the group actually began meeting it seemed difficult for the women to connect with each other. No one was willing to talk openly about their feelings or what led up to episodes of drinking. Linda is a good example of how the group is feeling; she sits, staring at her lap, saying very little. Every time I pushed them

into what seemed to be work, it became obvious that the women moved into fight or flight; Linda did not show up the week after revealing personal information. It appeared that eight weeks was too short a time, so the group was extended and the women still could not connect. No matter how hard I reached, the group did not seem to be able to talk about feelings.

3. *Summary of the Work with Process Excerpts:*

(First Session) I noticed that the women entered the room silently. Each one seemed to be very guarded and apprehensive. The women took their seats; each one was looking down and very sad. Since this was a time-limited group, I had planned the use of the Ungame as a way to break the ice and facilitate discussion. However, at this point I thought we needed to spend some time talking about the group. I opened the group by talking about the common bond that each member of the group shared. I was hoping to lessen some of the shame associated with failed attempts at sobriety.

I stated the purpose of the group. "As all of you know, this is the women's coping skills group. Everyone in this group has had difficulty remaining clean and sober; each of you has also had some type of trauma in your life. The trauma may be different. Some of you may have experienced childhood trauma, or possibly an abusive relationship as an adult, or you may have been raped. What you all have in common is that you all have intense and overwhelming feelings that lead you to drink or drug. Each one of you has expressed a desire to stop using substances and has tried on more than one occasion. When you stop drinking or drugging, the feelings flood in and then you have no ways to deal with them other than to return to numbing those feelings with alcohol or drugs. In this group we are going to talk about other ways that you can deal with the feelings and hopefully increase your ability to tolerate the feeling of being overwhelmed."

While the worker is direct about the purpose of the group and even acknowledges the underlying pain, she will fail to reach for the signals from one member that she was feeling the pain in the moment. The worker comments that she was not sure that the group members were ready; yet in my view, it was the worker who was not ready.

As I spoke, I noticed that all but one of the women raised their heads and began to glance around at the other women. However, after a brief glance, each would return to looking at the table. Only two of the women looked up at me. One woman continued to stare at her lap. She appeared to be on the verge of tears. I knew that this would be a good time to address the pain that Linda was expressing and the entire group was probably feeling, but I chose not to because I feared it was too soon. I am not sure what would have happened if I had talked about the pain. It is possible the group could have responded by identifying with it or they could have fled from it as in Bion's fight-or-flight theory.

I asked the group if they would like to introduce themselves to each other at this point, telling them that they could say as much or as little as they felt comfortable with. Carol started. She seemed a little hesitant but told the group that she had relapsed (drank) two days before. Each woman took a turn; all had drunk in the previous week except Dot, who said she had not drunk in about a month.

When it was Linda's turn, she continued to look down and only said, "I'm Linda, I drank yesterday." I wanted to say, "You really seem to be in a lot of pain, Linda," but I did not. I let the group move on. I was not sure how to handle Linda's pain, so I ignored it. As the next woman was speaking, I noticed that Linda had tears in her eyes.

After the introductions we went on to play the Ungame. In this game, the players draw cards and answer the question on each card. I continued to pay close attention to Linda. She answered all of her questions with as few words as possible, and I never saw her look up. I did not comment on Linda's answers or her obvious discomfort. I was afraid of making her more uncomfortable and afraid that she might not return to the group. Looking back, I could have acknowledged her pain by talking about the pain and frustration anyone feels when they try repeatedly to do something and fail and how much more painful it is when that something is trying to stop drinking.

(Third Session) Carol opened the group by talking about her recent relapse. Dot, who is still sober, tried to encourage Carol by telling her about a women's AA meeting where she feels she gets a lot of help. Cindy began to cry at that point and talked about drinking over the weekend. I asked the group if they could identify an event or feeling that led to drinking. Three of the women said that they thought it was hanging out with friends who drink. I acknowledged that friends are certainly a powerful influence and asked if they could remember exactly what it was they hoped to get from drinking. Carol responded by saying, "Yeah! It makes it easier to talk and I feel more at ease when I've had a few." I am hoping that at least one of the women will begin to talk about her feelings just prior to drinking. I do not want to lead the women in identifying their feelings, I just want to head them in that direction. At this point I am not sure where to go, so I remain silent. After a few moments of silence, Linda tentatively began to speak. She said she was embarrassed to admit it, especially now that she had kept quiet for so long, but she had relapsed. Linda then began to speak about her ex-boyfriend whom she is still very attached to. He is a cross-dresser and she does not feel that she can live with this, so they recently split up. Now every time she talks to him she ends up drinking. Linda started crying when she began to speak. I wanted to give the group a chance to respond and identify with Linda's pain, so all I did was get up and get a box of tissues.

Dot, who had become the leader, spoke up and said, "I know how you feel. When my boyfriend left and I lost my kids, I drank every time I saw him and it seemed like I was always seeing him since he lived in the same area that I did. Now I still see him but I call my sponsor instead of drinking." The group did not seem to be picking up on the feelings. I realize this is my agenda and that they may have a different agenda, but I chose to pursue it anyway. I asked, "When you see your ex-boyfriend or talk with him what is the feeling you are left with?" The group was silent for a few moments, then Dot said "lonely." I was watching Linda and she nodded in agreement. Cindy said that she usually drinks because she is feeling lonely. Carol denied that she ever felt lonely. I realized that the group was doing what looked like work but was really only doing what they thought was expected of them. I wonder if it would have made a difference if I had picked up on Linda's pain more, or is it still too early?

In retrospect, the worker could have taken some time at the end of this meeting to discuss the impact on all of the members, especially Linda, of sharing such painful material. Such a discussion might have made it easier for Linda to return for the next session.

(Fourth Session) Linda did not come to group today. I wonder if it is because she revealed so much last week. Carol opened the meeting by telling the group she relapsed again. Dot told her about meetings again. I know I have an agenda for this group, but it is a time-limited group and the purpose is learning new coping skills. I

am feeling pushed for time; we only have four more weeks, so I push ahead. I ask if anyone in the group can tell us what they go through before picking up a drink. Celia, who has not spoken before, offers that she drinks because she thinks it's going to make her feel better. I ask if anyone else drinks to feel better. Most of the group seems to identify. They seem ashamed to answer. No one openly said yes. However, there is a lot of muttering that sounds like agreement. I respond by asking how they respond to overwhelming feelings. I am hoping to move this group into the work phase of the group. It may have been too soon, but at this point I did not think it would send them into fight or flight. Dot was the first to answer. She said, "I used to. I would feel overwhelmed with loneliness or sadness so I would drink to feel better. Now I go to a meeting or call my sponsor." Dot continued talking about how she stays sober; no one else responded. I think I pushed too soon, or maybe I should not have pushed at all. The group knew the purpose. I think I should have let it go this group meeting and will begin the next meeting by reviewing the purpose of the group.

The group leader made the not-uncommon mistake of failing to share her thoughts and feelings with the group. If she wonders if it is "too soon" to push, why not ask the group members? If she was concerned about Linda's absence, why not raise it with the group? Over and over, in workshop after workshop, when I ask the worker what she or he felt or was concerned about, it becomes obvious that sharing it honestly with the group members is the best intervention.

After four sessions with this group, I can see that eight sessions is not enough to work with women who are trauma survivors and need new coping skills to stop drinking. I went to my supervisor to see if this group could become an ongoing group with new members being added at specific times. He agreed, since I will be staying with the agency after graduation.

(Fifth Session) I open the group meeting by telling the members that the group will not end after eight weeks, it will go on for as long as we can keep it going. Carol asks if the present members can keep coming. I told her that they can. There was almost an audible sigh of relief. I asked how they felt about the group continuing. I was still hoping that someone would begin to talk about how hard it is to learn new coping skills and how hard it is to use them. Carol was the first to answer. She said that she was really glad to hear that the group would not end because she knows she needs more time. Carol seems to be the spokesperson for the entire group. She is the deviant member in that she expresses the feelings everyone else is afraid of. In a way she is saying that she is afraid she cannot stay sober. She is able to say what the others are feeling. Linda surprised me when she spoke; she said she was relieved to hear that the group will not end because she really wants to stop drinking and nothing has helped before so she is hoping that this group will make a difference. Others in the group agreed.

Now that I know that the group is not limited to eight sessions, maybe I can let the group work at its own pace. It is possible that my having an agenda every meeting has kept the group from doing the work that they need to do in the way that they need to do it. I think they are only giving the appearance of work when they are really in the beginning stages of the group.

(Sixth Session) The women have begun to function as a group. I want to encourage them to continue to share their experiences with only a minimum of direction

from me. Carol opens the meeting once again by telling the group that she relapsed over the weekend. This time when Dot responded to Carol, she did not sound as patient. She confronted Carol with the fact that she hangs out with people who drink. She said, "How can you expect to stay sober when all the people you hang out with are drunks? You never go to meetings so you can meet sober people. Then you drink and wonder why." I think Dot is the gatekeeper; every time anyone in the group gets too close to feelings, Dot starts talking about AA. When she does, the group seems to stop feeling.

While Dot is talking, I look around to see how the rest of the group is taking this confrontation. Linda has tears in her eyes. This time I want to draw Linda in and acknowledge her pain. I say, "I wonder if some of you are feeling like it's hard to make new friends, especially while you're sober?" Linda remains quiet and withdrawn, but I feel like I am beginning to reach her. Now she is openly crying. The group is silent so I try to reach out to her. I say, "This seems like a very painful topic. Would anyone like to talk about their pain?" Linda surprised me by starting to talk, but I am a little afraid she'll scare herself and not return next week. She continued to cry and said very quietly, "I can't make friends, no one ever likes me. That's why Jack was so important to me. He liked me. I just can't stand his cross-dressing, but he's still my friend. That makes it really hard." The group remained silent. It seems like the group is having a hard time sitting with Linda's feelings. I want to bring the feeling of not being good enough to the group, so I say, "I'm wondering if others in this group feel like Linda?" It is almost like the group as a whole has been holding its breath and now begins to breathe again. Cindy, while hanging her head, mumbles, "Yeah." I can feel the pain in the room and want to keep it on the table, so I say, "It must hurt a lot to think no one really likes you." Linda nods. Dot gets the box of tissues. Cindy and Celia are crying now. Carol seems to be avoiding feeling anything; she stares up at the ceiling. I do not want to lose this moment, so I say, "I know how hard it is to talk about this; maybe we could spend some time talking about just how hard it is to talk." I am hoping that the group will move from talking about how hard it is to talk to talking about how hard it is to feel unlikable. The group seems more comfortable with this. Cindy, still crying, says that she has always had a hard time talking about some things. Dot, who always seems to be full of helpful advice but never really joins the group, began talking about AA and how it has helped her to learn to talk. I can really see how Dot is the one who stops the group from feeling. Every time the group gets too close to talking about how they feel, Dot diverts the feelings by talking about AA. I may send Dot into fight or flight, but I decide to take a chance and bring this to her attention. I say, "Dot, I know AA has been very helpful to you and that you have learned a lot about staying sober, but I'm wondering how you feel about talking about difficult things." Dot just sort of looked at me for a moment as if she was not understanding what I had just said. Then she responded by telling me that even though she has learned to talk about a lot of things it's still hard to feel it.

(Eighth Session) The group is now working a little better together and seems to be gaining some degree of trust. I am hoping to draw Linda into the group more. Linda is still more withdrawn than the rest of the group and appears sad all of the time. I am not sure how to draw her out. She is difficult to engage and resists connecting with the group. This can be seen in her remaining separate from the group before and after the group session when the other women come and go together. Sometimes I feel like the group is leaving Linda behind. I am not sure that she is the scapegoat; however, she

does serve a function in the group. She is like the part of each member that they all want to get rid off.

I am going to take a chance and ask the group how they feel about Linda's separateness from the group. I need to be very careful that Linda does not get attacked, or at least not more than she can handle. Carol responds by saying that she has noticed that Linda is quiet most of the time and it makes her nervous. She is afraid that Linda is judging her. I reach for the pain. I ask Carol what she thinks the feeling is. Carol thinks for a moment and then says, "fear." I am still reaching, so I ask whose fear. Carol replies, "both of our pain." This is more what I am looking for, so I stick with it. I ask Linda how it feels to hear Carol talking about her. Linda finally looked up and said that she is really afraid of how she feels and what the group thinks of her because she cannot seem to stop drinking. Other members of the group pick up on what Linda has said. I think the group is coming together.

4. *Where the Problem Stands Now:* The group is beginning to come together. Linda's looking up at the other members of the group was a good sign. It seemed that when the group thought they would only be together for eight weeks, they felt it was too risky to share painful information. After the members found out that they could continue longer, some members began to take some chances and talk about their pain. I was also able to give up my agenda to some extent and let the group set its own pace. The group reflected this when Linda talked about how much she wants to get sober. Each week there is a little progress. They begin to talk about their fear. This is real progress. Then when I confronted Dot with talking about AA but not feelings she was able to hear me and recognize what she is doing.

The group has not yet been able to begin talking about their intense feelings and how those feelings lead to drinking. They are still working on developing a group culture where it is safe to talk. Linda does a lot of testing this out. Dot also tested it when she confronted Carol with drinking every weekend. Other members are very tenuously experimenting when they pick up on what someone else has said. Once the members find that it is safe to talk, they can move into talking about the overwhelming feelings that lead them to drink, and then we can begin to talk about ways to cope with those feelings.

5. *Specific Next Steps:*

1. I will continue to allow the group to move into the work phase at their own pace, not at a pace I want them to move.

2. I will work toward making the group a safe place for the members to share their feelings, their failures, and successes.

3. I am going to take Celia and Linda aside individually outside of group to see if I can find out why they are so quiet in group. Possibly I can then help them to become more active members of the group.

4. I want to encourage the members to discover that one thing they all have in common is that they drink to numb overwhelming feelings.

5. I will keep the work focused on feelings and how to cope with them while watching for flight or fight behavior.

6. While I want the members to explore their overwhelming feelings that stem from childhood trauma, I will limit their discussion about the actual trauma.

7. I will continue to keep a watchful eye on all the members in order to help anyone who might become a gatekeeper, or feel ashamed and thus remain silent.

Facing painful feelings is not the only threat to recovery. Most clients fight the recovery battle while still remaining in a community or family situation that may encourage relapse. In the excerpt that follows, one woman describes the drug dealer she had to deal with on her way to the meeting. The focus of the group is assertiveness, which is exactly the quality she will need.

Women's Recovery Group: Fending Off the Dealers

Purpose: Assertiveness group with ten members.

Gender: All female; *Age Range:* 18–42. All Caucasian.

Susan talked about the frustration she was having in getting into a holding. I asked what a holding is. The group members explained that a holding is an unstructured, safe and sober place they can stay before going to a halfway house. Diane then talked about the long waiting lists to get into halfway houses. I asked the group for suggestions on how to deal with these wait lists. Linda spoke about calling every day to show her interest in the houses. She also said that she stays clean by living in a shelter and coming to day treatment. Robin responded by saying that she would never stay in a shelter because of the "lice, dirt and rows and rows of cots." I asked Robin if she had been to a shelter like that. She said she had not but could just imagine it. Karen and Julie spoke about their positive experiences with specific shelters. Linda also said that the shelter she is at is clean, but that the neighborhood has a lot of drug activity. I responded by saying, "That must be very difficult for you." Linda then shared a story about being approached by a dealer while she was on her way to day treatment this morning. She described how she got very nervous and gave him a comical and lengthy explanation of where she was going. The group (including myself) laughed at her story.

I then asked, "How did you feel after you said that?" Linda said that she was tempted and is nervous about how easy it would be to go back "to the streets." Linda also spoke about feeling in control and proud of herself about her decision. Wendy and Tricia said that they would not be able to live so close to the drugs because they would use. Chris said that she thought she'd be able to do it because even if she lives where there aren't any drugs, she knows where to get them. The entire group agreed. There was a brief silence. I asked if anyone wanted to share their plans about dealing with the easy access to drugs. Chris spoke about her living situation with a boyfriend who uses and how this situation may be impossible to continue if she wants to stay clean.

Maintaining recovery requires energetic and active work on the part of the client at all times. In many day-treatment programs, recognition that the weekend poses a particular threat to recovery has led to a focus on recovery-maintenance issues on Fridays. In the next example, the group leader deals with a number of common problems associated with such a group. First, it is one of five during the day. Second, it meets only once per week and because of the open-ended nature of the group (and the program), keeping the contract clear can become a problem. These problems often lead to an illusion of work, as the student co-leader of this group discovers.

Weekend Planning to Remain "Clean and Sober"

Type of Group: This group is called "Weekend Planning." It is an open-ended group that meets one time per week on Fridays. The purpose of this group is for the members to be able to come up with a solid plan for their weekend that will enable them to remain clean and sober. About an hour before the group begins, the members are given a sheet of paper to write down their plans for Friday afternoon through Sunday evening. This group is a place where they can talk about possible crisis situations that they might encounter and how they will handle them. Other members and staff have the opportunity to give feedback in response to an individual's plan.

The members also write down interpersonal goals for themselves for the weekend. During this time, the people who are finishing the program get a chance at the end of the group to talk about the plans they have made for aftercare, self-help meetings, and anything else they have arranged in order for them to have a healthy recovery. They are also to read a good-bye letter if they prepared one; if not, they just talk about the program or anything else they feel is important to share with the group.

Age Range: 21 to 68 years old

Gender and Ethnic/Racial Composition: The members of the group are gender-mixed, primarily white working-class people. The individuals are from various ethnic groups. They have all been diagnosed with having a drug and/or alcohol addiction. In addition to that diagnosis, some of the members also have some sort of mental illness.

Dates Covered in Record: 10/13 to 11/17 (five sessions; the program was closed on Veteran's Day)

Group Task: Internal structure issue

Description of the Problem: The problem this group faces is that it is one of five for the day. Members often struggle with the issue of it being "just another group." Another problem is that since the group only meets once a week, and the group is open-ended, members tend to be unclear regarding its purpose. The purpose of this group has to be stated (recontracting) at the beginning of each meeting. Another problem is that the members are presenting their plans by just reading them instead of sharing them in order to learn and get helpful feedback. They usually only look to me (the leader) for a sign that their plan is okay and someone else can go, or for me to comment.

The problem that I face is to find a way to state the purpose of the group so that they can see the importance of sharing rather than presenting, and to have them see that it is helpful to have a concrete plan to go by, especially for people who are in early recovery.

How the Problem Came to My Attention: After sitting in on several groups and then finally leading my first one on October 6, I noticed that the members did not take this particular group very seriously. They would slouch on the couches, yawn, and often they would even carry on conversations with other members of the group while someone else was talking. Members would also look only to me for input or a go-ahead that their plan was okay and I didn't have any comments to add. Another way that this problem came to my attention was that members sometimes asked what the purpose of the group really was. I realized that in order for the group to understand the importance of this particular meeting, some of these issues would have to be addressed.

Summary of the Work with Process Excerpts:

October 13 (First Session) The first session was a flop. All I did to prepare for leading this group was to watch the other clinicians lead it for 3 to 4 weeks. The first session was full of anxiety that the group was feeling, and I ignored that because I could not handle my own feelings of anxiety. The members of the group were not used to me doing or saying anything in the group because, up until this session, I was solely observing. When I walked into the room, everyone was lounging on the couch and chairs. Beth asked me where Rob (a clinician/group leader) was so that the group could get started. I explained to Beth and the rest of the group that Rob would be coming in later, and that I was going to lead the group. A few of the members looked excited for me to be leading the group, while others expressed what I felt was anxiety. I too was anxious, so I was unsure of how to handle the situation, and I ignored it, and began the group by sitting down and saying, "Okay, who wants to go first?" The group took control at this point because it was very obvious that I was not going to do much.

The group was going along quickly, mainly because I was frozen and also because I did not pose any questions or even make any comments as to what they were saying. Rob fortunately could see that I was "stuck," so he began asking questions and making comments about the group's weekend plans.

As the session went on, people started to lean back in their seats more and become very "comfortable." As they became more comfortable, their weekend plans had bigger and bigger gaps. If I had picked up on it, I could have pointed out the danger in feeling too comfortable all the time. I passed up a moment where we could have gotten a lot of work done. At this time, I still had the belief that their solely talking about their plans was the work. This was an illusion of work for me and for the group.

October 20 (Second Session) I walked into the room and there were ten members present: seven were on the couches and three were in chairs. As soon as I walked into the room, William said, "Okay, let's get this over with so that we can get out of here." I should have asked him why he was in such a hurry to leave before the day was actually over. Instead, I told him that we had to wait for Bob before we could get started. Had I asked him specifically what was going on for him, I would have understood that he was feeling anxious and sad because one of the members he had become close with was completing the program after this group. At this point, I should have also stated the purpose of the group so that William and the rest of the members would have known that this group is a safe place to talk about saying good-bye and feeling worried about the people who are leaving. Fortunately, I realize that I will have the opportunity to state the purpose of the group next week.

Once Bob came into the room, I began the group by saying, "Okay, before we get started, I just want to remind everyone that we have to leave time at the end because this is Carly and Shelly's last day and we want them to be able to say their good-byes. So, who wants to begin?" David began talking about his weekend plans, and I realized that he and a few other people in the group did not write anything down on their weekend planning sheets. I asked David why he didn't write anything down. He told me it was because he had it all in his head; thus, he didn't need to write it down. Since it was only my second time leading this group, I was still afraid of potential conflict, so I backed down and didn't say anything. I should have gone further with the dialogue and explained to David the importance of having a concrete plan written down so that in a crisis it would be there for him to refer to. Once again, I found myself and the group members unsure of the purpose of this particular group. As people were talking about their plans and becoming more relaxed, I found myself reclining with them. People were yawning and not very invested in the content of the group.

After everyone in the group talked about their plans, Carly and Shelly were given time to say their good-byes to the group and the counselors. At this time, I asked Carly and Shelly if they were nervous about leaving. I was wondering if they were feeling a sense of loss. They answered saying that they were just going to miss the people in the program and just coming to the program itself because it is safe for them. I forgot to think of the group as my client too. Had I remembered that, I would have picked up on the members' feelings of abandonment and loss too. Now I am able to see why William was so anxious to leave. He did not want to talk about people leaving. Unfortunately, by not confronting him and the rest of the group, I let them take flight, not in body, but in mind. On the other hand, the group's feelings regarding abandonment and loss have been, and still will be, talked about in future groups at the program.

October 27 (Third Session) Once again, I came into the same room and did not state the purpose. Part of the reason for this is because I was unsure of the exact purpose. As I mentioned earlier, these groups are open-ended, and today in particular, this group looked to me specifically when describing their plans for the weekend. I saw that this affected the group because hardly any of the members were giving feedback besides me. As John was going over his plans for his weekend, he mentioned that he might go to his house in New Hampshire for the weekend. I confronted John because the group members remained silent. I asked him if he thought that this was a safe situation for him to be in, because he had told us before that that's usually where he gets drunk. John did not respond, and I noticed many of the people in the group were looking very thoughtful. Since I know that some of the members would be helped by expressing their concern and anger, I asked if anyone in the group had anything to say to John about his plans. This opened up a new door for the group because they were able to talk about unsafe places for them, and how they would handle themselves in those situations. The group was able to benefit from John's risky situation, because they came up with various crisis plans that they could all use. Finally, I was able to see the group as a whole and experience the group as providing mutual aid for one another through direct confrontation. This was also a way of showing how important this group is without having stated the purpose.

November 3 (Fourth Session) Kristen began the group by asking me what "I" wanted her to put down on "her" weekend planning sheet. I sensed that many of the members of the group were wondering the same thing, so I explained the purpose of the weekend planning sheets in order to clarify the purpose. "As you know, this group is called weekend planning. This sheet is not for you to put down things that I want, it is for all of you to be able to have concrete plans for this weekend. The sheet goes day by day, and asks you to write down crisis plans and interpersonal goals. Seriously, keep in mind that the more concrete your plan is, and the less gaps that it has, the lower your risk for relapse will be. Does anyone have any questions?" It was amazing. After I spoke, some of the members sat up straighter and began to write down their plans so they could be ready when it was their turn to talk about their plans.

As the group continued, some members were looking at me and then at certain members of the group, and kept rolling their eyes, but I failed to receive their underlying message. I was unable to tune into the group as a whole and see that, although clarifying the purpose helped some members get work done, others were still dealing with the issue of the relaxed environment. Some were reading the newspaper, doodling on their weekend planning sheets, and just lying back in a reclining position until the session concluded. If I had tuned in, I would have been able to understand what was holding people back. I was too invested in the progress of work finally getting done, rather than finding out what was behind their eye-rolling. The members of the group were trying to tell me something by their actions, but I failed to respond to them appropriately.

November 17 (Fifth Session) I offered a more structured environment. This session was held in the conference room around a long table with chairs. I clarified the purpose of the group to the members. "This group is called weekend planning. As you know, we asked you to fill out the weekend planning sheets. This is a tool to help all of you think about a concrete plan for your weekend. We encourage you to write your plans down so that you are able to refer to them and remind yourself over the weekend what you need to do to remain clean and sober. This is also a time in which people will give and receive feedback on their individual plans. It is also a time to think about different plans that you would have if you were facing a crisis situation. Another important aspect to add is interpersonal goals that people have for themselves. For example, people often neglected self-care while they were using, and now is a good time to resume self-care. Remember that no one plan is right or wrong, but it can always be strengthened by closing the gaps in your plans. Does anyone have any questions? No. Okay, who wants to start?"

Frankie began by stating his plans and possible crises. He said, "I might go to A's (club/bar) to hang out this weekend." I said, "Will that be a crisis situation for you?" Frankie said, "No. I won't go if I feel unsafe." Tom asked, "What will you do if you feel unsafe once you are there?" Frankie answered, "I will just leave." Don commented, "Yeah, I know I wouldn't be able to go because I wouldn't be able to leave if I felt unsafe. I would end up just standing in a corner shaking because of my nerves." I asked the group if they had any suggestions for Frankie regarding his plans for the weekend, because they seemed to be concerned. Frankie's voice began to rise when he said, "I just won't go if I feel unsafe. And I'll just leave if I do go and feel unsafe once I get there." I feel that the rising of his voice put me in a position to confront his ambivalence towards hearing suggestions from members of the group, or to go on because he is not interested. Instead of pushing it any further, I wimped out. I hoped that he knew that we were concerned and just trying to help him get out of a possibly dangerous situation.

Where the Problem Stands Now: Even though I have only had one session in which I changed rooms and stated the purpose at the beginning of the session, I can see a big difference in the way the group responds to the weekend planning group. I feel the difference, which in turn helps the members to feel different. I am more comfortable in the structured environment. Members of the group do not seem so relaxed and uninvolved with the process. The room change, along with stating the purpose at the beginning of every group, has helped me and the group to understand the purpose of the group and take it more seriously. Some staff members look to the changes that I have made as "taking the group too seriously." I see the changes as a positive asset to the milieu that the program strives to create.

Specific Next Steps:

1. I will continue to state the purpose at the beginning of every group session.

2. I will continue to have the weekend planning group meet in the conference room.

3. I will keep emphasizing the idea of mutual aid to the members of the group.

4. I will try to provide more structure by writing on the board while they write on their sheets.

5. I will try much harder to concentrate on the group as a whole, rather than focusing solely on individuals.

6. I will try to be more in tune to cues from the members of the group.

7. I will keep learning from my mistakes as a leader so as to make fewer and better mistakes in the future.

8. Finally, I will continue to try to enlighten the staff as to the positive aspects of recontracting at every session and changing to a more structured setting.

This example provides a fairly common and accurate picture of a new group leader's "learning curve." Her strength lies in her honesty about her own feelings and struggles to assert her leadership role. Progress is evident each meeting as she makes "active mistakes" that allow her to deepen her learning and skill development. She will also need to consider carefully the meaning of the staff members' comments about taking the group too seriously. This is the equivalent of her group members' rolling their eyes, and she should explore and pay attention to the underlying meaning of these signals from the agency—her second client. This role will be explored in more detail in the next two chapters. In the next section, we will examine the impact of more than one diagnosis on the group development and process.

GROUP WORK WITH CLIENTS WITH A DUAL DIAGNOSIS

As illustrated in the previous sections, substance abuse often accompanies another diagnosis such as post-traumatic stress, mental illness or, as in one of the groups in this section, AIDS. It is important for the group leader to recognize that the group should not get stuck in focusing on the independent impact of each diagnosis on the life of the members. There is a joint effect that needs to be explored—the specific impact of the substance abuse on the second diagnosis, and vice versa.

In the first example in this section, a group of women discuss the impact of mental illness and substance abuse on their lives. In the second example, members of a group I recently co-led at first avoid discussing the painful interaction between AIDS and their prolonged, poly-substance abuse. It is only in response to recontracting and a demand for work that they finally begin to address the concerns related to self-image and stigmatization.

A Dual-Diagnosis Group: Mental Illness and Substance Abuse

March 4 (8th group)

Present: Worker, Barbara, Gloria, Rita, Pam, Nancy, and Theresa.

After reading the opening, Gloria took an opportunity to read, "Accepting Differences."

Theresa: I want to comment on the last sentence that says we would leave our fear, secrecy, and isolation. I have felt isolated over the last few weeks, and several issues of abuse have come up for me over the last two weeks. I feel like I'm struggling. I really want to stay home.

Worker: I wonder how other people are feeling about their ability to share their secrets in this group.

Theresa: I notice that I am very tired and that I have been holding onto things for a long time. I feel like I am very ashamed and I am finally now getting angry.

Nancy: Being tired is a symptom of anger. I notice that when I am feeling ashamed I am often angry.

Barbara: I notice that when I am angry lately and very irritated at the people at the House and I'm muttering under my breath, "You're an asshole," I don't know quite what to do with my anger because I can't really tell people in the AA community about it because most of my anger is about my mental illness. The other night when I was on a commitment (a trip to an AA meeting at which members from another group share their stories) with some other people with me in the car, the men started saying that people who are on psychotropic medications are not allowing themselves to go through their experience of being an alcoholic. They are taking medications, using the soft approach. I couldn't believe that they mentioned this right in the car when I was there, knowing that I take medication. I felt as though they were isolating me, and I find myself more and more angry that I have to take the medication, that I have to take it on time, that I have to check it with the pharmacist, and see my doctor. It is so much easier to be a drunk. All I have to do is stop drinking and show up to a meeting.

Gloria: I feel very ashamed of my alcoholism, and I don't really tell anybody my story in AA either. I can't imagine standing up and telling people that I have a mental illness and alcoholism.

Nancy: I feel as though some of the meetings would be accepting.

Barbara: I'm just not sure where those are, and I am not willing to take the risk of being put down.

Worker: What do you do about your anger?

Barbara: I don't do anything about it. I sometimes can call my sponsor, but he tells me to stop whining.

Nancy: I ignore it. I swallow it, pretend it's not there. I don't really know what to do with it.

Theresa: I swallow it. I used to self-medicate. Self-medication was easy for me. I would use any substance to make me not feel anger.

Rita: I ignore it.

Worker: I tend to think that anger is an energy and that if you leave it inside after a while it will just get more and more strong and want to get out. Some of us have rage attacks, others will feel the need to self-medicate. I even believe that the anger can turn into physical complications.

Theresa: I agree, but I don't have anywhere to go with it. It doesn't feel safe. I have a lot of anger about the abuse that I went through as a kid, but it doesn't feel right to yell and scream at my parents. But I do feel angry about what happened.

Barbara: I still feel very angry at the mental illness. For a long time I was angry at life and my drinking habit. But I've noticed now that it has switched. I am very comfortable not drinking, but I am very much in denial about my mental illness.

Rita: I've accepted it.

Nancy: I still don't feel very comfortable with mine, although over the years I have grown to accept the mental illness. I remember once that I had a therapist who helped me a lot with my mental illness, but she wanted me to become a productive member of society and I felt like she was pushing too hard and wasn't listening to me. It encouraged me to be mad at it.

Worker: I wonder if other people in the group feel angry at their mental illness. What do you think, Pam?

Pam: I sometimes feel angry at it because I really want to work. I want to contribute and have my own apartment, and I feel like my mental illness stops me from really being out there and working.

Barbara: I want to work also. I don't know what I want to do, but I guess I could flip a few hamburgers or something.

Rita: I guess I just want to redefine work. I am volunteering now, but I can only volunteer about six hours a week and then I am very tired.

Theresa: I don't feel like I am working, either, and I can't imagine being in the work force for a long time. I am so anxious.

Worker: I wonder if there is a way to redefine contribution. What is it like to be a worker or a participant right here in the group? What is it like to be a contributor? Rather than seeing ourselves as having to produce things, maybe being active contributors right here or in other parts of your treatment is enough work.

Barbara: I find work pretty easy because I am a manic and I can just keep doing and doing and doing.

(The group members laugh.)

Worker: When we feel like we are not contributors, isn't that what brings up our fear and isolation and secrecy that we talked about earlier and started the group with? Is that how we get the stigma that may be attached to the mental illness in the community and our alcoholism?

(The group members nod.)

Gloria: I feel as though I have a lot of shame. I notice that I'm angry that I can't really work as much as I would like to. I started a new job and I'm not able to manage it because it is too much.

Nancy: It's so much like the therapist who tried to get me to be an active participant as a worker. I just couldn't imagine being able to do it. It would be really nice to redefine contribution.

Worker: It's 10:00 and we need to close the meeting. Who would like to read the closing?

Group Work with Persons with AIDS Who Are in Early Substance Abuse Recovery

Agency: AIDS Action Committee

Setting: Independent living for persons with AIDS (alcohol- and drug-free housing)

Co-Leaders: Full-time, African-American substance abuse counselor working for AIDS Action; the author, a white social work professor

Group Purpose: A mutual aid support group for persons with AIDS who are also in early recovery from substance abuse. The focus is on the interaction between recovery and living with AIDS. Survivor issues emerged as central to the struggle for each of the members.

Timing: Eight initial sessions, 90 minutes each, with an agreement to consider renewal at the last session

Members: Jake (late thirties, African-American man), Gerry (early thirties, African-American man); Tania (early forties, white transsexual woman); Theresa (late twenties, white woman); Kerry (late twenties, white gay man)

Each of the members has met individually with my co-leader prior to the first meeting. My co-leader is a substance abuse counselor and brings a background in 12-step groups to the session. We have agreed that we would be exploring how to integrate the mutual aid approach central to my work with the structured recovery (12-step) approach designed to help the members maintain their recovery. As the "outsider," I felt it was important that I cede the initial lead role to my co-leader. We had met prior to the session to work out our understanding of the group and how we would share the leadership role. Tania, Kerry, and Jake are residents in the housing unit, a "clean and sober" residence for persons with AIDS. Both Tania and Kerry had relapsed recently and acted out. They were required to attend some form of recovery group and reluctantly decided on this one since it was conveniently held in the house. The early themes include their anger and suspicion as well as the difficulty of dealing with the holidays. The authority theme is also central as Tania takes on the role of testing the leaders.

(*First Meeting*) John (my co-leader) began the meeting by welcoming everyone and saying he thought it would be helpful to go over the rules for the sessions. He gave each member a list of ten rules and asked them to read them and comment. The members responded positively, with Tania saying that she liked the one about confidentiality. She went on in a hyper manner, saying that she could deal with a lot, but she couldn't deal with anybody ratting on her—that if someone rats on her, she is out of here.

Jake picked up on Tania's theme with anger in his voice. He described an incident over the weekend, where a still active (drug-using) girlfriend visited him. When things got "out of hand," he told her to leave his room. He then imitated his girlfriend going to the staff office in the lobby and telling them that he had hit her. The police were called and he refused to answer his door. The others were listening intently as he, with a lot of anger, said that the incident was written down in his book and that he didn't understand what this was all about. If this was independent living, this was his apartment, and he could do what he wanted in his apartment.

Kerry and Tania, who also had apartments in the house, added their anger towards staff. I said that they seemed to be saying that they were living in independent housing, but that they didn't really feel they were independent. Members nodded and agreed.

John returned to the contracting and asked if each one would initial or sign the contract. After they signed, I asked Tania whether she was concerned, not just about being ratted on by members of the group, but also concerned about what John and I would share with staff. She said she was, and then went on at some length about how she didn't have to be here and could leave if she wanted to.

John suggested that I explain the confidentiality rules that we would be following. I told them we had met with the house staff and we had agreed that we would keep discussion in the group confidential, with the exception of any information they shared that indicated to us that they were personally at risk or that someone else was being put at risk. I also explained that any activities in the house that were illegal, like selling dope, would also have to be shared. Other than that, there would be no disclosures to staff. I went on to say that, since this is an early recovery group, in which there was always the possibility of relapse, staff and we had agreed that relapse incidents would not be reported. The group members nodded in agreement when I made this comment.

I went on to tell them that the staff had also agreed that the only information they would share with us about resident activity at the house would be information which they felt indicated that a resident might be in danger of harming himself or herself.

Other than that, we would meet with the staff in about four or five weeks to discuss how the group was going. Tania, with great agitation, said, "Well, that sounds good, but we'll have to see." She said that she had too many people in the past give her assurances and then not come through. I laughed and said, "Maybe we should sign the contract, as well." The group members laughed and agreed that would be a good idea. I told Tania that I thought she was right not to trust us, since she had just met us, and that trust would be something we'd have to earn over time. She nodded her head in agreement.

My co-leader returned to the issue of group purpose. However, he did not sharply focus on the issue of the interaction between AIDS and recovery. I decided I would have to come back later in the session to clarify specific purpose.

John said that having clarified the rules, we should talk about the group. He told them that he saw this as their group, and that what we did in the group would be decided by the members. He said that he had some ideas about things that we could talk about, including, for example, issues around the medications they were taking. He suggested he could bring a medical person in to answer their questions. Personal and family issues would also be relevant. Tania interrupted, as she did often throughout the evening, and said, "Family issues—forget it." Thanksgiving was coming up, and, as far as she was concerned, she had no family.

Jake jumped in and said he wanted to tell a story about what had happened over the weekend. He had gone home to visit his family in another town in the state. He said, "I couldn't stay. They started to make me crazy right away. Everyone there was drinking and drugging, and I knew, if I stayed, they would pull me in, and I can't let them pull me in. I have to fight that. I know I can't control this. If I take one drink or use drugs once, I'm going to be back to going into the bar at 8:00 in the morning and staying right through until 2 A.M. drinking myself to death."

I said that it sounded like, in addition to giving up the drinking and drugging, he was also having to give up his family. He agreed. Kerry said that he had been in a bar in the last week and had had two drinks. He said, "I can handle that. Just because I have two drinks doesn't mean I am going back to where I was a year ago. I know you people are going to say I am in denial, but it's not true. I know I can handle this." John said that we had to understand that recovery was different for each person and that we had to make room in the group for people to feel safe and not defensive as they described their own ways of handling recovery. I nodded in agreement. The rest of the group did, as well.

Theresa jumped in at that point and said that she was not living at this house. She was living in a single-room-occupancy building two blocks away. She said that most of the people in that building were active users and, for her, it was a fight every day to make sure that she didn't get pulled in. She said that she knew that she didn't want to go back to all the drinking and drugging she had been doing. She told us that she had gotten out of the penitentiary after a five-year sentence, and that in the penitentiary she had dried out and learned not to use. She said that she didn't want to go back to when she hated herself and she would spend her time on street corners sucking old men's dicks in order to get enough money for a shot of crack.

Tania agreed and said that, when she thought of some of the things she did for the ten-year period that she was drinking and drugging all the time, she couldn't believe she had actually let herself do those things. Theresa said, "I still have to deal with the housing, even though I am not in this residence; but I know the real question is how we deal with ourselves. For me, religion has been the answer." And then she quickly said, "I know, John, you said that this isn't a religious group, but I can't help it. For me, religion is the answer." I told Theresa that I thought she'd misunderstood John. John wasn't saying that religion and spirituality couldn't be a part of what they talked about if that was what was important to them. He just wanted to make it clear that the group was not organized as a religious group. John agreed that that's what he had meant.

Theresa said she had a boyfriend now. She went back to visit her family just last weekend and she was really surprised that her father had actually invited the boyfriend into the house. She went on to say that her boyfriend was black and that her parents had a hard time accepting that. She said that her mother, in particular, was racist and couldn't believe she was going with a black boyfriend. Theresa said that this guy had been special to her and that it would have hurt a lot if her family had not accepted him.

She pointed out that he did not have AIDS and was not actively using and that he was very helpful to her. But she knew that she had to take responsibility for herself and that was why she made sure that they had safe sex. Her boyfriend, however, had had a lot of losses in life, including the death of his wife, and he felt afraid of having more losses.

Tania, still speaking with the same level of tension, said that the holidays were going to be impossible. Tania told us she was a part-time stand-up comic and did routines. She almost delivered her comments in the group as if it were a stand-up routine. I knew I was going to have to point that out at some point, but this first session was not the right time.

Tania went on about all the parties that were going on, and how difficult it was for her now to party. She said, "I don't know how to party without first drinking and drugging. As I looked at the people at this party I attended last week, through clean and sober eyes, I said 'My God, was this me? Was this the way I lived my life?' I left the party when they started passing around the cocaine, because, if I had stayed, I might have given in." (Tania was only one month into her recovery and still obviously very shaky about it.) She commented, "I know you all know what I'm talking about, since you're in recovery as well, although I don't know about them" (pointing towards us).

I decided to use this as an opportunity to address the authority theme. I pointed out that Tania had mentioned a couple of times her concern about confidentiality, and also she had raised the question indirectly about whether we were in recovery. I said that I would have to speak for myself. "I'm not in recovery so I am an outsider." I went on to say that I thought the issue of trust in me and John was a major one for them today, and they were worried about what we might share, and for three of them, whether or not what we might share could affect their ability to continue in the housing. They agreed that they wanted to hold onto their apartments, which were the best of this type available to them in the city. Theresa indicated that she was hoping to get into one of the apartments.

I told them that I was a social worker and that I taught social work at the University. I told them I had asked John and AIDS Action if it would be possible for me to co-lead this group because I thought it was important, as a teacher, that I continued to work directly with people. Tania exploded and said, "I thought you were a narc." I laughed and said, "A narc? You mean I look like a narcotics detective?" She continued, "I thought you were just going to sit there, take notes and, right after this session, you were going to march me off to the police station and that I'd be arrested." I laughed again and said, "Look (holding my sweater up), no wire and no badge." They all laughed. I said, "I'm not a narc, but it's going to take a while for you to really believe and trust that we will keep what you raise here confidential, except for those conditions I mentioned earlier. I'm hoping we can earn your trust." All their heads were nodding in agreement.

At this point, I wanted to bring them back to the purpose of the group. I also wanted to reinforce the AIDS issue, which appeared to be in the background as they focused on recovery issues. I attempted to partialize the issues they had raised to begin forming an agenda for our work together.

I said, "Let's talk a little bit more about what the group is about." I pointed out there were groups for people in recovery, and there were groups for people who had the virus. I said, "The unique thing about this group is that you have the virus and also are in early recovery. I don't want to lose sight of the fact that we need to also look at how having the virus affects your ability to deal with your recovery. That's a powerful issue, and we should make sure we don't ignore it." There was a silence in the room at that point, and Theresa said, "You bet it affects our recovery."

I said, "This should be a place we can talk about that." I continued, "Thus far, I've heard you raise a number of issues. You have some concerns about what goes on in the house and your relationship with staff. If that's an area we discuss, we can talk about what you can do and the way you deal with staff around these issues that have caused you a great deal of concern.

"You have also pointed out that you've had a lot of losses. Not only have you lost the drinking and the drugging, which had been important to you, but you're also facing the loss of family members and friends who are associated with the drinking and drugging. These are powerful changes. You feel you've lost your independence. That's another issue we can discuss. My guess is, with Thanksgiving coming up in just a few weeks, how you deal with the holiday must also be a big concern."

Tania jumped in and said, "I'm scared stiff. From now until Christmas it's going to be non-stop beer ads, drinking ads, parties—I'm not sure I know how I'm going to get through." Theresa said, "I know what you mean. That's a tough time, but, if you want, I'd be glad to help. I'll give you my telephone number and, if at any point, you feel you're really up against it and you just need someone to talk with about it, you can give me a call." Tania nodded her head, smiled and said, "Thank you." Theresa went on to say, "However, if you're active and you're using when you give me the call, I will have to call someone else from AA in order to have someone to help me deal with the issue. I'd like to help you, Tania, but I don't want to get pulled in with your struggle. Mine is tough enough." Tania shook her head, then nodded in agreement.

I pointed out that a little earlier in the discussion I thought Kerry had wanted to get in, but hadn't had a chance, and I wondered if there was something he wanted to say. Kerry was thoughtful for a moment and then said that he agreed with a lot of what was being said here, that the holiday times were pretty hard for him as well. He said he had boyfriends, but having the virus made it difficult for him. He described a trip he had just taken, and some of the difficulties he ran into with his partner. (Kerry looks gaunt, and along with Tania shows the most physical evidence of having AIDS.) Kerry went back to the issue of his being able to have a drink or two, and not feeling he was out of control. Jake said that, for him, one or two drinks would be the end of it.

My co-leader, John, said that different people approach recovery in different ways: "When I first began doing these groups, I would tell you, Tania, that just going to these parties is asking for trouble and that you should try to find clean and sober parties." Tania said, "I wish I could. I wouldn't know what to do at one of those." John continued, "Everyone has a different way of dealing with their recovery, and we have to make this a safe place for them to talk about it." Everyone agreed. John then pointed out that it was close to the end of the session and suggested that it might be useful to just go around the room and have each person comment on what they thought. He reminded them of the first step in the 12 steps, taking responsibility, and asked them to address that in a personal manner. Each member responded in turn.

Kerry raised the question of the timing of the group. He attended a free dinner from six to seven, and thought we should end the group earlier. John pointed out that we ended at six. If Kerry had to leave a little bit earlier, that was his choice. Tania pointed out that, if Kerry really wanted to come, he could be a little late for dinner. She said, "If you're worried about that, we can cook you something upstairs." Kerry laughed and said, "Okay," although both John and I felt there was some hesitancy on his part about attending the group.

Jake said he thought this meeting was a good start and he had found it helpful to talk to other people like himself. Theresa said she knew her way to salvation was through God, but that she also needed other people to help her. I commented that maybe this group could make up a bit for the lost friends and family. They nodded their heads. Tania said, "As long as no one rats on me, this will be okay, but I want to let you know, if someone rats, you're going to hear from me, and I can be a mean bitch."

John picked up on that right away and said, "We can only tell you that we're not going to be sharing information, except under certain circumstances. But I also think, Tania, we ought to make it clear that this group should not be a place where there are any threats or intimidation." Tania said that she was sorry and that she hadn't meant it to be threatening.

When it was my turn, I said that I had appreciated their allowing me to join them in the group, and I looked forward to continuing to meet with them each week. John suggested that we end the group with the serenity prayer.

While in the first session we had clearly stated the purpose of the group as focusing on the interaction between AIDS and recovery, a pattern developed over the next few sessions of avoiding the AIDS element of the work. My co-leader and I identified this unstated norm of the group and agreed to confront it and make a demand for work on this taboo subject at the fifth meeting. My co-leader was ill for that meeting, so I had to lead the group by myself for the first time. I felt some trepidation related to my ability to help the members keep recovery in the forefront as they explored the painful issues associated with the "virus."

December 9 (Session 5) Kerry, Jake, and Tania were in the lobby when I arrived. Tania was angry because John (my co-leader) was not going to be there that evening. She said she had business with him. I pointed out that I had passed along her concerns and that he would be there next week. She angrily said, "I don't think I'm coming to the meeting." She was in a bathrobe and looked terrible. She said she wasn't feeling well but said she would come just for the beginning. I spoke to Kerry, who was sulking as well, saying he could only come for the first half hour. I discussed his holidays with him for a few minutes and, at one point, he complained about the group as being just "bitching sessions." And then he said, "Some people" (and he secretively pointed towards Tania) "talk too much." I told him I understood what he was raising and that I would be dealing with it today. Jake was talking to another resident during this time. He joined us when we went upstairs.

Theresa arrived. Tania said, "Maybe we should fill the people who weren't here in on what happened last week." Then she turned to me and said, "But I'm doing your job, aren't I?" I told her I could take all the help I could get. So she filled in both John and Theresa about the discussion they had around the house and some of their issues about the group. I said I wanted to raise a question right at the beginning. I had spoken to John and we felt it was important to find out whether or not there was a real commitment to the group, in spite of the fact that some people had been asked to come or felt they were made to come at the risk of losing their housing. Tania said, "I suppose it helps to sit around and bitch each week. I guess that makes me feel a little bit better."

I told her that was not the purpose of the group, and that I wanted to restate the purpose and to see whether or not we had some agreement on it. I pointed out, once again, that it was a group for people who were dealing with both the virus and early recovery, and how those two conditions affected each other. Tania said she didn't think that was the group's purpose. Theresa said, yes, that was exactly what she understood it to be, a place where she could deal with the impact of having the virus.

I went on to tell them that, unless this group could become a place where they could be helpful to each other, where they could make connections and be supportive to each other, it would not succeed. I told them that the purpose of the group was to help each of them figure out how to deal with some of the difficult issues in their lives, not just to complain about them. I said I knew it was hard to set aside some of your own concerns and invest yourself in someone else's issues, but that's what the group was about. I thought all of them had had problems in their lives in trying to get close and make connections to people, and that this group was a place for them to learn to do that. I went on to say that the group would not be valuable unless they could learn to really care for each other, and that since most of them had experiences where either they were exploited by people or exploited people, and where their only connection in recent years that was serious was the one they had with drugs and booze, this was what the struggle was all about.

Theresa enthusiastically said that that's why she wants the group; that's what she needs help with. She said she wanted to talk about her boyfriend and the impact of her HIV on their relationship. As she was talking, Tania interrupted her and started to complete her sentences. I stopped the group and pointed this out. I said, "Tania, you know, you haven't let Theresa finish a sentence." I said, "I could be wrong, but I think you get very anxious about these discussions and that talking is a way of dealing with it." She said, "Oh, did I?" and made as if to zipper her mouth and put her hand over it. I told her I would help her because I thought she had a lot to give, but I thought other peopled needed the chance to get involved as well. Tania accepted this and, for the rest of the evening, actively tried to catch herself when she was jumping in, cutting people off, or not leaving room for others to comment.

Theresa started to talk about her concerns. She said she was 18 months clean and sober, and so she was in the middle of the second year, which was a "feelings year." She went on to describe that this was the period when she and, she thought, everyone in recovery, started to face all those feelings they had been running from. She said it was a complex and difficult time, and that it was hard to sort things out. She went on to say that her boyfriend had trouble sharing his feelings with her. When she wanted to talk to her boyfriend about issues like her AIDS, he pulled back and told her it was too painful. As a result, she backs off. She knows he's experienced a lot of losses, including the death of his wife from illness fairly recently, and she realizes he is still early in recovery, but she had things she wants to talk to him about. She has a closeness she wanted to achieve. She has some commitments she wants from him, and she is afraid that he can't make commitments at this point. He's holding back. I asked the others in the group if they had any advice for Theresa on this issue.

Kerry, who usually sits quietly at the meetings, and who indicated that he was going to leave as soon as he could, jumped right in. Kerry said he thought that her boyfriend was having trouble dealing with his losses and it wasn't easy. He described a very close relationship with his partner, Billy, that ended two years ago, when his partner died of AIDS on Christmas day. He said he still didn't think he'd come to grips with all the feelings that he had and the loss that he'd experienced. I said that must make each Christmas even more difficult for him, and he agreed. He went on to talk about how he had been raised by an extremely physically abusive mother and that his grandmother was the only person who had provided him with any support and love. He said he didn't think he had gotten over her dying either. He told Theresa that she had to realize that the grieving process takes a long time and that it might not be that easy for her boyfriend to even discuss it with her, because he knew it wasn't easy for him to discuss his loss with other people. (As Kerry talked, I saw a sensitive and caring side of him that he keeps covered up with his abrasive, angry front, his consistently telling us he doesn't need anybody and, if they don't care about him, "the hell with them.")

Theresa acknowledged his comments and thanked Kerry for sharing that with her, as did the other members of the group. Tania came in at that point and reinforced what Kerry had been saying. Jake was shaking his head as if he understood that difficulty as well.

Theresa then took us to the issue that she was facing at the moment. She related an incident which had led to a major fight with her boyfriend. They were in a car together and she was in the back seat. There was another woman in the front seat whom she experienced as coming on to her boyfriend. The woman was asking him when they could get together and saying how much she'd like to "bump and grind" with him on the dance floor. Every time Theresa described this woman's comments, she did an imitation of her, making it sound flirtatious and seductive. Theresa went on with a great deal of anger, saying that her boyfriend didn't even acknowledge that she was in the back seat and that she was his woman. Therefore, this woman, a friend of his, was going on right in front of her, which she felt was disrespecting her. She thought her boyfriend was disrespecting her by not stopping the woman and not being aware of her feelings.

I asked if she had talked to her boyfriend about this, and she said she had, but he had just told her that she was "insecure." Tania intervened at this point, and asked if the other woman was a black woman. Theresa said she was. Tania said, "I thought so." She said, "My first husband was a black man, and I can tell you all those black women just hated the fact that he was going out with me, As far as they were concerned, I was his 'trophy,' and I was invading their turf and taking away their man from them." She said, "It didn't matter what I did or what I said or how I tried to be nice or how I tried to connect up with his family, they never accepted me as a white woman taking a black man."

As Tania was speaking, with much feeling, I noticed Jake, who was sitting next to her, rolling his eyes and looking up to the sky. Jake is usually very quiet, so I reached for him and asked what he was thinking. I said I realized that he wasn't able to speak for all black men, but he was the only black man in the room at this time. He went on to agree that there was a big issue when a black man dated a white woman, and that people in the black community, in the black family—the black girlfriends—did resent it. He said he had found that when he had been dating white women, every time he did, there was a similar reaction from his family and others.

Theresa said, "Look, I don't know how to deal with this. I try to use a prayer I know from the 12-steps program, that maybe I can pray he can change. But I don't think he's going to change because, even though he is in a 12-step program, I don't think he's really committed to it. I think he can talk the talk, but he doesn't walk the walk. He's got all the words, but he doesn't practice any of it. I'm not sure he's going to change at all."

Theresa continued, "I realize for both of us this is our first 'recovery relationship,' and I know I have to be patient because he's not where I am in recovery, but still it's hard to sit in the car and have him disrespect me in that way." She said that she was absolutely furious at this woman and that maybe she ought to go have a talk with the lady. She had a great deal of anger as she described the fact that she was just recently released from the penitentiary, and there she had learned how to fight (pointing to her two missing lower teeth). She said, "I can ask this lady nicely first, but, if I don't get anywhere, then it's my boot up her ass."

I asked Theresa if that would solve the problem, since it might get rid of this woman, but if she doesn't resolve the issue with her boyfriend, wouldn't there just be another one? She agreed and seemed a bit deflated. I said that it seemed to me she had to talk to her boyfriend. Also, her anger was so strong that if she did take physical action against this other woman, she might be risking her own recovery and even her own freedom, and the last thing she wanted to do was to end up back in prison on an assault charge. She nodded her head and said, "I know it would mean I'd be losing control of my recovery and giving it to someone else, but I don't know if I could talk to him or if he'll listen to me without just putting me off."

By identifying Tania's pattern of interrupting because of her anxiety, and then actively helping her to monitor the process during the meeting, I believed I was helping her to begin to take control over her feelings. As she did so, she was able to invest herself in the thoughts, feelings and concerns of the other group members. In the remainder of this record we see her focusing in on Theresa's struggle and providing significant emotional and cognitive support. As she is helping Theresa, she is also helping herself and the other members of the group.

Tania came back in and spoke with great feeling about what an important and wonderful person Theresa was, and that she deserved respect and that, if she respected herself, which Tania thought she did, then she should stand up for herself and not let this guy get away with this. She had to tell him directly that she wanted him to make a commitment to her, to recognize her as his woman. Also, if there were these kinds of issues, she had to deal with them out in the open and couldn't let them just fester where she would get angrier and angrier. She said, "If you continue to get this angry, you're just going to hurt yourself, you're going to get sick and eventually you're going to threaten your recovery." Theresa agreed that this was going to be a problem for her.

I intervened and asked Theresa why she let him back off when she asked him to talk about the losses and these other issues and he said they were too painful. She said, "Well, he told me it was hard to talk about." I said to Theresa, "Well, you could have asked him what made it hard. So why do you back off when he resists conversations with you?" There was a long silence and then Theresa's face softened and she said, "I guess I really don't want to hear." Everyone in the room nodded their head in agreement. I said, "Good for you, Theresa. Now you're taking some responsibility for your part. What are you afraid you're going to hear?" She went on and said, "I'm afraid I'm going to be rejected."

Theresa's comment on her fear of rejection resonates with Jake, who takes us to the heart of their struggle over AIDS.

Jake jumped in at that point, with a lot of emotion, and said, "That's the problem when you've got the virus. People reject you." He went on and talked about his own family and how he'd gotten in trouble with the law over a fight and, he was in court and nobody knew him in that court, and he was about to get released without having to do jail time because of the fight. He said, "My own mother was in the court and she hurt me deeply—she really pained me—when she stood up and told the judge that I was HIV. Well, that changed everything, these people got real angry at me, and they didn't want a guy getting into fights who was HIV-positive, who had the AIDS bug, and they said: 'Go to jail.'" He said, "I couldn't believe the rejection I felt from my mother, and I tried to explain it to her later, and she didn't understand that I didn't want her telling people I was HIV, not in those circumstances." He then turned to Theresa and said, "So, I can understand why you're afraid of that rejection." He said, "I think we're all afraid of what people will do once they know we've got the virus."

Tania had been very quiet, although I could tell she wanted to speak. At one point, I stopped and said, "I think Tania wants to get in here, and she's been well-behaved this session, we have to give her a chance." She smiled and jumped in, telling Theresa how much she admired her, and how much strength she had, and that she hoped that she could handle her recovery in the way that Theresa was handling it. She told Theresa that she just deserved a lot more.

Theresa now starts to zero in on the core of her current struggle—the impact of her AIDS on how others view her. She begins with an indirect cue associated with a question. Later in the session, when she returns to this theme, I am able to understand it more clearly and to reach for the underlying feelings.

Theresa asked Tania whether she thought she was an attractive person. There was a silence, and Tania said, "I think you're a beautiful young woman and you could have any man you want." Theresa went on at some length about how men come on to her and, if she wanted to, she could "bump and grind" with them as well. But she didn't want that. She wanted one relationship. She wanted a serious relationship. She said she was getting older now and she wanted a commitment from someone and this was just not enough, and that was what the issue was all about.

At this point, Kerry had to leave to go to his dinner, and I said just before he left, "Kerry, I want to raise the question of commitment." I said, "I think you worked really hard today and I think you gave an important gift to Theresa and to the whole group when you shared some of your own pain over the loss of Billy." I added, "I think you could get and also give a lot of help in the group, but you really have to commit to it, so I have to ask you: Is this something that you want to keep on coming to?" He hesitated and then he said he would. He said he thought this was a helpful session but that he had to go.

We returned to Theresa, and I said, "Is the question really, Theresa, that you're afraid that he might not stay with you, that, if you actually confront him on this issue of the other woman, that he might leave you?" She agreed that it was her concern. At this point, I wondered if it might help Theresa to figure out what she might say to her boyfriend. Theresa said that would be helpful because she didn't know when and how to say it. Then she laughed and said, "Maybe I should say it in bed." Tania said, "Oh no. Don't say if before sex and don't say it after sex." And I added, "And don't say it during sex." Everyone laughed at this point and Tania did an imitation of having a conversation with Theresa's boyfriend, while pumping up and down as if she were in bed having sex with him.

Tania said, "You have to find a quiet time, not a time when you're in the middle of a fight, and you have to just put out your feelings." I asked Tania if she could show Theresa how she could do that. She started to speak as if she were talking to Theresa's boyfriend. I role-played the boyfriend, and said, "Oh, but Theresa, you're just insecure, aren't you?" Tania did a very good job of not letting me put her off and, instead, putting the issue right where it was—whether or not I was prepared to make a commitment or if I was too insecure.

Theresa said, "I know I have to talk to him, but you know, he's told me that he's not sure he wants to be tied down, that he likes to have his freedom." Jake nodded his head and said, "Yeah, that's the problem, they want their freedom and they don't want to make a commitment, and you're afraid, if you push him, he'll leave you because you got the virus." Theresa said she realized she had to sit down and talk to him because it couldn't keep up the same way. She would just get too angry and do something crazy and screw up her recovery. She said when she had a fight with him on Thanksgiving, he did call his sponsor and came back much more gently. She felt she had gotten through to him, but she had to find another way to get through to him and talk to him. Otherwise, this thing was just going to continue and it was going to tear her up inside.

As Theresa explores confronting this problem with her boyfriend, my concerns about the impact of such a discussion on her recovery emerge. Almost as if my co-leader's voice is reminding me about keeping recovery first in the work, I explore the availability of support. This brings from Tania a heartfelt offer to help as well as a poignant statement of what she was getting from the discussion. When Theresa returns to her question of her looks, I am ready this time and reach for the underlying core theme of the session.

I said, if she did confront him, it was going to be very rough for her, especially with the holiday times, and I wondered whom she'd have for support, especially if he said he didn't want to continue the relationship. She said she had her sponsor, and

Tania said, "You also have me. You can call me anytime you want." Tania said, "I didn't realize when I started this group there were people who have lived lives just like me, who had feelings just like me, who had struggles just like me. You—you're a woman—you've really helped me see that I'm just not the only one going through this. I'd do anything I could to help you."

Once again, Theresa asked Tania how she looked. She said, "You're a woman. I know, as a woman, you will be honest with me and just tell me what you think. Do you think I look okay?" Tania seemed confused and said, "Well, sure, you look wonderful." I said, "I wonder if Theresa is really asking, 'Am I pretty enough? Am I attractive enough? If my boyfriend leaves me, can I find someone else who could love me even though I have AIDS?'" She said, "That's it," and came close to tears. She said, "I'm so afraid, if I lose him, I won't find anyone else." She said, "I know I could have guys, and I could have sex, and I like the sex. I sure missed it during the time I was in prison, but can another guy love me?"

The group members tried to reassure her that she was a wonderful person. Tania said, "It's not what you look like on the outside, it's what you're like on the inside." And she said, "And you, honey—you've really got it where it counts."

I asked then, as we were coming to an end, what they thought about the evening. I pointed out it was already six o'clock, and some had been saying they thought one hour was too long for a group, and yet we had gone an hour-and-a-half, and the time had flown by. Theresa said everybody was really very helpful. Tania said, "You know, I didn't want to come, but, you know, it's turned out really to be okay." Jake said he really enjoyed tonight and he liked my leading the group. He said, "You let us talk. You're not as serious about the rules." Tania got angry again, remembering her argument with my co-leader.

I said, "Look, we can discuss this next week. I think you ought to talk directly about this when John is present. We can talk about what kind of group really is the best group for us." I told them I knew that John had a real commitment to them, and to their success in their recovery, and coping with AIDS, and I'm sure he'd be open to any discussion to help make the group work more effectively for them. I pointed out that they were all extremely helpful this evening, even though, for some of them, they didn't want to be there. I credited Tania for her ability to contain herself, even though many times she felt like just jumping in and speaking. I told her I thought she had been very helpful and supportive in her comments, and then I also credited Theresa for taking a big risk and sharing her problem with us. The meeting ended.

I was chatting with one of the staff members downstairs when Tania came down to sit down in the lobby area, and she said to me, "This was a really good meeting," and held out her hand for me to give her a high-five slap, which I did. I left the session feeling we had experienced an important turning point in the group's development.

GROUP WORK WITH THE SUBSTANCE ABUSER'S SIGNIFICANT OTHERS

Substance abuse takes its toll on everyone connected with the abuser. The impact of an addicted family member can emerge even years later to profoundly affect the ability of the survivor to create and maintain intimate relationships. The physical abuse often associated with the use of alcohol and drugs will also have profound consequences for those who have been abused as well as those who have only watched the abuse take place. In the following section we examine work with three common categories of significant others. The first is a group for adult daughters of alcoholics who struggle to revisit the pain of their traumatic childhoods and its impact on their current relationships. The second is a group for women who are currently living with abusers and who are experiencing physical abuse related to the substance use. The third example involves children living in homes where substances are or have been abused. In this example, we see clearly the struggle of a beginning worker as she tries to reach past the acting-out behavior that represents a flight/fight reaction and attempts to create a culture where the girls can feel safe enough to discuss the "family secret."

Adult Daughters of Alcoholics: Lowering the Walls of Denial. Children growing up in a family with an alcoholic parent are used to maintaining the family secret. They have observed widespread denial of a problem as a mechanism for avoiding pain and responsibility. When joining a group specifically for adult children of alcoholics, they take a first step toward public recognition of the problem and acknowledgment of the need to deal with it. In the record of service that follows, the worker attempts to help such a group begin to change the group culture that supports the notion that all of the pain and problems were in the past, the feelings have been resolved, and any current problems are usually the fault of significant others.

> **RECORD OF SERVICE**
>
> *Client Description and Time Frame:* A support and stabilization group for adult daughters of alcoholics. The purpose is for members to share with each other the experiences of growing up in an alcoholic home and, through the use of mutual aid, to help each other look at their behavior today and understand how it has been affected by past experiences.
>
> *Age Range of Members:* Approximately ages 26 to 54. These are white, middle-class and working-class women.
>
> *Dates Covered in Record:* From 10/9 to 11/20
>
> *Description of the Problem:*
>
> The group is resistant to the discussion of painful past experiences having to do with growing up in alcoholic homes. They have difficulty sharing current or past problems without externalizing them by focusing on the faults and character defects of others. They refer to personal "issues," such as low self-esteem, as having been problems in the past, but not any more. The problem facing the group and the leader lies in creating a culture for work and mutual aid in which the members trust each other enough to reach out and open up. The worker's task is to facilitate this intimacy by helping the members talk about and understand how they developed certain behaviors and how those behaviors currently affect themselves and others.
>
> *How the Problem Came to the Attention of the Worker(s):*
>
> On 10/23—the third session—the group began discussing **ACOA (Adult Children of Alcoholics)** issues that were listed on a sheet I had handed out. One of the members stated with some anger that she "never lies"—a characteristic common to many ACOAs. Most everyone agreed that they, too, never lie, but said that their husbands or other alcoholics they know lie all the time. Another member (Jane) pointed out that she agreed that adult children lie often—she said that she used to do it all the time, but that when she joined Alanon and began the 12-steps program she was forced to get honest. After this, the group continued discussing different degrees of lying, and

individuals slowly admitted to exceptional situations in which they had "lied." They generally denied having any behaviors possibly perceived as "bad." It seemed like it was too painful for them to examine and admit to any of their own maladaptive behaviors because it might mean looking back at a painful past where they learned these behaviors in order to cope.

On 10/26, a few days after the third session, Jane called to talk about the group and to tell me that she didn't think she was going to return. She felt that people were not talking about what they were in the group for. She felt everyone had been focusing on the problems of living with their alcoholic husbands instead of looking at their childhoods and being raised by alcoholic parents. She felt that people were not being honest about their feelings. I explained that the group was still new and that the members were testing each other out. I encouraged her to give it another trial period because I was pretty sure she had a lot to give and also a lot to receive if she would allow it in. She agreed to return for a few weeks.

Summary of Work:

October 23rd (Third Session)

Paula tried to set an agenda for work, so I reached for elaboration. Paula stated that she had a problem with some of the statements on the worksheet. Ginnette quickly said she had seen this list before in something she's read. I asked Paula if she could talk a little bit about what she was having problems with on the sheet. She said she didn't like the statement about ACOAs lying when it is just as easy as telling the truth. She said she never lied, adding, "I'm so honest I can't stand it." Kate quickly agreed, saying that it's the alcoholic who lies all the time because he's always making excuses for himself. There were nods of agreement as other members joined in the talk of not being "liars." A brief silence. *I missed a chance to reach for the indirect cues—that they were not willing to be honest until they felt safe enough to trust the group.* They still seemed to be checking it out and were afraid to admit responsibility for their own less-than-ideal behavior.

Then Jane said she could see what the worksheet was talking about because she used to lie all the time, until she was 30 years old (24 years ago). She continued to say that it definitely had to do with growing up with an alcoholic parent. She said there was a lot of shame—she would never have friends over because they might find out how things were for her—she would lie about how things were. Brief silence.

I tried to reach for the underlying feelings and to help Jane make a demand for work. In making this intervention, I missed the opportunity to explore what would be so awful about people knowing how bad things were. I was going along with the assumptions—partly from my own background—that you don't think about what it means to keep the secrets, you just do it. I asked Jane what happened then to make her change. She talked about being unhappy in a marriage with an alcoholic until she sought help through counseling and Alanon. She said the steps in Alanon (the 12 steps) made her look at her lies and why she was telling them. At this point I failed to help her get more specific about her thought/feeling. I went with the illusion of work (in part because there was no chance to say anything). The other members got into a discussion of the 12 steps. Kate and Jane talked about how the steps are hard because they make you admit that you've done something wrong. Paula nodded and mentioned the step about making amends—said that because of it she has gotten good at apologizing. The others all nodded and smiled in agreement as Paula continued to tell a couple of stories to illustrate how she always "swallows her pride" and apologizes. She said that people always tell her that she's too honest.

I tried to help identify obstacles to communication. I commented that everyone seemed to get defensive about the idea of lying. I said I wondered what "lying" means to everybody—that maybe it means different things for different people. Diane looked at me and said that she used to have to lie for self-protection. I asked if she could say something more about that. She said that while growing up her father used to get crazy and violent about things, so if she'd done something she thought he wouldn't like she would lie to protect herself and her siblings. Kate and Ginnette agreed about self-protection lies. Others began sharing experiences of being a child and having to protect oneself—quick examples and lots of identification with each other. The focus evolved again to their alcoholic husbands and reasons why their husbands lied.

I tried to bring them back closer to their own feelings. I commented that it seemed difficult keeping the focus on themselves and their behavior. Then Diane admitted that now she find herself telling "little white lies" when she is trying to get herself or others out of a situation. People agreed about telling these kinds of lies and talked about feeling guilty after having told them. Paula and Kate shared stories about enabling by lying to cover for their husbands when they were drunk. Jane, who had been frowning, stated disbelief that Paula is in Susan's group (a family group offered at the same agency) and gets away with behavior like that. She chuckled rather smugly and said that she herself never would have gotten away with that ten years ago. I had been feeling annoyed with everyone's goody-goodiness and their unwillingness to "fess up." Then I felt angry at Jane for acting so smug and righteous. I did not share my feelings, but in looking back, I see where it might have been helpful if I had been more open about them.

October 30th (Fourth Session)

The theme of this session seems to still be trust. The members are still trying to get to know me and each other. Throughout the session they talk about what it means to look or feel normal, and they worry about making mistakes. They seem to be wondering how they can express themselves here and feel safe.

I attempted to let the group answer Paula's demand for work. Paula brought up the phrase about "guessing at what normal is." She seemed angry and stated that she thinks she's normal. She said it makes her mad when "they" are made to sound like they all have the same problems. Kate said that she's just the opposite—that she likes reading it because it lets her know that she's not the only one who experiences these things, but that she also knows that they may not all apply to her. Jane agreed about how it makes her feel that she's not alone. Then she talked about this book being written about the experiences of many adult children and their issues—everything doesn't necessarily apply to everyone. Kate said that she does guess at what is normal, in a way—said she watches how other people do things and then tries to do what they do.

I attempted to encourage Kate to elaborate by validating what she was saying. I also tried to connect the content to the purpose of the group, but Kate was already doing it. Instead, I cut her off and sent the discussion in another direction. I commented that we usually learn behavior by watching others. If we didn't learn it from our parents, we usually learn it by watching others' behavior that we think works. Ginnette said that she worries about it because she is afraid of repeating her parents' mistakes since she doesn't know any other way. Paula shared some of her worries that because of her husband's drinking she did terrible things to her sons while raising them. I missed the chance to reach for their underlying feelings and fears and to help put them into words. I let the group continue with the illusion of work. Kate and Diane both identified with these fears about raising their children. Kate and Paula began talking about their husbands—how they had met them, when they came to realize they were alcoholics, and how they haven't been able to leave them. The members also talked about how their kids' fathers are not very available, but how, in the long run, it's probably better than being around and drunk.

I let my feelings of annoyance at the women's denial of their own faults hinder my ability to make interventions. I was unable to share my feelings openly in a way that could have been useful to the group, so I stayed silent. Kate and Paula continued to lead the group in discussion of the difficulties in living with their husbands.

November 6th (Fifth Session)

I attempted to allow the members to establish a structure and, at the same time, reach for feelings about the work to be done. When the session began, there was some small talk about the election. Then people got quiet, looking around at each other and at me expectantly. Paula commented that our "starter" isn't here. (Diane usually gives the group a cue to start with.) I said I wondered what someone else would say if they were to start the group. People seemed puzzled and asked what I meant. I asked what they would like to say—how they would like to start us off. Jane said she had an idea. She said she'd been thinking about last week's group and she'd like to relate people's troubles in their lives now to troubles when they were growing up. Kate said that she didn't have anything bad happen as a child. I reached for elaboration from Jane. Jane said that since this is an ACOA group, she would like to hear people talk about experiences as children and how those experiences affect us now. She said that she realized this week that there was a similar pattern between her mother's behavior while drinking and her ex-husband's. Silence.

I tried to connect what she had said to the rest of the members. I asked if anyone could see similarities between her husband's and parents' drinking. Ginnette began talking about how her father's drinking had affected her self-esteem, although it is better now. Said she wasn't sure why—"It's not like I was physically abused or anything—my parents never hit me...they told me I was stupid all the time." I tried to support her in a taboo area and tried to get the group to stay with the feelings around this experience. I recognized that emotional abuse can be just as painful and longer lasting than physical abuse. Diane talked about how she also used to have low self-esteem because of things at home, but that it's higher now. I asked what kinds of things happened at home.

Diane talked about her father's violent behavior while drunk and his complete emotional absence when sober. Diane told stories very animatedly and said that she knows it's weird, but that she used to feel excitement around these awful events. She said humor was the way to deal with the emotional and physical abuse. Ginnette said that she just felt shame and wanted to be invisible to everyone. Diane said she didn't—she felt like the commotion her family caused was a form of attention and any she could get was okay. She said it's sort of like, "Look at me! Look at me!" Silence.

I tried to reach for a sense of mutuality. I asked if anyone else remembered what it felt like when the alcoholic was drinking or when either parent was being abusive. Paula spoke up by saying she didn't really remember her childhood, but she began unfolding some of her childhood story anyway. Said she used to idolize her mother and she hardly knew her father because he was more like a boarder than anything. Told about her mother going out to get drunk then returning, sick and crying, wanting to tell all her troubles to young Paula. Paula said she hated it but she'd listened because she loved her mother. She talked about her father and how he didn't speak to anyone in the house—he would just stay out drinking until he came stumbling home and went to his room where he lived off canned food.

As we have seen so often in the examples in this book, the worker's capacity to share her own feelings helps the group members deepen their work. In the next excerpt, the worker also demonstrates being able to "see" the group and monitor its emotional development, while simultaneously tracking the involvement of individual members. The worker notes that Jane "looks" as if she is ready to say something and reaches out to Jane to help her into the conversation.

I shared my feelings and tried to reach for Paula's underlying feelings. I said that this is really painful to hear. It must have been a lot of pain for a child to carry—never having a father who would recognize her and wanting so much to have his attention; having to take care of her mother's physical and emotional needs. Paula responded that she'd never really thought of it as sad or painful—that's just the way it was. I had noticed that Jane looked like she'd been wanting to say something, so I commented on that. Jane said she could relate to what Paula had said about not talking or questioning anything at home. She said at her house it was like having an arm cut off and no one saying anything.

I failed to acknowledge the intense pain in her powerful statement. It could have been an opportunity to say more about what it felt like rather than explaining what her situation looked like. Jane went on to talk about never having known her father and never being able to ask her mother any questions about him. She described her mother's reaction when she read about his death in the newspaper—all the anger and hurt came out. I said that it sounds like she has had to carry her mother's anger and shame for a long time.

Near the end of the session, Diane brought up that she had been planning to call her mother tonight and break three months of silence. But she said now she feels too angry. Said she feels a lot of anger at the mothers who weren't drunk but who sat there and watched the kids suffer. We were almost at the end of the session, so I wanted to validate Diane's anger and to acknowledge the heavy sharing of feelings that had gone on. I summed up the things that were shared. I said that I appreciated that people could be so honest tonight and bring up such painful memories. I said that there had been a lot of talk about childhood abuse and neglect. I said there had also been some minimizing of the neglect and I just wanted to point out that it is abusive to a child when her needs—emotional and physical—aren't met. I said to Diane that she had shared experiences of having been hurt so I wasn't surprised that she was feeling angry. The members continued talking until I told them we had to clear the room for the next group.

November 13th (Sixth Session)

Ginnette said that she wanted to discuss intimacy and affection—that it had been on her mind. She said it's difficult to show affection towards anyone except her kids and that she has a hard time receiving it. Paula said she could relate to that. She cried as she told about the absence of intimacy and affection in her marriage—said there's nothing left between her and her husband. She said she's really been thinking about it and almost didn't come tonight because she had been depressed. She talked about an argument with her husband over the weekend. Talked about how his inability to show affection toward her has been a disappointment from the beginning. Silence. People tried to comfort Paula by assuring her that he is acting this way because she is making positive changes without him.

I brought them back to Ginnette's demand for work. I asked how others felt about intimacy in their lives. There was much discussion about lack of affection and intimacy growing up and now with spouses. Members talked about what it means to love someone and to say and show it. Throughout the bulk of the session I kept trying to help them get from general answers/talk to specific memories and feelings. I asked what it means to say or think that you love someone. They asked what I meant. I tried to clarify by asking how it feels to love. Paula said, "Well, I always thought it meant sex." People discussed their frequent confusion between sex and love. Kate related the inability to achieve intimacy after growing up without it. I reached back to her comment and put it out to the group. If you grew up "in the gutter" and never experienced intimacy, could you experience it now? Jane said yes, and Paula asked for a definition of intimacy.

In a beautiful example of synthesizing content and process, the worker asks the group members to relate their conversation about intimacy in their lives to the intimacy in the group. The group is a microcosm of their world of relationships, and if they can face their fears of intimacy with each other, they increase their chances of taking risks with significant others in their lives.

After a lengthy conversation about the definition of intimacy, I realized there was a lot of indirect communication. I pointed it out to the group and related it specifically to what was happening in the group. I said that I was hearing several words mentioned around intimacy—vulnerability, trust, no judgment. Kate mentioned fear that people wouldn't understand. I said I wanted to make an observation. I was wondering if people have been talking all this time about not getting intimacy and not having their needs met because they're really afraid that they won't have them met here and they won't be able to trust each other or that they will make themselves vulnerable and be judged. Kate immediately said she was glad I had brought that up because something had happened two weeks ago that had made her very uncomfortable. Said she was so worried about coming last week that she convinced herself that she was sick. She told the group that she had felt judged by a few people about something she had shared about herself. The members all talked about it, and Kate was given positive feedback about her courage to bring it up.

Current Status of the Problem:

The group has begun to deal with some sensitive issues in a much more open, honest way. They continue to externalize problems to focus on safer issues, like their husbands. However, they are beginning to examine the role their own behavior plays in perpetuating the difficulties in their lives. For example, in the most recent session I pointed out the connection between the way they communicate in the group and their frustration with never having their needs met "out there." They were able to start talking about it. They focused first on the lack of communication they get from their husbands, but with direction they looked at the patterns of communicating in their families of origin. Finally, they were able to start looking at their own communication skills and how that affects relationships.

At this point in the group—after eight sessions—the members seem to have developed some trust and are ready to do more work. With this population of women ACOAs, it will always be a challenge to keep up a culture for work because of their eagerness to agree and to avoid conflict. As the group leader I am feeling more comfortable with my role. I feel more willing to take risks to challenge them to work.

Strategies for Intervention:

1. To stick to the group purpose and to continue to make a demand for work.

2. To continue reaching for underlying feelings and pushing the members to recognize them.

3. To work on recognizing projective identification and using it to express my own feelings to enhance the work of the group.

4. To point out patterns of avoidance or "flight" and help the group identify obstacles to their communication.

The illustration points out how crucial it is for the worker to play an active role in pointing out what appears to be happening in the group. If the worker had shared her own feelings earlier, the group process would have been speeded up. The other striking observation is how often the second client, the group, responded with silence at crucial moments in the conversation. Reaching inside of the silences and exploring them might have been another way for the worker to move the group more quickly into its work. The worker's astuteness about how the group process related to the content of their work helped her develop more effective strategies.

In the example that follows, the group members are currently living with the addicted partner and in most cases are experiencing physical or emotional abuse. The example also introduces the variation on the theme introduced by the open-ended nature of the group. We clearly see the impact of members' being at different stages in the group process (beginning, middle, and end/transition) and the importance of the group leader's sensitivity to the associated issues. A second issue is the fact that group members are at different stages in dealing with their problems: denial, passive acceptance, and for some, the "taking action" stage that means ending the abusive relationship. It is important for the group leaders to acknowledge and respect the struggle for each member and to create a safe place for all of the women. Finally, a third element nicely illustrated in this group is the issue of co-leadership with one's supervisor. Once again, we see a sensitive handling of this dynamic by the student and a wonderful openness by the supervisor to the student's ideas and suggestions.

A Women's Open-Ended Codependent Group

Type of Group: Support and education group for women who are "codependent." The group is ongoing (has been meeting approximately six years) and open-ended. Some members have been in the group since it began. The leader of the group is my supervisor. She asked if I would like to co-lead the group as part of my field work. This is the first time my supervisor has ever co-led a group.

Age Range of Members: From 20 to 63 years

Gender, Ethnic, or Racial Information: All Caucasian: Italian, Portuguese, Greek, Irish, French-Canadian, Polish. Most members are Catholic.

Dates Covered in Record: From 10/6 to 11/17

Group Task: Structure-maintenance

1. *Problem:* The women in the group almost constantly focus on their partners' behaviors and feelings instead of on their own. Sometimes they discuss their reactions to their partners' behaviors. When feedback is given from one member to another, it is usually advice on how the person can "fix" her partner. The members are resistant in exploring who they are as individuals, what their individual goals are (separate from their partners'), and awareness of their own feelings. The contract aims to move the focus of the work off of the partners and onto group members.

2. *How the Problem Came to My Attention:* In my first meeting, members talked about how supported they felt by other women in the group, and they described the group as special time for themselves. Yet after a few meetings, I realized that little time was spent on their feelings. Whenever either leader tried to shift the focus away from partners and onto exploration of members' feelings, the subject was quickly changed. Members became quiet, and it seemed, full of shame. They either defended their partners or blamed themselves. They seemed secure in talking about their husbands' addictions. But it was clear to me that they had deep issues of insecurity and low self-esteem. They said things like, "But I'm always nagging him," or "I don't want to take up too much time talking tonight." I felt it was important to try to help them get at their root feelings of worthlessness.

3. *Summary of the Work with Process Excerpts:*

In my first session with the group, I did not say much and basically observed. But at the second meeting, I knew if I did not speak up, I would be going along with a norm that implied "the student is an observer." The group got started, and as usual, each woman took her turn to speak. By the time the third woman got into her story, I felt ready to make an intervention.

Laura spoke at length about her husband, who is a compulsive gambler. She was highly agitated as she talked about how he gambles away his paycheck each week. She shared with the group how he had "pushed her onto the floor" during an argument over the weekend. This was the first time there had ever been any aggressive physical contact between them. She expressed concern about this incident. She said she had made a contract with herself that if he ever got physical with her, "that would be it, he would be out." She said she knew the statistics, that if it happened once, it was bound to happen again.

Suddenly, Celia (the scapegoat) could not contain herself any longer. Before my supervisor had a chance to respond, Celia jumped in. She said, "Well, is he out? Did you keep your contract, or is he still living with you?" Laura responded with her voice trailing off. "No, he's not out. He's still living at home." She seemed ashamed to have to admit it.

I knew it was my time to jump in as well. I said, "Celia, it was great that you could challenge Laura on such a hard subject, as I'm sure it was really hard for you, Laura, to talk about such an upsetting incident with the group." I was validating Celia's confrontation of Laura. My intervention said it was okay for members to respond to other members, that they did not have to get feedback from the designated leader only. I was trying to alter the structure and norms of the group.

There was a real shift in the room. Celia beamed a large smile, while other members glanced around at one another and at my supervisor. I did not look at my supervisor because I was focused on what I was doing. Laura looked tentatively at me and then continued her discussion with Celia. Laura said, "I know I should have kicked his ass out right then and there, but I didn't. Instead I got up and pushed him back." Celia responded to Laura, "I know it's hard to keep to your bottom line. Believe me, I've broken mine many times...like when...."

The discussion continued, and I felt great! For the rest of the session, members were more actively engaged with each other. There seemed to be a great relief that they could now talk to one another instead of just to the leader. At the end of the session, I made a process observation to the group. I commented on what a great job they were doing in addressing each other's problems.

In the next meeting, the members engaged in significantly more interaction. The taboo of physical violence had been broken the week before and now Mary, the most timid member of the group, spoke up. She talked about an emotional/physical abuse situation that had taken place during the middle of the night, while she was in bed with her husband. Mary said, "He had been drinking all day and into the night. I just kept my distance from him most of the day and that night too. A couple of times he snapped at me and I just ignored it. Then, of course, it was time for bed and I got in. I knew he was still very drunk." Mary is quite light-skinned and I could see the fear creep over her in the form of deep, red blotches on her neck.

She said he passed out and she eventually fell asleep. Then, at around 3:30 A.M., he woke up and started calling her names. She said she was half asleep, and said some things she probably shouldn't have. Then the next thing she knew, he had backed her up against the bedroom wall and he had his fist placed ever so gently under her chin. She kept saying over and over, "He never hit me, he just held his fist under my chin." She made a fist and mimicked for the group what it was like.

My supervisor led a discussion around what constitutes physical abuse and tried to broaden Mary's and the group's definition of abuse. Other members jumped into the discussion, and they all intellectualized on the true meaning of physical abuse and domestic violence. There was a pause, and I caught Mary's eye. "Were you scared?" I asked gently. A hush fell over the room. Mary's eyes welled up with tears, and her face flushed bright red. "Yes," she said, "I was scared."

I reached for the underlying feeling of fear that I knew Mary must have felt at that moment. I was sure the others had felt this fear with their partners and could relate to Mary's feeling. It was the first time I had ever heard anyone talk about any feeling in the group. I was pleased that we were getting at what the work was about, focusing on the members and their feelings.

Mary went on to describe her situation as "not even having a marriage." She was strong in her conviction that because he really didn't hit her, it wasn't physical abuse. But she commented several times that she "could no longer go on living this way." Celia challenged Mary on her bottom line and expressed concern for Mary's safety.

After the meeting, my supervisor told me it was excellent that I could get at Mary's feelings. She said she had been alone with the group for so long that sometimes she gets caught up with them. She encouraged me to continue the "feelings work" with the group.

Betsy, also a timid woman, had lived for twenty years with an abusive alcoholic husband. He was also sex-addicted and had openly cheated on Betsy throughout their marriage. They have two sons together, a 17-year-old and a two-year-old. A year ago (she's been in the group since it began), Betsy had found the courage to ask for a separation from him because she had found him in their bed with another woman. He begged her for forgiveness, and eventually she took him back. Then one night, he came home violently drunk, and he raped her.

Betsy is now filing for divorce. She has a restraining order on her husband, although he has visitation rights to the children. Somehow, Betsy got caught up in the oppression of the legal system and agreed to supervise her husband's visits with their young son. She says there was all kinds of pressure from different lawyers and DSS and she felt she had no other choice. Part of me believes she truly felt this way, and another part of me believes that at an unconscious level, she's not quite ready to let go of him.

Betsy talked about seeing her husband during one of the supervised visits. She said, "It's really bothering me that I have to see him at those visits with Matt. He keeps on talkin' about it, you know, that night. I ain't listenin' to him, I ain't! I know what he did to me that night! He keeps on trying to tell me it didn't happen, but I know what happened! Then I did something stupid. I'm so stupid. It just slipped out at the end of the day and it was stupid."

My supervisor said, "What, Betsy, what did you do that you feel was stupid? Even though we all know you're not stupid, you're smart." Betsy looked hesitant, and then in a whisper she said, "I told him I loved him. I said, 'I love you, Tim.'" She lowered her head, and there was a long pause. I said, "Betsy, it's only natural to feel that way. You did live with him for 20 years and have two boys with him. Of course you still love him. But that doesn't mean you can still live with him." She looked at me. Then I added, "I'll bet you're feeling very lonely these days." Betsy began to cry, "I am lonely. It's lonely in that big house with just me and Matt. And I'm startin' to have more nightmares about that night."

I wanted to get at Betsy's feelings of grief and loss. She seemed relieved as she let it all out. The other members were silent and afraid. All this expression of buried feelings was new behavior for the group. Betsy is also living the other members' worst fears. She is leaving her husband this time, and feeling the pain of what it means to let go and say goodbye. Even though it's an unhealthy relationship, it is indeed the only "love" she's ever known.

The group is open-ended, so when a long-term member terminates, a new member is added to the group. In this last excerpt, I will discuss the group's process and structure around saying good-bye to an old member and saying hello to a new member. In this particular session, it was Faith's last meeting and Donna's first.

Faith spoke at length about how supportive the group has been for her and how much she will miss all the members. She said she would like to continue phone contact with a few people she had gotten close to. She reported many changes in herself and realized that she had reached the goals she had set for herself when she started the group, especially getting her driver's license. She acknowledged that her husband would never stop drinking and that she had come to terms with that fact. She also knew she was not ready to leave him.

The group focus was clearly on Faith and her leaving. Donna sat quietly and listened. She seemed nervous and self-conscious and for good reason. Finally, my supervisor turned the attention to Donna. She introduced her and then asked all members to introduce themselves and tell Donna something about their situations.

This rang an old bell for me as this was the same process that was used when I first entered the group. I knew how uncomfortable the members and I had felt about doing introductions this way. There was a long silence. I knew it was time to speak up, "It must be hard for people to reveal personal things to someone they don't know. Maybe you could just share something you feel comfortable about with Donna?"

Everyone smiled and breathed a sigh of relief. I was trying to take the pressure off of them by recognizing how hard it is to share personal information with a stranger. I was also trying to change the group culture that my supervisor had set up around introductions. Several women spoke about how hard it is for them to speak in groups. They also tended to share more positive things about themselves than when they introduced themselves to me. I hoped this was a beginning change that would continue when new members entered the group.

I think a termination should be done separately, without a new member present. I had so many mixed feelings with trying to say good-bye to Faith and hello to Donna. I'm sure the members also had lots of confusing feelings. Separation is a big issue for the women in the group. They need time to really feel the loss of a respected member. I would recommend a couple of sessions after the member left to discuss what it is like without her before a new member begins. This process would be beneficial for new, terminating, and current members.

4. *Where the Problem Stands Now:*

The women in the group are still focused on their partners' behaviors and feelings, though not quite as much. They have made progress in allowing themselves to experience more of their own feelings. This is typically done via the context of the relationship with their partner. This seems only natural as they take small steps in their emotional movement away from their partners.

The most significant change the group has made is in its structure and maintenance. The members have truly shifted from one-on-one therapy with the leader, to dynamic group work. There is considerably more interaction amongst members. This interaction is no longer in the form of one-on-one advice-giving on how to "fix" partners. Instead, it takes the form of open-ended questioning of other members. There also seems to be more genuine caring for other members.

The group is avoiding their deepest fear of abandonment and the loneliness that accompanies it. Although one member is beginning to openly work on it, the other women seem to communicate a "that's not me" attitude. They are dancing around the physical abuse issue, and I also believe that their feelings of worthlessness result from childhood sexual abuse. Perhaps this isn't the right forum for those issues to be worked on, but at some point, they need to be faced.

5. *Specific Next Steps:*

1. It is important that the women continue to focus on themselves and their feelings. I plan to push for feelings and make it a norm in the group to name them and express them. I think the group needs continual encouragement in the area of confronting each other. They need to see this skill modeled.

2. The group could use some practical coping techniques. They need behavioral strategies on relaxation and distancing. They need skill building around communicating, problem solving, and decision making. They need to learn how to set goals and take steps to achieve them. Since the group is on-going, it will continue after I'm gone. Still, I need to remind the group that I'll be leaving in May.

While many of the principles of leading a group for significant others are similar across populations, there are significant differences as well. For example, in the adult groups just presented, the members' "flight" was subtle and hard to immediately recognize. In the children's group described below, the acting out is more direct. These less-verbal children will need help in learning to articulate their feelings rather than acting them out. The worker begins directly with a recognition of the issue of substance-abusing parents but does not provide examples or "handles for work" that would help the members connect to purpose in a more solid manner. When acting out starts, the worker first relates to the underlying feelings of the group members. When the behavior escalates, the worker shifts to the "teacher/police" role rather than simultaneously setting limits and connecting to purpose. Her analysis of her own work reveals an astuteness and honesty about the impact of her own stress and anxiety that will be helpful in her continued development.

Children of Substance Abusers

Support and Stabilization Group

Members: seven females, aged 9–13; four African-American, two Caucasian, one Hispanic; lower-income; parents are substance abusers

Dates of Service: 10/7 to 11/11

Group Task: Structure and maintenance

1. *Problem:* The problem is getting the girls to talk about their issues and feelings. This will require establishing a group culture that is a supportive environment. There are a lot of feelings and issues in this group, but talking about them is hard. Some of the girls are not even sure how to talk about them, so the feelings get acted out. Other times, issues seem to get expressed indirectly, and they have to be recognized and acknowledged. Part of this task is working on the relationship of the girls to the group worker. As children of substance abusers it will be hard for them to trust adults, but there will also be a need to be kept safe and be taken care of. Whatever coping mechanisms have been used in the family will be brought out in the group. Denial, stony silence, parentification, clowning, and others can all be explored.

2. *How the Problem Came to My Attention:* The problem was demonstrated in early sessions by members engaging in horseplay, twirling around in swivel chairs, throwing popcorn, and other acting-out behaviors when the workers clarified the purpose of the group. When asked what they would like to do in the group, one member responded, "I want to run up and down the halls!" Three other members, who know each other outside of the group, consistently gossiped among themselves. At times when a sustained conversation did get going, members seemed to try to outdo each other in their badness, toughness, or misconduct.

3. *Summary of the Work:*

(First Session) I arrived with three of the girls on time, but my coworker did not arrive with three other girls (one was absent) until 45 minutes later. During our wait, the girls began to horseplay. This suddenly became physical and then there were Nerf™ balls flying around the room. Certainly this reflected their anxiety at being in a new place with new people and no structure. I attempted to help them refocus and get the girls interested in some art work in order to provide some structure. However, I was feeling anxious at the absence of my coworker and her carload of girls, and so were the girls that were in the group room with me. With every sound in the hallway, one of the girls would jump up to run to see, "Is it them?" I asked the girls what they would like to do in the group and got answers like "Let's run up and down the halls." "Let's bring in some boys." It was an uncomfortable situation in that I really did not feel like I could start without the rest of the group. I was growing impatient and con-

cerned in the wait and the children were right with me! I felt like the situation was slipping out of my control, and as it slipped the children got more out of control. Glue got spilt on the table. The Nerf™ balls were out again.

Finally, I did what I probably should have done about a half hour earlier. I started the group, and I reached for their feelings about the situation. I acknowledged to the girls, "This feels really odd to start without the others. It must feel sort of odd for you too. I said there was going to be another counselor here and 3 other girls, and they are not here." Donna answered, "I gave up on them." I empathized, "I guess I can understand that. If someone does not do what they say they are going to do, how can you trust them?" What I did not consider at the time was that I was the one that had told her that they would be at the group. I was the one that had misled her! The conversation was then deflected by Eddy. She had been in a group the year before. She suggested that we go around the room, say our names and how old we were. I went right along with this. In retrospect, it is interesting how skillfully Eddy brought out the group mentality of not talking about issues! As we went around the room, it felt cozy and comfortable as we munched on popcorn.

It was just as we finished this go-around that the other members walked in. The energy level went back up as the giggling and silliness began again. As the coworker explained why she was late, the children were teasing Deb about her hair. I felt uncomfortable with the teasing, but I did not express this to the group. Instead I began contracting with the group. While I presented to the group the purpose of the group, the silliness continued. I felt myself getting angry as the girls spun around in the swivel chairs. I recognized that this was resistance and tried to make the connection for the children between their feelings and their actions. This brought from Eddy the comment that her mother still was using drugs. However, when asked by the other children, she retreated from saying more about her mother. I supported Eddy by acknowledging that it is difficult to talk about personal issues in a new group. The group was then distracted again by Donna, who took on a clown role. My anger was more on the surface and I attended to some structure maintenance and suggested we get down some rules! Ann agreed to write down the rules, and then we put them up on the bulletin board. My coworker suggested that we close the group by "being serious" and going around the room and saying one thing that we liked about ourselves. Donna was once again quite silly during this process and kept the girls laughing.

By the end of the group, I was sure that I never wanted to go back. I had wanted to "do a group." But I had forgotten all the feelings and demands that would be involved. I am sure that the girls probably felt the same way. But they did all come back.

(Second Session) It felt like a new group. It felt so rewarding to have six out of seven girls on time and all in our seats at starting time. I began by recontracting. This time I tried to be more specific about what some of the potential issues were for this group. I then asked for feedback. Joan began talking with Ann about a boy. My coworker suggested to them that talking about boys was not an issue for this group. I felt uncomfortable with this, but did not address it directly with my coworker. I think that she might have been concerned about the pairing that was going on between these two, but I wondered if it was a relevant issue that the girls were expressing indirectly. I tried to reframe the issue and I asked Ann and Joan, "How do issues around boys get worked out with your parents? Is it a problem?" Ann replied, "Yes! I get into trouble all the time with my mom about boys."

The girls offered stories about problems that they have with their parents about going out with friends. This then moved into issues with violence in their community and the use of drugs among peers. My coworker and I both asked questions to get the girls to elaborate. Donna, who had begun to get wound up, withdrew and began to play with a doll house in a corner. This felt fine to me. I did not want to deal with her resistance and disruptive behavior. It just felt fine to me to be chatting away, but as the group went on I realized that we were talking about all these serious topics, but no one was really talking about how it felt. We were all a bit removed, just as Donna was. Deb was talking about a boy who was angry at her and who carried a knife. I realized how scary this sounded and reached for Deb's feeling about this. I said, "That sounds sort of scary to me. Does it worry you?" Deb's response was abrupt and rough as she denied any such feelings. I wondered whether it was hard for her to admit feeling scared in this group of peers, and I asked her what she did feel about the situation with this boy. When I said this, Donna, who had been playing quietly with the playhouse, sent a wooden figure sailing through the air, that just missed my head! I was not happy about this. The other members then let their anger show! It was focused on scapegoating Donna. Joan, Ann, and Deb, led by Tina, began to ask why Donna was not sitting with the rest of the group: "What is wrong with her?" With this flight/fight, we never got back to feelings about living with violence. I asked Donna to come back and join us for the activity. We drew trees and told stories about them.

In this group a lot was said, but it was said indirectly or only partially, without the feelings. Even the pictures and stories were sidestepping sensitive issues. It felt like we were walking on eggshells.

(Third Session) All members were present for the first time. We began the group by making sure that the members all knew a bit about each other. They shared information on which schools they attended, their ages, and where they lived. This was spontaneous among the girls. The data sharing seemed to help them get to know each other. I wanted to reorient the girls back to the purpose of the group, so I reviewed the contract and reached for feedback. This seemed particularly relevant as there was a new member in the group. It seemed like the room was suddenly flooded with problems. Each of the girls reported something that had happened that had upset them. Everyone had something that was pertinent and pressing. It did not seem like the girls were listening to each other, but were looking to my coworker and me for help. I felt overwhelmed by the dependency in the group. These girls must also have been feeling overwhelmed by all their own individual needs. Now that they were talking about issues, I felt flooded, did not know where to begin to proceed, and felt totally inadequate! I shared my feelings with the group and encouraged them to consider mutual aid. I said, "Wow, there are so many strong feelings here today with all that is going on for everyone. Does anyone have something that they would like to say to somebody to help them with their problem?"

I almost felt that when I let them know they were talking about relevant issues, they decided very quickly to not talk about these problems anymore. The group culture shifted here from dependency to fight/flight. The group worked together, not in mutual aid, but in mutual avoidance. Lauren got into Deb's space, and a bout of pushing began. The group centered on talking to Donna about the cast that she had on her leg. It allowed them each to talk about physical injuries from their past, but we were well clear of the painful events they had related earlier. Tina, who emerged as a leader in the group, may also have been feeling the leftover feelings. She suggested,

"Can we draw or something?" Drawing seems to be a safe way for these girls to express their feelings. My coworker and I presented the activity, which was to make masks. It turned out to be a very messy activity with lots of arguing about sharing supplies of glitter, feathers, stickers, etc. In retrospect, this process reflected the earlier stage of this group session, when individual needs were emphasized and members vied for the workers' attention.

The girls took turns sharing about their work, and their stories revealed something about their inner lives. The glitter that we used had run, so all of the masks appeared to be crying. Each girl told a story about why her mask was crying. I tried again to point out this common ground from the stories that they told and remarked that there were a lot of feelings in the room. The girls responded with a bit of silliness that was revealing. Starting with Tina, a leader in the group, the girls rattled off a list of feelings that they were experiencing, such as "happy," "sad," "angry," "silly," "tired," "wild," "funny," "bad."

It was time to end the group. The room was swirling with all these emotions. The room was a mess from snack and our project with globs of glitter drying. Much had been shared in the group, but it seemed predominantly a dependent culture.

(Fourth Session) Because of traffic, I arrived late with four of the girls to this meeting. When I say down in the group room, my coworker commented, "I think you sat down in a good place. There is a lot of energy over there." I had sat down between Ann and Joan. Joan began to talk about having been suspended from school. She said a number of things under her breath to Tina. Donna told a silly story and made lots of faces about getting suspended from her school. Donna made fun of Deb's hair. Eddy stood beside her chair and jumped up and down several times. Ann sat beside me with a face of stone. First, I pointed out the flight, hoping to give the girls an opportunity to comment on the uncomfortable energy. I said, "This reminds me of the first group when everyone was so nervous. What is going on?" This seemed to only get the resistance going stronger. My coworker began to try to get the girls focused by asking questions about their families and substance abuse. The whole thing did not feel right to me. It was apparent that Tina and Joan were ignoring Ann. I shared my feelings, saying that I was very uncomfortable. I suggested that if there was a conflict it could be talked about. Tina then began to tell the story, but it was vague and used third-person pronouns as if the people involved were not in the room. I asked her to get more specific. She then told more of the story. It was about a fight between Ann and Tina and Joan. I asked Ann and Joan if they had any comments. These two exchanged some brief, fierce words. There was a brief silence. Then Deb said, "Can I talk about my fight with my mother now?" It felt unsure where to go at this point. This seemed like flight rather than addressing the conflict that was presented. But Deb wanted to talk about her conflict with her mother. I put it before the group by asking, "Does anyone have anything they want to say about this conflict before we go on?" No one wanted to say anything. Though I still felt unsettled, Deb began her story. There were a lot of interruptions and jokes during her story. Deb also was laughing. My coworker intervened and reminded the group about the rule of not interrupting, and she suggested we stay focused on family issues. Lauren responded by saying, "I guess that no one here has any problems with their families."

I was feeling frustrated at this point, and felt like giving a push. I challenged the girls to work by saying that I thought they all had problems with their families. There was a silence, and then Eddy told the group that her family might get their phone service cut off. The group asked Eddy questions to get her story. I reached for Eddy's feelings, which she was able to share. I expressed the common theme of having money problems, and asked the other members if they had similar experiences. Other members shared stories. This felt like a good exchange. Eddy expressed her wish to have a money tree, and the other members were supportive in response to her needs. But Ann was withdrawn, and I felt uncomfortable. While Eddy's input was sincere, I could see how she was trying to save the group here, both by distracting the members from the conflict in the room and placating me (the authority) in my demand for work.

During our art activity, I raised again my concerns about the conflict in the group. I was feeling very uncomfortable with Ann's withdrawn posture and her not participating in the group. I expressed my feelings and asked the group members how they felt. The other members were not admitting to feeling as I felt. The group ended without addressing the conflict in the group, or how the group felt about the conflict.

(Fifth Session) Only three members were present at this group. One member was absent because of the Veterans' Day holiday, but Tina, Ann, and Joan were certainly absent because of the conflict from last week. What happened among the three members present was indicative of the struggle in the group for the survival of the group. We talked a lot about the purpose of the group. Eddy, the placater, stated several times that she wanted to talk about her family problems, and that it helped her to feel better to talk in the group. Deb, on the other hand, made frequent references to the missing girls, and took the position that she wanted to be like them and just talk about boys. I tried to acknowledge Deb's concerns. However, it seemed that regardless of what I said, she felt the group was "a waste of time." I was feeling very much like a failure and was wondering if the other girls would come back. Another part of me was able to see that Deb was pushing me, and that she was also feeling abandoned by the other three girls. I reminded her of the contract and the purpose of the group. She told me that she did not like the faces that I made or all the positive comments that I made to the members.

(Sixth Session) All members, except for Ann, were present. As the other members talked about their report cards, Donna began to antagonize the others. She stuck her foot in Deb's face, and she held on to Eddy's chair so that she could not swivel. Donna's behaviors were irritating me. And from the way my coworker and the other group members looked, they were also irritated. The group also seemed unfocused. Tina talked about her argument with Ann, but I did not feel that anyone was listening as the attention was focused on Donna's acting out. She had begun to tear apart some cards and then was throwing them on the floor. I confronted Donna. I asked her, "What is going on with you today? It seems like something is bothering you." Donna shrugged her shoulders, and then Joan said, "She is angry about something. That is how I act when I get angry." This seemed like a golden moment for me. Joan seemed to be acknowledging her own experience of pain and offering understanding to Donna. I asked Donna if she was feeling angry. Donna shrugged and stared hard at the card in her hand. Lauren asked, "Did something happen?" Donna still did not respond, and the group drifted on to other topics. I was not sure how to get Donna to tell the group what was bothering her. She continued to act it out. She continued to pick quarrels with Deb and Eddy. She got into a pushing match with Lauren. The group seemed to be dominated by this behavior. I was feeling angry, frustrated, and distracted from what was being talked about as Donna seemed to demand my attention. I felt that the group felt stressed because of Donna's

aggression, and several complained of stomachaches. There seemed to be a lot of needs in the group, but no one was really saying how they felt. I tried to pull the group together. I asked how many had stomach aches and when five or six girls raised their hands, I asked why. They were hungry. They wanted snack. What a wonderful reply from a dependency culture!

As we settled down with our snack, Lauren found part of a marijuana cigarette on the floor of the group room. I felt even more stressed at this point. The girls discussed where it could have come from. I could really see their defenses come out as they constructed elaborate stories about someone breaking in and planting the joint there before the group started. I gently challenged this flight, but it was easier to go with the flight than to have to cope with the fact that it likely came from someone in the room. (I had set up the group room before the group and it had not been there, and it is unlikely that anyone else had been in the room.) I asked how the girls were feeling. Tina thought it had been a strange group, while others said they were tired. Deb said that she could not wait to get home. I pointed out the connection between how they were feeling and what was going on in the group. I wondered out loud if it might not feel very safe. The girls agreed. By this time the joint had been discarded and the focus seemed to disintegrate again. Donna tried to leave the room several times and began knocking over buckets of toys. She distracted the group, and in particular she distracted my coworker and me from paying attention to the rest of the group.

In retrospect, there were so many ways the appearance of the joint could have been processed. It seems like a very clear message from someone in the group who is trying to break through the group's taboo on talking about drugs. The dynamic of the group allowed us to not talk about it, just as it might in a family where there is drug abuse. I, too, was caught up in the emotions.

4. *Where the Problem Stands Now:* The problem of not talking about problems and feelings has been played out in many different dramas and conflicts in the group. It became clear that there is a range of issues that interfere with members talking about their feelings and life experiences. Donna is in some ways the most expressive member of the group. But all her feelings come out in acting out that has been frustrating and difficult to contain. Eddy gets it out and says what is bothering her. But there is part of me that notices that she does this to please the group workers. The other girls have reached out to her, but at other times I sense that they resent her. She is breaking the group mentality of avoiding talking about real issues. Deb, like Donna, tends to act out her feelings. Her need to be accepted by the group and its influence on what she talks about is also the most obvious in the group. I have less of a sense of who Lauren is. She lets very little escape that would indicate to the group that something is wrong in her life. Joan and sometimes Tina are better able to express their feelings and talk about what is bothering them. As internal leaders they have reached out to other group members. It is hard to work with such a diverse group. However, the group has worked on sharing information with each other, and Joan was a good support and model for Donna in the last session. The group dynamics are really moving this group along. They seem committed, despite all the strong emotions that get stirred up. It feels like a big job for me to be constantly reflecting back all these strong feelings.

6. *Specific Next Steps:*

1. Revisit episode of finding pot in the room. In particular, the experience for the group, how each member felt, and how we all coped can be explored. This can be related to experiences that the children have had at home.

2. Do outreach to Ann, and try to get her back into the group. Try to continue to process the conflict in the group. My coworker and I have considered trying to meet individually with the three girls involved.

3. Continue to work with Donna about expressing feelings in a less destructive and disruptive fashion.

4. Continue to make connections between what is happening in the group and how members are feeling.

5. Continue to be aware of my feelings in the group.

6. Continue to meet weekly with my coworker to process the group and to clarify our roles and expectations of the group.

7. Be aware of when relevant issues are raised indirectly.

GROUP WORK AND SUBSTANCE ABUSE PREVENTION

Group work is a modality of choice when considering substance abuse prevention approaches. The many ways in which mutual aid can occur in the group—for example, sharing of data, the "all-in-the-same-boat" phenomenon, and the opening of taboo areas—lend themselves to the learning process. As children and youth come to grips with the impact of substance abuse on their own lives and the lives of significant others, as they attempt to cope with the pressures of growing up that may encourage conformity to unhealthy substance abuse norms, and as they experiment and learn to use substances in a controlled and limited manner, having an opportunity to meet with other youth experiencing similar struggles and having an adult who does not judge nor lecture them, may make all the difference in their successful negotiation of this vulnerable stage of life.

Substance Abuse Prevention

The first example, which involves a teen group in a school, raises the not-uncommon issue of confusion on the part of the school and the worker about group purpose. The school authorities have had bad experiences in the past when students have resisted substance abuse educational groups. Instead of considering that the source of resistance may be found in the way in which the group was conducted, the school staff suggests offering a "class." The worker's confusion is evident as she struggles to lead a "class" when she really believes it should be a "therapeutic group." In its strict sense, the term *therapy* implies something is wrong and needs to be fixed or cured. The alternative of offering the teens a group that can help them deal with the impact of substances on themselves and others, a group that can include educational content as well as mutual support and problem solving, is not part of the initial conceptualizing. However, since this is what the clients really need, this purpose becomes evident as the group takes its members where they need to go.

Educational Substance Abuse Group in a High School: Is It a Class or a Group?

Group Purpose: Group members are 15 to 17 years old; one white female and six males (five white and one Puerto Rican); *Dates Covered in Record:* 9/19–10/24

Group Problem: Relationship to the environment

Problem Statement: I am currently leading an educational substance abuse group with adolescents at an alternative high school. My assessment of the group problem involves its hidden agenda or "presented purpose." In the past, the school has had difficulty creating an effective therapeutic group regarding substance abuse issues. Considering the tremendous need for a group of this type, as an alternative, the school has integrated a substance abuse class within its health science curriculum. Every Tuesday morning, during the students' health science period, I "teach" a substance abuse "class."

The school requested that I approach this as a class, not a therapeutic group, in fear of the students becoming defensive and rejecting the topic of substance abuse entirely. I believe that the school's desire for me to approach this group as a "class" hinders the development of a therapeutic group. I believe the "classroom structure" puts a barrier on the sharing of feelings during this class period. This presented purpose of the "class" negatively impacts the contracting of the group, as well as the content, amount, and purpose of the students' participation.

How the Problem Came to My Attention: My first hint of the hidden agenda or presented purpose dilemma surfaced the first day of my field placement, when my supervisor informed me of the "class" I would be "teaching" the next day. At that time, I sensed that "teaching a class" rather than "leading a group" would limit the growth of a therapeutic environment and overall experience. It was not until after teaching a couple of classes that the tremendous impact the classroom theme/structure had on the therapeutic development of the class became apparent. I began to notice that the students (4 out of 7) whom I see individually were beginning to utilize and treat the class as a therapeutic group, while others continued with the "presented purpose." This split confused the purpose of the "class" and exacerbated the problem that the "class" approach had on the therapeutic development of the group as a whole.

Summary of the Work with Process Excerpts:

(First Session) I entered the first "class" with both enthusiasm and uncertainty. It was the second day of my field placement and my first experience teaching a class. I had short notice to prepare a lesson plan and to prepare for my first session. I did not know what to expect. After briefly meeting the students the previous day and hearing an abundance of "horror stories" from the staff, my greatest fear was that the students would misbehave. As I explained to the students what this class was all about, I kept in mind the school's request to approach it as a class, not a group.

"Hi, guys, thanks for settling down so we can get started. As Mrs. Haft explained, I will be working with you every Tuesday at this time. This class will be focused on learning about substance abuse. I want everyone to know that any questions and/or comments you may have are welcomed." I wanted to say something in regards to confidentiality and respect for others, but I felt that was appropriate for a therapeutic group, not a class, and the school would disapprove. The students remained silent. I was relieved that they were being well-behaved, but I was hoping for some sort of interaction or feedback.

"Does anyone have any questions so far?" I questioned. A student asked what we would be learning about. I proceeded to briefly state that we would be covering everything from cigarettes to alcohol to cocaine, and that we would begin with substance abuse in general. Jason laughed as he asked, "Do we get to experiment with some stuff in class?" The other students laughed and watched for my response. As I smiled and shook my head, I responded, "I don't think so, Jay, but we can definitely discuss any experiences anyone has with drugs or alcohol." Jason replied, "Cool. Rock on," as he nodded his head. I smiled and nodded my head as well. I quickly learned that "rock on" was a popular phrase among the students and had several meanings. I was glad a student had interacted. Jason's question allowed me to invite personal experiences into the class.

Now looking back, I realize that would have been the perfect opportunity for me to mention the importance of confidentiality and respect within the class. Although I missed the boat, I realize that if I had not, I would have deviated from the school's request to approach it as a "class," not a "group." We moved from the purpose and agenda of the class to the day's lesson. I provided the students with some information on substance abuse in general, gave them some time to complete a worksheet, and then we went over it together. Overall, the students were well-behaved, fairly attentive, and somewhat enthusiastic. The atmosphere was that of a "class," something I enjoyed, but something to which I would have to get accustomed.

(Second Session) I entered the second "class" with a sense of confidence. I had adequate time to prepare a lesson, a good idea of what would occur, and had begun to develop a relationship with four of the seven students that I had seen individually. "How's everybody doing?" I questioned as I entered the classroom. A few students responded as they settled into their seats. "What are you going to teach us about today?" questioned Derik. "I thought we would start with alcohol," I responded. "Are we going to talk about drunk driving and stuff?" asked Michael. "I hadn't planned on covering drunk driving until next week, but if that is something you want to discuss today, we can. Anytime anyone has something they want to discuss, please feel free to bring it up," I responded. I wanted to emphasize that we could talk about what they wanted, and that we did not have to abide strictly by the lesson plan.

Although I made a point to let the class know that we could discuss what they wanted, there were a couple of "things" I thought of later on, but had missed at the time. For instance, I did not realize that Derik (a student whom I do not see individually) asked what I was going to *teach* them, while Michael (a student whom I do see individually) asked what we were going to *talk* about. Already, only into the second class, Michael was beginning to view the class as a place to talk, while Derik viewed it as a place where I would teach. Another instance where I missed the boat was my opportunity to bring in the importance of confidentiality and respect after Michael's question regarding drunk driving. At that moment, I thought about mentioning confidentiality and respect, but felt it would deviate from the school's desired plan and intent for the class.

As the class continued, I lectured about alcohol and repeatedly invited comments and questions. Several students responded; however, no student fully crossed the "academic line" and shared a very personal experience. After several comments and questions, I found myself holding back interventions and attempts to bring about any sort of sharing of an experience in a therapeutic sense. Now as I look back, I can see not only myself but the class as a whole beginning to struggle with and/or question the "class" vs. "group" dilemma.

In the next excerpt, the student worker begins to renegotiate the contract with her supervisor. Her honest sharing of her dilemma helps the supervisor respond positively. It also would have been helpful if she could have been as direct with her group members, thus helping them to address group purpose and the working agreement.

(Third Session) After spending a great deal of time thinking about the last class, I expressed my opinion to my supervisor regarding the "class" vs. "group" dilemma. I explained that I understood where the school was coming from, but that I had a strong feeling that the students would be willing to participate in and benefit from an

integration of educational material into a therapeutic group regarding substance abuse. My supervisor was very supportive as well as pleased to openly bring a therapeutic aspect into the students' substance abuse course. After all, a therapeutic substance abuse course had been the school's original desired goal. My supervisor and I discussed a couple of ideas about carefully moving away from the educational aspect and incorporating a therapeutic aspect as the predominant aspect of the "group." I entered the third session with my eyes and ears wide open for reasons as well as opportunities to begin the shift. I felt prepared, supported, excited, and somewhat anxious. "Okay, is everybody settled?" I questioned, as an attempt to get all of the students in their seats. "Last week we went over various facts about alcohol and issues related to it. We also completed some worksheets and had an opportunity to discuss questions some of you had in regards to alcohol. I thought today we could all talk about some reasons why you think people drink and abuse alcohol." As I looked around the classroom, I noticed heads nodding in agreement, but no one said a word. For a moment, I began to have doubts about making the "shift."

I contemplated recontracting, but felt it was too soon and I needed to observe a desire among the students to express personal experiences before I recontracted. However, I thought this was an appropriate time to mention the importance of confidentiality. Not only to protect the rights of the students, but to increase the comfort level for sharing within the entire "group." "I just want to let all of you know that anything anyone shares in this class is confidential, and is left in this classroom among the group. Does anyone have a comment, concern, or question about any of this?" All of the students felt good about the idea, especially the confidentiality.

The student worker's first instinct to "recontract" was a good one. If she was concerned that it might be too early in the group, she could have shared that as well. Her handling of the group during the first sessions has built up a sound working relationship that she could draw upon if she were direct with the members. As is often the case, the discussion of confidentiality is incomplete and unintentionally misleading. There are some things which, if shared in the group, the social worker is mandated to report. She would have been more accurate to limit confidentiality by explaining exceptions to that rule. She provides one exception in response to a question; however, there are others as well. For example, she would have been mandated to report illegal activity, such as drug dealing, and to report if a member were in danger from others (e.g., experiencing sexual or physical abuse).

"Also, guys, it is important to remember to have respect for someone when they are taking. How does that sound to everyone?" I looked around the room for a response. All of the students nodded in agreement, and some commented "cool" and "sounds good." Paul (a student whom I see individually) questioned, "No matter what we say, you won't tell our parents?" "No, not unless you express harming yourself or someone else...and that is for your protection." "Rock on," commented Jason. I glanced over at Jason and, as I smiled, commented, "Jay, maybe you can start out and tell us a reason why you think people drink and/or abuse alcohol?" "To get drunk and forget about shit, ya know," responded Jason. Jason's response was the true beginning of the shift. As the class/group continued, I got a strong sense the "group" atmosphere was truly developing among the students. Each student added something to the discussion. However, I noticed that the students whom I see individually expressed much more personal experiences than the others. I think their comfort level and therapeutic relationship with me may have something to do with it. As the period was about to end, I reminded the students about the confidentiality and thanked everyone for sharing.

I asked the group if they would like to see the movie, *When a Man Loves a Woman,* next week in the lounge, and afterwards discuss issues, thoughts, and feelings around it. They all appeared to be enthusiastic about the idea. I gave them permission slips to watch the movie and asked that they be returned by Friday. Overall, I thought this group session went well. Students began to share, some "group rules" were established, and the plan for next week's group was a direct move toward the therapeutic aspect of the group, and the students seemed to be enthusiastic as well as comfortable.

In the next session, the worker makes a significant shift by recontracting with the members. Although she may feel that the members are now ready, in reality, she is the one who is ready. Her clarity about purpose sends the message to the group members that she is ready.

(Fourth Session) I discussed the content and outcome of the third session with my supervisor. Again, she was pleased and very supportive. We discussed my recontracting in the fourth session. I entered the classroom with enthusiasm and a bit of anxiety. Shortly after entering the classroom, when the students were settled, I stated, "Okay, are we all ready to move into the lounge to watch the movie?" The students responded positively, and we all moved into the lounge. After everyone was seated, I stated, "Each of you know that today we're going to watch *When a Man Loves a Woman.* This is kind of a 'tear-jerker' and may hit on some areas that are tough for some of you, but that is what the discussion with the group afterward is for. If anyone feels they need to leave, feel free and you can go to Mrs. Crawford's room." As I looked around, the students nodded their heads in agreement.

"Some of you may have noticed that we've been doing a lot more talking in this class lately, and sort of developed into a group. I think it is important to learn about substance abuse, but the feelings involved and the effects of it are just as important as the factual information, if not more. It seems that substance abuse in some way affects just about everybody's life." (As I spoke, I noticed the students were listening intently.) "I think it is important to have a place where these effects and feelings can be shared and expressed as well as comforted and supported. How do you guys feel about having this class be a group where that can happen?"

I sensed that the students would be interested and very accepting of my suggestion, but I was feeling somewhat anxious while awaiting their response. "It sounds pretty good, I like that anything we say doesn't leave the room," responded Nicole (a student whom I do not see individually). I nodded my head empathetically and in agreement as she spoke. "Yes, the confidentiality is extremely important in a group like this...it helps to really develop trust, respect, and comfort which make sharing a little bit easier," I responded. Derik commented, "I would still like to have you teach us some stuff, but I think it's pretty cool to talk about a lot of stuff, ya know." "Does that sound okay to everyone? That we can learn some facts and then have a discussion as well?" I questioned, and then looked around the room for a response. I observed several nods and "yeahs." The shift seemed to be unanimously desired among the group. "Rock on, let's get the movie going," shouted Jason. The students laughed and then focused on the television. I started the video and thought about what had just occurred. I was pleased with the "recontracting" and thought the gradual shift was appropriate as well as successful. I also felt that the combination of the factual information and the discussion is a good mix for this particular population.

As the movie ended, and the discussion developed, I felt the atmosphere of a "therapeutic group" strengthen among the students. Some students appeared to be apprehensive at first, but as others shared, more students opened up. As the group ended, I went over the "recontracting" and the content of that day's group. I also checked in with the students that everyone was "okay" with the group. It seems as if all the students were comfortable with the shift and had already begun to form a bond. I was glad, and I felt really good about the session. The bell rang, and the students proceeded to their next class. I thought about the session and realized how much more comfortable I felt leading a group than I did teaching a class. This thought reinforced and strengthened my desire to be a social worker.

Where the Problem Stands Now: I felt watching the movie in the lounge aided in shifting the group as a whole from the academic mode to a therapeutic mode. I noticed the physical atmosphere of the lounge (plants, couches, pictures, etc.) positively influenced the comfort level of the students' sharing. However, I strongly believe that it was the recontracting that had the greatest impact on the shift. I believe the recontracting clarified and strengthened what the group was really about as well as increased the amount of sharing among the group. After each group session, the discussions have grown in length and depth. It seems that the students neither feel threatened nor accused; rather, they seem to feel comfortable and have developed a sense of belonging. The atmosphere and content of the last couple of months of the group sessions leads me to believe that the integration of educational information in a therapeutic group has developed an environment conducive for a successful therapeutic group. Since the shift, comments made by several staff members lead me to believe that they are pleased with the shift, and they often offer their support.

Specific Next Steps:

1. I will continue to integrate educational information into the therapeutic group.

2. I will continue to reiterate the elements of the "recontracting" in hopes of emphasizing and strengthening the "new purpose" of the group.

3. I will continue to attempt to provide a safer, trusting, and comfortable environment for the group.

4. I will continue to welcome and encourage the sharing of feelings and personal experiences within the group.

5. I will attempt to strengthen the feeling and view that the students are part of a group, rather than simply a class.

6. I will accept the staff's offered support for the group, and keep them informed of its development.

CHAPTER SUMMARY

Our discussion of group work practice in relation to substance abuse brings to a close the group work section of this book. Parts I, II, III, and IV have been designated to aid you in thinking about your own practice with individuals, families, and groups, and to help you identify more clearly what it is you do that works well, as well as what you might want to do differently. In Part V of this book, we will examine the worker's skill in dealing with the larger systems clients must negotiate, as well as communities and other macro systems. You will note that the dynamics and skills identified thus far will be just as useful in describing this other aspect of the helping professional's functional role.

GLOSSARY

abstinence model An approach to recovery suggesting that complete abstinence from the use of drugs or alcohol is required for achieving and maintaining recovery.

ACOA (Adult Children of Alcoholics) A recovery movement organization for people with alcoholic parents, designed to help them deal with the long-term emotional impact of growing up in a household with an alcoholic parent.

addictive voice A concept from the rational recovery movement suggesting that thoughts and feelings involving the desire to abuse substances represent a part of the individual that attempts to subvert recovery.

contemplation stage The second stage in the addiction change model suggested by DiClemente (1991), in which the addicted person is considering his or her use of substances and exploring the possibility of the existence of an addiction problem. This stage precedes any efforts at change.

disease model The belief that addition is inherently a disease and should be treated as such.

enabler A person in the life of a substance abuser whose behavior, often including acceptance of the abuse, tends to preserve the status quo, thus enabling the abuser to maintain the addiction.

harm reduction An approach to substance abuse that attempts to help addicted persons to minimize harm to themselves and others (e.g., use of clean needles to avoid becoming infected with AIDS).

pre-contemplation stage One of the stages in the addiction change model suggested by DiClemente (1991). In this stage, the addicted person has not even begun to contemplate the idea that there may be an addiction problem.

relapse The loss of recovery through the use of substances. Relapse is seen as a potential step along the way to a more permanent form of abstinence-based recovery if the abuser can learn from the relapse experience.

triggers Events in a person's past or present life that create thoughts or emotions "triggering" relapse or a desire to abuse substances.

12-step model A model of recovery in which the participants follow 12 clearly defined steps to achieve recovery from drug and alcohol abuse. Although this model is closely associated with the Alcoholics Anonymous movement, it has been used in other recovery programs as well.

NOTES

1. Alanon is a group for significant others of persons with an alcohol addiction. The 12-step program is designed to help addicted persons, or those involved in codependent relationships, to systematically deal with the causes.

PART V

Social Work with the System

Part V consists of three chapters that focus on the social worker's role in attempting to influence the system, system representatives, and the community. In Chapter 18 we will explore the worker's efforts to help the client negotiate the system. The skills and dynamics described in the first four parts of the book reappear in the analysis of working with other professionals. Our focus in Chapter 19 is on the social worker's responsibility to have a professional impact on his or her own setting, the community, and the larger society. In Chapter 20, which concludes the book, we describe the function of the social worker in various settings within the community.

18

Helping Clients to Negotiate the System

CHAPTER OUTLINE

Introduction

The Individual-System Interaction

Mediating the Individual-System Engagement

Confrontation, Social Pressure, and Advocacy

In Parts I to IV of this book, we explored the helping model in the context of work with individuals, families, and groups. Much of the emphasis was on preparing and assisting clients to deal with important systems. In Part V, we will consider another level of interaction—the relationship between clients and the social institutions with which they come into contact, such as schools, hospitals, housing agencies, political systems, residential care centers, community organizations, and social agencies. As we examine this interaction and the worker's function and skill required to facilitate it, we will see that much of the material already presented is applicable by analogy. The use of an approach based on systems theory makes this possible: since different levels of systems have universal properties, insights into one level can serve as hypotheses for understanding another.

INTRODUCTION

Chapter 1 introduced the **systems or ecological approach** as a general framework for viewing the client in his or her broader social context. Parts II, III, and IV have focused upon the worker's efforts to help the client negotiate the various important systems in her or his life (e.g., family, school, the mutual aid group). It was suggested that the worker always had two clients—the client and the system—and that many of the principles developed in work with one would be applicable in work with the other. Practice examples included illustrations of social workers attempting to have professional impact on doctors, residential care workers, other social workers, and so on. In this chapter and the next, work with other professionals and the system comes to the foreground of the discussion for special focus. It is this level of systems work, an essential element of all practice, that distinguishes social work as a unique profession.

Hearn (1962) was one of the first social work theorists to describe the potential value of general systems theory to the development of a unified social work practice theory. He said,

> If there are principles which apply to **organismic systems** in general, and if individuals, groups, organizations, and communities may be regarded as such systems,

then these principles collectively might find their place in a unified theory of practice. This would provide a common framework for conceiving the individuals, groups, organizations, and communities as "clients," or as the means by which service is rendered to "clients" (p. 67).

Hearn is suggesting that we use our understanding of one level of system to better understand another level. An example of an application of this idea would be the functional role of the deviant member. In Parts II and III of this book, we examined the dynamics between a family and its deviant member, suggesting that often, the behavior evidenced in this role was sending a message for the family as a whole. This same idea was revisited in Part IV when we examined the functional role of the deviant member in the small group. In this chapter and the next, we will take the same concept of the role of the deviant member and apply it at the organizational and community levels. For example, in my consultations with large organizations, such as hospitals, there is always a service that is considered the deviant member of the system. This is the department that is constantly in turmoil, faces frequent staff changeovers, is in conflict with other departments, and so on.

Application of the deviant member constructs from smaller systems has led me to analyze the behavior of such a department as an entity in the larger organizational system, playing the same functional role as an individual in a group. Thus, as hospitals come under increasing stress because of cost-containment efforts resulting from managed care, the stress of the whole system may be acted out by specific departments. As with the small group and the family, the deviant member is usually the unit that is having the most difficulty coping with the general stress. In hospitals, it is often the emergency room, the intensive care ward, or the surgical service that plays this role. These parts of the system normally have high-stress operations. In a larger entity, such as a state or a province, a statewide agency, such as the child welfare service, may send the signal of stress for all of the other human services systems. As another example, scapegoating is also common, as some social service systems regard others as "less professional" and project their own problems onto the workers in that system.

Once this systems approach is integrated into a social worker's theoretical framework, all levels of systems are viewed dynamically and as potential targets for intervention. In addition, this point of view gives direction to conceptualizing the social worker's function and identifying the required skills. In this chapter, we will examine the individual-system interaction in much the same terms used thus far and will use the mediation function to describe the social worker's role. Examples from a number of settings will show work with clients who sometimes individually and at other times in groups are endeavoring to negotiate systems and their representatives (e.g., teachers, principals, doctors, housing authority administrators). Many of the skills already identified will prove to be as helpful in dealing with system representatives as they were with clients. Since confrontation with the system and social pressure are also part of the way change takes place, these processes will also be illustrated. The worker's mediation function will be defined broadly and will include advocacy as one method of implementing it. In Chapter 19, we will look at the worker's responsibility for having professional impact on her or his own agency and other settings. The illustrations in that chapter demonstrate how a worker can use experiences with clients to guide efforts to affect agency policies, structures, procedures, and programs to better meet the needs of clients. We will be arguing that it is this specific responsibility to influence the larger systems—the second client concept—that is rooted in our history as described in Chapter 1 and gives the social work profession its unique and crucial role in our society. The reader will be urged to stop complaining about the system (e.g., school, hospital, agency, community) and to start doing something about it.

THE INDIVIDUAL-SYSTEM INTERACTION

In a modern, industrial, and largely urban society, the relationship between individuals and society has taken on a very complex character. A large number of institutions and agencies have been established to deal with the individual on behalf of society. For example, welfare agencies were originally designed to care for those who were unable to support themselves (although more recent efforts at "welfare reform" have brought that function into question); schools were developed to provide the education needed for individuals to become integrated into the community and to play a productive role; hospitals were established as centers for medical care for physical illness; and psychiatric centers were set up to treat those with emotional disorders. As is often the case, the very institutions set up to solve problems became so complex themselves that new problems were generated. Social, medical, and educational systems can be difficult to negotiate even for individuals who are well equipped to deal with them, let alone those with limited education and resources. The services established for people are often so complex that it is difficult for individuals to make use of them.

In addition to complexity, there are other factors that compound the individual-system interaction. For example, many services inherently approach clients ambivalently. Thus, while welfare is established to meet the needs of the poor, it is often administered in a way that reflects a judgmental and punitive attitude. For example, welfare recipients are often made to feel that their checks are public "doles," gifts from a generous community rather than a right, and that acceptance of welfare is a sign that the individual is neither a productive nor an important member of society. More recent changes in the welfare legislation have reinforced such views. Anecdotal reports indicate that "welfare-to-work" efforts may be helpful for some recipients, in a good economy, when appropriate day care, training and other supports are in place. These reports also suggest that the undifferentiated application of the new rules to families and individuals who are not able to make the transition may result in unacceptable hardships for the most vulnerable members of our population.

A third factor contributing to breakdowns in the individual-system relationship is the size of a bureaucracy. For example, finding the right department in a large government agency can be a frustrating, even overwhelming, task. Entering a large high school as just one student in a class of 2,000 can easily lead to getting "lost" in the system, thus not getting the special help needed for successful completion of a program. Another complication is the difficulty of human communication. For instance, a student may, even in a small setting such as a specific class, feel that the teacher does not care, and the teacher, in turn, may feel the same way about the student. Both may well be mistaken. In another example, a student of color may experience a white teacher as racist and punitive. In some cases this perception may be accurate. In others, it may reflect the tremendous complications involved in relationships between members of different races and cultures. The reader can surely provide numerous examples in which the size and complexity of a system, difficulties in communications, or the ambivalence of the system towards its clients cuts them off from services they require. Since the individual who needs to use the system is also complex, feels some ambivalence towards the service, and has difficulty in communications, breakdowns become almost inevitable.

One fact of life we can all acknowledge from our own experiences is that simply establishing a service to meet a need is no guarantee that the need will be met. Recognizing this reality led Schwartz (1961) to propose the function of the social work profession to mediate the individual-social engagement. He suggests that this is the historical reason for the development of the social work profession: to stand as a buffer between clients and the systems they needed to negotiate. Other professionals (psychologists, nurses, etc.) may appropriately play this role; however, it is only the social work profession, according to Schwartz, that has this unique functional responsibility.

MEDIATING THE INDIVIDUAL-SYSTEM ENGAGEMENT

One of the major problems facing workers in implementing this role is their own feelings. They often tend to over-identify with the individual client against the system and its representatives. In our earlier discussion of work with the family and work with scapegoats in the group, we saw how workers, because of their own life experiences, often identify with one side in an engagement. Since we have all known complex bureaucracies, authoritarian and insensitive administrators, teachers who seemed not to care, and the like, it is not difficult to understand such an initial reaction to a client's problem with a system. I have seen workers develop a fine sense of tolerance for deviant behavior on the part of clients, an ability to see past a facade and reach for clients' underlying strength, and an understanding of clients' ambivalence. Yet these same workers lack tolerance for deviant behavior, are fooled by facades, and cannot accept ambivalence when they see these same characteristics in a system or representatives of the system.

There are times when anger is the only appropriate response, and workers may be faced with a situation in which confrontation is the only answer. However, workers often respond in this way before they have attempted to understand the dynamics involved and so may respond to teachers, doctors, welfare workers as if they were stereotypes. At the point when a client needs the worker's help in negotiating a system, the worker may be responding in a way that further cuts off the system from the client. The worker may then point to the system as impossible rather than examining personal feelings and critically analyzing his or her own part in the proceedings.

A striking example of this process was brought home to me in a workshop I conducted for Indian women who work as social aides for their local bands. Their job was to help the members of the band in their dealings with many white-dominated agencies and institutions (e.g., schools, welfare). One worker presented an example of her efforts to help an Indian teenager who was on his way to failing a course taught by a white teacher. This worker had often attacked the inadequacy of the school. The following record presents the conversation between the worker and the white teacher.

> **Worker:** I hear you're having problems with Albert's English.
> **Teacher:** It's not my problem, it's his.
> **Worker:** I do think you're leaning on him too hard.
> **Teacher:** Look, if he wants to get anywhere, he'll have to shape up. I really don't
> have the time to argue. If he wants to pass English, he'll have to try harder.
> **Worker:** Speaking about time, we do pay some of your wages, you know. I do
> think you could be a little more lenient.

Teacher: I'll try to keep that in mind.
Worker: You do that.

In discussing this brief interchange, the workshop participants, all Indian workers, felt that the presenter had come on too hard with the teacher. Both appeared to be defensive: the teacher may have felt the worker wanted her to let Albert pass in spite of his poor performance, and the worker felt that the teacher did not really care about Albert. There was consensus in the group that the relationship between the worker and the teacher was in poor shape and that, as a result of the interview, there was not much hope for an improved relationship between the teacher and Albert. The teacher had not gained a better idea about Albert's feelings in the class or towards the subject or a sense of what might be making it difficult for Albert to learn. In addition, the worker interpreted the teacher's expectations for Albert's performance as a rejection of him, even though many workshop members pointed out that some teachers made no demands on Indian youngsters at all. They just passed them along, a real form of rejection. The workshop group members strategized how the worker might go back to meet with the teacher and negotiate a contract for their relationship and try to begin again. Although the worker seemed to agree, I sensed her hesitation, particularly in respect to the part of the strategizing in which her fellow workers suggested she admits to the teacher that she had come on too strong. I reached for her feelings:

> **Workshop Leader:** You seem hesitant. I get the feeling you're not anxious to go back and try again. Am I right?
> **Worker:** (After a very long silence) It would hurt my pride to go back and talk to that teacher. (Another long silence)
> **Workshop Leader:** Could you explain why it would hurt?
> **Worker:** I don't think you understand. Thirty years ago, I was one of the first of five Indian children to go to that school when it was all white…

What followed was a description of her experiences in a white-dominated school in which she and other Indian students were made to feel ashamed of their race and their heritage. They had been forbidden to speak their native language, were ridiculed by teachers and white students for their poor dress and manners, and were generally made to feel like outsiders. One example of the cultural shock was related to the use of silence. When asked questions in class, Indian students would take a long time to respond because they were thinking about the answer (as was the custom in conversations they heard in their families) or trying to translate into their native language and then back to English. Teachers who did not understand the importance of silence would often interpret the delay as indicating the student did not know the answer, and would move on to another student. After a while, the Indian students did not even try to speak, and the teacher failed to ask. Others in the workshop group added their own experiences. Some participants gently pointed out that things were not the same today and that some of the white teachers tried hard to understand their students. I tried to acknowledge the feelings of the worker.

> **Workshop Leader:** I guess every time you walk into that school it must bring back a great deal of pain and feelings of humiliation. I can understand now why you would feel it would be a blow to your pride. I'm not sure if I can help right now. What is hitting me hard is that for you to work differently with this teacher, you have to deal with your feelings about the white world—all the hurt you have experienced—and that's a tall order.

Other workshop members moved in at this point, and the discussion focused on how they needed to avoid the tendency to see the world of today's Indian teenagers as being exactly the same as the one they had dealt with. There were still many similarities, and evidence of ongoing prejudice and oppression clearly existed. The anger they felt toward present injustices was clearly stated. Nevertheless, if they were to help things be different for their kids, they had to do something to try to change things themselves.

In this specific case, the workshop members felt it would not help Albert if the worker were simply to give up on the school. If Albert were to make it, someone had to open up communications between him and his teacher. The worker agreed that she could see this and said she would have to think about what she would do. I pointed out that this example opened up a larger question about the relationship between the children of the band and their parents and the staff of the school. Had they thought about the possibility of trying to do something on a band- and school-wide basis? Were other Indian parents also feeling somewhat intimidated by the school? Perhaps the school staff felt cut off and somewhat intimidated by the band. Would this be an area to explore? Discussion continued on the implications of this specific case for the general problems of Indian children in the school. This line of work—moving from the specific example to more general problems—will be illustrated in the next chapter. For now, the important point is that the worker's feelings can have a powerful effect on perception of the system and its representatives. If the worker only sees that part of the system that shows resistance, then the worker may fall into the trap of missing the part of the system that is still reaching out.

It is, of course, not necessary to have experiences such as those described by these Indian women to feel intimidated by a school seeing. One graduate student of mine described his first day of field work. He was placed as a student social worker in the same school he had attended as a child. On his first morning he met his former fourth-grade teacher in the hall, and she said, "Terry, what are you doing here?" He replied, "I'm the new student social worker." He described her face as broadening into a maternal smile as she said, "Isn't that nice." He blushed and felt that his possibilities of doing any effective work with this teacher were finished. A first step, therefore, in functioning more effectively in systems work is for the worker to become aware of her or his personal feelings about a system's representatives, particularly those in positions of authority. This is essential.

Work with the School System

The following example is part of a record of service to a youngster who has been suspended from school. It illustrates the mediation role in action. The worker demonstrates her ability to be with both the youngster and the system representatives in the engagement. This was the key to her success. The client was a 61-year-old woman who had contacted the worker at a community psychiatry department of the local hospital. The worker had been seeing her son in a group at the hospital, and the client, Mrs. Jones, had called to inform the worker that she was not able to get her son Bobby accepted into school, despite a court order requiring her to do so. The worker described the client as being somewhat inept at handling school matters and vague about why the school was failing to comply with the court order. The worker felt that Mrs. Jones was worried and depressed about the school problem. She visited the client at her home to help her talk about her problem.

Summary of the Work:

Worker: I know that with all of the criticism you have had regarding your children, it is very hard for you.

Mrs. Jones: (looking depressed) I am trying my best. I don't want the courts to send Bobby away, but the school won't let him return and he is getting into more trouble.

Worker: It's like going around in circles—everyone's telling you what to do, and no one is showing you how.

Mrs. Jones: Now they will say I'm neglecting Bobby. (In an exasperated manner) The court says put him in school; the school says he can't go. I don't know what to do!

She continued to talk about her inability to understand why the school has refused to allow Bobby to return. While we were talking, the other children were yelling and screaming. Mrs. Jones was very edgy. Several times she grabbed the little ones to make them be quiet. I said she seemed overwhelmed and asked how I could help. She said I could do better if I talked to the school. She didn't understand "those people." Maybe I could. She explained how difficult it is for her to travel to school with all the other children. I said I would speak to the school and keep in close contact with her as to what was happening. She seemed relieved and thanked me.

I later talked to Bobby to see how he was feeling. He was out on the block when I spoke with him, and he seemed unhappy but perked up a little when he saw me. His immediate comment was, "You going to get me in school?" I gave him some information about the steps I had in mind and added that I knew he and his mother had been trying very hard. My comment led to further discussion.

Bobby: I know why the school doesn't want me.

Worker: I'd like to know why.

Bobby: The teachers don't like me, and they don't want me in that school.

He was sulking and seemed quite torn inside. He looked at me, and his eyes were watery. I reached out and probed for what he was feeling.

Worker: I know it's hard, but get it out of you; tell me what you are feeling.

Bobby: (Who was crying) I want to go back into school. There's nothing to do on the block! The court is going to send me away, and my mother keeps hollering at me!

We talked at great length about his feelings, and he continued to express his fears about getting into school. If he gets into school, he is not sure he will do well. He is afraid the same experiences will repeat themselves. Mostly, I just listened, giving support where I could.

Worker: I know it's hard, Bobby. I want to help you by trying to help your parents as well as the school to see that you want to do the right thing. But it's not easy. You'll have to help me do this.

Bobby: I'll try.

Worker: You're trying already. It must have been very hard for you to tell me what you were thinking.

Bobby was silent, but I felt he understood what I was saying. When I was leaving, he reminded me of the group's trip that evening, and I said I would be there.

The worker had begun the process by contracting with Mrs. Jones and Bobby about how she could help. She tried to get a sense of how they saw the difficulty and attempted to encourage their expression of feeling about the problem. After these conversations it would have been easy to understand if the worker had gone to the school to do battle for Bobby. With a court order in the background, the worker might have tried to use the power of the court to force Bobby back into school. This effort might have worked, but the worker recognized it would have been a short-lived victory. If the problems between Bobby and the school system were not dealt with, they would just return to haunt him later, and he would soon be suspended again. In addition, while the worker might have been able to force the school to take Bobby back, she wanted more from them—she wanted them to work to help Bobby stay in. To enlist their aid, she needed to treat the staff at the school as allies in the struggle to aid Bobby, not as the enemy.

Instead of creating a "self-fulfilling prophecy" by attacking the school representatives and provoking a defensive and negative response, the worker began the first contact with the school guidance counselor by contracting, employing the skill of clarifying purpose. Often, because of their hidden agendas, workers begin their systems work without a clear and direct statement of what they are about. Lack of clarity as to purpose can be just as threatening and unproductive with systems representatives as it is in work with clients. She also encouraged the guidance counselor to elaborate her perceptions of the problem. A worker who saw the counselor as the enemy might have begun a "counter-attack" after the counselor's first responses. Returning to the worker's record of service,

> I visited the school for the purpose of getting clarification on the reasons why Bobby was not allowed in school and to trace the source of his difficulty there. I met Ms. Gordon, the guidance counselor, and after briefly describing my involvement with the family, I told her what I was after.
>
> **Worker:** The court has requested that Bobby be returned to school. Mrs. Jones has informed me that the school has refused to readmit him.
>
> **Ms. Gordon:** I know that the court has ordered Bobby back to school. However, when he was suspended, it was done by the district superintendent. Therefore, only that office can admit him to school.
>
> I then asked for some clarification as to the meaning of Bobby's suspension. I wanted to know if it were common for suspended pupils to have to wait so long for readmission. She said Bobby's situation was different because he had been so disruptive (emphasis on *disruptive*) in school. She was emphatic about his fight with the lunchroom teacher last year. Further discussion revealed that there was a possibility that Bobby had been provoked. This came out when I shared with her Bobby's feelings about the situation. I revealed some of Bobby's characteristics that I felt the school should know about. My purpose was twofold: (1) I knew Bobby's record at that school would follow him, and I wanted to clear it up; (2) because of the demands placed on teachers, a child's struggles with the school and himself can often go unnoticed.

In response to the worker's direct statement of purpose and her willingness to listen, the guidance counselor began to open up with the worker. The worker listened and attempted to empathize with the counselor and her difficulties. It is in this sense that the worker tries to be "with" the client and the system at the same time. It would be easier not to hear the problems facing the system, but just as with any relationship, there must be genuine understanding before it is possible to make demands.

> **Ms. Gordon:** I have noticed that Bobby is a sensitive boy, and under all his toughness there's a scared child.
>
> Ms. Gordon seemed frustrated by her inability to reach for the positive aspects that Bobby has, and I suspected that she was feeling defeated and threatened by my

probing into the particulars surrounding Bobby's suspension. I said to her, "There's probably a desire on your part to be more responsive. You probably feel uncomfortable about not reaching Bobby." Miss Gordon, in a sincere but hesitant manner, had this to say:

Ms. Gordon: Many of the teachers are insensitive, and there is a lack of cooperation on the part of the principal. Also, there is a large population of disruptive children who are frequently sent to the office. The lack of sufficient personnel for these children inhibits us from doing our job.

She continued for some time, talking about her frustrations. I made several unsuccessful attempts to refocus the discussion on Bobby. I then decided it was best to allow her to ventilate her feelings. I listened while she told me how she tries to help the children and how in the past she has had some real struggles in terms of getting the teachers to relate to the disruptive students. In an exasperated manner, she said, "The pupils do need help, but it is hard for the teachers to give it to them—especially with so many!" I chose this opportunity to get back to Bobby's problem.

Worker: Ms. Gordon, I can understand how frustrating it is for you and the teachers, but it is also frustrating for Bobby. He wants to belong to the school, and I know that the school wants to help him.

Ms. Gordon: (Very concerned) I will not send any record of this to Bobby's new school. I wouldn't want to prejudice the teachers against him. I will write in the records that Bobby is a sensitive boy who is bright and capable but who need some special help. I feel this will give him a better chance of adjusting.

Ms. Gordon then gave me some names of people to contact at the district office. She said she had enjoyed talking to me because it is rare that she gets a chance to talk about her frustration. I suggested that we could talk some more, and this comment led to a long discussion about obtaining a social worker for the school.

Because of the worker's stance and skill, the guidance counselor became an important ally in the effort to get Bobby back into school. Workers often wonder about the use of empathic skills on other staff. They ask, "Isn't it like 'social working' a staff member, and won't they resent it?" I believe that when they say this, they are using the term *social working* in its worst sense and that what they are referring to is an insincere, ritualistic empathic response, which the other staff members quickly experience as an attempt to manipulate them. In this case, there are real difficulties in dealing with children like Bobby in a school system, and if the worker expects the counselor and the staff to "listen" to Bobby, to "understand" his difficulties, and to "empathize" with his feelings, she must do the same with them. Of course, the guidance counselor and other staff people at the school are not "clients," and the worker needs to keep in mind that they are professional colleagues, each with different functions in relation to the same client. However, mutual respect and understanding between colleagues and a willingness to understand the complexities of a situation are important if the worker is to help Bobby and his mother, as well as have a positive effect on the Bobby-school interaction. When analyzing numerous process recordings of work with systems representatives, one often finds the worker running into trouble in the session just after the point where the problems in the system start to be shared. Workers demand empathy for clients despite refusing to empathize with a colleague.

The worker in this example next approached the supervisory level for further information. She sensed that there might have been some reactions to her involvement; therefore, she reached for possible negative reactions.

At the district office, my strategy was to find out just what or who was preventing Bobby's return to school. I spoke with Ms. Reardon, guidance coordinator. Upon introducing myself, I was told that she had heard of me. I was surprised and asked what she had heard. She said she had seen my name on several court reports as the family social worker for St. Luke's Hospital. Ms. Gordon had also called and told her I was coming. Ms. Reardon seemed nervous, and I decided to explore her feelings about my involvement:

Worker: Here I am trying to get a child back in school who has been out for a long period of time. You must feel somewhat annoyed by my efforts.

Ms. Reardon: At first I felt that way, but my conversation with Ms. Gordon changed my mind. I am impressed with anyone who is interested in listening to problems of the school as well as the child.

Worker: You must have had some bad experiences with social workers?

Ms. Reardon: (With some irritation) Too many social agencies attack the schools. They make a big stink, and when the child is returned to school, they drop out of the picture. I don't like the fact that Bobby has been out of school so long, but I am waiting for a report from Child Guidance before returning him to school.

I began to reach for her positive feelings.

Worker: I know you want the best for Bobby as well as for any child. With so many demands on counselors, it is easy for a child to get lost.

Ms. Reardon: This is true. There are so many students like Bobby who have been out of school long periods of time. The parents think we don't care; but the children need so much and the teachers are unable to give it. We need help!

I then attempted to focus on Bobby's situation and at the same time recognize the global problems of the school system. I said I knew how difficult the school situation is.

Worker: We need social workers and psychiatrists right in the school, and most of all we need sympathetic teachers. But I am concerned with what we can do together for Bobby.

Ms. Reardon: (Seeming rather embarrassed) Oh! Forgive me! It's just that I had said to Ms. Gordon that I would explore the possibility of getting social services in at least one of the schools in the district.

I invited her to a meeting that Ms. Gordon and I were having to work to secure services for the school. I then made some suggestions about what we could do for Bobby. I asked her to call Child Guidance to determine when the report would be ready. When she phoned, she discovered that Child Guidance was under the impression that the court was going to do a psychiatric evaluation. Ms. Reardon then phoned the court and spoke to the probation officer, who informed her that their psychiatric evaluation was to be done on the parents only, and Child Guidance was to do the one on Bobby. Ms. Reardon told me, frustrated, "No one really communicates with each other." She angrily phoned Dr. Bennet, head of Child Guidance, and obtained a commitment to do a psychiatric on Bobby.

After acknowledging the problems, the worker made a demand for work by concentrating on the immediate problem facing Bobby. The supervisor's conversation with the probation officer was one illustration of how the complexity of the system can often lead to clients falling through the cracks. In the following excerpt the worker senses the coordinator's underlying ambivalence and reaches directly for the feelings. She wanted to be sure that her conversation with the coordinator was "real," because any unexpressed doubts would return to haunt Bobby later. An important additional step is the worker's recognition that she would have to begin a working relationship with the staff in Bobby's new school; she thus suggested modifications in the coordinator's description of the worker's role to prevent misunderstanding.

> I told Ms. Reardon of my earlier conversations with Bobby and Mrs. Jones and expressed their desire to have him back in school right away. Ms. Reardon said she also wanted him in school immediately, but I sensed some reservations. I reached for her ambivalent feelings.
>
> **Worker:** Part of you seems to want him back, and part of you doesn't.
>
> **Ms. Reardon:** You're right. I'm concerned about what school to send him to. Most of the other schools in the district are loaded with problem kids. There is one school that is better than others, but they are somewhat rigid. I want Bobby to have the best possible chance, but that's the only school that has room for him.
>
> I offered a plan of action and reached for some feedback:
>
> **Worker:** If you could introduce me to the principal of the new school, perhaps we could work together with the teachers in a supportive role to broaden the chances of Bobby making a satisfactory adjustment.
>
> Ms. Reardon felt that this was a good plan. She thought the school would appreciate my help. However, she suggested that I work with the school social worker and the teachers because they might resent my working directly with the principal. I said that I didn't fully understand what she was trying to tell me. She explained that the principal and the teachers have a "pretty rocky relationship," and she didn't want to get in the way of my attempts to help. She wrote a letter to the principal explaining who I was and what role I would have in working closely with the school to help Bobby. She ended the letter by stating that I should be consulted before decisions were made regarding anything Bobby has become involved in. I suggested that the letter be reworded so as not to give the impression of taking away decision powers. I told her to simply ask that I be involved as a resource person to enable them to make more informed decisions.
>
> I gave recognition to Ms. Reardon for her assistance in getting movement on the reinstatement of Bobby.
>
> **Worker:** I know it isn't an easy decision to return Bobby to school, but I will be around to help when you need me.
>
> As I was leaving, Ms. Reardon said I should contact her about the meeting to get social services in Ms. Gordon's school.

This worker recognized that getting Bobby back into school was just the beginning of the work, certainly not the final solution to the problem. She managed to keep in contact with the school and to monitor Bobby's progress so that when trouble arose, she would be there to help. In this important part of her work, her earlier efforts to develop a positive working relationship with the school staff paid dividends, giving her a basis of trust from which to work. The following is the worker's assessment of where things stand.

> *Current Status of the Problem:*
>
> Bobby is in school. He is feeling quite nervous because the school is new, and he is having difficulty adjusting to a structured setting again. So far, he has not made any friends, and his relationship with classmates is strained. Bobby's teacher is kind of

rigid, but she has begun to use me when she feels he is heading for difficulty. She is somewhat overexcited and afraid of not "bringing Bobby around." Her preoccupation with having a good class is strong, and she lets it get in the way of reaching for and understanding Bobby's needs.

The social worker in the school is in a rather precarious position. She is the only social worker in the school and is walking a rather thin line by trying to please everyone and "not rock the boat." She is also frustrated because she has strong feelings about teachers' insensitivity. Mrs. Jones is worried that Bobby might not continue in school. Therefore, she is constantly threatening him. Her threats seem to discourage Bobby and put ideas into his head about "playing hooky."

The worker continued by identifying her next steps in this case.

Strategies for Intervention:

1. Meet on a regular basis with the teacher to talk with her in an attempt to help her see that her feelings about success are preventing her from reaching Bobby.

2. Work with the social worker who is in a bind and torn between the demands of the teachers and the children. I would like to see her work more closely with Bobby.

3. Point out to Mrs. Jones that her negative attitude toward Bobby's progress in school can only complicate things for him—as well as for herself.

4. Continue to encourage Bobby to talk about his fears and anxiety about being in a new school. Also, support him when things are going rough and let him know I am available to him.

5. Secure tutorial help for Bobby.

These first steps by the worker, predicated on the assumption that it was best to reach for the system's strength and to "talk softly" rather than begin with a confrontation, led to the client's reconnection to the school system in a new way and more helpful way. In addition, the worker made a major contribution toward strengthening not only her own professional relationship with the school system, but also, the relationship between her agency and the schools. She would likely find important benefits from this careful systems work if she needed to deal with this school system again. In addition, the worker's recognition of some responsibility for working with other professionals around the larger issue of availability of resources for children like Bobby reflects the broader social work function in action. Examples in the next chapter illustrate the steps involved in moving from Bobby's "private troubles" to the "public issues" affecting all of the children like Bobby.

Finally, although the worker was acting appropriately in working for Bobby's mother to overcome the immediate roadblocks to Bobby's readmission to school, it would be important that the worker take some steps to try to strengthen Mrs. Jones in her relationship with the school system. Other problems will come up and the worker may not always be available. Mrs. Jones's description of the school's staff as "those people" should be further explored. Mrs. Jones was an African-American, and the worker was not. There is at least the possibility of an underlying issue of racism—or at least, the perception that an African-American parent would not be respected by a largely white school system. Mrs. Jones may have found it difficult to be direct about this issue with the worker, and the worker may have been uncomfortable about raising it.

Work with the Hospital System

The next excerpts in this section are drawn from work in a hospital setting. In the first example, the context is an assertiveness training group for women in an inpatient psychiatric hospital. These women have been admitted for a variety of emotional illness problems. This particular group comes at the end of the day after a full day of group sessions. Early in the group it becomes clear that many of the issues the women wish to discuss are hospital-related. At first, the student worker attempts to acknowledge the women's frustrations while trying to defend the hospital staff. She quickly begins to understand that in an inpatient setting, assertiveness is taught by helping the women assert themselves within their immediate environment—the hospital ward and even the assertiveness group itself. The group leader demonstrates a keen understanding of the "two-client" concept as she intervenes as skillfully with the staff as she has with the patients.

A Women's Assertiveness Training Group: Dealing with the Hospital as the Second Client

Type of Group: Assertiveness issues, inpatient, open-ended

Age Range of Members: 17–43

All female members representing a variety of ethnicities and races, but group is primarily Caucasian.

Dates Covered in Record: 9/28 to 11/16

1. *Problem*

The task this group faces is how to get their needs met within the hospital system. The difficulties these female patients must deal with are feelings of disempowerment, feeling forced to cooperate with the hospital staff, and being subject to the rules and regulations of the hospital. This is seen in their daily interactions with the nurses, psychologists, and social workers. Another related problem is the high expectations of the staff on the women's unit for them to attend several groups throughout each day regardless of the individual needs of the client. As the group leader, my problem is creating a safe atmosphere within the group that will enable these women to discuss their feelings of disempowerment within the hospital. I must help them discover ways to become their own advocates and feel that they are being listened to. Ultimately, these women will become empowered as they make their concerns known to the administration and staff and we learn to work together to make an impact on the hospital system.

2. *How the Problem Came to My Attention*

There have been several incidents with different patients and in separate group situations which have occurred and led to this assessment. Patients have described feeling helpless in not knowing when or where they will be discharged. Many times the patients have wanted to get out of group early, are asleep and skip the group altogether, or expressed feeling frustrated that other people were not attending the group. Group members have described feeling intimidated and angry with their therapist, or at times expressed feeling controlled by the nurses. I realized that these issues were surfacing in a variety of ways as women entered and left the unit. Dealing with the problem has become central to working with this group. My role is mainly in providing a safe place where these women can discuss their conflicts, their feelings of disempowerment, and support and help each other in problem solving to find ways to have their needs met within the hospital.

3. *Summary of the Work with Process Excerpts*

(*Second Session*) There was confusion on the unit because an Overeaters Anonymous meeting was being held at the same time and in the same room as this group. I avoided airing any feelings from the members concerning the confusion and being forced to switch rooms and began the group be saying that I was sorry about all the confusion. I then stated the purpose of the group. Only three women had showed up and the rest were in the other meeting. Diane said, "I am really upset that they are holding the OA group at the same time as this one. It is not fair because this group started here first and there are other women on the floor who need this group." I agreed with her and asked the group what I should do. Instead of asking the women what they could do, I took on the responsibility of talking to the nurses for them. Feeling eager to make them feel better and wanting to get on with the group process, I failed to open the conversation up, which may have raised some of their feelings and concerns. Carlene said, "You should let the nurses know that two groups should not be scheduled at the same time." Rather than working with the group and encouraging them to talk to the nurses themselves, I took over the work for them. I missed this important opportunity to have the women express their feelings to the staff and empower themselves to make changes on the unit. Instead, I said that I would talk to the nurses and try to straighten this out, which I did when the group ended.

(*Third Session*) I made the opening statement and asked if anyone had situations from the hospital or from home that they would like to discuss. Jenny said, "I am really angry right now at the hospital administration because Irene left today but she was never told her discharge date." Cindy jumped in, saying, "I want to have some notice before they discharge me so I can prepare for it." And Jenny said, "I would at least like to have the time to call someone to pick me up." She was laughing as she said this. She then questioned whether there was a policy on letting people know their discharge date by a certain time in advance. There was silence. I said, "I don't blame you for feeling concerned because leaving the hospital is a difficult transition to make and I understand that you would want to have time to prepare for leaving." They all agreed. My intervention here was on target. I was empathizing with these women and expressing that I understood where they were coming from.

The next excerpt reveals the worker caught up in the "which side am I on?" dilemma as she tries to explain away the staff's behaviors. Her instinct not to simply identify with the patients versus the staff is on target. The key to avoiding this trap is to recognize that the real issue is not the policy on discharge information, but rather, the poor communications between patients and staff. If she stays focused on improving this line of communication she can be with both clients—the patients and the system—at the same time. The silence of her group members is the signal that she is seen as trying to diffuse the conflict rather than deal with it.

While I was right to empathize with their feelings, I blew it later when I said, "I think the hospital would let you know in advance if they know the date, but sometimes the insurance company changes its mind and things become less clear for the hospital staff." There was silence. I was unable to sit with their fear of the uncertainty and started to stand up for the hospital staff! This reveals my anxiety in my role as I initially supported the women and really understood how they felt and then went on to support the staff. I could have continued to validate them and said that still, the hospital should take responsibility for informing the patients in advance to let them prepare for the discharge. After this incident I did mention this to my supervisor, who said that usually the patients are informed of discharge as soon as the psychologist is informed, but she recommended that I talk to the nurses about the anxiety of the patients around this issue.

The next day I did talk to the nurses and explained what had happened in the group, and they said that maybe it would alleviate the uncertainty if they were to write the discharge date next to the patient's name as soon as it was determined. Then, each patient could look on the board and know when she is leaving. This will enable the other patients to also prepare for women leaving the unit. In talking to the nurses about this problem, I was taking the first step in establishing a relationship with the staff. I also sent a message to the women that they were being listened to and that by expressing their needs, they could have an impact on the system.

(*Fourth Session*) I stated the purpose of the group. Mickie said that she has a situation she would like to discuss but she does not want to role-play. I said that if she feels more comfortable talking about her issue that is fine. Mickie said that she is "terrified" of her therapist and doesn't know what to do. She said her therapist begins each session with a relaxation technique that is not helpful. The rest of the session she is so terrified she has nothing to say. The group asked her who her therapist is, and whether she has told her how she feels. One woman recommended that she switch therapists if she does not find her helpful. Mickie said that she likes her therapist but that she is afraid of her. She described feeling that her therapist has authority and power over her. The group continued encouraging her to get a new therapist, while Mickie maintained that she likes her. Finally, I said, "It sounds as if it doesn't matter who the therapist is, really, but that you will feel afraid of any of them." Mickie nodded in agreement.

I was using the information I knew about her and my previous interactions with her in the groups to express the idea that switching therapists would not matter. I was trying to help the group understand the real issue for Mickie, which is her fear of people, and was attempting to create an atmosphere of mutual aid. Another woman in the group said, "I bet you will be surprised how nice and understanding your therapist is once you let her know how you feel." Another woman encouraged her to say something rather than continuing this way because she is not going to get better if her therapist is unhelpful. There was silence. I tried to clarify what was said by the other women. I said, "Sometimes just expressing your feelings aloud may enable you to overcome your fear." These women were supporting Mickie, encouraging her and problem-solving together. It was wonderful to watch them begin to take control of the group process as they become engaged in relating to and helping each other.

(*Fifth Session*) I was empathizing with the patient and creating a safe place within the hospital where hospital-related issues could be discussed. Mary said that she is having a hard time in the hospital and described herself as going backwards since her baby came in today. She said she is feeling completely overwhelmed and lost and that while she is physically in the group, her mind is outside on the baby. I asked her if she was feeling concerned about the baby to the point where she is unable to take care of herself as she was before. I was restating what she said to be sure I understood how she was feeling. She said, "Yes," and began to cry. She said, "The nurses are watching over me when I put diapers on Tony and they make me really nervous. I never had a problem putting diapers on before, but suddenly I feel really anxious doing it." The group empathized with her and encouraged her to talk to the nurses about how she is feeling. One woman offered to go with her for support, after the group. Mary accepted the offer, stopped crying, and appeared comforted by the support of the group. A few minutes later the group ended. Laurie walked with Mary to the end of the hall, and I could hear Mary talking to the nurses.

The next day I asked her how things were going, to find out if talking to them had been helpful and express my concern, and she said that she was feeling much better.

She said she had spoken to the nurses and told them how she was feeling and that they have been leaving her alone more with Tony. I tried to empower her to express her needs and emphasize that she does have control over some of what happens in the hospital. I said that it is wonderful she was able to talk to them and assert herself. She said that it felt really good to let them know how she was feeling. Rather than handling this situation in terms of one individual's experience, I could have used it as an opportunity to broaden the issue of having the group members' needs met within the hospital system. This would have shown them that my group is a safe place to discuss hospital concerns, their feelings of disempowerment, and it would have normalized Mary's experience and shown her that she is not alone in her feelings.

In the next session, a member raises an issue with the group leader in another group. Concern is expressed about the lack of emotional involvement by the therapist. The silent "observer" who occasionally comments on the discussion is experienced by the group members as a total outsider who requires that they risk themselves, express feelings, and be vulnerable while the therapist models the opposite. This is related to the issues of use of self raised in Chapter 1 of this book, when we discussed the impact of the medical model on our practices. This group leader astutely realizes that the patient is also raising a confrontation to the worker in the current moment in the current group.

(*Sixth Session*) I tried to encourage the group to discuss any issues within the hospital by saying, "This is the assertiveness issues group, and it is a time to bring up any issues from within the hospital or outside the hospital that you would like to talk about." After my opening statement, Lisa asked if she could role-play her situation with someone. She said that there is another group that she has a hard time sitting in on because she can't connect with the group leader. She has told her individual therapist this. She continued saying, "I have agreed to sit in on this group anyway even though I will not say anything. My therapist is setting up an appointment with the group leader, and I want to practice what I will say to her." I said that I thought it was a good idea and that maybe working though it in the group will enable her to feel more comfortable for the real thing. I then proceeded to organize the role-play for the group, but if I had asked them to set it up themselves, it could have been empowering for them by giving them a chance to control what happens in the group. The role play began with Lisa telling the group leader that she is really angry at her because she is unable to connect with her. The other woman in the group who was playing the group leader was silent. Lisa said, "I know exactly what she will say to me. She will say that the group is supposed to do the work and help each other." I asked her how she will feel if the group leader says this to her. I was trying to reach for her underlying feelings in the group. She said she will be really frustrated because it is hard to sit in a group and feel that you are supposed to open yourself up when the leader sits back, says nothing, and watches you. She then said, "You are in the group (which is true, I observe it) and don't say anything, but I feel like you are involved."

I was about to say that my role in the group is to observe it, but instead of responding in a defensive way I wanted to validate her feelings and confront them directly. I said, "It sounds as if you feel like you are being judged by us in the group because we don't talk much." Lisa agreed. Looking back on this, I believe that Lisa was avoiding confronting me and I was unsure how to raise this issue to the surface. Thus, when I validated what she said, I said "us" to include myself because she is probably feeling judged by me as well. I should have confronted her more directly and told her that it is O.K. to let me know if she doesn't like something I am doing, because then I can change it. This would help Lisa and the rest of the group see that conflict can be productive and useful and help them realize that sometimes articulating their feelings will be helpful to the people who are unaware of how their actions or inaction are affecting others.

(*Seventh Session*) There were only three women in group today while there were about sixteen on the unit. In rounding everyone up for the group, many of the women were sleeping or said they did not feel like attending today because they were too tired or wanted to smoke. There were three women in the room waiting to begin, so I decided to start the group. After my opening statement there was a long silence. These women seemed drained, slouched back in the chairs with their faces drawn. I tried to empathize with the women and to express in words what seemed to be occurring in the group. I said, "Everyone is so quiet. I wonder if this is because it is late in the day. You have been attending groups since this morning." Sandy said that she was really tired because she had been going to groups all day. The other women nodded in agreement. Gail said, "I am really tired of talking about my problems." There was silence again. Finally, Pat began to talk about a problem from her past. I went along with the group's avoidance of work and felt relieved that someone had a problem outside of the hospital setting that they wanted to focus on. The session continued, and ultimately the other two women joined in and contributed to helping Pat problem-solve.

In the next excerpt, we see the worker taking the next step of raising the issue with staff. She consults her supervisor, who provides the support she needs to deal with the staff. Her tuning in and strategizing lead her to approach the team with the issue as what I would call a "technical problem." She is asking her colleagues to consider the concerns raised by the group members and to jointly explore their meaning with her. She is not raising it in a manner that would be experienced by other team members as her siding with the patients versus staff. This would only raise defensiveness and defeat the purpose of the intervention.

A few days later I met with my supervisor and told her what had happened. She recommended that I bring the issue up at the team meeting with the director of the women's unit, the nursing staff, and the psychologists who work individually with the patients. I did so the following week. I said, "I lead the assertiveness issues group at four o'clock on Tuesdays, and recently the women have expressed feeling tired from attending groups all day." I explained that I wanted to raise this problem to see if this had happened before and to find out what was done, or to see if they had any ideas of what could be going on. The psychologists said that this has happened in the past and that by four in the afternoon these women have had a long day. They said that the last time this had happened, they had recommended specific groups to their patients depending on those they thought they should really attend according to their treatment plan. This way they do not become overloaded on groups but are attending those they really need. I said that would be really helpful and asked them if it is possible that with the holidays coming up the women are reacting to that as well. The nurses and psychologists said that may definitely be affecting them as well and then realized that they really hadn't been discussing the holidays with the women at all. The social workers began to say that they should begin taking about this in their groups as well because this is usually a very difficulty time for the patients. Suddenly it appeared that I had raised an important issue, and possibly it was the weight of the season that was keeping these women from attending the group as well. I was making an impact on the system, and it felt wonderful.

In assessing this situation, it is clear that something was occurring within the hospital, possibly with the staff, which may have resulted in the women not wanting to attend the group. My intervention strategies entailed talking to the nurses and the staff in order to understand what they perceive to be happening on the unit, and I engaged them in paying attention to the issues that may be arising for these women. After conferencing with the staff, I arranged for them to attend a community meeting with the women on the unit to facilitate the interactions between these women and the hospital. This incident has clearly improved my relationships with the staff. They interact with me more and ask about my experiences with the patients in the groups.

4. *Where the Problem Stands Now*

Overall, the group has been very successful in having their needs met within the hospital system. The staff has altered its way of relating to the patients, which has enabled the women to feel empowered. I have noticed more interactions between the staff and the patients whereby they are being informed of discharge as soon as the date is known, and it is written on the board consistently now. The psychologists have begun to create a schedule with each patient as to which groups will be helpful given their specific issues.

As the group leader, I have successfully created a safe atmosphere that encourages and supports the discussion of hospital issues. These are becoming a significant and central focus of group discussions. Staff has become more respectful of me as a social worker as I understand my role more clearly and am making it clear to the staff through my interactions and relationships with them. The patients are continuing to raise their issues within the hospital because they are realizing the changes and the impact they can have on the system.

My work as a mediator is essential now, as the holiday season is upon us and the hospital staff are not doing enough to recognize the impact this time of year has on the patients. By creating open communication with the nurses, therapists, and patients, I hope to change the way the system is relating to patients on this issue. Ideally, the staff will bring it to the forefront and talk about it openly, encourage the patients to talk about their feelings in my group, and ultimately, use the holidays as a means to encourage more positive interactions between the staff and the patients.

5. *Specific Next Steps*

1. I will continue to create a safe and supportive atmosphere in the group and encourage the discussion of hospital issues.

2. I will continue working with the larger system—nurses, doctors, therapists—to sensitize them to some of the issues, feelings, and needs of the women.

3. I will continue to establish stronger working relationships with the staff to reach for their feelings within the hospital and gain knowledge about the problems experienced before, what has worked and what has not worked in the past.

4. I will encourage women to use the group to air their concerns and enable them to support and encourage each other to make an impact on the system themselves.

5. I will continue to work to maintain open communication between the patients and the hospital system to create a healthier environment for them.

6. I will work to empower these women as individual members of the group as well as the group as a whole.

7. I plan to continue working on my intervention strategies as a group worker and will continue to grow and create change in my newfound identity as a "mediator" within a complex system.

In our final example from a hospital setting, we see the classic conflict between professionals over "who owns the client." As the worker comes to grips with her feelings of anger toward a psychiatrist and works to clarify her role in her own mind and with her colleagues, she begins to play a more effective third-force role.

Helping an Individual Deal with the Hospital System
Description of the Problem:

Cynthie is a 23-year-old woman, diagnosed schizophrenic, with whom I worked intermittently over a course of six months. Her medical records revealed no less than eleven psychiatric admissions since the age of fourteen, three of these being at this hospital. During the time I knew her, she had in fact been discharged and readmitted to our ward twice with a serious suicide attempt in between. To say the least, the ward staff considered Cynthie to be a chronic patient. It seemed clear that they had pretty well given up on her. They felt discouraged, exasperated, and disillusioned with what they interpreted as her lack of motivation, her lack of compliance to treatment (specifically, medication) and her recurrent re-admissions. In my view, Cynthie had also taken on much of their discouragement and pessimism, which compounded her already hopeless and depressed view of her life.

My task, in the narrowest sense, was to find a suitable placement for Cynthie upon discharge. However, as time progressed, I soon realized that placement was the least of Cynthie's problems. I became aware that if I was to be of any help to her at all, it would be necessary for me to re-define the problem as follows: First, by virtue of her admission to hospital, Cynthie had been thrown into a complex maze of hospital life. Within six months, she had been subjected to no less than three psychiatrists, two psychiatrists-in-training, two psychologists, four primary nurses, an agency social worker, the ward social worker, three boarding home coordinators, two day-care program coordinators, two occupational therapists, two student nurses, and myself. She had been spared being assigned to medical students only because her "case" was considered chronic and thus not very interesting from a psychiatric point of view. Here was a multi-layered hierarchy of staff, difficult for even the well-equipped person to deal with, let alone a frightened, depressed, sometimes-psychotic and definitely over-medicated woman like Cynthie. Second, two further issues became crucial: Cynthie's medication (and her refusal to take it) and Cynthie's plea (revealed to me in an interview with her) that, and I quote, "I just want to be a normal human being."

Over and above the placement problem, my task became at least threefold: First, to help Cynthie negotiate this complex hospital system to her advantage: a system whose representatives were making demands of her (e.g., insistence on medication) that Cynthie saw as being incompatible with her goal of becoming "normal." Second, to help the system reach past their image of Cynthie as a chronic, unmotivated, and hopeless patient. Third, to persist in my efforts to reach out to both these "clients": to Cynthie, on the one hand, who much of the time was so withdrawn, depressed, and uncommunicative that it was very difficult for me to reach her; and to the staff, on the other hand, often resistant and rigid in their view of Cynthie as "sick" and definitely short of "normal." The following record of service highlights some of my attempts and many of my misses in my effort to stand as a buffer between Cynthie and the system.

Summary of the Work:

Early Attempts to Reach for Cynthie's Feelings. Our first few meetings revealed an image of Cynthie not unlike the one described in her chart: depressed, withdrawn, rigid in posture, and almost mute. She rarely spoke, and when she did, she answered my questions with one or two words at best. I entered her room, having tuned in to her possible concerns, or so I thought. I asked if I could talk with her. No response. I sat beside her, gave a brief introduction, and stated my purpose: "Cynthie, I'm the so-cial work student. I'll be helping you find a place to stay when you leave the hospi-tal." (My sense of role was not clear yet.) Silence. "Have you thought about where you might live?" Long silence, not even looking at me. (I'm missing the boat here, I thought. Probably the hospital's concern, not hers.) "I'm sorry, Cynthie, I guess a place to stay is the least of your worries right now." No response. I continued, "I know it's been scary for you, being in hospital." No response, but now looking at me, although rather vacantly.

I reached rather hesitantly, for the taboo issue: "I know about Jean-Paul too, Cyn-thie, and I'm so sorry." (Three weeks prior to my arrival on the ward, Cynthie had been abruptly informed by a social worker that her four-year-old son, Jean-Paul, had been permanently taken into care. The loss of her son had compounded Cynthie's anxiety and depression and had precipitated two solid weeks of pacing up and down the ward's corridors, screaming and wailing, "I want my son back" and prostrating her-self on the corridor floors, refusing to move, particularly when offered medication.) I felt torn: reluctant, on the one hand, to broach the subject of Jean-Paul knowing that the ward staff discouraged Cynthie's outbursts and fearing that I would precipitate one; and, on the other hand, feeling she had little opportunity to express her grief. There was no outburst. (I admit to having felt relieved about that.) Just a long silence and then, looking at me, she simply said, "Can I have my son back?" She looked so sad. I didn't know what to say. "No, Cynthie, you can't." It sounded so blunt. "I'm sorry," I said…. Long pause…I shared my feeling and made an offer: "I feel sad too, Cyn-thie…Do you want to talk about Jean-Paul?" No response. Long pause. "Or maybe you'd like to be alone now?" Another long pause. Finally, she said, "I'm okay, I'll be okay." I reassured her that I wanted to talk to her about Jean-Paul, if that's what she wanted. Long pause. "Perhaps tomorrow then," I said.

Making Demands for Work. In my later meetings with Cynthie she continued to show little response. Her affect was blunted, her face was mask-like and vacant. Oc-casionally she would say "I'm sad," sometimes "I'm okay." *I continued making efforts to put her feelings into words, to reach inside of silences (of which there were many), largely to no avail.* I felt I was getting nowhere. Finally, I said, "I feel frustrated, Cyn-thie. I don't know what you're thinking. I don't know what you're feeling. I'd like to help you, Cynthie, but if you never talk to me I don't know how I can." Long si-lence. What was to come showed me a side of Cynthie I hadn't seen; one I would later convey to her psychiatrist on her behalf. "I just want to be a normal human being," she said. Now I was silent. Actually, I was floored. She said it without emotion. It sounded so pathetic and tragic. And not much to ask for, really. The least she de-served. I felt like saying, you're in the wrong place for that, Cynthie. (My resentment towards her treatment was surfacing.) But I didn't want to cut her off from the help she might get here. I believed, perhaps naively, that this system could help her be normal. I sensed her feelings of being stuck and overwhelmed. Or maybe these were my own feelings. I partialized her concern: "It's just hard sometimes to know where to start," I said. I asked for clarification: "What would *normal* mean to you, Cynthie?" to which she replied rather solidly, "No more psychiatrists, no more mental hospitals, no more medication."

Identifying with Both Cynthie and Her Doctor. It was unlikely I could help her negotiate these goals within the context of this system. But perhaps in some small way, I wanted her to know that there was a next step. I know Cynthie had become less and less compliant to taking her meds—a going concern for the staff. Having experienced a round of anti-depressants myself at one time, I recalled my own feelings: feeling numb, deadened, unreal, not myself, slowed down, too numb to talk or care. In short, not normal. I wondered if Cynthie was feeling the same way. I shared this experience and reached for her feedback. Long pause. "The pills make me crazy," she said. "I'm scared.... They're trying to kill my brain. They're killing my brain." I acknowledged her fear and tried, with difficulty, to be with her and the system at the same time: "The side effects are scary, Cynthie—I had them too—Like you can't control your own body. But the doctor gives you the pills to help you, not to kill you. Remember how you felt before?" I hoped to help Cynthie see that the pills had helped. She said, "Before, I thought I was Jesus. I thought demons were crawling on my body. I covered my body in paint. I felt crazy." Cynthie was unable to talk to her doctor about her fear of the pills. We agreed that I would talk to her doctor and that I would help her talk to him.

Helping Cynthie's Doctor to Understand Her Feelings. First, some background: My first encounters with Dr. Renton were something short of positive. I found him patronizing and condescending and wondered if Cynthie experienced him in a similar way. He was the patriarch on the ward, with the nurses—all women—seemingly willing to jump at his every command. Everyone knew their place, and although there were resentments, these were never directly expressed (including my own).

From the moment I was introduced as the social work student, I sensed he had written me off as brainless. He rarely missed a chance to "put in a dig." Like the time in rounds, when we were discussing Tourette's (a central nervous system disorder). I'd studied Tourette's and know of its treatment. To which Dr. Renton asked, "Oh, did you see that on Quincy, or something?" I rose to the bait, responding defensively, "No, actually, Dr. Renton, I read it in Harrison's" (a well-known and standard textbook in internal medicine). That shut him up. I had won the point, but not the war.

Dr. Renton insisted on seeing me as "the placement person." Therapy, as he called it, was psychiatry's domain. It frustrated him, he said, that "everyone around here wants to do therapy." He actually approached me one time while I was talking with Cynthie in her room and demanded to know what we were talking about. I was beginning to wonder who was more paranoid, patient or doctor? Dr. Renton's argument was that the only one qualified to understand the patient's "complete clinical picture" was the psychiatrist. And one could not understand the so-called complete clinical picture, according to Dr. Renton, without medical training, of course. It started looking like a contest of "Who knows the patient best?"

It also really bothered me that Cynthie's case was always presented last or close to last in Dr. Renton's rounds. This indicated to me the low degree of Cynthie's interest or importance to him, or maybe his level of frustration. The focus rarely shifted from diagnostic issues and from endless discussions about which medication and in what dosage to use. Cynthie's feelings were always overlooked.

In retrospect, two things were clear: First, I had let my resentment toward Dr. Renton get in the way of any real work with him. I had written him off as a "jerk" and refused to reach for his feelings, convincing myself that he probably had very few. Second, I missed every opportunity to clarify my role (mostly because I wasn't yet clear on what that role was). If I didn't want to be seen simply as a "placement person," it would be my responsibility to tell Dr. Renton exactly how I could help. Cynthie's medication problem gave me this chance, as the following dialogue shows.

I approached Dr. Renton and asked if he had a few minutes to talk to me about Cynthie. "I'm still working on a placement for her," I said, reminding him. "You know, I guess I've never said it this way" (in an attempt to clarify my role) "but I also think an important part of my work with Cynthie is to help you help her, and that's why I need to talk to you." Crediting his work, I continued, "I know how hard you've been working to stabilize Cynthie on her medication," then empathizing with his situation, "and how frustrating it must be for you and for the nurses with Cynthie acting out all the time and refusing her pills." I had his full attention. "Well, that's true," he said, "it isn't easy." Sharing my own experience, I said, "I find it hard to reach her at the best of times too, but while I was talking to her today she said some incredible things I thought you should know about...about not taking her pills." "Oh, like what?" he asked. "Well, this probably won't surprise you, but she's really scared. She's scared of taking her pills. And do you know why?" (He shook his head to say no.) "She thinks we're trying to kill her brain." "Did she say that?" he asked. "Yes, she did. I wouldn't take them either, if I thought that, would you?" "Obviously not," he said.

I continued, "She also said—and this was really sad—that all she wants is to be a normal human being. Do you think she'd feel more normal without side effects? I was wondering if you thought she might be toxic?" "Well, I think you have a point. I'll check into it today," he said, "and we'll get this cleared up." I suggested a three-way meeting between Dr. Renton, Cynthie, and myself. "I've had some luck getting her to talk about her medication," I said, "but I think she needs some reassurance from you." He agreed.

Ignoring the Lurking Negative and Paying for It Later. All the while, I continued to look for a suitable placement for Cynthie. I soon came to realize that Cynthie's "private trouble" was indeed a "public issue": There was a serious shortage of suitable homes for women like Cynthie, and those that did exist had incredible waiting lists. Finally, en route to a home that was willing to take her, Cynthie announced to me, "I want to live with Jurgen" (her ex-husband). Oh no, I thought, I don't want to hear this, here we go again: Cynthie had bounced back and forth from Jurgen to hospital to Jurgen to hospital. At one point, Jurgen even had Cynthie prostituting herself. I felt she needed a supportive environment, some stability in her life...something she'd never had. "Cynthie," I said, "I can't force you to go to the boarding home, but I really think you should give it a try." What I failed to do was reach for her feelings. She was probably scared stiff. Living in the boarding home was my agenda, not hers. Besides, what gave me the right to make that decision for her anyway? Five days later Cynthie was back in hospital, having stabbed herself in the abdomen with a kitchen knife at the boarding home, missing all her vital organs, thank God. I came away feeling that I had set her up for failure.

Sabotaged by the System. The final blow came in early February. Cynthie, it had been decided, would be transferred to another hospital. "She's too chronic for our ward," announced Dr. Renton. "She needs long-term care, so I'm transferring her. And I've decided that she's not to be told." The orders were written in the chart, just like that. I was furious and shared my feelings with Dr. Renton: "I can understand the transfer, Dr. Renton (I guess I had rationalized that perhaps they could help her) but not preparing her for it! I think that's pretty crummy! She deserves at least that, don't you think?" "Look, I know it seems crummy," he started. I interrupted, "It doesn't *seem* crummy, it *is* crummy." He went on, "Look, in my opinion, she's a serious suicide risk, and if she's told now, she'll probably elope and kill herself. I can't and won't risk that." "I see your dilemma," I said, "but I can't agree with your decision. I think you're shortchanging Cynthie." (Actually, I also felt shortchanged and ripped off. Without choice, my ability to help her had been cut off.) Dr. Renton and I agreed to disagree.

I was on the ward when they came to get Cynthie. She cried when they told her. Within ten minutes, she was gone. I did manage to stop her in the hall on her way out. I felt like a traitor. I gave her a hug. "I'm sorry you're going, Cynthie," I said. "It's okay," she said to me, exactly as she had many times before. And off she went.

Current Status of the Problem:

Cynthie is out of the hospital and back with her parents, in another city. Fran, the student nurse who was also working with Cynthie, took it upon herself to phone Cynthie's parents. Up until now they had been unsupportive and had "written Cynthie off." Fran was "severely reprimanded" by her nursing supervisor for having acted in an unprofessional way and for putting her own needs ahead of Cynthie's. I thought what Fran did was great, and surprisingly, so did Dr. Renton.

Strategies for Intervention:

1. To continue "working on" Dr. Renton. I think he has potential.

If the worker is going to be able to tap the "potential" she sees in Dr. Renton, she will have to tune in to the implications of patient suicides in a psychiatric setting. The strong reactions of the system to Cynthie's suicide attempt can be viewed as a signal of serious, unresolved issues in this area. It is not unusual for helping systems to be very unhelpful to their own staff members at times of stress. Instead of providing support through some form of mutual aid, the defensiveness in the system is heightened by a crisis, and this can result in an effort to place blame. Chapter 19 explores ways in which a worker can move from a specific example, such as this case, to trying to deal with the underlying problem in the system.

CONFRONTATION, SOCIAL PRESSURE, AND ADVOCACY

If we think of agencies and institutions as social systems, employing the organic model used earlier to describe the group, then some of the processes observed in small groups may also apply to larger systems. One such idea is Lewin's (1951a) description of systems as maintaining a **quasi-stationary social equilibrium** in which "customs" and "social habits" create an "inner resistance" to change. This resistance to change is found in the individual, the family, the group, the community, agencies, and institutions. In the model presented thus far, the worker has endeavored to open up communications between clients and relevant systems in order to help overcome the obstacles to the inherent common ground (e.g., the individual and the group). The worker has at all times been reaching for the desire for change of both the client and the system.

Because of their inherent resistance to change, systems and their representatives do not always respond with a willingness to deal with the obstacles. Even with a worker who is understanding of the system's problems and who makes every effort to influence the system in a positive manner, there may be no progress. In such situations the use of confrontation and social pressure is required. Some additional force is needed to overcome the system's resistance to change and to bring to its attention the need to respond in new ways to the client's needs. This additional force upsets the "quasi-stationary equilibrium" and makes the system more open to change.

This argument is not unlike ideas of crisis theory which suggest that individuals and families are most open to change when a crisis makes maintenance of a situation untenable. Under conditions where negotiation has failed or has not even been given a chance, something is needed to upset the dysfunctional equilibrium. The resistance part of the system's ambivalence is so strong, it dominates the interaction. In the next section of this chapter, I describe an example in which this type of intervention proved necessary. It illustrates how a worker acted as an advocate for an overwhelmed client facing a housing crisis without receiving help from housing agencies.[1]

Client Advocacy: Helping a Client Negotiate the Housing System

In this example, a worker found it necessary to take the role of advocate of a client's right to housing when that client was ignored by an unyielding bureaucracy. As with the previous example, the worker was not hired as a client advocate, but rather, considered advocacy part of his role as a worker. In this case, the worker was employed by a child welfare agency in a large Canadian city. His client was a woman of 35, French-speaking, a single parent with four children. She had requested placement of her children with the agency because of severe depression after her husband left her. After a number of interviews, it appeared to the worker that one precipitating crisis was that the client, Mrs. Belanger, had been forced to move twice within the past six months because of changes in ownership of the buildings she lived in. Adequate and affordable accommodations were not available. As an alternative to accepting the children for placement, the worker proposed the following plan: Mrs. Belanger would continue seeing a psychiatrist to help her with her depression; the worker would arrange for homemaker services to give her some assistance with the children; he would also work with her to try to solve the housing problem. The client agreed. The worker felt this was a good example of a situation in which, with personal support and help in dealing with the housing system, the client had the strength to maintain herself and her children. The problem seemed to be partially the responsibility of society for not providing adequate housing for this family. Thus, the worker began a four-month odyssey that provided a lesson in the complexity of the housing system and evidence of the power of persistence.

As a first step, after consulting with Mrs. Belanger, the worker addressed a letter to the city housing authority. An excerpt from that letter follows:

Sept. 26th

This letter is on behalf of Mrs. Belanger and her application for a 3-bedroom unit.

Certainly this is a matter of urgency, as Mrs. Belanger and her children have been obliged to move twice in a very short time as her landlords have sold out. There is cause for serious concern, as Mrs. Belanger's health demands a stable environment.

Due to the limits of her financial situation and her health, her choice of adequate shelter depends on your assistance.

Mrs. Belanger, as I know her, is a quiet, reserved woman with very good house-keeping standards and well-behaved children. It is my opinion that she would be a very good tenant.

To keep her family together and maintain the home, it is imperative that she relocate to a suitable unit in a French-speaking area of her choice as soon as possible.

Thank you for whatever assistance you can offer to the Belanger family.

As the worker developed his case for Mrs. Belanger, he enlisted the aid of allies. The first was the psychiatrist who was treating the client. The psychiatrist's letter to the placement manager read as follows:

Sept. 26th

The above-named client, who is on your waiting list for housing, has been under my direct care for two years. She has exhausted her own possibilities in seeking housing for herself and her four children. It is imperative and urgent that suitable accommodation be found this month, as otherwise her mental health may decline once again with repercussions for herself and the children.

A return letter indicated that the client did not meet the residency requirements for housing within the city limits. The area Mrs. Belanger lived in was technically in another municipality surrounded by the larger city. The placement manager suggested he contact the provincial government housing authority for help. The worker repeated the letters to the housing authority of the smaller municipality. Because of a shortage of housing in the French-speaking area—a shortage that the municipality had done little to rectify—the only help available to Mrs. Belanger was an apartment in an English-speaking area. Since Mrs. Belanger could not speak English, she would have been socially isolated in this area, which would have compounded her problems. The worker made sure to consult with Mrs. Belanger at each step of the process to be sure she understood and agreed with the next steps. She felt identified with her present housing area and feared moving into an English-speaking housing project. They agreed to try to have the residency requirements waived to obtain housing in the city. A second letter was sent to the placement manager of the city housing authority with additional letters of support from the homemaker service. In addition, the worker arranged a meeting with the mayor of the smaller municipality, at which time he raised the problem of Mrs. Belanger and received assurances that the mayor would do his best to help.

Although there were promises of help, the months dragged on with no action. The worker arranged a meeting with the placement officer of the city housing authority and his client. His impression was that the officer was not as interested in the client's dilemma as he was in applying the regulations. As the worker encountered one frustration after another, he noted his increasing depression. After only two months in the shoes of the client attempting to negotiate government bureaucracies, he felt it would not be long before he began to show clinical symptoms of depression. This increased his anger at the way his client and her children were lost in the complexity of agencies supposedly established to serve their needs. With the agreement of Mrs. Belanger and his supervisor, the worker wrote the following letter to the federal government representative (member of Parliament):

Nov. 21st

I am writing on behalf of one of your constituents, Mrs. Belanger, who is having serious difficulty in finding adequate accommodations within her budgetary limitations.

The enclosed letters indicate a series of steps that we have taken on behalf of the Belanger family in support of her application for low-rent housing. I urgently requested that her doctor and visiting homemaker outline their involvement to support the request. Letters were delivered and immediate personal interviews were held with the mayor, Mrs. Johnson of the Provincial Ministry, and Mr. Rolf of the Housing Authority. Unfortunately, we have come to a dead end.

As you will note in the accompanying letter from Mrs. Helflin, Mrs. Belanger has exerted many frustrating efforts on her own behalf. She, too, has been unsuccessful. She has been forced to move twice within the past year, due, in both cases, simply to change of landlords through sales. Another move will occur at the end of the month, as she has received a notice to vacate.

These necessary moves due to no fault of Mrs. Belanger and her children are very seriously affecting her health, as is documented in the attached letters written by various agencies on her behalf. Needless to say, the housing problem and a resulting depression of the mother can only have negative consequences for the children. Our concern is to prevent what will inevitably occur as Mrs. Belanger's health deteriorates further: placement of her children in foster homes.

I am asking that you intervene immediately on behalf of your constituent. I have no doubt that you will be far more effective than my efforts have been.

Over the telephone, the secretary of the member of Parliament promised to look into the situation. The urgency of the problem increased as Mrs. Belanger received an eviction notice. She was to be out of her apartment by the end of the week. It was at this point in the process that the worker presented this case at a workshop I was leading for his agency's staff on systems work—the skills involved in helping clients negotiate agencies and institutions. He reviewed his efforts to date, reading excerpts from the letters and describing his interviews from memory. At the end of the presentation, he shared his utter frustration and anger at what was happening to his client and his feeling of powerlessness to do anything about it. I could tell from the reactions of his colleagues, and the looks on their faces, that they too were feeling the same sense of impotency as they reflected on similar cases on their own caseloads. An excerpt from the workshop follows.

Workshop Leader: I can tell this case has come to mean a great deal for you. It probably symbolizes all of the cases where you feel deeply about the injustices your clients face and how little you seem to be able to do about it. It must hurt and make you feel bitter.

Worker: What good is all the talk about systems work if Mrs. Belanger ends up with lousy housing and depressed, and then turns her kids over to us?

Workshop Leader: I don't think it is over yet. There is always some next step you can take. Does anyone have any ideas?

Workshop Participant: The only thing I would feel like doing is screaming about how mad I am about this.

Workshop Leader: Well, why don't you? If Mrs. Belanger is willing, isn't it time somebody brought her problem to the public's attention? How are they going to know about this kind of thing happening to people if you don't tell them?

Worker: I'm a representative of the agency. How can I go to the papers?

Workshop Leader: Sounds like you need to do some work within the agency to gain support for taking a more public step. Have you spoken to the agency director about that possibility?

Worker: No, I haven't. I assumed the agency wouldn't want this kind of publicity.

Workshop Leader: Why don't you ask your director? He's right here.

In the conversation that followed, the director indicated that he felt social pressure was needed at times, and that this seemed to be one of those times. He defined the parameters within which he felt his staff could operate. He wanted to be informed about cases as they progressed and to be assured that all steps had been taken before going to the press. After that, he would cooperate with staff if they felt that public awareness was the only step left. The director and the worker agreed to meet after the workshop to plan how to use the media in this case. What I found interesting is that the worker had assumed, without asking, that the agency administration would reject going public.

Workers often take this position, and in some cases they would indeed run into stiff opposition. This means that they have some work to do within their own agency systems to obtain allies and to try to change a policy that categorically rejects the use of agency social pressure on behalf of the client. If they are unsuccessful, then they may have to consider changing jobs or taking other steps designed to bring about changes in agency policy. It would be a mistake, however, to assume the rejection in advance without even trying. This constitutes a way of avoiding getting involved in a confrontation while being able to blame the agency for the problem. Workers have said that it takes a lot of courage to challenge their own agency system, and I agree. The process of social change is not an easy one. However, a sense of professional identification that extend beyond affiliation as an agency staff member requires that workers take some risks along the way.

After the discussion with the client in which she agreed with the strategy, the worker contacted the local reporter who covered the social services in that city. The following edited excerpt is from the newspaper story on the case of Mrs. Belanger.

Nov. 29th
"TAKE MY CHILDREN," MOM PLEADS

If Mrs. B. doesn't get help within the month, she will be forced to turn her children over to the Children's Aid Society.

Ron Strong, a Children's Aid Worker, said the separated woman's plight is critical as she and her four children continue to survive on a $464-a-month mother's allowance she receives.

This has been her only source of income since her husband left in April.

The problem is housing. The family finds itself forced to move this weekend for the third time this year because the house in which they are living has been sold.

She has two boys and two girls between the ages of eight and 12 and needs a three-bedroom accommodation that will not eat up half the monthly income, Mr. Strong said.

An added problem is that Mrs. B. only speaks French and must live in a French-speaking area. She has been living in _____, which, Mr. Strong said, is causing her another problem.

In living outside the community boundary, technically she is not eligible for a housing unit under the Housing Authority until she has been living in the city for a year.

"And the Provincial Housing Corp. has no units in other sections of the city—only further out—and even then they haven't offered her anything," Mr. Strong said.

"She has given up all hope," he said. She has already asked the Society eight times if they will take the children.

"The Society is trying to prevent taking them," Mr. Strong said. "I have been working almost full time to find some solution to the problem."

Is there a solution?

"City Housing can waive the eligibility in December, and they must do it—there is no other route to go," he said. "If it doesn't happen, the Society will have to take the children."

"She is a good mother and tenant," Mr. Strong said. "But another month and the situation will move to emergency proportions."

A few days after the appearance of this article, the worker and Mrs. Belanger met with the federal representative, the member of Parliament, who was somewhat upset at the publicity. Nevertheless, he offered his support. A call was received soon after from the placement officer of the city housing authority informing the worker that the one-year residency requirement was being waived. Soon after, Mrs. Belanger was offered a suitable apartment. It was interesting to note that the psychiatrist treating Mrs. Belanger reported that during the time she and the worker were involved in the fight for housing, a period of almost four months, her psychotic symptoms disappeared. There was something very therapeutic about acting in her own self-interest and starting to affect others, rather than being passively acted on by the system. The experience appeared to be good for the worker as well, as some of his symptoms of depression, sometimes known as the "child welfare worker blues," were also relieved.

This example has demonstrated that there are situations in which mediating between a client and the social system may require the worker to act as an advocate for the client. In this example, the worker made sure that the client was involved in each step of the decision-making process. In dealing with the system (the agencies), he was acting as if he believed they could provide the services if social pressure were employed. In a sense, he used pressure to make a demand for work and reached for the strength of the system. Another key factor was that he acted openly and honestly along the way. My view is that while tactics involving deceit may seem helpful in the short run, they always return to haunt the worker in significant ways. The worker involved allies wherever he could (the psychiatrist, homemakers, etc.). He was persistent and did not give in after encountering the first obstacles. Nor was he fooled by the system's efforts to "cool him off" by passing the buck or making vague promises of action. He made sure to involve and inform his own agency system, so that his agency (the director, supervisors) would feel part of the process. And most important, he maintained a belief in the idea that there is always some next step that can be taken.

It is unfortunate that there were no detailed process recordings of the conversation between the worker and the representatives of the systems he dealt with. It is not possible to analyze the skill use, or lack of skill use, that characterized the work. This would have enriched our analysis of this example. Heyman (1971) addressed the questions related to worker skill use and the ability to establish a relationship with the systems representative at points of conflict. Using the example of a social worker identified with tenants about to implement a rent strike, he describes in detail the way a worker attempted to play a mediating role and provide assistance to the landlord, which in turn could prove helpful to his clients. The key to the worker's effectiveness was that he was always open to the side of the landlord's ambivalence that ran counter to the strong forces of resistance to accepting his help. As long as the system is not viewed as completely closed, one-dimensional, and without ambivalence, then there is always the possibility of employing all of the helpful skills identified thus far.

The earlier example with the housing system raised another area of concern for the agency. Mrs. Belanger was one example of a client experiencing problems with public housing. There were many poor people in town who were not clients of the agency but who were also having these problems. This worker had invested a great deal of time in this case, something that clearly would not be possible for every case on a worker's caseload. What would happen to a Mrs. Belanger who did not have a worker-advocate? Thus, the individual example of the problem facing Mrs. Belanger raised for the agency and its professional staff the general problem of housing for the poor. Almost every individual case raises some issue of public policy. Workers cannot tackle all such issues at one time; however, they have a responsibility to deal with some of them. In this agency, a social policy committee was established to provide leadership in identifying and developing staff programs for dealing with the social policy implications of the problems facing individual clients. In the next chapter, we will explore this aspect of the professional's dual responsibility for both clients' private troubles and society's public issues.

CHAPTER SUMMARY

In this chapter, we examined the social worker's role in mediating the engagement between her or his client (individual, family, or group) and the systems that are important to them. Examples of mediation between clients and the school, hospital, and housing systems illustrated the "two-client" concept, in which the worker attempts to work effectively with both the client and representatives of the systems. At times, advocacy and confrontation were viewed as necessary strategies in order to "unfreeze" systems that proved to be unresponsive.

GLOSSARY

Organismic model A metaphor used to describe a phenomenon in reality. An organismic model suggests a capacity for growth and emergent behavior. These terms—*growth* and *emergent behavior*—describe a process in which a system transcends itself and creates something new that is more than just the simple sum of its parts.

Quasi-stationary social equilibrium A term used by Lewin (1952a, p. 254) to describe a stage in the change process which a person is in balance with his or her social environment. This balance can be upset by external or internal forces, resulting in a state of "disequilibrium" that can lead to change and a new quasi-stationary equilibrium.

Systems or ecological approach A view of the client that takes into account his or her dynamic interaction with the social context.

NOTE

1. For discussion of the advocacy role, see R.M. Kramer and H. Specht (eds.), *Readings in Community Organization Practice* (Englewood Cliffs, NJ: Prentice-Hall, 1969); C.F. Grosser, *New Directions in Community Organization* (New York: Praeger, 1973).

19

Professional Impact on the System

CHAPTER OUTLINE

Introduction

From Individual Problems to Social Action

Professional Impact and Interstaff Relationships

In this chapter we will discuss ways in which social workers can have professional impact on policies and services within their own and other agencies and institutions as well as on broader social policies that affect clients. We will also examine how social workers can bring about positive change in the inter-professional relationships within a setting and between settings. Illustrations of social workers attempting to influence larger systems, professional teams, and so on will demonstrate the functional role of mediation that is at the core of the interactional model.

INTRODUCTION

The term **professional impact** is defined in this chapter as the activities of social workers designed to effect changes in the following two major areas:

1. Policies and services in their own agency and other agencies and institutions, as well as broader social policies that affect clients;
2. The work culture that influences interstaff relationships within their own agency and with other agencies and institutions.

This breakdown is somewhat analogous to the division cited earlier between the "content" of the work and the "process" (way of working). Interest in the first area emerges directly from the worker's practice experience. As workers address the concerns of individual clients, they become aware of general problems affecting categories of clients. For example, in the illustration of the work with Mrs. Belanger, the client who was being evicted and could not find suitable alternative housing (discussed in Chapter 18), it became clear to the worker that Mrs. Belanger's particular difficulty was a specific example of the general problem of inadequate public housing. The worker's attempt to heighten his agency's interest in the problem of housing and his efforts to influence housing policies as part of his role as agency worker and as a member of a professional association are examples of professional impact on the agency, community institutions, and social policies. Similarly, a worker who brings to the attention of the agency administration a negative effect of an agency policy on service to his clients is also attempting to have professional impact within the system.

The second arena for professional impact is the work culture that exists within the agency staff system and between staff members of different agencies. As workers deal with clients, they are constantly brought into contact with other professionals. Services to clients are directly affected by how well interdependent staff members are able to work with each other.

The staff system in an agency develops a culture similar to that of a group. The barriers to the effective development of staff culture are also similar. In fact, my observations of staff systems have indicated that difficulties between staff members often occupy the greatest portion of staff time and energy. When one inquires what the prime source of frustration is for staff members (particularly in large and complex systems and especially if the staff is interdisciplinary), the answer is usually "interstaff relations." Similar problems often exist between staff members of different agencies within the community that are supposed to be working in partnership to meet clients' needs. It is not impossible to discover clients who are suffering because workers in two settings are no longer talking to each other. Efforts on the part of staff members to improve interstaff relationships and to create a more productive culture for work constitute the second area for professional impact.

In addition to provision of direct service to clients, helping professionals have a functional responsibility for attempting constructive impact on these two major areas—policies and services, and the work culture of the system. Of course, it is not possible to deal with every social policy, program, or staff interactional issue that emerges from the work; indeed, it would be a major task even to identify all of the concerns. Nevertheless, it is possible to tackle a limited number of issues, one at a time. For instance, a number of colleagues can begin working on an issue even though it may take months or even years to resolve. It was argued in Part II that the process of taking a problem and breaking it down into smaller parts (partializing) and then attacking the problem by taking a first step, followed by a second, and so on, is helpful for clients. This same process is also useful for tackling questions of professional impact.

Nonetheless, it is important to acknowledge that attempting professional impact is not easy. Let us review some of the factors that can make it hard. In addition to the magnitude of the problems, workers have to deal with many of their own feelings about change. Workers often bring to their work situation an apathetic attitude that reflects their view of themselves as incapable of exerting meaningful influence. Our socialization experiences have generally encouraged us to conform to social structures. Families, schools, peer groups, and work settings do not always encourage individual initiative. While all systems have a profound stake in encouraging members to differentiate themselves and to make contributions by challenging the system and asserting their individuality, they have not always been aware of this need or acted upon it. Encouraging members to be an integrated part of the system is an important imperative; however, the system often achieves this at the expense of individual initiative. Efforts to integrate individuals can develop system norms that encourage conformity.

The life experience of many workers tends to make them view taking responsibility for professional impact as a major change in their relationship to systems in general and to people in authority in particular. Even if workers are willing to involve themselves in striving for social change, experiences in agencies often discourage any further efforts. When workers face resistance to their first attempts, they may often fail to recognize the agency's potential for change and give up. The same worker who skillfully deals with resistance from a client, understanding that resistance is a central part of the change process, forgets this insight when dealing with the agency system. The potential for change is there, but it may require persistence on the worker's part to effect change. If workers remember that agencies are dynamic systems, open to change but also simultaneously resistant, then an initial rebuff does not necessarily mean closure to the worker's effort. Timing is also important. Workers are mistaken if they believe their agency is static and unchanging. An attempt to deal with a problem at one point in an agency's life may be blocked, while at a later stage in the agency's development the same effort might be welcomed.

In many situations, workers are simply afraid to assert themselves. If the agency culture has discouraged previous efforts, if workers feel they will be viewed as "troublemakers" and that their jobs may be on the line, then they will be reluctant to raise questions about services or policies. There are times when for a number of reasons, such as the extreme defensiveness of administrators or political pressures on the agency, these fears are well-founded. Workers in such situations have to decide for themselves, in light of their personal situations and their feelings about the professional ethical issues involved in the problem, whether they are willing to take the risk. If an effort to bring about change is risky in a particular setting, then workers would be wise to be sure that they have allies before they try.

While I have advocated the above views over the years in my teaching and writing, I have done so from a relatively safe position as a tenured faculty member in a university. The very nature of tenure is designed to create the freedom to take risks in teaching, research, and participation in university governance. More recently, while acting in a faculty leadership role in a university whose employment I left, all of my theories, practice principles, and skills related to professional impact were put to the test over an issue of university-wide academic freedom. After exhausting all avenues of negotiation, the Faculty Council I chaired was faced with the need to release a controversial report. When I received a letter from the university administration containing a thinly veiled threat to revoke my tenure and fire me if I proceeded, I felt the full impact of the risks involved in attempting to confront an unyielding system. The report was issued without execution of the threat. While my position on the responsibility of the social worker to improve her or his system has not changed, this recent experience has helped me to be more understanding of why in some situations it is just not possible to act.

In some situations I have observed workers who did not get involved because they held preconceived notions about the administration, not because any actual experience in the agency had led them to fear reprisals. Still, one should not minimize the fact that trying to make a professional impact often requires courage. Lack of time is also a serious factor. In some agencies in which caseloads are maintained at an impossible level, the idea of becoming involved in agency or social change seems completely unrealistic. In such settings, the first efforts at social action might deal with the working situation. Often outside organizations such as professional associations or unions are the best media for effecting such changes.

In summary, the complexity and magnitude of issues tend to discourage professional impact efforts. Workers' general feelings about asserting themselves, as well as specific experiences in agencies, may act as deterrents. Fear of losing their jobs or experiencing other retribution may also be an obstacle to involvement. And finally, unrealistically high caseloads may obstruct workers' attempts at professional impact.

FROM INDIVIDUAL PROBLEMS TO SOCIAL ACTION

Schwartz (1969), in developing his position on the function of the social work profession, argues that the worker must be concerned with both the specific problems faced by the client and the social issues raised by those problems.[1] Objecting to a trend he perceives in the profession of splitting these two concerns so that some professionals are involved only in dealing with the problems of the individual (clinicians) while others are concerned solely with problems of social change (activists), he argues that every professional has a responsibility for addressing both concerns. He cites C. Wright Mills (1959) as one who refused to accept this dichotomy between individual concerns and issues of policy:

> In our own time, C. Wright Mills has seen most clearly into the individual-social connections identified with social struggle. He pointed up the distinction between what he called the "personal troubles of milieu" and the "public issues of social structure," and noted that trouble is a private matter, while issue is a public one. Most important, he stressed that each must be stated in the terms of the other, and of the interaction between the two (Schwartz, 1969, p. 37).

Schwartz rejects the notion of splitting responsibility within the social work profession for serving individual needs or dealing with social problems, and he points out that such a split is impossible if "we understand that a private trouble is simply a specific example of a public issue, and that a public issue is made up of many private troubles." Recognizing that agencies and social institutions can be complex and ambivalent, he suggests the worker's function should be to act as a "third force" or a "hedge against the system's own complexity."

> Where...such a function originates within the agency itself, the image is that of a built-in monitor of the agency's effectiveness and a protection against its own rigidities. From such a position, the social worker moves to strengthen and reinforce both parties in the client-agency relationship. With the client—and with mutual aid systems of clients—the worker offers the agency service in ways designed to help them reach out to the system in stronger and more assertive ways, generalizing from their private experiences to agency policy wherever possible and avoiding the traps of conformity and inertia. In many instances, the activity thus produced is similar to that desired by the advocates—except that the movement is towards the service and the workers are interested in the process rather than having lost faith in it. With the system—colleagues, superiors and other disciplines—the worker feeds in his direct experience with the struggles of his clients, searches out the staff stake in reaching and innovating, and brings administration wherever possible into direct contact with clients reaching for new ways of being served (Schwartz, 1969, p. 38).

In the previous chapter, we saw a number of examples of workers helping clients reach out to the system "in stronger and more assertive ways." The following examples show the worker raising general issues with the system that result from his or her experience with clients.

Illustrations of Agency Change

The worker who is alive to the dynamic tension between clients' needs and the agency service will be looking for opportunities to generalize from direct practice experience to policy issues. Noticing a particular problem emerging regularly in the caseload may be the signal for a modification in agency service.[2] For example, one worker who dealt with groups of unmarried mothers noted the strain that seemed to be felt by the unwed mothers' parents. She shared her observations with other workers in her department, and the result was the development of a highly successful experiment in group service for parents of the clients. A number of illustrations of this process follow.

Hospital Emergency Room Service. For a hospital worker, repeated comments from patients in his ward group about the strains of their first contact in the emergency room (e.g., lack of attention for hours, which heightened their anxiety and that of their relatives, and difficulty in getting information) led to her exploration of the problems with the emergency room staff. The record of the start of this work follows.

> I asked for a meeting with the head nurse of Emergency. I met Ms. Thomas at the end of her shift, and I commented on how tired she looked. She told me it had been a particularly rough day complicated by two car accidents with four victims. I acknowledged that I could see it was really hectic and thanked her for taking some time to talk with me. I explained that I had been meeting with ward groups on 2 East and that a common theme had been patients complaining about their entry into the hospital through the emergency room. I told her I was raising this because I thought she would want to know about the problems and also I wanted to better understand the difficulty from the staff's points of views so I could handle this issue when it arose at meetings. Ms. Thomas seemed irritated at my statements, stiffened physically, and said she and her staff didn't have time to sit and talk to patients the way social workers did.
>
> I quickly reassured her that I was not coming down to criticize her or her staff. I told her that I had worried that she would misinterpret my intentions, and I thought that she had done just that. Would she give me a chance to explain? I said, "I realize it's no picnic down here, and part of the reason I stopped in was to see if there was any way social service could be of more help. Working under pressure the way you do is rough." Ms. Thomas seemed to relax a bit, and I asked how I might be able to help. She said she thought it would be helpful to have a social worker around more often. I told her that might be one way. I wondered if we could arrange a meeting with the other staff members where I could share the feedback and get their reactions. I had no set ideas yet but perhaps if we put our heads together, we could come up with some. She agreed, and we set a time to meet.

The worker's directness and statement of purpose helped to clarify the boundaries for the discussion. She responded directly to the indirect cues of defensiveness by sharing her own concerns. By acknowledging the real difficulties and offering to examine how she, in her function as social worker, might help, the worker quickly changed the situation from one staff member criticizing another to one in which two staff members, each with their own function, carry on the work of using patient feedback to examine their services. The meeting that followed was successful, with staff members having an opportunity to tell the social worker about the difficulties they were facing. In addition, they were able to identify certain changes they could make in response to the patient feedback. The worker, for her part, offered to develop an open-ended group in a quiet corner of the waiting room area for relatives and patients who were awaiting treatment. The group met for half an hour at midmorning to allow patients and relatives to ask questions and to deal with some of their anxieties about the emergency situation. Both staff and patients found the group to be helpful.

At a later date, the worker suggested that occasional meetings be held with patients before they left the hospital to discuss their experiences in the emergency room and to provide feedback for hospital staff. The meetings were instituted on a bimonthly basis and were effective. Both the social worker and the other staff members in Emergency approached other parts of the hospital to enlist their aid when required. For example, a trial program was established with young volunteers to man a children's group in the adjacent outpatient clinic waiting area to cut down the problem of bored children roaming the halls.

In both the case of the group for parents of unwed mothers and the example of the emergency room problems, the workers' sense of their dual responsibility for dealing with the specific problems and the policy issues led them to take their first steps. In these examples, the workers made use of direct client feedback in their efforts to influence service. There are times when the feedback is more indirect and the worker has to examine the relationship between client problems and agency service closely to observe the connections. Interestingly enough, in such situations, some of the dynamics used to understand processes in the group and family can also be applied to more complex systems such as an agency or institution. For example, earlier chapters pointed out how deviant group members may be signaling a problem in the group-as-a-whole. Problems in a system, such as irregular or deviant behavior on the part of groups of clients, may also be providing an indirect form of feedback.

Rehabilitation Institute for Paraplegics. One example of using principles from group work to understand more complex systems is drawn from a rehabilitation institution for paraplegics. The institution had a rule against patients going home on weekends because of a government policy that paid for a patient only on days they slept at the hospital. Systematic work by the staff and administration, including organizing feedback by patients to government officials, led to a change in the policy, and weekend passes were authorized. Three months after implementation of the new policy, the administrator called in the worker to raise a problem. He pointed out that patients were returning to the hospital with serious bedsores and that if this continued, he would have to suspend the pass program. Before instituting such a change, however, he asked the worker to meet with the patients' council to discuss the issue. The administrator had been criticized before when he had instituted changes without patient consultation and was thus hoping to avoid another confrontation.

The following excerpt is from the worker's meeting with the patient council.

> **Worker:** Dr. Mansfield met with me and told me that many patients are returning with bedsores. He is deeply concerned about this and feels he may have to revoke the weekend-pass policy.
>
> **Louis:** (With great anger) He can't do that. If he takes away that privilege, we will wheel down to his office, and he'll have a sit-in on his hands.
>
> **John:** Who does he think he is anyway? We fought hard for that right, and he can't take it away. (Others murmur in angry agreement.)
>
> **Worker:** I can understand why you are so angry. The pass is really important to you. It's important to see your families. But, tell me, I don't understand: why is it so many people come back with bedsores? (Long silence)
>
> **Terry:** (Speaking slowly and staring at the floor as he does) Here at the center the nurses turn us in our beds all the time. When we get home, our families do not.
>
> **Worker:** (Suddenly understanding) And you're too ashamed to ask them, isn't that it?

In the discussion that followed, the group members talked poignantly about their feelings concerning their new-found dependency. Many felt they had lost their "manhood" and were ashamed to need help suddenly for going to the bathroom and for turning in their beds.

So, they simply did not ask for help. As they discussed their families' reactions, it emerged that their wives were often too embarrassed to ask what kind of help they needed. It soon became clear to the worker that the problem of bedsores was an indirect communication to the center of an important new area for service to patients and their families: addressing the problem of dependency, patients' and family members' feelings about it, and how to handle it. The worker's next step was to ask for a meeting of the various department heads to report back on her session with the council.

> **Worker:** A most interesting issue was raised when I talked to the patients about the bedsores, and I wanted to share it with you to get your reactions and ideas.

After the worker recounted the discussion, there was silence at the staff meeting as the department heads thought about the implications of this feedback for their areas. The worker suggested it might be helpful to explore this question of dependency as it was handled throughout the institution and to see if some special attention could be paid to the problem. Once again, the stance taken by the worker was one of involving her professional colleagues in mutual discussion of an issue relevant to their work. From this discussion emerged a plan for raising the issue in the various departments and developing new services to deal with the problem, such as groups for relatives of recently paralyzed patients that would specifically focus on their reactions to the accident and their questions about their ongoing relationships, particularly how to handle the feelings of dependency they were sure to encounter. Programs for patients were also developed, and staff training implications were discussed. Because the worker was open to the idea that her setting was a dynamic system and that change was possible, she was able to enlist the aid of her colleagues to set important changes in motion.

Sexuality in a Home for the Aged. Another example in which a worker's mind-set dramatically affects how she may describe a problem is taken from a home for the aged. At a staff conference, a ward aide raised a problem concerning one patient who was constantly sitting in public places and openly masturbating. This was affecting both staff and other residents, and the social work student was asked to speak to her about the problem. The discussion at the staff meeting was brief, and the discomfort of staff who had noticed this behavior and had been at a loss as to what to do was evident. The student was not happy about having to see the woman and was not sure what she could do, but after some discussion with her supervisor, it began to dawn on the student that her discomfort, and the discomfort of the staff, was related to the fact that sexual issues were never raised at the home. In fact, the staff system operated as if all of its residents were past the point of sexual interest. This had a great deal to do with the staff's view of the aged and their embarrassment about even considering the question. The result was lack of attention to the real sexual needs of residents. This was, in many ways, a form of institutional oppression. In entering an institution, the adult resident was cut off from opportunities to engage in any form of sexual activity.

The student began to check out her hunch that this was a signal of a larger issue by approaching various staff members and raising her feelings. She was amazed to find that she had unlocked a number of major issues with which the staff had not dealt. Staff members were uncomfortable about this area and had not known how to raise the question. For example, there were elderly senile men who continually tried to get female residents and staff into bed with them. Staff joked about these occurrences, although their real feelings were marked by discomfort. After a preliminary survey, the student returned to the meeting with her findings.

The result was a decision by staff to develop a survey to identify the problem as seen by staff and residents, to discuss ways to deal with the feelings of the staff, and to develop new approaches for handling the issue with residents. A workshop for staff using outside consultants was held on the issue of geriatric sexuality. The student social worker's sense of the connection between "private trouble" and a "public issue" opened up important work in a formerly taboo area.

Social Action in the Community

Workers' contacts with clients often put them in a unique position in relation to community and social policies. Their first-hand experiences can provide insights into client needs, gaps in services, and the impact of existing policies that need to be brought to the attention of the community and policy-makers. The complexities of our society often make it difficult for the wider community to know what is happening with the many "left-out" groups. In addition, society has some stake in not finding out the real nature of the problems. Once again, the functional role of mediating between the client and the system—this time, the community—can provide direction for the worker's efforts. These can consist of letters to newspapers, briefs for government bodies prepared by the worker as an individual or as part of a professional organization, organized lobbying efforts in relation to specific legislation, and many other actions.

One illustration of this process comes from my early practice in a small, suburban community on the outskirts of a large city. I was a youth worker in a Jewish community center serving a middle-class population. Over a period of time I noticed two teenagers attending our lounge program who were not members of the center's client population. After I made contact with these youngsters and a working relationship developed, the boys began to discuss their gang activities in town. It became obvious that they were coming to the center in an effort to move away from their peer group because of fear of getting seriously hurt or in trouble with the law. As a new youth worker in town, I had not been aware of the existence of this problem and had not seen any reference to it in the local press. Conversations with other teenagers in the program confirmed the extent of the problem.

At about the same time, I was invited to participate in a mayor's committee on youth that had recently been established to plan the town's priorities in the area of youth programs. More than one hundred workers and volunteers in local youth organizations attended the first meeting. As I listened to the presentations, it became clear that each organization was presenting a brief in support of its own activities. It was also clear that the gang youth population was not going to be part of the discussion. In fact, because of their difficult behavior, these youngsters were usually barred from participating in the organizations represented at the meeting. I attempted to raise the issue and was naively surprised by the reluctance of the group to admit the problem. My notes of the session describe the process.

> After being recognized by the chair, I said we were missing an important youth problem in town. I pointed out that no one had mentioned the gang problem, and yet it was one that must be troubling all of our organizations. There was a long silence. The chairman of the committee, a town councilman, said that he didn't think the town had a gang problem. He felt the gang trouble was usually caused by kids who came over from a neighboring town and that perhaps those were the youngsters I was referring to. He turned to the planning and research coordinator for the county government and asked if they were aware of any serious juvenile delinquency problem or gang problem in this town. He pulled a folder from his briefcase and outlined statistics that in-

dicated very little difficulty in this area, with the exception of some limited informal gang activity in the neighboring town. The chairman of the committee then suggested that since I was new in town, it might explain why I believed the spill-over problem from the neighboring town was really our concern.

I sat down, resolving to keep my mouth shut in the future. I can still remember the embarrassment I felt in response to the patronizing tone of the chairman. A week later, after some reflection, I realized that a community was not much different from a family and that admitting a problem was not easy. Many of the members of the group were unaware of the extent of the problem, and reassurance from the officials was all they needed to return to questions such as the adequacy of the number of baseball diamonds in town. Some were aware of the problem but chose to deny the extent of the difficulty. I decided to strategize before the next committee meeting to develop a way of bringing the problem to their attention more effectively. I also decided that I needed both allies and some initial ideas about how to deal with the problem. When the two teenagers met with me that week, I explained what had happened at the meeting and asked how they felt about audiotaping a conversation with me about their gang activities in which I would maintain confidentiality, leaving their names out; they agreed to help me. I also inquired if there were any other people in the community with whom they had good relations and who might be helpful in convincing the committee that the problem really existed. They mentioned a police sergeant who had been involved with the kids when there was trouble and who most of the youngsters felt was okay. I called the sergeant and met with him for lunch. My notes of that meeting follow.

> I detailed my involvement in this issue, including my abortive attempt to raise the problem. He told me that he had heard about it the next day and had a good laugh at the response. When I asked him why, he told me he had been raising this issue with City Hall for two years and getting nowhere. I asked him what he thought needed to be done. He felt the town very badly needed a youth bureau that could concentrate on working directly with the gang kids. He tried to make contact, but this was not officially part of his job, and his being a police officer created real conflicts. I told him I thought this mayor's committee might be a great place to bring pressure to bear on City Hall, which would have a hard time ignoring a recommendation from its own committee. I asked if he would support me at the next meeting when I played the tape and raised the issue again. He said he could not raise the issue himself, for fear of sanctions, but he would attend. If the committee asked him questions directly, then he could respond. We agreed that I would raise the problem and he would respond.

My next step was to record a one-hour conversation with the two youngsters. In the first part, I asked them to discuss the gang structure and activities in town. In the second, I asked them to talk about themselves, their hopes and aspirations, the problems they faced in trying to accomplish them, and what they thought might be helpful. I felt that it would be important for the committee members not only to be shocked out of their complacency but also to gain a sense of these youngsters as the community's children who needed their help. We reviewed the tape together, with the youngsters editing out parts they felt might reveal too much about themselves and strategizing with me about which parts I should play for the committee so as to achieve maximum effectiveness. I then made an appointment to play the tape for the police sergeant to alert him to its content. At the next session of the mayor's committee, I explained what I had done and requested time to play the tape excerpts. The committee members were intrigued and agreed. They listened with attention as the two boys, in response to my questioning, described in intricate detail the gang structure in town, the names of each gang, whether they were white or black, the number of members of each gang, their relation to larger gangs in the county, and the internal structure of the gangs. They then reviewed a number of gruesome incidents in town of recent gang fights at movie theaters, in pizza parlors, and at the local high school. They gave detailed descriptions of their involvement in "stomping" kids with currently popular hob-nail boots. I asked them how they felt about all of this, and one responded, "Lousy, but what can I do? If I don't go along with the gang, I would be on my own, with no one to back me up." The boys then talked about their future plans.

> **Worker:** What kind of work would you like to do?
> **Tom:** I'd like to be something like a bank clerk, or work in an office somewhere—
> but you need high school for that, and I don't think I'm going to make it out.
> **Worker:** What do you think you will end up doing, then?
> **Tom:** Probably, I'll end up like my brother—going to jail.

At the end of the tape there was another silence in the room, but this time the expressions on the committee members' faces indicated that they were stunned by the detailed description of the gang structure and moved by Tom's fatalism. One committee member asked if all the gang fights that had been described had actually taken place. The police sergeant was asked if he knew about these fights, and he confirmed that they had occurred. He was then asked if he knew about the gangs described, and in response detailed his experiences over the past two years with gangs. The chairman of the committee asked him what he thought they could do about the problem. The police sergeant described the possibility of a youth bureau such as had been created in other communities. The story of the gang groups received front-page publicity in the town paper the next morning, along with an editorial stressing the importance of dealing with this problem. A number of recommendations emerged in the final report of the commission, including the establishment of a youth bureau and the development of special programs at the other youth organizations and activity centers that would make them accessible to the gang population. The youth bureau was funded in the town's next budget, and the police sergeant accepted the job as the first director with a field staff of two.

In this instance I had the advantage of dealing with a small town that was more open to influence, the availability of a very effective ally in the sergeant, the existence of the ready-made forum provided by the mayor's committee, the support and encouragement of my agency administration and board, and the willingness of two youngsters to risk themselves. In other situations, moving from identifying a problem to changing policy might not be as easy.

PROFESSIONAL IMPACT AND INTERSTAFF RELATIONSHIPS

The second area of professional impact concerns the work culture that influences staff relationships both within and between agencies. This is partially analogous to the "process" aspect of the helping relationship, but I am referring here to the way in which staff members relate to each other. It is important to be clear on a number of points. First, I am concerned with working relationships. Staff members need to deal with each other effectively while pursuing their own functions. Personal friendships may develop within a staff system, and they may enhance the working relationship, but it is not necessary to be friendly with a colleague in order to work well together. When interstaff relationships are poor within a system, however, there is usually a strong negative effect on the provision of services to clients. For example, an interesting research project by Stanton and Schwartz (1954) indicated an association between staff tensions and evidence of psychiatric symptoms on the part of patients in a psychiatric hospital. In addition, the emotional drain on staff members and the amount of time and energy expended on such issues can be extraordinary.

Second, the responsibility for strengthening staff working relationships and for dealing with obstacles that block effective collaboration rests with supervisory and administrative staff. If one thinks of the staff system as a group, then the discussion in Part II of this book can be employed to develop a model of the supervising and administrative functions. In workshops I have conducted for administrative staff, I have helped participants analyze problems in the staff system by using many of the constructs and models described earlier. For example, in staff systems there is often a "deviant" member who plays the same role as the deviant in the client group. In larger systems, a whole department or section may take on the scapegoat role, and one can see how the system avoids dealing with its problems by projecting them onto its weakest part. Through analysis of process recordings, audio- or videotapes, it is possible to identify all the skills described thus far—contracting, elaborating, empathy, demand for work, and the rest—as useful for staff management functions. Helping staff members to develop a positive working culture is thus analogous to dealing with the "intimacy" theme described in Chapter 13. A discussion of the use of this model in staff management is beyond the scope of this book, but the essential point is that the functional responsibility for dealing with problems in the staff system rests with the administrative staff.[3] Nonetheless, in spite of this general position, each member of a staff system can make a contribution to effective staff interaction. This is part of his or her responsibility for positive professional impact.

The Agency as a Social System

In one of my earlier publications, I described the agency as a social system and argued for the importance of paying attention to interstaff relationships:

> The complex organism called "agency" consists of two major subsystems: staff members and clients. The client subsystem is further divided into smaller units, such as families, groups, wards, cottages. The staff subsystem is subdivided along functional lines. We have administrators, social workers, supervisors, clerical staff, and so on. In order to analyze a part of a complex system we must set it off with a boundary—an artificial divider which helps focus our attention. In social work, it has been the client subsystem. We study family dynamics, ward behavior, group process, and so forth. While this is necessary, there is the danger that we can take this boundary too seriously. We examine our client interactions as if they were in a "closed" system in which interactions with other subsystems did not have significant impact. For example, we will try to understand the deviant behavior of some hospital patients as their problem rather than seeing this behavior as a signal of a problem in hospital care. Or we will describe our clients as "unmotivated" when they stop coming to our agencies rather than interpreting their dropping out as "voting with their feet" against poor service.
>
> If we view our agencies as open, dynamic systems in which each subgroup is somewhat affected by the movement of the other subgroups with which they come in contact, then we cannot isolate our clients as discrete entities. Instead, we must see the

total interaction between clients and staff as an essential part of the helping process. In turn, to the degree that staff interactions have a direct impact on the agency service, they must also be placed on our agenda. The way in which staff members' relations affect the "productivity" of the agency is thus directly connected to issues of client service (Shulman, 1970, p. 22).

Staff relations can have a profound impact on service. The cultural barriers that prevent open discussion of problems in the staff system are similar to those described earlier in our discussion of group work. In any complex social system there are bound to be conflicts of interest, hidden agendas, residues of bad feelings, misunderstood communications, and so forth; the system, however, treats discussion of these concerns as taboo. The organizational theorist Argyris (1964) describes how the formal organization stresses "cognitive reality" (as opposed to expressions of real feelings), unilateral control in human relations, and the artificial separation of "process and task." He points out how this interferes with genuine interpersonal feedback; openness to new ideas, feelings, and values; owning one's own views and tolerating others; experimentation and risk taking—all factors that vitally affect the productivity of an organization. Organizations continue to function in spite of these problems, operating under what Argyris calls a **pseudoeffectiveness** that corresponds somewhat with the previously described illusion of work. The most important conversations about the real problems in the system then take place in the halls, over lunch, or within subgroups gathering over beers on Friday afternoons to complain about staff members they find impossible to work with. Obviously, client service must suffer under such conditions.

There has been a growing recognition of the importance of paying attention to the way in which staff members work with each other. Braeger and Holloway (1978) wrote an excellent book dealing with this area of practice. They focused on the problems involved in effecting "changes from below" and explored forces affecting stability and change, the initial assessment stage, and the change process itself.

In a contrasting approach, agency efforts to deal with such problems have included using approaches borrowed from the "sensitivity training" movement, such as weekend retreats, encounter groups, and ongoing T-groups (training groups). Outside organizational development experts are often enlisted to assist staff in developing more authentic communications. Under some circumstances, these efforts can pay important dividends, but often they create more problems than they solve. Staff members may be stimulated in the artificial atmosphere created by the trainer to share thoughts and feelings with which other staff members or administrators are unable to cope. When the session has ended and the trainer has left, the ongoing repercussions of this honesty can deepen any rifts and intensify the bad feelings. In addition, staff members who may have felt "burned" by the experience are confirmed in their views that any attention to process is destructive, and their resistance to any form of open discussions of interstaff relationships is heightened. Periodic opportunities for a general review of the working relationships in a setting can be helpful only if the setting is already operating at a sophisticated level of open communication on an ongoing basis.

Because most staff systems are not operating on that level, an alternative process is needed. Rather than attempt a full-scale analysis of the working relationships in a system—a very threatening process at any time—it is often more helpful to focus on specific problems directly related to service issues. By this I mean that the discussion should not deal with the general question of "How do we work together?" but rather the question of "How do we work together on this particular case or in this area of agency concern?" This discussion needs to be built into the ongoing operation of an agency, as opposed to being reserved for special retreats or meetings. By keeping the discussion related to specific issues, one can avoid the trap of becoming personal (i.e., staff members dealing with each other's "personalities"), which is inappropriate for a staff session. Agency staff meetings are not "therapy" sessions, and staff members have a right to relate to each other in their own, unique ways. The only issues appropriate for discussion must be directly concerned with the business of the agency. It is precisely the fear that sessions will turn into personal encounter groups that generates resistance on the part of staff members to a discussion of process.

Focusing on specific issues on an ongoing basis allows a staff to develop the skills needed to be honest with each other at their own pace. As staff find they can risk their feelings with productive results, they will gradually lower their defenses, building on the first experiences to increase their capacity for authentic communications. As stated earlier, this process is greatly facilitated when administrative and supervisory staff are skilled in assisting staff members to deal with each other. Of course, this is not always the case. In either situation, staff members can develop their own skills in relating to others individually and as a group in order to improve the agency culture for work. While the process is speeded up with strong leadership, change can begin anywhere in the system, as will be illustrated in the examples that follow.

Four examples have been selected that typify common situations faced by social workers. In the first, a staff member tries to sort out her relationship with another staff member who shares work with her with a particular client. In the second, a unit in a large organization takes a first step at opening up communications in a system and is surprised to find that this leads to major changes. In the third example, staff members in one system face their responsibility for developing a better working relationship with staff in a related agency. The final example deals with the problem of discovering that a particular client is being served by a multitude of agencies and workers, none of which ever talk to each other. Each of these problems will probably be familiar to some readers.

Interdisciplinary Work with a Client: Who Owns the Client?

A common area of tension between staff members occurs when different workers deal with the same client. The strains are often intensified if the workers are from different disciplines. One variation of this struggle appears in the form of a contest over "**who owns the client?**" (Of course, it is the client who owns the client, in the last analysis.) In larger systems it is not unusual for one group of professionals to become quite concerned if they believe their role is being impinged upon by another group. Status issues are often at stake. More recently, with cost-containment efforts in full force, loss of a professional responsibility can have serious consequences in terms of threats to the continued employment of a whole professional group.

In one example, when nurses began to lead ward groups in a hospital, other professionals felt their traditional territory threatened. This type of conflict has emerged with new force recently as the impact of managed care has led various professional groups to attempt to carve out their "territories." Efforts in this example to discuss the questions of role in order to resolve the conflict failed because of the vagueness and generality used by the two professional groups when asked to describe what they did.

Interdisciplinary meetings often take place at which not a single sentence is spoken that is not full of jargon. When a professional group is clear about its function and the way in which that function is implemented in a particular setting and with particular clients, there is much less defensiveness and little need to resort to jargon. Interprofessional conflicts over territory are often signals of lack of functional clarity within each group. A first step towards resolving such conflicts is for each professional group to work on developing its own sense of role and then attempt to share this, not with reams of jargon, but by sharing specific examples of their work in action. In this way, different groups can become more aware of what they do with clients that is similar and what is different. Division of labor within a system can emerge from a joint discussion of what the clients' needs are and how each group can play the most effective role in meeting those needs.

Cooperation Between the Social Worker and the Psychiatrist. Give-and-take can begin on an individual staff level as members of different professional groups clarify how they will work together with specific clients. In the example that follows, a social worker dealing with Cindy, a 17-year-old girl attending a hospital clinic, is concerned about the lack of cooperation between herself and the doctor on the case. She feels he does not respect her contribution to the work, a complaint often voiced in interdisciplinary settings. Rather than simply complaining to colleagues, the worker confronts the doctor with the issue.

> I was alarmed that Cindy would cut off all contact with the clinic and thus a potential source of help. I was also concerned with how the doctor viewed the case, what his intentions were, and if he felt that my role and opinions in the case were relevant.
>
> I confronted him with these concerns and initially he reacted defensively, stating that he felt she needed an experienced psychiatrist and not a social worker. I replied that perhaps he was correct but that I felt at present she was having enough difficulty in accepting and receiving the aid of doctors, social workers, and school counselors, let alone a psychiatrist. (She had expressed some very strong and negative feelings about psychiatrists.) He calmed down, and I empathized with his difficulty in dealing with her during the interview. I then attempted to get some clarification of our roles in relation to a treatment program. We discussed at length where we might cross each other up and confuse her and decided that we would consult one another before tackling certain problem areas involved in the case.

The important result of this discussion was not that the two professionals no longer experienced conflicts in their work but that they began to develop a working relationship in which the conflicts could be anticipated or raised with each other more quickly. The worker's taking the first step of raising the question had lifted the strong taboo against direct discussion in this sensitive area. If staff members begin joint work with the understanding that there is bound to be some conflict and confusion, then they will be more likely to establish a maintenance system for early self-correction.

Interdepartmental Communications in a Large System

A common problem in large systems is for subgroups of professionals, such as departments, to identify all the problems in the system that are caused by the inadequacies of other departments. It is even possible to observe one group of staff members being identified as scapegoats or serving the "deviant member" function as a way of avoiding facing the system's problems. Because of rules or politeness, as well as the fact that each department has some stake in maintaining the status quo, formal discussion of the problems and the "problem" department usually are not held. The talk in the informal system often consists of speculations on how things would be much better "if only the other department straightened out." When the problem department is expressing a widely held concern, then its members will continue to bring the problem to the system's attention through indirect means. When this department finally starts to affect other departments directly, the response is often to deal just with the content of the issue. This is a mistake, since even if the specific issue is resolved, it will be replaced with another issue if the underlying problems are not addressed.

Having an Impact on the Residential System. To illustrate this process and the way in which staff can use a specific confrontation to deal with the larger question of staff relations, I will draw upon an experience I had as a field instructor for a school of social work with a unit of graduate students placed in a residential institution for adolescents diagnosed as mildly retarded.[4] After three months in the setting, the students and I had observed many practices with which we disagreed, particularly the control procedures used by the cottage staff. The cottage life department had responsibility for general resident supervision and for maintaining the rules of the institution. Staff in this department were not professionally trained, and a serious communication gap existed between them and the professionals (e.g., social workers, psychologists, educators, counselors). Distaste for some of the more restrictive policies was commonly expressed by professionals in the informal system but never directly raised in formal meetings. Our unit went along with this state of affairs, content to carve out our area of service while ignoring the general problems.

This **quasi-equilibrium** was upset when a cottage supervisor refused to allow group members to attend a session led by one of my students. Some of the residents were on restriction (a punishment for behavioral offenses), and the cottage staff viewed the club group as a reward. The supervisor informed my student that he could only see his members one at a time and that he was to use the session to "give them a good lecture on how to behave." Our first reaction at our unit meeting the next day was shock at being instructed how to do our job. After reflection, however, and by applying a systematic analysis of the staff system of which we were a part, it began to be clear that this incident was a symptom of a larger problem of lack of communication between departments.

While we could have easily won the battle of gaining permission to see our group members on our terms, since the administration wanted to maintain student training programs at the institution, we would have further alienated cottage staff and would probably have found our program subverted in indirect ways. We chose, instead, to attack the larger communication problem, using this incident as a specific example. It was apparent to us that a major obstacle was a split in the institution between the training and therapy services.

> The combination of overlapping boundaries and underdeveloped communications resulted in areas of conflict with limited opportunities for resolution. In such a situation, staff frustration grew, and a process of withdrawal was becoming evident. Instead of increasing lines of communications, those that were open were made less meaningful by avoiding discussion of conflict issues. Cottage Life staff, who bear the brunt of implementing the control function in the institution, became the convenient target for criticism. It became more difficult to mobilize the potential within the staff to

make those adjustments which would keep the system in a "steady state." The most serious consequence of these problems was the blocking of "feedback" essential for system adjustment (Shulman, 1968a, p. 45).

Our strategy for action involved three lines of approach. First, I requested permission to attend a weekly meeting of department heads on the training side of the institution. This was the first formal bridging of the therapy-training gap and provided a forum for the discussion of conflict issues. By disregarding the taboo against real talk, I was able to raise concerns directly, and the resultant discussions served to clear up mutual misconceptions. It became clear that staff in all departments were reacting to people in other areas as if they were stereotypes, which led to consistently missed communications. Face-to-face contact made it more difficulty for staff to dismiss each other out of hand. As communications opened up, the interdependence of department heads began to emerge, and the group became an arena for mutual aid. Members found they could help each other with their problems, particularly those in relation to the administration.

In a second line of work, each student in the unit requested weekly meetings with respective cottage attendants to help bridge the communication gap. One result of these meetings was that students could get a more balanced perspective on the problems faced by cottage attendants in dealing with residents. They found that their stereotypes of the attendants, developed by hearing only the residents' point of view and hardened by the general attitude towards cottage staff held in the institution, quickly faded as cottage attendants were able to share their "binds" in trying to do their jobs. Students also took turns coming in on a weekend to get a sense of the issues facing staff and residents at these less structured times. As the students began to listen and to understand, cottage staff dramatically changed their views about student social workers. As the students better understood the realities of the attendants' jobs, they were perceived as "having their feet on the ground." This outreach effort was continued with other areas of the system. For example, to gain a greater appreciation of the problems in the vocational training areas, students took turns helping to prepare meals or working in the center's laundry.

The third line of work had the most dramatic impact. In an effort to break down the isolation experienced between departments, we decided to make an effort to improve communications with the social service department itself. I outlined the problem in a meeting with the head of social service, as indicated in my notes:

> I explained to Mrs. Paul that I was concerned because the students felt they were an enclave in the institution and that they were even cut off from social service. I told her that we felt that we had contributed to this isolation by not attending meetings and by not raising these feelings earlier. I asked if a meeting could be held with the department staff to discuss this and to see what might be done to rectify the problem. Mrs. Paul told me she was glad I raised this, since she had always felt uncomfortable about the lack of connection but wasn't sure about what to do to correct it. She said she was always afraid to raise it. I asked her why, and she indicated that she didn't feel she could make demands on the unit as she would her staff, so she didn't want to seem to be pushing us for more involvement. I laughed and pointed out how we were both worried about the same thing but afraid to raise it. She agreed that other staff members might feel the same way and we decided to make it an agenda item at the next social work meeting.

The meeting provided an excellent clearing of the air as the staff members in the department and the students were able to raise their mutual concerns and to discover a number of misconceptions about each other's attitudes towards student involvement. Specific strategies were discussed for more meaningful student involvement in the work of the department. I moved to generalize the question by pointing out that we felt an estrangement between social services and the rest of the institution, particularly cottage life. I gave the example of our recent experience of a cottage supervisor withholding permission from residents to attend a meeting and shared our beginning efforts to open up better communications. I asked if others felt the same way, and a flood of examples and feelings emerged. It became clear that we were articulating common feelings held by the department members but never expressed. The balance of the meeting consisted of strategizing how we might reach out to the cottage life department to discuss the working relationship between social workers and cottage attendants. An invitation was extended to the head of Cottage Life and his supervisors to discuss this problem, and a date was mutually agreed upon. As the time approached, word of the meeting spread quickly, and comments in the informal system revealed some clues as to why such a meeting had not been held before. It was variously described as a "showdown," a "shooting match," and a "confrontation," and all staff members were tense when the meeting time arrived. To our surprise, the heads of all of the other departments also attended the meeting on their own initiative.

Three meetings were held, and those expecting fireworks were not disappointed. Many work issues were aired for the first time, often with great feeling. It was interesting to note that my attending the training department heads' weekly meetings paid dividends at this point. A beginning working relationship had been developed that led various department heads to offer support when a particular area was under attack, including the activities of my student unit. As we owned up to the ways in which we helped to make the work of others more difficult and as we attempted to be nondefensive, the defensiveness of the other staff members lessened. The focus of the discussion soon shifted from recrimination to identifying common problems, some needing to be dealt with by the departments and others requiring policy changes by the administration. As the list of concerns was drawn up, it became obvious that much work needed to be done even to begin to attack it. The group decided to form four task forces to deal with each general category of problems. Line and supervisory staff from each department sat on each task force so that all opinions could be represented in the discussions. A steering committee was formed with a department head or supervisor from each area to monitor the process, and a deadline was set for reports.

At this point the administration was approached and official support of this ad hoc effort requested. Some staff members had been concerned that the administrator might not value their efforts to institute change. They had developed a stereotyped view of the administrator as being someone who would object to anything that would disrupt the status quo, but when he was approached, his response was, "I'm always besieged by people telling me about all of the problems. It's a relief to have the staff coming to me with some solutions, for once." A memo to all staff clearly outlined his support for the project. What had begun as our student unit raising questions about our relationship to the social service department had become an institution-wide, formally sanctioned effort to attack long-standing problems. In addition, a new structure was developed that greatly enhanced interdepartmental communication at department head, supervisor, and line staff levels.

Thirty-eight recommendations for changes in policy and structure eventually emerged from the task forces. After the reports were reviewed and supported by line staff in each department, the changes were instituted. A sample of the recommendations provides a sense of the range of the topics:

1. Establishment of a representative resident council to meet monthly with the superintendent of the institution and department heads.
2. Elimination of a "gold-card" system that rated residents on their behavior and controlled their access to the recreation program. This system had been generally described by staff as ineffective.
3. A change in the dining room procedures to allow for coed dining.
4. Allowing residents to have a degree of choice in selection of on-campus work assignments.
5. The expansion of social services into evening and weekend time when the greatest need was felt by staff and residents.
6. The combining of the training and therapy services committee into one committee.

Of course, not all of the problems in the institution were solved by these changes. The crucial result was that staff members discovered that they could talk to each other and that doing so might yield positive results. Structural changes (e.g., resident council, combining training and therapy committees) would also increase the chances for better feedback on an ongoing basis. Most important, the experience released a flood of staff energy that had been suppressed by apathy and a related feeling of hopelessness. Staff learned that change could begin anywhere in the system and that they had to risk and invest themselves for those things they really wanted. The lesson was not lost on the social work students or their instructor.

Impact on Relations with Staff at Other Agencies

While providing services to clients, workers are brought into contact with staff from agencies who are also working with their clients. After repeated contacts, patterns of staff relationships develop. When these relationships are positive, they strengthen the cooperation between professionals. When they are negative, because of either direct or indirect cues of hostility or lack of mutual trust, barriers are erected that may cut a client off from the required service. In one example presented at a workshop, emergency service workers described how they had been cut off from using the services of a hospital psychiatric department that was refusing to accept their clients with drug-related psychotic episodes when they brought them to the hospital. A number of workers had undergone similar experiences or had experienced hostility on the part of the hospital staff, and as a result the agency had written off the hospital as being noncooperative and no longer attempted to use it as a resource. A negative judgment about staff members of another agency can quickly become part of the agency culture. New staff members, who have had no experience with the other setting, are warned not even to try. In another illustration of this process, parole officers would not suggest that their parolees use a particular government employment service because of past experiences that they felt had indicated a bias against their clients.

When the example of the uncooperative psychiatric service was examined in some detail and the actual conversations between workers and the hospital staff analyzed, it was obvious that the workers had approached the hospital staff as if they expected to be rejected.

Their aggressiveness in dealing with the nursing staff, for example, was answered by hostility and defensiveness. It was clear that the nursing staff was viewing workers in an equally stereotyped way and that both sides began each encounter ready for a fight. When I inquired if any efforts had been made, either individually or as an agency, to explore this poor working relationship, I was not surprised to find that the answer was no. The workers sensed the tension and hostility during the encounters, but they never directly reached for it to explore the reason for the difficulty. As a staff group, it had never occurred to them to ask for a meeting with the hospital staff to discuss the obvious difficulties in communication. As often happens, the staff of each setting had decided, in advance, that the situation was hopeless.

Analysis of numerous examples of institutionalized conflict between different staff groups leads to an observation that the root of the problem lies in the stress each group experiences in its work. The stress may come from the nature of the client's problem. For example, dealing with teenagers who have had drug-related psychotic episodes is difficult, and because of the issue of suicide, this is a frightening line of work. Lack of support for front-line workers in these high-stress jobs often leaves them unable to tune in to the feelings and concerns of workers in other settings. The conflict between staff members often represents the "flight-fight" syndrome, described earlier in the text, when running from a problem or angry confrontation becomes a maladaptive means of coping with pain. During times of cutbacks in funds and services—so-called "restraint" programs—tensions between overworked, threatened, and unappreciated front-line staff escalate. The unfortunate result is that social services staff are cut off from each other just at the time when they need each other's support and help the most. The cycle can be broken, however, if staff members begin to examine the process systematically rather than viewing the conflicts as personality-based.

After the analysis in our workshop of the example dealing with teenagers and drug abuse, a meeting was held with the hospital staff. The skills of tuning in, contracting, and the rest were all used in developing a strategy for opening up honest discussion without backing the hospital staff into a corner. Reports from workers after this session indicated that the hospital staff had been equally upset about the state of the relationship with this agency. They had sensed the workers' hostility and particularly the workers' lack of understanding of the fact that they were understaffed and somewhat overwhelmed by the cases brought in by the workers. The workers, in turn, were able to share their problems when faced with such cases on the emergency shift. Many of their problems were similar to those faced by the hospital staff (e.g., providing help to a spaced-out youngster, receiving a report of child abuse in progress, and being expected to be involved in both cases at the same time).

The results of the session were a better delineation of the mutual responsibilities of the two settings and the working out of a system for handling the immediate problems when either system was under strain. In addition, an agreement was reached to cooperate in bringing the staffing problem to the attention of the respective agency administrations and supervisory government bodies. While the problems were not solved immediately, the hospital was once again open to agency workers. In the earlier example with the parole officers and the employment agency, a joint meeting resulted in better understanding on both parts about the special problems involved in finding jobs for parolees and the establishment of a special group of workers to handle these referrals and to provide liaison with the parole service.

What becomes clear in many of these examples is that workers can become so overwhelmed by the demands placed upon them that they have little patience with problems in other systems. Communication breakdowns lead to the formation of stereotypes, which then become self-fulfilling prophecies. Client service suffers in the end. Workers will argue that they do not have time for these efforts to improve working relationships between agencies, yet close analysis reveals that poor communication often results in greater expenditures of time than would be needed for efforts to face and attempt to resolve the problems.

A final example of professional impact concerns the common problem of "too many cooks." The following excerpt provides a good illustration. One worker reported an interview with a young mother of six children who was seen by the worker because of her potential for child abuse. After a good contracting interview, the worker tried to arrange a second session but, much to her amazement, she discovered another problem faced by the mother:

Worker: I'm glad you found this interview helpful. Can we get together on Friday?

Client: I would love to, but I'm afraid I'm seeing Ted's probation officer Friday morning.

Worker: OK, how about in the afternoon?

Client: No, I have an appointment with the visiting nurse who is helping me out with my youngest.

Worker: Would Monday be OK?

Client: I don't know, the homemaker comes then, and the family support worker is here as well.

Worker: (Beginning to feel a bit frustrated) Can you tell me your schedule next week, and maybe I can find a time?

Client: Well, Tuesday I'm supposed to see Leslie's psychiatrist at the mental health center, and Wednesday the family court worker wants to speak to me, and...

Worker: My God, when do you have time for yourself?

Client: You know, it's a real problem—but some of these people I *have* to see, and others are so nice, I don't want to hurt their feelings.

Worker: Mrs. T., I wonder if all of these people know that you are seeing the others?

Client: Probably not.

Worker: Would it help if I tried to call a meeting of all the workers you are seeing, just so we can all find out what is going on with you, and perhaps work out some way to cut down on all of this?

Client: Please! Anything would help.

This interview is not unusual. Families with many problems often find themselves involved with such a complicated and intricate system of services that they need a worker just to help them sort it out. This worker called a meeting with the mother in attendance. Everyone was shocked to discover fourteen different services and workers involved with the family, some of whom were providing overlapping services. A plan was developed for the social worker to serve as **key worker** for the mother and for her to help coordinate the other services as needed. Discussions were also held as to how the services could do a better job of using registries to stay informed of each other's work with the same families.

CHAPTER SUMMARY

In this chapter, we have urged that the worker pay attention to opportunities for professional impact both to improve agency and community social policy and to promote better interstaff relationships. Common themes in the examples have stressed the need for workers to overcome initial feelings of apathy and hopelessness, to avoid being overwhelmed by the enormity of problems, to have faith in the potential of systems to change, and to use interpersonal skills in improving relationships.

When I have discussed issues of professional impact in training workshops, I have noted a pattern of response from workers. First, there is a tendency to externalize and place complete blame for the problem on the "others" in the system. When I challenge this, there is usually a great deal of defensiveness and anger. Often there are charges that I simply "don't understand the particular situation." Detailed examination of the specifics of the interactions often leads to a lowering of defenses, particularly if I can be genuinely empathic with the difficulties involved and the feelings generated in the workers. Recognition that they may have had some part to play in the proceedings often leads to expressions of guilt about past or present experiences that workers feel they could have handled differently. This is followed by a renewed enthusiasm about the possibilities for action.

Situations that seemed hopeless may remain very hard to deal with, but some possible next steps are evident. Workers are reassured when they realize that they need only take responsibility for their next steps and that the systems have responsibility for their own. I have come to realize that workers very much want to believe that there is a next step and that they can have some impact. Even though they may fight this idea initially, they would be very disappointed if I agreed with their apparent fatalism. I don't think I need to motivate workers to attempt professional impact on their systems. Rather, I need to reach for and free their existing impetus toward action.

GLOSSARY

Key worker   A worker, usually in a residential setting, who has particular responsibility for providing continuity of service to a particular client.

Professional impact   The activities of social workers designed to effect changes in the policies and services in their own agency and other agencies and institutions as well as broader social policies that affect clients, and the work culture that influences inter-staff relationships within their own agency and with other agencies and institutions.

Pseudoeffectiveness   Defined by Argyris (1954) as the ability of the organization to create the illusion of effective operation.

Quasi-stationary social equilibrium   A term used by Lewin (1951, p. 254) to describe a stage in the change process at which a person is in balance with his or her social environment. This balance can be upset by external or internal forces, resulting in a state of "dis-equilibrium" which can lead to change and a new, quasi-stationary equilibrium.

Who owns the client?   A maladaptive struggle in which helping professionals appear to fight over "ownership" of functional responsibility for a client.

NOTES

1. This position is also argued by Schwartz in a one-hour videotape program, "Program Two: Private Troubles and Public Issues," Lawrence Shulman (producer), *The Helping Process in Social Work: Theory, Practice, and Research* (Montreal: Instructional Communications Centre, McGill University, 1976).

2. For examples of efforts at systems change, see Z.P. Foster, "How Social Work Can Influence Hospital Management of Fatal Illness," *Social Work, 10* (October 1965): 30–35; H.K. Weiner, "The Hospital, the Ward, and the Patients as Clients: Use of the Group Method," *Social Work, 4* (October 1959): 57–64.

3. For further elaboration of the interactional model of supervision and management, see L. Shulman, *Interactional Supervision* (Silver Springs, MD: National Association of Social Workers, 1992).

4. For a full report on this work, see Shulman (1968a).

20

Social Work in the Community

In this chapter we examine the role of the social worker as she or he works with clients in the community. The concept of *community* will be applied broadly, including neighborhood communities as well as milieu communities (e.g., residential institutions, psychiatric wards). This form of practice is often termed "macro," in contrast with clinical direct practice, which is called "micro." Many social work activities are included under the term **macro practice**. For example, a social worker may undertake social policy research designed to influence legislation. The social worker may never actually work directly with clients. This would be an example of what is called **indirect macro practice**. In contrast, working to organize tenants in a housing project to help them influence their housing conditions is an example of *direct* macro practice. Our focus in this chapter will be on **direct macro practice**, in which the social worker is engaging and working with clients in pursuit of community goals and objectives.

NEIGHBORING AND NEIGHBORHOODS

Confirmation of increased professional attention to community concepts can be found in the social science literature as growing interest has been evidenced in the concept of "neighboring" and its social, cognitive, and emotional components. Unger and Wandersman (1985) reviewed the literature from several disciplines, including social psychology, environmental psychology, community psychology, and sociology. The authors define *neighboring* as involving "...the social interaction, the symbolic interaction, and the attachment of individuals with the people living around them and the place in which they live" (p. 141). They review research findings that identify a number of important areas of social support:

> *Personal/Emotional Support.* The extent to which neighbors are willing to greet and visit with each other can serve as a source of social belonging and reduce feelings of social isolation often fostered within cities.
>
> *Instrumental Support.* Neighbors may serve as informal helpers for one another.

Informational Support. Neighbors provide information to each other as they interact. This information may be helpful in locating needed resources.

Personal Social Networks. Neighbors establish linkages with key individuals in their neighborhoods for individual benefit. They use these connections to find and further link themselves to resources in their neighborhood and wider community to solve problems.

Neighborhood Social Networks. Neighborhood social networks are the linkages developed by a group of neighbors. (142–149)

The authors also describe "cognitive mapping" as "an activity neighbors routinely engage in. It has significant implications especially in transient and unstable neighborhoods for determining where neighbors feel safe to travel and where they choose to socially interact with others" (p. 150).

Finally, Unger and Wandersman address the affective bonds within a neighborhood.

> Being a neighbor involves an affective dimension. As neighbors live in interaction or isolation within their neighborhood, various feelings often develop which characterize their relationship to neighbors and the neighborhood. These feelings may affect residents' satisfaction with their neighborhood and may influence their motivation to become involved in ways to solve neighborhood problems....Three affective bonds are suggested: (a) a sense of mutual aid, (b) a sense of community, and (c) an attachment to place (p. 154).

COMMUNITY ORGANIZING PHILOSOPHY AND MODELS

Social work, drawing upon practice wisdom, has from its inception as a profession recognized strengths in neighborhoods and has attempted to define a role that includes working with communities. In an early effort to conceptualize community organization, Rothman (1979) pointed to the peripheral nature of the practice to social work and other human relation fields. He also described a "considerable degree of variation, transition and confusion" in the theory development at that time (p. 25). In an effort to more clearly conceptualize this practice, he described three orientations to purposive community change:

> Model A, locality development, presupposes that community change may be pursued optimally through broad participation of a wide spectrum of people at the local community level in goal determination and action....
>
> Model B, the social planning approach, emphasizes a technical process of problem solving with regard to substantive social problems, such as delinquency, housing and mental health.... Community participation may vary from much to little, depending on how the problem presents itself and what organizational variables are present. The approach presupposes that change in a complex industrial environment requires expert planners who, through the exercise of technical abilities, including the ability to manipulate large bureaucratic organizations, can skillfully guide complex change processes....
>
> Model C, the social action approach, presupposes a disadvantaged segment of the population that needs to be organized, perhaps in alliance with others, in order to make adequate demands on the larger community for increased resources or treatment more in accordance with social justice or democracy. It aims at making basic changes

in major institutions or community practices. Social action as employed here seeks redistribution of power, resources, or decision-making in the community and/or changing basic policies of formal organizations (pp. 26–27).

The area of community practice focused on in this chapter could be described as a hybrid of Models A and C. Another term commonly used to describe such a model is "grassroots organizing." Staples (1984) provided a manual for organizers that elaborated an organizing model starting with a basic philosophy and then describing strategies for implementing an organizing effort. After providing examples of government and corporate actions that directly and adversely affect people in disadvantaged communities, he suggests that

> These are typical problems faced by low- and moderate-income people across America. They exist because people do not control the institutions that affect their lives, because there is an unequal distribution of power, money, and prestige in our society. This is true at the local level as much as in the state and national arenas. Inequality is a fact of life.
>
> To solve problems, people need to get some control over the concrete circumstances of everyday life. Organizing seeks to do this. The person who acts alone has very little power. When people join together and organize, they increase their ability to get things done. The goal is to strengthen their collective capacities to bring about social change (p. 1).

The community organizing model of social work practice is emphasized in Specht and Courtney's (1993) critique of a trend in the social work profession to abandon its traditional mission of working with the poor and the disenfranchised. They call for a return of the social work profession to its historic and "unfulfilled" mission:

> to build a meaning, a purpose, and a sense of obligation for the community. It is only by creating a community that we establish a basis for commitment, obligation, and social support. We must build communities that are excited about child care systems, that find it exhilarating to care for the mentally ill and the frail aged, that make demands upon people to behave, to contribute, and to care for one another (p. 27).

Examples of community-based social work interventions are emerging that address a number of problem areas. For example, Mulroy (1997) describes an effort to build neighborhood networks to prevent child abuse and neglect. Mulroy and Shay (1997) illustrate how neighborhood-based collaboration of nonprofit organizations can lead to innovative prevention programs for child maltreatment. Amodeo, Wilson, and Cox (1995) described lessons learned in an effort to develop a community-based alcohol and drug abuse prevention effort in a multicultural urban setting. These are just a few examples that reflect a growing interest in how problem-specific community organizing efforts can enhance traditional treatment approaches.

THE NEIGHBORHOOD AS COMMUNITY

As in the earlier discussions of social work with individuals, families, and groups, the first question to be addressed is the role of the worker. In working with communities, the worker's role is often more complex because it must be modified in a "task-focused" group that has a formal structure. For example, if the group has a member who serves as a chairperson or president, and that person leads the discussion, what does the social worker do? While we pointed out earlier that all groups informally develop internal leaders, in these task-focused community groups the internal leader may be elected, with well defined responsibilities spelled out in the group's charter. So what is the role of the community social worker?

Staples (1984) addresses the distinction between leading and organizing:

> It is the organizer's job to get *other* people to take the lead. They have to be motivated and recruited, encouraged and convinced that they can really do it. Their knowledge and skills must be developed, their self-confidence bolstered, and their commitment to collective action deepened....Whoever acts as organizer shouldn't be a formal officer or the organization's public voice. S/he shouldn't make policy decisions or tell people what to do (p. 8).

In the excerpt that follows, we will look at worker interventions with an antipoverty action group that was formed to encourage poor people to use strength in numbers to try to change some of the local welfare and school policies that affected their lives. More than 50 members signed up at an initial organizational meeting. The need for structure was evident, since 50 people cannot operate in a cooperative manner without some form of organization. One early task was to identify roles required for effective operation. The term *roles* is used here more narrowly, relying on Hare's (1962) definition: "The expectations shared by group members about the behavior associated with some position in a group, no matter what individual fills the position, are called roles" (p. 24).

A small steering committee met to draft an outline of the group's structure and to identify functional tasks that needed to be carried out by group members: leadership (a chairperson), responsibility for relations with other community groups (a co-chairperson), responsibility for the group's funds (treasurer), and responsibility for maintaining the group's records and correspondence (secretary). As the group developed, other roles became necessary and were created (e.g., committee chairpersons for special projects). By creating these roles, the group was dividing the labor among group members so that each member carried some part of the burden. When **division of labor** and responsibility are not handled well—for example, when a chairperson attempts to do all of the work—the overworked member can become overwhelmed while the other group members feel angry, left out, and apathetic. The greater the apathy, the more the chairperson feels the need to "take responsibility."

In these circumstances, clarity about the worker's function is crucial. In addition to helping the members develop a structure for effective operations, the worker must monitor how well the structure is working and bring any problems to the attention of the members. This group task, called **structure and maintenance**, refers to the work done by group members to examine and maintain in good working order their structure for work. In the example of the chairperson who does not share responsibility, the worker's function would be to mediate the engagement between the chairperson and the other group members.

A Citizen's Antipoverty Action Group: The Role of the Worker. The following example illustrates this work in a steering committee session of the antipoverty action group described above.

> I had gotten signals from a number of members that they were upset with the way things were going and especially with Sid's leadership. He had taken responsibility for a number of follow-up items and had not handled them well. As a result, the group

faced some serious problems on a planned sit-in action that weekend. The meeting began as usual, with Sid reading the agenda and asking for any additions. There were none. Discussion began on a number of minor items. It finally reached the question of the plans for the action, and I could feel the tension growing. Sara began, "Is it true, Sid, that we may not have the buses for Saturday?" Sid replied abruptly, "I'm working on that, so don't worry." There was silence. I said, "I think there is something going on here. What's up?"

Sara continued, "Look, Sid, I don't want you to take this personally, but there are a number of things screwed up about this Saturday and I'm really worried." Sid responded defensively, "Well, what do you expect? You know I have a lot of responsibility to carry with not very much help." Terry broke in, "Every time we try to give you some help, you turn us down." Sid looked hurt. I intervened: "I think there has been a problem going on for some time, and you folks have not been able to level with each other about it. Sid, you feel you have to carry a lot of the burden around here and the group members don't really appreciate how hard it is for you. Am I right?" Sid nodded in agreement. I turned to the others. "I think the rest of you feel that you would like to pick up a piece, but you sense Sid seems to hang on—so you don't offer. Then you feel angry later when things don't work out." They nodded as well. I said, "Look, I know it's hard, but if we get this out, maybe we can work out a way of sharing the responsibilities that would be more helpful for the group."

The community social worker needs to be clear that his or her function involves helping group members work on their tasks. It is not unusual for workers with such groups to be just as uncomfortable about confrontation as the members. As a result, they may try to use indirect influence, or to take over some of the chairperson's functions, or even try to get the group to replace the chairperson. This reflects a lack of understanding about group developmental tasks. It is not at all unusual for groups to run into such problems in maintaining their structures for work. Indeed, if the group could work easily, without such obstacles, it would not need a social worker. The real problem for a group such as this one arises when the members cannot openly discuss these difficulties as they emerge. This is the work of the helping professional: not the details of the structure itself, but the way in which group members develop and maintain their structure. In helping the group to explore this area, the worker is conscious that feelings have a great deal to do with most communication problems and that skills in this area can prove helpful.

Although they were uncomfortable, they agreed to take some time to discuss the problem. I asked the group members why they had not leveled with Sid before. Rudy said, "Sid, we all like you a lot. That's why we asked you to be chairman. I didn't want to hurt your feelings. Since you became chairman, you seemed to forget the rest of us—and frankly, I started to get pissed off." I said, "Did you get the feeling, Rudy, that you weren't needed?" Rudy: "That's it! All of a sudden, Sid was gong to do the whole ball game himself." I asked Sid how come he felt he had to take all the responsibility. He said, "Look, this is my first time chairing anything. None of us has much experience at this stuff—I'm worried that we will fall on our faces. I've asked some people to do things, and they have screwed up, so I don't ask anymore, I just do it." I said, "Are you worried, Sid, that you're going to fall on your face?" He was silent and then said, "You bet." I waited.

Rita said, "I'm probably one of the people you feel let you down, aren't I?" Sid nodded. She continued, "Well, I meant to follow up and hold that subcommittee meeting. I just kept putting it off." I asked, "Have you ever chaired a meeting before?" Rita said, "No." I continued, "I guess you were probably nervous about it." She agreed that she had been nervous. Rudy said to Sid, "Look, Sid, I can understand your feeling worried about the group. We all feel the same way. But you really don't have to carry it all on your back. That's not what we expect of you. We can help out, and if we flop, we all flop." Sid relaxed a bit and said, "It would make it easier if I didn't have to feel completely responsible." I pointed out that the whole group was probably feeling shaky about their jobs and how well they could do them—just like Sid and Rita pointed out. "I don't think that's so unusual—in fact, I think that the fact that you are talking about this is a great sign. At least you can do something about the problem and not let it tear your group apart." They agreed that it was a start and spent the next 20 minutes analyzing the jobs to be done and redistributing the responsibilities.

In addition to overcoming division-of-labor problems, groups must develop formal and informal communication patterns. In the example of the community group, decisions had to be made about who reported to whom, how often various subgroups would meet, who would get copies of the minutes, and how communications at meetings would be governed. Another task required the development of a decision-making process that would be efficient and at the same time make sure that individual members felt involved. In addition to the work described on the formal structure, the worker could observe the informal system at work. For example, shortcuts in communication were found that facilitated the coordination of subgroups within the structure. This had to be monitored because the informal communication system could also serve to subvert the formal system, thus becoming an obstacle in itself.

The worker could also observe the informal assignment of status to various members of the group. Members who performed their functions well and demonstrated the most admired skills in the group would be assigned higher status, and their contributions to discussion tended to carry more weight because of this fact. Differential status can be a source of friction in the group, and the members' reactions to this also can be monitored by the worker.

In a sense, the worker is assigned the special responsibility of paying attention to the way in which the group works on these important structural tasks, monitoring the process to pick up cues signaling any difficulties as they emerge and helping the group members pay attention to these problems. It is not uncommon for community group workers to ignore these critical group tasks and instead concentrate on a strategy of action in relation to the outside systems (e.g., the welfare department, the school board, government officials). These workers may find that after a period of time, the internal struggles of the group have become so devastating that the strength of the group has declined. This results in a loss of group **cohesion**, the property of the group that describes the mutual attraction members feel for each other. Attempts to develop greater cohesion through social activities (e.g., group parties), or as is even more common, by attacking another system and trying to unite members against a common enemy, are only useful in the short run. There are striking similarities between work with community (task-focused) groups and the work carried out with growth and development, support and stabilization, or therapeutic groups. The developmental group tasks are similar, and the skills required by the worker to assist this second client, the group, are similar as well.

In the following example, we broaden the role of the community social worker to examine how it is implemented in helping the group to deal with its formation tasks. The example addresses many of the contracting issues and skills first raised in earlier chapters. Of particular interest is the social worker's skill in dealing with the underlying fears and anxieties of the potential group members. This step is often overlooked, with the community organizer taking over the tasks of the members rather than exploring the barriers to organizing.

A Tenants' Group in Public Housing. In the following example, a social worker contracts at a first meeting of public housing tenants he is attempting to organize. Public housing tenants are usually economically oppressed. They may also be members of minority groups or may face gender discrimination as single mothers. When they accept public housing, they may find themselves treated as second-class citizens, lacking even basic tenants' rights. Poor housing, inadequate maintenance, and non-responsive bureaucracies add a new level of oppression and increase their sense of hopelessness.

As described in our discussion of oppression theory in Chapter 2, oppressed people may internalize the negative self-image, leading to acting out the violence (physical or emotional) imposed upon them. This violence is often acted out on each other. Thus, they may become "autopressors as they engage in self-destructive behaviors injurious to themselves, their loved ones and their neighbors" (Bulhan, 1985, p. 126). In turn, oppression theory would suggest that the oppressors use this self-destructive behavior as a justification for additional oppression.

The cycle can be broken only by helping such clients to find their common ground and to assert themselves by confronting the oppression. The tenant's group was seen as a way of helping the tenants to deal with both the results of the oppression (such as their inter-neighborhood conflicts) and the oppression itself. The examples of the problems raised in the first meeting can be seen in new ways when viewed through the prism of oppression theory.

The social worker in this example has done his preliminary phase work through door-to-door contacts and interviews, thereby gaining a sense of the issues of concern to the tenants. The meeting has been publicized by circulars and posters. Natural leaders in the housing complex have been identified through the interviews, and the worker has requested their help in getting a turnout for this first session. Since the first session began without a structure in place, the worker made the opening statement to a room full of 45 tenants.

> After introducing myself, I explained that I was a community social worker employed by the local neighborhood house and that my job was to work with citizens' groups to help them organize themselves to improve their community—that included their housing, schools, recreational services for kids, etc. After spending some time in this housing project, it became clear to me that the tenants had a number of gripes which they felt the management was not doing anything about. The purpose of tonight's meeting was to discuss these gripes and to see if they felt it would help to organize a tenants' group to deal with the management more effectively. I would try to help them get started, and would stick with the group to try to help it operate effectively. However, it would have to be their group, since I couldn't do anything for them by myself. I asked what they thought about that.

The discussion began with group members starting to identify complaints about poor maintenance, a haughty administrator who ignored simple requests, and so on. There was a great deal of anger in the room, which the worker acknowledged while he kept track of the issues raised. He did little to intervene other than to assist the group members to speak in some order, and, at other times, to encourage members to respond to each other when it seemed appropriate. After a while, the members were speaking more to each other than to the chair. The discussion also moved to complaints tenants had about each other (e.g., noise at night, loud radios, littering) and about gaps in service for kids (e.g., no safe place to play). The discussion was animated. When the list seemed complete, the worker returned to the question of his role.

> "You have a number of issues here which I think can be dealt with if you organize yourselves as a group. There are issues with management, issues between each other, and new services you feel are needed. Now I told you at the beginning that I was getting you started, but that you would have to form your own group to deal with these concerns. I would like to recommend that you select a steering committee tonight that could meet to discuss next steps. For example, they could discuss whether you need an association: if yes, what kind should you have, etc. What about it?" There were murmurs of agreement. I then asked for volunteers and was greeted by silence.

As another demonstration of the importance of process in dealing with groups and the importance of using the skills described thus far, in the remainder of the excerpt we will see how the worker reached into this silence for the underlying concern to which he had tuned in prior to the meeting. If it were easy to get together as a group to take on these problems, why hadn't the tenants done so on their own? The worker had tuned in to the residents' fear of reprisals if they became identified as "troublemakers" in the housing project and decided to reach for it at this point.

> As the silence continued, I asked why they seemed hesitant to volunteer. With no response, I risked my hunch and said, "You know, I was thinking about this before the meeting, and I wondered if you might be concerned about reprisals if you get organized. You know you are dependent on this place for housing, and if you were afraid that management might be upset, I could understand that." Mrs. Cain, who has been identified as one of the community leaders, spoke up at this point, "You know, Mr. Brown used to raise a ruckus and complain all the time. He got drunk a while back and they used that to get him." I asked if they were afraid that this might happen to them. Discussion began to explore what might happen, their mutual fears, etc. Mrs. Cain finally said, "I guess we do take a chance, but if I knew you other folks would stand behind me and not run for cover if it got hot around here, I would think about doing it."
>
> At this point, others indicated they would help out on the committee. I said, "It seems like some of your neighbors are willing to take some responsibility for leading this off and getting the group organized, but they want to know that you will back them up." Another member, a tall, older man with gray hair who hadn't spoken all evening, said, "It's about damn time we stood up to the bastards!" Laughter broke the tension of the moment, and one could sense an agreement had been reached. I wanted to complete my contracting on my role before I finished the evening. "I want to be clear that I will help you folks get yourselves organized and help you work together, but it will have to be your group. You will need your own chairperson, you will have to make your own decisions." Group members murmured agreement to this. "We can discuss this later, but perhaps I might be able to speak to management at a later point and help them see how the group could be in their interest as well." The meet-

ing ended as I complimented them for making a great start and set up a brief meeting with the steering committee to get ourselves organized.

The principles of contracting, clarifying purpose, clarifying role, and reaching for feedback were central to the effective start of this group. In addition to the contracting skills, the worker's tuning in and effective elaborating and empathy skills helped the group members to examine and overcome a major obstacle to their formation. I would argue that if the worker had ignored their fears, tried to overcome them with a lecture on "strength in numbers," or simply jumped in and agreed to take the responsibility for the next steps *for* them instead of *with* them, then the group development that is central to the worker's purpose would have been seriously delayed. Instead, his empathy and demand for work helped them to find their own strength.

Another important distinction needs to be addressed in working with a task-focused, community organization group. That has to do with the need to clearly define the boundary between individual problems and the work of the group. For example, if a group member raised a specific problem related directly to the member's child (e.g., drug issues, getting into trouble after school, getting suspended for behavior problems in school) it would be a mistake to turn the group into a problem-solving support group for the parent. In a sense, the group member would be subverting the group for his or her own purposes, and the task of the group would be lost in this conversion of group goal. It would be important for the worker to allow for acknowledgment of the specific problem and even offer to talk with the client after the meeting. During the meeting itself, however, the individual problem should be addressed as a larger issue appropriate for the group's task. For example, should the group be working on drug prevention activities for all children? Should the shortage of after-school recreational opportunities be on the agenda for discussion? Is there a need to open up a dialogue with the local school principal on the issue of suspensions and how parents and the parent group can collaborate with the school to help children in trouble? Any of these issues can be included in a task-focused community organizing group (if relevant to the group's purpose) without subverting the group's task. It is the role of the social worker to help "guard" the contract when personal problems are raised in a task-focused group.

In the next example, we broaden our definition of the worker's role even further by focusing on how she or he helps the members to negotiate their environment. In this case, the group consists of welfare mothers in a public housing setting somewhat similar to the one described in the previous example. This time we will explore the "third force" role as the social worker attempts to work between the group and the systems that they must negotiate. In this example, we will see how the worker's mediating role can include confrontation and advocacy when the system representative is not responsive.

Welfare Mothers and the Housing Agency. The group was established by the state welfare agency to explore the problems faced by welfare families and to provide help with these problems when necessary. (This example of practice preceded the recent welfare reform act and the welfare-to-work movement.) Seven women, aged 23 to 45, made up the group's membership. Discussion during the group's second session indicated that their problems with the housing authority and the housing project in which they all lived were central concerns. Examples of these concerns are included in the following excerpt from the worker's record of that meeting.

Mrs. Brown: I don't have any complaint about the building or rent, but if we get more money from welfare for any reason, they (Housing Authority) raise our rent. But if our checks are reduced, they say they can't break our lease to reduce the rent.

Mrs. Melton: They also make us pay for things that people not on welfare do not have to pay for.

Worker: Like what?

Mrs. Smith: During the summer a man from the gas company came and put a tube on my stove so that I could move the stove, and the Housing Authority sent me a bill for $26.00.

Worker: Did you call the gas company for repairs on your stove?

Mrs. Smith: No, he just came.

Worker: Did you discuss this with the office?

Mrs. Melton: That doesn't do any good.

Mrs. Smith: I told them I couldn't pay the bill because I didn't have the money. They said I broke the pipe, so I had to pay the bill or move. So I paid it. But I didn't break any pipe.

Mrs. Lesser: Last summer the children were playing in the court and broke four windows in my apartment, and I had to pay for them. I called the office when they were broken and told them how they were broken, but I had to pay for them anyway.

Mrs. Smith: There is no such thing as wear-and-tear items that most landlords have to replace for tenants when you live in the project.

Mrs. Brown: That's what they tell us.

Mrs. Melton: If they come into your apartment and see the shades are worn, we have to pay for them.

Worker: Do you know of any repairs or replacements that the Welfare Board will pay for?

Mrs. Smith: Yes, Miss D. told us to send in these bills and the welfare would pay for plumbing, shades, oven doors, and things like that.

Worker: What does your lease say that the Housing Authority is responsible for replacing or repairing?

Mrs. Smith: It has all "don't" on the back and nothing else.

Mrs. Melton: They make us pay for everything, and I don't think this is fair.

Worker: Do you have a tenants' group that takes complaints to the office?

Mrs. Smith: Yes, but they [Housing Authority] choose the officers, and they don't do anything about the complaints. They call us troublemakers and try to keep us out of meetings.

(Group members all agree.)

Worker: Would you like for me to invite Mr. Murray [housing project manager] to one of our meetings so that you can find out just what the Housing Authority is responsible for and what your responsibilities are?

Mrs. Melton: It won't do any good. He's great for listening and taking no action on complaints.

Mrs. Smith: Yes, let's ask him. But I don't think he'll come.

Worker: Do you want him to come, or not?

(Group members all indicate yes.)

As they discussed their relationship to the housing project, they found they shared many of the same complaints. Strength in numbers made them believe some change might be possible in spite of their past experiences. In her enthusiasm for moving the work forward, however, the worker missed the underlying fears and doubts only hinted at in the conversation. If it were going to be so easy to take on the housing project, why had they not done so before? At the next session, the worker corrected her mistake and began by trying to determine if the housing issue was still the central concern.

It is important to note that the worker has not taken it upon herself to determine which issues the group members should tackle. A common error in community organizing is for workers to determine, in advance, what issues citizens should be concerned about. They see their work as applying direct or indirect influence to convince the members to act on the hidden agenda. Rather, the driving force for the work must emerge from the client's sense of urgency. The encounter may be a rough one, and the clients need to feel a commitment to the issue to carry them through. At the next meeting, their conversation reflected some of the fears and doubts that had occurred to them during the week. The silences hint at these feelings.

The worker redefined the purpose of the group and gave a brief summary of the concerns expressed in the last three meetings before the holidays to give the group some sort of perspective as to where the group was. The group members were asked on what topic they would like to focus their attention. They agreed that their problems with the Housing Authority needed immediate attention (14 welfare checks had been stolen from the mailboxes).

Worker: I called Mr. Murray's office and his secretary said that she thought Mr. Murray would be willing to meet with the group. Maybe we should use this time to plan for the meeting with him. Make a list of questions you want to ask and what approach to use.

Mrs. McIver: I would like to know if we can have more secure mailboxes or a different type of lock on them.

Mrs. Melton: Anybody could open these boxes—even a child with a stick or nail file.

Mrs. King: I'm there when the mailman comes, so no one gets my check.

Mrs. Melton: I can't sit by the box and wait for the man. I've got other things to do.

Mrs. Smith: Why should we have to wait? If the boxes were better, this would not be a problem.

Mrs. McIver: I've complained about those boxes, but they [Housing Authority] say we talk too much about our business. He said the thieves know who gets the most money and when the checks come.

Mrs. Smith: That's common knowledge that the checks come on the first.

Mrs. King: I'd never tell anyone I was on welfare.

Mrs. Smith: People assume that you are on welfare if you live in the project.

Mrs. Stone: Why can't the police be there on check day? Someone broke into my box, and I had to pay $2.50 for it.

Mrs. McIver: That's right. They [Housing Authority] say we are responsible for the boxes whether we break them or not.

Mrs. Smith: That's not fair. Why should we have to pay for something we did not do?

Mrs. McIver: Most people are afraid to call the police.

Mrs. Melton: You're right. You never know what those people [drug addicts] will do to you or your children.

Mrs. McIver: You remember when that brick was thrown through my window? It was because I called the office [Housing Authority] about those big boys hanging out in the halls.

Mrs. Melton: They can sure make it bad for you.

Mrs. McIver: The other tenants call you a troublemaker if you complain about noise or dirty halls or anything like that.

Mrs. Smith: I complain to the office all the time, not that it does any good. I don't care what the other tenants think. I've got my family to look out for.

Miss Brown: That's right, and look what happened to you last summer. (Laughter from the group)

Leader: What happened, Mrs. Smith?

Mrs. Smith: There were a lot of older boys outside my door making noise. I asked them to leave because my mother was sick, but they wouldn't do it, so I called the office. The police made them move, but they came back and turned on the fire hose and flooded my apartment. (Silence)

Mrs. Wright: They'll get you, all right. (The group agreed.)

The worker sensed the fear in the silences but did not reach for it. Workers in these situations are sometimes afraid to acknowledge underlying feelings of fear and ambivalence. One worker told me, "If I reach for it, I might get it, and then they would be so scared they would back out." This view underestimates the strength of people to face difficult and frightening tasks when they have a stake in the proceedings. Rather than frightening the group members off, the acknowledgment of the fears may provide the added strength needed to make the second decision about the confrontation. The first decision to act for their rights was made in the heat of the exchange of complaints. The second decision, the real one, must be made after the members have had a chance to react to their own bold steps. They must reflect on the risks involved and feel the fear that is associated with taking an action such as this. Workers who do not pay attention to helping clients with these feelings often find that when the crunch comes, clients are not ready to take the next step. It is then that a worker has to take over for the clients—for example, becoming the spokesperson in a confrontation—when, with more preparation, the clients might have handled the problem themselves. In this group, the housing manager's refusal to come to the meeting and a threat against one of the members by a local welfare rights group brings the issue to a head.

Plans had been made for Mr. Murray, manager of the Housing Authority, to attend this meeting. Worker told of her meeting with Mr. Murray and his refusal to come to the group's meeting. A general attitude of pessimism, disappointment, and "I told you so" was expressed by all members.

Mrs. Melton: I think we should go over his head, since he refused to come. (All agree.)

Mrs. Smith: Let's talk to Commissioner Long. He is black and just recently appointed to the Housing Authority Board. (All agree.)

At this point in the meeting, Mrs. King arrives late, appearing upset. In response to the concerns of the worker and the other group members, she reveals that because of her participation in this group she has been threatened by members of a welfare rights group to which she and others belong. This is an example of the problem of advocates taking the position that the system—in this case the Welfare Department and the welfare worker leading the group—is always the enemy. Rather than exploring the genuine common ground between their own group's goals and those of the agency, they attempted to coerce members into quitting the group.

Mrs. Melton: I told you, Mrs. Payne, that he would not come. He does not care about us. None of them do. (At this point Mrs. King came in, looking upset. She apologized for being late and stated that she almost had not come at all.)
Worker: I'd rather you be late than not come at all.
Mrs. Smith: What's the matter? Ronny [her son] all right?
Mrs. King: He's all right; that's not it.
Mrs. Melton: Don't you feel all right?
Mrs. King: (Silent for a few minutes)
Worker: If you'd rather not discuss it, we'll go on to our discussion about the Housing Authority.
Mrs. King: No, I'll tell you.

She then explained in detail how some members of the welfare rights group had come to her apartment and accused her of starting trouble with the people in the project by being in this group and told her that she should get out. She denied the charges but stated that she was upset when they left and was worried that they might cause trouble for her because of her participation in the group. She stated that this morning she got mad with herself for letting them boss her around, so she got dressed and came to the meeting.

Mrs. Melton: How can they cause trouble for you? They don't have any power.
Mrs. Smith: How did they know you belonged to this group?
Mrs. King: I don't know. I didn't know any of the people. I've seen two of them who live in my building. I don't bother anyone. I stay to myself and mind my own business.
Worker: Were any of you approached by this group? (All said no. Two of the five present belong to the welfare rights group.)
Mrs. Melton: Have they bothered you any more?
Mrs. King: I don't really know. I had two slips in my box to come to the office [Housing Authority]. The lady under me complained that I let water run down her walls from my apartment.
Mrs. Smith: I remember your telling me about that.
Mrs. King: I knocked over the pile of scrub water and it went through the holes between the radiator pipes. I said I was sorry, that it was an accident.
Mrs. Melton: They [Housing Authority] should close up the holes anyway.
Mrs. King: The other was that my son made too much noise.
Worker: Have you received complaints before these?
Mrs. King: No.
Group: (Long silence)

This time, the worker had strategized to reach into the silence and explore the group members' feelings and ask them to face the second decision.

Worker: I believe that this has troubled all of you, and I can understand your concern. Let's take a few minutes and think about the group and your participation in it. How do you feel about it? Are you getting anything from the group? (Silence)

Mrs. King: I've been thinking about it a lot. I'm not going to let people tell me what to do. I don't really know what I'm getting from being here. I like to come and I've been able to meet some new people. I think I understand your agency better.

Mrs. Melton: You see, Mrs. Payne, people are afraid of reprisals. I'm older so they don't bother me. I get a lot out of these meetings. Things are clearer to me. And you helped me with those bills from the Housing Authority. Besides, this gives me a chance to get out.

Mrs. Davidson: I've learned a lot. I think my attitude about the caseworkers has changed. I know now that they are not all bad, and it's my responsibility to see that they know what my family needs. Certain things that I did not know about came up and other policies were explained to me. I don't feel sorry for myself anymore because I see other people's problems are worse than mine.

Mrs. Melton: I like coming here; a lot of things that were on my mind about welfare are clear to me now. You have helped me a lot. Besides, if we can get somewhere with the Housing Authority about our complaints, that alone will be a great deal.

Mrs. King: I've learned a lot about welfare, too, that I did not know before. I enjoy the group and I'm going to keep coming. It's too bad more people don't come. It makes me mad to know that they will benefit from all our hard work.

Group: That's the truth.

Worker: Then I take it that you want to go on?

(All agree.)

Worker: I'll follow through and will let you know before the meeting if we will have a guest.

After contact was made with the city commissioners, the project manager, Mr. Murray, changed his mind about meeting with the group. The group members found that if they understood the political system, they could use it by applying pressure in the right places. Decisions concerning public housing are political in nature, and as long as there are no public complaints, problems can be ignored. Using the political system as a tool for citizens is an important step for change. All too often, members of poor and repressed groups have given up hope of trying to deal with the "system." An attitude of "you can't fight city hall" predominates, leading citizens to give up on the institutions, structures, and agencies established to meet their needs. The worker must convey the idea that there is always a next step. After the worker clarified the purpose of the meeting with Mr. Murray, the group members began their confrontation.

Mrs. Smith: I'd like to know what the Housing Authority considers wear and tear items. I don't think I should have to pay for shades that are worn when I came into my apartment or if they have been hanging for five years.

Mr. Murray: If the shades are worn when an apartment is vacant, we replace the shades. All apartments are in good order when you people move in.

Group: (All disagree.)

Mr. Murray: When you move in, you sign a statement that everything is in good order. If you don't agree, don't sign it.

Mrs. Smith: I wrote on the list that the shades were worn. You replaced them, but you charged me for them. Ask Mrs. Payne, she gave me the money for them.

Mr. Murray: You should not have been charged for those shades.

Mrs. McIver: You see, that's what we are complaining about. We don't know what we should and should not pay for. Your men make us pay for everything. Even if we disagree, you take their word for it.

Group: That's right.

Mr. Murray: You should come to me when you feel you are being charged unjustly.

Group: (Laughter)

Mrs. Smith: You're never there, and no action is taken if we leave a message.

Group: (Agreement)

As the meeting proceeded, the manager expressed his feelings about the tenants. It became clear that he had a stereotyped view of the tenants based on those who had damaged property and not maintained their apartments.

Mr. Murray: The problem is that you people don't take care of your apartments. You let your kids wreck the place because you don't own it. You've got a responsibility, too, you know.

Mrs. McIver: I resent that. Most of us keep our places clean. I know there are some people who don't care, but why should the rest of us have to suffer?

Mr. Murray: We clean the grounds, make repairs, paint the halls every four years. It's the tenants' responsibility to care for the upkeep of their agreements.

Mrs. Brown: Gin bottles, beer cans, and urine, stay in the halls for days, and your men don't clean it away.

Mr. Murray: Call me. I'll see that it gets done.

Mrs. McIver: What about the mailboxes? Can't we have better boxes with pick-proof locks? Our checks are always stolen and boxes broken into, and we have to pay for them.

Mr. Murray: There's no such thing as a pick-proof lock. I know the trouble you are having with your checks, and I'm sorry, but if we assume cost, then you people will break in every time you lose your key.

Mrs. McIver: I disagree. I don't think the tenants would deliberately break into boxes.

Mr. Murray: They do, and they will do it more often if I change that rule.

The white manager of this housing project with a majority population of persons of color was treating tenants in a racist and stereotyped manner. His offers to take care of things were largely efforts to disarm this group, probably due to his fear of the strength-in-numbers phenomenon. When the members felt they could not get past the defensiveness of the manager, they again resorted to political pressure, which had worked the first time. The manager responded by inquiring why they had not brought their complaints to him, and the issue of retribution was out in the open. The worker intervened to try to help the manager see that the residents were motivated to improve their living situation.

Mrs. Smith: Who makes appointments to the Housing Authority?

Mr. Murray: The city commissioners make the appointments.

Mrs. Smith: Can one of us go to the commissioners to let them know our problems?

Mr. Murray: My board meets once a month. It's open to the public. The board is autonomous. It sets its own rules within the federal guidelines. We will listen to your complaints.

Mrs. Smith: We want them to take some action, too.

Group: (All agree.)

Mrs. Melton: We don't feel that the building representatives represent us. I did not know about the elections of officers.

Mr. Murray: You were all told about the meetings, and I know it.

Group: (Disagreement)

Mrs. McIver: (Member of one of the committees) Maybe the representatives do not take the time to tell all the people in their buildings.

Mrs. Smith: That man in my building does not represent me. He's not qualified; besides, he does not care about us.

Mr. Murray: You people have lots of complaints, but you never bring them to the office.

Mrs. McIver: Most people don't complain because they are afraid of trouble from the office.

Mr. Murray: We have not put anyone out because of making complaints. I don't see why you should be afraid. There's no reason for it.

Worker: What the group is saying is that the office has ways to put pressure on these people. The fear is here and cannot be changed overnight. These people are not here to attack you personally but the people who make these unjust rules. These people are motivated—that's why they are here. They want to improve their living circumstances. It's up to you and your board to help them.

Mr. Murray: If the tenants think the representatives do not meet their approval, then I'll see to it that new elections are held.

Mrs. McIver: The people don't feel that you are willing to meet with them. They don't feel that you are interested.

Mr. Murray: I'll do what I can and take your complaints to the board. If you like, you may form your own committee.

Mrs. Smith: We will be at your next meeting.

The meeting had to be called to an end because it had run 45 minutes over the scheduled time. The housing manager's reaction to the confrontation was predictable—inspections were suddenly ordered for all apartments. At the next meeting, the worker again attempted to explore the members' feelings about the reactions to their assertive behavior.

Mrs. Smith: Everybody's talking about it (group's meeting with Mr. Murray) in the office. The janitor who came to inspect my apartment got mad because I refused to sign the inspection form. I told him why and he asked who had I been talking to, Mrs. Payne [the worker]?

Group: (Laughter)

Mrs. Brown: They think we are wrong. He [maintenance man] said that there were over $6,000.00 in repairs this year in the projects and that we were responsible for them.

Mrs. King: Andy [maintenance man] said it's about time someone spoke up. Some of my neighbors are blaming us for the inspection because they have not been inspecting apartments.

Group: (All agree.)

Mrs. Smith: I knew Mr. Murray would do something to get back at us.

Group: (All agree.)

Worker: Well, how do you feel about the things that are happening to you?

Mrs. Smith: I don't mind. I knew he would do something to get back at us. But with the agency (Welfare) behind us, he knows he cannot get away with these things anymore.

Mrs. Brown: I heard they were inspecting the apartments so I was ready for them. My apartment was really clean and in order.

Mrs. Melton: They [Housing Authority] have not inspected our apartments in two years or more. Why now?

Group: (Agreement. They seemed to make light of the situation and to take it as a joke.)

Worker: But you still have not told me how you feel about all this, the criticism and pressure from the Housing Authority and your friends and neighbors.

Mrs. Brown: I don't mind. Something had to be done, so we are doing it.

Mrs. Smith: I don't mind either being the scapegoat. I think we can still do a lot more. We will benefit if they [Housing Authority] approve some of our requests, as will those people who call us troublemakers. It's for them too, not just us.

Mrs. King: The only thing I did not like was their going into my apartment when I was not home.

Group: (All agree.)

Worker: Were you notified of the inspection?

Group: No.

Mrs. Smith: They [Housing Authority] can come into your apartment anytime they want—it's in the lease—as long as it's a reasonable hour.

Mrs. King: I still don't want them walking into my place.

Worker: Were non-welfare tenants' apartments inspected also?

Group: Yes.

Mrs. King: They wouldn't like it if it was their place.

Mrs. Melton: They did not miss a thing. We even had to pay for tassels on the shades and missing screws.

Worker: In other words, they went over your apartment with a fine-tooth comb.

Group: (Laughter, agreement)

Mrs. Brown: They even took the screens out of the windows to be cleaned and fixed. I asked the man not to take mine because those windows are high and the children might fall out, and he said I should put parachutes on all of my kids. I could tell he was mad.

(There was a great deal of conversation between members about what they did and did not sign for in regard to the inspection. Their general attitude was surprisingly light and gay.)

Worker: Am I correct in assuming that you want to go on with the plans for the meeting tomorrow?

Group: (All agree, saying, Of course, Why not? and so on.)

Mrs. Smith: We all have asked the tenants in our buildings, but most people won't come because they are afraid of reprisals. They are always asking what we are doing and are interested.

Worker: Are you afraid of the reprisals?

Group: (All chime in) No, of course not.

Mrs. Smith: No, I've always complained about things, not that it does any good. We think we are right. We are not asking for anything that is unreasonable.

Mrs. Brown: My friend said she would not come but would baby-sit so I could go. (Group all agreed that they were not afraid and would all be there Thursday night.)

The worker then suggested that they consider their strategy for the meeting. The members were concerned about speaking in public and asked the worker to read their requests. She refused, emphasizing the importance of tenants' speaking for themselves. The worker's belief in them was important. She offered to be there to help but said that it was their fight and she believed they could do it.

Worker: What approach are you going to use?

Mrs. Melton: Can't we do like we did at our meeting?

Group: (All agree.)

Mrs. Brown: Maybe one person should read the list of requests. Can't you do it, Mrs. P?

Worker: No, one of you should read it. The board will want to hear from you as tenants. What I will do is make a list of your requests and have one for each of you and the board members. Then they can ask you questions. I'll be with you and give you all the support I can, but it's up to you to present your side of the picture.

Mrs. King: That's a good idea, and it will help a lot if they ask us questions.

Mrs. Melton: Sometimes I get all confused and can't say what I want to say.

Worker: Let's all try to be calm and above all be polite.

Group: (Laughter. Personal joke on Mrs. Payne was told.)

Discussion continued about the painting of apartments; cheap quality of paint used; lack of color selection; penalties for not painting and differential treatment of some tenants. The meeting adjourned with plans to meet Thursday night at 8:00 for the board meeting.

At the meeting with the board the members acquitted themselves well, and the board immediately approved nine of their eleven requests. Two of the requests were complicated and required further study, but the board indicated a positive response would be forthcoming. The members of the group and the worker were elated. By using the political system, the members found they could exercise their rights. The balance of power shifted and the pattern of inaction and conformity because of fear was broken; other tenants were encouraged by the positive reaction to the first steps taken by this group. There were, of course, still many issues to deal with. The relationship with the project manager was still poor, but the worker strategized how to help him see that it was in his own interest to recognize tenants' rights. The problem of inter-tenant friction also needed to be attended to, since in the last analysis, peer pressure might well be the most important factor in getting tenants to take responsibility for better maintenance of the project. These next steps seemed more manageable to the group members after their initial success.

In addition to the roles described thus far, the community social worker with a task group has many of the same functions described in the earlier chapters on working with clinical groups. Many of the dynamics described earlier, such as the emergence of the "deviant member," are also evident in task groups such as the one described in the next example. This example also raises a fundamental issue common in community-based groups: "What if the worker has a strong opinion about an issue or the direction the group should go?"

Community-Based Citizens' Advisory Board: The Deviant Member in the Group. In previous chapters we saw how the deviant member in a group can be seen as a possible spokesperson, an ally for the worker rather than an enemy of the group. Stress was placed on the need for the worker not to identify with the group versus the individual but to maintain a focus on helping the "two clients." This clarity of role becomes particularly difficult when the deviant member expresses a point of view at variance with that of the worker.

One example of the functional role of the deviant member in a community group can be drawn from a community-based citizens' group charged with the responsibility of distributing a portion of community social welfare funds. Mr. Fisk has developed a reputation in the group for being outspoken, angry, and intimidating, and usually taking a minority conservative point of view on an essentially liberal board. Given that the worker usually agreed with the more liberal view of the majority, the strong temptation to work with the group against Mr. Fisk needed to be overcome. In the first encounters, the worker lost sight of this role and attempted to rebut Mr. Fisk, thus siding with the majority.

The purpose of the board was to represent community opinion in the distribution of funds. On the agenda the evening of the meeting was the funding of a local women's center that was both politically active and provided community social service. As the group worker expected, Mr. Fisk began by attacking the funding on the grounds that the group was essentially political. The worker, feeling a strong attachment to the work of the women's center, attacked his position by offering additional information in favor of the center. The debate between group members and Mr. Fisk continued, and he ended up losing the vote.

In a retrospective analysis of the process, the worker granted that when Mr. Fisk spoke, some members were silently nodding in agreement. Other members were obviously disagreeing. It was also clear that the group was uncomfortable about taking on Mr. Fisk because of the way he argued his point of view. As can easily happen, the worker was so intent on her agenda of getting the center funded that she ignored the communication problem in the group and jumped in to take sides. An alternative line of work might have been to help other members in the group express the feelings and thoughts behind the nonverbal signals, including those members who agreed with Mr. Fisk. The worker could bring out in the open the difficulty in discussion caused by Mr. Fisk's strong presentation but would do so in order to help the group members and Mr. Fisk in their communications.

With hindsight, it is easy to see that Mr. Fisk represented a larger body of opinion in the community, and if the board was to do its job effectively, then decisions had to be made that took into account a broad range of opinions. There was a good chance that some of the most ardent supporters of the women's center had some mixed feelings about funding the political action component, which was outside of the center's current mandate. In turn, Mr. Fisk and his supporters probably had a sense of the importance of the social service aspect of the center's work. If not, then the discussion would be enriched by a full debate on these ideas in which the worker helped the members from both sides say what they felt, as well as listen to those who disagreed with them. The worker would be free to add her own views on the matter, but she should not abandon the crucial function of group worker. Often, in an attempt to withhold personal views so as "not to influence the group," the worker ends up indirectly attempting to manipulate opinion to the desired outcome. The irony of this is that the same worker may feel and express a deep conviction in the importance of the "community decision-making process." Once again, the deviant member, Mr. Fisk, could have been helpful in strengthening the debate on a contentious issue.

In this next community group example, we examine a common type of program in which adolescents and teens in a housing project are organized to provide service to their community. The social worker's focus is on helping the teens to overcome their internalized sense of inadequacy, which has been reinforced by negative community stereotypes of their competency. The example also demonstrates that each individual member of such a group brings her or his own strengths and problems to the process and not all members will be able to achieve the hoped-for positive results.

Adolescent Peer Leaders: Relationship to the Environment

Type of Group: Task group for adolescent peer leaders

Age Range: 13–19 years old

Gender and Ethnicity: four African-American males, one African-American female, two Hispanic females, and one white female

Dates Covered: 10/15 to 1/13

Group Task: Relationship to the environment

1. Problem Statement: The peer leaders' lack of credibility in the community in which they worked and lived led to criticism from parents, the funding agency, the Housing Authority, and the Tenant Council. Few believed this group could organize positive events in this housing project, undermining the peer leaders' potential and purpose.

2. How the Problem Came to My Attention: During my twice-weekly training sessions with the peer leaders, the group would talk about the rumors and comments that their mothers, neighbors, Tenant Council, or Housing Authority Task Force were alleging against them. I watched the group go from joking about the newest rumor to growing discouraged, doubted their own abilities to create positive events. In late November I announced to the group that the funding agency was going to drop this project because of the negative press that this housing project was beginning to receive in relation to teenagers.

3. Summary of the Work with Process Excerpts:

Thirty teenagers from this small housing project interviewed for the peer leader position. Eight were hired: four males and four females. At the first formal meeting, during their first day on the job, the contract became the tool that disclosed the groups' task: negotiating its relationship to the environment.

Keith (17 years old, African-American) mentioned that Mary, the Tenant Council chair, probably would not let them use this community center every day. Amy (15 years old, African-American) elaborated on how the "green monster" yells and screams at them just for looking at her. I asked why they named her the "green monster." Bruce (15 years old, African-American) answered by pointing to a green partitioned office in the corner of the center. Everyone laughed. I asked if there were any rules connected with our use of the building. They all grunted and chuckled, and Lucy (19 years old, white) enlightened me by asking if I had all day to sit and listen to her list them. I was reaching for their perceptions of their own environment as well as conveying my willingness to learn from them.

As the group began defining the problems they wanted to tackle and the events to work on, they became more aware of what a peer leader group is. The group struggled, however, with the idea of serving as positive youth role models.

Jake (15 years old, African-American), Amy's twin brother, mentioned that there is nothing for a teenager to do in this city. "All we do is go to school, come home, and get into trouble." Gwen (14 years old, Hispanic) added that the weekends are boring, and "Someone needs to make some changes around here." I asked who they thought should make these changes. I wanted to assist them with connecting their purpose as peer leaders with the task of creating change. Bruce answered by insisting that the Housing Authority were the only ones who could create change because they had all the money. Danny (14 years old, African-American), Keith's younger brother, jumped in and said, "Yes, if they were the cops we'd all be in the state pen." They then went on to exchange stories about their bad encounters with the Housing Authority.

I asked if they thought they could make some changes. Once again, I was hoping to help them make the connection between themselves and their purpose. Karen (13 years old, Hispanic) nodded her head yes, vigorously. The Housing Authority was perceived to have all the power, and they continued to have a difficult time envisioning their own abilities to create positive changes. I too was feeling oppressed by this powerful organization, but also realized my need to know the Housing Authority Task Force so decided to attend meetings on an irregular basis.

In the excerpts that follow, the reality of living in a neighborhood in which crime, drug dealing, and murder are all too common is brought home dramatically to the social worker. The community environmental stressors are many for these teens, and the worker must have faith in their resilience to survive and thrive in the face of adversity.

In early November the group ran their first meeting with teenagers from the Project. Forty-five youth showed up for the meeting. The basic goals were to build an organization of youth, brainstorm ideas for future events, and establish themselves as leaders among their peers. On the following Monday I went prepared to process the success of their first organizing meeting; however, they came to work discouraged and quiet. I inquired about their gloomy faces. A few shrugged their shoulders, and then Danny looked over at Keith and said, "Just tell her."

Keith went on to tell me that he was arrested for assault on the weekend. I immediately responded by asking if Keith had been convicted. He informed me that he was given a court date in two months. I avoided details of the arrest intentionally because I did not want to set myself up as the moral teacher or the judge. Lucy, however, was upset with Keith and asked him how he ever thought the group was going to look good if they all went around beating up people. This conversation lasted for 45 minutes and ended with major changes on their work contract. They decided that they needed to be accountable as positive role models "twenty-four/seven" instead of just the two hours they worked each day. They also put in writing that, if any of them are arrested, caught in possession of illegal drugs, or caught carrying a gun, that they are immediately terminated. They all agreed that Keith should not be fired because he had not known about the rule.

During the last week of November, one of their friends, Jed, was shot seven times and killed in front of the community center. Jed was a local hero because he had just signed on with a record label and already had a rap album produced. He was also selling cocaine, resulting in his death, a fact that the group refused to accept verbally. They romanticized Jed's death. It appeared to me that Keith, Danny, and Jake were struggling internally with the decision to choose positive behavior over negative. The world that surrounds them daily is so full of pain and negative options. Their ambivalence about their role as peer leaders showed itself often in the group, putting them at higher risk for negative actions.

After an hour of talking about Jed's death, I asked them to think about how his murder affected them as a group. I saw this tragedy as an opportunity to clarify the need for peer leaders in this community. Keith said, angrily, that the world would do anything to keep the black man down. Jake agreed, adding that Jed was going somewhere, and someone had to go and "take him out." Once again I asked them to focus on the group as it related to Jed. I was aware of their avoidance to address the facts of the murder such as the drug charges and the sad reality that the killers were also black youth. It did not seem appropriate to address this at this time because their grief was so new. Therefore, I felt a deep need to look at the relationship between themselves as peer leaders and an environment where other youth are being killed.

After a brief silence, Gwen said that no one really gives a "fuck" about them. Danny jumped in and shared that his mother thought they were all a bunch of hoodlums and that she is surprised that any of them could even get out of bed in the morning. No one laughed. Bruce added that he thought the whole community was against them and that they all thought the members of this group were just like Jed. "We *are* just like Jed," blurted Jake. "I won't live past 18 years old." Silence fell over the group.

The silence was powerful. I was deeply affected by their comments. I was angry along with them. I was also sad as I felt their pain. "I'm tired of the killing," shouted Amy. "First my older brother is murdered, and then you (looking at Jake) were stabbed this summer, and now Jed, dead!" Amy turned to me and looked straight into my eyes and said, "Tina, no one gives a shit about us. What can we do to change anything?" "Amy, you can prove to yourself by proving to others that you care very deeply about life and you want to see it improve," I responded.

I could see a lot of hope in the anger that we were all feeling. I felt like we were closer to sharing a common vision than ever before. I could see some lights clicking on in the midst of the pain and a new energy for the work being rekindled. I also felt an urgency about our work. The time was now, and we needed to take the opportunity.

Instead of a teen dance, or party at Christmas, they decided to plan an event that would serve the whole community with an emphasis on celebration and healing. They needed money, credibility, and success. The Holiday Bazaar would offer international foods, raffles, free presents for all the children, Santa Claus, a craft corner, face painting, a graffiti wall, and speeches delivered by Amy and Keith. They sent out press releases to several newspapers and TV channels. They especially wanted Channel 7 news because they were the station that had covered the story on Jed. They liked the idea of the news team coming back to cover a positive story on youth. I overheard Amy telling the news reporter, "I believe youth need to be heard in America. We have a lot to say and a lot to give you adults, so listen closely."

During the event, the director of the Housing Authority stood behind the microphone, asked for attention, and proceeded to deliver a speech to the community about how crucial he felt these peer leaders were for this housing project, and how proud he was of them. He then announced to the group, in front of their parents, friends, siblings and neighbors, that the Housing Authority was giving the peer leaders $9,000 to continue their work. The group was stunned by this announcement. Lucy, Amy, Keith, and Bruce flew over to me confused and disoriented by the good news. They were firing questions at me, such as, "Did he say he was giving us money?" "Did you know about this?" "What does he mean?" "Did you hear all the cool things he said about us?" etc. I asked them how it felt to be such a success. I saw their shock at being delivered encouraging news from the Housing Authority, the very agency that they had felt so oppressed by during the past three months. I felt I needed to help them connect the director's announcement with their success. They were slow at internalizing good news, and I was hoping they could absorb the glory as they were experiencing it and not just in retrospect. Finally as the good news began to sink in, the peer leaders started hugging me and one another, exclaiming, *"We did it!"*

We all broke for the holidays for two weeks, then held our first meeting after our big event on January 6. Jake had taped the 7-minute excerpt from the local news the night of our event, so I arranged for us all to view it. We watched it two times and then discussed what our favorite part of the event was. "Being told we could continue working," said Lucy. "Yeah, I was shocked when the director got up there and said those cool things about us. I was scared that he was going to kick us out of the community center," Bruce commented. We all laughed. I then told them I had some more good news. Not only did the Housing Authority commit to donating money, but the drug prevention funding agency also donated some. In unison, they shouted, "How much?" I was so excited to tell them that the amount was $10,000. I really wanted them to absorb their success as a group so lingered in the details.

"That's $19,000," Bruce declared. "We were hoping to raise $200 from selling the food and sodas. Shit, we really showed them." "Who are *them?*" I asked. I hoped we could reconcile some of the pain that months of criticism had brought them. I was also hoping that they would really start seeing themselves as creative and positive people. Naming the "enemies" and realizing that they too could change could reveal to them some very important truths about their own personal power. We discussed every detail that was observed concerning their success as a youth organizing group.

During the next training session on January 13, we focused on our next big event. I started the group with a bit of new information that was being discussed in the Task Force meetings. "Because of your success as a group, the Housing Authority, in conjunction with the funding agency, wants to create five more peer leader groups in this city. They see the success of teenagers working to improve their own environments. Isn't that great! The youth voice in this city will be strong." I was personally so excited about this new development. From my perspective, this was the best news yet because it would provide more jobs for youth as well as reach a large constituency.

The group was silent. I was surprised that they did not seem excited. Lucy then blurted, "What about us?" I was lost and said, "What do you mean? It's because of you that this is happening." I really missed the point here. Lucy continued, "What about us?

They could be taking care of us and trying to improve our voice." "Yeah," Danny added, "they have completely forgotten about us." "We need a youth center," Bruce joined, "we can't keep meeting in this ugly building, on these metal chairs." "We can't even hang up a poster in here," Keith added. "They won't even let us have snacks in this center."

These comments went on for 15 minutes before I asked what was wrong. I felt there was something else going on that I wasn't aware of. They were back to being upset with the agencies and their surroundings. They continued talking about not wanted to be forgotten. I then asked if they would like to help train other peer leader groups. I was beginning to see how much they needed to be recognized on an ongoing basis and felt they were fearful of having their victory robbed. Perhaps if they were given some status among these other groups they might feel more in control.

They changed their tune completely after this comment. They started making plans on how to teach these other young rookies the ropes as youth organizers. They fantasized about their position as the top youth workers in the city and how the mayor would give them all outstanding citizen awards. I felt both sad and happy by their need to be accepted. I realized that the ongoing, daily reality of living as poor minorities in a housing project where they feared eviction was a very heavy burden that I so quickly forgot. Listening to them dream, however, was also beautiful. They had a very difficult time dreaming of a positive future.

4. Where the Problem Stands Now:

The problem still exists. However, the opportunity for the group to see agencies that felt so powerful and so oppressive to be affected by the peer leaders' dedication has made them realize that they do have some control over their environment. The ongoing struggle of daily life, however, feels like an endless battle for some of the youth. Danny was fired in late January because he was caught in possession of cocaine by his mother. The only reason she reported her son was to beat the eviction letter. If tenants confess their mistakes before the Council writes them a letter, they avoid eviction.

Jake is also struggling with his street-self. He was present when two of his friends were killed; he experienced the death of a brother, and another has recently been arrested; and he has experienced violence personally when stabbed in the summer. Rumor is floating around that Jake bought a gun. We have no proof, and Jake denies the allegation.

Keith, on February 8, was convicted of an assault that he committed in October. He will be on probation for a year. Lucy, two weeks before the Bazaar, married a 38-year-old man at the state penitentiary. He's been a "friend of the family" since Lucy was a child, and he is now serving time for rape charges.

These hard realities have certainly impacted upon the groups' newly attained credibility. One step forward, two steps back.

5. Specific Next Steps: I am now working three days a week with the peer leaders. We are currently planning a month of prevention in this city where the peer leaders will perform plays in the high schools, have a poster and essay contest, and a banquet/entertainment night where city officials and funders will be invited. The internal issues in the group, which are directly related to the environment in which they live, continue to undermine the group's work. However, much of my time is spent negotiating with parents and agencies to believe in these youth and encourage their efforts.

Dealing with the dysfunction and the group dynamics is an area that is demanding much more attention, requiring sensitivity and skill, but this is a whole new story.

What is so impressive about this example is the worker's never-failing faith in the capacity of the teens to overcome adversity. She understands the meaning of the "deviant behavior" that they have evidenced and still reaches for their strengths. In the example that follows, which involves work with a group of Jewish senior citizens, the worker also has to reach behind the anger and the acting-out behavior to be able to connect to the underlying pain of feeling abandoned. In this case, the group members feel rejected by their Jewish Community Center, which has moved to a more suburban community following the migration of the Jewish population. A service for these elderly clients who have chosen to remain in the old community continues; however, the relationship to the Center staff is strained. After overcoming the initial conflict associated with her replacing a beloved, long-term worker, this student focuses on helping to renew the connection between the group members and their community agency. This example also illustrates how other mediums such as singing, story-telling, and even joke-telling can be used to develop a working relationship as well as to help a group stay connected with their ethnic and spiritual community.

Senior Adults in a Jewish Community Center: A Changing Neighborhood and Feelings of Abandonment

Type of Group: Senior adults—educational/task oriented

Age Range of Members: 62–82

Gender, Ethnic, Sexual Orientation, Racial Information: Sixteen women and two men. All are white and Jewish, lower-middle-class and on fixed incomes.

Dates Covered in Record: 11/11 to 4/11

Group Task: Relationship to the environment

Introduction: This group of senior adults lives in the same urban neighborhood. Out of the 18 members, 15 are widowed, 2 never married, and one currently married. Her husband participates in the group. The other man never married and has some learning disabilities.

The "G" group has been meeting together for over 20 years. Their membership had 60 people, but over time many members have passed away, including most of the husbands. The group had the same leader for almost 20 years, who worked for the Jewish Community Center (JCC). The group loves her very much and was sad to see her leave. She retired abruptly, never terminating with the group. In addition, the "G" group believes that the JCC fired her or let her go.

Over time, the Jewish community has moved farther and farther out into the suburbs. The group's original meeting place was torn down, and they were forced to meet somewhere else until the new building was finished. In addition, their mobility had decreased over the years, leaving them isolated in their neighborhood and disconnected from their former community.

This group, which used to meet once a week, met with me three times a month at the Jewish Community Center's (JCC) satellite center. Two Mondays per month, I lead an activity and one Friday a month, the Center provides entertainment as part of the Shabbat Oneg (the celebration of the Sabbath) program. These meetings also always include a Center-wide senior adult luncheon.

When the previous leader retired, the group did not meet for about five months. When funds became available, I restarted the group and arranged transportation for them to get to the JCC.

1. *Problem Statement:* The task of the "G" group is one of dealing with their larger system, the JCC, to resolve their feelings of resentment over loss of a leader and abandonment by the JCC. The smaller system, the "G" group, and the larger system, the JCC, need to connect. The group acts as a dynamic system within the community center environment. The "G" group feels devalued by the JCC and therefore disempowered. The JCC did not recognize their strengths as a viable group serving an important need to its members and as an integral part of the Senior Adult program. The contributions the members made in their younger days had been forgotten.

Both systems serve as my clients, the "G" group being my first client and the JCC serving as my second client. My problem is to find a way for the two systems to interrelate. As a worker, I act as a mediator between the group and the environment.

In addition to the "relationship to the environment" issues, the group members also had issues related to meeting individual needs. The members were dealing with loneliness and abandonment on a larger scale. Most have lived alone since their spouses died. Their families do not live nearby anymore. The Jewish community, of which they had been an active part throughout their lives, has also moved away. Their health has deteriorated, and the group members no longer drive or own cars. They have lost their monetary wealth and live on fixed incomes. During the winter months they are trapped within their homes.

2. *How the Problem Came to My Attention:* Before I started the group I gained a sense of how the JCC described the members. The agency considered them a "pushy," difficult group. None of the paid workers offered to run the group when the first worker retired. This is how I, as an intern, gained the assignment. The JCC's Group Services Department viewed the "G" group as burdensome.

I had previously worked with other "less needy" senior groups within the agency. Recognizing that many senior adults have major life issues in common, I was warned by workers that this group was different. "G" group members were considered exceptionally difficult and needy. No worker wanted to resume the group, knowing the state of how the retired worker had ended her work with them. She did not clearly define boundaries nor properly terminate with the group. Therefore, the JCC knew that the "G" group would be angry, hurt, and upset.

Before my first meeting, I telephoned the group's president and other active members. They clearly expressed their anger over being forgotten and abandoned by the agency. They also showed their eagerness to begin the meetings again. On the phone, the members stated how open-minded they were to different activities and projects. They also added how excited they were to meet me and have a new, creative worker run their meetings.

At our first meeting, and many later meetings, I asked the group for some of their ideas and I suggested ideas for some long-term projects. They seemed excited and agreed to bring in materials for future group meetings but did not follow through. Every week they also mentioned how much they missed their previous JCC worker and how much they hated the Center and my supervisor for getting rid of her. In addition, they constantly complained abut being cut off from "everything Jewish" that had left their neighborhood, including the JCC.

3. Summary of the Work with Process Excerpts:
November 4—Meeting with Supervisor

At this meeting with my supervisor, the director of the department, I learned about the "G" group. She said that they were eager to get started again and that we had the funding to start them as soon as possible. In addition, a relative of one of the group members had been threatening to tell the press how the Center had abandoned the group.

I asked my supervisor if she would attend the first meeting to welcome them back. She said she would not attend that meeting but would come to one soon. My supervisor described the "G" group as a challenge. She described their history and the loss of their leader.

The assigned group is an example of what I call the "agency client"; that is, the individual, family, or group that everyone in the agency has worked with or won't work with. These are the clients they assign to students and new workers. At the end of her first meeting, this student will have a clear idea of why this is so.

November 11—First Session

I failed to tune in to the group members. I came to our first meeting with my own agenda. I had plans to introduce one another and come up with ideas of activities for future meetings. I started the group by introducing myself, stating that I was an intern and a student. I look very young, as well, so the members were confused if I was getting a master's degree or bachelor's degree. Next, I asked the members to introduce themselves to me. They each told me their names, how long they have lived in the community, if they had been married, how many children and grandchildren they have, and how long they had been members of the group. Next, I asked the group members what types of things they would like to do. They mentioned singing, dancing, Jewish trivia, current events, exercise (Tai Chi), and bingo. I suggested that they bring in some things such as current events for the next meeting.

I asked the group how they felt about not meeting for so long. I asked them about their feelings toward the agency. This opened up a very angry discussion. The group members bickered with one another and accused me as a representative of the agency for abandoning them. They mentioned how they wished they still had their previous worker and that things had never changed. They were very angry towards me, my supervisor, and the agency.

I had a hard time controlling the group. They all spoke at once and started to argue with one another. I could barely get their attention. I watched them unravel right before my eyes. Their discussion mainly focused on their anger towards the agency.

The group members' feelings of loss and abandonment can apply to many areas of their lives: grown children who do not call often enough; a community that has changed; loss of friends and family members; loss of their active lives as they had known them, and so on. All of these losses can be symbolized by the JCC leaving them and moving to the suburbs. It will take a while for the group to get past their anger to the pain of all of the losses. The young student is very distressed, but to her credit, she decides to stick with the group. She demonstrates a creative way of using activity—songs, dances, story-telling, and so on—to help the members connect to her, their Jewish culture and community, and eventually, the agency.

November 13—Meeting with Supervisor

I asked my supervisor to give the group to another worker. After my trying first group meeting, I did not feel comfortable or competent to run this group. I felt betrayed by my supervisor and other department workers, who had not truthfully warned me about the group. I had left my first group meeting in tears because they had been so rude and abrupt with me. After some discussion with my supervisor, I agreed to stick with the group at least for a month. In addition, I have never quit anything before, so I felt very uncomfortable asking not to run this particular group.

I set my short- and long-term goals for the group. My short-term goals were to develop a relationship with the group members, learn about the individual members, create a group that can work better together, and set rules, boundaries, and limits. My long-term goals included fostering growth over time, helping the members to feel reconnected to the JCC and the Jewish community, intertwining Judaism through cultural and religious activities and celebrations, and capturing their history. My supervisor noted that I did not set goals for myself.

December 16—Second Session

I set an agenda for the group to make the meeting flow more smoothly and to get some business out of the way. This included setting rules and boundaries, collecting dues, registering the members, choosing meeting dates, listing activity ideas, and going over group procedures.

We set some ground rules for the group. I told the group that the last meeting had been chaotic and difficult for me. I asked the members how we could engage in a calm, thoughtful discussion. The mentioned speaking one at a time, being considerate of what another person says, trying to listen instead of talking, and quieting down when I asked them. I agreed with these suggestions, adding that I expected we could have good discussions if we kept these rules in mind.

I re-registered the group members with the agency. The group members did not have to pay full agency dues, but I needed to reconnect them with the agency. Unfortunately, I had no way of getting them JCC membership cards with their pictures on them. Instead, I made special laminated "G" group membership cards with each of their names imprinted on them. The group had its own separate dues to cover refreshment costs.

I tried to connect with the group and link them to Judaism by singing Jewish songs with them. I surprised the group by bringing in my guitar and song sheets. I thought this might be a good way for the members to connect with me. We sang songs they already knew, and I taught them some new songs. The group members were very attentive and participatory. They really enjoyed singing, and some even danced. They asked me to bring my guitar in again for our next meeting.

January 6—Third Session

I used music to connect with the group again. We reviewed the songs they had learned the previous week and sang songs they already knew. One woman in the group played the piano in the room and the entire group sang with her. They played Yiddish songs and other "oldies" that I did not know. They taught me the songs and we all danced. They also showed me all of the line dances they knew, including the "Macarena."

I asked the group if they enjoyed the meeting. I told the group what a wonderful time I had and that I liked to learn from their experiences. They all said how much they enjoyed music and dancing. It seemed important for them to move around and teach me what they knew.

As a music teacher, I know how easy it is to create community and a sense of accomplishment through singing. In addition, I felt that my Jewish songs helped reconnect Judaism into their lives. I tried to demonstrate that they do not need a local Jewish butcher, bakery, or synagogue nearby to keep religion alive in their homes. They have the strength to maintain their identity from within themselves.

January 8—Recruitment of Guest Leaders

I spent this day calling agency workers to ask them to speak at my group meetings. Two workers committed to particular days. One is the Center's Jewish educator, and the other is an experienced senior adult worker. I confronted my supervisor as well. I reminded her that she had promised to visit at the beginning and never did. She said she could not commit to a particular date and I could use her as a last resort. The group had still expressed their anger toward her and the agency. I had already promised the group that she would attend a meeting so they could voice their concerns.

In addition, my supervisor stated that the woman who funded the group wanted to come and visit the group. This raised my anxiety level, knowing how angry the group felt. Also, I did not want to be observed in this capacity. I did not like this idea, especially because my supervisor did not say she would attend with her.

January 13—Fourth Session

I used humor to connect with the group. At the previous meeting we had agreed to all bring in jokes to tell at the next meeting. Only one person brought in a joke clipped from a newspaper. The rest of the members said that they had forgotten that we had agreed to bring in jokes. I brought in a Jewish joke book that I had borrowed. I read most of the book aloud and we all laughed. Many of the jokes were riddles, so the members tried to figure out the answers.

I used Jewish short stories to relate Jewish morals to the group's lives. Knowing that joke-telling would not fill an hour and a half's time, I brought in Jewish short stories. The stories were from the book, *Jewish Short Stories One Generation Tells Another.* The stories I chose were tales about Elijah the Prophet. Each person took turns reading aloud a part of the story. After the story we would discuss its moral and how it applied to our lives today.

I reached for personal short stories from the group members. I asked the group if they knew a short story they would like to share or an experience they had that has a moral. The president of the group shared a well-known Jewish short story. She talked about her childhood, when her father had read to her this story. Other group members recalled when they had heard it and what it meant to them.

February 3—Fifth Session

I brought in the group's first guest speaker, a social worker in my department at the agency. This worker is the agency's Jewish educator. The group had often complained of being cut off from their Judaism, in terms of culture, tradition, celebration, and community. The group also wanted guest speakers to come to the meeting and lead an activity. This worker engaged the group in a discussion about the losses in their lives and within their Jewish world. The group was livelier than usual. They all participated by answering the worker's questions and reading out loud the handouts he brought.

This meeting was the first one at which I had seen them so engaged, happy, and lively. They mentioned their resentment towards the agency, and this worker stayed with this for awhile. He linked this to the other losses they had experienced. His handouts were about Jewish individuals who work hard to practice their heritage and culture without many resources. Other handouts discussed aging and the Jewish religion. As the worker left, they thanked him many times. They also asked him to return soon and wanted to know when they might see him again. They inquired a lot about his personal life. He answered their questions without hesitation, openly and honestly.

I had brought a birthday cake for one of the group members. The whole group seemed very surprised that I remembered this woman's birthday. They all thanked me for the trouble I must have gone through to bake a cake. I told them numerous times that the chef at the agency made it, but they did not seem to hear me. I put candles in the cake and led singing of "Happy Birthday." The group brought a card for her that they had each signed. However, they did not give the card to me to sign. The members still might have been angry with me as a representative of the agency.

February 10—Sixth Session

I had the second guest leader this week. Martha, one of the agency's most experienced senior adult workers, led Yiddish bingo with the group. The group already knew Martha because she had been at the center for many years. Martha had also worked closely with the group's original leader. Martha will be taking over the group when I finish in April. The group really enjoyed using the Yiddish that they had learned as children with their parents. They also liked teaching me the words and playing the actual game. I felt that this game was a valuable experience for them. They connected with another agency representative and piece of their Jewish past that they might not have used in a while.

February 25—Shabbat Oneg (A Jewish Celebration to Welcome the Sabbath)

The male, unmarried group member sponsored this Oneg in honor of his birthday. The entire group brought a card for him and allowed me to sign it. The members were very excited that I had arranged for them to come on this day to see this entertainer. (The male member takes public transportation to the Center and comes to lunch there every day.) The entertainer sang songs in Yiddish, Hebrew, and English that they all knew. Some songs were related to Judaism, and some were familiar "oldies." The group had an opportunity to be with all of the senior adults for the luncheon and have a connection with their Jewish background.

March 3—Seventh Session

The group chose to watch a video, *Mrs. 'arris goes to Paris*. During our snack break, we talked about the movie. The group reminisced about the Jewish theater they used to travel to in the city. This led to a discussion about how much the city has changed and how Jewish restaurants and theater have dwindled. Most of the group members have lived their whole lives in the city and have witnessed the city's changes.

I asked the members what it was like to see a city change over the course of their lifetime. The members individually shared their experiences. This led to some life review, an important activity for people in this life stage. They talked about how their neighborhood had changed. The group always brings Judaism and being Jewish into their discussions.

March 31—Eighth Session

Martha came to run the group again. She brought a Yiddish folk story that had been translated into English. The story was written by Sholem Aleichem. Each of the members took turns reading paragraphs of the story. Martha would pause the reading to ask the members if they knew some of the expressions in Yiddish. They enjoyed practicing their Yiddish again. After the group finished the story, they discussed it. As they had done with other folk tales, the group identified this story's moral. Martha asked the group to relate the moral of the story to their lives and modern society. The group actively participated in the discussion and told her how much they enjoyed the activity. The group also thanked me for inviting her to lead a meeting again.

I brought in a special snack related to the Jewish holiday to spark a conversation around the holiday's traditions and its meaning in their lives. I brought in Hamentashen to celebrate Purim. We talked about the meaning of the food and the holiday. The group members told stories of when they were children how they celebrated the holiday. This included making Hamentashen at home, Purim carnivals, and dressing up like the story's characters.

April 7—Ninth and Last Session

I failed to terminate with the group properly, maybe recreating the situation with their previous worker. I started the session trying to discuss termination. However, the group had asked at the last meeting if they could watch *Brigadoon* at this meeting. When I began discussing how it was my last meeting with them, one member asked to see the video.

I did not continue to reach for feelings. The rest of the group agreed they wanted to get the movie started or they would not have enough time to watch the entire show. I gave up on trying to terminate. I did not challenge their resistance to this sad and difficult topic. They did not seem to want to get into the work, maybe because it would be too painful. Also, it might be uncomfortable for them to say good-bye. I would guess that most endings in their lives have been abrupt, without conversation around the feelings associated with the loss.

April 11—Last Shabbat Oneg

I terminated with the group. Normally I do not directly speak with my group for an extended period of time at the Shabbat Onegs. However, this week I spent a half hour with the group. I asked the group members what they had enjoyed about our time together. They mentioned my willingness to give them a chance and my perseverance. They added how much they had enjoyed my creativity in singing and dancing with them.

I asked the group members what they did not like about our group, or what I could have done better. The group members were silent. They said I did the best that I could do. I feel that I failed the group in many ways. I had wanted to capture their history on tape, video, or a scrapbook to demonstrate how active they had been in the Jewish community. The group members wanted more task and activity meetings, whereas I would have enjoyed more support group type meetings. I thought the group members would benefit more from working through their issues in that way. However, that is not the route they wanted to take to deal with their issues. Through some activities and discussions, we spoke about loss, abandonment, and resentment toward the agency. I had a difficult time always starting from where the group was.

I shared my feelings toward the group. When it was time to say good-bye, the group gave me a card which all of them had signed. They told me to save the card so I would always remember them. I asked if they were worried that I might forget about them. They said I might since I was graduating and getting a new job. I told them that I had a valuable experience working with them, and that I would not forget them. I honestly stated that I had often had a difficult time working with them, but that we had grown close over the past five months. The group members asked if I would visit the "old ladies" once in a while to update them on my life. I did not make them any promises, but I wished them all good luck in the future.

4. *Where the Problem Stands Now:*

I have observed a change in the way the JCC, its workers, and other senior adult members view the "G" group. The group has become an integral part of the senior program at the JCC. They are recognized by both the JCC workers and other senior members as an important part of the senior adult community. Agency workers greet group members when they are in the building. The "G" group's reserved lunch table used to be placed in the back of the room. Over time, the worker has moved their table to the front. Other senior adults join the "G" group members at their table for lunch and sometimes for their meetings. The agency worker who leads the luncheon has started to welcome the group members and thank them for attending.

When I approached workers in my department to volunteer to lead a program for the group, many accepted. They knew of the group's reputation and were pleasantly surprised by the members. The group members were participatory and interactive with the guest leaders and thanked them for their time. They conveyed how appreciative they were and always asked the leaders to return again soon.

One agency senior adult worker, Martha, has volunteered to take over my group when I leave the agency. She initially turned down the responsibility of running the group because they were a "tough" group and might have been too time-consuming. Because she has been at the JCC for a very long time, she has established a rapport with the group. The "G" group members are excited to have an experienced worker with whom they are familiar. I have begun to transition in this new leader and met with her several times to discuss the group. This worker had led a successful activity with the group when I invited her to serve as a guest leader.

The group is still working on getting what they want and expect from the agency. This includes respect and appreciation. They combat the agency (and societal) view of useless elderly people who should and can be discarded. The group strives to be valued by the Jewish community and fears abandonment by the community again in the future.

5. *Specific Next Steps:*

1. I will properly transition the group to the new worker they will be with when I leave the agency.

2. I will convey to the group that they are an important, integral part of the agency. As an agency representative, I will recognize the active role they currently have here and value their past active membership.

3. I will properly train the worker who will be taking my place as the "G" group leader and liaison to the agency.

4. I will, at every opportunity, convey to the group their importance to the agency.

5. I will describe to the group the impact they made on me, both emotionally and professionally.

6. I will encourage the group to always challenge the agency when they do not feel that they are being treated fairly or with respect.

7. I will describe to my supervisor, an important person at the agency, the positive experience I had with this group and the group's concerns.

8. I will also tell my supervisor the value of having this group as part of the agency and emphasize that they should not be taken for granted, scapegoated, or abandoned. This goes against the JCC's mission.

9. Lastly, I will be a better social worker as a result of my work with the "G" group. I will always function as a worker with two clients, my group and my agency. I will help these two systems negotiate with each other to empower my clients. I will never forget the important social work lessons this population and group taught me during the six months that I worked with them.

THE MILIEU AS COMMUNITY

In the final section of this chapter on community work, we will focus on the milieu as community. For many clients, their community may be a residential center or a hospital ward. While treatment programs may have some impact on their lives, the day-to-day experiences of living with and working with staff and other residents will always have the most powerful effects. If a treatment group teaches about life empowerment while its members feel they are disempowered in the setting, the real message reinforces weakness rather than strength, pathology rather than resiliency. In the example that follows, the social worker uses the medium of a ward newspaper to help psychiatric patients to negotiate their community more effectively. The newspaper becomes a vehicle for communication with staff as well as a means for the members to discover their own strengths. It also becomes a medium through which the members can communicate their inner feelings about having to deal with the oppression associated with mental illness.

Working with the Milieu as Community: The War Memorial Gazette

Members: White male veterans who are patients in a VA psychiatric setting.

Dates: 9/30 to 12/2

Group Task: Relationship to the environment

1. *Problem:* The task this group faces is one of negotiating the larger system in which it is situated, in order to produce a patient newsletter. Some of the challenges faced by the group are resistance from the larger system (the hospital), resistance within the group (fear of making waves), members' fear of retribution from staff, feelings of disempowerment, and suspicion from inside and outside of the group. The major problem is the feelings of disempowerment embodied by the group members. This is illustrated by the reluctance to express themselves honestly in the newsletter. A second, related, problem is the hospital's low expectations of the patients and the ambivalence of the hospital towards change. The problem I face is to find a way of mediating between these two systems.

2. *How the Problem Came to My Attention:* Several incidents occurred that led to this assessment. In beginning the newsletter, I observed a great deal of enthusiasm initially, both from group members and staff, but this enthusiasm began to falter after the first few meetings. Many of the members failed to complete the assignments they had volunteered for, and support from the outside system was not forthcoming, as had been promised. Staff members discussed the need to censor the newsletter before it was distributed, which heightened and reinforced group members' fear and reservations. I realized that some of these issues would need to be addressed if the group were to proceed any further.

3. Summary of the Work: The first session was exciting. It was filled with hope and expectations on the part of the worker as well as the members. It was a large group with 17 members in all. There was a sense of expectation in the air. I had been talking and preparing for the group for several weeks, and the newness of it was intriguing to the members. Most of the vets had gotten to know me well enough to suspect that something different was happening, that this group would be different from other groups at the program.

In the beginning of the session, I explained to the group what I had in mind for the newsletter in order to clarify its purpose. "As some of you already know, I had an idea to start a newsletter. The newsletter would be created by all of you. You would write the articles, decide what went into it, how often it would be published and things like that. In other words, it would be *your* newsletter. I also thought of it as a way of helping the members of this program to get connected with each other and to keep each other informed as to what kinds of things happen around here. We could send copies to your friends and families to let them know what kinds of things you do here. I would also contribute my own ideas from time to time and be available to help members with any problems they might have. There will also be some other students and volunteers who have offered to help in any way if you have trouble with writing. I'd like to hear from you now. Do you have any thoughts on this idea?"

Many members expressed interest and said it was a good idea, though I sensed some doubt on the part of the members. I had the vague sense they were just humoring me. Instead of confronting it directly I just went on, hoping in time they would become more invested. Had I confronted it then, it might have opened up the discussion and raised some of the concerns and doubts they were feeling.

We decided on a name for the newsletter, and people volunteered for jobs. There was much debate about what to call the newsletter. One member offered *The Elite Newspaper of the East* as a possible title. He seemed very angry. I added his title to the rest of the titles to be voted upon and commented that I thought it was an interesting name. He did not respond, and I went on collecting other titles. I realized I had not picked up the message he was indirectly sending me. I had missed the opportunity to address some of the anger he was feeling and I was not tuned in to what was urgent to him at that moment. I was unable to set aside my own agenda. Had I picked up on his anger, I would have been able to recognize that his feelings were representative of much of what the group was feeling. Fortunately for the group (and for me), this anger would surface again in later groups and help break through the illusion of work that had formed.

In the second session, the members volunteered one another for jobs. In a somewhat derisive manner, an older man named George volunteered Dana, one of the younger members, to be the editor. Dana was generally very quiet and reserved and seldom participated in other groups. I responded that I thought it was a great idea and asked Dana if he would consider accepting the position. He seemed pleased at this and accepted. Everyone applauded. At this point, Harold, another older man, said that, while he was in the army, he used to take a lot of pictures. I asked him if he wanted to be the photographer, and he agreed. The energy in the room seemed to increase, and everyone started volunteering for jobs. We decided to meet once a week as a group and to put the newsletter out once a month.

During the month, some of the members were very busy interviewing people and writing their stories. Others were not doing their jobs and were coming up with excuses for why they couldn't do them. I felt this was due to a lack of confidence in their abilities, so much of my work during this period focused on expressing my belief in their abilities to do the job. I began to recognize that a general theme was emerging on how disempowered the members were feeling.

During the fifth session, I noticed that many of the members were having difficulty concentrating and seemed completely disinterested in the group. I reached for what was happening. "What is going on today? Everyone seems to be having trouble focusing on the topic. You all look bored and tired." Dan responded, "We all just went out for a long walk, we are tired." Richard added, "They keep us too busy around here, all we do is go to groups. They never leave us alone." I asked if anyone else felt this way and if they wanted to spend a few minutes talking about this. Many members responded by agreeing that there were too many groups and they were feeling overwhelmed.

I tried to validate their feelings by saying that sometimes there were a lot of groups to attend, and then I asked if they had ever spoken to the staff and voiced their concerns. Jim, the member who had been so angry in the first session, responded by saying that it did no good, the staff didn't care what they wanted and that they treated them all like children. I knew I had to be careful here. My natural inclination was to side with the group members. I had often been angered by the patronizing manner in which these men were treated. It would have been easy for me to have jumped on the bandwagon and started criticizing the hospital, but I knew that would not have been useful. I responded instead by reaching for his feelings, saying, "It must feel pretty frustrating to be treated in this way. After all, you're not children, you're grown men."

This opened the door for a lengthy discussion about how it felt to be a psychiatric patient and to lose so much control over one's life. I tried to bring the conversation back into focus by suggesting that the newsletter might be a forum the men could use in order to voice some of their concerns. Roland, a member who I have always thought of as very ingratiating to the staff, eager and cooperative, fearful of making trouble and generally considered a "good" patient, said, "Oh no, we couldn't do that, they would never let us print it. Besides, it's not really so bad around here. The staff are all nice and they treat us well." Another member was made anxious by the interchange and completely changed the subject. Time was almost up, so I said that if the group wanted to, we could continue talking about this the next time we met.

The next session involved a field trip we had planned, and the session after that, the recreational therapist joined the group. Apparently, the news had gotten out about our discussion. I told the staff I was encouraging the members to write about things that were meaningful to them and that at times this might involve an expression of criticism towards the hospital. They joked about how I was getting the patients all riled up. I sensed some suspicion beneath the humor. I asked if they thought this was a bad thing. This brought the issue out to the surface and opened up the opportunity for me to speak with the staff about some of the feelings the patients were having.

During the next session we got back to the discussion and returned to the earlier topic. The members seemed distracted and uninterested. They were also having difficulties finishing the assignments they had volunteered for. I asked them what was going on. Jimmy, a member who attended only occasionally, responded, "How do you expect us to do anything? I can't write; look at my hands." He held up his hands, which were shaking visibly. "They keep us so medicated around here we can't even think straight." Jake agreed, "These doctors use us as guinea pigs. They try one medication after another on us. We are subjects in their experiments; they don't treat us like human beings." Roland began to get nervous. "Yes, but we need to take our medication, it helps us. I'm ready for my next shot. I get too agitated if I don't get my shot."

Jake responded, saying the medication didn't help him, that it had ruined his life. He spoke of how he was not able to have a relationship with women or to live a normal life. He said, "Any member in this room will tell you that the medicine make you impotent. How are you ever supposed to meet a girl or think about getting married?" Several of the men nodded their heads in agreement. I said that must be very difficult for them and asked if they had ever let the doctors know about the problems they had with the medications. Jake again responded, "They don't care. If you refuse to take the medications, they will just lock you up." He went on to tell of how he had been forcibly locked up in the hospital. Several other group members agreed, telling stories of how they had been locked in the seclusion room, been beaten up by orderlies, or were admitted to the hospital against their will. They said when they told someone, the doctors responded by saying it was just a symptom of their paranoia. Jake said that he was learning not to fight, that he was not a young man anymore. I empathized with the things that the group members had gone through and said it must be really difficult to always have someone questioning their reality. I then suggested that Jake might want to write about his experiences for the newsletter. I hoped to begin to help empower them and to show them a way to have their concerns heard. Jake expressed ambivalence about doing this. I said I could understand his reservations and said if he wanted to he could take some time and think about it or that he could do it anonymously. This all proved to be more than Roland could stand.

Under his breath, but loudly enough for everyone to hear, he said "Communist!" I was taken aback by this expression of anger from Roland. I was also not sure who he was talking to. Jake responded angrily, "What did you call me?" Roland looked in his direction and said, louder this time, "A communist. You're nothing but a communist. The doctors are just trying to help us. You're always going around trying to stir things up." Jake was very angry at this. A veteran considers this to be the worst kind of insult. Jake responded to Roland, "I'm no communist, and don't you call me that. I have a right to say what I feel." I was afraid the situation might escalate into violence, since Jake was extremely angry. (I also felt my maternal instincts surface.)

I interjected, "Roland, it seems as if you see the situation in one way and Jake sees it from a different perspective. But I don't think it is useful for us to call each other names." I had intended to try to create a culture in which discussions of such matters were allowed and also one in which members respected and listened to one another. But, in rushing to Jake's defense, I was sending a message that I didn't believe he could take care of himself and that he needed my protection. This was not a useful message to send to someone who already feels so oppressed. I might have done better if I had waited a little longer and allowed them to work things out themselves.

Roland apologized to Jake and said he was just a little "off" because he had not gotten his shot yet. Jake accepted this apology, and the conversation returned to a discussion of an article someone was writing for the newsletter. The session ended with me encouraging the members to consider writing about their hospital experiences for the newsletter.

4. *Where the Problem Stands Now:* I can safely say the newsletter has become firmly established as a part of the program. I've noticed more staff members be-

coming invested in its continuation. There has been discussion of who will take over the project after I am gone. The director of the program requested a copy of the newsletter to be sent with his semi-annual report, and another staff member included it in a presentation she was giving about the program. I have witnessed some change, in that the system now relates in a different manner towards the veterans. I notice some staff now saying "members" or "veterans" instead of patients. Positive change is occurring in that many staff members are viewing the veterans in a new light. Several have expressed surprise over the talent that the men are exhibiting. There is also less fear and suspicion about what kinds of things I am doing with the group. We are still working on the issue of censorship as I continue to advocate for as little as possible in order to make sure the newsletter remains within the patients' control.

The group is still working on how much they want to express themselves in the newsletter. Many of the members still feel very disempowered and alienated, but they have been receiving a lot of positive reinforcement from the hospital community, which has led to a tremendous boost in self-confidence and self-esteem. Some of the members of the newsletter group are working on submitting articles to a national journal that publishes works by disabled and hospitalized veterans. Others have expressed an interest in learning how to type so they can type the newsletter themselves. One member has decided to begin to study for his high school equivalency exam. This is truly an exciting process to watch.

Specific Next Steps:

1. I will continue to encourage the members to use the newsletter as a forum in which to voice their concerns.

2. I will attempt to create a safe atmosphere within the group where members can feel free to discuss things that are truly meaningful to them.

3. I will continue working with the larger system to sensitize it to some of the feelings, needs, and concerns of the veterans.

4. I hope to continue making the newsletter a project the members feel they can have ownership of.

5. I will continue to search for connections between the system and the group in order to help create more open systems and a healthier environment for the veterans.

6. At every opportunity, I will endeavor to empower the individual members as well as the group as a whole.

7. And lastly, I will continue to work on my skills as a group worker so I can "make more sophisticated mistakes" in the future.

It seems appropriate to conclude this last example of the book with some excerpts from the newspaper published by these veterans. Their first issue did not directly deal with some of their concerns and feelings about the hospital and the staff; however, they did appear to employ indirect communications. For example, the comedy section contained the following three jokes about psychiatrists.

War Memorial Gazette, First Issue (Comedy Section)
Jokes by Ed

1. What's the difference between a neurotic, psychotic, and a psychiatrist? A neurotic builds castles in the clouds. A psychotic lives in them. A psychiatrist collects the rent for them.

2. How many psychiatrists does it take to change a light bulb? One, but the light bulb has to be willing to change.

3. This guy went to the psychiatrist and he is talking to the psychiatrist, and the psychiatrist says, "You're crazy!" And the guy says, "I want a second opinion." And the psychiatrist says, "OK, I think you're ugly too."

As the members' confidence grew, they began to be more direct, including columns about their concerns over the ward policies and procedures balanced with interviews that highlighted members of the staff. In their third issue they included editorial and poetry pages, excerpts of which follow.

War Memorial Gazette, Third Issue

This newsletter is a project of the Community Support Program of this Veterans Administration Hospital. The opinions and views expressed within do not necessarily reflect those of the staff or administration of the Hospital.

(Editorial Page)

Politicians

We as an individual should not form our opinions of a politician by their rhetoric and exposure by the media, but rather by their actual voting record, which should be publicly displayed. What is their background educationally, religiously, and what special interest groups support them physically and financially? This will determine their voting records and real selves. The news media should take more objective responsibility in this area.

Personal Philosophy

I'm a Vietnam combat vet. I've been in and out of the Veterans' Hospital for many years for physical and mental problems. This doesn't mean I haven't got a good IQ or common sense.

On economics, it's about time we as Americans bought American products to put Americans to work. Our products are better, as good, or maybe not up to foreign products. Every individual makes our economy and jobs with their purchases.

On politics, it's about time we look at our representatives and the policies they put forward. Are they voting for money, people, and special interest groups or for the American people? Stop the political slander and get to the economic issues.

We have a beautiful system of checks and balances between the Congress, Presidency, and Supreme Court. We also have the right of petition if we disagree with what's going on. If we don't examine and vote, we stand a chance of losing this system.

(Poetry Page)

Tom

Feeling Blue
When I'm out under the trees
I watch the flowers dance in the breeze
I feel the pain and sorrow that surround me
All I want is the sun to shine, the rain to fall
And no one to be left standing small.

Saying Good-Bye
For you there are always tears, the well is never dry
People live sadly, they must die
Think of a deep, deep sleep
Think of the trees swaying in the breeze
Think of a cool mountain stream you may see

Only in a dream.
To find the answer you must be keen
Just be sure life was not just a dream.

Teddy Bear
I wish I was your teddy bear
I would squeeze away your tears
I would squeeze away your sorrows
I would squeeze away your fears
I would hug you ever so tight
Tell you I love you so
And
Never
Never let you go.

The War Memorial Gazette has continued to publish for more than five years. It has matured as a paper and has earned the respect and support of the staff. Of particular note is the fact that the patients decided to hold a five-year celebration of the inception of the paper. They invited the student who had helped them organize the paper to thank her for her initiative and her faith in their ability. I have chosen these excerpts to conclude this book on a positive note, serving as a tribute to the resilience and courage of our clients and to the profound impact of one student who refused to give up on them or the system, her second client. It sends an important and appropriate message to our profession during the year of publication of this edition, a year that marks the 100th anniversary of the founding of social work.

SUMMARY

In this chapter we have examined the specific role of the community social worker in working with task-focused community groups. *Community* was defined as the neighborhood, the ethnic community, and the milieu. Social work practice with community groups was described as macro practice, as compared to micro or clinical practice. Macro practice can include direct as well as indirect social work activity. The concepts of group dynamics and the skills of working with groups introduced in earlier chapters focusing on micro practice were reexamined and applied to work with community groups.

GLOSSARY

Cohesion The property of the group that describes the mutual attraction members feel for each other.

Direct macro practice Social work involving direct work with clients in pursuit of community goals and objectives.

Division of labor The development of group structure in which the tasks to be performed are distributed among members in a formal or informal manner.

Indirect macro practice Activities of a social worker on behalf of a community, such as research or legislative report writing, that do not involve direct work with clients.

Macro practice Social work with clients in the community.

Micro practice Social work with individual clients, families, or support groups in a clinical setting.

Structure and maintenance Structure (roles, rules, culture, and so on) must be created by a group before it can carry out its work. Maintenance involves monitoring and maintaining the structures.

■ *Epilogue*

This book has drawn on the practice illustrations provided by many students and workers. I have used process recordings, transcripts of audio- and videotapes, and summary devices, such as the "record of service." Each of these formats has provided insights into the moment-by-moment activities of workers in interaction with individual clients, small groups, families, or the representatives of systems important to clients. This book could not have been written without these examples.

I believe the detailed analysis of our work is essential if we are to deepen our understanding of the processes involved. Examination of practice recordings provides insights into the nature of a complex process, helps to keep practice theory development close to reality, and provides hypotheses that lend themselves to empirical research. In a cyclical fashion, these insights, theoretical constructs, and research findings help us return to the analysis of practice with increased clarity. The movement from practice to theory building and research and then back to practice is the key to our future development.

In a like manner, workers must be continually examining the details of their interactions with clients in order to strengthen their own practice models. Caseload realities usually make it impossible to record all practice; workers need to select some area of their work for special focus. The type of recording used for skill development can vary. The recordings shared in this book vary in type and level of sophistication. The best ones, however, usually included the following: some detail of both the beginning and the ending of the sessions described; summaries of the work, with expanded detail on key aspects of the interaction (efforts to write a complete process recording of an entire session can be overwhelming and self-defeating in the long run); identification of the worker as a participant in the action (it is not unusual for students to write their first process recordings with no mention of themselves in the interview); observations of the nonverbal signals as well as the conversation (e.g., June looked sad and seemed to turn away from the group); identification of the worker's and client's affects as integrated parts of the commentary; and, finally, the worker's analysis of the action described. The ability to record process after a session is a learned skill, with students usually moving from simple statements of the interaction to deeper and richer recordings, integrating the elements described earlier. Even in those situations in which more sophisticated devices for recording practice are available (e.g., video equipment), I think it is important to develop the process recording skills.

The wider availability of complex recording devices, such a videotape machines, is also having an important impact on our interest in the details of practice. We have the means of sharing our work with colleagues, and of exposing our practice to self-scrutiny and to our colleagues' scrutiny. Many of us who were not trained in a culture that encouraged this form of analysis have had to overcome our fears of risking in order to benefit from critical advice.

805

Many training institutions have recognized the importance of developing this capacity for sharing one's work and taking help from colleagues and have placed a priority on this aspect of student development. The use of student practice material throughout the school year reinforces this idea.

Workers can also tap another source of help for their continued learning—their clients. For example, questionnaires developed through research can provide feedback on skill use. Clients can also be asked to listen to tape recordings of interviews with workers (or watch videotapes) and to provide their reactions as a source of help for the worker's continued learning. Most clients are quite willing to act as consultants for their workers' training. The offering of help can be a complex procedure. Every helping professional can use all the assistance available—from clients, colleagues, supervisors, and teachers.

Research Methodology

SUMMARY OF THE DESIGN OF THE STUDY

This study was conducted in the Ministry of Human Resources of the Province of British Columbia, Canada.[1] (Since the completion of the study, the Ministry of Human Resources has been renamed the Ministry of Social Services and Housing.) The ministry was divided into five geographic macroareas administered by executive directors. Macroareas were further divided into 21 regions, each headed by a regional manager. Regions were divided into district offices headed by supervisors. Social workers working directly with families were based in these offices (see Figure A.1).

Ten (48 percent) of the 21 regions were selected for inclusion in the study, providing a representative sample of the province as a whole (e.g., urban, suburban, and rural). Project research assistants began visiting the 68 district offices in February of 1983 to review family files that had been opened (or reopened) in the office since December of 1982. Field staff returned to read new files in April and again in June of the same year. By the end of the research intake period 1,056 families were identified as potential subjects for the study.

Of the total identified, 348 (33 percent) of the families agreed to participate. Initial analysis of the 67 percent of the families that did not agree (nonrespondents) did not reveal significant differences between the participating and the nonrespondent groups. Forty-three families were dropped from the sample for a variety of reasons (e.g., social worker nonparticipation, unsuitability, or inability to trace after a move). The final sample consisted of 305 families with 449 children.

Two-thirds of these families are of the type of child welfare case that involves physical or sexual abuse, neglect, or the inability of parents to care for their children (e.g., health problems). Most of the children in this group are 12 years of age and under. About one-third of the families could be described as having teen-parent conflicts. In these cases, abuse or neglect may not be present. In the Province of British Columbia this type of family problem was increasing at the time of the study. The provincial percentages matched those of our sample (one in three cases).

Most of the data of the study were gathered during the spring of 1983. Home interviews were conducted with the parent(s).[2] Similar procedures were followed with a sample of 62

FIGURE A.1 Six Levels of the Study Sample

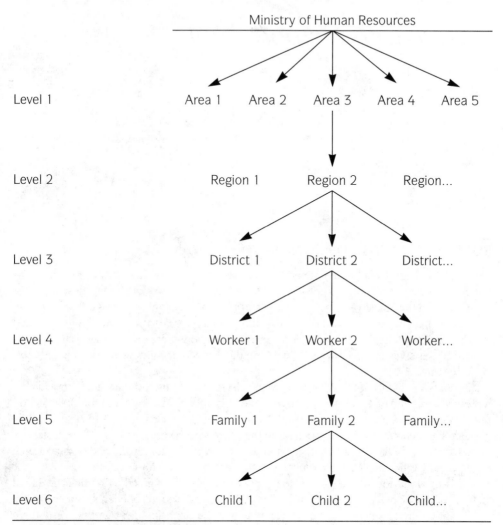

Note: This figure illustrates the nesting of each level within the one above it. Each of the 449 children in the study (Level 6) is nested in one of the 305 families (Level 5) assigned to a specific worker (Level 4) located in a district office (Level 3). The office is within a region (Level 2) that is part of a macroarea (Level 1).

teenagers from these families. A general survey of staff at all levels was conducted at the same time. When a family agreed to participate in the study, a family information questionnaire was sent to its social worker.

Project staff also read client files to obtain case information. If a child was placed in alternative care, the residential worker or foster parent was sent a questionnaire. The data obtained during this time period, the first five months of 1983, will be referred to as Time 1 data. Much of the analysis is based on this information.

Follow-up data were obtained through mailed surveys to clients, staff, and foster parents at various times in the study over the next 15 months. The family files were reviewed by project staff every three months. Regional data were also obtained from the ministry reports.

DATA ANALYSIS

Data analysis was conducted using the SPSSX (Statistical Package for the Social Sciences, 1988) on an IBM mainframe computer (SPSS, 1986). Summary statistics were computed for all variables and a range of statistical analyses was employed. For those analyses in which the number of cases exceeded 200, we were able to use causal path analysis using the program *Lisrel 7* (Jöreskog & Sörbom, 1988).

LIMITATIONS

It is important to recognize a number of limitations in the study design that affect our ability to make inferences from the findings. These limitations offer the possibility of reasonable alternative explanations for the results.

One limitation is the self-selection of the families involved. We recognized that our sample might represent a biased group, which would affect our ability to generalize to a larger population. However, research ethics in working with human subjects require that full and informed consent be received before a client can be included. We did attempt to determine if our included sample differed significantly from the potential population using some data from our initial reading of agency files. This information included the age of the parent, the number and age of the children, the degree of seriousness of the problem, race of the family, referring source, and the district office and region. In general, we found our sample to be similar to the nonresponding group. Of course they were dissimilar in one major way in that they agreed to be in the study.

Another major limitation of the study emerges from a traumatic event: the introduction of a restraint program and cutbacks in staff and services during the study. Rumors of these cutbacks began to circulate in June of the first year of the study, six months after the commencement of the project. Major cutbacks were announced that summer. These cutbacks were part of a broader program of restraint that affected the entire civil service and programs in health, welfare, education, human rights, and so on.

Since much of the study data was gathered during Time 1, which preceded these events, these data were not affected. In addition, because of the existence of a freeze in hiring that preceded these cutbacks, we had incorporated items on staff questionnaires that attempted to gauge the impact of this moderate restraint program. This proved to be fortuitous because it provided baseline data that could be used when assessing the cutback impact during the next two years. Rather than abandoning the second phase of the study, we attempted to be opportunistic by incorporating this variable into the design. The detailed data gathered on the impact of cutbacks on social services may be one of the more important unplanned results of the study. For all data gathered after the Time 1 period, these events must be considered as limiting the validity of the findings.

Finally, let me comment on the *Lisrel* causal path analysis program used to test some of the propositions of the theory. Essentially, the analysis performed tests on how well the theoretical models fit with the data. It is not a true test of the theory. It would be important to continue to treat findings tentatively, giving more weight to those that replicate earlier findings. As the model is tested with different populations in further studies, our confidence can be strengthened. Thus, we may be able to identify theoretical generalizations that apply across populations, problems, settings, and modalities of practice.

SUMMARY OF THE DESIGN OF THE STUDY

A brief summary of the design of this early study (Shulman, 1978), and its limitations is provided here so that the reader may put the findings discussed in the text in proper perspective. The central line of inquiry of the study was to examine social work practice skill and the relationship between what workers did in their interviews and the development of a positive working relationship with clients as well as the worker's helpfulness. One of the instruments developed in the study was the Social Worker Behavior Questionnaire. This consisted of 27 items, each describing a particular skill. The questionnaire was designed to be completed by clients who would be reporting on their workers' frequency of use of these behaviors. Eight of these items were included in the 1991 study.

A second instrument, the Service Satisfaction Questionnaire, obtained clients' perceptions on the content of the work as well as their perceptions of their relationships with the worker ("How satisfied are you with the way you and your worker get along?") and the worker's helpfulness ("In general, how helpful has your worker been?"). These two key items were used as dependent variables and were included in the 1991 project. The instrument-development stage included the testing of both questionnaires for reliability and validity.

The total staffs of the two Canadian child welfare agencies participating in the study were included in the sample. The entire caseload (active at the time of the study) for each of the 118 workers was identified, and all clients over 14 years old were sent either a Social Worker Behavior Questionnaire or the Service Satisfaction Questionnaire. Random assignment was used to determine which of the two questionnaires a client received, so that each client had an equal chance to report on either worker's behavior or satisfaction with the relationship and the worker's helpfulness. This procedure was followed so that filling out one questionnaire would not influence the results on the other. (The reader should note the difference in methodology used in this study as compared to the more recent research described earlier in this appendix. In that study, our concern about independence of measures was dropped and the same client rated both the worker's skills and relationship and outcome measures.) Questionnaires were mailed to potential respondents. The return rate was 53 percent, with a respondent sample of 1,784.

Average scores were computed from the returns for each worker on each questionnaire. These scores were then assigned as the worker's score. Pearson correlations were computed to determine the association between specific behaviors and the outcome measures of relationship and helpfulness. In addition, a partial correlation procedure allowed for interesting inferences about which skills contributed to relationship building, which ones to helpfulness, and which ones to both. Findings were then used to make inferences about the original practice framework.

In addition, mention is made in this text of the findings of a subdesign of this study in which videotapes of the practice of 11 workers in one of the agencies were analyzed by trained raters. The raters used an observation system developed during the study that allowed them to make systematic observations of the interactions between workers and clients, recording their observations every three seconds. From four to six individual sessions of each of the 11 workers were videotaped and analyzed in this manner. The resultant data rated 120 hours of practice and provided over 99,000 discrete entries for computer analysis (Shulman, 1981).

NOTES

1. For a full report of this study see L. Shulman, *Interactional Social Work Practice: Toward an Empirical Theory* (Itasca, IL: F.E. Peacock Publishers, 1991).

2. Many of the families lived in areas of the province that were difficult to visit. When it was not possible to make a return visit for the interview or an appointment was missed and another visit was not feasible, a version of the home interview designed to be self-administered was mailed to the family. Data on 26 families were obtained in this manner.

APPENDIX B

Codes of Ethics

NASW Code of Ethics*

OVERVIEW

The *NASW Code of Ethics* is intended to serve as a guide to the everyday professional conduct of social workers. This *Code* includes four sections. The first section, "Preamble," summarizes the social work profession's mission and core values. The second section, "Purpose of the *NASW Code of Ethics*," provides an overview of the *Code*'s main functions and a brief guide for dealing with ethical issues or dilemmas in social work practice. The third section, "Ethical Principles," presents broad ethical principles, based on social work's core values, that inform social work practice. The final section, "Ethical Standards," includes specific ethical standards to guide social workers' conduct and to provide a basis for adjudication.

PREAMBLE

The primary mission of the social work profession is to enhance human well-being and help meet the basic needs of all people, with particular attention to the needs and empowerment of people who are vulnerable, oppressed, and living in poverty. A historic and defining feature of social work is the profession's focus on individual well-being in a social context and the well-being of society. Fundamental to social work is attention to environmental forces that create, contribute to, and address problems in living.

Social workers promote social justice and social change with and on behalf of clients. "Clients" is used inclusively to refer to individuals, families, groups, organizations, and communities. Social workers are sensitive to cultural and ethnic diversity and strive to end discrimination, oppression, poverty, and other forms of social injustice. These activities may be in the form of direct practice, community organizing, supervision, consultation, administration, advocacy, social and political action, policy development and implementation, education, and research and evaluation. Social workers seek to enhance the capacity of people to address their own needs. Social workers also seek to promote the responsiveness of organizations, communities, and other social institutions to individuals' needs and social problems.

---

*This Code of Ethics was revised in May 1996 and is presented here with the permission of the National Association of Social Workers (NASW).

The mission of the social work profession is rooted in a set of core values. These core values, embraced by social workers throughout the profession's history, are the foundation of social work's unique purpose and perspective:

- *service*
- *social justice*
- *dignity and worth of the person*
- *importance of human relationships*
- *integrity*
- *competence.*

This constellation of core values reflects what is unique to the social work profession. Core values, and the principles that flow from them, must be balanced within the context and complexity of the human experience.

PURPOSE OF THE NASW CODE OF ETHICS

Professional ethics are at the core of social work. The profession has an obligation to articulated its basic values, ethical principles, and ethical standards. The *NASW Code of Ethics* sets forth these values, principles, and standards to guide social workers' conduct. The *Code* is relevant to all social workers and social work students, regardless of their professional functions, the settings in which they work, or the populations they serve.

The *NASW Code of Ethics* serves six purposes:

1. The *Code* identifies core values on which social work's mission is based.
2. The *Code* summarizes broad ethical principles that reflect the profession's core values and establishes a set of specific ethical standards that should be used to guide social work practice.
3. The *Code* is designed to help social workers identify relevant considerations when professional obligations conflict or ethical uncertainties arise.
4. The *Code* provides ethical standards to which the general public can hold the social work profession accountable.
5. The *Code* socializes practitioners new to the field to social work's mission, values, ethical principles, and ethical standards.
6. The *Code* articulates standards that the social work profession itself can use to assess whether social workers have engaged in unethical conduct. NASW has formal procedures to adjudicate ethics complaints filed against its members.[1] In subscribing to this *Code*, social workers are required to cooperate in its implementation, participate in NASW adjudication proceedings, and abide by any NASW disciplinary rulings or sanctions based on it.

The *Code* offers a set of values, principles, and standards to guide decision making and conduct when ethical issues arise. It does not provide a set of rules that prescribe how social workers should act in all situations. Specific applications of the *Code* must take into account the context in which it is being considered and the possibility of conflicts among the

---

[1]For information on NASW adjudication procedures, see *NASW Procedures for the Adjudication of Grievances.*

Code's values, principles, and standards. Ethical responsibilities flow from all human relationships, from the personal and familial to the social and professional.

Further, the *NASW Code of Ethics* does not specify which values, principles, and standards are most important and ought to outweigh others in instances when they conflict. Reasonable differences of opinion can and do exist among social workers with respect to the ways in which values, ethical principles, and ethical standards should be rank ordered when they conflict. Ethical decision making in a given situation must apply the informed judgment of the individual social worker and should also consider how the issues would be judged in a peer review process where the ethical standards of the profession would be applied.

Ethical decision making is a process. There are many instances in social work where simple answers are not available to resolve complex ethical issues. Social workers should take into consideration all the values, principles, and standards in this *Code* that are relevant to any situation in which ethical judgment is warranted. Social workers' decisions and actions should be consistent with the spirit as well as the letter of this *Code*.

In addition to this *Code*, there are many other sources of information about ethical thinking that may be useful. Social workers should consider ethical theory and principles generally, social work theory and research, laws, regulations, agency policies, and other relevant codes of ethics, recognizing that among codes of ethics social workers should consider the *NASW Code of Ethics* as their primary source. Social workers also should be aware of the impact on ethical decision making of their clients' and their own personal values and cultural and religious beliefs and practices. They should be aware of any conflicts between personal and professional values and deal with them responsibly. For additional guidance social workers should consult the relevant literature on professional ethics and ethical decision making and seek appropriate consultation when faced with ethical dilemmas. This may involve consultation with an agency-based or social work organization's ethics committee, a regulatory body, knowledgeable colleagues, supervisors, or legal counsel.

Instances may arise when social workers' ethical obligations conflict with agency policies or relevant laws or regulations. When such conflicts occur, social workers must make a responsible effort to resolve the conflict in a manner that is consistent with the values, principles, and standards expressed in this *Code*. If a reasonable resolution of the conflict does not appear possible, social workers should seek proper consultation before making a decision.

The *NASW Code of Ethics* is to be used by NASW and by individuals, agencies, organizations, and bodies (such as licensing and regulatory boards, professional liability insurance providers, courts of law, agency boards of directors, government agencies, and other professional groups) that choose to adopt it or use it as a frame of reference. Violation of standards in this *Code* does not automatically imply legal liability or violation of the law. Such determination can only be made in the context of legal and judicial proceedings. Alleged violations of the *Code* would be subject to a peer review process. Such processes are generally separate from legal or administrative procedures and insulated from legal review or proceedings to allow the profession to counsel and discipline its own members.

A code of ethics cannot guarantee ethical behavior. Moreover, a code of ethics cannot resolve all ethical issues or disputes or capture the richness and complexity involved in striving to make responsible choices within a moral community. Rather, a code of ethics sets forth values, ethical principles, and ethical standards to which professionals aspire and by which their actions can be judged. Social workers' ethical behavior should result from their personal commitment to engage in ethical practice. The *NASW Code of Ethics* reflects the commitment of all social workers to uphold the profession's values and to act ethically. Principles and standards must be applied by individuals of good character who discern moral questions and, in good faith, seek to make reliable judgments.

ETHICAL PRINCIPLES

The following broad ethical principles are based on social work's core values of service, social justice, dignity and worth of the person, importance of human relationships, integrity, and competence. These principles set forth ideals to which all social workers should aspire.

Value: *Service*

Ethical Principle: *Social workers' primary goal is to help people in need and to address social problems.*

Social workers elevate service to others above self-interest. Social workers draw on their knowledge, values, and skills to help people in need and to address social problems. Social workers are encouraged to volunteer some portion of their professional skills with no expectation of significant financial return (pro bono service).

Value: *Social Justice*

Ethical Principle: *Social workers challenge social injustice.*

Social workers pursue social change, particularly with and on behalf of vulnerable and oppressed individuals and groups of people. Social workers' social change efforts are focused primarily on issues of poverty, unemployment, discrimination, and other forms of social injustice. These activities seek to promote sensitivity to and knowledge about oppression and cultural and ethnic diversity. Social workers strive to ensure access to needed information, services, and resources; equality of opportunity; and meaningful participation in decision making for all people.

Value: *Dignity and Worth of the Person*

Ethical Principle: *Social workers respect the inherent dignity and worth of the person.*

Social workers treat each person in a caring and respectful fashion, mindful of individual differences and cultural and ethnic diversity. Social workers promote clients' socially responsible self-determination. Social workers seek to enhance clients' capacity and opportunity to change and to address their own needs. Social workers are cognizant of their dual responsibility to clients and to the broader society. They seek to resolve conflicts between clients' interests and the broader society's interests in a socially responsible manner consistent with the values, ethical principles, and ethical standards of the profession.

Value: *Importance of Human Relationships*

Ethical Principle: *Social workers recognize the central importance of human relationships.*

Social workers understand that relationships between and among people are an important vehicle for change. Social workers engage people as partners in the helping process. Social workers seek to strengthen relationships among people in a purposeful effort to promote, restore, maintain, and enhance the well-being of individuals, families, social groups, organizations, and communities.

Value: *Competence*

Ethical Principle: *Social workers practice within their areas of competence and develop and enhance their professional expertise.*

Social workers continually strive to increase their professional knowledge and skills and to apply them in practice. Social workers should aspire to contribute to the knowledge base of their profession.

ETHICAL STANDARDS

The following ethical standards are relevant to the professional activities of all social workers. These standards concern (1) social workers' ethical responsibilities to clients, (2) social workers' ethical responsibilities to colleagues, (3) social workers' ethical responsibilities in practice settings, (4) social workers' ethical responsibilities as professionals, (5) social workers' ethical responsibilities to the social work profession, and (6) social workers' ethical responsibilities to the broader society.

Some of the standards that follow are enforceable guidelines for professional conduct, and some are aspirational. The extent to which each standard is enforceable is a matter of professional judgment to be exercised by those responsible for reviewing alleged violations of ethical standards.

1. SOCIAL WORKERS' ETHICAL RESPONSIBILITIES TO CLIENTS

1.01 Commitment to Clients

Social workers' primary responsibility is to promote the well-being of clients. In general, clients' interest are primary. However, social workers' responsibility to the larger society or specific legal obligations may on limited occasions supersede the loyalty owed clients, and clients should be so advised. (Examples include when a social worker is required by law to report that a client has abused a child or has threatened to harm self or others.)

1.02 Self-Determination

Social workers respect and promote the right of clients to self-determination and assist clients in their efforts to identify and clarify their goals. Social workers may limit clients' right to self-determination when, in the social workers' professional judgment, clients' actions or potential actions pose a serious, foreseeable, and imminent risk to themselves or others.

1.03 Informed Consent

    (a) Social workers should provide services to clients only in the context of a professional relationship based, when appropriate, on valid informed consent. Social workers should use clear and understandable language to inform clients of the purpose of the services, risks related to the services, limits to services because of the requirements of a third-party payer, relevant costs, reasonable alternatives, clients' right to refuse or withdraw consent, and the time frame covered by the consent. Social workers should provide clients with an opportunity to ask questions.

(b) In instances when clients are not literate or have difficulty understanding the primary language used in the practice setting, social workers should take steps to ensure clients' comprehension. This may include providing clients with a detailed verbal explanation or arranging for a qualified interpreter or translator whenever possible.

(c) In instances when clients lack the capacity to provide informed consent, social workers should protect clients' interests by seeking permission from an appropriate third party, informing clients consistent with the clients' level of understanding. In such instances social workers should seek to ensure that the third party acts in a manner consistent with clients' wishes and interests. Social workers should take reasonable steps to enhance such clients' ability to give informed consent.

(d) In instances when clients are receiving services involuntarily, social workers should provide information about the nature and extent of services and about the extent of clients' right to refuse service.

(e) Social workers who provide services via electronic media (such as computer, telephone, radio, and television) should inform recipients of the limitations and risks associated with such services.

(f) Social workers should obtain client's informed consent before audiotaping or videotaping clients or permitting observation of services to clients by a third party.

1.04 Competence

(a) Social workers should provide services and represent themselves as competent only within the boundaries of their education, training, license, certification, consultation received, supervised experience, or other relevant professional experience.

(b) Social workers should provide services in substantive areas or use intervention techniques or approaches that are new to them only after engaging in appropriate study, training, consultation, and supervision from people who are competent in those interventions or techniques.

(c) When generally recognized standards do not exist with respect to an emerging area of practice, social workers should exercise careful judgment and take responsible steps (including appropriate education, research, training, consultation, and supervision) to ensure the competence of their work and to protect clients from harm.

1.05 Cultural Competence and Social Diversity

(a) Social workers should understand culture and its function in human behavior and society, recognizing the strengths that exist in all cultures.

(b) Social workers should have a knowledge base of their clients' cultures and be able to demonstrate competence in the provision of services that are sensitive to clients' cultures and to differences among people and cultural groups.

(c) Social workers should obtain education about and seek to understand the nature of social diversity and oppression with respect to race, ethnicity, national origin, color, sex, sexual orientation, age, marital status, political belief, religion, and mental or physical disability.

1.06 Conflicts of Interest

(a) Social workers should be alert to and avoid conflicts of interest that interfere with the exercise of professional discretion and impartial judgment. Social workers should inform clients when a real or potential conflict of interest arises and take reasonable steps to resolve the issue in a manner that makes the clients' interests primary and protects clients' interests to the greatest extent possible. In some cases, protecting clients' interests may require termination of the professional relationship with proper referral of the client.

(b) Social workers should not take unfair advantage of any professional relationship or exploit others to further their personal, religious, political, or business interests.

(c) Social workers should not engage in dual or multiple relationships with clients or former clients in which there is a risk of exploitation or potential harm to the client. In instances when dual or multiple relationships are unavoidable, social workers should take steps to protect clients and are responsible for setting clear, appropriate, and culturally sensitive boundaries. (Dual or multiple relationships occur when social workers relate to clients in more than one relationship, whether professional, social, or business. Dual or multiple relationships can occur simultaneously or consecutively.)

(d) When social workers provide services to two or more people who have a relationship with each other (for example, couples, family members), social workers should clarify with all parties which individuals will be considered clients and the nature of social workers' professional obligations to the various individuals who are receiving services. Social workers who anticipate a conflict of interest among the individuals receiving services or who anticipate having to perform in potentially conflicting roles (for example, when a social worker is asked to testify in a child custody dispute or divorce proceedings involving clients) should clarify their role with the parties involved and take appropriate action to minimize any conflict of interest.

1.07 Privacy and Confidentiality

(a) Social workers should respect clients' right to privacy. Social workers should not solicit private information from clients unless it is essential to providing services or conducting social work evaluation or research. Once private information is shared, standards of confidentiality apply.

(b) Social workers may disclose confidential information when appropriate with valid consent from a client or a person legally authorized to consent on behalf of a client.

(c) Social workers should protect the confidentiality of all information obtained in the course of professional service, except for compelling professional reasons. The general expectation that social workers will keep information confidential does not apply when disclosure is necessary to prevent serious, foreseeable, and imminent harm to a client or other identifiable person or when laws or regulations require disclosure without a client's consent. In all instances, social workers should disclose the least amount of confidential information necessary to achieve the desired purpose; only information that is directly relevant to the purpose for which the disclosure is made should be revealed.

(d) Social workers should inform clients, to the extent possible, about the disclosure of confidential information and the potential consequences, when feasible before the disclosure is made. This applies whether social workers disclose confidential information on the basis of a legal requirement or client consent.

(e) Social workers should discuss with clients and other interested parties the nature of confidentiality and limitations of clients' right to confidentiality. Social workers should review with clients circumstances where confidential information may be requested and where disclosure of confidential information may be legally required. This discussion should occur as soon as possible in the social worker–client relationship and as needed throughout the course of the relationship.

(f) When social workers provide counseling services to families, couples, or groups, social workers should seek agreement among the parties involved concerning each individual's right to confidentiality and obligation to preserve the confidentiality of information shared by others. Social workers should inform participants in family, couples, or group counseling that social workers cannot guarantee that all participants will honor such agreements.

(g) Social workers should inform clients involved in family, couples, marital, or group counseling of the social worker's, employer's, and agency's policy concerning the social worker's disclosure of confidential information among the parties involved in the counseling.

(h) Social workers should not disclose confidential information to third-party payers unless clients have authorized such disclosure.

(i) Social workers should not discuss confidential information in any setting unless privacy can be ensured. Social workers should not discuss confidential information in public or semipublic areas such as hallways, waiting rooms, elevators, and restaurants.

(j) Social workers should protect the confidentiality of clients during legal proceedings to the extent permitted by law. When a court of law or other legally authorized body orders social workers to disclose confidential or privileged information without a client's consent and such a disclosure could cause harm to the client, social workers should request that the court withdraw the order or limit the order as narrowly as possible or maintain the records under seal, unavailable for public inspection.

(k) Social workers should protect the confidentiality of clients when responding to requests from members of the media.

(l) Social workers should protect the confidentiality of clients' written and electronic records and other sensitive information. Social workers should take reasonable steps to ensure that clients' records are stored in a secure location and that clients' records are not available to others who are not authorized to have access.

(m) Social workers should take precautions to ensure and maintain the confidentiality of information transmitted to other parties through the use of computers, electronic mail, facsimile machines, telephones and telephone answering machines, and other electronic or computer technology. Disclosure of identifying information should be avoided whenever possible.

(n) Social workers should transfer or dispose of clients' records in a manner that protects clients' confidentiality and is consistent with state statutes governing records and social work licensure.

(o) Social workers should take reasonable precautions to protect client confidentiality in the event of the social worker's termination of practice, incapacitation, or death.

(p) Social workers should not disclose identifying information when discussing clients for teaching or training purposes unless the client has consented to disclosure of confidential information.

(q) Social workers should not disclose identifying information when discussing clients with consultants unless the client has consented to disclosure of confidential information or there is a compelling need for such disclosure.

(r) Social workers should protect the confidentiality of deceased clients consistent with the preceding standards.

1.08 Access to Records

(a) Social workers should provide clients with reasonable access to records concerning the clients. Social workers who are concerned that clients' access to their records could cause serious misunderstanding or harm to the client should provide assistance in interpreting the records and consultation with the client regarding the records. Social workers should limit clients' access to their records, or portions of their records, only in exceptional circumstances when there is compelling evidence that such access would cause serious harm to the client. Both clients' requests and the rationale for withholding some or all of the record should be documented in clients' files.

(b) When providing clients with access to their records, social workers should take steps to protect the confidentiality of other individuals identified or discussed in such records.

1.09 Sexual Relationships

(a) Social workers should under no circumstances engage in sexual activities or sexual contact with current clients, whether such contact is consensual or forced.

(b) Social workers should not engage in sexual activities or sexual contact with clients' relatives or other individuals with whom clients maintain a close personal relationship when there is a risk of exploitation or potential harm to the client. Sexual activity or sexual contact with clients' relatives or other individuals with whom clients maintain a personal relationship has potential to be harmful to the client and may make it difficult for the social worker and client to maintain appropriate professional boundaries. Social workers—not their clients, their clients' relatives, or other individuals with whom the client maintains a personal relationship—assume the full burden for setting clear, appropriate, and culturally sensitive boundaries.

(c) Social workers should not engage in sexual activities or sexual contact with former clients because of the potential for harm to the client. If social workers engage in conduct contrary to this prohibition or claim that an exception to this prohibition is warranted because of extraordinary circumstances, it is social workers—not their clients—who assume the full burden of demonstrating that the former client has not been exploited, coerced, or manipulated intentionally or unintentionally.

(d) Social workers should not provide clinical services to individuals with whom they have had a prior sexual relationship. Providing clinical services to a former sexual partner has the potential to be harmful to the individual and is likely to make it difficult for the social worker and individual to maintain appropriate professional boundaries.

1.10 Physical Contact

Social workers should not engage in physical contact with clients when there is a possibility of psychological harm to the client as a result of the contact (such as cradling or caressing clients). Social workers who engage in appropriate physical contact with clients are responsible for setting clear, appropriate, and culturally sensitive boundaries that govern such physical contact.

1.11 Sexual Harassment

Social workers should not sexually harass clients. Sexual harassment includes sexual advances, sexual solicitation, requests for sexual favors, and other verbal or physical conduct of a sexual nature.

1.12 Derogatory Language

Social workers should not use derogatory language in their written or verbal communications to or about clients. Social workers should use accurate and respectful language in all communications to and about clients.

1.13 Payment for Services

(a) When setting fees, social workers should ensure that the fees are fair, reasonable, and commensurate with the services performed. Consideration should be given to clients' ability to pay.

(b) Social workers should avoid accepting goods or services from clients as payment for professional services. Bartering arrangements, particularly involving services, create the potential for conflicts of interest, exploitation, and inappropriate boundaries in social workers' relationships with clients. Social workers should explore and may participate in bartering only in very limited circumstances when it can be demonstrated that such arrangements are an accepted practice among professionals in the local community, considered to be essential for the provision of services, negotiated without coercion, and entered into at the client's initiative and with the client's informed consent. Social workers who accept goods or services from clients as payment for professional services assume the full burden of demonstrating that this arrangement will not be detrimental to the client or the professional relationship.

(c) Social workers should not solicit a private fee or other remuneration for providing services to clients who are entitled to such available services through the social workers' employer or agency.

1.14 Clients Who Lack Decision-Making Capacity

When social workers act on behalf of clients who lack the capacity to make informed decisions, social workers should take reasonable steps to safeguard the interests and rights of those clients.

1.15 Interruption of Services

Social workers should make reasonable efforts to ensure continuity of services in the event that services are interrupted by factors such as unavailability, relocation, illness, disability, or death.

1.16 Termination of Services

(a) Social workers should terminate services to clients and professional relationships with them when such services and relationships are no longer required or no longer serve the clients' needs or interests.

(b) Social workers should take reasonable steps to avoid abandoning clients who are still in need of services. Social workers should withdraw services precipitously only under unusual circumstances, giving careful consideration to all factors in the situation and taking care to minimize possible adverse effects. Social workers should assist in making appropriate arrangements for continuation of services when necessary.

(c) Social workers in fee-for-service settings may terminate services to clients who are not paying an overdue balance if the financial contractual agreements have been made clear to the client, if the client does not pose an imminent danger to self or others, and if the clinical and other consequences of the current nonpayment have been addressed and discussed with the client.

(d) Social workers should not terminate services to pursue a social, financial, or sexual relationship with a client.

(e) Social workers who anticipate the termination or interruption of services to clients should notify clients promptly and seek the transfer, referral, or continuation of services in relation to the clients' needs and preferences.

(f) Social workers who are leaving an employment setting should inform clients of appropriate options for the continuation of services and of the benefits and risks of the options.

2. SOCIAL WORKERS' ETHICAL RESPONSIBILITIES TO COLLEAGUES

2.01 Respect

(a) Social workers should treat colleagues with respect and should represent accurately and fairly the qualifications, views, and obligations of colleagues.

(b) Social workers should avoid unwarranted negative criticism of colleagues in communications with clients or with other professionals. Unwarranted negative criticism may include demeaning comments that refer to colleagues' level of competence or to individuals' attributes such as race, ethnicity, national origin, color, sex, sexual orientation, age, marital status, political belief, religion, and mental or physical disability.

(c) Social workers should cooperate with social work colleagues and with colleagues of other professions when such cooperation serves the well-being of clients.

2.02 Confidentiality

Social workers should respect confidential information shared by colleagues in the course of their professional relationships and transactions. Social workers should ensure that such colleagues understand social workers' obligation to respect confidentiality and any exceptions related to it.

2.03 Interdisciplinary Collaboration

(a) Social workers who are members of an interdisciplinary team should participate in and contribute to decisions that affect the well-being of clients by drawing on the perspectives, values, and experiences of the social work profession. Professional and ethical obligations of the interdisciplinary team as a whole and of its individual members should be clearly established.

(b) Social workers for whom a team decision raises ethical concerns should attempt to resolve the disagreement through appropriate channels. If the disagreement cannot be resolved, social workers should pursue other avenues to address their concerns consistent with client well-being.

2.04 Disputes Involving Colleagues

(a) Social workers should not take advantage of a dispute between a colleague and an employer to obtain a position or otherwise advance the social workers' own interests.

(b) Social workers should not exploit clients in disputes with colleagues or engage clients in any inappropriate discussion of conflicts between social workers and their colleagues.

2.05 Consultation

(a) Social workers should seek the advice and counsel of colleagues whenever such consultation is in the best interests of clients.

(b) Social workers should keep themselves informed about colleagues' areas of expertise and competencies. Social workers should seek consultation only from colleagues who have demonstrated knowledge, expertise, and competence related to the subject of the consultation.

(c) When consulting with colleagues about clients, social workers should disclose the least amount of information necessary to achieve the purposes of the consultation.

2.06 Referral for Services

(a) Social workers should refer clients to other professionals when the other professionals' specialized knowledge or expertise is needed to serve clients fully or when social workers believe that they are not being effective or making reasonable progress with clients and that additional service is required.

(b) Social workers who refer clients to other professionals should take appropriate steps to facilitate an orderly transfer of responsibility. Social workers who refer clients to other professionals should disclose, with clients' consent, all pertinent information to the new service providers.

(c) Social workers are prohibited from giving or receiving payment for a referral when no professional service is provided by the referring social worker.

2.07 Sexual Relationships

(a) Social workers who function as supervisors or educators should not engage in sexual activities or contact with supervisees, students, trainees, or other colleagues over whom they exercise professional authority.

(b) Social workers should avoid engaging in sexual relationships with colleagues when there is potential for a conflict of interest. Social workers who become involved in, or anticipate becoming involved in, a sexual relationship with a colleague have a duty to transfer professional responsibilities, when necessary, to avoid a conflict of interest.

2.08 Sexual Harassment

Social workers should not sexually harass supervisees, students, trainees, or colleagues. Sexual harassment includes sexual advances, sexual solicitation, requests for sexual favors, and other verbal or physical conduct of a sexual nature.

2.09 Impairment of Colleagues

(a) Social workers should have direct knowledge of a social work colleague's impairment that is due to personal problems, psychosocial distress, substance abuse, or mental health difficulties and that interferes with practice effectiveness should consult with that colleague when feasible and assist the colleague in taking remedial action.

(b) Social workers who believe that a social work colleague's impairment interferes with practice effectiveness and that the colleague has not taken adequate steps to address the impairment should take action through appropriate channels established by employers, agencies, NASW, licensing and regulatory bodies, and other professional organizations.

2.10 Incompetence of Colleagues

(a) Social workers who have direct knowledge of a social work colleague's incompetence should consult with that colleague when feasible and assist the colleague in taking remedial action.

(b) Social workers who believe that a social work colleague is incompetent and has not taken adequate steps to address the incompetence should take action through appropriate channels established by employers, agencies, NASW, licensing and regulatory bodies, and other professional organizations.

2.11 Unethical Conduct of Colleagues

(a) Social workers should take adequate measures to discourage, prevent, expose, and correct the unethical conduct of colleagues.

(b) Social workers should be knowledgeable about established policies and procedures for handling concerns about colleagues' unethical behavior. Social workers should be familiar with national, state, and local procedures for handling ethics complaints. These include policies and procedures created by NASW, licensing and regulatory bodies, employers, agencies, and other professional organizations.

(c) Social workers who believe that a colleague has acted unethically should seek resolution by discussing their concerns with the colleague when feasible and when such discussion is likely to be productive.

(d) When necessary, social workers who believe that a colleague has acted unethically should take action through appropriate formal channels (such as contacting a state licensing board or regulatory body, an NASW committee on inquiry, or other professional ethics committees).

(e) Social workers should defend and assist colleagues who are unjustly charged with unethical conduct.

3. SOCIAL WORKERS' ETHICAL RESPONSIBILITIES IN PRACTICE SETTINGS

3.01 Supervision and Consultation
(a) Social workers who provide supervision or consultation should have the necessary knowledge and skill to supervise or consult appropriately and should do so only within their areas of knowledge and competence.
(b) Social workers who provide supervision or consultation are responsible for setting clear, appropriate, and culturally sensitive boundaries.
(c) Social workers should not engage in any dual or multiple relationships with supervisors in which there is a risk of exploitation of or potential harm to the supervisee.
(d) Social workers who provide supervision should evaluate supervisees' performance in a manner that is fair and respectful.

3.02 Education and Training
(a) Social workers who function as educators, field instructors for students, or trainers should provide instruction only within their areas of knowledge and competence and should provide instruction based on the most current information and knowledge available in the profession.
(b) Social workers who function as educators or field instructors for students should evaluate students' performance in a manner that is fair and respectful.
(c) Social workers who function as educators or field instructors for students should take reasonable steps to ensure that clients are routinely informed when services are being provided by students.
(d) Social workers who function as educators or field instructors for students should not engage in any dual or multiple relationships with students in which there is a risk of exploitation or potential harm to the students. Social work educators and field instructors are responsible for setting clear, appropriate, and culturally sensitive boundaries.

3.03 Performance Evaluation
Social workers who have responsibility for evaluating the performance of others should fulfill such responsibility in a fair and considerate manner and on the basis of clearly stated criteria.

3.04 Client Records
(a) Social workers should take reasonable steps to ensure that documentation in records is accurate and reflects the services provided.
(b) Social workers should include sufficient and timely documentation in records to facilitate the delivery of services and to ensure continuity of services provided to clients in the future.
(c) Social workers' documentation should protect clients' privacy to the extent that is possible and appropriate and should include only information that is directly relevant to the delivery of services.
(d) Social workers should store records following the termination of services to ensure reasonable future access. Records should be maintained for the number of years required by state statutes or relevant contracts.

3.05 Billing

Social workers should establish and maintain billing practices that accurately reflect the nature and extent of services provided and that identify who provided the service in the practice setting.

3.06 Client Transfer

(a) When an individual who is receiving services from another agency or colleague contacts a social worker for services, the social worker should carefully consider the client's needs before agreeing to provide services. To minimize possible confusion and conflict, social workers should discuss with potential clients the nature of the clients' current relationship with other service providers and the implications, including possible benefits or risks, of entering into a relationship with a new service provider.

(b) If a new client has been served by another agency or colleague, social workers should discuss with the client whether consultation with the previous service provider is in the client's best interest.

3.07 Administration

(a) Social work administrators should advocate within and outside their agencies for adequate resources to meet clients' needs.

(b) Social workers should advocate for resource allocation procedures that are open and fair. When not all clients' needs can be met, an allocation procedure should be developed that is nondiscriminatory and based on appropriate and consistently applied principles.

(c) Social workers who are administrators should take reasonable steps to ensure that adequate agency or organizational resources are available to provide appropriate staff supervision.

(d) Social work administrators should take reasonable steps to ensure that the working environment for which they are responsible is consistent with and encourages compliance with the *NASW Code of Ethics*. Social work administrators should take reasonable steps to eliminate any conditions in their organizations that violate, interfere with, or discourage compliance with the *Code*.

3.08 Continuing Education and Staff Development

Social work administrators and supervisors should take reasonable steps to provide or arrange for continuing education and staff development for all staff for whom they are responsible. Continuing education and staff development should address current knowledge and emerging developments related to social work practice and ethics.

3.09 Commitments to Employers

(a) Social workers generally should adhere to commitments made to employers and employing organizations.

(b) Social workers should work to improve employing agencies' policies and procedures and the efficiency and effectiveness of their services.

(c) Social workers should take reasonable steps to ensure that employers are aware of social workers' ethical obligations as set forth in the *NASW Code of Ethics* and of the implications of those obligations for social work practice.

(d) Social workers should not allow an employing organization's policies, procedures, regulations, or administrative orders to interfere with their ethical practice of social work. Social workers should take reasonable steps to ensure that their employing organizations' practices are consistent with the *NASW Code of Ethics.*

(e) Social workers should act to prevent and eliminate discrimination in the employing organization's work assignments and in its employment policies and practices.

(f) Social workers should accept employment or arrange student field placements only in organizations that exercise fair personnel practices.

(g) Social workers should be diligent stewards of the resources of their employing organizations, wisely conserving funds where appropriate and never misappropriating funds or using them for unintended purposes.

3.10 Labor–Management Disputes

(a) Social workers may engage in organized action, including the formation of and participation in labor unions, to improve services to clients and working conditions.

(b) The action of social workers who are involved in labor–management disputes, job actions, or labor strikes should be guided by the profession's values, ethical principles, and ethical standards. Reasonable differences of opinion exist among social workers concerning their primary obligation as professionals during an actual or threatened labor strike or job action. Social workers should carefully examine relevant issues and their possible impact on clients before deciding on a course of action.

4. SOCIAL WORKERS' ETHICAL RESPONSIBILITIES AS PROFESSIONALS

4.01 Competence

(a) Social workers should accept responsibility or employment only on the basis of existing competence or the intention to acquire the necessary competence.

(b) Social workers should strive to become and remain proficient in professional practice and the performance of professional functions. Social workers should critically examine and keep current with emerging knowledge relevant to social work. Social workers should routinely review the professional literature and participate in continuing education relevant to social work practice and social work ethics.

(c) Social workers should base practice on recognized knowledge, including empirically based knowledge, relevant to social work and social work ethics.

4.02 Discrimination

Social workers should not practice, condone, facilitate, or collaborate with any form of discrimination on the basis of race, ethnicity, national origin, color, sex, sexual orientation, age, marital status, political belief, religion, or mental or physical disability.

4.03 Private Conduct

Social workers should not permit their private conduct to interfere with their ability to fulfill their professional responsibilities.

4.04 Dishonesty, Fraud, and Deception

Social workers should not participate in, condone, or be associated with dishonesty, fraud, or deception.

4.05 Impairment

    (a) Social workers should not allow their own personal problems, psychosocial distress, legal problems, substance abuse, or mental health difficulties to interfere with their professional judgment and performance or to jeopardize the best interests of people for whom they have a professional responsibility.

    (b) Social workers whose personal problems, psychosocial distress, legal problems, substance abuse, or mental health difficulties interfere with their professional judgment and performance should immediately seek consultation and take appropriate remedial action by seeking professional help, making adjustments in workload, terminating practice, or taking any other steps necessary to protect clients and others.

4.06 Misrepresentation

    (a) Social workers should make clear distinctions between statements made and actions engaged in as a private individual and as a representative of the social work profession, a professional social work organization, or the social worker's employing agency.

    (b) Social workers who speak on behalf of professional social work organizations should accurately represent the official and authorized positions of the organizations.

    (c) Social workers should ensure that their representations to clients, agencies, and the public of professional qualifications, credentials, education, competence, affiliations, services provided, or results to be achieved are accurate. Social workers should claim only those relevant professional credentials they actually possess and take steps to correct any inaccuracies or misrepresentations of their credentials by others.

4.07 Solicitations

    (a) Social workers should not engage in uninvited solicitation of potential clients who, because of their circumstances, are vulnerable to undue influence, manipulation, or coercion.

    (b) Social workers should not engage in solicitation of testimonial endorsements (including solicitation of consent to use a client's prior statement as a testimonial endorsement) from current clients or from other people who, because of their particular circumstances, are vulnerable to undue influence.

4.08 Acknowledging Credit

    (a) Social workers should take responsibility and credit, including authorship credit, only for work they have actually performed and to which they have contributed.

    (b) Social workers should honestly acknowledge the work of and the contributions made by others.

5.   SOCIAL WORKERS' ETHICAL RESPONSIBILITIES TO THE SOCIAL WORK PROFESSION

5.01 Integrity of the Profession

    (a) Social workers should work toward the maintenance and promotion of high standards of practice.

    (b) Social workers should uphold and advance the values, ethics, knowledge, and mission of the profession. Social workers should protect, enhance, and improve the integrity of the profession through appropriate study and research, active discussion, and responsible criticism of the profession.

(c) Social workers should contribute time and professional expertise to activities that promote respect for the value, integrity, and competence of the social work profession. These activities may include teaching, research, consultation, service, legislative testimony, presentations in the community, and participation in their professional organizations.

(d) Social workers should contribute to the knowledge base of social work and share with colleagues their knowledge related to practice, research, and ethics. Social workers should seek to contribute to the profession's literature and to share their knowledge at professional meetings and conferences.

(e) Social workers should act to prevent the unauthorized and unqualified practice of social work.

5.02 Evaluation and Research

(a) Social workers should monitor and evaluate policies, the implementation of programs, and practice interventions.

(b) Social workers should promote and facilitate evaluation and research to contribute to the development of knowledge.

(c) Social workers should critically examine and keep current with emerging knowledge relevant to social work and fully use evaluation and research evidence in their professional practice.

(d) Social workers engaged in evaluation or research should carefully consider possible consequences and should follow guidelines developed for the protection of evaluation and research participants. Appropriate institutional review boards should be consulted.

(e) Social workers engaged in evaluation or research should obtain voluntary and written informed consent from participants, when appropriate, without any implied or actual deprivation or penalty for refusal to participate; without undue inducement to participate; and with due regard for participants' well-being, privacy, and dignity. Informed consent should include information about the nature, extent, and duration of the participation requested and disclosure of the risks and benefits of participation in the research.

(f) When evaluation or research participants are incapable of giving informed consent, social workers should provide an appropriate explanation to the participants, obtain the participants' assent to the extent they are able, and obtain written consent from an appropriate proxy.

(g) Social workers should never design or conduct evaluation or research that does not use consent procedures, such as certain forms of naturalistic observation and archival research, unless rigorous and responsible review of the research has found it to be justified because of its prospective scientific, educational, or applied value and unless equally effective alternative procedures that do not involve waiver of consent are not feasible.

(h) Social workers should inform participants of their right to withdraw from evaluation and research at any time without penalty.

(i) Social workers should take appropriate steps to ensure that participants in evaluation and research have access to appropriate supportive services.

    (j)   Social workers engaged in evaluation or research should protect participants from unwarranted physical or mental distress, harm, danger, or deprivation.

   (k)   Social workers engaged in the evaluation of services should discuss collected information only for professional purposes and only with people professionally concerned with this information.

   (l)   Social workers engaged in evaluation or research should ensure the anonymity or confidentiality of participants and of the data obtained from them. Social workers should inform participants of any limits of confidentiality, the measures that will be taken to ensure confidentiality, and when any records containing research data will be destroyed.

  (m) Social workers who report evaluation and research results should protect participants' confidentiality by omitting identifying information unless proper consent has been obtained authorizing disclosure.

   (n)   Social workers should report evaluation and research findings accurately. They should not fabricate or falsify results and should take steps to correct any errors later found in published data using standard publication methods.

   (o)   Social workers engaged in evaluation or research should be alert to and avoid conflicts of interest and dual relationships with participants, should inform participants when a real or potential conflict of interest arises, and should take steps to resolve the issue in a manner that makes participants' interests primary.

   (p)   Social workers should educate themselves, their students, and their colleagues about responsible research practices.

6.   SOCIAL WORKERS' ETHICAL RESPONSIBILITIES TO THE BROADER SOCIETY

6.01 Social Welfare

Social workers should promote the general welfare of society, from local to global levels, and the development of people, their communities, and their environments. Social workers should advocate for living conditions conducive to the fulfillment of basic human needs and should promote social, economic, political, and cultural values and institutions that are compatible with the realization of social justice.

6.02 Public Participation

Social workers should facilitate informed participation by the public in shaping social policies and institutions.

6.03 Public Emergencies

Social workers should provide appropriate professional services in public emergencies to the greatest extent possible.

6.04 Social and Political Action

   (a)   Social workers should engage in social and political action that seeks to ensure that all people have equal access to the resources, employment, services, and opportunities they require to meet their basic human needs and to develop fully. Social workers should be aware of the impact of the political arena on practice and should advocate for changes in policy and legislation to improve social conditions in order to meet basic human needs and promote social justice.

(b) Social workers should act to expand choice and opportunity for all people, with special regard for vulnerable, disadvantaged, oppressed, and exploited people and groups.

(c) Social workers should promote conditions that encourage respect for cultural and social diversity within the United States and globally. Social workers should promote policies and practices that demonstrate respect for difference, support the expansion of cultural knowledge and resources, advocate for programs and institutions that demonstrate cultural competence, and promote policies that safeguard the rights of and confirm equity and social justice for all people.

(d) Social workers should act to prevent and eliminate domination of, exploitation of, and discrimination against any person, group, or class on the basis of race, ethnicity, national origin, color, sex, sexual orientation, age, marital status, political belief, religion, or mental or physical disability.

CASW Code of Ethics[†]

DEFINITIONS

In this Code,

Best Interest of Client

means
(a) that the wishes, desires, motivations, and plans of the client are taken by the social work-
     er as the primary consideration in any intervention plan developed by the social worker
     subject to change only when the client's plans are documented to be unrealistic, unrea-
     sonable or potentially harmful to self or others or otherwise determined inappropriate
     when considered in relation to a mandated requirement,
(b) that all actions and interventions of the social worker are taken subject to the reasonable
     belief that the client will benefit from the action, and
(c) that the social worker will consider the client as an individual, a member of a family
     unit, a member of a community, a person with a distinct ancestry or culture and will
     consider those factors in any decision affecting the client.

Client[1]

means
(a) a person, family, group of persons, incorporated body, association or community on
     whose behalf a social worker provides or agrees to provide a service
     (i)   on request or with agreement[2] of the person, family, group of persons, incorporated
           body, associations or community, or
     (ii) as a result of a legislated responsibility, or
(b) a judge of a court of competent jurisdiction who orders the social worker to provide to the
     Court an assessment.[3]

Conduct Unbecoming

means behaviour or conduct that does not meet standard of care requirements and is therefore
subject to discipline.[4]

Malpractice and Negligence

means behaviour that is included as "conduct unbecoming" and relates to social work practice
behaviour within the parameters of the professional relationship that falls below the standard

---

[†]This Social Work Code of Ethics, adopted by the Board of Directors of the Canadian Association of Social
Workers (CASW) is effective on January 1, 1994 and replaces The CASW Code of Ethics (1983). The Code is
reprinted here with the permission of CASW. The copyright in the document has been registered with Consumer
and Corporate Affairs Canada, registration No. 427837.

of practice and results in or aggravates an injury to a client. Without limiting the generality of the above,[5] it includes behaviour which results in assault, deceit, fraudulent misrepresentations, defamation of character, breach of contract, violation of human rights, malicious prosecution, false imprisonment or criminal conviction.

Practice of Social Work

includes the assessment, remediation and prevention of social problems, and the enhancement of social functioning of individuals, families, groups and communities by means of
(a) the provision of direct counselling services within an established relationship between a social worker and client;
(b) the development, promotion and delivery of human service programs, including that done in collaboration with other professionals;
(c) the development and promotion of social policies aimed at improving social conditions and equality; and[6]
(d) any other activities approved by CASW.[7]

Social Worker

means a person who is duly registered to practice social work in a province or territory or where mandatory registration does not exist, a person practising social work who voluntarily agrees to be subject to this Code.

Standard of Practice

means the standard of care ordinarily expected of a competent social worker. It means that the public is assured that a social worker has the training, the skill and the diligence to provide them with professional social work services.

NOTES

1. A client ceases to be a client 2 years after the termination of a social work service. It is advisable for this termination to be clearly documented on the case file.

2. This sub-paragraph identifies two situations where a person may be considered a voluntary client. The person who requests a social work service is clearly a voluntary client. A person also may originally be receiving services as a result of the actions of a court or other legally mandated entity. This person may receive a service beyond that originally mandated and therefore be able to terminate voluntarily that aspect of the service. A situation where a person is referred by another professional or family member clearly falls into this "voluntary service" relationship when that person agrees with the service to be provided. This type of social work relationship is clearly distinguishable from the relationship in sub-paragraph (ii) where the social worker does not seek or have agreement for the service to be provided.

3. In this situation, the social worker is providing an assessment, information or a professional opinion to a judge of competent jurisdiction to assist the judge in making a ruling or determination. In this situation, the relationship is with the judge and the person on whom the information, assessment or opinion is provided is not the client. The social worker still has some professional obligations towards that person, for example: competence and dignity.

4. In reaching a decision in *Re Matthews and Board of Directors of Physiotherapy* (1986) 54 O.R. (2d) 375, Saunders J. makes three important statements regarding standards of practice and by implication Code of Ethics:
(i) Standards of practice are inherent characteristics of any profession.

    (ii)   Standards of practice may be written or unwritten.

    (iii) Some conduct is clearly regarded as misconduct and need not be written down whereas other conduct may be the subject of dispute within a profession.

5. The importance of the collective opinion of the profession in establishing and ultimately modifying the Code of Ethics was established in a 1884 case involving the medical profession. Lord Esher, M.R. stated:

> "If it is shown that a medical man, in the pursuit of his profession, has done something with regard to it which would be reasonably regarded as disgraceful or dishonourable by his professional brethren of good repute and competency", then it is open to the General Medical Council to say that he has been guilty of "infamous conduct in a professional respect".

6. This definition except paragraph (d) has been taken from *An Act to Incorporate the New Brunswick Association of Social Workers*, chapter 78 of the Statutes of New Brunswick, 1988, section 2.

7. The procedure for adding activities under this paragraph will be established as a bylaw by the CASW Board of Directory.

PREAMBLE

Philosophy

The profession of social work is founded on humanitarian and egalitarian ideals. Social workers believe in the intrinsic worth and dignity of every human being and are committed to the values of acceptance, self-determination and respect of individuality. They believe in the obligation of all people, individually and collectively, to provide resources, services and opportunities for the overall benefit of humanity. The culture of individuals, families, groups, communities and nations has to be respected without prejudice.[8]

    Social workers are dedicated to the welfare and self-realization of human beings; to the development and disciplined use of scientific knowledge regarding human and societal behaviours; to the development of resources to meet individual, group, national and international needs and aspirations; and to the achievement of social justice for all.

Professional Practice Conflicts

If a conflict arises in professional practice, the standards declared in this Code take precedence. Conflicts of interest may occur because of demands from the general public, workplace, organizations or clients. In all cases, if the ethical duties and obligations or ethical responsibilities of this Code would be compromised, the social worker must act in a manner consistent with this Code.

Nature of this Code

The first seven statements in this code establish ethical duties and obligations. These statements provide the basis of a social worker's relationship with a client and are based on the values of social work. A breach of any of these statements forms the basis of a disciplinary action. The remaining three statements are characterized as ethical responsibilities and are to be seen as being different from the ethical duties and obligations. These ethical responsibilities are not likely to form the basis of any disciplinary action if breached. However these sections may form the basis of inquiry. These ethical responsibilities may be used in conjunction with breaches of other sections of this code and may form the basis of necessary background information in any action for discipline. Of equal importance, these ethical responsibilities are desirable goals to be achieved by the social work profession which by its nature is driven by an adherence to the values that form the basis of these desirable ethical behaviours.

NOTE

8. Taken from: *Teaching and Learning about Human Rights; A Manual for Schools of Social Work and the Social Work Profession;* U.N. Centre for Human Rights, Co-operation with International Federation of Social Workers and International Association of Schools of Social Workers, United Nations, New York, 1992.

SOCIAL WORK CODE OF ETHICS

Ethical Duties and Obligations

1. A social worker shall maintain the best interest of the client as the primary professional obligation.
2. A social worker shall carry out her or his professional duties and obligations with integrity and objectivity.
3. A social worker shall have and maintain competence in the provision of a social work service to a client.
4. A social worker shall not exploit the relationship with a client for personal benefit, gain or gratification.
5. A social worker shall protect the confidentiality of all information acquired from the client or others regarding the client and the client's family during the professional relationship unless
   (a) the client authorizes in writing the release of specified information,
   (b) the information is released under the authority of a statute or an order of a court of competent jurisdiction, or
   (c) otherwise authorized by this Code.
6. A social worker who engages in another profession, occupation, affiliation or calling shall not allow these outside interests to affect the social work relationship with the client.
7. A social worker in private practice shall not conduct the business of provision of social work services for a fee in a manner that discredits the profession or diminishes the public's trust in the profession.

Ethical Responsibilities

8. A social worker shall advocate for workplace conditions and policies that are consistent with the Code.
9. A social worker shall promote excellence in the social work profession.
10. A social worker shall advocate change
    (a) in the best interest of the client, and
    (b) for the overall benefit of society, the environment and the global community.

CHAPTER 1—PRIMARY PROFESSIONAL OBLIGATION

1. A social worker shall maintain the best interest of the client as the primary professional obligation.
1.1 The social worker is to be guided primarily by this obligation. Any action which is substantially inconsistent with this obligation is an unethical action.
1.2 A social worker in the practice of social work shall not discriminate against any person on the basis of race, ethnic background, language, religion, marital status, sex, sexual orientation, age, abilities, socio-economic status, political affiliation or national ancestry.[9]
1.3 A social worker shall inform a client of the client's right to consult another professional at any time during the provision of social work services.
1.4 A social worker shall immediately inform the client of any factor, condition[10] or pressure that affect the social worker's ability to perform an acceptable level of service.
1.5 A social worker shall not become involved in a client's personal affairs that are not relevant to the service being provided.
1.6 A social worker shall not state an opinion, judgment or use a clinical diagnosis unless there is a documented assessment, observation or diagnosis to support the opinion, judgment or diagnosis.
1.7 Where possible, a social worker shall provide or secure social work services in the language chosen by the client.

NOTES

9. This obligation goes beyond grounds of discrimination stated in most *Human Rights Legislation* and therefore there is a greater professional obligation than that stated in provincial legislation.

10. The term condition means a physical, mental or psychological condition. There is an implied obligation that the social worker shall actively seek diagnosis and treatment for any signs or warnings of a condition. A disclosure under this section may be of a general nature. See also 3.4.

CHAPTER 2—INTEGRITY AND OBJECTIVITY

2. A social worker shall carry out his or her professional duties and obligations with integrity and objectivity.[11]
2.1 A social worker shall identify and describe education, training, experience, professional affiliations, competence, and nature of service in an honest and accurate manner.
2.2 A social worker shall explain to the client her or his education, experience, training, competence, nature of service and action at the request of the client.
2.3 A social worker shall cite an educational degree only after it has been received from the institution.
2.4 A social worker shall not claim formal social work education in an area of expertise or training solely by attending a lecture, demonstration, conference, panel discussion, workshop, seminar or other similar teaching presentation.[12]
2.5 A social worker shall not make a false, misleading or exaggerated claim of efficacy regarding past or anticipated achievement with respect to clients.
2.6 The social worker shall distinguish between actions and statements made as a private citizen and actions and statements made as a social worker.[13]

NOTES

11. The term objectivity is taken from the Québec Code of Professional Conduct. See Division 2: Integrity and Objectivity (6.0 Québec) November 5, 1979 Vol. 2 No. 30. The term objectivity is stated in the following: 3.02.01. A social worker must discharge his professional duties with integrity and objectivity.

12. The provincial associations may regulate the areas of expertise to be stated or advertised by a social worker. This will vary in each province according to its enabling legislation. Where there is not sufficient legislative base for this regulation, the claim of an expertise without sufficient training may form the basis of a determination of unprofessional conduct.

13. Even with a distinction made under this section, a social worker's private actions or statements may be of such a nature that the social worker cannot avoid the responsibilities under this Code. See also 6.2 (c).

CHAPTER 3—COMPETENCE IN THE PROVISION OF SOCIAL WORK SERVICES

3.   A social worker shall have and maintain competence in the provision of a social work service to a client.

3.1   A social worker shall not undertake a social work service unless the social worker has the competence to provide the service or the social worker can reasonably acquire the necessary competence without undue delay, risk or expense to the client.

3.2   Where a social worker cannot reasonably acquire the necessary competence in the provision of a service to a client, the social worker shall decline to provide the service to the client, advising the client of the reason and ensuring that the client is referred to another professional person if the client agrees to the referral.

3.3   The social worker, with the agreement of the client, may obtain advice from other professionals in the provision of service to a client.

3.4   A social worker shall maintain an acceptable level of health and well-being in order to provide a competent level of service to a client.[14]

3.5   Where a social worker has a physical or mental health problem, disability or illness that affects the ability of the social worker to provide competent service or that would threaten the health or well-being of the client, the social worker shall discontinue the provision of social work service to a client

(a)   advising the client of the reason and,[15]

(b)   ensuring that the client is referred to another professional person if the client agrees to the referral.

3.6   A social worker shall have, maintain and endeavor periodically to update an acceptable level of knowledge and skills to meet the standards of practice of the profession.

NOTES

14. This section should be considered in relation to section 1.4 and involves proper maintenance, prevention and treatment of any type of risk to the health or well-being of the social worker.

15. It is not necessary in all circumstances to explain specifically the nature of the problem.

CHAPTER 4—LIMIT ON PROFESSIONAL RELATIONSHIP

4.   A social worker shall not exploit the relationship with a client for personal benefit, gain or gratification.

4.1   The social worker shall respect the client and act so that the dignity, individuality and rights of the person are protected.

4.2   A social worker shall assess and consider a client's motivation and physical and mental capacity in arranging for the provision of an appropriate service.

4.3   A social worker shall not have a sexual relationship with a client.

4.4   A social worker shall not have a business relationship with a client, borrow money from a client, or loan money to a client.[16]

4.5   A social worker shall not have a sexual relationship with a social work student assigned to the social worker.

4.6   A social worker shall not sexually harass any person.

NOTE

16. Where a social worker does keep money or assets belonging to a client, the social worker should hold this money or asset in a trust account or hold the money or asset in conjunction with an additional professional person.

CHAPTER 5—CONFIDENTIAL INFORMATION

5.   A social worker shall protect the confidentiality[17] of all information acquired from the client or others regarding the client and the client's family during the professional relationship[18] unless
   (a) the client authorizes in writing the release of specified information,[19]
   (b) the information is released under the authority of a statute or an order of a court of relevant jurisdiction, or
   (c) otherwise authorized under this Code.

5.1   The requirement of confidentiality also applies to social workers who work as
   (a) supervisors,
   (b) managers,
   (c) educators, or
   (d) administrators.

5.2   A social worker who works as a supervisor, manager or administrator shall establish policies and practices that protect the confidentiality of client information.

5.3   The social worker may disclose confidential information to other persons in the workplace who, by virtue of their responsibilities, have an identified need to know as determined by the social worker.

5.4   Clients shall be the initial or primary source of information about themselves and their problems unless the client is incapable or unwilling to give information or when corroborative reporting is required.

5.5   The social worker has the obligation to ensure that the client understands what is being asked, why and to what purpose the information will be used, and to understand the confidentiality policies and practices of the workplace setting.

5.6　Where information is required by law, the social worker shall explain to the client the consequences of refusing to provide the requested information.

5.7　Where information is required from other sources, the social worker
　　(a)　shall explain the requirement to the client, and
　　(b)　shall attempt to involve the client in selecting the sources to be used.

5.8　The social worker shall take reasonable care to safeguard the client's personal papers or property if the social worker agrees to keep the property at the request of the client.

Recording Information

5.9　The social worker shall maintain only one master file on each client.[20]

5.10　The social worker shall record all relevant information, and keep all relevant documents in the file.

5.11　The social worker shall not record in a client's file any characterization that is not based on clinical assessment or fact.

Accessibility of Records

5.12　The social worker who contracts for the delivery of social work services with a client is responsible to the client for maintaining the client record.

5.13　The social worker who is employed by a social agency that delivers social work services to clients is responsible
　　(a)　to the client for the maintaining of a client record, and
　　(b)　to the agency to maintain the records to facilitate the objectives of the agency.

5.14　A social worker is obligated to follow the provision of a statute that allows access to records by clients.

5.15　The social worker shall respect the client's right of access to a client record subject to the social worker's right to refuse access for just and reasonable cause.

5.16　Where a social worker refuses a client the right to access a file or part of a file, the social worker shall advise the client of the right to request a review of the decision in accordance with the relevant statute, workplace policy or other relevant procedure.

Disclosure

5.17　The social worker shall not disclose the identity of persons who have sought a social work service or disclose sources of information about clients unless compelled legally to do so.[21]

5.18　The obligation to maintain confidentiality continues indefinitely after the social worker has ceased contact with the client.

5.19　The social worker shall avoid unnecessary conversation regarding clients.

5.20　The social worker may divulge confidential information with consent of the client, preferably expressed in writing, where this is essential to a plan of care or treatment.

5.21　The social worker shall transfer information to another agency or individual, only with the informed consent of the client or guardian of the client and then only with the reasonable assurance that the receiving agency provides the same guarantee of confidentiality and respect for the right of privileged communication as provided by the sending agency.

5.22　The social worker shall explain to the client the disclosure of information requirements of the law or of the agency before the commencement of the provision of social work services.

5.23   The social worker in practice with groups and communities shall notify the participants of the likelihood that aspects of their private lives may be revealed in the course of their work together, and therefore require a commitment from each member to respect the privileged and confidential nature of the communication between and among members of the client group.

5.24   Subject to section 5.26, the social worker shall not disclose information acquired from one client to a member of the client's family without the informed consent of the client who provided the information.

5.25   A social worker shall disclose information acquired from one client to a member of the client's family where

    (a) the information involves a threat of harm to self or others,[22]

    (b) the information was acquired from a child of tender years and the social worker determines that its disclosure is in the best interests of the child.[23]

5.26   A social worker shall disclose information acquired from a client to a person or a police officer where the information involves a threat of harm to that person.

5.27   A social worker may release confidential information as part of a discipline hearing of a social worker as directed by the tribunal or disciplinary body.

5.28   When disclosure is required by order of a court, the social worker shall not divulge more information than is reasonably required and shall where possible notify the client of this requirement.

5.29   The social worker shall not use confidential information for the purpose of teaching, public education or research except with the informed consent of the client.

5.30   The social worker may use non-identifying information for the purpose of teaching, public education or research.

Retention and Disposition of Information

5.31   Where the social worker's documentation is stored in a place or computer maintained and operated by an employer, the social worker shall advocate for the responsible retention and disposition of information contained in the file.

NOTES

17. Confidentiality means that information received or observed about a client by a social worker will be held in confidence and disclosed only when the social worker is properly authorized or obligated legally or professionally to do so. This also means that professionally acquired information may be treated as privileged communication and ordinarily only the client has the right to waive privilege.

Privileged communication means statements made within a protected relationship (i.e. husband–wife, professional–client) which the law protects against disclosure. The extent of the privilege is governed by law and not by this Code.

Maintaining confidentiality of privileged communication means that information about clients does not have to be transmitted in any oral, written or recorded form. Such information, for example, does not have to be disclosed to a supervisor, written into a workplace record, stored in a computer or microfilm data base, held on an audio or videotape or discussed orally. The right of privileged communication is respected by the social worker in the practice of social work notwithstanding that this right is not ordinarily granted in law.

The disclosure of confidential information in social work practice involves the obligation to share information professionally with others in the workplace of the social worker as part of a reasonable service to the client. Social workers recognize the need to obtain permission from clients before releasing information about them to sources outside their workplace; and to inform clients at the outset of their relationship that some information acquired may be shared with the officers and personnel of the agency who maintain the case record and who have a reasonable need for the information in the performance of their duties.

18. The social worker's relationship with a client can be characterized as a fiduciary relationship.

In *Fiduciary Duties in Canada* by Ellis, fiduciary duty is described as follows: ...where one party has placed its "trust and confidence" in another and the latter has accepted—expressly or by operation of law—to act in a manner consistent with the reposing of such "trust and confidence", a fiduciary relationship has been established.

19. The "obligation of secrecy" was discussed by the Supreme Court of Canada in *Halls v. Mitchell*, (1928) S.C.R. 125, an action brought by a disabled CNR worker against a company doctor who had disclosed the employee's medical history, to the latter's detriment. Mr. Justice Duff reviewed the duty of confidentiality:

We are not required, for the purposes of this appeal, to attempt to state with any sort of precision the limits of the obligation of secrecy which rests upon the medical practitioner in relation to the professional secrets acquired by him in the course of his practice. Nobody would dispute that a secret so acquired is the secret of the patient, and, normally, is under his control, and not under that of the doctor. Prima facie, the patient has the right to require that the secret shall not be divulged; and that right is absolute, unless there is some paramount reason which overrides it.

Thus the right of secrecy/confidentiality rests squarely with the patient; the Court carefully provided that there is an "ownership" extant in the confidentiality of the personal information. Duff J. continued by allowing for "paramount" criteria which vitiates from the right:

Some reasons may arise, no doubt, from the existence of facts which bring into play overpowering considerations connected with public justice; and there may be cases in which reasons connected with the safety of individuals or of the public, physical or moral, would be sufficiently cogent to supersede or qualify the obligations prima facie imposed by the confidential relation.

Duff J. continued:

The general duty of medical men to observe secrecy, in relation to information acquired by them confidentially from their patients is subject, no doubt, to some exceptions, which have no operation in the case of solicitors; but the grounds of the legal, social or moral imperatives affecting physicians and surgeons, touching the inviolability of professional confidences, are not, any more than those affecting legal advisers, based exclusively upon the relations between the parties as individuals.

20. The master file refers to all relevant documents pertaining to the client consisting of such information as demographics, case recordings, court documents, assessments, correspondence, treatment plans, bills, etc. This information is often collected through various means including electronic and computer-driven sources. However the client master file exists as one unit, inclusive of all information pertaining to the client, despite the various sources of the recording process. The description and ownership of the master file is most often defined by workplace standards or policies. The client's master file should be prepared keeping in mind that it may have to be revealed to the client or disclosed in legal proceedings.

21. A social worker may be compelled to reveal information under the section when directly ordered by the court to do so. Before disclosing the information, the social worker shall advise the court of the professional obligations that exist under this section of the Code and where reasonably possible inform the client.

22. The case of *Tarasoff v. The Regents of the University of California et al.* (1976), 551 p.2d 334 (Cal. Supreme Court) focused on the obligation of a psychiatrist to maintain the confidentiality of his patients' statements in their discussions. In that case the patient told the psychiatrist that the patient had an intention to kill a certain woman. When the patient actually did kill this woman, her parents brought suit alleging that the psychiatrist owed a duty to tell the woman of the danger to her.

It was held that the psychiatrist did have a duty to tell the woman of the threat. The court recognized that the psychiatrist owed a duty to the patient to keep in confidence the statements the patient made in therapy sessions, but held there was also a duty to care to anyone whom the psychiatrist knew might be endangered by the patient. At a certain point the obligation of confidentiality would be overridden by the obligation to this third person. The psychiatrist's knowledge itself gave rise to a duty of care. What conduct would be sufficient to fulfil the duty to this third person would depend on the circumstances, but it might be necessary to give a warning that would reveal what the patient had said about the third party. The court in this case held that the psychiatrist had a duty to warn the woman about the patient's stated intention to kill her, and having failed to warn her the psychiatrist was liable in negligence. Moreover, the court stated that the principle of this duty of care belonged not just to a psychiatrist but also to a psychologist performing therapy. It would follow that the principle would also apply to social workers performing therapy.

23. For the purpose of this Code, a child of tender years shall usually be determined to be a child under the age of seven years subject to a determination by a social worker considering the child's social, physical, intellectual, emotional or psychological development.

CHAPTER 6—OUTSIDE INTEREST

6.   A social worker who engages in another profession, occupation, affiliation or calling shall not allow these outside interests to affect the social work relationship with the client.

6.1 A social worker shall declare to the client any outside interests that would affect the social work relationship with the client.

6.2 A social worker shall not allow an outside interest:
(a) to affect the social worker's ability to practise social work;
(b) to present to the client or to the community that the social worker's ability to practise social work is affected; or
(c) to bring the profession of social work into disrepute.[24]

NOTE

24. This section brings the social worker's outside interest and personal actions in line with the professional duties and obligations as set out in this Code.

CHAPTER 7—LIMIT ON PRIVATE PRACTICE

7.   A social worker in private practice shall not conduct the business of provision of social work services for a fee in a manner that discredits the profession or diminishes the public's trust in the profession.

7.1 A social worker shall not use the social work relationship within an agency to obtain clients for his or her private practice.

7.2 Subject to section 7.3, a social worker who enters into a contract for service with a client
(a) shall disclose at the outset of the relationship, the fee schedule for the social work services,

(b) shall not charge a fee that is greater than that agreed to and disclosed to the client, and

(c) shall not charge for hours of service other than the reasonable hours of client services, research, consultation and administrative work directly connected to the case.

7.3   A social worker in private practice may charge differential fees for services except where an increased fee is charged based on race, ethnic background, language, religion, marital status, sex, sexual orientation, age, abilities, socio-economic status, political affiliation or national ancestry.

7.4   A social worker in private practice shall maintain adequate malpractice, defamation and liability insurance.

7.5   A social worker in private practice may charge a rate of interest on delinquent accounts as is allowed by law.[25]

7.6   Notwithstanding section 5.17 a social worker in private practice may pursue civil remedies to ensure payment for services to a client where the social worker has advised the client of this possibility at the outset of the social work service.

NOTE

25. This rate shall be stated on all invoices or bills sent to the client.

CHAPTER 8—ETHICAL RESPONSIBILITIES TO THE WORKPLACE

8.   A social worker shall advocate for workplace conditions and policies that are consistent with the Code.

8.1   Where the responsibilities to an employer are in conflict with the social worker's obligations to the client, the social worker shall document the issue in writing and shall bring the situation to the attention of the employer.

8.2   Where a serious ethical conflict continues to exist after the issue has been brought to the attention of the employer, the social worker shall bring the issue to the attention of the Association or regulatory body.[26]

8.3   A social worker shall follow the principles in the Code when dealing with

(a)   a social worker under the supervision of the social worker,

(b)   an employee under the supervision of the social worker, and

(c)   a social work student under the supervision of the social worker.

NOTE

26. In this situation the professional obligations outweigh any obligations to a workplace.

CHAPTER 9—ETHICAL RESPONSIBILITIES TO THE PROFESSION

9.   A social worker shall promote excellence in the social work profession.

9.1   A social worker shall report to the appropriate association or regulatory body any breach of this Code by another social worker which adversely affects or harms a client or prevents the effective delivery of a social service.

9.2   A social worker shall report to the association or regulatory body any unqualified or un-licensed person who is practising social work.

9.3   A social worker shall not intervene in the professional relationship of a social worker and client unless requested to do so by the client and unless convinced that the best interests and well-being of the client require such intervention.

9.4   Where a conflict arises between a social worker and other professionals, the social worker shall attempt to resolve the professional differences in ways that uphold the principles of this Code and the honour of the social work profession.

9.5   A social worker engaged in research shall ensure that the involvement of clients in the research is a result of informed consent.

CHAPTER 10—ETHICAL RESPONSIBILITIES FOR SOCIAL CHANGE

10.   A social worker shall advocate change
      (a) in the best interest of the client, and
      (b) for the overall benefit of society, the environment and the global community.

10.1   A social worker shall identify, document and advocate for the elimination of discrimination.

10.2   A social worker shall advocate for the equal distribution of resources to all persons.

10.3   A social worker shall advocate for the equal access of all persons to resources, services and opportunities.

10.4   A social worker shall advocate for a clean and healthy environment and shall advocate the development of environmental strategies consistent with social work principles.

10.5   A social worker shall provide reasonable professional services in a state of emergency.

10.6   A social worker shall promote social justice.

■ *Bibliography*

Ackerman, N. (1958). *Psychodynamics of family life*. 3rd ed. New York: Basic Books.

Addams, J. (1961). *Twenty years at Hull House*. New York: Signet. (Original edition published in 1910.)

Albert, J. (1994). Rethinking difference: A cognitive therapy group for chronic mental patients. *Social Work with Groups, 17*: 105–122.

Alexander, R., Jr. (1997). Social workers and priviledge communication in the federal legal system. *Social Work 42*(4): 387–391.

Alissi, A. S. (1980). *Perspectives on social group work practice*. New York: Free Press.

American Association for Counseling and Development. (1989). *Ethical guidelines for group counselors*. Alexandria, VA: American Association for Counseling and Development.

Amodeo, M., Grigg-Saito, D., & Robb, N. (1997). Working with foreign language interpreters: Guidelines for substance abuse clinicians and human service practitioners. *Alcoholism Treatment Quarterly, 15*(4).

Amodeo, M., Wilson, S., & Cox, D. (1995). Mounting a community-based alcohol and drug abuse prevention effort in a multicultural urban setting: Challenges and lessons learned. *The Journal of Primary Prevention, 16*(2): 165–185.

Argyris, C. (1964). *Integrating the individual and the organization*. New York: John Wiley & Sons.

Asch, S. E. (1951). Effects of group pressure upon the modification and distortion of judgments. In H. Guetzkow (Ed.), *Groups, leadership, and men* (pp. 177–190). Pittsburgh: Carnegie Press.

Baldwin, J. M. (1911). *The individual and society: Or psychology and sociology*. Boston: Gorham Press.

Bales, R. (1958). Task roles and social roles in problem-solving groups. In E. E. Maccoby et al. (Eds.), *Readings in social psychology*. New York: Holt, Rinehart & Winston.

Bandler, R., Grindler, J., & Satir, V. (1976). *Changing with families*. Palo Alto, CA: Science & Behavior Books.

Barker, R. (1991). *The social work dictionary*. Silver Springs, MD: National Association of Social Workers.

Bateson, G., Jackson, D., Haley, J., & Weakland, J. H. (1956). Toward a theory of schizophrenia. *Behavioral Science, 1*: 251–264.

Bavelas, A. (1950). Communication patterns in task-oriented groups. *Journal of the Acoustical Society of America, 22*: 725–730.

Beck, A., Rush, A., Shaw, B., & Emery, G. (1979). *Cognitive theory of depression*. New York: Guilford Press.

Beck, J. C. (1985). *The potentially violent patient and the Tarasoff decision in psychiatric practice*. Washington, DC: American Psychiatric Press.

Bell, N. W., & Vogel, E. F. (1960). The emotionally disturbed child as the family scapegoat. In N. W. Bell & E. F. Vogel (Eds.), *A modern introduction to the family* (pp. 382–397). New York: Free Press.

Bennis, W. G., & Shepard, H. A. (1956). A theory of group development. *Human Relations, 9*: 415–437.

Berlin, S. B. (1983a). Cognitive-behavioral approaches. In A. Rosenblatt & D. Wald Fogel (Eds.), *Handbook of clinical social work* (pp. 1095–1119). San Francisco: Jossey-Bass.

Berlin, S. B. (1983b). Single-case evaluation: Another version. *Social Work Research and Abstracts, 19*(1): 3–11.

Berlin, S., & Kravetz, D. (1981). Women as victims: A feminist social work perspective. *Social Work, 26:* 447–449.

Berman-Rossi, T. (Ed.) (1994). *The collected writings of William Schwartz.* Itasca, IL: Peacock.

Berman-Rossi, T., & Cohen, M. B. (1988). Group development and shared decision-making: Working with homeless mentally ill women. In J. A. Lee (Ed.), *Group work with the poor and oppressed* (pp. 63–74). New York: Haworth Press.

Bernstein, S. (1965). *Explorations in group work.* Boston: Boston University School of Social Work.

Bernstein, S. (1970). *Further explorations in group work.* Boston: Boston University School of Social Work.

Bernstein, S. (1976). *Explorations in group work.* Boston: Charles River Books.

Bernstein, S. (1984). *Explorations in group work.* Hebron, CT: Practitioners Press.

Besharov, D. J. (1985). *The vulnerable social worker.* Silver Springs, MD: National Association of Social Workers.

Bion, W. R. (1961). *Experience in groups.* New York: Basic Books.

Block, J., & Haan, N. (1971). *Lives through time.* Berkeley, CA: Bancroft Books.

Borland, J. (1981). Burnout among workers and administrators. *Health and Social Work, 6:* 73–78.

Bowen, M. (1961). The family as a unit of study and treatment. *American Journal of Orthopsychiatry, 31:* 40–60.

Bowen, M. (1978). *Family therapy in clinical practice.* New York: Jason Aronson.

Braeger, G., & Holloway, S. (1978). *Changing human service organizations: Politics and practice.* New York: Free Press.

Breton, M. (1988). The need for mutual-aid groups in a drop-in for homeless women: The sistering case. In J. A. Lee (Ed.), *Group work with the poor and oppressed* (pp. 47–60). New York: Haworth Press.

Brown, L. N. (1991). *Groups for growth and change.* New York: Longman.

Brown, S. (1985). *Treating the alcoholic: A developmental model of recovery.* New York: John Wiley & Sons.

Bulhan, H. A. (1985). *Frantz Fanon and the psychology of oppression.* New York: Plenum Press.

Burke, A. C., & Clapp, J. (1997, November). Ideology and social work practice in substance abuse settings. *Social Work, 42*(6): 537–632.

Butler, K. (1997). The anatomy of resilience. *Networker* (March/April): 22–31.

Chestang, L. (1984). Racial and personal identity in the black experience. In B. White (Ed.), *Color in white society.* Silver Springs, MD: National Association of Social Workers.

Clay, C., and Shulman, L. (1993). *Teaching about practice and diversity: Content and process in the classroom and the field.* (A series of two videotaped programs produced and distributed by the Council on Social Work Education.)

Collins, B. (1993). Reconstructing co-dependency using self-in-relation theory: A feminist perspective. *Social Work, 38*(4): 470–476.

Congress, E. P. (1994). The use of culturagrams to assess and empower culturally diverse families. *Families in Society, 75*(9): 531–540.

Connell, J. P., Spencer, M. B., and Aber, J. L. (1994). Educational risk and resilience in African-American youth: Context, self, action, and outcomes in school. *Child Development, 65:* 493–506.

Council on Social Work Education. (1992). *Curriculum policy statement.* New York: CSWE.

Coyle, G. (1948). *Group work with American youth.* New York: Harper & Brothers.

Curriculum guide for field education, 11th ed. (1990). Boston: Boston University School of Social Work.

Daly, A., Jennings, J., Beckett, J. O., & Leashore, B. R. (1995). Effective coping strategies of African-Americans. *Social Work, 40*(2): 240–248.

Daley, M. R. (1979). Preventing worker burnout in child welfare. *Child Welfare, 58:* 443–450.

Davidson, K. W. (1985). Social work with cancer patients: Stresses and coping patterns. *Social Work in Health Care, 10*(4): 73–82.

Davis, L. E. (1979). Racial composition of groups. *Social Work, 24:* 208–213.

Davis, L. E. (1980). When the majority is the

psychological minority. *Group Psychothera-py, Psychodrama, and Sociometry, 33*: 179–184.

Davis, L. E. (1981). Racial issues in the training of group workers. *Journal for Specialists in Group Work:* 155–160.

Davis, L. E. (1984). *Ethnicity in social group work practice.* New York: Haworth Press.

Davis, L. E., & Proctor, E. K. (1989). *Race, gender, and class: Guidelines for practice with individuals, families, and groups.* Englewood Cliffs, NJ: Prentice-Hall.

Day, L. G. (1991). Counseling for women: The contribution of feminist theory and practice. *Counseling Psychology Quarterly, 5*(4): 373–384.

Dean, R. G., & Fenby, B. L. (1989). Exploring epistemologies: Social work action as a reflection of philosophical assumptions. *Journal of Social Work, 25*: 46–54.

Deutsch, M. (1949). An experimental study of the effects of cooperation and competition upon group process. *Human Relations, 2*: 199–232.

Devore, W., & Schlesinger, E. G. (1991). *Ethnicsensitive social work practice.* 3rd ed. New York: Macmillan.

Devore, W., & Schlesinger, E. G. (1996). *Ethnicsensitive social work practice.* 4th ed. New York: Macmillan.

Dewey, J. (1916). *Democracy and education: An introduction to the philosophy of education.* New York: Free Press.

DiClemente, C. C., Prochaska, J. O., Fairhurst, S. K., Velicer, W. F. (1991, April). The process of smoking cessation: An analysis of precontemplation, contemplation, and preparation stages of change. *Journal of Consulting and Clinical Psychology, 59*(2): 295–304.

Douglas, T. (1995). *Scapegoats: Transferring blame.* New York: Routledge.

DuBray, L. (1985). American Indian values: Critical factors in casework. *Social Casework, 66*: 30–37.

Egeland, B., Carlson, E., & Sroufe, L. A. (1993). Resilience as process. *Development and Psychopathology, 5*(4): 517–528.

Elkin, I., Parloff, M., Hadley, K. S., & Autrey, J.

(1985). NIMH treatment of depression collaborative research program. *Archives of General Psychiatry, 42*: 305–316.

Ephros, P. H., & Vasil, T. V. (1988). *Groups that work.* New York: Columbia University Press.

Erikson, E. H. (1950). *Childhood and society.* New York: W. W. Norton.

Faden, R., & Beauchamp, T. (1986). *A history and theory of informed consent.* London: Oxford University Press.

Falck, H. (1988). *Social work: The membership perspective.* New York: Springer.

Fanon, F. (1968). *The wretched of the earth.* New York: Grove Press.

Fedele, N. (1994). *Relationships in groups: Connection, resonance, and paradox.* Wellesley, MA: Stone Center Working Papers.

Fisher, J. (1973). Is casework effective? A review. *Social Work, 18*: 5–20.

Flanders, N. A. (1970). *Analyzing teaching behaviors.* Reading, MA: Addison-Wesley.

Focus. (1996, November). Boston: Massachusetts Chapter of the National Association of Social Workers.

Fonagy, P., Steele, M., Steele, H., Higgitt, A., & Target, M. (1994). The Emanuel Miller Memorial Lecture 1992: The theory and practice of resilience. *Journal of Child Psychology and Psychiatry and Allied Disorders, 35*(2): 231–257.

Freeman, D. S. (1981). *Techniques of family therapy.* New York: Jason Aronson.

Frey, L., & Meyer, M. (1984). Exploration and working agreement in two social work methods. In S. Bernstein (Ed.), *Exploration in group work.* Hebron, CT: Practitioner's Press.

Fried, B. (1967). *The middle-age crisis.* New York: Harper & Row.

Galper, J. (1976). Introduction to radical theory and practice in social work education: Social policy. *Journal of Education in Social Work, 12*: 3–9.

Galper, J. (1979). Research and writing for radical social work. *Catalyst, 4*: 37–50.

Gambrill, E., & Pruger, R. (1997). *Controversial issues in social work ethics, values, and obligations.* Boston: Allyn & Bacon.

Garfield, G. P., & Irizary, C. R. (1971). Recording the 'record of service': Describing social work practice. In W. Schwartz & S. Zalba (Eds.), *The practice of group work* (pp. 241–265). New York: Columbia University Press.

Garland, J. A., Jones, H. E., & Kolodny, R. L. (1965). A model for stages of development in social work groups. In S. Bernstein (Ed.), *Explorations in group work* (pp. 17–71). Boston: Boston University School of Social Work.

Garland, J. A., & Kolodny, R. L. (1965). Characteristics and resolution of scapegoating. In S. Bernstein (Ed.), *Explorations in group work.* Boston: Boston University School of Social Work. (Published later under the same title by: Boston: Charles River Books, 1976; Hebron, CT: Practitioner's Press, 1984.)

Garmezy, N. (1991). Resilience and vulnerability to adverse developmental outcomes associated with poverty. *American Behavioral Scientist, 34*(4): 416–430.

Garmezy, N. (1993). Children in poverty: Resilience despite risk. *Psychiatry, 56*: 127–136.

Garmezy, N., Masten, A. S., & Tellegen, A. (1984). The study of stress and competence in children: A building block for developmental psychopathology. *Child Development, 55*: 98–111.

Garvin, C. (1969). Complementarity of role expectations in groups: The member-novice contract. In *Social Work Practice 1969* (pp. 127–145). New York: Columbia University Press.

Garvin, C. (1981). *Contemporary group work.* Englewood Cliffs, NJ: Prentice-Hall.

Garvin, C. (1987). *Contemporary group work.* Englewood Cliffs, NJ: Prentice-Hall.

Gary, L. E., & Leashore, B. R. (1982). High-risk status of black men. *Social Work, 27*: 54–58.

Germain, C. B. (1977). Teaching an ecological approach to social work practice. In *Teaching for competence in the delivery of direct services* (pp. 31–39). New York: Council on Social Work Education.

Germain, C. B., & Gitterman, A. (1980). *The life model of social work practice.* New York: Columbia University Press.

Germain, C. B., & Gitterman, A. (1996). *The life model of social work practice.* 2nd ed. New York: Columbia University Press.

Getzel, G. (1989). Group work with gay men with AIDS. *Social Casework, 2*: 172–179.

Gilgun, J. F. (1996). Human development and adversity in ecological perspective. Part I: A conceptual framework. *Families in Society*: 395–402.

Gilligan, C., Lyons, N., & Hammer, T. (1990). *Making connections.* Cambridge, MA: Harvard University Press.

Gitterman, A. (1991). *Handbook of social work with vulnerable populations.* New York: Columbia University Press.

Gitterman, A., & Shulman, L. (1994). *Mutual aid groups, vulnerable populations, and the life cycle.* New York: Columbia University Press.

Glaser, B., & Strauss, A. (1967). *Grounded theory.* Chicago: Aldine.

Glassman, U., & Kates, L. (1990). *Group work: A humanistic approach.* Newbury Park, CA: Sage.

Gochros, H. (1984). Teaching social workers to meet the needs of the homosexually oriented. In R. Schoenberg, R. Goldberg, & D. A. Stone (Eds.), *Homosexuality and social work.* New York: Haworth Press.

Googins, B. (1984, March/April). Avoidance of the alcoholic client. *Social Work, 29*(2): 161–166.

Grosser, C. F. (1973). *New directions in community organization.* New York: Praeger.

Gutheil, I. A. (1992). Considering the physical environment: An essential component of good practice. *Social Work, 37*(5): 391–396.

Gutheil, T., & Appelbaum, P. (1987). *Clinical handbook of psychiatry and the law.* Washington, DC: American Psychiatric Press.

Hacker, A. (1992). *Two nations: Black and white, separate, hostile, unequal.* New York: Charles Scribner's Sons.

Haley, J. (1963). *Strategies of psychotherapy.* New York: Grune & Stratton.

Haley, J. (1973). *Problem solving therapy.* San Francisco: Jossey-Bass.

Haley, J. (1984). *Ordeal therapy.* San Francisco: Jossey-Bass.

Hardesty, L., & Greif, G. L. (1994, July–September). Common themes in a group for female IV drug users who are HIV-positive. *Journal of Psychoactive Drugs, 26*(3): 289–293.

Hardy, K. V., & Laszloffy, T. A. (1992). Training

racially sensitive family therapists: Context, content, and contact. *Families in Society, 73*(6): 364–370.

Hare, P. A. (1962). *Handbook of small group research*. New York: Free Press.

Hartford, M. (1972). *Groups in social work*. New York: Columbia University Press.

Hearn, G. (1958). *Theory building in social work*. Toronto: University of Toronto Press.

Hearn, G. (1962). *The general systems approach to understanding groups*. Health Education Monographs, no. 14. New York: Society of Public Health Educators.

Hearn, G. (Ed.). (1969). *The general systems approach: Contributions toward an holistic conception of social work*. New York: Council on Social Work Education.

Hegel, G. W. F. (1966). *The phenomenology of mind*. London: Allen & Unwin.

Herrenkohl, E. C., Herrenkohl, R. C., and Egolf, B. (1994). Resilient early school-age children from maltreating homes: Outcomes in late adolescence. *American Journal of Orthopsychiatry, 64*(2): 301–309.

Heyman, D. (1971). A function for the social worker in the anti-poverty program. In W. Schwartz & S. Zalba (Eds.), *The practice of group work*. New York: Columbia University Press.

Hidalgo, H., Peterson, L., & Woodman, N. J. (1985). *Lesbian and gay issues: A resource manual for social workers*. Silver Springs, MD: National Association of Social Workers.

Ho, M. (1984). Social group work with Asian/Pacific Americans. *Social Work with Groups, Special Issue: Ethnicity in social group work practice, 7*: 49–61.

Hollis, F. (1964). *Casework: A psychosocial theory*. New York: Random House.

Holmes, M., & Lundy, C. (1990). Group work for abusive men. *Canada's Mental Health, 38*: 12–17.

Homans, G. (1950). *The human group*. New York: Harcourt Brace Jovanovich.

Horne, A. M., & Passmore, J. L. (1991). *Family counseling and therapy*. 2nd ed. Itasca, IL: Peacock.

Huber, J. (1973). *Changing women in a changing society*. Chicago: University of Chicago Press.

Ivanoff, A., Robinson, E. A., & Blyth, B. J. (1987). Empirical clinical practice from a feminist perspective. *Social Work, 32*: 417–423.

Jaffee v. Redmond. (1996). s.Ct., U.U. Lexis 3879.

Johnson, M. D., & Fawcett, S. B. (1987). Consumer-defined standards for courteous treatment by service agencies. *Journal of Rehabilitation, 53*: 23–26.

Jordan, J. (1991). Empathy, mutuality, and therapeutic change: Clinical implications of a relational model. In *Women's growth in connections: Writings from the Stone Center*. New York: Guilford Press.

Jordan, J. (1993). *Challenges to connection*. Work in Progress, No. 60. Wellesley, MA: Stone Center Working Paper Series.

Jöreskog, K. G., & Sörbom, D. (1988). *Lisrel 7: A guide to the program and applications*. Chicago: SPSS.

Keith, D. V., & Whitaker, C. A. (1982). Experiential/symbolic family therapy. In A. M. Horne & M. M. Ohlsen (Eds.), *Family counseling and therapy*. Itasca, IL: Peacock.

Kerr, M. E., & Bowen, M. (1988). *Family evaluation: An approach based on Bowen theory*. New York: Norton.

Kirk, S. A., Siporin, M., and Kutchins, L. (1989). The prognosis for social work diagnosis. *Social Casework, 70*: 295–304.

Klein, A. F. (1972). *Effective group work*. New York: Association Press.

Konopka, G. (1971). *Social group work: A helping process*. Englewood Cliffs, NJ: Prentice-Hall.

Kramer, R. M., and Specht, H. (1969). *Readings in community organization practice*. Englewood Cliffs, NJ: Prentice-Hall.

Kropotkin, P. (1925). *Mutual aid: A factor of evolution*. New York: Alfred A. Knopf.

Kubler-Ross, E. (1969). *On death and dying*. New York: Macmillan.

Kuhn, T. H. (1962). The structure of scientific revolution. Chicago: University of Chicago Press.

Lee, J. A. (1988). *Group work with the poor and oppressed*. New York: Haworth Press.

Lefco, H. (1975). *Dance therapy: Narrative case histories*. Chicago: Nelson-Hall.

Levine, B. (1967). *Fundamentals of group treatment.* Chicago: Whitehall Press.

Lewin, K. (1935). *Field theory in social science: Selected theoretical papers.* New York: McGraw-Hill.

Lewin, K. (1951). *A dynamic theory of personality: Selected papers of Kurt Lewin.* New York: McGraw-Hill.

Lewis, E. (1992). Regaining promise: Feminist perspectives for social group work practice. *Social Work with Groups, 15*(2–3): 271–284.

Lidz, C. (1984). *Informed consent.* New York: Guilford Press.

Loewenberg, F., & Dolgoff, R. (1996). *Ethical decisions for social work practice.* 5th ed. Itasca, IL: Peacock.

Lum, D. (1982). Toward a framework for social work practice with minorities. *Social Work, 27:* 244–249.

Lum, D. (1996). *Social work practice and people of color: A process-stage approach.* 3rd ed. Pacific Grove, CA: Brooks/Cole.

Mailick, M. D. (1991). Re-assessing assessment in clinical social work practice. *Smith College Studies in Social Work, 62*(1): 3–19.

Malluccio, A., & Marlow, W. (1974). The case for contract. *Social Work, 19:* 28–36.

Masten, A. S., Best, K. M., & Garmezy, N. (1990). Resilience and development: Contributions from the study of children who overcome adversity. *Development and Psychopathology, 2*(4), 425–444.

Matano, R. A., & Yalom, I. D. (1991, July). Approaches to chemical dependency: Chemical dependency and interactive group therapy: A synthesis. *International Journal of Group Psychotherapy, 41*(3): 269–293.

Mead, G. H. (1934). *Mind, self, and society.* Chicago: University of Chicago Press.

Miller, J. B. (1987). *Toward a new psychology of women.* 2nd ed. Boston: Beacon Press.

Miller, J. B. (1988). *Connections, disconnections, and violations.* Work in Progress, No. 33. Wellesley, MA: Stone Center Working Paper Series.

Miller, J. B., & Stiver, I. P. (1991). *A relational framing of therapy.* Work in Progress, No. 52. Wellesley, MA: Stone Center Working Paper Series.

Miller, J. B., & Stiver, I. P. (1993, August). A relational approach to understanding women's lives and problems. *Psychiatric Annals, 23*(8): 424–431.

Miller, W. R., & Rollnick, S. (Eds.). (1991). *Motivational interviewing: Preparing people to change addictive behavior.* New York: Guilford Press.

Mills, C. W. (1959). *The sociological imagination.* New York: Oxford University Press.

Minuchin, S., & Fishman, H. C. (1981). *Family therapy techniques.* Cambridge, MA: Harvard University Press.

Mirkin, M. P. (1990). *The social and political contexts of family therapy.* Boston: Allyn & Bacon.

Mulroy, E. A. (1997, May). Building a neighborhood network: Interorganizational collaboration to prevent child abuse and neglect. *Social Work, 42*(3): 255–264.

Mulroy, E. A., and Shay, S. (1997, September). Nonprofit organizations and innovations: A model of neighborhood-based collaboration to prevent child maltreatment. *Social Work, 42*(5): 515–524.

Murphy, G. (1958). *Human potentials.* New York: Basic Books.

National Association of Social Workers. (1996). *National Association of Social Workers Code of Ethics.* Washington, DC: NASW.

Navajits, L. M., Weiss, R. D., & Shaw, S. R. (1997, Fall). The link between substance abuse and posttraumatic stress disorder in women: A research review. *The American Journal of Addictions, 6*(4): 273–283.

Ness, J. A., & Ladicola, P. (1989). Toward a definition of feminist social work: A comparison of liberal, radical, and socialist models. *Social Work, 34:* 12–21.

Norman, E., & Mancuso, A. (1980). *Women's issues and social work practice.* Itasca, IL: Peacock.

Northen, H. (1969). *Social work with groups.* New York: Columbia University Press.

Nugent, W. R. (1991). An experimental and qualitative analysis of cognitive-behavioral intervention for anger. *Social Work Research and Abstracts, 27*(3): 3–8.

O'Brien, P. (1995). From surviving to thriving:

The complex experience of living in public housing. *Affilia, 10*(2): 155–178.

Oei, T. P. S., & Shuttlewood, G. J. (1996). Specific and nonspecific factors in psychotherapy: A case of cognitive therapy for depression. *Clinical Psychological Review, 16*(2): 83–103.

Palazoli, S., Boscolo, L., Cecchin, F. G., & Prata, G. (1978). *Paradox and counterparadox.* New York: Jason Aronson.

Perlman, H. H. (1957). *Social casework: A problem-solving process.* Chicago: University of Chicago Press.

Philips, H. (1957). *Essentials of social group work skill.* New York: Association Press.

Philips, M. H., and Markowitz, M. A. (1990). *The mutual aid model of group services: Experiences of New York Archdiocese drug abuse prevention program.* New York: Fordham University Graduate School of Social Work.

Pilsecker, C. (1979). Terminal cancer: A challenge for social work. *Social Work in Health Care, 4*: 369–379.

Pincus, A., & Minahan, A. (1973). *Social work practice: Model and method.* Itasca, IL: Peacock.

Polansky, N., & Kounin, J. (1956). Clients' reactions to initial interviews. *Human Relations, 9*: 237–264.

Pope, K., & Bouhoutsos, J. (1986). *Sexual intimacy between therapists and patients.* New York: Praeger.

Potok, C. (1976). *My name is Asher Lev.* New York: Alfred A. Knopf.

Potter, S. J., & Darty, T. E. (1981). Social work and the invisible minority: An exploration of lesbianism. *Social Work, 26*: 187–191.

Pottick, K. J. (1988). Jane Addams revisited: Practice theory and social economics. In J. A. Lee (Ed.), *Group work with the poor and oppressed.* New York: Haworth Press.

Prochaska, J. O., & DiClemente, C. C. (1982). Transtheoretical therapy: Toward a more integrative model of change. *Psychotherapy: Theory, Research, and Practice, 19*: 276–288.

Proctor, E. K., & Davis, L. E. (1994). The challenge of racial difference: Skills for clinical practice. *Social Work, 39*(3): 314–323.

Radloff, L. (1977). The CES-D Scale: A self-report depression scale for research in the general population. *Journal of Applied Psychological Measurement, 1*: 385–401.

Rak, C. F., & Patterson, L. E. (1996, March/April). Promoting resilience in at-risk children. *Journal of Counseling and Development, 74*: 368–373.

Reamer, F. G. (1990). *Ethical dilemmas in social services.* 2nd ed. New York: Columbia University Press.

Reid, K. E. (1991). *Social work practice with groups: A clinical perspective.* Belmont, CA: Brooks/Cole.

Reid, W. J., & Shyne, A. W. (1969). *Brief and extended casework.* New York: Columbia University Press.

Reitzes, D., & Reitzes, D. (1986). Alinsky in the 1980s: Two contemporary Chicago community organizations. *The Sociological Quarterly, 28*(2): 265–283.

Reusch, J. (1957). *Disturbed communication.* New York: W. W. Norton.

Richards, M., Browne, C., & Broderick, A. (1994). Strategies for teaching clinical social work practice with Asians and Pacific Islanders. *Gerontology and Geriatric Education, 14*(3): 49–63.

Richmond, M. (1918). *Social diagnosis.* New York: Russell Sage Foundation.

Richters, J. E., & Martinez, P. E. (1993). Violent communities, family choices, and children's chances: An algorithm for improving the odds. *Development and Psychopathology, 5*(4): 609–627.

Roback, H. B., Purdon, S. E., Ochoa, E., & Bloch, F. (1992). Confidentiality dilemmas in group psychotherapy: Management strategies and utility of guidelines. *Small Group Research, 23*(2): 169–184.

Robinson, J. B. (1989). Clinical treatment of black families: Issues and strategies. *Social Work, 34*: 323–329.

Rogers, C. R. (1961). *On becoming a person.* Boston: Houghton Mifflin.

Rogers, C. R. (1969). *Freedom to learn.* Columbus: Charles E. Merrill.

Rose, S. D. (1977). *Group therapy: A behavioral approach.* Englewood Cliffs, NJ: Prentice-Hall.

Rosenberg, M. (1978). *Logic of survey analysis.* New York: Basic Books.

Rothman, J. (1979). Three models of community organization practice: Their mixing and phasing. In F. M. Cox, J. L. Erlich, J. Rothman, and J. E. Tropman (Eds.), *Strategies of community organization.* 3rd ed. (pp. 25–45). Itasca, IL: Peacock.

Sandel, S. (1975). Integrating dance therapy into treatment. *Hospital and Community Psychiatry, 26*: 439–441.

Sands, R., & Nuccio, K. (1992). Post-modern feminist theory and social work. *Social Work, 37*(6): 489–494.

Sarri, R. C. (1985). Federal policy changes and the feminization of poverty. *Child Welfare, 64*: 235–247.

Satir, V. (1967). *Conjoint family therapy.* Palo Alto, CA: Science & Behavior Books.

Saulnier, C. F. (1996). *Feminist theories and social work: Approaches and applications.* New York: Haworth Press.

Scannapieco, M., & Jackson, S. (1996). Kinship care: The African-American response to family preservation. *Social Work, 41*(2): 190–196.

Schaefer, D. S., & Pozzaglia, D. (1986). Living with a nightmare: Hispanic parents of children with cancer. In A. Gitterman & L. Shulman (Eds.), *Mutual aid groups and the life cycle.* Itasca, IL: Peacock.

Scherz, F. H. (1970). Theory and practice of family therapy. In R. W. Roberts & R. H. Nee (Eds.), *Theories of social casework.* Chicago: University of Chicago Press.

Schiller, L. Y. (1993). *Stages of group development in women's group: A relational model.* Paper presented at the XV Annual Symposium of the Association for the Advancement of Social Work with Groups, New York, NY.

Schwartz, W. (1961). The social worker in the group. In *New perspectives on services to groups: Theory, organization, practice* (pp. 7–34). New York: National Association of Social Workers.

Schwartz, W. (1962). Toward a strategy of group work practice. *Social Service Review, 36*: 268–279.

Schwartz, W. (1968). Group work in public welfare. *Public Welfare, 26*: 322–368.

Schwartz, W. (1969). Private troubles and public issues: One social work job or two? In *The Social Welfare Forum, 1969* (pp. 22–43). New York: Columbia University Press.

Schwartz, W. (1971). On the use of groups in social work practice. In W. Schwartz & S. Zalba (Eds.), *The practice of group work* (pp. 3–24). New York: Columbia University Press.

Schwartz, W. (1976). Between client and system: The mediating function. In R. W. Roberts & H. Northen (Eds.), *Theories of social work with groups* (pp. 44–66). New York: Columbia University Press.

Schwartz, W. (1977). Social group work: The interactionist approach. In *Encyclopedia of Social Work*, Vol. 11. New York: National Association of Social Workers.

Seebalt, D. A. (1988). Ethical dilemmas in social work practice with groups. In M. Leiderman (Ed.), *Roots and new frontiers in social group work* (pp. 191–202). New York: Haworth Press.

Sherif, M. (1936). *The psychology of social norms.* New York: Harper & Brothers.

Sherif, M., & Sherif, C. W. (1956). *An outline of social psychology.* New York: Harper & Row.

Shulman, L. (1967). Scapegoats, group workers, and the pre-emptive intervention. *Social Work, 12*: 37–43.

Shulman, L. (1968). *A casebook of social work with groups: The mediating model.* New York: Council on Social Work Education.

Shulman, L. (1970). Client, staff, and the social agency. In *Social Work Practice*, 1970 (pp. 21–40). New York: Columbia University Press.

Shulman, L. (1971). Programs in group work: Another look. In W. Schwartz & S. Zalba (Eds.), *The practice of group work* (pp. 221–240). New York: Columbia University Press.

Shulman, L. (1978). A study of practice skills. *Social Work, 23*: 274–281.

Shulman, L. (1979a). *A study of the helping process.* Vancouver: University of British Columbia, School of Social Work.

Shulman, L. (1979b). *The skills of helping* (videotape series). Montreal: Instructional Communications Centre, McGill University.

Shulman, L. (1980). Social work practice with foster parents. *Canadian Journal of Social Work Education, 6*: 58–71.

Shulman, L. (1981). *Identifying, measuring, and teaching helping skills.* New York: Council on Social Work Education and the Canadian Association of Schools of Social Work.

Shulman, L. (1982). *The skills of helping individuals and groups.* Itasca, IL: Peacock.

Shulman, L. (1984). *The skills of supervision and staff management.* Itasca, IL: Peacock.

Shulman, L. (1991). *Interactional social work practice: Toward an empirical theory.* Itasca, IL: Peacock.

Shulman, L. (1993a). *Interactional supervision.*

Shulman, L. (1993b) *Teaching the helping skills: A field instructor's guide.*

Shulman, L., & Buchan, W. (1982). *The impact of the family physician's communication, relationship, and technical skills on patient compliance, satisfaction, reassurance, comprehension, and improvement.* Vancouver: University of British Columbia.

Shulman, L., & Clay, C. (1994). *Teaching about practice and diversity: Content and process in the classroom and the field* (videotape series). Alexandria, VA: Council on Social Work Education.

Shulman, L., Robinson, E., & Luckyj, A. (1982). *A study of content, context, and skills of supervision.* Vancouver: University of British Columbia.

Siporin, M. (1975). *Introduction to social work practice.* New York: Macmillan.

Smalley, R. E. (1967). *Theory for social work practice.* New York: Columbia University Press.

Smith, A., & Siegal, R. (1985). Feminist therapy: Redefining power for the powerless. In *Handbook of feminist therapy: Women's issues in psychotherapy.* New York: Springer.

Solomon, B. B. (1976). *Black empowerment.* New York: Columbia University Press.

Specht, H. (1988). *New directions for social work.* Englewood Cliffs, NJ: Prentice-Hall.

Specht, H., & Courtney, M. E. (1993). *Unfaithful angels.* New York: Free Press.

Srebnik, D. S. (1994). Feminist cognitive-behavioral therapy for negative body image. *Women & Therapy, 15*(2): 117–133.

Stanton, A. H., & Schwartz, M. F. (1954). *Mental hospital: A study of institutional participation in psychiatric illness and treatment.* New York: Basic Books.

Staples, L. (1984). *Roots to power: A manual for grassroots organizing.* New York: Praeger.

Stark, F. (1959, April). Barriers to client-worker communications at intake. *Social Casework, 40*: 177–183.

Staudinger, U. M., Marsiske, M., & Baltes, P. B. (1993). Resilience and levels of reserve capacity in later adulthood: Perspectives from life-span theory. *Development and Psychopathology, 5*(4): 541–566.

Stern, S., & Smith, C. A. (1995). Family processes and delinquency in an ecological context. *Social Service Review*: 703–731.

Stevens, J. W. (1994). Adolescent development and adolescent pregnancy among late age African-American female adolescents. *Children and Adolescent Social Work Journal, 2*(6): 433–453.

Stiver, I. P., & Miller, J. B. (1993, August). A relational approach to understanding women's lives and problems. *Psychiatric Annals, 23*(8): 424–431.

Strean, H. (1978). *Clinical social work theory and practice.* New York: Free Press.

Swigonski, M. E. (1994). The logic of feminist standpoint theory for social work research. *Social Work, 39*(4): 387–393.

Taft, J. (1933). Living and feeling. *Child Study, 10*: 100–112.

Taft, J. (1942). The relation of function to process in social case work. In V..P. Robinson (Ed.), *Training for skill in social casework.* Philadelphia: University of Pennsylvania Press.

Taft, J. (1949). Time as the medium of the helping process. *Jewish Social Service Quarterly,* 26: 230–243.

Thayer, L. (1982). A person-centered approach to family therapy. In A. M. Horne & M. M. Ohlsen (Eds.), *Family counseling and therapy* (pp. 175–213). Itasca, IL: Peacock.

Thornton, S., & Garrett, K. (1995). Ethnography as a bridge to multicultural practice. *Journal of Social Work Education, 32*(1): 67–74.

Thyer, B. A. (1987). Contingency analysis: Toward a unified theory for social work practice. *Social Work*: 150–157.

Thyer, B. A., & Thyer, K. B. (1992). Single-system research designs in social work practice. *Research on Social Work Practice, 2*(1): 99–116.

Tracy, E. M., & Whittaker, J. K. (1990). The social network map: Assessing social support in clinical practice. *Families in Society, 72*(8): 461–470.

Trimble, D. (1986). Confronting responsibility: Men who batter their wives. In A. Gitterman & L. Shulman (Eds.), *Mutual aid groups and the life cycle.* Itasca, IL: Peacock.

Trimble, D. (1994). Confronting responsibility: Men who batter their wives. In A. Gitterman & L. Shulman (Eds.), *Mutual aid groups, vulnerable populations, and the life cycle.* 2nd ed. (pp. 257–263). New York: Columbia University Press.

Trimpay, J. (1996). An overview of AVRT and rational recovery. In *Rational Recovery* (pp. 29–44). New York: Simon & Schuster.

Tropp, E. (1969). *A humanistic foundation for group work practice.* New York: Selected Academic Readings.

Truax, C. B. (1966). Therapist empathy, warmth, genuineness, and patient personality change in group psychotherapy: A comparison between interaction unit measures, time sample measures, and patient perception measures. *Journal of Clinical Psychology, 71*: 1–9.

Unger, D., & Wandersman, A. (1985). The importance of neighbors: The social, cognitive, and affective components of neighboring. *American Journal of Community Psychology, 13*(2): 139–169.

Vannicelli, M. (1992). *Removing the roadblocks: Group psychotherapy with substance abusers and family members.* New York: Guilford Press.

Vastola, J. Nierenberg, A., & Graham, E. H. (1994). The lost and found group: Group work with bereaved children. In A. Gitterman and L. Shulman (Eds.), *Mutual aid groups, vulnerable populations, and the life cycle.* 2nd ed. (pp. 81–96). New York: Columbia University Press.

Vinter, R. D. (Ed.). (1967). *Readings in group work practice.* Ann Arbor: Campus Publishers.

Weakland, J. H., Fisch, R., Watzlawick, P., & Bodin, A. M. (1974). Brief therapy: Focused problem resolution. *Family Process, 13*: 141–168.

Weaver, H. N., & White, B. J. (1997). The Native American family circle: Roots of resiliency. *Journal of Social Work, 2*(1): 67–79.

Weaver, H. N., & Wodarski, J. S. (1995). Cultural issues in crisis intervention: Guidelines for culturally competent practice. *Family Therapy, 22*(3): 213–223.

Weick, A., & Vandiver, S. (1982). *Women, power, and change.* Silver Springs, MD: National Association of Social Workers.

Werner, E. E. (1989, April). Children of the garden. *Scientific American, 260*: 106–111.

Westermeyer, J., Kopka, S., and Nugent, S. (1997, Fall). Course and severity of substance abuse among patients with comorbid major depression. *The American Journal on Addictions, 6*(4).

Whitaker, D. S., & Lieberman, M. A. (1964). *Psychotherapy through the group process.* New York: Atherton Press.

Whyte, W. F. (1943). *Street corner society: The social structure of an Italian slum.* Chicago: University of Chicago Press.

Williams, E. E., and Ellison, F. (1996). Culturally informed social work practice with American Indian clients: Guidelines for non-Indian social workers. *Social Work, 41*(2): 147–151.

Wilson, G., & Ryland, G. (1949). *Social group work practice: The creative use of the social process.* Boston: Houghton Mifflin.

Wilson, S. J. (1982). *Confidentiality in social work.* New York: Free Press.

Wilson, W. J. (1973). *Power, racism, and privilege: Race relations in theoretical and sociohistorical perspectives.* New York: Free Press.

Wong, Mary. (1988). Unpublished student paper.

■ *Index of Case Examples*

Case examples used in this text are cross-indexed to facilitate the reader's use of them. Examples have been indexed by problems (e.g., addiction, AIDS); population (e.g., pregnant teenagers, married couples); settings (e.g., medical, residential, child welfare); processes (e.g., acting out, resistance, scapegoating); and skills (e.g., contracting, demand for work). In addition, the client level (e.g., individual, family, group, institution) is indicated for each subreference (following a colon).

Name Index

Aber, J.L., 69
Ackerman, N., 237, 275, 275n1, 474–75
Addams, J., 17
Albert, J., 31
Alexander, R., 85–86
Alinsky, S., 18
Alissi, A.S., 318n2
Amodeo, M., 655, 766
Angelou, M., 67
Appelbaum, P., 92n19
Argyris, C., 753, 762
Asch, S.E., 557

Barker, R., 89
Baldwin, J.M., 37n9
Bales, R., 581
Baltes, P.B., 71, 72
Bandler, R., 275n1
Barker, R., 19, 34, 76, 89, 90, 145, 197, 198, 239, 275
Bass, B.M., 533n6
Bateson, G., 275n1
Bavelas, A., 581
Beauchamp, T., 92n22
Beck, A., 30, 31
Beck, J.C., 92n19, 92n22
Beckett, J.O., 69
Bell, N.W., 477
Benne, K.D., 532n1
Bennis, W.G., 535, 537, 538, 542–43, 592, 593, 594n1
Berlin, S.B., 8, 22, 131
Berman-Rossi, T., 29
Bernstein, S., 133n1, 318n2, 342n4
Besharov, D.J., 92n19
Best, K.M., 91n13
Bion, W.R., 441, 471, 557, 558, 560, 592, 593
Bloch, F., 80
Block, J., 199n2
Blyth, B.J., 37n17
Bodin, A.M., 275n1
Borland, J., 199n3
Bouhoutsos, J., 92n15
Bowen, M., 237–38, 243, 275n1

Braeger, G., 37n13, 753
Breton, M., 29
Broderick, A., 127
Brown, L.N., 318n2, 341n1
Brown, S., 655
Browne, C., 127
Buchan, W., 52, 161, 428
Bulhan, H.A., 8, 11, 12, 61, 63, 65, 66, 91n7, 770
Burke, A.C., 654
Butler, K., 67

Carlson, E., 70
Casey, 70
Cham-kun, L., 594n5
Chestang, L., 91n10
Cheung, Y.F., 594n5
Clapp, J., 654
Clay, C., 47, 127
Clinton, W.J., 12
Cohen, M.B., 29
Collins, B., 29
Congress, E.P., 119
Connell, J.P., 69
Courtney, M.E., 766
Cox, D., 766
Coyle, G., 18

Daley, M.R., 199n3
Daly, A., 69
Darden, C., 67
Darty, T.E., 91n11
Davidson, K.W., 523
Davis, L.E., 120, 123, 126, 127, 134n4, 276n2, 332
Day, L.G., 38n17
Dean, R.G., 37n16
Deutsch, M., 581
Devore, W., 120, 276n2, 456, 517, 573
Dewey, J., 36n7
DiClemente, C.C., 407–8, 709
Dolgoff, R., 76, 78, 79, 82, 83
Douglas, T., 477, 533n2
DuBray, L., 91n10

■ *Subject Index*

work with, 717–23
See also Adolescents; Children; High school
School setting
adolescent acting-out boys' group in, 402–5
contracting with 12-year-old boys in, 405–6
family support work in, 290–96
group for parents of children in alternative public
day school, 429–31
scapegoating adolescent girls in, 480–86
ten-year-old girls in, 394–400
School social worker, contracting by, 103
Self, inner and outer, 475
Self-analysis, 248, 386–87
Self-determination, 77
Self-disclosure, by worker, 47, 165
"Self in relation" theory, 7, 29
Self-interest
in group work, 313
as obstacle to interaction, 14
Sender, 41
Senior citizens. *See* Elderly
Sensitivity, to differences between workers and clients,
74
Sentiments, Homans on, 589
Services, worker impact on, 743
Sessional contracting, 137, 145–48
in group, 438–55
Sessional ending and transition skills, 137, 192–97,
470–72
Sessional tuning in, 136, 138–45
Setting
family counseling and mandate of, 277–78
and groups, 334, 427–31
See also Context of practice; specific settings
Setting limits. *See* Limits
Settlement house movement, 17–18
Sexism
psychological payoffs to, 12
See also Women
Sexual abuse
ending of group for adult survivors of, 607–14
group work and, 307
involuntary groups and, 407
teenage residents acting-out behavior and, 446–47
Sexuality
attraction between worker and client, 166–67
in home for aged, 748–49
Sexual orientation, sensitivity to, 47
Sexual taboos, 176, 562–63
Sharing data, 138
for mutual aid, 303–5
skills for, 185–91
Sharing worker's feelings with client, 45, 137, 161–68
ending feelings and, 209
issues in, 165–67

research on, 167–68
Shelter, pregnant teens in, 400–401, 486–90
Short-term practice
family support work, 236
open-ended groups, 631
Significant other, of substance abuser, 685–703
Silence
in group sessions, 348, 505–8
See also Reaching inside of silences
Single-parent family
and Big Brothers service, 296–99
family support work with, 254–61
Record of Service with, 256–61
Single-session group, 628–31
informal event group for remembering Holocaust,
630–31
information group for foster parent recruitment,
629–30
Single-System Research Design (SSRD), for outcome
evaluation, 131–32
Skill factor, 136
Skills
defined, 4
for demand for work, 171
for determining indirect cues in taboo areas,
60–61
elaborating, 148–55
of endings, 201–12
of generalizing, 193–94
for helping clients manage feelings, 167–68
for helping clients manage problems, 94, 104–5
identifying doorknob communications, 196–97
of identifying next steps, 194–95
initial interviews for groups and, 337–40
of rehearsal, 195–96
for sessional ending and transition, 192–97
for sharing data, 185–91
of social work, 22–25
for strengthening worker-client relationship, 57–59
of summarizing, 193
supporting clients in taboo areas as, 178–79
of transitions, 212–21
See also Skills in work phase; specific skills
Skills for Helping Clients to Manage Their Feelings
scale, 58
Skills for Helping Clients to Manage Their Problems, 60
Skills in work phase, 135–97
contracting as, 145–48
data-sharing, 185–91
demand for work as, 168–81
elaborating as, 148–55
empathic, 155–61
helping client see life in new ways as, 191–92
identifying process and content connections as,
181–85

THE SKILLS OF HELPING INDIVIDUALS, FAMILIES, GROUPS, AND COMMUNITIES
Fourth Edition
Edited by Janet Tilden
Production supervision by Kim Vander Steen
Designed by Lucy Lesiak Design, Park Ridge, Illinois
Composition by Point West, Inc., Carol Stream, Illinois
Paper, Lynx Opaque
Printed and bound by Quebecor Printing, Fairfield, Pennsylvania